NEW AGE

ENCYCLOPEDIA

Also published under the title of
Encyclopedia International

Lexicon Publications

VOLUME 7

EXPLOSIVES

GHANA

Library of Congress Cataloging in Publication Data

Main entry under title:
ENCYCLOPEDIA INTERNATIONAL

   Includes bibliographies and index.
   Summary: Thirty thousand alphabetically arranged articles
designed especially to meet the needs of the family and students
at various levels. Includes cross-references throughout and an
index in the final volume.
   1. Encyclopedias and dictionaries. [Encyclopedias and
dictionaries]

AE5.E447 1978   031   77-13344
ISBN 0-7172-0709-9

PRINTED
IN
U.S.A.

More than 4,000,000 pounds (1 815 000 kg) of explosives were detonated in this copper mine blast in Arizona.

EXPLOSIVES, compounds or mixtures capable of decomposing rapidly to produce heat and large volumes of gas.

Properties. Explosives fall into two classes—high explosives, which function by detonation, and low explosives, which function by deflagration. Detonation, a very fast reaction, is initiated by and in turn supports a supersonic shock wave. Examples of detonating explosives are dynamite, TNT (trinitrotoluene), lead azide, PETN (pentaerythritol tetranitrate), and nitroglycerin. Deflagration is a burning reaction in which the flame front traversing the explosive material moves at subsonic speed. Examples of deflagrating explosives are black powder and smokeless powder.

Many substances are capable of detonating under certain circumstances. The natural gas used in cooking and in heating houses, for example, can explode with devastating effect when mixed with the proper amount of oxygen. Ammonium nitrate, most often used as a fertilizer, has enormous explosive potential when mixed with proper amounts of carbon. These and many other substances can be made to explode under particular circumstances—producing useful work if handled properly, causing tragedy if the explosion is unintentional or carried out improperly.

Uses. Explosives have many industrial uses. For centuries they have been employed in mining operations, quarrying, and construction of many kinds. They have been a mainstay of such diverse undertakings as canals, railroads, highways, water conservation and irrigation projects, and site preparation for major building construction.

Use of commercial explosives generally involves drilling a series of boreholes, into which the explosive charge is placed. These boreholes usually range in diameter from 1 to 12 inches (2.5–29.5 cm). Their depths may be as little as several feet or more than 100 ft (30.5 m). For the occasional large blast involving hundreds of thousands or even millions of pounds of explosives the boreholes may in fact be tunnels dug into a hillside.

Detonators. In any controlled blast the "charge" consists of both the main explosive and an initiating, or detonating, system—a small explosive device, or devices, designed to activate larger amounts of explosives in a planned manner. Depending on the explosive being used, the detonating system may consist solely of one or more blasting caps properly placed in the charge, a combination of cap(s) and detonating cord, or a high explosive "primer" charge, which itself is detonated by a blasting cap or detonating cord system.

Electric blasting caps are the most commonly used initiating devices. They are used either by themselves, placed directly within a cartridged explosive, or in conjunction with a high explosive primer or detonating cord. Primers generally are either a normal cartridged explosive (a cast primer) or a plasticized PETN explosive about the size of a man's thumb. Detonating cord usually contains granulated PETN packaged in a tough, flexible tubular package. The cord itself is nearly ¼ inch (6.4 mm) in diameter and may be hundreds of feet long. The cord can be detonated by a single blasting cap and may be used to detonate a large number of charges placed on branch cords tied into the main trunk line. Detonating cord may be used by itself to initiate charges of cartridged explosives or, in conjunction with a primer, bulk explosive compounds.

A variety of millisecond delay devices—electric and nonelectric—can be used to control the sequence of detonations in the boreholes in a multicharge blasting operation. Proper sequencing of the charges in a blast makes it possible to detonate thousands of pounds of explosive with minimal ground vibration.

Because of their small size and curious appearance, blasting caps sometimes present unplanned hazards to the public. Despite strenuous efforts to maintain strict controls over explosive devices, blasting caps occasionally are lost and may subsequently be found by children. If found, they should not be handled except by trained fire department or police personnel. Although blasting caps look harmless, they are dangerous. Accidental detonation of a cap can cause serious injury.

Commercial Types

Three basic types of explosives dominate the commercial explosives industry: ammonium nitrate-fuel oil (ANFO) mixes; bulk slurry, or water gel, formulations; and small and intermediate diameter (less than 4 inches, or 10 cm) cartridged explosives, including both dynamite and the newer water gels. Black powder, the first explosive, is now rarely used for commercial blasting. Trinitrotoluene (TNT) is used extensively in military applications and for cast primers by the commercial explosives industry. Other, lesser known explosives, such as PETN, find a wide variety of applications, particularly in blasting caps, primers, and detonating cord.

Ammonium Nitrate-Fuel Oil (ANFO) Mixes. ANFO, a free-flowing mixture, is the workhorse of the commercial explosives industry. As the least expensive and one of the least sensitive of commercial explosives, it offers advantages in many applications. Its major disadvantage is that it is strongly hydroscopic and therefore not suitable for use in wet conditions. It is comparatively insensitive (difficult to detonate) and, accordingly, must be primed with a high explosive for reliable detonation. It is easily packaged in bags, which can be emptied either directly into a borehole or into a loader and then blown into the hole.

Ammonium nitrate prills (small spherical pellets) also can be delivered to the blast site in a bulk truck and mixed with the fuel oil on site as it is pumped from the truck into the borehole.

While ANFO does not have so high a detonation velocity as the water gels or dynamites, its explosive "punch" is adequate for many applications and, properly primed, it can sustain detonation in boreholes down to 2 inches (5 cm) in diameter. As a result, ANFO is most commonly used in open pit mining and large construction jobs where water is not present. It is also used extensively in underground mining—except for coal mining, in which explosives designed specifically to produce a flame of small volume, short duration, and low temperature are required to lessen the risk of a gas or dust ignition inside the mine.

Bulk Water Gels or Slurries. The water gels are an alternative to ANFO when conditions of wetness or need for higher detonation velocity make use of ANFO impractical. The basic ingredient of the water gel explosive is, again, ammonium nitrate—normally about 50% by weight. The sensitizers used for bulk water gels have included smokeless powder, TNT, powdered aluminum, and monomethylamine nitrate (MMAN). These ingredients are mixed in an aqueous gel to give them a consistency not unlike that of a granular pudding. The gel form makes the explosive water resistant. It also makes the product easily amenable to packaging in plastic sacks or to delivery in bulk trucks for pumping into the borehole.

Because of their relatively low sensitivity, bulk water gels, like ANFO, are comparatively safe in transportation, storage, and use. They must be primed with a high explosive charge for reliable detonation. Bulk water gels are normally used in boreholes of 4 inches (10 cm) or more in diameter where their advantages of higher detonation velocity and water resistance justify their higher cost. Often they are also used in conjunction with ANFO, with the water gel, for example, loaded in the bottom of the borehole, where water is present, and the ANFO loaded in the dry portion of the hole.

Cartridged Explosives. This packaging form generally is limited to diameters of less than 4 inches (10 cm), the most common diameter being from 1 to 2½ inches (2.5–6.4 cm). Until recently dynamite was the only commonly used cartridged explosive—because nitroglycerin was one of the few known economically viable sensitizers capable of enabling a small diameter cartridged explosive to sustain detonation reliably. Nitroglycerin's use in efforts to develop cartridged water gel explosives was ruled out in part because nitroglycerin, an oily liquid, is immiscible in the water gel formulations. Additionally, its use was precluded by the major motivation for developing a cartridged water gel explosive—the greater margin of safety offered by non-nitroglycerin explosives.

In the early 1970's monomethylamine nitrate was identified by Du Pont Company scientists as an effective sensitizer for use in water gel explosives in cartridges as small as 1 inch (2.5 cm) in diameter. Because of the added margin of safety offered by the water gels in manufacture, transportation, storage, and use, Du Pont, then the largest dynamite producer in the United States, decided in 1974 to replace its sales of dynamite with sales of a cartridged water gel. In 1977, Du Pont shut down its last dynamite production line, ending a 97-year history of dynamite manufacture. Simultaneously other manufacturers have added water gels to their lines.

A bagged water gel explosive is loaded into a borehole in an underground iron mine.

E. I. du Pont de Nemours & Co.

Historical Development

The discovery or "invention" of explosives is elusive. Evidence suggests that the first explosive, black powder, may have been developed by the Chinese, Indians, or Arabs. The first explosive of record in the West was noted in the 13th century. Instructions on how to make it are contained in surviving writings of the English scholar Roger Bacon.

Apparently Europeans initially used black powder only to fire guns and cannon. The idea of using it for industrial purposes was accepted only slowly—and only then in the 17th century. For example, the use of black powder in mining was proposed in Saxony as early as 1613, but the suggestion appears to have been ignored until 14 years later, when the explosive powder was used successfully to blast ore in the royal mines at Schemnitz. By 1689 the British were blasting ore in the tin mines of Cornwall using black powder.

The use of black powder eventually spread to other operations—for example, digging canals and building railroads. Moreover, as the industrial revolution progressed, demands for more coal, minerals, and building stone inexorably increased the demand for explosives.

In 1846 an Italian scientist, Ascanio Sobrero, discovered the explosive properties of nitroglycerin, and in 1866, Alfred Nobel, a Swedish scientist, harnessed them in dynamite. (See DYNAMITE.) At the time of Nobel's invention of dynamite, blasting operations in the United States were consuming more than 25 million pounds (11 340 000 kg) of black powder annually. By the end of the 19th century more than 85 million pounds (38 555 000 kg) of dynamite per year were being used in mining and construction applications with each pound of dynamite doing five times the work of a pound of black powder.

In the later 1970's more than 3.2 billion pounds (1.44 billion kg) of explosives were being used commercially each year in the United States alone. Of that total, black powder, the first explosive, represented an almost invisible fraction. Morever, use of dynamite, the second explosive, had fallen from a peak of 860 million pounds (390 089 000 kg) in 1956 to less than a quarter that amount in 1976—a period which saw the total consumption of explosives more than triple from the 1956 level of a billion pounds. ANFO accounted for about 82% of the commercial explosives consumed in the United States; bagged or bulk water gels accounted for 9%; and cartridged explosives filled the remaining 9%.

JOHN A. ROBERTS

EXPONENT [ĕks-pō′nant], in mathematics, symbol placed above and to the right of another symbol. Its meaning varies with its usage. Thus, 5^3 means $5 \times 5 \times 5$, or 125. In the expression b^x the exponent is x; b is called the base. If x is a symbol for a positive integer, then x is the number of times b is used as a factor. If x and y are exponents and both have positive integers as values, then $b^x \cdot b^y = b^{x+y}$. By definition $b^0 = 1$ and $b^{-x} = \dfrac{1}{b^x}$.

When the exponent is a positive rational number, say $\dfrac{p}{q}$, then $x^{\frac{p}{q}}$ is defined as $(x^{\frac{1}{q}})^p$. It follows that $x^{\frac{q}{q}} = (x^{\frac{1}{q}})^q = x^1$, or x. Hence, $x^{\frac{1}{q}}$ can be interpreted as one of the qth roots of x. In all of these instances $q \neq 0$, and 0^0 are left undefined. The same definitions are used when the exponent is a negative rational number.

When the exponent is an irrational number, such as the $\sqrt{2}$, it is interpreted as a number trapped between two rational numbers.

JOHN L. KINSELLA

EXPORT-IMPORT BANK OF WASHINGTON, a U.S. banking agency created by Congress in 1934. The bank's purpose is "assisting, supporting and encouraging overseas trade of U.S. free enterprise." The bank pursues these objectives by granting credits to finance specific sales and purchases, notably of U.S. capital equipment for public and private projects abroad, by making loans to foreign governments "to relieve critical dollar exchange stringencies," and by insuring U.S. exporters against war and expropriation risks.

EXPORTS AND IMPORTS, goods and services exchanged in international trade. Nations trade because many of the goods desired by the inhabitants of a country cannot be produced within its boundaries or can be produced more cheaply abroad. Even if a country can produce a wide range of goods cheaply and efficiently, it still may be advantageous to import some items because the country's productive efficiency in other fields is even greater. Interdependence has increased in the 20th century.

EX POST FACTO [ĕks pōst făk'tō] **LAW.** Any criminal statute enacted and applied against a person who acted prior to its effectiveness is an ex post facto law, and if in any manner it inures to that person's detriment, it cannot be enforced against him (Art. 1, secs. 9–10, U.S. Const.). In the case of *Calder* v. *Bull* (1798), the U.S., Supreme Court enumerated four categories of ex post facto laws: "1st. Every law that makes an action done before the passing of the law, and which was innocent when done, criminal; and punishes such action. 2d. Every law that aggravates a crime or makes it greater than it was, when committed. 3d. Every law that changes the punishment and inflicts a greater punishment, than the law annexed to the crime, when committed. 4th. Every law that alters the legal rules of evidence and receives less, or different, testimony, than the law required at the time of the commission of the offense, in order to convict the offender." The Supreme Court declared that all these and similar laws were manifestly unjust and oppressive.

GERHARD O. MUELLER

EXPRESSIONISM, movement in art, literature, and music that originated in Germany prior to World War I.

Art

Expressionist art elicits a heightened emotional response from the viewer by distortion of form, color, drawing, or space. These characteristics are also found in some of the older art of those northern European countries that were little influenced by the classical civilization of Rome and the Italian Renaissance—for example, the figureheads of Viking ships, French Romanesque sculpture, and the painting of the German Matthias Grünewald. The art of Vincent van Gogh in the 19th century has expressionist qualities, as does that of the French fauve painters in the first decade of the 20th century.

The typical subjects of the pre-World War I German expressionist artists were suffering or emotionally isolated people, mood-evoking landscapes, and penetrating psychological portraits. The painters, who exhibited jointly, formed into groups. In Dresden there appeared *Die Brücke* (The Bridge), comprised of such artists as Ernst Ludwig Kirchner, Emil Nolde, Max Pechstein, and Karl Schmidt-Rottluff, who emphasized distortion of drawing and dissonant color. In Munich appeared *Der Blaue Reiter* (The Blue Rider), its members being Wassily Kandinsky, Franz Marc, Paul Klee, Alexi von Jawlensky, and others. Their pictures tended to be more rhythmic in composition and lyrical in color.

Other modern expressionist artists are the Norwegian Edvard Munch and the Belgian James Ensor, both of whom preceded the German movement; the Lithuanian-born Chaim Soutine; and the Austrian Oskar Kokoschka. Georges Rouault of France is also described as an expressionist. A post-World War I movement in Germany, called the *Neue Sachlichkeit* (New Objectivity), continued certain aspects of the expressionist style. Its members were Otto Dix, George Grosz, Max Beckmann, and others.

Consult Dube, Wolf-Dieter, tr. by Whittall, Mary, *Expressionism* (1973); Willett, John, *Expressionism* (1971).

HERSCHEL B. CHIPP

Literature

Originating in painting, expressionism soon spread to other arts and provided technique, attitude, and subject to literature. Never important for greatness of works produced, literary expressionism nevertheless stimulated virtually every worthwhile writer after 1910. The movement began as a late manifestation of romanticism and centered in German drama just before and after World War I. By the mid-1920's its tricks of distortion, symbolism, and exaggeration alienated the public; the sequence of events in a play was no longer clear because dramatists appeared to have confused technique with purpose.

Inspired by the philosophy of Henri Bergson, novels of Fyodor Dostoyevsky, plays of Frank Wedekind and August Strindberg, and psychology of Sigmund Freud, German dramatists (and then poets and novelists) tried to explore deeper meanings of reality than their 19th-century inheritance of rationalism and materialism could furnish. They mingled past and present time, showed man as a machine in an industrial society, and animated inanimate objects. To make form dynamic, they shortened scenes and whirled the plot from one event to the next. Scenery was unrealistic, the wall in a madhouse twisting and turning to mirror an inmate's state of mind. Characters were types, such as the Soldier or the Tailor, because the major theme became Man versus Society, with Man in the Mass as the protagonist.

Attracted by the immediacy of communication that literary expressionists like Franz Werfel had achieved, T. S. Eliot in poetry, James Joyce in the novel, and Eugene O'Neill in drama sought to project their inner visions of reality by disintegrating and distorting outer experience and employing objects as well as words for symbols. A host of minor authors followed their use of montage, dreams, and stream-of-consciousness in place of realism and logic. Later, Sean O'Casey, seeking to dramatize modern life as futile and meaningless while rousing viewers to moral indignation and hope in a better future, revitalized expressionism by fusing it with realism.

Consult Rose, Ernst, *A History of German Literature* (1960).

ARTHUR BERINGAUSE

Expressionist Paul Klee distorts form and color in "Scene of an Arab City." Born in Switzerland, Klee studied art in Munich and in 1912 became associated there with expressionists known as *Der Blaue Reiter* (The Blue Rider). The course of his work was affected greatly by a 12-day painting trip to Tunisia in 1914.

Galerie Berggrien et Cie

Music

The phrase "musical expressionism" applies to the post-romantic style in 20th-century music that was initiated around 1909 by the extraordinary work of Arnold Schoenberg (*Three Piano Pieces*, Op. 11). As a general aesthetic, expressionism endeavored to give shape to the inner vision and the subconscious experience; organic forms of nature were distorted into a "dream-like grotesqueness and nightmare and were forced into abstract patterns," in the words of the great music historian Curt Sachs. Specifically, aside from this general outlook, in music this meant a disintegration of traditional tonality, irregular rhythms, melodies with wide leaps and jagged outlines, laconic and often strict forms (canon, rondo, passacaglia, and so on), disembodied textures, significant rests and silences, an orchestration of extreme pointillism that almost totally abolished the orchestral pedal (sustained sound), and *Sprechstimme*—a manner of half speaking and half singing on indicated pitches. It is also significant that, as an adjunct to the music, words of vocal works were frequently given an irregular accentuation; furthermore, the texts and plots chosen by Schoenberg and his disciples usually focused on such aberrational subjects as murder, violence, hysteria, hallucination, and madness so as to achieve an extreme range of intensity and dynamics.

This phase of musical expressionism found its fullest and most elaborate demonstration in such pivotal, yet radically different, works as Schoenberg's *Pierrot Lunaire* (1912), Alban Berg's *Wozzeck* (1921), and Anton von Webern's *Five Pieces for Orchestra* (1913).

In the next phase Schoenberg sought a logical and systematic governing principle that would resolve what he held to be a tonal crisis and approaching dead end in his own and in his pupils' works. He thus devised the system of composing with 12 tones, first used partially in his *Five Piano Pieces* (Op. 23, 1923). Although Schoenberg and his pupils now showed a radical change in the organizational

aspect of their music, and although there developed a marked shift in Schoenberg's own philosophical views, as reflected in his opera *Moses and Aaron* (1932) and in his Jewish liturgical music, the general impetus and psychological outlook of their work retained its expressionistic stamp.

Consult Leibowitz, Rene, *Schoenberg and His School* (reprinted, 1970); Payne, Anthony, *Schoenberg* (1968); Rosen, Charles, *Arnold Schoenberg* (1975).

ALBERT WEISSER

EXPRESSWAY, a highway designed to meet particularly high standards, including a divider strip or wall, limited access, and grade separations for faster and safer travel through intersections.
See also HIGHWAY.

EXTENSION EDUCATION, courses and services provided by universities and colleges for people who cannot enroll in regular programs of study. In the United States the universities of Chicago, Michigan, and Wisconsin pioneered in this form of adult education. Universities and colleges in the United States now devote as much as 5% of their total expenditures to extension work. The National University Extension Association has more than 100 member institutions, with more than a million students engaged in extension study on their campuses and in extension centers or in part-time or correspondence study. Many courses are taught in the evenings or on Saturdays; others are conducted by mail and by television. Some courses yield credit toward a degree.

Extension services include the agricultural and home economics educational and advisory services provided by land-grant colleges and universities and by county agents of the Cooperative Extension Service. Federal funds for these services were authorized by the Smith-Lever Act of 1914.

FRANK KLASSEN

COMMON HOUSEHOLD PESTS

PEST — CONTROL	(NOT TO SCALE)	WHERE FOUND	HABITS
CARPET BEETLES Contact spray.		Dark secluded places—under carpets, trunks, luggage, furniture.	Scavengers—attack woolen fabrics, furs, carpets.
MOTHS Contact spray.		Dark hidden places—on clothes, carpets, furs, furniture.	Adults fly, deposit eggs on materials. Larvae eat fabrics.
TERMITES Contact spray.		In soil; infests wood members of house.	Adult workers build tubes in wood and attack by dark; shun light.
RATS AND MICE Rat-proofing with lath and cement; poison bait and traps.		In outdoor burrows near houses. In holes in wall and floor. Near garbage.	Attack food stuffs and may spread disease.
COCKROACHES Contact spray or powder.	AMERICAN GERMAN	In kitchens, bathrooms, and sewers.	Nocturnal—hide in cracks under sink, behind shelves.
SILVERFISH Contact spray.		Boiler room, bathroom walls, around ceiling light fixtures, on plastered walls.	Feed on animal and vegetable matter —especially starch.
BEDBUGS Contact spray.		In tufts of mattress, springs, joints of bedlegs, behind loose wallpaper, behind moldings.	Will bite man.
ANTS Contact spray or powder.		Outdoors, indoors, behind moldings, in closets.	Behind moldings, on floor; search for food particles.
TICKS Direct sprays.		Brought in by dogs from outdoors, especially from areas of high grass, bushes.	Hide in homes in furniture, moldings, beds, books. Will bite man.
FLEAS Contact spray; insect powder, moth flakes and Para crystals.		On cats and dogs; eggs found under carpets, moldings.	Feed on blood of cats and dogs. Will also bite man.

Material by Charles Pomerantz — Bell Exterminating Company

EXTERMINATION, HOUSEHOLD-PEST. Common household pests include several species of insects, several arachnids (spiders, scorpions, mites, and ticks), two common rodent pests (rats and mice), and a varied group of bird and animal wildlife pests (bats, pigeons, sparrows, squirrels, skunks, and snakes).

Control Methods. Methods commonly employed in household pest control are:

Sanitation, the elimination of sites or materials in which pests can breed, either within the home or in areas surrounding the home.

Mechanical barriers, the use of screens to prevent entry by flies and mosquitoes.

Space application of insecticides, the spraying of oil solutions of insecticides into the air by a hand atomizer. Newer application methods develop smaller particles which give better distribution and a longer period of suspension for the particles. The most common example is the aerosol spray, which uses the evaporation of a liquefied refrigerant-type gas to suspend fine particles of insecticide solution in the air. Fine-particle dissemination of insecticides in air also is accomplished by means of mechanical devices, steam, or thermal aerosol generators (fogging devices).

Residual application of insecticides, placement of an insecticide residue on a surface on which the pest will walk or rest. Oil solutions or water emulsions of the insecticides are painted or sprayed on such surfaces. Dusts or water suspensions are effective, but leave visible residues. Gas-propelled residual formulations also are marketed. Residual insecticides may be used to establish chemical barriers to pest entry.

Fumigation, the introduction of a fumigant gas into the atmosphere of an enclosed area and maintenance of a sufficient concentration for the time necessary to kill the pest. Fumigant gases are highly toxic to humans. Fumigation should be done only by a professional exterminator following accepted procedures to ensure safe operation.

Repellents, the use of liquids or aerosol sprays which can be applied to the skin or clothing to repel mosquitoes and biting flies.

Protective treatments, the application of mothproofing agents to fabrics.

Baits, the incorporation of a toxicant with a material attractive to the pest, usually food or water.

Traps, the method most frequently used for control of rodents or wildlife pests.

Insecticides. Insecticides commonly used in households are:

Pyrethrins, used extensively in space sprays because of its rapid knock-down action and very low toxicity to mammals. Allethrin is similar in properties and uses.

Organic thiocyanates, used as knock-down agent in space sprays.

Chlorinated hydrocarbons, used chiefly as residuals. Those safe for specific household uses and most commonly used are methoxychlor, DDT, chlordane, lindane, and dieldrin. Also used as soil toxicants to establish chemical barriers against termites and ants are chlordane, dieldrin, aldrin, and heptachlor.

Organic phosphates, used chiefly as residuals. Malathion, ronnel, Diazinon R, and DDVP are safe for specific household uses.

Rodenticides. Those preferred for household use are the anticoagulants, such as warfarin or pival. Low concentrations in baits are effective in control of rats or mice if fed upon repeatedly (for example, each day for 4 to 5 days). The low acute toxicity from a single feeding makes them relatively safe for household use. Rodenticides with high acute toxicity, such as antu, phosphorus, arsenic trioxide, strychnine, zinc phosphide, thallium sulfate, should be used only with the greatest care in a home.

Almost all communities are served by professional exterminators or pest control operators, who will eliminate pest infestations or provide service for their prevention.

Pests. The following groups include the various species generally recognized as household pests.

Insects. Four species of roaches (German, brown-banded, American, and Oriental) are common household pests. All are annoying by their presence, but their only proved health hazard is their common association with filth. They are controlled by residual insecticides.

The fabric pests include the clothes moths and the carpet beetles. The larvae of these species will feed upon and damage materials made of wool, hair, feather, or horn. Good housekeeping and cleaning garments before summer storage are basic preventive measures. Populations in discarded or overlooked garments, and in floor cracks or other places of lint accumulation, should be eliminated. Thorough application of a residual chlorinated hydrocarbon is usually effective. Rugs may be protected with a mothproofing application. Fumigation is effective, but necessary only with the worst infestations.

The pantry pests are the bran beetles (in grain prod ucts), carpet beetles and larder beetles (in high-protein materials), drugstore beetles and cigarette beetles (in herbs and spices), weevils (in dried beans and peas, grains, and macaroni products), and the flour moths (in flour and cereal mixes). The control measures are to get rid of the infested material and apply a residual insecticide to the adjacent shelf areas.

Fleas are usually associated with dogs or cats. Control necessitates treatment of both the infested area and the pet.

The housefly breeds in decaying wastes and is a proved transmitter of disease. Control measures are sanitation to eliminate breeding media, screening to prevent entry, and regular use of space sprays, supplemented by residual applications or baits.

Mosquito-breeding is associated with accumulations of water, which may be as small as in a tin can in the back yard, or as large as a marsh or swamp area. Basic control involves elimination of breeding areas, but this may require municipal action. Screens to prevent entry and space sprays for elimination in the home are effective. Repellents for application on skin or clothes will give outdoor protection.

Subterranean termites may invade homes from colonies in the soil. Good construction will do much to prevent their entry, but treatment of the soil with a toxicant will give more positive protection and is the most commonly used corrective treatment.

Arachnids. Spiders may be annoying but usually are considered beneficial. Two species, the black widow and the brown spider, may inflict highly poisonous bites. The brown dog tick may infest a home in large numbers. Mites may invade from birds or rodents living in or near the home. Scorpions are common in the Southwest.

Rodents. The Norway rat finds food, water, and shelter in many home environments. Control is by sanitation to remove these. They may be blocked out by screens and rat-proofed doors, and are killed by trapping or by baits.

The house mouse commonly associates himself with man. He normally lives in a restricted area of about a 10-ft. radius. He must have food, but can get along well without water. The most common control method is by trapping. Exterminators may use baits or residual rodenticidal dusts.

Wildlife Pests. The wildlife pests require rather special control techniques. Repellents are used to drive them out of or keep them off a home. Their re-entry may be blocked mechanically. They may be trapped and removed to distant areas.

RALPH E. HEAL, Executive Secretary, National Pest Control Association

EXTRACT FLAVORINGS, food concentrates used separately or in combination to season foods. Obtained from the leaves, fruit, nuts, stems, roots, or flowers of plants and from animal tissue, these flavoring agents are available in liquid, cube, or granular form. Liquid plant extracts such as vanilla, lemon, and almond are commonly used in dessert recipes; while animal (beef or poultry) extracts give added flavor to soups, gravies, and stews. Liquid beef extract also lends a rich, smooth color to combination meat dishes and gravies.

Also available on the market is a large variety of synthetic, or artificial, flavorings. Many of these are adequate substitutes. However, the consumer should always read the label on the container to identify the source of the extract's ingredients.

EXTRACTION, in chemistry, a process of shaking together two layers of liquid to cause a solute originally dissolved in one layer to distribute itself into both layers. By separating the layers and repeating the shaking with fresh batches of the second solvent, the solute is gradually removed from the original solution. If two substances are present in a solution, they can often be separated by an extraction solvent selected so that only one of the two dissolves in it. The process is important in organic chemistry and is used in a variety of ways. Components of solid mixtures can also be extracted by use of the proper liquid solvent. Extraction also describes the process of physically pressing liquids out of solids, with or without heat as in the production of oils from seeds.

EXTRADITION, in international law, the surrender of a criminal or an alleged criminal by one country on whose territory he is found, to another on whose territory he has been convicted or accused of a criminal offense. There is no obligation incumbent upon nations to extradite under customary international law. Most states, however, are involved in binding treaty networks to extradite criminals for specified crimes. In principle, the treaties exclude political criminals from extradition. Among authorities, a difference of opinion exists regarding what should be considered a "political crime," particularly when it is mixed with acts in violation of penal law, such as murder and arson. Extradition treaties also stipulate that extradition must be requested with such evidence as constitutes a prima facie case against the accused, and that the accused may not be tried for crimes other than the one for which he was extradited or for those which are listed in the treaty.

THOMAS CHENG, Florida Normal and Industrial
Memorial College

Extradition In The United States

Extradition, in the United States, involves the surrender of an individual accused of crime by one state to another state competent to try or punish him. The Federal Constitution provides that any person charged with crime who shall "flee from justice, and be found in another State, shall on demand of the executive authority of the State from which he fled, be delivered up, to be removed to the State having jurisdiction of the crime." (Art. 4, sec. 2). Congress has passed a statute providing for a removal procedure. The duty to surrender fugitives under the federal statute is, however, a moral duty only. In *Kentucky* v. *Dennison* (1861), the Supreme Court held that the federal government had no power "to impose on a State officer, as such, any duty whatever and compel him to perform it."

The states of the United States have themselves passed laws setting up extradition procedures which make the task of extradition easier than it is under the federal statute. They authorize the surrender of a person even though he has not fled from, or was not physically present in the demanding state at the time of the offense. Thus, it would be possible to extradite an accused to a state in which he had caused a criminal act to take place, but into which he had not actually gone.

Federal law makes it a crime to go from one state to another to avoid prosecution for certain crimes. If a state police officer, in violation of law, crosses a state boundary and forces an accused to return with him, the power of the state to try him is not affected. Many states have authorized the peace officers of neighboring states to follow suspects across the state line while in "hot pursuit" and to make legal arrests in the state to which the suspect has fled.

MONRAD C. PAULSEN,
Columbia University School of Law

See also ASYLUM.

EXTRAPOLATION [ĕks-trăp-ə-lā-shən], in mathematics, the process of finding from known terms of a sequence other terms outside the range of the given sequence. The methods used are similar to those used in interpolation. If, for example, observed data are plotted and an equation for the resultant curve obtained, new terms can be obtained by substituting values in the equation. There is a greater chance for large errors to occur in extrapolation than in interpolation.
See also INTERPOLATION.

EXTRASENSORY PERCEPTION (ESP). *See* PARAPSYCHOLOGY.

EXTRATERRESTRIAL LIFE. *See* LIFE.

EXTRATERRITORIALITY [ĕks-trə-tĕr-ə-tôr-ē-ăl' ə-tē], **OR EXTERRITORIALITY.** The exemption from the operation of local laws accorded to foreigners is called extraterritoriality. It is universally recognized that in consequence of its territorial sovereignty, a nation enjoys exclusive control over all persons and property within its territorial limits. To this general principle there are, however, a number of exceptions where certain foreign nationals or foreign property must be treated as if they were not within the territorial limits of the host state.

Heads of foreign states are not subject to local jurisdiction, fiscal regulations, or any civil proceedings when visiting the host state. Local police or other officials may not enter houses occupied by them without express permission. They, together with their personal suite, enjoy these privileges and immunities even when traveling incognito. Diplomatic representatives also enjoy various privileges and immunities as do the premises on which diplomatic functions are carried out.

The armed forces of a friendly foreign power are, as a whole, not subject to local jurisdiction. However, since World War II, it has been a general practice to subject foreign troops to the criminal jurisdiction of local courts. Exceptions exist where the crimes committed are directed either against the sending state or against another member of the forces or result from any act or omission perpetrated in performance of a legal duty.

The warships of a friendly foreign power in port remain under the exclusive jurisdiction of that power. However, this exemption from local jurisdiction does not justify unlimited freedom of action. The ships are expected to comply voluntarily with all regulations relating to such matters as customs and sanitation. Failure to comply or the commission of an act of violence may lead to their expulsion or restraint by force.

By special treaties, known as capitulations (q.v.), several European powers and the United States obtained from Turkey, China, and other Asian and African countries the right to exercise civil and criminal jurisdiction over their nationals in the territories of the host states. This practice began in the early 16th century when the Ottoman rulers granted the French Kings the right to exercise jurisdiction over Frenchmen in the territory of the Ottoman Empire. Most of these treaties are now abrogated.

THOMAS CHENG, Florida Normal and Industrial Memorial College

EXTREME UNCTION (Lat. *unctio extrema*, "last anointing"), in the Roman Catholic and Eastern Orthodox churches the sacrament administered to those so ill as to be in danger of death. Such an anointing is prescribed in the Epistle of St. James (Jas. 5:14–16) as a means of raising up the sick man and freeing him from his sins. In the Roman Catholic Church, the priest administering the sacrament dips his thumb in blessed oil and makes a small sign of the cross on the eyes, ears, nose, lips, hands, and feet of the sick person, saying each time in Latin: "Through this holy anointing and by His most tender mercy may the Lord pardon whatever sins you have committed by your sight (hearing, smelling, taste and speech, and so forth)." Before and after these anointings, appropriate prayers are said for the spiritual and physical health of the suffering person. This sacrament is now called the anointing of the sick.

FREDERICK P. MANION, S.J., Xavier University, Cincinnati

EXTROVERSION or EXTRAVERSION. *See* INTROVERSION-EXTROVERSION.

EXTRUSION, in metallurgy, a process in which a metal is formed into a continuous cross-sectional shape by forcing through a shaped die. The first patent for an extrusion process was granted, in 1797, to Joseph Bramah, in England, who made lead pipe in seamless lengths. The chief use for extrusion, for many years, was the application of lead sheathing to wires. The process has now grown to the point where the die inventory of an extrusion firm may contain several thousand dies and the diversity of shapes is nearly countless.

Essentially, an extrusion press, which may be either horizontal or vertical in construction, is a fairly simple mechanism. The metal to be shaped is usually in the form of a cylindrical billet of varying size, depending on the size of the finished part and the capacity of the machine. Although some soft metals such as lead and tin may be extruded cold, the billets are usually preheated to bring them to a plastic condition. The billet is then placed within an enclosure and a cylindrical ram, activated either mechanically or hydraulically, exerts the pressure

to force the metal through the die. Collapsible tubes, for tooth paste, for example, are made by impact extrusion, a cold process in which a nonferrous slug is placed into a confining die and struck with a punch. The metal flows up around the punch.

Extrusion processes produce complicated shapes which otherwise could be obtained only by costly machining operation, often replace an assembly of components with a single extruded part, replace castings or forgings, and give desirable mechanical properties to the items extruded. In addition to metals, plastics and rubber are extruded into a variety of products.

PAUL B. EATON, Purdue University

EYCK, JAN VAN. *See* VAN EYCK, JAN.

EYE, the organ of vision. The eye is a sphere approximately one inch in diameter. It consists essentially of a transparent front portion which bends, transmits, and focuses light onto a light-sensitive layer in the rear (the retina). The optic nerve conducts impulses from the retina to the visual portion of the brain where the work of perception is completed.

The Structure of the Eye

The Outer Layers. The outermost layer, or fibrous tunic, forms the sclera, or "white of the eye." It is opaque throughout its extent, save for a circular transparent section in front (the cornea).

THE OUTER LAYERS OF THE EYE

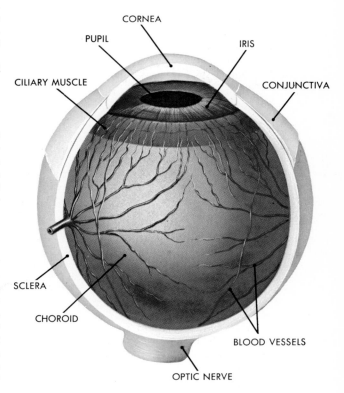

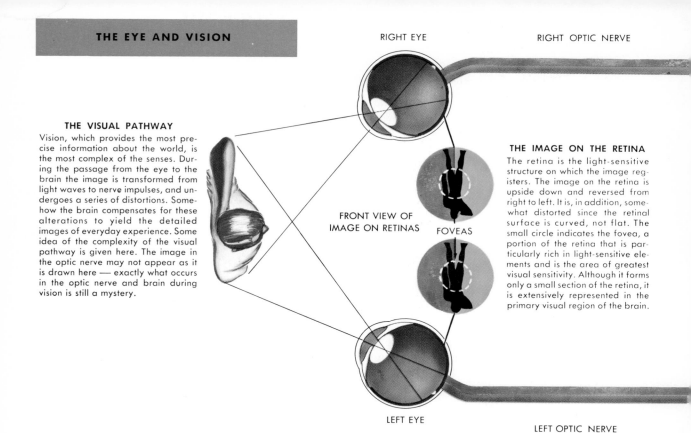

RIGHT EYE

RIGHT OPTIC NERVE

THE VISUAL PATHWAY

Vision, which provides the most precise information about the world, is the most complex of the senses. During the passage from the eye to the brain the image is transformed from light waves to nerve impulses, and undergoes a series of distortions. Somehow the brain compensates for these alterations to yield the detailed images of everyday experience. Some idea of the complexity of the visual pathway is given here. The image in the optic nerve may not appear as it is drawn here — exactly what occurs in the optic nerve and brain during vision is still a mystery.

FRONT VIEW OF
IMAGE ON RETINAS

FOVEAS

THE IMAGE ON THE RETINA

The retina is the light-sensitive structure on which the image registers. The image on the retina is upside down and reversed from right to left. It is, in addition, somewhat distorted since the retinal surface is curved, not flat. The small circle indicates the fovea, a portion of the retina that is particularly rich in light-sensitive elements and is the area of greatest visual sensitivity. Although it forms only a small section of the retina, it is extensively represented in the primary visual region of the brain.

LEFT EYE

LEFT OPTIC NERVE

SOME DETAILS OF EYE STRUCTURE

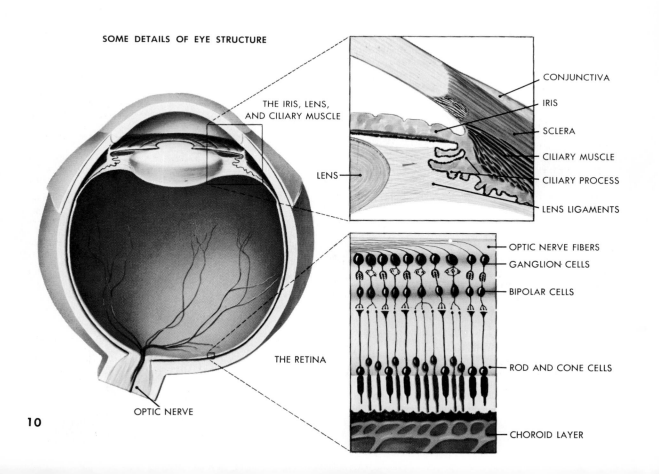

THE IRIS, LENS,
AND CILIARY MUSCLE

LENS

CONJUNCTIVA

IRIS

SCLERA

CILIARY MUSCLE

CILIARY PROCESS

LENS LIGAMENTS

OPTIC NERVE FIBERS

GANGLION CELLS

BIPOLAR CELLS

ROD AND CONE CELLS

THE RETINA

CHOROID LAYER

OPTIC NERVE

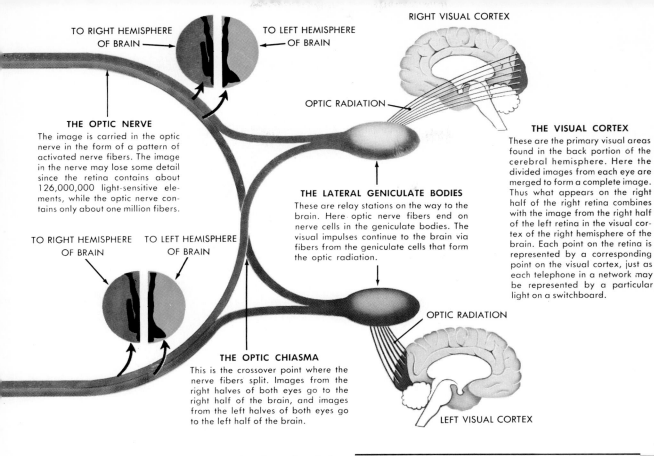

TO RIGHT HEMISPHERE OF BRAIN ← → **TO LEFT HEMISPHERE OF BRAIN**

RIGHT VISUAL CORTEX

OPTIC RADIATION

THE OPTIC NERVE

The image is carried in the optic nerve in the form of a pattern of activated nerve fibers. The image in the nerve may lose some detail since the retina contains about 126,000,000 light-sensitive elements, while the optic nerve contains only about one million fibers.

THE VISUAL CORTEX

These are the primary visual areas found in the back portion of the cerebral hemisphere. Here the divided images from each eye are merged to form a complete image. Thus what appears on the right half of the right retina combines with the image from the right half of the left retina in the visual cortex of the right hemisphere of the brain. Each point on the retina is represented by a corresponding point on the visual cortex, just as each telephone in a network may be represented by a particular light on a switchboard.

TO RIGHT HEMISPHERE OF BRAIN — **TO LEFT HEMISPHERE OF BRAIN**

THE LATERAL GENICULATE BODIES

These are relay stations on the way to the brain. Here optic nerve fibers end on nerve cells in the geniculate bodies. The visual impulses continue to the brain via fibers from the geniculate cells that form the optic radiation.

OPTIC RADIATION

THE OPTIC CHIASMA

This is the crossover point where the nerve fibers split. Images from the right halves of both eyes go to the right half of the brain, and images from the left halves of both eyes go to the left half of the brain.

LEFT VISUAL CORTEX

Underneath the fibrous tunic is the choroid, a dark-brown layer, richly supplied with blood vessels. In the back of the eye, this pigmented tissue acts like the layer of black paint inside a camera, which absorbs excess light and prevents internal reflections.

The Iris and Pupil. The iris, or colored part of the eye, is a circular curtain with a hole in its middle (the pupil). Blue eyes receive their color from two layers of pigmented cells in the rear of the iris. In brown eyes the front layers of the iris are also pigmented. The pupil acts as a light-adjusting mechanism, opening wide under conditions of low illumination, and contracting in bright daylight.

The Lens and the Ciliary Muscle. The lens lies directly behind the iris. The surrounding ciliary muscle helps to focus light on the retina by adjusting the shape of the lens.

The Retina. The retina is the light-sensitive membrane in the rear of the eye which corresponds to the film of a camera. It consists basically of three layers of cells: the rods and cones; an intermediate layer of conducting bipolar cells; and the ganglion cells, which conduct nerve impulses along the retina to the optic nerve. From the viewpoint of the approaching light ray, the retina is upside down, since light must pass through the upper layers to reach the light-sensitive rods and cones in the lower layer.

Knowledge of the anatomy of the retina provides interesting insights into the mechanism of vision. If the retina is compared to the film in the camera, the analogy can be extended to note that the quality of the picture obtained depends upon the grain—the number of individual light-sensitive points in the film. The finer the grain, the more

THE EYE AND VISION **STUDY GUIDE**

The topic of vision is related to a range of other subjects. This Study Guide directs the reader to articles in the Encyclopedia on a number of related topics.

Light. The phenomenon of light is treated from the physicist's viewpoint in LIGHT and related articles such as REFLECTION, REFRACTION, and OPTICS. The physical properties of color are dealt with in COLOR as well as in the other entries pertaining to light.

The Eye. The article EYE discusses the functions of the eye, the anatomy of the retina, the optic nerve, and the mechanisms of vision, including day and night vision and depth perception.

The Perception of Objects and of Color. The article EYE introduces such problems as how the size of an object is correctly perceived at varying distances. Further consideration of these problems can be found in SENSATION. BRAIN and NERVOUS SYSTEM provide additional information. Poor vision at night is the subject of NIGHT BLINDNESS. Distorted perception is discussed in OPTICAL ILLUSIONS and MOON ILLUSION.

Physiologists and psychologists have devoted years of effort in an attempt to explain how humans perceive color. COLOR VISION takes up theories of the functions of the cones in color perception. Full-color illustrations accompanying COLOR present theories of color vision. Color blindness is covered in the article on color vision.

Blindness. The article BLINDNESS has two sections, the first being concerned with the causes and treatment of visual defects from a medical viewpoint. The balance of the entry cites figures on the incidence of the problem and then discusses the education and rehabilitation of the blind. Related articles include BRAILLE; EDUCATION: *Education of Exceptional Children;* and HANDICAPPED, REHABILITATION OF THE.

EYE MOVEMENTS AND FOCUSING

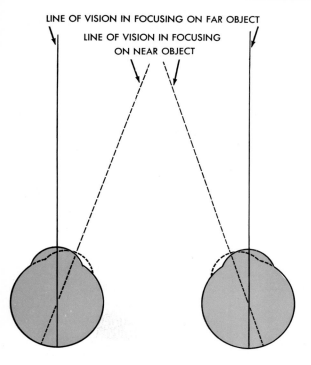

LINE OF VISION IN FOCUSING ON FAR OBJECT

LINE OF VISION IN FOCUSING ON NEAR OBJECT

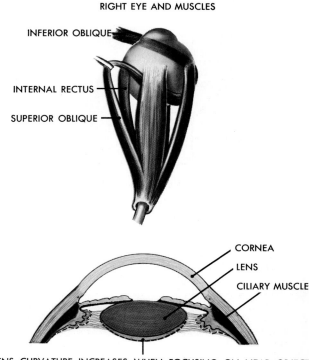

RIGHT EYE AND MUSCLES

INFERIOR OBLIQUE

INTERNAL RECTUS

SUPERIOR OBLIQUE

CORNEA

LENS

CILIARY MUSCLE

LENS CURVATURE INCREASES WHEN FOCUSING ON NEAR OBJECT

detailed the image. The grain of the retina is supplied by approximately 126 million separate light-sensitive elements called rods and cones (about 120 million rods and 6 million cones). This excellent grain is lost, however, since the optic nerve which conducts visual impulses to the brain contains only about one million individual fibers. A further limiting factor is the number of cells (bipolar and ganglion) which link the rods and cones to the optic nerve fibers. In the periphery of the retina many rods must share a single ganglion cell, while in the center, where vision is sharper, more ganglion cells are available.

From the Eye to the Brain

Visual impulses travel from the optic nerve to the occipital portion of the brain.

Prior to reaching the visual cortex half of the fibers cross at the optic chiasma and travel to the opposite side of the brain.

Thus the images are fragmented so that the left side of both visual fields travels to the right side of the brain and the right portion of the fields reaches the left half of the brain.

The Mechanisms of Vision

Directing the Eyes to the Object. The eye is fixed on its target by contractions of the ocular muscles which move the eyeballs.

Focusing is accomplished by the ciliary muscle which alters the shape of the lens.

The Double Function of the Retina—Day and Night Vision. If a person suddenly passes from the sunlit outdoors into a dark room he finds that while at first he can see

FROM THE EYE TO THE BRAIN

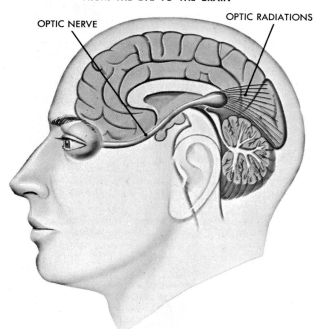

OPTIC NERVE

OPTIC RADIATIONS

nothing, objects gradually become visible over a period of time. If this process of "dark adaptation" is plotted on a graph, a distinct rapid increase in sensitivity is noticeable.

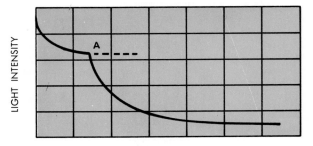

TIME IN DARKNESS

At the point of sudden inflection, the rods, which function more effectively in poor illumination, take over function from the cones, which are active principally under daylight conditions. The rods and the cones differ in other important respects: (1) the rods are found chiefly in the periphery of the retina; (2) rod vision is not as clear as cone vision (that is, side vision is not as sharp as central vision); and (3) rods do not participate in seeing color. The cones are found in greatest concentration in a small patch of the retina called the fovea. Cone vision is sharper, since, as we noted before, the cone section of the retina is more densely supplied with the ganglion cells which generate impulses to the optic nerve. For this reason, when the eye fixes on an object it focuses the image on the fovea for clearest perception. Another difference between the two types of light receptors is their sensitivity to different "kinds" of light. The cones are more sensitive to red, while the rods are more sensitive to blue and green.

The difference in sensitivity becomes evident during dark adaption when function shifts from the cones to the rods. This is known as the Purkinje shift, and accounts for the changes in colors observed when the eye becomes dark-adapted. Among the color changes associated with the shift is the well-known phenomenon in which red flowers appear black at twilight, while blue flowers appear gray or white. Purkinje shift night blindness occurs when the rods do not function properly.

How Light Stimulates the Retina. The remarkable sensitivity of the retina may best be appreciated by considering that the light given off by a single candle would be visible at a distance of one mile, if the intervening air were perfectly transparent. Light acts upon the rods of the retina by bleaching the pigment visual purple, or rhodopsin, which is derived from vitamin A. It is probable that photosensitive pigments are also present in the cones.

Binocular Vision. If one reflects upon the matter it becomes evident that each eye sees a different image.

In some unknown manner these images are fused in the brain to yield a single image. Although it has been suggested that binocular vision gives depth to the image, this cannot exclusively account for three-dimensional perception, since the third dimension does not vanish if the world is seen through one eye. Other factors have

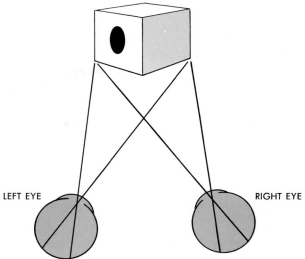

LEFT EYE   RIGHT EYE

BOX AS SEEN BY LEFT EYE   BOX AS SEEN BY RIGHT EYE

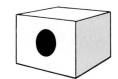 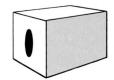

been cited as playing a role in depth perception. These include knowledge of the world acquired through experience, such as the actual size of objects seen at a distance, the apparent change of color of distant objects, and the role of interposition of objects. Physiological factors, such as the differences in muscle sensation developing from focusing on near as opposed to far objects, have also been invoked in explanation of depth perception.

Other Problems in Vision. The eye and the brain manage to see objects as they really are despite great variations in the position and the lighting conditions in which the objects appear. Consider the example of a piece of white paper, which is seen as white when under bright light and when in shadow, although the total quantity of light reaching the eye differs greatly under the two conditions. This is called "brightness constancy" and has been explained as resulting from the constant "ratio" of reflected light between the object and its surroundings. Other "constancies," that is the tendency to see objects in a particular way under a wide variety of conditions, remain largely unexplained. These include "size constancy" (a 6-ft. man appears 6-ft. tall whether seen at a distance of 4 ft. or 40 ft., even though the size of the image on the retina differs greatly in the two cases); and "shape constancy" (a table-top is seen as rectangular from all points of view, although its image on the retina is not always rectangular).

ROBERT S. COLES, M.D.

See also BLINDNESS; CATARACT; COLOR VISION; GLAUCOMA; NIGHT BLINDNESS.

EYE BANK. *See* CORNEAL TRANSPLANT.

EYEBRIGHT, common name for several low-growing, flowering plants of the genus *Euphrasia*, in the Scrophulariaceae, or figwort family. The best-known species is *E. officinalis*, found in the northern parts of Europe, North America, and Asia. Formerly used as a remedy for certain eye diseases, from which it derives its common name, this eyebright grows as a parasite on the roots of grasses, sedges, and other plants. It is usually found in meadows and heaths and bears small white or purplish flowers on leafy spikes.

EYEGLASSES. Although used in China prior to the 13th century, it is not known whether eyeglasses were worn at that time to improve vision or to bring good fortune. Beginning in the 13th century in Europe eyeglasses were worn as an aid to vision. The early lenses were convex and helped older people to see close objects. Concave lenses for the nearsighted probably did not appear until the 16th century. Prismatic lenses, used in cases of cross-eyedness, were developed in the 1850's. Cylindrical, or toric, lenses for the correction of astigmatism did not come into common use until around 1900.

Benjamin Franklin invented the first bifocal lens, which consisted of the top half of one pair of lenses and the lower half of another in the same frame. In this way the upper lens can be used for distance vision and the lower for reading and close work. Trifocal lenses, which incorporate three different lenses, are also available. Eyeglasses can be made to include different principles of correction in the same lens: the lens may be concave to correct nearsightedness, toric, to correct astigmatism, and prismatic, to correct the tendency to cross-eyedness.

MONROE J. HIRSCH, O.D., PH.D.
See also ASTIGMATISM; CONTACT LENSES; FARSIGHTEDNESS; NEARSIGHTEDNESS.

EYRE [âr], **EDWARD JOHN** (1815–1901), British colonial official. A clergyman's son, he immigrated to Australia in 1832 and won a reputation there as an explorer and friend of the aborigines. As a result, he became lieutenant governor of New Zealand in 1846. After holding other posts in the British colonial service, he was appointed commander in chief in Jamaica and four years later Governor. In 1865, when serious disturbances broke out among the Negro population, he approved the imprisonment, flogging, and execution of a large number of people and of the abrogation of the popular constitution. In Britain his actions were either warmly defended or bitterly criticized. Suspended from office, he was praised for his promptitude by a royal commission, but rebuked for his severity. Legal proceedings against him failed in 1867 and 1868. John Stuart Mill was a chief critic, and Thomas Carlyle, John Ruskin, and Alfred Tennyson leading supporters. In 1872 the government reimbursed him for his expenses, pensioning him in 1874.

ASA BRIGGS, University of Leeds

EYRE, LAKE, shallow saline lake of south-central Australia, occupying the lowest part of the Lake Eyre Basin, in the state of South Australia. At an elevation of 39 ft. below sea level, the lake is the focus of an area of interior drainage in the driest part of the Australian continent. Area, 3,700 sq. mi.

EZEKIEL [ĭ-zē′kē-əl], a priest of Jerusalem deported with Jehoiachin to Babylon in 597 B.C., where he was called to a prophetic ministry (593–571 B.C.) among the Jewish exiles. Ezekiel is known only from the book which bears his name. Here he is presented as combining the traditions of priest and prophet—an austere figure subject to abnormal psychological experiences and given to a vigorous and bizarre way of speaking and writing. Our assessment of his personality must depend upon critical analysis of the book of Ezekiel.

EZEKIEL, BOOK OF, third and last of the major prophetic books of the Old Testament, consisting of 48 chapters precisely dated between 593 and 571 B.C. The first half records Ezekiel's call to the prophetic ministry (chaps. 1–3) and his oracles of doom on Jerusalem (4–24). The second half contains prophecies of judgment on foreign nations (25–32), prophecies of the redemption of Israel (33–39), and a detailed "blueprint" of the restored Jerusalem in the coming new age, with its Temple and ordered ministry (40–48). The composition of this work is still a disputed question. Although Ezekiel's entire ministry is placed among the Babylonian exiles, scholars have argued that Jerusalem was the scene of a part, or even the whole, of the prophet's work (4–24). Much of the second half of the book has been ascribed to a Babylonian editor, especially 38–39 and 40–48. The book's characteristic teaching on the majestic holiness of God and the responsibility of the individual is closely related to the critical situation of Israel in the 6th century B.C.

E. W. HEATON, Oxford University

EZRA [ĕz′rə], priest and scribe who obtained a decree from King Artaxerxes I (458 B.C.) to introduce Biblical law as the constitution of the re-established Jewish commonwealth in Palestine. As expounder of the law, he was the first of the scribes, a precursor of rabbinic Judaism. Modern scholarship, beginning with Spinoza, sees his hand in the editing of the Pentateuch.

EZRA, BOOK OF, in the Old Testament, the continuation of the Books of Chronicles, further continued by the Book of Nehemiah. The first six chapters describe the decree of Cyrus, the Persian King, freeing the Jews from their Babylonian captivity, the subsequent return of the exiles to Judah, and the rebuilding of the temple in Jerusalem (c. 516 B.C.). In chapter 4 may be seen the beginning of the conflict with the Samaritans (cf. II Kings 17:24–41; Neh. 4:1–9; 6:1–14; Luke 9:51–53; John 4:9). The last four chapters (7–10) tell the story of Ezra, a priest and scribe, who came from Babylon to Jerusalem during the reign of Artaxerxes, King of Persia, to institute reforms in the Jewish community, especially with regard to improper religious observances and mixed marriages. A problem of dating arises because it is impossible to tell whether Artaxerxes I or II is intended. Some think that the story of Ezra should follow that of Nehemiah.

W. F. STINESPRING, Duke University

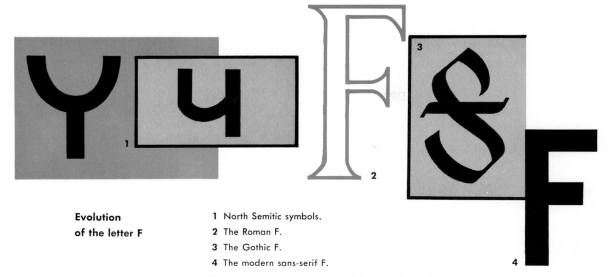

**Evolution
of the letter F**

1 North Semitic symbols.
2 The Roman F.
3 The Gothic F.
4 The modern sans-serif F.

F, sixth letter of the English alphabet. The spelling of the sound is most varied (*philosophy*, *laughter*, *rough*, *lieutenant* in British English, and *affray*) or *f* may be silent (*halfpenny*, pronounced hāp'nĭ). At first it was difficult to write the *f* sound in Latin and actually FH was used in the oldest Latin inscriptions. It was properly a bilabial, not a labiodental spirant. But the *h* symbol was simply dropped, and F came to be used alone, as in the English alphabet.

There is frequent alternation between *f* and *v*, partly a grammatical shift (*loaf* and *loaves*, *theft* and *thieve*), partly dialectal (*fox* and *vixen*). In the Cockney dialect *f* is substituted for *th*, as in the Russian *F*yodor (for *Th*eodore). In *few* and *refute* the modern English pronunciation is *fy*. The word *sheriff* has *f* in place of older *v(e)* as in *reeve*.

Indo-European had no *f*. English *f* in words of Indo-European origin (such as *f*ather and *f*our) always has arisen from some other sound (compare *pater*, *quattuor*).

JOSHUA WHATMOUGH, Harvard University

See also ALPHABET.

FABER [*fā'bər*], **FREDERICK WILLIAM** (1814–63), Roman Catholic priest, spiritual writer, and hymnologist. He left the Anglican ministry, was received into the Catholic Church by Cardinal Newman, and later became an Oratorian priest. He composed many popular Catholic hymns and wrote numerous books on the spiritual life. Among his many extremely popular hymns are *The Land Beyond the Sea* and *Pilgrims of the Night*.

FABERGÉ [*fà-běr-zhā'*], **PETER CARL** (1846–1920), Russian jeweler. As court jeweler to Tsar Alexander III, he made jeweled eggs, which the monarch presented to his Tsarina each Easter morning. These ingenious eggs opened, revealing a tiny peacock, coronation coach, or some other miniature. Fabergé fled Russia in 1918, and at his death was buried at Cannes, France.

FABIAN [*fā'bē-ən*], **ST.,** Pope (236–50). He enlarged and beautified the Cemetery of Calixtus and made repairs in the catacombs of Rome. After a period of peace he guided the church through the fierce persecution under the Emperor Decius in which he was martyred.

FABIAN SOCIETY, a British socialist society taking its name from the Roman general Quintus Fabius Maximus, known as "the Slow-goer" for his tactics against the Carthaginian general Hannibal. It was founded in 1884. The society's first object was the gradual reconstruction of society on socialist lines. It spurned revolutionary methods and placed its trust in propaganda, education, discussion, and permeation of other bodies. Fabian tracts were written on a variety of subjects, many of them concerned with the practical problems of central and local government, and *Fabian Essays* (1889) was a book with great long-term influence. The essayists included George Bernard Shaw, Annie Besant, H. G. Wells, and Sidney and Beatrice Webb. The Webbs were indefatigable Fabians, and played an important part behind the scenes in the development of the British labor movement. The Labour party's 1918 program, *Labour and the Social Order*, was drafted by Sidney Webb and remained the basis of Labour party policy until the general election of 1950. *New Fabian Essays* (1952) reflected new currents in British socialist thinking. Fabian influence, largely nondoctrinaire, was always considerable outside the Labour party and can be traced in Edwardian Britain in particular and in the development of later British social policy. The society still functions as a research institution, but it is no longer considered a major social and political agency.

ASA BRIGGS, University of Sussex

FABIUS MAXIMUS RULLIANUS [*fā'bē-əs măk'sĭ-məs rŭl-ē-ā'nəs*], **QUINTUS** (fl. about 300 B.C.), Roman leader prominent in Rome's struggle to control Italy. He is best known for his defeat of the Samnites, Gauls, and Etruscans at Sentinum in 295. He was consul five times between 322 and 295, and also served as dictator, master of horse, proconsul, censor, and chief of the Senate.

FABIUS MAXIMUS VERRUCOSUS [*věr-ŏŏ-kō'səs*], **QUINTUS** (died 203 B.C.), Roman politician and general. As leader of the conservative faction, he was appointed dictator in 217 B.C. after Hannibal's victory at Lake Trasimene. Recognizing Hannibal's military genius, Fabius avoided a set battle and adopted harassing tactics, hoping to force

15

the Carthaginians to leave Italy for lack of supplies. This policy ("Fabian tactics") earned him both the epithet *cunctator*, the Delayer, and the suspicion of more impatient and aggressive Romans who forced the unusual appointment of a second dictator, Minucius Rufus.

In 216 B.C. the consuls decided to engage Hannibal in formal battle at Cannae and suffered a catastrophic defeat. For the next ten years Fabius' strategy was followed, leading to a stalemate. However, over Fabius' strenuous opposition, the Romans allowed P. Cornelius Scipio (later called Africanus) to lead an invasion of Africa in 204 B.C., designed to draw Hannibal home to defend Carthage. His death in 203 B.C. prevented Fabius from witnessing Hannibal's defeat at Zama in 202 B.C.

GERALD E. KADISH, State University of N.Y. at Binghamton

FABLE, brief narrative, either in prose or verse, conveying a moral through the frankly fictitious but still believable actions of gods, men, animals, or inanimate objects. Fables are usually realistic in the use of details and ironic in their view of human affairs. They often end with an epigrammatic statement of a moral. The characters are most frequently animals, and when this is true the stories are called beast fables. Fables are a common expression of folk wisdom, and constitute a major aspect of folklore.

The fable probably originated in ancient Babylonia or Assyria. The Greek poet Hesiod (fl.8th century B.C.) wrote beast fables. By far the most famous fables, however, are those ascribed to Aesop, a Greek slave living c.600 B.C., whose beast tales were told orally. The first written collection of fables appeared about 300 B.C. Phaedrus and Babrius (both probably lived in the 1st century A.D.) produced verse fables, giving the form its first literary expression. Fables were very popular in the Middle Ages, when they were assembled into long poems known as beast epics, the most famous of which was the *Roman de Renard*, a 12th-century French work dealing with Reynard the Fox. The most famed of English medieval beast epics was Chaucer's "Nun's Priest's Tale" in *The Canterbury Tales*.

The best-known of modern fabulists is La Fontaine, a 17th-century Frenchman. Other important users of the form include John Gay in England, Gotthold Ephraim Lessing in Germany, and Ivan A. Krylov in Russia. Rudyard Kipling's "Jungle Books" (1894–95), Joel Chandler Harris' Uncle Remus stories (1880–1918), George Orwell's *Animal Farm* (1945), and James Thurber's *Fables for Our Time* (1952) represent recent examples of a form which has been a time-honored medium for commenting on the follies of mankind.

C. HUGH HOLMAN, University of North Carolina
See also FAIRY TALES; FOLK TALES.

FABRE [fä′br′], **JEAN HENRI** (1823–1915), French entomologist noted for his accurate observations on the life histories, habits, and instincts of many insects. After a brief teaching career Fabre retired in 1870. His most important work was done after this time. He was an exceptionally careful observer and was particularly interested in bees, ants, beetles, grasshoppers, and spiders. Fabre was unsympathetic to the evolutionary theory. He considered the apparently purposeful acts characteristic of insect be-

havior to be automatic rather than reasoned, and emphasized their difference from the intelligent behavior of man in support of his anti-evolutionary beliefs. Among his many published works were *Social Life in the Insect World* (1912), *The Life of the Fly* (1913), and *Bumble Bees* (1915).

FABREVILLE, residential town of Quebec, Canada, on Jesus Island (Île Jésus), about 12 mi. northwest of downtown Montreal. Inc., 1957; pop., 5,213.

FABRICIUS [fä-brē′tsē-ŏŏs], **JOHANNES** (1587–1615), German astronomer and physician who discovered that the sun rotates on its axis. In 1610, while a medical student in Wittenberg, he discovered sunspots at about the same time that Galileo discovered them. Fabricius noted that sunspots move, and he concluded that the movement was caused by the sun's rotation. He was the son of David Fabricius, also an astronomer.

FABRICIUS HILDANUS [fə-brĭsh′əs hĭl-dā′nəs], also known as Wilhelm Fabry of Hilden (1560–1634), German physician, called "the father of German surgery." Among his numerous contributions were the first classification of burns, the introduction of the tourniquet into surgical practice, and the use of a magnet to extract iron splinters from the eye.

FABRICIUS LUSCINUS [lŏŏ-sī′nəs], **GAIUS,** Roman statesman and soldier. While consul in 282 and 278 B.C. he won important battles over the Bruttians, Lucanians, Samnites, and Tarentines. In negotiating with Pyrrhus of Epirus during the war with Tarentum he refused a bribe, and likewise reported to Pyrrhus the offer of a traitor to kill him. He was distinguished for his stern simplicity and moral probity and served as an exemplar of old Roman virtue.

FACIES [fā′shēz], in geology, the appearance or aspect of sedimentary deposits, based upon such features as stratification, grain size, mineral composition, and contained fossils. Usually the term is applied to areally segregated parts of a single sedimentary unit when its various parts were deposited under different environmental conditions. Correlating various facies in terms of geologic time is a basic concern of stratigraphy.
See also GEOLOGY.

FACTOR, one of several constants or variables, multiplied together to give a product. For example, since $12 = 1 \times 12 = 2 \times 6 = 3 \times 4$, the positive integral factors of 12 are 1, 2, 3, 4, 6, and 12. Every natural number has as factors itself and 1. If it has no other factors, it is a prime number. Factoring, that is, breaking up a product into its component factors, is used in algebra to transform polynomials and rational expressions into equivalent ones; for example, $a^2 - b^2 = (a + b)(a - b)$ and $4x^3 - 10x^2 = 2x^2(2x - 5)$.

FACTORY, a building or group of buildings equipped with tools and machinery for the manufacture of one or more products. The term is also used in a broader sense to include the organization of the people (labor and manage-

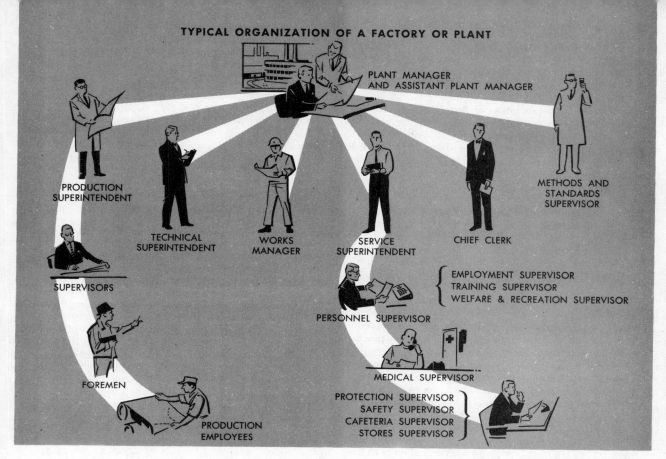

TYPICAL ORGANIZATION OF A FACTORY OR PLANT

PLANT MANAGER
AND ASSISTANT PLANT MANAGER

PRODUCTION
SUPERINTENDENT

TECHNICAL
SUPERINTENDENT

WORKS
MANAGER

SERVICE
SUPERINTENDENT

CHIEF CLERK

METHODS AND
STANDARDS
SUPERVISOR

SUPERVISORS

FOREMEN

PRODUCTION
EMPLOYEES

PERSONNEL SUPERVISOR

EMPLOYMENT SUPERVISOR
TRAINING SUPERVISOR
WELFARE & RECREATION SUPERVISOR

MEDICAL SUPERVISOR

PROTECTION SUPERVISOR
SAFETY SUPERVISOR
CAFETERIA SUPERVISOR
STORES SUPERVISOR

ment) engaged in producing and marketing the goods manufactured. The success of the enterprise depends largely upon the skill of its management.

Evolution of the Factory. The evolution of the factory system has been natural. It is easy to envision people on the frontiers of civilization, even today, producing only for their family needs. As they created excess goods and had desires for other goods produced by neighbors near and far, they found means of satisfying their wants by barter. It was only another step before money was used as the medium of exchange, and people discovered the advantages of specializing in some type of production or the distribution of goods. In the next phase a merchant with a sufficient accumulation of capital would buy raw materials which he would distribute to some workers in their homes for conversion into finished goods to be sold in turn by the merchant.

With the advent of heavy machinery, it became necessary for the workers to gather in one central location to do their work. This gave birth to our modern concept of the factory. The factory movement began before the turn of the 19th century, in the period of the industrial revolution, a quickening of events which included important inventions for the production of power and its use, especially in the textile industry, plus agricultural improvements in animal breeding and the utilization of land.

The depressing early factories with their dirt floors, small windows, dangerous machines, contaminated air, and general unsanitary conditions have been described in literature of the past. But factories have gone through an evolution of improvement. Today's modern factory is fre-

quently constructed in the pleasant surroundings of a rural area and every consideration is given to making it a good neighbor in its community. The building itself is frequently a single story structure of modern design, with ample natural and artificial light. It is not uncommon to find part or even all of a factory air-conditioned. Employee welfare is taken into consideration in the antiseptically clean cafeterias, recreation programs, and sometimes piped-in music to reduce the monotony of the working hours.

The factory movement, which was born in England and on the Continent, was soon adopted by the struggling colonies of North America and it was there that some of the greatest improvements in factory operations and production were made. Eli Whitney made an unusually important contribution with his innovation of interchangeable parts for easy assembly. Later, Henry Ford contributed the idea of transporting materials past the workers in his efforts to perfect the assembly line. Hundreds of improvements in factory management were made. Foremost among these were the time-and-motion studies of Frederick W. Taylor, who developed scientific management to increase production efficiency.

Today's factory organizations have felt the impact of automated machinery. Computers and better methods of data processing are also causing widespread changes in the operation of factories through improved scheduling and forecasting of production. This means that the laborer is taking a subordinate position, and the emphasis is upon the highly skilled technician who can maintain the computer and manipulate it to his will. This is an indication of the direction in which factory management is moving. The inevitable result will be a change in factory operations as we know them.

A Working Organization of People. The goods produced in factories are extremely varied, ranging from farm equipment to pharmaceutical products and from pipes to pipe organs. Because of this, it would seem improbable to expect any common characteristics among different factories. Yet some exist, based on worker organization.

The typical factory structure can be compared to a pyramid—the production employees forming a broad base and the manager at the apex. Small groups of employees work under the direction of supervisors or foremen; their areas of authority are referred to as departments.

Level of Authority. The supervisor or foreman is responsible to a higher authority, such as the superintendent who also is responsible to still another higher authority, and so on, until the most central authority is reached.

The entire organization, working within this framework of authority, can be divided into two groups: staff and line. Line organization is concerned directly with production, and the staff acts in an advisory capacity. In practice, the distinction between line and staff is difficult to draw because of overlapping duties caused by one person having two superiors—one on staff and one on line.

Staff. Staff departments lace the factory with networks of formal and informal systems of communication to plan, direct, and control production. There may be a staff group for developing and maintaining work schedules in line with production goals. Planning groups formulate budgets, which are later compared with actual costs to keep production in line with planned expenditures. Other staff activities may include store, shipping, tool design, maintenance, and time-and-motion study departments within a factory. There are also departments for sales, finance, purchasing, and product design, which must be consulted on production policy matters. In factories where employees are represented by a union, there is a provision for settling labor grievances and disputes with management.

An Organization of Machines. Machines will naturally vary with the nature of the manufacturing process. But regardless of what they are for, all factory machines are grouped in two general classes. The first, called a "job shop," is organized for a specific type of work; the second, based on the sequence of steps required in production, is called either a "production line" or a "continuous production shop." Factories often employ a combination of these.

The reasons for grouping machinery in these two ways vary. It may be for placing heavy machinery where the floor is sufficiently strong to withstand the weight, or to isolate some operations because of heat, noise, or fumes. Production processes for beer, cheese, and some chemicals operate satisfactorily only as continuous batch processes. Probably the most important reason for using a production line is the fact that the process will run for a long time before any radical changes are made. Placing the equipment in sequence minimizes the cost of materials handling, and saves time that can result in inventory savings on materials in process.

The job shop is more versatile and is equipped with machinery capable of working on different types of production jobs. On the other hand, more instruction is re-quired for the operators since they may be doing different tasks from day to day, and the machines must be scheduled to use them efficiently.

In the job shop where a variety of products are produced, the machinery that can be adapted to a variety of tasks is used, whereas in a production line, more special purpose machines can be found. Although the initial cost of the special purpose machine might be great, its greater production speed will mean a lower cost per unit.

JAMES H. GREENE, Purdue University
See also INDUSTRIAL ENGINEERING; MASS PRODUCTION; STANDARDIZATION; TIME AND MOTION STUDY.

FACTORY SYSTEM. Before the industrial revolution goods were manufactured by people working in their own homes. Following such inventions as the spinning jenny, the power loom, and the steam engine, technology improved and a new system of production became possible. Businessmen with capital (or entrepreneurs) began to build factories in which goods could be produced more rapidly and in larger quantities than in the homes of individual workers. In England and Scotland during the late 18th and the 19th centuries, the textile, leather-tanning, and other manufacturing and finishing industries began to abandon the domestic system and to consolidate operations in centralized locations, in one or a group of buildings devoted exclusively to work. The buildings and the equipment in them were owned and supervised directly by the entrepreneurs. This was the actual factory. The "system" that it nurtured and that in turn fed it was vastly more complex. It changed the whole economic and social structure of Great Britain and other nations.

Although a phenomenon of industrial life all over Europe, the system got its real start in England and Scotland, and the social legislation regulating it also began there. The early operation of the system is almost universally condemned as abusive, exploitive, and dehumanizing—which indeed it was—but it is less often examined in its proper historical setting, its relation to the technology itself, or with regard to those traits of modern industrial life which are its direct descendants.

By 1725 rudimentary steam engines were already in use; but these, like the Newcomen engine introduced in that year, were pumping engines used primarily to raise water. As yet no one had devised a means of making them impart rotary motion to the wheels and gears of other machines. Moreover, these engines were so inefficient that they were used only where large deposits of coal were at hand. Even in the 1780's the primary sources of power were water, wind, and draft animals; and the small machines of craftsmen were either foot-treadle operated or turned by an assistant. The early factories were bound to either natural falls or artificially dammed water. The early textile mills, including those using Richard Arkwright's water frame for cotton spinning, were scattered widely over the countryside, often in remote areas like the Scottish Highlands. Most factories were small simply because the water supply was small and uncertain. In an age of rudimentary transportation and poor roads, problems of labor supply and product distribution were aggravated by the lack of engineering accomplishment.

Great technological changes began with the designing

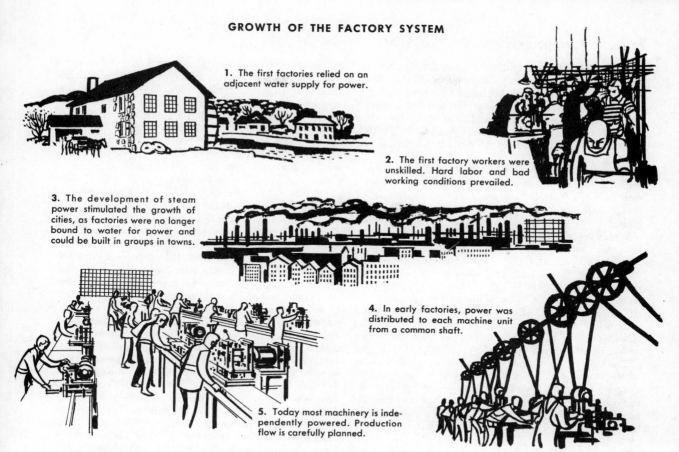

1. The first factories relied on an adjacent water supply for power.

2. The first factory workers were unskilled. Hard labor and bad working conditions prevailed.

3. The development of steam power stimulated the growth of cities, as factories were no longer bound to water for power and could be built in groups in towns.

4. In early factories, power was distributed to each machine unit from a common shaft.

5. Today most machinery is independently powered. Production flow is carefully planned.

by James Watt and others of steam engines that could translate piston motion into rotary motion, and whose speed could be regulated for uniform production. These improvements freed factories from geographical restrictions, and this in turn had a major effect on the growth of towns and cities. Factories were now built in towns, which were reservoirs of cheap labor, and the towns in turn swelled with newcomers seeking employment. Towns were also a ready market for factory products and were transportation hubs. Urbanization and industrialization are separate socio-economic phenomena, but almost universal concurrence began with the factory system.

The steam engine also determined the very shape and structure of factory buildings themselves; and this in turn lent itself to the inhumanly cruel working conditions. Early machines were driven from a single long shaft, called a line shaft, from which belts transmitted power to the machines. Machines were strung out in straight lines under these shafts, and as close together as possible. This arrangement combined with other ideas to suggest workflow arrangements, and also revealed the advantages of assigning men and machines to repetitive tasks that required a minimum of machine adjustment and worker training. Today, virtually all new machines are individually motorized, but there are still many small factories using old equipment operating from electrically driven line shafts and which are laid out like the factories of old.

The nature of the factory system was also influenced by the financial problems of early entrepreneurship. Markets were unstable, there was acute competition among manufacturers, and lack of transportation limited distribution.

Most important of all, prior to about 1850 the only major source of capital for expansion was profits. Under the aforementioned circumstances, the accumulation of profits was difficult, and so wages and expenditures for improving working conditions were regarded by the factory owners as major drains. By about 1850 the joint-stock company became popular as a means of raising funds; but by this time the pattern of employer-employee relations had already been firmly established. "Industrial relations," in the broad and complicated sense in which we apply the term today, began to be a problem at that time.

Another aspect of the system was the nature of the work force. Machine-operating skills could be taught—the serious fault, from the employers' point of view, was that it was an "undisciplined" labor force. At worst, factory hands were former farmers or herdsmen; at best they were still bound by tradition to the rigorous but "flexible" routines of rural life. Regular working hours, at a steady pace and with no respite and no variation, were the antitheses of all past work experience. Under the unremitting pressure to regard time as money and to waste nothing, absenteeism was rampant, labor turnover was high, resentment was passionate, and sabotage not infrequent. Workers were fined and even discharged for the slightest infraction of rules. With the religious rationalization that idleness was a vice and industriousness a virtue, workers were often locked in hot, airless, flammable factories from dawn to dusk, forbidden to "waste time" even to drink water or attend to natural functions.

In England, the first factory acts and other social reform legislation were directed against the employment of women and children, and unsanitary and dangerous working conditions. Factory acts were passed in 1833 and 1844, and in 1847 the Ten Hours Act limited the working hours for women and children. However, this legislation applied only to the textile industries, and enforcement was lax. Real reforms followed the Reform Act of 1867, which gave the vote to a broad segment of the English urban working class.

Yet it must be recognized that the conditions in the factories, and in the sea of urban slums surrounding them, were only concentrated and more obvious expressions of the general values of the day and of the level of technological development. Sanitation and ventilation did not suddenly become human problems for the first time with the rise of modern industry. The labor of children and women had been an integral part of peasant life and of the domestic system. Early critics romanticized the happy peasant, and depicted the guild shop as not unlike the workplace of Santa's Helpers. But pastoral poverty was still poverty, feudal justice was capricious, and the guild system had its own oppressions. Despite its numerous other assaults on bodily and spiritual integrity, the factory system raised the consumption level of most of the people.

The evils of the system have been the subject of many novels, stories, and essays. Charles Dickens, George Eliot, Benjamin Disraeli, Elizabeth Gaskell, Charles Kingsley, and others were the "industrial novelists" of the Victorian era. Critics of the 20th-century aspects of industrialization include D. H. Lawrence, Upton Sinclair, and Harvey Swados.

Consult Bendix, Reinhard, *Work and Authority in Industry* (1956).

SAMUEL E. GLUCK, City University of New York
See also AGRARIAN REVOLUTION; DOMESTIC SYSTEM; ENCLOSURE MOVEMENTS; FACTORY; INDUSTRIAL REVOLUTION.

FACULTY PSYCHOLOGY, the point of view that the mind is an aggregate of specific powers, such as memory, will power, judgment, and imagination. Such a view is frequently implied by laymen in their use of these and similar words: "He has imagination but no will power." In scientific psychology such terminology is considered a form of "word magic" which lacks explanatory usefulness. To say that some behavior illustrates a person's good memory does not explain the behavior, but only calls it by a different name and adds nothing to the original observation. Memory does not seem to be a single factor, for while a person may long remember some things he may have considerable difficulty remembering other things.

Phrenology, a pseudoscience that attained popularity in the 19th century, represented the most elaborate form of faculty psychology. Phrenologists made charts of the head showing areas believed to control faculties and traits. Subsequent advances in knowledge about the structure and function of the brain have rendered such theories untenable.

LAWRENCE R. BOULTER, University of Illinois

FADIMAN [făd′ə-mən], **CLIFTON** (1904–), American essayist and radio and television performer, born in Brooklyn, N.Y. He was an editor (1929–35) for Simon and Schuster, book publishers, and book editor (1933–43) of *The New Yorker.* He was master of ceremonies of the radio show Information Please from 1938 to 1948 and subsequently appeared on similar radio and television programs. He edited *The American Treasury* (1955) and wrote *Party of One* (1955) and *Enter, Conversing* (1962).

FAERIE QUEENE, THE, English allegorical poetic romance written by Edmund Spenser to celebrate the reign of Elizabeth I and to teach men the way to true glory and human perfection. The literal narrative consists of a series of knightly adventures in the manner of medieval tales of chivalry. Each legend of this complex political and moral allegory is intended to portray a specific virtue in action. Of the 12 cantos Spenser projected for his widely influential poem, he had completed at the time of his death in 1599 only the first 6 (containing the legends of holiness, temperance, chastity, friendship, justice, and courtesy), plus a fragment of the seventh.

FAEROE [fâr′ō] **ISLANDS,** group of volcanic basalt islands in the north Atlantic Ocean, situated between Iceland and the Shetland Islands. They are a self-governing community within the kingdom of Denmark. There are 18 inhabited islands, including Streymoy, Eysturoy, Vágar, Suduroy, Sandoy, and Bordoy. The capital is Thorshavn on Streymoy. The economy is based upon fishing; frozen and dried cod and cod-liver oil are exported. There are small home industries such as spinning and knitting, but agriculture is of minor importance. The official language is Faeroese, which resembles Icelandic and Norwegian.

FAFNIR, brother of Regin and Oter. He transformed himself into a dragon and was slain by Sigurd according to a tale in the *Volsunga Saga* (q.v.).

FAGIN [fā′gĭn], teacher of young thieves in Charles Dickens' *Oliver Twist.* His pursuit of young Oliver gives the book its moral suspense.

FAHRENHEIT [fä′rən-hīt], **GABRIEL DANIEL** (1686–1736), German physicist and instrument maker, originator of the Fahrenheit temperature scale. Born in Danzig, Fahrenheit settled in Amsterdam, where he constructed meteorological instruments. Though not the first to suggest it, he introduced the substitution of mercury for alcohol in the thermometer tube and devised his thermometric scale with two fixed reference points: the freezing point of water, 32°, and normal, human body temperature, 96° (actually 98.6°). Fahrenheit was elected to the Royal Society in 1724 and contributed papers to its *Philosophical Transactions.*
See also FAHRENHEIT SCALE; THERMOMETER.

FAHRENHEIT [fär′ən-hīt] **SCALE,** temperature scale named after Gabriel Fahrenheit, of Danzig and Amsterdam, who devised a mercury thermometer in 1714. In this scale the freezing point of water is taken as 32° and the boiling point as 212°. Thus the two points are separated by 180 Fahrenheit degrees. Absolute zero is at about $-459.6°$ F.

The Fahrenheit scale is commonly used in the United States and Great Britain for expressing meteorological temperatures. Conversion to the Centigrade scale may be performed by the formula $T°_C = (5/9)(T°_F - 32)$. For example, $86°$ F. $= (5/9)(86 - 32) = (5/9)(54) = 30$ C. *See also* CENTIGRADE SCALE; HEAT; TEMPERATURE.

FA-HSIEN [*fä'shē-ĕn'*] **or FA-HIEN,** (c.340 A.D.–?), Chinese Buddhist monk and writer. Born in Shanshi Province, he entered a Buddhist monastery while still a child. After his ordination, he lived as a monk until 399, when he left China and traveled to India. Arriving there in 402, he visited the traditional holy places, spent three years in Pataliputra learning Sanskrit, went to Ceylon for two years, and returned to Nanking by way of Java c.413. Greatly interested in *Vinaya*, or Discipline, he brought back the rules of two sects: the Mahasanghika, which he translated, and the Sarvastivadin. His *Record of Buddhist Countries*, written in 415, became a favorite classic of the Far Eastern Buddhist communities.

FAÏENCE [*fä-ĕns', fä-äns'*], any earthenware covered with a tin glaze, that is, a lead glaze made white and opaque by the addition of tin oxide. True examples of faïence are the early majolica made at various Italian cities, including Faenza, from which the term is derived. Others are the English and Dutch earthenwares and those with decorated white or colored grounds made at various places in France, such as Rouen, Nevers, and Marseille. The term is sometimes misapplied to white-bodied wares.

FAINTING or SYNCOPE, impairment of consciousness, accompanied by muscle weakness and an inability to stand upright. It is a condition of abrupt onset and brief duration. At the beginning of a fainting attack, the person has a sensation of giddiness. He has spots before his eyes, his vision dims, and his ears ring. His face becomes ashen and he may feel nauseated. The depth and duration of unconsciousness varies. Sometimes the person can hear the voices around him and see blurred images. In other cases there is a total inability to respond. The pulse is thin, blood pressure low, and breathing almost imperceptible. Upon regaining consciousness, if he arises too soon, another faint may occur. Often headaches, drowsiness, and mental confusion follow an attack.

The most common cause of fainting is a reflex action which opens the blood vessels in the trunk and legs. Blood collects in these dilated vessels, and the supply to the brain becomes insufficient. Pain, anxiety, excessive hunger, or a sudden shock can trigger this reflex. More serious forms of fainting are caused by changes in the heart and pulse rate, in blood pressure, or with bleeding and severe anemia. Fainting is effectively treated by lying flat with the head below the level of the rest of the body and the feet elevated.

E. CARWILE LEROY, M.D.

FAIR, JAMES GRAHAM (1831–94), American financier born in Belfast, Ireland. Fair emigrated to the United States when he was 12 years old, and while he was still in his teens joined the California gold rush in 1849. Later he was active in Nevada mining. With his associates, including John W. Mackay, he organized the Bank of Nevada in an attempt to wrest control of Nevada mining operations

from San Francisco bankers. When Fair and his partners hit the gold and silver pocket of the Consolidated Virginia Mine, they started feeding silver bullion into the American market so fast that coinage of silver became a national monetary and political issue. Between 1873 and 1879 the Consolidated Virginia owners realized more than $100,000,000 from their holdings. By the time the mine played out, Fair had invested his profits so judiciously that he escaped unhurt. In 1881 he was elected from Nevada as a Democrat to the U.S. Senate and served one term.

JOE B. FRANTZ, University of Texas

FAIRBANKS, CHARLES WARREN (1852–1918), American lawyer and politician. Fairbanks, born in Union County, Ohio, rose from poverty to establish himself as the foremost railroad attorney in Indiana. The work took him naturally into politics. By 1896, with control of the state's Republican party, he abandoned business to take (1897–1905) a seat in the U.S. Senate. Fairbanks became very close to President William McKinley, and after McKinley's death he represented Republican conservatives in the Senate and as Vice President, in the second administration (1905–9) of President Theodore Roosevelt. Thereafter Fairbanks continued active in politics both in Indiana and nationally. He was the unsuccessful Republican candidate for Vice President in 1916.

FAIRBANKS, DOUGLAS (1883–1939), American actor, born in Denver. He was among the first well-known stage actors to gain fame in films, which he entered in 1914. His early screen roles were in comedies, but his fame was achieved as the athletic, swashbuckling hero of costume romances, including *The Three Musketeers* (1921), *Robin Hood* (1922), *The Thief of Bagdad* (1924), and *The Gaucho* (1927). He was one of the founders of the producing firm United Artists in 1923. His son, **DOUGLAS (ELTON) FAIRBANKS, JR.** (1909–), also was a prominent screen actor.

FAIRBANKS, second-largest city of Alaska, located near the geographical center of the state, 400 mi. north of the Gulf of Alaska, 175 mi. south of the Arctic Circle. The city is located on the banks of the Chena River, near its junction with the Tanana River, and serves as an agricultural market for products from the Tanana River valley. Fairbanks is a mining center for gold and other minerals, and is also the northern terminus of the Alaska Highway and the Alaska Railroad. Commercial activity at the Fairbanks International Airport is second in Alaska only to Anchorage. Two large U.S. Air Force bases, Ladd Field and Eilson Field, are located southeast of the city. Fairbanks has several hotels, television stations, and the farthest-north golf and country club in the world. Winters are cold, with a $-11.6°$ F. average January temperature and a minimum of $-66°$ F. Summers are hot, with a July average of $60°$ F. and a maximum record of $99°$ F. Long hours of sunlight make grain ripen in spite of the short frost-free growing season. The University of Alaska (estab., 1915) and the Fairbanks branch of the University Agricultural Experiment Stations are located at College, 3 mi. north of the city.

The city was settled as a result of a gold strike in 1902. The early gold stampeders named the new community Fairbanks in honor of statesman Charles Warren Fairbanks, who became Vice President of the United States in 1905. Inc., 1903; pop., 14,771.

LUCY MICK, League of Alaskan Cities

FAIRBORN, city of southwestern Ohio, a suburb northeast of Dayton. Wright-Patterson Air Force Base is adjacent. Manufactures include cement and machinery. The city derived its name when two communities, Fairfield and Osborn, were consolidated in 1950. Inc., 1867; pop., 32,267.

FAIRBURY, city of southeastern Nebraska, and seat of Jefferson County, on the Little Blue River. It is a processing center for meat, dairy and poultry products, grain, and fertilizers, and produces metal castings. Inc., 1872; pop., 5,265.

FAIR EMPLOYMENT PRACTICES COMMITTEE (FEPC), U.S. government body established in 1941 by President Franklin D. Roosevelt to eliminate arbitrary discrimination against minorities and so help alleviate the shortage of manpower during World War II. It worked with some success among the war industries, but was more important in encouraging over a dozen states and nearly 50 cities to pass laws more or less similar to the federal model. The committee ceased to function in 1946. The spirit of the FEPC was revived in 1953 with the formation by President Dwight D. Eisenhower of the Committee on Government Contracts, which promoted nondiscriminatory employment practices in businesses doing work for the government. Its functions terminated in Mar., 1961, when it was absorbed by the newly created Committee on Equal Employment Opportunity. The Civil Rights Act of 1964 gave the United States a federal fair employment practices law for the first time. The act prohibits discrimination based on race, color, religion, sex, or national origin by employers, employment agencies, and unions. An Equal Employment Opportunity Commission was established to administer the provisions of the law.

JAMES W. KUHN, Columbia University

FAIRFAX, THOMAS FAIRFAX, 3D BARON (1612–71), English general. A vigorous leader and excellent disciplinarian, Fairfax was one of the outstanding Parliamentary generals during the English Civil War. His first success was the capture of Leeds (1643). Soon after he distinguished himself at Marston Moor (1644). When the army was reorganized, he became (1645) commander in chief. Realizing that the best strategy was to destroy the Royalist army, he sought it out and decisively defeated it at Naseby (1645). During the second Civil War he successfully besieged Colchester (1648). Soon after the execution of Charles I, he resigned as commander in chief (1650), and was succeeded by Oliver Cromwell. In 1659 he emerged from retirement to join George Monck against the radicals who wanted a republican regime. He led the commissioners sent to Holland to invite Charles II home (1660).

J. JEAN HECHT, Stanford University

FAIRFAX, THOMAS FAIRFAX, 6TH BARON (1693–1781), colonial landed proprietor, heir of the Culpeper estate, Northern Neck, Va., known in the 18th century as the Fairfax Proprietorship. As a reward to his loyal followers, exiled King Charles II in 1649 granted to several nobles, including the first Baron Culpeper, a massive tract of 5,000,000 acres of Virginia. This grant descended to the second Baron Culpeper, grandfather of Lord Fairfax, who took sole title to it in 1719. After defending his proprietary rights against Virginia land speculators, Fairfax settled in Virginia in 1747 and built an estate (Greenway Court, 1752) in the Shenandoah Valley, where George Washington surveyed some land for him. He lived there in relative isolation, undisturbed even by the American Revolution.

FAIRFAX, residential city of western California, 20 mi. north of San Francisco, in Marin County. Inc., 1931; pop., 7,661.

FAIRFAX, residential town, Fairfax County, Virginia, incorporated as county seat in 1799. The clerk's office in the county courthouse contains the wills of George and Martha Washington. Pop., 21,970.

FAIRFIELD, city of north-central Alabama, and an industrial suburb of Birmingham. Here are located various works of the Tennessee Coal & Iron Division, United States Steel Corporation. It was founded in 1910. Inc., 1919; pop., 14,369.

FAIRFIELD, city of western California, and seat of Solano County, adjoining Suisun City. Its plants process and can prunes, almonds, peaches, and pears, as well as tomatoes and asparagus, from surrounding orchards and truck farms. Travis Air Force Base is located nearby. Pop., 44,146.

FAIRFIELD, town of southwestern Connecticut, principally a residential community. Truck farming and the manufacture of drugs, machinery, and textiles are also carried on. The town was burned during the American Revolution, but it was rebuilt to become an example of New England charm and beauty. Fairfield University is located here. Settled, 1639; included in Connecticut Colony, 1685; pop., 56,487.

FAIRFIELD, city of southeastern Illinois, and seat of Wayne County. It is an agricultural center for grain, livestock, and redtop seed. Industries include the manufacture of auto accessories and clothing. Oil wells are nearby. Settled before 1820; inc., 1840; pop., 5,897.

FAIRFIELD, city of southeastern Iowa and seat of Jefferson County. Manufactures include farm equipment, laundry equipment, and work clothing. Parsons College (estab., 1875) is here. Pop., 8,715.

FAIRFIELD, city of southwestern Ohio, a residential suburb just south of Hamilton. There is some manufacturing of automobile bodies, chemicals, boxes, and machine tools. Inc., 1954; pop., 14,680.

FAIRHAVEN, town of southeastern Massachusetts, located on Buzzards Bay, in the Fall River–New Bedford metropolitan area. It was a whaling port during the mid-18th century. It has light manufacturing, fishing, and boatbuilding. Settled, 1664; separated from New Bedford, 1812; pop., 16,332.

FAIR HAVEN, residential borough and resort of eastern New Jersey, located on the south bank of the Navesink River. Boat building and repair are major industries. Inc., 1912; pop., 6,142.

FAIR LABOR STANDARDS ACT. *See* LABOR LAWS.

FAIR LAWN, borough of northeastern New Jersey, and residential and industrial suburb of Paterson. The well-planned 185-acre Industrial Park has attracted a number of diversified industries to Fair Lawn. Inc., 1924; pop., 37,975.

FAIRMONT, city of southern Minnesota and seat of Martin County. In addition to being a trade center, the city processes frozen vegetables and manufactures railroad-maintenance equipment. A Sioux uprising occurred here in 1862. Inc., 1878; pop., 10,751.

FAIRMONT, industrial city of north-central West Virginia, and seat of Marion County, on the Monongahela River at the confluence of the West Fork and Tygart rivers. The city is a mining center in the heart of the Fairmont coal field, and has industries producing fluorescent tubes, glass containers, aluminum, coke, fabricated metals, and corrugated boxes. Fairmont State College (estab., 1867) is here. Originally known as Middletown, the city has been called Fairmont, a contraction of Fair Mountains, since 1843. Laid out, 1819; inc. 1899; pop., 26,093.

FAIR OAKS, unincorporated area of northwestern Georgia, a residential suburb situated northwest of Atlanta. Pop., 21,899.

FAIR PLAIN, town of extreme southwestern Michigan, in Berrien County, located just south of Benton Harbor. Pop., 3,680.

FAIRPORT, village of western New York, on the New York State Barge Canal. Fairport manufactures ordnance accessories. Inc., 1867; pop., 6,474.

FAIRS AND EXPOSITIONS are held today for the same basic reasons that they were held in ancient Europe and Asia: (a) to advertise and sell the products displayed; (b) to give prestige to exhibitors; (c) to encourage excellence by awarding prizes; (d) to stimulate local business; and (e) to entertain and educate visitors.

Agricultural fairs, held in most parts of the world, feature the produce and livestock of local farms, along with native handicrafts and homemaking accomplishments. In the United States about 2,000 counties and larger areas sponsor agricultural fairs during the late summer and autumn. The games, shows, and rides of traveling carnivals add their usual kind of entertainment.

Specialized trade fairs or shows are limited to one kind

Below, a huge cowboy welcomes visitors to the Texas State Fair in Dallas. (PHOTO RESEARCHERS) **Right,** a vegetable and preserve exhibit at a fair in Pennsylvania. (H. ARMSTRONG ROBERTS)

A weight-pulling contest for horses at the Iowa State Fair. (MAGNUM)

FAIRS AND EXPOSITIONS

The Century of Progress Exposition, Chicago, 1933–34. This cable car gave the visitor a panoramic view of the fair. (UPI)

Interior of the Crystal Palace as it appeared during the World's Fair, London, 1851. (ILLUSTRATED LONDON NEWS)

Below, the Trylon and Perisphere symbolized the theme of the World's Fair, New York, 1939–40. **Right,** Canada's Centennial of Confederation featured Expo 67, an international fair held on two islands in Montreal. (KINNE-PHOTO RESEARCHERS)

IMPORTANT FAIRS AND EXPOSITIONS

NAME, PLACE, AND DATE	THEME OR FEATURE	NAME, PLACE, AND DATE	THEME OR FEATURE
World's Fair, London, 1851	Housed in the glass and iron Crystal Palace.	Panama-Pacific Exposition, San Francisco, 1915	Celebrated the opening of the Panama Canal and the 400th anniversary of the discovery of the Pacific Ocean.
Universal Exhibition, Paris, 1867			
International Exhibition, Vienna, 1873		Tokyo Peace Exposition, Tokyo, 1922	
International Centennial Exposition, Philadelphia, 1876	Commemorated the 100th anniversary of the Declaration of Independence. First public exhibition of the telephone.	Century of Progress Exposition, Chicago, 1933–34	Commemorated 100th anniversary of Chicago's founding.
		International Exposition, Paris, 1937	
Universal Exposition, Paris, 1889	Commemorated the 100th anniversary of the French Revolution. Eiffel Tower built for the occasion.	Golden Gate International Exposition, San Francisco, 1939–40	
World's Columbian Exposition, Chicago, 1893	Commemorated the 400th anniversary of the discovery of America. Electric lighting extensively used for first time.	World's Fair, New York, 1939–40	The World of Tomorrow.
		Festival of Britain, London, 1951	Commemorated 100th anniversary of 1851 World's Fair. The Atomic Age.
Universal Exposition, Paris, 1900		Brussels Universal and International Exhibition, Brussels, 1958	
Pan-American Exposition, Buffalo, 1901		Century 21 Exposition, Seattle, 1962	
Louisiana Purchase Exposition, St. Louis, 1904	Commemorated the 100th anniversary of the acquisition of the Louisiana Territory.	World's Fair, New York, 1964–65	Peace through Understanding.
		Expo 67, Montreal, 1967	Man and his World.
Brussels Exposition, Brussels, 1910		Expo 70, Osaka, 1970	Progress and Harmony for Mankind.

of business or manufactured product. Annual trade shows featuring housewares, automobiles, antiques, business machines, boats, food products, or electronic equipment are among the most popular. Specialized trade fairs are nearly always going on in the United States, whereas general trade fairs are customary in Europe. At general trade fairs many kinds of manufactured goods are displayed by international exhibitors.

World's fairs and exhibitions show the best and the most typical of man's past and present, as well as the latest inventions and discoveries which foretell the future.

JAMES GREGORY, The New York Historical Society

FAIRVIEW, borough of northeastern New Jersey, located on the summit of the Palisades. It is one of the nation's embroidery centers, with 52 firms engaged in this activity. Pop., 10,698.

FAIRVIEW, village of southeastern New York, adjoining Poughkeepsie. Pop., 8,517.

FAIRVIEW PARK, city of northeastern Ohio, a residential suburb situated south of Cleveland. Inc., 1910; pop., 21,681.

FAIRWAY, residential city of northeastern Kansas, and part of the Kansas City, Kansas-Missouri, urbanized area. Old Mission, established in 1829 to serve the Shawnee Indians, is here. Inc., 1949; pop., 5,133.

FAIRY, broad category of supernatural beings, similar to humans in appearance save for their diminutive size. Often invisible at will, they lived in caves, hills, or the depths of forests. They were supposed to possess magic powers and to meddle continually in human affairs for both good and evil purposes. They took human lovers and kidnaped human children. If wronged, fairies would spoil crops, curdle milk, or start fires. They could also be helpful, bringing gifts to children and food and money to the poor. Fairies are common throughout the world, but more frequently observed in Western and Asiatic cultures.

FAIRY RING, fanciful term describing the naturally occurring circles of mushrooms found growing in grassy places. This unusual pattern of growth begins with a single mushroom that spreads its spores outward in all directions. The parent plant dies out, leaving a small ring of offspring. In this way the ring is gradually enlarged by successive generations. New growth does not occur in the center of the ring because previous plants have absorbed the soil nutrients.

FAIRY TALES, term applied loosely to traditional folk tales and also to modern literary fairy stories. The folk tales have no known authors; they simply developed through the centuries. Surprisingly, the same stories with variations appeared in a great many countries. Among more than 300 variants of *Cinderella*, for example, are the version which has come down from ancient Egypt, the French peasant version which Charles Perrault (1628–1703) reworked in the mannered court language of his time, and the American-Indian version which is entitled *The Little Scarred One*. Identical themes crop up again and again throughout world folk literature: the supposedly stupid youngest brother who proves cleverer than his elders; the maligned girl whose virtue turns the tables on her persecutors; the kindly youth who is aided by magically gifted animals; the peasant whose wits win him an undeserved reward.

These stories were collected by pioneer scholars such

as Perrault of France, the brothers Jacob Grimm (1785–1863) and Wilhelm Grimm (1786–1859) of Germany, and Peter Asbjørnsen (1812–85) and Jørgen Moe (1813–82) of Norway. In the late 19th century Andrew Lang (1844–1912) collected and edited many tales in his much-loved "color" fairy books: *The Blue Fairy Book*, *The Green Fairy Book*, and others; and Joseph Jacobs (1854–1916) made collections of English, Celtic, and oriental Indian fairy tales.

The modern literary stories are created by individual authors, sometimes with plots based on folk themes. Hans Christian Andersen of Denmark (1805–75) is perhaps the greatest writer of fairy tales. His poignant and lovely stories include *The Ugly Duckling*, *The Little Mermaid*, *The Nightingale*, and *The Little Match Girl*. Outstanding English writers of fairy tales are Walter de la Mare (1873–1956) and Eleanor Farjeon (1881–1965). Irish-born Oscar Wilde (1854–1900) wrote *The Happy Prince* and other delicately beautiful tales. The robust, amusing, and rhythmic *Rootabaga Stories* of Carl Sandburg (1878–1967) are American to the core, while the stories in *Pepper and Salt* and *The Wonder Clock* by his fellow American Howard Pyle (1853–1911) are scarcely distinguishable from European folk literature.

ETHNA SHEEHAN

See also FOLK TALES; LITERATURE, CHILDREN'S.

FAISAL [fī'säl] **I,** Also Faysal, Feisal (1885–1933), king of Iraq. Faisal was the third son of Husein ibn Ali, sharif of Mecca and later king of the Hejaz. Born in Arabia, he grew up in Istanbul, where later he represented Hejaz in the Ottoman Assembly. He commanded a force under his father in the Arab revolt of World War I. Acclaimed king of Syria in Mar., 1920, he was expelled by the French in July of that year. The British favored him for the Iraqi throne, however, and he was formally invested as king of Iraq in Aug., 1921, after a popular referendum. Faisal I proved a skillful, energetic ruler; his statecraft eventually achieved Iraq's independence.

FAISAL II (1935–58), third and last Hashimite king of Iraq. The only son of King Ghazi, Faisal was educated privately in Iraq and later in England. He succeeded his father in 1939. His uncle, Crown Prince Abdul Ilah, acted as regent until 1953. In Feb., 1958, he became head of the Arab Federal Union between Iraq and Jordan. He was assassinated in 1958 when the monarchy was overthrown.

FAISAL (1905–75), king of Saudi Arabia. A favorite son of King Ibn Saud, Faisal was sent on important military campaigns and diplomatic missions beginning in his early manhood. After the accession in 1953 of his elder half-brother Saud, the cosmopolitan Faisal became crown prince. Appointed premier in 1958, he subsequently was the actual ruler of Saudi Arabia except for a period in the early 1960's when Saud reasserted his prerogatives. He advocated moderate social and political reforms and economic development. In Nov., 1964, King Saud was dethroned by royal and religious authority, and Faisal was proclaimed king. He was shot and killed by his nephew at an official reception in his palace in March 1975.

FAITH HEALING, the practice of curing physical and spiritual ills or alleviating suffering by the supposed use of supernatural force or the exorcism of evil spirits. Medicine men, shamans, witch doctors, saints, priests, and faith cultists, both in primitive and advanced societies have, on occasion, effected such cures. Psychosomatic medicine today recognizes faith as a factor in certain types of cures. The effectiveness of these "miracle cures" is accounted for psychologically by the state of mind developed in the subject through the power of suggestion.

FAIYUM [fī-yōōm'], **EL-,** city of northern Egypt and seat of El-Faiyum Province, located 55 mi (88 km) south-southwest of Cairo. It is the gateway to the agriculturally rich oasis of El-Faiyum and is an important market and distribution center for grains, livestock, and fruits. The principal industries are textile spinning and weaving, cigarette manufacture, and tanning. El-Faiyum marks the site of a Pharaonic town known as Crocodilopolis by the Greeks. To the north of the city are the mounds of the Ptolemaic town of Arsinoë.

FAJARDO [fä-här'thō], town of Humacao district, Puerto Rico, near the northeastern coast, 32 mi (51 km) east of San Juan. Sugar and tobacco are the main crops of this fertile and well-watered area, but oranges and pineapples are extensively cultivated, too. Founded in 1774, the town is a busy commercial center; it stands 1 mi (1.6 km) from a large well-sheltered bay. Fajardo saw action during the Spanish-American War, when U.S. forces took it from the Spaniards, lost it, and then regained it. Nearby is Roosevelt Roads, a large American naval base with airport facilities.

FALANGE [fə-lǎnj'], Spanish political movement, fascist in inspiration and character, founded in 1934. Its first leader was José Antonio Primo de Rivera (d.1936), son of the dictator Miguel Primo de Rivera (1923–29). Advocating land reform, new social services, and the subordination of private interests to a corporate and authoritarian state, the Falange provided a political basis for the "Nationalist" regime launched by the army revolt of July, 1936, against the second republic. Its "26 points" won adoption in Apr., 1937, as the official program of Nationalist Spain, which still lacked a civilian government or structure. The party, turning the political vacuum to account, created national services, a national council, and a *Junta Política* with some of the functions of ministries, Cortes (Parliament), and Cabinet respectively, which later sought to intertwine themselves with those regular bodies as they developed. Gen. Francisco Franco, head of the state, became also *Caudillo*, head of the party. The 26 points defined Spain as a one-party totalitarian state imbued with a will to empire and a military spirit, and repudiated capitalism, Marxism, and separatism alike. When the civil war ended (1939), the Falange became influential particularly in the fields of labor organization, education, provincial government, press, and propaganda. The movement's program became a liability to the regime after the defeat of Italy and Germany in World War II and contributed to the indictments of Spain at the Potsdam and San Francisco conferences in 1945. Another source of trouble was the Falange's steady opposition to Franco's view, increasingly popular, that the monarchy should eventually be restored. The party never succeeded in winning unconditional support from the army. After 1945, when Franco told the foreign press that "the Falange no longer wielded any political power in Spain," its influence and prerogatives declined notably though it remained the one legal party in Spain.

Consult Payne, S. G., *Falange* (1961).

WILLIAM C. ATKINSON, University of Glasgow
See also CIVIL WAR, SPANISH; FASCISM.

FALCÓN, state bordering the Caribbean Sea between the gulfs of Venezuela and Triste, in northwestern Venezuela. The southern half is in the low Segovia Highlands; the northern part is mostly lowlands. The climate is semiarid except in a few eastern valleys in the path of the trade winds. Goats and cattle are raised throughout; some coffee and cacao are produced in the wetter eastern valleys. Large oil refineries, the only significant source of income, receive petroleum via pipelines from the Maracaibo Basin oil fields. Coro is the capital. Area, 9,-575 sq. mi.; pop., 340,450.

FALCON, common name for about 60 species of birds of prey in the falcon family, Falconidae, which also includes the hawks and eagles. Falcons have long, pointed wings that enable them to fly at great speed. The beak has a toothlike projection on its upper tip, an adaptation for tearing flesh. Although many falcons capture and eat such birds as ducks, pigeons, and sparrows, they also prey on rodents and insects. Falcons have great courage and for centuries various members of the family have been trained for hunting. The largest falcons such as the caracara, or Mexican eagle, *Polyborus cheriway*, and the gyrfalcon, *Falco rusticolus*, of Arctic regions, may have a

A falcon perches on its trainer's well-protected arm.
Roche-National Audubon Society

wingspread of 4 ft. and weigh about 4 lb. The smallest falcon is the sparrow hawk or American kestrel, *F. sparverius*, with a wingspread of 2 ft. and a weight of under 1 lb. The peregrine falcon, *F. peregrinus*, is able to dive at a speed of over 150 mph. This species is found throughout the world and is the one most often trained for hunting. Other members of the family are the prairie falcon, *F. mexicanus*, of western North America; and the kestrel, *F. tinnunculus*, a European relative of the sparrow hawk.

CLARENCE J. HYLANDER, Author, *Feathers and Flight*

See also:

CARACARA	PEREGRINE FALCON
GYRFALCON	PIGEON HAWK
KESTREL OR WINDHOVER	PRAIRIE FALCON
MERLIN	SPARROW HAWK

FALCONBRIDGE, SIR WILLIAM GLENHOLME (1846–1920), Canadian jurist. Born in Drummondville, Upper Canada, he attended the University of Toronto (B.A., 1866; M.A., 1871). While lecturing at the university, he began the study of law and was called to the Ontario bar in 1871. He was a successful practitioner and became a Queen's counsel in 1885. In 1887 he was appointed judge of the Queen's Bench division and in 1900 Chief Justice. He was knighted in 1908. His opinions are noted for their fluency and precision. He was the last Chief Justice of the King's Bench.

FALCONET [făl-kô-nĕ'], **ÉTIENNE MAURICE** (1716–91), French sculptor in the classical style. In 1766 Catherine II called him to Russia where he executed a great equestrian statue of Peter the Great (Leningrad). Among his surviving works is "Woman Bathing" (Louvre, Paris). He is also remembered for his statuettes, which he made to be executed in Sèvres porcelain.

FALCON HEIGHTS, village of eastern Minnesota, a suburb north of St. Paul. It is the site of the Minnesota State Fair Grounds and the College of Agriculture, Forestry, and Home Economics of the University of Minnesota. Inc., 1949; pop., 5,507.

FALCONRY, sport of training and employing falcons to capture game. Sometimes other birds, including short-winged hawks and eagles, are used. The sport is of ancient origin and was a popular method of hunting small game until the introduction of firearms. In modern times it is practiced mainly in Germany, England, Canada, and the United States.

The birds must be captured from the nest or trapped in migratory flight, since they do not breed in captivity. Only the females are used in falconry. The training of the bird is a long and complicated process. Well-trained falcons hover high over the prey and then swoop down to snatch it from the ground or while it is in flight. Hawks are flown from the fist, and their prey include grouse, ducks, pheasants, woodcocks, hares, rabbits, and squirrels.

FALERII [fə-lĭr'ē-ī] (modern *Civita Castellana*), ancient stronghold in southeast Etruria, 18 mi. east of Viterbo, Italy. Its inhabitants, the Falisci, spoke a Latin-type language but enjoyed Etruscan culture. They strongly supported the Etruscan city of Veii against Rome until Veii's capture in 396 B.C., whereupon they, too, submitted (394 B.C.). Rebelling against Rome in 241 B.C., they were swiftly subjugated and forcibly transferred. to an indefensible site 3½ mi. away, Santa Maria di Falleri. Ancient Falerii was reoccupied in medieval times, and the modern town has excellently preserved Roman walls.

FALFURRIAS [făl-fōōr′ē-əs], city of southern Texas and seat of Brooks County, in an agricultural and oil-producing area. Processing of dairy products and the manufacture of carbon black and gypsum products are principal industries. Pop., 6,355.

FALKENHAYN [fäl′kən-hīn], **ERICH VON** (1861–1922), German general in World War I. Appointed chief of the general staff in Nov., 1914, he took Antwerp but failed in his effort to drive to Calais. With the western front stalemated, he turned east and in October moved four corps to help the Austrians, but setbacks followed early success. Though convinced that France was the decisive theater, he helped plan the 1915 summer offensive against Russia and made possible the breakthrough in south Poland in May. He organized operations with the Bulgarians to overrun Serbia during the winter of 1915–16, thus opening a direct road to Turkey. In 1916 he initiated the Verdun battles that almost exhausted both sides. Relieved in August and then given command of the Ninth Army, Falkenhayn, with Field Marshal August von Mackensen, conquered Rumania by Jan., 1917. Later that year, he took over the Asiatic Corps in the Caucasus. In 1918 he headed the Tenth Army in Lithuania.

MARTIN BLUMENSON

FALKENSEE [fäl′kən-zā], residential village of the northeastern German Democratic Republic (East Germany) in the government district of Potsdam, just west of Berlin. There is some manufacturing of chemicals and electric equipment. Falkensee consists of two former villages, Falkenhagen and Seegefeld. The nearby wood of Brieselang attracts tourists.

FALKIRK [fôl′kûrk], burgh in Stirling County, Scotland. Its main industries are iron, aluminum, and chemical works. The annual Falkirk trysts once were among the greatest livestock fairs in Britain. Two battles were fought nearby: the Scottish leader Sir William Wallace was defeated at Bannockburn by English King Edward I (1298); and the Young Pretender Prince Charles Edward defeated government forces under the command of Gen. Henry Hawley (1746).

FALKLAND [fôk′lənd] **ISLANDS** (Sp. **ISLAS MALVINAS**), group consisting of 2 large and about 200 small islands in the South Atlantic 250 mi. off the coast of Argentina. A British crown colony, the group is claimed by Argentina. East Falkland, the largest island, is 90 mi. long by 55 mi. wide; West Falkland, second largest, is 80 by 45 mi. They are separated by narrow Falkland Sound. The islands are bleak, treeless (attempts to grow trees have failed), and hilly. The highest point is Mount Adam (2,315 ft.), on West Falkland. A strong, wet, cold wind blows almost

continuously. Only scant crops of barley, oats, and potatoes can be grown. The meager economy rests on sheep raising and the export of wool, meat, skins, and tallow.

The group was discovered in 1592 by the English navigator John Davis. But it was nameless until 1690 when an English captain, John Strong, thus honored Viscount Falkland, treasurer of the Royal Navy. The first settlers were French, in 1764, at Port Louis on East Falkland, but they were driven out by the Spanish in 1766. During the 1770's the English and the Spanish disputed the territory and mutually abandoned it. Argentina claimed it in 1826 and sent Louis Vernet to develop a colony. However, he seized three U.S. sealing vessels in 1831, which brought on an attack by the U.S. corvette *Lexington*, destroying the colony. In 1833 the British returned, and the following year Stanley, the present capital, was founded. The colony also includes the Falkland Island Dependencies: South Georgia and the South Sandwich Islands. Since 1962 South Orkney and South Shetland islands and the Antarctic Peninsula, Antarctica, have been a separate colony, British Antarctic Territory. It is administered from the Falkland Islands (whose governor acts as high commissioner). Area, 4,618 sq. mi.; pop., about 2,000.

MELVIN MORRIS

FALL, ALBERT BACON (1861–1944), American politician. He was born in Frankfort, Ky., but moved to New Mexico, where he held offices in the territorial government and was elected to the U.S. Senate in 1912. He remained in the Senate until Mar., 1921, when he resigned to enter President Warren G. Harding's Cabinet as Secretary of the Interior. Two years later Fall resigned his secretaryship following an investigation of his role in the leasing of tracts in California and in the Teapot Dome reserves in Wyoming to private oil interests. He was convicted of accepting a $100,000 bribe and served a year in prison.

FALL, THE, Biblical account of the origin of evil given in Genesis 3. Yahweh had created man and woman in a state of innocence and placed them in the Garden of Eden. They were permitted complete freedom, except that they were not to eat from "the tree of the knowledge of good and evil." Genesis 3 relates how the woman was approached by "the serpent," who in a very subtle way tempted her to disobey God's prohibition. She yielded to the temptation, and so did her husband after her. The two were punished by immediate expulsion from Eden, by the loss of immortality, by the knowledge of pain, and by the need to labor throughout life for their bread.

The story is etiological in character; that is, it seeks to explain for later generations how sin entered the world, and why we are troubled by death, pain, the necessity of hard labor, and other evils. Disobedience to God is the answer given. The narrative can hardly have been considered as history: such concepts as a "tree of life" or a serpent standing upright (if indeed the story does imply this) and talking are patently either mythological or allegorical. Allegory is the more likely, since recognized mythological elements in the story are few; even the serpent was a common symbol for shrewdness (Gen. 3:1). The story has no close parallel in any other literature.

The doctrine of sin in Jewish and Christian theology is

based ultimately on this chapter. St. Paul (Rom. 5:12–21) contrasted the actions and position of Adam with those of Jesus.

Consult Ryle, H. E., *The Book of Genesis* (1921).

D. F. PAYNE, The University, Sheffield, England

FALLA [fä′yä], **MANUEL DE** (1876–1946), Spanish composer, born in Cádiz, Andalusia. He studied piano and composition in Madrid. In 1905 he won a prize for his opera *La Vida Breve* and two years later left for Paris, where he was befriended by Debussy, Ravel, and Paul Dukas. He returned to Spain following World War I, but left in 1939 to live in Argentina until his death.

Of all the composers to emerge during the modern Spanish musical renascence it was De Falla who made the most lasting impression on the musical world. Somewhat akin to Bartók in his transformation of authentic folk materials into a personal style, De Falla was one of the genuinely warm and attractive nationalists of the 20th century. The works which won him wide acclaim are Andalusian in character and utilize rhythms, modes, figures, and a guitar-like orchestration evocative of that area. Among these works are *Nights in the Gardens of Spain* (1909–15); *El amor brujo* (Love the Sorcerer, 1915), containing a masterly use of 7/8 rhythm in the Pantomime; and *The Three-Cornered Hat* (1919). Not to be overlooked are the opera *Master Peter's Puppet Show* (1923) and the neo-classic *Harpsichord Concerto* (1923–26), which search out with marked individuality other areas in Spanish music. The unfinished oratorio *La Atlántida* (1928) was performed with great success in Barcelona in 1961.

Consult Trend, J. B., *Manuel de Falla and Spanish Music* (1929); Chase, Gilbert, *The Music of Spain* (2d rev. ed., 1959).

ALBERT WEISSER, Brooklyn College

See also SPAIN: *Spanish Music.*

FALLEN TIMBERS, BATTLE OF, a decisive battle (Aug. 20, 1794) in the struggle for the Old Northwest, fought near the site of present-day Defiance, Ohio. The Indians of the Ohio-Indiana country, supported by British agents, sought to keep settlers south of the Ohio River. Armies sent against the Indians in 1790 and 1791 met defeat. But in the summer of 1794 Gen. Anthony Wayne led a third army to the Maumee River, near the spot where the Indians had taken up defensive positions in a tangle of fallen trees. Knowing that the Indians fasted before a battle, Wayne let it be known that he would attack on Aug. 17, then deliberately waited until Aug. 20. By then most of the hungry red men had drifted away to nearby Fort Miami, a British outpost. He soundly defeated the remainder. The battle convinced the Indians that they could not stop white encroachment and assured peace on the frontier for over a decade.

RAY A. BILLINGTON, Northwestern University

FALLING BODIES, LAW OF, in physics, law stating that a body falling freely under gravity and in the absence of air resistance accelerates or gains speed in the direction of the center of the earth at a rate of approximately 32 ft. per second per second, or 980 cm. per second per second. The exact value of the acceleration due to gravity, or g, varies

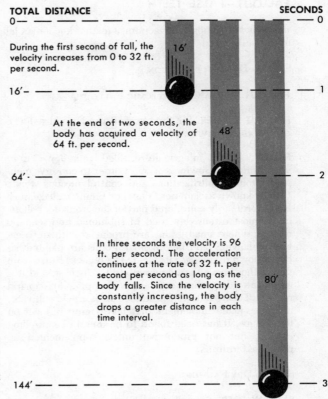

TOTAL DISTANCE — **SECONDS**

During the first second of fall, the velocity increases from 0 to 32 ft. per second.

At the end of two seconds, the body has acquired a velocity of 64 ft. per second.

In three seconds the velocity is 96 ft. per second. The acceleration continues at the rate of 32 ft. per second per second as long as the body falls. Since the velocity is constantly increasing, the body drops a greater distance in each time interval.

THE LAW OF FALLING BODIES

In a vacuum, heavy and light bodies fall with the same velocity and acceleration because of identical ratios between the respective masses and the forces required to move them.

slightly from place to place due to altitude and latitude. The latitude variation results from a combination of the fact that centrifugal force due to the earth's rotation is greatest at the equator and the fact that the earth is not exactly spherical. The variations are not large; for example, the equatorial sea-level value is about 32.086, the value at New York City, 32.160, and at the North Pole, 32.258.

Starting from rest, a falling body will attain a speed of 32 ft. per second at the end of the first second, 64 ft. per second at the end of the second second, 96 ft. per second at the end of the third, and so on. The distance traveled will be the time multiplied by the average speed, which for uniform acceleration is one-half of the final minus the initial speeds. Thus, the body falls 16 ft. during the first second, 48 ft. during the second second, and so on. The total distance, d, fallen, starting from rest, is one-half g times the square of the time in seconds, t, or $d = \frac{1}{2}gt^2$.

The preceding analysis disregards air resistance. If air resistance is taken into account, any body will rapidly attain a constant terminal velocity, the exact value of which depends on the shape and mass of the body and the atmospheric pressure at which the experiment is conducted. A feather or a small piece of paper, for example, attains an extremely low terminal velocity in a small fraction of a second; a man falling out of an airplane attains a terminal velocity of somewhere between 60 and 90 mph in four or five seconds; and a well-streamlined rocket, much higher values. In a vacuum, a feather and a man fall at the same speed.

SERGE A. KORFF

See also DYNAMICS; MOTION.

FALLOUT, ATOMIC. *See* ATOMIC FALLOUT.

FALLOUT SHELTER. *See* SHELTERS, BOMB FALLOUT; FALLOUT RADIOACTIVITY.

FALLOW [făl'ō], in agriculture, tilled land allowed to lie idle during the growing season in order to conserve moisture, promote nitrification, and control noxious weeds. Usually known as summer fallow, or summer tillage, such land is ordinarily considered part of the cropland. Fallowing is most extensively used in subhumid and semiarid regions, where small grains are produced without irrigation. Fallowing land before small grains are planted has been shown to increase its yield. The higher returns from the method more than compensate for its cost, and it is more rewarding than continuous cropping in semiarid regions. Trashy fallow is produced with a field cultivator or sweep-blade implement that leaves crop residues on the surface. It has been found to be useful in controlling erosion, but not productive unless supplemented by nitrogen fertilizers.

HOWARD F. ROBINSON

See also DRY FARMING.

FALLOW DEER, a small deer, *Cervus dama*, introduced into northern Europe by the Romans. The palmate antlers and yellowish-brown coat dappled with white are distinguishing features of this deer, which stands about 3 ft. at the shoulders. Once native to southern Europe and Asia Minor, the fallow deer is now known only as a captive species. These deer fare well in zoological parks and on large estates. In captivity fallow deer are gregarious, forming large herds. Confinement has not at all dulled their wild traits: the bucks attack humans with occasional fatal results.

FALL RIVER, industrial city of southeastern Massachusetts on Mount Hope Bay, and one of the three seats of Bristol County. Soon after the War of 1812, cotton spinning began here and Fall River became one of the nation's largest cotton-milling centers. During the 1920's many of the mills went bankrupt. The subsequent southward migration of the industry lessened further the city's importance as a textile center. Present manufactures are diverse.

The site of the city was settled in 1656 and was the scene of much fighting during King Philip's War. First called Pocasset and later Troy, Fall River received its present name in 1834. The city is governed by a mayor and a council. Chartered, 1854; pop., 96,569; urb. area, 139,392.

FALLS, CHARLES BUCKLES (1874–1960), artist and book designer, born in Fort Wayne, Ind. For his daughter he designed the popular *A B C Book* (1923), appealingly illustrated with animal pictures. In *The Modern A B C Book* (1930) he used machine-age symbols ranging from airplane to zeppelin.

FALLS, town of northeastern Pennsylvania on the Susquehanna River, 10 mi. west-northwest of Scranton. Pop., 29,082.

FALLS CHURCH, city of northern Virginia, and residential suburb, 7 mi. west of Washington, D.C. and 4 mi. south of the Potomac River. The city was named for the Falls Church (built, 1767–69) in which George Washington and his family worshiped. Inc. as town, 1875; inc. as city, 1948; pop., 10,772.

FALLS CITY, city of southern Nebraska, and seat of Richardson County, on the Nemaha River, in a farming area. It has meat, dairy, and poultry processing plants, and industries manufacturing trailer homes and fertilizers. Inc., 1858; pop., 5,444.

FALMOUTH [făl'məth], town of southern Maine, situated on Casco Bay, just north of Portland. It is a residential suburb and a yachting center. Settled about 1632, it is one of Maine's oldest settlements and until 1786 included the area of Portland within its limits. Inc., 1718; pop., 6,291.

FALMOUTH, resort town at the base of Cape Cod, Massachusetts. It was once a famous shipbuilding, whaling, and fishing center. Otis Air Force Base, the Woods Hole Oceanographic Institution, and Marine Biological Laboratory are located here. A bell cast by Paul Revere is in the Congregational Church. Settled, 1660; inc., 1686; pop., 15,942.

FALSE DECRETALS, THE, a canonical collection of about 100 apocryphal papal decretal letters interspersed among authentic letters and genuine decisions of church councils. The letters were forged in France by Isidore Mercator in the middle of the 9th century to strengthen the authority of the episcopacy which had been weakened by Carolingian state interference. Though quoted and used as authentic by Popes, canonists, and jurists, their forged character was finally established by David Blondel in the 17th century.

FALSE IMPRISONMENT is the wrongful confinement of a person within limits fixed by the actor and accomplished by force or a show of force. The force may be minimal. Examples are locking a person in a room or taking away a boat which is the only means of escape from an island.

False imprisonment includes false arrest, which may be effected by simply touching the person and using words of arrest if the person arrested submits. An arrest is lawful if made pursuant to a warrant valid on its face or where the person arrested commits a crime in the presence of the person making the arrest. A peace officer may arrest without warrant for a felony actually committed out of his presence where he has reasonable grounds to believe the person arrested is the felon. Unless an arrest is lawful it constitutes false imprisonment and thus gives rise to a civil action for damages.

FLEMING JAMES, JR.

FALSE TEETH. *See* DENTISTRY.

FALSTAFF, SIR JOHN, one of Shakespeare's greatest comic characters. A braggart, rogue, drunkard, and thief, Falstaff is nevertheless so lively and amusing that he wins the hearts of most audiences. He appears in *Henry IV* and *The Merry Wives of Windsor;* his death is movingly reported in *Henry V.*

FAMAGUSTA [fä-mə-gōōs'tə], chief port of Cyprus, situated on the east coast of the island, 6 mi (9.6 km) south of the ruins of ancient Salamis. It is the only harbor on Cyprus capable of accommodating ocean-going vessels. Citrus fruits are the principal export. Famagusta is on the site of ancient Arsinoë, built in the 3d century B.C. by Ptolemy II. Othello's Tower, a sea-front citadel, dates from the late 12th century. Massive stone walls with their moat hewn out of solid rock surround the town. The 14th-century Gothic cathedral of St. Nicholas, converted to a mosque after the Turkish conquest in 1571, is the most remarkable and best preserved of its numerous old churches and palaces. Excessive humidity makes life in the walled city uncomfortable. To the south the suburb of Varosha is being developed for both residential and business purposes.)

FAMILIAR SPIRIT, supernatural assistant of a human being. This superstition is associated with such varied phenomena as European witchcraft, the witch's familiar taking on the shape of a black cat, or spiritualist mediums, who have their "controls." Diviners among South African tribes are believed to be assisted by familiar spirits, as are the priests of the voodoo cult of Haiti. Medicine men and shamans are frequently thought to have familiar spirits. While this belief seems to be associated with direct contact with supernatural beings, as in shamanism and spiritualism, it is also associated with magic in the case of witchcraft. Aladdin's genie might also be considered a type of familiar spirit.
See also MAGIC; SHAMAN; VOODOO CULT.

FAMILY, probably the oldest human social institution. It has existed, insofar as anthropologists can ascertain, among all peoples in all ages. The reasons for the universality of the family are not hard to find. The human sex urge is a powerful one, and if the urge were not channeled into socially acceptable forms, chaos would result. In a very meaningful sense, therefore, the family is man's solution of the sex problem.

Studies by sociologists and psychologists also indicate that human beings need close associations with other human beings. The need to communicate, to share experiences and laughter, to elicit sympathy and comfort, to love and be loved are apparently lasting needs for the average person. And these "primary group" needs, as they are called by sociologists, can best be gratified within the family situation.

The family, of course, is also the biological and social unit for procreation and child rearing, the latter having come to be a most seriously regarded function in civilized

---

FAMILY	STUDY GUIDE

Family life is a concern of historians, lawyers, home economists, child psychologists, and students of many other fields. Anthropologists and sociologists make comprehensive studies of family patterns, functions, and problems. The entry on these pages — a sociological article — covers the following topics.

Background Factors. Behavior of male and female mammals toward offspring. Maternal instinct in lower animals and mother love in human beings. Importance of social, religious, and other cultural factors in human families.

Cross-Cultural Variations and Uniformities. Similarities in family patterns found by comparing societies, such as stress on the importance of marriage. Variations: monogamy and polygamy (polygyny and polyandry); conjugal and consanguine family systems.

Historical Perspective. Patriarchal families of ancient Hebrews, Greeks, and Romans, with woman subservient. Emancipation of women and decline of family life in the later history of Rome. Strengthening of family life under the influence of Christianity.

The American Family (Colonial Period). Importance of the husband-wife team in colonizing America. The farm family. The father as head of the household. Severe penalties for offences against the family.

The Changing Nature of the American Family. Emancipation of women. Change in function from a family as a self-sufficient economic and social unit.

The Modern American Family: Strengths and Weaknesses. Two views: On the one hand, weakened family ties, rising divorce rate, sex problems, and juvenile delinquency. On the other hand, continued importance of the family institution; problems seen as arising from urban-industrial living rather than from weakness of the family system. Agencies concerned with family life.

The reader who wants to know more about the family as it is studied by anthropologists and sociologists can turn to such articles as KINSHIP, CLAN, and TRIBE. The role of the consanguine family in Chinese society is discussed in CHINA: *Republic of China — Social Conditions.* A topic closely related to family structure and function is covered in WOMEN, STATUS OF. Other pertinent articles are COURTSHIP CUSTOMS, CHILD MARRIAGE, and MARRIAGE. The last-mentioned entry deals with monogamous and plural marriages, the history of marriage, and then with marriage rates and with legal considerations.

A fuller discussion of laws relating to marriage and the family is in FAMILY LAW. This article, prepared by a legal expert, deals with such topics as eligibility to marry, void and voidable marriages, the obligations of family members to one another, and with divorce, separation, alimony, and custody of children. The historical, sociological, and legal aspects of family dissolution are treated in DIVORCE.

The present Encyclopedia, moreover, has devoted considerable space to information useful for dealing with life's practical problems. In the area of the family, there are such articles as HOME MANAGEMENT, HOME ECONOMICS, FOOD FOR THE FAMILY, CLOTHING FOR THE FAMILY, and BUDGET, FAMILY. There are also articles entitled INFANT CARE, CHILD DEVELOPMENT, ADOLESCENCE, and ADOPTION.

The importance of families in a variety of ways is shown in many other articles. Families have ruled states or even empires for generations—see, for example, HABSBURG, STUART, STEWART OR STEUART, or the articles on LOUIS XIV and other Bourbon kings of France. Many nonroyal family names are illustrious — ADAMS, BACH, and MEDICI, for example.

FAMILY and other major articles conclude with lists of standard reference works on the subject of the family. Additional information can be obtained in many sources available in the library.

Family groupings developed early in the story of mankind. This Neanderthal group, tensed for impending danger at the mouth of their cave shelter, lived in the Old Stone Age. The painting is by Charles R. Knight.

societies. Inheritance and property rights, lineage, protection, care of the aged and infirm, and the transmission of societal values are additional factors making for the apparent inevitability of the human family system. Its importance has always been recognized, but the family has become an object of scientific study only recently.

Background Factors. Among the mammals, noticeable differences appear between the behavior of males and females. The male animal is clearly the sexual aggressor, whereas the female is generally passive. It is the male animal who, fighting off all intruders, attempts to collect a "harem" of females for his exclusive use. Monogamous animal species are numerically rare. Nowhere but among humans is a polyandrous mating system found, that is, one involving a single female and several males.

Due to a variety of social and physiological factors, the human female is deeply concerned with affectional and familial ties. There are hundreds of societies, for example, in which men take plural wives (polygyny), whereas the number of groups permitting women to take plural husbands (polyandry) is negligible.

In the mammalian world there is a sharp contrast between male and female animals regarding the feeding, training, and protection of the young. In practically every mammalian species, care of the offspring is a task falling to the mother animal rather than to the father. In fact, the mother animal not only fulfills her maternal obligations faithfully, but also often protects her young at the risk of her own life. The mammalian father, on the other hand, is anything but protective. Indeed, the males of some species devour their offspring whenever the opportunity arises. It should be pointed out that the maternal role among lower animals is an instinctive behavior pattern. That is, it is a behavioral reflex over which the female animal has little or no control. In the laboratory the maternal instinct can be either induced or terminated by the injection of hormones. In general, though, there is no paternal instinct in the mammalian class.

At the human level, also, it is obvious that child care is more the province of the mother than the father. Throughout the ages "mother love" has had a special meaning, whereas "father love" has had less social impact. In this instance, cultural factors undoubtedly have much to do with maternal and paternal roles, and there is little doubt that innate factors have less influence as one ascends the phylogenetic scale. Nevertheless, it is entirely possible that traces of a maternal instinct still exist at the human level. Recent research, for example, has disclosed that the strength of maternal feeling is related to various phases of the menstrual cycle.

At any rate, societies have generally tried to take advantage of these innate differences between human males and females. In view of the pattern of male sex-aggressiveness and female passivity, and in further view of the female's maternal proclivities, it is the woman rather than the man who is encouraged to uphold the moral codes more strongly, to preserve family ties, and to be instrumental in the ethical and religious training of the children.

Although these innate factors help to explain the mainsprings of the human family system, it has been even more strongly influenced by historical, social, religious, and legal forces. It is these cultural factors, rather than any biological attributes, which have been of primary interest to research sociologists.

Cross-Cultural Variations and Uniformities. Family systems vary from one society to another, and most books on the family are replete with illustrations of these differences. It is also true that certain familial uniformities run through all societies, and it is important to keep the variations and uniformities in proper perspective. The uniformities include the prohibition against marrying close blood relatives (the incest taboo). Also, practically all societies oppose extramarital sex relations, or adultery. Homosexuality generally meets with disapproval, although penalties vary in severity among cultures. The general topic of sex is a rather sensitive one in most societies, and it is often difficult to procure cross-cultural information relevant to sexual practices. It is self-evident, nevertheless, that in

---

Domestic scene from a Greek vase painting. Greek families were patriarchal. Women had little legal status and were expected to obey the orders of their fathers or husbands.

Culver Pictures, Inc.

virtually all societies the male is permitted more sexual leeway than the female. The latter, conversely, is accorded more freedom in the area of physical attractiveness and beautification.

Marital separation, divorce, and desertion are condemned in nearly all societies. Generally speaking, societies the world over tend to prohibit or disapprove of those activities which impinge upon the bonds of matrimony. To put it somewhat differently, all societies consider marriage a most important institution and take pains to impress this fact upon their members, who are expected to marry. In general there is little difficulty in fulfilling the expectation: in most societies marriage rates are high.

In addition to the similarities, certain cross-cultural variations also occur. Some societies permit only monogamy (one husband, one wife). There are even more societies, however, which allow a man to take plural wives (polygyny), and a few societies which even permit a wife to take plural husbands (polyandry). Among most civilized peoples, premarital sex relations are considered immoral, illegal, or both, but in many primitive groups sex before marriage is permitted and in some cases even encouraged. In some societies marriage is considered to be religious in nature, whereas in others it is regarded as secular. Kinship structure often varies from group to group, as do attitudes toward such familial problems as child rearing and care of the aged.

One variation worthy of particular mention, since it is so different from American practice, is the matter of consanguine family organization. Most Americans, in thinking of marriage and family life, envision a pattern of dating and falling in love, a wedding ceremony followed by a reception and honeymoon, and finally a setting up of the new home. The new home, in both an actual and symbolic sense, marks a break with the older parental ties, for in our society most couples are reluctant to marry and live with their parents. This total system is referred to by sociologists and anthropologists as a conjugal family system.

Many primitive societies, however, have rejected conjugal emphasis in favor of a consanguine family system, that is, one based on blood ties rather than on an affectional relationship. In a consanguineous system, the marrying couple do not start their home anew, but return to live with the husband's (patrilocal) or wife's (matrilocal) family, depending on whether descent is reckoned in a patrilineal or matrilineal manner. Children are integrated into the larger kinship group, or extended family. Family allegiance, therefore, is to one's original family, which over the years often grows to a fairly large size. An example of such a family would be the traditional Chinese family, in which the sons brought their wives to their father's house.

The conjugal family is structurally weaker, inasmuch as the family itself may be broken by death or divorce. The consanguine family can stand a variety of illnesses, deaths, and marital dissolutions, and still preserve its functional utility and identity. On the other hand, consanguine families often get so large that it is difficult to satisfy the primary group needs of the individual members. Also, unlike the conjugal system, the consanguine family organization takes little cognizance of the romantic inclinations of its young people, a block which must upon occasion give rise to frustrations and inhibitions.

Historical Perspective. Many modern family patterns originated among the ancient Hebrews, Greeks, and Romans. In all three of these groups the family was patriarchal in character and women were under the legal control of their husbands. Hebrew women, for example, could not inherit property or indulge in commercial or political activities. They were forced to dress conservatively, to make sure that their bodies were well covered, and to wear veils. Whereas the husband could procure a divorce for whatever reason suited him, the Hebrew wife had no legal right to divorce. Although the Hebrew patriarch had extensive familial power, the community expected him not to abuse his authority. Along with his patriarchal privileges went responsibilities; that is, he was expected to be a good husband and father, to provide food and shelter for his family, and to protect them from danger. Husbands who did not fulfill their familial obligations faced public criticism. Although the husband had the right to divorce his wife for any reason, the community did not look kindly upon men who procured a divorce on trivial grounds. Unless the cause was considered a just one, such as adultery or sterility, the husband would not receive the support of the community. Sterility was considered a serious ground because family names were important. Childbearing was a sacred obligation, and it was considered sinful to let family names die out; in fact, barrenness or sterility was interpreted as an omen of God's disapproval. The ancient Hebrews practiced tribal endogamy, or marriage within the group.

Adultery was considered a heinous offense by the Hebrews, particularly on the part of the wife; the death penalty was prescribed, although it is not clear how often it was actually imposed. Sex relations on the part of single people was also considered a sin, though it is referred to much less often in the Old Testament than is adultery. Nevertheless, virginity was practically mandatory on the part of a bride-to-be, and violators received harsh punish-

A peasant family of the 15th century on its way to market, from an engraving by the German artist Martin Schongauer (1445?–91). Most medieval families were poor and lived in rural areas.

"The Father of the Family," by the 18th-century French artist Jean Baptiste Greuze. The transmission to children of religious and social values is one of the major functions of the family.

ment; the death penalty might even be imposed. For virtually all sex offenses, violations by the female were considered more serious than those committed by the male. This double standard of sexual behavior has existed at all times among virtually all peoples.

Like the ancient Hebrew families, Greek and Roman families were patriarchal in organization. Women were subservient, modest in dress and manner, and sexual violations on their part were harshly treated. However high they might be on a maternal plane, legally and politically they were insignificant. During the later Roman period, however, there came a change in the social order. The start of the "new order" is usually placed at the 2d century B.C., the period of the Punic Wars, a conflict which lasted for several decades. Roman men were engaged in battle for an extended period, and women began to acquire independence. As male dominance declined, rich women became the objects of matrimonial attention, and marriages were often made for political and economic gain. More important, large numbers of both sexes refrained from marriage altogether. And among those who did marry, the divorce rate rose spectacularly. Adultery was practiced in an all but open manner. Prostitution and concubinage flourished. Inevitably, the birth rate fell as the desire for children and the wish to perpetuate the family name became less significant. Abortion and infanticide were common, and large numbers of babies were abandoned.

In addition to the emancipation of Roman women, another factor which may have contributed to the decline of family life was the rapid rate of growth of the wealth of the empire. Slaves and servants were plentiful, and women were no longer concerned with household tasks. As a result, groups of ladies of leisure developed, and preoccupation with food and fashion became the hallmark of the good life. Sexual morality and family life, on the other hand, simply went out of style. Governmental attempts to stem the moral and familial degeneration were to no avail.

With the rise of Christianity, family life was strengthened in many respects. Monogamy was the only form of marriage sanctioned by the Christians. All sex relations outside of marriage were prohibited and divorce was opposed. The status of children was raised and abortion and infanticide were forbidden. The Christians were especially severe regarding sex deviations, which they regarded as a major evil. Many of the early Christian leaders felt that the immoralities surrounding them derived from the abuses of sex.

Throughout the Middle Ages the status of women remained low. The family became firmly entrenched as the recognized social and procreative unit, but it remained patriarchal in character and organization.

The American Family

Early Beginnings. The early American family was strongly rooted in European traditions, although circumstances necessarily changed the general style of life. The first settlers at Jamestown (1607), Plymouth (1620), and Massachusetts Bay (1628) were of middle-class English background, and were poorly equipped for the wilderness living which faced them. In spite of the harsh New England climate and topography and the deplorable living conditions, the Puritans and Pilgrims had one unforeseen advantage over those settlers who had made their way to the James River in Virginia. Both the Pilgrims and Puritans had settled as families, in contrast to Jamestown, which was an all-male settlement. In spite of the pleasant Virginia weather, the Jamestown colony was marked by quarreling and general unpleasantness. Conversely, the Plymouth and Puritan settlements grew, both in numbers and in vigor, despite the environmental handicaps. The Jamestown group did not begin to thrive until shiploads of young women arrived from England to be wives for the male settlers.

The lesson learned from the sex ratio, or male-female balance, was to be repeated many times in the early history of the United States. All-male groups seemed destined

A rural American family of the mid-19th century gathered around the hearth. Children of past ages entertained themselves with simple amusements such as games, books, and pets. (BETTMANN ARCHIVE)

to erupt into lawlessness and violence, whereas family settlements made for stability and growth. The contributions of women in the development of colonial America can hardly be overestimated. In a very real sense the colonization of America was accomplished through the efforts of husband and wife teams prevailing over a hostile environment.

Over the years this family unit tended to become economically self-sufficient. It should be kept in mind that as late as 1790, 95% of the population was rural. Up to this time families often cleared their own land and built their own houses and barns. Although his main occupation was that of farmer, the average man was forced to be a Jack-of-all-trades, making and repairing his own furniture, equipment, and tools. The wife's task was to make usable products from the raw materials: spinning and weaving garments, making candles, and cooking and preserving food. Children were expected to help their parents; the girls assisted their mothers in the various household duties, and the boys worked along with their fathers. In an era when the family provided its own housing, food, furniture, and clothing, children were considered economic assets.

Family Roles. In accordance with Mosaic laws, the Puritan husband and father was the undisputed head of the household. Once the marriage vows were taken, the wife's property, including her personal effects, fell largely under the legal control of the husband, to be disposed of in whatever manner he wished. Legally, it was the husband who could determine where the couple should live. The law also gave him the right to insist on obedience from his wife. He could not, however, abuse her physically, and the law required him to support his family. Under the primitive conditions of the period, childbearing took its toll, and the maternal mortality rate was high. Women often died when they were quite young, and according to the custom of the day, the husband was expected to remarry rather quickly. Large families, of course, were quite common, and in view of her various household duties, the colonial wife had little time for leisure activities.

Colonial common law followed English common law; women had comparatively few property rights, and the field of education was held to be a male province. Girls were originally not permitted to attend school, and women were not encouraged to read.

Many men left their families for the gold rush to Alaska in the 1890's. They greet their wives after long separation (*right*). (BROWN BROTHERS)

Parading suffragettes in New York in 1920 display a sign quoting President Woodrow Wilson, who supported their cause. The right to vote, an important freedom in itself, also had an indirect effect on family life by encouraging women to participate in activities outside the home.

Colonial children were under the virtually absolute control of their fathers, and strict obedience was expected by both the family and the community. Some of the colonies even had laws which decreed the death penalty for willfully disobedient children, although no instance is recorded where the extreme penalty was ever invoked. The infant death rate in this early period was alarmingly high, and it was not uncommon for half of the children in a given family to die before reaching maturity.

Sexual Offenses. The colonists considered the family to be a most important institution, both in a sacred and a secular sense, and they took pains to prevent whatever they considered to be encroachments on the family. Nonmarital sex activity was clearly an encroachment, and the colonies in general, and the New England Puritans in particular, punished it severely. The Puritans belived that the function of sex was that of procreation within marriage, and any other form of sex expression was severely penalized. The crime of fornication was not taken lightly, and convicted persons, female as well as male, could be fined and given "stripes," or lashes. Interestingly, the Connecticut Code Laws of 1650 included compulsory marriage for fornication in its consolidated list of punishments.

The Puritans considered adultery a more serious offense than fornication; in most of the New England colonies adultery was punishable by death, though the death penalty was seldom imposed. Whipping and branding were more typical penalties, and women offenders were more severely punished than men. The "scarlet letter," made famous by Hawthorne's novel, was apparently a common punishment.

The Changing Nature of the American Family

After the Revolutionary War and during the 19th century, the American family underwent vast changes. The typical agricultural family of the pre-Revolutionary period slowly changed as America became industrialized and urbanized. At the end of the Civil War the change accelerated, and after World War I the American family system developed into one unlike any the world had ever seen.

The Emancipation of Women. Some of the most important changes in family organization resulted from the emancipation of American women. Prior to 1850 women had no legal control over their own property; they could not vote; their education was largely neglected; their job opportunities were few, and professional occupations were all but closed. At a convention in Seneca Falls, N.Y., in 1848, however, the women's rights movement was launched with the aim of procuring for women the same educational, economic, and political rights enjoyed by men..

By and large, the movement ultimately was successful. Women were admitted to universities and professional schools in large numbers. Legally and politically, women today have nearly equal status with men; women can own property, negotiate contracts, vote, and hold political office.

The effects on the family of this new feminine freedom were not long in making themselves felt, both in a positive and a negative sense. On the positive side, wives no longer considered themselves intellectually inferior to their husbands. Whereas once she was looked upon primarily as a homemaker and bearer of children, the young woman enters marriage today much better equipped to become a companion to her husband, and in this sense the family has undoubtedly been strengthened. The expanding job market for women has enabled wives to help with the economic support of the family. In fact, there are innumerable cases where families have been held together only because of the wife's financial contributions.

On the negative side, the fact that so many of today's wives are college graduates tends to create a certain amount of dissatisfaction and frustration. Young women who have had the benefit of a college education in literature, art, and the social and physical sciences, sometimes find it difficult to adjust to what they consider the humdrum existence of married living. To some women, the term "housewife" signifies a low-status position, with the result that they turn to careers other than marriage. That most jobs are not "glamorous" or "career" jobs, but are of the more routine clerical and office variety, does not alter the basic fact that for the first time in history the job market is competing with the marriage market insofar as many women are concerned. The extent of this competition becomes clear when it is realized that the majority of American working women are married. A sizable proportion of these women have minor children.

Changing Family Functions. The early American family was a functional institution. In an economic sense the husband-wife-children team was a self-sufficient producing unit, making its own home, furniture, and clothing, and raising its own food. The colonial family also served the educational function; that is, boys and girls were trained at home in the skills they would one day be called upon to perform, homemaking for girls and farming for boys. The religious function was likewise part of family life. Bible-reading, family prayers, grace before meals, and hymn singing were commonplace in the early American home, and in areas where there was no church, the family often held its own services, presided over by the father. The recreational function was another hallmark of the colonial family, with visiting, dancing, singing, and games of all kinds being thought of as family activities. Other family functions typical of this earlier period were those pertaining to health and medicine, protection, and care of the aged.

Increasingly, however, outside institutions and agencies have removed most of the traditional functions from the home. The modern American family has long since lost its function as a relatively complete economic and industrial producing entity. Organized churches now perform the spiritual and religious function. Schools and colleges have removed the educational function from the home. Commercialized entertainment, in the form of movies, night clubs, sporting events, and theaters, has tended to take over the recreational function. Police forces and fire departments have largely assumed the protective function. Doctors and hospitals now perform the medical and health services. And a variety of governmental agencies have for some time now been performing the function of caring for the aged, infirm, and handicapped.

The Modern American Family: Strengths and Weaknesses

No one can deny that the current family system is a far cry from the colonial or even the 19th-century American family. The changing nature of the family is a world-wide phenomenon, to be sure, but in few societies has the change been more pronounced than in America. Sociologists who specialize in the family field are divided on the question of whether the various changes have been for better or worse. One school of thought maintains that the present family system is not only weak but getting weaker. But the majority of family sociologists feel that the present family system represents a satisfactory change in keeping with societal realities.

Weaknesses. The present family system has been largely stripped of its traditional functions. The ties between husband and wife are functionally weaker. Young people marry today with the expectation of achieving love and happiness, and when these pleasures are not forthcoming there is often little compunction about getting a divorce. In consequence the divorce rate in recent periods has reached alarming proportions. At the rate of some 4,000,000 divorces per decade, it is estimated that close to one in four marriages contracted today will end in divorce. In urban areas separation and desertion are also problems of no small magnitude.

To the extent that the family has been man's answer to the sex problem, the increase in premarital and extramarital sex relations can also be viewed as a weakness in the family system. Concomitantly, figures released by the National Office of Vital Statistics show an increase in the illegitimate birth rate. Venereal disease, once believed to be headed for extinction, is apparently far from obliterated.

The general behavior of children has also been taken as an index of family disorganization. The "spare the rod" philosophy has become outmoded, and whether or not there is any causal connection, there can be no doubt that conduct problems associated with children have increased. Juvenile delinquency rates have not only increased steadily, but in many cities juvenile offenses represent a major proportion of all crimes committed.

Strengths. Not all of the family functions have been destroyed. The affectional function remains an important consideration. As a matter of fact, the family is still a very popular institution, with over 90% of both sexes marrying. A large majority, furthermore, stay married. Most couples desire children, and offspring are given a good deal of love and attention. If, in the process, behavioral problems arise, they may well be a reflection of urbanized, industrialized living rather than any inherent weakness in the family system. Similarly, the increase in sexual laxity might well reflect changes in morality which seem to go with the growth of a technological society. Some sociologists feel that as Americans become adapted to the urbanized, industrialized way of life, problems of sex and delinquency will tend to diminish.

It should also be mentioned that there are more agencies and institutions, both public and private, concerned with family life than at any time in the past. Family courts, marriage counseling agencies, child guidance clinics, family welfare organizations, the United States Children's Bureau, the National Council of Parents and

Members of an American family in 1915 depended largely on each other for entertainment. Conversation, reading, and looking at pictures through a stereoscope were among their diversions.

The Bettmann Archive

Teachers—all these and many others attest not only to the problems of, but, perhaps more significantly, to the high value placed on, the American family. Books, pamphlets, film strips, and newspaper articles dealing with family and child life find an eager audience. Year after year, marriage and family courses given in colleges and universities attract large numbers of students. And finally, family research has increased enormously since World War II. Social scientists today spend an enormous amount of time studying the institutional and interactive processes associated with family life. Their hope is that a fuller understanding will lead to a stronger family system.

Consult Morgan, E. S., *The Puritan Family* (1944); Ogburn, W. F., and Nimkoff, M. F., *Technology and the Changing Family* (1955); Clarke, H. I., *Social Legislation* (1957); Glick, P. C., *American Families* (1957); Anshen, R. N., *The Family: Its Function and Destiny* (rev. ed., 1959); *A Modern Introduction to the Family*, ed. by N. W. Bell and E. F. Vogel (1960); Cavan, R. S., *Marriage and the Family In the Modern World, A Book of Readings* (1960); Kenkel, William, *The Family in Perspective* (1960).

WILLIAM M. KEPHART, University of Pennsylvania
See also FAMILY LAW; KINSHIP; WOMEN, STATUS OF.

FAMILY COMPACT, in Canadian history, term used to describe the oligarchy that controlled the leading political offices in Upper Canada until the introduction of responsible government in 1848. Although its members were usually not related, they did form an exclusive group including the Anglican hierarchy, military staff officers, and, of course, the Governor, through whom they almost monopolized access to the British Colonial Office.

FAMILY LAW, as a distinct branch of the law, is essentially concerned with the institution of marriage, the rules governing its making, the rights and obligations arising out of it, and the provisions for its dissolution. In the United States each state is the final authority in these matters, except in situations involving the validity of divorces where federal constitutional law applies.

Marriage

Freedom of Choice. In the United States, as indeed in most of the other Western countries, persons eligible to marry are, for the most part, free from specific legal limitations on their choice of mates. Undoubtedly, there are many sociological and economic factors which affect individual choices; and attitudes of family and friends in the same status group naturally enter into such decisions. Anglo-American law, however, is particularly sensitive to protect young people from what are commonly regarded as improper restrictions. Thus when a man or woman arrives at majority, the parents have no legal power to dictate or restrict their choice in marriage. Even in many Asian countries as, for example, in India, arranged marriages with the economic influence of the dowry are disappearing. In England and the United States, contracts to procure or bring about a marriage are unenforceable in law. Although the professional marriage broker still has a limited function among certain ethnic groups, he operates outside the protection of the law.

Other collateral attempts by means of economic inducement to procure or prevent marriage are frowned upon by the law. General restraints upon marriage in contracts, wills, and deeds are void. Certain particular restrictions, however, are permissible. Thus, for example, courts have upheld provisions in wills which limit the estate devised to the widow so long as she remains unmarried. So, too, conditions in such documents restricting marriage to a certain national or ethnic group have been upheld. Subject to these and a few similar exceptions, freedom of choice in the selection of marriage partners among persons generally competent to marry is preserved.

The same policy, of course, requires that marriage consist of a consensual arrangement between the parties. A marriage brought about by physical force or threats of force is not valid, even though it is otherwise in strict compliance with the law. The same is true of consent induced by fraudulent misrepresentation of a material character which substantially affects the marital relation. This is not to say that trivial exaggerations and misstatements invalidate the marriage. Misrepresentation of important matters, however, may make the marriage vulnerable. It is also necessary that the parties be of sound mind. Insanity of either person at the time of the marriage will render it voidable by reason of the absence of real consent.

Formalities. In Western countries, and indeed in many others, certain ceremonial formalities are required by law. In the United States all jurisdictions have statutes providing for a marriage license to be issued by a designated official. Statutes also provide for ceremonies conducted by a clergyman, priest, rabbi, or judicial officer. Occasional exceptions are made for minor religious groups as, for example, the Quakers or the Mennonites. In addition to the procurement of licenses and health certificates, a waiting period and other conditions are frequently required by law.

In approximately one-third of the states, however, marriage is permitted without the statutory formalities. This is called common-law marriage. The requirements for such a marriage vary somewhat, but the one universal condition is that there be an agreement freely entered into between the man and the woman presently to become husband and wife. In some states this must be followed by cohabitation. In others there must be a "holding out" to the public as husband and wife. Although called common-law marriage, this form of union was in fact recognized in the Middle Ages by the Roman Catholic Church with the reasoning that it would prevent illicit relations and illegitimate children. In modern times, however, this type of marriage is disfavored by all Christian churches and is also falling into increasing disfavor in the secular law of countries which formerly recognized it.

Eligibility of Parties to Marry. Most modern nations, as well as all states of the United States, stipulate a minimum age for marriage. In American jurisdictions, the marriageable age varies from 16 to 21 years. Sometimes the girl is permitted to marry two or three years younger than the boy, and in many jurisdictions the parties may marry with parental consent two or three years before majority, after which the parents no longer have control.

Monogamy is the rule in North and South America, Europe, and many Asian and some African countries. Accordingly, a marriage in such countries between parties, one of whom is already married to a third person, is void and of no effect. Moreover, it is a criminal offense.

All societies in all ages appear to have customary or legal taboos with regard to marriages between persons within certain blood relationships. The rule in the United States varies from state to state. The dividing line is usually that which separates first from second cousins. Second cousins may marry in most of the states. First cousins are forbidden to marry in half or more of the states. Only one state, Rhode Island, permits marriages between aunt and nephew, or uncle and niece, and this exception is limited to persons of the Jewish faith.

Few countries prohibit marriages between persons of different racial origin. In a number of American states, however, marriages are forbidden between members of the Caucasian race and those of the Negro, Mongolian, or Indian races. The restrictions are not uniform.

Void and Voidable Marriages. Three classes of marriage may be distinguished: (a) marriages which are valid for all purposes, (b) those which are utterly void and of no effect, and (c) those which are voidable by one of the parties during the lifetime of both. In the last situation, the marriage has all the legal effects of a valid marriage, until it is avoided. A common example of such a marriage is a situation in which one of the parties is below the age of consent. Such party may disaffirm the marriage upon reaching the legal marriageable age. If, however, he or she fails to disaffirm within a reasonable time after reaching that age, it will be interpreted as a ratification, and thereafter the marriage is regarded as valid for all purposes. In some states the parent of the underage spouses may sue to have the marriage declared invalid. Likewise, a person induced to enter into marriage by fraudulent misrepresentation must disaffirm within a reasonable time after discovery of the fraud. Similarly, marriage by a temporarily insane person must be disaffirmed if and when sanity returns or the privilege to do so will be lost.

Annulment. Voidable marriages may be annulled at the instance of the party entitled to disaffirm. The decree of annulment was one originally rendered by the ecclesiastical courts under the canon law. Inasmuch as the decree invalidated the marriage as from the beginning, the parties were free to enter into a subsequent marriage under the law of the church. This is the rule under the secular law of all Anglo-American jurisdictions. An unfortunate, although logical, result of a decree of annulment is that it bastardizes any issue of the marriage. In New York and a few other states special legislation saves the children from this retroactive illegitimacy. Common grounds for annulment include nonage, fraud, duress, insanity, and impotency if, at the time of marriage, it is unknown to the wife.

Which Law Governs Marriage. The usual rule is that the law of the place where the marriage was entered into determines its effect—whether valid, void, or voidable. An exception to this rule is that a marriage valid where performed will be void if it violates a strong and deep-seated public policy of the state where either or both of the parties have their domicile or residence. For example, an American, already married, goes to an Asian country which permits polygamous marriages. After taking a second wife in that country, the parties return to his home. There, the subsequent marriage will be held invalid.

Obligations and Rights of Spouses. At the early common law, the husband was under an obligation to support his wife. This is still the law in the English-speaking world and many countries in Western Europe. In return the husband was entitled to his wife's services, and he became upon marriage the owner of all of her personal property and the income and profits of any real estate she might have owned. He also became liable on any prenuptial contracts which his wife may have made as well as liable for her negligence or other torts committed before their marriage.

In Great Britain and the United States the married woman has been largely emancipated. She may now retain the property which she owned before marriage, and she will have the sole dominion over property acquired by her after marriage. She may also enter into contractual relations with others, completely independent of her husband. She may own and operate a business, may sue and be sued in the courts, and exercise substantially the same legal rights as her husband. The husband, however, is still liable for her support.

In a number of states of the United States the wife may also become liable for the support of her husband if he is ill, unemployed, or otherwise indigent. This is the result of special legislation. By other statutes she is liable equally with her husband for "household expenses" as, for example, food, rent, and clothing for the family.

Under the early law in England and the colonies, the widow was entitled to a life estate in a portion of the real estate owned by her husband during their marriage. This was called dower, and he could not deprive her of this interest by sale, will, or other disposition of the property without her consent. The husband had a similar interest in his wife's real estate under certain conditions. Modern law has changed all this. Both the wife and husband have either an absolute right to share in the other's real estate at death or a right to inherit a share as any other heir might do. In most American states this right is protected by law against alienation without consent.

Other interests which the spouses have in their relationship with each other are identified by the technical name "consortium." This includes the interest in companionship, sexual relations, and the love and affection which presumably exists between them. Special rules of law protect these intangible interests against outside interference. Thus if a third person alienates the affections of either spouse from the other, he is subject to liability for damages at common law in an action by the injured party. If the alienation is accomplished by illicit sexual relations, the offender is liable to a further amount as determined by a jury in a civil action. Statutes in a number of states have abolished this action on the ground that it is against public policy. Although the wife is no longer obligated to render services to her husband outside the home, if she suffers physical injury by the wrong of another which disables her to attend to her normal household duties, the husband may recover damages from the wrongdoer and for any medical expenses incurred.

Obligations of Parents to Children. The father—and if he is unable to do so the mother—is liable for the support of their minor children. They are in turn entitled to the custody and services of their children. If a third person wrongfully injures a minor, the parent or parents may recover for the loss of the child's actual and anticipated services, as well as any medical or other expenses incurred by the parents on the child's behalf.

Although in the early stages of the law in England and in the states of the United States, the father was entitled to the custody of his children, he no longer has this exclusive right. In most states the parents have equal rights to the custody of their children. On dissolution of the marriage by divorce or annulment, the court will award such custody to the one or the other parent or to a third person according to the best interests of the child.

Family Disintegration

Divorce. In most nations the law provides for the dissolution of the marriage relation by divorce. This is true in all the states of the United States, but divorce policies vary widely among them. Only one ground for divorce is common to all of them, namely, adultery. In most states, desertion, cruelty, habitual drunkenness, imprisonment for serious crimes, and insanity constitute additional grounds. There are also many other incidental statutory grounds such as personal indignities, incompatibility, mental cruelty, nonsupport, vagrancy of husband, gross neglect of duties, drug habit, and others.

The general policy is that divorces are granted to "innocent" spouses against "guilty" spouses. In other words, divorce is based upon fault. Exceptions to this policy include, of course, divorce on the grounds of insanity, which is misfortune rather than fault. In a number of states provision is made for divorce after the parties have been separated and lived apart for a designated number of years, usually from two to seven. It is immaterial whether either is at fault. Occasionally a statute may provide for divorce if a spouse is absent and unheard of for seven years.

A great deal of confusion is created in the United States by reason of various decisions of the Supreme Court requiring domicile as the jurisdictional basis for divorce. This means that no state may render a divorce unless at least one of the parties, usually the plaintiff, is domiciled in that state. Domicile is the place where a person has his home. This, in turn, means that he must have a residence in the state with the intention of making that his home permanently or for an indefinite period of time. Temporary or transient residence is not enough. If, as is possible, a person has more than one home, his domicile is at the principal home. He can have but one domicile. In addition, legislation in all states but one requires that the person must have lived there for a minimum period of time (usually, 1, 2, or 3 years). In a few states this requirement is for a relatively short period, for example, three months in Florida, six weeks in Nevada and in the territory of the Virgin Islands.

When the requirement of domicile imposed by the Supreme Court is added to the local statutory residence requirement, the result is that to qualify for a divorce in any particular state of the United States, a person must have satisfied the local residence requirements and he must intend to continue to live there indefinitely. Thus a person does not acquire a domicile in Nevada if he leaves his home state to go there with the intention of returning as soon as he obtains the divorce decree. In such a case the decree is technically invalid or void. If either party subsequently remarries a third person, he becomes liable to prosecution for bigamy. If, however, the absent spouse participates in the proceeding, personally or by attorney, he or she may not subsequently attack the decree as invalid for any purpose. This is based upon the broad doctrine of estoppel. Since the plaintiff in the action is responsible for initiating it, he or she is likewise estopped. The net result, as a matter of fact, is that the divorce is for practical purposes effective as between the parties, but not as against the state in a criminal prosecution.

Alimony. The rule requiring the husband to support his wife applies only during marriage, unless the obligation is extended by judicial order. This extension is common in cases of divorce. The court may, if it appears equitable, decree continued support by the husband either by requiring him to convey to her some of his estate, to pay a cash lump sum, or, more usually, to pay monthly or weekly installments as alimony. Legislation authorizing such a decree usually leaves a wide discretion to the judge. He ordinarily will consider the wealth of the husband and his prospects for increased earnings, the age and health of the wife, the period of their marriage, and sometimes the fault of the parties in meeting their marital obligations. In some states the court is authorized to make an award of alimony to the husband, for example, where the wife is a woman of means and the husband ill or indigent. The general policy is to prevent either of the spouses from becoming a public charge, supported by the taxpayers. In most cases where alimony is required in periodic installments, the obligation ceases on the death of either party or on the remarriage of the woman if the award has been made to her. In cases where the decree provides for such periodic installments, the court retains jurisdiction to modify the decree as changed circumstances make it proper to do so. Thus, if the man's income is increased or decreased, the installments may be modified upward or downward as seems equitable.

Custody of Children. When a family with minor children is broken by divorce, it is necessary that the court make provision for the custody of the children. In so doing, the primary consideration is the welfare of the minors. Neither parent has a legal right to custody which is inconsistent with the child's welfare. If the judge finds that one of the spouses is utterly unfit morally or physically to have custody, the award will be made to the other parent, unless there is a similar finding of unfitness. In the latter case the children may be awarded to a relative, a social agency, or to the state welfare department. If the mother is a proper custodian, she would ordinarily obtain custody of children of tender age. Everything else being equal, the mother is preferred as the custodian of female children. If both parties are proper parents, the court may consult the desires of the child if it is of the age of discretion—perhaps 12 or 14 years, or older. All of these factors are taken into consideration. Where custody is awarded to one parent the other may be granted visitation rights at reasonable times and at reasonable intervals. A common pattern is to award the children to one parent for the school year, with rights of visitation, and to the other parent for the vacation period. Holidays are frequently divided between the parents. In cases of custody, as in alimony, the court retains jurisdiction and may modify the decree from time to time depending upon changed conditions.

The award of custody of minor children in cases of divorce is one of the most delicate judicial functions. Where there are strong feelings of acrimony and recrimination between the parents, the child frequently becomes the subject of continuous and repeated litigation, and changes from one parent to the other. Since decrees of custody are not permanent, and one parent may move with the children to another state, it is possible that the parties may relitigate the matter there as well as in the state where the decree was rendered. It is the general consensus among behavioral scientists that young children are the principal victims of divorce.

The father is ordinarily responsible for the support of children whether their custody is awarded to him or to the mother. In such cases the court will render a decree requiring the father to make periodic payments to the mother for support of the children and herself.

Separation by Agreement. The parties may simply agree between themselves to live separately and apart, and they may make an enforceable contract with respect to the conditions of their separation. Thus, the contract may provide for the division of property or for periodic installments for the support of the wife and children and for the custody of the latter. The contract must be fair to the wife and consistent with the welfare of the children. Such contracts are invalid if they are aimed at a separation in the future. If the parties subsequently become divorced and they mutually agree, the separation contract may be incorporated as a part of the decree.

Judicial Separation. In most of the states of the United States and many foreign countries, legislation provides for a decree of separation without the severance of the bonds of matrimony. In such a situation the parties are still married, but may live apart pursuant to such terms with respect to support and custody of minor children as are incorporated in the decree. Legislation of this type ordinarily stipulates the grounds on which one party may obtain such a decree against the other. The grounds may be coextensive with or different from those which will justify a decree of divorce.

Consult Madden, J. W., *Handbook of the Law of Persons and Domestic Relations* (1931).

FOWLER V. HARPER, Yale Law School
See also ALIENATION OF AFFECTIONS; BIGAMY; DIVORCE.

FAMILY SERVICE ASSOCIATION OF AMERICA,

voluntary federation of over 300 accredited social welfare agencies in the United States and Canada. The main service of the association is family casework by professional social workers in the fields of marriage counseling, home management, mental health, and family emergencies caused by illness and disabilities, unemployment, or death. The federated agencies also serve their communities through research and a variety of educational programs.

Organized in 1911 as the Family Welfare Association of America, the federation adopted its present name in 1946. Its headquarters are in New York. Member agencies are supported mainly through voluntary contributions by local United Funds, Community Chests, and sectarian federations.

Family Service publications are the magazines *Highlights* and *Social Casework*.

CLARK W. BLACKBURN, General Director, Family Service Association of America

FAN, device for circulating gases in a predetermined direction. Fans are used in heating and ventilating buildings, in dust-collection systems, in supplying air for combustion purposes, and in drying and cooling materials as well as distributing air within enclosed spaces. Fans are classified as either axial- or radial-flow, according to their air-flow characteristics. Axial-flow fans cause air to flow parallel to the fan axis. Propeller fans, in which the blades are designed as airfoil sections, and disc fans, in which a relatively straight blade is twisted near the hub, are common axial-flow fans. In radial-flow fans, air enters parallel to the impeller, or driving shaft axis, and is rotated 90°. Because of the rotational effect, the air is compressed. Hot-air furnaces often use radial-flow fans both for combustion and air distribution.

FANCY FREE, ballet in one act; music by Leonard Bernstein; choreography by Jerome Robbins; first performance Apr. 18, 1944, by the Ballet Theatre, Metropolitan Opera House, New York.

A lonely New York summer night finds three sailors on shore leave. They meet two girls at a bar and decide on a dance contest: the girls will choose the winners and the loser will leave. The sailors dance, but soon fists fly and the girls disappear. Friends again, they pursue a dazzling blonde. Bernstein's skillful score uses elements of American and Cuban dance rhythms, while Robbins stresses the enormous vitality and comic profile of his dancers.

FANDANGO [făn-dăng′gō], Spanish dance for one or two couples, in 3/4 or 3/8 time. Possibly of Phoenician origin, it was very popular throughout Spain from about 1710 to 1870 and was danced by people of all classes. It was sensual in content, depicting flirtation between man and woman, and the church tried, without success, to ban it. Tapping heels, probably added by the gypsies, was introduced into the fandango in the late 18th century. The choreographic pattern, set in three *coplas* (couplets), is similar to that of the *seguidillas*.
See also SEGUIDILLA; SPAIN: *Spanish Dance*.

FANEUIL [făn′əl, făn′yəl] **HALL,** historic public market and meeting hall, located in Boston, Mass. It is known as the Cradle of Liberty because of the many meetings convened there by patriots during the pre-Revolutionary period. The town meeting at which the Boston Tea Party was planned (1773) took place there. After the Revolution Faneuil Hall was the scene of orations delivered by many New England statesmen, including Daniel Webster and Charles Sumner. The original 2½-story brick building was erected in 1742 at the expense of the merchant Peter Faneuil and given to the city of Boston. The architect Charles Bulfinch added a third story in 1806. The ground floor continues in use as a market place, and the main hall, accommodating 3,000 people, can still be rented by civic groups for use as a forum. The building also contains an armory and museum that are open to the public.

FANFANI [fän-fä′nē], **AMINTORE** (1908–   ), Italian Prime Minister and economist. He was a professor of economic history and wrote extensively during the fascist period. He avoided politics but in 1943 had to take refuge in Switzerland. After World War II he held posts in several Cabinets headed by Alcide de Gasperi. As leader of the left wing of the Christian Democratic party, Fanfani consistently pressed for sweeping social and economic reforms. He was Prime Minister briefly in 1954, again in 1958–59, and for the third time from 1960 to 1963. His proposals for cooperation with the left-wing Socialists met strong opposition from conservative Christian Democrats. In March, 1965, he became Foreign Minister in Aldo Moro's cabinet, and though he resigned at the end of the year, he resumed office in February, 1966. He served as president of the Senate from 1968 to 1973.

FANGS, the long, pointed teeth of mammals, reptiles, and other animals. Fangs are found in carnivorous animals and are specially modified incisor teeth: the canine, or eye, teeth of dogs and cats are fangs. The fangs of reptiles may be solid or, as in the poisonous snakes, grooved or hollow for conduction of poison. Many pit vipers including the rattlesnakes have erectile fangs which spring into position when the mouth is opened.

The fangs of spiders and centipedes are specialized appendages of the head rather than teeth. Hollow and often swollen, they serve to inject poison into the prey. The fangs of the spider also conduct a digestive fluid to the body of the victim which reduces the tissues to semiliquid state for passage back through the fang canal.

FANNIN, JAMES WALKER (1804?–1836), Texas revolutionary hero. A Georgian, he entered Texas in 1834 and became a hot-headed leader in the revolt against Mexico. In 1836 he invaded Mexico despite the opposition of Gen. Sam Houston. Fannin drove south in January toward the Río Grande port of Matamoros, but failing to reach it and getting no reinforcements, he turned back in March. Caught by a Mexican advance, he surrendered his force of 420 near Goliad on Mar. 20. Gen. Antonio López de Santa Anna ordered 330 prisoners shot. Fannin was last to die.

FANON, FRANTZ (1926–61), French West Indian psychiatrist and social philosopher, who explored the psychological conditions of oppressed blacks and gained worldwide recognition with his books, *Black Skin, White Masks* (1952) and *The Wretched of the Earth* (1961). Fanon was born in Martinique and went to school there and in France. He studied medicine and psychiatry at the University of Lyon. In 1953 he became chief psychiatrist of Blida-Joinville Hospital in Algeria. Involved in the Algerian liberation movement, Fanon left his medical post to become editor of the Algerian National Front's newspaper. In 1960 the rebel provisional government made him its ambassador to Ghana.

Consult Genzier, Irene L., *Frantz Fanon* (1973); Zahar, Renate, Frantz Fanon: Colonialism and Alienation (1975).

FANTASIA, musical work which is based primarily on the composer's imaginative impulses or improvisatory fancies, rather than on restrictive formal principles. No single description of the fantasia is justified, because numerous composers from the 16th century on have applied the term to a wide variety of pieces for keyboard, small ensembles, and even for orchestra and chorus.

FANTIN-LATOUR [fäɴ-täɴ′la-toor′], **HENRI** (1836–1904), French painter. Although he associated with the advanced artists of his day, his own style tended to be academic. His still life and flower paintings are now popular, and he is also remembered for his notable group portraits of leading contemporary figures in the art and literary world. "Homage to Delacroix" (Louvre, Paris) shows Whistler, Baudelaire, Champfleury, and Fantin-Latour himself. In his later years he executed numerous lithographs.

FARABI [fä-rä′bē], **ABU NASR MOHAMMED AL-** (c.870–950), the founder and perhaps the greatest representative of that Islamic philosophic tradition which upheld the independence of philosophy and considered it to be the highest wisdom. He was born of Turkish parents in Turkestan, studied at Baghdad, lived for a time in Aleppo, and died in Damascus. His commentaries on Aristotle's *Organon* earned him the title of the Second Teacher. He recovered the original framework of Plato's philosophy and made use of the *Republic*, the *Timaeus*, and the *Laws* in his effort to define the relation between philosophy and revealed religion. His *Philosophy of Plato and Aristotle*, *Virtuous City*, and *Political Regime* inspired such later thinkers as Avicenna, Maimonides, and Averroës to understand the political role of philosophy. He was also an accomplished musician, and his *Great Book of Music* is the most important premodern contribution to musical theory.

MUHSIN MAHDI

FARAD [făr′əd], unit of electric capacitance. One farad is the capacitance of a capacitor (condenser) if 1 volt applied across its plates causes one coulomb of charge to accumulate on each plate. The unit is too large to be practicable: to produce one farad, two plates separated by 1 mm in air would have to be 44 sq mi (114 km^2) in area. Therefore the microfarad (one-millionth of a farad) and the micro-microfarad (one-millionth of a microfarad) are used.

FARADAY [făr′ə-dā], **MICHAEL** (1791–1867), English scientist, often called the greatest experimental genius in the physical sciences. He was born on Sept. 22, 1791, at Newington Butts, near London, in extreme poverty. "My education," he scribbled in his diary, "was of the most ordinary description, consisting of little more than the rudiments of reading, writing, and arithmetic at a common day school. My hours out of school were passed at home and in the streets."

At 14 Faraday became an apprentice bookbinder. He read many of the books, particularly the science books, avidly. An article on electricity in an encyclopedia and Jane Marcet's *Conversations on Chemistry* kindled Faraday's interest in electricity and chemistry. It was in these two areas that nearly all of his great work was done. In 1813 Faraday received a windfall—he became assistant to the noted chemist Humphry Davy. Thenceforth, nearly all of his time was spent in pure science.

Early Discoveries. By the 1820's the atmosphere of science had been charged by a series of significant discoveries in the new science of electricity. The two most important of these were Alessandro Volta's invention of the electric battery (voltaic pile) and Hans Christian Oersted's discovery that an electric current produced a magnetic field. Since electricity could produce magnetism, the central problem of science became: can magnetism produce electricity? If so, then how? This, indeed, became one of the greatest problems in the history of science.

Faraday worked sporadically on the problem. Meanwhile, in 1821, he made his first significant discovery. He found a way to make a wire revolve around a magnet, and vice versa. For the first time electric energy had been changed into mechanical energy—the principle of the electric motor.

For the next ten years Faraday concentrated on chemistry. He discovered benzene and butylene; he produced the first stainless steel; and he liquefied chlorine and many other gases. Yet the problem of getting electricity from magnetism (electromagnetic induction) continued to nag him. In 1822 he jotted down a note: "Convert magnetism into electricity." In 1824 and again in 1825 he tried and he failed. In 1831 he decided to switch for a while from chemistry to electricity, and on Aug. 29 he began the series of experiments that made him one of the immortals of science.

In the most famous of these experiments Faraday connected a coil of wire to a galvanometer, an instrument for measuring small electric currents. When he thrust a magnet into the coil, the galvanometer's needle deflected; when he withdrew the magnet the needle deflected in the opposite direction. In so simple a manner did Faraday obtain electricity from magnetism, by converting mechanical energy (the motion of the magnet) into electric energy—the principle of the electric generator. Faraday also succeeded in producing a continuous current by rotating a copper disc between the poles of a magnet.

In attempting to explain how electromagnetic induction occurred, Faraday imagined that the space surrounding the magnet and the coil was in a state of tension, like stretched rubber bands; he called these bands "lines of force." He believed that an electric current would be induced in a wire whenever the wire cut magnetic lines of force. This could happen if the wire moved through the magnetic field or if the magnetic field moved or changed relative to the wire.

Faraday went on to fill all space with these imaginary lines of force, and he believed that such space was basic to physical action. Here was a revolutionary concept, for Newton's theory would have it that particles (the magnet and the coil) and their mutual forces are fundamental, and that space and time are in the background. No, said Faraday; space and time are fundamental. If you know the properties of space and time, then you automatically know the properties of matter within that space and time. Today this approach is called the "field concept," and it forms the basis of Albert Einstein's general theory of relativity. Faraday's field concept is considered by many to be his outstanding contribution to science, and Einstein agreed that it "was the greatest creation of the scientific mind."

Later Discoveries. Many of Faraday's great discoveries, including electromagnetic induction, were made after he was 40 years old. In 1832–33 he formulated the two basic laws of electrolysis.

In 1837 Faraday found that the quantity of electricity that a capacitor could hold on its plates depended on the material between the plates. This effect that a material has on capacitance is called the dielectric constant of the material or, in Faraday's words, "the specific inductive capacity."

In the 1840's Faraday developed the hypothesis that light energy and electromagnetic energy were closely related. From this conviction he discovered in 1845 the magnetic rotation of the plane of polarized light (Faraday Effect). He also believed that gravitation and electromagnetism were somehow related, but he failed to find any connection. This became one of the deepest problems of science. Not until Einstein published his unified field theory was there any degree of success in establishing such a relationship. These hypotheses point to a significant aspect of Faraday's genius: although he knew nothing about mathematics, he was as creative in theoretical science as in experimental science.

Honors. In 1824 Faraday was elected to the Royal Society and in 1825 he became director of the laboratory of the Royal Institution. He was awarded many honors and medals during his life, but refused many of them, including the presidency of the Royal Society, in 1857.

In his later years Faraday suffered from loss of memory. Frequently he would perform an experiment that he had just completed successfully. On Aug. 25, 1867, he died peacefully, leaving the richest scientific heritage since Isaac Newton.

Consult Faraday, Michael, *Experimental Researches in Electricity* (3 vols., 1839–55); *Faraday's Diary*, ed. by Thomas Martin (7 vols., 1932–36).

HERBERT KONDO, New School for Social Research

FARADAY'S LAW. *See* ELECTROMAGNETIC INDUCTION.

FARAFRA [fə-rä'frə] **OASIS,** oasis in west-central Egypt in the Libyan Desert. Artesian water flows from the ground in a contact zone of Upper Cretaceous sandstones with Lower Eocene limestone. The chief caravan center is Qasr Farafra.

FARALLON [făr'ə-lŏn] **ISLANDS,** two small, dry, rocky Pacific island groups 26 mi. west of Golden Gate, belonging to San Francisco, Calif. Southeast Farallon, the only inhabited islet, has a lighthouse and U.S. Navy radio-beam compass and radar station. The islands, now a refuge for seals and birds, were once inhabited by Russian sealers.

FARANDOLE [făr'ən-dōl], communal chain dance of Provence, France. In extended line formation the dancers, linked together, follow the leader through the village, each dancer copying his antics. Occasionally, the first couple will form an arch under which the following couple will pass, this procedure being repeated down the line.

FARCE, comic dramatic form. The term, which derives from the French *farcir*, "to add stuffing to," was originally applied to comic playlets suitable for performance during the course of lengthy banquets. It now signifies a play that aims exclusively at arousing continuous laughter, often by means of overt physical action and absurd, even impossible, situations. The form, which dates from classical theater, tends to be shorter than comedy or tragedy, and usually has little literary value. Farce comedy is a form that includes elements of farce and comedy.

FAREHAM [fâr'əm], urban district in southeastern Hampshire, England, at the head of Fareham Creek, an inlet at the northwestern tip of Portsmouth Harbour. It is a center for retail shopping and such light industries as brickmaking and tanning. Building and repairing yachts have largely superseded shipbuilding and coastal trading. The district includes the settlements of Warsash, Titchfield, and Portchester. In Portchester is a fine Norman castle built in the northwestern corner of a large, walled Roman fortress.

FAREL [fȧ-rĕl'], **GUILLAUME** (1489–1565), reformer of French Switzerland. A zealous Catholic, Farel became a militant Protestant. In Basel in 1524 he publicly contended for reformed principles. A leader of the Reformation in Geneva, he tried to move too fast and withdrew three times when feeling ran against him. He was responsible for John Calvin's coming to Geneva, and relinquished to him the organization of the Genevan Church.

FAREWELL TO ARMS, A, novel by Ernest Hemingway, published in 1929, concerning the doomed love affair of a young American serving with the Italian forces in World War I and an English nurse. Written in the deliberately naïve, colloquial prose characteristic of Hemingway, the novel embodies both the familiar disillusionment of the postwar "lost generation" and a celebration of the "primitive" virtues of self-trust and courage in man's eternal struggle with death.

FARGO [fär'gō], **WILLIAM GEORGE** (1818–81), U.S. businessman who established a transcontinental express service as the American West expanded. He was born at Pompey, N.Y., and left school at the age of 13. In 1844 he and Henry Wells organized a carrying business (from the East to Chicago) that later became the American Express Company, with Fargo as secretary and later as president. In 1852, Wells and Fargo organized another express business, Wells, Fargo and Co., that took cargo to San Francisco, initially in stagecoaches and later in company coaches. Fargo was mayor of Buffalo, N.Y., from 1862 to 1866 and became a director in many corporations.

FARGO, largest city in North Dakota and seat of Cass County, located on the west bank of the Red River of the North. It is the major distribution center for the southern portion of the agricultural Red River valley and has food-processing and meat-packing plants. Leading industries are the manufacture of iron and steel, wood, glass, and concrete products. Fargo was settled in 1870 and named in honor of William G. Fargo, a founder of Wells Fargo Express Company. North Dakota Agricultural College is located here.

FARIBAULT [făr'ə-bō], city of southeastern Minnesota, and seat of Rice County, situated on bluffs at the confluence of the Cannon and Straight rivers. The city is an agricultural trade center and has a variety of manufacturing, including woolen mills, poultry processing, and vegetable canning. The city has a factory producing blue cheese, which is cured in caves along the banks of the rivers. Faribault was a missionary center during the 19th century. The Cathedral of Our Merciful Saviour, begun in 1862, contains a stained glass window which was a gift from the Sioux Indians.

FARINELLI [fä-rē-nĕl'lē], original name Carlo Broschi (1705–82), famous Italian male soprano or castrato. Born in Andria, he studied singing in Naples. After meeting with great success there as a boy and later in Rome (1721), he made several visits to Vienna and in 1734 became a favorite in London as a singer of non-Handelian opera. In 1737 he began a 22-year sojourn in Madrid, where, as court singer for King Philip V and later Ferdinand VI, he came to wield considerable influence and amassed great wealth. He was considered by his contemporaries the unequaled master of the art of florid, or coloratura, singing.

FARJEON [fär'jən], **ELEANOR** (1881–1965), English author of children's books, born in London. *Martin Pippin in the Apple Orchard* (1922), a whimsical fantasy about a youth and six maidens, has become a classic. *Poems for Children* (1951) contains verses published previously in four separate volumes; *The Little Bookroom* (1956) brings together some of her finest short stories. In 1959 she became the first recipient of the Regina Medal, conferred by the Catholic Library Association (U.S.) in recognition of her "distinguished contribution to children's literature."

FARLEY [fär'lē], **JAMES ALOYSIUS** (1888–1976), American politician. Born in Grassy Point, N.Y., he graduated from the Packard Commercial School in New York City in 1906. He was employed as a bookkeeper and sales manager. In 1926 he organized his own builders' supply company. He entered politics as town clerk in Stony Point, N.Y., in 1912 and served as chairman of the New York State Democratic Committee in 1930. He became chairman of the Democratic National Committee in 1932, and upon Franklin D. Roosevelt's election to the presidency, Farley was named Postmaster General. He resigned both positions in 1940 after having opposed Roosevelt's third term nomination and reentered business as board chairman and a director of the Coca-Cola Export Corporation. He wrote *Behind the Ballots* (1938) and *Jim Farley's Story* (1948).

FARLEY, JOHN MURPHY (1842–1918), Roman Catholic Archbishop of New York (1902–18) and Cardinal. He was born in Newtown-Hamilton, County Armagh, Ireland, and died in Mamaroneck, N.Y. After studying for the priesthood in America and in Rome, he served in the archdiocese of New York as episcopal secretary, pastor, vicar-general, auxiliary Bishop, and finally Archbishop. He fostered Catholic education, missionary activity, and apostolic work among immigrants. He was created a Cardinal in 1911.

FARMAN [fár-mäN'], **HENRI** (1874–1958), French pioneer pilot and aircraft designer and manufacturer. In 1908 he made the first circular cross-country flight in France and the first flight with passengers. In 1909 he made long-distance records. The same year he began to construct airplanes. Farman combat planes flew in World War I; after the war the firm built commercial airliners.

FARM BLOC, in American history, a combination of Western and Southern agrarian-minded Congressmen. Led by Senator Arthur Capper of Kansas, the farm bloc secured the adoption of measures to provide relief to farmers in the post-World War I agricultural depression. Its principal achievements were obtaining additional government farm credit and exemption of farmers' co-operatives from the provisions of the Sherman Antitrust Act. The bloc was most effective between 1921 and 1924, when it included some 14 Republicans and 10 or 12 Democrats in the Senate and perhaps 100 members of the House of Representatives.

FARM BUILDINGS. Developments in scientific agriculture have their parallel in more effective and economical farm structures. The objectives of modern buildings can only be attained by careful planning and the application of sound engineering principles to layout and construction.

The Farmhouse

The farmhouse is an inherent feature of most farms. Although relatively few are of recent construction, many older homes have been remodeled to include facilities for sanitation, light, and heat. The almost complete electrification of farms, especially in the United States and Canada, has served as an incentive to home improvement.

Farm housing has changed materially in the past few years. Instead of the multistory house with a surfeit of bedrooms, an attic, and a basement, the present trend is toward a one-story house with living room, dining room, kitchen, three bedrooms at the most, and a bath. The basement is no longer considered mandatory. Emphasis in planning is placed on ample storage space and a convenient arrangement of equipment and work units, particularly in the kitchen. Modern farmhouses have well-planned electric lighting, hot and cold running water, central heating, gas or electric cooking, and in warm climates very often have means for summer cooling. An index of the degree to which electricity contributes to modernizing the home is the 100-amp.-capacity entrance service recommended as a minimum in order to serve the requirements for cooking, laundry, water supply, refrigeration, lighting, ventilation, and radio and television. Increased entrance service may be required for those new farmhouses radiant-heated by electric energy or by the heat pump. Adequate insulation is specified for new construction to ensure comfort at lower cost through protection against the loss of heat and entrance of cold air.

Farm Outbuildings

Production or service buildings are required on most farms to house livestock and store produce. The advent of electricity and tractor power on farms, the economic necessity to reduce the labor cost of farming, and the resultant emphasis on farm mechanization in both field and chore work have resulted in an entirely new class of farm structures. Manufacturers have stimulated change by offering improved building materials, better equipment, and prefabricated buildings designed for specific purposes.

Dairy Buildings. Dairy farming requires its own specialized structures. Stall barns for the milking herd are tending toward one-story or one-and-one-half-story construction. The general use of baled or chopped hay and the increasing use of grass silage have outdated the large hay storage mows of the past. Many dairies have adopted the loose-housing system of management, utilizing an open-shed bedding area, structures for the self-feeding of silage and hay, a paved exercise yard, and a milking parlor equipped with pipeline milker and bulk tank storage for milk. This concentration of work and sanitation areas results in labor saving, adapts itself to changes in herd size, and may save on initial and subsequent construction costs. Structures for housing young stock, beef animals, sheep, and even hogs are tending toward open-shelter housing with completely mechanized feeding of both grain and forage and automatic water supply.

Poultry Farm Structures. Poultry housing and management have assumed the aspect of mechanized egg factories, through structural design incorporating mechanical feeding, controlled water supply, mechanized manure re-

Supplementary feeding of the green grains and grasses preserved by fermentation in the huge, air-tight silos keep this Indiana dairy herd's milk production at peak summer levels throughout the late fall and winter.

Jesse Lunger—Black Star

Marcel Cognac—Annan

In the modern hen house automatic devices control light, heat, sanitation, ventilation, feed, water, and egg removal.

moval, time-controlled lighting, and even equipment for gathering the eggs for centralized cleaning, grading, refrigeration, and packing. Poultry houses are insulated to avoid extremes in temperature, power ventilated to maintain fresh air, and are constructed of substantial, low-maintenance materials. The same functional planning and mechanization of heating, ventilation, and light control apply to the commercial broiler house. Climate may dictate the degree of weather protection, but the emphasis is on design that saves labor, provides the ultimate in bird health and comfort, and minimizes the cost of repairs and maintenance.

Storage Buildings. The farm storage of fruits and vegetables for commercial production has changed radically in recent years. Controlled-temperature storage is essential to maintain quality, and refrigerated storage buildings have almost completely replaced the traditional storage cellar. Buildings are heavily insulated for economy of operation. Sweet potato storage areas require heat for curing and the maintenance of moderate temperatures within close limits. Controlled hot-air heating systems under forced circulation satisfy these conditions. White potatoes are commonly stored in bulk in buildings which incorporate forced-air circulation to prevent bin heating and complete mechanization to fill and empty the storage. Vegetable and small fruit storages, which offer a hedge against temporary market gluts and the weekend closing of produce buyers, are generally well insulated and often cooled by mechanical refrigeration. A recent development is controlled-atmosphere storage for apples in which carbon dioxide content is maintained at a level for best

holding conditions. Such storages must be well insulated, of gas-tight wall construction, refrigerated, and equipped with air-composition controls.

Grain and Feed Storages. Mechanization of the grain harvest has materially changed design of grain storage buildings. The grain combine and increased use of the picker-sheller and the corn combine result in delivery of the harvest at a moisture content unsafe for keeping. Farm storages, therefore, are designed to dry grain and corn to a safe moisture content in the storage area itself, or mechanical driers are used prior to storage. Through the use of conveyors and blowers, materials are easily transported to taller storages, which are often fitted for gravity removal of the produce or equipped with mechanical means of transfer. Storages of wood construction are still common, but the cylindrical steel grain bin is often less expensive and more easily constructed.

Buildings for storing forage should be designed to save labor in filling and emptying. One-story construction for baled and chopped hay is common. Baled hay storage often flanks the feeding racks. Chopped hay can be self-fed from hopper-bottomed storages through swing gates or moved from storage to feed bunks by conveyors. Chopped, dry hay is sometimes stored in towerlike hay keepers similar to silos. These are designed to afford some degree of drying for hay brought in at unsafe moisture levels. The storage of corn and green forage in the form of silage offers succulent feed to animals during seasons when pastures are unproductive. Silos may be vertical cylinders of wood, concrete, masonry, or steel, 10 to 30 ft. in diameter, and 50 ft. or more in height. Variant forms of silo con-

Hays—Monkmeyer

Cylindrical steel bins provide storage for vast quantities of combine-threshed grains.

above ground, and the trench silo, a rectangular, horizontal structure, which is usually dug into a slope to afford earth insulation and enclosure.

Construction Materials

A wide range of construction material is offered the farmer: prefabricated steel buildings or steel structural components, such as trusses, joists, and girders, are readily available. Laminated wood construction for rafters, trusses, and beams simplifies the use of lumber for these elements. Both aluminum and steel in a wide variety of finishes are available for the surface enclosure of walls and roofs. Prefabricated wood panels of sandwich construction, including insulation for side wall and roof use, save time and work in building. Insulating materials include a wide variety of structural insulation boards that contribute stiffness to a building. Surfacing materials are offered in sheet form, and may be metal, asbestos-cement, or composition hardboard of organic origin. Glazed or baked enamel finishes are available on masonry units where sanitary construction is emphasized. Paints and allied finishes for wood, metal, or masonry are offered in a wide selection, according to the type of surface protection and appearance required. Each year new products or improvements in the present ones become available. Thus the farmer or builder has a wide choice of materials to best serve the purposes of the various structures.

WABUN C. KRUEGER, Rutgers University
See also AGRICULTURAL ENGINEERING.

FARMER, FANNIE MERRITT (1857–1915), American cookery expert who established the widespread use of level measurements and tested recipes. She attended and eventually became director of the Boston Cooking School (1889–1902). In 1902, she founded Miss Farmer's School of Cookery. Author of six books on the art of cooking and contributor to *The Woman's Home Companion,* she is best remembered for *The Boston Cooking School Cook Book* (1896).

FARMER, JAMES LEONARD (1920–   ), American Negro civil rights leader. Born in Marshall, Tex., he graduated from Wiley College there. He received a divinity degree in 1941 from Howard University but refused ordination because of segregation then practiced in southern Methodist churches. Turning to social action programs, he and a group of students founded the Congress of Racial Equality (CORE) in Chicago in 1942. As CORE leader until Mar., 1966, Farmer gained national recognition. In Feb., 1969, President Richard M. Nixon appointed him assistant secretary of health, education, and welfare, with special duties to act as a liaison with militant Negro youth.

FARMER-LABOR PARTY, in U.S. history, term applied to several minor political parties attempting to represent the interests of small farmers and urban workers. The most successful of these groups was the Farmer-Labor party of Minnesota, which grew out of the Minnesota Non-partisan League, an agrarian group organized in 1918. In 1922 the party elected Henrik Shipstead to the U.S. Senate. Floyd B. Olsen was elected to three terms as the governor of Minnesota on the Farmer-Labor ticket (1930, 1932, 1934).

In 1944, under the leadership of Hubert H. Humphrey, the party merged with the Democrats to become the Democratic-Farmer-Labor party.

The National Farmer-Labor party was organized in 1920 and nominated Parley P. Christensen for president. Christensen polled only 265,411 votes. After a disastrous 1923 convention, the party disintegrated. Many of the basic programs of the party, such as rural credit and tax reform, became law in the early days of the Franklin D. Roosevelt administration.

MURRAY S. STEDMAN, JR., Trinity College

FARMERS BRANCH, residential suburb adjacent to the northwestern limits of Dallas, Tex. Inc. as city, 1946. Pop., 27,492.

FARMING, the process of producing food and fiber from the land. Presently, there are about 3,000,000 farms in the United States, of which 95% sell more than $2,500 worth of farm products annually. The number of farms in the United States has been on the decline, while the average size of farms and annual sales per farm has increased.

The type of farming that is practiced in any area is determined by personal, physical, and economic factors. Personal factors include skills, customs, and mores of the people in the area. Physical factors are usually defined as the natural resources essential to farm production, such as climate, soil, topography, and water supply. The availability of markets, transportation and communication facilities, and public and private financial institutions, and the ownership and management patterns, are some examples of the economic factors. The interplay of all these forces underlies the formation of farming areas.

The type of farming in various areas in the United States and around the world is characterized by the products. While all areas specialize in certain products, they also produce others on a limited basis. For instance, over 50% of the income of North Carolina farmers is derived from tobacco, but fruits and vegetables, livestock, and peanuts are produced on a minor scale. In the discussion that follows, the main farming areas in the United States will be described.

Cotton Farming. The major cotton-farming areas are located in the southeastern and southwestern states, where the climate is warm. The producing area extends as far north as North Carolina in the east and California in the west. From cotton production we obtain cotton cloth, salad oil, shortening and margarine made from cotton seeds, and livestock feed. Cotton was originally produced mostly in the southeastern states, but it later shifted to the southwest.

Feed-Grain and Livestock Farming. The feed-grain and livestock farming area is located in 10 midwestern states. Beef and pork production thrive in the region, because they are based on corn, which is abundant. The distribution of rainfall, hot summer days, and warm nights com- struction are the bunker silo, an elongated bin erected

A STUDY GUIDE and a CAREER GUIDE dealing with farming and related topics accompany the article AGRICULTURE.

Fresh-picked spinach is loaded directly on a truck in the fields.
(R. GATES—FREDERIC LEWIS)

bine to create a favorable environment for the production of corn. Iowa, Illinois, Indiana, Minnesota, and Nebraska are examples of areas where feed grains and livestock farming are predominant. Considerable quantities of soybeans are also grown in this region.

Dairy Farming. Some dairy farming is practiced in every state, but Wisconsin, Minnesota, and New York are leading producers of milk, butter, and cheese. The cool climate in these states is favorable for the production of pasture and forage crops, which are necessary for successful dairy production. Highly productive dairy-farming areas are also found in California and Pennsylvania.

Wheat and Small-Grain Farming. The major wheat- and small-grain farming areas are located in the Great Plains, west of the feed-grain and livestock farming areas of the Midwest. Wheat is the most common of the small grains, with Kansas, North Dakota, Oklahoma, Montana and Washington its major producing states. Some important products from wheat and small grains are flour, cereals, and livestock feed. Small grains are also used as nurse crops in other parts of the United States.

Fruit, Truck, and Special-Crop Farming. Fruit, truck, and special-crop farming takes place in several scattered regions of the United States, the predominant areas being in the southern half of the nation. Although Arizona, California, Florida, Texas, Louisiana, and Mississippi are major producing areas, small specialized pockets are found along the Atlantic seaboard, around the Great Lakes, and in the Pacific northeast. Idaho, Maine, Florida, Alabama, and North Dakota have highly productive white-potato producing areas.

Tobacco and General Farming. Tobacco and general farming is practiced along the eastern seaboard from northern Florida to Connecticut and west to Pennsylvania, West Virginia, and Tennessee. A small quantity of tobacco is grown as far west as Wisconsin. In most cases, tobacco is the main enterprise in the southern states, being supplemented by livestock, fruits and vegetables, peanuts, soybeans, and other similar crops.

General Farming. In addition to those just mentioned, there are other general-farming areas, which are difficult to delimit due to their smallness. However, a more or less compact area can be found in the states of Ohio, West Virginia, Kentucky, Tennessee, Illinois, Missouri, and northern Arkansas, with small pockets in central and eastern Texas, Louisiana, and Alabama.

Range-Livestock Farming. More than one third of all the land in the United States grows nothing but grass. The major portion is known as the Western Grazing Region. Both private and public lands comprise this farming area, which is a very important source of food for all livestock, especially beef cattle. This type of farming is practiced to some degree in all parts of the United States.

HOWARD F. ROBINSON, Agricultural and Technical College of North Carolina

See also AGRICULTURE.

FARMINGDALE, village of southeastern New York, on western Long Island. Farmingdale is important for the manufacture of aircraft and missile parts and electronics equipment. It is about 30 mi. east of New York City. Settled, 1695; inc., 1904; pop., 9,297.

These adjoining fields of oats (*left*) and wheat on a farm in eastern Pennsylvania are ready for harvesting.   (HERBERT LANKS—PIX)

Young Herefords from the Western ranges are fattened in a Corn Belt feed lot.

FARMINGTON, town of central Connecticut, west of Hartford, on the Farmington River. It is a residential area with a few light industries, including the manufacture of steel balls and springs. One of the oldest towns in Connecticut, Farmington maintains its charm through old homes ranged along elm-lined streets. Miss Porter's School and the Hill-Stead Museum are located here. Inc., 1645; pop., 14,390.

FARMINGTON, a residential city of southeastern Michigan, a suburb northwest of Detroit. Inc., 1926; pop., 10,329.

FARMINGTON, city of east-central Missouri, and seat of St. Francois County, in a rich lead-mining area, 58 mi. to the south of the center St. Louis. Inc., 1879; pop., 6,590.

FARMINGTON, town of northwesten New Mexico, located on the San Juan River. Long the center of a fruit-producing area, Farmington grew rapidly after 1950,

Fed a well-balanced diet, an eight-month-old hog may weigh 300 lb.
Ewing Galloway

when gas, oil, and uranium production became important in the vicinity. Fifty mi. southwest of the town is Chaco Canyon National Monument. Inc., 1901; pop., 21,979.

FARM MACHINERY. The use of agricultural machinery is one of the distinguishing features of a progressive and highly developed nation. In a country with a high standard of living, which is itself largely the result of mechanization, the farmer without machinery for the preparation of the seedbed, for planting, cultivating, and harvesting, is severely handicapped.

Farm machines have been made longer lasting through rubber tires, better steel, better protection of working parts, and improved lubrication. Machines have been strengthened for use with tractors, have increased safety features, require less frequent lubrication, and are more easily handled than early machines. Tractors are lighter and faster for the same power, and engine and tractor performance are better.

Increasing adaptability of power and machinery to agriculture has made it possible to increase farm productivity with reduced manpower, releasing part of the labor force to industry. The following examples illustrate how mechanization has saved labor.

With sugar beets, a "stoop labor" crop, the customary hand blocking and thinning previously demanded about 25 man-hours per acre. Complete mechanical thinning, according to studies made by the U.S. Department of Agriculture, requires only 2.45 man-hours.

In corn harvesting, the 2-row picker is commonly used on farms where at least 100 acres of corn are planted. Plantings that yield 70 bushels per acre can be harvested with less than 1 man-hour an acre, while hand picking would require about 6¼ man-hours.

With a harvester-thresher combine, an acre of wheat requires 1 man-hour, whereas the binder and thresher method requires 4 man-hours. An acre of corn can now be produced and cribbed with about 5 man-hours of labor; in 1900 it required 15 man-hours. Cotton is the least mechanized of the major American crops, yet the man-hour requirement in a 40-year period has been reduced from about 100 to 70, although 75% of the crop is still picked by hand.

MODERN FARM MACHINERY

Ewing Galloway

Ewing Galloway

A combination drill seeds grain and fertilizes it in one operation.

A plowed field is tilled with a tractor-drawn, spring-tooth harrow and drag prior to planting.

The manure spreader distributes fragmented fertilizer over a wide area in a short time.

H. Armstrong Roberts

Modern farm machinery falls into six categories: (1) seedbed-preparation implements, such as plows, harrows, and other tillage machines; (2) planters, seeders, drills, transplanters, fertilizer distributors, and manure spreaders; (3) cultivators, weeders, and machines for the control of pests and diseases; (4) harvesters for cutting, gathering, digging, and threshing; (5) processing machines such as cotton gins, flax machines, feed grinders, corn shellers, balers, hay crushers, and forage harvesters; and (6) power sources such as trucks, tractors, electric motors, and engines.

Seedbed-Preparation Implements. A variety of tillage implements are available, ranging from the plow to equipment used in draining land, conserving rainfall, and preventing erosion. Recent changes in plow design have reduced draft and made plows more effective for turn-

ing under crop refuse—a considerable factor in controlling insect and weed pests. With the tractor as a source of power, different tillage implements are used together, for example, plows, disk harrows, and peg-tooth harrows, and sometimes even planters.

At Auburn, Ala., the Agricultural Engineering Research Division of the U.S. Department of Agriculture maintains the Tillage Machinery Laboratory. Here in tanks containing soils of various kinds, studies are made of the performance of tillage implements, improving their effectiveness.

Plows are used mainly for primary tillage and include moldboard, disk plows, and middlebreakers and listers. For secondary tillage, disk harrows, spike-tooth harrows, spring-tooth harrows, and rollers are used.

Even on small farms much plowing is done with light

tractors which pull 1- or 2-bottom plows. With such equipment a farmer can plow from 3 to 8 acres a day. And if secondary tillage tools are attached to a 2-plow or larger tractor, the land can be made ready for planting in a once-over operation. The advantage of this method is that the land is harrowed when it is most friable.

The spike-tooth harrow breaks clods. Spring-tooth harrows are more severe in their action, and disk harrows cut up very resistant soil. On lumpy soil, clod crushers or rollers are often used. On light and sandy soils, a roller is desirable to compact the seedbed.

Planting and Fertilizing Implements. Seeders, planters, transplanters, and combinations with fertilizer distributors are available in great variety. Drills for small grain consist of a long hopper on wheels, with spouts leading the grain down to the soil into furrows made by disks or shoes. The same type of planter is used for peas and some other crops.

Corn planters are made so that the corn, or other seeds, may be planted in drills cultivated only lengthwise in the field, or in check rows cultivated both ways. Planting plates in the bottom of the seedboxes are made with cells of different sizes to regulate the planting of different numbers of kernels of varying sizes and shapes. The wide use of hybrid corn has made seed corn more valuable, and planting plates have been made to conform with the practice of planting even the irregular kernels from the butts and tips of ears. Planters of this type are used for planting many crops such as peas, beans, and cotton. Improved sugar-beet planters drop single- or split-seedballs, which

Dusting machinery applies insecticide or fungicide to several rows of young tomato plants. (A. DEVANEY)

A mechanized picker strips the bolls from two rows of cotton plants. (INTERNATIONAL HARVESTER)

As the combine moves through the field, it cuts the wheat and threshes the grain, which is then piped onto the truck. (H. ARMSTRONG ROBERTS)

increase the number of single plants, reducing thinning work.

Transplanters consist essentially of a shoe, or disk, which opens furrows for the young plants and compacts the soil about them when they have been set in place by hand or by machine. Many transplanters have compartments for fertilizer and devices for placing it at the most advantageous location with respect to the seeds or transplants of a particular crop. Means are provided for supplying water or a liquid fertilizer to give the young plant a boost before its rootlets become established.

There are many types of fertilizer distributors which perform only this function. As a result of work done by the U.S. Department of Agriculture, by various state agricultural experiment stations, and by the fertilizer industry, distributors have been modified to place the fertilizer accurately in accordance with the needs and the peculiarities of crops and soils. Fertilizer placed 2 to 3 in. to the side of the row and 2 to 3 in. below the seed or root crown gives best results with a large number of crops, while other crops require closer placement of fertilizer for optimal results. Some seedlings are sensitive to strong fertilizer solution, and others are resistant. Attention to this knowledge has given noticeable increases in yields of potatoes, cotton, snap beans, tomatoes, and other crops without increasing the amount of fertilizer used. Manufacturers have modified their machines so that they can be used for many crops.

The manure spreader is in common use on dairy, livestock, and general farms for pulverizing and spreading manure, sometimes reinforced with chemicals. Spreaders, improved in durability and in ease of loading, consist essentially of a long box on wheels with an endless apron bottom or, more commonly, with a tight bottom, conveyor slats, and rotating beater at the rear. They are drawn by horses or tractor. Many tractor-mounted loaders are now available for loading spreaders where large amounts of manure are to be handled.

Cultivating Implements. Cultivation of crops is important largely because it controls weeds, thereby conserving soil moisture and plant food. With some crops it should begin even before the plants have come up and when it is convenient to cultivate without damaging the crop.

The cultivation of corn is typical of row crops. For early cultivation, a cultivator with a pair of rotary-hoe wheels near the row and six "sweeps" between rows has been found to be most efficient. In weedy corn, best results are obtained with a cultivator that has two pairs of disk hillers and one pair of sweeps per row. Sweeps are flat, knifelike shovels that cut off weeds just below the surface.

To thin sugar beets to a proper stand, modifications have been made in the seed itself, in the planting machines, and in the so-called blocking machines that may be set to leave the right number of plants. This may be either a cross-blocker or an in-the-row thinner.

An important development in the cultivation of commercial farm crops has been the multiple-row cultivator. Much corn and some other row crops are cultivated with cultivators that handle four or more rows. This development was speeded by the improvements in tractors. Some tractors are adapted to pulling cultivators, but more common use is made of the tractor-mounted cultivator. Even before the development of the tractor there were many 2-row horse-drawn cultivators.

Harvesting Machines. A wide variety of harvesters are available to meet the requirements of different crops. Farmers have found them profitable, and inventors and research workers continue their efforts to develop new harvesters and improve old ones. When labor is scarce, harvesting machines and other farm implements are especially in demand.

Haymaking has been more or less standardized for years except for an increase in the use of tractors and the appearance of the pick-up baler which bales the hay as it is automatically picked up from the windrow left by the side-delivery rake or swather. Common haying machines are the mower, now much improved in material and ease of handling; the side-delivery rake; the tedder; the loader; and the buck rake. Hay is commonly placed in rows or stacks by means of hayforks and heavy ropes, which pull large forkfuls along a steel track under the barn ridge or up to the peak of stacking poles.

The most conspicuous development in the harvesting of small grain has been the increasing use of 6-ft. threshers adapted to moderate-sized farms. There are about 1,000,000 harvester-thresher combines in the United States, and only a few grain binders remain in use on farms. Binders leave the grain in bundles so that it must be put up in shocks and threshed with the ordinary separator, either from the shock or from large stacks, whereas combines cut and thresh in one operation.

Some corn is still husked by hand from the standing stalks or from the shock, but large acreage is harvested with mechanical pickers which deliver the corn into wagons which are hauled to the crib with the same tractor that pulls the picker. Some corn is husked at the barn by husker-shredders. On many farms husked corn is elevated into the crib with a power-driven elevator. With modern machines it requires only about 1 man-hour to pick and crib an acre of corn.

Large acreages of corn are cut green with a binder, then chopped with an ensilage cutter, and stored as feed for dairy cows and other livestock. Since 1935 there has been a noticeable development in the use of grass for silage and in equipment for gathering and storing it. Field forage harvesters cut up green crops in the field ready to haul to the silo.

The emphasis placed on grassland farming, and the economy to the farmer of using silage as a major part of the animal ration, have encouraged the practice of making grass silage. The importance of reducing the time, labor, and cost of harvesting, storing, and feeding forage crops and, at the same time, conserving their maximum feeding value, has given added impetus to this trend.

Horizontal silos, both trench and above-ground types, are attracting wide interest because of their adaptability to low-cost mechanical forage harvesting, storage, and feed-handling methods, and to self-feeding.

Potatoes are commonly harvested with diggers which free the potatoes of dirt. In smaller fields, they are harvested with special plows. Some sugar-beet harvesting machines now do a good job of topping the beets in the ground, lifting and dropping the beets in a windrow or into a truck, and leaving the tops in piles.

The use of mechanical cotton harvesters is steadily increasing in the United States. A type of harvester known as a sled, or stripper, has been used in the drier parts of the Cotton Belt to snap off mature bolls, and under certain conditions this method has proved profitable. Several types of sugar-cane harvesters have appeared in recent years.

Processing Machines. The actual processing of some crops may be considered part of the farm operations. This is true of cotton ginning and of fiber flax processing. The hay baler, silo filler, feed grinder, corn sheller, stationary cornhusker-shredder, apple grader, potato grader, and other equipment all do primary processing.

The ginning of cotton has been greatly improved through the development of driers, cleaning and extracting equipment, and conveyors. Most of these processes are the direct result of new and improved harvesting machines which do not produce lint cotton, and match the quality formerly produced by hand picking.

Flax fiber is produced on a small scale in Oregon, where the U.S. Department of Agriculture and the Oregon Experiment Station have developed improvements in many of the machines and processes. The machines used are pullers, deseeders, tow-shakers, and cleaners. An improved cleaner makes low-grade tow marketable.

The growing of other fiber crops newly introduced into the United States has opened a new field in farm machinery development. For example, kenaf and sansevieria are being produced experimentally in Florida, and ramie is commercially grown on a small scale in that state. Kenaf is is a substitute for jute, and sansevieria has proved valuable in replacing Manila hemp as a cordage fiber. Ramie possesses qualities similar to those of cotton and flax. Machines for processing these crops are, on the whole, still in the experimental stages.

Consult Brodell, A. P., *Use of Tractor Power, Animal Power, and Hand Methods in Crop Production* (1948); U.S. Department of Agriculture, *Changes in Farm Production Efficiency* (1955); Brodell, A. P., and Cooper, M. R., *Power and Machinery on Farms* (1956); *The Yearbook of Agriculture, Power to Produce*, ed. by Alfred Stefferud (1960).

JERRY B. DAVIS, U.S. Department of Agriculture

See also:

FARM POWER. *See* RURAL ELECTRIFICATION.

FARM SAFETY. Agriculture has one of the poorest safety records of all occupations. In the United States there are over 12,000 accidental deaths to farm residents each year; almost 1,000,000 persons are injured, some crippled for life. The annual economic loss resulting from these accidents is almost $1,000,000,000.

Accidents in and around the home account for one-fourth of the total: falls lead the list; burns are next; suffocation, firearms accidents, and drowning follow in that order. Deaths associated directly with farm work number about 3,500. These result principally from contact with machinery or by the tipping of tractors. Motor vehicles take the lives of some 5,000 farmers per year. Blind driveway intersections with high-speed highways, slow-moving farm transports, and the lack of sidewalks in rural areas all contribute their share of hazard. Hunting, swimming, and boating account for 1,000 deaths a year, while farm fires add nearly another 800.

Farm safety cannot be legislated as it is in industry: there are no safety supervisors; there is no enforcement; the farm and its workers are independent. Safety, therefore, becomes an individual responsibility and safety consciousness has to be developed in the farmer, members of his family, and his help in order to reduce farm accidents. This requires a broad educational program.

The first concerted effort toward rural safety in the United States was the establishment in 1944 of the Farm Safety Committee by the National Safety Council. Most states now have their own rural safety committees and many employ a full-time agent to co-ordinate and promote safety efforts.

A general educational program for safety in agriculture involves three major interrelated steps. The first is to be able to organize hazards and weigh the possibility of a mishap. Farm safety check lists distributed by 4-H and Future Farmers of America organizations, and hazard hunts on farms contribute to the discovery of dangers that lurk around the farm and home.

The second objective of this integrated program is to persuade and train farm residents to eliminate those hazards that can be corrected. This involves a clean-up program to get rid of fire hazards, trash, obstructions, broken steps and ladder rungs, and guarding dangerous machine parts where function permits. Manufacturers are constantly making improvements to reduce machinery hazards, but maintenance of protective devices is the responsibility of the user. Too often, as with the tractor power-take-off shield, safety devices are removed and their protective value lost.

The third phase of the general accident-prevention program is to educate farm inhabitants to live with those hazards that cannot be eliminated. Such power-operated machines as the baler, corn picker, forage chopper, combine, and mower are inherently dangerous and cannot be guarded without destroying their function. In such cases, safety is dependent on training and educating the operator with insistence that manufacturers' operation instructions be closely followed. The difficulty of such instruction lies in the fact that farm workers must operate a wide variety of machinery under varying conditions, often for only short periods of time each year, and skill and experience are dulled by time.

Success in making the farm and farm home a safer place to work and play is dependent on the co-ordinated effort of all groups concerned with agriculture. All members of the farm family must be made safety conscious. This involves recognition of the danger areas, recognition of major hazards, appreciation of the risks in handling machinery and livestock, adequate maintenance of electric wiring and protective devices, constant vigilance in fire prevention, training in the use of approved fire extinguishers, and training in the use of first-aid practices.

WABUN C. KRUEGER, Rutgers University

FARNBOROUGH, urban district in northeastern Hampshire, England. It quarters the Royal Aircraft Establishment, center for aeronautic experimentation. In the Imperial Mausoleum of St. Michael's Roman Catholic Church, built (1887) by the former Empress Eugénie of France, are buried Napoleon III, Eugénie, and the Prince Imperial, Louis. Pop., 31,437.

FARNESE [fär-nā′zā], Italian noble family that flourished from the 15th to the 17th centuries. Although never very powerful politically, the Farnese family produced several distinguished soldiers and noted art patrons. The family's origins go back to the 10th century, and it began to play an important role during the 15th century, when several Farnese distinguished themselves in the military service of the Papacy. The family acquired considerable influence through the connection of GIULIA FARNESE (1474-1524) with Pope Alexander VI, but its great rise occurred after ALESSANDRO FARNESE became Pope Paul III (q.v.). Paul III used his power to enrich the family and created the independent Duchy of Parma and Piacenza for his natural son PIER LUIGI FARNESE (1503–47). Pier Luigi attempted to curb the privileged classes and was assassinated. Among his successors was ALESSANDRO FARNESE (1545–92), greatest soldier of the 16th century and a brilliant diplomat in the service of the Spanish crown, who prevented William the Silent from uniting the Netherlands in the struggle for independence from Spain. The dynasty declined in the 17th century and ended with ANTONIO FARNESE (1679–1731). However, his niece Elizabeth Farnese (q.v.), wife of Philip V of Spain, gained the succession for her sons, who founded the line of Bourbon-Parma. Though the Farnese never played a pivotal role in the history of Italy, despite their ambitions, they gathered valuable art collections and constructed numerous fine buildings, including the famed Palazzo Farnese in Rome.

ARMAND PATRUCCO, Queens College, New York

FARNHAM [fär′nəm], RUSSEL (1784–1832), American fur trader, born in Massachusetts. Farnham shipped around Cape Horn in 1811 as a member of the sea-borne party that met an overland group sent by John Jacob Astor to build a fur-trading fort at the mouth of the Columbia River. In 1813 the British forced Astor to sell the fort for $40,000 and Farnham was charged with bearing the money and records to Astor. The hardships of his winter journey on foot across Siberia and Russia to Europe and the United States tax the imagination, but he survived and continued working for the American Fur Company.

FARNHAM, city of Quebec, Canada, on the Yamaska River. It is an industrial and commercial city in an agricultural region, a railway center, and an important training center for the Canadian army. Woolen goods and men's clothing are manufactured. It was settled by American loyalists around 1790. Inc., 1876; pop., 6,354.

FARO, card game of European origin extremely popular in American gambling houses until about 1900. Any number of persons play against the house, which supplies a dealer and a casekeeper, who keeps track of the cards drawn during play. Betting consists in wagering that various denominations (numbers, or types of face cards, regardless of suits) will win or lose. Betting on such a number to lose is known as coppering one's bet and involves placing a copper token on the chips at stake. Chips are placed on a table whose top contains a layout representing the cards of the spade suit.

A 52-card deck is shuffled and placed face up in the dealing box. The top card (soda) does not count; it is removed to expose a card that loses; this latter card is then removed to expose a third card that wins. Thus ends the first turn; bets on the exposed numbers are settled, and unsettled bets remain. New bets are made prior to the start of another turn, which consists in the dealer's removing the previous winner from the stack of cards, exposing a card that loses, and then one that wins. The process continues until three cards remain under a winning one. Now bets are made on the order in which the three (whose ranks are known from the record of the previous cards drawn) will appear. Guessing this order is known as calling the turn.

Bets on a number to win or lose are settled on an even-money basis. The house collects half of the bets made on splits (numbers that are both winners and losers in the same turn). The house pays on a 4-to-1 basis to players successfully calling the turn. A pair (two cards of the same rank) among the last three cards in the box is known as cat-hop; winning bets on the order in which these two cards appear are settled on a 2-to-1 basis.

No skill is involved in the game, and the house percentage is so small that it is doubtful if an honest faro bank can exist.

FRANK K. PERKINS, Games Columnist, Boston *Herald*

FAROUK I. See FARUK I.

FARQUHAR [fär′kwər], GEORGE (1677?–1707), English dramatist. Born in Londonderry, he was educated there and in Dublin, where he soon left school for the stage. Turning to writing, he had his first play, *Love and a Bottle*, produced in London in 1699. *The Constant Couple* followed in 1700, and *Sir Henry Wildair* in 1701. A period of military service at this time was reflected in *The Recruiting Officer* (1706). His last play, considered by many as his best, was *The Beaux' Stratagem* (1707). While perhaps not so witty as Congreve's, his comedies have more human sympathy.

FARRAGUT [fär′ə-gət], DAVID GLASGOW (1801–70), U.S. naval officer. He was born near Knoxville, Tenn. and christened James Glasgow Farragut. He changed his name in honor of David Porter, who brought him up and sent him to sea at the age of nine. During the War of 1812 he served on Porter's ship, the *Essex*. During the cruise Farragut became master of a prize ship, though he was only 12 years old. He fought pirates in the West Indies (1823–24) and commanded a sloop during the war with Mexico (1841).

Upon the outbreak of the Civil War, Farragut moved his home from Virginia to New York. In Dec., 1861, he received command of the West Gulf Blockading Squadron, with orders to take New Orleans. On Apr. 28, 1862 Farragut took the city, having gone past defending forts

Admiral David Glasgow Farragut. (BROWN BROTHERS)

and defeated a Confederate flotilla. This feat made him the leading naval officer in the North, and he received the thanks of the government and promotion to rear admiral. Ordered to open the Mississippi River as far north as Memphis, Farragut ran past the active batteries of Vicksburg, saw that the town was impregnable against naval attack, and returned to New Orleans. He blockaded the Gulf coast and took Galveston, Corpus Christi, and Sabine Pass. In Mar., 1863, when he tried to take his fleet past the Confederate batteries at Port Hudson to help Grant at Vicksburg, only his flagship, the *Hartford*, and one gunboat succeeded, but he cut Confederate communications. In July, Port Hudson fell, and the Mississippi was open. Early in 1864 he attempted to capture Mobile Bay, its channel obstructed by mines, then called torpedoes. Farragut, in this successful engagement, answered "Damn the torpedoes!", to a warning cry of torpedoes ahead.

Farragut was promoted to vice admiral in 1864 and in 1866 was advanced to admiral. He retired in New York City and died at Portsmouth, N.H.

Consult Lewis, C. L., *David Glasgow Farragut* (2 vols., 1941–43).

MARTIN BLUMENSON, formerly, Senior Historian, Department of the Army

FARRAR [fə-rär'], **GERALDINE** (1882–1967), noted American soprano, born in Melrose, Mass. She made her first public appearance in concert in 1896. She subsequently studied with Lilli Lehmann and made her opera debut as Marguérite in *Faust* at the Berlin Staatsoper in 1901. She then sang at Monte Carlo in *La Bohème* with Caruso (1904) and made her American debut at the Metropolitan Opera as Juliette (1906). She sang *Madama Butterfly*, for the first of some hundred performances, at the Metropolitan in 1907, with Caruso and Scotti. Her repertoire also included *Tosca*, *Carmen*, *Thaïs*, *Suor Angelica*, and

Louise, among others. Between 1915 and 1919 she also made a number of silent films, including *Carmen*. She retired from the Metropolitan in 1922, but gave concerts for another decade. Besides having a voice of supreme quality, she was a superb actress.

FARRELL [făr'əl], **EILEEN** (1920–   ), noted American soprano, born in Willimantic, Conn. After little formal training she made her radio debut in 1941, continuing in her own featured program for six years. Engagements with major symphony orchestras throughout North and South America and successful appearances with the San Francisco and Metropolitan Opera companies followed, establishing her as one of the most brilliant American singers of her generation. Her rich voice is powerful, yet skillfully controlled through all degrees of shading and coloration. She is especially noted for her interpretations of Bach and Wagner and has also revealed talents as a singer of jazz and blues songs.

FARRELL, JAMES THOMAS (1904–   ), American novelist, known for naturalistic studies of city life. Born in Chicago, he was educated at the University of Chicago. His first major work was the *Studs Lonigan* trilogy—*Young Lonigan* (1932), *The Young Manhood of Studs Lonigan* (1934), and *Judgment Day* (1935)—a detailed picture of the destructive forces of a city working on a youth. His second major project was the Danny O'Neill series, paralleling *Studs Lonigan* in subject matter—*World I Never Made* (1936), *No Star Is Lost* (1938), *Father and Son* (1940), *My Days of Anger* (1943), and *The Face of Time* (1953). He has also published many volumes of short stories and literary criticism.

FARRELL, industrial city of extreme western Pennsylvania, near the Ohio state line. Originally known as South Sharon, it was renamed in 1911 in honor of a president of the United States Steel Company; the company's mills dominate the local economy. Inc. as city, 1932; pop., 11,022.

FARRUKHABAD CUM FATEHGARH [fə-rōōkн'ä-bäd-kŭm-fŭ-tä-gär'], city on the Ganges River in Uttar Pradesh State, India. Originally two cities, they now form a joint municipality comprising the capital of Farrukhabad District. As a trade center it handles agricultural produce; industries include the manufacture of brassware, copperware, and calico prints, and printing. At Fatehgarh is a government gun-carriage factory. The Afghan Nawab Mohammed Khan founded Farrukhabad about 1714. Southwest is the village of Sankisa, the scene of Buddha's descent from the heaven of the 33 gods and today a Buddhist pilgrimage site. The Marathas seized Fatehgarh in 1751, but in 1804 Lord Lake re-established British authority. In 1857 Sepoy rebels captured the fort and massacred many fleeing British. The British recaptured the city in 1858. Pop., 74,205.

FARSIGHTEDNESS or hypermetropia, common eye condition in which the eye cannot focus properly. In normal vision the image of the object is focused upon the retina, the light-sensitive surface in the back of the eye. In farsightedness the image of a distant object is focused behind the retina. The farsighted person can bring distant objects into clear focus by contracting the ciliary muscle which controls the curvature of the crystalline lens of the eye. The changed lens curvature projects the image on the retina. Although the young farsighted individual can see clearly by making this correction in lens shape, the ciliary muscle becomes overworked in the process, often causing headache and eye fatigue. The strain is even greater when looking at near objects since the ciliary muscle normally contracts in order to focus nearby objects; in the farsighted eye the muscle must produce a much greater contraction; consequently, farsighted persons experience more symptoms when doing close work.

At about the age of 40 the crystalline lens begins to harden and the ciliary muscle cannot change the lens curvature as easily as before. By the age of 60 or so the lens shape cannot be altered by muscle contractions and the farsighted person sees distant objects as blurred.

Eyeglasses correct the condition by focusing the image on, instead of behind, the retina. The need for glasses usually increases with age: the farsighted child may need them only when close work is being done. Older persons may require glasses to make the corrections which were earlier accomplished by muscular contraction.

MONROE J. HIRSCH, O.D., Associate Editor,
American Journal of Optometry

See also EYE; NEARSIGHTEDNESS.

FARUK [fə-roōk'] **I**, also **Farouk, Faruq** (1920–65), King of Egypt. The son of Fuad I, Faruk became King of Egypt on Apr. 28, 1936. A council of regency acted in his name until July, 1937, when he assumed his constitutional powers. Faruk's immense early popularity declined sharply during and after World War II, in consequence partly of his failure to resist British political control, partly because of the corruption of the court. After the revolution of 1952, he abdicated on July 26, 1952, in favor of his infant son, Ahmed Fuad II, and went into exile.

FASCES [făs'ēz], Latin name for a bundle of rods enclosing a two-headed axe which symbolized the authority of the higher Roman magistrates to order chastisement. Originally Etruscan, the fasces were borne by lictors, who accompanied the magistrates; the number of lictors varied according to the magistrate's rank. The emblem and name of Italian Fascism came from the fasces.

FASCHING [fäsh'ǐng], in the Germanic countries, the carnival preceding Lent. The name derives from *fasen, faseln,* "to talk nonsense," and the festival is characterized by burlesque songs and antics.

FASCISM [făsh'ĭz-əm], political movement that originated in Italy after World War I and ruled the country from 1922 to 1943. Similar movements in other countries, variously titled and reflecting special indigenous conditions, have also been called fascist.

Origins. The name "fascism" is derived from the Italian *fascio* ("bundle") and from the Latin *fasces,* the term for the Roman symbol of authority. *Fasci,* or political groupings for the achievement of some specific purpose, had

often been organized in Italy before, but Italian Fascism has come to be exclusively associated with the movement organized by Benito Mussolini in 1919. World War I, which Italy had entered in 1915, was far longer and more costly than anticipated, and Italy did not gain the expected benefits from it. The consequences were social unrest and national dissatisfaction. Some thought that these might be passing conditions, soon to be followed by a return to normality, but the strain proved too great for a weak economic structure and a relatively young and immature democracy. This state of affairs was reflected in the unsatisfactory operation of Parliament which in turn was manifested in a succession of weak and irresolute governments. Such conditions put a premium on illegality, and there was fear among the propertied classes that Italy might fall to the Communists.

Mussolini had been a prominent figure in the Italian Socialist movement until he broke with it in 1914 to advocate Italy's entrance into the war. A man of ability and ambition, in March, 1919, he organized the *fasci di combattimento.* The movement at first made little progress; in the election of Nov., 1919, Mussolini himself was badly defeated in Milan. But as conditions failed to improve in the country, *fasci* began to spread. Dedicated, as they purported to be, to the restoration of order and the authority of the state, they increasingly took matters into their own hands, resorting to violence against elements of the left. A truce with the Socialists in 1921 was short-lived, the Fascists depending ever more for support on the propertied classes and the forces of conservatism. In 1921 they elected 35 members to Parliament. The continued ineffectiveness of the regime and the persistence of disorder gave them their opportunity in Oct., 1922, on the occasion of a new Cabinet crisis. Fascist formations gathered at various points in the country, ready to "march on Rome." On the pretext of avoiding possible bloodshed and because of doubts about the attitude of the armed forces, King Victor Emmanuel III refused to institute martial law. Instead, he called Mussolini to the prime-ministership. In November his action was ratified by Parliament, which thereby signed its own death warrant.

Nature. Parliament was not dissolved, however, nor was the existing regime altered at first, and there was little public awareness of a revolutionary change; a *coup d'état* rather than a revolution had taken place. From Mussolini's numerous pronouncements it would have been difficult at this time to forecast the future course of Fascism. It was commonly expected that normality would shortly be restored. Rather than being an integrated system of thought, Fascism may be said to have gradually taken shape as a response to circumstances—those that had caused its birth and those that existed after Mussolini became Prime Minister. Only after Fascism had been in power for some years was a philosophy elaborated for it, Mussolini himself contributing the article entitled "Fascism" to the *Enciclopedia Italiana.* Nevertheless, the forces that shaped Fascism are easily discernible.

The designation National Socialism, the name of the fascist movement in Germany, is a far better appellation. Mussolini's own background was socialistic, and he was a man of the people. Although he broke with socialism—in fact became its worst enemy—the initial program issued by the Central Committee of the *fasci* in preparation for the 1919 election is revealing: the economic, social, and political reforms that it advocated—social security, higher wages, improved conditions of labor, female suffrage—were standard planks of any socialist platform. But, in addition, Mussolini endorsed the 1919 Fiume adventure of the nationalist author and soldier Gabriele d'Annunzio. It is this merging of what had traditionally been two antithetic tendencies, socialism and nationalism, that may be regarded as the original contribution of Fascism to the political thought and practice of our time.

In Fascism the Marxist concept of the class struggle was transposed to a different plane. The rich and the poor were to be found at the national level: there were "haves" (the United States, Great Britain, and France, for example) and "have nots" (Italy and Germany), with equal claims to places in the sun. Conflict between social classes dispersed and weakened national energies needed in the struggle against other nations. In Fascism the nation was the living political reality, wherein the individual fulfilled himself. Attempts to organize lasting peace, as within the League of Nations, were viewed with contempt, as being at best premature utopian hopes.

This outlook inevitably led to the exaltation of force, violence, even brutality—concepts ever congenial to Fascism. It had also the consequence of exalting the state, thus providing the third most important characteristic of Fascism: antidemocratic totalitarianism. The state was the supreme embodiment of the nation. All interests had to be subordinated to the strength and glorification of the state, and the state in turn supervised and regulated all the activities of its members. This led to the suppression of all opposition, to the legalization of the one-party state, and to the close identification of the Fascist party and the state. The structure of the party was hierarchical, authority descending from above, and dictatorship was the logical consequence. Mussolini was head of the government, though more commonly referred to as the *Duce* ("leader"). If he did not say *l'état, c'est moi* ("I am the state"), the slogan *Mussolini ha sempre ragione* ("Mussolini is always right") is of similar inspiration. The walls of Italy everywhere displayed that other slogan *Credere, obbedire, combattere* ("To believe, to obey, to fight")—an adequate summary of the Fascist philosophy.

In the economic domain Fascism adopted the concept of the corporate state, and eventually an attempt was made to organize the economic life of the country into 22 corporations comprising everyone engaged in the same industry or profession. Thus, for example, there was to be a "steel corporation," consisting of all those involved in the production of that commodity. The affairs of the steel industry were to be regulated by a body representing ownership, labor, and the state. There was, needless to say, no room for strikes, those wasteful manifestations of the outdated class struggle. However, the corporate state was never fully developed. The state inclined to the side of property, although some provisions were made for the general welfare of the people.

Domestic Affairs. When Mussolini became Prime Min-

Pix, Inc.

United Press International

Benito Mussolini addresses a civilian crowd of Fascist supporters.

International News

Il Duce, *right*, reviews a regiment of the goose-stepping Fascist army.

United Press International

An Italian Fascist display of power in 1935.

Fascism may be considered in two senses. In its strict sense it refers to a political movement that prevailed in Italy under Benito Mussolini from 1922 to 1943. In its wider meaning it may be applied to any totalitarian government—for example, that of Nazi Germany, Spain, and certain countries of Latin America. Articles dealing with Fascism can be grouped as follows.

Fascism in Italy. The article on these pages discusses Fascism as it existed in Italy between World Wars I and II, growing out of the first and helping to cause the second. The article describes the disorder in Italy following World War I that gave the Fascists their opportunity to take over the government. As Fascist power was established and a Fascist philosophy was created, three major characteristics of the movement could be discerned. First, it was nationalistic, exalting Italy above other countries. Second, it merged with nationalism some of the economic and social welfare policies of socialism. Third, it was antidemocratic and totalitarian, glorifying the state and making the individual in all ways subservient to it.

An over-all view of the rise of Fascism is provided in ITALY: *History,* and in the entry on the man whose name is virtually synonymous with Fascism, Benito MUSSOLINI. He exemplified the kind of rule described in ABSOLUTISM and traits of leadership described in CHARISMA. Some of his domestic economic policies are described in CORPORATE STATE.

Fascist Aggression and World War II. The aggressively nationalistic and militaristic policy of Mussolini's Italy was made clear by the events described in ITALO-ETHIOPIAN WAR. The failure of the LEAGUE OF NATIONS to stop Mussolini weakened that body, and the success of his ruthless policy took the world a step nearer to war. Mussolini next sent troops to Spain, as related in CIVIL WAR, SPANISH. His alliance with Germany is treated in the biography of Adolf HITLER, in NATIONAL SOCIALISM OR NAZISM, in GERMANY: *History,* and in AXIS POWERS. The threat of the Fascist and Nazi states to the democratic world is discussed in DEMOCRACY: *The Challenge to Democracy* and in WORLD WAR II.

Fascism, Communism, and Democracy. One of the best ways to study Fascism is to compare it with Communism. Fascism is often described as dictatorship of the extreme right, whereas Communism is dictatorship of the extreme left. Fascism rejects the Marxian concept of a classless society and tends to favor individuals of wealth and power. But there are many similarities between the two systems, as the article DICTATORSHIP makes clear by comparing the regimes of Stalin, Hitler, and Mussolini. Under such governments individual rights are suppressed, representative government is banned, political opposition is often beaten down by force, the national leader is glorified, and hatred of foreign countries is encouraged. Further understanding of the nature of Fascism, and its similarities with Communism, can be obtained by considering the values and institutions they reject—see DEMOCRACY, BILL OF RIGHTS, CIVIL RIGHTS AND LIBERTIES, and SPEECH, FREEDOM OF, for example.

Study of Italian history from World War I to World War II and of Fascism in general can be enhanced by reading books available in the library. Books dealing with Fascism and Communism should be chosen with attention to the qualifications of their authors. The school or public librarian may be a valuable guide in selecting titles.

---

ister, in Oct., 1922, the Fascist party was a small minority in Parliament. A new election in 1923 gave him the further sanction of a popular mandate. A scandal caused by the murder of the Socialist deputy Giacomo Matteotti in 1924 led to a tightening of Fascist control. Between 1924 and 1929 constitutional changes eliminated ministerial responsibility to Parliament. Instead, ministers were appointed and dismissed at the pleasure of the head of the government, who was in turn responsible to the King alone, the monarchy being retained despite some questioning of its desirability. Simultaneously, opposition was eliminated, and the one-party state emerged, leading to an interpenetration and a duplication of functions of the party and state, as well as to an inflated bureaucracy. The central governing body of the party, the Grand Council of Fascism, received constitutional standing in 1929. It was the real repository of power, though ever dominated by Mussolini himself, for no other personality emerged comparable to his own.

Without a doubt the Fascist regime re-established social and financial order in Italy, albeit through coercion, and the prestige of the country was enhanced. Those in opposition went either underground or abroad but remained essentially ineffectual; the regime was accepted at home with passivity rather than enthusiasm. Successes in the foreign field for a time strengthened its position in the country, but the alliance with, then the subservience to, Nazi Germany injured its popularity.

Foreign Affairs. Nationalism was the dominant element in Fascism, and Mussolini was dedicated to securing for Italy a larger place in world affairs. At first there was fear abroad that the advent of Fascism might initiate a policy of foreign adventures, but the early record of the new regime put these suspicions to rest, and the feeling came to prevail abroad that little more than talk and bombast was to be feared from Italy, whose foreign policy continued to be essentially moderate. Apart from the general assertion of claims, talk about the glory of Rome, and the effective reconquest of Libya, little was done during the first decade of Fascist rule, when emphasis was placed on domestic reorganization.

Things changed with the coming of the world crisis, which affected Italy as well as other countries. The advent of Nazism in Germany was welcomed by Fascist Italy for two reasons: Nazism and Hitler were paying Fascism and Mussolini the compliment of imitation (Hitler ever remained an authentic admirer of Mussolini); more important, the revival of German power promised to restore an equilibrium in Europe that Italy could exploit. In 1933 Mussolini proposed a four-power pact with Germany, France, and Great Britain that would have instituted a directorate of Europe, but the proposal foundered on the opposition of the defenders of the League—mainly France and the small powers.

Taking advantage of the uncertain European situation, Mussolini used the pretext of a border dispute to pick a quarrel with Ethiopia and in Oct., 1935, launched an attack against that country. Despite the intervention of the League, which declared Italy guilty of aggression but imposed only ineffective sanctions, the Italian campaign was successful; in May, 1936, Ethiopia was declared annexed, the King of Italy assuming the imperial title. The *fait accompli* was eventually recognized by the powers, and sanctions were lifted. This success enhanced the prestige of Fascism both abroad and at home, where it marked the high point of the regime's popularity.

When the Spanish Civil War broke out in July, 1936, Italy promptly intervened on the side of the Nationalist Gen. Francisco Franco. As the war continued, Italian involvement became ever deeper. This led to increasing cooperation with Germany, out of which was born the Rome-Berlin Axis, a partnership ostensibly dedicated to the reorganization of Europe and to its defense against the Communist menace. Germany made skillful use of the circumstances to enhance its own position, liberating itself from the remaining limitations imposed by the peace treaty of 1919, while Italy, heavily committed in Spain, was losing its freedom of maneuver. Thus the Axis combination was tightened, but the position of Italy in it was gradually changing from that of equal partner to subordinate or prisoner. This position was confirmed by the German annexation of Austria in 1938, which brought Germany to the Brenner Pass on Italy's border.

At the time of the Munich crisis, in Oct., 1938, Mussolini threw the weight of his influence on the side of accommodation, albeit on Germany's terms. In Sept., 1939, Germany launched World War II. Italy remained neutral at first, thereby recovering a measure of independence. The collapse of France in June, 1940, however, led Mussolini to believe that the war would soon terminate in a Nazi victory. In order to share in it he declared war against both France and Great Britain. This unpopular action and Italy's poor military showing once more increased its dependence on Germany. The war proved long and disastrous. In July, 1943, Mussolini was put in a minority in the Grand Council. He was arrested and the abolition of Fascism proclaimed to the accompaniment of widespread rejoicing. But the hope of the Italian people that they were extricating themselves from the war proved to be an illusion. After the new Italian government concluded an armistice with the Allies, the Germans occupied the country and for two years it continued to be a battleground. Meanwhile, Mussolini was rescued from his place of detention by German paratroopers and taken to the north, where he organized an Italian Social Republic. This episode is but a mean and sorry footnote to the Fascist interlude, the Social Republic being an impotent Nazi puppet that disappeared with the German collapse. Mussolini himself was captured and shot by partisans while trying to escape to Switzerland.

Conclusion. The words "fascism" and "fascist" have to a large extent become terms of abuse, and, even in Italy, there are few who would not disown the fascist label, which, changed to M.S.I. (Movimento Sociale Italiano), is acknowledged by only an insignificant group in postwar Italian politics. But it is well to realize that Fascism was in large measure born of the circumstances to which it adapted itself. The conditions of our time, when, in an increasingly complex society, the mass with increasing success clamors for recognition, tend to put a premium on organization, often at the expense of freedom. This is the common root of all totalitarian movements, of which Fascism is but one form. For that reason, what it stood for and expressed, under whatever guise or label, remains a living force.

Consult Finer, Herman, *Mussolini's Italy* (1935); Ebenstein, William, *Fascist Italy* (1939); Delzell, C. F., *Mussolini's Enemies* (1961).

RENÉ ALBRECHT-CARRIÉ, Barnard College

FASHER, EL-, capital of Darfur Province, Sudan, 500 mi. west of Khartoum. It is a market center for durra, sesame, and gum arabic and a caravan halt on the route from Khartoum to Fort-Lamy, Chad. Pop., 26,161.

FASHION, the artistic approach to designing, selling, and wearing clothes. To be in fashion is to conform to the constantly changing artistic ideal of the current day.

Modern fashion began at the end of World War I, when the invention of new industrial clothing machinery made the burgeoning of the now vast ready-to-wear industry possible. Before World War I, clothes were inspired by Paris but made with many personal interpretations by dressmakers all over the world. A situation in which two well-known women appeared at the same public event in the same dress would have been virtually impossible.

Although modern fashion may seem to outsiders to have moved capriciously in many directions since its beginning, its course has actually been uniquely simple and direct. Fashion has been tending steadily toward simplification and realism. All kinds of clothes are still in the process of shedding decoration, weight, and any trace of a specific seasonal look. Over a comparatively short period of time, considering how long women put up with them, fashion has managed to get rid of corsets, voluminous lingerie, long skirts, long hair, hats, and at least temporarily, sleeves. As clothes have eliminated decoration and become more basic in shape, color has assumed greater power in fashion. Only by her choice of color and fabric can a woman now prove her individual taste.

Fabrics have become consistently lighter in weight and more workable. Bantam weight is a selling point in everything from tweeds to elasticized girdles and bras. Dresses are advertised as weighing only a few ounces. Miracle drip-dry fabrics created a world-wide furor when they were invented in the early 1940's. The development of new stretch fabrics which move with the body have made clothes even more workable.

Fashion's most drastic change happened in the 1920's when, at the end of the war, women rebelled against restriction and artificiality. Almost overnight they shifted into the limp little short dress that was the flapper's uniform. Paris designer Gabrielle (Coco) Chanel sparked the fashion revolution. She also introduced wool jersey, the forerunner of the popular knit fashions.

The 1930's were probably the most charming era in modern fashion. Sportswear, at first very feminine, was born in answer to women's increasing freedom. Though clothes were becoming softer and simpler, they still kept some of their old-time personal mystery. Hollywood's film stars were a fashion power in the United States.

Paris in the 1930's was at a peak of creative activity. The snob appeal of buying original Paris designs, to be

A student designer examines one of his prize-winning outfits. The tendency for apparel firms to recruit designers from schools that offer specialized training in design is increasing.
(THE NEW YORK TIMES)

copied by American manufacturers, had begun. Paris was full of great names like Molyneux, Vionnet, and Mainbocher. The word chic, meaning the ultimate in fashion, became popular. It was personified in Elsa Schiaparelli, whose flippant, tongue-in-cheek fashion approach was canceled by World War II, which saw the fashion capital occupied by invading German armies.

During the years of World War II, American ready-to-wear fashion came into its own. Wartime fashions such as skimpy skirts and wide, padded shoulders resulted from L85, a government fabric restriction. Some of the famous American names developed through the period, though, were Gilbert Adrian and the great sportswear designer, Claire McCardell.

After the war, Christian Dior won back the fashion leadership for Paris when, in 1947, he launched the New

Look. The New Look, probably a subconscious rejection of uniforms and restrictions, detoured fashion into a romantic bypath. Although it did not actually change fashion's inevitable course, it was a persistent influence for seven years.

Through the 1950's, the two great Paris giants of creative fashion were Dior and Spanish-born Cristobal Balenciaga. Dior was the idol of the ready-to-wear industry, since each season he managed to produce a new fashion look that could be copied, promoted, and sold to outdate the one before. However, Balenciaga actually produced the decade's most influential fashions—the less fitted suit, the big, loose coat, and the unfitted dress. All these were milestones along the road to basic shape.

Italy made its first bid as a fashion center in 1951. Its extrovert mood has been strikingly successful, chiefly in

CAREER GUIDE

FASHION DESIGN

Characteristics of the Field. The designer creates original designs for new types and styles of apparel. Since designing is a creative job, designers usually work without close supervision but must produce a number of successful styles during a season. The designer of men's wear works wherever the factory is located. In the United States, women's wear designers usually work in New York City.

Qualifications and Training. A designer should have artistic ability, including a talent for sketching, a thorough knowledge of fabrics, a keen sense of color, and the ability to translate design ideas into a finished garment. Designers enter the industry in various ways. Many receive their training by working on the job with experienced designers. There is an increasing tendency for apparel firms to recruit designers from colleges that offer specialized training in design.

Prospects for Employment. Fashion design is a highly competitive field with a limited number of positions. In the 1970's the field of designing men's clothes holds the most promise for job openings.

Income. A designer's salary depends to a great degree upon his success in creating styles which will have a sizable market. Once a designer's reputation has been established the opportunity for large income is increased.

Sources of Information. The accompanying article gives an overall view of the world of fashion. General suggestions on career planning are given in VOCATIONAL GUIDANCE. Additional information can be obtained from the Clothing Manufacturers Association of U.S.A., 135 West 50th St., New York, N.Y. 10001, or Amalgamated Clothing Workers of America, 15 Union Square, New York, N.Y. 10003.

sportswear. Emilio Pucci's bold-colored silk print shirts and pants have been a world influence in fashion.

In the mid-1960's England went ahead in the fashion world with the introduction of "mod" and "mini" clothes. London's influence was also felt in men's fashions, which changed markedly in the late 1960's. As a result London began to compete significantly as a modern fashion capital.

The United States is not actually in competition with England, France or Italy, all of which it taps for creative ideas, simply because it likes to. Although the United States has its great creative designers like Norman Norell, James Galanos, and Pauline Trigère, it chooses to concentrate on successful production offering a wide range of types, sizes, and prices.

Now France, Italy, and England are all working ambitiously to develop their own ready-to-wear industries. They have a long way to go to catch up with U.S. production and sales methods. An incredibly wide range of types, sizes, and prices make American ready-to-wear the envy of the rest of the world.

EUGENIA SHEPPARD, Fashion Editor, New York *Post*

See also:

CASSINI, OLEG	DIOR, CHRISTIAN
CHANEL, GABRIELLE	DRESS, HISTORY OF
CLOTHING FOR THE FAMILY	GARMENT INDUSTRY
DACHE, LILLY	MAINBOCHER

FASHODA [fə-shō-də] **INCIDENT,** a clash (1898) between Great Britain and France over control of the Upper Nile, one of many such incidents during the period when the European powers were dividing up Africa. The British, already masters of Egypt, had pushed steadily southward up the Nile. In 1898 Gen. Horatio Herbert Kitchener defeated a Muslim army at Omdurman and established British control over the Sudan. Almost immediately, Kitchener learned that a young French officer, Capt. Jean Baptiste Marchand, leading a small expedition (120 men) from French Congo, had reached Fashoda, 400 mi. upriver. Kitchener went to Fashoda to request that Marchand withdraw. When Marchand refused, the conflict shifted to London and Paris. Britain and France then faced each other in a public test of strength. When the British hinted they would fight, the French, who regarded Germany as their principal enemy, backed down. A wave of anger swept over France, but the incident so impressed the government with the danger of diplomatic isolation that it undertook a policy of *rapprochement* with Britain that culminated in the Entente Cordiale of 1904.

JOHN G. SPERLING, Northern Illinois University

FAST, HOWARD MELVIN (1914–), American historical novelist, known for his fictional accounts of the search for human freedom. Born in New York City, he was educated in public schools and then roamed the country for several years working at odd jobs. His novels include *The Last Frontier* (1941), *The Unvanquished* (1942), *Citizen Tom Paine* (1943), *Freedom Road* (1944), *Spartacus* (1952), *Moses* (1958), and *Jews: A History* (1968). Fast has been politically active for many years, and his novels reflect his liberal social views.

FASTING (Anglo-Saxon *faestan*, "abstaining from food"), refraining from a certain quantity or quality of food for a period of time. Throughout history fasting in some form has been practiced as a sign of mourning, as an initiation to ritual acts, or as an ascetic practice. Two types of fasting most commonly observed in Christian churches are the ordinary penitential or lenten fast and the Communion or Eucharistic fast.

The penitential fast consists mainly in reducing the quantity of food, but in the Eastern churches the ordinary fast requires only abstinence from meat and dairy products. The Roman Catholic Church in the Latin Rite permits one full meal with meat and two small meatless meals. Eating between meals is forbidden on fast days, but those unable to observe the fast strictly may obtain a dispensation. In other churches fasting is not so minutely prescribed. In Jewish fasts, as on the Day of Atonement, one must refrain from all food and drink.

The Communion, or Eucharistic, fast is prescribed or encouraged in many churches. Often the communicant fasts from all food and drink from midnight of the day of Communion. But since 1957 Latin Rite Catholics must refrain from alcoholic beverages and solid food for only three hours before Communion and from nonalcoholic drinks (except water) for one hour.

JOHN P. MARSCHALL, C.S.V., Viatorian Seminary, Washington, D.C.

FASTOLF [făs'tŏlf], **SIR JOHN** (c. 1380-1459), English soldier, some of whose qualities Shakespeare embodied in his character Falstaff. Fastolf was of good family and took to soldiering early. After 1413 he served in France, first under English King Henry V, and by his service won appointment as governor of Maine and Anjou. His conduct at the battle of Patay (1429) caused him to be charged with cowardice, perhaps unjustly, but the taint endured. On returning to England in 1440 he managed his substantial properties, including the Boar's Head Inn at Southwark, and earned a reputation for greed.

FATA MORGANA. See MIRAGE.

FATEHPUR SIKRI [fŭ'tā-poŏr sē'krē], town in Agra District, Uttar Pradesh State, India. Founded by Mogul Emperor Akbar in 1569, it was the capital of the Mogul Empire until 1584. The town retains intact many Mogul buildings, including the Great Mosque with its mausoleum of the Muslim saint Salim Chishti, the palaces of Jodh Bai and Birbal, and the Turkish Queen's House. The main entry to the town is through the Gate of Victory, famed for its huge elephant statues. Pop., 8,196.

FATES, in classical mythology, the goddesses of destiny, called by the Greeks *Moirai* and by the Romans *Parcae*. They assigned a lot in life to everyone at birth. Sometimes Moira was conceived as an impersonal power whose decisions not even Zeus could alter. There were three Fates, often conceived as spinners: Clotho spun the thread, Lachesis measured it, and Atropos cut it at the proper time. They were daughters of Zeus and Themis or of Night. Their enduring influence in folk tales is reflected by the modern Greek *Mires* and Western fairies, who pronounce a child's destiny soon after his birth.

FATHER, THE, play (1887) by the Swedish dramatist August Strindberg. This powerful psychological study of the spiritual destruction of a cavalry officer by his dominating wife exemplifies Strindberg's antifeminism, pessimism, and realistic technique of his early creative period.

FATHER DIVINE (c.1875–1965), Negro cult leader, founder of the highly successful socio-economic-religious movement known as Father Divine's Peace Mission Movement, whose followers believe that he is literally God. His name was originally George Baker, and he began to gather followers in the countryside near Savannah, Ga., in 1899. Some accounts identify him as the "Son of Righteousness," who was active in that area in the early 1900's. As "The Messenger" he is said to have gathered followers in Valdosta, Ga., in 1913. Migrating to Baltimore, Md., he became a follower of one "Father Jehova." By 1915 he was in New York City participating in similar activities under the name of Major Morgan J. Devine (later Divine). He set up a communal center in Sayville, Long Island. Later, headquarters were moved to Harlem in New York City, and in 1926 his following was interracial, and his program stressed (1) happiness, health, and abundance; (2) equality and brotherhood of man; (3) peace. His followers, called "angels," greeted each other with the word "Peace," to which the response was "It's truly wonderful." The headquarters of the movement were subsequently moved to Philadelphia.

ARNA BONTEMPS, Fisk University

FATHERS AND SONS, Russian novel (1862) by Ivan Turgenev. Turgenev contrasted the ideas and way of life of the older landed gentry with those of their nihilistic offspring. Bazarov, the young nihilist, was concerned with destroying the old standards, the old morality. In presenting both views objectively Turgenev provoked a controversy as to where he stood.

FATHERS OF THE CHURCH, a title commonly used for certain eminent theologians and interpreters of the Bible in antiquity. Their study forms the principal substance of a branch of learning called patrology or patristics and includes a diverse range of writers extending from the Apostolic Fathers of the late first and early second centuries through Gregory the Great (d.604) in the West and John of Damascus (died c.749) in the East. Most of them wrote in Greek or Latin; a few used Syriac. Despite the unfavorable attitude of some of them toward philosophy, most of the Fathers betray considerable knowledge and use of Graeco-Roman philosophy in their expositions of Christian doctrine. Platonism exercised a predominant influence, but some of the Latin Fathers were more indebted to Stoicism.

The honorific title "Father" cannot be precisely defined, but in general it is limited to ecclesiastical writers whose doctrines are orthodox according to the creedal standards established by the ecumenical councils, beginning with that of Nicaea in 325. Yet certain opinions of some of the Fathers, such as Origen and Theodore of Mopsuestia, were condemned as heretical at these councils. The Latin Father Tertullian actually abandoned the Catholic Church in his later years to join the Montanist schism. A consensus of the Fathers' opinions concerning a specific doctrine or interpretation of Scripture is accounted to have theological authority second only to the Bible in the Eastern Orthodox churches, and is treated with utmost respect by Roman Catholic and Anglican theologians.

Most of the Fathers became Bishops, but their authoritative works were often written before as well as after their episcopal consecration. Some were priests (Clement of Alexandria, Origen, Tertullian, Jerome); one was a deacon (Ephraem of Edessa). A few laymen have also been accounted among the Fathers (such as Justin Martyr and Lactantius).

Consult The Ante-Nicene Fathers (10 vols., 1884–86); *A Select Library of Nicene and Post-Nicene Fathers,* 1st and 2d Series (28 vols., 1886–1900); Altaner, Berthold, *Patrology* (1960).

MASSEY H. SHEPHERD, JR., The Church Divinity School of the Pacific, Berkeley, Calif.

See also GREEK FATHERS, THE; LATIN FATHERS.

FATHER TIME, the personification of passing time, also death. An old bearded man, bald but for a forelock, holding a scythe and often an hourglass, he is depicted as the old year passing on life to the new baby year.

FATHOM, a measure of length. Originally, in ancient Egypt, it was equal to the length of the outstretched arms, or approximately 6 ft. It is now exactly 6 ft. and is employed in navigation, especially in measuring the depth of water.

FATHOMETER [fə-thŏm′ə-tər], also called sonic depth finder, instrument used to ascertain water depth. A

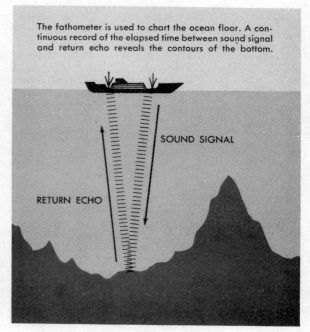

The fathometer is used to chart the ocean floor. A continuous record of the elapsed time between sound signal and return echo reveals the contours of the bottom.

SOUND SIGNAL

RETURN ECHO

sound signal is transmitted by a projector to the ocean or lake floor. The return echo is then detected by a receiver, and the elapsed time between the sending of the pulse and the reception of its echo is calculated by electronic means. In some fathometers, this elapsed time is calibrated directly, giving a reading in fathoms or feet. *See also* MARINE ELECTRONICS.

FATIGUE, term for the behavior of materials subjected to repeated cycles of stress or strain eventually resulting in progressive fracture. Fatigue behavior, although first encountered in metals, is also important in plastics, rubber, and concrete. It is characterized by loss in strength, loss of ductility, and most important, uncertainty in predicting service life.

Since fatigue failure generally originates on a material's surface, where stress is often greatest and boundary conditions are less than favorable, consideration is often given to means of improving the surface layer. Methods such as cold working of the surface are employed to increase resistance to fatigue.

Most elements of a structure or machine are also subjected to cycles of stress and therefore fatigue must be considered in their design. Such members may include motor shafts, springs, bolts, turbine blades, gear teeth, airplane and automobile parts, engines, railroad rails, wire rope, and axles.

ANTHONY VECCHIO, Brooklyn Polytechnic Institute
See also CREEP; DUCTILITY.

FATIGUE, MUSCLE. *See* MUSCLE.

FATIMA [fä'tĭ-mə, făt'ĭ-mə] (c.605–632), daughter of the Prophet Mohammed and Khadija. For later Shiite Muslims (members of one of the major branches of Islam) she embodied all that was noblest in woman, although little is known of her actual life. She was born in Mecca, went to Medina with Mohammed, and there married his cousin Ali about 623. Her sons Hasan and Husayn were, after Ali, the first of the imams (supernatural leaders) acknowledged by the Shiites and are ancestors of the sayyids and sharifs of today. The Shiite Dynasty of Fatimids in Egypt took its name from her.

FÁTIMA [fä'tē-mə], small Portuguese town about 70 mi. north of Lisbon. Its shrine of the Blessed Virgin Mary is a place of Catholic pilgrimage. Between May 13 and Oct. 13, 1917, three children between the ages of 10 and 13 saw a vision who identified herself as "the Lady of the Rosary." She urged the recitation of the Rosary, practice of penance, and devotion to the immaculate heart of Mary. Devotion to Our Lady of Fátima has several times been approved by papal authority.

FATIMID [făt'ĭ-mĭd] (909–1171), Caliphate which at the peak of its strength extended from North Africa to Iraq. It was established by an extreme Muslim sect of the Ismailis, themselves a sect of Shiite Islam. The latter regarded their Fatimid leaders as true descendants of the fourth Caliph, Ali, and his wife, Fatima (Mohammed's daughter). They believed the Fatimids were destined to replace the orthodox Abbasid Caliphate. Thus, apart from efficient military and administrative organization, the Fatimid Caliphate rested on strong religious foundations. As heads of the Ismaili sect, the Fatimid Caliphs held the position of infallible pontiffs endowed with supernatural attributes by divine ordination. Furthermore, an elaborate religious organization not only secured the inner cohesion of their regime but promoted the Fatimid cause by means of external missionary activities which culminated in a temporary proclamation of Fatimid sovereignty in Baghdad (1058–59).

After a period of consolidation in North Africa (909–69), the Fatimids captured Egypt, transferring their capital to the newly founded city of Cairo (969). The Fatimid Caliphate enjoyed a long period of cultural and economic development, particularly under the Caliphs al-Muiz (reigned 952–75) and al-Aziz (reigned 975–96). But in the second half of the 11th century the dynasty began to decline. It survived with difficulty a grave economic and social crisis under Caliph al-Mustansir (reigned 1036–94). Internally, the prestige of the Caliphs suffered from the emergence of military usurpers and from a major split in the Ismaili sect. Externally, the emancipation of North African provinces and the invasions of the Seljuk Turks and of the Crusaders reduced Fatimid possessions to Egyptian territory. In 1171 Saladin suppressed the Fatimid Caliphate and restored Egypt to her former Abbasid allegiance.

ANDREW S. EHRENKREUTZ, University of Michigan
See also SHIITE ISLAM.

FATS AND OILS. Edible fats and oils make up one of the three principal classes of food products, the others being carbohydrates and proteins. Fats are usually solid or semisolid at room temperatures and are obtained from the fatty tissues of hogs, sheep, and cattle by rendering. In dry rendering, the fatty tissue is heated to 225° F. to 250° F. and stirred in open or closed vessels. The fat melts, and is strained from the solid residue. In wet rendering, the tissues are put in pressure cookers, and the fat floats to the surface, where it is drawn off after about five hours.

Edible oils are liquid and are vegetable in origin, coming largely from seeds of corn and from cottonseed, soybeans, peanuts, and olives. The seeds are usually cleaned and hulled; the meats are separated from the hulls by screening, are ground or flaked to a small size, and are cooked before final processing. Continuous screw presses reduce oil content of the seed to about 5%. All but ¼% is then recovered by extraction with hexane. Refined oil can be chilled to crystallize solid materials, then filtered and deodorized. The process is called winterizing. Hydrogenation is an industrial process that increases the hydrogen atoms in the molecules of oil and makes them solid at ordinary temperature.

Nonedible fats and oils include castor oil, the purgative and lubricant; chaulmoogra oil, long used for treating leprosy; and neat's foot oil for preserving leather. Nonedible oils are frequently converted to edible fats by hydrogenation.

The substances described are known as fixed oils to distinguish them from another group called essential oils, which are odorous, highly volatile, and frequently have to be removed from edible oils to make the latter palatable. Grease is a name applied to petroleum oils that have a stiffening substance added for use where flow-resistant lubricants are needed.

FREDERICK C. PRICE, Assistant Editor,
Chemical Engineering

See also INDEX for individual fats and oils.

FATTY ACIDS, organic compounds with the formula RCOOH where R represents a hydrocarbon radical and COOH the carboxyl group. The lower members such as acetic and propionic acid, which are found in fruit esters and essential oils, were originally not included under the term but now are. The higher members, like palmitic, stearic, and oleic acids, occur in vegetable oils and animal fats as esters of glycerine. Some fatty acids are saturated, that is, they have no double bonds; others, like linoleic acid, are unsaturated and their oils, called drying oils, react with atmospheric oxygen to produce hard films. In the presence of alkalies, acids, or enzymes, water acts on fats and oils to break them down into glycerin and fatty acids. Potassium and sodium salts of these acids make soap. Important uses are in the manufacture of paints, cosmetics, soaps, detergents, plastics, and resins.

FATTY COMPOUNDS. *See* ALIPHATIC COMPOUNDS.

FAULKNER [fôk'nər], **WILLIAM** (1897–1962), American novelist and short-story writer, known especially for his stories about the South, the Civil War, and racial problems. He was born in New Albany and grew up in Oxford, Miss. His great-grandfather, William C. Falkner (a printer added a *u* to William Faulkner's name), was a notable figure—soldier, legislator, novelist—in north Mississippi. Faulkner drew upon his life and the lives of other members of his family for some of his characters. He attended the public schools in Oxford, but left high school after the 10th grade. He worked in his grandfather's bank and tried to become an artist. During World War I he received training in the British Royal Air Force, serving as a cadet in Canada. Like many of his contemporaries, he wrote novels about that war and its consequences.

As a veteran, Faulkner was allowed to enroll at the University of Mississippi, but stayed in school only a year. Odd jobs followed; he worked for a time in a bookstore in New York, then spent six months in New Orleans, where he knew Sherwood Anderson and began writing seriously. He spent six months touring Europe, and returned to find that *Soldiers' Pay* (1926), his first novel, had been well received. *Mosquitoes* (1927) is a satire about social life in New Orleans. In *Sartoris* (1929), Faulkner began to draw upon family legends and the history of his own region, which he was to call "Yoknapatawpha County." *The Sound and the Fury* (1929), published only a few months after *Sartoris*, established his reputation as an important novelist: a story about the decay of a family, it is generally held to be one of the great American novels. *As I Lay Dying* (1930), a serious yet comic novel about the burial of Addie Bundren, the wife of a poor farmer, was well received by critics. *Sanctuary* (1931), primarily about a sadistic gangster and a co-ed named Temple Drake, was an enormous popular success. It is a curiously comic as well as shocking book.

After publishing *Sanctuary* Faulkner occasionally worked in Hollywood, writing scripts, but mostly he lived and worked in Oxford. *Light in August* (1932), concerned with a lynching, is a deeply moving story about white-and-Negro relationships in Mississippi. Other significant Faulkner novels are *Absalom, Absalom!* (1936); *The Wild Palms* (1936); *The Hamlet* (1940), *The Town* (1957), and *The Mansion* (1959), a trilogy; *Intruder in the Dust* (1948); *A Fable* (1954); and *The Reivers* (1962). He was awarded the Nobel Prize for literature in 1950, and received the Pulitzer Prize in 1955 and 1963. Faulkner was preoccupied with man's compassion, courage, capacity for endurance, and ability to transcend his physical limitations. He was also a technical innovator, discovering many new ways of narrating a story.

Consult *The Portable Faulkner*, ed. by Malcolm Cowley (1954); O'Connor, W. V., *William Faulkner* (1959); *William Faulkner: Three Decades of Criticism*, ed. by Hoffman, F. J., and Vickery, O. W. (new ed., 1960); Howe, Irving, *William Faulkner: A Critical Study* (rev. ed., 1962); *Faulkner: A Collection of Critical Essays*, ed. by Warren, R. P. (1966).

WILLIAM VAN O'CONNOR, University of California

William Faulkner, American novelist who was awarded the Nobel Prize for literature in 1950. (ERISS—PIX)

FAULT, GEOLOGICAL, break or fracture, in rocks along which movement has occurred. Commonly, faults are represented by a zone of fractures rather than by a single break. Movement is parallel to the zone and it may range from an inch or less to many miles.

Faulting occurs because rocks are not strong enough to withstand stresses caused by movement of material within the earth or by adjustment of the earth's crust to internal expansion and contraction.

Faults are abundant in the upper crust of the earth, where they are generally recognized by the dislocation of rock strata. Movement of adjacent fault blocks causes friction, which in turn causes the strata to bend against the fault plane, producing drag folds. Commonly, rock within the zone of movement is broken, crushed, or even

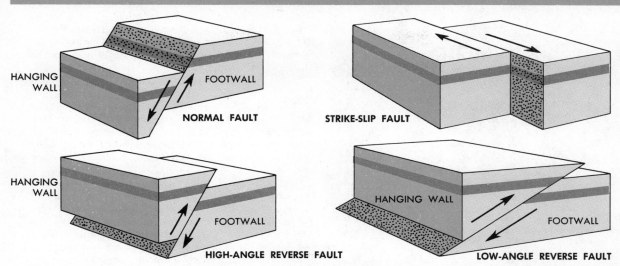

GEOLOGICAL FAULTS

HANGING WALL — FOOTWALL — **NORMAL FAULT**

STRIKE-SLIP FAULT

HANGING WALL — FOOTWALL — **HIGH-ANGLE REVERSE FAULT**

HANGING WALL — FOOTWALL — **LOW-ANGLE REVERSE FAULT**

pulverized. The plane of movement may be indicated by grooves and scratches called slickensides, and by highly polished surfaces.

Faults are classified on the basis of relative movement of the two blocks affected. The block above the fault forms the hanging wall, and the block below, the footwall. A fault in which the hanging wall is displaced downward relative to the footwall is a normal fault, or gravity fault. In contrast, if the hanging wall is displaced upward relative to the footwall, the fault is a reverse fault or thrust fault. A fault in which the relative movement of the blocks is horizontal is a strike-slip fault.

Vertical pressures commonly develop normal and reverse faults, such as those bordering the fault-block mountains in Nevada. Horizontal stresses (compression) cause thrust faulting. An example is the Lewis overthrust in Glacier National Park, Mont. This fault is probably more than 300 mi. long, and the upper block has moved several miles over underlying rocks. Lateral movement yields strike-slip faults, such as the San Andreas fault in California. Movement along this fault during earthquakes has caused considerable damage.

Robert E. Boyer, University of Texas
See also Diastrophism; Geology; San Andreas Fault.

FAUN, a Roman woodland spirit attendant upon the god Faunus, and identified with Greek satyrs (q.v.).

FAUNTLEROY [fônt′lə-roi], **LITTLE LORD,** central character in a children's novel (1886) of the same name by Frances Hodgson Burnett. Though generous and forthright in his behavior, he is best remembered for the long curls and sissified clothes that set a fashion in dress for small boys.

FAURE [fōr], **FÉLIX** (1841–99), French statesman. A wealthy Le Havre merchant and a moderate Republican, Faure was elected deputy in 1881. He became Under-Secretary of State for Colonies (1882–85; 1888) and Minister of the Marine (1894). He owed his unexpected election to the presidency in 1895 to a deep division in party ranks that forced the selection of a noncontroversial candidate. Faure's dignified presence on state occasions won him some popularity; but his unwillingness to see the Dreyfus case reopened delayed justice. He died of a cerebral hemorrhage while in office.

FAURÉ, GABRIEL URBAIN (1845–1924), French composer, born in Pamiers. A pupil of Saint-Saëns, he advanced to the post of chief organist at the Church of the Madeleine, Paris, in 1896. In the same year he became professor of composition at the Paris Conservatory, attaining the directorship in 1905.

Fauré's main strength (long-lined melody and striking harmony) appeared in nearly 100 songs, including Verlaine's cycle *La bonne chanson* (1892) and Lerberghe's *La chanson d'Ève* (1910). In addition to the operas *Prométhée* (Béziers, 1900) and *Pénélope* (Paris, 1913), he wrote incidental music to several stage plays, notably *Pelléas et Mélisande* (1898). His finest large work is the *Requiem* (1887), original in achieving an effect of innocence and sincerity by simplification of line and harmony. Active in chamber music, he wrote quintets, quartets, a trio, and a number of sonatas and lesser works for piano with violin, cello, or flute. Outstanding among his numerous piano pieces are the 13 barcarolles and 13 nocturnes.

In harmony, the most important feature of his style, Fauré anticipated the modal chords (based on the church scales) of Ravel and Debussy, though depending more on good part writing and logical, if often unexpected, modulations (key changes). Though fond of elaborate broken-chord accompaniments, Fauré could achieve expressive settings with chords as simple as those used for hymn tunes.

Consult Suckling, Norman, *Fauré* (1946).

Jan LaRue, New York University

Umrisse zu Goethes Faust, Part II (1836)

A 19th-century illustration by Moritz Retzsch for Goethe's *Faust*. As evil spirits lower Faust into the grave, the devil summons his helpers to prevent the escape of Faust's soul.

FAUST [foust]. The idea of a man who sells his soul to the devil to obtain knowledge and power dates from late antiquity. In the early 16th century the legend was connected with Magister Georgius Sabellicus Faustus, who lived in Germany and dabbled in magic. The most popular of the early accounts of his life is *Historia von D. Johann Fausten* (1587), translated soon afterward as *History of the Damnable Life and Deserved Death of Dr. John Faustus.* Christopher Marlowe based his play, *The Tragicall History of Dr. Faustus* (written shortly before his death in 1593 and published in 1604), on this work. In both the prose and dramatic versions, Faustus acquires the devil's service for 24 years of empty pleasures and, in spite of his attempted repentance, is damned because he preferred earthly to heavenly knowledge.

There existed during the next two centuries many German stage and puppet plays, one of which Johann Wolfgang von Goethe saw in his childhood. He started work on his famous play *Faust* in early manhood and finished Part II shortly before his death (1832), spending a lifetime on his favorite subject. He transformed Faust into a man who, although ever striving for spiritual insight, is constantly frustrated by earthly limitations. Faust turns from the pursuit of knowledge through books to a search for understanding through experience in actual life. To this end he commits himself to the devil (Mephistopheles), paradoxically realizing that happiness will never be his. Goethe added to the legend the story of the ill-fated love of Faust and Gretchen, which Charles François Gounod used as the text of his opera *Faust* (1859). In contrast to Marlowe's Faust, Goethe's Faust is saved because erring is implicit in the human condition which Faust fully accepts.

Goethe's play inspired many authors. But Thomas Mann's *Doktor Faustus* (1947; trans., 1948) goes back to the original book. A modern composer, Adrian Leverkühn, makes his own peculiar pact with a modern devil to be a great creative artist, writes at the climax of his career the music to Faust's Lament in the old Faust-

book, and becomes insane after having finished it. The question of his salvation is left open.

Among the authors and composers inspired by the Faust legend, or by Goethe's version of it, have been Gotthold Ephraim Lessing, Ludwig Spohr, Richard Wagner, Robert Schumann, Charles Gounod, Hector Berlioz, Heinrich Heine, Franz Liszt, Arrigo Boito, Gustav Mahler, Ferruccio Busoni, Stephen Vincent Benét and Douglas Moore, and Paul Valéry.

LISELOTTE DIECKMANN, Washington University

FAUST, opera in five acts by Charles Gounod; libretto by Jules Barbier and Michel Carré; first performance Mar. 19, 1859, Théâtre-Lyrique, Paris. In return for youth Faust sells his soul to the Devil. After his betrayal of the beautiful and innocent Marguérite, he is carried off to hell.

Gounod's *Faust* belongs to the genre called lyric opera —a form falling somewhat between grand opera and *opéra comique.* From the former it takes its serious subject, set numbers, large ensembles, ballets, and elaborate stage effects; from the latter comes its stress on graceful and flowing vocal lines, simple harmonic texture, and a dramatic procedure which is French in its refinement and lack of excess. Concerned primarily with the love affair in Part I of Goethe's drama, Gounod's work endures because of a special type of pathos that is to be found in its best pages, especially the brilliantly sustained Act III with its *Jewel Song, Salut! demeure,* and the *King of Thule* ballad.

ALBERT WEISSER, Brooklyn College

FAUSTA [fôs'tə], **FLAVIA MAXIMIANA** (289–326 A.D.), Roman Empress. The younger daughter of the Emperor Maximian I, she was married to Constantine the Great in 307, partly for political reasons. Her sons became Constantine II, Constantius II, and Constans I. Fausta was executed on her husband's orders because she had falsely accused her stepson Crispus of misconduct with her.

FAUSTIN I. *See* SOULOUQUE, FAUSTIN ÉLIE.

FAUSTUS OF RIEZ [fôs'təs; ryĕz], **ST.** (c.410–490 A.D.), Gallican theologian of British origin. As Abbot of Lerins, he was involved in the settlement of the rights of Abbots and Bishops at the Council of Arles in 455, and as Bishop of Riez (after 462) was a leader of Semi-Pelagianism.

FAUVISM [fōv'ĭz-əm], French painting movement of the early 20th century. Its members included Matisse, who was the dominant influence in establishing the style of painting and who came to be regarded as the leader of the group, André Derain, Maurice de Vlaminck, Albert Marquet, and others. Their paintings were distorted in drawing and painted in violent color with active brush strokes. The name "fauvism" came from the critic Louis Vauxcelles. Supposedly he saw a Renaissance-style statue of a baby in a room of their paintings, and remarked that it was in a cage of wild beasts (*fauves*). The fauves first exhibited as a group in 1905 in the newly organized Salon d'Automne in Paris. Raoul Dufy exhibited with them in 1906, and Georges Braque in 1907. By 1908 the group, which was never closely knit, had fallen apart as the painters developed in other directions or came under the influence of cubism. Fauve color and brush stroke were highly influential on succeeding movements, especially on German expressionism. Important examples of fauve painting in America are Matisse's "Joy of Life" (1905–06; Barnes Foundation, Merion, Pa.) and "Woman with a Hat" (1905; Walter A. Haas Collection, San Francisco).

HERSCHEL B. CHIPP, University of California

FAVRE [fä′vr′], **JULES** (1809–80), French statesman. Elected in 1848 to represent Lyon in the Constituent Assembly, Favre was a lifelong moderate Republican and a liberal. He opposed the *coup d'état* of 1851 which doomed the Second Republic; and in 1858, under the Second Empire, he won election to Parliament as one of five opposition deputies. A lawyer, he defended (1858) Felice Orsini, who had tried to assassinate Napoleon III. After the deposition of Napoleon III (1870), he became Vice President and Foreign Minister in the Government of National Defense. An inexperienced diplomat, he fared poorly in the armistice negotiations with German Chancellor Otto von Bismarck and lost his Cabinet post (1871). He remained a deputy until elected to the Senate (1876).

FAWKES [fôks], **GUY** (1570–1606), English soldier. Fawkes, a Catholic, played the key role in the Gunpowder Plot, a conspiracy designed to aid his coreligionists by blowing up Parliament and King James I. Born an Anglican, he became a zealous convert to Catholicism. Fawkes served for a time in the Spanish army in Flanders, distinguishing himself in the siege of Calais (1596). His military experience as well as his calmness and courage led the Gunpowder Plot conspirators to entrust him with the execution of their plan. Fawkes made the final preparations and was supposed to ignite the explosives. When caught (Nov. 5, 1605), he showed great fortitude, refusing to disclose his accomplices. Fawkes was tried with the other conspirators and executed (Jan. 31, 1606). The anniversary of the Gunpowder Plot is celebrated by English children much as Halloween is observed in America. Children build grotesque effigies of Fawkes and solicit from door to door asking "a penny for the Guy." On the evening of Nov. 5, they build bonfires and burn "the Guy."

J. JEAN HECHT, Stanford University

FAWKNER, JOHN PASCOE (1792–1869), Australian merchant, journalist, colonizer. In 1835, competing with John Batman, he led a party to the site of what is now Melbourne, where his group erected the first buildings. Fawkner launched several newspapers, was a member of the Australasian League, and served ably in the Legislative Council of Victoria.

FAYETTEVILLE [fä′ĭt-vĭl], city of northwestern Arkansas and seat of Washington County. The city is on rolling-to-hilly land in an important poultry, cattle, small fruit, and vegetable region. Chief industries of the city include the preparation of frozen and canned foods, garment manufacture, wood processing, and the manufacture of electronic organs. The University of Arkansas is located here. Fayetteville was a stop on the Butterfield Stage Route. The area was the scene of several engagements of the Civil War, including the battle of Pea Ridge. Inc., 1836; pop., 30,729.

FAYETTEVILLE, commercial city on Cape Fear River in eastern North Carolina, and seat of Cumberland County. In 1783 the Highland Scots settlements, Campbellton and Cross Creek, were incorporated as Fayetteville. Dock and terminal facilities have revived river trade, important in early days. Textile and lumber mills are the largest industries. Fayetteville State Teachers College is here. Nearby Fort Bragg has changed the appearance and tempo of this colonial town. Pop., 53,510.

FAYETTEVILLE, city of central Tennessee, and seat of Lincoln County. The city serves a general farming area, processes dairy products, and manufactures cotton textiles and work clothes. It is the historical site of Camp Blount, where Gen. Andrew Jackson mobilized the Tennessee militia to fight the Creek Indians, 1813–17. Inc., 1809; pop., 7,030.

FAZOLA [fə-zō′lə], **IRVING**, original surname Prestopnik (1912–49), American jazz musician, born in New Orleans. He played with Louis Prima, Ben Pollack, Gus Arnheim, Claude Thornhill, Glenn Miller, Muggsy Spanier, Teddy Powell, Horace Heidt, and Bob Crosby. His ability to adapt his limpid New Orleans style to the demands of the swing era made him one of the most sought-after clarinetists of his time.

FEAR, CAPE, cape on the southern North Carolina coast, located on Smith Island near the mouth of the Cape Fear River. The dangerous Frying-Pan Shoals extend into the Atlantic Ocean about 20 mi. south and southeast of the cape.

FEASTS, ECCLESIASTICAL, days set aside for the public worship of God, sometimes with special reference to the saints, angels, Our Lady, or to an event in the life of Our Lord. The Jews observe the Sabbath as a divinely appointed day of rest. Other feasts such as the Passover and Tabernacles commemorate significant events in Jewish history. The Day of Atonement is an important Jewish penitential feast.

In the Christian Church Sunday has been observed since Apostolic times in commemoration of Christ's resurrection. In 321 Constantine declared Sunday a general holiday. Martyrs were commemorated in the early centuries, and by the 5th century the number of feasts was very large. Some days, such as Pentecost and Ascension, are movable feasts because their celebration depends on the date of Easter, which is determined by the lunar cycle. Other feasts, such as Christmas and saints' days, have permanent dates for their celebration. Originally they were sometimes scheduled to counteract the effects of pagan festivals. A new classification of feasts according to their importance became effective in the Roman Catholic Church Jan. 1, 1961. A new calendar is

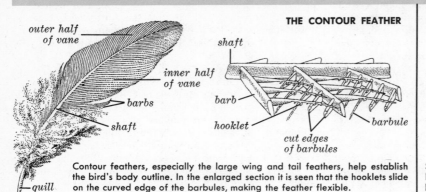

THE CONTOUR FEATHER

outer half of vane

inner half of vane

barbs

shaft

quill

shaft

barb

hooklet

cut edges of barbules

barbule

THE DOWN FEATHER

barbs

quill

shaft

Contour feathers, especially the large wing and tail feathers, help establish the bird's body outline. In the enlarged section it is seen that the hooklets slide on the curved edge of the barbules, making the feather flexible.

Soft, flexible down feathers provide insulation from heat and cold. They are found on newly hatched birds and beneath the contour feathers of waterfowl.

also being prepared by the Protestant Episcopal Church. *Consult* Harper, H. V., *Days and Customs of All Faiths* (1957); Weiser, F. X., *Handbook of Christian Feasts and Customs: the Year of the Lord in Liturgy and Folklore* (1958).

JOHN P. MARSCHALL, C.S.V., Viatorian Seminary, Washington, D.C.

FEATHER, an outgrowth of the outer layer (epidermis) of the skin of a bird. Feathers provide birds with a lightweight, heat-retaining, waterproof covering. They also serve for protective coloring in many instances and as a means of sex recognition during courtship. Several types of feathers make up a bird's plumage, the most important being the soft down feathers of newly hatched birds, and the contour feathers that cover body, wings, and tail of the adult bird. A typical contour feather is attached to the skin by a hollow quill that has an opening in its base to permit entry of blood vessels which furnish nourishment to the developing feather. When fully formed, the opening disappears and the feather becomes a dead structure. The quill extends as a shaft into the webbed or flattened portion of the feather, an intricate structure made up of hundreds of slender, parallel barbs. Each barb, in turn, has many tiny barbules projecting from it, which interlock to form an airtight supporting surface. The color of feathers is produced by pigments (red, yellow, or brown); by reflection of light; and by light refraction, which produces the effect of blue color and iridescence. When a feather becomes worn it is lost through molting, and replaced by new growth.

CLARENCE J. HYLANDER, Author, *Feathers and Flight*

FEATHER RIVER, river in north-central California, formed by the confluence of the North and Middle forks, which flows southwest to Sacramento River. North Fork's Feather River canyon is noted for spectacular scenery. The river basin yields gold and is a source of hydroelectric power. Work has started on the Feather River watercontrol project at Oroville Dam. Length, 80 mi.

FEATHER STAR, common name for a marine animal of class Crinoidea in the phylum Echinodermata, to which the starfish and sea urchins also belong. Feather stars have a body consisting of a slender stalk topped by many featherlike arms which sweep small organisms into a central mouth. Young feather stars are attached to the ocean floor; adults are free-swimming. Feather stars are found in shallow seas, especially near reefs. They are closely related to the sea lilies which were extremely abundant in the Paleozoic Era (about 500 million years ago). *Antedon tenella*, a common feather star, is found in cooler Atlantic waters from Newfoundland to Chesapeake Bay. *See also* CRINOID.

FEBRUARY, second month of the modern Western year. It has 28 days except in leap years, when it has 29. The name derives from the Roman god Februus, who eventually became god of the underworld, but was initially associated with purification. When the Romans added two months to their 10-month calendar they put Janu-

An old man warming himself by a fire represents February in the relief series of the months, Amiens Cathedral, France.

Jean Roubier—Rapho-Guillumette

ary at the beginning, February at the end, but c.452 B.C. they moved it to its present position.

FEBRUARY REVOLUTION, in French history, sudden uprising (Feb. 22, 1848) in Paris that overthrew the July Monarchy of King Louis Philippe. *See* REVOLUTIONS OF 1848.

FEDER [fā′dər], **ABE H.** (1909–), American lighting designer, born in Milwaukee. He first gained prominence as principal lighting designer for the Federal Theater Project in the late 1930's. Subsequently, he designed the lighting for many Broadway productions, including *Inherit the Wind* (1955), *My Fair Lady* (1956), and *Camelot* (1960). He was lighting designer of the U.N. building and New York Coliseum.

FEDERAL ART PROJECT, a part of the Works Progress Administration, established by the executive order of Franklin D. Roosevelt to help counter the economic depression. Conducted from 1935 to 1939, the program sponsored artists on a scale without precedent in the United States. At one time it employed, on a basis of financial need, over 5,000 artists. Such activities as teaching, the establishment of galleries, the preserving and recording of the country's art heritage, as well as the production of murals for many public buildings were embraced by the program.

FEDERAL AVIATION AGENCY (FAA), an independent U.S. government agency created by the Federal Aviation Act of 1958. Together with the Civil Aeronautics Board (CAB), it is responsible for the regulation of air commerce. The FAA and the CAB alike promote safe civil aeronautics development. The FAA, under the direction of its administrator, establishes safety regulations for the navigable airspace of the United States. Both civil and military operations are under its control, and a common system of air traffic control and navigation is provided for both. Consolidated research, with respect to air navigation, is

under the direction of the FAA, and consideration for the "public interest" is its guide in all such matters.

The FAA safety regulator's authority includes powers of inspection, certification, and rating of airmen. Regulations are promulgated covering such safety matters as manufacture and operation of aircraft, registration of aircraft ownership, flight inspection of air navigation facilities, and enforcement of safety regulations.

In addition, the FAA has responsibility for providing and operating federal aids to navigation and thus maintains emergency landing fields, flight aids, communications networks, and air traffic control tower equipment, while also administering grants-in-aid for public airports under the Federal Airport Act. The Agency also develops air traffic rules and regulations, assigns airspace, establishes aircraft routes, and encourages civil aviation abroad through technical aid and training programs. Its other services include airway modernization programs, assignment of allotments for civil aircraft under the defense production program, and the collection and dissemination of information relative to all aspects of civil aeronautics.

STUART GERRY BROWN, Syracuse University

FEDERAL BUREAU OF INVESTIGATION (FBI), agency established in 1908 as the investigative arm of the U.S. Department of Justice. It has headquarters in Washington, D.C., with field offices in 55 cities in the United States and Puerto Rico. The FBI, in general, is charged with enforcement of all federal laws not specifically delegated to other agencies. This includes approximately 168 violations in the areas of general investigations and domestic intelligence. The FBI is a fact-finding agency which does not recommend prosecution or evaluate investigative results. Information regarding investigations is submitted to the Attorney General or his representatives for prosecutive opinion. John Edgar Hoover was appointed FBI director in 1924.

All investigations are conducted by Special Agents. Applicants for the position of Special Agent must be male

Employees of the Identification Division of the FBI in Washington, D.C., search for names appearing on fingerprint cards. (FBI)

An instructor in an FBI training class for fingerprint technicians discusses the whorl pattern of finger markings. (FBI)

CRIME DETECTION METHODS

At the FBI laboratories in Washington, D.C., the latest scientific techniques are applied to the detection of crime. Thousands of specimens and millions of fingerprints are examined yearly by FBI specialists.

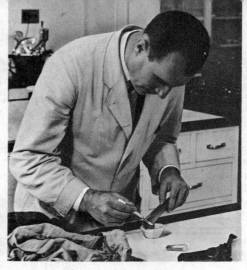

A serologist scrapes blood sample from a knife.

A fingerprint expert verifies an identification.

Safe insulation has adhered to the heels of a burglary suspect.

Wood is examined for marks left in it by a tool.

This spectrograph can detect minute quantities of chemicals.

citizens of the United States, 23 to 41 years old, in excellent physical condition, with a degree from either a resident law school or from an accounting school, and with at least three years' practical accounting experience after graduation. New agents receive 14 weeks of intensive training in Washington, D.C., and the FBI Academy, Quantico, Va., after which they must be available for assignment in any field office. Additionally, many nonagent administrative and technical assignments are available to qualified men and women. Political considerations are not involved in personnel appointments, and promotions are based solely on merit.

The FBI was charged by presidential directive on Sept. 6, 1939, with responsibility for domestic intelligence matters relating to espionage, sabotage, and subversive activities. This set the stage for World War II investigations which led to the identification and arrest in June, 1941, of 33 members of a Nazi espionage ring in New York City. In June, 1942, eight German saboteurs, landed by submarine on the east coast, were arrested within ten days of their arrival. As a result of this and other investigations, not a single successful act of enemy sabotage was committed in the United States during World War II.

An upsurge in crime after the war greatly increased criminal investigations conducted by the FBI. The effectiveness with which this challenge has been met is indicated by the fact that FBI investigations each year result in the convictions of more than 95% of the persons brought to trial, and in the apprehension of thousands of fugitives from justice.

A vital area of the FBI's operations is the cost-free service functions maintained to assist local enforcement agencies and other agencies of the federal government. The FBI laboratory provides scientific crime detection facilities to these agencies and annually conducts between 200,000 and 300,000 examinations on somewhat fewer specimens. Fingerprint cards, received yearly from local and federal agencies and processed by the FBI identification division, can be numbered in the millions. This division contains the world's largest known collection of fingerprints and serves as a national repository of data for purposes of fingerprint identification.

Police training schools in the field and the FBI National Academy, which was established in Washington, D.C., in 1935 to train selected local officers as executives and instructors, are further co-operative services designed to assist law enforcement. Various publications are also issued to provide continuing information concerning developments in the law enforcement field. The best known of these are the FBI *Law Enforcement Bulletin*, a monthly magazine composed in large part of instructive articles contributed by local authorities, and the *Uniform Crime Reports* bulletin, issued annually to reflect criminal trends throughout the country.

J. EDGAR HOOVER, Director,
Federal Bureau of Investigation

FEDERAL COMMUNICATIONS COMMISSION (FCC).

An independent agency of the federal government, the FCC is composed of seven commissioners, one of whom acts as its chairman. The commissioners are appointed by the President, with the consent of the Senate, for seven-year terms. The commission was created by the Communications Act of 1934 and administers that act, as amended. The purpose of the commission as stated in the 1945 statute is "regulating interstate and foreign commerce in communication by wire and radio so as to make available, so far as possible, to all people of the United States a rapid, efficient, nationwide, and worldwide wire and radio communication service with adequate facilities at reasonable charges. . . ."

The FCC's authority extends over standard, frequency modulation, television, international, auxiliary and experimental broadcast stations; and over citizens, amateur, and radio amateur civil emergency communications. Only the commission can authorize the discontinuance or reduction of a common carrier's operations or the extension of its lines. The commission is to regulate the common carriers so that they do not exact unfair charges or make unjust discriminations or offer unfair advantages. The commission can prescribe what are reasonable rates. Only the commission can license transmission of energy or communication and it is the commission which licenses the operators. It can also modify or revoke licenses, which in the case of broadcasting licenses last a maximum of three years. It prescribes the nature of the service offered by broadcasting stations and assigns frequencies.

The Communications Act provides that the general standard governing the commission's granting of licenses is "public interest, convenience, or necessity." No power of censorship over such communication systems is allowed by law. The commission's decisions may be appealed to the courts. By law, all legally qualified candidates for public office are entitled to equal opportunity in the use of a broadcast station if one such person is permitted to use that station. However, an act of Congress in 1960 exempted the radio and television stations during the 1960 presidential election campaign so that they could carry a nationwide series of debates between candidates Richard Nixon and John F. Kennedy.

STUART GERRY BROWN, Syracuse University

FEDERAL CONSTITUTIONAL CONVENTION,

meeting (May 25–Sept. 17, 1787) in Philadelphia that drafted the U.S. Constitution. A call for delegates from the various states to attend a meeting to revise the Articles of Confederation was issued in 1786 by the Annapolis Convention (q.v.). On May 25, 1787, the convention opened and immediately elected George Washington chairman. He was the most distinguished delegate, but among the 55 who eventually appeared there were many of great reputation and talent. Benjamin Franklin, old and in ill health, was there; Alexander Hamilton took part, and so did James Madison and John Dickinson. With the exception of Franklin and Washington and one or two others, they were a young group—mostly in their 30's and 40's. Yet almost all had substantial political experience, and many had fought in the Revolution. They were not radical men, nor did they count many rigid conservatives among their number. Instead, as the record of their debates reveals, they were saturated with the political theory of the Revolution —theory that emphasized the natural rights of man but also insisted upon the connection of liberty and property. The mood of this group was serious and determined:

the delegates knew that under the Articles of Confederation national power had ebbed away, that much of the old revolutionary purpose had been lost. Everyone agreed, according to Caleb Strong, a Massachusetts delegate, "that Congress are nearly at an end. If no Accomodation takes place, the Union itself must soon be dissolved." The Articles of Confederation had to be totally superseded by a new fundamental law.

For the most part the delegates were agreed on the form of the new government. Alexander Hamilton and John Dickinson admired limited monarchy, but they believed, with the other delegates, that only a republic was appropriate for the United States. Agreement extended much further than matters of political form. Most delegates favored a strong central government. They wanted to increase the powers of Congress—notably to tax and to regulate commerce—but they did not believe that Congress should continue to be the sole agency of government. The experience of state governments had taught them that a more complex structure, with power divided among different branches, was possible, and the failures of the Articles had demonstrated that it was desirable.

Agreed on the nature and structure of the proposed government, the delegates found in the Virginia Plan suggestions that, amplified and altered, became the Constitution of the United States. Written by James Madison, the Virginia Plan proposed that the government should consist of a two-house legislature, an executive, and a judiciary. Representation in each house of the legislature was to be proportioned either to population or to taxation. This provision frightened the small states. Reckoning representation by either population or the amount of taxes paid would diminish their influence in Congress, where under the Articles of Confederation each state cast one vote. Therefore they protested, offered a scheme of their own, the New Jersey Plan, and finally, when the convention rejected their scheme, threatened to leave the meeting. At this point what has since been called the "great compromise" was agreed upon—representation would be determined on the basis of population in the lower house, while in the Senate every state would be represented equally.

There were lesser divisions in the convention, too. One, which pitted North against South, concerned the slave trade. Some Northern delegates wished to abolish it, while Southerners urged that a guarantee that the new government would not interfere with it be written into the Constitution. The South won a partial victory, as the Constitution prohibited any legislative action against the slave trade until 1808.

The convention faced a delicate problem when it came to the question of what power was to be left to the states. One of the most distressing features of life under the Articles had been the propensity of the state governments to levy discriminatory customs duties, to issue paper money, and to act in other ways that threatened property. Hence the convention decided to write prohibitions against such activities into the Constitution, including one that forbade laws impairing the obligation of contracts.

To write these provisions and all others, the convention relied upon a number of committees. When a committee finished its work, the entire convention considered its suggestions and often sent the committee back to work. In this way the Constitution gradually took form. The final document was reshaped and polished by a Committee of Style and Arrangement. Its leading member, Gouverneur Morris, had an editor's pen: slashing, reorganizing, shortening, and rewriting, he improved the prose of the Constitution immeasurably.

Only slight changes were made when Morris and the committee submitted their work to the whole convention. Yet not all the delegates were pleased with the document. Several left the convention when it became apparent that the delegates meant to do more than alter the Articles of Confederation. A few—including George Mason, Elbridge Gerry, and Edmund Randolph (who had presented the Virginia Plan to the Convention)—refused to sign the Constitution.

But most liked it. Washington did and so did Franklin, whose words on the last day of the convention expressed the hopes of the majority. Madison reported the scene as follows:

"Whilst the last members were signing it, Dr. Franklin looking toward the President's chair, at the back of which a rising sun happened to be painted, observed to a few members near him that painters had found it difficult to distinguish in their art a rising from a setting sun. I have, said he, often and often in the course of the session, and the vicissitudes of my hopes and fears as to its issue, looked at that behind the President without being able to tell whether it was rising or setting: but now at length I have the happiness to know that it is a rising and not a setting sun."

ROBERT MIDDLEKAUFF, Yale University
See also CONFEDERATION, ARTICLES OF; CONSTITUTION OF THE UNITED STATES.

FEDERAL COUNCIL OF THE CHURCHES OF CHRIST IN AMERICA, first official association of Protestant denominations in America, organized in 1908. In 1950 it merged into the National Council of the Churches of Christ in the United States of America.

FEDERAL DEPOSIT INSURANCE CORPORATION (FDIC), a government corporation through which the United States insures bank deposits. The FDIC was created by the Federal Reserve Act of 1933 at a time when the banking system was in partial collapse. The corporation insures depositors of all insured banks against loss should a bank fail. It also acts as receiver for national banks in receivership and for state banks when it is appointed receiver. A further responsibility of the corporation is to prevent unwise banking practices from developing. There are three members of the board: one is the Comptroller of the Currency; the other two are appointed by the President with advice and consent of the Senate. The corporation is financed by assessments on insured banks and by income from its investments.

FEDERAL HALL MEMORIAL, historic building site in New York City. The Stamp Act Congress (1765), the Continental Congress (1785), and the inauguration of President George Washington (1789) took place in the original structure. The hall was torn down in 1812 and replaced in 1842 by the New Customs House, which housed the U.S. Subtreasury. The site was named the Federal Hall Memorial National Historical Site in 1939, and the building is now known as the Federal Hall National Memorial.

FEDERAL HOUSING ADMINISTRATION (FHA). Created in 1934 by the National Housing Act, FHA was made part of the new U.S. Department of Housing and Urban Development in 1965. Previously, from 1947, it was a constituent of the Housing and Home Finance Agency, whose programs and functions were absorbed by the new department. Headed by a commissioner, who is also Assistant Secretary for Mortgage Credit in the new department, the FHA improves housing standards, provides a system of mutual mortgage insurance, and helps stabilize the mortgage market. It does not lend money or engage in construction; it is limited to insuring privately financed residential building operations. It is self-financing, with its income derived from fees, insurance premiums, and interest on investments.

In addition to its original programs of insurance for home improvement loans, home mortgages, and multifamily rental housing, FHA administers land development mortgage insurance and the rent supplement program for private low-income housing.

JACK H. BRYAN, U.S. Department of Housing and
Urban Development
See also HOUSING AND URBAN DEVELOPMENT, U.S. DEPARTMENT OF.

FEDERALISM, a system of government in which several states have united for common purposes but retain their own identities. Under a federal system, powers are shared and divided between the central government and the constituent governments. Under a unitary system of government, all powers are exercised by a central government, and there are no constituent units with independent powers. The confederal system, on the other hand, leaves most powers to constituent states but gives limited powers to a central government.

The foremost problem in federalism is to determine how power should be distributed between the central government and the constituent units. In most systems, the central government handles problems common to the entire body, such as defense and foreign affairs, while the constituent units handle local matters. In the U.S. Constitution, powers not specifically granted to the federal government are reserved to the states; however, in interpreting the Constitution, the Supreme Court has frequently favored the central government over the states in the allocation of power. In Canada, the reverse is the case: all powers not specifically allotted in the Constitution are reserved to the central government. In spite of this fact, judicial interpretation of the Canadian Constitution has tended to favor the provinces in the distribution of power.

Although there were leagues of states in ancient Greece (notably the Aetolian and Achaean leagues) and commercial leagues in medieval Europe (such as the Hanseatic League), the federal principle was more fully expressed in the transformation of the American colonies into the United States. The U.S. government was established by the Constitution of 1787 after the American colonies had experimented with a confederation for over ten years. The Swiss adopted a federal constitution similar to that of the United States in 1848. They revised it in 1874, giving greater power to the central government.

A system of federalism served to unite the German states in the North German Union of 1867 and in the German Empire in 1871. Canada, also in 1867, formed a federal government under the British North America Act. Australia adopted a federal system in 1900. In 1909 South Africa formed a federation, but the power of the central government was so nearly complete that it can not be considered a genuine federal state. Several Latin American states, especially Argentina and Brazil, have federal governments.

After World War II several of the newly independent states formed their governments on the federal principle. India and Nigeria were the most notable examples, although there were numerous efforts to form federal systems in Asia and Africa. The British government imposed a federal system on the Federation of Rhodesia and Nyasaland (1953–63).

Although federal states are usually organized on the principle that the constituent governmental units are free to levy internal taxes and to borrow money, certain fields, particularly import duties, belong exclusively to the central government. Moreover, where both levels of government derive income from the same sources, the central government has priority. This characteristic has led to a concept called "new federalism."

Under "new federalism" there is a trend toward cooperation between different levels of government. For example, in an area of local problems such as housing, the national government of the United States provides funds and sets standards for municipalities dealing with housing problems. Thus, where the traditional emphasis of federalism was the guarding of prerogatives of each constituent government unit, "new federalism" emphasizes intergovernmental action.

There have been several movements to form a world federation composed of existing states. A more realistic, and moderately successful, scheme has been the formation of a Western European federation. The movement began with a series of co-operative steps on a functional basis. For example, Western European countries first proposed the Coal and Steel Community in 1950, and later projected other functional associations. A "common market" was developed with the purpose of creating an unrestricted flow of goods, capital, and labor between the common-market countries. Some statesmen believed that in time this might lead to political integration under a federal system.

Consult Wheare, K. C., *Federal Government* (3d ed., 1953); Anderson, William, *The Nation and the States* (1955); *Federalism, Mature and Emergent*, ed. by A. W. Macmahon (1955).

STUART GERRY BROWN, Syracuse University

FEDERALIST PAPERS, series of articles written (1787–88) by Alexander Hamilton, James Madison, and John Jay to urge ratification of the U.S. Constitution. The papers were first published in New York, where a powerful opposition to ratification had developed. Reasoned and restrained, the essays carefully expose the defects of the Articles of Confederation and analyze the Constitution, showing how it would strengthen the national government, but still reserve valued powers to the states. The papers also emphasized that the Constitution would safeguard minority rights against excesses of the majority and would provide the advantages of republican government in dealing with many conflicting interests and with the control of a large land area. Seventy-seven of the essays, titled *The Federalist* and signed "A Citizen of New York" and "Publius," were published (Oct. 27, 1787–Apr. 2, 1788) in the *Independent Journal*. Eight more essays were added when the articles were published in book form. Hamilton is generally credited with 51, Madison 29, and Jay 5 of the papers, which proved decidedly influential in winning adoption of the Constitution not only in New York but in other doubtful states, where they were widely distributed as pamphlets. Though strongly partisan, *The Federalist* eventually won universal praise for its literary excellence and its penetrating analysis of the American structure of government.

Consult The Federalist, ed. by B. J. Wright (1961).

ROBERT MIDDLEKAUFF, Yale University

FEDERALIST PARTY, American political party that flourished in the 1790's. The Federalist and Republican parties emerged during the presidency of George Washington. The Federalists supported the administration's centralizing financial policy and pro-British foreign policy, which was largely the work of Secretary of the Treasury Alexander Hamilton. The Republicans, led by Thomas Jefferson, distrusted centralized government and were sympathetic toward revolutionary France.

Merchants, professional men, large landowners—men of wealth and social position—supplied the Federalist leadership. For popular support the party relied principally upon farmers, especially prosperous farmers living near cities and engaged in commercial agriculture. Early in its life, the party could also count on some city voters —artisans, craftsmen, and small businessmen, all strong nationalists who admired and trusted the great symbol of union, George Washington. Separated from these groups by class, temperament, and mentality, Federalist leaders were determined to direct U.S. affairs according to their own lights. They despised democracy, and liked to repeat the aphorism that those who owned the country ought to run it. Human nature was, after all, untrustworthy—especially the nature of those humans who owned no property. It was up to themselves, to the better sort of people, they thought, to govern the mob in order to protect property and to preserve order. They were, in short, republicans —not democrats—convinced that the American experiment would profit the world only if it were kept within conservative limits.

Federalist political philosophy changed over the years, but slowly, and in a direction away from the course of national development. America was becoming more democratic, not less, but the Federalists opposed the extension of the franchise. At their worst they agreed with the crotchety Noah Webster, who urged that the minimum voting age should be 45 years and that every office-

holder should be at least 50 years old. The farmers who had rallied to them before 1800 soon learned that all they could expect from the Federalists was pious reassurance that the interests of business and agriculture were identical.

After Washington's retirement, the Federalists divided internally between Adams and Hamilton factions. President John Adams alienated Hamilton and his group forever in 1799 by deciding for peace with France rather than war. The next year the party lost the presidency and never regained it. By this time the Federalists had become a sectional party—New England voted solidly for them and the Republicans dominated the South, the West, and New York. Soon Federalist strength dwindled even in New England, and in 1804 they carried only Connecticut. Jefferson's economic measures hurt New England in the next few years and in the next election (1808) Charles C. Pinckney, the Federalist candidate, recovered all of New England except Vermont. The resurgence was temporary; the Federalist party was virtually dead by the end of the War of 1812.

Despite their failures, the Federalists had achieved much in their great years before 1800. They had made the government function according to the prescriptions of the Constitution; they had established administrative techniques that persisted long after their party's demise; they had stimulated American nationalism; and they had guided the new nation through a dangerous period of world affairs.

Consult Miller, J. C., *The Federalist Era, 1789–1801* (1960).

ROBERT MIDDLEKAUFF, Yale University

See also DEMOCRATIC PARTY.

FEDERAL MEDIATION AND CONCILIATION SERVICE, an independent agency of the U.S. government created by the Labor Management Relations Act of 1947 to aid both sides in labor-management disputes involving interstate commerce. It may enter such disputes on the invitation of the disputants or on its own initiative. When asked, it may also participate in the negotiation of first contracts between employer and employees. When participants in a labor-management dispute cannot reach agreement, the service assigns one of its 200 mediators to help them. It also maintains a roster of experienced arbitrators and upon request will furnish the names of other qualified arbitrators to disputants who seek arbitration of their differences. The service has its headquarters in Washington, D.C., and maintains 68 field offices. Its former name was the United States Conciliation Service.

FEDERAL POWER COMMISSION (FPC). In 1920 a U.S. Federal Power Commission was established, consisting of the secretaries of War, Agriculture, and Interior, to license hydroelectric projects on government lands and on navigable waters of the United States. Since 1930 the commission has been an independent agency, with five commissioners serving five-year staggered terms.

In 1935 the commission was given the power to control interstate wholesale electricity rates, and to regulate the security issues of private utility companies which were engaged in interstate commerce. In 1938 the commission was given statutory authority to regulate the transportation and sale of natural gas for resale in interstate commerce and to supervise those gas companies engaged in such commerce. In that same year the Flood Control Act extended the commission's jurisdiction to include planning for multipurpose dam sites and for hydroelectric power plants at government-constructed dams. The commission also has the authority to confirm and approve rates for electric power which is sold from governmentally controlled reservoirs and international hydroelectric plants, and the power to issue permits for construction of electric power and natural gas facilities which are located on the borders of the United States.

The activities of the commission include the regulation of rates, services, and general business practices of all public utility holding companies which supply either gas or electricity for sale in interstate commerce or which make use of the United States mails. Control over security issues, mergers, and sales of property by operating gas and electric companies engaged in interstate commerce are also within the commission's controlling authority. The five-man commission is responsible for making recommendations to Congress on proposed legislation relating to electric power or natural gas matters.

More substantively the commission's responsibilities require that it study, plan for, and advise on matters concerning multiple-purpose river basin development and development of the national water power resources. Licensing of dam construction on sites over which the commission has control, investigation to insure compliance with the terms of issued permits, and determination of rents, fees, and other costs for such privileges as the above are also counted among commission activities.

In the natural gas field the commission issues certificates covering construction, sale, or operation of interstate facilities and also rules on their abandonment, accounting systems, depreciation, rates, charges, and

services. Controversy over the commission's role in regulating the natural gas rate as the gas enters the pipeline has been the subject of considerable conflict among the Congress, the commission, the courts, and the operators.
— STUART GERRY BROWN, Syracuse University

FEDERAL RESERVE SYSTEM, in the United States, a group of financial institutions created by Congress in 1913, and charged with supervising the money supply in order to promote economic stability.

Structure

Most nations have one central bank. The United States, however, has 12 regional Federal Reserve Banks, co-ordinated by a central board of governors.

Member Banks. All national banks (chartered by the federal government) must become members of the system by joining the Federal Reserve Bank of their district. Other banks (chartered by state governments) may join if they meet certain standards. In 1961, there were over 6,000 member banks, less than half the total number of commercial banks, but they accounted for 85% of the country's commercial banking business. Nonmember banks are mostly too small to meet membership requirements.

Federal Reserve Banks. Each of the 12 Federal Reserve Banks is legally a separate corporation. Member banks must purchase stock in their district's Reserve Bank and are entitled to elect six of its nine directors. The board of governors appoints the others. The Reserve Banks handle the day-to-day operations of the system.

Board of Governors. The board of governors of the Federal Reserve System has supervisory authority over the whole system. It consists of seven members appointed by the President. The governors are somewhat independent of political pressure in that they serve 14-year terms and cannot be reappointed or dismissed.

THE FEDERAL RESERVE SYSTEM

ALASKA 12

HAWAII 12

━━ Boundaries of Federal Reserve districts
── Boundaries of Federal Reserve branch territories
★ Federal Reserve bank cities
• Federal Reserve branch cities
⊛ Board of Governors of the Federal Reserve System

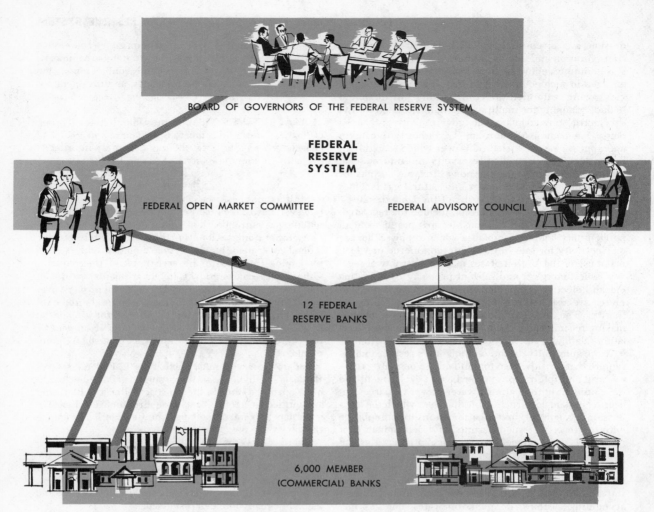

FEDERAL RESERVE SYSTEM

BOARD OF GOVERNORS OF THE FEDERAL RESERVE SYSTEM

FEDERAL OPEN MARKET COMMITTEE

FEDERAL ADVISORY COUNCIL

12 FEDERAL RESERVE BANKS

6,000 MEMBER (COMMERCIAL) BANKS

Open Market Committee. The Federal Open Market Committee consists of the seven governors plus five presidents of the Reserve Banks. This committee determines what securities the Reserve Banks shall buy or sell.

Federal Advisory Council. The Federal Advisory Council has 12 members, each of whom is a banker selected by the Reserve Bank of his district. It advises the board of governors but has no power to determine policy.

Operations

The routine operations of Reserve Banks resemble those of ordinary commercial banks, except that Reserve Banks deal primarily with other banks rather than the public, and have as their purpose monetary stabilization rather than profit.

Reserves. Member banks must maintain as reserves a specified percentage of their own deposit liabilities to customers—called the reserve ratio, or legal reserves. Reserves may take the form of cash in the bank's vault or deposits with the district Reserve Bank. A member bank makes a deposit by giving the Reserve Bank cash or checks that it has received—largely from its own depositors. The Reserve Bank then owes this amount to the member bank. The reserve requirement is higher for demand than for time (savings) deposits; it is higher for banks in big cities

than for banks in smaller communities; and it can be changed by the board of governors within statutory limits. Historically the rate has varied from 3% for time deposits to 26% for demand deposits of New York and Chicago banks. Since member banks can create money when their reserves exceed the requirement, an increase in the requirement restricts monetary expansion, while a decrease promotes it.

Clearing. Member bank deposits also make possible the Federal Reserve's clearing mechanism, which arranges payment for checks drawn on one bank and deposited in another. The transfer of funds is a bookkeeping rather than a physical shift.

Other Deposits. Reserve Banks accept deposits from the government, thus acting as its bank. They also do business with foreign central banks and accept deposits from nonmember banks who wish to use Reserve clearing facilities without becoming members.

Notes. The Federal Reserve Banks are the issuing authorities for Federal Reserve notes, the primary form of currency. The law requires that these notes be backed by a 25% gold reserve, but there has been considerable sentiment for eliminating this requirement as unnecessary. Normally the notes are paid out against checks written by member banks on their deposit accounts in the Federal

Reserve, and are retired when the Reserve Banks receive them from depositors.

Gold Certificates. The Reserve Banks hold title, in the form of certificates, to most of the country's gold. Because the government buys or sells its gold through the Federal Reserve, the gold certificate holdings of Reserve Banks reflect any changes in national gold stocks.

Open-market Operations. The primary assets of Reserve Banks are United States government securities. The Reserve does not buy securities directly from the Treasury; it deals instead with the general public in the open market. When the Reserve buys securities, it gives the seller a check drawn on itself, which he deposits in his own commercial bank. The commercial bank then redeposits the check in its Reserve Bank. Thus whenever the Reserve buys securities, it creates additional bank reserves, enabling banks to expand credit. When it sells securities, the process is reversed: banks lose reserves, and credit is restricted.

Discounts and Advances. Reserve Banks also lend directly to member banks that temporarily need additional reserves to meet a deficiency. The member bank may sell the Reserve certain assets (commercial paper); or, much more commonly, may give the Reserve its own promissory note. In either case the Reserve Bank charges interest, called the discount (or rediscount) rate. Changes in the discount rate are an instrument of monetary policy: low rates encourage, high rates discourage, additional borrowing. When member banks as a group borrow more from the Reserve Bank than they have in excess reserves (reserves above the legal requirement) they are said to have net borrowed reserves. If excess reserves of all banks exceed borrowing from the Federal Reserve, banks are said to have free reserves.

Technically, each Reserve Bank decides the discount rate for its district, subject to approval by the board of governors. In practice the rates are usually uniform.

Consult Kemmerer, E. W., and D. L., *The A B C of the Federal Reserve System* (12th ed., 1950); Bach, G. L., *Federal Reserve Policy-making* (1950); Goldenweiser, E. A., *American Monetary Policy* (1951); Board of Governors of the Federal Reserve System, *The Federal Reserve System: Purposes and Functions* (4th ed., 1961).

WALTER W. HAINES, New York University
See also BUSINESS CYCLE; ECONOMIC STABILIZATION POLICIES.

FEDERAL SAVINGS AND LOAN INSURANCE CORPORATION, a U.S. agency created by Congress in 1934 to protect savers and investors by insuring, up to $10,000, accounts in savings and loan institutions. The corporation derives its income largely from premiums paid by insured institutions and from interest on investments. Self-supporting, it has repaid with interest the funds it originally received from the U.S. Treasury and has also built up a large reserve. It insures over 4,000 institutions with 26,000,000 members and more than $67,000,000,000 in assets. The activities of the corporation are supervised by the Federal Home Loan Bank Board.

FEDERAL STYLE, American architectural style of the era 1775 to 1825. It is characterized by more complex plans and more delicate detail than the preceding Georgian style. Charles Bulfinch's Boston State House, Thomas Jefferson's University of Virginia, in Charlottesville, and Benjamin Henry Latrobe's Baltimore Cathedral exemplify its range.
See also UNITED STATES, ARCHITECTURE OF THE.

FEDERAL THEATER PROJECT, federally sponsored U.S. theatrical program (1935–39) directed by Hallie Flanagan as part of the Works Progress Administration. Using unemployed actors and technicians, it produced classic and modern plays in 40 states. Among its major contributions was the development of a Negro theater and the production of a novel form, called Living Newspaper, that effectively dramatized leading social and economic problems and employed elements of staging that became best known through Bertolt Brecht's "epic theater" (q.v.).

FEDERAL TRADE COMMISSION (FTC), independent regulatory agency of the U.S. government, created by the Federal Trade Commission Act of 1914. It absorbed such pre-existing agencies as the Bureau of Corporations. Originally the commission was to investigate and report, but it also had the power to issue "cease and desist" orders if, upon hearing a case involving industries engaged in interstate commerce, it found evidence of unfair business competition. These hearings and subsequent action by the commission did not have the force of a legislative or judicial decision and only occasionally achieved the desired effect.

The Federal Trade Commission was also empowered by the Clayton Antitrust Act of 1914 to prevent illegal price discrimination, interlocking directorates, tying contracts, and purchases of stock in competing corporations. The major purpose of this legislation was the maintenance of competition, the prevention of monopoly, and the furtherance of the free enterprise system. It was thought that the Sherman Antitrust Act of 1890 was inadequate in its definition and weak in both application and interpretation and that the economic system was in need of federal intervention in order to insure free and open competition in the national marketplace.

Eventually the commission set up a scheme whereby large corporations voluntarily sent representatives to a Trade Practice Conference wherein a co-operative definition of unfair business practices was evolved. The participation of large-scale industrial concerns insured that the standards thus established would more readily be followed by other businessmen. As a result of this plan a new era of self-regulation by industry seemed to be in effect. The role of the government in these proceedings was that of a representative of the consumer and a force aiming at the securing of public good. Much costly and time-consuming litigation was avoided through the use of this method and resort to the courts was seldom necessary.

However, by 1936 the inadequacies of the Conference method and the Clayton Act in general were clear. The Robinson-Patman Act passed in June of that year was devoted to further restraining monopoly practices and other undesirable activities lessening competition. Two years later the Wheeler-Lea Act amended the commission's powers to enable it to supervise advertising practices and give the commission's decisions the force of administrative law to be supported by suits brought by the Attorney General if the commission's cease and desist orders were ignored. Appeal to the courts was limited to a 60-day period, after which the decision was final.

Later amendments to the Federal Trade Commission Act gave commission decisions the force of law, with penalties to be applied in the event of their violation. The commission's powers to supervise advertising practices in the fields of foods, drugs, cosmetics, and therapeutic devices were later strengthened. Where fraud, criminal intent, or injury to health can be proved, criminal penalties are provided. A commission decision in these matters was to be supported by a temporary injunction issued by a federal district court and was to be effective until changed by the commission or set aside by the courts upon review. In practice, however, it is not so easy to obtain such an injunction and delaying action by corporations under commission censure is the usual order of the day. By slight modifications of censured advertising copy a new case can be presented for commission action.

The Federal Trade Commission has also received broad powers to review practices in labeling, handling of flammable fabrics, trademarks, and the like. The great bulk of the commission's time, however, is now spent in the area of supervision of radio and television commercials and in review of commercial advertising in periodicals. It can fairly be said that the commission has done much to raise standards in these fields and to reduce harmful practices which endanger public health or safety.

The commission is composed of five members appointed by the President with the advice and consent of the Senate. No more than three of these may be from the same party.

STUART GERRY BROWN, Syracuse University

FEDERAL WRITERS' PROJECT, relief program of the Works Progress Administration (1935–39), which provided employment for over 6,000 writers throughout the United States. The chief accomplishment of the program was the *American Guide Series*, a series of volumes covering the geography, history, and culture of the 48 states.

FEDERATED CHURCHES, local churches in which two or more denominations unite at the local level while in all other matters maintaining their respective denominational relationships.

FEDERATED MALAY STATES, the four Malay states of Perak, Selangor, Negri Sembilan, and Pahang, the first three on the west coast and the last on the east coast of the Malay Peninsula. By the Treaty of Federation (1896), these states, under British protection and advice, formed a federation centered in Kuala Lumpur which lasted until the Japanese invasion in 1942. *See* MALAYSIA.

FEEBLE-MINDED, EDUCATION OF THE. *See* EDUCATION: *Education of Exceptional Children;* MENTALLY RETARDED, THE.

FEEBLEMINDEDNESS. *See* MENTAL DEFICIENCY.

FEEDBACK, a method in which the output of a system is returned, or fed back, to influence the input. An example of feedback is the home heating system. When a thermostat is set it is "informed," in effect, of the temperature at which a room is to be maintained. When the room temperature falls below the set level, the thermostat transmits a signal to a furnace control which ignites a fuel; the heat is then conducted through ducts to the room or rooms. As soon as the desired temperature is again reached, another signal from the thermostat shuts off the furnace and the cycle is completed.

The adoption of the term "feedback" may have been suggested by the way in which block diagrams of such systems are usually drawn. The flow of information in a system is conventionally shown proceeding from left to right. But if a feedback path is present in which the output of the system is fed back to be compared with the input, that information flow path must be shown as proceeding backward, that is, from right to left.

It is important to distinguish the alternative to the feedback system. If the feedback path including the Indicator were missing from the system shown in the figure, the resulting system would have a straight-through information flow-path from input at the left to output at the right. Such a configuration may be referred to as an "open-chain" system, whereas the feedback system is a "closed-loop" system.

To illustrate this distinction, let us consider the control of the speed of an automobile in which the human driver serves as the controller. If the driver were to operate the car in an open-chain manner he would have to deprive himself of any indication of the speed of the car which could serve a feedback function. In that case he would control the speed simply by depressing the accelerator pedal to a position which he believes will result in the correct speed and hold it constant. In actual practice, however, the driver controls his speed in a feedback manner. He observes an indication of the actual speed, by glancing at the speedometer, for example, compares the indicated speed mentally with the desired speed, and adjusts the accelerator pedal up or down so as to reduce the error. In this case then, the driver serves the function of the Comparator and the Controller. The Controlled System is the automobile, and the Controlled Variable, speed, is indicated by the speedometer.

The feedback system enjoys several distinct advantages over the open-chain system in most applications. One is the possibility of faster response; other advantages are better regulation against disturbances and less dependence upon the characteristics of the system being controlled. These advantages accrue from the fact that the feedback controller, if intelligent enough, can manipulate the Actuating Variable in whatever manner seems necessary to achieve the desired result. The open-chain controller, since it has no indication of the results it is getting (that is, has no feedback from the Controlled Variable), must be a calibrated controller which can take little or no account of changes from standard operating conditions or of deviations of the Controlled Variable from the desired value. It is clear that a human being serving as the Controller in a feedback system can perform that function in a very intelligent way and thus realize these

THE FEEDBACK SYSTEM COMPARED TO THE OPEN-CHAIN SYSTEM

OPEN-CHAIN SYSTEM

The controller is set and the input remains constant as long as the system is in operation, regardless of changes that may occur in the controlled variable or operating conditions.

FEEDBACK SYSTEM

The feedback circuit returns some measure of the output to the comparator for comparison with the desired performance. If the indicator and the comparator are not in agreement, the controller automatically adjusts the input.

advantages to a very high degree. It is also true that man-made controllers for inanimate systems, though far simpler than the human mind, can also realize these advantages to a very important degree. For example, the feedback system which positions a large gun to correspond with the position of a small sighting bar can hold the gun with essentially no error in spite of a strong wind blowing across the gun and regardless of the fact that parts of the drive system may be worn. Also, the altitude controller and autopilot for an aircraft can control the vehicle to the desired altitude, and maintain it, regardless of the number of passengers on board even if one engine were to fail.

Stability. The major disadvantage in the use of feedback is the problem of stability. Because of lags in the cause-effect relationships within the loop, a closed-loop system may "overcontrol" and cause undesirable oscillations, even if it consists of elements which are all well behaved by themselves. The open-chain system is free from this problem of stability, which is the major consideration of the classical theory of feedback systems.

As has been evident from these illustrations, feedback systems are not only designed and constructed by man specifically for control functions, but they appear quite naturally in a broad variety of situations. Most human and other animal activities seem to be controlled by systems employing feedback. For example, an indication of the amount of light received in the retina of the eye is fed back to open or close the pupil and thus regulates the amount of light transmitted. There are many closed-loop situations represented in economic or business activity. For example, the general economic condition of a nation or region is a factor which helps to determine the potential for profit-making and thus influences the rate of business investment. But the rate of business investment in turn has an important influence on the economic condition of the region. The major difficulty in the application of feedback control theory to situations like these is the identification of the proper variables to consider and the determination of all the cause-effect relationships which are significant in the system. Once having complete data on the individual elements of the system, the evaluation of the characteristics of the complete feedback system and the recognition of potentially dangerous conditions is relatively easier.

Consult Wiener, Norbert, *Cybernetics* (1948); Ahrendt, W. R., and Taplin, J. F., *Automatic Feedback Control* (1951).

WALLACE E. VANDER VELDE, Massachusetts Institute of Technology

See also AUTOMATIC CONTROL; AUTOMATION; CYBERNETICS.

FEEDS. Prior to the 19th century, the nutritional needs of domestic animals were little understood and were met largely by "natural" means—milk for suckling young and pasture or forages for mature animals. These diets, however, are recognized even today as fairly complete nutritionally. The early investigations of scientific animal feeding that took place during the 19th century revealed that livestock required more or less specific amounts of protein, carbohydrate, and fat, referred to as "balance rations," with mineral requirements much less definitely established. The general need for salt was recognized, as well as that for other minerals such as calcium and phosphorus.

Research during the first 60 years of the 20th century has specified fairly precise amounts of all recognized nutrients and has noted the requirements of vitamins and the minor or trace minerals, especially iodine, cobalt, manganese, copper, iron, and zinc. During the 1940's and 1950's the growth- and production-promoting properties of so-called "additives" to rations became known, especially certain antibiotics and hormones. The manufacture of medicated feeds came into prominence in the 1950's. These feeds are designed to rid animals of internal parasites and other infections while providing adequate nourishment to the host animal. The greatly increased technological problems of feeding farm animals during the 20th century have brought about a corresponding development of the feed-manufacturing industry, exemplified in the manufacture of poultry feeds, but extending to feeds for all other farm animals.

TABLE 1.	BASIC DAILY NUTRIENT REQUIREMENTS (Feeding Standards)						
	BODY WEIGHT (lb.)	FEED (lb.)	DIGESTIBLE PROTEIN (lb.)	TOTAL DIGESTIBLE NUTRIENTS (lb.)	CALCIUM (gm.)	PHOSPHORUS (gm.)	CAROTENE (mg.)
DAIRY CALF[1]	400	11.0	0.80	6.5	13	12	16
BEEF CALF[2]	400	12.0	1.00	8.0	20	15	7
LAMB, FATTENING[3]	80	3.4	0.19	2.1	3	2.7	1.4
PIG, GROWING[4]	50	3.2	0.51*	2.4	9.4	7.3	2.4

National Academy of Sciences, National Research Council, Publication 464[1], 579[2], 504[3], 648[4]
*Crude, indigestible protein

TABLE 2.	ANALYSES OF TYPICAL FEEDS SUITABLE FOR "BALANCING" RATIONS[1]					
	DRY MATTER (%)	DIGESTIBLE PROTEIN (%)	TOTAL DIGESTIBLE NUTRIENTS (%)	CALCIUM (%)	PHOSPHORUS (%)	CAROTENE (mg./lb.)
FORAGES						
ALFALFA HAY	90.5	10.9	50.7	1.47	0.24	8.2
TIMOTHY HAY	89.0	3.0	49.1	0.35	0.14	4.4
CORN SILAGE	27.6	1.2	18.3	0.10	0.07	5.8
CONCENTRATES						
CORN (NO. 2)	85.0	6.7	80.1	0.02	0.27	1.3
OATS	90.2	9.4	70.1	0.09	0.33	—
SOYBEAN OIL MEAL	89.3	42.1	77.2	0.32	0.67	—
MEAT SCRAP	93.5	43.8	65.4	7.90	4.03	—

(1) National Academy of Sciences, National Research Council, Publication 464

Livestock Feeds. The two general classifications of livestock feeds are roughages (or forages) that have high fiber or cellulose content—about 18% to 40%—and concentrates that are low in cellulose—from 0% to about 15%. Forages may be classified as (1) dry forages, which include hay, straw, and fodder (mainly corn and sorghum fodder), and also stover, which is fodder without the ears of grain; (2) green forages from the above crops, with root crops also included; and (3) silages from nearly all of the foregoing forages and from additional crops. Concentrates include grains or seeds and their by-products, animal products and by-products, and miscellaneous feeds that are low in cellulose.

Livestock Feed Preparation. The preparation of harvested crops for feed preserves the feeds and also improves their palatability, digestibility, and efficiency. Feed preparation consists of drying where necessary (hay crops and unripe grain), grinding, chopping, rolling or crushing, pelleting, heating (potatoes, beans, and all oil-bearing seeds), soaking (grain), sprouting (grain), and ensiling (forage crops and various succulent feeds). The most common methods of preparation are drying, ensiling, grinding, chopping, and pelleting. A large part of the farm implement industry is devoted to the manufacture and sale of machinery for feed processing.

GUSTAV BOHSTEDT, College of Agriculture, University of Wisconsin

See also FORAGE PLANTS; GRAIN; HAY; PASTURE; SILAGE.

FEILDING, city of New Zealand, on North Island about 85 mi. north of Wellington. It is the trade and processing center for a sheep farming and dairying region. Pop., 8,172.

FEININGER [fi'ning-ər], **ANDREAS** (1906–), American photographer, known for his poetic pictures of cities and buildings and for enlarged studies of details of nature. Feininger was born in Paris, son of Lyonel, noted modern American painter. In 1939 he moved to New York, where he became a staff photographer for *Life* in 1943. His numerous books include *Successful Photography* (1954); *Successful Color Photography* (1954); and *The Creative Photographer* (1955).

FEKE [fēk], **ROBERT** (c.1705–c.1750), American painter, born probably in Oyster Bay, Long Island, N.Y. The best

Fogg Art Museum

"Isaac Royall and Family," a group portrait by the 18th-century American artist Robert Feke.

American-born portraitist before John Singleton Copley, Feke was influenced by the British-born John Smibert. Since he lacked Smibert's European training, Feke's style is naturally less sophisticated, his compositions less complex, but his best portraits show a sensitive appreciation of feminine charm and a superior perception of form and color. Feke's group portrait of the younger Isaac Royall and his family (1741; Harvard University, Cambridge, Mass.) is his masterpiece. His portraits may be seen in the Bowdoin College Museum of Fine Arts, Brunswick, Maine; the Museum of Fine Arts, Boston; and the Philadelphia Museum of Art; many are privately owned.

FELDKIRCH [fĕlt'kĭrkH], town of western Austria, located in the province of Vorarlberg near the Swiss border. It is a road and railway junction and a marketing center. Feldkirch is the starting point for the railway through the Arlberg Tunnel leading to the Tyrol. A 13th-century castle of the Montforts and a Gothic church are features of the town. Pop., 15,045.

FELDSPAR MINERALS, aluminosilicates of potassium, sodium, calcium, and rarely barium, comprising several related species. The common feldspars can be grouped into the potash and plagioclase feldspars.

The potash feldspars include two species, orthoclase and microcline, with the formula $KAlSi_3O_8$. Orthoclase and microcline resemble each other closely in all respects; even the crystals are similar, although orthoclase crystallizes in the monoclinic system and microcline in the triclinic. The mode of occurrence is somewhat different: orthoclase is present in potassium-rich igneous rocks such as granite, rhyolite, and syenite, whereas microcline is more common in veins and in coarse-grained quartz-feldspar bodies of igneous rock called pegmatites. The hardness (Mohs' Scale) is 6 and the density 2.56. The color is usually white, cream, or pink, but microcline is sometimes found in a beautiful green variety called amazonite. Clear orthoclase with a pearly opalescence, called moonstone, is used as an ornamental stone.

The plagioclase feldspars are arbitrarily divided into six species ranging in composition from pure $NaAlSi_3O_8$ to pure $CaAl_2Si_2O_8$. They are albite, oligoclase, andesine, labradorite, bytownite, and anorthite. The plagioclases are commonly white or gray, sometimes red or reddish-brown; labradorite often shows a beautiful blue-gray iridescence. The hardness is 6, and the density ranges from 2.62 in albite to 2.76 in anorthite. The plagioclases are important minerals of igneous and metamorphic rocks, and albite is common in pegmatites and veins.

The feldspars are the most abundant of all minerals, making up an estimated 60% of the earth's crust. The potassium- and sodium-rich varieties are important industrially as raw materials for the manufacture of glass and ceramics. Although feldspar is abundant in nature, workable deposits are confined to pegmatites. More than 1,000,000 tons of feldspar, mainly microcline and albite, are mined annually throughout the world; about half of this comes from the United States.

BRIAN MASON, American Museum of Natural History
See also CRYSTALLOGRAPHY; FELDSPATHOID MINERALS; MINERALOGY.

FELDSPATHOID [fĕld-spăth'oid], **MINERALS,** alkali-rich (mainly soda-rich) and silica-poor aluminosilicates. They commonly occur with, or take the place of, feldspars as rock-forming minerals. They are more or less restricted to igneous rocks that contain abundant sodium and potassium but do not contain sufficient silica to completely satisfy the feldspar demand for silica. Crystallographically, feldspathoids are framework silicates. They include the nepheline group, the sodalite group, leucite, analcite, cancrinite, and other less well-known varieties. The term is little used in modern chemical and structural classifications of minerals because feldspathoids do not constitute a distinct chemical group, nor do they have a unique crystal structure. Petrologists, however, find the term useful because the feldspathoids have significance in terms of rock origin. The presence of feldspathoids in igneous rocks indicates that the original magma was silica-poor.

PETER FLAWN, University of Texas
See also FELDSPAR MINERALS.

FELICIAN [fĕ-lĭsh'ən] **SISTERS,** a Roman Catholic congregation of Franciscan tertiaries founded in 1855 in Warsaw, Poland, by Sophia Truszkowska in honor of St. Felix of Cantalice, Italy. The first American mother house, established in 1874 in Polonia, Wis., was later moved to Livonia, Mich. About 5,000 sisters in the United States teach at the college, secondary, or elementary level and conduct orphanages, hospitals, and homes for the aged. The first Canadian foundation of the Felician sisters was established in Toronto in 1937. In Canada they do important work in helping to integrate immigrants from Eastern Europe.

WILLIAM A. DEHLER, S.J., Loyola University, Chicago

FELIDAE [fē'lĭ-dē, fĕl'ĭ-dē], a family of carnivorous mammals whose members, the cats, are characterized chiefly by their retractile claws and digitigrade feet (they walk on their toes). Felids have large canine teeth, effective as stabbing weapons; the hindmost molar of the upper jaw is bladelike and adapted for cutting flesh. Felids are almost entirely carnivorous, seeking their prey by stealth. Members of the family are found in all parts of the world except in the Australian region. They range in size from the domestic cat, *Felis catus*, which stands less than 1 ft. at the shoulders, to the lion, *Panthera (Leo) leo*, and tiger, *P. (Tigris) tigris*, both of which attain a shoulder height of over 3 ft.

See also:

BOBCAT	LYNX
CAT	OCELOT
CHEETAH	PANTHER
JAGUAR	PUMA
LEOPARD	TIGER
LION	

FELIX [fē'lĭks], **ANTONIUS,** a freedman of the Claudian House in Rome. Brother of Pallas, a favorite of the Emperor Claudius, Felix became governor or procurator of Palestine in 52–53 A.D. He was governor at the time of St. Paul's arrest (Acts 23:24–24:26). Tacitus (*Historiae*, Vol. IX) says that Felix "revelled in cruelty and lust, and wielded the power of a king with the mind of a slave."

FELLENBERG [fĕl'ən-bĕrкн], **PHILIPP EMANUEL VON** (1771–1844), Swiss educator, agriculturist, and philanthropist. To put into practice his belief that education could improve the way of life of the farming classes, he established schools at Hofwyl, near Bern, that combined elementary schooling with instruction in farming and trades. His pupils worked on the land, their produce helping to support their school.

FELLER, ROBERT WILLIAM ANDREW ("BOB") (1918–), American baseball player, born in Van Meter, Iowa. One of the great right-handed fast-ball pitchers in the history of the sport, he played for Cleveland of the American League from 1936 to 1956, except for a period (1941–45) when he served in the U.S. Navy. He won 266 games and lost 162 during his career. In 1938 he set a major league record by striking out 18 players in a 9-inning game; in 1946 he established a major league record for strike-outs in one season (348). He pitched three no-hit games, in 1940, 1946, and 1951. In 1962 he was elected to the National Baseball Hall of Fame.

FELLINI [fĕl-lē'nē], **FEDERICO** (1920–). Italian motion-picture director and writer, acknowledged as one of the great modern masters of the cinema. After World War II he was one of the first to write screenplays for neorealist films and was coauthor of the screenplays for Roberto Rossellini's *Roma città aperta* (Open City), 1945, and *Paisà* (Paisan), 1946. Fellini's first independent production was *Lo sceicco bianco* (The White Sheik), 1952. He also was coauthor and director of the successful *I Vitelloni* (The Wastrels), 1953; *La Strada* (The Road), 1954, which received an Academy Award in 1957; *La dolce vita* (The Sweet Life), 1960, which was awarded the 1960 Cannes Film Festival and New York Film Critic Circle awards; and *8½* (1963), another Academy Award winner. *Juliet of the Spirits* (1965) was his first film to make use of color. Fellini's *Satyricon* appeared in 1969. His films are notable for their perceptive social commentary and use of symbolism.

FELLOWS, SIR CHARLES (1799–1860), English traveler and archeologist. In 1827 he discovered the modern route up Mont Blanc in the French Alps. Between 1838 and 1841 he traveled and excavated in Asia Minor, discovering the sites of Xanthus and Tlos, two cities of ancient Lycia. He gave a number of marble sculptures to the British Museum.

FELLOWSHIPS, EDUCATIONAL. The term "educational fellowships," according to the U.S. Office of Education, should refer to financial aid given to graduate college students for which no service is required in return. Sometimes fellowships are confused with scholarships, a term which should refer only to financial aid given to undergraduate college students.

Fellowships are of two types: (1) those furnished by the institution in which the graduate student is enrolled, and (2) those furnished and administered by outside agencies.

The oldest extensive program of the second type in the United States is that of the American Association of University Women, which has awarded over 1,400 fellowships to women since 1890. The federal government offered extensive programs in the 1960's: those of the National Defense Education Act of 1958, providing for 2,500 three-year fellowships, paying $2,000 or more annually, in addition to over 500 foreign language fellowships; and those of the National Science Foundation, which awarded fellowships valued at $13,000,000 in one year.

Other outstanding fellowships programs, privately administered, include those of the Woodrow Wilson National Fellowship Foundation, awarding 1,000 per year under a grant of $25,000,000 made by the Ford Foundation in 1957; the John Simon Guggenheim Memorial Foundation, Rotary International, the Rockefeller Foundation, and the General Education Board.

Consult Eells, W. C., and Hollis, E. V., *Student Financial Aid in Higher Education* (1960); Schiltz, M. E., *Fellowships in the Arts and Sciences, 1960-61* (4th ed., 1960) which gives data on 20,000 available fellowships; UNESCO, *Study Abroad: International Handbook of Fellowships, Scholarships, Educational Exchange* (1960).

WALTER CROSBY EELLS, Educational Consultant
See also FULBRIGHT FELLOWSHIPS.

FELONY. *See* CRIMINAL LAW.

FELT. *See* TEXTILES: *Glossary of Textile Fabrics.*

FEMALE DISEASES. *See* GYNECOLOGY.

FEMINISM. *See* WOMAN SUFFRAGE; WOMEN, EDUCATION OF; WOMEN, STATUS OF.

FEMUR or THIGHBONE. *See* SKELETAL SYSTEM.

FENCE LIZARD, common name for several species of heavy-bodied lizards of the genus *Sceloporus*, in the family of New World lizards, Iguanidae, found throughout North America. Fence lizards, or swifts as they are often called, have large, rough, spine-tipped scales. They live on the ground or in trees and feed on insects. The common fence lizard, *S. undulatus*, is found in many parts of the United States and in northern Mexico. It grows to a length of about 7 in. and is grayish-brown in color. Males have patches of bright blue on the throat and underside.

FENCING, in its present form, a close-combat sport involving armed personal offense and defense between two persons using swords or foils.

Origin and Growth. Fencing originated long before the Christian era, as a form of life-and-death combat. As a sport, it got its start at the time when insults were avenged by means of duels fought with sabers or dueling swords. Although such duels are illegal throughout the present-day civilized world, the sport has become increasingly popular. Modern fencing dates from the 14th century and had its greatest early impetus in France, Italy, and Spain. Until 1952, France, Hungary, and Italy dominated the sport; since then the Soviet Union has successfully challenged France and Italy, and the United States and Poland have become strong contenders. The Soviet Union entered competitive fencing for the first time in the Olympic Games of 1952. In those of 1960 the Russians emerged

Action photograph shows a lunge performed by Michael Alaux, fencing master at New York Fencers' Club.

The art of fencing was revitalized when the Olympic Games were resumed in 1896. The international meet now includes individual and four-man-team contests in foil, épée, and saber for men and foil for women. In the United States this sophisticated sport is governed by the Amateur Fencers' League of America, and is popular in many educational institutions.

FENCING

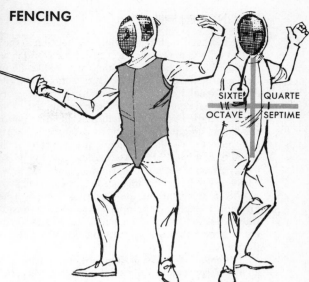

SIXTE QUARTE
OCTAVE SEPTIME

THE ON-GUARD POSITION

SIDE VIEW, SHOWING
TARGET AREA IN GRAY

FRONT VIEW, SHOWING
QUARTERS OF DEFENSE

LUNGE: from on-guard, fencer extends right arm and steps forward with right foot, left foot remaining in place.

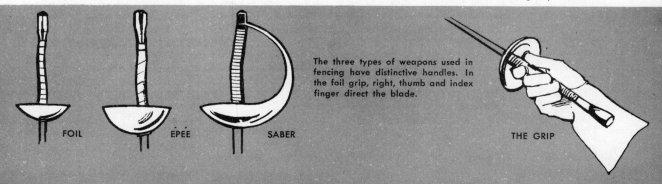

FOIL   ÉPÉE   SABER

The three types of weapons used in fencing have distinctive handles. In the foil grip, right, thumb and index finger direct the blade.

THE GRIP

as the most successful in over-all competition in the sport.

The growth of fencing throughout the world is best exemplified by the fact that in the early 1960's, 65 nations belonged to the Fédération Internationale d'Escrime (International Fencing Federation), governing body in international competition, and competed in the Olympic Games. In the United States, during the same period, the sport was taught and practiced extensively. Forty-two colleges competed in a tournament conducted by the National Collegiate Athletic Association, and 33 high schools took part in the annual tournament held at New York University. As a further indication of the growing strength of U.S. fencing, Miguel de Carpriles, former American Olympic fencer and champion, was elected president of the Fédération Internationale d'Escrime in 1960, thus becoming the first non-European to hold this highest post in the sport.

Equipment and Rules of Competition. Fencing is mostly an indoor sport and requires skill, stamina, grace, balance, speed, and a high degree of intelligence. Each participant wears a mask, glove, and uniform made of special cloth that affords maximum protection against injury. The blades of the weapons are flexible and the tips are blunt. Three weapons are used: foil, dueling sword (*épée*), and saber. Men use all three but women fence only with the foil. A bout takes place on a "strip" 40 ft. long and between 5 ft. 10⅞ in. and 6 ft. 6¾ in. wide, and is decided on the basis of five out of nine touches for men and four out of seven for women. There is a standard time limit of six minutes for each bout for men and five minutes for women.

The foil and *épée* are thrusting weapons, and touches can be scored only with the point of the blade. The saber is both a thrusting and cutting weapon so that valid touches are scored either with the point or with the cutting edge of the blade. Touches in all weapons count only if they are scored on the target area, which is different for each weapon. All matches are conducted under the supervision of a director. In foil and dueling-sword competition, the validity of a touch is determined with the aid of an electric machine connected to the specially wired weapons. Foil fencers wear over their uniforms a special vest made of metallic cloth and covering only the valid target area consisting of the trunk of the body and the groin. In dueling-sword competition the metallic jacket is unnecessary because the entire body is a valid target. The target in saber fencing is every part of the body above the imaginary horizontal line passing through the highest points of the folds in the thighs and trunk when the fencer is in the "on-guard" position.

The fencing strip is made of copper mesh and is grounded so as not to register touches that hit the floor. In saber fencing there is as yet no electric machine. The director is assisted by four judges, two of whom determine the validity of a touch. In the case of a disagreement each judge has one vote and the director has one and a half.

Actual fencing is preceded by the opponents saluting each other, the officials, and the spectators. Although the bout always starts from the basic position of on-guard, it immediately becomes a highly mobile sport within the confines of the strip. The basic aim is to hit one's opponent in the area of the prescribed target and to avoid being hit. This is achieved through a series of advances, lunges, and retreats. A sense of distance and timing is thus of the utmost importance.

Training. The development of a fencer is the responsibility of the coach or fencing master. The best masters have traditionally been developed in special academies in Europe, and they have carried the sport to the world. A fencer must spend a long period in perfecting his technique by working with a master before entering competition. A competitive peak is not usually reached until the early 30's, and it is not unusual to have fencers at the top level of competitive efficiency in their middle or late 40's. Loss of speed can be compensated for by experience.

GEORGE V. WORTH, Competing Manager, U.S. Olympic Fencing Team, 1948–52–56–60

FÉNELON [făn-lôN'], **FRANÇOIS DE SALIGNAC DE LA MOTHE** (1651–1715), French Catholic Archbishop and author. After university studies at Cahors and Paris, he was ordained a priest and joined the Society of Saint Sulpice. Sent to Saintonge to preach in the renewed effort to convert the Protestants after the revocation of the Edict of Nantes, he later was tutor of the young Duke of Burgundy (1689–95) and wrote his *Fables*, *Dialogues des morts*, and *Télémaque* to arouse that prince's interest in studies. Louis XIV rewarded this work by arranging for Fénelon to be given the Abbey of Valery, to be nominated to the French Academy, and finally to be installed as Archbishop of Cambrai. He lost favor at court, however, when he refused to sign Bossuet's condemnation of Madame Guyon's quietism. His *Explication des maximes des saints* (1697), written to explain his attitude, was condemned in France and at Rome. Fénelon submitted to the condemnation and continued to work in his archdiocese of Cambrai. He wrote strongly against the Jansenists but was accused of being too lenient with them in his archdiocese.

JAMES V. McGLYNN, S.J., University of Detroit

FENIAN [fē'nē-ən] **BROTHERHOOD,** secret society of Irish immigrants in the United States supporting the independence of Ireland from Great Britain. It flourished between 1858 and 1876. Under the leadership of John O'Mahoney, the Fenians attained a peak strength of 250,000, largely among residents of New York City. There they proclaimed (1865) the creation of the Irish Republic and sold bonds to finance their operations. Raids into Canada from New York and Vermont (1866, 1870) were frustrated by Canadian and U.S. troops. In Mar., 1867, the Fenians sent to Ireland the ship *Erin's Hope* loaded with arms and recruits. When captured by a British warship, the men claimed American citizenship. This incident and the failure of the U.S. government to punish the raiders because of political pressure from Irish voters complicated U.S. relations with Great Britain for several years. The Fenian movement declined rapidly after 1870 as a result of its failures, the opposition of the Catholic Church, and the tendency of its members to form splinter groups. After O'Mahoney's death in 1877 it disappeared from the American scene.

ROBERT E. ROEDER, University of Chicago

FENNEL, short-lived perennial herb, *Foeniculum vulgare*, in the carrot family, Umbelliferae, native to southern

Europe but now naturalized in North America. The wild plant grows from 3 to 5 ft. tall, has leaves divided into threadlike segments, and produces clusters of small yellow flowers. The cultivated varieties, *F. vulgare* var. *dulce* (Florence fennel or finocchio), and *F. vulgare* var. *piperitum* (Italian fennel or carosella), have, respectively, enlarged leaf bases and stems which are eaten as a vegetable. The leaves and seeds are frequently used in fresh or dried state as a condiment. Fennel may be easily cultivated as an annual from seeds sown in early spring, in moderately rich, well-drained soil.

FENNEMAN, NEVIN MELANCTHON (1865–1945), American geographer and geologist, born in Lima, Ohio. He took (1901) a Ph.D. in geology from the University of Chicago and spent most of his professional life at the University of Cincinnati as professor and chairman of the department of geology and geography, which he founded. His primary interest was in the regional physiography of the United States, and he is best known for the two-volume work, *Physiography of the Western United States* (1931) and *Physiography of the Eastern United States* (1938), in which he set forth a scheme of geological divisions regarded by scholars as the most complete and authoritative treatment of the subject.

FENNO, JOHN (1751–98), American journalist. Born in Boston, Mass., he founded (1789) and edited the Federalist *Gazette of the United States*. The paper was sponsored by U.S. Secretary of the Treasury Alexander Hamilton, a frequent contributor. Fenno was generally involved in acrimonious exchanges with Republican journals, especially Philip Freneau's *National Gazette*, and the paper gained a wide circulation. It experienced financial difficulties, however, despite loans from Hamilton and printing patronage from the U.S. Treasury.

FENRIS or the FENRIS WOLF, monstrous wolf in Norse mythology, son of the giant Loki. Chained by the Aesir, he will break loose on the doomsday of the gods, devour Odin, and be slain by Odin's son Vidar.

FENTON, village of eastern Michigan, a residential suburb south of Flint. Inc., 1863; pop., 8,284.

FENUGREEK, annual plant, *Trigonella foenum-graecum,* in the pea family, Leguminosae, native to southern Europe and western Asia. The plant grows to a height of 2 ft., has three-part leaves, and bears whitish flowers that ripen into sickle-shaped pods. The seeds of fenugreek are a main ingredient of curry and are also used medicinally; the plants are used for forage. Fenugreek is raised from seed and requires well-drained, loamy soil.

FEPC. *See* FAIR EMPLOYMENT PRACTICES COMMITTEE.

FERAL CHILDREN. *See* WOLF CHILDREN.

FERBER [fûr′bər], **EDNA** (1887–1968), American novelist and playwright, born in Kalamazoo, Mich. She first attracted general attention in 1924 with a best-selling novel, *So Big*. Other entertaining romantic novels, such as

Show Boat (1926), *Cimarron* (1930), *Saratoga Trunk* (1941), and *Giant* (1952) kept her work steadily before the reading public and proved equally popular on the screen. In 1927 *Show Boat* was transformed, by Jerome Kern and Oscar Hammerstein, into a perennially appealing operetta. She also collaborated with George S. Kaufman to produce several successful plays, among them *Dinner at Eight* (1932) and *Stage Door* (1936).

FERBER, HERBERT (1906–   ), American sculptor, born in New York City. A leading member of the abstract expressionist school, Ferber produces his works by soldering together pieces of various metals, such as brass, tin, or copper. His sculpture, "And the Bush Was Not Consumed," which decorates the façade of a synagogue in Millburn, N.J., is considered by critics as one of the finest pieces of architectural sculpture in the contemporary nonrepresentational style. Ferber is represented in the Metropolitan Museum of Art, the Museum of Modern Art, and the Whitney Museum of American Art, all in New York City, as well as other American galleries.

FER-DE-LANCE [fâr-də-läns′], large poisonous snake, *Bothrops atrox*, in the pit viper family, Crotalidae. The fer-de-lance occurs from southern Mexico to South America. It may reach a length of 8 ft. and is gray, olive, or brownish in color, crossed by darker bands with yellow or green margins. The head tapers to a point from the width behind the eyes and has the shape of a spear point—hence the common name. The bite of the fer-de-lance is usually rapidly fatal and is inflicted by two large fangs in the upper jaw that fold back when not in use.

The fer-de-lance is a poisonous snake of the New World tropics.

Dade W. Thornton—National Audubon Society

FERDINAND [fûr′də-nănd] I (1503–64), Holy Roman Emperor (1556–64). King of Hungary and Bohemia in his own right (1526–64), and successor to his older brother, Charles V, as Holy Roman Emperor, Ferdinand continued the Habsburg drive into eastern Europe, and to mobilize

support for that drive, sponsored a policy of conciliation within Germany. Raised in Spain and originally a loyal supporter of Charles' Imperial Catholic policy, Ferdinand received from his brother charge of all Habsburg functions in the east. Charles handed him the old Austrian duchies (1521); appointed him regent of all Habsburg German possessions, except Alsace (1521); and arranged his selection (1531) as German King (heir presumptive of the Emperor). Ferdinand fought a long, indecisive war (1526–38) against John Zápolya and the Turks in an effort to make good his title to Hungary. Convinced of the need to behave like a central European, Ferdinand remade himself in a German image. He learned the German language and German manners. He comported himself as a German constitutional ruler, and was increasingly accepted as such. And ultimately he opposed Charles' plan to bring the Spanish Habsburgs into the German Imperial succession. Further, it was he who negotiated the compromise religious peace in Germany embodied in the Treaty of Passau (1552) and the Peace of Augsburg (1555).

LEONARD KRIEGER, Yale University

FERDINAND II (1578–1637), Holy Roman Emperor (1619–37). As King of Bohemia (1617), King of Hungary (1618), and Holy Roman (German) Emperor, Ferdinand led the forces of the Catholic Counter Reformation in central Europe. Ferdinand early earned the animosity of the Protestants by persecutions in his own territories (Styria and Carinthia). By assuming the crown of Bohemia he touched off (1618) a Protestant revolt there that led to the Thirty Years' War. Ferdinand utilized his early victories not only to enforce Catholicism but to attempt the establishment of absolute rule in all Habsburg lands except Hungary. Urged by his allies, Spain and Bavaria, Ferdinand extended the war to Germany in 1621, and by 1629 had not only reversed the Protestant tide but threatened to transform Germany into a Catholic state under the authoritarian rule of the Emperor. But Imperial power soon ebbed, the Peace of Prague (1635) fell short of Ferdinand's objectives, and the war dragged on until 1648.

LEONARD KRIEGER, Yale University

FERDINAND V, called "the Catholic" (1452–1516), Spanish King. He became king consort of Castile and Leon (1474–1504) by his marriage to Isabella of Castile, and later King of Aragon (1479–1516) in his own right. The marriage opened the way to the fusion of the two realms into a unified Kingdom of Spain. With Isabella, he supported Christopher Columbus' voyage to the New World. Commanding Isabella's forces against Granada, last Muslim stronghold in Spain, he completed the reconquest in 1492 and proceeded to the task of enhancing Spanish prestige throughout Europe. He made diplomacy a science, creating a secretaryship for foreign affairs a century ahead of France and two ahead of England. His ambassadors, chosen and schooled with care and then admitted to his full confidence, consistently outwitted their opponents. He had recourse to war only when diplomacy failed: his campaigns in Italy, under the "Great Captain" Gonzalo de Córdoba, laid the foundations of Spain's military reputation over the next century and a half. His children he

married to the ruling houses of Portugal, the Holy Roman Empire, and England, thereby encircling France and making her Spain's implacable foe for two centuries. Ferdinand also recovered, largely by guile, Roussillon (1493), once part of Catalonia north of the Pyrenees; then, in 1504, the Kingdom of Naples, which Alfonso V had detached from Aragon in 1458. Navarre south of the Pyrenees, French for almost three centuries, he won back in 1512. In the countless political combinations of the age his hand was rarely absent. He owed his reputation for political deception to the need to cover every contingency in dealing with rulers unresponsive to his dream of a Christendom united against the infidel.

Ferdinand's plans and Spain's destinies were profoundly altered by the deaths between 1497 and 1500 of his son and grandson and of his eldest daughter (the Queen of Portugal) and her infant child, who had been formally accepted as heir to Castile, Aragon, and Portugal. When Isabella died in 1504, Ferdinand married Germaine de Foix, because his Aragonese subjects desired—the hope proved vain—a direct heir to Aragon. The Castilian crown fell to his second daughter, Joanna the Mad, whose insanity necessitated a regency under her Habsburg husband, Philip of Burgundy. Philip's death in 1506 recalled Ferdinand to power in Castile. In bequeathing Aragon and Castile to Joanna's Flemish son Charles (later the Emperor Charles V), Ferdinand left a united Spain,

During the reign of Ferdinand V, Spain became a major power.

Historical Pictures Service

86

transformed into a major European power, beginning its long and costly connection with the Holy Roman Empire.

Consult Prescott, W. H., *History of the Reign of Ferdinand and Isabella* (1837).

WILLIAM C. ATKINSON, University of Glasgow, Scotland

FERDINAND VII (1784–1833), King of Spain. Son of Charles IV and Maria Luisa of Parma, he grew up in an atmosphere of irresponsible intrigue. By forming an opposition party to the Queen and her favorite, Manuel de Godoy, he played into the hands of Napoleon, with whom he had presumed to plot. A mob rising in Aranjuez (Mar., 1808), as French forces occupied Madrid, extracted from Charles an abdication in Ferdinand's favor. Father and son were lured to Bayonne, where Napoleon intimidated both into renouncing their rights in his favor. Ferdinand spent the Peninsular War years (1808–14) in France, fawning on his captor. A tumultuous welcome on his return to Spain emboldened him to annul the constitution enacted in 1812 and to persecute mercilessly all liberal elements.

Six years of tyranny evoked (1820) the first *pronunciamiento* in Spanish history, when the army revolted in the name of the constitution. Ferdinand, capitulating abjectly, swore to abide by the constitution. The ensuing liberal triennium (1820–23) he ended by appealing to the Congress of Verona. It entrusted France with re-establishing "order," meaning the absolutist monarchical principle, in Spain. One hundred thousand French troops restored Ferdinand to absolute power, and another decade of persecution and reaction began with thousands fleeing into exile. French garrisons manned the fortresses until 1828. Dissensions so profound made impossible the subduing of the rebellious American colonies, and by 1824 Spain's New World empire had shrunk to the Caribbean islands. Because Ferdinand was still childless when he married his fourth wife, Maria Christina of Naples, in 1829, ultramontane and regionalist interests had identified themselves with his brother and heir, Don Carlos. When Maria Christina bore a daughter in 1830, these repudiated her title to the throne, and Ferdinand's death three years later unleashed the first Carlist War.

WILLIAM C. ATKINSON,
University of Glasgow, Scotland

FERGANA [fər-gä′nə], city of the U.S.S.R.; capital of Fergana Oblast of the Uzbek S.S.R. Located in the southern part of the Fergana Valley of Soviet Central Asia, Fergana is an important market center. Its basic industries involve the processing of local agricultural raw materials. These include cotton-ginning mills, textile manufacturing, the production of construction materials, and food processing. A recently constructed oil refinery handles petroleum from the oil fields in the western Fergana Valley. Founded in 1876, Fergana was first known as Novy Margelan; from 1907 to 1924 it was called Skobelev. The city's population has more than doubled in two decades as a result of its industrial growth. Pop., 80,000.

FERGUS, town of southern Ontario, 60 mi. west of Toronto. Flour mills and a domestic appliance factory are here. Inc., 1857; pop., 3,677.

FERGUS FALLS, city of western Minnesota, and seat of Otter Tail County, located at the falls of the Otter Tail River. The city is primarily a trade center for a large agricultural and resort area. Government is by mayor and council. Inc., 1872; pop., 12,443.

FERGUSON [fûr′gə-sən], city of east-central Missouri. It is a suburban community 10 mi. north of St. Louis. Matches are manufactured in the city. Settled, 1945; inc., 1894; pop., 28,759.

FERMAT [fĕr-mà′], **PIERRE DE** (1601?–1665), French mathematician and a leading figure in the theory of numbers. Independently of Descartes, he discovered the fundamental principles of analytic geometry; and before Newton, he invented a method of tangents equivalent to the differential calculus. He established, together with Blaise Pascal, the theory of probability. Two theorems bear his name: the "lesser Fermat theorem" and "Fermat's last theorem."

See also NUMBERS, THEORY OF.

FERMANAGH [fĕr-măn′ə], county of Northern Ireland, lying astride Upper and Lower Lough Erne. The county town of Enniskillen is strategically located on the crossing between the lakes. The land rises on all sides from boggy lowlands to heath-covered mountains and farming, its main occupation, is difficult. Area, 653 sq. mi.; pop., 50,700.

FERMENTATION, an energy-producing chemical reaction which occurs in living organisms. The true purpose and nature of fermentation was first grasped by Louis Pasteur, who stated that "fermentation is the consequence of life without air." While air-breathing organisms depend upon respiration for their energy, other organisms survive without air by using fermentations. Even in higher air-breathing organisms, however, fermentation may be used for special purposes, such as to supply quick energy for muscular contraction.

Fermentation v. Respiration. In both fermentation and respiration negatively charged electrons are transferred from one substance to another, a process known as oxidation-reduction. The chemical which loses the electrons is said to be oxidized, while the chemical which gains the electrons is said to be reduced. In respiration oxygen (an inorganic substance) is reduced. Another type of respiration, called "anaerobic respiration" because it proceeds in the absence of air, reduces other inorganic substances such as nitrate or sulfate. In fermentation organic substances are reduced.

The fact that fermentation involves only organic substances often makes it possible for the organism to carry out its energy-producing reactions using only one substance. Yeast can obtain energy from the fermentation of carbohydrates (sugars) without the necessity of using other materials to act as reducing agents. The yeast decomposes the carbohydrate into carbon dioxide (the oxidized product of the reaction) and alcohol (the reduced product of the reaction).

Many different organic compounds can be fermented by various organisms. Carbohydrates, such as sugars, are among the most readily and universally fermented substances. The products of different fermentations include carbon dioxide, hydrogen gas, methane (ordinary cooking gas, also known as marsh gas and sewer gas), alcoholic compounds, and a variety of organic acids.

Fermentation in Muscle. This involves the conversion of the starch glycogen, which is stored as a reserve material in muscle, to lactic acid. This fermentation makes energy rapidly available for muscular activity. The accumulation of the end-product, lactic acid, contributes to muscular fatigue.

Fermentation in Pickling, Sour Milk Products, and Food Storage. Long before the nature of bacteria or fermentations was known, man used the activities of certain bacteria in the preservation of food and the preparation of food products. The so-called "lactic-acid bacteria" are responsible for many of these activities. During their growth these organisms manufacture sufficient acid to kill or inhibit the reproduction of other bateria and are eventually destroyed themselves by their own waste products. Examples of natural lactic-acid fermentations include sauerkraut, pickles (of the dill type), and green and "ripe" olives.

Salt is added to the raw material and air is excluded to encourage the growth of the lactic-acid bacteria which are normally present on the vegetable matter. At first a variety of bacteria develop. Some of these remove the available oxygen while others produce large quantities of carbon dioxide and some hydrogen gas. Eventually, however, the lactic-acid bacteria outgrow all the other organisms and destroy them. In this way lactic-acid bacteria destroy the microorganisms in food products which might lead to spoilage.

Enrico Fermi in his laboratory at Columbia University, New York City.

Brown Brothers

Sour milk products, resulting from the activities of these bacteria, include cheese, yoghurt, and sour cream. Although bacteria that occur naturally in the environment can cause the souring of milk and cream, "starter cultures," or specially prepared colonies of selected bacterial strains, are used in modern industrial processes. These strains are chosen on the basis of their fermentative ability and because of the special flavors that they impart.

Fermentation in Brewing and Baking. Alcoholic beverages are produced by fermentation. Wine and hard cider result from the fermentation of the sugars present in fruit juice. In beer production the starch of the grain is first converted to the sugar, maltose, in the malting process. Maltose is then fermented, yielding alcohol. Rye, scotch, and other hard liquors are obtained after the fermentation of starches contained in various plants.

The other product of alcoholic fermentation, carbon dioxide, is essential to the leavening of bread. The dough is raised by the formation of minute bubbles of this gas. In order for the reaction to proceed, sugar must be present in the dough. Crude flour contains small amounts of enzymes that convert the starch of the flour to the sugar maltose, but in highly refined flour these enzymes have been destroyed and sugar must be added for the fermentation.

Butanol-Acetone Fermentations. Next to alcoholic fermentation, these are the most important of the commercial fermentations. In these reactions carbohydrates are converted to the industrially important solvents, acetone and butyl alcohol. Pure cultures of anaerobic bacteria are used for these processes.

Other commercial fermentations include the production of glycerine, butyric acid, and butylene glycol. The "propionic acid fermentation" is essential to the ripening of Swiss cheese. Putrefaction, which is the decomposition of proteins, involves a variety of fermentative processes, the products of which impart some of the characteristic odors to decomposing meat, fish, and to certain cheeses.

A number of processes in which products of commercial value are obtained through the action of microorganisms are commonly referred to as "fermentations," although they are not truly fermentative in nature. These include the manufacture of vinegar, which is based on the oxidation of alcohol to acetic acid by the "vinegar bacteria" and the production of citric acid from sugar by molds. Such processes are "incomplete oxidations" of organic compounds which depend upon the presence of air and should therefore be classed as respirations rather than fermentations.

MICHAEL DOUDOROFF, University of California
See also BACTERIA; MICROBIOLOGY.

FERMI [fĕr'mē], **ENRICO** (1901–54), Italian-born physicist and Nobel laureate. One of the most distinguished scientists of the first half of the 20th century and a leader in the field of nuclear physics, he has come to be known as the "father of the atomic bomb." He was born in Rome on Sept. 29, 1901, the son of a minor railroad official. Fermi developed an early interest in science, largely through self-study, and showed such ability while in high school that he was awarded a fellowship to the Reale Scuola Normale of the University of Pisa. After earning the degree of Doctor in Physics *magna cum laude* in 1922, Fermi studied in Göttingen and Leiden and in 1924 was appointed lecturer at the University of Florence.

Two years later he became a professor of theoretical physics at the University of Rome, where he remained until 1938. The period in Rome was his most productive. In 1926 he published his statistical theory of systems involving many identical particles, known as Fermi statistics. His theory of beta decay followed in 1934 and that same year he began the investigations on transmutation of the elements by slow-neutron absorption for which he won the Nobel Prize in 1938. These were the experiments which led others to the discovery of uranium fission and thus marked the beginning of the atomic age.

Upon leaving Italy to accept the Nobel award, Fermi decided not to return because of Mussolini's anti-Semitic acts. He went instead to the United States and eventually became a U.S. citizen. He continued his work, first at Columbia University and later at the University of Chicago, until his untimely death on Nov. 28, 1954. It was at Chicago during World War II that he directed a team of scientists who produced, on Dec. 2, 1942, the first self-sustained nuclear chain reaction. Later at Los Alamos he collaborated with other scientists in the development of the first atomic bomb.

Fermi's honors were world wide and included honorary degrees from the universities of Utrecht, Heidelberg, Co-lumbia, Yale, and Washington and Rockford College; the Franklin medal (1947) and the Barnard medal (1950); and election to the Royal Academy of Italy in 1929 and the Royal Society (England) in 1950. Two weeks before his death he received the first annual Atomic Energy Commission award and the following year element 100 was named fermium in his honor.

Consult Fermi, Laura, *Atoms in the Family* (1954).

MORRIS SHAMOS, New York University

FERMIUM [fĕr′mē-əm], a radioactive metal and element (symbol Fm; atomic number 100) of the actinide series; it is not found in nature. It was detected in 1952 among the debris of the first H-bomb explosion in the Pacific. In 1953 it was formed in the laboratory by exposure of plutonium to neutron bombardment within a nuclear reactor. Its longest-lived isotope is Fm^{253}, which has a half life of seven days.

FERN, perennial plant of the class Filicineae, in the phylum Tracheophyta, the vascular plants. Ferns have roots, stems, and leaves but do not reproduce by flowers and seeds. The stem of most ferns is a thickened, horizontal, underground organ, the rhizome, which produces a few erect leaves each year. The leaves, or fronds, borne on stemlike stalks, are usually lobed or subdivided into many small leaflets. The curled-up tips of young fronds,

SOME TROPICAL FERNS

The common maidenhair fern.

The Victoria brake fern.

The Boston fern.

A staghorn fern.

The bird's nest fern.

Walter Singer

known as "fiddleheads," can be cooked and eaten. Ferns reproduce by spores produced in spore-sacs (sporangia) which appear as dark clusters (sori) on the underside of the leaves in many species. Such sori are often mistaken for bugs or diseased tissue. Fern leaves are delicate structures, restricting the plants to shaded, damp habitats. They abound in cool, moist woods of the north temperate regions, but reach their maximum luxuriance in the humid tropics.

The life history of a fern includes an interesting alternation of a sexually reproducing plant (gametophyte) and an asexually reproducing one (a sporophyte). The reproductive sequence in the common boulder fern, *Polypodium*, is typical. The terminal portion of the frond bears many brown sori on the undersurface, each consisting of stalked sporangia whose capsules are filled with microscopic spores. These spores are unicellular, asexual reproductive structures. Each spore falls to the ground and, under suitable conditions, germinates into a tiny, heart-shaped, flat green plant known as a prothallus, which matures and develops a male sex organ (antheridium) and a female sex organ (archegonium). When moisture is present, the sperm swim to the archegonium and fertilize the single egg. The fertilized egg remains in place and develops into an embryonic sporophyte, which soon develops roots, stem, and a small frond. In time it becomes another mature boulder fern, capable of producing spores and repeating the cycle.

Class Filicineae includes about 9,500 species, and is divided into three orders. The majority of the temperate zone ferns belong to the order of true ferns, Filicales, whose several families have as members most of the common ferns. Polypodiaceae, the polypody family, is comprised of the brake, maidenhair, Christmas, Boston, boulder, sensitive, and other familiar ferns. Osmundaceae, the royal fern family, includes many large and ornamental species, such as the royal, interrupted, and cinnamon ferns. Cyatheaceae, the tree fern family, includes the giant tree ferns of tropical rain forests. Order Ophioglossales contains a single family, Ophioglossaceae, a small group of fleshy-stemmed ferns such as the grape and rattlesnake ferns. The ferns of order Marattiales are largely confined to tropical regions and are only occasionally seen out of their native habitat.

Ferns as a group are of little economic importance except for their use as ornamentals; however, in prehistoric geologic eras they played a major role in coal formation.

For outdoor planting, hardy ferns make excellent border and background plants, provided they are located in shaded areas, protected from strong winds, and planted in rich soil that retains an even amount of moisture. Most species need a firm soil since an excess of leaf mold is too porous for adequate root growth. Species of *Osmunda*, *Adiantum*, *Pteris*, *Onoclea*, *Polypodium*, and *Polystichum* can easily be grown outdoors in the cooler, more humid regions of North America and Europe. For indoor planting, the roots should be firmly compacted in a soil made up of 3 parts fibrous loam, 1 part peat, and 1 part leaf mold, with sand and charcoal added to ensure good drainage. The temperature should range between 55° F. and 70° F.; extremes of heat and moisture should be avoided. When the air is hot and dry, the leaves should be syringed

several times daily. On damp or rainy days, heat should be provided to prevent a saturated atmosphere. In a too-dry environment, ferns fall prey to various insect enemies— scales, mealy bugs, thrips, and red spiders. When overly moist, ferns turn black and rot as a result of fungous diseases.

CLARENCE J. HYLANDER

See also:

BOULDER FERN	QUILLWORT
BRACKEN OR BRAKE FERN	RATTLESNAKE FERN
CHRISTMAS FERN	ROYAL FERN
CINNAMON FERN	SENSITIVE FERN
CLIMBING FERN	SPLEENWORT
INTERRUPTED FERN	TERRARIUM
LADY FERN	TREE FERN
MAIDENHAIR FERN	WALKING FERN

FERNANDEL [fĕr-näN-dĕl'], professional name of Fernand Contandin (1903–71), French motion-picture actor. He made his debut in the early 1930's and won fame for his portrayal of seriocomic roles in which his talent for pantomime and range of facial expression were major factors. His films included *La Fille du Puisatier* (*The Well-Digger's Daughter*), 1940, and *Le Petit Monde de Don Camillo* (*The Little World of Don Camillo*), 1952.

FERNÁNDEZ DE LIZARDI [fĕr-nän'däs thä lē-sär'thē], **JOSÉ JOAQUÍN** (1776–1827), Mexican writer, born in Mexico City. As a young man he was imprisoned for supporting the independence movement. Under the pen name of El Pensador Mexicano ("The Mexican Thinker"), which also became the name of the revolutionary journal that he founded in 1811, he wrote several novels and many articles in support of political liberty. He is best known for a celebrated picaresque novel, *El periquillo sarniento*, 1816 (*The Itching Parrot*, 1942). The finest example of this genre since the 17th century in Spain, it also was the first important novel written in Spanish America.

FERNANDINA BEACH, city of northeastern Florida, and seat of Nassau County, situated on Amelia Island near the mouth of the St. Marys River. The French built a fort there in 1562. The city, long a resort, has large pulp mills and is the home of a fishing fleet.

FERNANDO DE NORONHA, offshore archipelago of volcanic origin, northeast of Cape São Roque in northeastern Brazil. It is a federal territory. Although prevailing ruggedness and a semiarid climate limit utilization, the territory has been used as a penal colony, settlement area for ex-convicts, and a military base. There are guano deposits on the islands. Area, 10 sq. mi. (26 sq. km.).

FERNANDO PO [fər-năn'dō pō'], island component of Equatorial Guinea, in the Gulf of Guinea, 25 mi. (40 km.) off the coast of Cameroun. It is of volcanic origin, with forested mountains rising to 9,449 ft. (2,880 m.) in Santa Isabel Peak. High temperatures and extreme rainfall give an unhealthy climate. Coffee, bananas, and cabinet woods are produced, and cacao is exported from Santa Isabel, the capital and chief city. The island was discovered by the Portuguese in 1471. Area, 779 sq. mi. (2,018 sq. km.).

FERNDALE, city of southeastern Michigan, and a suburb on the northern boundary of Detroit. It is a part of Detroit's metropolitan industrial area. Inc. as city, 1927. Pop., 30,850.

FERNIE, city of southeastern British Columbia, Canada, located in the coal-rich Elk River valley. Although its own vast coal mines closed in 1958, Fernie is still the center for the collieries of Michel and is developing a lumber industry. Inc., 1904; pop., 2,808.

FERN PALM. *See* SAGO PALM.

FERRARA [fə-rär'ə], city in northern Italy, capital of Ferrara Province in the region of Emilia-Romagna. Located in the fertile lower Po River Valley, it is the important market center for the region and also an important industrial city. Its products include flour, macaroni, beet sugar, hemp, machinery, soap, and candles. Enclosed by 15th-century walls, Ferrara possesses a wealth of medieval and Renaissance monuments. The 12th-century Cathedral of San Giorgio is filled with art treasures and is topped by a Renaissance campanile (bell tower). The Este Castle, in the center of the city, has four towers and is surrounded by a moat. The Palazzo Schifanoia now houses the collection of the Civic Museum. The Palazzo of Ludovico Sforza (Ludovico the Moor) contains the National Archeological Museum. The Palazzo de' Diamanti, faced with diamond-cut marble, contains the collection of the Municipal Picture Gallery.

Ferrara was ruled by the Lombards until 774, when it came under papal control. In 1101 it was seized by Matilda, Countess of Tuscany, and was ruled by several families until the Estes made it their family seat in 1208. It remained under the Estes until 1598, during which time it was a great cultural center. It was the home of poets Ludovico Ariosto and Torquato Tasso. The Dominican friar Savonarola was born in Ferrara. Its university, established in 1391, quickly became one of the most important in Europe. In 1598 Ferrara became part of the Holy See and remained so for the most part until it joined the newly established Kingdom of Italy in 1860. Although the city was bombed during World War II, most of its art treasures were undamaged. Pop., 152,654.

ANNA CROGNALE HANSEN, Italian Institute of
Culture, New York

FERRARA-FLORENCE, COUNCIL OF, continuation of the 17th general council, which originated in Basel in 1431. The growing radicalism of the theologians at Basel in their attempt to dominate the Papacy alienated their supporters. Pope Eugene IV, having temporized for several years, finally felt strong enough to order the council to transfer to Ferrara, where it would meet under his personal direction. Most Bishops and all but a single Cardinal complied. The council was solemnly reopened at Ferrara Jan. 8, 1438. In March a contingent of about 700 Greeks arrived, including Emperor John VIII and Patriarch Joseph II of Constantinople. The major item on the council's agenda was reunion of the Greek and Latin churches. Discussion concerned the points on which they differed: purgatory, the epiklesis (petition in the Eastern Eucharistic prayer asking the Father to send the Holy Spirit to change the bread and wine into the body and blood of Christ), unleavened bread, and papal primacy. Because of the plague, the council moved to Florence in 1439. On July 6, 1439, the decree *Laetentur coeli* officially announced the reunion, the end of the Great Schism. Subsequently, reunion was established with other dissident Eastern communities. However, the Orthodox synods refused to ratify the union, so the Schism continued. The decree *Moyses*, Sept. 4, 1439, embodied the first strong papal attack on the conciliar theory. Early in 1443 the council adjourned to Rome, where it ended between Aug., 1445, and Feb., 1447, without a formal dissolution.

RAYMOND H. SCHMANDT, Loyola University, Chicago

FERREIRA [fər-rā'rə], **ANTÓNIO** (1528–69), Portuguese dramatist and poet, perhaps the writer of greatest influence in the importation of Renaissance literary forms to Portugal. He adapted classical tragedy to Portuguese with his famous *Inés de Castro* (c. 1587), which was much imitated throughout Europe. His two comedies patterned after Plautus and Terence, *Bristo* and *O Cioso* (both 1622), were less successful. As a lyric poet he left a collection of delicate Italianate compositions (he introduced the ode to Portugal), posthumously issued as *Poemas Lusitanos* in 1598.

See also CASTRO, INÉS DE.

FERREL [fĕr'əl], **WILLIAM** (1817–91), American meteorologist who noted the relationship (now called Ferrel's law) between the earth's rotation and the movement of winds and currents. After teaching school for 12 years, he became associated with the *American Ephemeris and Nautical Almanac* and later with the U.S. Coast and Geodetic Survey. He made tidal analyses and invented a tide-predicting machine. From 1882 until 1886 Ferrel was with the U.S. Army Signal Corps, out of which grew the U.S. Weather Bureau. His many meteorological publications, especially the "Essay on the Winds and Currents of the Ocean," gave him a top rank among scientists.

See also ANTICYCLONE; CYCLONE.

FERREL'S LAW. *See* CORIOLIS FORCE.

FERRER [fə-rĕr'], **JOSÉ VICENTE** (1912–), American actor, stage producer, and director, born in Santurce, Puerto Rico. A versatile, bravura actor, he had leading stage roles in *Charley's Aunt*, 1940; *Othello*, 1943; *Cyrano de Bergerac*, 1946; and *The Shrike*, 1952, which he directed. In 1951 he also directed *The Fourposter*, and produced and directed *Stalag 17*. He won an Academy Award for his acting in the title role of *Cyrano de Bergerac* in 1951, and acted in the films *Moulin Rouge*, 1953, and *The Caine Mutiny*, 1954.

FERRET [fĕr'ĭt], common name for the domestic polecat, *Mustela furo*, a weasellike, European carnivore. The ferret was developed from a wild Asian species, *M. eversmanni*, and has long been used in Europe to hunt rabbits and rodents. It has a slender, yellowish-white body and is about 1 ft. long. It is a short-legged animal and can easily enter a rabbit burrow to drive out the occupants

The European ferret is the only domesticated weasel. (GATES PRIEST)

which are then set upon by dogs. The ferret has been domesticated for so long that it cannot survive in the wild.

FERRIC COMPOUNDS, compounds containing iron with oxidation number III, such as ferric oxide, or hematite, Fe_2O_3, used as a paint pigment, polishing agent, and jeweler's rouge. Ferric salts are produced when iron is dissolved in oxidizing acids or when ferrous salts (oxidation number II) are oxidized. The ferric ion Fe^{+++} combines readily with water to form hydrated ions which then behave as acids. Therefore an aqueous solution of a ferric salt is acidic and exhibits the yellowish, muddy appearance of colloidal hydroxide, $Fe(OH)_3 \cdot 3H_2O$.

Ferric chloride, one of the commonest salts and usually written $FeCl_3$, yields a hydrated ion and hydrochloric acid. It is used as a mordant for dyes and in etching metals. Ferric acetate and ferric oxalate are used in making blueprints, and ferric tannate is used in black inks. Natural waters with small amounts of dissolved ferric salts are called chalybeate and are esteemed as curatives for simple anemia. Double salts of ferric iron sulfate with alkali sulfates are called alums.

G. RAYMOND HOOD, Blackburn College

FERRIER, KATHLEEN (1912–53), English contralto born in Higher Walton, Lancashire. She did not begin formal vocal training until 1940. Within a decade, however, she had won a prominent place among the world's great singers. Her most memorable operatic role was Orfeo in Gluck's *Orfeo ed Euridice*, in which she appeared throughout Europe and America. Acclaimed as an unusually sensitive lieder specialist, she was also noted for her performances of Mahler's song cycles and arias by Bach and Handel.

FERRITE [fĕr′ĭt], in metallurgy, designates pure alpha-iron, the chief component of wrought iron and an important component of steel. In chemistry, ferrites are salts of ferrous acid, $HFeO_2$. They are insoluble substances of spinel type prepared by fusion of ferric oxide with basic oxides to yield such compounds as sodium ferrite, $NaFeO_2$, and calcium ferrite, $Ca(FeO_2)_2$. Ferrites occur naturally in minerals like franklinite (zinc ferrite) and magnetite, ferrous ferrite, $Fe(FeO_2) = Fe_3O_4$, the black oxide of iron.

FERROL [fĕr-rōl′], **EL, or EL FERROL DEL CAUDILLO** [fĕr-rōl′ thĕl kou-thē′lyō], naval base and fortress of northwestern Spain, on Ferrol Bay. An academy trains naval personnel, and there are facilities for building warships. Fishing and fish processing are important, and manufactures include electric equipment and furniture. Founded as an arsenal by Charles III, the city prospered after it was made a naval station in 1752. The name was changed from El Ferrol in 1939 to honor Generalissimo Francisco Franco ("El Caudillo"), who was born here. Pop., 47,388.

FERROMAGNETISM. *See* MAGNETIC MATERIALS.

FERROUS COMPOUNDS, compounds of iron in which the oxidation state of iron is 2; it is then said to have a valence of $+2$. Ferrous carbonate, $FeCO_3$, siderite, is found in nature, but most ferrous compounds are made in the laboratory. Important ones include ferrous hydroxide, $Fe(OH)_2$, ferrous chloride, $FeCl_2$, ferrous sulfate, $FeSO_4$, ferrous sulfide, FeS, ferrous oxalate, FeC_2O_4, and the stable complex ferrocyanides such as potassium ferrocyanide, $K_4Fe(CN)_6$. In the presence of moist air ferrous compounds are easily oxidized to ferric compounds. Thus the white hydroxide quickly changes to green and then to brown ferric hydroxide, $Fe(OH)_3$. Likewise, green ferrous sulfate solution changes to brown ferric sulfate solution. Hydrated ferrous sulfate, $FeSO_4 \cdot 7H_2O$, also known as green vitriol or copperas, is probably the most important ferrous salt. It is prepared by (1) the oxidation of moist iron pyrites, FeS_2, or (2) by the action of sulfuric acid on iron as in the pickling of steel. It is used as a disinfectant, in making dyes, inks, pigments, and as a wood preservative.

JOHN R. LEWIS, University of Utah

FERRY [fĕ-rē′], **JULES** (1832–93), French Republican politician. A trained lawyer, Ferry figured prominently in the Republican opposition to the Second Empire as editor of the prestigious daily, *Le Temps*. When the disastrous war with Prussia led to the collapse of the Empire in 1870, Ferry was made a member of the moderate Republican Government of National Defense. Later, as mayor of a Paris besieged by the Prussians (1870–71), he was held responsible for popular distress and suffered a temporary political eclipse.

From 1879 to 1885, Ferry held power either as premier or in one of several ministerial posts. He is significant in three areas—civil liberties, education, and French colonial expansion. He helped liberalize the Third Republic by a series of laws (1881–84) broadening freedom of assembly, press, and labor organization. He initiated a comprehensive system of free, compulsory, and secular elementary education. Ferry furthered French expansion by the annexation of Tunisia in 1881, occupation of part of Madagascar in 1883, establishing France's claim to the lower Congo in 1884, and an attempt to conquer northern Indochina in 1885. This last policy proved so unpopular that Ferry was ousted and never regained power.

PETER AMANN, State University of N.Y. at Binghamton

FERRY, any boat used for transporting passengers, vehicles, or both for short distances across waterways (usually inland). Ferries range from primitive rafts poled by a single oarsman to huge radar-equipped boats, and have figured prominently in man's transportation for countless centuries. Some ferries, in rivers where strong currents prevail, are guided by a chain to ensure reaching the proper destination. Today, most ferries are propelled by steam or diesel engines. They are usually double ended, with a propeller at either end enabling the boat to move in and out of the slip without turning. The famous Staten Island ferry line, owned by New York City, operates 10 ferries between Manhattan and Staten Island on a round-the-clock basis. This line carries more than 24,000,000 passengers and 1,700,000 vehicles a year.

FERTILE CRESCENT, term generally applied to the fertile agricultural and pastoral land running in a semicircle from west to east around the Great Syrian Desert. On the southwest it is bounded by the Mediterranean coast of Palestine, on the southeast by the Persian Gulf, on the north by the Taurus Mountains, and on the south by the Arabian Desert. In the last 40 years some Arab nationalists have considered the Crescent's geographical unity sufficient basis for political unity, although after its partition by Britain and France at the end of World War I, the Fertile Crescent scheme became a cause for contention among Arab rulers, especially in the 1940's. Nuri as-Said of Iraq suggested in 1943 a union between Syria and Iraq as a first step toward greater Arab unity, but the scheme antagonized Egyptian and Saudi leaders.

FERTILITY. *See* STERILITY.

FERTILITY GOD, a male deity associated with the fruitfulness of the earth or the seasons of the year. Fertility cults, very widespread in the agricultural civilizations of the ancient world, often had a male divinity whose waxing and waning strength, marriage, life, and death paralleled the growth and decay of nature. Ecstatic rituals and myths justifying these rituals grew up around this divinity. Worshippers performed magical rites to strengthen the god when he was weak (in the winter when no vegetation grows) or to bring him back to life (in the spring) or to celebrate his marriage and thus ensure fertility in the land.

Stories of dying gods who came back to life are very common in the mythology of these peoples. Among the most famous examples are the stories of Osiris, Tammuz, Adonis and Attis. Biblical stories like that of Samson and even the resurrection of Jesus have been taken by some scholars as reflections of earlier fertility god stories. The classic work on this subject is Sir James G. Frazer's *The Golden Bough* (12 vols., 1911–15).

MARSHALL HURWITZ, College of the City of New York

FERTILIZATION, a process characteristic of multicellular plants and animals during which the male and female germ cells are united. Fertilization may occur either externally or internally, depending on the species. In lower plants and animals it occurs in the external aqueous medium in which the organisms live. In the higher forms it occurs within the female tissues. Although the actual mechanism of fertilization varies in different species, the major features are the same. In animals, after the sperm and eggs have been introduced into the same medium, the sperm move toward the eggs. The paths of the sperm are random, and contact with an egg thus depends on chance. The chance that a meeting will occur, however, is greatly enhanced by the extremely large number of sperm released at one time. When a meeting occurs, the sperm usually stick to the egg. Chemicals from the sperm called lysins dissolve the external egg membranes in a small area so that the sperm can penetrate. If the external membranes are thick, as in the case in the eggs of fishes and insects, there is generally a special opening into the interior of the egg called a micropyle through which the sperm may pass.

Sudden changes occur in the egg when a sperm begins to penetrate the egg membrane. These changes begin at the point of sperm penetration and spread over the surface of the egg. In many species there is an immediate elevation on the surface of the egg. Shortly thereafter, the membrane becomes greatly reinforced and effectively prohibits further entry of sperm. In the sea urchin this blocking mechanism is completed within one minute after sperm penetration. The reinforced surface membrane is called the fertilization membrane. Thus, usually only one sperm is able to enter the cytoplasm of the egg. If more than one sperm happen to penetrate the egg—a condition known as polyspermy—the embryo usually develops abnormally, or only one sperm actually functions within the cytoplasm.

The penetration of the sperm also stimulates the egg to complete its meiotic divisions (cell divisions during which the number of chromosomes in the nucleus of the reproductive cell is halved) if it has not already done so. The haploid nuclei (the nuclei of cells that have undergone meiotic divisions) of the egg and sperm are at this stage called pronuclei. The pronucleus of the sperm enlarges and moves through the egg cytoplasm toward the female pronucleus. During the migration, the egg cytoplasm undergoes changes in preparation for the first mitotic division (normal cell division producing two identical cells) of the newly formed organism. The pronuclei unite to form a diploid nucleus (a cell nucleus containing the number of chromosomes characteristic for the species). After fusion of the pronuclei the cell is called a zygote. The zygote then undergoes successive divisions as a developing embryo.

The details of fertilization in plants differ from those in animals in the events which precede and follow the fusion of the pronuclei. In flowering plants, for example, the sperm nuclei are discharged into the embryo sac where fertilization takes place. After fusion of the pronuclei, changes take place in the surrounding parts of the flower—some structures that are no longer of use wither away; other structures which will be important to the developing embryo are stimulated to grow. As in animals, the zygote then begins a series of cell divisions.

THOMAS H. RODERICK, Roscoe B. Jackson
Memorial Laboratory

See also CHROMOSOME; EGG; EMBRYOLOGY; MEIOSIS; MITOSIS.

FERTILIZER

FERTILIZER, any inorganic or organic compound containing one or more plant nutrients that is applied to soil (directly or mixed with other media) to increase plant growth.

Inorganic Fertilizers

Inorganic fertilizers contain higher percentages of nitrogen and other inorganic materials than do organic fertilizers. Nitrogen, phosphorus, and potassium salts are the principal materials of inorganic fertilizers. However, calcium, magnesium, sulfur, copper, manganese, boron, zinc, iron, and molybdenum are also essential plant nutrients, and are generally applied (alone or in varying combinations with nitrogen, phosphorus, and/or potassium) to produce optimum plant growth on particular soils.

Nitrogen-containing Fertilizers. Among the important nitrogen compounds used as fertilizers are sodium nitrate, ammonium nitrate, calcium nitrate, ammonium sulfate, urea, ammonia, and calcium cyanamide. Most fertilizers are manufactured using atmospheric nitrogen: cyanamide is made by combining nitrogen with calcium carbide to form calcium cyanamide; ammonia is made by combining nitrogen and hydrogen in contact with a catalyst under high pressure. (Ammonia also is produced as a by-product of the coke industry.) Urea is formed by combining ammonia with carbon dioxide under high pressure. Ammonium nitrate is produced by oxidizing ammonia to nitric acid and neutralizing the nitric acid with ammonia. Ammonia also is combined with sulfuric acid to form ammonium sulfate, or with phosphoric acid to form ammonium phosphate. A small quantity of nitrogen is combined with

oxygen when air is passed through an electric arc. The nitric acid produced by this process is used to make calcium nitrate. Synthetic nitrate of soda is produced by combining nitric acid and sodium carbonate.

Ammonium nitrate applied over a period of years will make a soil acid. The same quantity of sodium or calcium nitrate applied to adjacent land will not increase soil acidity. Ammonium nitrate, calcium nitrate, and urea are hygroscopic and must be treated to prevent rapid absorption of moisture when the fertilizer is exposed to a highly humid atmosphere. Because of this, these fertilizers are packaged in moisture-proof bags.

The nitrogen content of various inorganic nitrogen fertilizers is as follows: sodium nitrate, 16%; ammonia nitrate, 33%; urea, 44%; calcium cyanamide, 22%; ammonium sulfate, 20%; monoammonium phosphate, 11%; diammonium phosphate, 20%; calcium nitrate, 15%.

Phosphate-containing Fertilizers. Among the most important phosphate fertilizers are superphosphate, double superphosphate, mono- and diammonium phosphate, and finely ground rock phosphate. Ordinary superphosphate containing 18% to 20% P_2O_5 (phosphoric anhydride) is produced by treating finely ground rock phosphate with sulfuric acid that contains a sufficient quantity of water to produce a dry product when the chemical reaction is complete. Double superphosphate containing from 43% to 48% P_2O_5 is produced by treating rock phosphate with sufficient sulfuric acid to convert all of the phosphorus to phosphoric acid. The phosphoric acid is removed from the gypsum and other mineral matter by leaching with water and, after concentration, is mixed with finely ground rock phosphate to produce monocalcium phosphate. Finely ground rock phosphate contains from 28% to 34% P_2O_5. Calcium and potassium metaphosphates and fused tricalcium phosphate, made in experimental studies by the Tennessee Valley Authority at Muscle Shoals, Ala., are

Organic fertilizer is incorporated into topsoil with a spade.

USDA

Two bands of fertilizer flank a central seed furrow.

USDA

utilized more readily by plants grown on acid soils in humid regions than on nonacid soils in a subhumid environment.

Potassium-containing Fertilizers. Important potassium fertilizers are muriate of potash, sulfate of potash, and a double salt of potassium and magnesium sulfate. Potassium chloride is separated from sodium chloride in sylvanite by flotation and by crystallization from an aqueous solution. The potassium in potassium chloride is equivalent to 60% K_2O (potassium monoxide). Potassium sulfate is made by adding a strong solution of potassium chloride to a concentrated solution containing a double sulfate of potassium and magnesium. Potassium sulfate contains about 48% K_2O. Potassium salts that contain low percentages of potash are not used extensively in fertilizer at the present time.

Uses of Inorganic Fertilizers. A fertilizer grade is a mixture of fertilizer materials containing a guaranteed percentage of nitrogen, phosphoric acid, and/or potash. A fertilizer grade such as a 10-20-10 contains 10% nitrogen, 20% phosphoric acid, and 10% potash. Fertilizer grades vary in the percentages of nitrogen, phosphoric acid, and/or potash because they are made to supply nutrients that are not present in a soil in sufficient quantity to produce a maximum crop yield. Low analysis grades are made with ordinary superphosphate. High analysis grades are made with treble superphosphate or ammonium phosphates. Since mixed fertilizers are frequently applied in the row when row crops are planted, fertilizers containing a high percentage of soluble salts applied at high rates per acre must be placed 1 or 2 in. from the seed to prevent injury to young roots. Less injury to germination occurs when a fertilizer high in nitrogen and potassium is drilled in rows 7 in. apart, as compared with the same quantity of fertilizer applied at the same rate per acre in rows 42 in. apart. When potassium fertilizers are applied at a high rate per acre, they usually are scattered over the soil before or immediately after a crop is planted. When a highly soluble form of nitrogen, such as nitrate nitrogen, is applied before plant roots are well established, it may be carried into the deeper subsoil during periods of abundant rainfall, especially on sandy land. Consequently, fertilizers high in nitrate nitrogen are applied after a young crop is growing rapidly. Potassium, phosphorus, and ammonium ions are rapidly absorbed on the surface of clay particles. Consequently these plant nutrients are not removed as rapidly from soils during periods of high rainfall as nitrates or sulfates. The rate of fertilizer application is regulated by the ability of the soil to supply various nutrients, the average climatic possibility for crop production, and the fertilizer grade. Optimum economic fertilization should supply the nutrients required to raise the natural productive capacity of a soil to the productive capacity that the average climatic environment will permit. The quantity of fertilizer applied should be increased as the natural crop-producing capacity of a fertile soil gradually declines from continued cultivation. Trace elements including salts of boron, manganese, copper, molybdenum, magnesium, sulfur, and zinc may be mixed with fertilizers containing nitrogen, phosphorus, and/or potassium, or applied alone to supply available nutrients not present in an available form in sufficient amount to produce maximum crop yields.

Organic Fertilizers

Organic fertilizers from plant or animal residues that are commonly used for soil improvement usually contain from 2% to 8% nitrogen and much smaller amounts of phosphorus and other plant nutrients. Common types of organic fertilizers are neutral peat, acid peat, various animal manures, compost, oilseed meal, and sewage sludge. The latter material, when produced by anaerobic digestion (fermentation in the absence of free oxygen) contains about 2% nitrogen. The availability of nitrogen in this material is low. Activated sewage sludge is made by an aerobic process (fermentation in the presence of free oxygen). The total nitrogen in this material may exceed 5%, and a high percentage of the nitrogen is changed rapidly to nitrate when this material is mixed with soil. Neutral peat contains more nitrogen than acid peat. The nitrogen in neutral peat is liberated at a more rapid rate than the nitrogen in acid peat. Barnyard manure varies in fertilizing value depending upon the amount of decomposition or leaching that has occurred before the material is applied to a soil. Highly weathered barnyard manure applied at a high rate per acre will improve the physical condition of a soil but will not provide much nitrogen for plant growth. Oilseed meals made from soybeans, cotton, flax, or rapeseed contain from 6% to 8% nitrogen. These materials provide nitrogen for plant growth at a slow rate over a long period of time when soil conditions are favorable for the growth of microorganisms. Urea-formaldehyde mixtures also have been made which release nitrogen slowly when applied to a soil. The nitrogen in calcium cyanamide and in urea is present in organic form and is changed to ammonia very rapidly when these fertilizers are placed in a warm, moist soil.

HORACE J. HARPER, Oklahoma State University

See also:

ANAEROBE
COMPOST
FERMENTATION
LEAF MOLD
LIMING
PEAT

PHOSPHATES
POTASH
SOIL
SOIL CONDITIONER
SOIL CONSERVATION

FÈS or FEZ, city of northern Morocco, one of the largest cities of the country and the oldest of the religious and commercial capitals. The older part of the city (the Medina, or Fès el-Bali) has narrow, crooked streets and closely packed buildings with flat roofs. It is built on the slopes of two valleys. Two streams, the Fès and its tributary, the Zitoun, cross the city, but in most places are covered by paved streets or buildings. Many mosques, palaces, and gardens are enclosed within the old city. The main business areas, or *souks*, are narrow, with small stores and handicraft shops that open directly on the street.

Fès is noted for its mosques and Muslim universities and is the main center of religious teaching and Islamic culture in northwestern Africa. The religious schools, Arabian art and architecture, and handicraft articles such as metalwork, pottery, jewelry, tapestries, and silverware, attract students, traders, and tourists. Tanneries and leatherworking shops are noted industries of the old city.

The modern French, or new, city dates only from 1916 and lies to the southwest of old Fès. The central business district has broad boulevards, banks, modern hotels, restaurants, and stores. Residential quarters, parks, hospitals, barracks, public buildings, and the railroad station complete the new city. Between the old and new cities is Fès Djedid, with the Sultan's palace, and crowded residential areas with narrow streets.

Although it is probable that older towns existed on the site, old Fès was established in 808 A.D. It was the capital for a succession of Moroccan dynasties. The French protectorate over Morocco was established in 1912, and remained until 1956. The modern portions of Fès, as well as railway and road connections to other cities of North Africa, were established under French control. Pop., 224,865.

BENJAMIN E. THOMAS, University of California

FESCENNINE [fĕs'ə-nīn] **VERSES,** coarse Roman songs of Etruscan origin. They supposedly came from the Etruscan town of Fescennium and were rustic lampoons sung at weddings and other feasts by actors with masks or painted faces. They survived in ribald verses sung by wedding attendants, and by soldiers at a general's triumph to deflate any excessive pride.

FESCUE [fĕs'kū], common name for plants of the genus *Festuca* in the grass family, Gramineae. Fescue grasses are native to temperate regions. Of the approximately 100 species, some are cultivated as lawn, meadow, or pasture grasses, and a few are used as garden ornamentals. The genus includes both annual and perennial species that are mostly low-growing, usually have slender, rather stiff leaves, and narrow clusters of sparse bloom. Among the most important species are meadow fescue, *F. elatior*, commonly grown in pastures and meadows; red fescue, *F. rubra*, also found in meadows; and sheep's fescue, *F. ovina*, often used in lawn mixtures for shady locations. *See also* GRASSES.

FESSENDEN, WILLIAM PITT (1806–69), American public official. Born in Boscawen, N.H., he graduated (1823) from Bowdoin College and became a prominent lawyer in Portland, Maine. He served as a Whig in the state legislature and in the U.S. House of Representatives before being elected to the U.S. Senate in 1854. Fessenden was a leading opponent of President James Buchanan's policies and assisted in organizing the Maine Republicans. Through most of the Civil War he was chairman of the Senate Finance Committee and was briefly (June, 1864–Mar., 1865) Secretary of the Treasury. Again in the Senate (1865–69) he was the principal author of the historic report (Dec., 1865) of the Joint Committee on Reconstruction that formed the basis of the Fourteenth Amendment and the governmental system set up in the South.

FESTUS, PORCIUS, Governor of Palestine, c.60–61 A.D. St. Paul was in prison at Caesarea when Festus took over from Antonius Felix (Acts 24:27ff.). Paul having appealed to Caesar, Festus arranged his hearing before Agrippa, and later sent him to Rome (Acts 25:1—26:32).

FESTUS, city of eastern Missouri, located on the Mississippi River. Shoes, textiles, and grain products are produced by industries located there. Founded, 1878; pop., 7,530.

FETISH (from Port. *feitiço*, "artificial"), man-made object that is treated with awe, an idol. The term is often used for objects of native religions: statues, charms, and symbols. Fetishes are considered sacred because they are thought to contain supernatural powers, either because of the ingredients of which they are composed (as in the case of the medicine bundles of the American Indian tribes of the Great Plains) or because of the manner of their manufacture or treatment (for example, woodcarvings of West Africa and the Congo basin). Because the term has been used uncritically and carries implications of savagery and barbarism, it is generally in disfavor with anthropologists. *See also* RELIGION, PRIMITIVE.

FETTERMAN MASSACRE, American frontier incident. As the winter of 1866 approached, Sioux warriors regularly attacked wood trains and construction gangs trying to build federal forts in the trans-Mississippi West. In Wyoming Capt. William J. Fetterman boasted that with 80 men he could "march through the whole Sioux nation." When, on Dec. 21, 1866, a wood train came under attack near Fort Kearny, Wyo., Fetterman violated orders and set out with troops to attack the Sioux. Two thousand Sioux, Cheyenne, and Arapaho under Crazy Horse trapped Fetterman's 80-man force and wiped it out before reinforcements could race to its relief. Fetterman apparently used his last bullet on himself rather than submit to capture and mutilation by the Indians.

FEUCHTWANGER [foiKHt'väng-ər], **LION** (1884–1958), German novelist and dramatist. Born in Munich of wealthy Jewish parents, Feuchtwanger was educated at the universities of Munich and Berlin. He went into exile from Nazi Germany, settling first in southern France (1933) and later in California (1940), where he stayed to the end of his life. His numerous novels probe deeply into the subconscious and often deal with modern political and social problems in a historical setting. In *Die hässliche Herzogin*, 1923 (*The Ugly Duchess*, 1928), a connection is drawn between physical repulsiveness and the thirst for power. *Jud Süss*, 1925 (*Power*, 1926), set in the 18th century, is the story of the rise of a conscienceless, power-hungry man, his change of attitude, and his final martyrdom. A historical trilogy, *Der Wartesaal* (The Waiting Room), is concerned with the era between 1914 and 1939, the first part, *Erfolg*, 1930 (*Success*, 1930), treating satirically the beginnings of the Nazi party, the subsequent parts, *Die Geschwister Oppenheim*, 1933 (*The Oppermanns*, 1934), and *Exil*, 1939 (*Paris Gazette*, 1940), dealing with the life of the Jews in Nazi Germany and the fate of the exiles. His Josephus trilogy deals with the struggle of the Jews against Rome in *Der jüdische Krieg*, 1932 (*Josephus*, 1932), *Die Söhne*, 1935 (*The Jew of Rome*, 1936), and *Der Tag wird Kommen*, 1946 (*Josephus and the Emperor*, trans. first, 1942). Feuchtwanger's other novels include *Der falsche Nero*, 1936 (*The Pretender*, 1937) and *Goya oder der arge Weg der Erkenntnis*, 1951 (*This Is the Hour*, 1951).

HUGO SCHMIDT, Bryn Mawr College

FEUDALISM, in European history, the system of government and of society in which political and social relations among freemen were determined by contract. The contract was a free agreement between two men of unequal social level, the greater of whom was called a lord and the lesser a vassal. This is the usage preferred today by most historians, but the term is much abused. A long tradition in historical writing has also sanctioned the use of "feudalism" in an economic as distinct from a political or social sense. Economic feudalism refers to a system of production based upon large estates or on some form of serfdom or servile obligations.

Lords and Vassals. Although it drew upon older institutions and practices, feudalism as a political and social system first fully emerged in western Europe in the late 9th and 10th centuries. Violence and disorders stemming from the disintegration of the Carolingian state and from the invasions of Northmen, Magyars, and Saracens confronted the individual freeman with the critical problem of ensuring his own personal security. In some areas of Europe, notably Scotland, Ireland, and Wales, the enlarged family, or clan, could assume responsibility for protecting the individual. Such areas did not develop real feudalism. In other regions of Europe, however, the family was not strong enough to extend needed protection, and the individual appealed for help to a stronger neighbor. This recourse seems especially characteristic of the lands between the Loire and the lower Rhine, where the classical forms of European feudalism developed. The weaker man, or vassal, seeking protection entered into a personal, moral relationship with the stronger man, or lord, able to extend it to him. This personal relationship reflected in part the German institution of the comitatus described by the Roman historian Tacitus, in which young warriors attached themselves to older and more experienced fighters as their leaders. Probably a more influential model for the personal bond of vassalage was the father-son relationship within the family.

Since vassalage was not established naturally, that is, by blood, it had to be established artificially, by contract. As in any contractual relationship, both the vassal and lord had mutual rights and obligations. To his lord, the vassal, like a dutiful son, owed primarily fidelity, or fealty. In time, the feudal obligations came to be defined with greater precision. The vassal had to provide his lord material help, or aid, and to give him advice, or counsel. Aid implied primarily military help, the amount and duration of which also came to be defined more precisely. The vassal, for example, would typically be required to serve 40 days a year on a local campaign—less in a foreign war—and to bring with him a fixed number of knights commensurate with his resources. Aid also meant financial help. Actually the vassal owed financial help whenever the lord needed it. By the 13th century, custom had established that the lord unquestionably needed it on four occasions, or "incidents": ransoming of the lord if captured, knighting of his eldest son, marriage of his eldest daughter, and departure on a Crusade. For other needs, the lord could ask his vassals for aid, but they retained the right to deny the request. The vassal was also required to entertain his lord a few days a year.

The obligation of counsel required that the vassal come to the lord's court certain days each year, typically on Christmas, Easter, and Michaelmas. There the vassal would advise the lord and sit with his fellow vassals to help judge cases before the lord's court.

The lord in turn owed his vassal two things: protection and maintenance. He had to protect his vassal in war and usually in lawsuits outside his own court. To maintain his vassal, the lord might keep him at his court

The Bettmann Archive

Left, Charles Martel and his forces defeating the Saracens at Poitiers in 732. Numerous such invasions afflicted the European continent and contributed to the development of feudalism. The engraving is after a painting by Karl Wilhelm von Steuben (1788–1865).

Below, the act of homage. A vassal vows to serve a lord in return for his protection.

The World We Live in and How It Came to Be, by Gertrude Hartman, Macmillan Co.

Walters Art Gallery

Knights are sent into battle, in the drawing "Giselbertus Autissiodorus," from the Austrian manuscript Threnos Jeremiae (c.1100).

as a "house knight." However, the difficulties of conveying large quantities of food and supplies for great distances severely limited the number of vassals the lord could maintain permanently at his own court. A second, more important, means of maintaining a vassal was to grant him an estate that he could manage and upon which he could live. This was the fief. The two ties, personal and property, vassalage and fief, made up the feudal bond and formed the heart of the feudal relationship.

The Fief. The "fief" may be defined as conditional, temporary, and nonhereditary land tenure, as distinct from the alodium, which was unconditional, permanent, and heritable tenure. In other words, the vassal was entitled to his fief only so long as he fulfilled his services to his lord. Should those services cease, the fief escheated, or reverted, to the lord. The origins of fief tenure probably go back to late Roman and Merovingian times and are associated with ecclesiastical landownership. The Church was forbidden by canon law to alienate its property. To abide by the letter of the canons, yet not be hamstrung by them, the Church developed the practice of granting the "use," but not the full ownership, of lands to favored laymen. The early Carolingians, wishing to use Church lands to support their soldiers, took to ordering churches or monasteries to make such grants to their knights. Apparently the true fief of the post-Carolingian period was modeled on such ecclesiastical tenures.

Initially, the fief was not hereditary, but in time custom granted to a vassal's heirs—even minors and women—the right to his fief lands. The lord, however, claimed a payment whenever the fief changed hands through inheritance. The lord also could appropriate the revenues of a fief during the minority of an heir, appoint the

minor's guardians or wards or, if the heir was a woman, select her husband for her. Custom also allowed a vassal to sell or alienate his fief, though the lord's permission was required.

Homage and Investiture. Since the feudal relationship was considered the most sacred of bonds, a veritable liturgy grew up around the symbolic acts by which it was created. The personal tie of vassalage was created by the act of homage, in which the vassal placed his hands within the hands of his lord. A pledge of fealty and a kiss of peace were sometimes added. The property relationship was created by the act of investiture, whereby the lord gave the vassal a twig or clod of earth as symbol of his fief. Usually, both ceremonies of homage and investiture were performed at the same time.

Political Feudalism. Although feudalism in origin reflected the spontaneous efforts of individuals to provide for their own security, feudal relationships grew more complex as the system extended. One man might become the vassal of several lords. In such a situation, he owed to one—his "liege" lord—primary allegiance. As the system extended, one man's lord would usually become another man's vassal, and medieval society came to be organized into a vast and complicated feudal pyramid, with the King at its apex and the poorest knight at its base.

In regard to government, feudalism is often taken as equivalent to decentralization and even to anarchy. Vassals typically obtained with their fiefs jurisdiction over the inhabitants of their lands. They and not their lords or the King were the chief judges and governors of the people within their estates. Still, the terms of the feudal contract, if effectively enforced, were incompatible with anarchy. The application of feudal principles and the enforcement of feudal obligations, in fact, brought about a considerable increase in royal power, particularly after the year 1000. In England, for example, after the Norman Conquest (1066), William the Conqueror insisted that all freemen take an oath to recognize him as their liege lord (the Salisbury Oath). He and his successors also insisted that all land in England be considered a fief of the King, which meant that all landowners could lose their property if they did not perform the services imposed upon them. By the work of its Norman and Angevin Kings, England became a model feudal state, and the English monarchy was the most powerful in medieval Europe. On the Continent, too, the policy of the French Kings aimed not at destroying feudalism but at forcing the great nobles to fulfill their obligations as vassals of the King. Of course, while the feudal monarch could be strong, he could not be absolute, as his government remained decentralized and he himself was limited by the terms of the feudal contract. Only in the early modern period were these limitations imposed by feudalism gradually overcome, and the way cleared for truly absolutist monarchy. But the later triumph of absolutism should not obscure the fact that feudalism brought a considerable increase in royal authority and public order. The rise of feudalism helped bring Europe out of the anarchy and chaos of the Dark Ages and represented a major step forward in the establishment of stable political order in the West.

Feudal institutions continued to have marked influence on later European political development. The right of a Parliament to control the purse strings is distantly related to the vassal's rights to refuse his lord's excessive demands for aid. The right to trial by one's peers declared in the Magna Charta derives from what was originally the duty of vassals to attend the lord's court and to help him judge cases involving his fellow vassals. The idea of government as founded upon a contract between rulers and ruled reflects the real practice of feudal government.

Economic Feudalism. In an economic sense, "feudalism" is used to describe an economic system based upon large estates (manorialism) or on some form of servile obligations (seignorialism). But the historical chronology of manorialism is not identical with that of feudalism considered as a system of government. Great estates were well established during Carolingian times before political feudalism was mature, and on the Continent the manor was declining by 1200, centuries before political feudalism began to ebb. Even with the disappearance of great manors, lords continued to claim seignorial dues from persons and lands. These dues included quitrents given to the seignorial overlord and tithes given to the Church. The lord could often claim the property of a peasant in the absence of heirs in the direct line and forbid its alienation, collect an inheritance tax, and require a payment for the land transfers he might permit. He also had the right to establish certain monopolies upon his property, such as the pressing of wine, milling, or baking. These payments were largely uncompensated, in the sense that the lord gave no real service in exchange for them. The "economic feudalism" which these dues constituted continued to exist long after political feudalism had faded. Such seignorial prerogatives were not abolished in France until the Revolution in 1789. In the revolutionary period the seignorial, or feudal, regime was similarly abolished in most of Europe.

In 19th-century histories, "feudalism" tended to mean the system of special privilege, largely economic, of the noble classes under the *ancien régime* which the Revolution abolished. Karl Marx adopted the term largely in this sense, for in his terminology "feudal" is used to describe the stage of economic development immediately preceding capitalism. The sense of the word has been further blurred by loose popular usage, in which it is

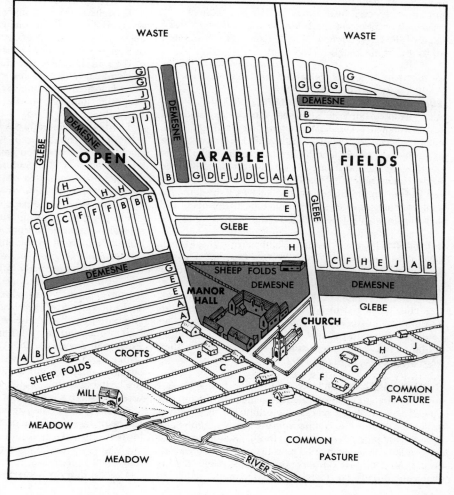

The feudal manor provided practically all of the necessities for the lord and his peasants. The manor hall was the lord's residence. Nearby were the church and the peasant cottages (designated here by the letters A through J). The crofts, or enclosed plots, near the peasant cottages were used to stack the hay gathered from the meadows. Animals grazed in the common pasture and sometimes in the "waste," where wood was cut for fuel, posts, and beams. Crops were usually grown on three open arable fields divided into strips allotted to peasants A–J, as well as on individual holdings (demesne) for the lord and fields (glebe) for the church.

Manor scene (c.1338), from frescoes by Ambrogio Lorenzetti, in Palazzo Pubblico, Siena. Agricultural activities are shown, and, at bottom right, a falcon hunt.

Alinari—Art Reference Bureau

taken as equivalent to "nonmodern," or "backward." These abuses of the term have, of course, no real connection with historic feudalism, one of the most important and influential institutions in Western history.

Consult Stephenson, Carl, *Medieval Feudalism* (1942); Ganshof, F. L., *Feudalism* (1952); *Feudalism in History*, ed. by Rushton Coulborn (1956).

DAVID HERLIHY, Bryn Mawr College
See also KNIGHTS AND KNIGHTHOOD; MIDDLE AGES.

FEUERMANN [foi'ər-män], **EMANUEL** (1902–42), Polish cello virtuoso, born in Kolomea. He studied with his father and with Anton Walter (of the Rosé Quartet), making his concert debut at the age of 11. He continued his studies at Leipzig, and he began teaching cello at the Cologne Conservatory in 1918 and later taught at the Berlin Hochschule für Musik (1930–33). In 1938 he settled in the United States, where he was known for his solo, concerto, and chamber music performances, and his recordings with Jascha Heifetz and Artur Rubinstein.

FEUILLANTS [fû-yäN'], political club during the French Revolution, consisting of conservative Jacobins who left the mother society in July, 1791, and met at the former Feuillant convent. Antoine Barnave was the leading figure, but the Marquis de Lafayette was also prominent. The club consisted of 250 deputies in the Legislative Assembly who stood for constitutional monarchy. The Feuillants lost control of the ministry to the Girondists in Mar., 1792. Thereafter associated with royalism, they were suppressed in Sept., 1792.

FEUILLET, OCTAVE (1821–90), French dramatist and novelist. His plays were highly successful during his time. In most of his works, including his best-known novel, *Le roman d'un jeune homme pauvre*, 1858 (*The Romance of a Poor Young Man*, 1859), Feuillet upheld a conventional and sentimental morality. Even the unsavory hero of *Monsieur de Camors* (1867; trans., 1868) hid his cynicism under the niceties of social decorum.

FEVER, an abnormal elevation of body temperature which usually develops in response to invasion of the body by microorganisms.

In health the average body temperature, which is usually given as 98.6° F., is maintained by an accurate balance between heat production and heat loss. Heat production is increased by exercise, shivering, and contraction of the muscles. The digestion of food and certain types of glandular activity also contribute to heating the body. Heat is lost by sweating, by vaporization of water from the lungs, and by radiation of heat from the surface of the body.

The body temperature is controlled by the heat regulating center of the brain which is located in a part of the brain called the hypothalamus. Infections bring about a disturbance in this center, resulting in increased heat production, diminished heat loss, and raised body temperature. The elevation of temperature is accompanied by an increase in the pace of activity of the tissues, including a greater production of white blood cells and special substances (antibodies) which combat the infection. A subnormal temperature in a patient with a severe infection is a serious sign, as it indicates that the body is not responding properly in its own defense. No attempt should be made to reduce body temperature unless it becomes excessive, in which case sponging, or immersion in tepid water is indicated. When the fever breaks, the patient perspires heavily so that heat loss exceeds heat production and the temperature returns to normal. Fever can develop without infection as in cases of heat stroke in which there is a disturbance of the heat-regulating mechanism, in injury to the brain which damages the heat-regulating center, or following the injection of foreign proteins into the body.

Fever Patterns. The pattern of temperature fluctuations can be of value in diagnosis. In lobar pneumonia and scarlet fever there is an abrupt temperature rise and fall; in typhoid fever the temperature rises and subsides gradually over a period of days.

Certain descriptive terms are applied to temperature

fluctuations. When the temperature reaches its maximum height and remains at that level it is described as "continued"; this is seen in typhoid and typhus fevers. A "remittent" temperature is an elevated temperature which fluctuates. Such a pattern is seen in tuberculosis. An "intermittent" temperature returns to normal or below normal in a 24-hour period, a characteristic feature of malaria. In brucellosis, or undulant fever, there is a prolonged remittent fever of several weeks' duration, interrupted by periods of normal temperature. In lice-borne and tick-borne relapsing fevers the clinical diagnosis is based on bouts of fever lasting several days and separated by fever-free intervals, during which the patient's condition improves. There may be three or more such relapses. A notable example of a disease in which the temperature is alternately elevated and normal is Hodgkin's disease, a disorder involving the lymph nodes.

Changes in Body Function in Fever. In fever there is a marked decrease in urine output. The pulse is rapid and the skin is hot and dry, owing to the suppression of glandular secretions. The activity of the body cells is increased so that more than the normal number of calories is consumed. The body may consume its own tissues (which consist of protein) in an attempt to meet the abnormal energy demands if the diet does not contain large amounts of energy-supplying carbohydrates.

JAMES H. LAWSON, M.D.

FEVERFEW, common name for a herbaceous perennial, *Chrysanthemum parthenium*, in the composite family, Compositae. Native to Europe and Asia, feverfew is now grown in many parts of the world. The plants are bushy, grow to a height of about 3 ft., and have the deeply cut leaves typical of many chrysanthemums. The flower heads are small with a yellow central disk and white rays. Feverfew is commonly used in garden borders and is grown from seed. The plants require well-drained soil and full sunlight.
See also CHRYSANTHEMUM.

FEVER THERAPY, treatment of disease through elevation of body temperature. Fever produces certain physiological changes in the body, such as an increase in the number of bacteria-fighting white blood cells, which enhance the ability of the patient to fight infection.

This technique has been used for centuries by the Chinese, Japanese, and American Indians, who employed steam baths (made by throwing water over heated stones), heated sand, and hot springs to raise the body temperature. Many of these techniques are still in use. Fever has been induced in syphilitic patients by injecting them with living malarial germs. Similar use has been made of typhoid vaccine. These methods have been supplanted by the use of antibiotic drugs in treating syphilis. Other procedures for inducing fever utilize cabinet electric-light baths, and high-frequency electric currents.

FEYNMAN, RICHARD PHILLIPS (1918–), American physicist, born in New York City. He shared the 1965 Nobel Prize in physics with Julian Schwinger and Shinichiro Tomonaga. The three, working separately in the 1940's, performed research in quantum electrodynamics and solved the difficulties of carrying out quantitative calculations of the interplay between charged particles. Their discoveries proved useful in describing nuclear forces and the understanding of elementary particles.

FEZ. *See* FÈS OR FEZ.

FEZZAN [fĕ-zăn'], southern region of Libya, and from 1951 to 1963 one of the federated provinces (the other two being Cyrenaica and Tripolitania) that made up the United Kingdom of Libya. The provinces were abolished when Libya became a unitary state in 1963. Fezzan is bounded on the north and east by the other Libyan provinces of Tripolitania and Cyrenaica, and on the south and west by Chad, Niger, the Algerian Sahara, and Tunisia. The Fezzan is all desert except for scattered oases such as Sebha, Murzuk, Zuila, and El-Gatrun. About 90% of the population of 50,000 live in the oases, which have irrigated gardens and about 300,000 acres of date palms. The people are mostly Tebu, Taureg, and Negro, and Arab.

FIBER, NATURAL. The term "natural fiber" applies to threadlike materials obtained from plant and animal tissues and from mineral sources. Although in recent years many synthetic fibers have been introduced, natural fibers are still of great importance. The significant animal fibers are hair, wool, and silk (from insect cocoons). The most important plant fibers are cotton, wood pulp, abaca (Manila hemp), sisal, jute, and flax. The only significant mineral fiber is asbestos.

Fabric Fibers. Natural fibers used for fabrics range from fine silk used for delicate wearing apparel, to jute and sisal used for coarse sacking and burlap. Cotton is not only the most widely employed fabric fiber but is also the most important commercial fiber in the world. It is grown in about 60 countries, but more than 80% of world production is concentrated in the United States, India, China, the U.S.S.R., Brazil, and Egypt. Cotton products include wearing apparel, decorative fabrics, and commercial and industrial textiles.

Jute follows cotton in world importance as a fabric fiber. About 97% of the total jute supply comes from India, where more than half of the raw fiber is processed into coarse materials such as burlap and sacking. Jute yarn is also used extensively for webbing, floor covering, and carpet backs. Flax, hemp, and ramie produce fine household and apparel fabrics, and, with sisal and istle (a fiber obtained from the leaves of wild pineapple and agave plants), are used in making industrial materials.

Sheep wool, used for woven goods, hosiery, and felts, is foremost among the animal fibers. In addition, hair and wool from Angora and Cashmere goats, vicuna, alpaca, llama, and camel are used in large quantities for fine-quality woven goods. The bulk of the world's apparel wool and over 80% of world wool exports come from Australia, Argentina, New Zealand, South Africa, and Uruguay.

Cordage Fibers. Natural fibers from the four corners of the earth are used to produce about 357 million pounds of rope and twine each year in the United States alone. Cordage products range from small string and tying twine to rope and cable 24 in. in circumference. These products perform essential tasks in industry, agriculture, and around the home. Abaca is the strongest of the vegetable fibers, has the most resistance to abrasion, and makes the strongest and most durable rope. Sisal (henequen) is also used for rope and almost exclusively in the manufacture of binder and baler twine.

Other cordage fibers are cotton, hemp, flax, istle, coir (a fiber obtained from the outer husks of coconuts), ramie, and esparto (a fiber obtained from esparto grass). These are used for making special-purpose ropes; fishing nets, lines, and twines; string; and commercial twines. Jute, in the form of twine, is extensively used for heavy bundling, and in the form of yarn is largely used in carpet making.

Brush and Braiding Fibers. Hair obtained from animals such as the horse, badger, camel, and sable are widely used for paint and shaving brushes. Various plant fibers are processed into baskets, brushes, mats, and rugs. Piassava, a palm fiber, is the most important fiber in the brush trade. It is primarily used for brooms and brushes. Palmyra palm fiber makes excellent street brushes. Jute is used for mats. Coir is used for mats and large brooms and brushes.

Stuffing Fibers. Stuffing materials used for mattresses, pads, cushions, and upholstery, and caulking fiber for ships, barrels, and pipes are made from kapok, cotton, jute, sisal fiber and sisal tow, hemp and hemp tow, istle, vegetable silk, and Spanish moss. Paper manufacturers use almost all kinds of vegetable fibers, alone or mixed with wood pulp, for making paper products.

STEWART G. RUSSELL, Columbian Rope Company

FIBER, SYNTHETIC. A relatively new development in the textile field, synthetic fibers have taken a large role in fabric production, particularly in the United States, where many of them were developed. They have come to enjoy a long and growing list of applications, ranging from clothing, blankets, and curtains to industrial uses, where the requirements are quite rigid.

There are several different trade names for the many synthetic fibers produced, and these often give no clue to what the fiber is made of. Therefore it is easier to divide these fibers into broad classifications first, as noncellulosic and cellulosic, then discuss them under their general chemical groups.

Noncellulosic. These are the true synthetic fibers, generally produced by chemical reactions in which relatively small molecules are converted into high polymers, or molecules with a very high molecular weight. They are made from petroleum and to a lesser extent, coal and vegetable products. The exception is glass fiber, made from inorganic materials.

Nylon, which is a polyamide, was the first noncellulosic fiber of commercial importance. It was introduced about 1940 by E. I. du Pont de Nemours & Co., which had spent more than $25,000,000 in perfecting the production process. It has since been licensed to other companies, and today nylon ranks second in production volume of all synthetic fibers. Several different types have been developed: nylon 66, nylon 610, and nylon 6. Nylon 66, the original nylon, is still the most important, but the others are also used in large quantities in garments,

tire cord, and industrial applications such as belt drives, ropes, coated fabrics, and brushes. Arteries for human circulatory systems have been fabricated of nylon and successfully implanted in several medical operations.

The acrylic fibers are known by the trade names of Orlon, Acrilan, Dynel, Zefran, Creslan, Verel, and Darvan. They are basically acrylonitrile polymers or copolymers with other materials. They have excellent resistance to sunlight, moths, acids, and solvents, and are used in blankets, sweaters, and garments otherwise made of wool, as well as in tents, awnings, and protective clothing for extreme weather conditions.

Polyester fibers, known by the trade names of Dacron, Teron, Terylene, Vycron, and Kodel, also have a wide range of textile applications in clothing as well as in industry.

Glass fiber, which can be classed as a synthetic fiber, has been widely used as curtain material and in other home furnishings. Another application, which is rapidly growing, is in the production of glass-reinforced plastics. Research has been conducted into other inorganic materials to develop fibers that withstand high temperatures, such as those experienced in space travel.

Cellulosic Fibers. The cellulosic fibers are produced by modification of the cellulose occurring in nature, primarily from wood pulp and cotton linters. They are not truly synthetic for this reason but may be classed as synthetic fibers because they are chemically reconstituted.

Rayon is the most important of these fibers and is also the first, in production volume, of all the synthetic fibers. Its largest uses are in textile fabrics, tire cords, industrial belting, and hosing. The acetate, or cellulose acetate, fibers have fewer industrial uses than rayon, and are primarily used in garment fabrics.

Cotton and wool, which are basically natural fibers, are quite frequently chemically modified or treated in order to improve their properties. As a result the final products can be considered as partially synthetic.

LYLE F. ALBRIGHT, Purdue University
See also ACRILAN; DACRON; DYNEL; NYLON; ORLON; PLASTICS; RAYON.

FIBER OPTICS, branch of optics based on the phenomenon that light entering one end of a bundle of extremely fine, flexible glass fibers is conducted, without loss of energy, through the fibers and emerges at the other end. The flexibility of such a bundle of fibers can be made use of in medical instruments to view, for example, the inside of the heart and stomach. Other applications are in astronomy and television.

Light normally travels in a straight line; one cannot see around a corner. However, light follows a zigzag pattern through a glass rod or fiber, bouncing repeatedly from surface to surface due to the phenomenon known as total internal reflection. If the fibers are bent or curved in a spiral, they enable one to see around a corner.

Although the basic phenomenon of light conduction along transparent dielectric (nonconducting) cylinders has long been known, the fundamental studies of their properties and techniques relative to the field of fiber optics were started in 1952 by N. S. Kapany and his associates in England.

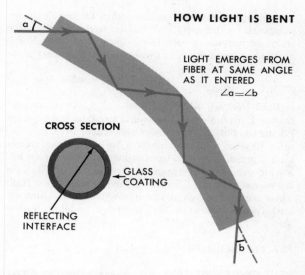

HOW LIGHT IS BENT

LIGHT EMERGES FROM
FIBER AT SAME ANGLE
AS IT ENTERED
∠a =∠b

CROSS SECTION

GLASS
COATING

REFLECTING
INTERFACE

The total reflection of the light ray at every point of contact (the interface) between the fiber and the coating causes the ray to "bounce" through the fiber.

The light conductors used in fiber optics consist in general of two parts: (1) a cylindrical glass fiber with a high refractive index, encased in (2) a coating formed of a thin layer of glass with a low refractive index. Total reflection occurs at the interface of the two media. The glass coating serves as a permanent protection for the reflecting interface; separates the individual fibers to prevent "coupling" between them; and provides the interstitial medium in vacuum-tight, fused fiber assemblies. Glass-coated glass fibers have considerable flexibility and as optical elements they allow the transmission of images along flexible axes. They can accept a wider cone of light (they have a larger angle of acceptance) than most existing optical systems, and therefore have a higher photometric efficiency. When the fiber diameter is small they act as dielectric wave guides having similar properties as microwave wave guides.

The field of fiber optics has found varied forms of applications in medicine, astronomy, television, cryptography, high-speed photography, guidance, and reconnaissance. For example, flexible assemblies of appropriately aligned fibers have given rise to development of a number of instruments for remote viewing in medicine and engineering. In particular, their application as endoscopes for viewing the interior of the human heart, stomach, urinary tract, ear, nose, throat, and other regions has most valuable diagnostic potential.

In conventional stellar spectroscopy a large fraction of the light in the star image gathered by the telescope is wasted at the spectrograph slit. However, with the use of a fiber assembly with circular cross section at the input end and rectangular cross section at the output end, a large amount of light is gathered at the telescope and passed without loss at the spectrograph slit.

Because of the large acceptance angle of high refractive-index fibers, these fibers can transport an image from a phosphor to a photosensitive surface with greater efficiency and ease than is possible with other optical sys-

tems. Such fused-fiber plates have found valuable use in cathode-ray-tube photography and coupling of multistage image intensifiers.

A large number of other possibilities exists in the field of fiber optics, and recent developments indicate the extension of these principles to ultraviolet and infrared regions of the spectrum. With the combinations of some known principles in solid-state physics and nuclear physics it would be possible to evolve high-energy particle tracking chambers and a number of photosensitive devices.

N. S. KAPANY, Optics Technology, Inc.

FIBIGER [fē'bē-gər], **JOHANNES ANDREAS** (1867–1928), Danish pathologist who was awarded the Nobel Prize in 1926 for his research on cancer. He was the first to attempt to produce cancer experimentally (1913) and claimed to have caused cancer in the fore-stomach of rats by infesting them with the worm *Gongylonema neoplasticum* (then called *Spiroptera*). He served as director of the Institute of Pathological Anatomy of Copenhagen, Denmark, and as chairman of the International Union for Cancer Research.

FIBRIN [fī'brĭn] **AND FIBRINOGEN** [fī-brĭn'ə-jən], substances involved in the clotting of blood. Fibrinogen is a protein which is produced in the liver and is normally present in circulating blood. During clotting the soluble fibrinogen is converted into fine threads of fibrin which form the matrix of the blood clot. In the rare congenital blood disease, afibrinogenemia, bleeding tendencies result from absence of fibrinogen. Fibrinolysis, or the dissolution of the fibrin threads, occurs normally to some extent but may cause hemorrhages when excessive amounts of fibrin-dissolving enzymes are present in the blood. This sometimes occurs in cases of cancer of the prostate and in certain abnormalities of pregnancy.
See also BLOOD.

FIBROMA [fī-brō'mə], a noncancerous tumor of fibrous tissue which may develop spontaneously anywhere in the body but is most common in the skin and subcutaneous tissue. Unlike cancerous tumors, fibromas are separated from the surrounding tissue by a capsule and do not tend to spread to other parts of the body. The tumors may be excised, but tend to recur if not removed completely. Rarely, fibromas may become cancerous and invade other parts of the body.
See also TUMOR.

FIBROSITIS [fī-brō-sī'tĭs], a rheumatic condition involving stiffness, pain, and swelling of the soft tissues, most commonly affecting the neck, shoulders, and back. The cause of the condition is unknown, although it has been associated with chilling, dampness, and sudden changes in temperature. Psychological factors are also suspected. Stiffness in the involved part usually increases after rest and can be relieved by activity. Specific painful, "trigger" points can sometimes be located. The general health is unaffected. The condition does not become worse with time and patients are rarely incapacitated. Treatment consists of heat and exercise.

FIBULA. *See* SKELETAL SYSTEM.

FICHTE [fĭκн′tə], **JOHANN GOTTLIEB** (1762–1814), German philosopher. He was a professor at Jena and was a leading spirit in founding the University of Berlin. The turning point of his life came when, after a youth of poverty, he published an anonymous *Critique of All Revelation*, which was at first attributed to Kant, and which was highly praised by the great philosopher. Fichte went on to develop Kant's thought into a form of absolute idealism. The ultimate reality he conceived as a divine will, which manifested itself through individual minds in the degree to which their thought and action were controlled by reason. Fichte was an eloquent orator, and some of his most influential works were presented as lectures to Berlin audiences, notably *The Vocation of Man* (1800) and *The Nature of the Scholar* (1805). His passionate patriotism helped to rally the German people against Napoleon. A good literary interpretation of his thought is to be found in the writings of Thomas Carlyle.

BRAND BLANSHARD, Yale University

FICINO [fē-chē′nō], **MARSILIO** (1433–99), Italian philosopher. He is important for his Latin translations of Plato and Plotinus. His *Platonic Theology* combines traditional Christian notions with Neoplatonism.

FICTION. *See* NOVEL; SHORT STORY.

FIDDLE, colloquial term for violin. It also designates a group of medieval and Oriental ancestors of the violin. *See* LIRA; REBEC; VIOLIN.

FIDDLER CRAB, name for several species of small crabs of the genus *Uca*, in the order Decapoda of class Crustacea. The males have one claw greatly enlarged and it is from this that the common name is derived. Fiddler crabs live on dry sandy beaches and are found in many parts of the world. Their mottled, light-brownish color blends in well with the sandy background. They live in burrows dug in the sand and feed on small pieces of organic matter. Although the adults spend most of their time on land, fiddler crabs are aquatic animals; they breathe by means of gills which must be kept continually moist.

FIDELIO [fĭ-dā′lē-ō], opera in two acts by Ludwig van Beethoven; libretto by Joseph von Sonnleithner, based on Bouilly; first performance, in three acts, Nov. 20, 1805, Vienna; revised versions in collaboration with Stephan von Breuning (1806) and Georg F. Treitschke (1814); first American performance in English, Sept. 9, 1839, New York.

Leonore, disguised as a page, Fidelio, seeks to rescue her husband Florestan, who is a political prisoner of Pizarro, a tyrannical Governor. With a pistol she prevents Pizarro from stabbing Florestan, who is finally rescued.

Beethoven's mastery of dramatic effects produces unforgettable moments such as the dankly atmospheric introduction to Florestan's great dungeon aria and the suspenseful rescue scene. Unfortunately, his powerful development of musical forms is often carried beyond the timing appropriate for the stage action. Of four overtures composed for the opera, only the last is used normally for stage performances, but the *Leonore* Overture No. 3 (1806) has become one of the best-known concert overtures.

JAN LaRUE, New York University

FIEDLER [fēd′lər], **ARTHUR** (1894–   ), American conductor. Born in Boston, he studied music in Berlin before joining the Boston Symphony Orchestra in 1915. In 1929, after 15 years with the orchestra, he inaugurated its annual Esplanade series of free outdoor concerts. In the following year he was appointed conductor of the then 45-year old Boston "Pops," given in Symphony Hall. These concerts of light music, during which refreshments are served, have become very successful under his leadership.

FIEF. *See* FEUDALISM.

FIELD, CYRUS WEST (1819–92), American merchant, promoter of the transoceanic cable. Born in Stockbridge, Mass., he retired (1853) from the paper business with a moderate fortune, which he used to finance a scheme for laying a transatlantic cable to England. After five attempts (1857–58) the cable was secured, transmitting the first message on Aug. 16, 1858, but breaking four weeks later. Field's company, bankrupted by the Panic of 1857, reorganized, and in 1866 re-established the cable. Field, widely acclaimed for his accomplishment, subsequently sponsored cable communications with the other continents.

FIELD, EUGENE (1850–95), American poet and journalist, born in St. Louis. After serving on the staffs of several Western newspapers, he became a columnist for the Chicago *Morning News* (1883–95). His column, called "Sharps and Flats," was distinguished by his whimsical humor and sentimental verse. He is best remembered for his poems of childhood, such as "Little Boy Blue" and "Wynken, Blynken, and Nod."

FIELD, JOHN (1782–1837), Irish composer and pianist, famous for his nocturnes, which influenced Chopin. In 1794 he became the pupil of Muzio Clementi in London and later settled permanently in Russia. The poetic quality of his playing, as of his best music, anticipated Chopin. His works include 18 nocturnes, seven concertos, and four sonatas for piano.

FIELD, MARSHALL (1834–1906). American merchant and philanthropist, born in Conway, Mass. Field entered (1856) a Chicago drygoods business, which promoted him to general manager (1861) and to president (1881), and which became Marshall Field and Company, one of the world's great department stores. His bequests especially aided the University of Chicago, the Art Institute of Chicago, and the Chicago Museum of Natural History. MARSHALL FIELD II (1868–1905) was prevented by poor health from being active in his father's business. MARSHALL FIELD III (1893–1956) retired in 1935 from the investment field to pursue other interests. He published (1940–

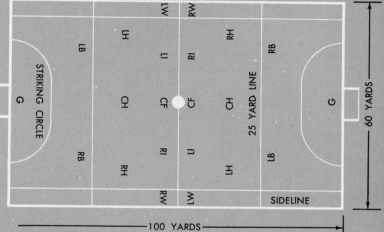

FIELD HOCKEY

Below, team positions at the start of play. Each team has five forwards, three halfbacks, two fullbacks, and one goalkeeper. The letters "L," "R," and "C" refer to left, right, and center. Right, two opposing players match speed and endurance as they race for the ball during the Women's International Hockey Competition in Sydney, Australia. (AUSTRALIAN NEWS INFORMATION BUREAU)

<table>
<tr><td colspan="2">STRIKING CIRCLE</td><td>LB</td><td>LH</td><td>LW</td><td>RW</td><td>RH</td><td>RB</td><td></td></tr>
<tr><td>G</td><td></td><td></td><td>LI</td><td>RI</td><td></td><td>G</td></tr>
<tr><td></td><td>CH</td><td>CF</td><td>CF</td><td>CH</td><td></td></tr>
</table>

25 YARD LINE

60 YARDS

100 YARDS

SIDELINE

48) the liberal New York daily *PM*, and the Chicago *Sun* (after 1948, the *Sun-Times*) from 1941 to his death. He was active in philanthropic causes. MARSHALL FIELD IV (1916–65) was head of Field Enterprises, Inc.

FIELD GLASS, portable, low-power, monocular or binocular telescope designed for military or other outdoor use in viewing objects. The basic Keplerian telescope presents an inverted image to the eye, a peculiarity that is of no consequence in astronomy but is inconvenient for viewing terrestrial objects. For this reason, an essential part of any field glass is a lens or prism system arranged to erect the image.

Early field glasses were of the spyglass type, a tube of telescoping brass sections with an objective lens at one end and an eyepiece at the other. Modern field glasses usually are binocular, presenting a separate image to each eye. The erecting system, placed between the eyepiece and the objective lenses, also enables the instrument to be made more compact, because the light path is folded back upon itself. Good binocular field glasses give the observer enhanced stereoscopic perception of distance, provide a wide field of view, and also enable him to see into dense shade or other dimly lighted areas.

JOSEPH H. RUSH, National Center for
Atmospheric Research

See also BINOCULAR; LENS; TELESCOPE.

FIELD HOCKEY, game played by two teams of 11 persons each. The modern game originated in England about the middle of the 19th century. Though field hockey, an Olympic sport, is popular with both men and women in many parts of the world, in the United States it is played almost exclusively by women.

Each player uses a curved stick to advance a ball toward —and into—the opponents' goal. The object of each team is to score more goals than the other in the 60-minute playing time (divided into halves). A goal counts one point.

The playing area is a rectangular turf field with side lines 100 yd. long and goal (end) lines 60 yd. wide. Two lines 25 yd. from the goal lines and a center line divide the field into quarters. The goal cage in the center of each end line has a mouth 4 yd. wide. A semicircle with a radius of 15 or 16 yd. (15 for women) marks off a striking area in front of each goal cage. Goals count only when the ball is hit from within this striking circle.

The end (head) of the curved wooden stick is rounded on its right side and flat on its left. Only the flat surface may be used to hit or stop the ball. In advancing the ball, a player may not raise any part of the stick higher than his shoulders. The ball, weighing about 5½ oz., has a cork center and leather or plastic cover.

Five members of each team comprise a forward line, three a halfback line, and two a fullback combination; the 11th player is the goalkeeper. All players may hit and pass the ball in any direction and stop the ball with stick, foot, or hand. The goalkeeper alone may kick the ball.

The game starts and restarts after each goal by putting the ball in play in the center of the field. If an attacker hits the ball over the goal line without a goal being scored, the ball is put in play on the nearer 25-yd. line. If a defender accidentally hits the ball over the goal line, the umpire awards the attackers a corner hit. For this infraction the defenders must stand behind the goal line until an attacker drives the ball in play from the corner of the field while his teammates are outside the striking circle. If a defender hits the ball over the goal line intentionally or commits a foul within the striking circle, the umpire awards a penalty corner hit. An attacker takes this hit from the goal line, 10 yd. from the nearer goal post. For other fouls, the team fouled receives a free hit at the spot where the infraction occurred. If the ball goes over the side line (out of bounds) a player opposed to the one who last touched it rolls it back into play by hand.

An umpire is stationed in each half of the field. Umpires may refrain from calling fouls if, through enforcement of the penalty, the offending team would gain an advantage.

JOSEPHINE T. LEES, Coauthor, *Field Hockey for Players, Coaches, and Umpires*

FIELDING, HENRY (1707–54), English novelist, playwright, and journalist. Fielding came of an aristocratic family and was educated at Eton, but for most of his life he was harassed by money worries. His first appearance on the literary scene was as the author of ingenious burlesques, farces, and comedies, the most memorable of which are the burlesque *Tom Thumb* (performed 1730) and the comedy *Don Quixote in England* (performed 1734). He edited newspapers of strong party bias, and many of his farces are political satires directed against the ministry of Sir Robert Walpole. In 1740 Fielding was admitted to the bar. In 1748 he became a London magistrate, the pay for which he regarded as "the dirtiest money upon earth." He sailed for Portugal in June, 1754, in hopes of recovering his shattered health, but died within a few months of landing.

Fielding's fame rests upon his novels. In *Shamela* (1741), a work which he never formally acknowledged, he lampooned the prurience of Samuel Richardson's *Pamela* (1740). *Joseph Andrews* (1742) was begun with the intention also of burlesquing *Pamela*. In the course of writing, however, Fielding warmed to his characters, and the book became a comedy of manners rather than a literary parody, the characters belonging to the burlesque intention fading before such freely invented characters as Parson Adams. The sudden revelations and melodramatic reversals in the last section of *Joseph Andrews* represent the lingering traces of the comic playwright. Fielding's experience as a playwright accounts as well for the skillful organization of the diversified episodes of *Tom Jones* (1749), which Coleridge considered one of the best-plotted works in all literature. Basically a picaresque novel, *Tom Jones* takes its hero through adventures in which his manly good nature triumphs over hypocrisy and ostentatious virtue.

The most lovingly portrayed character in *Tom Jones* is the softly feminine, affectionate, independent Sophia Western, modeled on Fielding's first wife Charlotte Cradock. The heroine of *Amelia* (1751) represents a fuller portrait of the same woman. Fielding preferred the hastily written *Amelia* to *Tom Jones*, but most readers find the feckless Booth, Amelia's husband, an unsympathetic character and many of the scenes of domestic struggle merely vulgar.

Interspersed in *Tom Jones* are essays on literary theory, in one of which Fielding describes his novel as "a comic epic in prose." His insistence on the epic affinities of the novel gave dignity to the genre, in the same way that Fielding's ingenious plotting demonstrated that the novel was capable of both form and diversity. What principally

The History of Tom Jones, Derby & Jackson

Novelist Henry Fielding, from an engraving after a picture by William Hogarth.

distinguishes Fielding's novels and what accounts for much of their charm is the tone of the author—his high spirits, geniality, sympathy, and his patent dislike of people and actions that are pretentious or ungenerous.

ALBERT B. FRIEDMAN, Claremont Graduate School

FIELD MOUSE, name for several small, plump-bodied rodents of the genus *Microtus*, in the rat family, Muridae. Found in meadows and grasslands in many parts of the world, field mice, or voles as they are often called, live in grassy nests built on the ground and feed on seeds, grass, and other plant foods. The short-tailed field mouse, *M. agrestis*, occurs in Europe and western Asia. The yellow-nosed vole, *M. chrotorrhinus*, is found throughout North America.

FIELD OF THE CLOTH OF GOLD, pageantlike meeting (1520) near Calais, France, between English King Henry VIII and French King Francis I, who paraded their wealth and might, and greeted one another like brothers. Henry, seeking prominence in European diplomacy as intermediary between Francis and the Holy Roman Emperor Charles V, hoped that his display at the meeting would impress both. The meeting achieved nothing, and later that year Henry signed a treaty with Charles V providing for an English invasion of France.

FIELDS, DOROTHY (1905–   ), American lyricist and librettist. She was born in Allenhurst, N.J., the daughter of comedian Lew Fields. With composer Jimmy McHugh, she wrote the score for *Blackbirds of 1928*. Later she collaborated with Jerome Kern, Sigmund Romberg, Arthur Schwartz, and Fritz Kreisler. With her brother Herbert, she wrote the librettos for *Let's Face It!* (1941), *Up in Central Park* (1945), *Annie Get Your Gun* (1946), and other musicals. Some of her best-known songs are *I Can't Give You Anything But Love, Baby, On the Sunny Side of the Street, A Fine Romance*, and *The Way You Look Tonight*.

FIELDS, GRACIE (1898–   ), English comedienne and vocalist. She had her first success in English music halls and revues, including *Mr. Tower of London* (1918). She made her first U.S. stage appearance in 1930. Through English and U.S. films, television, and recordings, her songs and sketches, invariably about the indomitable Lancashire working girl, have attracted wide audiences.

FIELDS, W. C., professional name of William Claude Dukenfield (1880–1946), American actor, born in Philadelphia. Beginning as a juggler, he incorporated comedy in his act, which became a favorite in vaudeville and in five editions of the *Ziegfeld Follies* between 1915 and 1921. He gained his greatest fame in radio and films through his caustic wit and talent for mimicry. His films included *If I Had a Million* (1932), *David Copperfield* (1935), and *The Bank Dick* (1940).

FIELD SPANIEL. *See* SPANIEL.

FIELD TRIALS, competitions for sporting dogs in actual performance. Field trials are a formalized development of natural hunting with dogs. There are almost as many kinds of trials as there are kinds of hunting dogs, and each is adapted to a particular breed. There are competitive events for the pointing breeds, whose developed talent is pointing out where game birds hide; for spaniels and retrievers, whose functions are similar in some respects; and for various breeds of hounds, which pursue rabbits and hare according to their own particular code. The dogs are alike only in their common desire to bring game to the hunter. In no breed does it matter how the dog looks, as in bench-show competition; only results count in field trials. The dogs are entered in stakes according to age and experience. These are usually designated as puppy, derby, or all-age events, in that progression.

Bird-dog trials originated in 1874 with a competition held in Memphis by the Tennessee State Sportsmen's Association. Spaniel trials began in England in 1899 and spread to the United States in 1924. The most popular breed in U.S. field trials is the beagle, for which the first competition was held in Salem, N.H., by the National Beagle Club in 1890.

Conduct of Trials. As in bench-show competition, beagles run in two divisions according to size—those 13 in. and under and those measuring up to 15 in. at the shoulder. They run either in pairs, when pursuing rabbits, or in packs, when hare is the game. They are required to find game and then drive it "in an energetic and decisive manner and show an animated desire to overtake it," according to the American Kennel Club rules, which govern most contests for beagles. Speed and flashy driving are less important than accuracy in trailing, endurance, starting ability, style, and obedience to the handler's commands.

Trials for pointing breeds require the dogs to cover a great deal of ground in "races." Handlers and judges follow on horseback. A time limit (usually about 30 minutes) is imposed on each brace of dogs. At the end of the course is a special area of five acres or more, called the bird field or bird lot, where birds are planted. Pointers and setters are the chief breeds in this form of competition. The most important event is the national bird-dog championship in Grand Junction, Tenn., where three-hour heats and the

A field trial between a pointer and a setter begins as the two sporting dogs receive commands from their masters.

Percy T. Jones—F. Lewis

country's most severe competition bring out the utmost in the dogs' capacities.

The function of the retriever is to seek and retrieve fallen game when ordered to do so. The dog should sit quietly in line or in the blind, walk at heel, or assume any station designated by his handler until sent to retrieve. When ordered, the dog should retrieve quickly and deliver with great care. (Birds must be delivered to hand.) Retrievers that bark or whine while awaiting orders are penalized. Dogs are judged on the basis of intelligence, attention, control, perseverance, and style. The usual trial consists of a specified number of land and water events.

Spaniel trials are similar to those for retrievers, but the dogs find and flush game, in addition to retrieving, and work close to the hunter. Emphasis is on land competition, although a test on water is frequently required. Handlers and judges follow on foot instead of on horseback. There is no bird field. Spaniels find their game anywhere along a course having considerable length and breadth.

JOHN RENDEL, New York *Times*

See also HUNTING.

FIENNES, WILLIAM. *See* SAYE AND SELE, WILLIAM FIENNES, 1ST VISCOUNT.

FIESOLE [*fyâ'zō-lā*] (anc. *Faesulae*), hill town in Tuscany, Italy. Popular tradition insists that Fiesole founded Florence, 840 ft. below and three mi. away, but proof is lacking. Originally Etruscan, Fiesole was under Roman domination before 225 B.C. It received Roman citizenship in 90 B.C. and a colony of Romans in 80 B.C. This Romanized town became headquarters for Catiline's military operations against the Roman government (63–62 B.C.). Although a bishopric and still a strong fortress during Belisarius' campaign against the Goths (6th century A.D.), Fiesole dwindled into insignificance in medieval times as Florence burgeoned. Its antiquities include town walls and a vaulted subterranean cistern (both Etruscan), a temple (Etrusco-Roman), a theater and baths (both Roman), an 11th-century Romanesque Cathedral, and a Franciscan church and convent.

FIFE or FIFESHIRE, county of eastern Scotland, forming a peninsula between the Forth and Tay estuaries. The Cleish and Lomond hills provide upland grazings, but the greater part of the county is excellent arable land; dairy cattle are also kept and seed potatoes are a specialty in the north and east. In the west and south is an important coal field, centered in Cowdenbeath, Lochgelly, Glenrothes, and Methil. Once one of the most important regions of Scotland, and still referred to as the "Kingdom" of Fife, the county has a remarkable number of small towns, many of these seaports and royal burghs. Dunfermline and Kirkcaldy are large industrial towns, known for linen and linoleum respectively; St. Andrews is a university town and resort, famous for its golf. Among the small coastal towns, Crail, Pittenweem, St. Monance, and Culross are particularly well-preserved examples of 16th- and 17th-century burghs; Culross is largely preserved by the National Trust for Scotland. The shire dates from the 15th century. Area, 505 sq. mi.; pop., 325,000.

H. A. MOISLEY, The University, Glasgow, Scotland

FIFE, ancient form of the transverse, or cross, flute, widely used in the late Middle Ages. Of cylindrical shape, with six finger-holes, it was mainly employed as a military instrument. In the 16th century the extremely narrow bore of the fife, which caused a shrill sound, was gradually enlarged so that the instrument could be utilized in regular musical composition.

FIFTH COLUMN, term for those who contribute to the destruction of a country from within. It was first used during the Spanish Civil War to describe Nationalist agents within Loyalist Madrid (1936). General Emilio Mola spoke of four columns marching on the city and of a fifth column that would rise up within the city itself. The term now broadly applies to enemy agents who may spy, sabotage, or agitate, and also to those who aid the enemy by spreading his propaganda.

FIFTH MONARCHY MEN, in English history, a fanatical millenarian sect that arose among Anabaptists during the English Civil War. The Fifth Monarchy Men anticipated a fulfillment of Biblical prophecy through the establishment on earth of the rule of Christ and the saints as successors to the Assyrian, Persian, Macedonian, and Roman empires. Some held that they ought to hasten events by forcibly destroying the remnants of the existing order. A group of these led by Thomas Venner plotted a rising (1657), which was frustrated by discovery, and attempted a second (1661), which proved abortive. Others counseled a passive role, seeing society as divinely destined for destruction at an appointed time.

FIFTH REPUBLIC, in French history, regime that succeeded the Fourth Republic, brought down by disorders in Algeria in May, 1958. Its constitution, written under the direction of Gen. Charles de Gaulle, sought to remedy the Cabinet instability chronic under the Third and Fourth Republics by drastically cutting the power of the legislature and greatly increasing the power of the executive, both President and Premier. The nation ratified the constitution in a referendum in Sept., 1958, and shortly afterward De Gaulle was elected President.

FIG, common name for several trees of the genus *Ficus* in the Moraceae, or mulberry family, but referring especially to the botanical varieties of *F. carica*, the edible fig. This species is native to the Mediterranean region and has been successfully introduced into many of the warmer regions of the world. The tree is densely branched, has large, lobed leaves, and grows to a height of from 15 to 30 ft. The fleshy "fruit" of the fig tree is actually a hollow receptacle (a syncarp) within which the flowers develop. The true fruit are the "seeds" that line the syncarp. Fruit formation depends on pollination of the syncarp by a small insect, the fig wasp, whose larvae develop only in the fruit of the wild Capri fig (*F. carica* var. *sylvestris*). For this reason some Capri fig trees are always planted in stands where other varieties are grown. Figs have been grown for over 5,000 years in the Near East and Mediterranean region. They were introduced into California during the 18th century by Spanish missionaries, and since that time have been extensively cultivated there and along the Gulf Coast of Texas. Fig trees do well in many kinds of soil but require very warm summer temperatures and cannot tolerate prolonged freezing.

CLARENCE J. HYLANDER,
Author, *The World of Plant Life*

See also POLLINATION.

FIGHTING FISH, common name for a popular aquarium fish, *Betta splendens,* in the family Anabantidae, native to Thailand. In the natural state it is a dull-colored creature of retiring disposition, but has been domesticated and cultivated for over 100 years. This has resulted in greater size, exotic coloration, and enhanced fighting qualities. Females may be kept together, but males will fight and tear each other's fins.
See also FISH, TROPICAL.

FIGURATE [fĭg′ yər-ĭt] **NUMBERS,** system of expressing numbers as geometrical arrangements of dots. Thus 1, 3, 6, and 10 are the first four triangular numbers; and 1, 4, 9, and 16, the first four square numbers. Figurate numbers were originated by the earliest Pythagoreans and form a link between geometry and numbers.

FIGURES OF SPEECH are departures from the normal construction or meaning of language in order to achieve freshness of expression, description through analogy, or the revelation of similarities in seemingly dissimilar things. Figures of speech are of two kinds: tropes (literally "turns"), in which the words undergo a change in meaning; and figures of thought, in which the words retain their literal meaning but their usual rhetorical pattern is changed. The principal tropes are the simile, an explicit comparison between two things ("he is as strong as a lion"); the metaphor, in which two objects are compared by identification or by substitution of one for the other ("he is a lion in strength"); synecdoche, a kind of metaphor in which a part represents the whole; metonymy, a kind of metaphor in which the name of one object or idea is substituted for another with which it is closely associated; personification, in which an inanimate object or an abstraction is given human characteristics; pun, a play on words that have identical or nearly identical sounds but different meanings; hyperbole, which is a conscious and extravagant exaggeration of fact for effect. Among the important "figures of thought" are paradox, in which a statement that appears to be contradictory is assumed to be true; apostrophe, a sudden shift to direct address; rhetorical question, a question asked for emphasis rather than to elicit a reply; irony, which implies attitudes or judgments different from those directly expressed; antithesis, a balancing of one term against another for emphasis or rhetorical effect.

C. HUGH HOLMAN, University of North Carolina

See also IRONY; METAPHOR; PUN; SIMILE.

FIGWORT, common name for a botanical family, Scrophulariaceae, of flowering herbs, shrubs, and small trees of world-wide distribution. Members of the family include such well-known garden plants as foxglove (*Digitalis*) and snapdragon (*Antirrhinum*), the popular greenhouse flower *Calceolaria,* and the Kenilworth ivy (*Cymbalaria*). The plants specifically known as figworts belong to the genus *Scrophularia,* which consists of about 150 species of annual and perennial herbs of the north temperate region. Figworts are tall, erect plants and have a strong, unpleasant odor. The small flowers are borne in loose branching clusters and may be greenish-purple, purple, or yellow. Most species are too weedy for use as ornamentals.

FIJI [fē′ jē] **ISLANDS,** independent member of the Commonwealth of Nations, situated in the southwest Pacific Ocean, about 1,200 mi. north of New Zealand.

The Land. The country is made up of some 300 islands, most of which are of volcanic origin. The major ones are mountainous—Viti Levu, the largest island, rises to 4,341 ft.—and hot springs still attest to volcanic activity. Many of the smaller islands, such as the Lau group, are made of coral and limestone. The Fijis have a tropical climate, pleasantly influenced by the prevailing southeast trade winds. About half the total area of 7,036 sq. mi. is covered with forests, but there are also grasslands, and the soil is generally fertile.

The People. Only 80 of the islands are inhabited. Some 53% of the population of nearly 500,000 are descendants of workers brought from India to help cultivate sugarcane. The native Fijians, a Melanesian, dark-skinned, athletic people with bushy hair, make up about 42%. The remainder are of British, Chinese, Polynesian, or Micronesian origin. The principal products are sugarcane, coconuts, rice, and bananas. A number of sawmills are operated, and there is also goldmining and a variety of light industries. The largest city is Suva on Viti Levu. It is the capital, commercial center, and principal port of the islands. The University of the South Pacific, the first in the South Seas, was opened here in 1968.

History and Government. The Fijis were discovered by Tasman in 1643. After some bloody internal wars the islands were annexed and pacified by England in 1874. The British then developed large sugar plantations and thus launched commercial agriculture. The Fijians, however, always retained some measure of self-government, and this was gradually increased before and after World War II. Independence was achieved on Oct. 10, 1970.

RALPH A. HLADIK, Chicago State College

Fiji Islanders in a semiannual communal fishing drive. (ANI)

FILARIASIS [fĭl-ə-rī′ə-sĭs], infection by one or more species of threadlike roundworms. Infection begins when the worm larvae are deposited in the skin by infected insects. They mature in the human body where they produce pain, swelling, and other disturbances.

Wuchereria bancrofti is the most important filarial parasite. It is carried by several varieties of mosquitoes. The organisms tend to collect in the lymph glands and in the lymphatic vessels which conduct fluid from the body tissues. The worms may produce an inflammatory reaction with fever, chills, headache, vomiting, and localized areas of redness and swelling on the arms and legs. The filaria may obstruct the lymph vessels, causing massive swelling of the arms, legs, or other parts of the body, a condition known as elephantiasis.

Loa loa (African eye worm) is limited to west and central Africa. The adult worms migrate throughout the body. The worms may pass immediately under the skin of the face and the covering of the eye (the conjunctiva), causing considerable pain, irritation, swelling and congestion. Characteristic swellings (calabar), sometimes approaching the size of a hen's egg, are seen in the skin, particularly on the wrists and arms. The worm is carried by the mango fly.

Onchocerca volvulus is found in Africa and certain parts of Central and South America. The worms frequently invade the eye and sometimes cause blindness.

Filarial infestations can often be diagnosed by examining the peripheral blood or urine for the presence of the small microfilarias, the prelarval form of the worms. A remarkable feature of some of the infections is that the microfilarias appear in the peripheral blood only at night.

The microfilarias may be destroyed by the drug diethylcarbamazine (Hetrazan). Surgery is often required to relieve the swellings seen in elephantiasis and to remove adult worms from the eye or worm-infested nodules from under the skin.

HAROLD TUCKER, M.D.

See also ELEPHANTIASIS; ONCHOCERCIASIS.

FILBERT. *See* HAZELNUT.

FILENE [fĭ-lēn′], **EDWARD ALBERT** (1860–1937), American merchant. Born in Salem, Mass., Albert Filene with his brother Lincoln (1865–1957) pioneered in scientific management and progressive labor relations, and brought William Filene and Sons Company, Boston, to prominence in the retail merchandising field. He was chairman of the War Shipping Committee in World War I, helped organize the Boston Chamber of Commerce and U.S. Chamber of Commerce, and founded the Twentieth Century Fund. Lincoln Filene succeeded him as president of Filene's, expanded the firm into a specialty chain, Federated Department Stores, Inc., and in the 1930's became an adviser to the U.S. government.

FILIBUSTER [fĭl′ə-bŭs-tər], in parliamentary tactics, a device used particularly in the U.S. Senate to frustrate the passage of measures strongly opposed by a minority. Under Senate rules debate is unlimited unless two-thirds of the Senators present vote to close debate (cloture). Thus an intransigent minority can prolong debate indefinitely and thereby indefinitely postpone action on the measure to which they are opposed. The "debate" may consist of reading books or articles aloud, demanding a roll call of the Senate, or making speeches on almost any subject; and it may be carried out by a group of Senators taking turns at speaking. The simple threat of a filibuster is sometimes sufficient to prevent passage of a measure or keep it from coming before the Senate for a vote. While the Southern Senators have frequently used the filibuster or threat of filibuster to forestall certain kinds of civil rights legislation, they are by no means alone in their employment of the tactic. Northern liberals like Robert M. LaFollette, Sr., and Wayne Morse have established records by maintaining the floor for many continuous hours in efforts to prevent Senate action. Over the years a number of efforts have been made to alter the Senate rules so that a simple majority could vote to close debate. But these efforts have failed, at least in part because of the pride taken by most Senators in the free debate traditional in the Senate.

STUART GERRY BROWN, Syracuse University

FILIBUSTERING EXPEDITIONS, in U.S. history a term applied to groups of adventurers, Westerners, soldiers of fortune, and freebooters, who made armed incursions into Spanish Texas, Latin America, and the Caribbean in the 19th century. Aaron Burr might be considered the first prominent leader, and his failure was an omen of the future. Dozens of expeditions were attempted and failed in Texas between 1807 and 1830. The expeditions of Narciso López against Cuba in 1850–51, and those led by William Walker against Sonora, Mexico, in 1853–54 and against Nicaragua in 1855–58, were the best known. These and other self-appointed liberators and leaders of "manifest destiny" caused foreign governments to distrust the United States. Following Walker's capture by the British navy and his subsequent execution by the Honduran government in 1860, filibustering never again regained its former importance. The growing sense of maturity and responsibility of the U.S. government gradually made such behavior insupportable.

W. EUGENE HOLLON, University of Toledo

FILIGREE [fĭl′ə-grē], decorative work in fine wire. Filigree, now chiefly confined to jewelry, is made by bending, arranging, and soldering gold or silver wire with beads or platelets to form delicate designs. The technique has an ancient history, having been practiced by the Etruscans of the 6th century B.C., the Hellenistic Greeks, and the Romans. Ecclesiastical vessels of the Middle Ages were richly jeweled between areas of filigree, Bernward's Chalice at Hildesheim being a significant example. Benvenuto Cellini has left a description of the process as practiced in the 16th century. In China under the Manchus (1644–1912) filigree headdress or bracelets might represent a bride's dowry. The silver wire was gilded and shaped into a complexity of floral and animal patterns interspersed with colored stones. The city of Cuttack in India has produced some handsome filigree jewelry, and Malta and Portugal have long been noted for their filigree work.

JEFFERSON T. WARREN, The John Woodman Higgins Armory

FILIPINO. *See* PHILIPPINE PEOPLES.

Library of Congress

Fillmore presides as Senate debates Fugitive Slave Law

Library of Congress

Abigail Powers Fillmore

MILLARD FILLMORE

13th PRESIDENT OF THE UNITED STATES

1850-1853

Perry departs on mission to Japan, Nov., 1852

FILLMORE, MILLARD (1800–74), 13th President of the United States (1850–53). Born in Locke, N.Y., he had little formal schooling, but he read law in his spare time and was admitted to the bar in 1823. He opened his own law office and became active in politics. Under the patronage of Thurlow Weed, the leader of the Anti-Masonic party, Fillmore was elected to the New York state legislature (1828) and to the U.S. House of Representatives (1833). Later he followed Weed into the Whig party and, as a Whig, served three consecutive terms in Congress (1837–43). He belonged to the Whig faction led by Henry Clay, although he maintained an independent attitude on several issues. As chairman of the House Ways and Means Committee (1840), he was chiefly responsible for the high protective tariff passed in 1842.

Fillmore failed to secure the vice presidential nomination in 1844 and became the Whig candidate for Governor of New York. Unsuccessful because of a party split over the slavery issue, he attributed his defeat to the "Abolitionists and foreign Catholics." Three years later he was elected New York state comptroller. His staunch support of Henry Clay helped gain him the Whig nomination for Vice President (1848) on the ticket with Zachary Taylor. Elected, he succeeded to the presidency in 1850 upon Taylor's death.

The new President believed in upholding a middle-of-the-road policy, a course he had consistently pursued while presiding over the Senate as Vice President. He was a persistent advocate of compromise in closing the widening gap between North and South. His principal domestic achievement was the Compromise of 1850. The leading feature of this controversial legislation was the Fugitive Slave Law, which required the return of escaped Negro slaves to their owners. Unmoved by the harsh criticism of the abolitionists, Fillmore spared no effort in enforcing the unpopular law. But bitter feelings about the measure helped destroy the Whigs as a powerful national party.

During Fillmore's administration Matthew C. Perry was selected to negotiate a treaty opening Japan to American trade. When Perry sailed in 1852 he carried with him a letter from President Fillmore to the Emperor of Japan containing proposals for an agreement. The success of Perry's mission proved to be one of the most significant diplomatic developments of the 19th century.

At the Whig convention in 1852 Fillmore had the cordial support of the Southern Whigs, but he was unable to muster enough backing among the Northerners. The nomination went to Gen. Winfield Scott, an avowed enemy of slavery. Fillmore abandoned the disintegrating Whig party for the American, or Know-Nothing, party, hoping thereby to save the Union. In 1856 he accepted its nomination for the presidency, and in his campaign he stressed the value of moderation and the dangers of sectionalism. He ran a poor third in the election, winning but one state. Retiring from active politics, he retained a keen interest in the issues of the day and devoted himself to many educational and civic enterprises. He opposed Abraham Lincoln's administration in its conduct of the Civil War and supported the Reconstruction policy of President Andrew Johnson.

Fillmore was a large man who made an impressive platform appearance. His personal manner was gracious and kindly. Though not an outstanding President, his honesty and integrity were unquestioned. He was married twice. His first wife, Abigail Powers, died in 1853, and five years later he married a widow, Mrs. Caroline McIntosh.

Consult Rayback, R. J., *Millard Fillmore: Biography of a President* (1959).

JAMES P. SHENTON, Columbia University

FILM, PHOTOGRAPHIC. *See* PHOTOGRAPHY.

FILMER, SIR ROBERT (d.1653), English political theorist. Filmer is noted for his strenuous defense of the right of Kings to rule. In his *Patriarcha* (published posthumously in 1680) and other writings, he traced the origins of government to the patriarchal organization of families and tribes. He maintained that Kings rule as fathers over their families. Their right to rule is by "nature," by the will of God, and by inheritance, not by the consent of the governed. Although he derived many of his ideas from Thomas Hobbes (1588–1679), he attacked Hobbes' theory that sovereignty is established by a contractual agreement among the people. The Tories espoused Filmer's theories after his death; his views, however, have endured largely because of John Locke's criticism of them.

FILTER, ELECTRIC, combination of components used in electric circuits to discriminate between frequency bands, thus permitting one group of frequencies to pass through while rejecting others. Filters are classified as low-pass filters, which allow the lower frequencies to pass through while rejecting or attenuating the higher frequencies; high-pass filters, which pass high frequencies and reject low frequencies; and band-pass filters, which allow a band of frequencies to pass through while attenuating all frequencies that are below or above the desired band.

Most filters consist of coils and capacitors connected in a circuit designed to provide the desired frequency selectivity. Four terminals are provided, a pair for the input signal and a pair for the output.

Band-pass filters are used in radio receivers to select the band of frequencies corresponding to the desired program. Low- and high-pass filters are often used in high-fidelity loudspeaker systems to direct the low frequencies to one speaker and the high frequencies to another.

WILLIAM C. VERGARA, Bendix Corporation

FILTERING MEDIA. A filtering medium is a barrier that cleans a fluid stream by mechanically blocking dirt particles and thus allowing only a pure fluid to pass. Broadly, there are two types of mechanical filtering media—surface and depth. In the surface media filters, dirt is removed by a plane surface with fairly uniform orifices such as wire mesh, membrane, or simple edge-types. Depth media filters depend upon a rigorous path the fluid must pass in order to remove impediments. These filters include paper, felt, glass fiber, sintered powders, matted wool, and wound spools.

Filters can be made in almost any desirable form, including cartridges, wadding, sheets, and beds. Absolute performance is measured by a minimum particle size positively blocked by the filter. A woven fibrous cloth, for example, will block all particles larger than 25 microns (1

micron equals approximately 1/25,000 in.). A fritted glass porous-plug filter will stop particles larger than a fraction of a micron. Flow rates and allowable pressures are determined by the physical construction of the filter support and not so much by the filtering media themselves.

FRANKLIN D. YEAPLE, TEF Engineering Company

FILTRATION, process of separating a solid from a liquid or a gas. The solid is held on a supporting material that has fine pores, through which the liquid or gaseous filtrate can pass. Various types of supporting materials, or filter media, are used. Paper is the most common for small-scale filtration, although other materials such as porous porcelain, glass wool, sintered or fritted glass powder, asbestos fibers on a metal screen, or porous metals prepared by sintering may be used. Vacuum filtration is frequently used both in the laboratory and industry. Ultrafiltration is a process in which minute particles, such as bacteria, are filtered through media, such as porcelain, which have extremely fine pores.

For large-scale filtration, cloth or canvas is frequently used as the medium, and the liquid is forced by pressure through the bed of solid that collects. A common method of large-scale filtration is the purification of water by collecting suspended matter on a bed composed of coarse gravel covered with finer layers of sand. The water sinks through the gravel and is run off by gravity. Cake filters, rotary drum filters, filter presses, and systems of baffles and screens are common adaptations of the principle for special commercial needs.

HERBERT A. LAITINEN, University of Illinois

FINANCE. *See* BANKS AND BANKING; BUSINESS; CREDIT; PUBLIC FINANCE.

FINBACK WHALE, large marine mammal, *Balaenoptera physalus*, in the suborder Mysticeti of toothless, or whalebone, whales. The finback has a long, tapering body, a wedge-shaped head, and grows to a length of 80 ft. Finbacks occur in all seas and are commonly seen in western Atlantic waters. The roof of the finback's mouth is equipped with many frayed plates of baleen that serve to strain out the planktonic shrimp on which the whale feeds. *See also* WHALE; WHALING.

FINCH, group name of many members of the songbird family Fringillidae. Certain other birds, resembling them superficially, are likewise called finches. Finches eat seeds and fruit. They usually have a rather conical bill and nine primaries (flight feathers on the outer part of the wing). They are considered among the most recently evolved group of birds. From the typical shape the bill varies to the heavy structure of grosbeaks, used to crack hard seeds, and to the crossed mandibles of crossbills, used to extract seeds from pine cones.

Most authors include the subfamilies Fringillinae and Carduelinae in the family. The former includes the Old World chaffinch and brambling. The Carduelinae, a large group of somewhat frugivorous (fruit-eating), mainly arboreal, birds, often with red or bright yellow, includes the Old World goldfinches and greenfinches; canaries and serins; bullfinches; hawfinches; northern redpolls and linnets; siskins and American goldfinches; purple, rose, and house finches; crossbills; and the evening grosbeak and its allies. Most American authors also consider as members of the Fringillidae the Old World buntings and New World sparrows (Emberizinae), and the New World cardinal-grosbeaks (Cardinalinae). The Galápagos, or Darwin's, finches (Geospizinae) are probably closely allied to these American groups. Many finches are excellent songsters, and this, combined with the colorful plumage of some species, makes them favorites in aviculture.

Eugene Eisenmann, *American Museum of Natural History*

FINDLAY, city of northwestern Ohio and seat of Hancock County. It has varied manufactures and was formerly the center of a large oil and gas field. Findlay College (estab., 1882) is located here. Settled, 1821; inc., 1838; pop., 35,800.

FINE ARTS, a term generally used to distinguish the major arts, particularly painting, sculpture, and architecture, from the minor decorative, or applied, arts. It is commonly used in its French form, *beaux arts*. Supposedly in the fine arts the aesthetic qualities such as composition, expression, and decoration dominate or even exclude practical or utilitarian considerations, whereas the converse is true in the minor arts. Such a distinction is nebulous at best and may be misleading. It is quite possible for a Persian rug, a Chinese vase, or a Hepplewhite chair to have as fine aesthetic quality as a painting, a work of sculpture, or a building. However, the aesthetic scope of the fine arts is less limited than that of the applied arts. The term sometimes includes literature, music, dancing, and acting.

FINE ARTS, UNITED STATES COMMISSION OF, an agency of the U.S. government established in 1910. Its purposes are to give advice on aesthetic questions to other agencies of the government and to oversee the development of the National Capital district of Washington. The various agencies which are responsible for parks, public buildings, and other facilities in Washington are required to obtain the approval of their plans by the Commission of Fine Arts before proceeding. The seven members, chosen for their qualifications as judges of art, are appointed by the President and serve without pay for terms of four years.

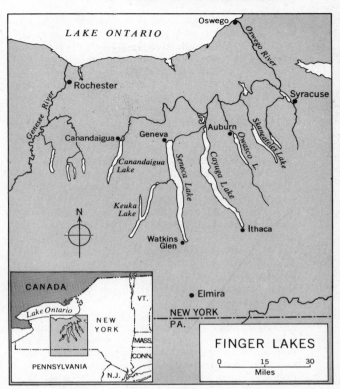

FINGER LAKES, group of long, narrow, north-south-oriented glacial lakes on the northern edge of the Allegheny Plateau in west-central New York. West to east they are Conesus, Hemlock, Canadice, Honeoye, Canandaigua, Keuka, Seneca, Cayuga, Owasco, Skaneateles, and Otisco. They occupy stream valleys that were considerably modified by continental glaciation during the Ice Age. Glaciers deepened the lake basins and deposited moraines across their southern ends, thus impounding the water. There is no satisfactory explanation for the depths below sea level (up to 180 ft.) of some of the lake basins.

FINGERPRINTING, the procedure of recording and comparing impressions of the lines and patterns on the inner

Examples of the three categories of fingerprint patterns.

PLAIN ARCH

PLAIN WHORL

LOOP

An expert uses a soft brush and powder to discover fingerprints.

Fingerprinting can be done quickly and easily (*above*).

The FBI stores the world's largest collection of fingerprints.
(FEDERAL BUREAU OF INVESTIGATION)

FINLAND

surface of the last joint of a thumb or finger. There are three categories of print patterns: arch, loop, and whorl.

In 1823 J. E. Purkinje cited the diversity of patterns and made the first attempt to classify fingerprints. Sir William Herschel (1833–1917) was first to use fingerprints as a means of civil and criminal identification. Sir Henry Faulds (1843–1930) published in 1880 the first article on the use of fingerprints for criminal identification.

The modern system is based mainly on the work of Sir Francis Galton (1822–1911) who established the uniqueness, indestructibility, and immutability of fingerprints. His system, elaborated by Sir Edward Henry (1850–1931), was adopted by Scotland Yard in 1889 and is now used in all English-speaking countries. A modified form of the Henry System was introduced at Sing Sing prison in New York state in 1903. The system was adopted by the federal government at the federal prison in Leavenworth, Kansas, in 1904.

The procedure is simple and the apparatus inexpensive. Printer's ink is rolled onto a metal or glass sheet or block with a rubber-covered roller. The fingers are thoroughly cleaned of grease, inked, and the impression is made on a fingerprint blank.

During World War I, the U.S. government fingerprinted members of the armed forces. This practice led to the use of the method by the Civil Service Commission and other agencies and organizations. Many states have established identification bureaus, and the U.S. Federal Bureau of Investigation in Washington, D.C., has more than 150 million sets of prints on file.

Consult Spatz, J. W., *The Science of Fingerprinting* (1946); Browne, D. G., and Brock, A. S., *Fingerprints: Fifty Years of Scientific Crime Detection* (1953).

JOSEPH S. ROUCEK, University of Bridgeport
See also CRIME DETECTION.

FINIAN'S RAINBOW, musical play, with music by Burton Lane; lyrics by E. Y. Harburg; book by Harburg and Fred Saidy; New York première, Jan. 10, 1947. The book was a combination of Irish whimsy and social commentary, with its musical score adding greatly to the atmosphere of lightness and fantasy. The theme is brotherly love and the locale is Rainbow Valley, Missitucky, where Finian McLonergan has come to plant a crock of gold that he has stolen from a leprechaun.

FINISTERRE [fin-is-târ'], **CAPE,** rocky promontory of extreme northwestern Spain, on the Atlantic coast in La Coruña Province. Its name derives from Lat. *finis terrae*, "land's end."

FINK, MIKE (1770?–1822), American frontier hero. A keelboatman on the Missouri and Ohio rivers, he was also a backwoodsman, Indian fighter, rifleman, and teller of tall tales about his own prodigious powers. When steamboats superseded flatboats, he became a trapper and joined fur trader William Ashley on his first expedition. He is said to have died in a wilderness gunfight. Much of the American folklore of exaggeration derives from roistering frontier characters like Fink.

Consult Blair, Walter, and Meine, F. J., *Mike Fink, King of the Mississippi Keelboatmen* (1933).

AREA	Approx. 130,120 sq. mi.
ELEVATION	
Highest point (Mount Haltia; Finn. Haltiatunturi)	4,343 ft.
Lowest point	Sea level
POPULATION	Approx. 4,497,000
PRINCIPAL LANGUAGES	Finnish, Swedish
LIFE EXPECTANCY	Approx. 66 years
PERCENTAGE OF LITERACY	More than 99%
UNIT OF CURRENCY	Markka
NATIONAL ANTHEM	*Maamme* ("Our Land"), words by J. L. Runeberg, music by F. Pacius
CAPITAL	Helsinki
PRINCIPAL PRODUCTS	Barley, oats, hay, potatoes; copper, iron, zinc; food products, light machinery, textiles, wood products

FINLAND [fin'lənd] (Finn. **SUOMI**), a republic of northern Europe extending about 720 mi., from north to south, with the U.S.S.R. as its eastern neighbor. One-fourth of Finland lies north of the Arctic Circle. There are numerous coastal islands, especially in the southwest, the Åland Island archipelago being the largest.

The Land

Physical Features. The terrain is mainly lowland around the western and southern coasts, and, farther inland, moderate plateau (400–600 ft.). This rises to the Scandinavian highland in the north. The highest peak is Mount Haltia (4,343 ft.), on the Finnish-Norwegian frontier. The Kemi, the Oulu, the Kymi, and the Vuoksi are the largest river systems; some 55,000 lakes, most of them small, constitute about 10% of the country's area. Narrow strips of land, often tree-covered, wind across the waters, sometimes creating involved lake systems like the Saimaa. More than one-fifth of the country consists of marsh and moor, and lichen-covered upland. There is some tundra in the north.

Climate. On Finland's northeastern frontier, arctic sub-zero temperatures may be encountered in winter. The country as a whole, however, has a surprisingly moderate climate for such a northerly latitude. This is partly due to the extensive forest and marsh cover; also, westerly winds, warmed by the Gulf Stream, prevail in Finland for much of the year. Average temperatures in February are 7° F($-14°$ C) in the north and 24° F($-4°$ C) in the south; and in July, 56° F($13°$ C) and 62° F($17°$ C). Average annual rainfall in the north is 16 in (41 cm) and in the south roughly twice that amount. Only in the southwest does snow fall for less than 90 days a year; Lapland has snow for about three-fifths of the year. Coastal waters freeze, and in severe winters only Helsinki and, perhaps, one other port, Turku, in the south can be kept open with icebreakers.

Natural Resources, Vegetation, and Wildlife. Finland's greatest natural resource is forest, which covers some 70% of the country, the highest percentage in Europe. Over half the stand is pine, over one-fourth spruce; birch ranks third, growing mainly in the north. Leaf trees are fairly common in the south, notably oak, with some ash and hazel. Finland's principal mineral resource is copper, and there are lesser quantities of iron, zinc, silver, and nickel, although the largest nickel deposits lay in the area ceded to the U.S.S.R. in 1947.

In the forests of the north the bear, the wolf, and the lemming are still encountered, but the arctic fox and the reindeer are disappearing. Mosquitoes swarm over the northern marshes, and wild geese and swans frequent many waters. Hedgehogs are plentiful, and seal are hunted in the coastal waters.

The People

The Finnish Character. The northern part of Finland has continuous daylight for several weeks during the short but brilliant summer, and during midwinter, an equally long period of darkness. Stamina and other qualities of the frontiersman are needed, therefore. Finnish athletes have

Pix, Inc.

A ship steams past a wooded island off the coast of Finland.

excelled in such sports as long-distance running and skiing. Endurance is called for on the national level, too, for Finland is strategically situated, and has been an area of contention between Muscovite and Swede over the centuries. The country defends itself with a sense of commitment to the Western, or Latin, tradition. To Finland, it seems, has fallen the historic task of defending the northeastern bastion of that heritage.

Ethnology. Most of the national stock is composed of Finns, but there is also a small but important Swedish element. Swedish infiltration began about the 12th century and led to the virtual integration of Finland into the Swedish realm. This domination lasted until the early 19th century, during which time Swedes supplied the core of political, social, and economic leadership. Swedish settlements were concentrated in coastal areas, particularly around Vaasa and Helsinki. In 1880 the Swede-Finn con-

Finland has been called the northeastern bastion of the Western powers. Its location makes it both a buffer and a bridge between the Scandinavian countries and the Soviet Union. Finland, which formed part of Sweden for centuries, was ceded to Russia in 1809 and declared its independence in 1917. Following World War II Finland had the difficult task of maintaining independence and coexisting with the U.S.S.R. The nature of Finland's situation is discussed in the article on these pages, which surveys the geography, people, economy, government, and history of the country. Many articles in the present Encyclopedia supplement this main entry.

The article EUROPE provides the continental setting in which Finland is placed, and SCANDINAVIA describes the cultural, political, and ethnological area adjacent to Finland. Geographical features of Finland such as ALAND ISLANDS OR AHVENANMAA, PORKKALA PENINSULA, BOTHNIA, GULF OF and FINLAND, GULF OF receive separate treatment, as do important cities such as TURKU, HELSINKI and TAMPERE. Parts of northern Finland have the characteristics described in TUNDRA.

Finland has long been a bilingual nation, with FINNISH and SWEDISH as the principal languages. Finnish belongs to the FINNO-UGRIC LANGUAGES subfamily. The Lapps in the north speak Lappish. FINNISH LITERATURE notes the influence of both Finnish and Swedish traditions. KALEVALA describes the national epic. LUTHERANISM deals with the established religion. Many Finns have contributed to both national and world culture, including the poet Johan Ludvig RUNEBERG and the anthropolo-

gist and philosopher Edward Alexander WESTERMARCK. Frans Eemil SILLANPAA won the Nobel Prize for literature in 1939 and Artturi Ilmari VIRTANEN won it for biochemistry in 1945. The composer Jean SIBELIUS made great contributions to the world of music and paid lasting tribute to his homeland in his tone poem *Finlandia*. The contributions of Finnish architects like Eliel SAARINEN are noted in the article ARCHITECTURE, MODERN.

The climate and the historic problems of Finland have required that the people show stamina and endurance. They have fought the cold and the Swedes and the Russians. Aspects of their history are provided in the history sections of articles on their neighbors, SWEDEN and UNION OF SOVIET SOCIALIST REPUBLICS. Finland's defeat in the RUSSO-FINNISH WAR (1939-40) and loss of extensive territories caused it to join Germany in the campaign against the Soviet Union. Defeated again, Finland resorted to force to expel German troops toward the end of WORLD WAR II. The Finnish army was led by Baron von MANNERHEIM, who became a national hero and was elected President of Finland. Väinö Alfred TANNER led the Social Democrats and rallied the anti-Communist forces in Finland.

Many articles conclude with lists of selected books through which the reader can extend his study of Finland. These and other sources may be available in the library. To keep abreast of economic and social developments and political events that occur from year to year, the reader can consult such sources as the annual supplement to this Encyclopedia.

Preparing to milk a reindeer cow, a Lapp herder of the far north ropes it and ties it to a tree stump. (WERNER BISCHOF—MAGNUM)

Expert with a lasso, a Lapp ropes a reindeer out of the herd. (PIX, INC.)

stituted some 14% of the population, but subsequently declined to about 8%. Until the mid-19th century the language of culture and public life was Swedish, but the use of Finnish increased despite public debate against it. A separate political party continues to represent the Swede-Finn interest. The population of the Åland Islands is almost entirely Swedish in background and was accorded special guarantees after World War I, partly because of the islands' strategic importance. Small minorities in Finland include about 2,500 Lapps, some of them still nomadic, and a scattering of gypsies. (*See* FINNO-UGRIC LANGUAGES.)

Population and Chief Cities. Finland's annual rate of population increase is only slightly over 1% and density of population is rather low, approaching 35 persons per square mile. Much settlement in the north is of fairly recent date, and the southern half of the country has six-sevenths of the inhabitants. About one-fourth of the population is urban, the largest city being the capital, Helsinki. Other important cities are Turku (Åbo) and Tampere.

Religion. The established church of Finland is the Evangelical Lutheran, to which about 96% of the population belongs. The Archbishop of Turku serves as Primate, although a number of Swedish parishes are under the leadership of the Bishop of Borgå. Laymen are well represented in the Ecclesiastical Congress which meets every five years. The government appoints the higher clergy and supports religious instruction in public schools. Local parishes enjoy wide autonomy. Minority groups, which enjoy freedom of worship, include Finland's Free Church, Jehovah's Witnesses, and certain Adventist bodies. There is a relatively large Greek Orthodox community, whose Archbishop has his see at Kuopio. Most of the small Jewish population lives in Helsinki.

Education. Literacy is almost universal, with eight years of compulsory education, though instruction may be pri-

vate. After four or six years of primary schooling pupils may shift to junior secondary schools for five or three years. This stage includes some practical courses and the beginning of at least one foreign language. Many students then proceed to higher secondary education or to vocational training.

Adult education in Finland is promoted by more than 80 folk high schools and folk academies and as many workers' institutes. Advanced technical instruction is available in colleges of forestry, agriculture, navigation, and business. Helsinki has the oldest university, founded in 1640 at Turku, and transferred in 1827. Later two new universities were opened at Turku, one Finnish speaking (1922) and the other Swedish speaking (1918). Finland has an extensive public library system.

Cultural Life. Swedish was for many years the language of culture, and even scholars and writers of Finnish background used Swedish as their medium. The naturalist Peter Kalm, who left a lively description of his visit to North America in the 18th century, brought early renown to his country. Three generations later, this was enhanced by the epic poet, J. L. Runeberg. By the second half of the 19th century, however, at about the time of the appearance of the great national epic *Kalevala*, compiled by

Two Finnish farm children are delighted with a friendly colt. (WERNER BISCHOF—MAGNUM)

Tuberculosis Sanatorium in Paimio, designed by Alvar Aalto, one of Finland's most influential architects.

Ducks and sea gulls congregate in winter in the frozen square in front of Helsinki's city hall (*left*).

Elias Lönnrot, the Finnish language began to assert itself; the novelists F. E. Sillanpää and Mika Waltari, and the anthropologist E. A. Westermarck were among those who brought international renown to Finnish letters in the 20th century. There is much local dramatic activity, and both painting and sculpture are widely cultivated. Finland has also made a significant contribution to architecture in the works of Alvar Aalto, and of Eliel Saarinen and his son Eero. The country's rich heritage of folk music has influenced its musical tradition. Choral singing is popular, and both the opera and the state orchestra in Helsinki maintain high musical standards. An academy of music appropriately bears the name of the country's most illustrious composer, Jean Sibelius.

The Economy

Agriculture and Forestry. Less than 9% of Finland's area is cultivated and even this includes much hay and meadowland. A short growing season further limits the growing of crops—the most important of which are oats, followed by barley. Yields of wheat and rye are not adequate for domestic consumption. The chief root crops are potatoes and sugar beets. The better farm lands lie on the coastal plains and are often interspersed among semi-wooded tracts. Though some large holdings remain in the southwest, farms are generally of modest size. Mechanization has begun. Dairying is sufficiently extensive to allow for the export of butter and cheese. Beef cattle are also raised, as well as smaller numbers of sheep and hogs. Nearly 45% of the population is employed in farming, forestry, or fishing. Many farmers are also engaged in forestry, the most important single sector of the economy. More than half of the forest lands are in private hands, owned chiefly by individual farmers. About one-third is publicly owned, principally by the central government, and most of the remainder is controlled by companies.

Industry. Finland's industrial expansion was underway by the end of the 19th century. Despite heavy losses of power facilities to the U.S.S.R. after World War II, the production of electricity, mostly from water power, has in-

creased rapidly. The mining industry is also growing and produces considerable quantities of copper from the state-owned mine at Outokumpu, as well as some zinc, iron, nickel, silver, and gold. More than one-fourth of the population is employed in manufacturing and construction work, most workers being engaged in the processing of wood products. Sawn lumber is exceeded in value by paper-pulp, newsprint, and packing materials. The textile industry is also important.

The manufacture of machines and transport equipment, particularly ships, was somewhat artificially stimulated by reparations payments to the U.S.S.R. after World War II; when these were completed in 1952, special trade treaties

ECONOMIC RESOURCES OF FINLAND

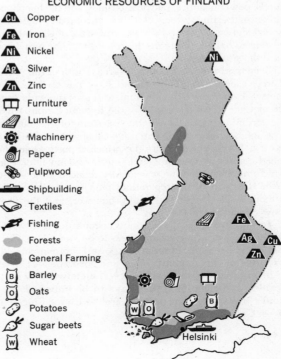

- Cu Copper
- Fe Iron
- Ni Nickel
- Ag Silver
- Zn Zinc
- Furniture
- Lumber
- Machinery
- Paper
- Pulpwood
- Shipbuilding
- Textiles
- Fishing
- Forests
- General Farming
- B Barley
- O Oats
- Potatoes
- Sugar beets
- W Wheat

Helsinki

A Finnish athlete races over floating logs. (PIX INC.)

with the U.S.S.R. and Communist China were arranged to reduce the dislocation of the Finnish economy. The processing of dairy and fish products is increasing. Skilled craftsmanship is well represented in copperwares, glass, and ceramics.

Co-operatives, Labor, and State Control. Both producers and consumers are well organized in co-operatives. Agricultural marketing and purchasing, the wholesale and retail trades, manufacturing, housing, insurance, and savings and loan associations are all represented. The Social-Democratic party operates a co-operative primarily for urban workers; various co-operative efforts promote adult education. Collective bargaining in the industrial field is extensive. Comprehensive agreements governing labor and production conditions are negotiated by the Central League of Finnish Trade Unions (SAK) and other labor unions, and the Finnish Employers' Confederation (STK).

The state shares substantially in the ownership of forest lands, power facilities, railways, airlines, and the telephone and broadcasting systems. But through a broad program of social legislation, the power and resources of the state are also used to help maintain the freedom of the individual and the small-holder.

Transportation. All populous areas south of the Arctic Circle except the Åland Islands have rail services. The network covers nearly 5,000 mi. and uses the wide-gage track since Finland was part of the Russian Empire when construction began. The highway system totals about 40,-000 mi., and there is an extensive canal system. Helsinki, Kotka, Turku, and Pori are the principal ports. Oulu, the chief port for northern Finland, is icebound in winter. Finland's merchant marine was greatly reduced after World War II as part of the reparations payments to the Soviet Union. Replacement was rapid, however, and the fleet now exceeds 1,000,000 tons.

Foreign Trade. Wood products account for nearly 70% of the value of exports and appear to be increasing. Copper, dairy products, hides and furs, and ceramics are also exported in some quantity. Coal and coke, fuel oils, sheet iron and steel, some machinery and metalwares, wheat, textiles, and some foodstuffs have to be imported. Finland's principal trading partners are the United Kingdom, West Germany, and the U.S.S.R.

Government

Structure of Government. Finland is a republic governed under the constitution of 1919. Later supplements included a law of 1928 regulating the parliament, or Diet (*Eduskunta*, or *Riksdag*). The executive is a president, elected for six years by 300 electors, chosen for each occasion by popular vote. He governs with a council of state (cabinet), whose members must have the confidence of parliament. He may dissolve a regular parliament, through appointment of a new cabinet if necessary, and he may call or dissolve special sessions. He possesses delaying veto power on legislation, and exercises wide appointive power. The unicameral legislature, the *Eduskunta*, has 200 members, chosen by universal suffrage, the voting age being 21 years. Parliamentary safeguards include a special committee of 45 members, which reviews proposed bills before they are submitted to parliament. Also, if one-third of parliament so wishes, a law may not be effective until a newly elected parliament confirms it by a regular majority.

The judicial system owes much to Swedish law, codified in 1734, and to later Scandinavian example. Lay judges often assist the presiding judge in courts of first instance. There are appellate courts at Turku, Vaasa, Kuopio, and Helsinki; the final court of appeal is the supreme court at Helsinki.

Local Government. Finland is divided into 12 provinces, administered by governors appointed by the president. The locally elected communal councils and other organs of local government enjoy considerable autonomy. The Åland Islands have their own legislative body, the *Landsting*, whose concurrence the national Parliament may need in certain matters.

Political Parties. The major political parties are the Social-Democratic, the Finnish People's Democratic League, the Agrarian, and the Conservative. There is also a Finnish People's party of liberal orientation, and a Swedish People's party. The Social-Democratic party came to prominence early in the 20th century, and first held office in 1926 under Väinö Tanner; its support comes from urban labor and small farmers. Under pressure from the Soviet Union, the party was kept out of all Finnish cabinets from 1958 until 1966, when it again formed a government, with the inclusion of the Finnish People's Democratic League (SKDL). The latter, formally an association of leftist forces, is actually dominated by the Communists.

INDEX TO FINLAND GENERAL REFERENCE MAP
Total Population 4,497,000

History

Early History. Man's first appearance on Finnish soil may date back to 6000 or even 8000 B.C. Artifacts have been found from each of the Stone, Bronze, and Iron ages. Among early settlers were the nomadic Lapps in the north and Germanic peoples in the southwest, but about 100 A.D. the Finns began to arrive from the shores of the East Baltic and the Vistula. The Suomi, who later gave the country its name, settled in the southwest, the Tavasts (Häme) slightly farther north, in the center, and the Karelians in the southeast.

These distinct groupings were not wholly united until the 16th century, under the early Swedish Vasas. In the meantime, however, many powers had sought control over the Finnish peoples. The Swedish Crusade of Erik the Saint in the mid-12th century, and that of Birger Jarl a century later, imposed Roman Catholicism upon the western and central Finns, but among the Karelians the Novgorodian or Greek Orthodox influence made headway. This rivalry was somewhat stabilized in 1323, when Karelia was partitioned and the frontier between Sweden and Novgorod was defined.

Swedish Rule. For more than half a millennium the Finns shared the history of the Swedish people. With them they formed part of the Kalmar Union of Scandinavian states until Sweden withdrew early in the 16th century, and later shared in the Reformation and the building of a Baltic empire. The Finn acquired much of his cultural heritage from the Swede. Although the term "grand duchy" was usually applied to Finnish territory after 1581, no country-wide political institutions existed to give separate identity to Finland as such.

By the 16th century Sweden was again thrusting eastward, thus precipitating new rivalry with Russia. In 1595 the Peace of Täyssinä moved the northern end of the frontier eastward from the Gulf of Bothnia to the White Sea, while the Treaty of Stolbova (1617) brought all of southeastern Karelia, as well as Ingria (Ingermanland) on the south side of the Gulf of Finland, under Swedish control. However, the Northern War, ended by the Treaty of Nystad in 1721, cost Sweden much of Karelia, all of its possessions south of the Gulf of Finland, and most of those in northern Germany. An ill-starred attempt at revenge 20 years later brought further losses on the Karelian front.

By the late 18th century there were those who felt that Finnish interests were not adequately served within the Swedish-Finnish state. Their opposition (chiefly nobles) was expressed in the Anjala League. Yet when Alexander I of Russia sought to absorb Finland in 1808 he found the mass of Finns loyal to Sweden. Finland was ceded to the Tsar by the Treaty of Hamina in 1809, but the Russian ruler found it prudent to treat his newly won subjects with solicitude.

Russian Rule. Instead of being incorporated into the Russian empire, Finland was organized as a grand duchy with Alexander as its Grand Duke. As such he assured the Finns that their traditional political rights (a heritage of the Swedish connection) would be preserved, and a surprising degree of autonomy was granted in domestic affairs. The Diet did not meet after 1809, however, and political regression rather than progress resulted by the mid-19th century. In 1863, in the reign of Alexander II, the Finnish Diet finally assembled again and met more frequently thereafter. The functions of local government

The fortress of Olavinlinna, built in 1475. Damaged by fire in 1860, it was rebuilt and is now a popular tourist attraction.

Pix, Inc.

ARCTIC OCEAN

FINLAND

Territory ceded to the U.S.S.R. in 1944

*Leased to the U.S.S.R. for 50 years, but returned to Finland in 1956

0   150
Miles

NORWAY

SWEDEN

Petsamo

KARELIA

U.S.S.R.

GULF OF BOTHNIA

FINLAND

*PORKKALA NAVAL BASE

SAIMAA CANAL

Vyborg

Lake Ladoga

GULF OF FINLAND

were extended and freer trade policies adopted. The grand duchy received its own currency in 1865, its own military establishment in 1878. The last decades of the century were marked by material improvements, early industrialization, and the beginnings of social legislation.

The 19th century, moreover, had seen a marked development of Finnish nationalism. Already in the 18th century the scholar H. G. Porthan had insisted that the Finns had a history and a language of their own, distinct from the Swedish heritage. In the 19th century Elias Lönnrot revealed the Finnish folk heritage in the national epic *Kalevala*, while J. L. Runeberg was creating a national literature in which Finn and Swede-Finn could share. The philosopher J. V. Snellman urged that nationalist aspirations should also involve political and social life. But Russia soon intensified its Russification policy, and the February Manifesto of 1899, which met with widespread resistance, was a frontal attack on the autonomous constitutional status of Finland.

Independence. The Bolshevik upheaval in Russia in 1917 finally enabled Finland to declare its independence. But left-wing elements were now reluctant to sever the tie with Russia, and in 1918 a bitter civil war broke out between Reds, who supported Russia, and Whites, or Finnish nationalists. Both sides received foreign help, and the Whites, supported by Germany, finally prevailed under Gen. C. G. E. Mannerheim. However, the collapse of German arms late in 1918 ended plans to enthrone a German Prince as ruler of the new state. A republican constitution was adopted in June, 1919, and the Treaty of Tartu (Dorpat) with Russia in 1920 confirmed the country's independence.

The Finns immediately set about making the most of their independence. Parliamentary government, including female suffrage (1906) had already been established. An agrarian law of 1922 increased the number of moderate-sized farms, thus reducing the marginal peasant population. The world depression of the 1930's affected Finland severely, but gave further impetus to a broad program of social insurance. Finland was the only European country that met its war-related debt obligations to the United States. A general political amnesty in 1926 helped to heal some of the bitterness left by the civil strife of 1918. But the extreme right-wing Lapua movement and the expansionist aims of the Academic Karelian Society in the 1930's continued to be disturbing factors for some time.

The outbreak of World War II introduced a difficult period for the young republic. The Finns' heroic defense against the Soviet Union in the Winter War, or Russo-Finnish War (1939–40), evoked the admiration of the non-Axis world, and its sympathy when defeat came. An opportunity for redress occurred when Hitler attacked the Soviet Union, and Mannerheim led an army far into Soviet Karelia, though the Finns always insisted that they were fighting a separate war. An armistice signed in 1944 entailed a third war, lasting nearly nine months, with their erstwhile military associate, Germany.

The terms agreed upon in 1944 and confirmed by the Treaty of Paris in 1947 were harsh indeed. Only token military forces were allowed henceforth (a term, which was modified in 1963, when Finland was permitted to build up and modernize its military forces). Territory ceded to the Soviet Union in Karelia, including the important city of Vyborg (Viipuri), at Petsamo, and on the northeastern frontier amounted to more than 11% of the country's area, including 10% of its arable land, 11% of its forests, and 10% of its industries. In addition, Finland had to shoulder a reparations load of $300,000,000. About 7% of the working population had been killed, and the Germans had devastated north Finland. Over 425,000 persons from the ceded territories had to be settled in what remained of independent Finland. The cost of resettlement, the repair of war damage, and economic dislocation caused by reparations payments all had their share in stimulating inflationary tendencies, which sometimes severely tested the stability of the democratic procedure.

Postwar Policies. Finnish postwar statesmen, such as President Paasikivi (1946–56) and his successor, Urho Kekkonen, were painfully aware of the fact that their country existed in the shadow of its vast Soviet neighbor. Their task, often against great odds, was to preserve Finland's independence and democratic ways, while placating the Soviet Union in order to maintain tolerable relations with it. Thus, Finland could not benefit from the Marshall Plan in 1948, and plans for a possible Scandinavian defense union (1948–49) did not envisage Finnish participation. Facing realities, the country in 1948 signed a mutual assistance treaty with the U.S.S.R. and in 1955 agreed to a 20-year prolongation. In return, the Soviets in 1948 extended the deadline for payment of reparations and agreed (1956) to the return of the Porkkala naval base, which they had leased for 50 years. Again, in 1961, when Finland became an associate member of the European Free Trade Association (EFTA), it guaranteed the Soviet Union the same preferential treatment on exports to Finland as that given to EFTA members.

At the same time, Finland sought closer relations with the West, particularly with its Scandinavian neighbors. By 1955, the country had become a member of the Norden (Scandinavian states) Council and joined the United Nations. It contributed troops to the U.N. forces at Suez in 1956 and on Cyprus in 1964.

Pressures from the giant neighbor were varyingly felt on the domestic political scene. The Soviets were long wary of hostility within the powerful Social-Democratic party. Diplomatic pressure thus kept the latter out of all Finnish governments from 1958 until the party's victory in the elections of 1966. In the coalition then formed by the Social-Democrats the Communists were included. This time, however, the political mood was much less tense than when last (1944–48) they shared in coalition government.

Consult Platt, R. R., *Finland and Its Geography* (1955); Mazour, A. G., *Finland Between East and West* (1956); Jakobson, Max, *The Diplomacy of the Winter War* (1961); Jutikkala, Eino, *A History of Finland* (1962).

OSCAR J. FALNES, New York University

FINLAND, GULF OF, arm of the Baltic Sea extending eastward about 260 mi. between Finland and Estonian S.S.R. Its width varies from 45 to 85 mi.; at the eastern end it narrows and flows into Kronshtadt (Kronstadt) Bay. Principal cities on the gulf are Helsinki, Finland, and Vyborg, Leningrad, and Tallinn in the Soviet Union.

FINLAY [fēn-lī′], **CARLOS JUAN** (1833–1915), Cuban physician, of Scottish and French ancestry. Finlay studied medicine in the United States, Cuba, and France. While engaging in general practice in Havana, he sought to determine the cause and to trace the spread of yellow fever, long endemic in Cuba. A paper he wrote in 1881 pointed to the mosquito as the carrier of the disease. Finlay's hypothesis contributed to the spectacular work of Walter Reed and colleagues two decades later. Although Finlay at the time received insufficient credit, he later won many Cuban and foreign decorations and other honors.

FINLAY [fin′lē] **RIVER,** river in north-central British Columbia, Canada. It rises in the Stikine Mountains and flows south and east, joining the Parsnip River to form the Peace River. The Finlay is considered the ultimate headwater of the Mackenzie River. Length, 210 mi.

FINLETTER, THOMAS KNIGHT (1893–   ), American public official, born in Philadelphia, and educated at the University of Pennsylvania. An Army captain in World War I, Finletter practiced law (1920–41) in Pennsylvania and New York before serving (1941–44) as assistant to Secretary of State Cordell Hull. He was consultant at the United Nations Charter Conference (1945), chairman of the Air Policy Commission (1947–48), and Air Force Secretary (1950–53). Finletter was appointed permanent U.S. representative to the North Atlantic Treaty Organization in 1961.

FINLEY, JAMES (1762-1828), American suspension-bridge pioneer. In 1801 he built the first modern suspension bridge over Jacob's Creek, in Pennsylvania, "under contract to build a bridge of 70 foot span, 12½ feet wide, and warrant it for 50 years (all but the flooring) for $600." Finley estimated tension by testing weighted models to determine the size of bars to be used. Wood towers supported the linked chain-bars, from which the timber floor was suspended while trussed side members served both as guard rails and in distributing the load over an inherently flexible structure. There is no record of any of his bridges having failed.

FINNEGANS WAKE. *See* Joyce, James.

FINNISH, member of the Finnic branch of the Finno-Ugric subfamily of the Uralic language family. Nearly all speakers of the language live in Finland. The Finnish alphabet, which has 13 consonants and 8 vowels, is well suited to the language, as there is one letter for each of its 21 sounds and one sound for each letter. In pronunciation the stress always falls on the first syllable of a word. In grammar the words have numerous variations of endings; long words are formed by joining several short words. The following proverb is a sample of Finnish:

Parempi pyy pivossa kuin kymmenen oksalla.

A grouse in the hand is worth ten on the branch.
See also Finno-Ugric Languages.

FINNISH LITERATURE. Literature in Finland has reflected and continues to reflect the fact that the population of the nation has been bilingual since time immemorial. About nine-tenths of the population is Finnish-speaking and a fraction less than 10% is Swedish-speaking. There is much bilingualism; many educated people speak both languages. Literature understandably reflects the language situation: it falls into two unequal parts, the Finnish and the Swedish. Their beginnings do not occur much before the 19th century. Finland's Swedish-language literature is in a sense a part of Swedish literature, but it is also, to a significant degree, a particularly provincial branch of the general culture of Finland. Much of it has risen, however, above mere provincial concerns. Swedish-language writers such as Johan Ludvig Runeberg (1804–77) and Zacharias Topelius (1818–98) were as truly Finnish as any of their contemporaries in exalting love of country and consciousness of nationality. The same applies to many of the Swede-Finn writers of the past half century.

Outstanding among the early contributors to Finnish literature during the past century is the towering figure of Aleksis Kivi (1834–72). A dramatist as well as a novelist, he used in his work, among other things, materials from the national epic, the *Kalevala*. Finnish realism, which appeared in the 1880's, reflected Scandinavian and especially Norwegian influence. One of its outstanding representatives was Juhani Aho (1861–1921); Aho also serves as a connection with the neoromantic school, whose main spokesmen were Johannes Linnankoski (1869–1913) and Volter Kilpi (1874–1939). The finest lyric poet, Eino Leino (1878–1926), reflected the same orientation. The outstanding Finnish novelist since 1918 is Frans Eemil Sillanpää, 1939 Nobel Prize winner in literature. Mika Waltari and Väinö Linna stand out among today's talented writers. The former's historical novels, especially those published since 1945, have become well known abroad through translations. Outstanding among them is *Sinuhe, Egyptiläinen*, 1945 (*The Egyptian*, 1949). Linna is a "worker-author" of exceptional talent whose important works have appeared since 1954, when his *Tuntematon Sotilas* (*Unknown Soldier*, 1957) was published. This two-volume novel on the Finnish war of independence (1918), which was also a civil war, has secured his place among the front-rank writers of modern Finland.

John H. Wuorinen,
Columbia University

FINNISH MUSIC. *See* Scandinavian Music.

FINNISH-RUSSIAN WAR. *See* Russo-Finnish War.

FINN MAC CUMAILL [fin măk-cŭm′əl], supreme extratribal hero of Celtic mythology. His father, Cumall, leader of a *fián*, or independent warrior band, was killed by Goll mac Morna. Finn was brought up in hiding; while still a boy, he ate the Salmon of Knowledge and thus acquired supernatural insight and wisdom. Finn killed Goll and gained the leadership of the *fián*. Oisin, or Ossian, the father of Oscar, was Finn's son by his first wife. An accomplished poet, Ossian gave his name to the Ossianic Cycle, which celebrated the exploits of the *fiana*. Finn's betrothed second wife, Grainne, daughter of Cormac mac Art, forced Diarmaid, one of Finn's warriors, to elope with her.

After many years during which Finn pursued the couple, hoping for a chance at vengeance, peace was made, but Finn treacherously caused the death of Diarmaid in a hunt. Oscar and a great part of the *fián* were killed in the Battle of Gabra. There are several versions of Finn's death; the best-known is that of his fall in the Battle of Ventry, fought against the forces of the King of the World.

JOHN MACQUEEN,
University of Edinburgh

See also MYTHOLOGY, CELTIC.

FINNO-UGRIC [fin'ō-ōō'grik] **LANGUAGES,** subfamily of the Uralic language family. The members are divided into two branches. The most important languages of the Finnic branch are Finnish, Estonian, the Lapp languages of Scandinavia and northern Russia, and a few minor languages of European Russia—Mordvinian, Udmurt (or Votyak), Mari (or Cheremiss), and Komi. The Ugric languages are Hungarian and two minor languages of western Siberia, Ostyak (or Khanty) and Vogul (or Mansi). The Finno-Ugric languages seem to have been spoken in northeastern Europe by about 3000 B.C. Today for the most part the languages are geographically isolated from one another and have diverged widely, so that, for example, only a linguistic specialist can demonstrate a relationship between Finnish and Hungarian.
See also URALIC LANGUAGES.

FINSEN, NIELS RYBERG (1860–1904), Danish physician who was awarded the Nobel Prize in 1904 for his use of concentrated light rays in the treatment of tuberculosis of the skin (lupus vulgaris). He investigated the action of ultraviolet light on the skin and observed particularly its bactericidal effect. The Finsen lamp, which used a carbon arc as a light source, is the forerunner of the modern ultraviolet, or "sun," lamp.

FIORD [fyôrd], also fjord, a deep, narrow, steep-sided arm of the sea. Fiords are found where a coast underlain by very hard rocks has been uplifted, cut by stream valleys, glaciated, and partly submerged. Tributary streams usually form cascades and waterfalls. Coasts with many fiords include those of Norway, Greenland, Labrador, Alaska, British Columbia, Chile, and New Zealand. The height of the cliffs above the sea in many fiords exceeds 3,000 ft., and the depth of water is comparably great. Some Norwegian and Chilean fiords are more than 4,000 ft. deep. The floors of many fiords are basinlike, some having been excavated directly by a glacier, others made by glacial moraines deposited near the valley's mouth.
See also COASTS AND COAST LINES; GLACIERS AND GLACIATION.

FIORE, IL. *See* DANTE.

FIORELLO! [fē-ə-rĕl'ō], musical play, with music by Jerry Bock; lyrics by Sheldon Harnick; book by Jerome Weidman and George Abbott; New York première, Nov. 23, 1959. Enhanced by a score notable for its deft satirical commentaries on New York City politics, the story was based on the career of Fiorello La Guardia, from the time

he decided to run for Congress just before World War I until he became mayor in 1933. The musical won the Pulitzer Prize for drama.

FIR [fûr], common name for about 40 species of tall forest trees of the genus *Abies*, in the pine family, Pinaceae. Firs are evergreen trees, usually of conical growth habit, and occur chiefly in the north temperate regions of North America, Europe, and Asia. The height of various species ranges from about 80 ft. (the Spanish fir, *A. pinsapo*) to 250 ft. (the red firs, *A. magnifica* and *A. nobilis*). Firs have needlelike leaves that leave a circular scar on the branchlet when they fall. The thin gray or brownish bark is smooth on young trees and marked by prominent resin-containing blisters. The erect, seed-bearing cones of firs are oval or cylindrical in shape. Young firs make handsome ornamental trees. Species widely cultivated include *A. veitchi*, the Japanese fir, and *A. concolor*, the white or

Above, balsam firs, native to Canada and northeastern United States. (GIRARD NURSERIES) **Below,** purplish cones are 2 to 3 in. long and the flat needles are rounded at the tip. (U.S. FOREST SERVICE)

Colorado fir, which is especially suited to park planting. The soft, perishable lumber obtained from many species is used for building construction, crates, and pulpwood. Resin obtained from the bark has medicinal and optical uses. Firs are commercially the most widely cut Christmas trees and are valuable for landscaping.

GEORGE A. CARLE, Assistant Landscape Architect, New York City Department of Parks

FIRBANK, (ARTHUR ANNESLEY) RONALD (1886–1926), English writer. He was highly precious and affected in his mode of living. Firbank wrote his short novels chiefly by collecting witty sayings on individual scraps of paper; this hoard was raided when sustained composition began. Among his best novels are *Vainglory* (1915), *Valmouth* (1918), and *Concerning the Eccentricities of Cardinal Pirelli* (1926). His work is sometimes disconcertingly episodic, but it has nevertheless been consistently admired by a small public, and has influenced some later writers. Although occasionally degenerating into silliness, Firbank's output reveals an impressive comic power.

FIRDAWSI [fir-dou'sē] **or FIRDUSI** [fir-dōō'sē], pseudonym of Abu'l-Qasim (c.940–c.1020), renowned Persian epic poet. Author of Iran's greatest epic, the *Shahnama* (Book of Kings), he is reputed to have spent 30 years (980–1010) on its 60,000 rhyming couplets. Virtually nothing certain is known of his life, but Firdawsi was an impoverished country gentleman of northeastern Iran, the area most resistant to Islam and to Arab influences generally. Doubtless a good Muslim, he yet embodied in his poem all his countrymen's pride in their ancient, pre-Islamic civilization. He drew on oral traditions and earlier writings to present, in the purest Persian, all Iranian legend and history from the beginning of time to the fall of the Sassanian Dynasty (c.652). Iranians of all classes have always loved to sing from their great national song. Western critics who complain of its monotony and stereotyped style often overlook passages of wit, urbanity, beauty, and narrative power. *The Shahnama of Firdausi* (9 vols., 1905–25; trans. by A. G. and E. Warner) is the latest annotated translation.

G. M. WICKENS, University of Toronto

FIRE, rapid combustion characterized by high temperatures and flame. The first great discovery of prehistoric man, as told in the legends of most peoples, was how to make fire. To the ancients and alchemists, fire, earth, water, and air were the four elements from which all matter was made.

In order to produce fire, a combustible material and oxygen must be present and in contact at sufficiently high temperatures to initiate combustion. Oxygen and fuel must continue to be available and in contact for combustion to continue. It follows that a fire may be extinguished by removal of any one of these constituents—oxygen, fuel, or heat.

The combustibility of a substance depends on its chemical composition and its physical state. If the source of oxygen is air, then the molecules of any flammable gas escaping into the air will mix with oxygen molecules and, at ignition temperature, will burn. A flammable liquid must first be vaporized and its vapor mixed with oxygen before it will burn. Solids must usually be liquefied and vaporized, or at least reduced to small particles, with large surface area, but if they are porous this may not be necessary. All solids burn more readily as the size of the solid particle decreases and the total surface area exposed to oxygen increases. Very severe fires result from a mixture of air and oxidizable dusts, such as flour, metal powder, or powdered coal. If such a mixture is in the right proportions it will burn explosively.

Every material must be raised to its specific ignition temperature before a fire will occur, though oxidation of the material may take place below this temperature. Above it, the heat of oxidation does not dissipate fast enough, and raises the next area of unburned fuel to ignition temperature. Except for very finely divided materials, therefore, the ignition temperatures of solids are higher than those of liquids. Generally liquids are more flammable the lower their boiling point.

A fire heats the air immediately around it, causing it to expand and rise, pulling into its place colder air from regions farther away. This chimney effect assures a continuous new supply of oxygen to support the fire. When a fire covers an area as large as a forest or city, the inward rush of cold air is a wind with considerable velocity.

The visible flame of a fire is caused by unburned particles that are incandescent. The color of the flame depends on the elements in the fuel. Ideal burning will produce an almost colorless flame.

There are reactions which produce flame and heat, for example the combination of sodium and chlorine, but the term "fire" is used only when oxygen is one of the reactants.

MELVIN J. ASTLE, Case Institute of Technology
See also COMBUSTION; FLAME.

FIRE ALARM. *See* ALARM SYSTEM.

FIRE ANT, a small red ant, *Solenopsis geminata*, of the family Formicidae, found in southeastern United States and Mexico. The insects inflict painful stings that feel like jabs from red-hot needles. Fire ants are an enemy of bobwhite quail and poultry. They bore into the eggs just before the young hatch, or attack the newly hatched young, stinging the prey to death and then feeding on their bodies.
See also ANT.

FIREARMS, or small arms, originated in Europe during the 14th century, and spread to the Orient at a later date. Gunpowder, on the other hand, was first known in the Orient at a much earlier period, but was never used as such. Probably as a result of contact with the Orient, the Crusaders brought the knowledge of this mixture back to Europe and eventually its use was applied in warfare. This resulted in the cannon, which appeared in the first half of the 14th century. The earliest cannons were comparatively small pieces, used mostly during the siege of castles or fortified towns. Later, about 1370, some were so large and heavy that once they were placed in position, they remained there through the siege. Others were small enough to be carried by two or three men. It was from this small type of cannon that handguns came into being.

The early handguns were smaller counterparts of the cannon and appeared in one of two forms. The first were constructed of a series of iron bars placed side by side and welded in a manner to form a tube, bound together with iron hoops. At times there was an extra housing of rope, leather, or a combination of both to cover the outside. The second type was formed of a one-piece tube. These handguns had barrels about 8 in. to 2 ft. in length and a bore of ¾ in. to 2 in. Most of these guns were made to load from the muzzle, having a plug at the breech end. The early guns were provided with a touchhole on top of the barrel. A burning match cord (rope made of hemp soaked in a saltpeter solution and dried) was held in a shooter's hand and used to ignite the priming powder in the touchhole. At a later date, about 1440–50, the touchhole was moved to the side to provide a little more protection for the priming powder. About the same time a movable cover for the pan came into use, in an attempt to keep the pan dry in wet weather. It also enabled a man carrying the handgun to have his piece ready primed, as necessity indicated that this was advisable.

Improved Firing Mechanisms. The first improvement in firing mechanisms appeared in the second half of the 15th century. This, known as the matchlock, was an arrangement whereby a piece of burning match cord or fuse rope was attached to the gun by means of a curved, movable mechanism near the breech. This mechanism was connected with the trigger in such a manner that when the latter was pulled, the burning match cord ignited the priming powder in a flashpan which in turn fired the charge inside the barrel.

Matchlocks had their disadvantages. Rain would put out the burning match cord or wind would blow sparks from one match cord to the powder in the priming pan of a gun held by a man nearby. Then too, if soldiers tried to launch a surprise attack, the enemy might see the smoke from the burning match cords during the day or the glowing ends at night. Consequently, early in the 1500's an improvement called a wheel lock was developed in Germany. This system had a steel wheel which was wound against the tension of a powerful spring. As the trigger was pulled the friction of the spinning wheel against a piece of sulfide of iron, held in the jaws of a piece called the cock, provided a shower of sparks which fired the gun. Wheel locks were complicated, quite expensive to make, and thus impractical. They were used extensively for sporting purposes and the matchlock continued to be used for military purposes.

About 1580 a device called the snaphance was incorporated in the firing mechanism of firearms. A gun was fired by having a piece of pyrites or flint held in the jaws of a movable member, called a hammer, or cock. When the trigger was pulled, the hammer moved forward, causing the flint to strike a piece of steel, called a frizzen, which was placed over the priming pan, making a shower of sparks and firing the gun. The snaphance mechanism had a priming pan cover which slid back and forth over the pan.

The name "snaphance" was derived from the German word *schnapp hahn* meaning a "snapping or pecking fowl." In firing the gun, the motion of one of the parts of the lock called a cock (now known as the hammer) was similar to that made by a pecking or snapping fowl. Another suggested source of the name is from the Dutch word *snap-hahn* referring to a chicken thief, or hen snatcher. The connection between snaphance, the name of the gun, and *snap-hahn*, the name for chicken thieves is thought to be that this type of lock was developed by thieves. As is obvious, such an occupation is best pursued after dark and the glow of the burning match of a matchlock might easily have led to detection. For this purpose the matchlock was impractical and the wheel lock too expensive. Therefore, they designed their own gun mechanism, little thinking that with slight modifications it would remain in use for about 250 years.

Contemporaneous with the introduction and subsequent development of the snaphance was the development of a type of lock called a miquelet, apparently originating in Spain. This name is said to have been derived from an old Spanish word meaning "robber" or "highwayman." The miquelet was also supposed to have been developed as a result of circumstances similar to those under which the snaphance was developed.

In some respects the miquelet was an improvement over the snaphance. In the miquelet, the sliding pan cover, separate from the striker or frizzen, was done away with, and the striker was made in the form of a right angle piece working on a screw pivot with its base covering the flashpan. The miquelet mainspring, which activated the hammer when the trigger was pulled, was on the outside of the lock plate. About 1630 the mainspring was moved to the inside, and other improvements were made which resulted in a new type of lock known as a flintlock. Flintlocks continued in use until about 1840.

Early Firearm Manufacture. Up to about 1840–50 guns were made by hand. Most barrels were made from low-carbon steel and were formed by hammering a flat strip around a mandrel forming a tube which was then welded or brazed along the seam. These tubes were then straightened and reamed smooth on the inside. The shoulder stocks were made much in the same manner that a cabinetmaker would make a piece of fine furniture. The various small parts were hammered and filed by hand until they fitted properly.

In 1798, near New Haven, Conn., Eli Whitney established a shop with some crude machine tools to manufacture guns with interchangeable parts. From that time to about 1850 machine tools gradually came into use. During the Civil War guns were made by machinery, and the day of the small independent gunsmith was past,

In 1807 an English patent was granted to a Scotch clergyman, Alexander John Forsyth, for a gunlock that was destined to have a great effect on the development of firearms. Called the percussion lock because a blow from the hammer fired the gun, it eliminated the use of flint and steel. The lock plate and the internal working parts of the lock remained the same. The hammer was made with a blunt noselike part which, when the trigger was pulled, struck a small plunger placed where the priming pan had previously been. Beneath the plunger, on a small lug at the breech of the barrel, was placed a

BASIC FIRING MECHANISMS BEFORE THE BRASS CARTRIDGE

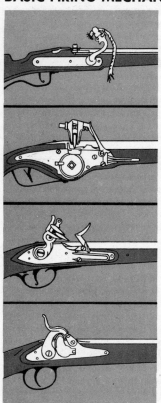

MATCHLOCK

The improved version was developed in the 15th century. When the trigger was pulled, a curved hammer thrust the burning match cord into the touchhole, igniting the primer.

WHEEL LOCK

Pulling the trigger released a clock-type, hand-wound spring. This spun a steel wheel against a piece of flint or iron pyrites and the primer was ignited by a shower of sparks.

FLINTLOCK

A simple spring snapped the hammer down when the trigger was pulled. A piece of flint or pyrites, fastened in the hammer jaws, struck sparks from a steel pivot set over the priming pan.

PERCUSSION LOCK

The catch holding the hammer at cock was released by the trigger. The hammer exploded a small percussion cap in the lock, which detonated the main charge.

The matchlock originated in the 14th century as a small, unwieldy cannon. Little improvement was made in the gun for almost 100 years. The early 16th-century wheel lock was too expensive for general use. The flintlock, invented about the same time, endured for nearly 250 years. It was replaced by the forerunner of modern arms, the percussion lock.

REMINGTON ROLLING BLOCK CARBINE

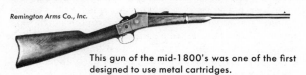

Remington Arms Co., Inc.

This gun of the mid-1800's was one of the first designed to use metal cartridges.

HANDGUNS

The revolver has a cylinder that revolves mechanically to bring each cartridge into firing position. The "automatic" pistol is autoloading, cartridges being fed from a magazine in the grip.

Colt Patent Fire Arms Mfg. Co., Inc.

small quantity of extremely sensitive detonating or percussion powder made of fulminate of mercury. When the plunger was driven down by a blow from the hammer, the percussion powder was exploded, the flash passing through a small hole in the lug and firing the gun.

The first percussion locks used loose percussion powder, which was dangerous. Several safer methods were tried. First, the percussion powder was placed in little pellets or tubes called pellet or tube locks. These, however, were simply variations of the percussion locks. By the 1820's the most common type of percussion lock had come into use. In this type, a small, tubelike piece, referred to as a nipple, was screwed into the lug at the breech. On the nipple was placed a small percussion cap shaped similar to a tiny thimble and containing fulminate of mercury. When the hammer struck it, the fulminate ignited, firing the gun. The percussion lock was commonly used until 1865. From percussion caps evolved the modern types of cartridges, containing their own priming. This made possible the making of practical breech-loading guns. Up until this time most guns had been muzzle-loading although some breechloaders had been made but not perfected.

Modern Firearms. During the late 1800's various types of single-shot and repeating firearms came into use. The most common actions are lever, bolt, slide or pump, and automatic. Lever action repeaters are made with the cartridge magazine in the buttstock, in the form of a tube under the barrel, or with a box magazine in front of the trigger guard. The lever for operating the mechanism forms the trigger guard. It is operated by moving it down and forward to open the breech and up and back to close it.

Slide or pump actions have the magazine below the barrel, and are operated by moving a part called an action slide handle backward and forward along the outside of the magazine tube. In the bolt action the breech bolt is similar to a door bolt. By moving the handle upward and back, the breech is opened and by moving the handle forward and down, the breech is closed.

Early in the 1900's a type of action called automatic, or self-loading, came into being. In these the energy from the recoil or burning powder gas operates the mechanism. This action comes in two types, automatic and semiautomatic. In the semiautomatic the trigger must be pulled for each shot. In the full automatic the gun continues to fire as long as the trigger is depressed and there is ammunition in the magazine.

Consult Gluckman, Arcadi, *U.S. Martial Pistols and Revolvers* (1939); Held, Robert, *The Age of Firearms* (1957); Chapel, C. E., *Gun Collectors Handbook of Values* (5th ed., 1960).

THOMAS E. HALL, Curator, Winchester Gun Museum
See also PISTOL; RIFLE.

FIREBALL. *See* METEOR.

FIREBIRD, THE, ballet in one act; music by Igor Stravinsky; choreography by Michel Fokine; first performance June 25, 1910, Diaghilev's Ballets Russes at the Paris Opéra. The story concerns Prince Ivan's rescue, with the help of the firebird, of a princess enchanted by the demon Kostchei. The harmonic scheme is so organized that diatonic themes (based on a 7-note scale) are associated with the human elements and chromatic themes (based on a

CURRENT FIREARMS

Self-priming metal cartridges made breech-loading guns practical. Breech loading, in turn, made possible the development of the great variety of loading and firing mechanisms available in both military and sporting guns.

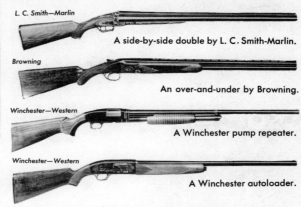

U.S. Army

Above, military lightweight M-14 automatic rifle, fitted with a muzzle brake. Other accessories include the sling, magazines, shells, and *(top to bottom)* a grenade launcher, a grenade, a bayonet, and a bayonet scabbard.

A side-by-side double by L. C. Smith-Marlin.

An over-and-under by Browning.

A Winchester pump repeater.

A Winchester autoloader.

HOW THE BOLT ACTION WORKS

As the handle is raised and the bolt drawn back, the spent shell is ejected and the gun cocked.

A spring lifts the next shell into line, and the forward thrust of the bolt forces it into the chamber.

The handle is lowered, locking the breech. The gun is fired, and the cycle is repeated.

12-note scale) with the magical. Two folk songs from Rimsky-Korsakov's collection (1876) are used in the Princess' round and the finale. Quite extraordinary is the rhythmical invention (especially the syncopation in the Firebird's Dance) and colorful orchestration that stresses the individual timbre of each instrument.

FIRE BLIGHT, disease of fruit trees that causes serious damage to pear and apple orchards and also affects such ornamentals as quince, hawthorn, and fire thorn. Fire blight is caused by the bacterium *Erwinia amylovora,* which winters at the base of diseased tree limbs, and appears in oozing droplets in the spring to be carried to other trees by insects. Blighted trees have brown or blackened branches with dead, persistent leaves, and appear to have been scorched by fire. Control of fire blight consists of removing diseased branches and spraying the trees (especially during periods of bloom) with copper- or streptomycin-containing solutions.
See also PLANT DISEASES.

FIRECRACKER, a small paper cylinder containing a mixture of black powder which is ignited by a fuse. If properly handled the explosion which results is more noisy than dangerous. Possession by private individuals is illegal in many states in the United States.

FIREDAMP, combustible gas that forms in mines. When coal or other carbonaceous material decomposes, it gives off a gas, or damp, principally methane (CH_4), that burns like domestic natural gas. Many coal-mine fires and explosions are caused by accidental ignition of firedamp. It is

not to be confused with chokedamp (blackdamp), a non-explosive concentration of carbon dioxide.

FIRE-EATERS, in American history, a term used before the Civil War to describe Southerners who advocated destruction of the Union. They justified their stand by claiming that the North was systematically denying the just aspirations of the South. They pressed for federal support of the expansion of slavery into the territories and the suppression of antislavery agitation. As free-soil sentiment grew in the North, they called for secession as the final assertion of the supremacy of the state over the federal government. Prominent "fire-eaters" included William Lowndes Yancey of Alabama, Edmund Ruffin of Virginia, Robert Toombs of Georgia, and Robert Barnwell Rhett, James Henry Hammond, and William Gist of South Carolina.

FIRE ENGINE. *See* FIRE FIGHTING AND PREVENTION.

FIRE ESCAPES, stairways, ramps, or slides of fire-resistant material that allow safe exit from burning buildings. Most familiar are the iron or steel "fire escape" stairways, either return-platform or straight-run type, seen on the exterior of older buildings. The enclosed tower stairway, considered the safest, is a separate brick or concrete structure from the street to the roof of a building. Open-air balconies on each floor lead to the tower's firedoors, which open in the direction of exit. Enclosed interior stairways in modern office and apartment buildings are similar in construction to the tower stairways. Other fire escapes include outside metal stairs, slides, chutes, and horizontal exits (fire doors leading to another building).

Equipped with aerial ladder trucks, pumpers, and other sophisticated equipment, a metropolitan fire department battles to save lives and reduce property losses in a multiple-alarm fire.

FIRE FIGHTING AND PREVENTION. From earliest times, the fire that empowered man to cook food, drive off animals, shape tools, and survive intense cold, has also been an everlasting hazard to all who used it. Forest fires have always been a threat. When men began to live in villages and later to build cities the possibility of a blaze spreading into a conflagration increased. Rome was the scene of the first large fire about which there is extensive information. In the reign of Nero, A.D. 64, it destroyed much of the city. The Great Fire of London, recorded in Samuel Pepys' diary for 1666, devastated the city in five days. Moscow in the great conflagration of 1812, Hamburg in 1842, Chicago in 1871—all suffered tremendous loss from fire. In the present century, Chelsea, Mass., was destroyed by fire in 1908. In 1949 a fire in the crowded city of Chungking, China, killed 1,700 people.

To cope with this constant threat, municipalities and the industries they encompass maintain fire departments that stand ready with trained personnel and an array of specialized fire fighting equipment. The departments offer continuing schooling and stress careful planning.

Most fires are caused by carelessness. Thoughtless acts, such as allowing children to play with matches, tossing away lighted cigarettes or matches, overloading electrical wiring, and accumulating flammable rubbish, are typical examples of practices that sooner or later will call for the services of the fire department.

Home Fires

The menace of fire is present in every home. There are many precautions, however, that can be taken to minimize the danger. Many fire departments have established Fire Prevention and Fire Prevention Education Programs. A major effort in many departments has resulted in standardized inspection procedures, establishments of speakers' bureaus, and dissemination of fire-prevention information through news media, schools, and places of employment.

The National Board of Fire Underwriters lists the three most common causes of home fires as (1) carelessness with lighted matches and with smoking, (2) misuse of electricity, and (3) lightning. Some major causes of home fires include faulty television sets, defective heating and cooking equipment, and accumulation of rubbish. Knowing how to recognize a potential fire hazard, along with learning the precautions to take, can save lives and property. Some of the precautions are:

Matches and Smoking. Large, noncombustible ashtrays, instead of the use of plastic coasters as ashtrays. When emptying an ashtray, make sure there is no live ash left in it. Emptying ashtrays into a garbage pail or wastebasket may cause a fire. It is preferable to empty them into metal containers with a tight lid.

When discarding a lighted match, hold it for a second or so after blowing it out and then put it into an ashtray, never a wastebasket. Never carelessly toss away a lighted match or cigarette.

Never strike a match in, or carry a lighted candle into, closets, attics, or other confined spaces where combustible materials are stored. Use a flashlight.

Do not smoke while working near gasoline, oil drippings, or combustible vapors.

Never smoke in bed. It is too easy to fall asleep and drop a lighted cigarette. Toxic gases from a fire can render one unconscious before the heat has a chance to waken a sleeper.

Never leave small children where they can gain access to matches. A high incidence of fire and loss of life has resulted from fires started by unattended children playing with matches.

Misuse of Electricity. A large percentage of home fires are of electrical origin. Overloading of wires causes them to heat, and a fire may result. To be safe, one can do the following:

Have a competent electrician repair defective wiring. Install electric wiring and electric service adequate for equipment used in the home.

Buy only electrical appliances and cords approved by Underwriters Laboratories, Inc., a nonprofit organization that tests thousands of products for safety.

Use proper size fuses in the home. Generally, no larger fuse than 15 amps is required for the lighting needs in the average home.

Avoid the excessive use of extension cords and multiple plug outlets, which increase the chances of overloading electrical circuits. By checking lamp and extension cords frequently and replacing worn or broken cords, fires caused by short circuits can be prevented.

Do not run wires under rugs, over nails, or where they may be subjected to mechanical damage.

Disconnect electric irons when not in use.

Always remove cords from electric sockets by grasping the plug, not the wire.

Be sure wiring is adequate for such heavy appliances as air conditioners and electric stoves.

Television Sets. Do not make home repairs on television sets. Fire or shock may result.

TV sets generate considerable heat and should have adequate ventilation. Do not obstruct ventilation.

In some areas, TV antennae increase the danger of lightning striking the home. This can be prevented when setting up the antenna by the installation of lightning conductors.

Heating and Cooking Equipment. Furnaces, as well as chimneys and all flues, can be fire hazards when they are clogged. They should be cleaned regularly.

Qualified heating-service firms should be utilized when cleaning, adjusting, or repairing automatic heating units.

Ashes should not be placed in cardboard or wooden containers, only in metal cans.

Keep a metal fire screen in front of every fireplace to prevent sparks escaping.

Be sure your kitchen stove is in good repair. Do not hang curtains, towels, or other combustible materials near or in the stove.

Oven, broiler, and burners should be kept free of grease, and grease containers should be stored away from the stove.

There should be a sufficient clearance between stoves and combustible walls.

If the gas leaks, call the gas company immediately.

Never leave the house when the stove is lit.

Be sure the pilot light works properly.

Keep children away from the stove.

Turn off portable oil or gas heaters, before retiring. Place portable heaters where they cannot be easily tripped over or overturned. They should be kept away from combustible materials, such as bedding and furniture. In some cities, portable appliances, using flammable liquid mixtures for fuel, have been outlawed and can no longer be used legally. Avoid their use entirely.

Areas near furnaces should be free of combustible materials such as rubbish and paints.

Never throw flour or dust from the vacuum cleaner or dustpan into an open fire. Dust is explosive—wrap it up and dispose of it safely. Also, tenants in large city apartment buildings who dispose of trash in incinerator flues should first wrap up the refuse.

In case of a home fire, it is vital to know how to conduct oneself. The safety-conscious person will realize the urgency of notifying the fire department, so that he will be assured professional help is on the way. He should also get everyone out of the house immediately. These are two most important steps and it is essential that they be carried out at once.

Every family should have periodic fire drills to teach each member how to act in an emergency. Everyone in the family should be aware of two possible routes of escape from each room in the home. The telephone number of the local fire department should always be available near the telephone, and family members should learn the proper way to notify the fire department by telephone. They should also know the location of the fire alarm box nearest to the home and how to operate it. These are practices endorsed by the International Association of Fire Chiefs.

When reporting a fire, one should be calm, speaking slowly and clearly. Tell the fire department the location of the fire, and do not hang up until certain that it has the correct location. If one does not know the number of the local fire department, and it is not posted near the telephone, do not waste time searching for it. Dial the operator and say, "I want to report a fire." She will then connect you with the fire department.

In the event of fire in places of public assembly, the same rules apply as at home. Leave the premises as quickly and as calmly as possible. Notify the fire depart-

---

FIRE FIGHTING

Characteristics of the Field. Fire fighters, or firemen, at the call of an alarm must be prepared to go to a fire and handle any emergency they find there. On the scene a fighter has his assigned duty, such as connecting hose to a hydrant, or putting a ladder into place. In addition, he must be able to respond to the directions of the officers in charge, taking on new tasks as assigned, as well as handling emergencies on his own as they arise.

Fire fighters must also be adept in fire prevention, making inspections of public buildings and educating the public. While not actually fighting fires they have such duties as maintenance work at the station, studying fire manuals and textbooks, and participating in practice drills.

Every city and town of size has its fire department staffed by full-time paid employees. Some fire fighters also find employment with other governmental or private institutions. The many citizens who in small communities offer their services as volunteer firemen generally do so as a civic duty and are not professionals.

Qualifications. The hiring of city fire fighters is governed by local civil service regulations. In most cases applicants must pass a written test as well as a physical examination that determines strength, stamina, and agility. Most communities require a 21-year age minimum.

Education. A high school diploma is the customary academic requirement for becoming a fire fighter. Once on the job, the beginner in a large fire department receives a few weeks training in a fire service school. Here he studies firefighting techniques, building codes, fire prevention, first aid, and other related subjects.

Prospects for Employment. A large number of openings for professional fire fighters is expected annually. Newcomers will be needed just to replace those who die, retire, or leave the field for other work. Competition, however, is likely to remain keen, and in most cities there will be more applicants than job opportunities. Some industrial firms also hire fulltime fire fighters.

Income. The average earnings of firemen are not impressive, though some variation is found both geographically and by size of city. Generally the beginner receives salary increases annually during his first few years of service, as well as an allowance for protective clothing and equipment, and perhaps even for a dress uniform. In large departments the line of promotion is to lieutenant, then to captain, battalion chief, assistant chief, and chief, with pay increases each step along the way. In most cases a man has to be in the service five years or longer before promotion to lieutenant. Firemen tend to work a long week, though this is compensated for by considerable time on the job to pursue personal interests. Advantages of the profession are liberal pension plans, vacation pay, and other fringe benefits, including provision for retirement at half pay at an early age.

Sources of Information. In addition to the accompanying article on FIRE FIGHTING AND PREVENTION, the reader may want to turn to VOCATIONAL GUIDANCE for suggestions on career planning. Further information and reading materials may be obtained from the International Association of Fire Fighters, Washington, D.C., and the International Association of Fire Chiefs, Washington, D.C.

Fireboats spray a burning wharf, reaching areas inaccessible to standard fire-fighting equipment. (AUTHENTICATED NEWS INTERNATIONAL)

ment of the location of the fire, either by telephone or from the nearest fire alarm box. When entering a building, such as a theater or a restaurant, make note of an alternate way out. This can be done by remembering secondary stairway locations, exit signs, and the location of fire escapes. It is vital to remain calm, remembering that one can be crushed to death in a panicked mob. Act quietly and with a clear head.

How to Escape a Burning Building

Ten points to keep in mind when caught in a building fire are:

1. *Alternate Exit:* Use the nearest exit that is available and safe.

2. *Get Out:* It is always dangerous to remain in a burning building. Fires often spread rapidly and cut off escape, and are likely to generate poisonous gases.

3. *Keep Calm:* If there is a panicked rush for the main exit, keep out of the crowd and attempt to find other means of escape.

4. *Hold Breath—Keep Low:* If forced to remain in a smoke-filled building, remember that the air is usually better near the floor. If you must make a dash through smoke or flame, hold your breath.

5. *Seek Refuge:* Call for help. A temporary refuge may be secured behind any closed door. Try to pick a room with a window to the outside. Open the window at the top and bottom. Air comes in at the bottom, and smoke and heat will escape at the top.

6. *Do Not Jump:* Do not jump from upper-story windows, except as a last resort. Many people have jumped to their deaths, even as firemen were bringing ladders to rescue them.

7. *Evaluate the Situation:* Feel closed doors with the palm of the hand. If a door is hot, do not open it. If you feel no heat, the door may be opened carefully. Keep your body behind the door, with one hand held at the opening. If the air is hot, or if you feel pressure, slam the door shut.

8. *Closed Doors:* If you leave a room that is on fire, close the door behind you. This limits the amount of oxygen available to the fire and keeps the hall free from heated gases and fire.

9. *Caught In Smoke:* If you are caught in smoke, take short breaths, breathe through the nose. Crouch or crawl along the floor to escape, remembering that heated gases rise, and in the area nearest the floor the air is most likely to be cooler and more breathable.

10. *Do Not Return:* Take no chances by re-entering a burning building to save property. Only the saving of lives justifies taking a personal risk. Leave the job of fighting the fire to firemen.

If one's clothing catches fire, he should cross his arms across the chest, so that the right hand touches the left shoulder, and the left touches the right shoulder. He should drop to the floor and slowly roll over and over. Lying on the floor and folding the arms keeps the flame away from the face. Rolling over will help cut off the air and put out the fire. Never run! That stirs more air toward the flames, causing them to intensify.

In case of a fire in an automobile while it is in motion, do not slam on the brakes suddenly, thus risking being hit by a following car. Pull off to the side, turn off the ignition, and leave the car. If the fire is small and there is a portable fire extinguisher, use it, spraying the contents at the base of the flames. Otherwise, notify the fire department. Most automobile fires are electrical in origin, though some are caused by carelessly dropped cigarettes and others by mishandling of fuel.

Industrial Fires

Industrial fires, like home fires, are usually caused by carelessness. However, the danger of fire is considerably greater in an industrial installation, and the dollar loss is much higher.

Today, most industrial plants observe strict safety regulations. Many have their own safety departments, employing personnel who are well trained in the fire-safety field. Plant maintenance and operational safety are closely supervised by safety inspectors. Machines are adequately spaced apart from each other to permit cleaner and safer work areas and allow easier inspection. Smoking is forbidden in areas where flammable materials are present. Fireproof doors (usually self-closing, on a fusible link) are used to separate work areas. These doors are kept free of obstructions and are generally kept closed at night.

Many modern plants are equipped with fire-fighting apparatus and appliances, and they employ their own firemen. These plants usually have the latest fire-detection systems, including alarm systems which are connected, either directly or indirectly, to the local fire department, and interior alarms as well.

Automatic sprinkler systems are effective fire-extinguishing devices, when properly installed and supplied with water under pressure. The reliability of such a system also depends upon proper maintenance and periodic inspection. The sprinkler system is usually connected to a signaling system that automatically notifies a central

---

MAJOR CAUSES OF INDUSTRIAL FIRES

1. Combustible materials in boiler rooms.
2. Accumulations of lint, dust, and dirt on top of steampipes that ignite and spread flame throughout the plant.
3. Spontaneous combustion of soft coal, rags, or leaves.
4. Improperly lubricated machinery that causes the bearings to overheat and ignite.
5. Improperly wired or insulated electrical installations for power, heat, or lighting.
6. Improper use of chemicals. Lime, for example, builds up heat when it gets wet, and often causes fires. Among chemicals that require special precautions are: nitrates, chlorates, inorganic and organic peroxides, carbon disulfide, picric acid, nitroparaffins, and hydrazine.
7. Gas leaks resulting from improperly installed gas heaters and appliances.

---

agency, whenever the system is activated. These systems are also equipped with facilities, usually a siamese connection on the exterior of the building, to allow the fire department to supply water to the system when necessary. The sprinkler heads in such a system are installed on piping which can carry the water to any area of a fire. These sprinkler heads are similar to a faucet or garden sprinkler that, when open, allows the water to pour out. The head is held closed by a fusible link, usually a bismuth alloy, that melts at a pre-set temperature. When heat melts this soft metal, it opens the sprinkler head aperture and allows the water to flow. The sprinkler head is usually fitted with a deflector that causes the flowing water to spray over a wide area. The area covered and the spray pattern are determined by the type of deflector. The spray pattern can be upward or downward, square or circular, right or left. The spray is thrown over and on the fire, either extinguishing it or helping to control it and prevent its spread.

In areas where the sprinkler pipes might freeze, dry pipe (containing no water) sprinklers are used. These may be found on open piers, in unheated freight sheds, and in refrigerated areas, like those in a food-processing plant. The pipes in this system contain air under pressure that holds back the water in the lines. When a sprinkler head fuses because of heat, the sprinkler head opens, the air rushes out, and the water flows through the pipe. It is sprayed over the fire area to extinguish or control the fire.

Many industrial plants also have a complement of auxiliary fire-fighting equipment to assist the sprinkler systems. This equipment includes various types of fire extinguishers and sand or water pails. The type of plant generally governs the auxiliary equipment used. Carbon dioxide extinguishers are employed where there is electrical equipment. In some types of occupancies, such as gasoline stations or garages, dry chemical, carbon dioxide, or foam extinguishers are desirable. Pressurized water or soda and acid extinguishers, or water pails, are desirable where common rubbish fires may occur. Sand pails are common in plants where there is a danger that small flammable liquid fires may break out. The use of sand pails, however, is limited. They are of no value in controlling flammable liquid fires in deep pans or vats. In plants where water may be best used to extinguish a fire, yard hydrants or standpipe systems, equipped with hoses, usually are found.

Fire Extinguishers

Fire is a combination of heat, fuel, and oxygen (air). This is known as the Fire Triangle. All three are necessary to have a fire. The action of the fire extinguisher is either to cool the burning substance to below its ignition temperature, or to exclude air supply, or a combination of both. These are quenching, cooling, and blanketing effects.

Fires are generally classed as Class A, Class B, or Class C, and the class of fire determines the type of fire extinguisher to be used. There is also a special class of fires, known as Class D.

Class A Fires are fires of ordinary combustible materials, such as paper, wood, or cloth. The quenching and cooling effects of quantities of water, or solutions containing large percentages of water, are of first importance. An example is a rubbish fire, or a fire in a wastebasket. The extinguishers that would be used are a soda and acid type, a pressurized water type, or a water tank and pump type.

Class B Fires are fires of flammable liquids, greases, or related materials. Examples are fires in open vats of flammable liquids and gasoline spills. In fighting them a blanketing, or smothering, effect is essential. A water extinguisher would have little effect on the fire, and would tend to spread it by floating the burning liquids. On Class B fires, a carbon dioxide, dry chemical, or foam extinguisher is most effective. These extinguishers have a smothering effect, and by excluding oxygen from a fire, will extinguish it.

Class C Fires. In fires in electrical equipment, as in an electric generator motor, the use of a nonconducting extinguishing agent is of prime importance. Carbon dioxide or dry chemical extinguishers are the best. Their agents are nonconductors of electricity. It can readily be seen that a water-type extinguishing agent would be most dangerous around electrical equipment.

Class D Fires comprise a special class recognized by the National Fire Protection Association. These are fires in

Fire inspectors on the job. Fire prevention is a primary function of any fire department. (NEW YORK CITY FIRE DEPARTMENT)

Classroom instruction for student firemen. They are learning how to handle a burning railroad tankcar. (MERRIM-MONKMEYER)

A mobile fire-fighting unit in action. It carries its own water, and sprays it with its own power. (AUTHENTICATED NEWS INTERNATIONAL)

such metals as magnesium, potassium, powdered aluminum, zinc, sodium, titanium, and zirconium, which require careful fire attack, with special extinguishing agents. One of these agents is "Pyrene" G–1, which is composed of screened graphitized foundry coke, to which organic phosphate has been added. The graphite reduces the temperature and smothers the fire. This is only one of several commercially available extinguishing agents for fire in combustible metals.

Vaporizing liquids, such as carbon tetrachloride, were

Fighters try to stop a forest fire by making a break between the burning and untouched areas. (AUTHENTICATED NEWS INTERNATIONAL)

popular some years ago as extinguishers of petroleum and electrical fires. However, it was found that when applied to hot metal, such as a stove top, a chemical reaction converted the carbon tetrachloride into a deadly gas, known as phosgene.

Forest and Brush Fires

Forest fires are difficult to fight and usually rage out of control for long periods before they are extinguished. Often covering large areas that are almost inaccessible, they cannot be fought with the fire-fighting strategy used in cities and towns. Large numbers of men, much equipment, and thousands of gallons of water and chemicals must be brought into play. Chemical borate solutions, containing wetting agents, are dropped from airplanes and helicopters to penetrate and coat the trees, thus slowing down the fire and extinguishing it. Breaks are made between stands of trees to stop the spread of the flame. A break is a clearing of trees over a large space between the burning area and the untouched area as an attempt to cause the fire to burn itself out because of lack of fuel. Sometimes, controlled backfires are used to stop the spread of a forest fire. Forest fires sometimes burn across the tops of trees. These are known as crown fires. Forest fires can burn with great intensity and, aided by winds, become conflagrations, which can spread over large areas, causing great loss of property.

Fire wardens are employed as fire spotters in order to try to detect and stop incipient forest fires. They utilize high towers, airplanes, and helicopters in a fire watch which, in especially hot dry weather, is constantly maintained. Airplanes and helicopters are used to bring men, as speedily as possible, to locations where fires are spotted, in order to control them before they spread out of control.

Brush fires are also a high hazard in suburban areas, and in parkland and undeveloped areas within cities.

They are usually fast burning, and in California spectacular fires have caused the loss of many homes. They are fought by local fire departments with water and rattan brooms. Some brush may grow taller than a man, and when it catches fire is difficult to control. Here, heavy streams may be necessary to control the fires.

Forest fires are generally started through carelessness by hunters and campers, who do not properly extinguish campfires or who carelessly toss away lighted cigarettes. Lightning can also be a cause of forest fires.

Brush fires start in much the same way. In New York City the fire department has found, from experience, that the greatest number of brush fires occur after school hours and during holidays—periods when children are out of school. This indicates that children, through carelessness or pranks and vandalism, are a large contributing cause to the many brush fires.

Fire Alarms

Methods of transmitting alarms vary. In large cities, fire alarm boxes are located on street corners and are generally connected to a central office by a telegraph cable. The central office in turn retransmits the alarms to the fire houses in the city, which are assigned by a predetermined plan.

In some areas where there are volunteer fire departments, the fire alarm boxes are attached to horns or sirens. When an alarm is sent from the box, the horn or siren emits a coded number, notifying the fire department or volunteers that there is a fire, and its location.

In complex cities, such as New York City, the fire department has a Bureau of Fire Communications, which is responsible for all fire alarm, telegraph, telephone, radio, and voice facilities. Every year this bureau handles many thousands of street box alarms, verbal alarms, and building box alarms.

Radio communications have become a large part of the modern-day fire department. Fire companies are dispatched to alarms for fire via radio. In a large city, fire companies may be out of quarters on inspectional and educational programs; or, they may be in the process of returning to quarters from a previous alarm; or, they may be at the scene of a fire alarm, but available for response to other alarms. These companies can be dispatched by radio to alarms of fire received while they are not accessible to telegraph communications. Fire companies are always available, because they are in constant communication with the central fire alarm office. This gives the fire department greater mobility and efficiency.

In New York City, street fire alarm boxes are connected to the central station by a closed telegraph circuit. When an alarm is transmitted by a citizen (generally by pulling an outer handle on the alarm box), a signal is transmitted to the central office over a closed telegraphic circuit, giving the location of the fire alarm box. The dispatcher at the central station then notifies the companies who are assigned to this area by retransmitting the signal over a telegraph circuit, with which all fire houses in the city are connected. If the companies are not in quarters, or are in the process of answering a previous fire alarm, but are available to respond, the central office dispatcher can

notify them to respond to the later alarm via radio communications.

At the scene of a fire, the senior officer, generally a chief officer, is in command. If the fire cannot be controlled by the companies answering the initial alarm, the chief may transmit additional alarms. This is generally done by radio communications, or else the telegraph circuit on the fire alarm system can be utilized. That is, additional alarms can be transmitted from the alarm box by use of a telegraph key in the interior of the box. All officers in the fire department in New York City are provided with an alarm box key. However, this method of transmitting greater alarms has been largely outmoded by radio communications.

When greater alarms are transmitted because of a large fire, the protective machinery of the fire department is set into motion. Companies relocate from other areas of the city into the quarters of companies that are operating at the fire. Thus, the facilities of the fire department are spread out to cover the entire city and provide maximum fire protection to the public. No area is stripped of fire protection coverage because of a large fire in progress.

Fire-Fighting Equipment

The equipment used by a fire department varies in accordance with the type of fire it is likely to encounter. Small towns do not usually require trucks equipped with aerial ladders. They would be more likely to emphasize pumpers, water tankers, and hose trucks equipped with portable ladders. They would have most use for pumping engines capable of moving water over long distances. The New York City Fire Department has equipment designed to meet the particular problems encountered in a city so complex and huge.

Pumping engines and aerial ladder trucks are the two most common types of fire apparatus generally used by a fire department. A pumping engine, usually called a pumper, carries several hundred feet of hose, and assorted equipment, such as axes, hooks, extinguishers, wrenches, nozzles, and hose fittings. Ladder trucks usually are equipped with several types of ladders, forcible entry tools, nets, ropes, and hooks. Aerial ladder trucks, of the type found in a large city such as New York, are generally equipped with hydraulically operated ladders. The aerial ladder generally can reach a height of about 100 ft (30 m). There is a variety of other types of fire-fighting apparatus, such as foam trucks, rescue vans, salvage company trucks, and special type pumpers.

A city with diverse problems such as New York City has special equipment, such as the tower ladder units. This is essentially a mobile, exterior, hydraulic elevator that operates by a system of controls. The platform is attached to a boom which telescopes so that the platform can be raised or lowered.

Some cities located on harbors equip their departments with fireboats. The New York Fire Department has a Marine Division, which is equipped with fireboats, a fireboat tender, and a special boat unit for use in shallow water. This division of the fire department protects the Port of New York and is responsible for approximately 650 mi (1 050 km) of usable waterfront, serviced by ranks of piers that handle oceangoing vessels.

A fireman checking with his communications bureau. For him, prompt, dependable contact is essential.

Fireboats are equipped with powerful pumps to draw water from the harbor and shoot it under great pressure, at ranges of several hundred feet. They have large turret-type monitor nozzles for use on ship and pier fires. They can also pump water to land fires to help augment the land engine companies' supply of water.

Among the most valuable pieces of equipment the modern fire department utilizes is the two-way radio apparatus, including walkie-talkie type units that are invaluable at the scene of a fire. They have vastly increased the efficiency of the fire fighter.

Another valuable advance in modernization for the fire fighter is the development of self-containing breathing equipment. It allows firemen to enter smoky buildings without fear of suffocation. The fireman carries his own air, or oxygen, supply in a tank fitted to a face mask.

There have been other advances in the development of fire-fighting equipment with safety advantages for the fireman, such as protective eye shields that are an integral part of the fire helmet.

There is constant testing and development of new types of equipment, such as fire-protective clothing and various power saws to aid in ventilating, searching, and overhauling at fires. New types of lightweight hose have been developed to assist in more efficient operations.

History of Fire Fighting

Rome. The ancient Romans were the first to organize a resistance to the terrible menace of fire. Rome was the first city to organize a regular fire-fighting force—numbering over 7,000. The homes of the poorer Romans, in the most populous area of the city, were usually built of wood and straw. Each family maintained a fire on a small altar in honor of the domestic gods. Fires frequently broke out.

In those days, long before the discovery of electricity, there were human alarm boxes, officially called nocturns. These nocturns were strategically stationed throughout the city. The alarm was relayed from one nocturn to another until it reached the nearest castra, which we know as a firehouse. The duty of the nocturn was then to rush to the scene of the fire, driving back crowds and establishing fire lines. Then would come a centurion leading a company of firemen, complete with leather trousers, jackets, and helmets. They were equipped with wooden hand pumps that worked like bellows or syringes (siphons), axes, hammers, saws, iron bars, and short ladders, so made that the ends could be clamped together to reach the roofs of buildings.

Following these came hundreds of aquarii, carrying light earthenware jars or vases. The aquarii formed chains from the nearest cistern, supplied from the great aqueducts leading into the city, and presently the jars would begin emptying a stream of water in the siphons for application to the fire. The prefectus vigilum, equivalent to the fire chief of today, would take command of the fire on his arrival. Surgeons, too, would be in attendance. Usually three were attached to each castra (firehouse). Also, pillow bearers in groups of four, carrying huge leather pillows, 4 ft (1.2 m) square and stuffed with feathers, would respond. Their purpose was to rescue people trapped at upper windows of buildings. As the forerunner of today's fire marshall, the questionarius was also on the scene. His job was to question the people and try to ascertain the cause of the fire. Roman law at that time demanded that responsibility be fixed for every fire. The questionarius established a board of inquiry before the flames had died.

London. From the late 1500's to the 1700's, the people of London endeavored to build effective fire-fighting equipment in the form of huge syringes operated by three men. Each syringe had a capacity of about a half gallon of water. They provided the people of London with a false sense of security. On Sept. 2, 1666, a fire broke out which raged for five days and virtually destroyed the city. From the embers of the Great London Fire came the world's first organized fire department since the time of the Romans. Within a year of the fire, the world's first fire insurance policy was written.

Colonial America. Ten years after the fire of London, merchants in Boston ordered fire-fighting equipment from England to protect their city from a like disaster. In 1679 the colonies had their first paid fire department, their first firehouse, and, for the first time, men were paid to put out fires. Boston was divided into five fire districts, and wardens were appointed to patrol each district. The fire wards, as they were called, could order any resident to help in fighting fires. In 1718 the first fire society was organized, thus beginning a long era of volunteer firemen, which has carried over into modern times.

Benjamin Franklin organized Philadelphia's first fire company in 1736, and cofounded America's first successful mutual fire insurance company 16 years later. Philadelphia passed fire laws aimed at poorly constructed or dirty chimneys, providing a fine of 40 shillings should one "be so foul as to take fire." Other laws ordered every house to have at least one fire bucket ready for use. Laws also ordered "no person should presume to smoke tobacco in the streets, either by day or night."

The history of organized fire fighting in New York began in 1648, when, during the administration of Governor Peter Stuyvesant, the first fire ordinance was adopted by the Dutch settlement of New Amsterdam. The act provided that any funds realized from fines levied for dirty chimneys would be used for the maintenance of buckets, hooks, and ladders. It also established a fire watch of eight wardens and required that each male citizen stand watch in turn.

In Dec., 1731, the schooner Beaver arrived in New York bearing two hand-drawn pumpers from distant London. These pumpers were the first engines to be used in the colony. With the arrival of the pumpers, all able-bodied citizens were required to respond to alarms and perform duty under the supervision of aldermen. The roster of the first two engine companies reveals the names of many prominent and wealthy citizens of the time.

Professional Departments. With the colony fast growing northward, the General Assembly, in Dec., 1737, passed an act which established the Volunteer Fire Department of the City of New York. This organization was to continue under this name for 128 years, until in 1865, after the close of the Civil War, it was superseded by the paid Metropolitan Fire Department.

In 1853 the city of Cincinnati introduced the first steam fire engine. This was really the beginning of the trained, professional fireman. Instead of pulling the engines by hand, professionals used horses; instead of hand pumpers, they used heavy steam pumpers.

In 1908 gasoline engines began to replace the horse as a means of propelling the large steam pumpers. As the internal combustion engine was further developed, it was soon to replace the steam engine as a means of driving the pumps. The romantic day of the steam pumper, pulled by charging horses, was nearing an end. Soon other forms of modernization, such as aerial ladder trucks, aluminum ladders, stainless steel fittings and hose connections, and a variety of chemical extinguishers, replaced old-fashioned equipment.

In 1904 a fire in Baltimore, Md., brought fire companies from many communities. Unfortunately, in those days, all hose couplings were not the same and did not fit Baltimore's hydrants. As a result, a great many fire trucks could not be utilized. They stood idly by while the fire took a greater toll than necessary. This brought hose manufacturers, hydrant makers, and fire departments together to establish a code of standards.

Recent years have seen many improvements in fire-fighting methods, fire prevention, and fire protection. Fire losses have spiraled through the years, with the development and expansion of population and industry. But with much credit to the modern fire department, the number of fires has not increased in similar proportions.

Today, the fire department has become a complex of men and equipment. It features rigorous training, home and buildings inspections, and careful planning. Fire fighting is only one of its many responsibilities. Other functions include fire prevention, public relations and education, administration, training of officers and men, and maintenance of equipment, fire alarms, and communications systems.

The public over the years has become more aware of the importance of the fire service. In the United States the continuing observance of Fire Prevention Week, the oldest of the presidentially proclaimed "weeks," is an example of this. The idea originated in small Midwest

SOME OF THE WORLD'S NOTABLE FIRES

64	A.D. Rome—burned for 8 days; consumed 70% of the city.
798	London—destroyed most of the city.
1137	York—destroyed the entire city.
1666	London—"The Great Fire." Burned for five days and consumed 13,200 buildings.
1728	Copenhagen—city nearly destroyed; 1,650 houses burned.
1756	Constantinople—15,000 houses destroyed.
1812	Moscow—Russians burned city to drive out Napoleon. In five days, 90% of the city was razed; 30,800 houses destroyed.
1822	Canton, China—city 85% destroyed.
1825	New Brunswick, Canada—forest fire destroyed 4,000,000 acres, killed 160 people.
1835	New York City—530 buildings (13 acres) destroyed; loss $15,000,000.
1842	Hamburg—4,219 buildings burned; 15% of the city destroyed.
1845	Pittsburgh—1,100 buildings destroyed.
1871	Chicago—"The Great Chicago Fire." 250 people killed; 98,500 persons homeless; 17,430 buildings destroyed; loss, $175,000,000.
1871	Peshtigo, Wis.—forest fire destroyed 1,280,000 forest acres; 1,152 people killed.
1872	Boston—"Great Fire of Boston." 776 buildings destroyed; loss, $75,000,000.
1904	New York City—excursion steamer *General Slocum* burned; 1,030 people killed.
1906	San Francisco—earthquake and fire; 75% of the city burned; 28,000 buildings destroyed.
1923	Tokyo and Yokohama—fires following earthquakes destroyed 70% of Tokyo and most of Yokohama.
1942	Boston—Coconut Grove nightclub fire killed 492 people.
1961	Niteroi, suburb of Rio de Janeiro—circus fire; 326 people killed.
1974	São Paulo—fire caused by defective air conditioner in bank building killed 189 people.
1977	Southgate, Ky.—Beverly Hills Supper Club fire killed 161 persons.

communities, where clean-up campaigns to lessen the incidence of fire and beautify homes and gardens had taken hold. As a result of such activities there were fewer fires, and communities soon began to refer to "clean-up" day as Fire Prevention Day. On Oct. 9, 1911, the 40th anniversary of the Great Chicago Fire, President Woodrow Wilson issued the nation's first Fire Prevention Proclamation. President Warren G. Harding proclaimed Fire Prevention Week 11 years later.

The week set aside always contains the date of the Great Chicago Fire of Oct. 8–10, 1871. The week marks the anniversary of one of America's biggest fires, which destroyed 17,430 buildings and resulted in the death of 250 persons and losses of more than $175,000,000.

Consult Bauer, Jeraldine, *Fire Engines Past and Present* (1975); Erven, Lawrence W., *Fire Company Apparatus and Procedure* (1974); International City Managers Association, *Municipal Fire Administration* (7th ed., 1967); Kirk, P. L., *Fire Investigation* (1969); Walsh, Charles V., *Firefighting Strategy and Leadership* (1963).

ROBERT O. LOWERY

FIREFLY, elongated, flattened beetle, also known as the lightning bug, in the family Lampyridae. Fireflies are found in Europe and North America. *Photinus pyralis*, a common North American species, has dark-brown forewings, often with a lighter margin. Its head is hidden beneath a projection of the thorax. In many species the females are wingless and resemble larvae. During the day fireflies hide in grasses and vegetation, and appear at night to form a twinkling array of flashing lights. Most adult fireflies do not feed at all. The females lay eggs, in damp locations, that hatch into brown larvae known as glowworms. The larvae feed on snails, slugs, and cutworms and can be used to control these garden pests. Both adults and larvae possess luminous, yellowish-green segments in the abdomen. Firefly light is "cold" light—it is produced by an almost complete conversion of potential energy into light. The light is caused by the oxidation of a substance called luciferin, which takes place through the action of an enzyme, luciferase. The flashing mechanism is considered a mating response, each species having a characteristic flashing rhythm by which it can be recognized.

CLARENCE J. HYLANDER, Author, *Insects on Parade*

FIRE ISLAND, narrow, 30-mi.-long barrier beach off the south-central coast of Long Island, New York, between Great South Bay and the Atlantic Ocean. There are summer colonies here and at the western end a state park. Fire Island, sometimes called Great South Beach, is reached by ferries and automobile bridge from Long Island. Length, about 30 mi.; width, ¼ to ½ mi.

FIRENZE. *See* FLORENCE.

FIREPLACE, hearth for heating and cooking by fire. Although it was once essential to man's living habits, the fireplace has become a decorative as well as practical feature in today's homes.

History. In primitive shelters the fireplace was nothing more than a burning clump on the floor and a hole through the roof for the escape of smoke. It was not until the 11th century that fireplaces were set against the wall next to a vent. The first chimneys that followed the wall fireplaces were unsatisfactory. They guided smoke out through the roof but also permitted downdrafts which interfered with combustion. Since the heat given off was limited to the radiation from the fire itself, the medieval fireplaces became huge areas built so that several persons could sit around them comfortably absorbing the fire's heat. Then in the 1600's a French physician, Louis Savot (1579–1640), invented an air inlet placed beneath the hearth. It provided better combustion but still did not increase the heat radiation. This problem was solved when another Frenchman, Nicolas Gauger, in 1713 devised a fireplace with a hollow metal form surrounding the back and sides of the fire. As the air circulated around the hot metal, it became warm and then passed into the room. In 1745 Benjamin Franklin introduced an inverted flue that gave still more heated surface with which to heat the air. His flue was a long metal pipe curved up and down and through which hot air passed. Franklin, in essence, created a stove rather than a fireplace and his ideas led to the familiar finned heating radiator.

The most significant contribution to modern fireplace design was made by the Englishman Benjamin Thompson (Count Rumford, 1753–1814) in the early 19th century. By sloping the side walls of the firebox and the upper half of the back wall inward he increased the heat reflections; he also created the smoke shelf at the bottom of the flue. The smoke shelf deflected cold downdrafts and allowed a smoke-free operation. Modern fireplaces are based on Count Rumford's innovations.

Fireplace Design. The opening of the fireplace is usually slightly wider than it is high, and the depth is one-half the height of the opening. The width of the back wall is two-thirds of the front width. The throat of the opening formed next to the smoke shelf is where the damper is installed. Above this is the smoke dome which tapers into the chimney flue. Fireplace linings are of fire-brick and the flue lining of fire clay, preferably glazed. The hearth and the facing of the fireplace can be brick, flagstone, or dec-

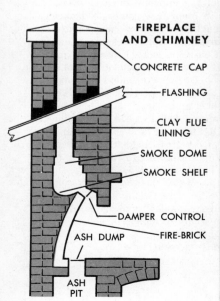

FIREPLACE AND CHIMNEY

CONCRETE CAP

FLASHING

CLAY FLUE LINING

SMOKE DOME

SMOKE SHELF

DAMPER CONTROL

ASH DUMP

FIRE-BRICK

ASH PIT

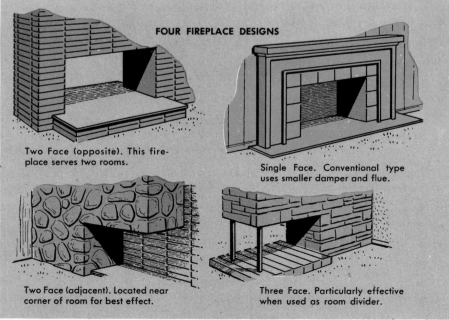

FOUR FIREPLACE DESIGNS

Two Face (opposite). This fireplace serves two rooms.

Single Face. Conventional type uses smaller damper and flue.

Two Face (adjacent). Located near corner of room for best effect.

Three Face. Particularly effective when used as room divider.

orative tile. Steel fireplace forms require only a masonry exterior and a flue. Some are double-walled so that the flow of air passing between raises the heat output. Prefabricated fireplace units, together with prefabricated chimney units, require no masonry work and can be quickly installed.

Modern architecture often calls for a fireplace with front and back openings between two rooms, or openings on three sides. These steel forms, containing damper, smoke shelf, and smoke dome, require a masonry exterior and chimney.

JOHN ENNEY, Editor, *Family Handyman*

See also CHIMNEY.

FIRESTONE, HARVEY SAMUEL (1868–1938), American industrialist, founder of the Firestone Tire and Rubber Company. Born in Ohio, Firestone started his company in 1900 in Akron, and from the outset supplied automobile manufacturers with tires. In 1923 Firestone introduced the balloon tire that became standard on motor vehicles. He established huge rubber plantations in Liberia and promoted the development of rubber production in South America and the Philippines. Firestone was president of his company from 1903 to 1932 and chairman of the board from 1932 until his death. He wrote *America Should Produce Its Own Rubber* (1923) and, with Samuel Crowther, *Men and Rubber* (1926).

FIRE WALKING, walking through flames or over hot stones or coals as part of a religious ritual or a religious ordeal. This practice was found in ancient India and in modern times has been reported in India, Japan, Mauritius, New Zealand, Fiji, Tahiti, Trinidad, Haiti, and Bulgaria. Somewhat akin to fire walking was the fire dance of the North American Indians, in which barefoot dancers stamped on glowing embers. Fire walking is taken by believers in the ritual as proof of supernatural presence or assistance. The phenomenon is usually associated with states of trance in which the walker is anesthetized by psychological means rather than by drugs. This is no more mysterious than other types of psychologically induced resistance to pain, although little is known about the bodily processes involved.

To the wonder of his Ceylonese audience a fire walker treads over glowing coals. He is one of a cult whose members travel from village to village throughout the year.

Ewing Krainin

Authenticated News International

Skyrockets bursting over the Rhine River illuminate the ancient German fortress of Ehrenbreitstein, in Coblenz.

FIREWORKS, variety of devices used for religious or entertainment purposes. They contain incendiary compounds that produce sound, color, smoke, or movement, or combinations of these. The ingredients consist of fuels, oxidizers, and modifying agents. The fuels used are charcoal, sulfur, antimony sulfide, and powdered metals. Chlorates and nitrates usually provide oxygen for the reaction, since fireworks do not use atmospheric oxygen. Various colors are obtained from metal salts. Sodium produces yellow; copper, blue-green; calcium, red; strontium, scarlet; and barium, green. Picric acid or sulfur tends to intensify the colors, and ammonium salts increase the shades obtainable. Addition of iron and aluminum powder provides sparks and fiery displays. The craft of blending mixtures and packaging them is an ancient one in China, where fireworks are used for religious purposes. In Europe fireworks for entertainment have been manufactured since the 13th century. In many places throughout the United States and Canada the sale of fireworks is restricted by law because of the danger of injury.

FIRKUŠNY [*fír-kŭs′nē*], **RUDOLF** (1912–   ), Czech pianist. Among his teachers were Leoš Janáček and Artur Schnabel. After a concert appearance in Prague in 1920 he toured Europe and in 1929 was soloist in Prague in his own piano concerto. He made his New York debut in 1938 and in 1943 toured South America. Though excelling in the interpretation of standard works, he is particularly known for his playing of major piano works by contemporary composers, among them Martinů and Menotti. He appears occasionally with leading chamber music organizations and major symphony orchestras.

FIRST AID

FIRST AID refers to the immediate, temporary care of limited extent given to the victim of an accident or sudden illness before the arrival of a physician. Immediate action is required only (1) when there is severe bleeding (hemorrhage); (2) when breathing has stopped for any reason; (3) when poison has been swallowed; and (4) when irritating chemicals come in contact with the skin or get in the eyes. Should any of these situations confront one who has had even elementary first-aid training, he may be able to save a life.

In first aid the words "signs" and "symptoms" are frequently used. Signs refer to what can be seen either with respect to the body or at the accident scene. Symptoms refer to the feelings of the victim. For example, in shock, signs are perspiration, dilated eyes, shallow and irregular breathing, weakness or absence of pulse, and so on. Symptoms are feelings of weakness, nausea, dizziness, and the like.

Remedial First-Aid Action

Control of Bleeding: *Hemorrhage.* When a large artery or vein is severed, a person can bleed to death in a minute or so. In cases of severe bleeding, always be concerned first with applying pressure *directly* over the bleeding part, preferably with a clean cloth but, if necessary, with the bare hand. If the cloth held on the part becomes saturated with blood, do not remove it, but place another on top of it. Removal of the saturated cloth will disturb the normal clotting processes. At two places on each side of the body large arteries lie close to the surface along one of the long bones. There are instances when pressure on the supplying blood vessel combined with direct pressure on the part may be helpful in controlling profuse bleeding. For example, pressure on the artery in the area about midway between the armpit and the elbow will sometimes reduce the flow of blood into the part below. If pressure is exerted on the artery where it crosses the groin, the flow of blood should be lessened in the part below that point.

Tourniquet. The tourniquet is mentioned principally to discourage its use. Its application usually causes tissue injury, and many times it is applied needlessly. Its function is to shut off the *entire* blood supply to the area immediately adjacent to the point where it is applied. Use of the tourniquet is justified only when all other attempts to control life-threatening bleeding fail, or where there is partial or complete severance of an arm or leg.

If it is decided to use a tourniquet, it should be placed close above the wound, toward the heart, but not at the wound edge. There should be normal uninjured skin between the tourniquet and the wound. If the wound is near a joint, the tourniquet should be applied at the nearest practical point above the joint. Make sure that the tourniquet is applied tightly enough to stop bleeding. If improperly applied, it is likely to increase venous bleeding.

Improvised tourniquets should be made of flat material about 2 in. wide. Avoid using ropes, wires, or sash cords, since they will cut into and damage the underlying tissues and blood vessels. To apply an improvised tourniquet: (1) wrap the material tightly twice around the limb, if possible, and tie a half knot; (2) place a short

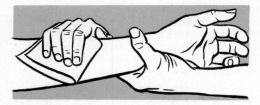

Clean cloth applied to wound with direct pressure controls bleeding.

Finger pressure on brachial artery will reduce bleeding of arm wound below pressure point.

Pressure on femoral artery crossing groin lessens bleeding of leg wound.

A tourniquet should be used as a last resort *only if all other methods to stop profuse bleeding have failed.* Application: Tourniquet strip is tied. Stick is twisted, and secured to halt bleeding.

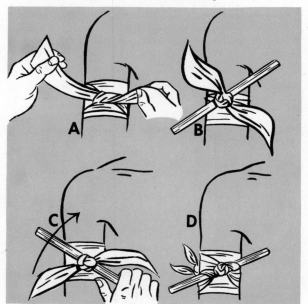

stout stick or similar article on the half knot and tie a full knot; (3) twist the stick to tighten the tourniquet until the flow of blood ceases; (4) secure the stick in place with the loose ends of the tourniquet or another strip of cloth.

Once a tourniquet is applied, the victim should be taken as soon as possible to a physician. Only a physician who is prepared to control hemorrhage and replace lost blood volume should release it. Experience has shown that a properly applied tourniquet can be left in place 1 or 2 hours without causing undue damage. However, a note should be attached to the victim, giving the location and the hour of application of the tourniquet if the first-aider does not accompany him to the hospital or physician's office.

Wounds in Which Bleeding is Not Severe. The best source of information concerning home care for minor cuts and scratches is your family physician. Lacking such advice, the following procedure is recommended: (1) wash the hands thoroughly with clean water and soap; (2) cleanse the wound thoroughly, using plain soap and boiled water cooled to room temperature or clean running tapwater and soap; (3) use a sterile or, at least, a clean piece of cloth to apply the soap and water; (4) apply a dry sterile dressing or a dressing made from clean cloth and bandage it snugly into place; (5) be sure to tell the victim to see his doctor promptly, especially if soreness develops.

Stoppage of Breathing. A person may cease to breathe as a result of disease or accident. If breathing stops as a result of disease, body conditions may not permit life, and artificial respiration efforts are of questionable value. On the other hand, if breathing has been suspended due to accidental causes, it is often possible to revive the person if artificial respiration can be given in time.

The causes of asphyxiation may be divided into four categories.

1. Complete shutting off of air (drowning, choking, strangling).
2. Insufficient supply of oxygen in the air (in abandoned ice boxes, empty silos, vats, wells, and cisterns).
3. Displacement of oxygen from the circulating blood (carbon monoxide poisoning, certain combinations of gases).
4. Paralysis or depression of the breathing center (electric shock, sleeping drugs).

Because nonmedical people are usually not equipped to distinguish between suspension of breathing as a result of disease and that resulting from accident, it is best to apply some form of artificial respiration in all cases until the condition can be identified by a physician.

An open airway from the lungs to the mouth must be maintained if any form of artificial respiration is to be successful. Thus, it is important to free the throat if it is blocked by foreign matter and to be able to keep the mouth clear at all times. If the person is discovered quickly and artificial respiration started, his muscles usually retain sufficient tone, so that opening an airway is not a major problem. Alternately increasing and decreasing the size of the chest will move air in and out of the victim if there is no obstruction. If air is not quickly moved in and out of the lungs and the person revived, the throat begins to close from an internal source. When muscle tone is lost, the base of the tongue, which weighs approximately a quarter of a pound, relaxes against the windpipe and shuts off entry and exit of air. Since the tongue is attached to the lower jaw, when the first-aider tilts the head of the victim backward and stretches the neck muscles as tightly as possible, a small opening is created that permits passage of air. In addition when the rescuer lifts the lower jaw upward the air passage will usually open completely.

Once a passage for air has been guaranteed, any action that alternately increases and decreases the size of the chest cage will revive the person if body conditions permit life. This increase and decrease may be accomplished by blowing directly into the lungs through the mouth or nose or by alternately compressing and expanding the chest. The oral or mouth-to-nose technique of artificial respiration is now considered to be the most practical for emergency use (*see* ARTIFICIAL RESPIRATION).

Ingestion of Poisons. Poisonous substances—household cleaners, disinfectants, medicine, and many other things—are taken accidentally by hundreds of people. In all instances diluting the poison by having the victim drink large amounts of plain water or milk is the first step. Generally, the antidote for the poison is on the label of the container and should be administered if it is available. Diluting the poison will usually be sufficient until medical advice can be obtained. If there is a delay, it may be wise to induce vomiting, except when the victim is known to have taken an acid, an alkali, or a petroleum product such as kerosene. In these cases vomiting should not be provoked. If an acid has been taken, it should be diluted and a weak alkali given to counteract the acid. If an alkali has been taken, giving a weak acid is indicated. If a petroleum product has been taken, it should be diluted only. It is more dangerous to take a chance on fumes entering the lungs than it is to allow the poison to pass through the digestive tract and be absorbed into the blood stream.

Rescuer may roll shock victim off exposed live wire with a dry stick.

In cases where the poison is unknown and no directions are available, a universal antidote is recommended. Made up of magnesium oxide, activated charcoal, and tannic acid, it is available commercially in most parts of the country. It can also be improvised by using one part milk of magnesia, two parts crumbled burned toast, and one part strong tea measured in terms of volume rather than weight (see POISONS).

Many chemicals are dangerous even if they only come in contact with a body surface, especially with the eyes. The part affected by an irritating substance should be washed thoroughly with large amounts of "running water." Putting salve, ointment, or other medications on the skin or in the eye is not recommended as a first-aid measure: (1) because it will obstruct the physician's view of the damaged areas, and (2) the presence of medication makes the physician's cleansing of the area more painful than it would otherwise be.

Shock. Nearly all accidental injuries are accompanied to some degree by a condition called shock. This reaction to injury should not be confused with electric shock or the temporary shock of simple fainting or with neurogenic shock, previously called shell shock. If the injury involves loss of blood, the circulatory system sets up an automatic, self-regulating action that tries to keep the blood in the deeper parts of the body near the vital organs. The skin often becomes cold, wet, and clammy.

First aid to deal with shock and prevention of shock are the same. The most important single first-aid measure is to keep the patient in a lying-down position and thus help the flow of blood to the brain. Unless there are head or chest injuries, the victim may be placed with his head somewhat lower than his feet.

In treating shock, the over-all objective is to prevent a large loss of body heat. Good judgment and observation should dictate whether or not external heat should be applied to the body surface. The victim should not be warmed to the extent of sweating.

If there must be a long interval between the onset of shock and medical care and if the patient is conscious, it may be beneficial to give him a mixture of common baking soda and table salt, one-half level teaspoon of each in a quart of water. This mixture may be administered in small sips at 15-minute intervals. All handling of the victim should be as gentle as possible; rough handling will add to shock.

First-Aid Supportive Action (Protection)

Injuries to Bones, Muscles, and Joints: *Fractures.* A fracture is a break in the continuity of the bone. If there is no wound associated with the break, it is called a simple fracture. If there is a wound associated with the break, it is called a compound fracture. In all fractures the broken bone ends, as well as the adjacent joints, must be kept immobile. If materials are available and if the first-aider is skillful, he may wish to splint the injured limb. The best splints are made of rigid materials, such as wood of varying thicknesses. Magazines, newspapers, and even pillows may be used as temporary substitutes. In almost every instance the broken bone ends can be kept from moving by the hands alone, and if ambulance service and a physician are near at hand, it is usually best to use only the hands.

Signs: Odd position of limb; distortion.
Symptoms: Pain on movement of part.
Dislocation. Dislocations are difficult to identify because they often resemble simple fractures. Normally the same supportive care is given, with the part being kept as quiet as possible until the arrival of the physician. Do not attempt to reduce dislocations, except possibly of the lower jaw and the first joint of the fingers and toes.
Signs and symptoms: Similar to those in fractures.
Sprains. The word "sprain" should be associated with the word "joint" since sprains occur at joints, most frequently at the ankle and at the wrist. As many of the same symptoms are present, sprains are often mistaken for fractures. Hence, sprains should be treated like fractures until properly identified. The part should be kept as quiet as possible. No serious damage will result if this is done.
Signs: The joint is greatly enlarged and sometimes discolored.
Symptoms: Pain if the joint is moved.
Strains. Strains occur when muscles are overstretched. Although uncomfortable, they usually are not serious. Application of heat and bed rest will generally be sufficient.
Signs: Usually not evident.
Symptoms: Soreness and discomfort when the muscle area is touched or when movement is attempted.

Burns

Thermal Burns. When the skin comes in contact with heat, either moist or dry, the skin reddens, becomes blistered, or is charred, depending upon the degree of heat and the length of the contact. The severity of the burn is judged by the degree or damage to the tissues and by the extent of the burn. A burn is said to be of limited extent when less than 10% of the body surface is involved; when there is 10% or more involvement, the burn is referred to as extensive. Those with extensive burns need hospitalization as soon as possible.

The most essential job for the first-aider is to reduce pain and the possibility of infection. Cover the part as quickly as possible with layers of clean, dry, lint-free material to exclude air and protect the burned area from contamination. If there are blisters, wrap the part so that you do not break them. If the part such as a finger, arm, or leg, is merely reddened, quick relief can be given by letting cold running water cover the burned area. First-aiders should not apply ointments, salves, butter, or lard to burned areas. Such coverings may not only be absorbed into the subcutaneous tissues but they also invariably interfere with the physician's examination of the burned area and his choice of treatment.
Signs: Reddening, blistering, and charring of the skin.
Symptoms: Intense pain, nausea, fear.
Other Conditions Associated with Heat: *Sunburn* is caused by exposure to ultraviolet rays. The small blood vessels in the skin dilate, and the skin becomes red. Prolonged exposure to the rays of the sun may even cause blisters to appear.

Commercial preparations of varying degrees of efficacy are available to protect the skin from the effects of ultraviolet rays. Some are highly effective but may cause allergic reactions. The best first-aid practice is to prevent overexposure. Long initial sunbathing periods especially should be shunned, and length of exposure gradually increased.

Heat Exhaustion, although more prevalent in hot weather and among the aged, the obese, and those with systemic diseases, can affect anyone working under conditions that cause profuse perspiration and loss of body fluids and certain minerals. Persons working for long periods in poorly ventilated areas should increase the intake of water. Taking extra salt occasionally may be helpful. A well-balanced diet also helps prevent heat exhaustion. A person suffering heat exhaustion should have a period of bed rest.

Signs: Profuse perspiration; pale, damp skin; nearly normal body temperature; rarely unconsciousness.

Symptoms: Unusual fatigue; occasionally headache and nausea.

Heatstroke. Elderly people are more prone than others to develop heatstroke, a condition which may be caused by overexposure to the sun. The body temperature may rise as high as 109° F. Medical attention should be given as soon as possible. While awaiting the arrival of the physician or the ambulance, bring the patient indoors, provide bed rest, and sponge the body freely with alcohol or lukewarm water to reduce the temperature. If a thermometer is not at hand, the only guide may be the pulse rate. A rate below 110 per minute usually means a temperature the body can tolerate.

Signs: Dry skin, rapid pulse, temperature well above normal.

Symptoms: Headache, dizziness, nausea, unconsciousness in severe cases.

Cold Injuries. Heat affects the skin surface and so does cold. Parts of the body distant from the heart—the nose, ears, fingers, and toes—are most frequently affected by what is known as frostbite. Formerly it was believed best to warm frostbitten and frozen parts slowly. It is now known that they should be warmed quickly as long as they do not come in direct contact with heat.

As the victim himself usually is not aware of the onset of frostbite, companions should note the color of one another's ears and noses. If any of these parts have become grayish-white, warming should start as soon as possible, even with warm scarves and clothing. If possible, the frostbitten part should be immersed frequently at short intervals in water not exceeding 90° F. to 100° F. If the victim's entire body is affected, bring him into a warm room and wrap him in warm blankets. If he has stopped breathing, give artificial respiration. If water is available, immerse him in a tub of warm (78° F. to 82° F.) water; then dry the body thoroughly. When he reacts, give him a hot drink.

Transportation

Transporting accident victims is a difficult task and may be harmful if done improperly. Safe transportation of an injured person calls for good group co-operation and understanding of the problem involved and the parts of the body affected. The objectives are to avoid disturbing the victim and to prevent the injured parts from twisting or bending. Therefore, if a person "must" be moved and no help is available, pull him by the ankles or at the armpits but do not try to lift him. When assistance is available, it is best to use a cot or a litter.

Bandages and Dressings

A dressing is a sterile or clean piece of cloth that is placed directly over the wound. A bandage is a piece of cloth or other material used to hold a dressing in place. Bandage compresses combine the benefits of both in that a large gauze pad is affixed to strips of cloth which may be used to encircle the part in opposite directions. A sterile compress of this type can be applied as snugly or as loosely as one desires. The chief danger in bandaging injuries is making the bandage too tight and thus interfering with the circulation of the blood in the part.

First-aiders should not have to learn intricate bandaging skills. It is sufficient for them to know how to cover a dressing so that it will stay in place until medical aid can be reached. It is necessary to know how to do a circular turn, how to anchor the bandage, and how to tie it off when completed.

If the body surface to be covered is tapered, such as a forearm, a closed spiral turn is used.

If the part tapers sharply, the turn will have to be an open spiral. In this, gaps will appear, but as long as it holds the dressing in place it is satisfactory.

If the body part to be covered is angular, a figure-of-eight turn—two loops crossing each other in opposite directions—should be used. Knees, elbows, shoulders, and the like can best be covered by this type of turn.

If an irregular surface—fingers, toes, or head—must be covered, a recurrent turn is first used; that is, the bandage goes back and forth over the ovoid surface and is held in place by a circular turn.

Anchoring bandage: (A) Strip end is angled so that (B) top flap can be turned down over first winding and (C) secured by second.

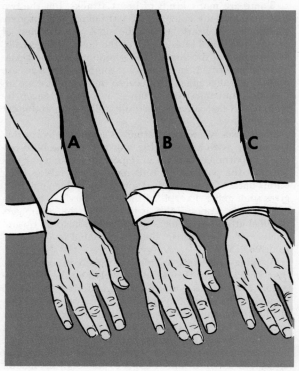

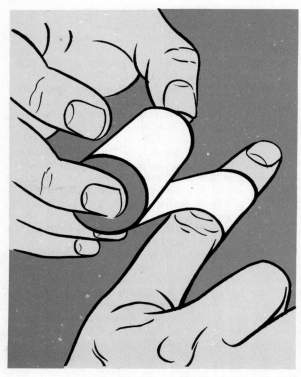

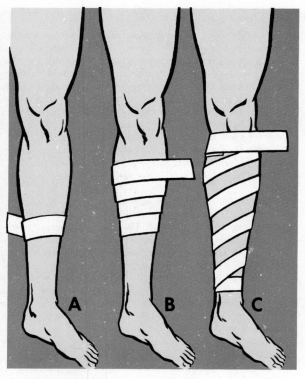

Circular turn of the bandage, layer upon layer, is useful for wrapping body parts of uniform width, as finger, neck, or head.

(A) Anchoring spiral turn on the calf. (B) Closed spiral, strips overlapping. (C) Open spiral, more oblique, no overlap.

Common Emergencies

There are many kinds of heart attacks, but the two most common are congestive heart failure and coronary thrombosis. In heart failure, the signs are shortness of breath, occasional bluish color of the lips and fingernails, and swelling of the ankles. The symptoms are chest pain and extreme fright. In coronary thrombosis, the signs are quite often negligible, but because the symptoms are indigestion and nausea, the illness is often mistaken by friends and first-aiders for simple indigestion and upset stomach.

In all cases where heart attack is suspected, reassuring the victim with encouraging words is probably of primary importance. Second in importance is to allow him to select the position he finds most comfortable—lying on his back or propped up at any comfortable angle that gives some relief. Except for these two services, the first-aider's main responsibility is to see that the victim gets medical attention. If he is taken to the hospital by ambulance or other vehicle, the driver should be instructed to drive SLOWLY.

Apoplexy (Stroke). Apoplexy is usually brought about by a blood clot or hemorrhage involving a vessel of the brain. The victims are often those suffering high blood pressure. The signs of apoplexy are paralysis on one side of the body and possibly unconsciousness and heavy breathing. Again, this disorder calls for prompt medical attention. While awaiting the arrival of the physician, keep the victim as quiet as possible and lying down, face up or face down. If mucus tends to collect in the mouth,

put him slightly on his side and turn his head completely to the side to allow the fluids to drain out.

Simple Fainting. Simple fainting is a reaction of the nervous system that results in a temporary lack of sufficient blood supply to the brain. It can be caused by injury, by the sight of injury, or by lack of sufficient concentration of oxygen in a room.

Recovery can be effected by bending the victim over or laying him down so that his head is lower than his heart. From time to time many kinds of medication have been recommended. It may help to give aromatic spirits of ammonia and the like or to hold smelling salts under the victim's nose at the onset of fainting.

If recovery of consciousness is not prompt, medical attention is needed because the underlying cause of the unconsciousness is more serious than simple fainting.

Epileptic Seizures. In epilepsy episodes of unconsciousness may appear for only a moment or they may be of long duration and be accompanied by convulsions involving the entire body. Epileptics who recognize the symptoms that precede an attack usually seek a quiet place and lie down with something between their teeth to prevent injury to the tongue. If a victim is found during an epileptic seizure, his convulsive motions should not be restricted. Try to keep him from injuring himself and, if possible, gently place something—a book cover or a spoon handle wrapped with clean cloth—between the teeth. When the convulsive motions have ceased, loosen the clothing about his neck and allow him to lie flat with his head turned to one side to prevent aspira-

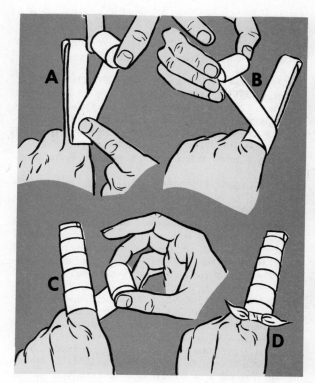

(A) Recurrent turn on opposite side of finger. (B) Circular turn holds bandage and (C) continues along finger. (D) Finished bandage.

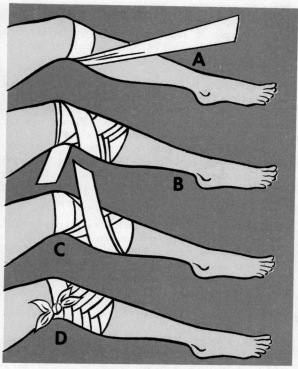

Figure-of-eight turn, useful for a joint or whole limb. Spiral turns, one up and one down, cross each other and then are secured.

tion of food and other stomach contents that may have been regurgitated and are in the mouth. Allow him to rest undisturbed during the deep sleep that follows a seizure.

Unconsciousness—Cause Unknown. Unconsciousness is associated with many injuries and illnesses, but when its cause is unknown, the only classifications a first-aider can make are: (1) cases requiring artificial respiration and (2) cases where breathing is adequate. The accident scene nearly always provides a good clue to the cause of unconsciousness. If it does not, the first-aider, in the presence of reliable witnesses, should search the victim for a statement concerning specific diseases that may be the cause, such as diabetes, heart disease, or others.

If breathing is not adequate, start artificial respiration immediately and have someone notify a physician or police officer.

Foreign Body in the Eye. Injuries to the eye include damage to the soft tissue around the eye, scratching of the eye surface, and puncturing of the eyeball. No matter what the injury to the eyes may be, first-aid care should be held to a minimum. If the soft tissue about the eye is damaged place a fairly tight bandage over the eye and the affected area after giving normal first-aid care for wounds. When the eye itself is involved, cover it with moist cotton held in place with a bandage until medical assistance can be obtained.

Occasionally small foreign bodies become lodged on the inner surface of the upper lid. These may be removed by pulling the upper lid outward and downward over the lower lid so that the small object will be picked up on the outer surface of the lower lid.

Foreign Body in the Throat or Air Passage. If a foreign body lodges in the throat or air passage, violent choking and spasm will likely occur. These reactions alone often eliminate the object, but in other cases it must be removed by a bronchoscope or operation.

Let the victim first attempt to cough up the object. Do not probe with the fingers down the throat because you may force the object deeper. If breathing ceases, give artificial respiration and have someone get medical assistance quickly.

Foreign Body in the Food Passage. Most foreign objects that have been swallowed pass harmlessly along and are excreted. However, some objects require extraction either by special instruments or by operation. Medical care, therefore, should be obtained as soon as possible. Remain calm and do not excite the victim. Do not give him a cathartic nor, in general, any food. If the victim is an infant or small child and feeding is necessary do not give cereal or other bulky foods.

Suggested First-Aid Supplies	
1-in. gauze roller bandage	Cleansing agent—rubbing
2-in. gauze roller bandage	alcohol, plain soap
3-in. × 3-in. gauze pads	Eye dropper
Plain gauze, ½ sq. yd.	Hot-water bottle
Absorbent cotton—½-oz. box	Flashlight

American National Red Cross

FIRST EMPIRE, in French history, regime established in 1804 by Napoleon Bonaparte; interrupted by his defeat and abdication in 1814; revived during the Hundred Days (1815); and ended by his defeat at the Battle of Waterloo and his exile to the island of St. Helena.

FIRST REPUBLIC, in French history, radical democratic period of the French Revolution. It began on Sept. 21, 1792, when the newly elected National Convention decreed "the abolition of monarchy." France was not officially proclaimed a republic until a year later. The terminal date usually given is Nov. 9, 1799, when the Consulate of Napoleon Bonaparte replaced the Directory. Sometimes the First Republic is taken to include the Consulate, which ended with the proclamation of the First Empire (1804).

FIRUZABAD [fə-rōō′zə-băd], ancient ruined city in south Iran, capital of the Sassanian Empire. Built by the Sassanian Ardashir I (reigned 226–41 A.D.), and called Gur, it was surrounded by mud-brick walls with semicircular bastions and contained a great domed palace, a fire temple, and tower.

FISCAL POLICY. See ECONOMIC STABILIZATION POLICIES.

FISCHART [fish′ärt], JOHANN (c.1546–c.1590), German satirist. His vocabulary is unusually rich, but his writings lack form. In many of his satires Fischart fought against the dangers threatening the Reformation. His humor is best seen in *Das glückhafft Schiff von Zürich* (The Lucky Ship from Zürich), 1576. In his *Geschichtklitterung* (1575), he translated the first book of Rabelais' *Gargantua* and expanded it to three times its original length with a conglomeration of puns, grotesque exaggerations, and moralizing against vices.

FISCHER, EMIL (1852–1919), German organic chemist who discovered the constituent parts of many compounds needed by animals and plants. He explained the basic structure of the sugars and the purines (such as caffeine and uric acid). He showed how proteins are formed and explained the chemistry of the tannins. He taught at various universities, was recognized as the foremost organic chemist of his day, and received the Nobel Prize in 1902 for his work in this field.

FISCHER, ERNST KUNO BERTHOLD (1824–1907), German historian of philosophy. A celebrated scholar and literary critic, he established the history of philosophy as a distinct and central philosophical discipline. His *History of Modern Philosophy* (10 vols., 1897–1904), revealing his Hegelian idealism, comprises separate studies of Bacon, Descartes, Spinoza, Leibniz, Kant, Fichte, Schelling, Hegel, and Schopenhauer.

FISCHER, HANS (1881–1945), German organic chemist noted for his synthesis of the blood pigment, hemin. He received degrees in chemistry and in medicine, and taught chemistry at the universities of Innsbruck and Munich. His work on the structure and synthesis of hemin also explained the nature of the pigments in the bile. The chemical structure of hemin is related to that of chlorophyll, the green pigment of plants, and he worked out the relation between these substances. He received the Nobel Prize in 1930 for his work.

FISCHER-DIESKAU [fish′ər-dēs′kou], DIETRICH (1925–   ), German baritone, born in Berlin. Joining the Berlin State Opera in 1948, he became the company's leading baritone. By the mid-1950's he was recognized internationally as perhaps the finest lieder, or concert song, specialist of his generation. He projects his warm voice with a blending of power, delicacy, and impeccable enunciation.

FISCHER-TROPSCH PROCESS, in chemical engineering, a process for making liquid fuels from gases. It was developed in 1933 in petroleum-deficient Germany. Water gas (carbon monoxide and hydrogen, obtained from coal and steam) is combined with hydrogen in the presence of catalysts to form a mixture of liquid hydrocarbons well suited for diesel fuel. Its octane rating can be raised sufficiently to make satisfactory synthetic gasoline.

FISH, HAMILTON (1808–93), U.S. politician and diplomat. He was born in New York City and practiced law after graduation from Columbia University. Fish became active in politics as a Whig. He served single terms in the U.S. House of Representatives (1843–45), as governor of New York (1849–51), and in the U.S. Senate (1851–57), where he was a member of the Foreign Relations Committee. After the Whig party broke on the slavery issue, Fish became a Republican with hesitation, deploring the sectional basis of the new party. Although he took office reluctantly, as a temporary duty, Fish served for eight years as Secretary of State under Ulysses S. Grant.

His personal qualities enabled him to shield American diplomacy from some of the impulsiveness which threatened its integrity under Grant. Fish argued for a moderate course on the issues of relations with Britain in regard to British violations of neutrality during the Civil War, as well as on the question of the annexation of Santo Domingo. The principal opponent of Grant's policies was Charles Sumner, chairman of the Senate Foreign Relations Committee. The third major issue, relations with Spain over revolution in Cuba, presented further complication. By acquiescing in the Santo Domingo project, Fish managed to avoid a hasty recognition of the Cuban revolutionists, which would have been inconsistent with American claims against Britain and would probably have led to war with Spain. After the Santo Domingo treaty was blocked by Sumner in the Senate, Fish found that the break between Sumner and Grant cleared the way to a settlement with Britain. The Treaty of Washington (June 17, 1871) established friendly relations between the United States and Great Britain as an enduring monument to Fish's career.

Consult Nevins, Allan, *Hamilton Fish* (1936).

WHITNEY T. PERKINS, Brown University

FISH. Fishes are the most numerous of all vertebrates. Over 25,000 species are known. In their forms and habits they show a diversity equal to that of any group of land animals. Water, the natural habitat of fishes, covers more

FAMILIAR AQUARIUM FISH

The Double Swordtail Guppy is one of many domestic varieties developed from the wild guppy, a fresh-water native of Trinidad.

The Veiltail Goldfish was developed from the wild goldfish, which is native to fresh waters in Asia.

The Banded Distichodus, a native of fresh water in central Africa, belongs to the characid family.

The Neon Tetra, a fresh-water native of South America, also belongs to the characid family.

The Silver Hatchetfish, of the Amazon basin in South America, can actually fly above the water by moving its pectoral fins.

The Sailfin Mollie occurs in brackish and fresh water in warmer parts of North America.

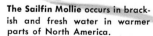

The Siamese Fighting Fish is native to fresh water in Thailand. The wild species is dull-colored and has small fins.

PLATE 1

MARINE GAME FISH

The Atlantic Salmon occurs on both sides of the North Atlantic. At maturity it swims upriver to spawn.

The Atlantic Sailfish is found in western Atlantic waters as far north as Cape Cod. It fights spectacularly when hooked.

The Tarpon, commonest in tropical western Atlantic waters, may occur in summer north to Cape Cod. It is prized as a fighting fish.

The Common Pompano swims in warm waters along the Atlantic coast of the Americas. It is prized as both a food and game fish.

The Bluefish occurs in all temperate and tropical waters except the eastern and central Pacific. It travels in large schools.

The Striped Bass, originally native to the Atlantic coast of North America, has been introduced along the Pacific coast.

The Swordfish is found in temperate and tropical seas throughout the world. It may use its flattened sword to impale small fishes.

PLATE 2

FRESH-WATER GAME FISH

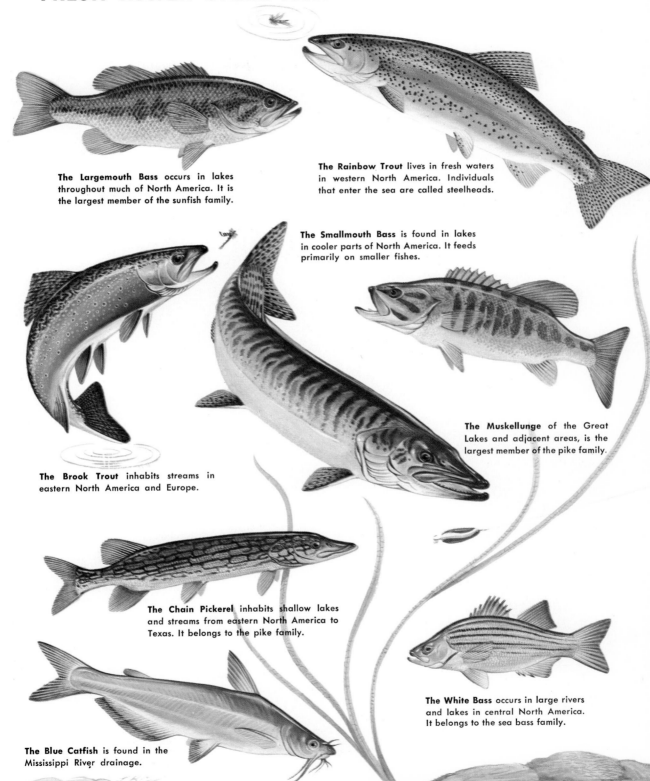

The Largemouth Bass occurs in lakes throughout much of North America. It is the largest member of the sunfish family.

The Rainbow Trout lives in fresh waters in western North America. Individuals that enter the sea are called steelheads.

The Smallmouth Bass is found in lakes in cooler parts of North America. It feeds primarily on smaller fishes.

The Brook Trout inhabits streams in eastern North America and Europe.

The Muskellunge of the Great Lakes and adjacent areas, is the largest member of the pike family.

The Chain Pickerel inhabits shallow lakes and streams from eastern North America to Texas. It belongs to the pike family.

The White Bass occurs in large rivers and lakes in central North America. It belongs to the sea bass family.

The Blue Catfish is found in the Mississippi River drainage.

PLATE 3

CURIOSITIES OF THE FISH WORLD

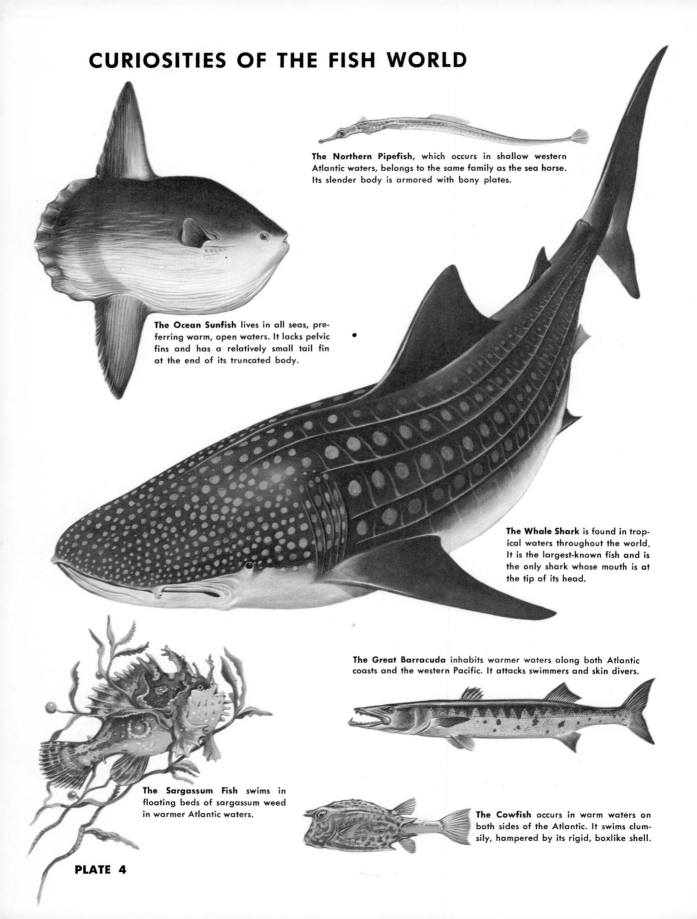

The Northern Pipefish, which occurs in shallow western Atlantic waters, belongs to the same family as the sea horse. Its slender body is armored with bony plates.

The Ocean Sunfish lives in all seas, preferring warm, open waters. It lacks pelvic fins and has a relatively small tail fin at the end of its truncated body.

The Whale Shark is found in tropical waters throughout the world. It is the largest-known fish and is the only shark whose mouth is at the tip of its head.

The Great Barracuda inhabits warmer waters along both Atlantic coasts and the western Pacific. It attacks swimmers and skin divers.

The Sargassum Fish swims in floating beds of sargassum weed in warmer Atlantic waters.

The Cowfish occurs in warm waters on both sides of the Atlantic. It swims clumsily, hampered by its rigid, boxlike shell.

PLATE 4

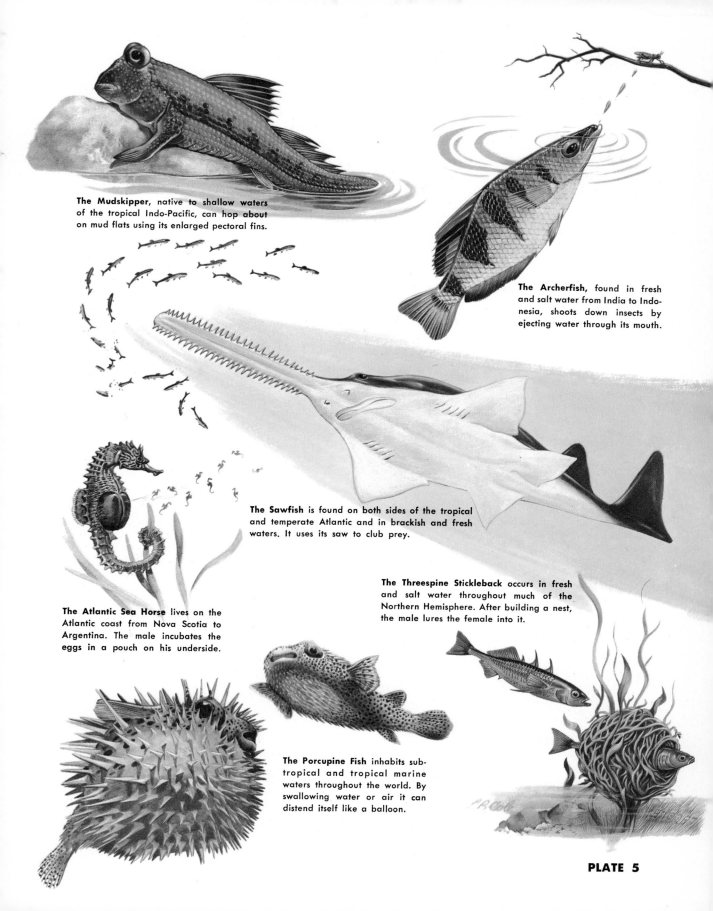

The Mudskipper, native to shallow waters of the tropical Indo-Pacific, can hop about on mud flats using its enlarged pectoral fins.

The Archerfish, found in fresh and salt water from India to Indonesia, shoots down insects by ejecting water through its mouth.

The Sawfish is found on both sides of the tropical and temperate Atlantic and in brackish and fresh waters. It uses its saw to club prey.

The Threespine Stickleback occurs in fresh and salt water throughout much of the Northern Hemisphere. After building a nest, the male lures the female into it.

The Atlantic Sea Horse lives on the Atlantic coast from Nova Scotia to Argentina. The male incubates the eggs in a pouch on his underside.

The Porcupine Fish inhabits subtropical and tropical marine waters throughout the world. By swallowing water or air it can distend itself like a balloon.

PLATE 5

MARINE FOOD FISH

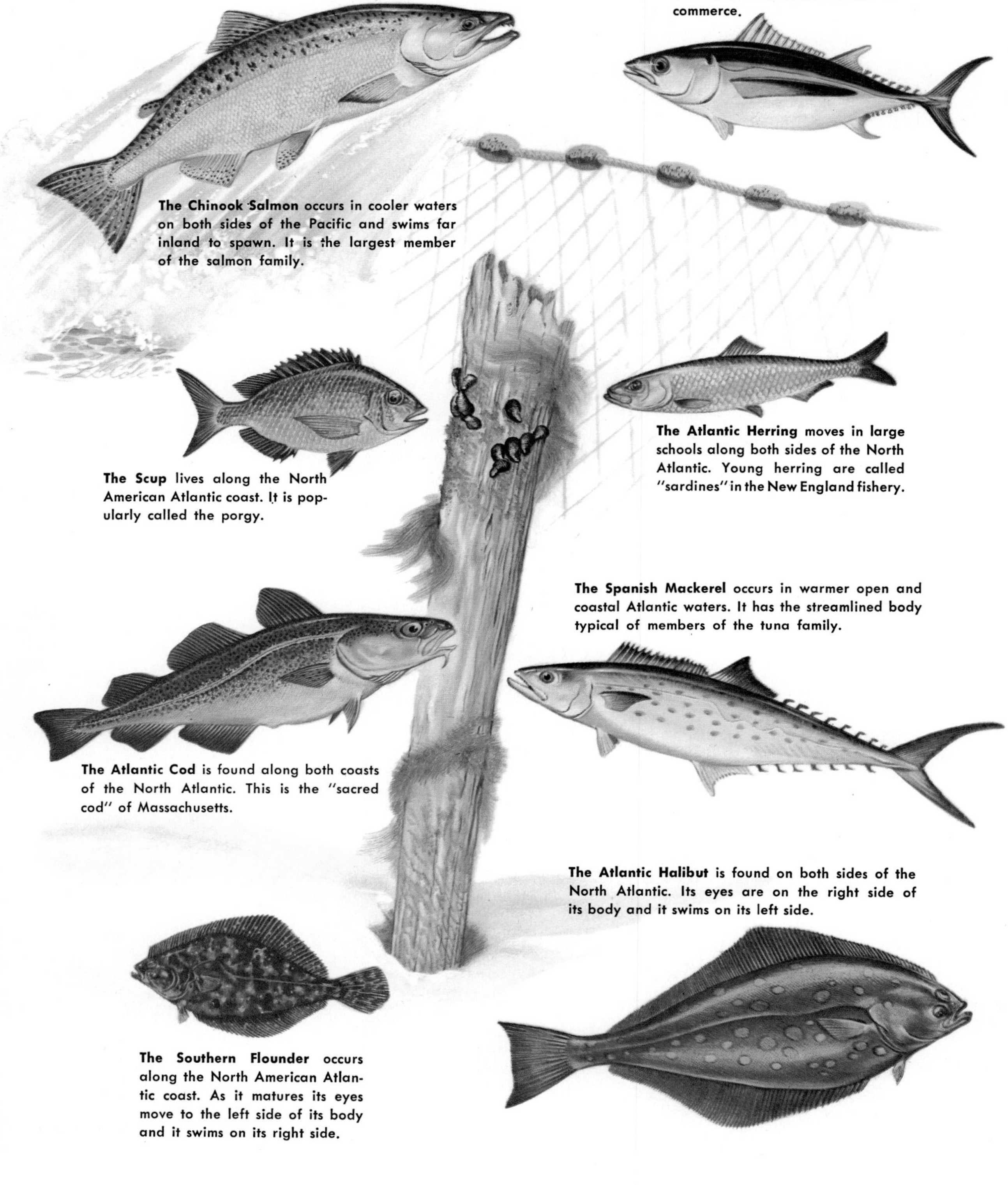

The Albacore is found in offshore Atlantic and Pacific waters. Its flesh is the "whitemeat tuna" of commerce.

The Chinook Salmon occurs in cooler waters on both sides of the Pacific and swims far inland to spawn. It is the largest member of the salmon family.

The Scup lives along the North American Atlantic coast. It is popularly called the porgy.

The Atlantic Herring moves in large schools along both sides of the North Atlantic. Young herring are called "sardines" in the New England fishery.

The Spanish Mackerel occurs in warmer open and coastal Atlantic waters. It has the streamlined body typical of members of the tuna family.

The Atlantic Cod is found along both coasts of the North Atlantic. This is the "sacred cod" of Massachusetts.

The Atlantic Halibut is found on both sides of the North Atlantic. Its eyes are on the right side of its body and it swims on its left side.

The Southern Flounder occurs along the North American Atlantic coast. As it matures its eyes move to the left side of its body and it swims on its right side.

PLATE 6

FRESH-WATER FOOD FISH

The Lake Trout inhabits deep lakes in Canada and northern United States. Its numbers in the Great Lakes have been reduced by the parasitic sea lamprey.

The Channel Catfish occurs in clear, moving rivers through central North America. Its spotted markings usually disappear at maturity.

The Lake Whitefish lives in larger lakes in Canada and northern United States. The sea lamprey has reduced its numbers.

The Northern Pike is found in cool streams and lakes in North America and Eurasia. It is also a popular game fish.

The Walleye lives in lakes and streams in eastern North America. It is a member of the perch family.

The Cisco occurs in the same region as the lake whitefish, to which it is closely related. Ciscos swim in large schools, usually near the water's surface.

The Carp, native to the region between the Black and Caspian seas, has been introduced into fresh water throughout the world.

The Lake Sturgeon inhabits large lakes in temperate North America. It swims on the bottom, sucking in small invertebrates with its tubular mouth.

PLATE 7

TROPICAL REEF FISH

The Queen Angelfish inhabits coastal reefs from the Gulf of Mexico to Brazil. Young fish have blue stripes on their sides.

The Ocean Triggerfish is found among reefs from Florida to the West Indies. It is able to lock its first two dorsal spines in erect position, preventing predators from removing it from a coral reef crevice.

The Green Moray lives among coral reefs along the warmer western Atlantic coast. It attacks viciously if disturbed.

The Longspine Squirrelfish occurs in western Atlantic reefs from the Carolinas to Colombia. It was named for its squirrellike eyes.

The Rainbow Parrotfish, found in tropical and subtropical reefs on both sides of the Atlantic, was named for its parrotlike "beak."

PLATE 8

than two-thirds of the earth's surface, providing fishes with enormous space for development. Fish are found in the coldest and in the warmest seas, living from the surface down to depths as great as 7 mi.; they are found in still ponds, lakes, and in fast-moving streams and rivers.

What Is a Fish?

Because of their tremendous diversity of form and color, and their wide range of habits and habitats, it is difficult to find a definition that will include all fishes and exclude all other animals. To define fishes as scaled animals, for example, is of no help since certain fishes have no scales and some reptiles do have them. Nor is it possible to say that fishes are gill-breathing animals because this method of respiration is also employed by most amphibians, and is not used by certain lung-breathing fishes that have only vestigial gills. Similarly, it is not significant to say that fishes are finned creatures that live in water —some fishes lack fins and a few fishes live at least as much on land as in the water.

The Physical Characteristics of Fishes

What criteria can be used to distinguish a fish from all other creatures? We can say that a fish is a backboned, cold-blooded animal with a two-chambered heart. Aside from these facts, no other statements can be made that will apply to all fishes, but there are many characteristics that are found in almost all fishes.

Most fishes have scales, which are hard, more or less curved, overlapping plates, covering their bodies outside the skin proper. However, many catfishes are entirely scaleless or are covered by overlapping bony plates. Eels are either scaleless or have minute scales buried in the skin. All fishes, except perhaps the sharks, are covered with a mucoid substance that acts as a lubricant in the water, and protects them against bacterial and other infections.

Almost all fishes seem to be equipped with at least five senses—sight, hearing, touch, taste, and smell—but again there are exceptions.

The Sense of Sight. There are quite a number of fishes that have no eyes at all, for they live in dark caves where light never enters. However, experiments have been performed in which eyeless fishes, kept in well-lighted aquaria with sighted fishes, seemed able to compete for the available food without trouble. Apparently their other senses compensate for their blindness.

Sighted fishes possess varying degrees of visual acuity. Sharks seem to use their eyes little in finding food, while trout fishermen are quite positive that a trout can distinguish not only the form of a fly but its color as well. One attribute of the eyes of many fishes, including the trout, is the ability to compensate easily for the refraction of the air-water surface. If a straight rod is held through the surface of the water, it appears to the human eye to bend just at the surface so that the distant end of the rod appears to be in a place other than we know it to be. A fish jumping for a fly must be able to correct for this distortion immediately. We know that some fish can do this. For example, the archerfish, which squirts drops of water at airborne insects, can hit a target at least 10 ft. away.

The Sense of Smell. Although keen sight is of great value in clear water, it has little value in murky water or at night, when a sense of smell is far more useful. We do not know how keen the sense of smell is in most fishes, but in some it is extremely acute, curiously enough in cases where there is apparently no great need for it. Sharks, for instance, although they live mainly at or near the surface of normally clear water, depend much more upon their noses than on their eyes. A shark with one nostril plugged will go around a piece of bait in ever-narrowing circles (on the unplugged side) until it reaches the bait, even though the bait has been in plain sight all the while. If the plug is removed and the other nostril plugged, the shark repeats its circling, but in the opposite direction. If both nostrils are plugged the shark may never find the bait.

The Sense of Taste. In human beings the sense of taste is intimately associated with that of smell. In fact, in mammals there is close juxtaposition between the organs of these sensations. In fishes there may also be close position-

Fishes are a subject of scientific study, a major item of food, an article of commerce, and an object of sport. Articles in this Encyclopedia deal with all of these aspects of the topic of fish.

Biological Classification and Study. The article FISH first seeks to categorize fishes—not a simple matter since many of the characteristics associated with fishes are not found in all species. Not all fishes breathe through gills, some lack fins, and a few live partially out of water. The article then deals with the physical characteristics of fish. The section on the activities of fishes discusses locomotion, feeding habits, and reproduction. The article concludes with an account of the evolution of fishes.

The article ANIMAL provides an illustrated animal classification. Under phylum Chordata, group Craniata (vertebrates), the three classes of living fishes are shown: Cyclostomata, the roundmouthed fishes like the LAMPREY (see CYCLOSTOME); CHONDRICHTHYES, the cartilaginous fishes like the SKATE; and OSTEICHTHYES, the bony fishes like the TROUT and many other food and game fishes. Individual articles include BASS, BLINDFISH, CLIMBING PERCH, DOGFISH, GUPPY, ELECTRIC FISH, SHARK, and TARPON.

Fish as a Source of Food and Other Products. The article FISHERIES provides data on the extent of fishing by various nations, the expansion of fishing after World War II in an effort to make the food supply keep pace with population growth, and the need for conservation. A later section of the article is devoted to the fishing industry in the United States. It should be noted that this article discusses shellfish and other aquatic animals that are not fish. On the other hand, fish such as the ANCHOVY, COD, HERRING, MACKEREL, MENHADEN, SALMON, SARDINE, and TUNA have great commercial value. The need for careful use of marine life is covered in NATURAL RESOURCES, CONSERVATION OF. "Fish farming," or raising pond fish for food, is treated in one portion of FISH CULTURE. FOOD PRESERVATION, FISH AND SHELLFISH COOKERY, and JAPANESE COOKERY deal with other aspects of fish as food.

Sport and Recreation. FISHING describes the history of the sport and the development of modern tackle, discusses types of fresh- and salt-water fishing, and lists noted fishing areas in the United States and Canada. One section of FISH CULTURE deals with hatching fish to stock streams and ponds. Keeping fish as a hobby is discussed in FISH, TROPICAL.

THE THREE CLASSES OF LIVING FISHES

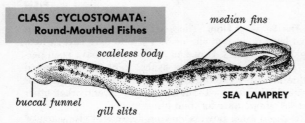

CLASS CYCLOSTOMATA:
Round-Mouthed Fishes

median fins
scaleless body
buccal funnel
gill slits
SEA LAMPREY

The round-mouthed fishes (lampreys, hagfish, and slime eels) are the most primitive living vertebrates. They lack jaws and scales and their skeleton is composed of cartilage. Their fins are median, rather than paired as in more advanced fishes.

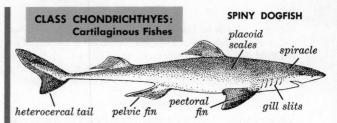

CLASS CHONDRICHTHYES:
Cartilaginous Fishes

SPINY DOGFISH
placoid scales
spiracle
heterocercal tail
pelvic fin
pectoral fin
gill slits

The cartilaginous fishes (sharks, rays, and chimaeras) have movable jaws and skin covered with toothlike (placoid) scales. They have a gill-like opening (spiracle) behind each eye. Their tail is heterocercal (the vertebrae extend into the larger dorsal lobe).

CLASS OSTEICHTHYES:
Bony Fishes

The bony fishes have a skeleton composed largely of bone. Their bodies are covered with ganoid (bony, enamel-covered), cycloid (smooth), or ctenoid (spiny) scales. Most species have both median and paired fins supported by cartilaginous or bony fin rays.

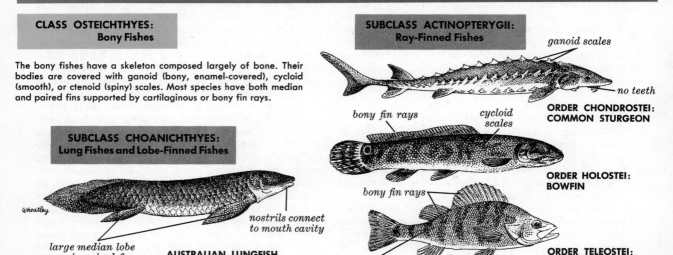

SUBCLASS ACTINOPTERYGII:
Ray-Finned Fishes

ganoid scales
no teeth
bony fin rays
cycloid scales
ORDER CHONDROSTEI:
COMMON STURGEON

bony fin rays
ORDER HOLOSTEI:
BOWFIN

SUBCLASS CHOANICHTHYES:
Lung Fishes and Lobe-Finned Fishes

Wheatley
nostrils connect to mouth cavity
large median lobe in paired fins
AUSTRALIAN LUNGFISH

ctenoid scales
ORDER TELEOSTEI:
YELLOW PERCH

ing, but this is not always true. Catfish, for instance, have taste buds scattered over their skins, and particularly along the flanks. This is useful when they are grubbing around in muddy water looking—or perhaps tasting—for food. Not all fishes are so well equipped, of course, but all can taste the water around them to some extent.

The Senses of Hearing and Touch. The hearing organs of fishes are entirely internal. They also serve as a balancing mechanism, a fact that is especially important to an animal supported from all points, not just below, and one that can move in three dimensions without difficulty. The hearing organs also seem to be associated with the sense of touch, which is perhaps to be expected of an animal living in so dense a medium as water.

Along the sides of most fishes is found one or more solid or incomplete lines that usually extend from the gill plates to the tail, but sometimes extend forward on the head to the snout. These lateral lines are a series of pores that penetrate each scale along the line and connect with a duct running beneath. In many fishes there is actually a tube along which dye can flow, in others it appears to be blocked. In any case, the fish appears to be able to "hear" sounds through these connected pores, the sound being translated into pressure waves in the water. It is probably this sense that enables blind cave fishes to avoid collisions with walls and rocks, and indeed to survive at all.

Since the surrounding temperature of the water is of importance to a fish, it is not surprising that they are able to distinguish fine differences of temperature. So sensitive are herring to temperature variation that they will not cross from one body of water to another if the adjoining water differs by as little as two-tenths of a degree in temperature from the one they are in.

Noise *per se* seems to be of some moment in the lives of many fishes, for a great many make sounds of some sort—grinding their teeth, grunting, or drumming by vibrating parts of the swim bladder. The ocean is full of sounds, many associated with particular fish, a considerable number still unidentified. There does not seem to be any particular reason for the noise, but whole schools will start sounding off simultaneously. Drumfish do this; croakers seem just to call and reply to each other without taking further action.

The Sixth Sense. There is at least one more sense with which some fishes are provided, which may not be a discrete sense, but is possibly a modification of the sense of touch. This is the ability of some fishes to detect minute electric currents, and to be guided by them. Fishes capable of doing this are provided with organs that generate electricity by the action of one chemical on another. These fishes can emit a series of electric discharges into the surrounding water and are guided by the echo of the electricity. So acute is this sensitivity to electricity that some of the knifefishes of the Amazon, which swim backward or forward with equal facility, can swim backward through a hole with less than ⅛ in. clearance on each side without touching the sides of the hole.

The Activities of Fishes

Locomotion. Fishes swim through the water in a variety of ways, but essentially by a sort of sculling motion of their fins, their whole bodies, or both. Eels have extremely flexible bodies and move with an undulating side-to-side motion produced by rhythmic contractions of the myomeres (the flaky muscles running from the backbone to the sides of the fish). The electric eel, although it is not related to the true eels, and has a long, fairly inflexible body, moves in a somewhat similar fashion. It translates the same kind of motion into its long anal fin, which ripples backward from the head, pushing the fish forward. Ripples that start at the tail, on the other hand, produce a backward movement. Fishes that live inside a hard shell—seahorses, trunkfish, boxfish—swim by a sculling movement of their pectoral, ventral, dorsal, anal, or tail fins, whichever seems best and most workable.

Feeding Habits. Most fishes are carnivorous, depending mainly upon other fishes for nourishment. Predatory species get their food simply because they are faster than their prey. Once seized, the food is usually swallowed whole, but in rare instances, it may first be torn apart. A very few fishes resort to subterfuge to get food, even to the extent of developing "fishing rods" that attract other fish within reach of the jaws. This curious feature is found in the angler fish. Other feeding methods are found in the electric fishes which capture their prey by paralyzing them with electric discharges.

Reproduction. Fishes generally reproduce by eggs, released into the open water by the females, which are then fertilized by milt, released simultaneously by the males. The fertilized eggs are seldom given the slightest care. Some fishes produce living young, and in certain species the eggs are fertilized before release from the body. A few fishes make nests for the reception of the eggs. These "nests" may merely be cleared and cleaned pieces of rock, or they may be assembled from bits of vegetation, excavations in the sandy or gravelly bed of the water, or bubbles "blown" by the fish. Some of the fishes that build nests attend carefully to the eggs and hatched young; others make the nest and then abandon it and the eggs. When there is parental care it is usually the male that is most active.

The Evolution of Fishes

The earliest-known vertebrate animals were fishes. They first appeared about 500 million years ago and were mostly small, bottom-dwelling, fresh-water creatures. These ostracoderms, as they are called, lacked jaws and were covered by bony plates. Their only direct descendants are the present-day lampreys, hagfishes, and slime eels of class Cyclostomata—the most primitive of all modern vertebrates. The cyclostomes are jawless, but lack the armored body covering of their ancient ancestors.

At a time (about 400 million years ago) when the ostracoderms were declining, the first fishes with movable jaws appeared. These were the placoderms, a group of predom-

inantly marine fishes. Placoderms had body armor like many of the jawless fishes, but their main distinction was the possession of paired fins—an evolutionary advance over the cyclostomes. The placoderms gave rise to two main groups: class Chondrichthyes, whose members had skeletons composed of cartilage, and class Osteichthyes, fishes whose skeletons were composed of bone. Class Chondrichthyes is today represented by the sharks, rays, and chimaeras (or ratfish). From the ancestral forms of class Osteichthyes, arose three distinct branches. Subclass Palaeopterygii, the ancient bony fishes, is a group represented today by such primitive forms as the sturgeon, spoonbill, and bichir. The second subclass, Neopterygii, includes most of the modern and familiar fishes—the teleosts—such as the herring, salmon, trout, pikes, carps, minnows, flying fishes, eels, catfishes, seahorses, cod, perch, mackerel, tuna, and many others. The third branch of class Osteichthyes, subclass Choanichthyes, is of extreme significance as far as the evolution of forms beyond the fishes is concerned. Within this subclass are two superorders.

The lungfishes of superorder Dipnoi are interesting because they have lunglike structures that enable them to breathe air. Some species, in fact, will drown if held under water for any length of time. The second superorder, Crossopterygii, is represented today by a single known genus—*Latimeria*. This strange-looking fish, better known as the "coelacanth," is the sole survivor of a group that is believed to have given rise to all land animals. The ancient crossopterygian fishes did not have the flattened fins characteristic of bony fishes, but had instead paired, fleshy lobes, within which were bones. One bone of each lobed fin attached to the shoulder girdle. At the far end of this bone were two more bones, side by side; and beyond these was a branching series of smaller bones. This basic skeletal pattern is like that of the fore or hind leg of a land animal. In addition to these distinctive skeletal features, crossopterygian fishes also had a lung as well as gills and were able to breathe both on land and in the water. For these, and other more technical reasons, it is believed that the earliest amphibians owe their ancestry to some lobe-finned fish whose shallow, fresh-water stream dried up, forcing the fish to breathe air and to move about on land with some sort of waddling gait, using its armlike fins.

Consult Schultz, L. P., and Stern, E. M., *The Ways of Fishes* (1948); Curtis, Brian, *Life Story of the Fish* (1949); Herald, E. S., *Living Fishes of the World* (1961); Jordan, D. S., *A Classification of Fishes* (1963); Hylander, C. J., *Fishes and Their Ways* (1963); Norman, J. R., *A History of Fishes* (rev. ed. 1963).

C. W. COATES, Director, New York Aquarium

See also:

FISH, TROPICAL. The term "tropical fish" includes any small fresh-water fish other than goldfish which may conveniently be kept in a domestic fish tank. Fishes from the tropical rivers of Africa, South America, India, and the Indonesian area are true tropicals, but certain fishes from

PREPARING AN AQUARIUM

Eric Akerman

An attractive, well-planned aquarium housing a variety of fish.

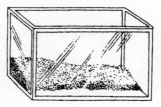

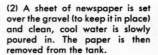

(1) After rinsing the tank in warm water, gravel is added to a depth of 1 in. The gravel should slope toward the front of the tank.

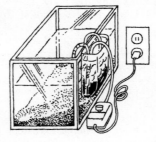

(2) A sheet of newspaper is set over the gravel (to keep it in place) and clean, cool water is slowly poured in. The paper is then removed from the tank.

(3) An outside filter is mounted on the rear edge of the tank. The filter aerates the water and circulates it, maintaining an even temperature.

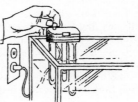

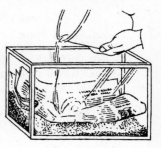

(4) A heater unit is also mounted on the rear edge of the tank. It should be adjusted to maintain a temperature of at least 72° F.

(5) Aquatic plants and small rocks are added to simulate a natural habitat. The plants should first be washed to remove insect pests.

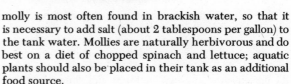

(6) When the tank is completely set up the fish are added. A lighted reflector is put in place to cover the aquarium.

southeastern United States, Japan, China, Argentina, Australia, and even Europe, are also called "tropicals."

Although fishes of one sort or another have been kept both as pets or raised as food fishes since antiquity, the rise of tropical fish keeping can be dated to about 1860 when the theory of a "balance" between fishes and growing aquatic plants in the same tank was developed. This theory holds that since fish need oxygen to live, and in the process of living produce carbon dioxide as a waste product, and since plants need carbon dioxide to live and produce oxygen in their metabolic process, the two kinds of life, fish and plants, can be kept together and will complement each other. It is a nice, convenient theory, but it is not quite true because the number of plants that would be required to provide the oxygen needed by a few fish, in a given confined space, would be so great as to leave no room for the fish.

However, since aquatic plants make attractive settings for the fishes, provide protective cover for smaller and weaker individuals, and do no damage to fishes, the theory, true or false, has done no harm. On the contrary, it has helped to increase the popularity of tropical fish keeping to the point where there are at present literally millions of people in Western Europe, North America, and other regions who derive considerable pleasure from this pastime.

Kinds of Tropical Fish

Not all tropical fishes are suitable for home tanks, only those that have learned to tolerate still, relatively stagnant water, and to eat foods that differ considerably from their natural diet. Of the possibly 1,000 kinds of fishes brought in by the collectors from the Amazon and Congo drainages, and the rivers and swamps of India and Indonesia, not more than 150 are really good "tropicals." The others do not feed well in captivity, or cannot adjust to tanks.

Among the most easily cared-for tropical fish is the guppy (*Lebistes*). Guppies are live-bearers, live for as long as 5 years, are available in a variety of colors, and thrive on almost any commercial fish food. Mollies (*Mollienisia*) run a close second to guppies in popularity as aquarium fish. They also occur in a wide range of forms and colors but demand slightly more care than guppies. The wild

molly is most often found in brackish water, so that it is necessary to add salt (about 2 tablespoons per gallon) to the tank water. Mollies are naturally herbivorous and do best on a diet of chopped spinach and lettuce; aquatic plants should also be placed in their tank as an additional food source.

The angel fish (*Pterophyllum*) is one of the handsomest tropicals. Larger than most aquarium fishes (up to 6 in. long), angel fish prefer ample vegetation, fairly warm water, and full sunlight.

Siamese fighting fish (*Betta*) are perhaps the most spectacular of all aquarium tropicals. Their splendid and varied coloration and flowing fins make a fine addition to the hobbyist's collection. However, the males are extremely pugnacious and cannot be kept together in the same tank.

Other popular tropical fish are the swordtail (*Xiphophorus*), zebra fish (*Brachydanio*), and the danios (*Danio*).

The Home Aquarium

The equipment usually considered necessary for the successful maintenance of tropical fish consists of a container, or tank, which has glass sides and a glass or slate bottom; a tank cover of glass or a metal hood, provided with a light source; an automatically controlled, submersible heating unit; and a low-pressure pump to pump air into the tank where, after passing through a porous filter, it is released in fine bubbles. Sometimes, and usually advisedly, the water in the tank is itself passed through a filter of some sort. This serves to break up stratification in the water, clearing it of gross particles, and also aerates it. If both an air pump and a water filter are used, the number of fish that can be kept in the tank will be at least two times, and usually three or four times, as great as in the same tank lacking such equipment. The best shape of tank, for the benefit of the fishes, is a rectangle of such proportions that the width is greater than the depth. If this is not possible a tank of any shape and size can be used if it is equipped with pump and filter.

The bottom of the tank should be covered with some loose, heavy material. Sand is commonly used but it must be coarse enough to allow the growth of plant roots. Crushed quartz, glass, and gravel are also widely used for this purpose. Soil is the least satisfactory bottom cover. It is good for plants but makes the water dirty and is difficult to hold in place even when kept in pots and covered with sand.

Pieces of rock are often placed in the tank both for decorative purposes and to provide natural shelter. In freshwater tanks rocks of limestone, marble, coral, or any metallic ores should not be used because they will pollute the water for many fishes. However, if particularly desirable rocks of undesirable composition are available, they may be sealed with a spray of clear, inert, synthetic resin which prevents any action by water.

The Salt-Water Aquarium. A vast number of small, colorful fishes inhabit the inshore reefs along all warm sea coasts. Their attractiveness and small size have prompted many tropical fish hobbyists to attempt keeping them. The essentials of marine fish maintenance—tanks, pumps, filters, and controlled heating elements—are all available, but good sea water is not always so readily obtained. Natural sea water, unless changed very frequently, tends to break down. The acid wastes of the fishes, for example, buffer out the necessary alkalinity of sea water in a short time. The use of coral or coral sand in the tank helps to control this but it is usually necessary to change or add to the water at more or less regular intervals. A change of 10% of the water once a week will add considerably to the life of most marine tropicals. Sea water for a marine aquarium should be obtained from a clean beach and if stored in sealed glass containers in the dark, will keep for several months. If it is not possible to get good natural sea water, there are several commercially available salts which, when mixed with water (preferably distilled), are fairly

good substitutes. Artificial sea water has the advantage that fish parasites do not thrive in it, but like natural sea water, it must be changed periodically following the directions of the supplier. Because salt water, either natural or artificial, is extremely active chemically, some fresh-water tanks are unsuitable for this use. The marine fish hobbyist should be certain that the tank selected will survive exposure to salt water.

Consult Coates, C. W., *Tropical Fishes as Pets* (1950); Axelrod, H. R., and Schultz, L. P., *Handbook of Tropical Aquarium Fishes* (1955); Axelrod, H. R., and Vorderwinkler, William, *Encyclopedia of Tropical Fishes* (1957).

C. W. Coates, *Director, New York Aquarium*
See also Angelfish; Fighting Fish; Guppy; Neon Tetra; Swordtail; Zebra Fish.

FISH AND SHELLFISH COOKERY. A wide variety of both fresh- and salt-water fish can now be purchased either fresh, frozen, canned, or cured. All of the common varieties, with the exception of some lake and game fish, are available in frozen form at chain grocery stores. Canned fish, such as sardines, salmon, and tuna, are standards on most pantry shelves. Cured fish—smoked, dried, or pickled—include herring, chug, salmon, whitefish, and mackerel.

Fish. The most important rule to remember when preparing fish is that it should not be overcooked. The one exception to this rule is lake trout; like pork, it must always be well cooked. Lake trout suffers from a liver fluke which can only be killed by cooking the fish until well done.

All fish may be baked, broiled, barbecued, planked, poached, or sautéed. However, fat fish (shad, butterfish, herring, mackerel, catfish, salmon, lake trout, tuna, and whitefish) are at their best when baked, broiled, or planked, as their fat content keeps them from drying out. Lean fish (cod, flounder, halibut steaks, pike, swordfish, and haddock) are better when poached or sautéed, for their flesh remains firm and does not crumble easily. Lean fish may also be broiled or baked. However, when these two methods are employed, the fish must be basted frequently with melted, unsalted butter. Salt in cooking toughens protein foods.

Shellfish and shellfish sauces complement lean fish. For example, flounder fillets are vastly improved when served with a delicate cream sauce accented with shrimp bits or a dash of sherry or both. Mushrooms or hard-cooked eggs may be substituted if shrimp is not available.

Baked or broiled fish should be dressed with colorful garnishings. A liberal sprinkling of paprika, sprigs of fresh parsley or watercress, radish roses, lemon slices, red pepper strips, truffles, or small mushroom caps add not only to the attractiveness of the dish but lend an extra flavor dimension.

When poaching fish the accepted method is in carefully seasoned court bouillon. The cook may, however, add white wine to the court bouillon when preparing a fish to be served cold, such as salmon. Or she may, when poaching small whitefish or halibut, use a broth of half water and half milk.

Shellfish. Generally, fresh shellfish is eaten raw, boiled, steamed, or French fried. Oysters and hard-shelled clams are particularly delectable in their natural state. Lobster is usually boiled or broiled. Shrimp is boiled and served with a cocktail sauce or converted into creamed dishes. In French frying shellfish, one should start with the raw product rather than boiling it first.

Such is the delicacy and adaptability of shellfish that it lends itself to truly great dishes: lobster thermidor, oysters Rockefeller, seafood newburg, shrimp creole, paella, hearty clam chowders, bouillabaisse, clam bisque, and oyster stew. Shellfish combines happily with cream or piquant sauces, with sherry or Madeira. In many recipes its delicate flavor is accented or complemented by such spices as saffron, nutmeg, curry, or paprika.

Cooking Fish. Fish is naturally tender and becomes tough only when overcooked. It should be cooked quickly at high temperatures, and salted only after it has been removed from the heat. Nutritionally, the protein in fish contains all of the biologically essential amino acids as well as minerals and other inorganic compounds necessary for good health. Whole fish, fillets, or steaks can be prepared by any of the following methods.

Baked. Place fish on a bed of chopped carrots, onions, and lettuce in the bottom of a pan. Cover with bacon slices and bake at 425° F. in a preheated oven. Fish is done when it flakes easily with a fork.

Whole fish	8 to 10 min. per lb.
Fillets	20 min. total time
Steaks ¾-in. thick	30 min. total time

Broiled. Heat broiler 10 min. Then oil pan and lay in fish. Baste fish often during broiling with melted, unsalted butter.

Fillets: Cook 2 in. from heat 5 to 8 min., depending upon thickness of the meat. Do not turn.

Steaks: Cook 2 in. from heat 6 to 10 min. on each side.

Whole Fish: Cook 3 in. from heat 3 to 5 min. on first side, and 3 to 8 min. on second side.

Deep-fat Fried. Heat fat to 375° F. on thermometer. Fry batter-dipped fillets or small whole fish 3 to 5 min. depending upon size. Be careful not to overcook.

Grilled over Charcoal. Heat a hinged grill and coat it well with oil. Lay in whole fish, steaks, or fillets. Cook each side 2 to 3 min. over very hot coals. Baste often.

Pan Fried. This is a particularly good method for small whole fish or fillets. Dip fish first into milk and then into a mixture of flour and cornmeal. Heat unsalted butter in a skillet. Add fish and brown on both sides. Serve with a sauce of melted butter and chopped fresh parsley.

Poached in Court Bouillon. To prepare court bouillon, cook the following ingredients together for 30 min.: 2 qts. water, 3 carrots, 2 onions, and 2 stalks chopped celery all chopped; ½ cup vinegar, 5 cloves, 1 bay leaf, ½ tsp. thyme, 4 sprigs of parsley, and 1 tsp. salt. When bouillon is ready, wrap fish in cheesecloth and lower into bouillon. Simmer, do not boil, until done.

Whole fish: Cook 6 to 8 min. per lb.

Fillets: Cook 4 to 6 min.

Frozen fish and shellfish should be thawed in the refrigerator prior to cooking. Smoked fish may be served as is, poached, or baked. Salted fish must be soaked overnight in cold water before being cooked.

ALMA LACH, Food Editor, Chicago *Sun-Times*

FISH CULTURE, the artificial propagation of fishes. It began as a simple husbandry in ancient China and has since developed into a complex art and science that requires the skills of trained technicians and scientists. Modern fish culture produces fish for sport fishing, for aquarium hobbyists, for use as bait, and for food in countries where other forms of animal protein are in poor supply.

In the United States fish culture is practiced at about 500 hatcheries which produce many millions of sportfish each year. While these hatcheries primarily produce the salmonlike fishes, especially the many species of trout, they also have large outputs of catfish, walleye pike, sunfishes, and bass. These fishes are grown and stocked in waters to supplement existing natural fish populations. Fish may also be stocked in waters where natural reproduction is severely limited; where introductions of new species are desired; and where "put and take fishing" (stocking fish with the intention that they be caught immediately) is required. In the late 1800's many eggs and newly hatched fry were stocked. Current trends are not only toward stocking fewer, larger fish, but also include environmental improvement and expanded research programs.

A typical example of the fish culturist's hatchery activities may be seen in the production of rainbow trout. In the early spring trout with mature eggs and milt (the male reproductive secretions) are selected from the brood stock. The eggs and milt are extruded into a moist pan by applying gentle pressure to the sides of the brood trout. Each female trout produces about 750 eggs per lb. of body weight. The eggs and milt are thoroughly mixed in the pan. After a few minutes water is added to the pan and the fertilized eggs are placed in troughs of cool, running water. The eggs are kept meticulously clean and dead eggs are immediately removed from the trays. The eggs hatch in 30 days at a water temperature of 50° F. The young are fed as soon as their yolk sacs are absorbed. When the trout become too large for the troughs, they are placed in nursery ponds.

A hatcheryman must regulate the nutrition of his fishes and attempt to minimize loss through disease and other causes. The nutrition of trout is a complex technology that requires the proper blending of such food items as cattle and sheep livers and other viscera; fish meal; brewer's solubles such as yeast; and vitamins, minerals, and antibiotics. The feeding of dehydrated food in the form of pellets is popular but often must be supplemented by fresh foods. Outbreaks of disease may result in severe fish losses. Diseases may occur in the eggs or infect the hatched fish at any age. Some diseases are nutritional, others may be viral, bacterial, fungal, or protozoan in character. In addition, parasitic worms occasionally reach epidemic levels in hatcheries and may cause losses. For treatment of disease, fish culturists use various organic dyes, antibiotics, drugs, chemicals, and modification of water flow and temperature.

Fish culture also includes the breeding and rearing of aquarium fishes. Because the tropical fishes and goldfish which are commonly kept in home aquaria are not native to North America, many species are cultured on a local basis to avoid the high cost of importation. Most of the tropical fish farms in North America are located in southeastern United States. Some of the tropical fish are even easy for the amateur to breed because they bear their young alive. These live-bearers include the well-known guppies, platies, swordtails, and mollies. Egg-laying tropical fishes are often much more of a challenge to the culturist since their breeding may require rigid control of temperature, water hardness, and acidity. Examples of egg-layers are the zebra danio, the neon tetra, and the angel fish.

The fish culturist is also concerned with selective breeding and the improvement of brood-fish stocks. The popular goldfish is an excellent example of the results of selective breeding. The wild goldfish is an olive-colored fish with a body shape much like that of the common carp to which it is related. Throughout the ages the fish culturist has selected those offspring of the wild-type goldfish with unusual colors or body shapes, and by careful breeding of these mutants (new types of offspring resulting from spontaneous genetic changes) has developed new strains and varieties. Thus, selective breeding has produced orange-gold, pinkish-white, and jet-black goldfish. Some of the body shapes produced through selective breeding include those with flowing three-lobed tails (veiltail strain), huge, bulbous-headed varieties (liontail strain), and upward, rather than laterally directed eyes (Chinese celestial goldfish).

The final aspect of fish culture is pond culture. In North America pond culture is utilized for rearing warm-water fish such as the largemouth bass; for raising fish that will be used for bait (for example, the golden shiner and fathead minnow); and in farm ponds for obtaining a sustained yield of a variety of fishes. Farm ponds are usually managed for bluegill, sunfish, and largemouth bass although in cooler regions trout are raised successfully.

In Asia, Europe, and Africa many tons of carp, mouthbreeders, and milkfish are cultured and harvested for food. Intensive management practices, such as fertilization, may result in yields of several thousand pounds of fish per acre per year, providing valuable animal protein food in areas where it is in poor supply.

Consult Atkins, C. G., and others, *Manual of Fish Culture* (1900); Davis, H. S., *Culture and Diseases of Game Fishes* (1953); Dobie, John, and others, *Raising Bait Fishes* (1956); Lagler, K. F., *Freshwater Fishery Biology* (1956); Wickler, Wolfgang, *Breeding Aquarium Fish* (1966); Hickling, C. F., *The Farming of Fish* (1968).

BRIAN J. ROTHSCHILD
See also FISH; FISHERIES; FISH, TROPICAL.

FISHER, ANDREW (1862–1928), Australian Prime Minister (1908–9, 1910–13, 1914–15). Fisher, a Scottish immigrant, served in the first Labor government in Queensland (1899). In 1901 he won a seat in the federal Parliament. He held the portfolio of Minister for Trade and Customs in the first federal Labor government under John Christian Watson (1904). In 1907 he became leader of the party and Prime Minister the next year. Under Fisher, Labor carried through (1910–13) perhaps the most constructive legislative program in its history. As Prime Minister, he gave unhesitating support to Britain upon the outbreak of World War I (1914). Re-

signing in 1915, he later went to London as high commissioner (1916–21). A trusted party leader, Fisher ranked also as a national leader at a time when Labor's policy dovetailed with Australian national sentiment and social aspiration.

FISHER, CHARLES (1808–80), Canadian statesman. Born in Fredericton, New Brunswick, he studied law and in 1837 won a seat in the provincial legislature, where he distinguished himself as a reformer. In 1848 he entered the government. Six years later he expelled his colleagues from office and formed his own government. He held the premiership until 1861, when a minor scandal drove him from politics. Returning in 1864 as a champion of union with Canada, Fisher attended the Quebec and London conferences, thus becoming a Father of Confederation. He sat in the first Dominion Parliament but resigned (1868) to become a judge on the New Brunswick Supreme Court.

FISHER, DOROTHY CANFIELD (1879–1958), American author, born in Lawrence, Kans. In France during World War I she worked with the wounded and displaced and then returned to America, where she settled permanently on the Canfield family farm near Arlington, Vt., with her husband, James Redwood Fisher. Here she lived a life of combined domesticity, writing, and scholarship. *The Squirrel Cage* (1912) was the first of her books to attract attention; her best-known novels include *The Brimming Cup* (1921) and *The Deepening Stream* (1930). Typically, she wrote sympathetically and well of the people she knew best—New England villagers, college faculty members, French peasants.

FISHER, GEOFFREY FRANCIS (1887–1972), Archbishop of Canterbury (1945–61). An Oxford graduate, Fisher was headmaster of Repton School (1914), Bishop of Chester (1932), and Bishop of London (1939) before succeeding William Temple at Canterbury. A shrewd administrator and ecclesiastical statesman, he encouraged ecumenical relations, particularly with the Eastern Churches, was president of the World Council of Churches (1946–54), and created history and some controversy by his visit to the Pope in 1960. On his retirement he became Baron Fisher of Lambeth.

FISHER, JOHN ARBUTHNOT FISHER, 1ST BARON (1841–1920), British sailor. Born in Ceylon, Fisher entered the Royal Navy in 1854 and served in the Baltic Fleet during the Crimean War. He became vice admiral in 1896, full admiral in 1901, and Second Sea Lord in 1902, when he began a major reorganization of training methods. On Trafalgar Day, 1903, he became First Sea Lord. In this office he advocated, often by unorthodox methods, the building of a large and effective fleet to counter growing German naval power. The Dreadnought construction program, which drew him into the thick of political controversy, was the result. He resigned in 1910 but returned at the outbreak of World War I (1914). Hostile to government policy, particularly in the Dardanelles campaign, he resigned in 1915, thereby precipitating a government crisis.

FISHER, ST. JOHN (1469–1535), English Roman Catholic prelate. Educated at Cambridge, he was ordained a priest in 1491, and in 1497 he was confessor to Lady Margaret Beaufort, mother of Henry VII, through whose generosity he founded Christ's and St. John's colleges at Cambridge. In 1504 he was appointed Bishop of Rochester, counselor to the King, and chancellor of Cambridge, and it was during his chancellorship that Fisher brought Erasmus to Cambridge. As confessor and counselor to Queen Catherine, Fisher championed her cause against Henry VIII's divorce and England's subsequent breach with the Pope, in consequence of which he was imprisoned in the Tower of London in 1534, and beheaded in 1535. He was made a Cardinal just before his death; was beatified in 1886; and in 1936 was canonized by Pius XI. His feast day is June 22.

ABBÉ GERMAIN MARC'HADOUR, Université Catholique,
Angers, France

FISHER, large weasellike carnivore, *Martes pennanti*, in the family Mustelidae, found in Canada and northern United States. Fishers grow to a length of 3 ft., have a bushy 1½-ft.-long tail, and are dark-brown in color. They live in damp forested areas, spending much time in the trees, and hunt at night for birds, small mammals, and some plant foods. Fishers are in turn hunted or trapped for their valuable pelts.

FISHER, FORT, sand dune fortification near Wilmington, N.C. Late in 1864, during the American Civil War, it guarded that city, then the Confederacy's last seaport. Two different Union expeditions were sent against the fort. The first expedition (Dec. 7–27, 1864), led by Gen. Benjamin F. Butler, returned without attacking. The second (Jan. 6–15, 1865), a joint enterprise of Gen. Alfred H. Terry and Adm. David D. Porter, succeeded after a heavy naval bombardment and an infantry attack.

FISHERIES. The world's fisheries have been an important source of food for maritime nations and indirectly for other countries from the earliest times. In recent years their primary importance as a food supply has been supplemented by the valuable contributions of their by-products to arts and industries. Fish meal is widely used in poultry and swine feed; and fish oils and fats are used in the manufacture of margarine, paints, soaps, munitions, linoleum, insect sprays, cosmetics, and many other products. Also derived from the fisheries are fine jewelry, buttons, and many useful and ornamental objects made of pearls or mother-of-pearl or coated with the lustrous pearl essence derived from herring scales.

The World's Fisheries

The world catch of fish and shellfish totals over 80,-000,000,000 lb. annually. Japan, China, the United States, the U.S.S.R., Peru, and Norway produce about half of this harvest. In addition to these nations, countries whose annual catch normally exceeds 2,000,000,000 lb. are Canada and the United Kingdom. Japan leads by a wide margin in the production of fishery products with a yearly catch of over 13,000,000,000 lb. Marine species account for 88% of the world catch, and fresh-water items the remaining 12%. The principal fishes taken are herring, sardines, anchovies, and other related species, which account for 25% of the total catch. These fish are found in large numbers in many temperate areas, and are the basis of important fisheries in all major fishing countries.

Members of the cod family, which includes the hakes and haddock, are the second most important group, accounting for about 13% of the world catch. These fish are largely bottom-dwellers and are taken principally by trawling and with hook and line. They are the basis for an important fresh- and frozen-fish industry. Large quantities of cod are salted and are sold especially in tropical and semitropical countries. The cod fishery in the northwest Atlantic off the coast of Canada is one of the world's great fisheries. In the 16th century the abundance of cod in these waters prompted fishermen from France, Spain, Portugal, and England to extend the economic frontiers of Europe to the New World. In 1958 two North American and ten European nations took nearly 2,000,-000,000 lb. of cod from these waters. About two-thirds of the catch was taken by European fishermen.

Fresh-water fishes comprise about 12% of the world catch. An important part of the supply of these fish is taken from fresh-water ponds and waters over rice farms, particularly in the Orient, where unusual success has been achieved in raising fish in impounded waters. In the United States, the once-great lake trout and white-fish fisheries of the Great Lakes have almost been destroyed by the sea lamprey, which found its way into the lakes through the Welland Canal. The disappearance of lake trout from all but Lake Superior and great declines in the abundance of whitefish and other species have caused the Great Lakes fishing industry great hardship and spurred efforts to find measures to eliminate or reduce the sea lamprey population. Since the lamprey spawns in fresh-water streams emptying into the lakes, an effort was made to find chemicals which would destroy young lampreys in the stream bed. Over 4,000 compounds were studied and one that proved highly toxic to the young lamprey larvae was finally found. An effective chemical control program was developed which is expected to permit recovery or reintroduction of stocks of lake trout and whitefish into the Great Lakes.

Rapid changes are taking place in inland fisheries. Pollution and the silting of streams and lakes destroy fish populations in many areas. However, programs for the construction of power, navigation, and flood-control dams have created large bodies of water suitable for fish life. With proper management, it can be expected that increasing quantities of fresh-water fish will be taken from streams and lakes.

The world tuna fishery has grown from a position of relatively minor importance at the beginning of the 20th century to one of the world's major fisheries. Tunas are a world resource found in tropical and temperate waters throughout the world. They are the principal edible species taken by U.S. fishermen and are one of the more important fishes taken by the Japanese. Japanese fishing vessels range the Pacific and Atlantic oceans in search of tuna and take about 800,000,000 lb. annually. Large quantities of these fish were found late in the 1950's off the west coast of Africa and an important tuna fishery is developing in that area.

Information assembled by the Food and Agriculture Organization of the United Nations indicates that about 43% of the world catch of fish and shellfish is marketed fresh, 20% is cured, 17% is reduced into meal and oil, 9% is canned, 8% is frozen, and 3% is used for miscellaneous purposes. In individual countries the pattern of disposition shows great variation from these percentages. In the United States, for instance, nearly half of the catch is used in the manufacture of fish meal and oil, 30% is marketed fresh or frozen, 19% is used for canning, and less than 2% is cured.

The need for increased supplies of food to feed the world's growing population has resulted in rapid expansion of the fisheries in all oceans. The total world catch of about 45,000,000,000 lb. annually, in the years immediately following World War II, increased to over 83,000,000,000 lb. in 1960. Many countries have increased the size of their offshore fishing fleets. The greatest growth of long-range fishing fleets has taken place in Japan and the U.S.S.R. Japan, because of its limited land area, looks to the sea for much of its food supply. Its fishing craft operate over a wider area than those of any other nation. In the years since the end of World War II, the U.S.S.R. has greatly expanded its fishing operations to the western and southern Atlantic and eastern Pacific oceans. Murmansk has become the world's greatest fishing port with landings of from 1 to 2 billion lb. annually. The most rapid growth of a major fishery has occurred in Peru, where the Humboldt Current supplies the minerals necessary for the growth of a rich plant life. This provides food for tremendous numbers of anchovies which have long been the main food supply of the great flocks of sea birds that reside on Peru's offshore islands. In the mid-1950's regulations restricting the anchovy fishery were removed and the world's largest fish-meal industry developed along Peru's coast. The Peruvian catch of fish increased from 184,000,000 lb. in 1950 to 772,000,000 lb. in 1957, and then to about 6,000,000,000 lb. in 1960. Expansion of Peru's production of fish meal from a few thousand tons to 300,000 tons in 1959 and about 600,000 tons in 1960 disrupted the world market for fish meal. As a result the Peruvian producers have placed a quota on production and limited the construction of new processing plants in an effort to stabilize the market.

Because of the tremendous expansion of fisheries throughout the world, and recognition that the oceans are not an inexhaustible source of fish, a number of international conventions for the conservation of sea fisheries have been formed. Conventions to which the United States belongs include those having to do with the resources of the north Pacific, the halibut fishery off the west coast of North America, the Fraser River salmon fishery, the tuna fishery off the west coast of North and Central America, the shrimp fishery off the east coast of Florida, the groundfish fishery off the east coast of New England and Canada, and the world whale fishery. One of the most successful conventions for the conservation of an ocean resource is the fur seal treaty presently in force among the United States, Canada, Japan, and the U.S.S.R. This treaty has restored the depleted Pribilof Island seal herd from slightly over 100,000 animals in 1911 to a present population of several million animals, and at the same time has permitted an annual yield of over 2,300,000 sealskins.

Another example of successful conservation of an off-shore fishery resource is that of the Pacific halibut, where the annual catch had declined from about 65,000,000 lb. to less than 45,000,000 lb. Through proper management, the stock of fish was restored and the annual catch increased to over 70,000,000 lb.

One of the more serious problems confronting the fisheries is the lack of uniformity in the width of territorial limits and jurisdiction over the fisheries claimed by various nations. Attempts by the United Nations to solve the dilemma through international agreement have resulted in failure, leaving the claims of the various nations—of 3, 6, 9, 12, 15, and even 200 mi.—unresolved.

United States Fisheries

Between 4 and 5 billion lb. of fish, shellfish, and miscellaneous aquatic animals are landed annually at the fishing ports of the United States. Making due allowance for the waste of inedible materials, the annual consumption of fishery products is between 10 and 11 lb. per capita. Actually, people in coastal sections, where large quantities of fresh fish are available, eat as much as 32 lb. of fish a year, while those in inland sections eat as little as 6 lb. However, nationwide, more than twice as much fish as lamb and mutton, and 40% more fish than veal is consumed. Only pork and beef supply a greater quantity of animal protein.

Of the 200 items reported in catch statistics, only a few are taken in large quantity. The fact that normally only 10 items account for about three-quarters of the total catch shows that the United States is unfamiliar with the great variety of fishes in its waters. Fishing is the regular or part-time occupation of 130,000 Americans, and closely related industries provide employment to additional thousands. The average annual catch per fisherman is over 35,000 lb., but ranges as high as 400,000 lb. in the menhaden fishery.

Major Fishing Areas. The Atlantic and Pacific oceans and the Gulf of Mexico supply the United States with almost the entire yield of fish and shellfish. Compared to the enormous quantities taken from salt water, the fishery crop of the lakes and rivers is insignificant. The Atlantic coast provides about 50% of the total catch, the Gulf coast 26%, the Pacific coast 21%, and the Great Lakes and the Mississippi River system 3%.

The food fishes on which the great commercial fisheries depend are not distributed uniformly throughout the oceans, but are mostly confined to the comparatively shallow water (600 ft. or less) over the continental shelf. Fish such as haddock, cod, halibut, and flounder are especially abundant on the submerged plateaus, known as banks, which are shallower than surrounding waters. The Grand Bank, southeast of Newfoundland, is celebrated in legend and literature as a great fishing region, but only a few U.S. vessels fish in these distant waters, taking principally cod and ocean perch. Georges Bank, east of Nantucket, is a very productive fishing ground, on which New England fishermen catch as much as 100,000,000 lb. of haddock, cod, flounder, pollack, and other fishes each year. It is also a center of the scallop fishery.

Herring, sardines, mackerel, tuna, swordfish, and similar fishes are typical inhabitants of the upper layers of the sea. The smaller pelagic fishes like herring, menhaden, and mackerel travel in large schools that may extend almost as far as the eye can see. Most of the fish that support canning industries and reduction plants for the preparation of meal and oil belong in the class of pelagic fishes.

Such fish as salmon, shad, and alewives, which spend most of their lives in salt water but return to coastal streams to spawn, are another important group, and one that probably has suffered the greatest depletion.

Major Fisheries. Over 40% of the total yield of U.S. fisheries consists of a single species, the menhaden. This foot-long member of the herring family ranges the Atlantic and Gulf coasts from Texas to Maine. Annual catches of menhaden during the past decade have averaged nearly 1,750,000,000 lb. Practically the entire catch of menhaden is used in the manufacturing of fish meal and oil.

The California sardine supported the major U.S. fishery for many years, yielding catches averaging over 1,000,-000,000 lb. annually from 1934 to 1944. Following 1944 the catch declined sharply, due to the disappearance of the fish from California waters, and in 1953 it totaled less than 10,000,000 lb.—an outstanding example of the decline of a major ocean fishery. In the seven years following 1953 the catch averaged 105,000,000 lb., or less than 10% of the 1934–44 average.

The salmon, one of the best-known fish in the United States, and for many years the second species with respect to total volume caught, declined in abundance during the years following World War II. The catch during the years from 1950 to 1960 was only slightly over half that taken during the 1930's. Most of the present catch is canned and yields an annual pack of about 3,500,000 cases, of which approximately 75% come from Alaska. Choicest of the five Pacific salmons for canning is the red, or sockeye, salmon, a red-meated fish caught in greatest numbers in Bristol Bay. The highly prized Chinook or king salmon is most abundant in the Columbia River and is widely utilized in the fresh or smoked state, although an excellent canned product is also prepared from this species. Other Pacific species are the pink, chum, and silver salmon.

Five species of tunas and tunalike fishes provide an annual yield of nearly 300,000,000 lb., 99% of which come from the Pacific coast. Tuna fishermen take only a small proportion of their catch off the coast of the United States,

COMMERCIAL FISHING METHODS

Clam Fishing. The clam dredge is dragged on the ocean bottom in water 30 to 40 ft. deep. Water passes under pressure through jets in the dredge, exposing clams beneath the bottom sand. The clams are scooped up by the dredge blades and pass into the sled.

Salmon Trolling. The salmon troller has four outriggers to which tackle (lines, hooks, and sinkers) is attached. The pull of hooked fish on the line releases the line from the clamp, indicating to the ship's crew that the line should be pulled in.

Swordfish Harpooning. Swordfish and other large, nonschooling species are caught by harpooning. The striker stands on the ship's pulpit and thrusts the harpoon into the fish. The fish is hauled in by the retrieving line which is attached to a buoy.

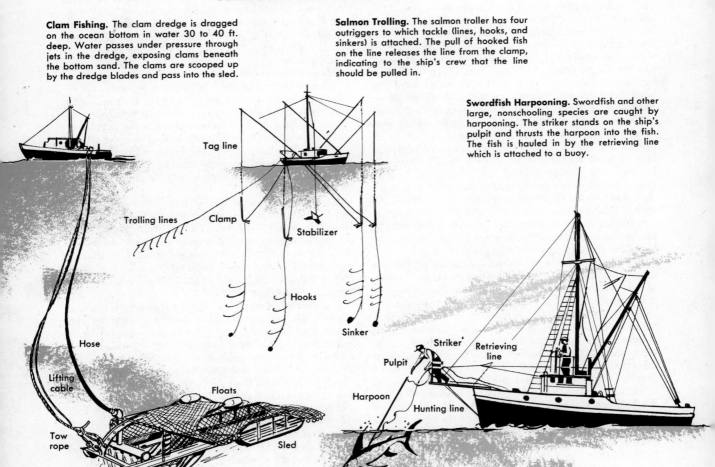

fishing extensively off Mexico and Central America, and ranging south of the equator to the vicinity of the Galápagos Islands and Peru. The entire catch of tuna is delivered to canneries, which turn out a product well known in all parts of the United States.

Mackerel, commonly associated with New England and the picturesque Gloucester schooners of a bygone era, actually come chiefly from the Pacific coast. Atlantic and Pacific mackerels are distinct species, although they belong to the same family.

Shrimp, found chiefly off the south Atlantic, Gulf, and Pacific coast states, ranks third in productivity among all U.S. fisheries. Shrimps are the most valuable product taken, yielding an annual catch valued at about $60,000,000.

The ocean perch, little known before 1935, has been caught since that year in tremendous quantities by New England fishermen. It has supplanted haddock as the leading Atlantic coast food fish. The entire catch of ocean perch and the major portion of the production of haddock and cod are the basis of the New England fillet industry.

Fish sticks and fish portions, manufactured largely from cod fillets imported from Canada, Iceland, and Norway, are important new fishery products. They are breaded, precooked, and frozen, and their pleasing flavor and tex-

ture have made them popular with American consumers. The production of fish sticks, first manufactured in 1953, has increased from 7,500,000 lb. in that year, to 50,000,000 lb. in 1954, and to 65,000,000 lb. in 1960. Fish portions are similar to fish sticks except that they are larger and are intended principally for institutional feeding. They were first manufactured in volume several years after the production of fish sticks was begun. However in 1960, production amounted to over 48,000,000 lb.

Consult Gregory, H. E., and Barnes, Kathleen, *North Pacific Fisheries; With Special Reference to Alaska Salmon* (1939); Innis, H. A., *Cod Fisheries: The History of an International Economy* (1940); Ackerman, E. A., *New England's Fishing Industry* (1941); Russell, E. S., *The Overfishing Problem* (1942); Tressler, D. K., and Lemon, J. M., *Marine Products of Commerce* (1951); Food and Agriculture Organization of the United Nations, *Fishing Boats of the World* (1955); *Modern Fishing Gear of the World* (1959); and *Yearbook of Fishery Statistics, 1960* (1961); Fish and Wildlife Service, Department of the Interior, *Commercial Fisheries Review* (issued monthly).

E. A. POWER, Chief, Branch of Statistics, Bureau of Commercial Fisheries, U.S. Department of the Interior

See also WHALING.

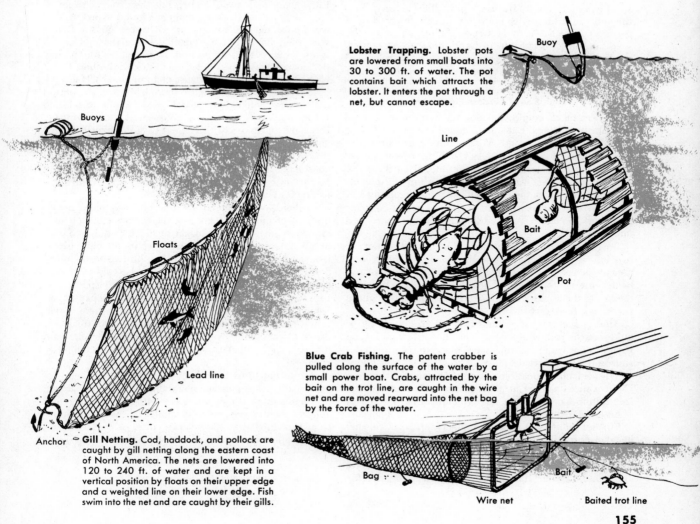

Lobster Trapping. Lobster pots are lowered from small boats into 30 to 300 ft. of water. The pot contains bait which attracts the lobster. It enters the pot through a net, but cannot escape.

Buoy

Line

Bait

Pot

Buoys

Floats

Lead line

Anchor — **Gill Netting.** Cod, haddock, and pollock are caught by gill netting along the eastern coast of North America. The nets are lowered into 120 to 240 ft. of water and are kept in a vertical position by floats on their upper edge and a weighted line on their lower edge. Fish swim into the net and are caught by their gills.

Blue Crab Fishing. The patent crabber is pulled along the surface of the water by a small power boat. Crabs, attracted by the bait on the trot line, are caught in the wire net and are moved rearward into the net bag by the force of the water.

Bag

Bait

Wire net

Baited trot line

FISHER'S HILL, BATTLE OF, engagement (Sept. 22, 1864) near Strasburg, Va., during the Shenandoah Valley campaign in the American Civil War. Union Gen. Philip H. Sheridan defeated Confederate Gen. Jubal A. Early.

See also CIVIL WAR, AMERICAN.

FISHERS ISLAND, island in eastern Long Island Sound, forming part of New York State. It is 11 mi. northeast of Orient Point, the northeastern tip of Long Island, and 7 mi. southeast of New London, Conn. A ferry links the island, primarily a summer resort area, to New London. Length, 8 mi.; width, 1 mi.

FISH HAWK. *See* OSPREY OR FISH HAWK.

FISHING, as a sport or recreational activity, dates from prehistoric times. Early man in search of food found that he could devise means of catching fish, first by seizing them with his hands, then successively by spearing them, securing them in nets woven from grass, and hooking them with pieces of baited bone attached to strips of leather or lines woven from hair. One day he discovered that such activity yielded fun and excitement along with food, and sport fishing was born. There are accounts of sport fishing that date from Egypt in 2000 B.C. Angling, the sport of fishing with hook and line, is referred to in passages of the Bible, in the Greek of Plutarch, and in the works of numerous writers of Latin literature. A famous treatise on the subject was published in English in 1496 constituting a part of the second edition of the *Boke of St. Albans.*

Evolution of Modern Equipment

The first tackle employing hook and line was discovered in prehistoric caves. Early man coiled the primitive line at his feet, swung a length of it in a circle, and flung the baited hook out into the water. When the wheel was invented, the early angler placed the line, or cord, on the wheel; thus the reel was born. The evolution of the modern fishing rod from the early pole cut from a sapling and the growth of accessories has been a matter of constant brainwork, precision workmanship, much experience, and unending tests.

Basic Tackle and Refinements. The basic elements of modern tackle include the rod, by which the bait, or lure, is cast; the reel, on which the line is wound; the line and leader (used to join line and hook), employed in bringing the fish to the angler's station; and baits and lures, whose function is to attract the fish.

Among the earliest refinements was the addition of guides to the rod, which employed the basic winch-type reel. For convenience, rods were made in takedown design employing ferrule joints. Later the single-action-winch reel made possible faster retrieving of the line. Devices such as drags, attached to the reel to prevent too free spinning of the drum, gave the angler better control of his equipment.

Further refinement came as anglers found they needed heavy rods for throwing bait and lures (which simulate the animals on which fish feed, though they do not necessarily bear physical resemblance to such animals) made of metal and wood. Limber, thin, and light rods were needed for casting artificial flies (hooks fitted with feathers and yarn to simulate actual flies) and very light baits. In salt-water fishing, catching tuna and marlin called for very heavy rods and lines and for reels with great capacity. The early years of the 20th century witnessed the greatest advancement in the machining of reels and metal parts for rods and in precision cutting and matching of split bamboo for rods. Such developments were followed by the introduction of numerous accessories—such as gaffs (barbed spears or hooks used in securing heavy fish), elaborate boxes for tackle, and wading equipment.

Fishing Literature and Its Influence. Coincident with the development of specialized equipment was the emergence of fishing experts whose writings comprise both an exciting history of the sport and an invaluable body of practical information, ranging from the philosophical (Izaak Walton's *The Compleat Angler,* 1653) to the latest in "how-to-do-it" books. These works, moreover, had direct influence on actual practice of the sport. In England, for example, the 19th-century writer Frederic M. Halford was among the first to detail the art of fishing with dry flies, which simulate insects on the water's surface (in contrast with wet flies, which serve the same purpose when submerged). His works dealt with fishing for trout in English and European waters, but they spread to many corners of the earth where trout are found. North American fly-fishing (fresh-water or salt-water surface fishing with flies, natural or artificial) became the epitome of sport. Such present-day authors as Theodore Gordon, Ray Bergman, Charles M. Wetzel, Art Flick, and Albert J. McClane have furthered the cause championed by Halford.

In trout-fishing circles, the snobbishness of the period put the dry-fly man in a special class. Anyone who fished with a sunken fly or bait was considered a social outcast. It was only after the British expert G. E. M. Skues brought out several treatises on nymph fishing, employing artificial flies in imitation of insect larvae, that the sunken fly was considered fair tackle among expert fishermen. Fly-fishing for Atlantic salmon went through the same evolution as fishing for trout.

Further Developments. An important step in the development of modern tackle was the introduction of lures known as plugs (wooden or plastic objects equipped with hooks and painted to represent wounded bait fish or frogs). They were introduced in the Midwestern United States by James Heddon for use with relatively short bait-casting rods having multiplying reels (with spools that turn four times for every revolution of the reel handle), in fishing for large- and small-mouth bass. Another innovation was the use of artificial bugs in imitation of small bait fish or insects. These were heavier than large dry flies and lighter than the smallest plugs, and were cast with long fly rods.

Two other lures have become standard—spoons, revolving objects of polished metal that give the appearance of fish in motion as they are drawn through the water; and spinners, which are generally similar in design and function, and which, like spoons, can either be cast or trolled behind a boat or canoe.

Types of Fishing

Fishing is generally divided into two broad categories:

ROD-AND-REEL FISHING

(PHOTO RESEARCHERS, INC.)

FLY-CASTING

 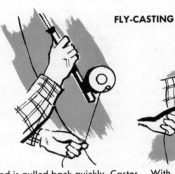  

Left hand holds loop of line in readiness, but pulls line taut on rod to tense rod action.

Rod is pulled back quickly. Caster pauses while back-cast line straightens.

With wrist locked, caster brings rod forward so line is driven parallel to water surface.

When forward movement of rod is halted, left hand releases reserve line, which shoots out.

SPINNING

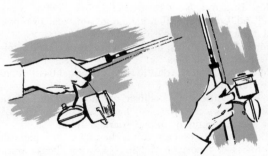  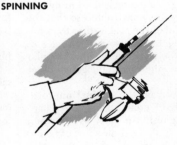 

Rod is pointed toward and above target. Line is held by tip of forefinger, not by joint.

Rod is quickly drawn to vertical. It reaches maximum flex, and caster begins forward push.

Caster stops rod in forward position. Line feeds out as lure shoots toward target.

In follow-through rod is dropped toward target. Caster halts line with forefinger against spool.

BAIT-CASTING

Cast begins with rod pointed toward target, with wrist turned so reel handles are topside.

Rod is raised to vertical, momentarily halted, then allowed to drift back for forward push.

Rod is brought forward. Reel is released. Caster extends arm to lessen line friction on guides.

Reel is stopped by thumb. Rod is moved to left hand, where reel is palmed for retrieve.

157

FISHING

fresh-water and salt-water. The fresh-water variety is subdivided into surface (fly) fishing; mid-water fishing, employing moving bait that is either natural (small fish) or artificial; and bottom fishing, employing bait (such as worms or paste) placed at or near the bottom of the water. Although they are not as sharply defined in salt-water fishing, these subdivisions also apply to that major category.

Fly-Fishing. This most highly developed variety is practiced in both fresh and salt water, in the former in fishing for trout, salmon, bass, and pan fish, and in the latter in catching bonefish, tarpon, snook, striped bass, bluefish, and pompano. The standard gear includes a fly rod of two or three sections, constructed of split bamboo or glass fiber; single-action reel; hard-finish, braided line of nylon or silk; and tapered leader of translucent monofilament nylon. Both wet and dry flies, and a variety of more specialized lures such as nymphs (in imitation of insect larvae) and streamers and bucktails (which resemble minnows), are employed. Fishing is done by wading in streams and lakes, casting from shore or boat, or trolling from boat or canoe.

Bait casting, by which live bait or artificial lures are cast and retrieved, requires a light line, relatively heavy lure, short rod, and reel that rotates with a maximum of ease; fly casting, in contrast, demands a very light lure.

Spin Fishing. One of the most important developments in the modern U.S. sport has been the introduction of "spin fishing," which actually was practiced in Europe as early as the 17th century. Spinning tackle came to America from Switzerland, France, and Italy in the 1930's and proved the most revolutionary development in the history of sport fishing in more than 100 years. Designed for use in both fresh and salt water, it employs a reel with a spool that remains fixed in casting. Unlike reels used in fly and bait casting, the spinning reel is constructed so that the line literally spins off the end of the reel, rather than unwinding. By making fishing technique much easier to master, such gear caused the sport to become popular with millions who otherwise might not have come under its spell.

Salt-Water Fishing. Aside from the gradual improvement of hand lines, nothing of great consequence happened in this form of fishing until the early 1900's when anglers such as Zane Grey popularized the sport of taking mighty game fish—swordfish, marlin, and tuna—with heavy gear from yachts. Soon thereafter, the International Game Fish Association was formed by sport fishermen and scientists eager to learn more about the habits and growth of salt-water species. Michael Lerner, S. Kip Farrington, Jr., Van Campen Heilner, Louis Mowbray, and many other present-day experts made big-game salt-water fishing a sport of international proportions, while other anglers helped to popularize the catching of bonefish and other smaller game fish. As a result, salt-water sport fishing is also a major business; entire communities make their livelihoods through fishing tournaments and contests.

Other Varieties. Still fishing, the most simple of all varieties, involves merely the lowering of baited hook into water; in contrast, casting requires both the specialized equipment described above and a highly developed technique involved in throwing out bait and lure and then retrieving them. A somewhat more advanced form of still fishing makes use of trotlines stretched across a stream and equipped with baited hooks. Trolling involves use of hook and lure drawn along or through the water by the fisherman in a boat or canoe.

Extent and Locales of North American Sport Fishing

In the 1960's more than 30,000,000 Americans participated in sport fishing, and the figure does not take into account the countless numbers (including salt-water anglers) who are not required to get licenses or permits, or who do not observe the requirement. With the industrialization of many parts of the country, fishing began to decline near centers of great population; consequent pre-emptying and polluting of streams presented a major problem to anglers. They have responded by forming conservation organizations designed to protect and promote the sport through research and law enforcement. In this effort they have been joined by government agencies on all levels.

The following is a guide to U.S. and Canadian areas noted for fishing, and to some of the types of fish for which they are famous:

Pacific Northwest: Pacific salmon, steelhead trout, smallmouth bass

Oregon, California: striped bass, trout, many salt-water varieties

Mountain states and adjoining Canadian areas: trout

North Central states and adjoining Canadian areas: musky, pike, largemouth and smallmouth bass

New York State, New England, Ontario, Quebec: musky, pike (including wolf-eyed pike), pickerel, trout, salmon (including landlocked salmon), largemouth and smallmouth bass

New England, New Brunswick, Nova Scotia, Newfoundland, Labrador: Atlantic salmon, squaretail or brook trout, tuna, pollack, bluefish, weakfish

North Atlantic states: fluke, bluefish, tuna, marlin, dolphin, shark, striped bass

Central and South Atlantic states: channel bass, many salt-water varieties

South Atlantic states: sailfish, wahoo, blue and white marlin, amberjack, albacore, barracuda, bonefish, sea trout, snook, tarpon, pompano, shark, dolphin

Midwestern states: bass, trout, channel catfish, pan fish

Tennessee, Georgia, Alabama, Florida: largemouth bass, crappie

Gulf Coast states: all but the deep Atlantic Ocean varieties.

Consult Caine, L. S., *North American Fresh Water Sport Fish* (1949); Farrington, S. K., *Fishing the Atlantic* (1949); Bates, J. D., *Streamer Fly Fishing in Fresh and Salt Water* (1950); Camp, R. R., *Fishing the Surf* (1950); Bueno, Bill, *American Fisherman's Guide* (1952); La Monte, F. R., *Marine Game Fishes of the World* (1952); Brooks, J. W., *Complete Book of Fly Fishing* (1958); Bergman, Ray, *Trout* (1959); Ovington, Ray, *Young Sportsman's Guide to Fresh Water Fishing* (1961) and *Young Sportsman's Guide to Salt Water Fishing* (1961).

Ray Ovington, Author, *The Young Sportsman's Guide to Fresh Water Fishing*

FISHING, COMMERCIAL. *See* FISHERIES.

158

FISH LOUSE, common name for many small marine and fresh-water crustaceans of the subclass Copepoda. Fish lice are found throughout the world. They are external and internal parasites of fish. All have flattened, jointed bodies and many have hooklike appendages that aid them in clinging to the skin of the host fish. The mouth parts of fish lice are highly modified for piercing. Common genera of fish lice include *Caligus*; *Choniostoma*, parasitic on larger crustaceans; and *Salmincola*, a parasite on the gills of trout.

FISH OILS, oils obtained from pressing the entire fish. The principal sources are the menhaden, sardine, and herring. To obtain the oil, large quantities of fish are subjected to high pressures. Foreign insoluble matter is removed from the oil by filtration, and it is then placed in settling tanks. The stearin, the solid portion of the oil, settles out; olein, the liquid portion, is removed. Both the solids and liquids are used in currying leather, in making resins, paints, and linoleum, and in foods. The scrap remaining from the fish is used as fertilizer and in animal feeds.

FISHWAY, structure permitting fish to pass a barrier in a stream. Fishways, also called fish ladders, are common accessory features to dams. Of the several types in use, the channel fishway, which has internal baffles to dissipate the energy of the falling water and create temporary resting places for the fish, is most efficient. Another type is the pool-and-jet fishway. In its simplest form this is a series of overflowing, stepped pools up which active swimmers such as trout and salmon can fight their way. Entrances or leads to fishways should be near the base of the dam or barrier where the fish are stopped in their upstream travels. Experience has shown that if the fishway opens too far downstream, few fish will find it. To solve this problem some engineers double back or reverse their fishways. Conservationists advocate legislation making fishways mandatory for all structures which block streams.

FISK, JAMES (1834–72), American stock manipulator, born in Bennington, Vt. He was a peddler and circus manager before he prospered during the Civil War as a cotton dealer in occupied areas and as a salesman abroad of Confederate bonds. After becoming a Wall Street broker in 1866, he collaborated with Daniel Drew and Jay Gould in wresting control of the Erie Railroad from Cornelius Vanderbilt. He then proceeded to plunder the road by stock market manipulations. Fisk and Gould, in attempting to corner the gold market, precipitated the notorious "Black Friday" scandal on Wall Street (1869). Fisk invested in both steamboat and ferry lines and bought Pike's Opera House in New York City. In his final years he lived on a grand and gaudy scale foreshadowing the "Gilded Age." He was fatally shot by Edward S. Stokes, a business associate.

FISKE, JOHN (1842–1901), American philosopher and historian, born in Hartford, Conn. He demonstrated great intellectual powers as a boy. At Harvard he was strongly influenced by the evolutionary philosophy of Herbert Spencer. After graduation (1863) he studied law and continued his philosophical interests. He gave public lectures and wrote widely on science, religion, and the Darwinian theory. Later he turned to American history; in this field his most influential work was the *Critical Period of American History* (1888). Fiske commanded a charming and lucid literary style, but he is chiefly remembered as an able popularizer rather than as a profound or original thinker.

FISKE, MINNIE MADDERN (1865–1932), American actress, born in New Orleans. As Minnie Maddern, she achieved success as a child actress and ingénue prior to her marriage in 1890 to the playwright-critic Harrison Grey Fiske. As Mrs. Fiske, she became a leading actress, noted for the naturalism of her performances and her pioneer work in playing Ibsen heroines for U.S. audiences. Her other famous roles were in *Becky Sharp*, *Tess of the D'Urbervilles*, and *Salvation Nell*.

FISSION, asexual form of reproduction characteristic of one-celled plants and animals. When such an organism reproduces, it merely divides into two approximately equal halves. First the nucleus divides, then the surrounding cytoplasm constricts and the two new individuals are formed. This method of reproduction is properly called binary fission. In some one-celled organisms the nucleus divides into more than two parts so that more than two new individuals result. This is known as multiple fission, or sporulation, and is the characteristic method of reproduction of protozoans of the class Sporozoa—parasitic one-celled animals such as *Plasmodium* (which causes malaria) and *Eimeria* (which causes coccidiosis).
See also REPRODUCTION.

FISSION, NUCLEAR. *See* ATOMIC ENERGY.

FISTULA [fĭs'chŏŏ-lə], an abnormal communication between the skin surface and a body cavity or internal organ (external fistula), or between two internal organs (internal fistula). The opening may be present from birth or result from injury or disease. External fistulas include communications between the skin and the abdominal viscera. Internal fistulas may develop between the stomach and the large intestine, between adjacent loops of the small bowel, or between the rectum and the bladder. Arteriovenous fistulas are connections between an artery and a vein. Fistulas frequently interfere with normal function and are usually corrected by surgery.

FITCH, (WILLIAM) CLYDE (1865–1909), American playwright, born in Elmira, N.Y. The first success among his voluminous writings was *Beau Brummell* (1890), commissioned and frequently played by Richard Mansfield. From historical plays like *Nathan Hale* (1898) and *Barbara Frietchie* (1899), he turned to comedies, including *The Climbers* (1901) and *Captain Jinks of the Horse Marines* (1901). His later plays, although weakened by melodrama, embody some realism and social commentary; they include *The Woman in the Case* (1905), *The Truth* (1907), and *The City* (1909).

FITCH, THOMAS (c.1700–1774), colonial Governor of Connecticut. Born in Norwalk, Conn., he became a lawyer and served in the Connecticut general assembly (1726–30). He was assistant (1734–35, 1740–50) and later deputy governor (1750–54). In 1754 he set a Connecticut precedent by defeating an incumbent (Roger Wolcott) for Governor. During his administration he enthusiastically promoted the British cause in the French and Indian War, inducing Connecticut to exceed its recruitment quotas almost every year. He vigorously opposed the British effort to pay for the war through a stamp tax, but he deemed it his duty to enforce the tax act after it was passed. Consequently he was defeated for re-election in May, 1766, and never again held public office.

FITCHBURG, industrial city of central Massachusetts, on the Nashua River. Paper and machinery are manufactured here. Settled, 1740; inc. as town, 1764; as city, 1872; pop., 43,343; Fitchburg-Leominster urb. area 78,053.

FITZGERALD, BARRY, professional name of William Joseph Shields (1888–1961), Irish actor. Early in his career he was a leading stage actor at the Abbey Theater, Dublin, where he created the role of "Capt." Jack Boyle in *Juno and the Paycock* in 1924. He made his U.S. stage debut with the Abbey troupe in 1934. After 1936 he devoted himself to character and comedy roles in U.S. films, including *Going My Way* (1944), for which he won an Academy Award, and *The Quiet Man* (1952).

FITZGERALD, LORD EDWARD (1763–98), Irish patriot, son of James Fitzgerald, 1st Duke of Leinster. He began his career in the British army (1779) and fought in the American Revolution. He served briefly in the Irish Parliament (1784), traveled in North America, and returned home during the first enthusiasm for the French Revolution. In 1792 he visited Paris and was cashiered from the army for displaying prorepublican sentiments. He returned to Ireland and again resumed his parliamentary career. The repressive policies of Britain turned him from a light-hearted patriot into a dedicated and disciplined conspirator. In 1796 he joined the United Irishmen and worked to prepare the "Rising of '98," but he was captured before the event and died of wounds received at his arrest.

FITZGERALD, EDWARD, original surname Purcell (1809–83), English translator and poet. He received the surname FitzGerald in 1818, when the family adopted his mother's maiden name. After education at Trinity College, Cambridge, he became a rather retiring country gentleman, devoting himself chiefly to translating masterpieces of Greek, Spanish, and Persian literature. Though *Six Dramas of Calderon* (1853) and *The Downfall and Death of King Oedipus* (1880) are accomplished translations, his only really significant work is *The Rubáiyát of Omar Khayyám*, based on the quatrains of the 12th-century Persian poet. Consisting of 75 quatrains when it first appeared in 1859, it was expanded to 110 quatrains in 1868. In subsequent editions the stanzas were rearranged and reduced in number to 101. The poem stands, as a translation into English, beside Chapman's Homer and Jowett's Plato. It is a very free translation which captures the spirit rather than the letter of the original. *The Rubáiyát's* pessimism and exoticism had a great influence on late 19th-century aestheticism.

Consult Terhune, A. M., *The Life of Edward Fitz-Gerald* (1947).

JAMES K. ROBINSON, University of Cincinnati

FITZGERALD, ELLA (1918–), American jazz singer, born in Newport News, Va. In 1934 she was heard at a Harlem amateur show by orchestra leader Chick Webb, and subsequently sang with his orchestra for several years. After 1940 she toured various foreign countries and appeared with small groups in night clubs and theaters. Her voice increased in range throughout the years and retained its celebrated clarity and sureness of pitch. Although not considered a traditional jazz singer, she is a fine melodic improviser who understands the rhythmic modes of jazz and who projects extraordinary zest into her work.

FITZGERALD, FRANCIS SCOTT KEY (1896–1940), American novelist and short-story writer, born in St. Paul, Minn., and educated at Princeton. Two relatively immature novels, *This Side of Paradise* (1920) and *The Beautiful and Damned* (1922), were followed in 1925 by *The Great Gatsby*, a beautifully finished study of a young Midwesterner who capitalizes on but is ultimately destroyed in the ruthless, amoral business society of New York during the prohibition era. Other works were *Tender Is the Night* (1934), a rich, complex picture of American expatriates in the 1920's; *The Last Tycoon* (1941), an unfinished, posthumously published novel about Hollywood; and several notable collections of short stories, including *All the Sad Young Men* (1926) and *Taps at Reveille* (1935). Fitzgerald's unhappy last years, clouded by alcoholism and the mental illness of his wife Zelda, were the basis of Budd Schulberg's novel *The Disenchanted* (1950). Celebrated in his lifetime primarily as the laureate of the Jazz Age, whose life and work represented the disillusioned, reckless, frenetic spirit of youth in the 1920's, Fitzgerald has since received widespread critical attention for his subtle, economical prose style and his probing, compassionate portraits of Americans searching for self-realization in a pushing, acquisitive society.

Consult Mizener, Arthur, *The Far Side of Paradise* (1951).

SEYMOUR RUDIN, University of Massachusetts

FITZGERALD, GEORGE FRANCIS (1851–1901), Irish physicist whose theories contributed to the development of the theory of relativity. Educated in Dublin, he was a professor at the University of Dublin and did research in electrical phenomena. To explain the results of the Michelson-Morley experiment (that the earth's motion through a hypothetical medium, called the ether, exerts no influence on the speed of light; and that there is no ether drag, or relative motion of earth and ether), FitzGerald proposed that matter contracts in the direction of its motion through the ether. The Dutch physicist H. A. Lorentz also put forward this idea and it is known as the FitzGerald-Lorentz Contraction.

See also MICHELSON-MORLEY EXPERIMENT; RELATIVITY, THEORY OF.

FITZGERALD, city of south-central Georgia and seat of Ben Hill County. It is a market for tobacco, peanuts, and other farm products. Industries include meat packing and the manufacture of naval stores and fertilizers. Nearby Jefferson Davis State Park commemorates the site of the Union capture of the Confederate President on May 10, 1865. Inc., 1896; pop., 8,187.

FITZHERBERT, MARIA ANNE (1756–1837), wife of King George IV of England. She was descended from a Catholic gentry family and twice widowed. A woman of singular charm and beauty, she captivated George IV when he was Prince of Wales. She married him secretly in 1785, but their union was declared invalid. Nevertheless she was widely received as his wife until she finally ended their relationship in 1803.

Consult Leslie, Shane, *Mrs. Fitzherbert* (1939).

FITZPATRICK, DANIEL ROBERT (1891–   ), American editorial cartoonist, born in Superior, Wis. His brilliant cartoons attacking social evils and governmental corruption and misrule helped to impart a crusading tone to the St. Louis *Post-Dispatch*, which he served from 1913 until he retired in 1958. He won Pulitzer prizes for cartooning in 1926 and 1954.

FITZPATRICK, THOMAS (c.1799–1854), U.S. mountain man, guide, and Indian agent. Born in Ireland, Fitzpatrick came to America before he was 17 and moved westward to Missouri. He joined William H. Ashley's expedition up the Missouri River in 1823 to trap and trade for furs. After two disastrous years Ashley sent a party to the Crow Indian country to recoup losses. Co-leaders Fitzpatrick and Jedediah Smith made the effective discovery of South Pass in Wyoming in 1824. After a summer's trapping in the rich Green River area, Fitzpatrick packed the fur harvest to Missouri. News of the catch lured trappers to the central Rockies and led to complete exploration of the region. In 1830 Fitzpatrick became head of the Rocky Mountain Fur Company.

When the beaver trade declined sharply because of depletion and a drop in price, Fitzpatrick began his second career, as a guide. In 1841 he led the first emigrant train toward Oregon and California. The next summer he escorted the second caravan west from Fort Laramie. He guided John C. Frémont, called the "Pathmarker," on his most important exploration tour—to Oregon and California in 1843–44. Next year he led Stephen W. Kearny and J. W. Albert on their western expeditions. With the outbreak of the Mexican War, Fitzpatrick guided Kearny's "Army of the West" to New Mexico and returned with dispatches to Washington.

Fitzpatrick's third career began as first agent to the Indians of the upper Platte and Arkansas. He helped negotiate a treaty with hostile Kiowas and Comanches. His excellent reports and wise recommendations exhibited high ability. While on official business he died in Washington, D.C. The Indians long remembered him as "Broken Hand, the best Agent we ever had."

Consult Hafen, L. R., and Ghent, W. J., *Broken Hand* (1931).

LeRoy R. Hafen, Brigham Young University

FITZROY, ROBERT (1805–65), British meteorologist and hydrographer who, in 1858, organized the first storm-warning service using weather maps based on telegraphic reports. He graduated from the Royal Naval College in 1819 and served in surveys of the Mediterranean Sea and the South American coast until placed in command of H.M.S. *Beagle* in 1828. In 1839 he published *Narrative of the Surveying Voyages of H.M. Ships Adventure and Beagle, 1826–1836* in three volumes. Charles Darwin, who participated in voyages of the *Beagle*, wrote the third volume of this famous work. Fitzroy was named a member of Parliament from Durham in 1841 and he was Governor of New Zealand from 1843 to 1845. He was appointed chief of the meteorological department of the Board of Trade in 1854. He is noted also for having devised the first practical marine barometer.

FITZSIMMONS, JAMES E. ("SUNNY JIM") (1874–1966), American thoroughbred-horse trainer, born in Brooklyn, N.Y. He trained two winners of racing's "Triple Crown" (the Kentucky Derby, Preakness, and Belmont Stakes): Gallant Fox (1930) and Omaha (1935). From 1954 to 1956 he also trained Nashua, who won $1,288,565 before being retired.

FITZSIMMONS, ROBERT PROMETHEUS ("BOB") (1862–1917), boxer, born in Cornwall, England. He went to the United States in 1890 and won the world's middleweight championship in 1891 by knocking out Jack Dempsey, "the Nonpareil." In 1897 he won the heavyweight title by knocking out James J. Corbett and lost it in 1899 via a knockout by James J. Jeffries. Fitzsimmons won the light-heavyweight title from George Gardner in 1903 and lost it in 1905 to "Philadelphia Jack" O'Brien.

FIUME. *See* Rijeka.

FIVE CIVILIZED TRIBES, five groups of North American Indians—the Cherokee, Chickasaw, Choctaw, Creek, and Seminole—originally of the southeast but forced to move to Oklahoma Indian Territory in the 1830's. *See* Indian Tribes, North American; Oklahoma.

FIVE DYNASTIES. *See* China: *History*.

FIVE FORKS, BATTLE OF, last important engagement (Apr. 1, 1865) of the American Civil War. Union Gen. Philip H. Sheridan repulsed an attack by Confederate Gen. Robert E. Lee's right wing, commanded by Gen. George E. Pickett, 15 mi. southwest of Petersburg, Va.

FIVE NATIONS, the five North American Indian tribes making up the Iroquois Confederation: Cayuga, Mohawk, Oneida, Onondaga, and Seneca. *See* Indian Tribes, North American; Iroquois.

FIXATION, term used in psychoanalysis to describe an arrest in psychic development at some infantile level. According to Freudian theory, an excessive amount of psychic energy remains attached to some phase of early development, interfering with the normal process of personality growth, and leading to neurosis in adult life. For example, an overly dependent adult is said to be fixated at the oral level, the earliest psychosexual stage, when dependency is normal and at its height. Fixation is distinguished from regression, in which an individual who has progressed beyond a particular stage subsequently returns to it.

See also PSYCHOANALYSIS.

FIXED OILS. *See* FATS AND OILS.

FIZEAU [fē-zō'], **ARMAND HIPPOLYTE LOUIS** (1819–96), French physicist noted for his experiments to measure the velocity of light. One of the first to obtain a relatively accurate measurement of the velocity of light through air, Fizeau also measured its velocity in moving water. The results of this experiment provided support for the wave theory of light. Fizeau was a member of the French Academy of Sciences and on the staff of the École Polytechnique.

See also LIGHT.

FLAG, common name for several plants of the genus *Iris*, in the iris family, Iridaceae. Flags are found in the north temperate regions of Europe, Asia, and North America. The plants have sword-shaped leaves and flowers resembling those of the cultivated iris. The common blue flag, *I. versicolor*, is a wildflower of swamps and pond margins in Canada and northern United States. It is a stout-stemmed plant, and bears showy purplish flowers marked with yellow and white. A related species, *I. prismatica*, the slender blue flag, is native to damp habitats in eastern North America. The water flag, *I. pseudocorus*, is a yellow-flowering species native to Europe but naturalized in eastern North America. All species of flag are hardy and are easily grown as ornamentals around pools and in garden borders.

See also IRIS.

FLAG, a piece of cloth or bunting, of varying sizes, shapes, and colors, usually attached by one edge to a staff or cord, designating a community, armed force, country or other political body, or any organization or institution.

Flags may be used to send messages as well as to represent a state or organization. Ships relay messages by international code flags, and signaling in armies and navies is often done with flags. An inverted flag indicates distress. A flag at half-mast indicates mourning. Truce is represented by a white flag, mutiny or revolution by a red flag, piracy by a black flag, and infectious diseases by a yellow flag. A white flag with a red cross has been used by the International Red Cross in wartime to indicate hospitals and medical units.

The history of the flag can be traced back to the early days of Egypt. Egyptians and Assyrians placed sacred emblems and other objects on standards. Attached to these were streamers of diverse colors, shapes, and designs, identifying a group or military unit. Later the Romans attached replicas of eagles, wolves, horses, and bears on standards, helmets, and armor, again often with streamers attached to the standards. The Roman cavalry flags most closely resemble present-day flags.

The use of flags by Saracens was later copied by the Christians who, during the Third Crusade in the late 12th century, carried flags figured with the Christian cross. But the flag as representing a principality or specific group did not come into general use until centuries later. Flags were employed in medieval times, sometimes bearing an emblem of religious significance. Later, kings had personal flags, but in time flags were established to represent the country itself. After the French Revolution, the tricolor, a flag with three broad stripes of different colors, came into prominence, thereafter symbolizing republicanism.

American Flags. Until the American Revolution, British flags were flown in the colonies. Local banners and flags appeared soon after the outbreak of the Revolution, and one of the earliest battle flags was that of the Bedford minutemen who opposed the British at Concord. During the Revolution each state adopted a flag of its own, such flags often containing the symbol of a pine tree, for example, or a rattlesnake and the inscription, "Don't tread on me."

The first flag with 13 stars flew over the armed schooner *Lee* in 1775. It included a blue canton containing 13 five-pointed stars and a blue anchor in the center of the flag. At its top was inscribed the word "Hope."

Prior to the Declaration of Independence, the Continental Congress desired to show that it did not seek independence despite the hostilities. Thus, on Jan. 1, 1776, the day the new Continental Army came into existence, the new flag displayed by the American troops besieging Boston included 13 red and white stripes and a canton in the middle of which was the British Union Jack.

There is a tradition that a seamstress, Betsy Ross, made the first American flag of stars and stripes. However, the historical authenticity of this has been questioned. In June, 1777, the Continental Congress approved a design for a new flag. It was resolved that the flag of the United States should have 13 stripes, alternate red and white, with a union of 13 stars of white on a blue field, "representing a new constellation." The replacement of the Union Jack by the constellation of stars represented the only change from the earlier flag.

On Jan. 13, 1794, with the admission of Vermont and Kentucky to the Union, two more stars were added to the flag. When other states had been admitted, Congress in 1818 decided to prescribe general rules governing the flag and the changes to be made in it when new states were admitted. The Act of Apr. 4, 1818, provided that the flag would have 13 alternate red and white stripes representing the first 13 states, and 20 stars, white in a blue field. One star would be added to the flag on the admission of every new state to the Union, the addition to take effect on the 4th day of July following each admission.

On Mar. 4, 1861, the seceding states of the Union approved a flag for the Confederate States of America. It became known as the Stars and Bars and was first flown over the state house in Montgomery, Ala.

The number of stars (and states) remained at 48 from 1912, when New Mexico and Arizona were admitted to the Union, until 1959 when Alaska became the 49th state. The next year, with the admission of Hawaii to statehood, the number of stars was increased to 50.

The flag of the United States contains 13 horizontal stripes, 7 red and 6 white, with red stripes at the top and

FLAGS OF NORTH AND CENTRAL AMERICA

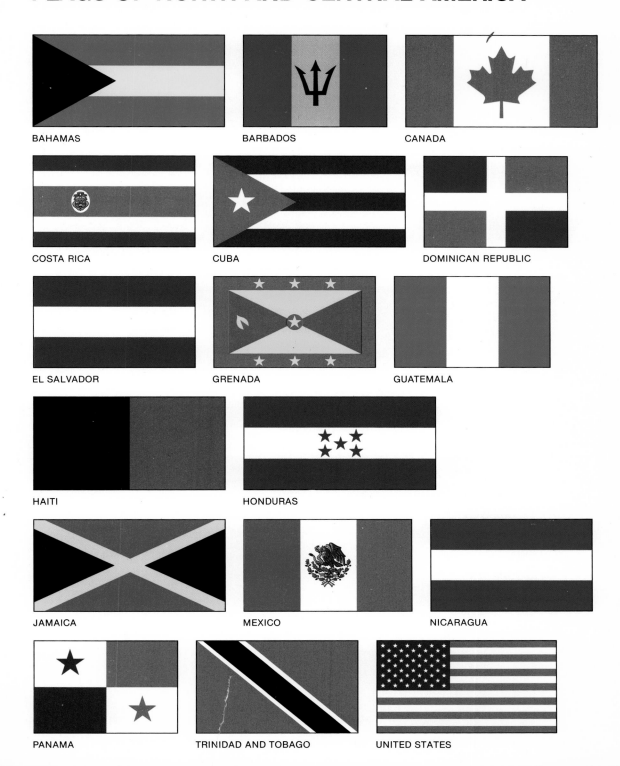

BAHAMAS

BARBADOS

CANADA

COSTA RICA

CUBA

DOMINICAN REPUBLIC

EL SALVADOR

GRENADA

GUATEMALA

HAITI

HONDURAS

JAMAICA

MEXICO

NICARAGUA

PANAMA

TRINIDAD AND TOBAGO

UNITED STATES

FLAGS OF SOUTH AMERICA

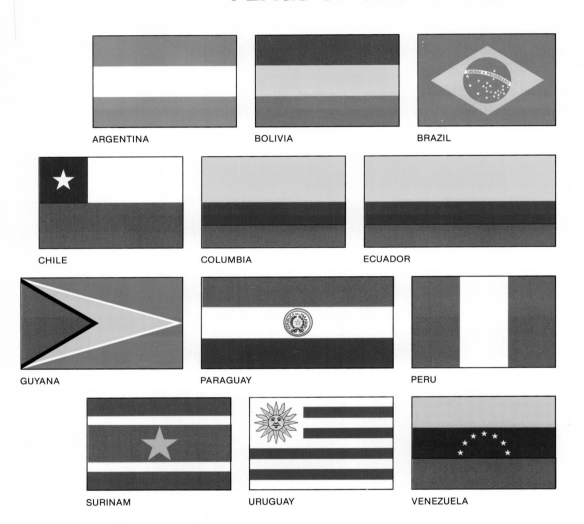

ARGENTINA

BOLIVIA

BRAZIL

CHILE

COLUMBIA

ECUADOR

GUYANA

PARAGUAY

PERU

SURINAM

URUGUAY

VENEZUELA

FLAGS OF EUROPE

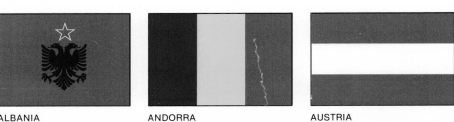

ALBANIA

ANDORRA

AUSTRIA

BELGIUM

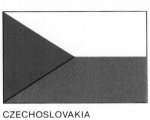

BULGARIA

CZECHOSLOVAKIA

DENMARK

FINLAND

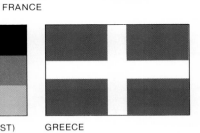

FRANCE

GERMAN DEM. REP. (EAST)

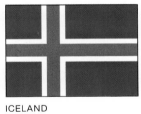

GERMANY, FED. REP. OF (WEST)

GREECE

HUNGARY

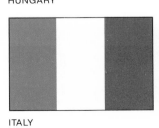

ICELAND

IRELAND

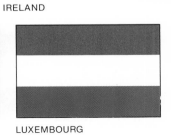

ITALY

LIECHTENSTEIN

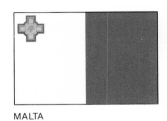

LUXEMBOURG

MALTA

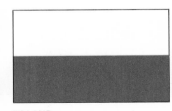

MONACO

NETHERLANDS

NORWAY

POLAND

PORTUGAL

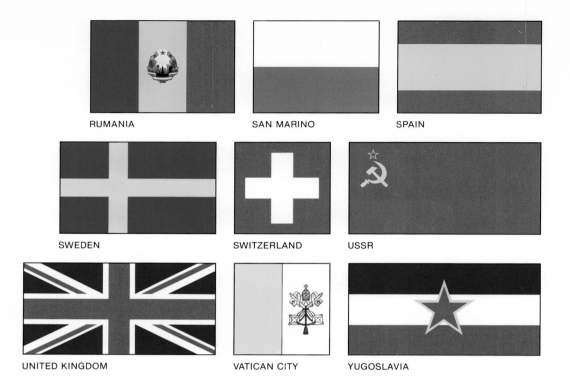

RUMANIA

SAN MARINO

SPAIN

SWEDEN

SWITZERLAND

USSR

UNITED KINGDOM

VATICAN CITY

YUGOSLAVIA

FLAGS OF ASIA

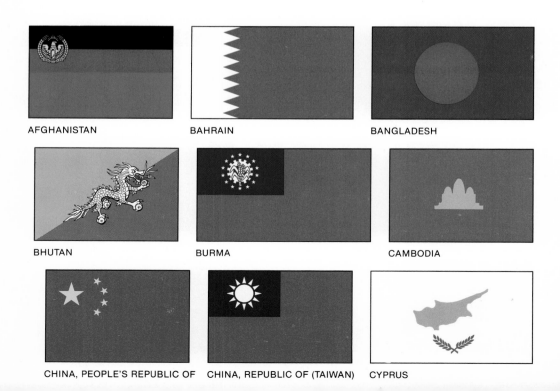

AFGHANISTAN

BAHRAIN

BANGLADESH

BHUTAN

BURMA

CAMBODIA

CHINA, PEOPLE'S REPUBLIC OF

CHINA, REPUBLIC OF (TAIWAN)

CYPRUS

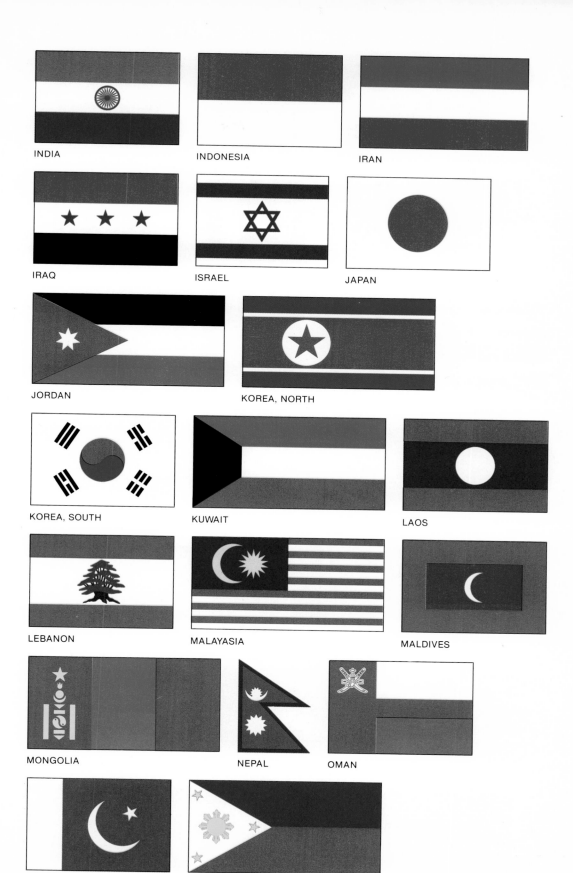

INDIA

INDONESIA

IRAN

IRAQ

ISRAEL

JAPAN

JORDAN

KOREA, NORTH

KOREA, SOUTH

KUWAIT

LAOS

LEBANON

MALAYASIA

MALDIVES

MONGOLIA

NEPAL

OMAN

PAKISTAN

PHILIPPINES

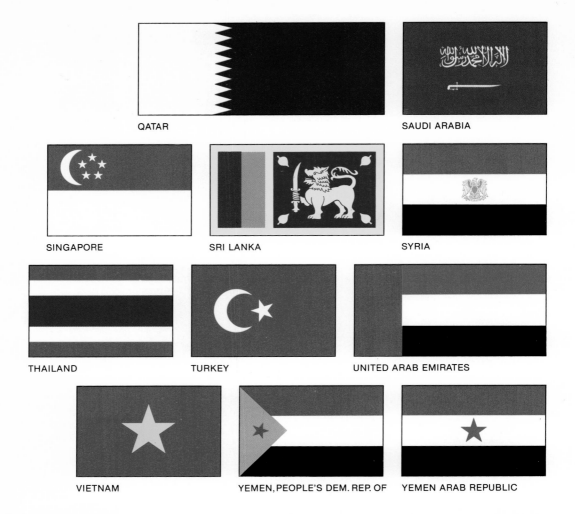

QATAR

SAUDI ARABIA

SINGAPORE

SRI LANKA

SYRIA

THAILAND

TURKEY

UNITED ARAB EMIRATES

VIETNAM

YEMEN, PEOPLE'S DEM. REP. OF

YEMEN ARAB REPUBLIC

FLAGS OF AFRICA

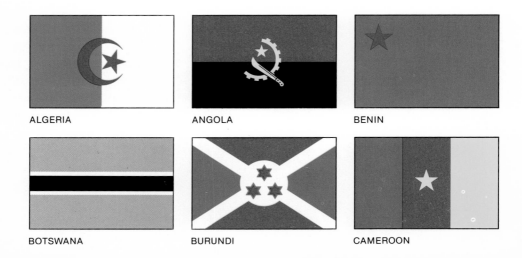

ALGERIA

ANGOLA

BENIN

BOTSWANA

BURUNDI

CAMEROON

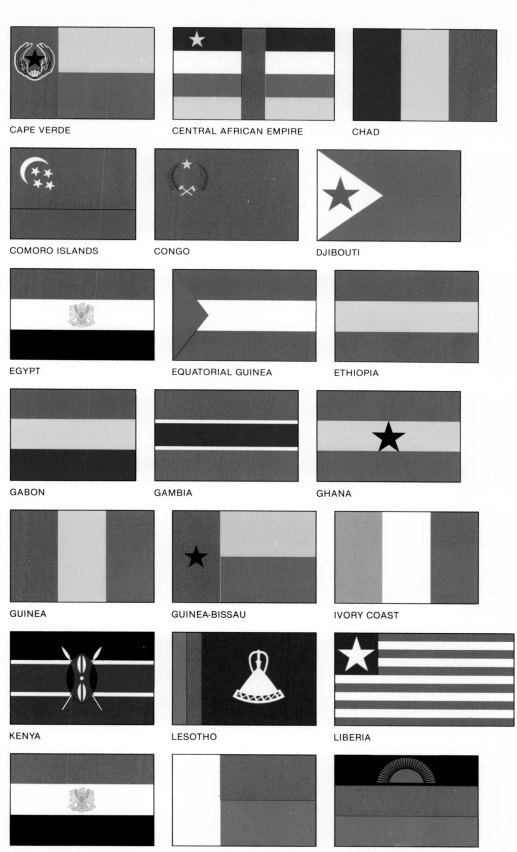

CAPE VERDE

CENTRAL AFRICAN EMPIRE

CHAD

COMORO ISLANDS

CONGO

DJIBOUTI

EGYPT

EQUATORIAL GUINEA

ETHIOPIA

GABON

GAMBIA

GHANA

GUINEA

GUINEA-BISSAU

IVORY COAST

KENYA

LESOTHO

LIBERIA

LIBYA

MADAGASCAR

MALAWI

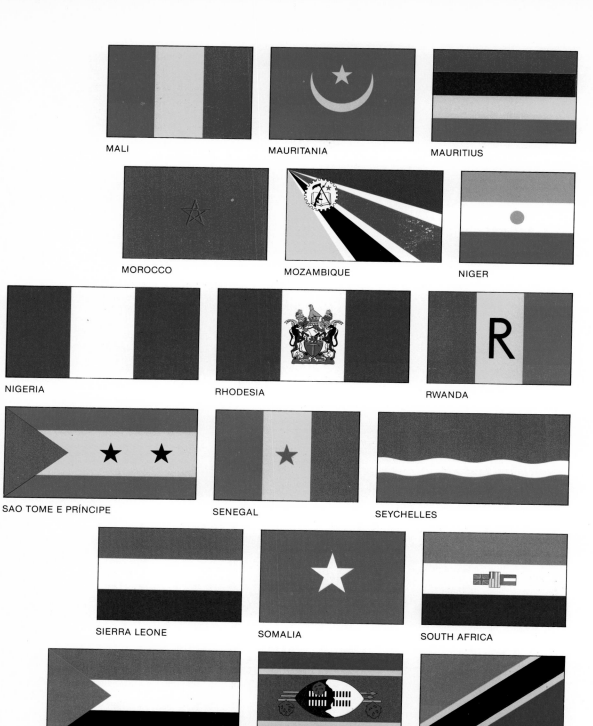

MALI

MAURITANIA

MAURITIUS

MOROCCO

MOZAMBIQUE

NIGER

NIGERIA

RHODESIA

RWANDA

SAO TOME E PRÍNCIPE

SENEGAL

SEYCHELLES

SIERRA LEONE

SOMALIA

SOUTH AFRICA

SUDAN

SWAZILAND

TANZANIA

TOGO

TUNISIA

UGANDA

UPPER VOLTA

ZAIRE

ZAMBIA

FLAGS OF OCEANIA

AUSTRALIA

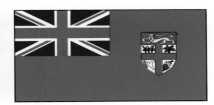

FIJI

NAURU

NEW ZEALAND

PAPUA NEW GUINEA

TONGA

WESTERN SAMOA

FLAGS OF THE STATES

(With date of admission and order of admission of each state.)

ALABAMA, DECEMBER 14, 1819 (22)

ALASKA, JANUARY 3, 1959 (49)

ARIZONA, FEBRUARY 14, 1912 (48)

ARKANSAS, JUNE 15, 1836 (25)

CALIFORNIA, SEPTEMBER 9, 1850 (31)

COLORADO, AUGUST 1, 1876 (38)

CONNECTICUT, JANUARY 9, 1788 (5)

DELAWARE, DECEMBER 7, 1787 (1)

FLORIDA, MARCH 3, 1845 (27)

GEORGIA, JANUARY 2. 1788 (4)

HAWAII, AUGUST 21, 1959 (50)

IDAHO, JULY 3, 1890 (43)

ILLINOIS, DECEMBER 3, 1818 (21)

INDIANA, DECEMBER 11, 1816 (19)

IOWA, DECEMBER 28, 1846 (29)

KANSAS, JANUARY 29, 1861 (34)

KENTUCKY, JUNE 1, 1792 (15)

LOUISIANA, APRIL 30, 1812 (18)

MAINE, MARCH 15, 1820 (23)

MARYLAND, APRIL 28, 1788 (7)

MASSACHUSETTS, FEBRUARY 6, 1788 (6)

MICHIGAN, JANUARY 26, 1837 (26)

MINNESOTA, MAY 11, 1858 (32)

MISSISSIPPI, DECEMBER 10, 1817 (20)

MISSOURI, AUGUST 10, 1821 (24)

MONTANA, NOVEMBER 8, 1889 (41)

NEBRASKA, MARCH 1, 1867 (37)

NEVADA, OCTOBER 31, 1864 (36)

NEW HAMPSHIRE, JUNE 21, 1788 (9)

NEW JERSEY, DECEMBER 18, 1787 (3)

NEW MEXICO, JANUARY 6, 1912 (47)

NEW YORK, JULY 26, 1788 (11)

NORTH CAROLINA, NOVEMBER 21, 1789 (12)

NORTH DAKOTA, NOVEMBER 2, 1889 (39)

OHIO, MARCH 1, 1803 (17)

OKLAHOMA, NOVEMBER 16, 1907 (46)

OREGON, FEBRUARY 14, 1859 (33)

PENNSYLVANIA, DECEMBER 12, 1787 (2)

RHODE ISLAND, MAY 29, 1790 (13)

SOUTH CAROLINA, MAY 23, 1788 (8)

SOUTH DAKOTA, NOVEMBER 2, 1889 (40)

TENNESSEE, JUNE 1, 1796 (16)

TEXAS, DECEMBER 29, 1845 (28)

UTAH, JANUARY 4, 1896 (45)

VERMONT, MARCH 4, 1791 (14)

VIRGINIA, JUNE 25, 1788 (10)

WASHINGTON, NOVEMBER 11, 1889 (42)

WEST VIRGINIA, JUNE 20, 1863 (35)

WISCONSIN, MAY 29, 1848 (30)

WYOMING, JULY 10, 1890 (44)

DISTRICT OF COLUMBIA, ESTABLISHED 1790.

AMERICAN SAMOA

FLAGS OF THE TERRITORIES

PANAMA CANAL ZONE, ACQUIRED 1904 (GOVERNOR'S FLAG)

PUERTO RICO, CEDED TO U.S. 1898

U. S. TRUST TERRITORY OF THE PACIFIC ISLANDS

VIRGIN ISLANDS, PURCHASED 1917

INTERNATIONAL CODE FLAGS

Certain combinations of letters and numbers
have meanings understood by seamen of all nations.

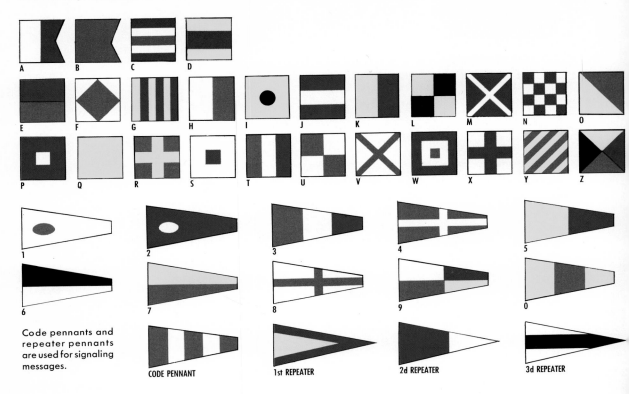

Code pennants and
repeater pennants
are used for signaling
messages.

CODE PENNANT   1st REPEATER   2d REPEATER   3d REPEATER

WEATHER BUREAU FLAGS

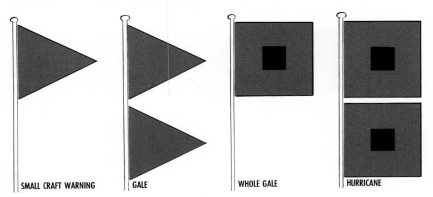

SMALL CRAFT WARNING   GALE   WHOLE GALE   HURRICANE

FLAGS USED AS
WARNING SIGNALS

AMBULANCE   DANGER   QUARANTINE   SHIPWRECK   TRUCE

bottom. In the upper left hand corner is a canton of blue which contains 50 stars arranged in nine rows, a row of six stars alternating with a row of five stars.

Legislation Pertaining to the American Flag. The laws pertaining to the flag include: the original proposal of June 14, 1777; the resolution of 1818; the Trade-Mark Act of 1905, which prohibits the display of the nation's flag or coat of arms on trade-marks; the Act of 1914, which authorized official display of the flag on Mother's Day; the Act of 1917, which fixed penalties for the desecration of the flag; the Act of 1918, by which federal employees may be dismissed for criticizing the flag in an abusive manner.

A codification of the rules and customs on the use and display of the flag was passed by Congress on Dec. 22, 1942. Included in the resolution are three sections on the display of the flag: "No other flag should be placed above the flag of the United States of America," although exceptions are made for certain church services. "When the flags of states, cities, or localities, or pennants of societies are flown on the same halyard with the flag of the United States, the latter should always be at the peak. . . . When flags of two or more nations are displayed, they are to be flown from separate staffs of the same height. The flags should be of approximately equal size. International usage forbids the display of the flag of one nation above that of another nation in time of peace." (In 1953 Congress authorized the display of the U.S. flag below that of the United Nations at the U.N. headquarters; it also permitted other national flags to be flown with equal prominence there.)

Other customs commemorated in the 1942 resolution are as follows: "It is the universal custom to display the flag only from sunrise to sunset. . . . However, the flag may be displayed at night upon special occasions when it is desired to produce a patriotic effect. . . . The flag should be hoisted briskly and lowered ceremoniously. . . . The flag, when flown at half-staff, should be first hoisted to the peak for an instant and then lowered to the half-staff position. . . . During the ceremony of hoisting or lowering the flag or when the flag is passing in a parade or in a review, all persons present should face the flag, stand at attention and salute." The flag should never touch the ground. It should be carried "aloft and free," never flat or horizontally. If the flag is no longer in good condition for display, it should be destroyed in a dignified way, preferably by burning.

Canadian Flags. For nearly 100 years Canada had no official flag because of early identification with the British Union Jack. In 1924 Parliament designated that the Red Ensign fly over Canadian buildings abroad, and it eventually was accepted as the national, if unofficial, standard. French Canadians, however, resented the Red Ensign with its Union Jack in the upper (mast) corner because it reflected only the British influence in national history. In Dec., 1964, Prime Minister Lester B. Pearson won Parliament's approval of a distinctive official flag with a red maple leaf on a white ground, flanked by vertical red bars. It was first raised on Feb. 15, 1965.

Nova Scotia, Quebec, British Columbia, and Prince Edward Island have their own official flags, authorized in 1621, 1948, 1960, and 1964 respectively.

STUART GERRY BROWN, Syracuse University

FLAGELLANTS [flăj'ə-lənts, flə-jĕl'ənts], bands of men in the Middle Ages who scourged themselves in public processions. During the reform of Western monasticism in the 11th century, self-whipping appeared in the penitential books as an efficacious means of penance, and was later preached as such by the Franciscans, who incorporated the rope into their habit. In the mid-13th century flagellant societies appeared throughout Europe. Processions of penitents, including priests carrying crosses and religious banners, paraded the streets chanting prayers and lashing themselves until blood was drawn. In a bull of Oct., 1349, Clement VI declared the movement heretical. Strong measures were taken to suppress it, but traces of the movement continued into the 19th century.

FLAGELLATES [flăj'ə-lĭts], protozoans belonging to the class Flagellata, or Mastigophora. The name means "whip-bearing," and all flagellates have at least one flagellum, a long, thin, whiplike filament. When viewed through a microscope this flagellum can be seen thrashing back and forth, as it propels the protozoan through the water.

Flagellates are an extremely varied group. Some are quite plantlike, some are animal-like, others combine both characteristics. *Euglena*, common in green pond water, has a red eyespot sensitive to light. Its body contains chlorophyll, the green pigment found in plants, and like many flagellates, it is able to manufacture foodlike plants. Dinoflagellates, having two flagella, are mostly marine. Some species are luminescent. In waters where *Noctiluca* is abundant, the waves glow at night with a strange light. Another species of flagellate is found in melting snowdrifts of high mountains. When numerous, they may color the snow pink. Some flagellates are parasitic. Many live in invertebrates, but some invade larger animals, including man. African sleeping sickness is caused by flagellates, known as trypanosomes. They live, apparently causing no harm, in many animals and then are carried to humans by the bite of the tsetse fly.

BARBARA NEILL, American Museum of Natural History
See also PROTOZOA.

FLAGEOLET [flăj-ə-lĕt'], type of whistle flute similar to the recorder, used mainly in European folk music; it was also used in 18th-century art music. It is blown at the end (rather than through the side) and has four finger holes on the upper side, two thumb holes on the lower side.
See also FLUTE; RECORDER.

FLAGLER, HENRY MORRISON (1830–1913), American businessman. He was born in Hopewell, N.Y., and engaged in the grain and salt business before becoming a partner of John D. Rockefeller in oil refining. Their firm, Rockefeller, Flagler and Andrews, was incorporated in 1870 as the Standard Oil Company. He left Standard Oil in 1911 with a sizable fortune and invested over $40,000,000 in hotels, railroads, and steamship lines in the state of Florida. He contributed to hospitals, churches, and educational institutions.

FLAG OF THE UNITED STATES, PLEDGE TO THE. The pledge of allegiance, as authorized and amended by Congress in 1954, is as follows: "I pledge allegiance to the flag of the

United States of America and to the republic for which it stands, one nation under God, indivisible, with liberty and justice for all." It is often carried out as a patriotic act in public schools, by civic and fraternal orders, and at public gatherings. Although recognized by most people as symbolic of national unity, the flag salute has been controversial. In 1940 two children were expelled from public elementary school in Pennsylvania for refusing to salute the flag (by state law, part of a daily school exercise) because of their religious tenets as Jehovah's Witnesses. The U.S. Supreme Court, in *Minersville School District* v. *Gobitis* (1940), held that the Pennsylvania law was constitutional. Later, however, in a similar case (*West Virginia State Board of Education* v. *Barnette*, 1943), the court overruled that decision on the grounds that such a law violated the spirit of the First Amendment.

ERWIN L. LEVINE, Skidmore College

FLAGSTAD, KIRSTEN (1895–1962), celebrated Norwegian soprano, born in Hamar. She received her early education from her mother and made her operatic debut in 1913. Very slowly she developed into the foremost dramatic soprano of her time. In 1933 she sang for the first time in Bayreuth, but had only small parts. When she made her debut at the Metropolitan Opera in 1935 as Sieglinde in *Die Walküre* she was still little known in musical circles. However, her success was so immediate that she has been credited with the renaissance of the Wagnerian repertoire (in which she specialized) at the Metropolitan. She remained there for six seasons and then returned to Norway. After World War II she gave mainly song recitals. Especially famous for her interpretation of Isolde in Wagner's *Tristan und Isolde*, she possessed a rich, ringing voice, not unlike many cellos playing in unison, which could soar above the full Wagnerian orchestra.

HENRY MARX, Staats-Herold

FLAGSTAFF, city of north-central Arizona, and seat of Coconino County. Its industries include sandstone quarrying, firebrick manufacturing, and lumbering. The city is a tourist center for a scenic region that includes Sunset Crater, Wupatki, and Walnut Canyon national monuments. Also located in or near Flagstaff are Arizona State College, Lowell Observatory, the Museum of Northern Arizona, and Navaho Ordnance Depot. The Nahohi, or Indian powwow, is held here annually in July. Founded, 1881; pop., 26,117.

FLAHERTY [flä′ər-tē], **ROBERT JOSEPH** (1884–1951), American motion-picture director and producer, born in Iron Mountain, Mich. He was one of the pioneers in, and outstanding contributors to, documentary films. His first film, *Nanook of the North* (1922), an enduring account of Eskimo life made in northern Canada, typifies Flaherty's concern with man's relation to nature, usually in a rather primitive state. Subsequently he directed *Moana of the South Seas* (1926), an idyllic picture of Samoan life; *Tabu* (1931), based on Polynesian customs and made with F. W. Murnau; *Industrial Britain* (1932), made with John Grierson; *Man of Aran* (1934), a documentary about islanders' struggle for a livelihood against the odds of the sea; *Elephant Boy* (1937); *The Land* (1941); and *Louisiana*

Story (1948), which describes the impact of oil drilling in Louisiana on a Cajun family.
See also MOTION PICTURES.

FLAME, hot, luminous gases or vapors resulting from rapid combustion. The luminosity may be greatly increased by the presence of incandescent solid particles such as dust and carbon. When a flammable mixture of gases is ignited at a point, the flame is propagated in the form of an expanding spherical shell, but the pattern is considerably distorted by convection currents. The propagation of a flame in a moving gas depends upon the rate of flow of the gas. At velocities approaching the rate of flame propagation, the flame will move only in the direction of flow, and at higher gas velocities the flame will be extinguished.

Flame temperatures vary with the nature of the substance being burned. Natural gas flames reach temperatures of about 1,860° C. (3,380° F.), oxyhydrogen flames about 2,800° C. (5,072° F.), and oxyacetylene flames about 3,300° C. (5,972° F.). Salts of various metals placed in the flame give characteristic colors.

Cold flames are frequently obtained when a substance such as ether, acetaldehyde, carbon disulfide, and some hydrocarbon vapors are burned with limited amounts of air. They are characterized by a rise in temperature of not much more than 100° C. to 200° C. (212° F. to 392° F.), and travel slowly through the medium. Decomposition of the compounds occurs without complete combustion to oxides of carbon and water.

MELVIN J. ASTLE, Case Institute of Technology

FLAME HARDENING, surface-hardening process in which steel or cast iron is flame-heated, then immediately water-quenched. The result is a maximum hardness to a depth of about 0.30 in. The technique is widely used to surface-harden gears, shafts, cams, crankshafts, bearings, and other parts which must have wear-resistant surfaces.

FLAMENCO [flə-měng′kō], type of dance and music typical of the gypsies of Spain. The term "flamenco" is of uncertain origin. Flemish mercenary soldiers, drinking and singing in the taverns, may have caused Spaniards to use the epithet "flamenco" for noisy behavior, the term being eventually applied (c.1871) to the equally noisy gypsies.

Forms of Flamenco. The flamenco song (*cante flamenco*) probably has been influenced by both the Arab and the Hebrew, especially in the elaborate melodic coloraturas and in the scale structure. However, the gypsy has brought to it so much spontaneous creative genius that it is not comparable to any other musical form. Only certain flamenco songs may be danced. Notable exceptions are types of the older *cante jondo* (deep song) of Andalusia, such as the *saetas, martinetes, carceleras, deblas,* and *tonas,* all of which are sung without guitar, rhythmic accompaniment being provided by fingers, palms, and heels.

Flamenco dancing is characterized by the heel-beats (*taconeo*) of the performer and the sinuous, Oriental movements of body, arms, and hands. Dances are built in sections divided by *desplantes*. These sections vary in length, according to the mood of the dancer. The *desplante* is a signal to the guitar accompanist, and the number of bars, or beats, varies according to the dance form. A leading *desplante* heralds a new section of the dance; a closing *desplante* ends the dance.

Not until the 20th century did the gypsies adopt the Spanish castanets, and for a decade or more only women used them, the men considering them too feminine.

The repertory of flamenco dances changes constantly. Since 1920 the *zambra* (of ancient Moorish origin) and the *garrotin* (adapted for the music halls at the end of the 19th century) have fallen out of fashion, while *zapateados* and *seguirillas* have become popular.

True gypsy dancing is spontaneous and improvised; thus, a given dance-form is never twice the same. The pure *jondo* style is found only in emotional improvisation.

La Meri, Author, *Dance as an Art Form*

See also Alegrias; Farruca; Seguidillas; Seguirillas; Tango.

FLAMEOUT, a term describing the extinguishing of the flame in a turbojet engine's combustion chamber. There are two major causes of flameout. One is the interruption or improper metering of the fueling into the combustion chamber. The other is the interruption or surging of the air being pumped through the combustion chamber by the compressor. Flameouts are most apt to occur during violent maneuvers and during flights at high altitude.

FLAME TEST, method of qualitative analysis based on the production of characteristic color in a gas flame. A drop of the test sample solution is usually placed on a small loop at the end of a platinum wire the other end of which is sealed into a glass tube that serves as a handle. When the sample is placed in the flame, the presence of various elements is indicated by characteristic colors; for example, sodium is orange, potassium is violet, lithium is red, and barium is green.

Quantitative analysis is carried out by means of a more elaborate form of flame test known as flame photometry in which a solution sample is atomized into a flame at a definite rate and the intensity of the flame color is measured. The measurement is calibrated by comparison with similar measurements on a series of solutions of known concentration. To distinguish between different elements, advantage is taken of the fact that each element emits light of a characteristic wave length or color. Flame photometry is a simplified version of spectroscopy, and differs from it in using a flame instead of an electric arc or spark.

H. A. Laitinen, University of Illinois

FLAME THROWER, device that shoots a high-pressure stream of burning fuel. It consists of a hose and nozzle, and tanks for fuel and a propellent gas. Developed for use in warfare, flame throwers are also employed in agriculture to destroy insects and weeds. Early models used oil or gasoline, and in World War I they served mainly to demoralize troops. In World War II, however, using gelled gasoline made with a thickener called napalm, they provided a means of penetrating tank ports and bunkers. Gelled gasoline gives greater range and it sticks to whatever it hits.

See also Napalm.

A pair of flamingos, habitual wading birds well adapted for feeding in shallow waters. (ANGERMAYER—PHOTO RESEARCHERS)

FLAMINGO [flə-mĭng′gō], name for the 6 species of tropical wading birds that constitute the flamingo family, Phoenicopteridae. Flamingos are found chiefly in the Mediterranean region, Asia, South Africa, and the American tropics, but one species occurs in the Peruvian Andes. They are long-legged, long-necked birds with webbed feet and an unusual bill bent downward at the tip. Their plumage is rosy-pink or pinkish-white, with black wing margins evident when the wings are spread in flight. The common flamingo, *Phoenicopterus ruber*, is a colorful pinkish-red bird. It stands about 4 ft. tall, has a wingspread of 5 ft., and feeds on marine mollusks which it swallows whole. While feeding underwater, the head is bent so that the submerged beak is inverted. In this position, the bent, upper portion of the beak becomes an efficient scoop. The common flamingo is found in the Mediterranean region and in the Bahama Islands, Cuba, and northeastern South America. It was formerly abundant in Florida. Other species of flamingo are *P. antiquorum*, found in South Africa and Asia, and the Andean flamingo, *Phoenicoparrus*, which inhabits the shores of Lake Titicaca.

Clarence J. Hylander, Author, *Feathers and Flight*

FLAMINIAN [flə-mĭn′ē-ən] **WAY,** principal northern Roman road, built by the censor Gaius Flaminius (220 B.C.). Augustus restored it and rebuilt almost all its bridges. Beginning at the foot of the Capitoline Hill, it ran due north to cross the Tiber at the Milvian Bridge, followed the Tiber, traversed difficult country in Umbria and across the Apennines to the Adriatic, then followed the coast to Rimini (209 mi. originally, later 215). The line of the road is still followed in large part; and the arch of Augustus, which marked its end at Rimini, and part of his high bridge at Narni still stand.

FLAMININUS [flăm-ĭ-nī′nəs], **TITUS QUINCTIUS** (c.230–c.174 B.C.), Roman general and statesman. He became consul in 198, and in 197 defeated Philip V of Macedon at Cynoscephalae. The Senate kept him in Greece as proconsul to arrange the peace. In 196 he proclaimed to the Greeks assembled at Corinth for the Isthmian Games that henceforth all Greek city-states were to be free. The implementation of this proclamation gave the Romans much trouble.

FLAMINIUS [flə-mĭn′ē-əs], **GAIUS** (d.217 B.C.), Roman general and statesman. In 232 B.C. he secured passage of a law to distribute public land in small lots to landless citizens. This law offended senators who wanted to lease the lands profitably. As censor in 220, he built the Circus Flaminius and the Via Flaminia. In 218 he supported a measure designed to keep senators out of trade, since landowning seemed less likely to conflict with the interests of government. In 217 B.C. popular favor brought him to command against Hannibal, but at Lake Trasimeno he lost his army and his life.

FLAMSTEED, JOHN (1646–1719), English astronomer who in 1675 was named the first astronomer royal by Charles II, who founded the Greenwich Observatory. In the new observatory Flamsteed began work on star catalogues and lunar tables based on observations more accurate than any up to that time. He devised new methods of observational astronomy, and he determined the co-ordinates of the vernal equinox. The results of his work were published in 1712 in his *Historia Coelestis* (Celestial History), which contains descriptions of his observations of fixed stars, planets, comets, sunspots, Jupiter's satellites, and the co-ordinates of 2,884 stars.

FLANAGAN, EDWARD JOSEPH (1886–1948), Catholic priest and youth worker. A naturalized American citizen of Irish origin, Father Flanagan founded the Boys Town orphanage near Omaha, Nebr. After winning national fame for developing leadership in his boys, he was sent by the U.S. government to Europe and the Far East following World War II to help establish similar orphanages.

FLANDERS, former country in the Low Countries, now divided between the Belgian provinces of East and West Flanders, the French Départment du Nord, and the Dutch province of Zeeland. Its main cities were Ghent and Bruges. From the 12th century on, Flanders was a major cloth-making area, and cloth is still an important Flemish industry. Flanders also contains large coalfields and is a rich farming area, much land having been reclaimed from the sea.

The first count, Baldwin I, married the daughter of Charles the Bald, King of France, and received Flanders as a hereditary fief in 862. He and his successors defended Flanders against Viking raids and added to their territory. By the 11th century, Flanders was one of the richest and best-governed French states. The rise of the cloth industry in the 12th and 13th centuries led to the prosperity and independence of the Flemish towns. Flanders was united with Burgundy in 1384. During the next three centuries, under the dukes of Burgundy and, later, the Hapsburgs, Flanders became a major art center, developing such painters as Van Eyck, Bosch, Breughel, and Rubens. In the 16th century, Flanders revolted unsuccessfully against Hapsburg rule and was devastated. Part of northern Flanders was ceded to the Netherlands in 1648, while Louis XIV of France acquired southern Flanders, between 1659 and 1678. The remainder was given to Austria in 1714. It was occupied by France from 1795 to 1815, when it was awarded to the Netherlands. In 1830 Flanders became part of Belgium.

ROBIN S. OGGINS, State University of N.Y. at Binghamton

FLANNER, JANET (1892–   ), American writer, born in Indianapolis, Ind. She is best known as Genêt, Paris correspondent for *The New Yorker* magazine. Her letters from Paris reflect the temper of contemporary French life as seen in the capital. She has published a novel, *The Cubical City* (1926), and has translated Colette's *Claudine à L'Ecole* (1930) and *Chérie* (1929), and Georgette Le-Blanc's *Souvenirs* (1932). Her essays and articles are collected in *American in Paris* (1940); *Pétain* (1944); *Paris Journal 1944–1965* (1965); and *Men and Monuments* (1957), a volume of art criticism.

FLAP, AIRCRAFT, a movable surface hinged under the trailing edge of an aircraft wing, and normally extending from the fuselage to the inboard side of the aileron. The pilot controls its position from the cockpit. When the flap is partially extended it increases the wing lift by expanding the total wing area, allowing slower and safer speeds for landing and take-off. When fully lowered it also acts as an air brake, allowing steeper and slower glides.

FLARE, SOLAR, bright, irregular area on the sun. A typical flare may increase to about five times the normal brightness of the solar disk in a period of 5 to 10 minutes, then fade to normal brightness in about a half hour. Flares vary greatly in size, often exceeding 30,000 mi. in diameter. They occur almost exclusively in association with active sunspots.

Large flares often produce, or are associated with, tenuous streams of matter that escape the sun at high velocity. The presence of these streams is evident in radio-telescope observations of the sun; only rarely can they be seen. In their flight through space many of these particles strike the earth. The more energetic arrive a few minutes after the flare, and they cause increases in cosmic ray activity. The less energetic arrive one to three days later, and they may produce polar blackouts in radio communication, low-latitude auroral displays, and geomagnetic storms.

R. GRANT ATHAY, High Altitude Observatory, Boulder, Colorado

See also SUN.

FLASH POINT, in chemistry, the lowest temperature at which a liquid will become a flammable gaseous mixture. It occurs at a lower temperature than the fire point, or burning temperature, required to maintain steady combustion. The fire point determines, for example, the safety of a lubrication oil. The flash point, the temperature at which the oil will decompose and cease to act as a lubricant, determines its efficiency as a lubricant.

FLATEYJARBÓK [flät-ā-yär′bōk], a compilation of old Norwegian Kings' sagas in a beautifully illuminated codex, made in 1380–90 on the island of Flatey, off the western coast of Iceland and preserved in the Royal Library in Copenhagen. It contains many short tales of Icelanders, an Eddic lay, and the *Saga of the Greenlanders*, which relates their voyages to North America. It was presented by Bishop Brynjólfur Sveinsson (d.1675) to King Frederick III of Denmark, and it was edited in facsimile in 1930 to celebrate the millennium of the founding of the Icelandic Parliament.

FLAT FEET. *See* FOOT.

FLATFISH, name for members of several families of bottom-feeding, marine shore fish that constitute the order Heterosomata. Flatfish are unusual in that the young individuals swim in a normal fashion, and have an eye on each side of their head. As they mature, however, one eye migrates over the top of the skull to lie next to the other. The adult fish then spends the rest of its life lying on its blind side and swims with its body parallel to the surface of the water. Most species of flatfish lack pigment on the blind, or underside; many species, such as the flounder, halibut, sole, and turbot, are important food fish.
See also FLOUNDER; HALIBUT; SOLE; TURBOT.

FLATHEAD LAKE, largest natural lake in Montana. Glacial in origin, the lake occupies a structural depression in the northern Rocky Mountains. It is both fed (north) and drained (south) by the Flathead River. Its waters are used for irrigation and hydroelectric power. Length, 30 mi.; max. width, 15 mi.; area, 189 sq. mi.; surface elev., 2,885 ft.; depth, 220 ft.

FLATTERY, CAPE, cape of northwestern Washington, on the south shore of the entrance to Juan de Fuca Strait, an arm of the Pacific Ocean. It was discovered by Capt. James Cook in 1778.

FLATWORM. *See* PLATYHELMINTHES.

FLAUBERT [flō-bâr′], **GUSTAVE** (1821–80), French novelist, born in Rouen, the son of a wealthy surgeon. Flaubert studied law before taking up a literary career. As a young man he traveled to Italy and North Africa. Between 1841 and 1850 he had periodic seizures resembling epilepsy; after 1846 he lived and worked mostly at Croisset, near Rouen.

Flaubert's greatest works are *Madame Bovary* (1857; trans. by Francis Steegmüller, 1957); *L'éducation sentimentale* (1869; trans. by Anthony Goldsmith, 1941); and *Trois contes* (1877; *Three Tales*, trans. by Arthur McDowall, 1924). The first two novels treat in realistic detail the essential banality and monotony of life: *Madame Bovary* in the provinces, *L'éducation sentimentale* in the capital. Emma Bovary's tragedy is that she failed to reconcile her romantic aspirations with everyday reality. Some critics believe this theme reflects the dualism of Flaubert's own nature and his hesitancy between romanticism and realism; it is true he once remarked, "*Madame Bovary, c'est moi*" ("Madame Bovary is myself").

The Bettmann Archive

Gustave Flaubert, great French prose stylist.

Although he is generally known as a realist, Flaubert's romantic side reveals itself in his *La tentation de Saint Antoine* (1874; trans. by Lafcadio Hearn, 1910), a poetic, at times hallucinatory portrayal of the saint's struggle against evil, and *Salammbô* (1862; trans. by E. P. Mathers, new ed., 1950), a tale of ancient Carthage. Always critical of the middle class—his battle cry was "*Épatez le bourgeois!*" ("Shock the bourgeois!")—he satirized its smugness and conventionality in his *Dictionnaire des idées reçues*, 1913 (*Dictionary of Accepted Ideas*, trans. by Jacques Barzun, 1954) and *Bouvard et Pécuchet* (1881; trans. by T. W. Earp and G. W. Stonier, 1954).

Flaubert's chief aesthetic principles were objectivity and *le mot juste* (the exact word). His *Correspondance* (1926–33) affords a fascinating insight into his intense struggle for artistic perfection.

Consult Steegmüller, Francis, *Flaubert and Madame Bovary* (1939); *Selected Letters*, trans. by Francis Steegmüller (1953).

JOHN C. LAPP, University of California at Los Angeles

FLAVELLE [flə-vĕl′], **SIR JOSEPH WESLEY, 1ST BART.** (1858–1939), Canadian financier and industrialist. He was born in Peterborough, Ontario, and made his fortune in the meat-packing business in Toronto. He later became governor of the University of Toronto and the head of the Royal Ontario Museum. Flavelle was created a baronet for his services as chairman of the Imperial Munitions Board of Canada (1914–20). As chairman of the Grand Trunk Railway (1920–21), he planned the organization of the Canadian National Railway. In 1925 he endowed the Flavelle Medal awarded annually by the Royal Society of Canada to an outstanding scientist.

FLAVIAN [flā′vē-ən], **ST.** (d.449), Christian martyr, Patriarch of Constantinople. A defender of orthodoxy in the Eutychian controversy, Flavian was defrauded and murdered at the Robber Synod of Ephesus (449). His feast day is February 18.

FLAX, a slender-branched, herbaceous annual, *Linum usitatissimum*, in the flax family, Linaceae, widely grown in Europe and Asia for its stem fiber, from which the fabric linen is made. It is also cultivated in North America for its seeds, from which linseed oil is derived. The plant grows from 1 to 4 ft. tall and bears small blue or white flowers that ripen into seed capsules or "bolls." Each boll contains up to 10 very smooth, shiny seeds. The bark of the stem is made up of long, tough fibers.

Flax was grown for fiber and probably for food long before the earliest historical records. It probably originated in the Mediterranean region or southern Asia. In comparatively recent times much of the crop has been grown solely for its seed.

The plant requires a moderate-to-cool climate, with frequent light showers and high humidity throughout most of the growing season. It grows best on fertile, well-drained soil of medium-to-heavy texture with good moisture-holding capacity. Flax is a poor competitor with weeds, so it is usually planted on new land or in rotations where it follows a clean-cultivated crop.

FLAX

A bundle of flax with the seed capsules still attached.

Harvesting flax by hand (*top*) and by machine (*bottom*).

Irish Linen Guild

The crop is spring-seeded in the cooler temperate regions, but in more southern regions may be seeded in late fall and grown as a winter annual. Seeding rates of from 30 to 50 lb. per acre, depending on climate, are common in seed-producing areas. Fiber flax is planted at 75 to 80 lb. or more per acre to ensure tall, nonbranching stems. Flax grown for fiber is more exacting in its climatic and soil requirements than seed flax. It is necessary, however, to have a good, firm seedbed for successful growth of both types. The most serious cultural problem is always weed competition.

Seed flax is harvested when the majority of bolls are ripe. If moisture content of the seed is too high (above 10%), due to uneven ripening or a high weed content, it is necessary to cut and field-dry the crop before threshing or combining. Fiber flax is harvested after most of the stems have turned yellow and the lower leaves have fallen. Then one-third to one-half of the seed bolls are yellow or brown. Earlier harvesting produces fine and silky but weak fibers, while late-harvested fibers are coarse and brittle.

Flax seed contains from 32% to 44% oil, which is extracted by steaming and pressing. Linseed oil meal, a by-product of the extraction, is used for livestock feed. The oil is used in the manufacture of paints, linoleum, and printer's ink. Fiber flax is processed by retting (rotting away the wood tissues and gums) and breaking them away from the fiber. The fibers are then scutched (all woody portions are removed by scraping). The resulting linen fibers are used for producing linen cloth and in the manufacture of fine papers.

MARTIN E. WEEKS, University of Massachusetts
See also FIBER, NATURAL.

FLAXMAN, JOHN (1755–1826), English draftsman and sculptor, especially influential in reviving an interest in classical models. He studied at the Royal Academy and went to Rome in 1787, where he spent seven years. His drawings for the *Iliad* and *Odyssey* and for Aeschylus and Dante won him international acclaim. In 1800 he became a member of the Royal Academy. Among his sculptural works are monuments to Lord Mansfield (Westminster Abbey) and to Sir Joshua Reynolds and Lord Nelson (St. Paul's Cathedral, London).

FLEA, name for the more than 200 species of small, wingless insects, of world-wide distribution, that constitute the order Siphonaptera. Almost all fleas are parasites at some stage of their life cycle, and some species feed on the blood of mammals and birds. Their narrow, laterally compressed bodies and absence of wings enable them to move easily through fur or feathers. The body bears many small, rearward-projecting bristles; unusually long legs give fleas their jumping prowess; the mouth parts are of the piercing-sucking type. Fleas leave their hosts to lay their eggs in dirt, debris, or the nests of birds. Flea larvae are small, white, legless, and armed with a pair of hooks on the last segment of the body. The pupa is protected by a silken cocoon. Some species, such as the human flea, *Pulex irritans*, and the dog flea, *Ctenocephalides canis*, are merely annoying; others are carriers of disease. Bubonic plague and marine typhus are transmitted to humans by the Indian rat flea, *Xenopsylla cheopis*. The chigoe flea, *Tunga penetrans*, is a parasite that burrows into the skin, usually between the toes or under the toenails, and causes a painful sore.

CLARENCE J. HYLANDER, Author, *Insects on Parade*

FLEABANE, common name for about 200 species of annual or perennial herbs of the genus *Erigeron*, in the composite family, Compositae. Fleabanes are found in many parts of the world, particularly in temperate and mountainous regions. The flower heads resemble those of wild aster and have yellow disks surrounded by rays of white, yellow, red, or purple. Certain species, such as *E. coulteri* and *E. speciosus*, are suited to planting in garden borders; others, such as *E. alpinus*, *E. compositus*, and *E. multiradiatus*, make especially fine rock garden plants. Fleabane does well in ordinary soil and is usually propagated by division.

FLEA HOPPER, name for several small, short-winged insects in the family Miridae of order Hemiptera, the true bugs. Flea hoppers are found throughout the world and are agricultural pests, feeding on the juices of tender plant parts. *Psallus seriatus*, the cotton flea hopper, is common in southern United States, and damages the buds and leaves of cotton plants.

FLEDERMAUS [flā′dər-mous], **DIE** (The Bat), operetta by Johann Strauss, Jr.; lyrics and libretto by Haffner and Genée; based on *Le Réveillon* by Henri Meilhac and Ludovic Halévy, and *Das Gefängnis* by Roderich Benedix; Vienna première, Apr. 5, 1874; it was presented on Broadway as *The Merry Countess* (1912), *A Wonderful Night* (1929), *Champagne Sec* (1933), and *Rosalinda* (1942). In 1950 an English version with lyrics by Howard Dietz and libretto by Garson Kanin became part of the Metropolitan Opera repertory. The story involves Baron von Eisenstein, his wife Rosalinde, and her lover Alfred. The lilting music is the epitome of the waltz era and continues to have great appeal.

FLEET STREET, street in London, England, which runs along the north bank of the Thames River from Ludgate Circus, in the east, to the Strand and the West End. It is the site of many newspaper offices and in the early history of London was notorious as a refuge for criminals.

FLEETWOOD, municipal borough of Lancashire, England, on the Irish Sea, north of Blackpool. It is the major fishing port of England's western coast, and has marine engineering and modern industries, including the manufacture of plastics, and nylon and other fabrics. Fleetwood has grown steadily since the railway reached here in 1840. Pop., 27,760.

FLÉMALLE [flā-mál′], **MASTER OF,** Flemish painter, one of the key figures in the development of the realistic style in Flemish painting of the 15th century. Known as the Master of Flémalle because of works supposed to have been painted in Flémalle, near Liège, he is considered by many scholars to be Robert Campin of Tournai. Campin was active at Tournai as early as 1406, and the earliest

extant works of the Master of Flémalle date from about 1415 to 1420. Another view, which is less likely, holds that the works now ascribed to the Master of Flémalle were actually the youthful works of Rogier van der Weyden.

Down to earth in approach, the Master of Flémalle is known for his observations of subtle effects of atmosphere, of light, and of the varied textures of objects. He pioneered also in the couching of traditional medieval symbolic allusions in objects that appear at first sight to be simply natural elements of the setting, such as the pitcher and towel (symbolic of Mary's purity) in the so-called "Mérode Annunciation," now in The Cloisters Museum, New York. He and his great contemporary Jan van Eyck appear to have influenced each other, and he had an even more pervasive influence on Rogier van der Weyden.

HOWARD M. DAVIS, Columbia University

FLEMING, SIR ALEXANDER (1881–1955), Scottish bacteriologist who shared the Nobel Prize in physiology and medicine with Ernest Boris Chain and Howard Walter Florey in 1945 for his discovery of penicillin. Fleming's first significant discovery was lysozyme, a bacteria-destroying enzyme which is normally present in body fluids, such as tears and saliva. In 1928, while working in St. Mary's Hospital in London, he neglected to cover some culture dishes containing staphylococci bacteria. An airborne mold grew in the culture and inhibited the growth of the surrounding bacteria. Fleming subsequently determined that the mold secreted a substance (penicillin) which interfered with bacterial reproduction. He attempted to use this substance as a dressing for infected wounds, but the results were discouraging, owing to the low potency of the natural material. Fleming's description of the antibiotic effect of penicillin would have remained buried in the literature were it not for the efforts of Florey and Chain in refining and developing penicillin for practical medical use.

CLAUDIUS F. MAYER, M.D.

See also ANTIBIOTICS.

FLEMING, SIR JOHN AMBROSE (1849–1945), English electrical engineer and inventor of the Fleming valve (the electron tube). Born in Lancaster, Fleming was educated at Cambridge, and in 1884 became professor of electrical engineering at University College, London. In 1904 Fleming invented the electron tube, called a valve in England, for use in radios. Fleming made many contributions to the development of telephony and wireless telegraphy and became a fellow of The Royal Society.
See also ELECTRONICS.

FLEMING, SIR SANDFORD (1827–1915), Canadian railroad engineer. Called the father of Canadian engineering, he was born in Scotland and went to Canada at the age of 16. His earlier work included the Intercolonial Railroad which, when completed in 1876, connected Quebec with the Atlantic port of Halifax. The admission of British Columbia to the Dominion in 1871 obligated Canada to complete the railroad system from Windsor to the Pacific Coast, and in 1871 Fleming was appointed chief engineer.

The first sod of the Canadian Pacific was turned in 1875, but difficulties held up work until 1880. The line was completed in 1885 under the American William Van Horne.

FLEMING'S RULES, rules for determining the relation between current, motion, and field in the electric motor and the generator. The thumb, forefinger, and middle finger are held perpendicular to each other. In the left-hand rule (for motors) the forefinger is pointed in the direction of the magnetic field and the middle finger in the direction of the current, that is, from higher to lower potential. The thumb then points in the direction in which the conductor tends to move. In the right-hand rule (for generators) the thumb is pointed in the direction of motion and the forefinger along the lines of the field. The middle finger points in the direction of the induced current.

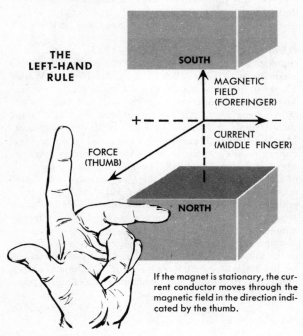

THE LEFT-HAND RULE

SOUTH

MAGNETIC FIELD (FOREFINGER)

CURRENT (MIDDLE FINGER)

FORCE (THUMB)

NORTH

If the magnet is stationary, the current conductor moves through the magnetic field in the direction indicated by the thumb.

FLEMISH, the name for Dutch in its use as a literary language in Belgium, and for the various dialects of Dutch spoken in the Belgian provinces of West Flanders, East Flanders, Antwerp, Brabant, Limburg, and in part of French Flanders. Its speakers number about 4.8 million. The early beginnings of the Dutch literary language in the 13th century are centered in Flemish territory, chiefly in western Flanders and Brabant. Only in the 16th century did the leading role shift to the province of Holland.

In Belgium, Flemish and French have now equal status before the law. In Flemish-speaking territory, Flemish is the sole language of administration. The great penetration of French in the 18th and early 19th centuries endangered the very existence of Flemish. The "Flemish movement" after 1838 resulted in a renaissance of the Dutch language in Flanders and in its gradually increasing recognition as the language of Belgian courts, science, schools, and universities.

HERBERT PENZL, University of Michigan

FLEMISH ART. The arts produced in the South-Netherlandish or Belgian provinces where the Flemish dialect was spoken originally are generally referred to as Flemish arts. Since the basic styles of Flemish art were formulated by the painters, sculpture and architecture are not discussed extensively here.

The Middle Ages

The earliest manifestations of a regional Flemish style appeared during the Late Gothic period (14th and 15th centuries) in the work of such painters as Melchior Broederlam. In general the art of the Late Gothic period displayed a highly detailed realism and an interest in presenting the traditional Biblical stories with local Flemish costumes, architecture, and landscape.

The first golden age of Flemish art was initiated by the brothers Hubert and Jan van Eyck, who settled in Ghent and Bruges in the early 15th century. The Van Eycks developed a style of realism so exacting that it appears microscopic in its execution. They accurately depicted all textures and details of figures and objects and mastered the illusion of deep space and natural lighting effects.

Also important for later Flemish painting was the system of disguised symbolism employed by Jan van Eyck. Every object, whether secular or religious, could assume meaning on two or more levels—meaning as a recognizable object of the natural world and meaning as a transcendental religious symbol. Although such symbolism was employed throughout the Middle Ages, Jan van Eyck intensified its usage. Thus in his "Annunciation" (National Gallery, Washington), the three windows behind Mary symbolize the Trinity realized at the moment of the Incarnation, the white flowers allude to Mary's purity at this moment, the zodiac designs on the tile floor under the angel designate the month of the Annunciation, while the lofty church interior itself becomes the physical embodiment of the role that *Notre Dame* (Our Lady) symbolized for the Gothic community.

The Van Eycks have been accredited with the invention of oil painting, a medium that enabled the artist to blend pigments easily and to achieve enamellike glazes over the flatter tempera colors. Among their numerous followers, Petrus Christus was the most notable.

A second current of early Flemish art was introduced by painters from the French-speaking province of Hainaut that borders Flanders and Brabant on the southeast. The most famous painter from Hainaut, Rogier van der Weyden, settled in Brussels, and there he developed a monumental style with elegant figures described in linear rhythms reminiscent of French Gothic sculpture. In works such as the "Deposition from the Cross" (Prado, Madrid), where Mary falls into a swooning posture that echoes her son's position, he showed himself to be a masterful composer. His graceful compositions were copied again and again by his numerous followers and imitators.

During the second half of the 15th century the styles of the Van Eycks and Rogier van der Weyden were assimilated. Dirk Bouts and Gerard David, both from the North-Netherlandish province of Holland, furthered the achievements of the Van Eycks in landscape painting. In his "Gathering of Manna" (St. Peter's Cathedral, Louvain, Belgium) Dirk Bouts executed one of the earliest works in

FLEMISH PAINTING

"Annunciation," painted about 1434 by Jan van Eyck, is rich in realistic detail.

National Gallery of Art, Mellon Collection, 1937

Bruckmann—Art Reference Bureau

"Hunters in the Snow," painted in 1565 by Peter Bruegel the Elder.

"Deposition from the Cross," painted about 1436 by Rogier van der Weyden.

Anderson—Art Reference Bureau

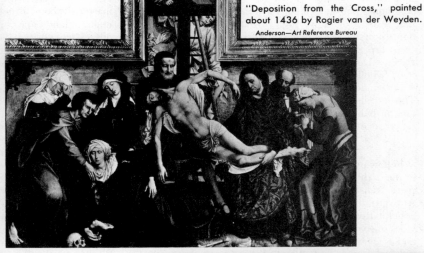

"Raising of the Cross" (1610) by Peter Paul Rubens (*right*).

A.C.L.—Art Reference Bureau

Landscape is a dominant element in "The Flight into Egypt" by Joachim Patinir (c.1485–1524).

A.C.L.—Art Reference Bureau

which the Biblical figures were reduced to insignificant figures in a deep Flemish landscape. Hugo van der Goes refashioned the microscopic realism of the Van Eycks with the intensity of an expressionist. In the "Portinari Nativity" (Uffizi, Florence), contrasts of courtly and humble figures, of heavy and fragile elements, together with the somber blue coloration, give his composition tensions and ambiguities that effectively convey the mystery of the lowly birth of a king of kings.

The first golden age ended with a dream and a nightmare. Hans Memling, a German immigrant, settled in Bruges after training under Rogier van der Weyden. Combining his own Rhenish mysticism with the grace of his teacher and the vigorous realism of the Van Eycks, Memling established a lyrical style that had a large following throughout the 16th century. In direct contrast to the quietism of Memling was the explosive art of Jerome Bosch. Bosch reacted fanatically to the religious crises that troubled Europe on the eve of the Reformation. His panoramic paintings record a frantic and violent society that leads itself unwittingly toward a torturous damnation. In many of his religious works, curious hybrid creatures are the antagonists, but in the huge "Garden of Earthly Delights" (Prado, Madrid) mankind surrenders itself wholly to the delights of the flesh and cavorts in wild abandon in a landscape of grotesque rock formations. The so-called Boschian surrealism had a lasting influence on the painting of the Netherlands, particularly during the years of the religious wars with Spain.

The 16th Century

Following the sudden impact of the Italian Renaissance in the early 16th century, Flemish art underwent a complete transformation. A new center of art emerged in Antwerp, the prosperous trading port at the mouth of the Scheldt River. Flemish culture of the 16th century provides one with images of both decadence and renaissance, and as an art period it can be described as an age of eclecticism, mannerism, and specialization. It was eclectic insofar as the artists freely borrowed from the earlier masters, and usually their paintings were so overworked that they were mannered caricatures of previous styles. The 16th-century artist, furthermore, was often a specialist in the execution of a certain kind of subject matter and worked under the guidance of one master who mass produced works of art for the new world market that Antwerp enjoyed.

The later works of Quentin Massys show the new character of Flemish art with the exaggerated sensuousness and the obvious borrowings of compositional motifs from such Italian Renaissance masters as Leonardo da Vinci. Massys headed a big workshop, and in some of his panels it is believed that he enrolled a specialist by the name of Joachim Patinir to paint the landscape backgrounds. Patinir, generally considered to be the first landscape specialist in Flemish art, painted countrysides he had never seen, panoramic views with fantastic mountains and deep gorges described from a high angle of vision. An example is his landscape "The Flight into Egypt" (Koninklijk Museum, Antwerp). In his sprawling landscapes, Patinir differentiated the spatial strata in terms of zones of color suggestive of the dimming atmospheric effects. Following

Patinir's formula, numerous Flemish painters, including Joos van Cleve and Henri met de Blès, painted themes whose religious subject matter could be submerged easily in an expansive landscape. The influence of Italian Renaissance art was particularly evident in the works of the artists of the Romanist school, among whom were Bernard van Orley and Jan Gossaert. Not only did the Romanists turn directly to Raphael and Michelangelo for their models, but they often painted the same mythological themes that were popular in Italy.

An exceptional painter in the 16th century was Peter Bruegel the Elder. Working from the earlier traditions of Flemish art, Bruegel created a fresh and vigorous manner of painting that anticipated the style of the 17th century. Bruegel frequently painted secular themes that revolve about the life of the peasants. With the visual accuracy of the Van Eycks, he depicted the robust Flemish farmers working or having fun, and he placed his big figures in space with the boldness of the later Flemish master, Rubens. Bruegel's major contribution was in the realm of landscape painting, where he devised new methods of composition for the somewhat incoherent panoramas of the mannerist tradition. In "Hunters in the Snow" (Kunsthistorisches Museum, Vienna), Bruegel employed diagonals to lead the spectator down the foreground hill of the broad valley that is clearly mapped out in square tracts of land. His interest in designing colorful silhouettes is evident here in the dark patterns of the hunters and their dogs seen against the snow-white background. His space compositions were followed by numerous landscape painters of the later Flemish and Dutch schools, including his sons Peter the Younger and Jan.

The 17th Century

Because the South-Netherlandish provinces had very close ties with the Roman Catholic countries in southern Europe, Flemish art of the second golden age developed a dynamic style closely related to the baroque art of Italy. In all spheres of art the influence of Italy can be discerned. Italian baroque architecture appeared in the new Jesuit churches in Antwerp and Louvain. The theatrical style of the Italian sculptor Bernini inspired the Flemish artist François Duquesnoy, who actually worked on the decoration of the new St. Peter's Church in Rome.

The leading painter, Peter Paul Rubens, spent many years in Italy and Spain, a fact that helps explain his love for highly dramatic compositions that pulsate with light and dark contrasts. His rich color and his fluid brushstroke no doubt owed something to the example of Titian. Rubens' own Flemish background emerged in his colorful landscape, rich in detail. In his religious works Rubens achieved the epitome of the Catholic Counter Reformation style. The painful drama of the "Raising of the Cross" (Antwerp Cathedral), intensified by bold, thrusting diagonals, contorted postures, and eerie lighting effects, evoked an image of struggle and pain in the spectator that effectively fulfilled the Counter Reformation demand for an art that would deeply move the worshiper. Rubens also formulated a new aristocratic style for later court painters. In the "Marie de Médicis Arriving at Marseille" (Louvre, Paris), painted for the French Queen's palace, Rubens introduced numerous mythological figures and personifications to aggrandize the momentous occasion of Marie's arrival in France to rule as the Queen of Henry IV.

Rubens, who produced large compositions in numbers, managed a veritable painting factory employing students and assistants trained for specialization in the painting of animals, fruits and flowers, and landscapes. Among his more famous assistants were Frans Snyders, who excelled in the painting of dead animals, and Anthony van Dyck, who later became a leading portrait painter. Aside from the overwhelming authority of Rubens' style, the influence of the more rugged realism of 17th-century Dutch painting can be noted in the works of Flemish painters such as Jacob Jordaens and David Teniers the Younger, both of whom often painted peasant genre.

The 18th and 19th Centuries

Flemish art displayed no new directions or original styles after the 17th century. Such painters as Willem Jacob Herreyns and Pieter Verhaegen continued the style of Rubens with mediocre success, while others turned to the Dutch and French schools for models. With the exception of a few artists, such as the realist sculptor Constantin Meunier, the history of 19th-century art belongs more to the study of the academic styles that developed in France and Germany. The latest Belgian contributions are significant ones, but they belong to a discussion of international art rather than the analysis of a Flemish regional style.

Consult Rooses, Max, *Art in Flanders* (1914); Panofsky, Erwin, *Early Netherlandish Painting* (1953); Friedländer, M. J., *From Van Eyck to Bruegel* (1956); Lassaigne, Jacques, *Flemish Painting* (1957); Wilenski, R. H., *Flemish Painters* (1960).

JAMES E. SNYDER, University of Michigan

FLEMISH LITERATURE. *See* BELGIAN LITERATURE; DUTCH LITERATURE.

FLENSBURG [flĕns′bŏŏrKH], city of northwestern Federal Republic of Germany (West Germany), near the Danish border, at the head of the Flensburg Fiord, 20 mi. from the Baltic Sea. It was the seat of the German government during the last phase of World War II in Europe. Flensburg is today a small port and commercial trade center. Through it passes a modern highway, known as Europastrasse 3, as well as the railway connecting Hamburg and northwest Germany with Denmark and Scandinavia. The main shopping street extends from the Südermark to the Nordermark, at the end of which stands the medieval city gate known as the Nordertor, in red brick with crow's-foot gables. In ancient times the city was a center of Baltic trade. Within the old town a number of late medieval merchants' houses survive, with half-timbered walls, pantile roofs, and steeply pitched gables. There is a historic castle, the Glücksburg, on the outskirts of the town. Among the modern buildings are the red brick "German House," a new teachers training college, and a theater. Industries include paper manufacture, brewing, and distilling. The surrounding countryside is dotted with windmills and thatched-roof farmhouses. Pop., 98,526.

ALICE F. A. MUTTON, University of London

FLETCHER, JOHN (1579–1625), English dramatist. He was the son of Richard Fletcher, later Bishop of London, who died deeply in debt when John was only 17. In 1607 Fletcher began his famous dramatic collaboration with Francis Beaumont (q.v.), which lasted until Beaumont's death in 1616. Beaumont and Fletcher exerted a strong influence on 17th-century English drama, especially through their popularization of tragicomedy. The two best examples of their joint work are *The Maid's Tragedy* (1608–11) and *Philaster* (1609–10). Fletcher, who became principal dramatist for the King's Men after Shakespeare's retirement, also may have collaborated with Shakespeare on *Henry VIII* (1613) and on *The Two Noble Kinsmen* (c.1613–16). He wrote 16 plays on his own, including an attempt to introduce a new kind of pastoral drama, *The Faithful Shepherdess* (c.1609). His forte, however, lay in comedies of manners such as *The Wild-Goose Chase* (c.1621) and *Rule a Wife and Have a Wife* (1624).

LAWRENCE V. RYAN, Stanford University

FLETCHER, JOHN GOULD (1886–1950), American poet and critic, born in Little Rock, Ark., and educated at Harvard University. From 1908 to 1933 he lived chiefly in Europe, where he became a leader in the imagist movement. He also experimented in polyphonic prose, but later adopted more conventional forms. After his return to the United States, he became associated with the southern Agrarian poets. His works include *Goblins and Pagodas* (1916); *Branches of Adam* (1926); *The Black Rock* (1928); *The Epic of Arkansas* (1936); *Selected Poems* (Pulitzer Prize, 1938); and *The Burning Mountain* (1946).

FLEURS DU MAL, LES. *See* BAUDELAIRE, CHARLES PIERRE.

FLEURUS [flû-rüs], town in Hainaut Province, southwestern Belgium, 7 mi. northeast of Charleroi. Here, during the Thirty Years' War, the Spanish were defeated (Aug., 1622); during the War of the Grand Alliance, the French defeated the Dutch, Spanish, and German troops (July, 1690); during the French Revolutionary Wars, French Republican forces defeated the Austrians (June, 1794). Pop., 7,320.

FLEURY [flû-rē′], ANDRÉ HERCULE DE (1653–1743), French statesman and Cardinal. He was the tutor of the future Louis XV and established a powerful influence over his pupil, ensuring his own political and social position at court. In 1726 he was elevated to the cardinalate and from that time virtually ruled the kingdom. Skillful and frugal management of finances created a surplus in the treasury that had been depleted by the extravagance of Louis XIV and the collapse of the system of Scottish speculator John Law. He succeeded in re-establishing the government's credit and made many internal improvements. The construction of roads and the development of the merchant marine resulted in increased French commerce. His severe measures toward the Jansenist religious dissenters made him unpopular. A pacifist, he was unwillingly drawn into the War of the Polish Succession, but he secured favorable provisions for France in the treaty of Vienna (1738).

RALPH H. BOWEN, Northern Illinois University

FLEXNER, ABRAHAM (1866–1959), American educator. After receiving degrees from Johns Hopkins and Harvard, he taught at Louisville (Ky.) High School and operated a preparatory school. In 1908 he became associated with the Carnegie Foundation for the Advancement of Teaching, and later served as secretary of the General Education Board of the Rockefeller Foundation (1917–25). From 1930 to 1939 he was the director of the Institute for Advanced Study at Princeton, which he helped to establish. His direction of philanthropies and his writings did a great deal toward the revamping of American medical education. Particularly influential was his 1910 report denouncing the unscholarly training then offered in medical schools. His writings also helped to create the Lincoln Experimental School of Teachers College, Columbia University. His books include *The American College: A Criticism* (1908), *Medical Education in the United States and Canada* (1910), *A Modern School* (1916), *Do Americans Really Value Education?* (1927), and *Abraham Flexner: An Autobiography* (rev. ed., 1959).

ROBERT D. HARTMAN, University of Illinois

FLEXNER, SIMON (1863–1946), American physician well known for his investigations of infectious diseases. He served for many years as director of the Rockefeller Institute for Medical Research in New York. Among his numerous contributions were studies of diphtheria toxin, isolation of one of the organisms responsible for bacillary dysentery (Flexner's bacillus), and investigations on the transmission of poliomyelitis in monkeys.

FLICKA. *See* MY FRIEND FLICKA.

FLICKER, name for several ground-dwelling birds of the woodpecker family, Picidae, native to North America. The northern, or yellow-shafted flicker, *Colaptes auratus*, is a speckled, brownish bird marked by a white rump and golden-yellow underwings. The male bears a red crescent on the back of its head, and a black "mustache" on either side of its bill. This species occurs throughout eastern and central North America, from Canada to the Gulf Coast. It frequents open fields and orchards in search of its favorite food—ants. It nests in a hole in a tree, like all woodpeckers. A related species, the red-shafted flicker, *C. cafer*, occurs west of the Rocky Mountains, from British Columbia to Mexico. It has salmon-red underwings and a red "mustache."
See also WOODPECKER.

FLIGHT, BIRD. During the course of animal evolution flight has been achieved four times by various groups: insects, reptiles, birds, and mammals. In all instances the wing serves both as an airfoil and as the propulsive mechanism. In this respect animal flight is very different from that of an airplane in which the wing serves only as an airfoil, and the propulsive mechanism is either a propeller or a jet stream. The flight "experiments" of reptiles terminated with the prehistoric pterosaurs. Mammalian flight has been perfected by only one small group—the bats. Birds, on the other hand, have become a numerous and highly successful group of flying vertebrates. This

FLIGHT MODIFICATIONS IN THE BIRD'S SKELETON

The skeleton of a bird shows many modifications from the basic vertebrate pattern. These modifications are directed toward the bird's special type of locomotion—flight. The most highly modified structure is the forelimb, or wing. Other, less obvious modifications are found throughout the bird's skeleton.

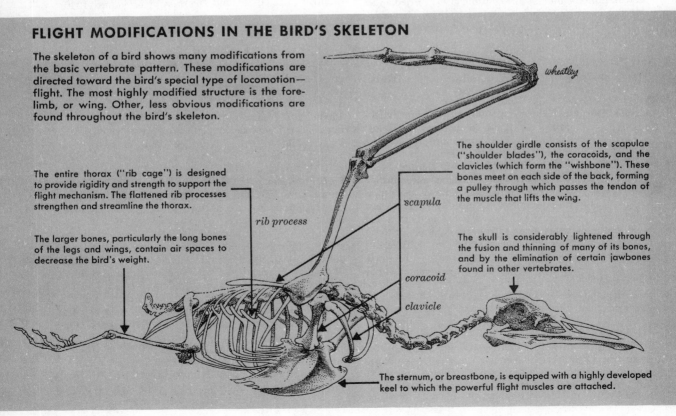

wheatley

The entire thorax ("rib cage") is designed to provide rigidity and strength to support the flight mechanism. The flattened rib processes strengthen and streamline the thorax.

The larger bones, particularly the long bones of the legs and wings, contain air spaces to decrease the bird's weight.

rib process

The shoulder girdle consists of the scapulae ("shoulder blades"), the coracoids, and the clavicles (which form the "wishbone"). These bones meet on each side of the back, forming a pulley through which passes the tendon of the muscle that lifts the wing.

scapula

The skull is considerably lightened through the fusion and thinning of many of its bones, and by the elimination of certain jawbones found in other vertebrates.

coracoid

clavicle

The sternum, or breastbone, is equipped with a highly developed keel to which the powerful flight muscles are attached.

success has resulted from a unique combination of many biological features which suit them for flight—a streamlined body, a lightweight skeleton, feathers as a covering for body and wings, forelimbs modified into wings, powerful breast muscles that bring about flight movements, and remarkable respiratory and digestive systems in which food can be rapidly and efficiently converted into power to operate the flight muscles.

Birds have developed three types of flight—flapping, gliding, and soaring. Flapping or powered flight is the most common, and is produced by an up-and-down movement (in an arc) of the wings, which both keeps the bird airborne and brings about forward or backward motion. The downward and backward portion of the arc is the power stroke, and is facilitated by the concave undersurface of the wing, the tightly closed position of the wing feathers, and the fully-extended wing position. The upward and forward portion of the arc is carried through with a minimum expenditure of energy because air slips readily over the upper, convex wing surface, and because the separation of the wing feathers permits air to pass through the wing. During the upward stroke, the wings are folded close to the body, further minimizing wind resistance.

Gliding flight is the simplest type of flight. It is also thought to be the earliest kind of animal flight—used by ancient reptiles which may have climbed into the trees to take off into the air with a gliding motion. Many birds use flapping flight to gain initial take-off speed, then change to gliding flight to travel as far as possible with little effort.

Soaring is a specialized type of flight that takes advantage of air currents and updrafts of air. Soaring birds have large, sail-like wings, as can be seen in gulls, pelicans, hawks, and eagles. Soaring vultures ride the air currents for miles without a movement of the wings except to provide balance.

The wingbeat of birds varies from fewer than 10 to 50 beats or more per second. Ducks have a slow wingbeat of 2 beats per second; sparrows and most songbirds have a wingbeat of 3 to 5 beats per second; hummingbirds, 50 to 75 wingbeats per second. The speed of bird flight varies from 15 to 25 mph for most songbirds to 40 or 50 mph for ducks and geese. Record speeds of over 100 mph have been noted for falcons and swifts.

CLARENCE J. HYLANDER, Author, *Feathers and Flight*

FLIGHT, THEORY OF. *See* AERODYNAMICS; AERONAUTICS; FLYING.

FLIGHTLESS BIRDS, term applied to birds of several orders that have lost the power of flight. Most flightless birds are large and heavy bodied and lack the keeled breastbone characteristic of flying birds. Flightless birds occur on all continents except Europe and North America. As a group, the following six orders of flightless birds are often classified as the superorder Palaeognathae, the walking birds. The order Apterygiformes includes the kiwi of New Zealand, which possesses rudimentary wings. Other living orders retain wing structure similar to the flying birds, but with wings of insufficient size or strength to make the bird airborne. The order Rheiformes includes the South American rhea. The order Struthioniformes includes the ostriches of Africa and Arabia. The order Casuariiformes includes the cassowaries and emus of Australia and adjacent regions. Two orders of flightless birds have become extinct within recent memory: Dinornithiformes, represented by the huge, ostrichlike moa of New Zealand; and Aepyornithiformes, represented by the elephant bird of Madagascar. Members of several orders of modern birds (superorder Neognathae) are also flightless. The penguins, of order Sphenisciformes, have wings modified into flippers which they use for a kind of "underwater flight." The great auk, of order Charadriiformes, and the dodo, of order Columbiformes, were modern flightless birds that became extinct in the 17th and 19th centuries, respectively.

CLARENCE J. HYLANDER, Author, *Feathers and Flight*
See also AUK; CASSOWARY; DODO; ELEPHANT BIRD; EMU; KIWI; MOA; OSTRICH; PENGUIN; RHEA.

FLIGHT RECORDER, a tape-recording device used on aircraft; it provides a continuous record of the plane's flight from take-off to landing. In the United States the Federal Aviation Agency requires that flight recorders be installed in turbine-powered planes of more than 12,500 lb. take-off weight and in planes which operate above a 25,000-ft. altitude. The flight recorder records time, altitude, airspeed, vertical acceleration, and heading; some also record maintenance data. Flight recorders are valuable for accident investigations and for analysis of various incidents, such as extreme vertical acceleration caused by air turbulence.

FLIGHT SIMULATOR, later development of the early Link Trainer by which pilots were taught the technique of blind flying, inside a hooded cockpit. The instructor sat at an adjoining table giving radio guidance and corrections from a chart that plotted the course a student was following. Modern flight simulators save time and the operating costs of actual airliners, and teach the aircrew to control a craft and correct pilot errors under severe weather conditions and mechanical failures. A replica of the flight deck of an airliner with all flight controls, radio, and navigational aids, functioning precisely as in flight, is mounted on a movable base which duplicates the pitch, roll, and yaw encountered in flying, landing, and takeoff. A wide view from the cockpit window reproduces a moving color panorama of terrain, runway approaches, airport lighting, and obstacles; it is accompanied by engine sounds and the squeal of tires in landing. The instructor is able to pose problems due to engine failures and radio and computer malfunctions, and can monitor the recovery measures taken by the pilot.

CLAYTON KNIGHT, O. B. E., Author, *The Story of Flight*

FLIGHT TESTING, the final testing phase for a new aircraft. It is preceded by many months of ground testing of the aircraft's structure and internal equipment. Since the early days of aviation, flight testing has grown from a highly dangerous and relatively unpredictable art into an exact science which is relatively safe, although never free from hazard. Steady progress in the understanding of airplane flight characteristics, better airplane structures and auxiliary systems, the extensive use of wind tunnels to test exact models of the new aircraft, and many years of flight work have all contributed to improving the predictability of flight testing. Along with advances in engineering and flight test methods, modern test pilots are almost without exception highly competent engineers who contribute to the design of the aircraft they test and who thoroughly understand them. Most test pilots of the past had only a rudimentary technical knowledge even though they were highly skilled aviators.

While modern flight testing is extremely complex its basic objectives are still the same as they were in the 1920's. A flight-test program can be divided into five distinct parts: first or shakedown flights, engine-cooling and vibration flights, basic stability check, detailed performance determination, and final stability check. During the shakedown phase the pilot familiarizes himself with the flight characteristics of the airplane and the operation of its systems during flight. Engine cooling and vibration are then checked at all speeds and altitudes to see if any shaking or overheating occurs. An analysis of basic flight characteristics follows. Performance demonstration consists of making precision measurements to determine exactly how fast the airplane will fly and climb, its range, endurance, take-off distance, and so on. Final stability checks are to establish what instabilities and unpleasant or dangerous motions the aircraft will go through during all possible maneuvers. JAMES J. HAGGERTY, JR.

FLINDERS, MATTHEW (1774–1814), British sailor, cartographer, and explorer. Courageous, persistent, and skillful, Flinders contributed heavily to authentic knowledge of the Australian coast. One of his early expeditions in association with George Bass produced the discovery of Bass Strait. In 1802 he surveyed the south coast of Australia. His next task was to fill in details of the eastern and northern coasts. Accomplishing much valuable work until his ship, the *Investigator*, became unseaworthy, he returned to Sydney and sailed (1803) for England. En route, he stopped at Mauritius where the French held him for seven years.

FLINDERS RANGES, system of folded and faulted mountains of southern Australia, extending for about 200 mi (322 km) northward from Spencer Gulf in the state of South Australia. Wheat is grown on the lower slopes and lignite coal is mined at Leigh Creek on the northwestern margin.

The highest point in the Flinders Ranges is St. Mary Peak (3,500 ft, or 1 067 m).

FLINDERS RIVER, river of northwestern Queensland, Australia, flowing northward for about 325 mi (525 km) to the Gulf of Carpentaria. Rainfall in its drainage basin varies from less than 20 inches (51 cm) in the headwaters area to 40 inches (102 cm) near the mouth.

FLIN FLON, town of western Manitoba, Canada, located on the Laurentian Plateau near the Saskatchewan border. It was founded in 1915 when copper- and zinc-ore bodies were developed in the area, and it is the most important mining and smelting center in Manitoba. Saw milling is of local importance. Tourists are attracted by excellent hunting and fishing and the exceptional scenery. The town is connected to southern Manitoba by rail and road, and there are daily flights to Winnipeg, 350 mi (563 km) southeast.

FLINT, city of southeast-central Michigan, on the Flint River. It is a highly specialized manufacturing city for the automobile industry. General Motors Corporation has major divisions for Buick, Chevrolet, Fisher Body, Ternstedt, and A C Spark Plug. Other manufacturers produce auto accessories, flour, cotton textiles, cement blocks, paints, furniture, and canvas products.

Michigan School for the Deaf is at Flint. General Motors Institute, Flint College of the University of Michigan, Flint Junior College, and Baker Business College are here. Chartered as city, 1855.

FLINT, municipal borough of Flintshire, Wales, located on the Dee estuary. The manufacture of rayon yarn and paper are leading industries. Flint was founded in 1284 and, though marred by industry, is a fine example of a grid-planned, fortified town.

FLINT, hard, tough, microcrystalline variety of quartz that occurs as nodules or beds in chalky limestones. Flint is usually brown, gray, or black. It breaks with a sharp edge, and it was used extensively by early man for cutting and scraping tools and for weapons. Before matches were invented fires were often started with sparks made by striking flint against steel; the same principle was used in flintlock firearms, common until the 19th century. Today flint is a source of silica for ceramics, and the nodules are used as grinding pebbles.

How flint implements were shaped by percussion flaking.

American Museum of Natural History

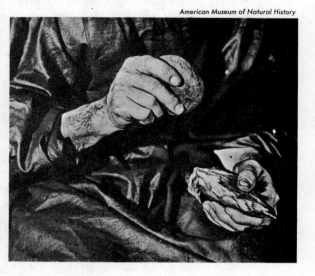

FLINT IMPLEMENTS. Flint is a form of silica, with a crystalline consistency, that is very hard—harder, in fact, than steel. Flint was a major material for tools and weapons during the Paleolithic (Old Stone Age) and Neolithic (New Stone Age). Flint may be broken and shaped into a wide variety of implements by varying the force and direction of the blow, the point of impact, and the quality of the material with which the blow is given. The most primitive technique, called percussion flaking, simply involves hitting one stone with another. In this way a sharp cutting edge can be produced on the core stone. In the mid-Paleolithic the pressure flaking technique appears: the flakes struck from a core are shaped into implements by removing small pieces of stone through the application of pressure by means of an awl-like tool of bone or antler. Toward the end of the Paleolithic a more elaborate technique is found: the core stone is shaped through percussion flaking to provide a striking platform and to give the core a prism shape. Long, uniformly shaped blades with parallel sides could be struck off such a core. They were then shaped by pressure flaking into lance points, arrow points, chisels, drills, gravers, and a variety of knifelike tools.

PHILIP L. NEWMAN

See also NEOLITHIC AGE; PALEOLITHIC AGE; TOOLS AND WEAPONS, PRIMITIVE.

FLINTLOCK, a mechanism for discharging a firearm by means of flint and steel. Flintlocks appeared in Europe about 1630 and continued in use until about 1840—a longer period of use than any other type of discharge mechanism. A piece of flint was held in the jaws of a hammer, or cock, in such a position that when the trigger of the gun was pulled, the flint struck a piece of steel, called a frizzen. This action caused a shower of sparks which ignited the priming powder in a small pan at the side of the breech end of the barrel, firing the gun.

FLINT RIVER, river in southwestern Georgia, formed by the confluence of Mud and Camp creeks, just south of Atlanta. It flows generally south, joining the Chattahoochee River in southwestern Georgia to form the Apalachicola River. It is navigable to Albany, Ga., and is dammed for hydroelectric power. Length, 330 mi (528 km).

FLINT RIVER, river in southeastern Michigan, formed by the confluence of North and South branches. It flows southwest to Flint, then northwest to join the Shiawassee River near Saginaw. Length, 71 mi (114 km).

FLOATING ISLAND, a mass of vegetation that has been detached from the sides of a river, lake, or ocean, or has risen from the bottom to the surface. Such islands vary greatly in size and are generally most common in rivers during floods. Floating islands are particularly common in flat regions where rivers or lakes are not well confined. Under these conditions reeds and grasses that flourish along the margins of rivers and lakes may float away when the water rises. Floating islands in the ocean are instrumental in spreading plant and animal life among remote islands. In the Arctic, detached ice forms floating ice islands.

FLODDEN FIELD, BATTLE OF, climactic battle (1513) in the first war that Henry VIII of England fought with Scotland. The English, led by Thomas Howard, later Duke of Norfolk, completely routed the Scots, killing their King and commander, James IV. Sir Walter Scott recreated the struggle in *Marmion.*

FLONZALEY [flŏN′zə-lā] **QUARTET,** one of the foremost string ensembles of its time (1904–29), founded (1902) by Edward J. de Coppet, a New York banker. Its members during most of its career included Adolfo Betti, first violin; Alfred Pochon, second violin; Ugo Ara, viola; and Iwan d'Archambeau, cello.

FLOOD, JAMES CLAIR (1826–89), a bonanza king of Nevada mining. He was born in New York City and at 23 joined the first gold rush to California. With William S. O'Brien, he opened a mahogany-bar saloon in San Francisco near the mining stock exchange. As miners and mining experts, influenced by liquor, talked freely of their knowledge, Flood and O'Brien listened, absorbed, and planned. Finally, with John W. Mackay and James G. Fair, they organized the Consolidated Virginia City Mine near Virginia City, Nev., from a number of smaller holdings on the Comstock Lode. Discoveries in 1873 and 1874 of the Big Bonanza made them millionaires overnight. With Flood as the financial expert, the group is supposed to have taken more than $150,000,000 in silver and gold from their Nevada mines, with their dividends aggregating $78,148,800.

JOE B. FRANTZ

FLOOD, THE, Biblical account of the Deluge (Gen. 6–9) relating how Yahweh decided to destroy mankind for its wickedness. The upright patriarch Noah, warned of the impending disaster, escaped with his family and a large number of selected animals by building a huge vessel, the ark. The floods exterminated all other living creatures, and then abated, depositing the ark on the mountains of Ararat (between the Caspian and the Black seas).

The story in many of its details bears comparison with several similar stories current in Mesopotamia during the 2d millennium B.C., particularly with the flood story of the Babylonian *Epic of Gilgamesh,* of which a certain Utnapishtim was the hero. It is highly probable that some historical event, perhaps a disaster affecting a large area in the Tigris-Euphrates Valley, gave rise to all these narratives. Excavations at Ur and other ancient Mesopotamian cities have proved that the area was subject to periodic flooding.

D. F. PAYNE

FLOODPLAIN, a smooth, flat plain bordering a river or stream that is flooded during periods of high water. The floodplain includes the channel, various kinds of bars, natural levees, abandoned channel segments known as oxbows, ox-bow lakes, sloughs, and swamps. Floodplains form (1) as a result of deposition on the inside of curves or meanders in the channel or (2) as a result of deposition by floodwaters flowing out of the channel. Floodplain deposits consist of channel sands and gravel and overlying silt and clay. They are really flat-topped bodies of sediment stored temporarily in a valley as the stream or river carries on the job of moving the sediment to a basin of deposition. Some floodplains are scarcely wider than the stream. Others, such as the Mississippi floodplain, are more than 100 mi (160 km) wide and hundreds of feet thick. Floodplains are prime agricultural land; soils are renewed by periodic deposition of fresh silt and mud during floods.

PETER FLAWN

See also LEVEE, NATURAL; RIVER.

S. V. Overshire—FPG

Douglas Dam on the French Broad River is one of the high dams behind which storage reservoirs are impounded on the upper branches of the Tennessee. Nine long dams equipped with locks create a continuous chain of smaller lakes on the main stream.

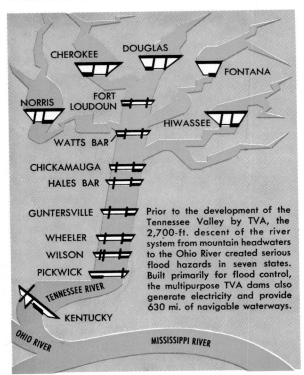

CHEROKEE DOUGLAS

FONTANA

NORRIS FORT LOUDOUN

HIWASSEE

WATTS BAR

CHICKAMAUGA

HALES BAR

GUNTERSVILLE

WHEELER

WILSON

PICKWICK

TENNESSEE RIVER

KENTUCKY

OHIO RIVER   MISSISSIPPI RIVER

Prior to the development of the Tennessee Valley by TVA, the 2,700-ft. descent of the river system from mountain headwaters to the Ohio River created serious flood hazards in seven states. Built primarily for flood control, the multipurpose TVA dams also generate electricity and provide 630 mi. of navigable waterways.

FLOODS AND FLOOD CONTROL. It is a common belief that man contributes to the magnitude and frequency of floods by cutting down forests and creating paved areas in the form of cities, airports, and highways. Except in special cases this is not true. Geologic studies and biblical and other ancient writings reveal that rivers have flooded almost since the earth was formed and that the material carried by prehistoric floods has formed plains, wide valleys, and river deltas. Traces of waterborne sediments have been found above the level of known floods. It is true that the removal of natural vegetal cover can contribute to soil erosion and cause increased deposition of sediments in lowlands. It is also true that the paved areas of cities and large airports can contribute to the rapid concentration of storm water, which if discharged into small streams can cause localized flooding.

The Cause of Floods

Flooding of land that is normally dry results from increases in the water level of adjacent rivers, lakes, swamps, and oceans. Floods from rivers are the most common cause of inundation, but disastrous coastal flooding may occur from increases in the levels of oceans and lakes.

River Floods. River floods occur when the supply of water to the normal channel exceeds the hydraulic carrying capacity of the channel. The channel requirements of river systems vary widely. A river which only receives water from distant melting snows may not need the same capacity as one subject to tropical storms, even though both rivers drain the same area in square miles. The natural carrying capacity of river channels is often reduced by works of man, such as buildings, bridges, highway and railroad embankments, and by land fills and waste disposal. In northern climates such obstructions may contribute to the formation of ice jams, which block the river channel and cause flooding even under moderate flows.

The flat areas adjacent to normal river channels and extending back to the bordering hills are called flood plains. It is common for the flood-carrying capacity of river valleys to be reduced by the construction of entire communities on flood plains which rivers have used for centuries to carry away floodwaters. In hilly and mountainous regions the normal river channel and the adjacent flood plain have always been natural routes of travel and inviting sites for settlements. As rivers claimed their floodways only at rare intervals, man boldly developed river valleys and the settlements became cities. The cities have remained, but at a great price in flood losses. In the United States, outstanding examples of such cities are Pittsburgh, Pa., located where the Allegheny and Monongahela rivers meet to form the Ohio River, and Kansas City, Kans. and Mo., where the Kansas and Missouri rivers meet.

River floods may result from the rapid melting of snow fields in the spring and summer, from extraordinary rainfalls, or from a combination of melting snow and heavy rainfall. Severe localized thunderstorms may cause floods on small streams. The basic cause of floods depends upon the latitude, altitude, and climate of a river basin and upon its position in relation to oceans, the principal source of moisture for great storm rainfalls.

Floods may be experienced at great distances from the sources of their cause. Floods on the Nile in Egypt, a desert country, come from rains that have fallen in equatorial Africa, 2,000 mi (3 200 km) away. In the same way the levees on the Mississippi River at New Orleans, La., must protect against floods sometimes originating 1,000 mi (1 600 km) away. However, the Mississippi River basin differs from that of the Nile in that main river floods may come from any part except the semiarid areas near the base of the Rocky Mountains.

Man has contributed to some of the greatest river flood disasters in history by building dams which later failed. There have been scores of such failures, but the most infamous example in the world occurred at Johnstown, Pa., on May 31, 1889, when a neglected 46-year-old earth dam broke and caused the death of at least 2,100 people.

Coastal Floods. Flooding from oceans is caused by two types of long-period waves or surges. One type is induced by earthquakes beneath the ocean floor. Such seismic waves have been popularly called tidal waves, but oceanographers have adopted the term "tsunamis" as these waves are not associated with tides. Coastal floods from ocean waves may be generated by earthquakes whose centers are thousands of miles away. The Chilean earthquakes in May, 1960, along the southwestern coast of South America, caused great seismic waves in the Hawaiian Islands, 7,000 mi (11 200 km) away.

The other type, which may occur on either oceans or lakes, results from wind forces piling water upon the shore, particularly during hurricanes. Wind-induced waves are augmented if they are coincident with the normal tide cycle. Shore areas inundated by wind-driven ocean waves usually suffer from destruction by both wind and water. All ocean wave phenomena are accentuated by movement through shallowing water toward the shore.

When flood waters reassert prior claim to a flood plain, there is nothing for dwellers in injudiciously located housing to do but clear out, abandoning what they can not carry.

Differences in atmospheric pressure over bodies of water may cause the surface to vary a few feet from the normal level. If the last-named cause is combined with increases due to wind forces, serious flooding may occur on windward shores.

Flood Control

Flood control measures fall into two general classes: (1) land treatment measures and (2) engineering structures. The first method consists of providing adequate vegetal cover to hold the soil, terracing of steep slopes, and providing small dams in gullies and brooks to check channel and stream bank erosion. Where it is necessary to cultivate slopes it is desirable to plow at right angles to the slope, a process called contour plowing, to provide resistance to overland flow. These so-called conservation measures encourage rain to infiltrate into the soil by providing resistance to overland flow. They thereby reduce the frequency of flooding from light or medium rainfalls equaling rates up to 1 inch (2.5 cm) per hour. However, these measures offer little protection against intense rainfall rates, which may exceed 2 inches (5 cm) in half an hour, or longer rains that amount to 10 inches (25 cm) or more in 24 hours. Such extraordinary rains saturate and erode the soil and may even destroy the conservation works. The areas where special land-use practices can be adopted are limited in extent and therefore the flood control benefits are confined to small river basins.

The second class of flood control measures, consisting

A floodwall bordering the Fall River protects Hot Springs, a South Dakota town, from flash floods.

of large engineering works, are the only means of providing protection against floods which result from extraordinary rainfalls. These structures fall in turn into two classes—(1) upstream storage reservoirs and (2) downstream channel improvements, or confining works such as dikes and levees. Reservoirs must be built in relatively confined valleys which afford good sites for dams and which provide basins for the storage of floodwaters. Ideal valleys are often in the most upstream parts of river basins and therefore reservoirs in such valleys are able to control the runoff from only a small portion of a major river basin. Storms over hundreds or even thousands of square miles of uncontrolled area below reservoirs can generate damaging floods. In order to obtain reservoir areas it may be necessary to flood valuable lands, highways, and railroads that occupy the valleys. The economic loss from taking upstream areas must be balanced against the downstream benefits from flood control.

Because reservoirs cannot always provide sufficient flood protection, it is necessary to provide downstream flood control works, usually at points where the potential damage is the greatest. On small rivers an enlarged channel may be dredged, lined with walls, and sometimes paved. Usually existing bridge openings must be enlarged and buildings close to the river moved or torn down. On large rivers lining of the channel, except for bank protection, is too costly, and only confining works such as walls around important structures or earth levees can be provided. These confining works may raise the water level above natural conditions and above the ground surface behind the levees. This creates drainage problems, and pumping stations must be provided to discharge storm water and sewage from the protected areas.

Flood control reservoirs, channel improvements, and levee systems are usually designed to protect against floods of the greatest magnitude ever known in the region and often to protect against even greater floods. However, at rare intervals still greater floods may occur because there is no known upper limit to rainfall depths

Pine and locust seedlings planted on a gullied North Carolina hillside provided thick watershed protection in 20 years.

Tennessee Valley Authority

and durations. The physical limitations of upstream valleys prevent constructing reservoirs that will contain the greatest flood that is likely to occur. The cost of complete downstream protection against large rivers is not only prohibitively expensive, but the height and size of the structures required may prove objectionable to the communities receiving protection. Therefore, it is not practicable to provide complete flood protection except against very small rivers.

One method of preventing flood damage which has been receiving increasing consideration over the years is to prohibit building in areas that are subject to known flood hazards. Flood plains may be reserved for public parks, for grazing lands, or for a purpose for which the known risk is willingly accepted.

Consult Briggs, Peter, *Rampage: The Story of Disastrous Floods, Broken Dams and Human Fallibility* (1973); Dougal, Merwin D., ed., *Flood Plain Management: Iowa's Experience* (1969); Hoyt, W. G., and Langbein, W. B., *Floods* (1955).

GORDON R. WILLIAMS

FLOORS. Since they are among the largest surfaces in a house and receive the most wear, floors must be durable, attractive, and easy to maintain. They should be able to keep their original appearance under hard use and should be resistant to abrasion from foot traffic and heavy furniture.

All these qualities cannot usually be found in a single flooring material, even though a wide variety of colors, patterns, and materials is available. Therefore the choice of flooring must be made by weighing the relative importance of each characteristic and deciding which ones are the most important. In a living-room floor, for example, one might compromise on durability and ease of cleaning for the sake of comfort and appearance.

In selecting a flooring material, there are several qualities to look for. A hard and tough surface will resist abrasion as well as stains or bleaches. The floor should not absorb dust or spilled liquids; otherwise soiled spots would show in between cleanings. The area covered should be simple in shape and the floor should join the wall in curved, rather than right-angle, molding. The floor's appearance will last longer if it has a pattern and dull finish that camouflages dust and scratches. Definite textures, glossy surfaces, and light or dark solid colors show dirt faster. Also, in general, the more resilient a floor is, the more comfortable it is to walk on and the less it tends to reflect noise.

Basic Floor. The basic floor, over which the finished floor is laid, can be made of either concrete or wood. Concrete floors are usually installed in the basement or in the bottom floor of the house, if there is no basement. If the finish flooring is to be wood, it can be nailed to wood strips, called sleepers, imbedded in the concrete or it can be glued with a special adhesive. For other types of flooring a moisture-proof membrane must be placed between the concrete and the finish floor. One of the major problems of concrete subfloors—the fatigue caused by hardness underfoot—can be reduced with a resilient flooring material or by heating or insulating the concrete slab.

A basic wood floor consists of a wood frame of parallel

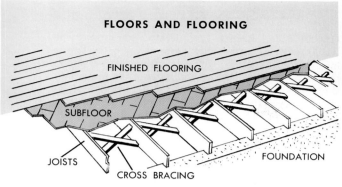

FLOORS AND FLOORING

FINISHED FLOORING

SUBFLOOR

JOISTS

CROSS BRACING

FOUNDATION

FLOOR CONSTRUCTION IN A SMALL HOME

For maximum strength, the subfloor is laid diagonally and the wood finish floor at right angles to the joists.

Tongue-and-groove machined finish flooring makes a tight, smooth surface. Overlapping grooves cover nails in adjacent tongues.

All photos: Weyerhaeuser Co.

Resilient floor tiles, such as these vinyl tiles, come in many materials and patterns. An adhesive bonds them to the subfloor.

joists sometimes braced to prevent squeaking. The subfloor is nailed over these joists and the finish floor fastened over that. Usually the subfloor is of parallel wood strips, but plywood or composition board is sometimes used instead.

Materials for Finish Flooring. For finish flooring, wood is still the most popular material, but resilient tiles and various types of masonry are coming into widespread use.

Wood flooring comes in strips and planks, which are laid in parallel, and in parquetry blocks which are laid in various patterns. Oak and maple are the most commonly used woods, with birch, beech, and pecan running a close second. In general, the top grades are the most attractive, but the lower grades, which are equally strong, can be used for floors where appearance is not so important, for example, in attics or closets, or as subfloors which are to be covered with another permanent flooring. Wood's long-standing popularity is due to its good appearance, warmth, and durability. Although it requires frequent waxing, it is relatively easy to refinish.

Resilient Floor Tiles. Of the many resilient flooring materials, vinyl is perhaps the best for all-round use, since it is tough, has an attractive finish, colors well, resists staining, and requires little upkeep. Cork and rubber tile, which also have a good appearance and are easy to main-

tain, rank next. Vinyl asbestos, another widely used material, is durable, low cost, and suitable for a wide variety of floors. Asphalt tile is brittle and tends to show stains and marks sooner, but can be laid directly over concrete and may be suitable for basement floors.

Linoleum. Still the most common of the resilient floorings, linoleum has an appearance that can be maintained easily and is relatively inexpensive, but it should not be used on concrete. Inlaid linoleum is the most durable because the color and pattern go all the way through.

Masonry. Although they are not used very extensively, masonry floorings are extremely durable, and easy to maintain. However, they are generally hard, noisy, and cold.

Concrete can be the least expensive of all flooring materials when used as a foundation, subfloor, and finish floor in one. But since it is not very attractive unless painted or otherwise colored, it is usually used as a base for other floorings or covered with rugs.

Stone. Because of their natural color and texture, stone floorings such as slate, flagstone, and marble are handsome when used outdoors or near entrances or fireplaces. They can also be used elsewhere in the house, except in the kitchen, where grease might cause spotting. Similarly, glazed and unglazed ceramic tile and brick are used in areas subject to hard wear, moisture, and dirt, although unglazed tiles and brick must be used carefully since both they and their surrounding grout absorb grease, are slow to dry after being washed, and, even with waxing, are difficult to free of stains.

Consult Berkeley, Bernard, *Floors: Selection and Maintenance* (1968); Edwards, J. K., *Floors and Their Maintenance* (1972); Karen, Jack, *Floor Stripping and Refinishing* (1976); Salter, Walter L., *Floors and Floor Maintenance* (1974); Schuler, Stanley, *The Floor and Ceiling Book* (1976). MARGARET FARMER
See also HOUSE.

FLOOR WAXES, polishes used on wood floors and on linoleum, asphalt, rubber, and other types of flooring. They may consist of waxes blended in an organic solvent in either a liquid emulsion or paste form. The wax content of the liquid type is not less than 12%, while it may be higher than 20% for the paste type. Wax polish emulsions, therefore, are more easily applied whether by manual or mechanical processes, and ordinarily require no hard buffing to produce a high-gloss film. Such emulsion-type liquid waxes may actually be self-polishing in that no buffing operations are necessary in their application. These are suitable for linoleum and synthetic vinyl-type floor coverings but not for wood. The wax ingredient may consist of substances such as carnauba wax, beeswax, ceresin, paraffin, natural resins, synthetic polymers of the type of polyethylene, and polystyrene. These preparations are water-thin or slightly viscous in appearance and dry to a hard, lustrous film with water-spotting resistance and high scuff and wear resistance. Such preparations are particularly suited to kitchen and bathroom floors.

The so-called solvent-type waxes are used for wood and linoleum floors, but not for asphalt or plastic tile compositions which would be attacked by solvents. The biggest drawback to this type of wax polish preparation is the difficulty entailed in application. However, such waxes usually exhibit tough film characteristics, high water resistance, and long-lasting finishes. Most solvents used in such preparations are high flash-point naphthas, aromatic solvents, and mixtures of these. The use of naphtha allows a quicker application period and a smoother film.

Another type of floor-wax preparation which requires a high expenditure of energy in its application is the paste-type solvent combination. Wax polish preparations require more time and labor for their application, and they frequently produce a harder high luster finish; these combine both polishing and cleansing action.

The most popular floor polishes contain both water and oil dispersed in a stable emulsion form. Water and soap alone would provide an unattractive surface. With the emulsion types, the soap has a detergency function, the water a diluent effect for oil and wax, and the wax ingredient leaves a lustrous, smooth, tough film or protective coating on the surface after drying.

For asphalt and rubber tile floor coverings either liquid, no-buffing wax or water-emulsion paste waxes should be used. The latter contains no petroleum or aromatic solvent, and the dried paste film can be buffed to a lustrous, water-resistant finish. WALTER A. COOK

FLORENCE (*Ital.* FIRENZE; *Lat.* FLORENTIA), historic city on the Arno River, central Italy. Surrounded by the Tuscan hills, Florence, widely regarded as one of the world's most beautiful cities, lies on both sides of the Arno where the river is relatively narrow and easy to bridge. Its location just south of the passes through the Apennine Mountains has, since its earliest history, contributed to its significance.

Florence has preserved much from the artistic genius that flourished there during the Italian Renaissance (13th to 16th centuries). Among the many Florentine artists of that era were Giotto, Filippo Brunelleschi, Donatello, Benvenuto Cellini, Sandro Botticelli, Lorenzo Ghiberti, the Della Robbia family, and Michelangelo. Great literary figures included Dante Alighieri, Petrarch, and Boccaccio. The explorer Amerigo Vespucci, from whose name America is derived, was a Florentine as was the statesman Niccolò Machiavelli. Today, the vernacular of Florence has become the modern written language of all Italy.

In the area just north of the Ponte Vecchio ("Old Bridge"), old Florence is still seen. In the center of this section, with its narrow, straight alleys laid out by the Romans, is the Piazza della Repubblica. To the northeast of this square is Florence's cathedral, Santa Maria del Fiore, where lie the tombs of Machiavelli and Galileo. The cathedral was begun in 1296 and crowned in the 15th century with the Dome designed by Brunelleschi. Inside are displayed works by Michelangelo, Ghiberti, Luca della Robbia, and others.

Beside the cathedral is the Campanile ("bell tower") designed by Giotto in 1334. Opposite the cathedral is the 11th-century, octagonal Baptistery of San Giovanni, famous for its three doors with bronze reliefs denoting Biblical scenes, the most beautiful of which is the East Door done by Ghiberti.

North of the Piazza della Repubblica stands the oldest church in Florence, Santa Maria Novella. To the southwest is the Church of Santa Trinità. South of the Piazza della Repubblica is the Palazzo Vecchio, also called the Palazzo della Signoria. In the 13th and 14th centuries it was the seat of the *signori*, elected representatives of the Republic of Florence, and today houses government offices. Nearby is the Loggia della Signoria, an open gallery containing art works that include Cellini's "Perseus." Each year, in the square in front of the Loggia, a 14th-century version of football (*calcio*) is played in period costume.

Florence has many other beautiful churches. The Church of San Lorenzo was designed by Brunelleschi who worked on it between 1442 and 1446; it was completed in 1460 by Antonio Manetti. In its New Sacristy designed by Michelangelo for the Medici are his famous statues, "Night and Day" and "Twilight and Dawn." The Franciscan Church of Santa Croce, rebuilt after 1294, is called the Pantheon of Florence because many notables are buried here. The church is decorated with frescoes by Giotto and works by the Della Robbia family.

The Palazzo degli Uffizi and the Palazzo Pitti were also built for the Medici. The Uffizi contains the most important art collection in Italy. Here are found works by most Italian painters and by many non-Italians. The Pitti's great art collections include the sumptuous display

Florence: at left, the Ponte Vecchio; center, tower of the Palazzo Vecchio; right, the domed cathedral.

in its Palatine Gallery.

Educational institutes in Florence include the Accademia della Crusca and the University, established in 1924 replacing one built in 1321 and later removed.

The most famous bridge of Florence is the Ponte Vecchio. Here one finds many jewelry, goldsmith, and other craft shops. When the Allies entered the city (1944) during World War II they were ordered not to destroy anything of artistic value. However, the retreating Germans mined all the stone bridges, except the Ponte Vecchio. Thus the Ponte Santa Trinità, with its statuary of the four seasons, was destroyed. It was rebuilt after the war, and the statuary recovered from the Arno.

History. Florence dates from the 2d century B.C. when it was a market village at the foot of a hill topped by the Etruscan town of Faesulae (Fiesole). The first important historical event occurred in 405 A.D. when the Roman general Stilicho drove out the besieging Visigoths. Under the rule of the Lombards, it was the capital of a duchy. In the 9th century it became a margraviate (frontier zone) of the Carolingian Empire. In 1054, Matilda, Countess of Tuscany, won the city. By the time of her death in 1115, it had become a center of commerce and had laid the foundations of representative government.

During the next century Florence assumed the leadership of the Guelph party. The Guelphs, loyal papists, opposed the Ghibellines, or feudal country nobility. They resented the attempt by the Ghibellines to give the ruling power to a few who would maintain their control with the help of foreign aid. By 1250 the Guelphs had gained control of the city and set up the free Republic of Florence. The government was run by the *consoli* (consuls) and the *signori* who came mainly from the merchant and artisan guilds. Conflict was renewed in 1260, but by 1266 the Guelphs had succeeded in expelling the Ghibellines from the government. Eventually two factions emerged within the Guelph party, the Neri ("Blacks") and the Bianchi ("Whites"). In 1301, Charles of Valois entered Florence with orders from the Pope to crush the Bianchi. Many were exiled including Dante.

The guilds, for the most part, maintained control of Florence until the early 15th century when the Medici family gained supremacy. In 1434, Cosimo the Elder took over the administration of civil affairs. His grandson Lorenzo the Magnificent assumed power in 1469. Lorenzo is considered the greatest of all art patrons; under his sponsorship many of the greatest works of the Renaissance were accomplished. Lorenzo's son, Pietro, however, was weak and soon removed from power. The Dominican friar Savonarola re-established the republic in 1494. The people, however, did not approve his ascetic rule, and in 1498 he was hanged on a cross and burned.

Giovanni de' Medici, with the aid of Spain, regained control of Florence early in the 16th century. But in

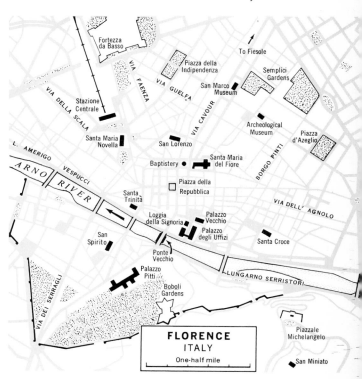

1527 the republic was again restored. In 1530 the Medici returned, and Florence became a duchy. When in 1569 the Grand Duchy of Tuscany was established Florence became its capital.

The Medici dynasty ended in 1737 when Florence fell to the House of Lorraine. During the Napoleonic wars it was occupied by France. In 1814 the Grand Duchy of Tuscany was restored, and the Lorraine Prince Ferdinand III became Grand Duke. In 1861 the Kingdom of Italy was founded and Florence was its capital from 1865 to 1870. Florence is now capital of the province of Florence and of the region of Tuscany.

A major incident in the long history of Florence occurred on Nov. 4–5, 1966, when the Arno flooded, killing 27 persons and causing inestimable damage to the art and architecture of the city.

Florentine iron and steel works produce automobile bodies, machinery, bicycles, and motorcycles. Other manufactures include chemicals, textiles, paper, furniture, soap, and plastics. It is also a market for wines, olive oil, flowers, vegetables, and fruits sent from the neighboring farming area, as well as headquarters of the fashion industry.

Consult Martinelli, Giuseppe, ed., *The World of Renaissance Florence* (1968); McCarthy, Mary, *The Stones of Florence* (new ed., 1976).   ANNA CROGNALE HANSEN
See also RENAISSANCE ARCHITECTURE; RENAISSANCE ART.

FLORENCE, an eastern South Carolina city that was founded in 1853 as a railroad junction. It is the Florence County seat, in the heart of a rich agricultural region, and the home of diversified industries. A branch of the University of South Carolina is located here. The Womack Gardens and Nursery are noted for their displays of azeleas and camellias.

FLORES [*flō′rās*], **JUAN JOSÉ** (1800–64), Ecuadorian soldier and President. Flores served Simón Bolívar bravely as military aide in fighting against the Spanish, but in 1830 led Ecuador, of which he had become chief administrator and military leader, to secede from Gran Colombia, Bolívar's project for a united northern South America. A Conservative, Flores held the presidency of Ecuador from 1830 to 1835 and then, after an arranged rotation with a Liberal, returned to it from 1839 to 1845, when a Liberal revolt ousted him. In 1832 he established Ecuador's claim to the Galápagos Islands. His administrations were moderately successful.

FLORES [*flôr′əs*], island of the Lesser Sundas in the Republic of Indonesia. Flores is situated east of Java between the Flores and the Savu seas. The Florinese are physically a Malay-Melanesian mixture, divided into eight major language groups. Historical and cultural ties link the area to Sulawesi (Celebes) and Java.

Flores was named by a Portuguese navigator in the 16th century and was sporadically subjected to the influence of the Dutch and the Portuguese during the following three centuries. The Netherlands Indies government established power there in the second half of the 19th century, consolidating its administration in the early part of the 20th century. Much of the economic life is on a subsistence basis, with maize, cassava, and vegetables the chief products. Some copra is exported. Area, 5,511 sq mi (14 273 km²).

FLORES, island, belonging to Portugal, in the north Atlantic Ocean. It is the westernmost island of the Azores, in the district of Horta. Flores is volcanic in origin and has a rugged terrain. It rises to a maximum elevation of more than 3,000 ft (914 m). Farming, cattle raising, fishing, and catering to tourists are the main occupations on the island. The major town is Santa Cruz das Flores. A famous naval engagement between Sir Richard Grenville's *Revenge* and several large Spanish vessels occurred near Flores in 1591. Area, about 55 sq mi (142 km²).

Sir Howard Walter Florey.

Camera Press-Pix

FLOREY, SIR HOWARD WALTER (1898–1968), British pathologist who shared the Nobel Prize with A. Fleming and E. Chain in 1945 for their work on penicillin. Born in Australia, Florey took his medical degree at the University of Adelaide and went to Oxford in 1921 as a Rhodes Scholar. After teaching and working at several other institutions, he returned to Oxford in 1935 as professor and head of the Sir William Dunn School of Pathology. There, with Ernest Chain, he studied the ability of the mold extract penicillin to inhibit bacterial growth, a property first discovered by Alexander Fleming in 1928. Florey and Chain succeeded in refining penicillin and demonstrated its therapeutic effects, first in animals, and later in men. Florey was knighted for his work in 1944.

FLORIANÓPOLIS [*flôr-ē-ə-nŏp′ə-lĭs*], city on the Santa Catarina Island in southern Brazil, the capital and chief seaport of the state of Santa Catarina. The city was founded in 1700 by settlers from São Paulo who chose the insular site for protection from hostile Indians on the forested mainland. Later some of the German colonists who settled in the state in the 19th century fled to Florianópolis to escape the Indians. Today, in addition to its political and educational functions, Florianópolis is an important exporting center for mainland agricultural products including coffee, sugar, rice, flour, and hides. It is connected to the mainland by a 2,788-ft (850 m) long bridge. Florianópolis was originally called Destêrro, later Floriano Peixoto, then Santa Catarina, and finally by its present name.

FLORIDA

| Capitol at Tallahassee | Sabal Palmetto | Mockingbird | Orange blossom |

CAPITAL	Tallahassee	**POPULAR NAME**	The Sunshine State
ADMITTED TO UNION	1845	**MOTTO**	In God We Trust
ORDER OF ADMISSION	27th	**FLOWER**	Orange blossom
POPULATION		**TREE**	Sabal palmetto
1970 (9th in Union)	6,789,443	**BIRD**	Mockingbird
1960 (10th in Union)	4,951,560	**SONG**	*The Swanee River* (or
AREA IN SQUARE MILES (22d in Union)	58,560		*Old Folks at Home*)
Land	54,262	**REPRESENTATION IN U.S. CONGRESS**	
Inland water	4,298	Senate	2
ELEVATION IN FEET		House	15
At highest point (in Walton County)	345		
At lowest point	Sea level		

Florida is the southeasternmost state of the United States, largely a peninsula thrusting in a generally southeastly direction into the Atlantic Ocean on the east and the Gulf of Mexico on the west and south. From the St. Marys River in the north, southward to Key West, the state is about 447 mi (715 km) long. From the Atlantic west to the Perdido River it is about 360 mi (576 km) wide. The general coastline extends 1,197 mi (1 915 km)—399 mi (638 km) on the Atlantic and 798 mi (1 277 km) on the Gulf of Mexico.

PHYSICAL GEOGRAPHY

Florida lies entirely within the Coastal Plain, a physiographic region which is, in turn, part of the greater Atlantic Plain of the United States. About two thirds of the state's area, including the peninsula and its coastal islands, is in the Florida section of the Coastal Plain. Except for a small area in the extreme northeast which is part of the Sea Island section of the Coastal Plain, the remaining strip across northern Florida is within the East Gulf Coastal Plain.

Surface Features. Although its average elevation of 100 ft (160 km) above sea level ties Louisiana's as second-lowest of the 50 states, Florida is not without profile.

Lavish hotels preempt the ocean front at Miami Beach.

Workers harvest oranges in a Florida citrus grove. Oranges have been grown commercially in the area since the mid-eighteenth century. (FLORIDA NEWS BUREAU)

An efficient way to begin the study of Florida is to examine the maps accompanying this article. They make it easy to follow the discussion, besides providing a great deal of information about the state. Rivers, surrounding waters, and other major features on the physical map are treated in separate articles, and the same is true of cities, larger towns, and important sites. Examples of related articles follow, grouped under the major headings of the main article.

Physical Geography. The geographical setting of the state is described in NORTH AMERICA and in SOUTHERN STATES. Surrounding waters and physical features receive individual attention in such articles as EVERGLADES; FLORIDA KEYS; TAMPA BAY; SUWANNEE RIVER; ST. JOHNS RIVER; ST. MARYS RIVER; OKEECHOBEE, LAKE; and MEXICO, GULF OF. Details on vegetation and wildlife may be found, for example, in CABBAGE PALM, MANGROVE, CYPRESS, MOCKINGBIRD, ALLIGATOR, and PUMA. An aspect of the climate of the area is treated in HURRICANE.

Economy. The varied resources and industries of Florida may be studied further in a number of articles. The economy of the general region is covered in SOUTHERN STATES. CITRUS FRUITS and TRUCK FARMING discuss many Florida crops. Mineral resources include LIMESTONE, PHOSPHATES, and RUTILE. A facet of the tourist industry is treated in HOTELS AND MOTELS. One of the world's foremost centers of research on rocketry and space exploration is at Cape KENNEDY.

People. Additional information on how and where Floridians live is in city articles such as JACKSONVILLE, TALLAHASSEE, ST. AUGUSTINE, and MIAMI. Statistics on institutions of higher education are furnished in the table in Volume 20. Popular sports and recreations are covered in SKIN DIVING, FISHING, and SWIMMING AND DIVING.

Other phases of Florida life are suggested by the list entitled Places of Interest. A famous tourist center is SILVER SPRINGS. Other famous recreation and tourist centers are mentioned in NATIONAL PARK SYSTEM, UNITED STATES. Resort areas include DAYTONA BEACH, FORT LAUDERDALE, WEST PALM BEACH, and MIAMI BEACH.

Government. Some of the problems with which Florida's governors and legislature have contended are discussed in FLOODS AND FLOOD CONTROL and LABOR LAWS.

History. The history section of the article UNITED STATES provides the background for Florida's history. Details can be filled in from many other articles. Indians of the region are discussed in INDIAN TRIBES, NORTH AMERICAN, in SEMINOLE, and in SEMINOLE WARS. Florida was discovered by Juan PONCE DE LEON and explored by Hernando DE SOTO. Acquisition of Florida by the United States is discussed in LOUISIANA PURCHASE and WEST FLORIDA CONTROVERSY. Florida's participation in the War Between the States is covered in CIVIL WAR, AMERICAN; CONFEDERATE STATES OF AMERICA; and RECONSTRUCTION.

One of the best ways to survey the history of the state, as well as its contributions to national and world culture, is to read biographic entries on the men and women who have been associated with the state. This does not apply only to historical figures such as Andrew JACKSON, who served for a while as military governor of Florida. It also applies to businessmen such as Henry M. FLAGLER and soldiers of World War II such as Joseph W. STILWELL. The books of Marjorie Kinnan RAWLINGS and MacKinlay KANTOR portray many facets of American life.

Basic statistics on agriculture, industry, population, education, and other aspects of the state are included in the Profile and in the body of the text. The growth and development of the state year by year can be followed in the annual supplement to this Encyclopedia and in sources available in the library. The library, moreover, provides books that give extended treatment of Florida's history, of the lives of its important men and women, and of other aspects of the state.

Parts of the north and northwest are hilly, rising in Walton County to 345 ft (105 m), the state's highest elevation. The south-central section is marked by a ridge which rises as high as 300 ft (91.4 m) and marks the division between streams draining to the east and to the west. A noteworthy feature of the land surface in north Florida is the occurrence of sinkholes caused by solution of the underlying porous limestone.

The state's extensive coast line is commonly divided into three unlike parts: the east coast, the southern end of the peninsula, and the west coast. Barrier beaches and lagoons fringe much of the eastern shore, but there are stretches in which the lagoons narrow into marshy swales. The remarkable width and gentleness of slope of the beaches have made them a major recreational asset. The coast line at the end of the peninsula is marked by the Florida Keys. A line of islands formed from a broken coral reef, the Keys extend about 150 mi (240 km) from Miami Beach in a curve southwestward to Key West. Along the west coast, from Cape Romano northward for about 180 mi (288 km), there are straight sandy beaches, many of them barrier islands. From Tampa Bay north and west to Franklin County, beyond Apalachee Bay, the shore line is largely marshy. From Panama City west to Pensacola there are excellent and dazzling white beaches.

Rivers, Lakes, and Springs. The Suwannee River, popularized by song, enters northeastern Florida from its source in the Okefenokee Swamp in Georgia and flows generally southward to the Gulf of Mexico. The 276-mi (442 km) St. Johns River is the state's most important. Rising southwest of Melbourne, it flows north to Jacksonville before turning east to empty into the Atlantic. In the course of its northward flow, eight wide places of sluggish current occur that are designated as lakes. Among other rivers are the Perdido forming the western boundary with Alabama, the Escambia, Blackwater, Choctawhatchee, Chipola, and Apalachicola in the northwest; the Ochlockonee and Aucilla in the central north; the St. Marys in the northeast, forming part of the Georgia boundary; the Withlacoochee, Kissimmee, Oklawaha, and Hillsborough, in central Florida; and the Caloosahatchee, Manatee, Peace, and St. Lucie, in the south.

Central Florida is dotted with a great number of lakes. There are said to be about 30,000 between Gainesville in the north and Lake Okeechobee in the south—some no bigger than pond size, others much larger. Florida lakes, including Lake Okeechobee, account for 4,298 sq mi (11 132 km^2) of inland water surface; many are exceptionally clear, with clean and sandy bottoms. Lake Okeechobee (700 sq mi, or 1 813 km^2) is the third-largest freshwater lake wholly within the United States. Reaching from Lake Okeechobee for over 100 mi (160 km) to the south is the Everglades, a vast, flat, fresh-water marsh covering about 2,500,000 acres (1 012 145 ha) clothed with saw grass and punctuated by occasional hardwood hammocks or clumps of sabal palmettos.

The giant limestone springs of Florida are a source of beauty and recreation. These surface gushings of underground waters are widely scattered, and some have extensive caves that dangerously challenge the skin diver to exploration. The water temperatures range from 69° to 75° F (20°–23° C), with slight seasonal variation. Of the 75 first-magnitude springs in the United States (those having a minimum flow of 100 cu ft, or 2.83 m^3, per second), 17 are in Florida. Two of the largest, Silver Springs and Rainbow Springs, have a combined average daily flow of 974,000,000 gal (257 304 liters).

Climate. Florida spans two climatic regions—its northern sections are subtropical; its southern sections, tropical. "The Sunshine State" is an apt nickname, bestowed because of the high average number of days the sun shines on Florida each year.

There is more regional variation in temperatures in winter than in summer. Average January temperatures, for example, range from 54° F (12° C) at Tallahassee and Pensacola in the northwest, to 60° F (16° C) at Orlando in the central interior, to 69° F (20° C) at Miami Beach in the southeast. July temperatures average between 80°–83° F (27°–28° C) throughout the state. Most of mainland Florida may receive frost, but it is a rare occurrence in the extreme south and has never been reported in the Keys.

The growing season for crops varies according to the sectional variations in climate. Starting at the extreme tropical south there are some winters without frost, and tender plants may be grown the year round. Moving northward the growing season becomes progressively shorter until, from the neighborhood of Gainesville north, the features of the southern subtropical zone are manifest.

Rainfall is quite varied both in annual amount and in seasonal distribution. Annual averages throughout the mainland vary from 50 to 65 in (127–165 cm), the highest occurring in the extreme northwestern counties and at the southern end of the peninsula. On the Florida Keys, annual averages drop to about 40 in (102 cm). On the peninsula rainfall is greater during the summer, a tendency more strongly marked in the south than in the north. The climate of Florida is generally humid. Inland areas with

Porpoises perform at Marineland, a noted tourist attraction south of St. Augustine.

Editorial Photocolor Archives

greater temperature extremes have slightly lower relative humidity, especially in hot weather. Areas removed from the coast also experience a greater nocturnal-diurnal range, with cooler nights.

Tropical storms, or hurricanes—most likely to occur in August, September, and October—produce Florida's principal high winds and are often destructive. The chances of hurricane-force winds occurring in any given year range from 1 in 50 in Jacksonville to 1 in 7 in Key West.

Soils. Florida's soil is chiefly sand. There are, however, some extensive areas of peat and muck that are richly productive with drainage control. Although there are significant differences in the composition of the sandy soils, a factor often of equal economic importance is whether they are well, excessively, or poorly drained.

Mineral Resources. Florida has long been the chief source of phosphate rock in the United States. Considerable amounts of limestone, sand, gravel, fuller's earth, kaolin, peat (used as soil conditioner), and heavy minerals also are found in the state. Although phosphate rock occurs in other parts of Florida, the deposits currently exploited are found in an area just east of Tampa. The peat is found principally in the southeast. The heavy minerals, consisting of ilmenite, rutile, zircon, monazite, staurolite, and garnet are found associated with some beach and dune sands. The other minerals are in deposits scattered about the rest of the state. No coal, very little petroleum, and no natural gas are produced.

Natural Vegetation. Florida's most abundant trees are slash pines. Other common trees are long-leaf pines, oaks, cypresses, mangroves, and cabbage palms. Commercial forest land, covering close to 60% of the state's total land area, is predominantly pine, although in recent years the acreage of hardwood forest has increased. The ground cover ranges from wire grass and saw palmetto in the well-drained lands to saw, switch, and reed grasses and sedges in the low-lying prairies.

There are marked differences in vegetation between the pine flatwoods of the north and the mangrove swamps of the south. In the warm climate of south Florida many trees flourish which are characteristic of the West Indies and other tropical areas. North and west Florida have trees characteristic of the other lower Southern states.

Wildlife. The game species of wildlife in Florida include the black bear, white-tailed deer, gray and fox squirrels, wild turkey, bobwhite quail, mourning dove, and a variety of waterfowl. Deer and turkey have been increasing in the state because of protection and other conservation practices. Florida is the only state east of the Mississippi in which the panther (variously called mountain lion, puma, or cougar) is known to exist. The range of the panther, now protected by law, is chiefly confined to the remote fastnesses of the Everglades. The cottontail rabbit, gray fox, raccoon, bobcat, and opossum are abundant. Alligators, once widespread, were placed under the protection of the Endangered Species Act in 1969, and Florida banned the sale of alligator products. Since mid-century the armadillo has spread over much of the peninsula.

The bird life of Florida, both upland and aquatic, is abundant and diversified. In addition to the native birds and those migrants to which Florida is a winter home, there are many other transient visitors in spring and early fall. Most conspicuous to the casual observer are the great number and variety of wading and aquatic birds. Of these, the egrets, herons, and pelicans are most frequently seen.

The state's fresh-water fishes include the large-mouthed black bass, many varieties of bream, or sunfish, crappie, pickerel, and catfish. Among the salt-water fish esteemed for sport or food are tarpon, kingfish, Spanish mackerel, bluefish, redfish, pompano, snook, mullet, and spotted trout, or weakfish. Offshore fishing for sailfish and marlin is a favorite sport for many anglers.

Zubli—Photo Trends

Wood ibises and spoonbills feed in Florida's Everglades National Park. The Everglades, a fresh-water marsh extending down the peninsula for more than 100 mi (160 km), is one of America's great wildlife preserves.

FLORIDA

TOPOGRAPHY

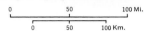

Florida's generously watered, low-lying farmland is ideal for citrus growing and truck farming on a large scale. The state's agriculture is dominated by corporate producers. View is of orange groves at Lake Placid.

ECONOMY

Dramatic population growth has marked the economy of Florida in the years since World War II. This surging inmovement of new residents has been paralleled by a great increase in the vacation business, which remains a primary factor in the economic activity of the state. Early in the 1950's the number of summer vacationers, earlier quite overshadowed by the winter visitors, showed substantial increase. This development continued until today the summer activity exceeds that of the winter. The number employed in trades and services and the proportion of personal income derived from this employment are correspondingly high in Florida, because this work is closely related to tourism.

Manufacturing has notably increased its share in employment and income and it now outranks agriculture, although the latter remains an important component of the economy. Construction, stimulated by the successive waves of new residents and the burgeoning vacation business, has become an important source of employment and income. The aerospace activities centered on Cape Kennedy also contribute significantly to the economy of the state.

Accompanying this growth, per capita income has increased in the state and, although below the national average, has for many years been higher than that of any other southeastern state.

The relative importance of broad divisions of activity in Florida can be indicated by the number of workers employed within each division. Measured in this way, trade stands first, government second, services and manufacturing compete for third and fourth places, construction is fifth, and agriculture, once first, is in sixth place.

Agriculture. Less than 5% of the civilian personal income of Floridians is derived from agricultural activities, and agriculture furnishes close to the same proportion of the total employment. In keeping with the national trend, there is a tendency for livestock and livestock products to form an increasing percentage of cash receipts from sales of all farm commodities. Nevertheless, the division of receipts is only about one-quarter for livestock and livestock products, and about three-quarters from all crops.

Oranges and grapefruit account for about 40% of the value of receipts from crops. Truck crops, including tomatoes, potatoes, sweet corn, snap beans, celery, and watermelons, are next in order of value. Field crops, among which tobacco, sugar cane, peanuts, and corn are prominent, are third. Flowers and horticultural specialties grown for national markets are a significant part of agricultural production.

Among livestock and livestock products, cattle and calves bring cash receipts which are about equal to those from dairy products (principally whole milk); eggs come next, followed by hogs.

Florida farms show a persistent slow decline in number, yet an increase in average size. Subsistence farms are dropping out, and there is a strong movement to large acreages and large aggregations of capital, especially in citrus, dairy, beef cattle, and truck crop production. This movement is reinforced by a tendency among citrus-concentrate and full-strength-juice processors to purchase citrus groves and thus create larger grove units with fewer owners. Producers of beef cattle have extensively replaced rough pasturage with improved pasturage and are improving the quality of their cattle. Although Florida's rainfall is abundant, its uneven seasonal distribution has brought about the increased practice of irrigation for truck crop and citrus growing throughout the state.

One of the most dramatic features of Florida agriculture is the necessity for precise timing in the marketing of its winter truck crops. Much of the production is at high cost and is planned to precede the marketing of similar crops from other states. If frost, drought, or flood greatly disturb this timing, the losses may be severe. Another dramatic element is in the production of truck crops in the Everglades' muck lands. Here as many as three crops from the same soil can be harvested in a favorable season. But the hazards of frost, flood, and drought are ever-present.

Fisheries. Employment in commercial fishing in Florida varies from year to year as well as seasonally. As a source of personal income, it typically accounts for less than 1% for the state as a whole, but in some areas it is an important fraction of economic activity. In terms of quantity, Florida usually ranks among the first 10 states in sea-food production, but higher in the value of the catch. The value of the shrimp landing far exceeds that of any finfish or other shellfish taken, such as blue crab, stone crab, oyster, and spiny lobster. Among the food fish, mullet and red snapper yield the greatest dollar receipts from sales. Mullet, spotted weakfish, bluefish, grouper, king mackerel, pompano, redfish, red snapper, and Spanish mackerel are the other principal food fish taken. Menhaden, processed to yield meal and fish oil, is an important nonfood fish. The once-active sponge fisheries have not recovered from the crippling disease that struck the beds in 1940, although some sponges are being harvested by boats out of Tarpon Springs.

In Florida the subject of fisheries cannot be dismissed without mention of sport fishing. Although it is an adjunct of the recreation and vacation business, the number of people directly or indirectly engaged in serving this industry, and the amount of capital investment in boats and the number of facilities for hire are impressive. Charter boats and party boats ply the waters from almost every suitable harbor, and marinas catering to boat-owners dot the Florida coast and waterways. The freshwater sport fishing is also a significant source of livelihood to guides and operators of fishing camps.

Forestry and Forest Products. During the 1960's there was a slight decline in forest acreage in Florida. The average volume of timber per acre, however, increased, so the total volume of growing-stock timber remains essentially unchanged. Cypress and slash pine continue to dominate the industry.

Of the approximately 200,000 acres of timber land lost since 1959, 58% went to expanding urban areas and 42% to citrus groves and pastures. Logging accounts for very little of the total tree removal in Florida, and during the late 1960's net growth exceeded removals by more than 50%.

Of the commercial forests in the state 32% (5,200,000 acres) is owned by the forest industry; 13% (2,100,000 acres) is publicly owned; and 55% (8,900,000 acres) is owned by farmers and assorted individuals and corporations.

Turpentine and rosin (naval stores), once a major activity, are now minor in the Florida economy. Gum from living pine trees, the chief source of production before World War II, has been largely replaced by other cheaper sources, including pitch-soaked stumps and by-products of the sulfate pulp-making process.

Manufacturing. Employment in manufacturing amounts to about 16% of nonagricultural employment and is the source of the same percentage of personal income paid to civilians for participation in production.

In the decade between 1960 and 1970, although manufacturing employment showed little change in the nation as a whole, it increased 59.2% in Florida. Although the rate of manufacturing growth has, since mid-century, surpassed that in any other Southern state, manufacturing employment and payrolls are still small in absolute amounts. Therefore, comparison of percentage increases with those of other states can be very misleading.

Food and kindred products are the most important single manufacturing industry group in Florida, followed

A prize bull being exhibited at an agricultural fair. Florida farmers are eager to improve the quality of their beef cattle. (THE TAMPA TIMES)

by chemicals and chemical products, paper and allied products, electrical machinery, transportation equipment, and fabricated metals. The relative importance of food products, however, is declining in favor of other manufacturing. One stimulus to this change is the increasing production of mobile homes in Florida. During the latter half of the 1960's only stone, clay, and glass products showed a decline in employment.

Mineral Production. Mineral production in the state is valued at about $300,000,000 annually. Florida has led the nation in phosphate production since the 1890's, and this industry alone accounts for 50% of the state's mineral value. More than 60% of the phosphate produced in Florida goes into fertilizer and stock feed.

Florida also quarries limestone, produces cement, and is a significant commercial producer of fuller's earth, kaolin, peat, and a group of heavy minerals, including ilmenite, rutile, (sources of titanium), zircon, monazite, staurolite, and garnet.

Limestone, cement, and other materials used in construction are chiefly marketed in Florida. The greater part of fuller's earth, kaolin, titanium, and zirconium

Children romping on a sandy beach. In many people's minds, Florida is synonymous with sun, sand, and sea. (FLORIDA NEWS BUREAU)

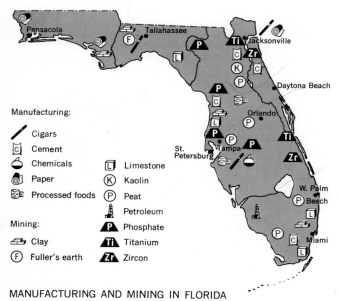

Manufacturing:

✐	Cigars
Ⓒ	Cement
◠	Chemicals
◓	Paper
▤	Processed foods

Mining:

◅	Clay
Ⓕ	Fuller's earth

Ⓛ	Limestone
Ⓚ	Kaolin
Ⓟ	Peat
⛏	Petroleum
◣P	Phosphate
◣Ti	Titanium
◣Zr	Zircon

MANUFACTURING AND MINING IN FLORIDA

concentrates are shipped out of the state for further processing and consumption.

For many years the sole producing oil field in Florida was in Collier County in the southwest, producing 25,000 to 40,000 barrels monthly. In 1970 a major strike was made at Jay (north of Pensacola). A year later, three wells at Jay were producing 180,000 barrels a month.

Power. Most of the electric energy produced and distributed in Florida is generated by steam plants fired by oil or natural gas; only about 1% by hydroelectric sources. Production and distribution are provided by four private utility companies and a large number of municipally owned and operated systems, including those of some large cities such as Jacksonville, Tampa, and Orlando. Fifteen co-operatives have contributed to the develop-

ment of rural electrification. The installed generating capacity totals about 11,000,000 kw., of which some 75% is provided by private utility companies and most of the rest by municipal systems, although there are a few co-operative groups. In terms of energy produced (kw-hr) the share of private utilities is somewhat more than 80%.

Electric power has been able to meet the growth requirements of the state, showing an enormous gain in generating capacity. The proportion of the total energy sold for residential use has increased, although commercial consumption still accounts for 56%.

Trade, Commerce, and Other Business. This broad category accounts for well over half of total employment and income in Florida. Retail and wholesale trades comprise the largest component and provide about 26% of total employment and 20% of personal income. These two trades, when combined with service trades and professions, generate 45% of total employment and a somewhat smaller proportion of personal income. The unusual share of trades and services in the Florida economy is largely attributable to the great volume of tourism to which it is closely geared. In addition to hotels, motels, restaurants, and amusement and recreation services, practically every service or trade activity is related to tourism. With more than 23,000,000 visitors a year, spending some $6,000,000,000 in the state, tourism is by far Florida's leading industry.

Employment in construction provides about 7.5% of total employment; transportation, communication, and public utilities, around 7%; finance, insurance, and real estate about 6%.

Transportation and Communication. There are 87,000 mi. of roads and highways in Florida, 47,000 of which are paved. Major arterial highways are Interstates 4, 10, 75, and 95 and U. S. Highways 1, 17, 19, 27, 41, 90, 301, and 441. The Florida Turnpike extends from Wildwood to Miami and is a toll facility. Approximately 4,000,000 motor vehicles are registered in Florida.

The Seaboard Coast Line, Florida East Coast, Louisville and Nashville, and Southern are the major railroads

The historic take-off from the Kennedy Space Center of Apollo 11, the first manned lunar landing mission, on July 16, 1969.   (NASA)

Phosphate stored beneath huge conveyor belts. Florida produces some 75% of the total U.S. output of this mineral   (FLORIDA NEWS BUREAU)

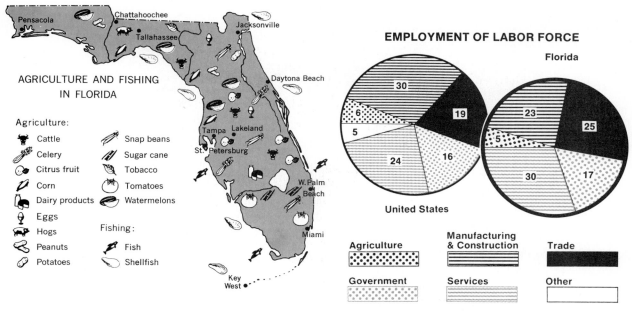

AGRICULTURE AND FISHING
IN FLORIDA

Agriculture:

- Cattle
- Celery
- Citrus fruit
- Corn
- Dairy products
- Eggs
- Hogs
- Peanuts
- Potatoes
- Snap beans
- Sugar cane
- Tobacco
- Tomatoes
- Watermelons

Fishing:
- Fish
- Shellfish

EMPLOYMENT OF LABOR FORCE

Florida

United States

| Agriculture | Manufacturing & Construction | Trade |
| Government | Services | Other |

of Florida. Of these the Seaboard Coast Line has the greatest trackage and handles most of the passenger traffic. Its principal lines into the peninsula are part of the Amtrak system. Total rail mileage is 4,348 mi.

Florida has 20 commercial airports (four of which are international), besides 110 public and 200 private airfields of smaller size. There are also many heliports, especially in metropolitan areas. Between 30 and 40 regularly scheduled air carriers serve the state. Several Florida cities, such as Miami and Jacksonville, have outstanding air terminals, and Tampa's $80,000,000 facility, completed in 1971, is among the most modern terminals in the world.

Major bus lines, as well as several local lines, operate within the state. A large number of truck freight carriers also serve the area.

Of the numerous rivers only the St. Johns River and the Okeechobee Waterway have much freight traffic.

The use of these and other waterways for boating is extensive.

Of Florida's many ports, seven (Palm Beach, Tampa, Miami, Jacksonville, Pensacola, Port Everglades, and Panama City) account for the principal tonnage. Other ports of lesser trade volume are Boca Grande, Fernandina Beach, Port St. Joe, and Key West. Although the tonnage moving in foreign trade has shown a steady increase, the domestic volume remains considerably greater. The export of greatest value and volume consists of phosphate fertilizers. The greater part of all port tonnage is bulk cargo, which is lower in value than general cargo.

In 1970 Florida had 54 daily newspapers, 11 semiweeklies, and about 125 weeklies. There are numerous magazines published in the state. Radio stations total 264 (75 of which are FM); there are 21 commercial TV stations and 9 educational channels, reaching some 95% of the state's population.

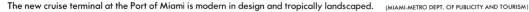

The new cruise terminal at the Port of Miami is modern in design and tropically landscaped. (MIAMI-METRO DEPT. OF PUBLICITY AND TOURISM)

Florida Times-Union and Jacksonville Journal

The skyline, on St. Johns River, of Jacksonville, now Florida's largest city.

PEOPLE

During the decade 1960 to 1970 Florida experienced a remarkable population growth, moving from 4,951,560 to 6,789,443, a gain of 37.1%. Only Nevada had a greater percentage rate of increase (71.3%) and only California gained more people. But the frantic growth rate of 1950–1960 (78.7%) has slowed. Florida is now the 9th largest state in population, having climbed from 10th in 1960, and 20th in 1950.

Population Distribution. The distribution of Florida's 1960–70 population gain between urban and rural residents was in accord with past trends. Approximately 75% of the population is urban, but only 2% of the total population lives on farms. About 70% of the population lives in 10 of the 67 counties, and it is estimated that by 1990 Florida will have 11 completely urban counties, containing 90% of the people. The state's major population concentrations are the lower southeast coast (about 2,000,000), the Tampa Bay region (about 1,000,000), the Jacksonville area (about 750,000), and the Orlando region (about 750,000).

Chief Cities. Seven Florida cities had populations of over 100,000 in 1970: Jacksonville, 528,865; Miami, 334,859; Tampa, 277,767; St. Petersburg, 216,232; Ft. Lauderdale, 139,590; Hollywood, 106,873; and Hialeah, 102,297. Orlando, with 99,006, almost made the 100,000 class, and six other cities exceeded 50,000. Tallahassee, the capital, had a population of 71,897.

These figures are somewhat misleading. Jacksonville, the state's largest city, consolidated with Duval County in 1968, and the population reflects this merger. Tampa, in a metropolitan county of 490,265, voted down a consolidation proposal in 1970 and appears to be half the size of Jacksonville. Miami's metropolitan area population is in excess of 1,250,000, most of which resides in satellite cities.

Population Composition. Continuing a trend prevailing since 1900, the proportion of Negro residents declined, constituting 17% of Florida's population in 1970. Of other nonwhite races, accounting for 0.1% of the 1970 population, the largest single component was Indian.

Religion. By virtue of early Spanish settlement the Roman Catholic Church is the oldest denomination in the state. The Methodist and Baptist churches have the largest memberships among the Protestant denominations in Florida. In Miami and adjacent areas there are large Jewish congregations.

Dennis Hallinan—FPG

The inlets, rivers, and man-made canals that thread Fort Lauderdale provide miles of navigable waterways and convenient berthing for flotillas of pleasure boats.

FLORIDA

COUNTIES

Alachua, 104,764 D 2
Baker, 9,242 D 1
Bay, 75,283 C 6
Bradford, 14,625 D 2
Brevard, 230,006 F 3
Broward, 620,100 F 5
Calhoun, 7,624 D 6
Charlotte, 27,559 E 5
Citrus, 19,196 D 3
Clay, 32,059 E 2
Collier, 38,040 E 5
Columbia, 25,250 D 1
Dade, 1,267,792 F 6
De Soto, 13,060 E 4
Dixie, 5,480 C 2
Duval, 528,865 E 1
Escambia, 205,334 B 6
Flagler, 4,454 E 2
Franklin, 7,065 B 2
Gadsden, 39,184 B 1
Gilchrist, 3,551 D 2
Glades, 3,669 E 5
Gulf, 10,096 D 7
Hamilton, 7,787 D 1
Hardee, 14,889 E 4
Hendry, 11,859 E 5
Hernando, 17,004 D 3
Highlands, 29,507 E 4
Hillsborough, 490,265 D 4
Holmes, 10,720 C 5
Indian River, 35,992 F 4
Jackson, 34,434 D 5
Jefferson, 8,778 C 1
Lafayette, 2,892 C 2
Lake, 69,305 E 3
Lee, 105,216 E 5
Leon, 103,047 B 1
Levy, 12,756 D 2
Liberty, 3,379 B 1
Madison, 13,481 C 1
Manatee, 97,115 D 4
Marion, 69,030 D 2
Martin, 28,035 F 4
Monroe, 52,586 E 7
Nassau, 20,626 E 1
Okaloosa, 88,187 C 6
Okeechobee, 11,233 F 4
Orange, 344,311 E 3
Osceola, 25,267 E 3
Palm Beach, 348,753 F 5
Pasco, 75,955 D 3
Pinellas, 522,329 D 4
Polk, 227,222 E 4
Putnam, 36,290 E 2
Saint Johns, 30,727 E 2
Saint Lucie, 50,836 F 4
Santa Rosa, 37,741 B 6
Sarasota, 120,413 D 4
Seminole, 83,692 E 3
Sumter, 14,839 D 3
Suwannee, 15,559 C 1
Taylor, 13,641 C 1
Union, 8,112 D 1
Volusia, 169,487 E 2
Wakulla, 6,308 B 1
Walton, 16,087 C 6
Washington, 11,453 C 6

CITIES and TOWNS

Alachua, 2,252 D 2
Alford, 402 D 6
Altamonte Springs■, 4,391 E 3
Altha, 423 A 1
Altoona, 800 E 3
Alturas, 468 E 4
Alva, 900 E 5
Anna Maria, 1,137 D 4
Anthony, 500 D 2
Apalachicola⊙, 3,102 A 2
Apollo Beach, 1,042 C 3
Apopka, 4,045 E 3
Arcadia⊙, 5,658 E 4
Archer, 898 D 2
Astatula, 388 E 3
Astor, 300 E 2
Atlantic Beach, 7,106 E 1
Atlantis■, 425 F 5
Auburndale, 5,386 E 3
Avon Park, 6,712 E 4
Azalea Park■, 7,367 E 3
Babson Park, 950 E 4
Bagdad, 850 B 6
Baker, 500 C 5
Baldwin, 1,408 E 1
Bal Harbour, 2,038 C 4
Bartow⊙, 12,891 E 4
Basinger, 300 F 4
Bay Harbour Islands, 4,619 B 4
Bay Pines, 1,100 B 3
Bayshore Gardens■, 9,255 D 4
Bayview■, 696 C 6
Beacon Squier■, 2,927 D 3
Bee Ridge, 2,100 D 4
Belleair, 2,962 B 2
Belleair Beach, 952 B 2
Belleair Bluffs, 1,910 B 3
Belle Glade, 15,949 F 5
Belle Glade Camp, 1,892 F 5
Belle Isle, 2,705 E 3
Belleview, 916 D 2
Biscayne Park, 2,717 B 4
Bithlo, 684 E 3
Blountstown⊙, 2,384 A 1
Boca Grande, 600 D 5
Boca Raton, 28,506 F 5
Bokeelia, 750 D 5
Bonifay⊙, 2,068 C 5
Bonita Springs, 1,932 E 5
Bostwick, 500 E 2
Bowling Green, 1,357 E 4
Boynton Beach, 18,115 F 5
Bradenton⊙, 21,040 D 4
Bradenton Beach, 1,370 D 4
Bradley, 1,276 D 4
Brandon, 12,749 D 4
Branford, 820 D 2
Briny Breezes, 481 G 5
Bristol⊙, 626 B 1
Broadview Park-Rock Hill■, 6,049 B 4
Bronson⊙, 698 D 2
Brooker, 340 D 2
Brooksville⊙, 4,060 D 3
Browardale■, 17,444 B 4
Brownsville, 20,924 B 6
Bryant, 400 F 5
Buena Vista■, 3,407 D 3
Bunche Park, 5,773 B 4
Bunnell⊙, 1,687 E 2
Bushnell⊙, 700 D 3
Callahan, 772 E 1
Callaway, 3,240 D 6
Campbellton, 304 D 5
Canal Point, 900 F 5
Candler, 500 E 2
Cantonment, 3,241 B 6
Cape Canaveral, 4,258 F 3
Cape Coral, 10,193 E 5
Carol City, 27,361 B 4
Carrabelle, 1,044 B 2
Carver Ranch Estates■, 5,515 B 4
Caryville, 724 C 6
Cassadaga, 250 E 3
Casselberry, 9,438 E 3
Cedar Grove, 689 D 6
Cedar Hammock-Bradenton South■, 10,820 D 4
Cedar Key, 714 C 2
Center Hill, 371 D 3
Century, 2,679 B 5
Charlotte Harbor, 990 E 5
Chattahoochee, 7,944 B 1
Cherry Lake Farms, 400 C 1
Chiefland, 1,965 D 2
Chipley⊙, 3,347 D 6
Christmas, 800 E 3
Cinco Bayou, 362 B 6
Citra, 500 D 2
City Point, 350 F 3
Clarksville, 250 D 6
Clearwater⊙, 52,074 B 2
Clermont, 3,661 E 3
Clewiston, 3,896 E 5
Cocoa, 16,110 F 3
Cocoa Beach, 9,952 F 3
Coconut Creek, 1,359 F 5
Coleman, 614 D 3
Collier Manor-Cresthaven■, 7,202 F 5
Colonial Hills■, 2,193 D 3
Combee Settlement■, 4,963 E 3
Concord, 300 B 1
Conway■, 8,642 E 3
Cooper City, 2,535 F 5
Copeland, 500 E 6
Coral Cove, 1,520 D 4
Coral Gables, 42,494 B 5
Coral Springs■, 1,489 F 5
Cornwell, 700 E 4
Cortez, 600 D 4
Cottagehill, 500 B 6
Cottondale, 765 D 6
Country Estates■, 1,950 D 3
Crawfordville⊙, 750 B 1
Crescent City, 1,734 E 2
Crestview⊙, 7,952 C 6
Cross City⊙, 2,268 C 2
Crystal River, 1,696 D 3
Crystal Springs, 300 D 3
Cutler Ridge, 17,441 F 6
Cypress, 266 A 1
Cypress Gardens, 3,757 E 3
Cypress Quarters, 1,310 F 4
Dade City⊙, 4,241 D 3
Dania, 9,013 B 4
Davenport, 828 E 3
Davie, 4,977 B 4
Daytona Beach, 45,327 F 2
Daytona Beach Shores, 768 F 2
De Bary, 3,154 E 3
Deerfield Beach, 17,130 F 5
De Funiak Springs⊙, 4,966 C 6
De Land⊙, 11,641 E 2
De Leon Springs, 1,134 E 2
Delray Beach, 19,366 F 5
Deltona, 4,868 E 3
De Soto City, 250 E 4
Destin, 1,536 C 6
Doctors Inlet, 800 E 1
Dover, 2,094 D 4
Dundee, 1,660 E 3
Dunedin, 17,639 B 2
Dunnellon, 1,146 D 2
Eagle Lake, 1,373 E 4
Earleton, 350 D 2
East Auburndale■, 2,621 E 3
East Lake-Orient Park, 5,697 C 2
East Naples, 6,152 E 5
East Palatka, 1,446 E 2
Eastpoint, 1,188 B 2
East Winter Haven■, 1,148 E 3
Eatonville■, 2,024 E 3
Edgewater, 3,348 F 3
Edgewood, 392 E 3
Egypt Lake, 7,556 C 2
Elfers, 500 D 3
Ellenton■, 1,421 D 4
Eloise■, 1,504 E 4
El Portal, 2,068 B 4
El Ranchero Village-Golf Lake Estates■, 1,859 D 4
Englewood, 5,182 D 5
Ensley, 2,400 B 6
Espanola, 300 E 2
Estero, 950 E 5
Eustis, 6,722 E 3
Everglades City, 462 E 6
Fairbanks, 380 D 2
Fairvilla, 950 E 3
Fellsmere, 813 F 4
Fernandina Beach⊙, 6,955 E 1
Fern Crest Village, 1,009 B 4
Five Points■, 1,214 D 1
Flagler Beach, 1,042 E 2
Florahome, 400 E 2
Floral City, 975 D 3
Florida City, 5,133 F 6
Florida Ridge■, 1,338 F 4
Floridatown, 297 B 6
Foley, 500 C 1
Forest Hills■, 1,215 D 3
Fort Denaud, 300 E 5
Fort Drum, 100 F 4
Fort Green, 300 E 4
Fort Lauderdale⊙, 139,590 C 4
Fort Lauderdale-Hollywood, ‡620,100 C 4
Fort McCoy, 900 E 2
Fort Meade, 4,374 E 4
Fort Myers⊙, 27,351 E 5
Fort Myers Beach, 4,305 E 5
Fort Myers Villas-Pine Manor■, 3,408 E 5
Fort Ogden, 700 E 4
Fort Pierce⊙, 29,721 F 4
Fort Walton Beach, 19,994 C 6
Fort White, 365 D 2
Fountain, 650 D 6
Freeport, 950 C 6
Frink, 275 D 6
Frostproof, 2,814 E 4
Fruitland Park, 1,359 D 3
Fruitville, 1,531 D 4
Gainesville⊙, 64,510 D 2
Geneva, 950 E 3
Georgetown, 687 E 2
Gibsonton, 1,900 C 3
Gifford, 5,772 F 4
Glen Saint Mary, 357 D 1
Glenwood, 400 E 2
Golden Beach, 849 C 4
Golden Gate, 1,410 E 5
Gomez, 400 F 4
Gonzalez, 750 B 6
Goodland, 500 E 6
Goulding, 500 B 6
Goulds, 6,690 F 6
Graceville, 2,560 D 5
Grand Ridge, 512 A 1
Grant, 500 F 4
Greenacres City, 1,731 F 5
Green Cove Springs⊙, 3,857 E 2
Greensboro, 716 B 1
Greenville, 1,141 C 1
Greenwood, 515 A 1
Gretna, 883 B 1
Grove City, 1,252 D 5
Groveland, 1,928 E 3
Gulf Breeze, 4,190 B 6
Gulf Gate Estates■, 5,874 D 4
Gulf Hammock, 300 D 2
Gulf Harbors, 1,177 D 3
Gulfport, 9,730 B 3
Gulf Stream, 408 F 5
Haines City, 8,956 E 3
Hallandale, 23,849 B 4
Hampton, 386 D 2
Harlem, 2,006 F 5
Hastings, 320 E 2
Havana, 2,022 B 1
Haverhill■, 1,034 F 5
Hawthorne, 1,126 D 2
Hernando, 524 D 3
Hialeah, 102,297 B 4
Hialeah Gardens, 492 B 4
Highland City, 900 E 4
High Point, 800 B 3
High Springs, 2,787 D 2
Hiland Park, 3,691 C 6
Hilliard, 1,205 E 1
Hillsboro Beach, 713 F 5
Hobe Sound, 2,029 F 4
Holden Heights■, 6,206 E 3
Holiday Gardens■, 2,132 D 3
Holiday Hills■, 1,657 D 3
Hollister, 500 E 2
Holly Hill, 8,191 E 2
Hollywood, 106,873 B 4
Hollywood Ridge Farms, 302 B 4
Holmes Beach, 2,699 D 4
Holt, 850 C 6
Homestead, 13,674 F 6
Homosassa, 850 D 3
Homosassa Springs, 550 D 3
Hosford, 975 B 1
Howey In The Hills, 466 E 3
Hudson, 2,278 D 3
Hurlburt■, 2,155 C 6
Hypoluxo, 336 F 5
Immokalee, 3,764 E 5
Indialantic, 2,685 F 3
Indian Harbour Beach, 5,371 F 3
Indian Rocks Beach, 2,666 B 3
Indian Rocks Beach South Shore, 791 B 3
Indiantown, 2,283 F 4
Inglis, 449 D 2
Interlachen, 478 E 2
Inverness⊙, 2,299 D 3
Islamorada, 1,251 F 7
Jacksonville⊙, 528,865 E 1
Jacksonville, ‡528,865 E 1
Jacksonville Beach, 13,326 D 1
Jan Phyl■, 1,340 E 4
Jasmine Estates■, 2,967 D 3
Jasper⊙, 2,221 D 1
Jay, 646 B 5
Jennings, 582 C 1
Jensen Beach, 975 F 4
June Park, 3,090 F 3
Juno Beach, 747 F 5
Jupiter, 3,136 F 5
Jupiter Inlet Beach Colony■, 396 F 5
Jupiter Island, 295 F 4
Kathleen, 900 D 3
Kendall, 35,497 B 5
Kenneth City, 3,862 B 3
Kensington Park■, 3,138 D 4
Key Biscayne, 4,563 B 5
Key Colony Beach, 371 F 7
Key Largo, 2,866 F 6
Keystone Heights, 800 E 2
Key West⊙, 27,563 E 7
Kinard, 450 D 6
Kissimmee⊙, 7,119 E 3
La Belle⊙, 1,823 E 5
Lacoochee, 1,380 D 3
La Crosse, 365 D 2
Lady Lake, 382 E 3
Lake Alfred, 2,847 E 3
Lake Butler⊙, 1,598 D 1
Lake Carroll, 5,577 C 2
Lake City⊙, 10,575 D 1
Lake Clarke Shores■, 2,328 F 5
Lake Como, 340 E 2
Lake Forest■, 5,216 B 4
Lake Hamilton■, 836 E 3
Lake Harbor, 300 F 5
Lake Helen, 1,303 E 3
Lake Holloway■, 6,227 E 3
Lake Jem, 314 E 3
Lakeland, 41,550 D 3
Lake Magdalene, 9,266 D 3
Lake Mary, 900 E 3
Lake Monroe, 500 E 3
Lake Park, 6,993 F 5
Lake Placid, 656 E 4
Lakeport, 375 E 5
Lake Ship Heights■, 1,114 E 4
Lake Wales, 8,240 E 4
Lakewood, 525 C 5
Lake Worth, 23,714 G 5
Lamont, 500 C 1
Land O'Lakes, 900 D 3
Lantana, 7,126 F 5
Largo, 22,031 B 3
Lauderdale-by-the-Sea, 2,879 C 3
Lauderdale Lakes, 10,577 B 4
Lauderhill, 8,465 B 4
Laurel Hill, 418 C 5
Laurel-Nokomis, 3,238 D 4
Lawtey, 636 D 1
Leesburg, 11,869 E 3
Lehigh Acres, 4,394 E 5
Leisure City, 2,900 F 6
Leto, 8,458 C 2
Lighthouse Point, 9,071 F 5
Live Oak⊙, 6,830 D 1
Lockhart■, 5,809 E 3
Longboat Key, 2,850 D 4
Longwood, 3,203 E 3
Lorida, 950 E 4
Loughman, 950 E 3
Lowell, 350 D 2
Loxahatchee, 950 F 5
Lutz, 950 D 3
Lynn Haven, 4,044 C 6
Macclenny⊙, 2,733 D 1
Madeira Beach, 4,158 B 3
Madison⊙, 3,737 C 1
Maitland, 7,157 E 3
Malabar, 634 F 3
Malone, 667 A 1
Mango, 950 D 4
Mangonia Park■, 827 F 5
Marathon, 4,397 E 7
Marco, 900 E 6
Margate, 8,867 F 5
Marianna⊙, 6,741 A 1
Marineland, 13 E 2
Mary Esther, 3,192 B 6
Masaryktown, 389 D 3
Mascotte, 966 E 3
Mayo⊙, 793 C 1
McDavid, 500 B 5
McIntosh, 287 D 2
Medley, 351 B 4
Melbourne, 40,236 F 3
Melbourne Beach, 2,262 F 3
Melbourne Village■, 597 F 3
Melrose, 950 D 2
Melrose Park, 6,111 B 4
Memphis, 3,207 D 4
Merritt Island, 29,233 F 3
Mexico Beach, 588 D 6
Miami⊙, 334,859 B 5
Miami, ‡1,267,792 B 5
Miami Beach, 87,072 C 5
Miami Lakes, 3,500 B 4
Miami Shores, 9,425 B 4
Miami Springs, 13,279 B 5
Micanopy, 759 D 2
Micco, 400 F 4
Miccosukee, 275 B 1
Middleburg, 950 E 1
Midway, 900 B 1
Midway-Canaan■, 2,060 E 3
Milligan, 950 C 6
Milton⊙, 5,360 B 6
Mims, 8,309 F 3
Minneola, 878 E 3
Miramar, 23,973 B 4
Molino, 850 B 6
Monticello⊙, 2,473 C 1
Montverde, 308 E 3
Moore Haven⊙, 974 E 5
Mount Dora, 4,543 E 3

⊙ County seat. ‡ Population of metropolitan area. ■ Name not shown on map.

All figures available from 1970 final census are supplemented by local official estimates.

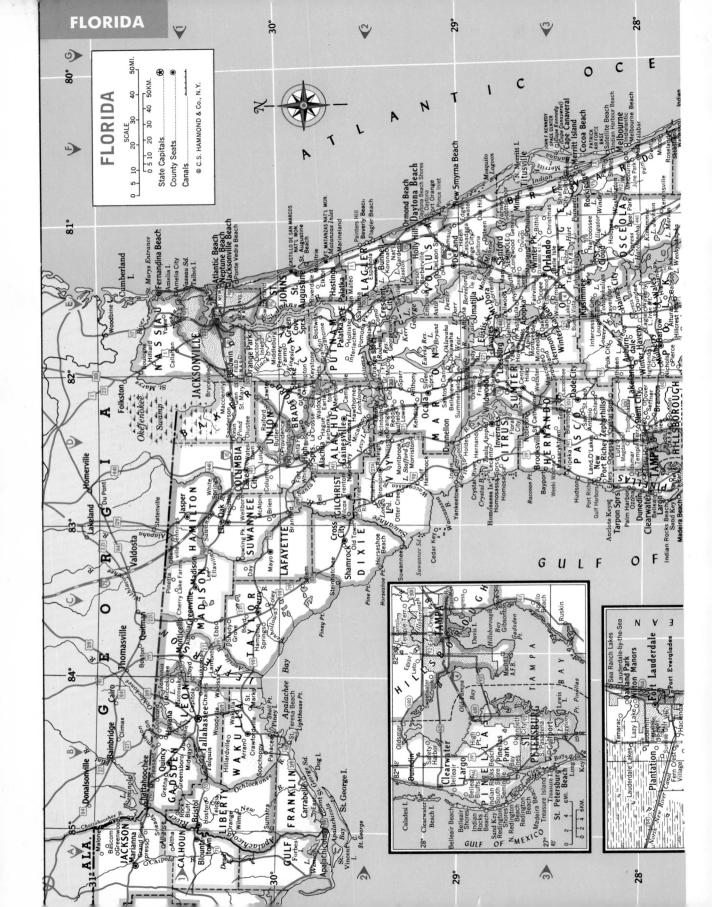

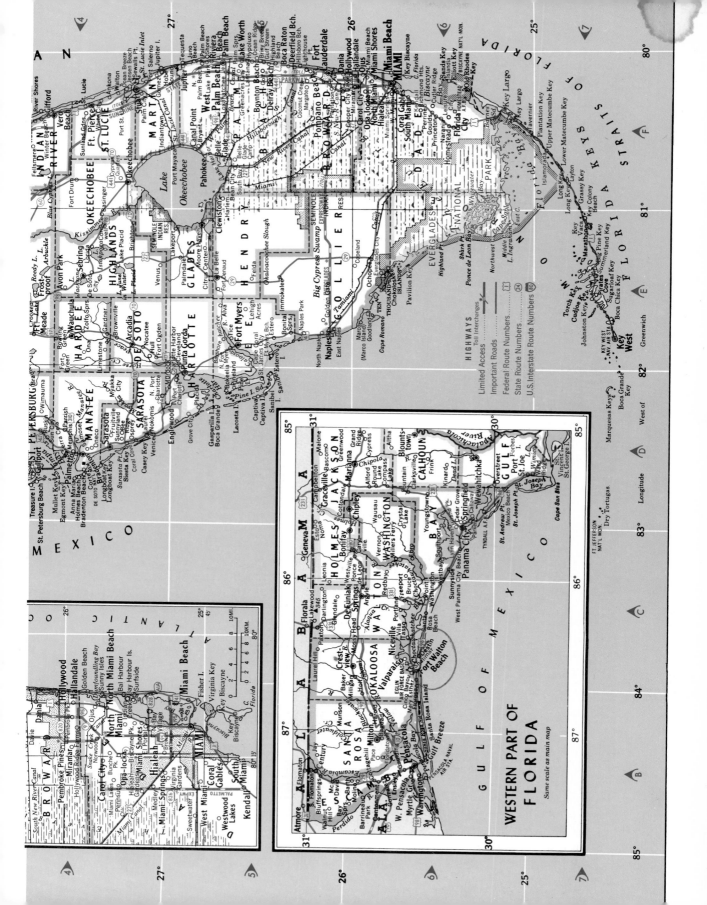

FLORIDA

The buildings of the old Tampa Bay Hotel, with their Moorish-style minarets, now house part of the University of Tampa. (A. DEVANEY, INC.)

Education. Though efforts to provide public schools were made as early as 1828, Florida's present system of public schools dates from the Constitution of 1868 and the school law of 1869. Attendance was made compulsory on a statewide basis in 1919, and today children of ages 7 through 15 are obliged to attend. The public education system was greatly improved by the establishment in 1947 of the Minimum Foundation Program, which strengthened the schools by a formula of state aid according to local "capacity" and assured a minimum 180-day term to children in all counties. All public schools are directed and controlled at the county level by a county school board. Textbooks are provided free to all students in grades 1–12, and school-bus service is available to all rural children residing two miles or more from the school. Many counties have programs for handicapped children, and a few have programs for the exceptionally advanced children.

In addition to the public school system, Florida supports the Florida State School for the Deaf and Blind

The chapel of Florida Southern College at Lakeland. The institution is old (estab., 1885), but its spirit is young. (FLORIDA STATE NEWS BUREAU)

at St. Augustine, 23 vocational-technical centers, 12 technical centers located in junior colleges, 28 junior colleges, and nine universities. There are also six private junior colleges and 21 private universities and colleges. Some 99% of Florida's population is within commuting distance of a state-supported institution of higher education.

Libraries and Museums. The University of Florida, with approximately 1,500,000 volumes, has the largest library in the state—public or university. The Florida State University library added its 1,000,000th volume early in 1971. The largest public libraries in Florida and their approximate holdings are: Miami-Dade Public Library (700,000), Jacksonville Public Library (400,000), Tampa Public Library (300,000), Albertson Public Library in Orlando (300,000), and St. Petersburg Public Library (250,000). There are a total of 98 public libraries in Florida and 26 bookmobile services.

The Florida State Museum in Gainesville, a component of the University of Florida, features outstanding archeological and biological exhibits. Art museums include the John and Mabel Ringling Art Museum in Sarasota, the Norton Art Gallery in West Palm Beach, and the Dade County Art Museum in Miami. The Beal-Maltbie Shell Museum at Rollins College has a large collection of shells; the Florida Citrus Museum at Winter Haven contains exhibits pertaining to the cultivation of citrus fruit. The Museum of the American Circus and the Circus Hall of Fame are in Sarasota.

The modern Coliseum at Jacksonville, pleasantly set in landscaped surroundings, has a seating capacity of 12,000 (FLORIDA TIMES UNION)

Cultural Life and Recreation. Several Florida cities, among them Orlando, Miami, Tampa-St. Petersburg, and Jacksonville have symphony orchestras of varying sizes. Visiting orchestras, chamber music groups, and vocalists are presented during the winter by civic music groups or universities in many communities. Little theater groups have flourished since the 1920's, and professional theaters are now established in Miami, Daytona Beach, Orlando, Sarasota, and Palm Beach. Among noteworthy gardens open to the public without charge are the Killearn Gardens State Park near Tallahassee, the Fairchild Tropical Garden in Coconut Grove, and the Bush Gardens in Tampa.

The cloisters and court of John and Mable Ringling museum of Art, located at Sarasota in west-central Florida. (A. DEVANEY, INC.)

Florida has experienced many phases in architecture. There are buildings of the Spanish period in St. Augustine and Southern plantation houses in northwest Florida. Between World War I and World War II, a Spanish and Mediterranean style was in vogue, reaching its full flowering in the designs of the Mizner brothers in Palm Beach. Adaptations of West Indian plantation styles were also favored. After 1946 the ranch house style became popular over the entire state.

Outdoor recreation is popular in Florida, in keeping with the mild climate and the features that have been magnetic for so many migrants. Boating, water skiing, swimming, salt- and fresh-water fishing, hunting, and gardening are among the most popular pursuits. Skin diving, or simply glass mask and snorkel diving for the less expert, enlist many to view the silent underwater world. Upland, marsh, and aquatic birds in abundance are a source of recreation for a large and rapidly growing number of bird-watchers and amateur ornithologists. A similar diversity of plant life engages the attention of amateur botanists. For the sports spectator, there are horse races at four tracks, greyhound racing at 14 locations, and six jai-alai frontons. There are numerous national and international competitions in golf, track and field, and tennis competitions in the state every year, besides boat and auto races (notably at Daytona Beach and Sebring).

Seventeen major league baseball teams hold spring training in Florida, and many cities have professional baseball throughout the summer. Florida also has professional football, hockey, and basketball, as well as college teams in these and many other sports.

Commercial attractions are countless, but they are dominated by Walt Disney World, an eastern Disneyland located just southwest of Orlando. Second in attendance is Busch Gardens at Tampa, where the visitor may view hundreds of exotic animals and birds and ride a monorail over a man-made African savanna.

The chairs in this mirror-lined corridor of the Tampa Museum may beckon a weary visitor, but they may not support him. (THE TAMPA TIMES)

Narrow, historic St. George Street in St. Augustine still retains some of the flavor of the Old World. (THE FLORIDA TIMES-UNION JACKSONVILLE JOURNAL)

The State Seal of Florida

The state seal of Florida was adopted in 1868. The rays from the sun over a distant highland illuminate an Indian woman scattering flowers and a cacao tree in the foreground, and hills and a steamboat in the background. The scenery represents the state's tropical climate. In the outer circle below is written the state motto, "In God We Trust."

GOVERNMENT

Florida is governed under the sixth constitution of its history, a document that became effective in 1968.

The governor and lieutenant governor are elected to a four-year term and may succeed themselves for one term. The constitutional cabinet is not appointive: the secretary of state, attorney general, comptroller, treasurer, superintendent of public instruction, and commissioner of agriculture are elected to four-year terms and may be reelected indefinitely. The governor controls nine departments of quasi-cabinet status: air and water pollution, community affairs, professional and occupational regulation, transportation, health and rehabilitative services, business regulation, commerce, administration, and citrus.

The legislature is bicameral and meets every year. The Senate has 48 members, the House of Representatives 119. Senators are elected for four years, representatives for two years.

The judicial system consists of a seven-man supreme court, four district courts of appeal, 20 circuit courts, and a host of county and municipal courts. Florida is, additionally, part of the Fifth Judicial Circuit of the Federal Court system and has three lower district courts. Above the county and municipal level, where most judges are elected to four-year terms, Florida judges are elected to six-year terms.

Florida has 67 counties, each administered by a five-member elected board of county commissioners.

Health, Welfare, and Corrections. Florida has approximately 200 hospitals, and one physician for every 590 people. There is one dentist for every 2,200 people and one registered nurse for every 270 people.

Medical schools are located at the University of Florida (Gainesville), University of South Florida (Tampa), and the University of Miami (Coral Gables). The state has four mental hospitals and operates three large training centers for the mentally handicapped and defective. Florida was the first state (1941) to establish a training and adjustment center for the adult blind.

In addition to the state penitentiary in Raiford there are several other prison establishments and a large number of convict road-work camps. There are four juvenile correctional institutions, two each for boys and girls.

A state welfare board of seven members appointed by the governor functions through a department of public welfare in the administration of laws, providing aid for the aged, the blind, the disabled, and dependent children.

Labor Legislation. Workmen's compensation for industrial injuries and deaths is administered by the Florida Industrial Commission together with the joint state-federal programs of unemployment compensation and employment service offices. In 1944 Florida adopted a right-to-work amendment to the constitution, the effect of which was to prohibit the closed shop in industry.

Conservation, Planning, and Development. The Central and Southern Florida Flood Control District, financed by federal and state funds, is a major conservation undertaking. In 1964 work was begun on a 107-mi. cross-Florida barge canal that was to connect the St. Johns, Oklawaha, and Withlacoochee rivers. However, in Jan., 1971, construction was halted by President Richard M. Nixon, pending further ecological studies. Advances have been made in controlling the waters of Lake Okeechobee and in draining sections of the swampy Everglades. In general, Florida has very strong environmental protection laws.

HISTORY

Discovered in 1513 by the Spanish conquistador Juan Ponce de León, parts of the east and west Florida coasts were explored by him and subsequently by his countrymen, Pánfilo de Narváez, Álvar Núñez Cabeza de Vaca, and others. In 1539 another famed Spaniard, Hernando de Soto, beginning a three-year exploration, landed at Tampa Bay and proceeded first northward and later westward. Spanish efforts to colonize Florida persisted after early notions of treasure had been dispelled, because the land afforded a refuge for ships from West Indian storms and Spanish occupation precluded its use by other nations as a base for attack on Spanish ships. A French Huguenot settlement under the command of René de Laudonnière was attempted in 1564 with the building of Fort Caroline a few miles up the St. Johns River. Pedro Menéndez de Avilés was then sent from Spain to destroy the French colony and to found a permanent settlement which he established at St. Augustine in 1565. Menéndez captured the French colony and in a later action largely destroyed the shipwrecked forces of French Admiral Jean Ribaut who had come with additional colonists for Fort Caroline.

Editorial Photocolor Archives

St. Augustine's formidable 17th century Spanish fortifications are fine examples of European fort architecture at its height. Fort Marion, on Mataneas Bay, is shown.

Menéndez and his successors then established forts, and Spanish Jesuits founded numerous missions, the Spanish holdings eventually being extended south into the peninsula, west toward Pensacola, and north into Georgia and the Carolinas. Although Spanish-French hostilities did not cease, the English subsequently became Spain's major opponents in Florida.

In 1586 Sir Francis Drake destroyed St. Augustine, and in 1607 the English were successful in expanding their Virginia Colony to include the northern part of Florida. St. Augustine was again plundered in 1665 by John Davis, an English buccaneer. In 1670 a boundary agreement between England and Spain permitted the English to establish a colony in the present-day area of Charleston, S. C. To prevent encroachments by the French from Louisiana, Spain erected (1698) Fort San Carlos near Pensacola. In 1702 the English besieged St. Augustine and in numerous subsequent raids with their Indian allies destroyed much of the Spanish mission system. By the mid-18th century Britain had won all the land once claimed by Spain from the St. Marys River northward to Maine. In 1762 Cuba also fell to the British, and in order to regain this prize, Spain finally ceded its Florida claims to Great Britain in 1763.

From 1763 until 1783 Florida was formally a British colony, divided and designated as East and West Florida—the latter including large parts of present-day Alabama, Mississippi, and Louisiana. Trade between Great Britain and her new overseas territory was begun; Florida was able to export lumber, oranges, and animal skins. With the defeat of the British by American colonists, however, Florida was returned to Spain in 1783 at the same time the independence of the United States was recognized.

During the second period of Spanish possession, 1783 to 1821, Spain's control was weakened not only by the expansionist ambitions of the United States and the aggressive activities of Indian traders from the United States, but by its own inability to keep order. By 1812 former West Florida lands had been annexed by the United States. Pensacola was taken by Andrew Jackson's forces in 1814. Finally, in 1819, Spain ceded the territory of present-day Florida to the United States. Upon final ratification of the treaty in 1821, Florida came under the American flag.

Twilight at Cedar Key, midway down Florida's west coast. The area rivals the Everglades as a sanctuary for wildlife.

Florida News Bureau

Fort Jefferson National Monument. (H. ARMSTRONG ROBERTS)

Lion Country Safari. (LION COUNTRY SAFARI)

Marineland. (FLORIDA NEWS BUREAU)

Mountain Lake Sanctuary. (JOHNNY JOHNSON—FLORIDA NEWS BUREAU)

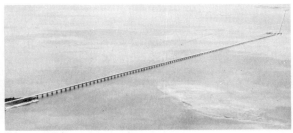

Overseas Highway. (FLORIDA STATE NEWS BUREAU)

FLORIDA PLACES OF INTEREST

APALACHICOLA NATIONAL FOREST, southwest of Tallahassee. Mixed forest of cypress, pine, magnolia, and other trees, with many streams and ponds. Hunting and fishing.

CASTILLO DE SAN MARCOS NATIONAL MONUMENT, St. Augustine. Oldest masonry fort in the United States, construction begun in 1672 by the Spanish. Indian leader, Osceola, imprisoned there during Seminole War.

DE SOTO NATIONAL MEMORIAL, west of Bradenton, commemorates Hernando de Soto's landing in 1539.

EVERGLADES NATIONAL PARK, southwestern Florida. Second-largest national park in United States. Subtropical vegetation, birds in great variety, wild animals, and game fish. Pine islands, tropical palm hammocks, and mangrove forests connected by an intricate network of waterways.

FORT CAROLINE NATIONAL MEMORIAL, east of Jacksonville. Historic site on the St. Johns River where French expedition in 1564 established first European colony in North America east of Mexico.

FORT JEFFERSON NATIONAL MONUMENT, Dry Tortugas islands (68 mi. west of Key West). Impressive ruin dating from 1846. Protected anchorage with landing wharf.

FORT MATANZAS NATIONAL MONUMENT, south of St. Augustine. Spanish fort built in 1737 to guard the rear entrance to St. Augustine.

LION COUNTRY SAFARI, Royal Palm Beach. African big-game preserve through which visitors can motor and enjoy face-to-face encounters with lions and other wild game while safely seated in their cars.

MARINELAND, south of St. Augustine. Aquarium housing a remarkable collection of marine creatures. Performances by trained porpoises.

MOUNTAIN LAKE SANCTUARY, near Lake Wales. Graceful Singing Tower (housing carillons) rising from a wooded hilltop.

OCALA NATIONAL FOREST, east of Ocala. Scrub pine forest, many clear lakes, several giant springs, and streams. Hunting, fishing, swimming, and boating.

OSCEOLA NATIONAL FOREST, northeast of Lake City. Timber production area dominated by long leaf and slash pine trees. Maintained as a federal experimental station in the production of naval stores, particularly turpentine. Good hunting.

OVERSEAS HIGHWAY, spanning the Florida Keys from Homestead to Key West. Unique highway providing a notable experience, especially when a day of sunshine and shadow accentuates the changing color of sky and shallow sea.

RAINBOW SPRINGS, near Dunnellon. One of Florida's largest springs, equipped with glass-bottomed boats for viewing underwater life. Swimming and canoeing popular.

SILVER SPRINGS, near Ocala. Large clear-water spring believed to be over 100,000 years old and, because of fossils discovered here, the watering place for prehistoric animals. Glass-bottomed boat trips for viewing turtle specimens, many varieties of fish, and rare underwater plants. Famous for swimming.

Organized as a territory of the United States in 1822, Florida was admitted to the Union in 1845. The northern region from St. Augustine to Pensacola had persistent growth from 1822 to 1861 despite the brutal Seminole Wars (1835–42), but expansion into the peninsula was slight.

In 1861 Florida seceded from the Union and joined the Confederate States of America, becoming an important supplier of salt and foodstuffs during the Civil War. The long Florida coast line provided havens to blockade runners, but most of the coast towns were captured by Union forces early in the war. During the Reconstruction period following the war Florida became part of the Third Military District and experienced government by Radical Republicans under Carpetbagger influence. The state was readmitted to the Union in 1868. In the election of 1876 the Democratic party made a sweep of the state offices.

In the 1880's two venturesome and imaginative capitalists, Henry B. Plant and Henry M. Flagler, built railroads down the peninsula and created hotels and entertainment facilities for tourists. This extension of transportation was the basis of the development of the peninsula. In the early 20th century Florida's population increased significantly, drainage of the Lake Okeechobee region was undertaken, and the citrus industry began to flourish. Although the collapse of Florida's real estate boom of the 1920's caused serious financial losses, as did the depression of the 1930's, the state continued to develop agriculturally and industrially.

Since World War II Florida's population has experienced explosive growth (chiefly from migration) with dramatic agricultural and industrial development, and accelerated urbanization. The missile-testing station at Cape Kennedy is the most widely known of the federal government establishments in the state. It was from this site that the first U.S. satellite, *Explorer I*, was launched into orbit (1958), the first American sent into space (1961), and the first man sent to the moon (1969). Many other defense establishments in Florida are contributing importantly to its growth. Although the peninsula has experienced the greatest development, north Florida—with the exception of a number of rural counties that have lost population—has shared in this growth at a lesser rate.

Politically, Florida has shown some departures from the traditionally Democratic Solid South; several Republican candidates have won election to the state legislature, and the proportion of Republicans in that body was greatly increased after reapportionment in 1963. Florida sends Republicans as well as Democrats to the U.S. Congress, and at times Republican presidential candidates have carried the state. A half-dozen populous counties are predominantly Republican. The first Republican governor since 1872 was elected in 1966. Although the Democrats regained the governorship in 1970, the facts suggest that a two-party system is emerging in Florida.

Consult Raisz, E. J. and Dunkle, J. R., *Atlas of Florida* (1964); Marcus, R. B., *A Geography of Florida* (1964); Cowles, F., Jr., *What to Look for in Florida and What to Look Out for* (1969); Morris, A. C., *The Florida Handbook: 1969–1970* (1969); Tebeau, C. W., *A History of Florida* (1971).

ROBERT H. FUSON,
University of South Florida

FAMOUS FLORIDA FIGURES

Irving Bacheller (1859–1950), popular novelist.

Rex Beach (1877–1949), popular novelist.

William D. Bloxham (1835–1911), twice Governor and a leader during Reconstruction.

Richard K. Call (1791–1862), twice territorial Governor and leader in Florida's early development.

William P. Duval (1784–1854), first territorial Governor; his administration held the confidence of the Indians.

Henry M. Flagler (1830–1913), railroad builder, promoter of tourism, and developer of east and southeast Florida.

Henry B. Plant (1819–99), railroad builder, promoter of tourism, and developer of central and southwest Florida.

Majorie Kinnan Rawlings (1896–1953), novelist and interpreter of the rural people of Florida.

David L. Yulee (1810–86), U.S. Senator and builder of first cross-state railroad.

A list of all the state's famous figures whose biographies appear in this encyclopedia will be found in the index in the supplementary biography listing.

IMPORTANT DATES IN FLORIDA HISTORY

1513	Florida coast discovered by Juan Ponce de León.
1539	Landing of Hernando de Soto at Tampa Bay.
1565	Settlement of St. Augustine by the Spanish.
1586	Destruction of St. Augustine by British Admiral Sir Francis Drake.
1698	Fort San Carlos near Pensacola erected by the Spanish.
1702	Invasion of Florida by the English.
1763	Florida ceded to Great Britain by Spain in exchange for Cuba.
1763 1783	Florida under British sovereignty.
1783 1821	Florida under Spanish sovereignty.
1819	Spanish cession of Florida to United States.
1821	Ratification of Florida's transfer to the United States.
1835	Beginning of Seminole War.
1845	Florida admitted to statehood.
1861	Florida's secession from the Union, entrance into the Confederate States of America and the Civil War.
1868	Florida readmitted to Union.
1876	End of Carpetbagger control.
1947	Minimum Foundation Program for public schools established.
1958	First U.S. satellite put into orbit from Cape Canaveral (now Cape Kennedy).
1961	First American sent into space from Cape Canaveral (now Cape Kennedy).

FLORIDA, STRAITS OF, channel between the Florida Keys and the north coast of Cuba and the Bahama Islands. It connects the Atlantic Ocean with the Gulf of Mexico and contains a major portion of the Florida Current, the beginning of the Gulf Stream. Max. width, 90 mi.; depth, main channel, about 600 ft.

FLORIDA KEYS, chain of coral islands curving southwestward from Miami around the end of the Florida Peninsula. Principal keys from northeast to southwest include Virginia, Biscayne, Sands, Elliott, Old Rhodes, Largo (largest, 30 mi. long), Plantation, Upper and Lower Matecumbe, Long, Grassy, Vaca, Big Pine, Torch, Ramrod, Summerland, Cudjoe, Sugarloaf, Boca Chica, and West. They comprise a popular resort area, reached by the 145-mi.-long Overseas Highway from Homestead to Key West. Fishing and farming are practiced. Crops include some 80% of U.S.-grown limes, other tropical fruits, and winter vegetables. Key West has a U.S. naval station. Length, 150 mi.

FLORISSANT [flôr′ĭs-ənt], suburb northwest of St. Louis. Chartered, 1857; pop., 65,908.

FLORODORA, English musical comedy (1889) with music by Leslie Stuart, book and lyrics by Owen Hall. It had a highly successful New York engagement beginning in 1900, and is best remembered for the song *Tell Me Pretty Maiden* and the legendary beauty of the sextet of girls featured in that number.

FLOTATION PROCESS, industrial process used to separate a particular solid from a group of solids. The process is used primarily to separate valuable minerals from their ores in the refining of gold, lead, zinc, and the like. The principle of flotation is based on the surface properties of the mineral or minerals to be separated. Thus, a mineral whose surface is not wetted by the water solution in which the process is conducted will tend to remain at the bottom of the solution while the wetted mineral will be buoyed to the surface.

Froth can be formed by bubbling air through the bath. Nonwetted particles will then attach themselves to the rising air bubbles and be carried to the surface. This method is called froth flotation.

FLOTOW [flō′tō], **FRIEDRICH, BARON VON** (1812–83), German opera composer, born in Teutendorf. He enjoyed popular acclaim for his light operas, beginning with his first successes in Paris in the 1830's and continuing with later works produced in Germany (for example *Alessandro Stradella*, 1844). However, his fame now rests upon his greatest success, *Martha*, produced in Vienna in 1847. A degree of superficiality and ineffective orchestration in his work are somewhat minimized by a freshness of melodic line.

FLOUNDER, name for several marine flatfishes of the families Bothidae (the left-eye flounders) and Pleuronectidae (the right-eye flounders). The approximately 60 species of flounder are found along the coasts of Canada and the United States. The summer flounder, or fluke, *Paralich-*

thys dentatus, is a popular game and food fish along the Atlantic coast of the United States. The winter flounder, *Pseudopleuronectes americanus,* is also found in western Atlantic coastal waters, but unlike the summer flounder's, its eyes are on what was originally the right side of its body. The starry flounder, *Platichthys stellatus,* is an important commercial species of the Pacific coast.
See also FLATFISH.

FLOURENS [floo-räNs′], **PIERRE MARIE JEAN** (1794–1867), French anatomist and physiologist, well known for his investigations of the central nervous system. He was among the first to locate properly the parts of the brain associated with sensation and voluntary acts, and demonstrated the importance of the cerebellum in the co-ordination of muscular movements. He also recognized the existence of a breathing center in the brain and studied the role of the spinal cord in carrying impulses to and from the brain. He was professor of comparative anatomy in Paris and was permanent secretary of the French Academy of Sciences.

FLOUR MILL, machinery for grinding cereal into flour. The highly complex modern flour mill is the product of thousands of years of evolution. Ancient Egyptian Pharaohs ate bread made from grain pounded in a crude mortar and pestle. By the time of Moses, milling had evolved into rubbing grain between two coarse, flat stones. Up to the 18th century the major improvements were the use of crude sieves and the replacement of slaves with animal and water power. Modern steel-roller mills were perfected in the 1860's in Austria and Switzerland and gradually supplanted stones as major grinding surfaces.

Flour mills grind any type of grain, such as corn, rye, and oats, but today they are most commonly used for grinding wheat. The grain's starchy inner part (endosperm) is separated from the tougher outer shell (bran) and the embryo (germ), then ground into flour.

Before milling, the wheat is carefully selected on the basis of quality. Hard, or high-protein, wheats are made into bread flours; soft wheats, into cake or pastry flours. The wheat is cleaned of sticks, stones, metal, chaff, and dust, then moisturized with water to soften the bran shell so that the endosperm can be more easily ground into flour.

The basic machinery of modern flour mills consists of large steel rolls, which turn toward each other at different speeds. As the grain passes between them, it is mashed and rubbed. The resulting mixture of bran, germ, endosperm, and flour is then sifted several times through coarse wire and then a silk mesh that permits only fine flour to fall through. The remaining mixture is reprocessed until all the endosperm is ground to flour. The bran and germ are collected to be later sold as animal feed.

In the bleaching process which follows, various chemical agents are used in an agitation chamber. Minerals and vitamins are added for enrichment at this stage. The milled flours may be blended into standard grades or selected for special flours with certain desired baking properties.

REUBEN WAITMAN, General Foods Corporation
See also BREAD.

FLOWER, botanical term for the reproductive structures of plants in class Angiospermae, the flowering plants. A flower is composed of several floral organs, and the different types of flowers are distinguished by the presence or absence of these organs. A complete flower is composed of four distinct whorls of floral organs. These consist of sepals, the outer group or whorl of floral organs; petals, usually the conspicuously colored parts; stamens, composed of the stalk or filament and the anther, the latter containing the pollen; and one or more pistils. All of the sepals together make up the calyx, while all of the petals together constitute the corolla. Calyx and corolla constitute the perianth. Since the stamens and pistils function in reproduction, they are referred to as the essential organs of flowers. Petals and sepals have no reproductive function and are called accessory organs.

Not all flowers are complete: some lack one or more of the four whorls of floral parts and are said to be incomplete. In some, petals are absent; in others, both sepals and petals are lacking. Incomplete flowers that lack stamens or pistils are said to be imperfect to distinguish them from perfect flowers in which both stamens and pistils are present. Imperfect flowers that bear stamens are said to be staminate, while those that contain pistils are called pistillate. In some plants, such as corn, oak, and walnut, both staminate and pistillate flowers are borne on the same plant. This condition is described by the term "monoecious." In other plants, such as willows and poplars, staminate and pistillate flowers are borne on separate plants. This condition is described by the term "dioecious."

A pistil is composed of the stigma, the style, and the ovary. Within the ovary are the ovules which develop into seeds. The transfer of pollen from anther to stigma is called pollination. The pollen grain germinates on the surface of the stigma, producing a pollen tube which penetrates the style and extends to the ovules. It then grows into an ovule, enters the embryo sac, and there releases two sperm nuclei. One sperm nucleus unites with the egg which is in the embryo sac. The union of sperm and egg is fertilization, and a young plant develops from the fertilized egg, or zygote.

SAMUEL L. MEYER, University of the Pacific
See also INFLORESCENCE; POLLINATION; REPRODUCTION: *Reproduction in Plants*.

FLOWERING MAPLE. See ABUTILON.

FLOWERING PLANTS. See SPERMATOPHYTE.

FLOWERS OF EVIL. See BAUDELAIRE, CHARLES PIERRE.

FLOW METER, an instrument that measures fluid flow. Water-distribution systems use a displacement type and a velocity type. The displacement meter, used primarily for small fluid flow, measures flow rate by recording the number of times a container of known volume is filled and emptied. The velocity meter registers, on a calibrated dial, the rate of flow past a cross section of known area. Other common flow meters are the Venturi meter and those based on a weir, an orifice, or a weighing tank in conjunction with a chronometer.

FLOYD, JOHN BUCHANAN (1806–63), American politician and Confederate general. Born in Virginia, Floyd received his early education at home, graduated from South Carolina College (1829), and moved to Arkansas to practice law and plant cotton. Failing in both endeavors, Floyd returned to Virginia and practiced law until he entered the state assembly (1847). A strong advocate of state improvements, especially railroads, Floyd won the governorship in 1849. He believed strongly in states' rights but rejected secession. After helping to secure the election of President James Buchanan, Floyd was appointed (1857) Secretary of War. Buchanan's refusal to withdraw Maj. Robert Anderson from Fort Sumter infuriated Floyd; he resigned (1860) and turned bitter secessionist. Buchanan maintained that he had requested Floyd's resignation because of misuse of $870,-000 in War Department funds. A Confederate brigadier general during the Civil War, Floyd commanded Fort

TWO KINDS OF FLOWERS

COMPLETE FLOWERS

There are four kinds of floral organs: sepals (the outermost circlet), petals (the circlet inside the sepals), stamens (which produce pollen), and pistils (which produce ovules). Complete flowers, such as the tulip *(right)* and plum *(below)*, possess all of these.

Walter Singer

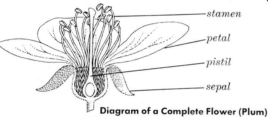

stamen
petal
pistil
sepal

Diagram of a Complete Flower (Plum)

INCOMPLETE FLOWERS

A flower that lacks any of the four floral organs is called incomplete. The tiny petalless flowers of the poinsettia *(right)* are surrounded by petallike bracts (modified leaves). The anemone *(below)* lacks petals, but has colorful sepals.

Walter Singer

petals
are
absent

stamen

sepal

pistil

Diagram of an Incomplete Flower (Anemone)

Donelson, Tenn. His withdrawal by night just before the fort was surrendered (Feb. 1862) led President Jefferson Davis, an old foe, to strip him of his command.

JAMES P. SHENTON, Columbia University

FLOYD, WILLIAM (1734–1821), American legislator, signer of the Declaration of Independence. Born to a wealthy landed family in Brookhaven, N.Y., Floyd served (1774–77; 1778–83) competently but without distinction in the Continental Congress. During the American Revolution he headed the Long Island militia and then was (1789–91) a representative in the first Congress.

FLU. *See* INFLUENZA.

FLUID, a substance composed of particles that readily change their relative positions. Fluid refers, therefore, to both gases and liquids, as contrary to solids. However, the distinction between highly viscous liquids and solids is sometimes difficult to make, since the same material acting as liquid under some circumstances may act as a solid under others. The important physical properties of a liquid are density, specific gravity, vapor pressure, surface tension, molecular-transport properties, viscosity, thermal conductivity, heat capacity, diffusivity, and compressibility.

An ideal fluid is one that is incompressible and frictionless. A frictionless fluid has zero viscosity; that is, it offers no resistance to shearing forces. Hence, the fluid pressure on any surface during flow and deformation is always normal to that surface. Although no such fluid actually exists, many real fluids have small viscosities, and the effects of compressibility may be small. The concept of ideal fluid, however, greatly simplifies the mathematical treatment of such flow cases.

All real fluids have finite viscosity, and in most cases of flow in ducts and over immersed bodies it is necessary to consider the viscosity and the related shearing stresses associated with deformation of the fluid. Real fluids are therefore also called viscous fluids.

Nonviscous fluids are those having zero viscosity, but they may or may not be incompressible. Flow of an ideal fluid is called nonviscous, incompressible flow, while flow of a real fluid is called viscous flow.

Fluids are classified as compressible or incompressible only on a relative basis. Gases are considered compressible. An incompressible fluid is actually nonexistent in nature. Liquids usually have very low compressibility, and for most practical purposes can be considered incompressible.

VEN TE CHOW, University of Illinois

FLUIDICS, engineering of control and computing devices which use gas or liquid streams as the energy medium. The first fluidic devices were announced in 1959 by U.S. army laboratories. These devices, while performing functions similar to those of conventional electrical and mechanical equipment, can operate under more severe environmental conditions. They are generally fabricated from stainless steel, special glass, ceramic, or composition materials and can operate at temperatures as high as 3,000°F. Fluidic computers are constructed from combinations of basic switching elements, which assume one of two states. A typical fluidic switch is constructed with a Y-shaped channel etched in a blank of glass, which is subsequently covered with a slide to form tunnels through the assembly. The supply medium, often air, enters the bottom of the Y and, due to built-in asymmetries in the structure, all the air flows out of the top right branch. The control air jet is injected on the right side of the Y near the junction. Application of the control signal switches the supply air from the right leg to the left leg. One important use of fluidics is in jet engine controls. The high-temperature environment of a jet engine, and the availability of exhaust gases which can be used as the supply medium, make this a natural application.

MARTIN L. SHOOMAN, Polytechnic Institute of Brooklyn

FLUID MEASURE, system for measuring liquid capacity, either in metric or common units. The basic units are the liter and the gallon, respectively. In the United States, 1 gal. is equivalent to 3.785329 liters or to 231 cu. in. The British, or Imperial, gallon, used in Canada, is equivalent to 1.2 U.S. gals. *See* WEIGHTS AND MEASURES.

FLUKE or TREMATODA are flattened, leaflike worms which are found as parasites on or within certain land and water animals. Flukes which infest humans have complex life cycles, during which time they infect two, three, or even four different types of animals. It has been estimated that there are approximately 148,000,000 cases of human fluke infestation throughout the world, principally in the Orient.

The most important infection is produced by blood flukes, which are contracted by working in or drinking water which has been contaminated by larva-infested snails. The worms attack the bladder, intestine, and liver (*see* SCHISTOSOMIASIS).

Other flukes also infect snails and enter the human body through the digestive tract. The parasites then mature in the intestine, liver, or lung. In the intestine, flukes may produce inflammations and ulcers with bleeding, severe diarrhea, nausea, and vomiting. Severe cases may be fatal. Liver fluke is contracted by eating contaminated raw, pickled, or smoked fish. The worms produce a chronic disease with symptoms varying from indigestion and stomach pain to diarrhea, enlarged liver, and swollen abdomen. Lung fluke may be acquired by eating contaminated uncooked crabs or crayfish. The patients may suffer from cough with bloody sputum, chest pains, fever, and shortness of breath.

A number of drugs are available for treating these conditions, but results are frequently unsatisfactory.

HAROLD A. TUCKER, M.D.

FLUORESCENCE [floo-a-rĕs′əns], emission of light by a substance while under excitation by radiation of a wavelength different from that emitted. Paraffin oil, for example, illuminated in a dark room with a beam of white light, produces a colored glow. In the fluorescent lamp, mercury vapor is electrically excited to emit invisible ultraviolet radiation which excites strong fluorescence at visible wavelengths in the special coating material inside the glass tube.

The incident radiation of certain wavelengths is absorbed by electrons in atoms or molecules, raising them to excited energy levels. Such an excited electron may return to its normal level in one step, emitting resonance radiation of the same wavelength as that of the exciting radiation; or it may return by several steps, each emitting fluorescent radiation. These processes occur almost instantaneously; that is, as soon as the illuminating source is turned off, the luminescence ceases. Thus fluorescence differs essentially from phosphorescence, in which electrons removed from atoms return with the emission of light after delays up to many hours.

The wavelengths of the fluorescent emission are independent of the wavelength of the exciting radiation. In a given substance, radiation longer than a certain critical wavelength does not excite fluorescence. Most fluorescence occurs at wavelengths greater than the critical excitation wavelength.

JOSEPH H. RUSH, National Center
for Atmospheric Research

FLUORESCENT LIGHT, form of illumination caused by the electro-chemical stimulation of phosphor. Two important applications of this property, known as fluorescence, are found in the television picture tube and the fluorescent lamp. The fluorescent lamp glows when electric energy is introduced into a closed, phosphor-coated tube containing mercury vapor. The electric current causes the vapor to emit ultraviolet energy, which in turn reacts with the phosphor coating, producing light.

Fluorescent light has advantages in its cool operation and wide distribution of light. Although it consumes less power to produce a given amount of illumination when compared with an incandescent lamp, fluorescent lighting has a higher initial cost.

See also CATHODE-RAY TUBE; ELECTROLUMINESCENCE;
FLUORESCENCE.

FLUORESCENT MINERALS, minerals that emit visible light when subjected to ultraviolet radiation. The invisible ultraviolet rays are absorbed by atoms in the minerals, and the energy of these rays is then released as visible light. In many such minerals it has been shown that the fluorescence is caused by foreign atoms that function as activators. In the mineral willemite (Zn_2SiO_4) the activating atom is manganese substituting for zinc; in scheelite ($CaWO_4$) it is lead substituting for calcium and molybdenum for tungsten. Other minerals that commonly fluoresce include fluorite (from which the phenomenon got its name), some calcite, and many secondary uranium minerals. The fluorescence of minerals has long been of scientific interest, and it has a number of practical applications. It is a valuable aid in prospecting and in mineral dressing for distinguishing ore minerals that have a characteristic fluorescence.

BRIAN MASON, American Museum
of Natural History

See also FLUORESCENCE.

FLUORIDATION [flŏŏr-ə-dā'shən], the addition of specific amounts of fluorine to drinking water for the purpose of preventing tooth decay. The earliest relationship noted between fluorine and dental health was mottling of the tooth enamel. This was strongly suggested in 1931 when it was demonstrated that the water in five localities, where mottling was present, contained fluorine in amounts ranging from 2.0 to 13.7 parts per million. Later studies proved that mottling of the enamel could be halted by lowering the fluorine content of the drinking water.

The role of fluorine in cavity-prevention first became evident when a new low-fluorine water supply was introduced in Bauxite, Ark. Children born after the water supply was installed showed a much higher incidence of cavities than those who were raised while the old water was still used. Following this, the U.S. Public Health Service undertook large-scale studies which indicated that a 50% to 66% reduction of cavities could be safely achieved by adding 1 part per million of fluorine to the drinking water.

Vigorous opposition to the fluoridation of public water supplies has been forthcoming from various groups, which contend that the safety of fluoridation is still in doubt, that it imposes unprecedented mass medication on the population, and that its efficiency in preventing caries is questionable. Both the American Dental Association and the American Medical Association have endorsed fluoridation. The U.S. Public Health Service reported that in recent years many American communities, with a total population ranging into the tens of millions, were using fluoridated water. In nonfluoridated areas many dentists use repeated applications of a 2% solution of sodium fluoride to the teeth to reduce caries: evidence indicates that this may help to reduce cavities by as much as 40%.

ALFRED CARIN, D.D.S.

FLUORINE [flŏŏ'ə-rēn], pale-yellow gas and a chemical element of the halogen group. Its most common ore is fluorite, which glows when exposed to short-wave radiation, giving rise to the term "fluorescence." Difficult to obtain in its elemental form, fluorine in compounds was discovered by C. W. Scheele in 1771, but was first isolated in 1886 by H. Moissan, who passed an electric current through a fluoride.

Best known of fluorine compounds is hydrogen fluoride, H_2F_2, which reacts with compounds of silicon, including glass, to form gaseous silicon tetrafluoride, SiF_4. Glass may be etched by first coating the surface with wax, scratching off the wax in any desired design, and exposing the glass to hydrogen fluoride. The wax-free area becomes permanently frosted.

Uranium hexafluoride, UF_6, is the only gaseous uranium compound and was used during World War II to separate the isotope U^{235} from other isotopes of uranium, by a diffusion process. Atomic energy projects also make use of compounds of fluorine and carbon, the fluorocarbons, which are highly resistant to the corrosive action of fluorine. Teflon, a fluorocarbon polymer, is a waxy plastic, high melting, and completely insoluble in most solvents. It is impervious to the action of almost all strong chemicals and is an excellent electric insulator. Freon, CF_2Cl_2, a nonflammable, nontoxic gas, is commonly used as a refrigerant in home air conditioners and refrigerators.

Although fluorine is not essential to life, small quantities (0.1% to 0.2%) are found in tooth enamel, and recent research indicates that it increases resistance to tooth decay. Programs of fluoridation, the addition of small quantities of fluorine to community water supplies, are being adopted by many cities.

Bones buried in soil slowly accumulate fluorides from their environment, the amount of fluorides absorbed being a measure of the age of the bone. This was one of the ways in which the hoax of the Piltdown man was exposed.

PROPERTIES

Symbol	F
Atomic number	9
Atomic weight	19.00
Density	1.69 g./liter
Valence	1
Melting point	−223° C. (−369.4° F.)
Boiling point	−188° C. (−306.4° F.)

ISAAC ASIMOV, *Boston University*
See also FLUORIDATION.

FLUORITE, calcium fluoride mineral, CaF_2. It usually crystallizes in cubes. Fluorite is transparent to translucent and is commonly purple, green, or blue-green. Under ultraviolet light many specimens are fluorescent. Fluorite is the commonest fluorine mineral and it is the raw material for making fluorine chemicals. It is also used as a flux in steelmaking, and as a constituent of white glasses and enamels. From 1,000,000 to 2,000,000 tons are mined annually. Important producers include the United States, Mexico, Germany, Italy, Spain, the Soviet Union, and China.
See also CRYSTALLOGRAPHY; FLUORESCENCE; FLUORESCENT MINERALS; FLUORINE; MINERALOGY.

FLUOROCARBON [floo-ə-rō-kär'bən] **PLASTICS,** group of plastics having excellent resistance to heat, chemicals, and electricity and which are marketed under the trade names of Teflon, Kel-F, RC-2535, and Tedlar. Although they are expensive to produce, their general inertness has made them useful in many applications where cost is not important.

Molded into mechanical parts, the fluorocarbon plastics exhibit very little friction. As bearings, they do not require lubrication. They have also been successfully used in other mechanical devices such as valves, compressors, and pumps. Teflon, the best known of the fluorocarbon plastics, has been made into a permanent coating for skis and also for cooking utensils, where it prevents food from sticking to the pan.

Interest in fluorocarbon plastics developed after World War II when there was a demand for materials to withstand extremely high temperatures. These plastics have proved to be superior electrical insulators especially when chemical and thermal stability are critical. Ways are being sought to make fluorocarbon into a rubber substitute and also into protective metal coatings. Another type of coating, a chromium complex of a fluorocarbon (known by the trade name Scotchgard), has been found that imparts ex-

cellent oil, water, and stain resistance to paper and various textiles. As the cost of producing fluorocarbon plastics and of fabricating products from them decreases, these polymers may be used to an increasing extent in place of other plastics, metals, and ceramics.

LYLE F. ALBRIGHT, *Purdue University*
See also PLASTICS; TEFLON.

FLUOROSCOPE, specially prepared screen that glows when exposed to X rays. A sheet of glass or other material that is transparent to X rays is coated with a substance, such as barium platinocyanide, that fluoresces (emits visible light) at a brightness proportional to the concentration of X-ray radiation upon it. By using such a screen, a physician, for example, can observe directly bones, foreign objects, or other details revealed in a body by the X rays. The fluoroscope has been supplanted almost entirely by the use of photographic film, except where rapid changes are being studied.
See also FLUORESCENCE; X RAYS.

FLUOROSCOPY. *See* X RAYS, DIAGNOSTIC.

FLUSHING. *See* VLISSINGEN.

FLUTE, wind instrument (aerophone) consisting of a cylindrical tube, open or closed at the lower end. The air inside is made to vibrate by a ribbon-shaped column of air which strikes a sharp edge at the upper end or side of the tube. This column of air is usually produced when the player blows through pursed lips. However, the whistle flute, the best-known representative of which is the recorder, has a built-in device (flue) for shaping the column of air coming from the player's mouth and directing it against the sharp edge. The whistle flute's mouthpiece resembles a beak. Flutes are held either vertically and blown from the upper end (as are whistle flutes) or horizontally and blown from a side hole (embouchure). The latter are called transverse or cross flutes. Pitch is changed and melodies are produced by overblowing, or blowing harder (particularly for the middle and upper range of the instrument), and by changing the length of the tube with the use of finger holes, which may be furnished with keys to facilitate covering them completely and rapidly.

Flutes are found in both high and nonliterate cultures on nearly all continents, and in all forms (factory-made and hand-made). They are made of bone, ivory, wood (most common), and metal. The number of finger holes varies greatly. Flutes without finger holes are sometimes combined into compound instruments such as Panpipes and the organ. The European flute, which is a transverse flute with a hole in the side 3 in. from the upper end, has been part of the standard orchestra since about 1750, when it also became an important solo and chamber music instrument. Before 1750 the recorder was equally important. The transverse flute now uses a system of finger holes devised by Theobold Böhm (1794–1881).

The modern flute exists in several sizes with corresponding differences in pitch and tone color. Most important, aside from the ordinary or soprano flute, is the piccolo, which is much smaller, plays an octave higher,

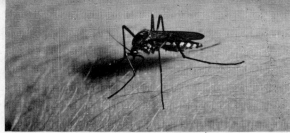

A mosquito feeding. Only the females have piercing mouth parts and are able to bite.

G. Ronald Austing—National Audubon Society

An adult housefly. Houseflies are the commonest of all fly species.

N. E. Beck, Jr.—National Audubon Society

A female midge with eggs attached to the underside of her abdomen.

Grace A. Thompson—National Audubon Society

A bee fly. Bee flies, named for their resemblance to true bees, live in communal hives and feed on flower nectar.

Hugh Spencer—National Audubon Society

and has a shrill and penetrating tone; it is used in symphony orchestras and bands.

Consult Miller, D. C., *The Flute and Flute-Playing* (1922); Fitzgibbon, H. M., *The Story of the Flute* (2d ed., 1929); Sachs, Curt, *The History of Musical Instruments* (1940).

BRUNO NETTL, Wayne State University
See also FLAGEOLET; RECORDER.

FLUX, material that, when added to the contents of a smelting furnace, tends to purge the ores of impurities and makes them less viscose. In the smelting of siliceous iron ore, limestone is added as a flux. It combines with the silica to lower the melting point of slag as well as to remove sulfur from the smelted iron. Fluxes are classified as basic (lime), acid (silica), and neutral (fluorspar).

FLY, name commonly given to many small, flying insects, but correctly applied only to members of certain families in the order Diptera, the true flies, characterized by a single pair of transparent forewings. The hindwings of flies are represented by a pair of knobby structures, the halteres, which function as balancing organs. Of the several thousand species of true flies, many are merely pests, but others pose a serious health threat as disease vectors. They have achieved this dubious distinction through their scavenging habits which enable them to pick up and transmit many disease-causing microorganisms. On the credit side of the ledger, some flies are useful as pollinators of crops; others destroy harmful insects.

The body of a fly consists of the usual division of head, thorax, and abdomen, typical of insects. The head is dominated by two compound eyes so large in some species that they almost touch each other. With these, a fly can detect the slightest movement and react accordingly to escape danger. Short antennae project between the eyes. The mouth parts form a beak. In the house fly, the lower lip is expanded to form two broad sucking lobes; in other species the beak is an effective instrument for sucking plant sap and blood. The flies with piercing-sucking mouth parts subsist on the blood of birds and mammals; others are scavengers, feeding on dead and decaying animal remains, thereby performing a valuable sanitary service. The fragile body is covered by a thin cuticle from which emerge bristly hairs; the padded feet are also covered with hairs. Flies vary in size from the almost microscopic midges and punkies to the large horse and deer flies. Flies are generally dull-colored, unlike the brilliantly hued beetles and butterflies. Flies pass through a complete metamorphosis in their development from egg to adult. The eggs are often laid in manure or other decaying organic materials, and hatch into wormlike larvae known as maggots. After a period of voracious eating, the maggots become pupae and, eventually, winged adults.

CLARENCE J. HYLANDER, Author, *Insects on Parade*
See also:

APPLE MAGGOT	HESSIAN FLY
BEE FLY	HORSEFLY
BLACK FLY	HOUSEFLY
BLUEBOTTLE OR BLOWFLY	MOSQUITO
BOTFLY	ROBBER FLY
CRANE FLY	TACHINA FLY
DROSOPHILA	TSETSE FLY
GADFLY	WARBLE FLY
GNAT	

FLY AGARIC [ə-găr′ĭk, ăg′ə-rĭk] **or FLY AMANITA** [ăm-ə-nī′tə], common name for a poisonous mushroom, *Amanita muscaria*, in the gill fungus family, Agaricaceae. Found throughout the world growing in open woods, the fly agaric reaches a height of about 8 in., and can be easily recognized by its orange-to-red umbrellalike cap, flecked with warty patches. The fly agaric is perhaps the most lethal of all poisonous fungi. In spite of this, it is made into a beverage by Siberian tribesmen. Ingestion of the extract produces hallucinations but it is apparently not taken in sufficient quantity to cause death.

FLY CASTING. *See* FISHING.

FLYCATCHER, common group name of many members of two very distinct families of perching birds—the Old World flycatchers, family Muscicapidae, and the American, or tyrant, flycatchers, family Tyrannidae. The best-known and most typical Old World flycatchers are the European spotted and brown flycatchers, genus *Muscicapa*—small, dull-colored birds, that sally from a fixed perch to catch flying insects. The pied flycatchers, sometimes separated in the genus *Ficedula,* with a number of brightly colored species, are found chiefly in Asia. Many of the flycatchers of Africa and Australia are boldly marked or endowed with vivid hues. Among the handsomest are the paradise flycatchers, *Tersiphone.*

The tyrant flycatchers are numerous and varied in the American tropics and in South America. A small number of species breed as far north as the United States. These are more or less migratory. All tyrants are mainly insectivorous. A few larger species take small reptiles and mammals, and occasionally birds. Most species seem to be colored for concealment, the plumage running to olive, grays, and browns, but often with bright yellow below. A number have a hidden red or yellow crown patch. This is notable in the royal flycatchers, *Onychorhynchus,* of tropical America, which reveal a magnificent fanshaped crest in a defensive display. Common North American groups, all also represented in tropical America by allied species, are the bold, aggressive kingbirds, *Tyrannus;* the water-haunting phoebes, *Sayornis,* often nesting under bridges or on other man-made structures; the pewees, *Contopus,* which derive their common name from the simple melancholy notes of the eastern bird; and the crested flycatchers, *Myiarchus,* which often put a piece of shed snakeskin in their nest hole. In South America flycatchers occur in all kinds of habitat. Many species glean from leaves and twigs; others feed only on the ground. More than 300 species are included in this family.

EUGENE EISENMANN, American Museum of Natural History

FLYING, the art of taking off, operating aloft, and landing an airplane, helicopter, airship, or motorless glider. Only winged, powered aircraft will be discussed here, but the same basic principles of aerodynamics apply to all types of heavier-than-air craft (*see* AERODYNAMICS).

From his seat in the cockpit, the pilot controls every movement of an aircraft by co-ordinating the power output of the engine with the movable surfaces on the wings and the tail assembly. Each engine has a throttle and other manual and automatic controls that vary power output.

Flight Controls. Flight controls consist of a vertical stick linked to the ailerons and elevators and of two pedals linked to the rudder. Flaps and tabs are auxiliary controls. The rudder pedals are operated by the pilot's feet. When the left pedal is pushed the rudder moves to the left into the slipstream which then pushes the tail of the plane to the right, so that the whole aircraft yaws or turns left. On small planes the rudder is the only steering device for taxiing on the ground. Large planes are steered by turning the nosewheel which is linked to the rudder.

The stick is placed between the pilot's legs. When it is moved to the left, the aileron on the left wing is raised into the slipstream while the aileron on the right wing is depressed an equal amount. As a result, the left wing drops, the right wing rises, and the plane tips, or banks, or rolls, to the left. If the rudder is moved to the left also, the plane will turn left smoothly without sideslip.

When the stick is moved forward, both elevators on the tail are depressed into the slipstream; the tail is forced up and the nose is pointed down. The plane descends. When the stick is pulled back, the elevators are raised up into the slipstream, depressing the tail and tipping the nose up. The plane climbs. Every movement of the stick in any direction should be co-ordinated with the rudder. In large aircraft the stick has a wheel and the ailerons are moved by turning the wheel, but the whole assembly is moved forward and back to descend or climb.

Trimming tabs are small hinged sections on the trailing edges of elevators, ailerons, and rudder and are set from the cockpit to adjust or trim the control surfaces for straight and level flight or periods of steady climb or descent. They hold the control surfaces at small angles into the slipstream.

Flaps are sections hinged to or slotted in the trailing edges of wings. They are usually located between fuselage and the inboard end of the aileron. By extending the flap downward or downward and to the rear, the pilot changes the camber of the wing in order to slow landing speeds. Some flaps are designed to provide quicker take-off and improved climb by enlarging the wing area.

Flight. After making a carefully prescribed cockpit check, the pilot taxis out to that end of a runway from which he can take off against the wind. He has already filed his flight plan and destination with the personnel in control of air traffic at the airdrome and has received traffic, wind, and last-minute weather information for his route, and take-off instructions. At large airports he is in radio communication with the control tower before he begins to taxi. Just prior to turning on the designated runway for take-off, the pilot stops and makes a final check of his engines, instruments, and controls in a careful sequence to make certain that everything is in operating condition. He then radios for permission to take off.

To take off, the pilot lines up the aircraft on the runway and opens the throttles fully to get all the power available. As the aircraft gains speed, he constantly adjusts all control surfaces to keep the plane following the center line of the runway and to keep the nose at the right attitude for take-off. At take-off speed the pilot gently pulls back on the stick and raises the nose just enough to lift the plane off the ground without risking a stall. Stalling on take-off can be fatal because the aircraft, having lost its lift in the stall, is out of control. It can re-

---

A STUDY GUIDE and a CAREER GUIDE dealing with the broad topic of aviation accompany the article AVIATION.

HOW A PILOT CONTROLS HIS AIRCRAFT

With the stick and the pedals the pilot operates the elevators, ailerons, and rudder, which control movement of the craft about the lateral, longitudinal, and vertical axes, respectively.

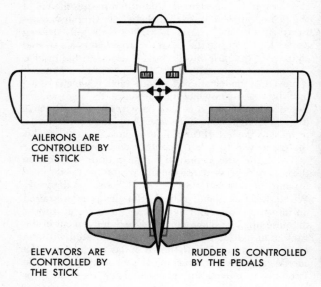

AILERONS ARE
CONTROLLED BY
THE STICK

ELEVATORS ARE
CONTROLLED BY
THE STICK

RUDDER IS CONTROLLED
BY THE PEDALS

LEFT TURN

Stick is moved left to raise left aileron and drop right one. Left pedal moves rudder left.

PEDALS

STICK
LEFT

This aileron position causes plane to roll to the left, but the greater drag on the right wing tends to pull the nose to the right. The rudder must be used to correct this adverse pull so that a smooth bank and turn may be accomplished.

gain lift only by diving and there is not enough altitude to gain sufficient speed in a drive to recover.

When the aircraft is airborne, the pilot retracts the landing gear, the pitch or bite of the propellers is increased, and engine power is reduced for the climb to cruising height. The pilot must be on constant alert for other traffic. On major airways, which he joins as quickly as possible, he is under constant supervision of the air-traffic control centers and, in high traffic density areas, is under the supervision of long-range radar. In this manner he is always informed of his position relative to nearby traffic.

When the pilot reaches the altitude set by his flight plan, he puts the plane into level flight headed on his compass course and cuts his engine power to cruising speed. A pilot without basic instruments can maintain level flight by watching the horizon and can navigate by following rivers, railroads, and other landmarks. However, most aircraft are equipped with altimeter, airspeed indicator, artificial horizon, and magnetic and gyro compasses.

During en-route flying, the pilot continuously makes control adjustments necessary to keep the aircraft on course and at proper altitude and airspeed. For example, if cross winds force the plane off the desired track along the ground, the pilot must yaw into the wind to offset the deviation or make periodic directional changes. Aircraft flying under the control of an automatic pilot requires no such attention since the adjustments are made automatically through power linkages between the controls and the instruments.

Instrument flying is known as IFR (instrument flying rules) and is resorted to when the pilot cannot see the ground. Then the pilot flies watching only his flight and engine instruments and co-ordinates his adjustments on the controls with their readings and with radio aid, beacon markers, visual omnirange, directional-measuring equip-

ment, instrument-landing system, and ground-approach control or precision-approach radar.

To prepare for landing the pilot calls the destination airport when he is about 25 mi. away for wind, weather, field, and traffic conditions; he receives his landing instructions and is then under the airport's orders. All incoming planes must join a traffic pattern under control of the tower personnel. Before taking his position in the traffic, the pilot always runs through a landing check of instruments, engines, and controls. At small airports without radio facilities the pilot flies over the field to get the direction of the wind from the windsock, check local traffic rules, and choose the proper runway, so that he may land into the wind. At any airport he must wait his turn to land, but generally a landing craft takes priority over craft waiting to take off.

To descend, the pilot throttles back, which reduces the thrust and hence the lift in such a way that it is necessary for the pilot to exert a backward pressure on the stick to maintain the desired attitude. As he nears the airport, he drops the wing flaps to provide a braking action, allowing slower air speeds to assure safety; and he then lowers the landing gear which adds further drag and also gives him time to discover trouble. As he turns into his final approach, the pilot maneuvers to line up the plane with the runway and to establish a glide path aimed at a touch down as close to the runway threshold as is practical. The engine is throttled almost to idling. If the pilot finds his landing may be short, he gives more power to the engines and pulls the stick back to restore level flight. When he feels he has a proper approach position he resumes his descent. If the pilot feels he will overshoot the runway, he may decide to climb up and go around again for a fresh approach or he may slow down and lose altitude by yawing, or side slipping, the plane. When the pilot reaches the runway he levels off and keeps pulling

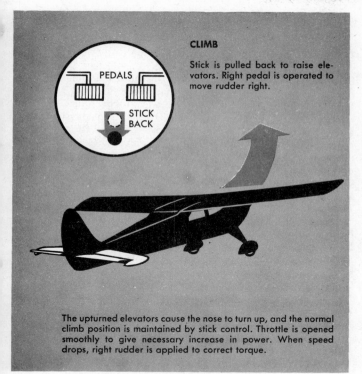

CLIMB

PEDALS

STICK BACK

Stick is pulled back to raise elevators. Right pedal is operated to move rudder right.

The upturned elevators cause the nose to turn up, and the normal climb position is maintained by stick control. Throttle is opened smoothly to give necessary increase in power. When speed drops, right rudder is applied to correct torque.

back smoothly on the stick, pulling the nose up as he loses airspeed and finally pulling the stick back sharply to make ground contact, and then returning it to a neutral position for taxiing. Although landing is accomplished primarily through use of the elevators, the pilot constantly works the ailerons and rudder so that the craft will retain proper balance. A wind blowing across the runway will make the plane drift and this must be counteracted. All planes are equipped with wheel brakes usually applied through the rudder pedals and used cautiously until the rolling speed has fallen off. Many planes have reversible pitch propellers that cause the blades to push against the onrushing air. Turbojet engines can also be reversed.

All maneuvers in the air must be conducted manually. An automatic pilot only keeps the plane on a selected course at a selected altitude. Normally, a plane properly rigged and with trimming tabs set tends to fly straight and level, and unless the air is rough, the pilot puts only brief pressures on stick and rudder. Loops, rolls, flying upside down, and other violent aerobatics are all accomplished with stick and rudder movements and engine handling, but only planes designed for it will allow such departure from conventional attitudes in the air. Many planes are designed with safety factors that prevent even stalls.

Basic piloting is relatively simple to learn. However, modern aircraft and modern navigational rules and systems, coupled with high speeds and heavy air traffic, impose severe responsibilities on a pilot. He must develop skill and alertness, and acquire experience and the same respect for the air that a sailor has for the sea.

Consult Gibbs-Smith, C. H., *A History of Flying* (1953); Caidin, Martin, *Let's Go Flying* (1960); Bergman, Jules, *Anyone Can Fly* (1964).

LAURENCE L. DOTY, *Aviation Week*
See also AEROBATICS; AERODYNAMICS; AERONAUTICS; AVIATION.

FLYING BOAT. *See* SEAPLANE.

FLYING BUTTRESS. *See* GOTHIC ARCHITECTURE.

FLYING DRAGON, arboreal lizard, *Draco volans*, in the family Agamidae of Old World lizards. The flying dragon is found in the Malay Peninsula. A slender-bodied, long-tailed creature, it grows to a length of about 12 in. By means of a fold of skin along each side of its body, which can be spread out like wings, the lizard can leap into the air and glide from branch to branch.

FLYING DUTCHMAN, THE (*Der fliegende Holländer*), opera by Richard Wagner, text by the composer, based on a Dutch legend. World premiere in Dresden, Jan. 2, 1843, composer conducting. American premiere in Philadelphia, Nov. 8, 1876.

Vanderdecken (the Flying Dutchman) has been condemned to sail the seas until doomsday for having sworn he would round the stormy Cape, even if it required eternity. He is allowed to land once every seven years, and the curse can be revoked only if a woman promises to love him faithfully forever. A storm drives the Dutchman and Captain Daland to the same shore. When Vanderdecken, disillusioned, returns to his phantom ship and sets sail, Daland's daughter Senta, obsessed by compassion for his suffering, leaps into the sea, "faithful unto death," and brings deliverance. As the Dutchman's ship sinks, Vanderdecken and Senta soar heavenward.

Wagner, inspired by a perilous North Sea voyage, depicted with astonishing force the howling winds and turbulent waters. Vanderdecken's desperation and Senta's exalted theme of redemption achieve tremendous impact, as Wagner inaugurated in this work new musico-dramatic ideas, transforming grand opera into music drama.

SIRVART POLADIAN, Music Division
New York Public Library

FLYING FISH, common name for members of several genera of marine fish in the family Exocoetidae, found especially in temperate seas but also in moderately cool waters of the Atlantic and Pacific coastal areas. Flying fish do not fly, but leap from the water (mainly to escape larger fish, such as tunas and mackerel, which feed on them) and glide for some distance. They are able to do this because of their tremendously enlarged pectoral fins which are often more than half as long as the body. On rising to the surface, the fish gives a powerful thrust with its tail, at the same time spreading its fins in order to remain airborne. Common species include the four-winged flying fish, *Cypselurus heterurus*, which has enlarged pelvic as well as pectoral fins; and the black-winged flying fish, *Prognichthys rondeleti*.

FLYING FOX, common name for the large, fruit-eating bats of family Pteropodidae, derived from the foxlike appearance of the head, with its slender snout and tapered ears, and the usually reddish coat. Flying foxes occur in Africa, Asia, and Australia. They are highly gregarious, hanging close together in large numbers from the branches of trees. They do extensive damage to cultivated fruits and poisoning of these bats in orchards is widely practiced. The kalong, *Pteropus vampyrus*, an Asian flying fox, is one of the largest of all bats. Its body length is about 16 in. and its wingspread may exceed 5 ft.

FLYING LEMUR, gliding mammal of the order Dermoptera, equipped with a greatly developed membrane stretching from wrists to ankles. Representatives of the single genus, *Galeopithecus*, live in the forests of the Malay Peninsula, Sumatra, Borneo, and the Philippines. Flying lemurs are strictly nocturnal, and feed on leaves and fruits. They glide from tree to tree by means of their extended, membranous "parachute."

FLYING PHALANGER, name for several squirrellike, arboreal marsupials in the family Phalangeridae, native to Australia. The three genera comprising the family are *Petauroides*, *Petaurus*, and *Acrobates*. Flying phalangers do not fly, but glide from branch to branch by spreading a web of skin that extends from their front to hind legs.

FLYING REPTILE. *See* Pterosaur.

FLYING SAUCER, also called unidentified flying object (UFO). A variety of objects or lights seen in the sky have been described as flying saucers. Some observers believe that they are of nonterrestrial origin; others claim that they are imaginary or that they are the result of unusual optical, meteorological, or other natural phenomena. The objects are usually described as bright and cigar- or disk-shaped, either almost stationary or moving at great speed; often they are ill-defined and featureless.

Objects that undoubtedly would be called flying saucers today have been reported at least since the time of the Old Testament. Ezekiel's vision of wheels, for example, is a good, although fanciful, description of sundogs and associated halos. Many reports from the Middle Ages and later times clearly refer to such phenomena as meteors, mock suns or moons, comets, and auroras. A rash of reports of saucerlike objects occurred during 1896 and 1897. The objects were hailed by many as airplanes, the invention of which was imminently anticipated; but these claims were not substantiated.

During the period 1947 to 1957 there were many reports of unidentified flying objects. Some of these were later admitted to be hoaxes. Others were too incomplete for the occurrence to be reconstructed. Most, however, can be attributed to weather balloons, lenticular clouds, mock suns, certain auroral forms, bright planets and stars, and the reflection from clouds of distant searchlight beams. Kites and newspapers, carried to great heights by winds, might be mistaken for flying saucers. Mirages caused by bending of light rays, as over warm pavement, often bring distant objects or lights into view. Radar reports of UFO's probably resulted from a similar phenomenon. The elusive "foo balls" and "foo fighters" seen accompanying or chasing airplanes, especially during World War II, are caused by reflections from irregularities in the wind flow over damaged wings. It is doubtful, therefore, whether any flying saucers can be convincingly attributed to nonterrestrial sources.

Helmut Abt, *Kitt Peak National Observatory*
See also Halo; Mirage; Mock Suns and Moons.

FLYING SICKNESS. *See* Motion Sickness.

FLYING SQUIRREL, name for a small broad-tailed, soft-furred rodent of subfamily Petauristinae, family Sciuridae, found in Europe, Asia, and North America. Flying squirrels are arboreal and glide through the trees by spreading a loose fold of skin that extends from wrists to ankles. They are sociable creatures and feed at night, chiefly on seeds and nuts. The American flying squirrel, *Glaucomys*, occurs in forested regions over much of North America; the Old World flying squirrel, *Sciuropterus* (*Pteromys*), is native to Europe and Asia; and species of *Petaurista*, *Eupetaurus*, and other genera are restricted to Asia.

FLYING TIGERS, popular name of the American Volunteers Group of the Chinese air force which fought against the Japanese during the early phase of World War II. Organized and led by a retired U.S. Army officer, Claire Lee Chennault, the Flying Tigers received the tacit approval of the U.S. government. Because the Neutrality Act was in effect, the group operated under extreme logistical difficulties in blockaded China. It was largely because of the superior flying skills of the group's pilots and the intelligence network provided by the Chinese government that the group was able to hold the far larger Japanese air force at bay. Shortly after the entrance of the United States into the war, the group was reorganized into the 14th Air Force of the U.S. Army.

FLYWHEEL, heavy-rimmed wheel used to maintain a constant speed in machines subjected to variable loads. When such a machine is driven at operating speed, the kinetic energy contained by the rotating wheel tends to overcome any sudden change in power or load. Flywheels are used in automobile engines as well as in single-cylinder piston engines where power strokes are delivered at relatively large time intervals. They may also be used in punch presses where high loads are applied suddenly. In each case the flywheel smooths out motion, preventing stalling.

FM. *See* Radio.

FOAM RUBBER, rubber compound made by adding air to latex and then heat curing it at 210° F. to 212° F. The resulting substance is a soft, spongy compound used in pillows, mattresses, seat cushions, and the backing of rugs.

Foam rubber is made by adding soap to latex, then whipping the mixture at high speeds. When about seven volumes of air have been added for each volume of latex, the froth is poured into metal molds and cured. A second process for making foam rubber was developed in 1935 by Joseph A. Talalay. Instead of using air, the Talalay process uses carbon dioxide as the blowing, or expanding, agent. Within each cubic inch of foam rubber there are about half a million tiny bubbles. The bubbles form a network of open, interconnecting cells. The foam can be varied in density from about 3 lb. per cubic foot to about 12 lb. per cubic foot. (Water weighs 62.5 lb. per cubic foot.)

The choice of the best rubber foam for specific uses is based upon its compression ratio. In pillows the compression ratio is about 8 lb.; in mattresses about 30 to 45 lb.

Foam rubber was developed in England by the Dunlop

Rubber Company in 1928 and commercialized in the United States in 1932.

GEORGE W. BLUM, The Goodyear Tire & Rubber Company

FOCH [fôsh], **FERDINAND** (1851–1929), French general. A corps commander at Nancy upon the outbreak of World War I (1914), Foch met defeat in his first engagement but made such a firm stand that his troops became known as the Iron Corps. Foch commanded an army in the first battle of the Marne (Sept., 1914) and held fast against the main effort of two German armies. He next (October) coordinated the allied forces in Flanders during the "race to the sea," though he lacked command authority over the British and Belgians. He led the French northern army group for two years. The near success of the Mar., 1918, German offensive led to the creation of the first unified Allied command under Foch. Assisted by a small French staff, and working closely with the national commanders, Haig, Pershing, and Pétain, Foch launched his crushing Aisne-Marne counteroffensive in July. Sensing victory late in September, he ordered the all-out drive that ended the war. On Nov. 11, 1918, Foch met with German representatives in his headquarters, a railroad car on a siding near Compiègne, and signed an armistice effective at 11 A.M. He became a marshal of France in Aug., 1918.

MARTIN BLUMENSON, Senior Historian, Department of the Army

FOCŞANI [fôk-shän'], city of eastern Rumania, in Galaţi Region, situated northwest of Galaţi near the Milcov River. Surrounded by vineyards, the city, together with the town of Odobeşti, is famous for its *galbenă* white wine. It is the home of the Unirea Symphonic Orchestra. Negotiations that led to the unification of the principalities of Walachia and Moldavia to form Rumania (1859–62) were held in Focşani. Pop., 28,244.

FOCUS, in mathematics, point associated with conic sections. For the ellipse it is either of two fixed points on the principal axis. It is related to the reflection properties of the conics. If a parabola, for example, is considered as a concave mirror, rays parallel to the axis are reflected to the focus.

FOEHN [fün], warm, dry, down-slope wind characteristic of mountainous areas. It results from the movement of air up and over a mountain range. As the air is forced upward it expands and cools, and its moisture condenses out. When the dry air moves down the lee side, it is warmed by compression. Several feet of snow can be melted overnight by a foehn. The name comes from Europe, where such winds are common in the Alps. Similar winds are the chinook of the Rocky Mountains, the *zonda* of Argentina, the *puelche* of the Andes, and the Canterbury northwester of New Zealand.

FOG, cloud of water droplets suspended in the air near the ground. By international convention visibility must be less than 1 km. (0.62 mi.) for the term "fog" to be applied. Fogs are formed when the relative humidity of the air is increased to the saturation point by cooling or by the ad-

MOIST AIR

COOLING GROUND

RADIATION OR GROUND FOG
Shallow layer of evening fog caused by contact between calm, moist air and rapidly cooling ground (left).

MOIST AIR

ADVECTION FOG
A persistent fog can be formed in moist, warm air blown over cold water or land (right).

COLD WATER OR LAND

COOL AIR

STEAM FOG
Rapid evaporation of warm water into cold air produces a dense, steamlike fog (left).

WARM WATER

dition of moisture. Water vapor then condenses on the minute particles always present in the air. On clear nights land areas lose heat by radiation; the ground in turn may cool the lower layers of air sufficiently to cause fog. Since cool air is relatively heavy this kind of fog, called radiation or ground fog, may be spotty in extent, concentrated in ditches, dips in highways, and other low areas.

Persistent fogs result when moist air moves over colder land or water. Called advection fogs, they are common in summer over cold ocean currents that flow near coasts. In winter and spring the flow, or advection, of humid air from over an ocean to a land area may cause dense, widespread fogs that seriously restrict air traffic.

Fogs sometimes occur when falling rain adds moisture to cool air. Moisture is also added when cold air moves over warm water, often forming so-called steam fog.

LOUIS J. BATTAN, University of Arizona
See also AIR POLLUTION; CLOUDS; CONDENSATION; HAZE; ICE FOG; MIST.

FOGAZZARO [fō-gät-tsä'rō], **ANTONIO** (1842–1911), Italian novelist and poet. He started as a poet, but found fame as a novelist. Writing as a Catholic, Fogazzaro portrayed the conflict between faith and reason and between reason and sensuality. The most popular of his seven novels were *Daniele Cortis* (1884; trans., 1887); *Piccolo mondo antico*, 1895 (*The Patriot*, 1906); and *Il santo*, 1905 (*The Saint*, 1906). Despite Fogazzaro's attachment to Catholicism, *Il santo* was condemned by the church for its advocacy of religious reform.

FOGGIA [fôd'jä], city in southeastern Italy, capital of Foggia Province in the region of Apulia. It is situated on the slopes of a mountainous promontory, the Gargano, which rises in the middle of the Tavoliere ("chessboard") plain where sheep and wheat are raised. At the tip of the Gargano, 23 mi. northeast of Foggia, is the city's Adriatic port, Manfredonia. Foggia is the chief grain market in

215

southern Italy, long famous for its underground store-houses. Cattle, wool, and olive oil are also traded. Besides macaroni and flour, Foggia produces chemicals, paper, and wines. Its importance as a transportation junction was greatly increased by the huge air base built during the Fascist regime.

The development of the Apulian style of architecture centered in Foggia. However, most examples of it were destroyed by an earthquake in 1731. The best existing Apulian structure in Foggia is the 12th-century cathedral. Foggia reached its height of splendor under the Swabian Prince Frederick II, the Angevin Dynasty, and the Aragonese. It was the birthplace of the opera composer Umberto Giordano. During World War II it was heavily bombed. In Sept., 1943, it was occupied by the British Eighth Army, and its air base became an important Allied aerial center. Pop., 118,608.

ANNA CROGNALE HANSEN, Italian Institute of Culture, New York

FOGG MUSEUM (William Hayes Fogg Art Museum), art museum of Harvard University in Cambridge, Mass. Its works illustrate the whole evolution of art, Eastern and Western, from ancient Egyptian to modern times. The collections of prints, drawings, Romanesque sculpture, Italian primitive paintings, French 19th-century paintings, and Chinese bronzes are particularly distinguished.

FOIL, METAL, metal sheet rolled to a thickness of 0.005 in. or less. Lead, tin, and aluminum have been made into foil, but aluminum has by far the widest number of applications. It can be rolled as thin as 0.0002 in. and is impervious to moisture or gas. Its main use is in food, tobacco, and pharmaceutical packaging. Metal foils of aluminum or lead are used in electric parts and can be stamped into a great variety of mechanical parts. Tin foil, which has a high production cost, has been supplanted by aluminum foil in packaging. Gold foil, mainly for decorative plating or gilding, is made by a beating process; other metal foils, however, are precision rolled to obtain a uniform thickness.

See also ROLLING MILL.

FOKINE [fô-kēn'], **MICHEL** (1880–1942), eminent Russian choreographer and dancer. Born in St. Petersburg, he studied there at the Imperial Ballet School under Petipa, Cecchetti, and others and joined the Maryinsky Theater company as soloist in 1898. Dissatisfied with existing ballet forms, he attempted without immediate success to introduce new ones under the influence of Siamese dance forms and Isadora Duncan. His first ballets (1905) were *Acis and Galatea* and *The Dying Swan*, the latter starring Pavlova. These were followed by several more, notably *Chopiniana* (1908) and *Une nuit d'Égypte* (1908), which later became famous in the Diaghilev Ballets Russes as *Les Sylphides* and *Cléopâtre*. From 1909 on he created several Diaghilev ballets, among them *Prince Igor* (1909), *The Firebird* (1910), *Scheherazade* (1910), *Petrouchka* (1911), *Le spectre de la rose* (1911), and *Daphnis and Chloë* (1912). In the 1920's Fokine and his ballerina wife Vera Fokina (1888–1958) toured the United States as a team. He subsequently created *Don Juan* (1936) and other

works for the Ballet Russe de Monte Carlo and *Bluebeard* (1941) and *The Russian Soldier* (1942) for Ballet Theatre.

A fine dancer and one of the great choreographers, Fokine possessed a breadth of style and subject that was enormous. His emphasis on the integration of dance, drama, and music greatly influenced the course of ballet.

GRANT CODE, former Curator, Brooklyn Museum Dance Center

See also BALLETS RUSSES.

FOKKER [fô-kēr'], **ANTHONY HERMAN GERARD** (1890–1939), Dutch pioneer aircraft manufacturer. He built his first plane in 1910. During World War I he supplied Germany with several famous combat-type airplanes and with a synchronizing device for firing a machine gun between the blades of a propeller. In 1922 he migrated to America, where he founded the Fokker Aircraft Corporation. Fokker was the first to build planes with fuselages of welded steel, and these planes were the first that were flown to the North Pole and across the Pacific. In 1931 he wrote an autobiography, *The Flying Dutchman.*

FOLCROFT [fôl'krôft], suburb 7 mi. southwest of Philadelphia, Pennsylvania. Its population increased substantially between 1950 and 1970. Inc., 1927; pop., 9,610.

FOLDING, EARTH. See DIASTROPHISM.

FOLEY, CLYDE JULIAN ("RED") (1914–   ), American singer of country songs, born in Blue Lick, Ky. Early in his career Foley broadcast from Chicago and later from Nashville. Among his recorded songs are the sacred *Just a Closer Walk With Thee* and *Keys to the Kingdom* and the country-styled *Goodnight Irene* and *Candy Kisses.*

FOLGER [fôl'jər] **SHAKESPEARE LIBRARY,** foremost research center for students of Shakespeare, located in Washington, D.C. It was opened to the public in 1932. Its collection of material on Shakespeare, the world's largest, was assembled by the American oil magnate Henry Clay Folger (1857–1930) and his wife Emily Jordan Folger. Upon his death it was willed to the American public, together with an endowment fund for its maintenance and expansion. The library also contains much material on the drama in general and ranks as the major American research institution for the European Renaissance and the whole of the Tudor and Stuart periods.

FOLIC ACID. See VITAMINS.

FOLIES-BERGÈRE [fô-lē' bĕr-zhâr'], a Paris music hall opened in 1869. Its revues, featuring nearly nude girls in lavish settings, have been a steady magnet for tourists. Outstanding performers who have appeared there include Maurice Chevalier, Mistinguett, Josephine Baker, and Fernandel.

FOLK DANCE signifies dance of the people. The term should not be limited to European and Euro-American recreational types; it should embrace all collective and solo dances that have passed the primitive stage but have not yet crystallized into conscious art. Throughout the

An energetic step from a Polish folk dance, brightened by traditional costumes.

Country Dance Society of America

William Kimber, modern English morris dancer. Morris dances were commonly performed in festivals during medieval times.

Gjon Mili

American square dance couples salute, swing, and change partners, as a caller directs steps.

Hy Peskin—Sports Illustrated

world the variations are more striking than the common elements.

Characteristics

Function. Folk dances often reflect present or former occupations of a locality. The English Abbott's Bromley Horn Dance descends from a prehistoric reindeer cult; the Hungarian haymaking and Swedish flax-reaping dances reflect harvest festivities; and the Portuguese tailor's dance represents urban work. Sometimes the dancers mime animals or occupational gestures; or they suggest the activity in geometric patterns, as in the Hebridean weaving lilt. More frequently such dances now serve purposes of sociability.

Style. While objectives vary with the general environment and degree of urbanization, local styles vary even more. Not only nations but adjacent villages or tribes develop special versions. Social class and sex also affect style and pattern.

The most important stylistic factors are the steps used, the body parts emphasized, type of posture, and dynamics, or energy expended. Some steps are almost universal, as the run and two-step. Others characterize special groups, as the Arab *debka* (foot twisting with jump), Scottish fling step, and Russian squat-fling step. Andalusians stress supple arm and hand motions which are absent in northern Europe. The English dance upright; Persians and Congolese sway and flex their torsos. Posture and dynamics change the quality of a step. The *pas de basque* (sideward leap and close) is light and precise in Scotland and Navarre, forceful and exuberant in the Ukraine. The *zapateado* (heel and toe stamping) of the proud Spaniard becomes earthen in the Mexican *jarabes*, or regional couple dances, with bowed posture in the least Hispaniolized places.

Patterns of ground plans for the individual dances relate to economic pursuits, hence to geographical location. Circuits usually proceed sunwise (clockwise) among former hunters of northwest Europe (English sword dance), Plains Indians (Ponca buffalo dance), and Siberian tribesmen (*ungkulatem* of the Yakuts). Long dance lines circle against the sun (counterclockwise) or meander, as among southern agriculturalists of the Balkans (kolo), of native America (Cherokee corn and snake dances), and of southern Asia (*gour* dance of Maharashtra farmers, *lai harouba* of Manipur). These distinctions tend to be somewhat blurred in folk dances of today.

Formations in straight lines, which especially appeal to some peoples, as the Ute Indians and the Irish, have a universal function in warrior and courtship contests; these survive in the morris dance and reel. Interweavings in the line are a specialty of modern western Europe and the United States, as in quadrilles.

The Sexes. The participants and their arrangement reflect the role of the sexes in society and also reflect the antiquity of the dance. Male supremacy is expressed in the fierce male and demure female actions of the Caucasian *lezginka*. More equal roles are evident in modern couple dances, as in the waltz. Dances derived from ancient rit-

217

uals assign special mime and special rounds to men and women, as in rites of the Iroquois and festivities of the Balkans. Joint participation in various groupings has been increasing since the Middle Ages.

Stylistic Areas

Stylistic variations suggest division of the world into choreographic areas. This process is complicated by factors that cut across geographical divisions, by interpenetration of dance styles, and by the simultaneous survival of contrasting dance types within localities. Certain dance types, however, have radiated from significant centers by means of migration, trade, or conquest. In chronological order such types emanated from Asia, the Near East, Europe, Africa, and the Americas.

Asia. Frenzy dances of Asia, performed in a trancelike state, have their roots in remote prehistory. The source is probably the whirling dance of the Siberian shaman, who communicates in a trance with supernatural powers to obtain cures or other benefits. In Mongolia and in the Arctic zone shamanism has retained its aboriginal character, but among sophisticated peoples it has changed, as in the trance dances by girls of Bombay and saber dances by Arab men. In Turkey the *Mevlevi* dervish dancing has borrowed the regional circle pattern in the rounds of whirling devotees. In the opposite direction, shamanism traveled with Paleolithic migrants to the tip of South America. Among more advanced Indian tribes, as the Chippewa, shamans have banded together in dancing societies, while the Salish of Washington adapted their trance dances to Christian customs in the circuits of their Shaker church.

Throughout India, while people of the lower classes leap in masked madness, the upper classes have developed the complex *Bharata Nâtya*, or classic gesture dances. The gesture code has influenced the theater dance of China, Japan, and Indonesia, while in Samoa and Hawaii gesture symbolism is incorporated in folk dances, as in the hula. In the western migration to Spain gesticulations lost their symbolism, though en route in Azerbaijan women adopted some mime. The quail, for example, is represented in their *turadji*.

Near East. The countries around the Aegean Sea were in constant interchange with India, North Africa, and South Europe. The legacy of Asia Minor is a blend of individual frenzy dances with chain-dances by groups with linked hands. Rituals represented the sacrifice and resurrection of an agrarian beast-god and depicted contests of dark and light. In ancient times agrarian resurrection drama climaxed in the Egyptian Osiris cult and the Greek Eleusinian mysteries. Such drama spread to Europe in various forms and survives as the Thracian *kalogheroi*, Rumanian *cǎluşari*, and English mummers. In Spain medieval theology renamed this drama form "the battle of Moors and Christians," and missionaries took these dramas to the New World and to the Philippines. The chain dance also was diffused through Europe as the Rumanian *hora*, Yugoslavian kolo, and French branle and farandole, with local steps and often with gestures for song words.

Europe. Early peoples of Europe mixed their native rites with such importations. Recent Europeans, however, have made their most conspicuous contribution in the couple dance. During the Renaissance, while courtly partners elegantly held hands peasants of Central Europe, notably Austria, began to dance their *Ländler* in a close embrace. Open holds still appear, as in the Polish *varsovienne* (derived from the mazurka), but the closed hold dominates the social dance, as in the waltz. Central Europe also contributed new steps, such as the Bohemian polka and Hungarian czárdás. On the threshold of Near Eastern influence, Croatian couples circle in orderly kolo-like rounds. In modern Israel dance, leaders have similarly combined couple circuits (a European importation) with Yemenite steps, as in the *dodili*.

Africa. Arab Africa retains Muslim religious rounds and dervish dances while entertaining tourists with male saber dances and female muscle dances, which are symbolic of fertility. Negro Africa's influences on the Mediterranean are lost in prehistory; its influences on the New World are well known, being evident in ritual, such as the Haitian *vodun*, and in modern ballroom dancing.

The Americas. Like Australian aboriginal rites, Amerindian rites have not left their mark on the Western world. These continents have been mainly on the receiving end, absorbing dances transplanted from Europe. In most cases British or Spanish immigrants have metamorphosed such dances as the quadrille in the new home; or their importations have been combined with the native styles, as in the Ecuadorian *sanjuanito*. After 1800 the importations were further mixed with African style in the habanera and jazz dances. These and other American-born ballroom dances have now invaded the rest of the world, rebounded to Europe and Africa, and have enthralled even the Japanese and the Eskimo.

Consult Spreen, H. L., and Ramani, Rao, *Folk-Dances of South India* (1945); Duggan, A. S., and others, *Folk Dance Library* (1948); Lawson, Joan, *European Folk Dance* (1953); Lekis, Lisa, *Folk Dances of Latin America* (1958); Mooney, G. X., *Mexican Folk Dances for American Schools* (1958).

GERTRUDE KURATH, Dance Research Center

See also:

AFRICA: *African Dance*
DANCE
EGYPT: *Egyptian Dance*
INDIAN TRIBES, NORTH AMERICAN: *Indian Dance*
LATIN-AMERICAN DANCE
NORTH AMERICAN DANCE
ORIENTAL DANCE
SPAIN: *Spanish Dance*
Entries for individual dances

FOLKESTONE [fōk'stən], municipal borough, Kent, England, located on the Strait of Dover where it is only about 20 mi. wide. It is a popular resort, fishing center, and important port for steamship traffic between Britain and France. Folkestone is situated at the foot of chalk cliffs along which is a promenade called the Leas. Here stands a memorial to William Harvey, discoverer of the circulation of the blood, who was born in Folkestone in 1578. There are Roman ruins nearby, and the town boasts the 12th-century Church of St. Mary and St. Eanswith. Several Martello towers, built for an expected invasion by Napoleon, stand along the coast. Parts of the city were badly bombed during World War II. Pop., 44,129.

FOLKLORE. The term "folklore," as used by most anthropologists and many folklorists, refers to the beliefs, sayings, poems, folk songs, ballads, tales, proverbs, and riddles that are preserved by oral tradition. The term may be expanded to include folk dances, folk art forms and techniques, and ceremonials that are transmitted from one generation to the next in an informal manner, without the benefit of books or formularized instruction.

Some folklorists in America and many European scholars expand this definition to include crafts, customs, beliefs, and superstitions that represent a view of life not held by the dominant modern society. The German folklorists who study peasant ways of stacking hay or the supposed perils of a black cat employ the expanded definition.

A third approach applies the term to "popular" stereotypes, as in the phrase "the folklore of capitalism." Serious folklorists find this third approach misleading.

Folklore in the first definition cannot be categorized as primitive, childish, or lacking in artistry. Folk songs may include both a popular ballad like *Barbara Allen* or tunes with "gapped," or incomplete, scales peculiar to the modern ear. In such tunes serious musicians (Béla Bartók, Franz Liszt) or popular entertainers (Susan Reed, Burl Ives, hillbilly singers) find creative inspiration, but their methods of performance depart widely from those common in a Kentucky or Ozark "folk" situation. Folk tales have been widely adapted by writers of juvenile fiction, but in their true setting they are told by adults to the whole community without euphemism or immature appeal. Folklore flourishes in a small cohesive community and is greatly influenced by that community, but each specimen tale or song or woven carpet is the work of an individual folk artist.

The serious student of folklore is first interested in its careful collection. Preferably he collects from the nonliterate cultures where memory is not aided by the printed page. In the past songs and tales were collected from American Negroes and from sailors and soldiers of many lands. Other sources have included convicts, Hungarian peasants, mountaineers, and primitive peoples like the Bhils of India, the Lolos of China, and various aborigines of America, Australia, and Africa. Among such peoples folklore is a functioning part of the total culture of the group.

In highly civilized societies there are always some carriers of the less dominant culture who remember tales or songs handed down from their grandparents. This material holds valuable clues, but it is less prized because less functional. The skilled collector seeks an "informant" or individual bearer of tradition, with a full repertory, like

---

"Folklore" is sometimes defined as oral literature, but as used in the article on these pages the term embraces traditional ballads and instrumental music, dances, ceremonies, crafts, customs, and superstitions as well as tales. An important and distinguishing feature of folklore can be illustrated in terms of literature. A favorite folk tale, *Hansel and Gretel,* was written *down* by the brothers Grimm, but it was not written *by* them nor is there any author known for it. Until the Grimms recorded the tale, it had been handed on by storytellers who knew it by memory. Norse myths, Scottish ballads, and American Indian ritual dances are part of the traditions of these people growing out of their lives and work rather than the products of individual authors, composers, or choreographers, educated in artistic technique.

Many articles appearing throughout this Encyclopedia deal with this worldwide field of study. They may be grouped under four headings.

The Study of Folklore in General. The article FOLKLORE defines the topic as including a variety of arts, literature, crafts, customs, and beliefs but stopping short of popular extensions as in "the folklore of capitalism." The article next stresses that folklore cannot be thought of as lacking artistry or as limited to a juvenile level. Other topics brought out in the article are the methods of collecting folklore; the international nature of the examples found; the classification of tales, songs, proverbs, and the like; and the comparative study of folklore. Comparisons help anthropologists understand patterns of culture and help scholars trace the influences of legends on writers and of folk songs on composers.

What anthropologists mean by culture and how they study it is discussed in CULTURE, ANTHROPOLOGY, ETHNOGRAPHY, and ETHNOLOGY. Theories relating myths to the cultures that produced them are treated in MYTHOLOGY. An anthropologist's view of beliefs that often appear in folklore is presented in MAGIC and WITCHCRAFT.

Myths, Legends, and Other Tales. A number of articles describe kinds of folk literature. MYTHOLOGY treats stories that typically deal with gods, heroes, and the origins of gods, men, the world, and customs. The Greek myths of the Olympian deities are cited as the best-known examples. Others are discussed in MYTHOLOGY, NORSE — which deals with such legends as the creation of the world, the battles of Thor with giants, and the eventual downfall of the gods — and MYTHOLOGY, CELTIC. A kind of tale found around the world is covered in CREATION MYTHS, and an almost equally widespread one in DELUGE MYTHS. CULTURE HERO deals with figures like PROMETHEUS, found among many peoples. Gods and heroes appear in the great national poems described in EPIC and other entries such as ROLAND, SAGA, and BEOWULF. Folk heroes of more recent date are ROBIN HOOD and PAUL BUNYAN.

Another kind of oral literature is discussed in FOLK TALES and FAIRY TALES. Examples include BEAUTY AND THE BEAST, CINDERELLA, RED RIDING HOOD, and RUMPELSTILTSKIN. NURSERY RHYMES and LITERATURE, CHILDREN'S are also pertinent articles. FABLE discusses a common expression of folk wisdom. REYNARD THE FOX is an instance of a folk fable. The fables of LA FONTAINE, on the other hand, are examples of literary productions freely adapted from old folk tales.

Folk Music. Folk stories and folk songs are combined in the BALLAD. A discussion of traditional music is presented in FOLK MUSIC. The entry ETHNOMUSICOLOGY deals with the descriptive and historical study of the music of various cultures—a combining of the interests of the anthropologist and the musicologist. Other pertinent articles are JAZZ and UNITED STATES, FOLK MUSIC OF THE.

Folk Dance. Folk songs may be related to work (sea chanties). Similarly, folk dance patterns may reflect harvesting, hunting, or other occupations as well as attitudes and beliefs characteristic of a people. The article FOLK DANCE explores the nature of this form of expression and contrasts styles of Asia, the Near East, Europe, Africa, and the Americas. Related articles include those on country and area styles, such as ORIENTAL DANCE.

Contes de Perrault, drawing by Félix Lorioux, published by Hachette, Paris

Illustration from a French version of Cinderella. Variations of this tale have been found in the folklore of many peoples.

The Oxford Dictionary of Nursery Rhymes

"High Diddle, Diddle, the Cat and the Fiddle," from the frontispiece of an 1816 English edition of *Mother Goose's Melody.*

Huddie Ledbetter, who was a source of songs for John Lomax, or the nurses who told fairy tales to Jacob and Wilhelm Grimm. He records every dialectical peculiarity and melodic line, every grace note and "squeeze" (a peculiar line-ending among American mountaineers), and gives credit with date, place, and biography of the informant. Such ideal procedures have been greatly aided by the phonograph and the tape recorder, and have led to a critical view of honest but more casual collectors of the past. Much of what is recorded is publishable, but because there are limits to the reproduction of large masses of tale and song, a favored way of preservation is the folklore archive. In such countries as Finland, Ireland, Hungary, and Yugoslavia such archives have been extensively developed; a nucleus for such an archive in the United States is now found in the Folklore Section of the Library of Congress.

One striking characteristic of folklore is its international nature. From the time of the Grimms it has been known that the skeleton of many folk tales is almost identical in such widely separated places as India, Germany, and North America. Cinderella and the story of the Deluge, for instance, are almost universal among mankind. The styles and sometimes the structures change from culture to culture, and regional variants are significant. To comprehend this continuity and contrast fully, students avail themselves of two major activities, classification and comparison.

Classification. Classification began in earnest with archivists like Kaarle Krohn of Finland, who made a census of published and unpublished materials. Such studies led to a cumulative *Types of the Folk-Tale* (1910) by Antti Aarne, revised by Stith Thompson (1927), which reduces the folk tales of the world to 2,499 numbers, including gaps allowing for additional entries. Such tales are international. Certain major classes emerge: the animal tale (How the Bear Lost His Tail by Fishing Through the Ice); "ordinary folktales," or *märchen*, which include tales of magic (Perseus or The Dragon-Slayer, Rapunzel, Red Riding Hood, Rumpelstiltskin, Aladdin, Tom Thumb); the religious tale (The Three Wishes, The Singing Bone, The Devil in Noah's Ark); the *novella*, or romantic tale (The Goose-Girl, Griselda, Oedipus); and jokes and anecdotes. The number of the last is legion; it includes numskull stories (tales of people who are stupid, or act stupidly, like The Three Men of Gotham); stories about married couples (Chaucer's *Miller's Tale*), women (Clever Elsie, The Matron of Ephesus), men (The Master Thief, The Brave Little Tailor), parsons or priests in various escapades; tall tales (Baron Munchausen and Paul Bunyan); and formula tales (This Is the House That Jack Built). Excluded from this classification are local legends, or *sage*, like the Pied Piper of Hamelin, which are not international, though the exact limits of *sage* and folk tales, or *märchen*, are hard to define.

Less successful has been the classification of folk songs. Modern study is built around the 19th-century collections of Francis James Child and Svend Grundtvig, who held to rather special theories about the genesis of folk song and the nature of the folk. In the 20th century valuable collections of the songs of all countries have been made. Notable in America is the work of Cecil Sharp, J. A. and Alan Lomax, Arthur K. Davis, John H. Cox, and Vance Randolph. This work has greatly expanded the number of folk songs and ballads available for study, and recent classifications, such as those by Margaret Dean-Smith for England, and Tristram P. Coffin and G. Malcolm Laws for America, merely began the work which Aarne did for the folk tale in 1910. Folk songs are not so widely international as folk tales, since the tie of text to tune hinders the migration so easy in the case of the folk tale skeleton. But the collaboration between the Danish Grundtvig and the American Child showed the kinship of British and Scandinavian ballads, and a ballad like *The Two Sisters* wanders freely, even at times as far as eastern Europe. The very English *Lord Randal* has a textually and musically brilliant Italian counterpart, *L'Avvelenato* (The Poisoned One).

Archer Taylor has notably begun the systematic study of proverbs and riddles. Superstitions, which may not, according to the strict definition, belong to the sphere of the verbal arts unless imbedded in formal verses, have been badly documented and carelessly studied, but the collections of Newbell Puckett and Wayland Hand have made headway. The folk dance has been ably studied by Gertrude Kurath and others.

Comparison. The main purpose of classification is comparison: the history of the kind of folklore under survey. One traces the migration of folk tales, not solely from India to the West as was argued in the 19th century, but from Europe to the Middle East and the reverse, from southern to northern Europe and the reverse, from the Middle East to Africa, from Europe and Africa to America, from India to the Pacific islands. History includes not only these major directions of movement, but also the transformations made in a tale or song on the way. A demon lover becomes a house carpenter, a horror tale like Red Riding Hood is "cleaned up," a fatalistic Muslim tale like The Seven Goats becomes simply an exercise in magic, a European tall tale is converted into the style of the American frontier, a Hindu jackal becomes a European fox or an American Br'er Rabbit. Style, structure, logic, and closing and opening formulas change. Various peoples show special preoccupations: Italy with woman's wiles, the Middle East with magic fantasies like a flying horse and a brazen castle with a whirling door, the Jews with moral tales and trenchant wit and humor, the Germans with numskull stories, Americans with tall tales, Celts with fairy lore.

Comparative cultural analysis leads to critical understanding of the individual work of folk art and provides a bridge to the area of custom and belief excluded by the favored definition. Thus the ballad demonstrates beliefs in such things as these: a separable soul, the other world of grave or fairy paradise, the ligature or knot with which witchcraft impedes pregnancy, blood brotherhood and the role of the sister's son, and the power of raising spirits from the dead. Much of this borders on mythology, a special division of folklore. Anthropologists like Melville Herskovits and Melville Jacobs find the folk tale a clue to the total culture and the individual personality, and the culture a clue to the tale. By such study the relationship of folklore to written literature is revealed (though the distinction is rigidly affirmed by the serious student). Scholars discover how the humor of Rabelais and Chaucer and Mark Twain owes much to the folklore of France, England, and America, how musicians are inspired by folk songs, how the proverb parallels the wise sayings of sages like Solomon, Seneca, and Aesop. The final ends of folklore study are not only history and the unwritten laws of human aspiration and expression, but criticism as well—the assessment by the student from a dominant culture of the values of widely separated peoples and subcultures.

Consult Grimm's Household Tales, trans. by Margaret Hunt (1892); Puckett, N. N., *Folk Beliefs of the Southern Negro* (1926); Wimberly, L. C., *Folklore in the English and Scottish Ballads* (1928); Taylor, Archer, *The Proverb* (1931); Gerould, G. H., *The Ballad of Tradition* (1932); Sharp, C. J., *English Folk Songs from the Southern Appalachians* (1932); Lomax, J. A. and Alan, *American Ballads and Folksongs* (1934); Thompson, Stith, *The Folktale* (1946); Leach, Maria, *Funk & Wagnalls Standard Dictionary of Folklore, Mythology and Legend* (2 vols., 1949); Haywood, Charles, *A Bibliography of North American Folklore and Folksong* (1951); Taylor, Archer, *English Riddles from Oral Tradition* (1951); Thompson, Stith, *Motif-Index of Folk Literature* (6 vols., 1955–58); Child, F. J., *The English and Scottish Popular Ballads* (3 vols., repr., 1956); Herskovits, M. J. and F. S., *Dahomean Narrative* (1958); Jacobs, Melville, *The Content and Style of an Oral Literature* (1959).

FRANCIS LEE UTLEY, The Ohio State University
See also FOLK MUSIC; FOLK TALES; MYTHOLOGY.

FOLK MUSIC is the traditional, collective music of a community. Such a community is either a folk (usually rural) culture within a high civilization or a primitive, preliterate culture. Quite often, music of the latter is termed "primitive music," and that of the former, "folk music."

Characteristics

Although the distinctions are not always clear-cut, and although there is some overlapping, folk music generally differs from art music in the following respects: (1) Folk music is transmitted orally, from generation to generation and from place to place, while art music usually relies upon a written notation. Occasionally folk music has also been written down and published, for research as well as for commercial purposes (examples of this are the English 16th- and 17th-century broadsides, or song sheets, and modern song books). Mainly because of its dependence upon memory, folk music is often re-created or reshaped through the years, so that a song, for example, may have multiple versions, or variants. (2) Despite the changes stemming from oral transmission, the basic style of a particular folk music is generally quite rigid and strongly molded by tradition. Art music, on the other hand, particularly Western, is essentially exploratory, continually seeking new stylistic paths of expression. (3) Folk music represents the communal personality, or collective spirit, and is therefore readily accessible to the mass of people. Although single individuals often create a piece, their names are usually forgotten as the piece becomes community property, moving through generations of performers who add their own variations. Art music, especially Western, is a personal idiom, the expression of an individual personality, and is not usually aimed at general group identification. Furthermore, the nonprofessional community at large can readily participate in the performance of folk music (although a few talented individuals may "lead"); art music, however, is designed primarily for select, professional performers. (4) Closely associated with daily life, folk music is a vehicle for ritual (songs of exhortation, prayer), work (sea chanties; mining, weaving, rice-pounding songs), dance, storytelling (ballads), historical transmission (legends, epics), and so forth. It is therefore more functional than art music, which, although in some respects functional (when associated with church ritual, for example), is designed primarily for aesthetic appreciation, generally in stage or concert performance. Ritualistic primitive music, however, usually has stronger connotations of magic and supernatural power than folk music in advanced cultures. (5) In over-all structure folk music tends toward the simple (with constant repetition of a short melody or section usually constituting a piece), while art music encompasses both the simple and the complex. In addition, theories of music with their complex mathematical, acoustical rules are conspicuously absent from folk music, although usually attached to most art music.

Despite the above differences, there has been extensive interaction between folk and art music. Not only have simple art songs occasionally been adopted by the people, but many composers of art music, such as Grieg, Sibelius, Mussorgsky, Copland, Bartók, and others have often been strongly influenced by national folk styles. Such influence was particularly evident during the rise of musical nationalism in the 19th century.

Functions and Styles

Two large areas, Europe and Asia, will serve to illustrate some of the functions and styles of folk music. (The music of the Americas is largely European-derived with African and Indian admixtures.)

Europe. In contrast to that of the United States, European folk music is in many areas still connected with ritual. Such ritual is associated with two main categories, the calendric, that is, festival celebrations at various times of the year, and the life cycle, that is, celebrations of the main life-events (birth, marriage, and so on). Many of the calendric festivals are vestiges of primitive vegetation and fertility rites, particularly the rites of spring planting, with their pantomime of the death and resurrection of a vegetation god. The May Day celebrations, the Shrovetide celebrations with their archaic sword dances, the midsummer solstice festivals featuring the circling of a bonfire, and the Whitsuntide hobbyhorse dances (such as the English morris dance) are remnants of ancient fertility and defense rituals. The death and revival pantomime frequently appears in these festival dances.

Song and instrumental dance music are a vital part of both the calendric and life cycle festivals, although the music is not considered as magical as it was in primitive times. Mixed choruses accompanied by drums and accordion sing during the Padstow hobbyhorse festival for May Day in England; at funerals "professional" wailers sing special laments (such as the Rumanian *bocet*, often accompanied by a flute, and Irish *ochone*, or keening song); during Christmas, processional songs (such as the Greek *kalenda*, Rumanian *colinde*, and Andalusian *saeta*) are a common feature in many parts of Europe.

Work songs, in which the music actually accompanies a particular occupation, are gradually vanishing. Notable examples are the Scottish *waulking* song, accompanying the softening and stretching of yarn for tweed making; the

Scandinavian and Swiss cattle calls, such as the florid Norwegian *lokk* and the Swiss *ranz des vaches*, or cowherds' song, sung or played on the alphorn; and the English sea chanty, a remnant of sail-hoisting days.

Music for general entertainment includes the lyric song, the narrative ballad (such as *Donna Lombarda*, *Lord Randal*, and *Edward My Son*), and music accompanying the dance (such as the Austrian *Ländler*, French *branle*, Ukrainian *hopak*, and Irish jig). Instruments such as the bagpipes, hurdy-gurdy, fiddle, drum, among many others, may provide the dance music, although the Scottish *port-a-beul*, or "mouth music," is a vocal diddling replacing instrumental dance music.

The epic song, serving as a substitute for written history (actual or mythical), may be included in the folk music category, although in earlier times it was in many cases sung by highly trained professionals such as the Celtic bards. Among the epic song types are the medieval Norwegian *kjempeviser* (of which some 300 are extant) dealing with knights and ogres; the Scottish Ossianic chant (Ossian was a Gaelic hero of the 3d century A.D.); the Russian *byliny*, Ukrainian *duma*, Yugoslavian songs of the *guslar*, or traveling epic singer; and Finnish *runo*. The famous story of the *Nibelungenlied* of the Middle Ages is still sung today in the Faeroe Islands.

Musical style varies throughout Europe, although most of it belongs to the Western folk tradition. This includes simple major, minor, and other diatonic scales (scales without gaps, containing only intervals of seconds, like the scale of C major or the medieval church scales), and some chasmatonic, or gapped scales (such as the five-note pentatonic scale A-C-D-E-G of Scotland). Some of the scales have spans smaller than an octave; this is especially evident in the recitative or chantlike melodies of certain epic songs (Ossianic chant, *guslar* epics), which revolve about tiny melodic nuclei of two or three notes (for example, C-D-E). Simple rhythms exist toward the north, 4/4, 2/4, 3/4, and 6/8 time being most prominent; 5/8, 7/8, 7/16, and more complex patterns are characteristic of Yugoslavia, Greece, and the surrounding area. (A notable northern example in 5/4 time is found in the Finnish *runo* epic.) Free rhythm appears in old Hungarian Magyar music and also in certain coloratura music of the south.

Harmony is not an essential part of European folk music, the emphasis usually being on the single melodic line. However, some exceptions exist in Russian choral singing; in the harmonization in parallel thirds (for example, C-E to D-F) in the German-speaking countries, in Italy, and in medieval England; and in the singing in parallel fifths (for example, C-G to D-A) in the Icelandic *tvísöngur* (twin-song). Instrumental music, of course, may include a simple harmony in various forms, such as drones, or continuous accompanying notes, and occasionally full chords (under the influence of art music). Simple rounds provide another form of rudimentary harmony.

In over-all form the folk melody (European and otherwise) contrasts most sharply with art music, usually being composed of simple, brief phrases and periods (groups of contrasting phrases, or verses) which are constantly repeated (often with slight variations). Verse-and-refrain types are quite common. More complex organizations, such as thematic development, are entirely absent. European singing style is essentially syllabic (one or two notes to a syllable). Florid, or coloratura, singing exists in the south (where it may have been of Oriental origin) and occasionally in some Celtic music (Brittany, Scotland, Ireland). Performance style tends toward the restrained and quiet (facial expressions are usually "dead-pan") in the north and is more visibly emotional and emphatic in the south and southeast.

Asia. Folk music within the high civilizations of Asia is somewhat more closely connected with religious ceremonial music than Western folk music, although general, secular music is of course common. Japan has its annual Bon festival (Buddhist festival of the dead), with costumes and masks and special songs and dances accompanied by drums, concussion sticks, flutes, and the banjolike shamisen. Although the Shinto dance ritual, *Kagura* (depicting the story of a hiding sun goddess), is associated with art music (such as the Noh theater drama), as well as with Shinto temples, it is also a folk dance with special folk songs. In China some of the songs of ancient Confucian rituals, which, like their Christian counterparts, were often blended with pagan ceremonies of the winter and summer solstices, are still found in rural communities as folk songs. In Assam the *Aliyai Ligang*, the seasonal Hindu village festival of planting paddy seeds, with its ritualistic sowing by the head of each family, contains special music and dance. In Islamic countries the rites of circumcision are the occasion for music-making and dancing, and special songs greeting pilgrims returning from Mecca are quite common.

The connection between art and folk music in Asia is more pronounced than in the West. Not only do both types of Asian music partake of "traditionalism" (that is, art music, as well as folk music, tends toward a marked stylistic durability through the centuries), but there are many overlappings in style. Thus the ritualistic *Kathakali* dance drama of Kerala in southwest India contains classic melody patterns (*ragas*) and rhythms (*talas*) requiring trained dancers, but also features many folk elements and is actually a popularized form of what was once exclusively a temple art. Related to *Kathakali*, but more folklike, are the dance dramas with very simple music and dance, the *Terukkuttu* of the Tamils of south India and the *Kuchipudi* of Andhra in southeast India. In Indonesia the aristocratic gamelan, or orchestra, is not the exclusive property of royalty and the upper class, but exists in simpler versions in the villages. The nay flute of the Islamic world is both a folk and art instrument, and the modern Islamic double clarinet *zummarah*, a folk instrument, corresponds almost exactly to the ancient Pharaonic double clarinet (*mat*).

In comparing Eastern and Western folk styles, the most striking differences are found in melodic ornamentation, singing style, and rhythm. Ornamented and florid melody (with grace notes, rapid turns, runs, glides) is vital to the style of the Middle East and India and to a much lesser extent of some Far Eastern music. (Gliding melody, however, is very common in the Far East.) The intense, emotional, nasal singing style of the Middle East and India becomes even more nasal and constricted in the Far East, while rhythmic complexity (asymmetric patterns such as 5/8, 7/8, as well as counter rhythms, or different rhythms

played against each other) in the music of the former area gradually gives way to a simple, four-square rhythmic style toward the latter area. The gapped, pentatonic scales are characteristic of China and Japan. (The Japanese today consider the pentatonic *Auld Lang Syne* a Japanese folk song, *Hotaru no Hikari*, or Light of Fireflies.) Ungapped seven-note and smaller diatonic scales (sometimes adopting the special tunings of art music, with tones smaller than a semitone) are more prominent in Middle Eastern and Indian folk music. Indonesia has a scale of five *equal* tones to the octave, although the source of this is art music. Harmony in the Western sense is not characteristic of Oriental music, although limited types of accompaniment exist (such as a continuous one- or two-note drone and heterophony, the simultaneous group variation of a melody, especially in the Indonesian gamelan).

Folk music research, begun mainly in the 19th century and reaching a scientific orderliness in the 20th century (as a branch of ethnomusicology), has had to contend with a fast-disappearing phenomenon. With modern urbanization, much of the rural (and hence more primary) folk music of the world will eventually be found only in archive repositories and in recordings. Among the most important U.S. archives are the Library of Congress Archive of American Folk Song and the Indiana University Archives of Folk and Primitive Music. European archives include the Phonogrammarchiv of the Austrian Academy of Science (Vienna), the Berlin Phonogrammarchiv, the Schallarchiv of the Institute of Musical Research (Regensburg), the Folklore Archives of the Athens Academy, and the archives of the Musée de l'Homme (Paris).

Consult Sachs, Curt, *The History of Musical Instruments* (1940); Karpeles, Maud, *Folk Songs of Europe* (1956); Nettl, Bruno, *An Introduction to Folk Music in the United States* (1960); Sachs, Curt, *The Wellsprings of Music* (1962).

ROSE BRANDEL, Hunter College
See also ETHNOMUSICOLOGY; FOLK DANCE; MUSICAL INSTRUMENTS; RHYTHM; SCALE; and entries on the music of individual countries.

FOLK TALES. When the human race was young, a body of unwritten literature gradually took form. This traditional literature, or folklore, includes myths, fables, hero stories, nursery rhymes, and folk tales. Many theories are held by scholars concerning the origin of folk tales, for it has been discovered that variants of the same story are told in widely separate parts of the world. For instance more than 300 versions of Cinderella have come down to us in many languages. Were the same stories carried from one area to another as tribes moved about? Did they arise spontaneously as people in different places tried to explain natural phenomena or seemingly supernatural occurrences? So far, no definite answers exist.

Folk tales are enjoyed by children because of their dramatic qualities and strong plots; they are important in developing the imagination, building ethical concepts, and providing understanding of racial customs and characteristics. Folk tales have been broken down into several categories: repetitive stories (*The Three Billy Goats Gruff*, Norway); accumulative tales (*The Old Woman and Her Pig*, England); beast tales (*The Traveling Musicians*, Germany); droll, or humorous, stories (*Contrary Mary*, Finland); and nursery or fairy tales, with magic as their theme (*Billy Beg and His Bull*, Ireland). The types overlap, for the same tale can include fairies, witches, animals, repetition, and humor. Some of the great collectors and adapters of folk tales were the Frenchman Charles Perrault (1628–1703), whose *Tales of Mother Goose* (1697) included such stories as *The Sleeping Beauty* and *Puss in Boots;* Jacob Grimm (1785–1863) and his brother Wilhelm (1786–1859), whose tales heard from the German peasants in the early 19th century included *Hansel and Gretel* and *Snow White and the Seven Dwarfs;* Peter C. Asbjørnsen (1812–85) and Jørgen Moe (1813–82), who first wrote down Norwegian tales such as *Why the Sea Is Salt* and *The Princess on the Glass Hill* in the mid-19th century; and James Orchard Halliwell (1820–89), who collected *Nursery Rhymes and Nursery Tales of England* (1845). In America Joel Chandler Harris (1848–1908) published his versions of American Negro tales (*Uncle Remus* stories) in 1880 and later.　　ETHNA SHEEHAN

FOLQUET DE MARSEILLE or MARSEILLA [fôl-kĕ′ də märsä′y′] (c.1160–1231), Provençal troubadour of Genoese origin. Folquet came of rich merchant stock and in his youth cultivated the poetry of the troubadours, following conventional love motifs. Later he renounced the world and, as Bishop of Toulouse, played a leading role in the Albigensian Crusade. He was revered as a saint by the orthodox. In the *Divine Comedy* Dante places him in Paradise. Folquet's poems are competently turned but of no special distinction.

FOLSOM, MARION BAYARD (1893–1976), U.S. businessman and public official who was chief architect of the 1935 Social Security Act. Folsom was born in McRae, Ga., and earned degrees at the University of Georgia and the Harvard Business School. He joined the Eastman Kodak Company in 1914 and remained with the firm except for periods of military and government service. He was a member of many economic policy bodies, including the Federal Advisory Council on Social Security. Folsom became a member of the Committee for Economic Development in 1942 and later (1950) its chairman. He served as undersecretary of the Treasury (1953–55), and Secretary of Health, Education, and Welfare (1955–58).

FOMALHAUT [fō′məl-hôt], also known as Alpha Piscis Austrini, white, first-magnitude star, the brightest in the constellation Piscis Austrinus (Southern Fish). In medieval astrology Fomalhaut, Regulus, Aldebaran, and Antares were called the Royal Stars. Only 23 light-years from earth, Fomalhaut is the 18th-brightest star in the sky.

FOMBONA [fŏm-bō′nä], **RUFINO BLANCO** (1874–1944), Venezuelan writer, born in Caracas. His first works were poetical and showed a strong sense of Nietzschean individualism. He was also a tireless pamphleteer against the Gómez dictatorship and the United States. He is best known, however, as a novelist and short-story writer, through such trenchant writings as *Cuentos americanos*

(American Stories), 1904; *El hombre de hierro* (The Man of Iron), 1907; and *El hombre de oro* (The Man of Gold), 1916.

FONDA, HENRY (1905–), American actor, born in Grand Island, Nebr. His first major success on the Broadway stage came in *The Farmer Takes a Wife* (1934), the screen version (1935) of which was his first film. His other movies include *Blockade* (1938), *The Grapes of Wrath* (1940), *The Ox-Bow Incident* (1943), *Twelve Angry Men* (1957), *Madigan* (1968), and *Sometimes a Great Notion* (1972). In his more than 70 pictures, he often portrayed a man of great warmth and integrity. His later Broadway appearances were in *Mister Roberts* (1948), *The Caine Mutiny Court-Martial* (1954), and *Two for the Seesaw* (1958). In 1974–75, he toured in *Clarence Darrow*.

Jane Fonda (b. 1937), his daughter, appeared in starring roles on Broadway and in several films. For her film performance in *Klute* (1970) she won the Academy Award for best actress. His son, Peter Fonda (b. 1939), a film actor-director-producer, had a notable success in *Easy Rider* (1969) as coauthor, producer, and actor.

FOND DU LAC [fŏn′ də lăk], city of east-central Wisconsin, and seat of Fond du Lac County, at the southern end of Lake Winnebago (whence the name, French for "bottom of the lake"). The city has railroad shops and is a dairy-products center. Food canning and the manufacture of machinery, shoe leather, and outboard motors are leading industries. The city was settled in 1835 by early French traders. Marian College of Fond du Lac is here.

FONSECA [fŏn-sā′kə], **HERMES RODRIGUES DA** (1855–1923), Brazilian soldier and politician. Fonseca, nephew of Brazil's first president, Gen. Manoel Deodoro da Fonseca, made the army his career but entered politics and won the presidency in 1910. His regime (1910–14), inept and harsh, led Brazilians to return to a civilian presidency after his term.

FONSECA, MANOEL DEODORO DA (1827–92), army officer and first President of Brazil. Fonseca had a distinguished military career but turned more to politics in the 1880's, advocating a republican government. He led the peaceful coup of Nov. 15, 1889, which overthrew the empire. He then served as provisional President until a constituent assembly elected him constitutional President in Feb., 1891. Inept, capricious, and arbitrary as President, Fonseca encountered increasing resistance. Yielding to pressure, he resigned in Nov., 1891.

FONSECA, GULF OF, sheltered inlet of the Pacific Ocean bordered by El Salvador, Honduras, and Nicaragua. Numerous volcanoes rise near its shores, and the Goascoran, Choluteca, Guasaule, and Est Real rivers enter its waters. The principal port is La Unión, El Salvador.

FONT, large stone or bronze bowl, often richly sculptured, that holds water sanctified for religious uses. The holy water font stands inside the church door; the baptismal font is in the aisle or transept of the church or in a special structure, the baptistery.

FONTAINEBLEAU [fŏn'tən-blō], town in the Seine-et-Marne Department, north-central France, about 35 mi. southeast of Paris. Some small manufacturing is done in the town: Gloves, porcelain, cabinets, and metalwork are the main products. The château at Fontainebleau, built (1528–31) by Francis I on the site of an older castle, was the principal royal residence for many years. Its interior was decorated by French and Italian artists, including Benvenuto Cellini; its grounds were planted with beautiful gardens. After the palace at Versailles was built, Fontainebleau was little used. Napoleon, however, preferred it. It was here that he first abdicated (Apr., 1814).

The forest of Fontainebleau extends 19 mi. covering an area of 66 sq. mi. Oak and pine cloak the knolls that rise above sandstone rocks deeply fissured into fantastic shapes. The village of Barbizon at the northeastern edge of the forest was the center of the 19th-century Barbizon School of painters. Fontainebleau has a School of Fine Arts for American students, founded in 1923. The Supreme Headquarters, Allied Powers, Europe (SHAPE) for Central Europe is located in Fontainebleau. Pop., 22,704.

JOHN FRASER HART, Indiana University

FONTAINEBLEAU, SCHOOL OF, group of artists established at the palace of Fontainebleau by Francis I (reigned 1515–47) to encourage Italian art in France. In addition to the Italians, the most prominent of whom were Il Rosso, Primaticcio, and Niccolò dell'Abbate, the school included French and Flemish artists. They created paintings and stucco decorations in the decorative mannerist style. The so-called Second School of Fontainebleau, established near the end of the 16th century, was more French in orientation.

FONTANA [fŏn-tä'nä], **DOMENICO** (1543–1607), Italian architect and engineer. Engaged by Cardinal Felice Peretti (later Pope Sixtus V), he built a chapel in the Church of Santa Maria Maggiore in Rome. His other works include the Vatican library; the Vatican palace; the royal palace at Naples; and, with his brother Giovanni, the Acqua Felice aqueduct and fountain in Rome. He helped Giacomo della Porta in building the dome of St. Peter's on the design left by Michelangelo. Fontana also erected the obelisk in front of St. Peter's, a feat that won him great fame.

See also ITALY: *Italian Architecture.*

FONTANA, city of southern California, at the foot of the San Bernardino Mountains, in an area of citrus groves and vineyards. One of the largest steel plants in the western United States, Kaiser-Fontana, is here. Inc., 1952; pop., 20,673.

FONTANE [fŏn-tä'nə], **THEODOR** (1819–98), German novelist and poet. Beginning his literary career as a writer of historical ballads, he turned to fiction in 1878. His novels are especially noteworthy for their depictions of Berlin life, which Fontane viewed with humor, keen understanding, and objectivity. His best works are *Irrungen, Wirrungen,* 1888 (*Trials and Tribulations,* 1917); *Effi Briest* (1895; trans., 1913–15); and *Frau Jenny Treibel* (1892).

FONTANNE [fŏn-tăn'], **LYNN** (1887–   ), actress. She was born in England, made her stage debut in London in 1905, and her first U.S. appearance in 1910. After 1924, with few exceptions, she appeared opposite her husband, Alfred Lunt, principally on the U.S. stage in both comedies and serious works, including *The Guardsman* (1924), *Reunion in Vienna* (1931), *Idiot's Delight* (1936), *Amphitryon 38* (1937), *There Shall Be No Night* (1940), *The Visit* (1958). She appeared without Lunt in *Strange Interlude* (1928). Her wit, grace, and high style contributed greatly to her place among leading modern actresses.

FONTENOY [fôNt-nwä'], village in Hainaut Province, southwestern Belgium, 4 mi. southeast of Tournai. Here, on May 11, 1745, during the War of the Austrian Succession, the French, under Marshal Maurice de Saxe, defeated the British and their Hanoverian allies, under the Duke of Cumberland, to prevent them from freeing the besieged fortress at Tournai. Pop., 666.

FONTEYN [fŏn-tān'], **DAME MARGOT** (1919–   ), British ballerina. Following studies in China, the United States, and London (with Serafina Astafieva), she made her debut in 1934 with the Vic-Wells Ballet; in 1938 she became the company's leading ballerina and later a star of the Royal Ballet. Noted for her impeccable ballet "line," meticulous technique, and versatility, her roles ranged from the gentle Odette in *Swan Lake* to the flashing Firebird in the ballet of the same name. She also scored notable successes in *The Sleeping Beauty, Giselle, Petrouchka,* and others. Among the ballets created for her, the most notable are Frederick Ashton's *Sylvia, Ondine,* and *Daphnis et Chloé.*

FOOCHOW [foo'chou'], also known as Minhow, city on the Fukien coast of south China, and capital of Fukien Province. It is located on the north bank of the Min River about 35 mi. above its mouth, at the head of an elongated delta.

The site of the city was occupied in ancient times by aborigines who worshiped the dog as their ancestor. In the Han Dynasty (c.206 B.C.–220 A.D.) it was known as Min Yueh. The city wall, 6 mi. in circumference, was built during the Ming Dynasty (1368–1644) when the city was the site of the prefectural government.

Foochow was one of the original ports opened to foreign trade by the Treaty of Nanking with Great Britain in 1842. The city became the center of much of the China tea trade in the 19th century, but the port declined after 1880. The Min River delta is not navigable by large ships owing to sand bars at its mouth and to shallows within the delta, but it remains a regional port for such products as tea, timber, lacquer, and silks. After 1952 the Communists began the development of major industries to turn Foochow into an industrial center. The completion of the railway linking Foochow with Nanping in western Fukien Province in Dec., 1958, there connecting with the main Chinese railway system, has lessened the isolation of the city from the rest of the country. Pop., 553,000.

JOSEPH E. SPENCER, University of California

The sketchy evidence available indicates that our ancestors ate what food came to hand — fruit, buds, grubs — just as they found it.

Meat — obtained by scavenging and perhaps hunting — was added to the diet. Stones may have been used to cut up carcasses, and sticks may have been used to dig for vegetable foods.

POSSIBLE DISCOVERIES and INVENTIONS

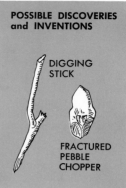

DIGGING STICK

FRACTURED PEBBLE CHOPPER

FOOD, any substance other than water that can be taken into the body of an organism for its maintenance, growth, and reproduction or to provide energy for other activities. Thus defined, it includes not only the familiar organic materials which form the bulk of human foodstuffs, but oxygen (carbon dioxide in the case of plants), inorganic salts, and traces of various elements which are ingested or absorbed by living things. In ordinary English usage, however, "food" has a more restricted meaning, and may exclude spices, beverages consumed for nonnutritive purposes, or even nutritious substances in liquid form. Here, food will be discussed in its relation to human culture and history. For chemical and physiological aspects of food, see the list of related articles at the end of this entry.

For hundreds of millions of years, plant and animal organisms have been competing for nutritive materials in the waters and on the land surfaces of the earth. Even though nutritive materials can be used over and over again, thanks to the use of the sun's energy by green plants, this competition for foodstuffs explains their relative scarcity. Another reason is that each species tends to expand its numbers toward the limits of its food supply. Man has been no exception to this, and as he has increased his ability to extract foods from the environment, his numbers have risen correspondingly. Until the last few centuries, a large part of human labor and intelligence went into the task of obtaining a food supply, leaving little time and energy for other activities. Usually the population of a given animal species comes into balance with the food resources of a rather limited area, or *niche*, as it is called in ecology. Man, with his high intelligence and ability to use tools and fire, has not confined himself to one region or environment, but has spread in the course of the last million years into all the major land environments of the planet, and has learned to exploit part of the aquatic environment as well. In each of these different environments he has had to develop a food supply, and he has been able to do so without fundamental biological changes, thanks to his developing culture. All major increases in the human population of any region beyond the tiny numbers able to subsist by simple wild-food gathering have required technological advances. Human history could be written in terms of foods and the techniques used to secure them, though, of course, this would be to focus on only one of many aspects. For

mankind, food is a many-layered topic, extending beyond nutrition to values, ritual, and social relationships—even to the level of what has been called the fine art of cookery.

Man is a mammal, and therefore lives in infancy on a special food secreted by the mother, milk. He is also a primate, an order of mammals which embraces tree shrews, lemurs, tarsiers, monkeys, and apes, in addition to man. As is the case with most primates, man's teeth and digestive system are adapted to a remarkably diversified diet consisting of fruits, berries, seeds, shoots, buds, stalks, leaves, roots, tubers, birds' eggs, insects and larvae, and the flesh of mammals, birds, reptiles, fishes, and many kinds of mollusks and other shellfish. Under natural conditions most primates are vegetarians, consuming animal foods only incidentally. Several million years ago our own primate ancestors were probably also chiefly vegetarian. Yet the primate's capacity to live on a highly varied diet, including meat, is of the utmost importance in explaining how the human body developed. Man's evolution has probably depended in part on dietary shifts related to environmental changes and migration into new regions. Modern mankind lives mainly on vegetable foods derived from grass seeds, legumes (peas and beans, for example), roots, and tubers. Most of man's foods are cooked and otherwise prepared in ways employed by no other animal.

Primate omnivorousness (ability to subsist on a very variegated diet) was not the only factor involved in the development of man. Others were the ability to manipulate tools and weapons, not only for hunting but also for butchering, for grubbing out wild plants, and to carry food burdens gathered from a wide area back to a central lair, where food could be chopped up at leisure. Out of this last habit the important human trait of sharing food among immediate family members may have arisen. Other primates are disinclined to share food. The fact that some carnivores share food suggests that it may have been big game hunting or regular stealing of carrion which initiated this important social change among the ancestors of man.

Phases in the History of Food-getting

Several phases in the history of man's food-getting can be described, though not all peoples or all world areas passed through all of them.

Men learned to use fire for cooking as well as for comfort. They developed rudimentary weapons with which they successfully hunted such big-game animals as wild horses, bison, and elephants.

DISCOVERIES and INVENTIONS

FIRE

KNOBBED CLUB

STONE-POINTED SPEAR

Seals, fish, and other marine life increased the quantity and variety of edibles. Weapons were improved. Baskets made systematic food gathering possible. Stones were used to grind seeds.

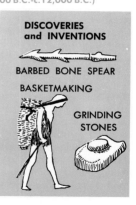

DISCOVERIES and INVENTIONS

BARBED BONE SPEAR

BASKETMAKING

GRINDING STONES

Phase 1. Several million years ago, during the Miocene Era, our ancestors lived on the same foods as modern monkeys and apes. This required no tools and little foresight or ingenuity.

Phase 2. At an indeterminate date, but perhaps on the order of 1 million years ago, certain man-apes called Australopithecines already adapted for bipedal, upright walking, were eating flesh and marrow of big game animals, which they were either hunting regularly or perhaps only stealing from the kills of lions or other predators. The onset of meat eating did not eliminate the gathering of wild plant foods, but it is possible that some very simple tools, such as digging sticks and fractured pebbles, were being used in the quest for vegetable food, as well as to help cut up the carcasses of wild animals. Food-sharing may well date from this epoch.

Phase 3: Hunting and Gathering. During the next 200,000 years, known to archeology as the Lower Paleolithic (the early part of the Old Stone Age), two specialized food-getting patterns were established, one much better known than the other. These were big-game hunting and systematic food-gathering. The animals hunted included bison, wild cattle, wild horses, antelope, deer, members of the elephant family, and rhinoceroses. Spears, clubs, and techniques such as stampeding, running down, and perhaps the fire-drive were used. Fire is known from a cave occupied about 250,000 B.C. by Peking Man, who presumably used it for cooking and heat. Man spread into different and cooler regions as his hunting became more skillful; between 100,000 and 50,000 years ago he managed to penetrate regions with severe winter climates; some archeologists consider this period to form the Middle Paleolithic. Not all the regions into which man expanded had great herds of wild game. In some areas, gathering plants and other wild foods (snails and other mollusks) was more important than big-game hunting. The gathering process had been gradually improved by the use of tools, and was probably carried on mostly by women and children. Both big-game hunting and wild-food gathering imposed a wandering existence, though within recognized territories or ranges. Cooking was apparently limited to broiling, roasting, and baking in hot ashes; there were no cooking vessels of pottery. Boiling with hot stones and the "earth oven" (a pit in which foods were cooked by hot stones) had probably not yet been invented.

Phase 4: Improved Hunting and Food-collecting. In the Upper Paleolithic, extending from about 50,000 to 12,000 B.C., big-game hunting continued with greater efficiency owing to the invention of projectile weapons such as the spear thrower, and perhaps also the bow and arrow. Fishing and sealing were made easier by the inventions of multibarbed spears and harpoons. Food-gathering methods were becoming still more efficient, and the term "food-collecting" is sometimes used to mark this change. More and more, the foods collected consisted of smaller seeds, nuts, and roots and tubers, many of which require special preparation before they can be eaten. Such preparation included grinding (milling), pounding, or mashing, with the resultant meal capable of being cooked as an unleavened bread. Hard seeds could also be made more edible by parching or popping. More effective harvesting required devices such as seed-beaters and containers such as bark, wood, or basketry trays. Fish and other aquatic foods also were becoming more important, a tendency that became even more noticeable in the succeeding Mesolithic Period.

More attention was paid to the harder-to-get foods in the environment, not only because in some regions big-game herds were diminishing (perhaps because man was becoming too efficient as a hunter), but also because the total population was steadily increasing, and people were being forced to move into regions where it was much harder to find enough to eat. During the Lower Paleolithic, man had probably been aware of the edibility of fish and shellfish, but was rarely placed in environmental situations where survival depended on finding efficient ways of living off such resources.

The Mesolithic was a widespread cultural phase in the Old and New Worlds which began at the end of the last glacial episode of the Pleistocene. This phase lasted a few thousand years in some regions until it was succeeded by the Neolithic, a period marked by the appearance of agriculture and animal husbandry. But in areas that agriculture or livestock raising did not reach, a Mesolithic way of life persisted until modern times, as in aboriginal Australia, the Kalahari Desert of South Africa, the southernmost part of South America, and in much of western and northern North America. In some of these areas big-game hunting continued, but in others it was the seed-collecting, shellfish-gathering, and fishing aspects of the Mesolithic that survived. The food economy of the California Indians and those of the Great Basin was until a few generations ago an excellent sample of Mesolithic subsistence. Even where agriculture and livestock raising were established, big-game hunting, fishing, and wild-plant gathering did not entirely vanish.

Phase 5: The Food-producing Revolution. The Neolithic, or food-producing revolution, beginning around 7000 B.C. or earlier, saw the emergence of agriculture and animal husbandry, or livestock raising. These innovations were in fact long-drawn-out processes of development and not sudden inventions. They meant that man could depend increasingly upon harvests from controllable and predictable sources, produced in fixed localities, and that up to a point, greater expenditure of human labor could produce greater amounts of food within a given area. Of course, many hazards and uncertainties remained. Nevertheless, people could settle down in permanent communities instead of moving about from one camp site to another. Another result of the food-producing revolution was a major expansion in the world's human population.

Food production was not a uniform procedure, however. The plants and animals that could be domesticated varied tremendously, as did the kinds of environment in which they could thrive. Many hundreds of plants were brought under cultivation, but only two dozen or so animal species turned out to be worth domesticating. Though the dog, probably the first domestic animal, was not primarily kept for food, dog flesh is eaten by various peoples. The most important domestic animals are hoofed animals, such as goats, sheep, cattle, donkeys, horses, camels, reindeer, and llamas; the first seven of these provide both flesh and milk, and the last six transportation as well as meat. Only the pig among major domestic animals is ordinarily neither milked nor used for transport or work. Among birds, only ducks, geese, chickens, and turkeys have much economic importance. No reptiles or amphibians have become regular domestic animals, but several fish species are raised in ponds and provide significant amounts of food for man in Southeast Asia and Indonesia. Among invertebrates, domestic animals include honeybees, silkworms

Food, like clothing and shelter, is a basic concern of mankind. Thus it is one of the most extensively covered topics in the Encyclopedia. This Study Guide directs the reader to groups of articles on aspects of food supply and food use ranging from the origins of farming to the handling of frozen meats. A logical introduction is the article FOOD, which has the broad scope shown by the following outline.

Phases in the History of Food-getting.
- Phase 1: Reliance on wild plants.
- Phase 2: Beginning of meat eating.
- Phase 3: Hunting and Gathering.
- Phase 4: Improved Hunting and Food-collecting.
- Phase 5: The Food-producing Revolution—the start of agriculture.
- Phase 6: Improvements in Producing and Distributing Food.
- Phase 7: The Spread of Foods over the World.
- Phase 8: Food Since the Industrial and Scientific Revolution.

Food Customs and Taboos. Social and religious significance of food; fasting and other religious observances; etiquette, manners, and methods of eating.

Food Supply and Technology. Famines and starvation; the population explosion and the world's food supply.

The reader who wants more information about the history of food-getting and the importance of the food supply in the history of human culture can turn to articles by anthropologists and archeologists: PALEOLITHIC AGE, HUNTING AND GATHERING STAGE, NEOLITHIC AGE, FOOD-PRODUCING REVOLUTION, BRONZE AGE, and CIVILIZATION.

Modern food raising is described in AGRARIAN REVOLUTION, AGRICULTURE, and many related articles such as DAIRY FARMING. Individual articles discuss major farm products, for example, DAIRY PRODUCTS, CHEESE, GRAIN, WHEAT, POULTRY, and APPLE. Another major food source is treated in FISHERIES and FISH CULTURE. Methods of preparing food products for storage and distribution are described in FOOD PRESERVATION; FOOD, FROZEN; FOOD FREEZER PLANT; and CANNING, COMMERCIAL. These articles and the discussion of the meat packing

industry in the article MEAT illustrate that food is a big business in the modern world. Beverages are also considered—COFFEE, TEA, and WINE, for example.

One major purpose of this Encyclopedia is to provide practical information for the homemaker. To fulfill this aim, home economists have written such articles as FOOD FOR THE FAMILY; CANNING, HOME; FOOD FREEZING, HOME; and MENU PLANNING. The preparation of food is discussed in COOKERY, FISH AND SHELLFISH COOKERY, POULTRY COOKERY, MEAT (see Meat Cookery), BARBECUING, VEGETABLE COOKERY, SPICE AND HERB COOKERY, SPICE (with a chart of names and uses), and WINE COOKERY.

Representative dishes of many lands are described in special articles: ARMENIAN COOKERY; CHINESE COOKERY; COOKERY, AMERICAN; FRENCH COOKERY; GERMAN COOKERY; HAWAIIAN COOKERY; INDIAN AND PAKISTANI COOKERY; JAPANESE COOKERY; KOSHER FOODS AND JEWISH COOKERY; MEXICAN COOKERY; RUSSIAN COOKERY; SCANDINAVIAN COOKERY; SPANISH COOKERY; and VIENNESE COOKERY. These articles may interest the menu planner and cook. They have additional value in that they show differences in food customs and in uses of materials in a variety of cultures.

Another aspect of the topic of food—one of importance to the homemaker—is discussed in NUTRITION and other articles such as DIGESTION, VITAMINS, CALORIE, CARBOHYDRATES, FATS AND OILS, and PROTEINS. There is also an entry called DIETETIC FOODS. Many articles stress proper care and handling of foods, and there is a special entry FOOD POISONING.

Finally, mention should be made of articles showing official concern on the national and international level for nutrition and food supplies. These include FOOD AND AGRICULTURAL ORGANIZATION OF THE UNITED NATIONS (FAO) and FOOD AND DRUG REGULATION. Protection and wise use of soil and other resources are discussed in NATURAL RESOURCES, CONSERVATION OF. This topic is of particular concern in view of the rate of increase of humans discussed in POPULATION.

Further reading about food, whether from the point of view of the home economist, gourmet, nutritionist, anthropologist, or conservationist, can be found in many books available in the library.

PHASE 5 The Food-producing Revolution (From c.7000 B.C.)

At widely different times, in widely different places, men began to settle down. Plants were brought under cultivation. Domesticated animals and poultry provided meat, milk, and eggs. Food processing began with butter, cheese, beer, and wine. Food preservation was accomplished by drying, smoking, or salt curing. Tools and pottery were improved aesthetically as well as practically.

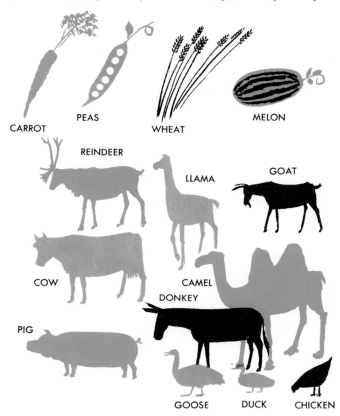

CARROT PEAS WHEAT MELON

REINDEER LLAMA GOAT

COW CAMEL DONKEY

PIG GOOSE DUCK CHICKEN

DISCOVERIES and INVENTIONS

SUN-DRYING SMOKE-CURING

BEER and WINE

MATTOCK

MILK, BUTTER, and CHEESE

SALT-CURING

(not used for food), and some types of oysters which are regularly "planted" and harvested in shallow waters.

The most important plant domesticates are of three main types: (1) grasses yielding small, hard seeds, such as wheat, barley, oats, millets, rice, and corn; (2) plants with starchy roots, tubers, or rootstocks such as the potato, sweet potato, yam, taro and manioc; and (3) legumes, such as peas, lentils, gram or chick-peas, and beans. The staple vegetable foods of the world's peoples consist mainly of some of these, plus oilseeds like rape or sesame, the peanut, banana or plantain, and squashes, melons, and cucumbers. Cultivated fruits, vines, berries, nuts, leafy vegetables, and the like, although of great nutritional importance, provide only a small portion of the food supply of mankind as a whole.

Brewing beer, an invention of Neolithic or possibly early metal-age agriculturalists, is another way of utilizing cereals. Fruits, berries, honey, and even milk can be made into alcoholic beverages, too, usually called wine. That prepared from honey is mead, and from milk—usually mare's milk, as in Central Asia—kumiss. A few types of naturally fermented fruit or berry juices may have been in wide use even before the development of agriculture.

Agriculture did not at first require many new tools. The digging stick of earlier times could also be used for planting and weeding. The adze, a stone-bladed implement like a mattock, developed in the Mesolithic for such purposes as woodcutting and chopping out dugout canoes, was also usable in agriculture. Clearing of land for crops was probably done much as it is in some primitive farming areas of the world today: by a combination of wood and brush cutting and burning known as "slash and burn." No really new tools were needed for food preparation, at least at first. The same kinds of milling and food-pounding stones used during the Mesolithic for wild seeds were used for cultivated grains. Bread could be baked in simple ovens or even ashes, but lengthy boiling of beans, of mushes and gruels, stewing, and brewing required not only watertight but also fireproof containers. Baskets could be made watertight, and liquids stored or carried in gourds, but Neolithic cookery led to the invention of pottery. This did not appear automatically wherever agriculture emerged or spread, but it certainly tended to accompany it. On the other hand, breakable pots were inconvenient for nomads,

PHASE 6 Improvements in Production and Distribution

This phase was marked more by improvements in methods than by new or different foods, although olives and olive oil gained great importance and pepper and spices were used as preservatives. Animals were used for plowing and transport. Levees and canals controlled water supplies and made irrigation possible. Metal was used for tools, such as sickles.

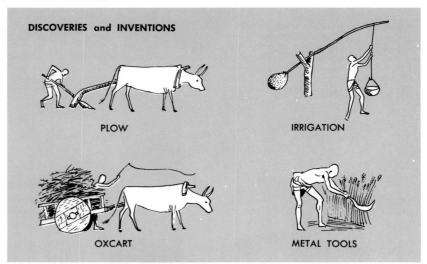

DISCOVERIES and INVENTIONS

PLOW

IRRIGATION

OXCART

METAL TOOLS

OLIVES

whether hunters and gatherers or pastoralists.

Experimentation with plant cultivation and animal breeding covered several thousand years, nor were such efforts limited to a few favored regions like the famous Middle Eastern Fertile Crescent. In most areas with suitable resources, such attempts at domestication probably occurred. Exceptions—lands suitable for agriculture or livestock raising, but whose inhabitants did not practice either until recent times—include the Pacific coast of North America, the Canadian Prairies, the southern grasslands of South America, and parts of South Africa and Australia. Significantly, in none of these areas has modern man found any wild plant or animal worth trying to domesticate which the native inhabitants overlooked.

Many early domesticated plants were species of what we now regard as weeds, quick-growing annuals that flourish on recently disturbed or cleared soil. Many were abandoned as crop plants when other species were found to be more productive or more palatable. It is no accident that most of the highly successful staple food crops produce seeds or roots that are easy to store for long periods in dry places. Regular food storage is characteristic of most, though not all, agricultural peoples. Meat and other animal food products can also be dried or otherwise preserved, as by salting, smoking, or packing in fat. Some of these techniques were probably developed in the Mesolithic or even in the Upper Paleolithic, others during the course of the Neolithic.

Taking milk from other mammals is in all likelihood a by-product of keeping flocks or herds as a handy source of meat and hides. It could well have started as a way of meeting emergency feeding needs of livestock sucklings or human infants whose mothers had died or could not provide enough milk for their offspring. She-goats may have been the first regularly milked, with cows, she-asses, mares, female camels, and female reindeer following in about that order. Other dairy products, such as curds, clabber, butter, cheese, and kumiss, would have come later, and their use reflects the difficulty of storing liquid whole milk. Dairying arose only in the Old World, and

even there did not spread to all peoples who kept cattle or other stock. It was virtually unknown until the last century in the Far East, Southeast Asia, and Indonesia. In the Americas, the only domestic animals that might possibly have been milked were the llama and alpaca in the Andean area of South America; but they were not milked, nor are they now.

Phase 6: Improvements in Producing and Distributing Food. The early metal ages (Bronze Age, early Iron Age) saw the rise and spread of civilization, which rested on the food-producing economy achieved in the preceding Neolithic. Few really new domesticated plants or animals stem from this period, which began in the Middle East about 3000 B.C. What was important from the food standpoint was a great improvement in food-processing and food-producing technology and in facilities for food transport. A major innovation was the plow, with the ox as power. Other applications of nonhuman animal power to the food economy were for grain threshing, lifting water for irrigation, turning grain mills, and transport—by pack animal and eventually by oxcart. An outstanding feature of most of the early metal-age civilizations was the development of elaborate irrigation systems, which greatly increased food production in suitably situated river valleys, for the first time permitting a significant fraction of the population to engage in nonagricultural work.

One result of this was to greatly expand trade relations, based partly on mining and handicrafts, but also on certain food commodities. The expanded trade intensified contacts between peoples, speeding the interchange, not only of ideas, tools, and luxuries, but of crop plants, spices, and animals. Much valuable crossbreeding between local varieties of domesticated species thus took place. The restricted food patterns of formerly isolated populations began to be enriched by borrowings from other cultures. Two foodstuffs—olive oil and grape wine—played an enormously important role in the trade of the Mediterranean from late Bronze Age times onward. Trade in tropical spices tied remote Indonesia, via India and Ceylon, to the Middle East and Mediterranean worlds in classical (Greco-

Roman) times. A similar trade, in which highly prized spices and other foodstuffs were involved, linked China with Southeast Asia and Indonesia. On a less extensive scale, trade in foods between tropical lowlands and interior highlands in Middle America (Southern Mexico and Guatemala) seems to have played an important role in the elaboration of civilizing contacts there, starting 2,000 or more years ago. Africa south of the Sahara was deeply affected in terms of its food supply by the spread there of various crops from India and of the humped breeds of Indian cattle. Honey from northern Russian forests was shipped south by river, along with Baltic amber and furs, to markets in the Middle East. An important element in the trans-Saharan trade, which was starting about the same time, was common salt.

The spread of city life during the early metal ages also was marked by the professionalization or commercialization of many food-processing and food-preparing operations which in earlier times had been home or family activities. Fishing and the collecting of other aquatic foods, the milling of grains and the baking of bread, and brewing and winemaking became businesses practiced by specialists. Taverns and eating houses, where meals could be had by paying for them, appeared in some ancient cities.

Not long before the onset of the next period, distillation to make beverages with higher alcoholic content, such as whiskies, brandies, and rum, was developed. It can be regarded as one of the first industrial-chemical food-refining processes.

Phase 7: The Spread of Foods over the World. The next food era, considering the subject from a world perspective, began about 1450–1500 A.D., and was characterized by a world-wide interchange of food resources and techniques, based on the new ocean routes pioneered by the Portu-

guese and Spanish to Africa, Southern Asia, and the Americas. The East Indian spice trade was a major factor in this epoch of exploration and discovery. The Portuguese found valuable sources of pepper in West Africa, even before rounding Africa and crossing to India. Though the gold of Mexico and Peru and the silks and porcelains of East Asia were more spectacular than foodstuffs, the European overseas expansion of the 15th and 16th centuries vastly changed the food patterns of much of the world. Sugar cane, rice, and the banana were brought to the New World by the Spanish and Portuguese, who also

PHASE 7 The Spread of Varieties of Food Throughout the World

DISCOVERIES and INVENTIONS
The establishment of sea routes during the 15th century between West and East, with the incidental discovery of the Americas, was encouraged by the highly profitable spice trade. Foods and techniques were exchanged on a world-wide basis.

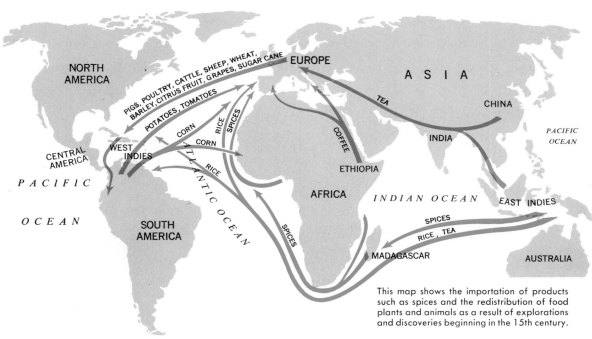

This map shows the importation of products such as spices and the redistribution of food plants and animals as a result of explorations and discoveries beginning in the 15th century.

introduced such Old World crops as wheat, barley, citrus fruits, wine grapes, and many vegetables to the New World areas they visited. They also brought pigs, chickens, horses, cattle, goats, sheep, and donkeys to regions where these domestic animals had not been previously known. From the Americas the Portuguese took corn to tropical Africa, where it spread with amazing rapidity, and to Southeast Asia. Other American food plants followed: New World beans and squashes, tomatoes, peanuts, pineapples, potatoes, and many more. It is now difficult even for botanists to be sure which direction some of these food plants traveled during this period.

In the 17th and 18th centuries Europeans began to consume formerly "exotic" foods in increasing volume. These included tea from Southeast Asia; coffee, originally from Ethiopia, but spread to other areas of Africa by the Arabs and other Muslims, who were forbidden by religion to drink alcoholic beverages; and the Mexican-Guatemalan cocoa, or chocolate. There was also an immense and growing demand for cane sugar, leading to a spread of the plantation system on which its production was based. Rum,

made from sugar cane, also became an important trade commodity in the Atlantic area. Corn and potatoes had harder going in gaining acceptance as foods in Europe, and even in the 20th century many Europeans still think of corn as an animal fodder. The potato, however, after encountering great opposition, was finally not only accepted but became the staple food of millions in Ireland and in Central and Northeastern Europe.

By the 18th century A.D. the main outlines of the world's present food pattern had been established as a result of the great era of intercontinental exploration and colonization and the trade relations then created.

Phase 8: Food Since the Industrial and Scientific Revolutions. The latest phase in the history of man's food supply began only about 200 years ago (1750–60) and has been one aspect of the industrial (and scientific) revolution. One of the first results of the new attitudes was the deliberate effort to improve livestock breeds and promote certain food crops (such as turnips) in Great Britain. The British blockade of Napoleonic Europe stimulated the development of extracting sugar from beets, beginning in

PHASE 8 The Industrial and Scientific Revolutions (1750 A.D.-Present)

Through selective breeding and hybridization, existing strains of livestock and plants have been improved and new strains have been developed. Modern inventions make more — and better — food available to ever-increasing numbers of people in all parts of the world.

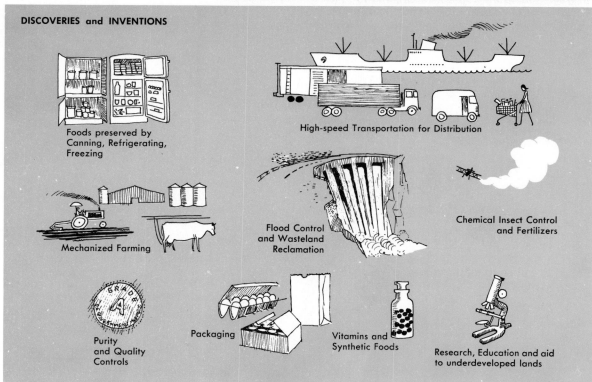

DISCOVERIES and INVENTIONS

Foods preserved by Canning, Refrigerating, Freezing

High-speed Transportation for Distribution

Mechanized Farming

Flood Control and Wasteland Reclamation

Chemical Insect Control and Fertilizers

Purity and Quality Controls

Packaging

Vitamins and Synthetic Foods

Research, Education and aid to underdeveloped lands

FEEDING THE WORLD

More than half of the world's population suffers from hunger or malnutrition, and population is increasing faster than the food supply. In these circumstances widespread famine will occur before the 21st century unless traditional farming methods and land use yield to a more efficient technology and organization. The peasant plowman in Mexico, above, working his own plot, and the farmers of Madras, India, at right, raising irrigation water by the bucketfull, cannot do the job. Some of the methods that may do it are shown on the next three pages.

PLATE 1

PHOTO CREDITS
TOP: UNITED NATIONS
BELOW LEFT: INTERNATIONAL RICE RESEARCH INSTITUTE
BELOW RIGHT: MARC & EVELYNE BERNHEIM—RAPHO GUILLUMETTE

PLATE 2

A revolution is occurring in food production that promises to increase enormously the world's food supply. Machinery has virtually replaced the man and beast of burden in industrialized countries and will do so elsewhere as capital formation permits. But overriding the mechanization of the farm is an emerging technological revolution in land use, fertilization, hybridization, irrigation and advanced husbandry that could increase the earth's potential several fold before the end of the 20th century.

Land reform must precede progress in countries where predominantly small holdings exist, for marginal farmers, such as those shown on Plate 1, have neither the capital nor the acreage to take advantage of the new techniques. But once that is accomplished, crop yields may be doubled and redoubled through the use of chemical fertilizers and new hybrid strains. At Los Banos in the Philippines (facing page, lower left), researchers have produced a short rice plant, Peta IR8, that produces two and a half times as much grain as the ordinary taller variety, and hybrid corn in India (facing page, lower right) has yielded unprecedented harvests.

Experiments in saline irrigation in Israel's Negev region, coastal Spain, Tunisia's arid Medjerda Valley (facing page, top), and elsewhere have indicated that salt water flooding can turn deserts into gardens. The potential for increasing livestock and poultry production (upper right) through improved feeding and controlled assembly-line rearing is enormous, and it goes without saying that the type of fish farming shown at right, on Luzon in the Philippines, is to ordinary commercial fishing what animal husbandry is to nomadic game hunting.

PHOTO CREDITS
TOP: OTIS FEED COMPANY
BOTTOM: TED SPIEGEL—RAPHO GUILLUMETTE

PLATE 3

Abundance alone will not solve the world's food problem unless the increase is registered in high-protein foods. At present the protein deficit effects more than one half of the human population. The deficit may be met in four ways—better use of plant proteins, particularly oilseeds; extraction of proteins from yeasts (shown in a microphotograph, below, being grown experimentally on a petroleum base), bacteria, algae, and other single-celled organisms; synthetic production; and increased exploitation of the sea. The sacks of fishmeal, shown at left, at Lima, Peru, will be added to ordinary animal feeds to hasten growth and boost protein content. High-protein oilseed meals, one-celled proteinoids, and, ultimately, synthetics can be added to ordinary foods for human consumption.

The combined efforts of rich and poor nations, scientists and farmers, government and industry will be needed to make the quantum leap to an adequate food supply for the world's people. But if the increase in population, which now exceeds the increase in the food supply, continues unabated, widespread famine will surely result.

PLATE 4

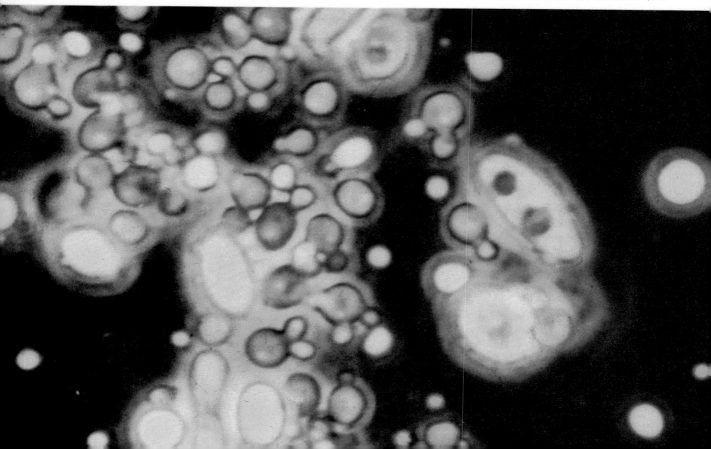

1801. Great progress was under way in sciences having a bearing on food industries. Studies of plant respiration and nutrition paved the way for later discoveries in applied biology, chemical fertilization, and soil science. Louis Pasteur demonstrated the role of microorganisms in fermentation and food spoilage, starting with wines, beer, and milk, in the 1860's. Toward the beginning of the 19th century, even without this knowledge, Nicolas Appert, a French chef, had started food canning, which has been an important factor in the modern food revolution. A science of nutrition emerged by the end of the 19th century, though some of its key findings, such as those relating to the role of vitamins, were to come in the early decades of the 20th century.

Population growth in urban industrial regions during the 19th century was accompanied by marked changes in food production and distribution. In the United States and Great Britain and somewhat more slowly in the industrial countries of continental Europe, staple foods came to be shipped and processed in bulk by commercial enterprises. Foodstuffs that had formerly been processed in the home or at most in small local shops began to issue more and more from food factories and packing houses. At first the commercially handled items were such things as wines, sauces, fancy teas, spices, candies, and biscuits. But a century and a half later, in the United States at least, all foods except fresh vegetables and some fruits were reaching the consumer in commercially packaged form or had been processed in the plants or stored in the cold-storage warehouses of great industrial food firms.

More rapid and dependable transport by railroad and by fast sailing ships and, later, steamships carried ever-increasing quantities of foodstuffs to markets in industrial areas from sometimes distant food-producing regions. Early in the 19th century natural ice was being used in some cities for cold storage. Mechanical refrigeration superseded this, and by the late 1870's, frozen meat was shipped from the United States to Great Britain in refrigerated ships. A few years later regular shipments of frozen meats were being made from Australia, and cold storage of dairy products was becoming common. After the U.S. Civil War, meat packing, centralized in a few cities, began to replace local slaughtering. Centralized grain milling was part of a pattern of industrialization of food processing which involved railroads, river and lake transport, and the building of elevators to facilitate grain handling. Barbed-wire fencing and improved windmills changed livestock herding methods. By the end of the 19th century producers in countries like the United States, Canada, Australia, Argentina, and Russia were supplying much of the grain, and some were also supplying much of the beef and mutton, consumed by the heavily industrialized zones of western Europe.

During the 19th century many governments organized ministries or departments of agriculture and agencies concerned with fisheries. Colleges and universities began to provide courses and research facilities to study the problems of agriculture, animal husbandry, and food technology. Systematic studies of weather and climate have also had an impact on man's food supply and on plans for expansion of it. Economists, agronomists, and other experts, in and outside of government, devoted their careers to food-supply questions. Though there had been sporadic study and writing on such topics in the past, and in ancient China even a Bureau of Agriculture, the attention devoted to food production in the 19th and 20th centuries by scientists, engineers, and government administrators has been without precedent. Also for the first time in history, international efforts to combat famines and malnutrition have been made by both private and governmental agencies.

Food Customs and Taboos

For human beings, foods fulfill more than physiological needs. Food consumption is often the focus of religious rituals and other social interactions, reinforcing group solidarity. Just as eating together may emphasize the closeness of those who join to break bread, not eating with people from other groups may serve to emphasize social distinctions, as in the caste system of India. Foods are the object of complex beliefs and values in most cultures. Most such ideas are prescientific in origin and without nutritional foundation. Among such traditions are customary mealtimes and the notion that certain kinds of foods are suitable for certain meals but not others. Foods are frequently offered as sacrifices to the supernatural. Cannibalism usually has a strong ritual aspect, and few known peoples who eat human flesh ever do so in a casual fashion, as if it were an ordinary food. Such group beliefs about foods, however, are not the explanation for individual food preferences and idiosyncrasies, which are more likely related to individual personality factors or to actual food allergies. Food notions are sometimes held tenaciously, even when it can be shown that customary food practices may lower or destroy important food values. Thus prolonged cooking of fruits and vegetables is common, even though it may eliminate many vitamins.

Food taboos are rules against eating certain foods, against taking any food for certain periods of time, against mixing certain foods, and so on. Familiar instances are the Jewish and Muslim prohibition on pork, the Jewish rule against mixing milk and meat dishes, and the special ways in which even acceptable meat animals must be butchered in order to be kosher. Most Europeans and Americans have a taboo on eating dog flesh, though there is no explicit religious rule against it. In fasts some or all food is given up for a specified time or until some desired result is obtained. Fasting varies from abstention from meat on Fridays among Roman Catholics, to the longer abstentions of Lent among many Christians, the daytime ban on food or drink among Muslims in the month of Ramadan, and the fasts undertaken by individuals or groups to fulfill vows or produce a political or other effect, as in hunger strikes. Several religions impose a vegetarian diet on their followers—notably Buddhism, Jainism, orthodox Hinduism (at least among members of the highest castes) and, among Christians, Seventh-day Adventists and some others.

Eating in most or all human groups involves some form of food etiquette, or manners, which may prescribe the order of serving food, when to start eating, what to say when one finishes, or whether to talk at all while at meals, whether men and women should eat together, and the proper way of handling food, with or without eating utensils. About half of mankind eat with their fingers and not with knives, forks, and spoons, or with chopsticks; yet food-handling etiquette may be meticulously prescribed even when only the fingers are used. In some cultures food is served in small bits, chopped in the kitchen into bite-size pieces suitable for chopsticks, as in China. In other cultures, the diner may be expected to do a considerable amount of food cutting at the table. Foods are served on leaves or sea shells, in their own skins, pods, or husks, wrapped in leaves or thin breads, or as liquids, pastes, powders, at room temperature, hot, cold, or even frozen. In the cultures where cooking is a fine art, much attention may be lavished on modes of serving or presenting food, including purely visual effects. About half the world's peoples eat their meals while sitting on the floor or ground, from mats or cloths, or from very low trays. Dining tables are found among European or Europeanized peoples, and among the Chinese.

Food Supply and Technology.

Most of mankind has suffered at one time or another from food scarcity, and in some parts of the world people are chronically undernourished or endure frequent famines. While starvation when it occurs is fairly obvious, food deficiencies resulting from insufficient protein, vitamin, or mineral intake may not be recognized as such by the victims of this deprivation.

Until the 19th century, little could be done to alleviate the effects of famines. Relief supplies could not be moved very rapidly in the days before railroads or steamships, and national and international agencies had not yet been organized to distribute food on a large scale. Chronic malnutrition was not universally recognized as a problem by the medical profession. Scurvy was the first major food-deficiency disease to be treated or prevented, through the use of citrus fruits or juice in the 18th century, but the discovery of its cause—insufficient Vitamin C—was delayed for over a century.

In the 19th century another deficiency disease, rickets, now known to be due to Vitamin-D deprivation, was treated or prevented by administering cod-liver oil. Beriberi and pellagra were later also found to be connected with food deficiencies. Still later, kwashiorkor, a widespread condition in infants with insufficient protein intake, was recognized. In fact, protein deficiency is probably the single most serious human dietary problem, particularly in the less developed tropical countries. Unfortunately, it has been much more difficult and costly to overcome massive protein deficiencies in large populations than insufficiencies in vitamins or trace minerals, and other essential elements such as iodine.

Increasing Man's Food Supply.

Until recent times, the problem of enlarging and expanding man's food supply mostly entailed putting more land under cultivation, and in the case of lands already cultivated, of improving the productivity of crops through better seed, more efficient tools, fertilizers, and comparable improvements in handling, storage, processing, packing, and distribution. Similar improvements could be made in animal husbandry, or in fisheries. The basic environmental resources on which all food production rests—air, soil, water, and sunlight—were generally looked upon as inexhaustible or endlessly renewable through natural processes. The fragility of the world's ecosystems was not yet perceived.

Although a few countries were already becoming overcrowded, it was assumed that man could go on expanding his numbers practically indefinitely in the vast, thinly populated "new" continents of the Americas and Australia. It was not, in fact, until 1798 that anyone set forth a more pessimistic hypothesis in unambiguous terms. The English economist Thomas R. Malthus, in his *Essay on the Principle of Population*, proposed that there were limits to man's expansion on the planet. Foreseeing war, famine, misery, and disease as the ultimate controls, he could only advise continence or self-control of man's reproductive instincts. Birth-control methods, which already existed, he regarded with dismay. He was opposed by various more optimistic thinkers, including the English writer William Godwin, who had confidence that science and technology would always find a way out of the Malthusian dilemma.

Actually, the world situation in Malthus' time was still far from critical. In 1800 there were less than one billion people on the planet. The world's population passed two billion early in the 20th century, three billion in the 1960's, and by 1970 had reached approximately 3.5 billion. Expert estimates tend to agree that by the year 2000 it will have reached, if not exceeded, 6 billion. Little more land suitable for cultivation remains, unless desalinization, that is the removal of salt from ocean or other salty waters, can be employed to permit the irrigation of existing desert or near-desert lands. A few more areas may be reclaimed by expanding irrigation, or by creating farmlands from coastal marshes or lowlands, as in the Netherlands, but these efforts are not likely to change the prospects substantially. Nor is the dream of being able to extract greatly increased amounts of food from the oceans very likely of fulfillment. Most experts are not very optimistic about the prospect of vast new harvests from the sea, whether of fish and other animal species not yet being exploited, or of the small plants (chiefly algae) on which fish and other sea animals subsist. Virtually no experts see much hope for circumventing future food shortages by improvements in animal husbandry. While meat, dairy products, and eggs are of great nutritional value, they are already a luxury for the vast majority of mankind. In the future we shall probably be able to afford relatively less, not more, of animal food products, which, acre for acre, are inherently less efficient than foods on which animals too must depend.

Technological Advances.

To be sure, the outlook for progress in meeting the world food problem is not entirely hopeless. We have seen remarkable improvements in certain staple crops, such as rice, wheat, and maize, as a result of both genetic research and advances in the technology of tillage, fertilizers, pesticides, and weedkillers. The age-old scourge of farming, unforeseen storms and droughts, and other adverse weather conditions, has been mitigated by great improvements in weather prediction. Efforts, still mostly experimental, suggest that man can hope to control some weather phenomena, such as local rain or hailstorms, and minimize the destructiveness of others, such as hurricanes. Worldwide "remote sensing of the environment" should also provide data on world farm crop prospects, far more accurate than the present piecemeal collection of statistics.

Pesticides, weedkillers, chemical fertilizers, and soil conditioners are steadily reducing risks for farmers, and more efficient controls over both plant and animal diseases also continue to flow from laboratories and testing stations. However, many of these improvements have undesirable side-effects, which may, even in the fairly short run, upset delicate environmental balances. Chemical pest and weedkillers, along with residues of chemical fertilizers, run off into streams and lakes and eventually reach the sea, where they combine with industrial and other pollutants. What may benefit farmers may destroy fisheries. At the food processing level, the effectiveness of some products may be enhanced by improved treatment and additives. Unfortunately, some of these technological improvements have great disadvantages, either to the consumer directly—as in the furor in the late 1960's over cyclamate sweeteners—or because along with masses of other trash they contaminate the environment, as has been the case with disposable or non-returnable containers.

On the other hand, faced with the increasing costs of meat, dairy, and other animal food products, we may have to depend on the ingenuity of food technologists for synthetic substitutes for such products. Some have already appeared on the market, though the impetus for their creation has come mainly from consumers with religious or other objections to animal foods. The first major substitution of this kind was oleomargine or margarine, a vegetable product designed to replace butter. Synthetic substitutes for coffee, cream, and whipped cream, and approximations of bacon, all from vegetable sources, are now available. Producers of animal food may resent these synthetics, but the hard economic facts suggest that their role in man's diet will steadily increase. It should be noted that even some vegetable foods may eventually become so expensive that substitutes made from cheaper sources may enter the market. Artificially flavored and colored "fruit-juice" substitutes have been available for many years, and orange-juice like products are sold in powdered form.

Environmental Perspective. All of the above problems came into much sharper focus around 1970 with a great growth of popular interest in ecology. Many of the technological improvements that had led to increased food production were seen to be double-edged, with polluting side-effects on the environment, or deleterious effects on living organisms in the food-chain.

Equally serious have been the problems of the less developed countries. After World War II, much was expected of planned economic development, guided by foreign experts and international agencies. Some spectacular advances were achieved in public health care—for example, in malaria control or in the realm of plant breeding. But many of the hopes of the development planners were undermined by political instability, ideological conflicts, and regional warfare. Unbridled urban growth and excessive expenditures for armaments have been some of the unexpected checks on rational planning to achieve modernization.

While a few of the underdeveloped countries have achieved an economic "takeoff" into modernization, most have not. Countries such as India and Pakistan do not offer great promise of overcoming the Malthusian dilemma in this century. Mainland China, which is likely to have a

billion people by 1985 and over two billion by 2000, is faced with a particularly ominous problem. China has not had a favorable record of meeting the food requirements of all its people over the past several centuries, and it is unreasonable to suppose that by 2000 A.D. the Chinese administrators, planners, and technologists can cope with a population in a single country which will approximately equal the 1930 world population.

The immense difficulties that are likely to confront even the most advanced countries in the next three decades—from avoiding disastrous international war to the maintenance of internal order and salvaging what remains of the environment—suggest that the food supply question will become a paramount problem for mankind. Until recently, the experts most concerned with food concentrated their attention on agriculture, animal husbandry, and fisheries, and the technical means to improve them. The present and presumably future prospects would seem to link this set of problems inextricably to those of demography, sociopolitical structures, and all the other factors which shape our environment, thus immeasurably complicating the search for solutions.

Consult Hardoldsen, E. O. (ed.), *Food, One Tool in International Development* (1962); Bennett, M. K., *The World's Food: a Study of the Interrelations of World Populations, National Diets, and Food Potentials* (1964); Myrdal, Gunnar, *Asian Drama: an Inquiry into the Poverty of Nations*, 3 vols. (1968); Cochrane, W. W., *The World Food Problem: a Guardedly Optimistic View* (1969).

GORDON W. HEWES, University of Colorado, Boulder

FOOD, FROZEN. Frozen foods in retail packages for home consumption were first introduced in Mar., 1930. As early as 1905 fruits and berries had been frozen in 50- and 100-lb. barrels for use by the bakery, preserve, and ice cream industries. The earliest history of commercial freezing of foods coincides approximately with the advent of mechanical refrigeration in 1880. Meat, poultry, and fish began to be frozen by this method for transportation over long distances.

The frozen meat, poultry, and fish available in the early 1900's were not too acceptable to the consumer as frequently only the poorest quality was frozen. Equipment was sometimes inadequate to freeze the material before spoilage set in, and storage temperatures fluctuated so greatly that off-odors and off-flavors developed. Since these products were usually available only at refrigerated warehouses, they were called cold storage meat, poultry, eggs, and so forth.

Clarence Birdseye (1886–1956) of Gloucester, Mass., is credited with being the "father of frozen foods." As a missionary, trapper, and U.S. Wildlife Service employee in Labrador, he discovered that fish caught and thrown onto the ice in extremely cold weather had markedly better eating quality than that frozen at higher temperatures. Using his natural inventiveness, in 1920 he developed the first machine that quickly froze foods either as bulk pieces or retail-size packages. This invention made possible better-quality frozen foods than those resulting from the slower, older methods. The process was called quick freezing; the products were called frosted foods, to distinguish them from the less acceptable cold storage items.

How to Freeze Foods. Freezing prevents foods from spoiling because at temperatures below 15° F. the spoilage agents—bacteria, yeasts, and molds—cease functioning. These microorganisms, in general, do not die but cease activity until returned to a more suitable temperature. Chemical changes resulting in discoloration, such as the browning of apple flesh and peach slices, and the development of off-flavors, such as rancidity, continue to take place, but the colder the temperature, the more slowly they occur. When foods are held at 0° F., these changes in quality do not develop for approximately a year. Therefore, freezing of foods and their distribution in the marketing channels is usually accomplished at 0° F.

When a food is frozen, the juices form into ice crystals similar to snowflakes. Rapid freezing results in small ice crystals, and slow freezing in large crystals. Since all foods are made up of liquid-filled cells, much like a honeycomb, the size of the ice crystals determines the amount of rupturing damage that is done to the cell walls. Even the smallest crystals do some damage, but larger crystals do severe damage, and the product on thawing is found to have lost its firm structure. This is why lettuce, celery, cabbage, tomatoes, and other foods that are eaten in part for their crispness are not recommended for freezing.

There is some misconception concerning the statement printed on frozen food packages that the product should not be refrozen after defrosting. There is no chemical substance formed in the defrosting and refreezing cycle that will make one ill; it is only that refreezing with equipment normally available in the home is not rapid enough, and a less desirable product results.

Prefreezing Precautions. The procedures for freezing foods of various types differ only in the prefreezing handling steps. Freezing does not improve a product. Therefore, only the best raw materials should be used. Fish, meat, and poultry need only to be cleaned, washed, and trimmed, as prepared for cooking in the fresh state. Fruits and berries are washed and prepared as if they were to be served fresh. When sugar is recommended, it is added to help retard the chemical changes such as browning that can occur even at freezing temperatures. Vegetables are prepared as for serving fresh and are then blanched (placed in boiling water or steam) until the centers of the pieces reach approximately 180° F. This heating aids in retarding the chemical changes that can take place subsequent to freezing. Prepared foods are usually cooked until three-quarters done and then the subsequent heating to serve finishes the cooking.

Packages for the foods in all cases should be sealable and the packaging material should be a moisture- and vaporproof barrier to prevent the food from drying out. "Freezer burn" is a term used to describe the surface of frozen poultry and meat that has dried out because of poor packaging. The surface has a mottled appearance as if burned, which is also a drying-out process. Freezing should be accomplished immediately after packaging and the product should be 0° F. within 24 hours to minimize losses in quality.

Frozen foods in general maintain their color and flavor better than foods preserved by other conventional methods, but they are still preserved foods, and some differences from the fresh product, including a difference in texture, have to be expected. Nutritionally, freezing retains vitamin values better than other conventional preservation procedures because high temperatures, damaging to vitamins, are not present. Minerals, fats, proteins, and carbohydrates are not impaired by the freezing process.

WALTER A. MACLINN, Refrigeration Research Foundation
See also BIRDSEYE, CLARENCE C.; FOOD FREEZER PLANT; FOOD FREEZING, HOME; REFRIGERATION.

FOOD ADDITIVE, a substance added to a foodstuff to improve its desirable properties or to suppress its undesirable properties. As an agricultural society yields to industrialization, families who once grew their own food become dependent upon the supermarket for what they eat. Food preparation has become centralized in large plants. The original long hours of home meal preparation have been shortened by the many convenience foods and mixes now on the market. Such changes have to a large extent been made possible by the development of food additives which perform the required functions.

Regulation. In 1958 the U.S. Congress amended the Federal Food, Drug, and Cosmetic Act to provide that anyone who wished to add a new substance to food had to submit a petition for clearance of the additive to the Food and Drug Administration (FDA) before marketing it. Certain substances already being used in food were not designated as food additives, and their use was permitted to continue without requiring the submission of a petition. These additives were classed in the "generally recognized as safe" (GRAS) and the prior-sanctioned substance categories.

A petition for a new food additive must include, among other things, scientifically developed data to establish that the proposed usage is safe and that the amount to be used is no more than that necessary to accomplish the intended effect. The amendment classes as food additives not only those substances which are added directly to food, but also substances whose use may otherwise affect the characteristics of the food or which may indirectly become a component of the food from contact with containers, packaging materials, and food-contact surfaces in general. Any source of radiation is also considered a food additive if used to irradiate food or food containers.

Pre-marketing clearance of new food additives assures that the risk of adverse effects from proper use of an approved additive is vanishingly small. In order to provide the same assurance for those substances exempted by the 1958 amendment, the FDA instituted a massive review of the safety of over 700 exempt GRAS and prior sanctioned items. This effort was aimed at establishing a scientific basis for evaluating the safety of all substances added to the food supply.

ALAN T. SPIHER, JR., Food and Drug Administration
See also PRESERVATIVES, CHEMICAL: SWEETENERS, ARTIFICIAL.

FOOD AND AGRICULTURE ORGANIZATION OF THE UNITED NATIONS (FAO), specialized agency of the United Nations. Its purposes are, according to its constitution, "raising levels of nutrition and standards of living, securing improvements in the efficiency of the production and distribution of all food and agricultural products, bettering the condition of rural populations, and thus contributing toward an expanding world economy." At a meeting called by President Franklin D. Roosevelt in Hot Springs, Va., in 1943, representatives of 44 countries formally proposed the establishment of the organization. The FAO officially came into being in Oct., 1945.

The scope of its activities is very broad, ranging from the collection, evaluation, and dissemination of information to practical projects such as the introduction of hybrid corn seed in a member country. Nutrition studies which aim at determining what foods in what quantity ensure man's health comprise one of the exciting fields of its activities. Similarly, forestry and fisheries and neglected crops in many areas of the world have come under intensive study by FAO experts to determine the maximum use of these gifts of nature. The spread of new ideas and techniques is also a matter of first priority.

The organization has no mandatory powers but seeks to advance its aims with individual states and on the international level by improving education, by suggesting and developing new techniques of processing, marketing, and distributing products, by stimulating conservation programs, by aiding the growth of agricultural credit facilities, and by aiding governments in the execution of international agricultural commodity agreements.

The policy-making body of the FAO is the Conference, which meets every second year, and allows each member nation one vote. The Secretariat, headed by a Director-General, is organized into five functional divisions: agriculture, forestry and forestry products, fisheries, nutrition, rural welfare and distribution; and three service departments: economics, statistics, and information.

Almost all of the nations of the world except the Soviet-bloc countries are members of the FAO.

WAYNE WILCOX, Columbia University

FOOD AND DRUG REGULATION is aimed at promoting the purity, standardization, and truthful and informative labeling of consumer products. From earliest times there have been regulations about food, often for religious reasons. The Old Testament prohibition against eating pork, for example, also had a basis in hygiene. Other laws were passed to halt sharp commercial practices. The Greeks and Romans punished the adulteration of wine. As food preparation moved from homes to the shops of urban artisans in the Middle Ages, both the guilds and governments began to regulate many consumer products.

By the early 1800's most countries regulated food and drugs, but through a hodgepodge of statutes and trade and professional rules. With the introduction of large-scale processing of foodstuffs in factories at this time, it became even more difficult for the consumer to be sure of what he was getting in either food or drugs. Adulteration and substitution were common. Labeling was often misleading. Unsafe preservatives were frequently used. In the case of drugs, a lack of standardization and certainty of purity was disturbing doctors.

Following a series of exposés beginning in 1820, the British passed the first general law on the adulteration of food and drink in 1860. Soon most industrial nations began to face seriously the difficult problem of protecting the public from injurious and falsely or inadequately represented food and drugs.

United States. A general dislike of government regulation, plus constitutional provisions dividing the regulation of commerce between the national government and the states, fostered a situation in which the United States followed rather than led most advanced nations in general food and drug regulation. After 1789 the early laws were mainly state laws directed against the adulteration of specific commodities, such as meat, fertilizer, milk, and certain drugs. Producers as well as consumers sought protection. Illinois passed the first general food law in 1874 and in the next 25 years most states passed food laws and provided for small staffs to enforce them.

Congress provided for food inspection in the District of Columbia by 1871, and enacted a general food and drug law for the district in 1888. The first national food law was the Oleomargarine Act of 1886, aimed at the adulteration of butter and the protection of dairymen. A series of similar laws, some using the taxing power to discourage adulteration, was passed in the next 20 years.

Meanwhile, Dr. Harvey W. Wiley, chief chemist of the Department of Agriculture, began the first systematic examination of food from a consumer point of view and published a series of bulletins on "Food and Food Adulterants," between 1887 and 1902. These gave much ammunition for a growing protest against the lack of consumer protection. A 1902 law forbade the importation of adulterated or mislabeled food, and another law of the same year authorized the Department of Agriculture to investigate and report on the use of food preservatives and coloring agents. Aided by volunteers, known as "the poison squad," Wiley's bureau frequently made headlines with its published findings of dangerous practices.

At the turn of the century, a series of dramatic articles in the popular muckraking magazines of the day further heightened public indignation. Not only food preparation but the practices of proprietary (patent) medicine purveyors and liquor distillers came under widespread condemnation. The powerful Women's Christian Temperance Union and the General Federation of Women's Clubs lent active support to reform. Then the publication of Upton Sinclair's *The Jungle*, a biting exposé of the meat-packing industry, came in 1906 at a critical point in congressional consideration of general food and drug legislation. The simultaneous report of a presidential fact-finding commission and the energetic support of President Theodore Roosevelt were added. The result was the passage of the Food and Drugs Act of 1906, effective the following year. This was the first general U.S. regulation of food and drugs. It was also notable for its concern about consumers, rather than producers.

Wiley's Bureau of Chemistry was charged with enforcement. The law gave considerable authority to control adulteration and mislabeling, but only in the case of drugs was there power to set standards of purity and quality. Control of advertising was a function of the Federal Trade Commission under earlier statutes. While administration of the new regulations faced a stormy course in the next few years and Wiley resigned in protest in 1912, considerable improvement resulted.

After 1906 further regulations came in a series of laws between 1909 and 1922 aimed at the control and distribution of narcotics, with administration under the Treasury's Bureau of Internal Revenue. By the early 1930's technological developments, adverse court decisions, and the low penalties set in 1906 suggested the time had come for further consumer protection. President Franklin D. Roosevelt recommended new legislation soon after his inauguration. This was introduced in 1933, but it took five years and wide publicity to overcome industrial pressure-group opposition. Nevertheless, a strengthened law—the Federal Food, Drug, and Cosmetic Act—was finally approved on June 25, 1938, and went into effect the following year. It increased penalties and gave more powers over labeling, standardization, potentially injurious foods and food additives, and initial marketing of new drugs. Cosmetics were included for the first time, factory inspection was strengthened, the power of injunction was granted, and the interstate movement of foods manufactured under unsanitary conditions was forbidden. This is still the basic U.S. law.

The administrative agency was the Food and Drug Administration of the Department of Agriculture, a descendant of the old Bureau of Chemistry. In recognition of the difficulty of operating in a department devoted mainly to the interests of those whom the food and drug laws are designed to regulate, the FDA was transferred to the Federal Security Agency by Reorganization Plan IV, effective June 30, 1940. The redesignation of the Federal Security Agency as the Department of Health, Education, and Welfare in 1953 made no change in the status of the FDA. Meat inspection, also a product of 1906, has remained with the Department of Agriculture.

After World War II there came renewed interest and concern about food and drug protection, and a number of Congressional acts resulted in controls for drugs, pesticides, food additives, as well as such foods as poultry.

A new FDA bureau was set up in 1966 to administer the new regulations. The Child Protection Act of 1966 gave additional protection against inadequate labeling of substances intended for use by children. While the FDA has inspected and tested drugs used for animals over many years, a new Bureau of Veterinary Medicine was created in Nov., 1966 to reflect the growing problems associated with veterinary products and medicated feeds. Also in 1966 the FDA contracted with the National Academy of Sciences-National Research Council to evaluate the effectiveness of 3,000 to 4,000 drugs. These drugs had been approved on the basis of safety alone between 1938 and the passage of the Drug Amendments of 1962, which added an effectiveness-testing provision.

The array of federal laws and regulations is supplemented by a wide variety of state laws applying to intrastate products, and by the supervisory activities of state, county, and municipal health agencies.

Canada. Canadian food and drug legislation dates back to 1874. The basic statute is now the Food and Drugs Act of 1953, with major amendments in 1962. There is also a Narcotic Control Act, revised in 1961. Administration is by the Food and Drug Directorate of the Department of National Health and Welfare. In general, the scope and nature of the regulations parallel U.S. practice, except that the Directorate also has powers over advertising and packaging, which are regulated by separate agencies in the United States. The Canadian laws are also more general. Detailed regulations having the force of law are issued by administrative officials. This makes for somewhat more flexibility in meeting new conditions.

International. The widespread importation of foodstuffs has led to several efforts at international agreement on standardization regulations. Little was done in the 19th century, but proposals for joint food control among the Scandinavian countries began in the 1920's. Since 1956 there has been an effort to develop a European Food Code to replace many national statutes. The Food and Agriculture and the World Health Organizations of the United Nations have co-operated on the development of international standards for the guidance of governments throughout the world.

Consult Thornton, Horace, *Inspection of Food* (2d ed., 1960); Gunderson, F. L., and others, *Food Standards and Definitions in the United States* (1963); Kleinfeld, V. A., and Kaplan, A. H., *Federal Food, Drug, and Cosmetic Act: Judicial and Administrative Record, 1961–64* (1965).

PAUL P. VAN RIPER, Cornell University

FOOD CHAIN, the transfer of food energy from its primary source—the green plants—through a number of steps, known as trophic levels, leading from herbivorous to carnivorous animals. When such a food chain includes scavengers and organisms that cause decomposition, a self-sustaining energy cycle results that makes the ecosystem a stable, living unit. An example of a food chain can be seen in a fresh-water pond. It includes green plants, herbivores, small carnivores that feed on herbivores, and large carnivores that feed on the small carnivores. The marginal vegetation, of rooted and floating aquatic plants, and the algal phytoplankton are the basic food sources. Many small herbivorous invertebrates and zooplankton feed on these aquatic pastures; they constitute a second step in the food chain. Some of the herbivorous invertebrates, especially the bloodworms, are eaten by small carnivorous fish like the bluegills; they constitute a third step in the food chain. At the end of the line are such large carnivorous fish as bass which feed on the smaller bluegills.

The flora and fauna of an ordinary field provide an example of a terrestrial food chain. Here the grasses are the basic producers. They are eaten by the many small herbivorous invertebrates which, in turn, become the food of carnivorous spiders, ants, and beetles. The last step includes the large carnivores—in this case birds and moles—which feed on the insects.

CLARENCE J. HYLANDER, Author,
The World of Plant Life

See also ECOLOGY; ECOSYSTEM; ENVIRONMENT.

FOOD FOR THE FAMILY. One of the primary concerns of the homemaker is how to feed her family well and efficiently within the family means. The health of her family, their mental and physical vitality, work capacity and productivity, and resistance to disease depend to a large degree upon her ability to meet this daily challenge. Equally important are the good (or bad) food habits to be learned by the younger family members, for these are the food patterns that they will carry into adult life.

The homemaker's tools for success in this daily venture are an awareness of her family's particular nutritional needs, organization in home management, imagination in meal planning, and resourcefulness in food shopping. These, combined with a knowledge of the basic nutrients necessary to good health, will result in attractive, nutritious meals and a well-fed, healthy family.

Planning for Sound Nutrition

Menus must be flexible enough to meet the needs of individual family members. Thus growing children may require two or more servings of some foods at mealtime, while adults need only small portions of each food served. Teen-agers' daily food requirements are generally greater than those of their parents. The head of the family, however, may require more meat and eggs (protein) in his diet to meet work demands. Family members with sedentary jobs burn up fewer calories and thus need lighter foods or smaller portions.

For a task as important as feeding a family, a plan is needed. The homemaker should know the foods and the minimum amounts of foods essential for the family's individual nutritional requirements. A nutritionally adequate diet includes those foods needed for growth, energy, and vigorous health.

Dietitians, nutritionists, and scientists think of nutritive needs in terms of about 50 chemical substances generally called *nutrients*. The basic nutrients are proteins, carbohydrates, fats, minerals, and vitamins. Some are sources of energy; some build and repair tissues; others regulate the biochemical reactions which take place within the body. The homemaker need not know the specific quantity or distribution of these individual nutrients in order to provide an adequate diet. She does need to be familiar, however, with the general food groups basic to good nutrition.

National diets vary the world around. Each general geographic region boasts its own food staples to sustain life. In many of the world's areas, the diet of the people is at little more than minimal subsistence level. The reasons are many, ranging from harsh climate and soil conditions to primitive farming methods or political unrest. Other regions are blessed with natural wealth, the benefits of technological advance, and a healthy economy.

In the Far East, rice and millet form a basic part of the people's diet. Australia and New Zealand produce an abundance of varied crops, with lamb and mutton forming an important part of the export economy of the two countries. Lamb and wheat products are standard fare in the Middle and Near East, while the staples of Africa range from the starchy, but nutritious, cassava to a bewildering array of fruits, vegetables, and meat in the prosperous and productive farm regions. Europe produces a wealth of foods. Here, regional staples may exist, but the palate —backed by an energetic economy—has a choice in the selection of a varied, nutritious diet.

Extreme variances in regional climate, soil conditions, and farming methods of Central and South America are reflected in diets ranging from the subsistence level to the most sophisticated fare. In contrast, the temperate climate of North America, combined with advanced farming methods and a sound economy, has resulted in a choice of foods available to the individual consumer that is all but staggering in its abundance and variety. Stock raising and farming contribute heavily to the strength of Canada's economy and play an important part in the country's export program.

Free choice of consumer selection, however, does not necessarily guarantee a balanced, nutritious diet. Aware of this, many nations have moved to educate the consumer public in sound nutrition, to establish regulatory laws, and to set standards of food production.

The "Basic Four" food plan, devised in 1958 by the Food and Nutrition Board of the U.S. National Research Council, lists the basic nutrient requirements for various groups with the added protection of a safety margin for stress and extra needs. Briefly, these requirements for a daily food plan are:

(1) Milk group (daily milk requirements)

Children	3 to 4 cups
Teen-agers	4 or more cups
Adults	2 or more cups
Pregnant women	4 or more cups
Nursing mothers	6 or more cups

(Cheese and ice cream can replace part of the milk.)
(2) Meat group (2 or more servings daily)
Beef, veal, pork, lamb, variety meats (such as liver, heart, or kidney), poultry, fish, eggs; with dry beans and peas and nuts as alternates.
(3) Vegetable-fruit group (4 or more servings daily)
A dark-green or deep-yellow vegetable (important for vitamin A) at least every other day.
A citrus fruit or other fruit or vegetable (important for vitamin C) daily.
Other fruits and vegetables including potatoes.
(4) Bread-cereals group (4 or more servings daily)
Whole grain, enriched, restored.

The above selections are based on what we know of people's needs for vitamins, minerals, proteins, and other nutrients. The number of servings indicated in the plan are necessary for an adequate diet. The "Basic Four" provides a framework for the meals of a day rather than a complete menu. However, if a homemaker chooses foods for her family's meals from these groups, the nutritional value of the diet is protected. Other foods may be added to this framework as desired if individual weight permits.

Determining Family Food Needs

A family's food needs are influenced by many factors: the size of the family, the ages of family members, family activities, family income, special health problems (such as obesity or allergies), storage space, whether or not some family members have lunch away from home, and whether or not the homemaker also goes to work.

The eating patterns of the family need first be considered when determining foods for a family. If a family member does heavy labor, he will require higher-calorie foods than other family members. The average American diet contains about 40% fat, which is thought to be too much by many nutrition authorities. Those who are obese should be limited to a low-calorie diet. Their daily food intake, however, must include satisfactory amounts of the basic food groups.

FOOD FOR THE FAMILY

Lunch and some snacks are often eaten outside the home. Nevertheless, they are part of the daily diet and should be carefully chosen from the "Basic Four" food groups. The homemaker should be aware of and plan for the extra items of food consumed in the home. A "snack shelf" of nutritious fruit, cheese, and milk in the refrigerator enables the family to nibble on foods that are good for them.

A high family income does not necessarily guarantee a good diet; the tendency is to include a greater amount of rich foods and desserts in the menu, and this is the way to obesity. On a low family income the homemaker must plan carefully for use of low-cost nutritious foods. Regardless of income the homemaker must evaluate her food plans in terms of the "Basic Four" food plan. It is applicable to all ages and types and is broad enough within its framework for adaptation to any taste or food pattern.

Marketing for the Family

How should the homemaker spend the family food dollar? This is determined in part by the composition of the family (number, age, sex), amount and type of activity, and size of family income. Family values also affect the way the food dollar is spent. Other factors to be considered are the amount of home food preservation and preparation, the amount and type of entertaining done in the home, personal preferences, special dietary needs, and existing marketing facilities.

The conscientious homemaker feeds her family according to a specific cost plan. In the United States, for instance, food budgets have been devised by the U.S. Department of Agriculture for this purpose. These budgets—low cost, moderate cost, and liberal—list the recommended amounts to be eaten in the different food groups for an adequate diet.

The conscientious homemaker chooses the plan which is best suited to her family's income. Then, with this in hand, she designs menus suitable to her family's nutritional needs. Newspaper grocery advertisements make excellent food cost guides for preparing budgeted family menus. Also, home-stored foods—particularly freezer foods—should be kept in mind when planning meals.

Once the menus have been drawn up, usually by the week, the homemaker is ready to compile a market order. Writing a market list is a simple operation. The menus and their recipes are checked and the needed items written down. The refrigerator, freezer, and pantry shelves should be checked for staples and seasonings which need replenishing. (Jotting down items as the supply dwindles and noting the price and the size of the package being discarded also decreases time involved in making a market list.) A shopping list of this type saves the homemaker both time and money. There will be fewer last-minute trips to the market. A well-organized list also helps the homemaker to resist tempting but unnecessary items. Buying on impulse is not conducive to staying within a budget.

Market items should be listed according to category, grouping like products. Thus, all dairy products are listed together, as are fresh fruits and vegetables, canned foods, cereals, bread items, cookies and crackers, spices, and other products. Being familiar with the store layout also helps to make a more efficient market list; food groups can then be jotted down in the order foods are stocked. A grocery list is particularly important when shopping by phone. When the food is delivered the items should be checked against the market order. Has every item ordered been delivered? Does the bill tally with the prices marked on the items?

Who does the actual marketing is a matter of personal choice. Some homemakers enjoy the opportunity to select their own perishables, such as meats, vegetables, and fruits. Others see it as a valid excuse to get out of the house. Still others elicit the co-operation of husbands or other family members to do the shopping for them.

Shopping by phone is not recommended and should be done only as a matter of necessity. The homemaker not only pays for the special phone and delivery service, but also has little or no opportunity for comparison shopping and purchase of unadvertised specials. (On the other hand, "impulse buying" is practically eliminated.) Telephone orders are usually possible only through independent stores, which are relatively expensive and limited in choice of merchandise. Because of the higher cost involved families on limited budgets should not use this type of service unless it is physically impossible for one of the family members to shop in person.

Food Quality and Consumer Protection

High standards in food quality have increasingly become the concern of responsible governments at both national and local levels. In Canada, supervision and development of farm products and methods are administered chiefly through the federal Department of Agriculture (established in 1868) and the 10 provincial agricultural departments. Federal acts and regulations require the grading of various foods, fair marketing practices, and food plant inspection. For instance, the Meat and Canned Foods Act requires the inspection of packing plants dealing in interprovincial commerce and the examination of meat and canned products.

In the United States consumers and food producers are also protected by legislation (federal, state, and local) which defines or regulates food quality. The Agricultural Marketing Service of the U.S. Department of Agriculture is responsible for developing standards on which grades for food are based. The agency also provides grading service in co-operation with state agencies. Food industry use of U.S. grades is voluntary; the grading service must be requested by individual users and a fee must be paid.

The abbreviation "U.S." precedes most grade symbols which are enclosed in a shield-shaped mark. A round, vegetable-dye stamp on meat with the message "U.S. INSP'D & P'S'D" indicates to the consumer that the meat is from healthy animals and was wholesome at the time of inspection, that it has been prepared for sale under safe and healthful conditions, and that it was suitable for consumption when it left the processing plant.

U.S. meat grades are based on such characteristics as juiciness, amount of fat, tenderness, flavor, and color. The color and marbling of fat and lean in the meat convey to the government graders the quality of the meat.

FOOD PLAN AT MODERATE COST:
SUGGESTED WEEKLY QUANTITIES OF FOOD FOR 19 GROUPS[1]

FAMILY MEMBERS	MILK, CHEESE, ICE CREAM (Qt.)	MEAT, POULTRY, FISH (Lb. Oz.)		EGGS (No.)	DRY BEANS, PEAS, NUTS (Lb. Oz.)		FLOUR, CEREAL, BAKED GOODS (Lb. Oz.)		CITRUS FRUIT, TOMATOES (Lb. Oz.)		DARK-GREEN AND DEEP-YELLOW VEGETABLES (Lb. Oz.)		POTATOES (Lb. Oz.)		OTHER VEGETABLES AND FRUITS (Lb. Oz.)		FATS, OILS (Lb. Oz.)		SUGAR, SWEETS (Lb. Oz.)	
	Qt.	Lb.	Oz.	No.	Lb.	Oz.	Lb.	Oz.	Lb.	Oz.	Lb.	Oz.	Lb.	Oz.	Lb.	Oz.	Lb.	Oz.	Lb.	Oz.
CHILDREN:																				
Under 1 year	6	1	4	6	0	0	0	12	1	8	0	2	0	8	1	8	0	1	0	2
1-3 years	6	1	12	6	0	1	1	0	1	8	0	4	0	12	2	12	0	4	0	4
4-6 years	6	2	4	6	0	1	1	12	2	0	0	4	1	0	4	0	0	6	0	10
7-9 years	6	3	0	7	0	2	2	0	2	4	0	8	1	12	4	12	0	10	0	14
10-12 years	6½	4	0	7	0	4	2	12	2	8	0	12	2	4	5	8	0	10	0	14
GIRLS:																				
13-15 years	7	4	8	7	0	2	2	12	2	8	0	12	2	4	5	12	0	12	0	14
16-19 years	7	4	4	7	0	2	2	8	2	8	0	12	2	0	5	8	0	10	0	12
BOYS:																				
13-15 years	7	4	12	7	0	4	4	0	2	12	0	12	3	0	6	0	0	14	1	0
16-19 years	7	5	8	7	0	6	5	0	3	0	0	12	4	4	6	4	1	2	1	2
WOMEN:																				
20-34 years	3½	4	4	6	0	2	2	4	2	8	0	12	1	8	5	12	0	8	0	14
35-54 years	3½	4	4	6	0	2	2	0	2	8	0	12	1	4	5	4	0	8	0	12
55-74 years	3½	4	4	6	0	2	1	12	2	4	0	12	1	4	4	4	0	6	0	8
75 years and over	3½	3	12	6	0	2	1	12	2	4	0	12	1	0	3	12	0	6	0	8
Pregnant	7	4	4	7	0	2	2	4	3	8	1	8	1	8	5	12	0	8	0	12
Lactating	10	5	0	7	0	2	2	12	5	0	1	8	2	12	6	4	0	12	0	12
MEN:																				
20-34 years	3½	5	8	7	0	4	4	0	2	12	0	12	3	0	6	8	1	0	1	4
35-54 years	3½	5	4	7	0	4	3	8	2	12	0	12	2	8	5	12	0	14	1	0
55-74 years	3½	5	0	7	0	2	3	4	2	12	0	12	2	4	5	8	0	12	0	14
75 years and over	3½	5	0	7	0	2	2	12	2	8	0	12	2	0	5	4	0	10	0	12

[1] U.S. Department of Agriculture, *Food: The Yearbook of Agriculture*

The official U.S. Department of Agriculture (USDA) grades, in their respective order for different kinds of meat, are:

Beef	*Veal*	*Lamb*	*Mutton*
Prime	Prime	Prime	
Choice	Choice	Choice	Good
Good	Good	Good	Good
Standard	Standard		
Commercial			
Utility	Utility	Utility	Utility
Cutter	Cull	Cull	Cull
Canner			

The lower grades of beef, USDA Cutter and USDA Canner, are not offered on the retail market, but are used by manufacturers of various luncheon meats.

The grading of fresh fruits and vegetables is used chiefly in the wholesale markets. The use of grades is optional. Wholesale grades may be U.S. No. 1, U.S. No. 2, and so forth, with 1 indicating the highest grade. For some foods, however, U.S. Fancy or U.S. Extra Fancy indicates top grades above U.S. No. 1. The grading system for the consumer is indicated by U.S. Grade A, U.S. Grade B, and so forth. These grades may be further divided, as U.S. Grade A-Large and U.S. Grade A-Small. Factors for determining grades are appearance, waste, and preferences.

An egg grading program was introduced by the U.S. Department of Agriculture in 1925. Grade labeling is the best consumer guide to egg quality. U.S. grades AA, A, B, and C describe the quality of eggs. The four weight classes usually available in retail stores are extra large, large, medium, and small. They represent the standard minimum weight in ounces per dozen, not including 2 ounces for the carton.

Labels on canned goods must carry a full description of the food, its quality, and the name of the producer or retailer who is responsible for the product. This is a regulation of the federal Food, Drug and Cosmetic Act of 1938.

The Food Additives Amendment (1960) to the federal Food, Drug and Cosmetic Act states that if additives are included in a product their names must appear on the food label. Additives are included in various food products to increase keeping quality, to enrich the products, or to heighten the products' appearance. The U.S. Food and Drug Administration, however, may forbid the inclusion of an additive if it is found to be harmful.

Deciding the Most Economical Food to Buy

Various factors must be considered when spending the food dollar. Living within the family food budget is indeed highly desirable. The conscientious homemaker, however, selects not only according to price but also takes into consideration the relative nutritive value of foods available. She selects those which will provide an interesting, varied, and flavorful diet high in nutrition. Orange juice may be more expensive than apple juice, but in comparison apple juice provides only a small amount of the important vitamin C. Tomato juice, a valuable and generally economical source of vitamin C, may be cheaper than orange or other citrus juices at certain times of the year. The shopper should be familiar with the food sources of important nutrients so that she can substitute a low-cost seasonal food for a more expensive item.

Meat, poultry, fish, and dairy products provide the necessary proteins for sound nutrition. Thus the homemaker bases her family's daily meals on a selection from this general group.

The principal meats are beef, veal, lamb (or mutton), and pork. Poultry provides a wide choice, including chicken, turkey, goose, and duck, while the variety of fish depends on both the locale and season. If groceries are bought by the week the homemaker can buy a selection of cuts from these three groups to allow for variety in both food and means of preparation. Planning by the week discourages food waste. Thus the roast served early in the week can reappear at a later date in the form of a stew or hash.

When comparing costs of meat cuts the number of edible portions must be the final basis for economy. Round steak may be more expensive than sirloin but will be more economical in cost per serving. Rump roast may run approximately twice the cost of short ribs by weight but be the more economical purchase of the two.

When the homemaker buys poultry she must decide on how many pounds to purchase in relation to edible portions. A whole chicken is about 30% edible meat. To obtain 1 lb. of meat the homemaker must purchase a 3-lb. chicken. These figures are important when comparing cost of chicken with that of other meats.

Dairy products, necessary to the diet in their own right, are excellent substitutes for the most expensive meat group. From soufflés and omelets to puddings and casseroles, as main dishes or desserts, milk, cheese, and eggs offer a welcome variety to family meals.

Cost differences in types of milk are dramatic. Protein from fresh milk costs approximately three times as much as that from nonfat dry milk and one-third more than evaporated milk. By using nonfat dry milk many families spend far less for milk yet receive all the important nutrients contained in milk except the fats.

Milk provides many opportunities to stretch the food dollar. A quart of unhomogenized milk yields about 1 cup of cream for whipping (if a day old) at one-third the cost of heavy cream. Top milk is an excellent substitute for half-and-half. Cultured sour cream may be substituted for heavy cream in many dishes, at one-half the cost. An increasingly popular dairy product, it may be used as a dessert topping, in casseroles, as a salad dressing base, and for sauces. Whipped evaporated milk or nonfat dry milk may also be used for whipped dessert toppings according to recipe.

In some communities "local" eggs are offered for sale rather than the more generally acceptable graded variety. However, graded eggs offer the greatest assurance of quality and freshness. The term "freshly laid eggs" is meaningless.

Savings on eggs are possible, although many consumers are unaware of or do not take advantage of cost differences. Grade B eggs are perfectly acceptable, particularly for baking. Although the yolk is fatter and the white thinner than a grade A egg, the grade B egg is definitely edible. Brown eggs and white eggs have the same nutritional value, flavor, interior color, and quality; the only distinction is in the color of the shell. If there is a difference in price by color, it is wise to buy the one having the lower price. According to U.S. weight classes, a 1-doz. carton of graded eggs marked "large" must weigh at least 24 oz., net; "medium," 21 oz.; and "small," 18 oz.

An economical stand-by for extending protein intake is the use of dried beans, peas, and nuts. It is desirable, however, to include some animal protein in at least two meals a day.

The wide variety of fresh fruits and vegetables available may well be confusing, but it is to the homemaker's advantage to be familiar with the bountiful selection. It is wise to buy at a store which carries a varied stock of fresh, high-quality produce. Fresh fruits and vegetables should be exactly that. They are perishable items at best; thus it is preferable to buy early, when the produce is fresh from the wholesaler, and in small quantity. A thorough knowledge of fruits and vegetables provides variety in the menu. Many are seasonal in nature, and it is the wise shopper who takes this into account.

Since fresh, frozen, and canned fruits and vegetables supply approximately the same nutrients, the consumer is faced with what is essentially an economical choice. She must learn to estimate the number of servings the different fruits and vegetables will yield, as her basis for decision will be made, in most instances, on cost per individual serving. For example, if spinach and carrots are selling at the same unit cost, the purchase of carrots is preferable for they will yield approximately twice as many servings as the spinach.

Convenience Foods

Today's convenience foods include new and improved forms of familiar products carrying various legends: "ready to eat," "heat and serve," "just add water," and "mix and bake." What the consumer is actually buying is food plus service in the form of partially prepared foods. Costs to the producer include the basic food materials; labor, plant, and machinery costs; and the cost of research by which these products are developed. In buying convenience foods the consumer buys (saves) time. This is time that she would ordinarily spend shopping for the individual ingredients, cleaning and trimming vegetables, cooking, and washing utensils. For the homemaker who is employed full time or part time outside the home or who has many family and community responsibilities, convenience foods are of significant value. If the homemaker actively dislikes cooking, the freedom gained through the use of a comparatively high amount of convenience foods is important. Mixes are also a boon to the inexperienced homemaker. They not only provide a variety of dishes beyond her immediate capabilities, but lend her encouragement to attempt new recipes on her own.

It is unwise, on the other hand, to rely too heavily on prepackaged foods. Mass-produced foods are prepared to appeal to a wide audience; thus, flavoring agents must be used cautiously. The homemaker also loses the opportunity to be creative. However, the most significant loss in excess use of these foods is in dollars and cents. The cost per portion is increased and in some instances even doubled. There are exceptions, of course. An excellent example is the angel food cake mixes. The price of the mix may alone equal the cost of fresh eggs needed for the cake

when made from a recipe. When comparing the cost of the various mixes, read the label to see what ingredients must be added in order to calculate the total cost of the cooked product.

The nutritive value of processed and convenience foods is frequently questioned. Food faddists contend that processors have refined foods beyond all reasonable limits. Food processing, however, is carried out under rigidly controlled conditions, and most processors replace food elements which have been destroyed or removed from a food in the refining process. Cereals and white flours are enriched with the B vitamins and iron. In some instances the convenience product is of higher quality than the "fresh" food. For instance, fresh broccoli, when crated and shipped long distances, may be bruised, dehydrated, improperly refrigerated, or stored for too long a time. By the time this product is served it has lost much of its original vitamin content. In contrast, prime broccoli picked and quickly frozen under carefully regulated conditions and cooked to specific directions comes to the family table high in nutritive value.

To determine which of the many convenience foods meet the family's needs and pocketbook, the homemaker must analyze the time available for food preparation, the comparative costs of foods made from basic ingredients and those completely or partially prepared commercially, the seasonal availability of unprocessed foods, and her own ability to cook.

Quantity Buying

The homemaker can save a substantial amount of money by giving careful attention to the size of the package she purchases. In general, as package size increases, the cost per ounce, pound, pint, and so forth decreases. (Cost decrease varies according to product and package size.) Although these cost differences appear to be negligible, the homemaker must remember that she makes hundreds of purchases each year, and many small savings add up to a considerable sum.

Purchasing canned food by the case shows a saving in contrast to buying a few cans at a time. Large families might buy by the case as a convenience as well as a saving. Quantity purchasing for the small family is often impractical due to infrequent use of the product or limited storage space.

Food Storage

The amount of home storage space determines the quantity of food that can be purchased at one time. Lack of such space often requires the apartment dweller to shop biweekly or even daily. However, the homemaker with adequate room for storing quantity purchases can do her shopping on a weekly basis. Such perishable items as green leafy vegetables and milk products may then be picked up when convenient and checked out at the supermarket's express lane.

The home freezer, usually measuring 12 or 15 cu. ft., provides space for a three-month supply of frozen foods for the average family. Freezer food plan corporations offer packaged quick-frozen meats, vegetables, fruits, juices, and "bake-and-serve" goods to the consumer by door-to-door service. These plans are timesavers for the

HOME-FROZEN STRAWBERRIES

Westinghouse

Remove stems with sharp knife. Place berries and sugar (2 tbsp. to 1 cup berries) alternately in polyethylene freezer bag.

Wash berries quickly but thoroughly. Drain on absorbent paper.

housebound homemaker with small children. Shopping is reduced to a minimum, and food preparation is simplified. This service, however, plus the cost of the home freezer and its operation, increases the cost of feeding the family. A more economical use of the home freezer is to take full advantage of market specials by buying sale meats and frozen foods in quantity.

Food Fads and Fallacies

With the rapid increase in scientific knowledge, quacks and food faddists have capitalized on the fact that people today are increasingly aware of the importance of the right foods for good health. It has been estimated that approximately 10,000,000 Americans waste $50,000,000 a year on quack diets, fake pills, and spurious "health" foods.

Not only are food fads costly in a financial sense, but they can cause injury to individuals through improper diet and neglect of proper medical care in time of illness. Food fads tend to undermine sound nutritional practices. The diet craze is an example. Any type of drug or pill advertised for weight control should be taken only under medical supervision. A number of reducing pills contain appetite depressants. Aside from the fact that indiscriminate use of these reducing pills may be injurious, they tend to divert attention from the main problem of overeating.

Food fallacies have many sources, from ancient superstition to deliberate misrepresentation by 20th-century "medicine men." Food fallacies range from the old wives' tale that eating carrots will curl your hair to the modern-day belief that improper diet causes most diseases.

The following are a few examples of fallacies and facts about foods and nutrition.

Fallacy: Home-ground or stone-ground flour is vastly superior to that which is commercially ground. *Fact:* Home-ground or stone-ground flour has the same food values as whole-wheat flour processed in a commercial mill.

Fallacy: White eggs are more nutritious than brown eggs. *Fact:* The nutritive value of an egg is not related to the color of the shell. Shell color is determined by the breed of hen.

Fallacy: Omit meat, eggs, and milk from the diet to cure arthritis. *Fact:* There is no evidence that any food will either cause or cure this disease.

Consult Justin, M. M., and others, *Foods: An Introductory College Course* (4th ed., 1956); American Dietetic Association, *Food Facts Talk Back* (1957); U.S. Department of Agriculture, *Food for Fitness: A Daily Food Guide* ("Basic Four") (Leaflet No. 424, 1958), *Shopper's Guide to U.S. Grades for Food* (Home and Garden Bulletin No. 58, 1958), and *Food: The Yearbook of Agriculture, 1959* (1959); Batjer, M. Q., and Atwater, M. A., *Meals for the Modern Family* (1961).

Hazel Addison, Hunter College

See also:

Budget, Family	Instant Foods
Consumer Education	Meat
Cookery	Menu Planning
Fish and Shellfish	Nutrition
Cookery	Poultry Cookery
Food Freezing, Home	Vegetable Cookery
Home Management	

FOOD FREEZER PLANT. The modern freezer plant is an assembly line for the preparation of foods for freezing. Depending on the food being frozen, the equipment in the line washes and husks, silks, shells, cuts, trims, pits, juices, slices, or stems. Visual inspection and grading is then done on long moving belts. Fruits have sugar or syrup added, and vegetables are subjected to steam or boiling water to retard chemical changes such as browning and off-flavor development that can occur during subsequent storage. Filling and sealing of packages is usually done by complicated machines designed for the purpose.

The freezing step is accomplished in one of three ways: by immersion or spraying of the packages with a low-freezing-point liquid such as a concentrated salt solution; by indirect contact with a refrigerant that flows through shelves or belts that may touch the bottom, or both top and bottom, of the packages; or by a cold air blast as the packages either move through a tunnel or as they are stacked in rooms. The equipment accomplishing the freezing is made in many different sizes and shapes, designed for small locker plants or for plants that can freeze a million pounds of a product per day.

Good operating procedures include selecting only the

Expel air from bag; twist, fold and secure top with band or string. Place in freezer immediately.

Thaw berries in refrigerator for several hours to retain firmness. Serve with frozen whipped cream.

varieties and strains of a product that have been known to freeze well, harvesting only at full maturity, culling out poor grade material, handling under sanitary conditions, and completing the entire procedure in the shortest time possible to retard quality losses.

WALTER A. MACLINN, Refrigeration
Research Foundation

See also FOOD, FROZEN; REFRIGERATION.

FOOD FREEZING, HOME. Home food freezers, in which raw or cooked foods are kept at 0° F. (−18° C.), prevent food spoilage, extend the use of out-of-season foods, and make possible cook-ahead meals and last-minute dinners.

Only foods which are high in quality should be selected for freezing. Fresh foods are frozen as quickly as possible and defrosted at the last moment to ensure freshness and good flavor. Many foods, properly packaged, will keep from two weeks to a year:

One year: beef, lamb, venison, rabbit, game birds, most vegetables (blanched and cooled) and fruits (packed dry or in sugar or syrup).

4 to 6 months: poultry, veal, lean fish.

6 weeks to 3 months: most cooked foods, ground beef, fat fish, smoked ham, commercial frozen foods.

4 to 6 weeks: leftovers, ground fresh pork, seasoned sausage, ice cream.

SAFE STORAGE IN HOME FREEZER

1 YEAR	BEEF, LAMB VENISON, GAME BIRDS MOST VEGETABLES, FRUITS
4-6 MONTHS	POULTRY VEAL, LEAN FISH
6 WEEKS TO 3 MONTHS	COOKED FOODS GROUND BEEF FAT FISH, SMOKED HAM, COMM. FROZEN FOODS
4-6 WEEKS	LEFTOVERS, GROUND FRESH PORK, ICE CREAM, SAUSAGE
UNDER 2 WEEKS	UNPACKED LEFTOVERS BREAD, BAKED GOODS, POTATO CHIPS, AND THE LIKE

Under 2 weeks (no need for freezer wrappings): Leftovers packed simply in covered refrigerator dishes; bread in wax wrappers; baked goods in cartons; packaged potato chips, crackers, and pretzels.

Once thawed, foods should not be refrozen but should be treated as fresh, perishable produce.

Foods for freezing should be carefully packaged in special moisture- and vapor-proof freezer wrapping. The food is placed in the center of a large piece of wrapping, and the two long ends brought together and folded over twice until snug against the food's surface. The ends are then folded under and the finished package tied with string or tape-sealed. A warm iron will seal cellophane ends. A stockinet or cheesecloth bag holds cellophane or pliofilm wrappings tight against the produce. Manufacturers' instructions should be followed when using waxed or aluminum-foil cartons, freezer jars, or plastic containers.

Packages for freezing should be labeled clearly with the name of food, date frozen, number of servings, and type of pack (dry, sugar, sugar syrup). It is wise to package foods in serving sizes suitable for family needs.

Practically all foods can be frozen and stored satisfactorily at 0° F. (−18° C.). Exceptions are cooked egg whites, custards, mayonnaise, French dressings, and vegetables high in water content which are to be served crisp and raw in salads or sandwiches. However, these vegetables may be frozen to serve in cooked form; raw lettuce, celery, tomatoes, and cucumbers are examples. Most freezer manufacturers publish handbooks giving directions for freezing specific foods.

SYLVIA SCHUR, Creative Food Service

See also FOOD, FROZEN.

FOOD POISONING most commonly results from contamination of food by bacteria or by toxic bacterial secretions. The term also includes disorders produced by consuming naturally poisonous substances and chemical poisons. Food poisoning should be distinguished from "ptomaine poisoning," which refers to the condition supposedly caused by consuming ptomaines, substances produced by the putrefaction of proteins. It is no longer believed likely that these substances can in themselves produce food poisoning.

Food poisoning resulting from consumption of food containing living bacteria is most commonly caused by organisms of the genus *Salmonella*, which includes the bacteria responsible for typhoid fever. An acute intestinal upset occurs from 6 to 48 hours after eating food that has been heavily contaminated. Fever, headache, abdominal pains, nausea, vomiting, and diarrhea appear suddenly and usually persist for a few days.

Toxins given off by bacteria may contaminate food and produce severe and sometimes fatal poisoning. One of the deadliest poisons known is manufactured by the *Clostridium botulinum*, a bacillus that cannot grow in the presence of air and which consequently thrives in home-canned foods which have been inadequately sterilized. The toxin can be completely destroyed by cooking the contaminated food at 80° C. for 10 minutes. Within 12 to 36 hours after the meal there is a sudden onset of dizziness and double vision. Other symptoms include difficulty

in breathing, talking, and swallowing. More than half the victims die, usually within three to six days. A specific antitoxin is available against the botulinum poison, but if it is to be effective it must be given before advanced symptoms appear.

The commonest type of food poisoning in the United States is that which results from eating food contaminated with the toxin of the staphylococcus bacteria. Inadequately refrigerated, perishable foods, such as chicken salad, potato salad, and cream-filled pastries may be responsible. Nausea, vomiting, retching, abdominal cramps and diarrhea occur within one to six hours after eating. Large amounts of fluid may be lost through the vomiting and diarrhea and, in rare cases, shock may result.

Other Types of Food Poisoning. Shellfish or mussel poisoning may occur because of toxic materials which form part of the shellfish diet. Certain types of poisonous mushrooms cause severe watery diarrhea, abdominal pain, vomiting, jaundice, convulsions, and in some cases, death.

JEROME D. WAYE, M.D.

See also BOTULISM; POISONING.

FOOD PRESERVATION. The preservation of foods, once the task of the housewife, has become chiefly the province of mass production. Scientific methods applied to quantity production have made these foods available to all. Today, such processes as home freezing, canning, and jellying are done more as an applied art of cookery than as a necessity. For information on these pertaining to the homemaker, *see* CANNING, HOME; FOOD FREEZING, HOME; PICKLING; PRESERVES.

Food preservation may be defined as the use of processing methods to delay or prevent decay, deterioration, and spoilage of foods used by man, thus making them available to him beyond the normal period of use. The basic principles of food preservation are to create conditions unfavorable to the growth or survival of spoilage microorganisms and to prevent deterioration by enzymes.

Early man was bound to his food supply and had to move with it according to the seasons. He had little independence from the supply because without it he starved. Until he learned to preserve certain items from time of plenty through time of need, he was unable to move into localities that could not satisfy all his food needs. He learned to sun and air dry grains to preserve them against molding and insect damage. An outstanding example of this was long-term storage of grains in ancient Egypt. Primitive man learned to sun-dry fruits and vegetables and to dry and smoke meat over a fire. He learned to preserve fruit products by fermenting them into wines and vinegars; he fermented milk into curds and cheeses and preserved certain vegetables by lactic acid fermentations. Gradually, over the centuries, these food preservation methods were perfected through trial and error until they became standardized procedures. The successful preservations gave man independence to move across the face of the earth and to populate what had been inhospitable lands. Although early methods had gradually been perfected, they still had severe limitations.

It was not until the evolution of the scientific approach that reasons for successful preservations were understood and technological approaches devised to accomplish ends

FRUIT AND VEGETABLE CANNING CALENDAR[1]

🎃 AVAILABLE　　🎃🎃 MIDSEASON　　🎃🎃🎃 PEAK SEASON (Can now)

FRUITS AND VEGETABLES	MAY	JUNE	JULY	AUGUST	SEPT.	OCT.	QUANTITY	QUARTS
APPLES		🍎	🍎🍎	🍎🍎🍎	🍎🍎🍎	🍎🍎🍎	1 bu. (40-50 lb.)	20-25
APRICOTS	🍑	🍑🍑	🍑🍑🍑	🍑🍑🍑	🍑		4-bkst. crate (20 lb.)	12
ASPARAGUS							1 crate (24 lb.)	6-8
BEANS (Lima)							1 bu. (28-30 lb.)	6-8
BEANS (Green or Wax)							1 bu. (28 lb.)	14-18
BEETS							1 bu. (50 lb.)	17-20
CHERRIES							16-qt. crate (22 lb.)	12
CORN							1 bu. (70 lb.)	8-12
PEACHES							1 crate (20 lb.) 1 bu. (40-50 lb.)	8-10 20-25
PEARS							1 peck (14 lb.) 1 bu. (50-60 lb.)	5-7 20-25
PEAS							1 bu. (30 lb.)	7-8
PLUMS							1 crate (15-18 lb.) 1 bu. (50 lb.)	8-11 28-30
TOMATOES							1 bu. (50-60 lb.)	16-20

[1] This chart is based on national supply in the United States rather than on regional crops.

previously thought impossible. In the early 1800's Nicolas Appert developed a method of sealing foods in "canisters" and preserving them by the systematic application of heat. He understood how spoilage could be prevented in almost any type of food by sufficient heating and by keeping the container tightly closed. Thus, the canning industry was born. However, it took Louis Pasteur to develop the concept that living microorganisms are responsible for spoilage and fermentation.

Heat. Nearly all types of food can be preserved for a considerable period of time by cooking. When raw foods deteriorate, it is through the action of the enzymes they contain and action of bacteria with which they become contaminated. Heating or cooking destroys or inactivates these enzymes thus preventing this type of deterioration. Cooking also destroys certain types of microorganisms that cause spoilage. In the home, cooking is used as a preservation method as well as a method to make food more palatable. However, ordinary cooking does not destroy all bacteria. Deterioration, although delayed, will come about through the growth of surviving bacteria.

Pasteurization. In this method of preservation, named for Louis Pasteur, foods are subjected to sufficient heat to kill most of the bacteria without markedly altering flavor or other characteristics. The food is heated in a closed system, rapidly cooled and then placed in covered or sealed containers to prevent recontamination. This method is generally used for liquids such as milk, fruit and vegetable juices, and beer. Pasteurization markedly extends the useful life of food products but is not intended for

long-term or extended storage. As a rule pasteurized products are refrigerated to get maximum benefits from the treatment.

Canning. Microorganisms may exist in two forms, a growing vegetative cell or an inactive form called a spore. Vegetative cells can be killed by rather mild heat (140° F. to 180° F.), depending upon the time of exposure. However, some spores can withstand boiling water for hours and after cooling still germinate into vegetative cells causing spoilage. Therefore, it is necessary to use much higher temperatures to kill spores in foods. The canning industry sterilizes foods by using steam retorts operating at 15 lb. pressure per square inch (psi) to obtain a temperature of 250° F., the time of exposure varying according to product requirements. For example, the more acid contained within a food, the shorter the exposure to heat required. Food products are heated to expel air, then sealed in containers of glass or tin-coated steel and heat-sterilized in retorts and cooled. The resulting product is altered in flavor and texture from that of the raw product but is preserved so that it can be shipped or stored for several years at ordinary temperatures.

Baking. Baking has a twofold purpose: developing a different type of food product from grains, then preserving it for future use. Grains for bread are ground into flour, then made into dough by fermentation with yeast to develop desirable flavors and textures. The dough is then subjected to heat. This coagulates the bread, reduces the moisture, and kills microorganisms that would otherwise cause spoilage. Cakes and other items owe their open structures to chemical leavening agents such as baking powder, or natural products such as beaten egg whites. Unless the heat used is sufficient to kill yeasts, molds, and spoilage bacteria, the product will spoil rapidly. If exposed to air these products have a short shelf-life, but in hermetically sealed containers keep very well.

Refrigeration. The rate of deterioration by naturally occurring enzymes and the rate of growth of microorganisms are progressively retarded by low temperature. Shelf- or storage-life of most fresh foods is prolonged by chilling or holding them at 32° F. to 45° F. In supermarkets fresh meat is displayed in a chilling case, and fresh poultry in crushed ice, as means of maintaining quality and retarding deterioration. Fresh fruits and vegetables are held in refrigerated warehouses regulated to obtain maximum storage according to product requirements. To extend storage-life, products such as butter, cheese, dehydrated eggs, and canned goods are stored in cooled warehouses. No change of form or texture is involved when products are simply cooled to retard deterioration.

Sun and Air Drying. In certain localities where warm sun and low humidity prevail, local fruit is dried on trays

SUN AND AIR DRYING

in the open. Rapid drying is essential to prevent molding and maintain quality. For fast drying and where sun drying is not practicable, mechanical air drying offers a solution. Fruit and vegetables are prepared, spread on perforated trays or belts, and passed through temperature-regulated air until dry. In some products, sulfur dioxide is applied to preserve color and retard deterioration. Some liquid foods such as milk, liquid eggs, and instant coffee are dried by spraying them into a rapidly moving current of hot dry air, then recovering the resulting powder. Drying on a rotating heated drum is also employed for certain products.

Vacuum Drying. In products where quality loss from heat or oxidation is encountered, a vacuum-drying process may be employed in batch or continuous flow. A high vacuum plus heat causes the product to dry rapidly by evaporation. Raising the temperature increases the rate of evaporation but this must be regulated according to product requirements. This method lends itself to the drying of certain fruit juices.

Freeze Dehydration. Certain products require a porous structure to facilitate rehydration, otherwise they may suffer heat or oxidation damage during drying—even at room temperatures. Products such as raw or cooked meat, fish, and certain fruits and vegetables are frozen, placed in a chamber, and subjected to a high vacuum. This causes the ice crystals to sublime or evaporate leaving small cavities. The spongy material takes up water rapidly during rehydration. To facilitate evaporation, heat is applied through the shelves upon which the frozen food rests. Temperature of the shelves must be regulated to increase the drying rate without melting the product. Many products can be dried in this way and very closely resemble raw products when rehydrated, yet will keep for long periods without refrigeration provided proper moisture-proof packaging is used.

Fermentation. Wines and beers are produced by adding yeasts to ferment the natural sugars. Because fruits and juices spoil through the action of many types of organisms, they are placed in a container to seal out air. Yeasts can utilize sugars even without oxygen and produce alcohol, which acts as a preservative. When the container is opened, acetic acid bacteria will oxidize the alcohol within the beverage, producing vinegar. Commercially, cider vinegar is manufactured by percolating yeast-fermented solutions of apple cider through tall towers filled with beechwood shavings or other filling material, where bacteria convert the alcohol to acetic acid which acts to preserve the vinegar or products to which it is added.

Buttermilk or other acid milks are fermented with lactic acid, producing bacteria to form a beverage. Bacteria fermentation produces the milk curd known as yoghurt. The curd of various milks is pressed to reduce the water content, then made into various types of cheeses, each requiring special treatment to encourage particular bacterial types responsible for the cheese variety. Quality control is governed by the type of fermentation to bring about the characteristic flavor.

When cucumbers are covered with salted water and allowed to undergo lactic acid fermentation, pickles are produced. They may be produced as natural dills or as an intermediate salt stock for processing into various types of commercial pickles through the use of vinegar.

Preserving, Concentration, and Carbonation. In jams, jellies, marmalades, and such, preservation is accomplished by addition of sugar, while concentration of products by the removal of water produces sirups and various fruit concentrates. Most of these products will keep without refrigeration, but some require cool storage to retain flavor. Such products add variety to the diet through use of this preservation method. Honey is a natural product owing preservation to soluble sugars gathered from flowers and concentrated by the bees.

Beverages are often preserved, and made more palatable, by use of carbon dioxide gas under pressure. The gas is soluble in the liquid and inhibits bacterial and mold growth. Fine filtration of raw fruit juices coupled with saturation with carbon dioxide under about 7 atmospheres pressure is used for long-term bulk refrigerated storage.

Salting, Curing, and Smoking. Meats, fish, and certain vegetables may be preserved by high salt concentration. The salt inhibits microorganisms and enzyme action. Products are later utilized by leaching the salt out with water. In curing ham, bacon, brined fish, and producing

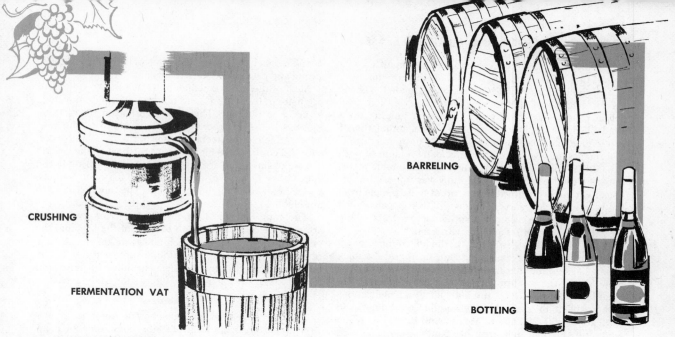

CRUSHING

FERMENTATION VAT

BARRELING

BOTTLING

pickles, the product is submerged in a solution of curing salts, allowed to undergo a "cure," then certain products are processed in a smokehouse by dry heat. Corned beef is cured in brine and distributed under refrigeration. Certain sausages, like salami, are made by adding small amounts of curing salts to control a fermentation that imparts characteristic flavors and exerts preservative qualities. These products are partially dehydrated in the smokehouse and are stable for a time without refrigeration.

Chemicals. In a limited number of food products chemical preservatives are used such as sodium benzoate to prevent fermentation in fruit juices, calcium propionate to retard mold growth in bread, sodium propionate in cakes, sulfur dioxide in dried fruits, and sodium nitrate and nitrite in certain meats. In the United States the use of such chemicals in food products is very strictly regulated under the Food, Drug and Cosmetic Act.

Irradiation. Energy imparted by atomic radiations can kill living cells and is used as a preservation method. This has been referred to as a cold sterilization method since it does not employ heat. Extensive work is now in progress employing gamma rays from radioactive cobalt 60, machine-accelerated electrons, and X rays. Used in small amounts, a pasteurizing effect can be obtained for short storage; or, by use of higher doses of energy, sterilization can be obtained. Certain low levels will inhibit sprouting of potatoes in storage. Use of this method is in the experimental stage, and extensive work is yet to be done to prove the commercial practicability and to assure safety and wholesomeness of products thus treated.

Dr. HARRY GORESLINE, Institute of Food Technologists
See also CANNING, COMMERCIAL; DEHYDRATED FOOD; FOOD, FROZEN; MEAT.

FOOD-PRODUCING REVOLUTION. The prehistoric development that added agriculture and animal husbandry to hunting and gathering as sources of man's food supply is known as the food-producing revolution, an analogy to the industrial revolution of modern times. Archeologists of the 19th century noted that after a certain time in the prehistoric period, stone implements were often finished by grinding or polishing instead of by chipping or flaking. John Lubbock, Lord Avebury (1834–1913), called the earlier epoch of chipped and flaked tools Paleolithic, or "Old Stone Age," and the epoch of ground and polished tools the Neolithic, or "New Stone Age." Later, archeologists adopted the concept of a Mesolithic phase, extending from the end of the Upper Paleolithic (variously dated from about 12,000 to 10,000 B.C.) to the start of the Neolithic (about 7000 to 5000 B.C.). However, in addition to detecting the change in stone-working techniques, which was neither universal nor complete, prehistorians observed that Neolithic sites often had pottery and indications of crop raising and animal husbandry. It was gradually realized by archeologists that the important thing about the Neolithic was the advent of food production by crop planting and livestock raising, and not the making of more smoothly finished stone tools.

Plant domestication, in particular, was conducive to more permanent village communities rather than nomadic camp sites and to population increases, since most land areas can support more people from farming than from hunting, fishing, and wild-plant collecting, however inten-

SMOKING OF MEATS AND FISH

sive. Thus the Neolithic Age came to be regarded as a period of fundamental transformation in economic life. V. Gordon Childe, a British prehistorian, made the clearest formulation of this food-producing revolution. The actual process was hardly revolutionary, judging from available evidence, but was rather a slow accumulation of experience in the care of a great variety of plant and animal species, in several and perhaps many regions of both the Old and New Worlds. In the long run, Childe maintains the food-producing revolution was important, not because it made possible the support of more people from the land in certain parts of the world, but because such population increases, along with other factors, fostered the growth of the first cities and of civilization.

In the Middle East, especially in the hill country which flanks the so-called Fertile Crescent, crop and livestock raising began sometime around 7000 B.C.–6000 B.C. In the New World the food-producing revolution came somewhat later, between 7000 and 5000 B.C., and civilizations comparable to the earliest in the Middle East did not arise until about 300–200 B.C. in Mexico and Peru. Just when agriculture first began in areas like Southeast Asia remains uncertain. The Pakistan-India area apparently derived agricultural techniques from the Middle East. North China, still more distant, possibly derived its agriculture and animal husbandry from the same source.

Consult Braidwood, R. J., *The Near East and the Foundations for Civilization* (1952); Childe, V. G., *New Light on the Most Ancient East* (1957).

GORDON W. HEWES, University of Colorado
See also BRONZE AGE; CIVILIZATION; FOOD; NEOLITHIC AGE; PALEOLITHIC AGE.

FOOL'S GOLD. *See* CHALCOPYRITE; PYRITE.

FOOL'S PARSLEY, extremely poisonous annual plant, *Aethusa cynapium*, in the carrot family, Umbelliferae, found in Europe, Asia, and North America. The plants are from 1 to 2½ ft. tall and have erect, branched stems, and glossy, much-divided leaves that resemble edible parsley.

FOOT, in human anatomy, mechanically intricate structure, composed of 26 small bones which are bound together by capsules, ligaments, tendons, and muscles into a strong, flexible organ of locomotion.

The bones of the foot bear the entire weight of the body, which is transmitted to them through the talus, or ankle, bone. The talus distributes this weight to the heel bone (calcaneus) and to the bones of the arches in front. The longitudinal arch runs from the heel to the heads of the long, slender metatarsal bones which form the ball of the foot. Muscles and bands of strong, fibrous tissue run from the heel bone to the metatarsal heads, being drawn across the arch like the string of a bow; the resiliency of these tissues gives the arch its spring. The metatarsal arch runs crossways across the foot, being formed by the metatarsal heads.

The long arch is depressed in flatfoot, a common condition often characterized by pain and fatigue following long periods of walking or standing. The height of the arch is extremely variable; in some feet it is normally depressed, while in others it is markedly high. Contrary to popular belief, a congenitally low-arched foot is usually strong and does not require treatment.

Most of the muscles which move the bones of the foot originate in the leg and send tendons alongside the ankle to insert in the foot. The largest and strongest of these muscles is the gastrocnemius-soleus group in the calf, which attach to the heel by means of the Achilles' tendon (the heel cord). These muscles raise the heel off the ground during walking and are responsible for the spring in the gait. Other muscles originating in the leg include those which bend and straighten the toes. The tendons of these muscles help to stabilize and support the ankle joint.

The foot receives its nourishment from two main arteries: the dorsalis pedis on the top of the foot and the posterior tibial, which runs behind the inside prominence of the ankle bone. The pulsation of these arteries can be felt by the fingers in the same way as the wrist pulse, and is used to test the adequacy of circulation in the foot.

Foot Disorders

The hard pavements and the constricting shoes of civilized living are responsible for the common foot complaints, such as corns, calluses, and bunions. Corns and calluses are the product of intermittent friction and pressure which stimulate the skin to thicken its outside horny layer. Shoes which are tight and pointed may bend the great toe, producing the deformity of the great toe joint, the bunion. Athlete's foot is caused by infection with certain fungi which produce itching and fissuring of the skin.

A number of disorders which affect other parts of the body also manifest themselves in the foot. Gout frequently attacks the first toe joint and the ankle. Infectious arthritis, such as that resulting from gonorrhea, may also attack the ankle joint. Diseases of the nervous system may damage the nerve supply to the feet so that the individual sustains constant damage to the skin of the foot without being aware of it. This occasionally develops in diabetes and in late syphilis and may result in deep, penetrating ulcers on the sole of the foot. Poliomyelitis may leave permanent muscle weakness, resulting in a characteristic limp and foot deformity.

A common and serious manifestation of a general bodily disease in the foot is impairment of the blood supply. Arteriosclerosis, or hardening of the arteries, often affects the arteries of the legs, reducing the blood supply to the foot and devitalizing its tissues. Individuals with advanced arteriosclerosis of the extremities are unable to resist infection effectively and comparatively minor injuries of the foot may lead to infection, gangrene, and eventually, amputation. This is especially true in diabetics, who for this reason should avoid home foot surgery, ill-fitting shoes, and the application of heat or harsh chemicals (iodine, for example) to the feet.

JOEL HARTLEY, M.D.

FOOT, unit of length in the English, or imperial, system of measure. In ancient times it was derived from the length of the human foot. In 1324 King Edward II defined the inch as "three barleycorns, round and dry" and the foot as 12 such inches. The foot is equivalent to 30.48 cm.

FOOT-AND-MOUTH DISEASE. *See* CATTLE: *Diseases*.

DISORDERS OF THE FEET

FOOT DISORDERS CAUSED BY IMPROPER FOOTGEAR, HARD WALKING
SURFACES, AND STRAIN TO THE MECHANICAL STRUCTURES OF THE FOOT.

ANKLE SPRAIN: Caused by strong lateral twist, often occurs when walking on rocky, uneven surfaces.

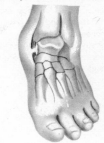

INGROWN NAIL: Nail cuts into soft tissue of toe. May be associated with tight-fitting shoes.

"CORNS," or HELOMA: Overgrowths of the upper layer of the skin caused by intermittent friction and pressure of shoe.

"BUNION," or HALLUX VALGUS: Deformity of the great toe caused by sharply-pointed shoes.

PLANTAR CALLUS: Thickening of skin on ball of foot may be caused by long hours of walking on hard surfaces in thin-soled shoes.

"FALLEN ARCHES" or "FLAT FEET": Depression of the long arch of the foot may be caused by excessive strain on a congenitally weak foot.

ACHILLES BURSITIS: Friction of the shoe against the heel tendon causes the development of a fluid-filled sac (bursa) at the point of irritation.

FOOT DISORDERS ASSOCIATED WITH DISEASES OCCURRING ELSEWHERE IN THE BODY.

DIABETES may impair functioning of nerves of foot and leg, causing deep, painless ulcers on sole of foot. In late syphilis, involvement of the spinal cord may produce the same condition.

KIDNEY DISEASE: Loss of proteins in certain kidney diseases permits fluid to escape into tissues, causing swollen ankles.

GOUT: Uric acid salts may be deposited in the joints, particularly at the base of the great toe.

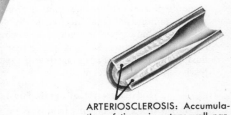

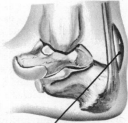

ARTERIOSCLEROSIS: Accumulation of tissue in artery wall narrows the arterial passage and reduces circulation to feet and legs. Symptoms include coldness of the feet and muscle cramps.

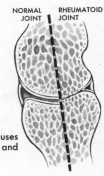

NORMAL JOINT   RHEUMATOID JOINT

TUBERCULOSIS may attack the bones of the foot.

RHEUMATOID ARTHRITIS causes inflammation of the joints and may result in joint deformity.

FOOTBALL

Football attracts vast crowds in the United States and Canada. Throngs come to see star running backs like Tony Dorsett perform. Dorsett (No. 33) makes excellent use of a University of Pittsburgh teammate's block against a Penn State defender.

Wide World

FOOTBALL, outdoor game played by two teams, each team attempting to carry or kick a ball over the other team's goal line. In most nations the word signifies soccer, rugby, or a variation of one or the other. In the United States football refers to a popular sport developed from soccer and rugby but with its own rules, traditions, and color. The same game, with some variations described later in this article, is played in Canada.

Football in the United States is played by hundreds of colleges and universities and by countless professional, semiprofessional, high school, grade school, and sand lot teams.

Large crowds are common at college and professional games. More than 100,000 spectators have seen contests in the Rose Bowl, Pasadena, Calif.; the Los Angeles Memorial Coliseum; the University of Michigan stadium in Ann Arbor; and the John F. Kennedy Memorial Stadium in Philadelphia, site of the annual Army-Navy game. Annual attendance exceeds 32,000,000 for college games and 10,000,000 for professional games. Millions more watch the college and professional contests on television.

The games are often only parts of colorful spectacles. Marching bands, cheerleaders, cheering sections, and card stunts (performed by students who sit together and flash colored cards at a signal to form a pattern) add to the festive air.

History of Collegiate Football

American football stems from soccer, which probably was first played in England in the 11th century. Until the 19th century the game consisted solely of kicking a ball.

In 1823 soccer was revolutionized during an interclass game at Rugby School in England. William Webb Ellis, frustrated because he had missed a kick, picked up the ball and ran down the field with it. His team captain was so angry and embarrassed that he apologized profusely to the opposing team for this utter disregard of the rules.

Ellis' breach of soccer etiquette, however, was not forgotten. Some Rugby students liked it and in 1839 invented the game of rugby, named for their school. Thus football became two sports—soccer and rugby.

Beginning of Intercollegiate Play. The first intercollegiate game of American football was played on Nov. 6, 1869, in New Brunswick, N.J. Rutgers defeated Princeton, 6 goals to 4. The game was actually soccer, and only kick-ing was allowed. There were 25 men to a team.

The sport caught on quickly. Columbia played in 1870, Harvard staged class games in 1871, Yale played in 1872, and Cornell formed a team in 1873. In 1873 Princeton, Rutgers, Columbia, and Yale drafted rules primarily drawn from soccer.

In 1874 Harvard and McGill University met, employing "Boston game" rules. Their contests combined soccer and rugby; the players not only kicked the ball but advanced it by running with it and by passing it to teammates. Harvard and Yale met in 1875 for the first time, thus beginning a famous series. Harvard won, 4 goals to 0, under rules drawn mostly from rugby. The American Intercollegiate Football Association was founded the next year, and Yale claimed the association's championship. Rugby rules prevailed.

The sport received impetus in 1880 from Walter Camp, a 21-year-old Yale senior who later became one of the great figures in football. He reduced the number of players from 15 to 11 per team. He also replaced the rugby scrum, a semichaotic method of putting the ball in play, with something resembling the modern scrimmage, or the action between opposing lines of players.

In 1882 signals, as a method of directing a team's play, were originated and positions were standardized. At the same time it was decreed that to retain possession of the ball a team must gain 5 yd (4.6 m) in three downs (plays) or not lose 10 yd (9.1 m) in that time.

During its early years football was almost a private possession of the Eastern colleges that later formed the Ivy League. Of the 132 places on the All-America teams from 1889, when the first All-America was chosen, through 1900, 107 were filled by players from Yale, Harvard, and Princeton and 21 others by University of Pennsylvania athletes.

Early Criticism and Reform. Serious obstacles to continued growth of the game arose in the 1890's. In 1894 Harvard and Pennsylvania withdrew from the American Intercollegiate Football Association. The organization disbanded in 1895, leaving the game without a governing body. Playing rules were again revised, but football almost disappeared from the American scene.

The low point was reached in 1905 and 1906. Mass plays, notably use of the flying wedge, stressed sheer force rather than skill and resulted in many deaths and crippling injuries. Some schools were ready to abandon the game. President Theodore Roosevelt was foremost among those who declared that football must be made safer.

New rules banned most mass formations and permitted throwing the ball in a forward direction. The forward pass was tried in 1906 by Wesleyan University against Yale. In a move to discourage power plays, which produced short gains, a team was required to gain at least 10 yd rather than 5, in three downs.

Football was saved, and it made rapid strides. In 1910 Glenn Scobey (Pop) Warner, then coach at the Carlisle (Pa.) Indian School, devised the single-wing formation, which became the basic offensive pattern for 30 years. In 1912 a team was given four downs to gain 10 yd, and a touchdown, or act of crossing the opponents' goal line while in possession of the ball, was valued at six points. These rules are still in effect. (Warner later coached at Pittsburgh, Stanford, and Temple.)

In 1913 the forward pass emerged as a potent weapon when Notre Dame upset Army, 35–7. Notre Dame scored one touchdown and set the stage for four others by em-

ploying passes. Its passing combination was Charles E. (Gus) Dorais to Knute Rockne. Rockne later became head coach at Notre Dame and was probably the most renowned coach the sport has seen.

Michigan, Washington, and Carlisle were among the leading teams early in the 20th century. Michigan's point-a-minute teams under coach Fielding H. (Hurry Up) Yost ran off plays with unbelievable speed. From 1901 to 1905 they played 56 games without a defeat. From 1908 to 1916 Washington went unbeaten in 61 straight games. Carlisle, a tiny school whose teams were led by the legendary Jim Thorpe, won against all comers.

The 1920's were the golden age of sports, including football. Notre Dame was the big team. Rockne was its coach, and its stars included the Four Horsemen. Although these four backfield men—Harry Stuhldreher, Jim Crowley, Elmer Layden, and Don Miller—averaged only 160 lb (73 kg), their running ability captivated the imagination of the public. This also was the era of Harold (Red) Grange of Illinois and Bronko Nagurski of Minnesota, runners without peer.

Renowned coaches include Knute Rockne, left, a forward-pass pioneer, and Pop Warner, below, who devised the single-wing formation.

Legendary players from football's early days include, clockwise from top right, Jim Thorpe, Harold (Red) Grange, and Bronko Nagurski.

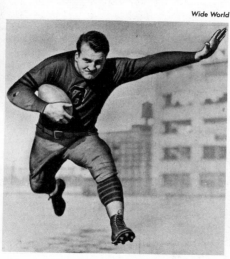

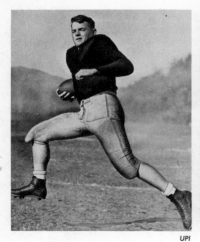 

UPI   UPI

Glenn Davis, far left, and Felix (Doc) Blanchard, called "The Touchdown Twins," made Army almost invincible from 1944 through 1946.

Major Developments. In 1940 came a major development, the return of the T formation. The T is an offensive formation, previously used and abandoned, in which the quarterback stands directly behind the center, who hands the ball to him. It offered deception in contrast with the single-wing formation's power. Clark Shaughnessy, in his first year as Stanford's coach, brought back the T and added a man in motion—a halfback running laterally before the ball is passed back from the center. The T soon became the basic offensive weapon of football.

In 1941 Don Faurot, then coaching at the University of Missouri, devised the split-T formation. It varies the T by allowing the quarterback to run laterally with the ball behind the line of scrimmage. The quarterback then has these options: he can continue to run, he can throw a forward pass, or he can hand off or pass the ball laterally to a teammate, depending on how the defense has committed itself. The split T achieved popularity after World War II through two of Faurot's coaching disciples, Charles (Bud) Wilkinson at Oklahoma and Jim Tatum at Maryland.

Another landmark of the postwar era was two-platoon football. Unlimited substitution of players became legal in 1941, but despite this apparent aid, about 350 colleges gave up the sport during the war. In 1947 Michigan was the first to take full advantage of free substitution. It used separate units for offense and defense. Army adopted this system, and many others followed.

Extra coaches, extra players, and extra equipment were needed under the platoon system. Some 50 colleges abandoned football because platooning made it too expensive. The free-substitution rule, which had grown more and more controversial, was dropped in 1953. Professional football retained it, however, with notable success, and the college substitution rule was progressively liberalized until platoon football and free substitution returned in 1965.

The outstanding teams in the 1940's and 1950's included Army, Notre Dame, Michigan, Alabama, and Oklahoma. Army dominated the game from 1944 through 1946, the years of its fabled "Touchdown Twins," Glenn Davis and Felix (Doc) Blanchard. Wilkinson's teams at Oklahoma won or shared the Big Eight (previously, the

Big Seven) Conference championship from 1947 through 1959, his first 13 years there.

In 1958 the first change in scoring values since 1912 was authorized. To increase interest, the conversion after touchdown, which had been worth one point, was altered. A team now has the option to try for one point, by place kick or drop kick, or two points, by a run or pass. The conversion attempt, previously made from the 2-yd (1.8-m) line, was moved back to the 3-yd (2.7-m) line. (See section on rules.)

In 1959 the colleges widened the goal posts from 18 ft 6 inches to 23 ft 4 inches, or 5.6 m to 7 m (inside measurements), to stimulate field-goal kicking, and the aim was quickly achieved.

Offensive formations changed slightly in the 1960's and 1970's. At least 90 percent of the college teams used some sort of triple-option offense—the veer, wishbone, split T, or wing T. The old single wing and double wing were no longer used.

The outstanding teams included Alabama, Nebraska, Ohio State, Notre Dame, Southern California, and Oklahoma. The most celebrated players were O. J. Simpson of Southern California, Archie Griffin of Ohio State, and Tony Dorsett of Pittsburgh, all running backs.

The cost of fielding college football teams rose dramatically. Most major colleges gave their players grants-in-aid (also known as athletic scholarships) that paid for tuition, books, room, and board. In 1974 the member colleges of the National Collegiate Athletic Association, the major governing body in college sports, voted economy restrictions. They limited the total number of football scholarships at each major college to 95 at one time and the number of new scholarships to 30 each year.

Rules and Progress of Game

The team that scores the most points is the winner. There are four types of scoring plays: touchdowns (worth six points each), conversions after touchdowns (one or two points), field goals (three points), and safeties (two points).

A touchdown is scored when a team advances the ball—by running, passing, or recovering an oppoenent's fumble—over the goal line defended by its opponent. Each touchdown is followed by an additional opportunity

Diagram of a standard collegiate football field.

Diagram labels: 100 YD. FROM GOAL TO GOAL · 53-FT. 4 IN. · END LINE 160 FT. · GOAL LINE · END ZONE · 10 YD. · G · 10 · 20 · 30 · 40 · 50-YARD-LINE · 40 · 30 · 20 · 10 · G · GOAL LINE · END ZONE · 53 FT. 4 IN. · 10 YD.

Diagram of a standard collegiate football field.

to score by the team that has made the touchdown—a conversion attempt from the 3-yd (2.7-m) line. The team attempting the conversion can try for one or two points.

A field goal is made from any place within the playing area by a place kick or drop kick that sends the ball between the goal-post uprights and over the crossbar.

A safety is scored by the defensive team when it tackles the ball carrier in his end zone, the area behind the goal line defended by his team. However, if the impetus that put the ball in the end zone came from the defensive team (via a kick, fumble, or intercepted pass, for example), it is a touchback, not a safety, and no points are scored.

The field, a rectangle of dirt covered by natural or artificial grass, measures 160 by 300 ft (48.8 by 91.4 m). In addition, there is an end zone 30 ft (9.1 m) deep at each end of the rectangle. The goal posts are stationed centrally on the back lines of the end zones. Each goal consists of two uprights, 20 or more ft (6 m) high, and a crossbar, 10 ft (3 m) above the ground.

The actual playing area is 100 yd (91.4 m) in length, from goal line to goal line; chalk marks, running from side line to side line and parallel to the goal lines, divide the playing area into 10-yd (9.1 m) segments, the distance necessary for a first down.

More than 100,000 persons crowd into the Rose Bowl at Pasadena, Calif., site of the oldest and most prestigious of the annual bowl games. The games often are accompanied by marching bands, organized cheering, and other festive activities.

UPI

FOOTBALL

The ball is a pointed oval, technically a prolate spheroid. It has a leather or composition surface. It measures 11 to 11¼ inches (28 to 28.5 cm) in length, 6.73 to 6.85 inches (17.09 to 17.40 cm) in width, and 28 to 28½ inches (71.1 to 72.4 cm) in circumference. It weighs 14 to 15 oz (400 to 425 grams) when inflated to a pressure of 12½ to 13½ pounds (5.5 to 6 kg).

Make-up of Teams. Each team has 11 players on the field, seven in the line and four in the backfield. The linemen are the left and right ends (or tight end and wide receiver), left and right tackles, left and right guards, and center. The backs are the quarterback, left halfback, right halfback, and fullback (or quarterback, flanker, and two running backs).

Both offense and defense operate from a variety of formations. On offense the backs run with, pass, or kick the ball. Passing may be either forward or lateral. The center snaps, or passes, the ball between his legs to a back and then attempts to block the forward progress of opposing players. The guards and tackles block, and the ends block or run downfield to be in a position to catch forward passes.

On defense, every player attempts to prevent the other team from advancing with the ball. The defense does this by tackling the ball carrier and by breaking up attempts by the opponents to pass the ball or by intercepting the pass. A defensive player who intercepts such a pass while it is still in the air is entitled to run with the ball and to attempt to score a touchdown.

A game consists of four periods of 15 minutes each, with intermissions of one minute between quarters and 15 minutes at half time. The teams change goals each quarter.

A complex code of rules governs play. To enforce these rules the officials can call more than 60 types of penalties. The most common penalties result in losses of 5 to 15 yd (4.5 m to 13.7 m) by the offending team. Some result only in the loss of a down. Severe infractions can result in the loss of the ball or disqualification of a player.

The team captains and game officials meet immediately before a game. The captain who wins the toss of a coin has a choice of (1) kicking off or receiving the kickoff or (2) defending either goal.

Conduct of Play. The game starts with a kickoff—an unobstructed place kick—from the kicking team's 40-yd (36.5-m) line (40 yd from the goal line it defends) to the opponent's territory. (In professional football, the kickoff is made from the 35-yard line.) The receiving team runs back the kickoff as far as possible, thus becoming the offensive team.

Then scrimmage plays start. The team on offense must advance the ball, by running or passing, at least 10 yd in four downs or lose possession at the point of failure. If it gains the 10 yd, it makes a first down and gets four more opportunities to make at least another 10 yd. The process continues until the offense scores points or loses possession of the ball.

If the offensive team faces loss of possession of the ball, it can surrender the ball by punting, or kicking, it. A good punt travels 40 yd or more in the air from the line of scrimmage (the point where the ball was put in play), so its advantage is obvious. When one team punts, the opposing team takes possession of the ball and seeks to carry it over the goal line defended by the team that has punted.

The offensive team loses possession if it (1) fails to make a first down, (2) punts, (3) fumbles the ball and fails to recover it, or (4) throws a pass that is intercepted (caught before the ball strikes the ground) by the defensive team. In each case, the teams exchange offensive and defensive roles.

In collegiate football a running play stops when any part of the ball carrier's body except his feet and hands touches the ground. In professional football such a play continues if the ball carrier slips or falls without being touched by a defensive player.

Offensive plays and defensive formations are rarely improvised. They are selected (the offensive play usually by the quarterback) in a huddle immediately before the play is run. Plays are chosen from an intricate set memorized by each player.

American Professional Football

Professional football's first 30 years were marked by failure upon failure. But in the late 1920's, with the aid of exhibition tours of the Chicago Bears' Red Grange and imaginative leadership, the game achieved great popularity and financial success. In the 1970's the National Football League lifted its average attendance per game to more than 55,000.

The professionals, who emphasize passing, are more skilled than the collegians. Leading players earn up to $450,000 a year. The rules generally follow college rules with two major exceptions. The pros allow free substitution, permitting the use of offensive and defensive platoons, and all successful conversion attempts count one point.

The pioneers of professional football would have been amazed at the game's eventual acceptance by the public. The professional game started quite inauspiciously. On Aug. 31, 1895, the Latrobe, Pa., team needed a quarter-

SOME COMMON REFEREE SIGNALS
The referee on the field indicates penalties and other decisions by means of signals. Learning to interpret these adds to a spectator's enjoyment of a game. Some frequently seen signals are illustrated at the right.

OFFSIDE   ILLEGAL POSITION OR PROCEDURE   UNSPORTSMANLIKE CONDUCT   ILLEGAL MOTION OR SHIFT

back for its game with nearby Jeanette. It persuaded John Brallier, a former college player, to fill the position and paid him $10. Thus he became the first man known to have accepted money for playing football.

In 1902 and 1903 professional teams were formed in Massillon, Canton, and other communities in northern Ohio. Their rosters eventually included many college graduates, among them Knute Rockne and Jim Thorpe.

Colleges looked down on professional football, however, and discouraged their players from entering it. In 1920 the American Professional Football Association was founded with Thorpe as president. Franchises were sold for $100 each. The American Professional Football Association failed after one season.

National Football League. In 1921, from the association's remnants, Joseph F. Carr of Columbus, Ohio, formed a new league which in 1922 became the National Football League. Franchises cost as little as $50 apiece. The attendance at one game was only 30. Twenty-three teams played in 1921, some dropping out during the season and others replacing them. The first league championship was won by the Staley Athletic Club of Decatur, Ill., owned and coached by George Halas. The team's quarterback was Charles Dressen, later a major-league baseball player and manager. The next year the Staleys changed their name to the Chicago Bears and became one of the greatest teams in the annals of the sport.

In 1925 the professionals achieved success. For three years Red Grange's running exploits for the University of Illinois had captivated the sports world. Halas signed Grange immediately after Grange's last college game, and a tour filled stadiums and made considerable money for Grange and the Bears. It also made the public conscious of professional football.

In 1933 the National Football League held its first championship play-off game involving sectional leaders; the Bears defeated the New York Giants, 23–21, in Chicago. In 1936 the league conducted its first draft of college players, now the standard procedure for allotting talent.

In 1946 the All-America Football Conference, a rival professional league, was formed. Both leagues bid for key players, and salaries rose accordingly. The Cleveland Browns dominated the new league, winning division and league championships in each of the league's four seasons.

Another major event in 1946 was the ascendance of Bert Bell, owner of the Philadelphia Eagles, to the office of National League commissioner. He held the post until his death in 1959 and was largely responsible for the growth of the professional game.

The war between the leagues cost millions of dollars on both sides. It ended on Dec. 9, 1949, when the All-America Conference disbanded. Three of its best franchises—Cleveland, San Francisco, and Baltimore—were absorbed by the National League, which now had 13 teams.

Growth. Professional football continued to grow. In 1957 a crowd of 102,368, a professional record, saw the Los Angeles Rams defeat the San Francisco Forty-Niners, 37–24, in the Los Angeles Memorial Coliseum.

The American Football League, a new rival of the National League, started play in 1960 with eight teams. Miami started play in 1966 as the ninth team. The new league lost more than $3,000,000 in its first season, but its financial stability was assured when in 1964 it signed a five-year television contract worth $36,000,000.

The two leagues fought bitterly to sign graduating collegians, sometimes paying bonuses that surpassed half a million dollars. The bidding war financially weakened teams in both leagues until the leagues reached a peace agreement on June 8, 1966. Effective in 1970, there would be one league (the National) composed of two conferences under one commissioner (Pete Rozelle, who headed the National League). The agreement also called for a common draft of college players and the Super Bowl game between the two conference champions annually. The American League teams agreed to pay indemnities to the National League of $18,000,000 over a 20-year period.

The National Football League gained wide acceptance in the 1960's during the Green Bay (Wis.) Packers' seasons under the celebrated coach, Vince Lombardi. The professional sport created new attention in 1969 when the New York Jets, champions of the American Football League, upset the Baltimore Colts, champions of the National Football League, in the Super Bowl, a victory the Jets' quarterback, Joe Namath, had "guaranteed."

With that impetus, and with the demise of the American Football League, the National League flourished in the early 1970's. The NFL-AFL merger had created a 26-team National League, and Seattle and Tampa Bay were added for the 1976 season. The three major networks paid $50,000,000 a year to televise games. Advertisers paid $225,000 per minute for commercials during Super Bowl telecasts. Franchises cost $16,000,000, and ticket prices ranged as high as $20.

But there were problems. One was the World Football League, a new major league that started play in 1974 with 12 teams. It signed such National League stars as Larry Csonka, but financing was inadequate and television and the public were not overly interested. The league collapsed midway through the 1975 season after losses estimated at $20,000,000.

CLIPPING

HOLDING

FORWARD PASS INTERFERENCE

INCOMPLETE PASS, PENALTY DECLINED

FIRST DOWN

TOUCHDOWN, FIELD GOAL

FOOTBALL FUNDAMENTALS

To function well as part of a team, the football player must spend hours on the field to develop the basic skills: passing, blocking, kicking, catching, and running.

PASSING

Passing can be a quick, spectacular means to a score. A passer needs poise and good judgment as well as accuracy.

(1) Delivery of ball begins as player, with arm cocked, begins pivot on ball of right foot to aid in stepping in direction of throw. (2) Left arm and hand extend at shoulder level in direction of target. (3) He begins transfer of weight to left foot. (4) Releasing ball, he has weight on left foot. (5) He follows through with forward, downward sweep of arm.

BLOCKING

Blocking is essential in offensive play. Blockers protect the passer and clear the way for the ball carrier.

(1) Head and shoulder block: player lunges forward and, elbows extended, pins opponent with neck and forearm. (2) Cross-shoulder block: blocker pivots, projecting shoulder into opponent. (3) Reverse body block: player pivots and whips body across front of opponent. (4) Double-team block: "post" man halts opponent, who is driven back by "drive" man's head and shoulder block.

PUNTING

A team failing to make a first down may choose to punt. A well-placed punt can reverse the direction of a game.

(1) Punter receives ball. (2) Holding ball with long axis parallel to ground, he takes short step with kicking foot. (3) He follows with natural step on nonkicking foot. (4) As kicking leg comes forward, ball is released below hips and close to kicking foot. (5) Kicking leg comes forward with knee flexed. (6) Leg snaps upward, and instep hits belly of ball.

PASS CATCHING

(1) Running receiver, fingers spread and palms open toward his face, is in position for ball. (2) After the ball is caught, receiver secures ball in the arm opposite the nearest opponent.

RUNNING

(1) Runner with ball tucked into his arm takes high steps to keep balance and pumps free arm naturally, like a sprinter. (2) When trapped, runner lowers shoulders for greater power.

Another problem arose when federal courts, in separate cases in 1975 and 1976, ruled that the draft of college players and the compensation clause (the so-called Rozelle Rule) violated federal antitrust laws. The NFL and its players association, after three years of negotiations, agreed in 1977 to a contract that modified the draft and compensation clause. In addition, the league agreed to pay $15,875,000 in damages to individual players.

Canadian Game. Canadian football closely resembles the American variety but is a more wide-open game. The sport is popular, especially on the professional and university level. Many outstanding college players from the

United States join professional teams in Canada; each professional team of 32 players may carry 15 American players, and play 14 in any one game. Many of the coaches of these teams were born and trained in the United States.

These are the major differences between American and Canadian football. In Canada:

1—Each team has a 12th man, at one time called a flying wing, now usually called a slot back.

2—The field is 30 ft (9.1 m) longer from goal line to goal line and 35 ft (10.7 m) wider.

3—The end zones are 25 yd (22.8 m) deep.

4—The offensive team has three downs, not four, in which to gain 10 yd (9.1 m).

5—A punt that lands behind the goal line must be run out from the end zone or the kicking team scores a rouge, or single, worth one point.

6—On punt returns blocking is allowed above the waist only.

7—There is no fair-catch rule for punt receivers, but opposing tacklers cannot come within 5 yd (4.6 m) of the receiver until he catches or at least touches the ball.

The Canadian Football League has an Eastern Conference (Hamilton, Montreal, Ottawa, and Toronto) and a Western Conference (British Columbia, Edmonton, Saskatchewan, Calgary, and Winnipeg). Conference winners meet each fall to contest for the Grey Cup.

High School. Football is played by thousands of high schools in the United States; hundreds of additional schools play six-man, eight-man, or nine-man varieties. High schools generally use college rules. Ohio, Pennsylvania, and Texas are the hotbeds of high school football.

High school football started in 1876 with a game between Andover Academy of Massachusetts and Exeter Academy of New Hampshire, actually preparatory schools. Since then football has become the major sport in high schools in every state.

Variations

Six-Man. Six-man football was originated by Stephen E. Epler in 1934 while coaching at Chester (Nebr.) High School. His idea was to reduce injuries and to make the game safe for smaller boys. The six-man game is played by many schools having small enrollments, small playing areas, or small budgets.

A six-man team has three backs and three linemen. The field is scaled down to 240 by 120 ft (73 by 36 m). The ball must be passed or kicked on every play. Otherwise the rules of the 11-man game generally are followed.

Eight-Man. Eight-man football is another variation favored by many smaller schools. Five men play in the line and three in the backfield. The field is the same size as that for 11-man football.

Touch. Touch football follows the rules of the 6-man, 8-man, or 11-man games except that tackling is not permitted. A play is ended when the ball carrier is touched by one or two hands (depending on ground rules) of a defender.

Any number of players may be used, and the field may be any size. Touch football is especially popular in intramural and sandlot competition. It gained considerable attention as the favorite participant sport of the family of President John F. Kennedy.

Wide World

O. J. Simpson, celebrated ball-carrier of the Buffalo Bills, cuts sharply to register a gain against the New England Patriots.

Association. Association football is the name used in Great Britain for the sport known in the United States as soccer, treated in a separate article in this encyclopedia.

Individual Skills

Blocking. This is planned physical contact with an opponent, designed to obstruct him. It is an offensive weapon used to clear a path for the ball carrier.

The basic blocks are the cross-body block, in which the body is thrown across an opponent's thighs, and the shoulder block, in which the shoulder does the work.

It is permissible to block a player from a position in front of, or to the side of, him, but usually not from a position behind him. A block from behind is called clipping and usually results in a 15-yd (13.7 m) penalty against the offending team. The blocker may not use his hands, but the defensive player may use his to ward off or escape the blocker.

Drop Kicking. In the early days of the game this was the principal method of scoring field goals and extra points; it has become a lost art and is now rarely seen. Instead, the place kick is used. The drop kick is made by dropping the ball and kicking it just after it has struck the ground.

Passing. Passing, which almost always refers to forward rather than lateral passing, is a prime offensive weapon, especially in professional football.

The passer grips the ball behind its middle, lifts it behind his ear, steps in the direction he will pass, and throws the ball with a snap of the wrist. He usually "leads" the receiver; that is, he throws the ball ahead of the man who will attempt to catch it.

Passes can be thrown for short or long distances, and a good passer can throw 40 yd (36.5 m) with accuracy. He normally throws the pass from 5 yd (4.5 m) or more behind the line of scrimmage, protected in a "pocket" of teammates blocking for him. The passer usually has about three

Coaches in action: Vince Lombardi of the Green Bay Packers observing play while linebacker Ray Nitschke stands alongside; Woody Hayes of Ohio State University uses a sideline phone to receive analysis from aides in the stands.

seconds to release the ball before the defensive team pours in.

Pass Receiving. A good passer will have only moderate success without capable pass receivers. The players eligible to receive a pass are the backfield men and the men at each end of the line of scrimmage (usually the ends).

The pass should be caught in front of the body and with both hands. The receiver must watch the ball in flight as long as possible. Speed is important for a pass receiver, but deception is more valuable in reaching an unobstructed place in which to catch the ball. In most cases the player passing the ball tries to have several available receivers; if his prime target has not been able to break away from the defense, he will then have other targets.

The receiver's duty is to elude his defender or defenders and get in the clear. If he can get behind his defender and then catch the pass, he may have an unobstructed path to a touchdown.

Place Kicking. The place kick is used for field goals and for one-point conversion attempts after touchdowns. It is also used for kickoffs.

For field goals and conversions the center snaps the ball to the holder who touches one of the ball's pointed ends to the ground. Then the kicker strikes it with his toe, aiming for a point just under the center of the ball. The ball rises in an end-over-end motion.

Place kickers in professional football seldom fail on conversion attempts. From 1959 through 1965, for example, Tommy Davis of the San Francisco Forty-Niners kicked 234 consecutive extra points before missing.

At times the ball is held on a kicking tee, similar to but larger than a golf tee. Kickoffs almost always are made from a tee without the use of a player to hold the ball.

Punting. This is primarily a defensive weapon, although it has a definite but infrequently used value in offense.

The punt is a kick made from the instep of the shoe after the kicker drops the ball and before the ball strikes the ground. The punter stands 10 to 15 yd (9.1 m to 13.8 m) behind the line of scrimmage in punt formation, a special alignment that offers maximum protection against the possibility of the punt being blocked by the defensive team.

A team normally punts when it faces the loss of the ball on downs, except when it is deep in enemy territory. By punting, a team loses possession but usually at a much more advantageous point on the field. The punt commonly is made on fourth down, although college teams sometimes punt earlier when deep in their territory.

There are two types of punts—spiral, in which the ball spins, and end over end, in which the ball rotates on its short axis. The punter strives for distance but also attempts to make the kick high so that his teammates, especially the ends, can race downfield and tackle the punt receiver before he can run back a sizable distance with the ball. When the punting team is close to midfield or in enemy territory, it often tries to punt the ball so that it lands or rolls beyond the side lines of the field. In that case the receiving team puts the ball in play at the point where the ball went out of the playing area; since it is deep in its own territory, the team is at a disadvantage. If the punt goes into the end zone instead of going out of bounds before the ball is touched by any player, the ball is put in play on the receiving team's 20-yd (18.2-m) line.

Running. The main method of advancing the ball is by running, also known as rushing. Each team has many offensive plays for various types of runs, some of which involve the handling of the ball by two or three players.

Good runners combine speed, power, and change of pace. They lift their knees high, making themselves difficult targets for the tackler.

Most plays provide interference for the runner. Interference consists of one or more blockers attempting to clear a path for the ball carrier. The successful runner makes the most of his interference, following it until he has a chance to break away and follow his own course.

When confronted by a tackler, the runner tries to elude him or to run past him. He may accomplish this by straight-arming—extending his arm and using it to push the tackler away.

Tackling. This and blocking are the two fundamental skills of football. Tackling is achieved by using the hands or arms to grasp or encircle the ball carrier. Ideally, the tackler hits the ball carrier with shoulder and body, then grasps him and pulls his legs from under him. Tackling is used only by the defensive team, and only the ball carrier may be tackled.

The purpose of tackling is to bring the ball carrier to the ground, thus ending the play and preventing him from gaining additional yardage. It is best, although often difficult, to tackle below the waist. In that manner the runner's legs are immobilized.

Formations Used in Play

Offensive. Basic offensive formations include the veer, wishbone, single wing, double wing, short punt, and the T with its variations. The T formation gave birth to the split

T, wing T, and slot T, among other variations. Standard formations often are varied by the flanking of backs and ends.

Defensive. Standard defensive formations include the 4-3-2-2 (the professional four), 3-4-2-2, 6-2-2-1, 6-3-2, 7-2-2, 7-1-2-1 (diamond), 5-3-2-1, and the 5-2-4. In each case the first figure represents the number of defensive players on the line of scrimmage, the next figure the number of line backers (players backing up the linemen), and the other figure or figures the number of defensive backs. Defenses may be changed from play to play, depending on what type of play the defensive team expects the offensive team to use next. A four-man or five-man defensive line is best when a forward pass is expected. More men play in the line when a running play is anticipated.

Players' Equipment

In the game's early days players wore tight pants and sweaters, later canvas pants and jackets. The modern player is dressed somewhat like an armored warrior. His knees, shoulders, hips, and thighs are protected by pads usually made of plastic. He wears tight knickerbocker pants and a jersey numbered on the front and back. His plastic helmet usually has a nylon nose and face guard. His leather shoes have cleated soles and heels to help provide secure footing.

Outstanding Games

Bowl Games. The first postseason bowl game was the Rose Bowl contest of 1902. Michigan's point-a-minute team routed Stanford, 49–0. The game, one feature of the Tournament of Roses in Pasadena, Calif., was dropped in favor of Roman chariot racing and other diversions until 1916, when it was renewed and retained. A West Coast team always has played in the Rose Bowl game, which attracts a crowd of 100,000 annually.

Other major bowl games are the Orange in Miami and the Sugar in New Orleans (both started in 1935), Cotton in Dallas (1937), and the Gator in Jacksonville, Fla. (1946). About 15 postseason bowl games are played each year, the major ones on or near New Year's Day. There were many more bowl games—47 in the 1946–47 postseason period alone—before the National Collegiate Athletic Association adopted restrictions.

Football Honors

All-America Teams. The first college All-America team was selected by Casper Whitney in 1889. For the first two years he was aided by his close friend Walter Camp. Camp chose the first All-America team under his own name in 1897 and picked a team each year until his death in 1925. His teams were regarded as official. Grantland Rice succeeded Camp as the major All-America selector, although many others started choosing such teams, too. In later years All-America teams were named by about 20 major selectors, notably newspapers, news agencies, magazines, and football publications. This practice continues today.

Hall of Fame. The Football Hall of Fame was begun in 1947. In 1954 it became the National Football Foundation and Hall of Fame with headquarters in New Brunswick, N.J. The foundation's purpose is to promote the values of college football and to keep college football records. The

Wide World

Rocky Bleier (No. 20) carries the ball as fellow Pittsburgh Steelers fan out to block the Oakland Raiders.

Professional Football Hall of Fame was dedicated in 1963 at Canton, Ohio.

Consult Buoniconti, Nick, and Anderson, Dick, *Defensive Football* (1973); Daley, Arthur, *Pro Football's Hall of Fame* (1971); Higdon, Hal, *Inside Pro Football* (1970); Liss, Howard, *Football Talk for Beginners* (1970); Nelson, David, *Illustrated Football Rules* (1976); Olson, O. Charles, *Prevention of Football Injuries: Protecting the Health of the Student Athlete* (1971); Treat, Roger, *Official Encyclopedia of Football* (14th ed., 1976).   FRANK LITSKY

As two Miami Dolphins bear down on him, quarterback Billy Kilmer (No. 17) of the Washington Redskins lofts a short pass.

UPI

FOOT BINDING, form of feminine mutilation practiced in China from about 600 A.D. It was supposed to have arisen as a custom because of the desire of the women of the imperial court to emulate the small feet of one of the Emperor's favorite concubines. The feet of females of the Mandarin class were compressed in infancy by extremely tight swaddling so that they were permanently stunted and walking became painful. This operation was performed, of course, only upon the children of the upper classes as a sign of social status and of their not having to work. Thus the custom forms an extreme instance of what the American economic philosopher Thorstein Veblen called "conspicuous leisure," a badge of socially consecrated waste, in this case waste of feminine work-value. The custom went out of fashion in the late 19th century and virtually disappeared in the 20th.

FOOT-CANDLE, measure of the amount of illumination. One foot-candle is the illumination falling on an object 1 ft (30.48 cm) from a source of one candle power of luminous intensity. The unit is used in rating photographic film. Some exposure meters are calibrated in foot-candles. *See also* CANDLE POWER.

FOOTE, ANDREW HULL (1806–63), American admiral. Born in New Haven, Conn., Foote attended Episcopal Academy of Connecticut. After a few months at West Point (1822), he turned to naval service. From 1849 to 1851 he combated slave trading on the African coast, and later wrote *Africa and the American Flag* (1854). In Canton, China, in 1856, he seized four forts in retaliation for anti-American acts. Commander of the Brooklyn Navy Yard when the Civil War began, he soon shifted to the West, where as Union naval commander on the upper Mississippi (1861–62), he cooperated skillfully with land forces in capturing forts Henry and Donelson and Island No. 10. Rewarded by promotion to rear admiral (1862) he later received command of the fleet at Charleston, S.C., but died en route to his post. A zealous teetotaler, Foote helped to end the navy's liquor ration.

FOOTE, ARTHUR WILLIAM (1853–1937), American composer, born in Salem, Mass. From 1878 to 1910 he was organist at the First (Unitarian) Church in Boston. His music belongs to the romantic tradition, and one of his best-known works is the Suite in E Major for strings (Op. 63, 1909). He also wrote numerous theoretical works, including the widely used *Modern Harmony* (1905).

FORAGE PLANTS, term used to describe any green, leafy plants that can be used for animal feed. The two main classes of forage plants are grasses and legumes, but certain weeds, truck-farming crops or their by-products, beet tops, and other vegetation can also serve as animal feed. Forage plants are often referred to as roughage because of their high-cellulose content, in contrast to grains, seeds, and their by-products, which are of low-cellulose content and are referred to as concentrates or high-energy feeds. Among the many forage plants are various pasture crops, tall-growing grasses, and legumes that can be used in a natural state or processed and stored for later feeding. *See also* FEEDS; HAY; PASTURE; SILAGE.

FORAKER [fôr'ə-kər], **JOSEPH BENSON** (1846–1917), American political leader. Born near Rainsboro, Ohio, he served in the Civil War, graduated (1869) from Cornell, and practiced law in Ohio. He was Republican Governor of Ohio (1885–89) and U.S. Senator (1897–1909); in 1904 he succeeded Mark Hanna as Republican boss of Ohio. As Governor, Foraker was a tax reformer, but in the Senate he was a noted conservative. He was an ardent imperialist and played a prominent part in the organization of territories acquired from Spain. His senatorial career ended when it was revealed that he was in the pay of the Standard Oil Company. He wrote the autobiographical *Notes of a Busy Life* (1916).

FORAKER, MOUNT, peak in south-central Alaska, located in the Alaska Range and in Mount McKinley National Park. The peak is always covered with ice and snow, and many glaciers radiate from its flanks. Crevasses, slides, and avalanches make access dangerous. Mount Foraker's elevation is 17,280 ft, or 5 307 m.

FORAMINIFERA [fô-răm-ə-nĭf'ər-ə], single-celled animals related to amoebas. They secrete shell-like skeletons called tests, which are found as fossils in rocks as old as Early Ordovician, deposited 500 million years ago. Most foraminifera are less than 1 mm in diameter, although some may be up to 100 mm across. Modern forms live mostly in shallow marine waters. The tests are made of chitinous, calcareous, or silicious materials, or of tiny, cemented sand grains, sponge spicules, or similar particles from the ocean bottom. Many tests are complex, and microscopic examination of cross sections is necessary to distinguish most genera. The family Fusulinidae clearly reveals an evolutionary sequence, which characterizes successive stratigraphic zones in rocks of Late Mississippian to Late Permian age (about 320 to 230 million years old) in the midcontinent region of the United States. Fusulinids and other foraminifera are valuable in petroleum exploration, for they can be retrieved from drill cuttings and used to correlate rock layers from well to well.

JEAN BUCHANAN SQUIRES

See also PROTOZOA.

FORBES, GEORGE WILLIAM (1869–1947), New Zealand statesman and Prime Minister (1930–35). Forbes entered Parliament in 1908 but did not obtain national office until the United ministry (1928–30). When the ailing Joseph Ward resigned (1930) as Prime Minister, Forbes formed his own ministry. Facing a severe economic crisis, he resorted to an orthodox but ineffective and unpopular program of retrenchment, increased taxation, and wage cuts. This quickly alienated the Labour party and forced Forbes into a coalition with the Reform party led by J. G. Coates. There followed a recovery program that included exchange devaluation, conversion of the debt, establishment of a central bank, coordinated agricultural marketing, and adjusted mortgage financing. But these measures, though sound, failed to win popular support, and the coalition ministry was defeated by the Labour party (1935). Forbes lost the leadership of the new National party the next year. He retired from Parliament in 1943.

PETER J. COLEMAN

FORBES, JOHN (1710–59), British general born in Scotland. He fought in Europe during the War of the Austrian Succession (1740–48). Early in the French and Indian War, William Pitt sent him (1757) to Pennsylvania to take Fort Duquesne, a job that Gen. Edward Braddock had died (1755) trying to do. Forbes faced two initial obstacles: stubborn terrain and stubborn Pennsylvania and Maryland legislators, who refused to vote him adequate funds and material. Anticipating a great struggle, Forbes hacked a highway west through the wilderness to supply his large army. En route, he conciliated the reputedly pro-French Indians. Despite difficulties, he advanced relentlessly. On Nov. 25, 1758, as Forbes approached, the French blew up the fortress and retreated. Forbes rebuilt the fort and called it Fort Pitt. Chronically ill and in pain during the entire campaign, Forbes was carried back to Philadelphia where he died. He had won control of the western approaches to Canada and struck a major blow against French hopes of maintaining a North American empire. The highway he cut through the forest later became a major route for English colonization of the Ohio country.

RICHARD M. ABRAMS

FORBES, WILLIAM CAMERON (1870–1959), American business executive and diplomat. Born in Milton, Mass., he graduated from Harvard University in 1892, entered his grandfather's banking house (J. M. Forbes & Co.), and became a partner in 1899. From 1904 to 1908 he was a member of the Philippine Commission and from 1909 to 1913 served as Governor General of the Philippines. President Warren Harding appointed him (1921) to the Wood-Forbes Commission that outlined the basis of U.S. policy toward the Philippines during the 1920's. He headed a committee to study conditions in Haiti in 1930, and during the Manchurian crisis of 1931–32 he was ambassador to Japan.

FORBES, city of Australia, in east-central New South Wales, on the Lachlan River. It is the marketing center for a region of wheat and sheep production.

FORBES-ROBERTSON, SIR JOHNSTON (1853–1937), English actor and theatrical manager. He made his stage debut in 1874, and during the next 40 years became one of the country's outstanding players of classic and modern roles, in association with such leading actresses as Helena Modjeska, Mary Anderson, and Mrs. Patrick Campbell. Especially noteworthy was his Hamlet, first seen in 1897, which gave him full scope for his refined intellectualism, penetrating grasp of character, and peerless elocution.

FORBIDDEN CITY (Chin. **TZU-CHIN-CH'ENG**), walled compound of some 40 imperial palaces, situated in the center of Peking and protected by an encircling moat, about 2 mi (3.2 km) in perimeter. Largely the creation of Emperor Yung-lu, the Forbidden City was started in 1406 and completed in 1420.

The basic architectural principle permeating the complex is symmetry and balance, blended in a magnificent display of color contrast. The main south entrance, known as the Noon Gate, leads to a huge courtyard featuring a set of five evenly spaced bridges. Farther on, the imposing Gate of Heavenly Peace leads to the Gate of Supreme Harmony, which opens to the grand view of three stately halls, known as the Hall of Supreme Harmony, the Hall of Intermediate Harmony, and the Hall of Insured Harmony. Imperial audiences, banquets honoring tributary missions, "palace examinations," and other important state ceremonies were held in any one of these three halls. On both sides, forming two subaxes, complementary groups of similar buildings, headed by the Hall of Literature on the west and the Hall of the Military on the east, stand in symmetrical contrast. With its red walls against the background of gold-tiled roofs, bright-colored pillars, and snow-white marble terraces, Forbidden City is one of the architectural wonders of China.

Y. T. WANG

FORCE, in physics, the push or pull on a body, which tends to change the momentum of the body on which it acts. This definition was formulated by Isaac Newton in 1687 and is still used in physics except for subatomic phenomena. It applies to magnetic, electric, and gravitational effects. If the mass m of the body does not change, which is usually true, the force F is given by $F = ma$, where a is the body's acceleration. For example, if a 2-lb. body is being accelerated at the rate of 3 ft. per second per second (3 ft./sec.^{2}) upward, it is said, by definition, that an upward force of six poundals must be acting on the body. Other sets of units for F, m, and a, respectively, in $F = ma$, are newton, kilogram, meters/sec.^{2}; dyne, gram, centimeters/sec^2; and pound (force), slug, feet/sec.^{2}.

The primary definition, or standard, of force, $F = ma$, is not an easy one to use in actual measurement of force. A secondary standard is therefore commonly used: weight of a body or the force exerted by a spring. The weight of a body of mass m is taken as equal to mg, where g is the acceleration of gravity, that is, the acceleration produced by the weight force. In Chicago, for example, $g = 9.803$ meters/sec.^{2} and on the moon $g = 1.67$ meters/sec.^{2}. Therefore the weight of 1 kilogram mass is 9.803 newtons in Chicago and 1.67 newtons on the moon. Once the relation between weight and mass at a given locality has been established, a spring balance can be calibrated by using weights; it will then read true in any locality.

Some of the consequences of defining force by $F = ma$ may be somewhat unexpected. A body moving at a constant speed in a straight line is not accelerated; therefore the net force on it is zero: if a car is pushed without accelerating it, the net force is zero because the force applied is exactly equal and opposite to the sum of the frictional forces. If an elevator is descending at a constant speed, so is a man in it, and the force of gravity on the man is equal and opposite to the force exerted on him by the floor of the elevator. If the elevator is descending at an increasing speed, for example, at the beginning of the descent, the man is accelerated downward, the force exerted by the floor is smaller than the man's weight, and the man feels suddenly light. If the elevator cable breaks, and the man is descending with the acceleration of gravity, g, the net force on him is equal to his weight, the floor exerts no force on him, the man exerts no force on the floor, and feels weightless.

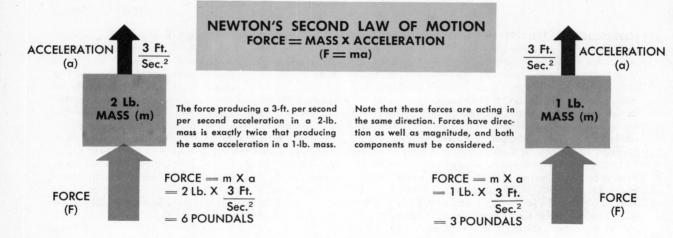

NEWTON'S SECOND LAW OF MOTION
FORCE = MASS X ACCELERATION
(F = ma)

ACCELERATION (a) — 3 Ft. / Sec.²

2 Lb. MASS (m)

The force producing a 3-ft. per second per second acceleration in a 2-lb. mass is exactly twice that producing the same acceleration in a 1-lb. mass.

FORCE (F)

$$\text{FORCE} = m \times a$$
$$= 2 \text{ Lb.} \times \frac{3 \text{ Ft.}}{\text{Sec.}^2}$$
$$= 6 \text{ POUNDALS}$$

Note that these forces are acting in the same direction. Forces have direction as well as magnitude, and both components must be considered.

$$\text{FORCE} = m \times a$$
$$= 1 \text{ Lb.} \times \frac{3 \text{ Ft.}}{\text{Sec.}^2}$$
$$= 3 \text{ POUNDALS}$$

3 Ft. / Sec.² — ACCELERATION (a)

1 Lb. MASS (m)

FORCE (F)

A body is accelerated not only when its speed changes, but also when its direction of motion changes. The force necessary to change a body's direction of motion without changing its speed is called the centripetal force. It can be shown that a body moving with a constant speed v along a circle of radius r has an acceleration equal to v^2/r which is directed toward the center. Such a motion must therefore require a centripetal F_c equal to mv^2/r. If a stone is whirled on a string, the string supplies the force. The equal and opposite force exerted by the stone on the string is called the centrifugal force. The equation $F_c = mv^2/r$ is true even if the path of a body is not a circle and the speed not constant, if v is taken as the instantaneous speed of the body and r is the radius of curvature of the path at the point where the body is. This equation is used in designing the banking of highways and in calculating the force on a pilot at the bottom of a dive.

LEO NEDELSKY

FORCE ACTS or ENFORCEMENT ACTS, in U.S. history, acts passed by Congress in May, 1870, and Feb., and Apr., 1871, to protect the freedoms guaranteed by the Fourteenth and Fifteenth Amendments. The first enforcement act sought to protect Negro suffrage, prohibit fraud in congressional elections, and provide penalties for infringement upon the right to vote. In 1876 the Supreme Court declared portions of this act void on the ground that the Fifteenth Amendment did not extend any positive guarantee of the franchise.

The second act placed congressional elections under federal supervision by requiring special deputies to verify voting lists, count votes, and keep the peace. This act retained its validity.

The third act, or Ku Klux Klan Act, was intended to levy penalties against persons (such as Ku Klux Klan members), conspiring to prevent Negroes from voting or exercising other rights granted to them by the Fourteenth and Fifteenth Amendments. The Supreme Court declared a portion of this act unconstitutional in 1883, and Congress repealed most of the other sections in 1894. In general, the presidents and attorneys general showed little disposition to use those portions of the acts not declared unconstitutional.

ELSIE M. LEWIS

See also KU KLUX KLAN.

FORCEPS, tonglike instruments used for grasping and pulling objects. Examples include hemostatic forceps used during surgery to grasp and close severed blood vessels, dental forceps for extracting teeth, and splinter forceps for removing splinters. Obstetrical forceps are occasionally used in childbirth to grasp and pull the baby's head.

FORCING, horticultural term describing the methods by which plants are brought into a blooming or fruiting stage out of their normal season. Among the several forcing methods, the one most frequently used is the application of heat and increased humidity to plants kept in greenhouses. Other greenhouse forcing techniques include the shortening of daylight exposure by shading the plants with black cloth or the addition of artificial light to lengthen the daylight period. In some cases forcing may be accomplished by the application of chemicals in liquid or gaseous form. Most forcing is done in greenhouses where such conditions as heat, light, and humidity can be easily controlled. Forcing plays an important role in commercial horticulture where the majority of seasonal gift plants must be caused to bloom ahead of their natural flowering time. The term "forcing" is sometimes erroneously applied to greenhouse horticulture in general where plants such as begonias and gloxinias are grown from seeds or cuttings during the cold winter months. Tulips and azaleas brought into bloom at Easter, on the other hand, are forced.

WALTER SINGER

FORD, FORD MADOX, originally Ford Madox Hueffer (1873–1939), English writer and editor. He is best known for his subtle psychological novels, which show the influence of Flaubert and Henry James. He collaborated with Joseph Conrad on *The Inheritors* (1901) and *Romance* (1903). In 1908 he founded the *English Review* and in 1924 the *Transatlantic Review*. One of his best novels is *The Good Soldier* (1915). His masterpiece is the "Tietjens tetralogy" (*Some Do Not*, 1924; *No More Parades*, 1925; *A Man Could Stand Up*, 1926; *The Last Post*, 1928), a vast panorama of Edwardian England receiving and reeling under the blow of World War I. In his consistently rich narrative prose Ford also wrote several volumes of reminiscences, including *Ancient Lights* (1911), *Thus to Revisit* (1921), *Return to Yesterday* (1931), and *Mightier Than the Sword* (1938).

FORD, GERALD RUDOLPH (1913–   ), 38th President of the United States (1974–77) and the first to assume the office after the resignation of a President. In a smooth and orderly transition, Ford was sworn in as President on Aug. 9, 1974, succeeding Richard M. Nixon, whose impeachment had been recommended by the House Judiciary Committee after hearings that stemmed from the Watergate burglary and cover-up.

Ford had been what he called the nation's "first instant vice president" only since Dec. 6, 1973, the first to be nominated and approved under the provisions of the 25th Amendment to the Constitution, ratified in 1967. The vice presidential vacancy had been created on Oct. 10, 1973, when Spiro T. Agnew resigned and pleaded *nolo contendere* to a charge of federal income tax evasion. Ford, then the minority (Republican) leader of the U.S. House of Representatives, was nominated by President Nixon on Oct. 12 to fill the Agnew vacancy. After an intensive investigation by the House and Senate—and while Nixon was facing threats of impeachment and calls for resignation—Ford was confirmed.

In 1976, Ford ran for election to a full four-year presidential term but was defeated by the Democratic nominee, James Earl Carter, Jr.

Early Life. He was born Leslie King, Jr., in Omaha, Neb., on July 14, 1913, and moved with his mother to Grand Rapids, Mich., two years later. His mother remarried, and her husband, Gerald Ford, Sr., owner of a paint and varnish sales firm, changed the boy's name to his by adoption. Young Ford played football at South High in Grand Rapids, winning a position on the all-Michigan team. He played center and linebacker on two undefeated national-championship teams (1932 and 1933) at the University of Michigan and was graduated there in 1935.

He earned a law degree from Yale University in 1941 after working part-time there as assistant football coach and freshman boxing coach. In 1942 he enlisted in the Navy as an ensign, serving 47 months as an aviation operations officer and rising to lieutenant commander.

Legislator. After a period of private law practice in Grand Rapids, Ford first won election to the House from the Fifth District of Michigan in a tough 1948 campaign in which he had the support of Sen. Arthur H. Vandenberg, also a Grand Rapids resident. In 1948–49, Ford served with Representative Nixon and the two became good friends. In 1965 he became House minority leader, replacing Charles A. Halleck, and, during the Nixon Presidency, Ford consistently supported Nixon's policies. He steadily emphasized a need for fiscal responsibility and a strong national defense. At a time when conservative members of Congress resented the Senate's defeat of two Nixon nominees for the Supreme Court, Ford worked unsuccessfully to impeach Justice William O. Douglas.

Ford's 25 years in the House were marked by strong party loyalty, dogged hard work, a complete absence of scandal, and a marked ability to get along with members of both political parties. In the House, he had a reputation as a boring public speaker but a highly effective vote trader and assiduous representative of his constituents. In a national atmosphere of scandal, disbelief, and disdain of politicians at the time he was nominated for vice president and then President, Ford was known as "Mr. Clean" to journalists.

Presidency. The circumstances of Ford's entry into office influenced the nature of his presidency. At his swearing-in ceremony he said, "Our long national nightmare is over." He added, "Our Constitution works. Our great republic is a government of laws and not of men. Here, the people rule."

One month later, Ford issued a "full, complete, and absolute" pardon to Nixon for any wrongs he committed or may have committed while President. Critics attacked Ford for failing to await an indictment and for treating Nixon specially. The issue was pushed by James Earl Carter, Jr., his Democratic opponent, in the 1976 presidential election. Carter said he would offer a pardon to persons who had refused to serve in Vietnam. Ford insisted that the question be settled by a program of earned clemency; he added that about 12,000 persons had been processed under his clemency program.

Ford called inflation "public enemy No. 1." The Congress, controlled by the Democrats, disagreed and put first

Wide World

Gerald R. Ford takes the oath of office as the 38th President of the United States in the East Room of the White House. The President's wife, Betty, looks on as Chief Justice Warren Burger administers the oath.

UPI

President Ford starts his 1976 State of the Union address to a joint session of Congress. Behind him and applauding are Nelson Rockefeller, left, chosen by Ford to succeed him as vice president, and Speaker of the House Carl Albert, a Democrat. Democrats had majorities in both the House and the Senate.

priority on lowering unemployment. The last Ford budget included a $69 billion deficit, the largest in the nation's history.

Defense spending passed the $100 billion per year mark. Carter promised to cut defense spending if he were elected. Ford insisted on the necessity of spending to modernize the Navy and to build new systems such as the B-1 strategic bomber, the Trident ballistic missile submarine, and the M-X land-based missile. Arms sales to foreign nations, particularly to oil-rich countries of the Middle East, escalated and formed a significant part of the U.S. balance of payments. Ford called a strong U.S. defense a guarantee against war and requisite for security.

Relations with the Soviet Union were conducted on the basis of detente, or "peace through strength," as Ford preferred to call it. Detente was threatened by the Soviet intervention in Angola in 1975 and by Soviet support of other "liberation movements" directed against Rhodesia and South West Africa (Namibia). A plan by Ford and Secretary of State Henry Kissinger for bringing peace to southern Africa was opposed by the U.S.S.R.

In the area of strategic arms, Ford pushed for a new SALT (Strategic Arms Limitation Talks) agreement on the basis of the Vladivostok Agreement. This was a protocol signed by Ford and Soviet leader Leonid I. Brezhnev in that Soviet city in December 1975. It stated that the two countries would negotiate to limit strategic launchers (intercontinental ballistic missiles, submarine-launched ballistic missiles, strategic bombers, and "other" delivery systems) to a total of 2,400 for each side. Of these launchers, 1,320 could be MIRVed (that is, could contain multiple independently targeted reentry vehicles). The development of the strategic cruise missile by the United States and the deployment of the Backfire strategic bomber and the Delta strategic submarine by the USSR complicated the negotiations. No SALT II agreement had been signed when Ford left office.

Energy policy for the country was debated between Congress and Ford throughout his administration. Ford recommended a program designed to achieve independence from foreign energy sources by placing high reliance on coal, nuclear energy, solar energy, and domestic sources of petroleum. Congress, however, did not provide Ford with the legislation he requested.

Ford oversaw the beginning of the reorganization of the intelligence services after extensive Congressional investigations of the Central Intelligence Agency, the Federal Bureau of Investigation, the National Security Agency, the Defense Intelligence Agency, and others. New heads were appointed to all these agencies.

Ford's campaign for election to the presidency was hotly contested from the beginning. In the Republican primaries his chief opposition came from Ronald Reagan, former California governor. Reagan narrowly missed being nominated but left his mark on the party platform, especially in areas that condemned the detente policy by implication and that praised Alexander Solzhenitsyn, the exiled Soviet writer critical of the policies of his homeland.

In the general election, millions of people around the world watched as Ford debated Carter three times.

Ford's impression on the office of the President was most visible in the area of integrity. He calmed the nation at a time of domestic upset over Watergate-related matters. He exhibited a public visage of honesty in a period of considerable public disenchantment with politicians and officials. While Carter ran on a platform asking for trust, Ford stressed his own performance. Ford also reflected a growing public dislike of bigger and bigger government by emphasizing the role of the private sector in defeating unemployment. He opposed higher spending levels and new federal programs. Ford said, "We should never forget that a government big enough to give us everything we want is a government big enough to take from us everything we have."

Family. Ford married the former Elizabeth Bloomer, a native of Chicago but long a Grand Rapids resident, in Grand Rapids on Oct. 15, 1948. They had four children—Michael, John, Steven, and Susan.

Betty Ford, earlier a professional dancer and model, expressed outspoken support for women's rights, including the right to abortion. She caused some stir when she told a reporter that she would understand if her daughter had a premarital "affair." She also supported more lenient marijuana laws and supposed that some of her children had had "experience" with marijuana. None of these views was publicly shared by her husband.

WALTER DARNELL JACOBS

FORD, HENRY (1863–1947), American automobile manufacturer. Born on a farm near Dearborn, Mich., Ford left school at 15 and went to Detroit, where he became a machinist and developed an interest in engines. He returned to the farm in 1888 to help his father, but spent his spare time trying to build an inexpensive steam tractor. Back in Detroit in 1891, he went to work for the Edison Illuminating Company as an engineer and machinist. Giving up the steam engine as impractical for light vehicles, he experimented at nights with internal combustion engines. He built his first car—a buggy body mounted on four bicycle wheels with a 2-cylinder gasoline engine—in 1892. He was chief engineer for the Edison Company when, in 1899, he resigned to found the Detroit Automobile Company. In the next three years he manufactured 20 cars, but then, disagreeing with his backers, who regarded the automobile as necessarily a custom-built, luxury item, he resigned.

Ford's ambition was to mass produce a simple, inexpensive car, and to that end he founded the Ford Motor Company in 1903. In 1908 the Ford Company introduced the 4-cylinder Model T and for 19 years thereafter concentrated exclusively on its production. To speed output Ford began in 1913 to develop the moving assembly line, where each worker performed a single operation as the cars moved past him. He also cut costs by acquiring iron and coal mines, steel mills, rubber plantations, and steamships, and eventually by shipping finished parts for assembling at branch plants in other cities and in foreign countries. As a result of these economies, Ford was able to reduce the price of the Model T every year. Ford produced 15,000,000 black Model T's between 1908 and 1927, when, under pressure of competition from other manufacturers, the car was discontinued. In 1927 he introduced the 4-cylinder Model A—in a variety of body styles and colors—and in 1932 the Ford V-8.

Along with efficient methods of mass production, Ford pioneered a labor policy of strict discipline and high wages. In 1914 he began to pay all his workers a minimum of $5 for an 8-hour day—more than twice the previous average wage in his plants. Ford continued to pay high wages during the depression, although he was a bitter foe of union efforts to organize his employees and a vigorous opponent of the New Deal. The history of attempts of the United Automobile Workers (UAW) to organize the Ford plants is punctuated by violence. A strike in Apr., 1941, and an election supervised by the National Labor Relations Board, finally compelled Ford to sign a contract in June, 1941, with the UAW-CIO.

Always an individualist, Ford from the beginning sought to keep control of his enterprise in his own hands. He refused to borrow money from banks, and in 1919 bought out minority stockholders for $75,000,000, thus vesting ownership of the company entirely in his family. In 1915 he sponsored the voyage of a peace ship to Europe in the vain hope that such a dramatic move might end World War I. He ran for the U.S. Senate as a Democrat in 1918 but was defeated.

In 1919 Ford became the publisher of the Dearborn *Independent* and was severely criticized for the paper's anti-Semitic policy. He was again criticized in 1938 when, on his 75th birthday, he accepted decorations from a number of governments, including one from Nazi Germany. Ford was an isolationist before World War II and refused to manufacture airplane engines for Great Britain. When the United States prepared for war, however, Ford converted his plants to the manufacture of airplanes, tanks, trucks, and other war materials.

In 1919 Ford turned over the presidency of his company to his son, Edsel Bryant Ford (1893–1943). Upon his son's death, he resumed the presidency, which in 1945 he finally turned over to his grandson, Henry Ford II.

Ford's influence has been incalculable. The technique of mass production pioneered by Ford revolutionized industrial activity throughout the world. The production of multitudes of cheap, efficient automobiles worked profound sociological changes in American life—ranging from the vast expansion of cities to new patterns of courtship. Ford himself became enormously wealthy and a symbol everywhere of American enterprise. The mammoth Ford Foundation, established in 1936 by Henry and Edsel Ford, continues to influence American life by its contributions to education and many other fields.

Consult Burlingame, Roger, *Henry Ford* (1970); Greenleaf, William, *Monopoly on Wheels: Henry Ford and the Selden Automobile Patent* (1961); Nevins, Allan, and Hill, Frank E., *Ford* (3 volumes, 1954–63); Rae, John B., editor, *Henry Ford* (1969); Sward, Kenneth, *The Legend of Henry Ford* (1968).   ROBERT A. ROSENBAUM

See also AUTOMOBILE.

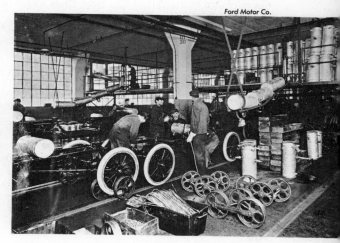

Ford Motor Co.

Henry Ford, pioneer in the mass production of automobiles (*left*). An early assembly line of the Ford Motor Company turning out the famous Model T in the plant at Highland Park, Mich. (*right*).

FORD, JOHN, professional name of Sean O'Feeney (1895–1973), American motion-picture director, born in Cape Elizabeth, Maine. He began directing films in 1917. A number of his pictures reveal his sure hand with Irish subject matter, including *The Informer* (1935), which won for him an Academy Award, *The Plough and the Stars* (1937), *The Quiet Man* (1952), for which he won an Academy Award, and *The Last Hurrah* (1958). Ford also is noted for films stressing strong dramatic action beautifully photographed against outdoor settings. Among these are *The Iron Horse* (1924), *Stagecoach* (1939), *The Grapes of Wrath* (1940), for which he received an Academy Award, *The Long Voyage Home* (1940), *How Green Was My Valley* (1941), another Academy Award winner for direction, and *They Were Expendable* (1945).

FORD, JOHN (1586–after 1638), English dramatist. Born in Devonshire, he studied at Exeter College, Oxford, and at the Middle Temple. Little else is known of his life. Ford, though he also collaborated with other playwrights, composed his best works by himself. These are psychological tragedies involving the conflict of love, often of a psychopathic kind, and the demands of morality or honor. They are subtle studies of complex states of mind and of involved character relationships. Among them are *'Tis Pity She's a Whore*, *The Broken Heart*, and the historical drama *Perkin Warbeck*, all written and acted between 1625 and 1634.

FORD, PAUL LEICESTER (1865–1902), American author, born in Brooklyn, N.Y. At the age of 11 he edited his first volume, a genealogy compiled by his great-grandfather Noah Webster. During the next 25 years he wrote or edited more than 70 works, including *The Writings of Thomas Jefferson* (10 vols., 1892–99) and *The True George Washington* (1896). His novels include *The Honorable Peter Stirling* (1894), based on his own political experience, and *Janice Meredith: A Story of the American Revolution* (1899). Promise of greater achievement was cut short when he was murdered by his brother shortly after his 37th birthday.

FORD CITY, borough of west-central Pennsylvania, on the Allegheny River. The city was named for John B. Ford, father of the U.S. plate-glass industry, who established major plants of the Pittsburgh Plate Glass Company— now the PPG Industries—here.

FORD FOUNDATION, private nonprofit corporation, established in 1936 by Henry Ford, founder of the Ford Motor Company, and his son Edsel. Until 1950 it granted funds for charitable activities of special interest to the Ford family. Then, as a result of substantially increased funds from the estates of its founders, it was reconstituted as a nationwide philanthropy.

The foundation seeks to strengthen American society by identifying problems of national importance and underwriting efforts—mainly of an educational nature— toward their solution. The foundation itself does not engage in research, teaching, or other direct operations. It pursues its objectives as a philanthropy through grants to other nonprofit organizations.

Foundation grants in the educational field are made to improve teaching and academic programs, and extend public understanding and support of education. The program parallels that of the Fund for the Advancement of Education, established in 1951 by the foundation as a separate organization.

Other grants are made for teaching and research in economics and business activities, in the humanities and arts, science and engineering, public affairs, urban and regional problems, youth development, and problems of the aged. In the international field, grants are made for aid to less developed countries, to improve international understanding, and to strengthen U.S. teaching and research in foreign-area studies. RICHARD MAGAT

FORDLÂNDIA, town on the Tapajós River in the state of Pará in north central Brazil about 135 mi (217 km) from the confluence of the Tapajós and Amazon rivers. Fordlândia was built by the Ford Company of Brazil on the company's rubber plantation established on land purchased from the state of Pará in 1927. The plantation was financially unsuccessful and was relinquished to the Brazilian government, which is now in charge of the operations of Fordlândia.

FOREIGN EXCHANGE. *See* TRADE, INTERNATIONAL.

FOREIGN LEGION, military organization composed of foreigners who volunteer their services to a country in peace or war and are rigorously trained to become tough, professional soldiers.

France, which had organized foreign volunteers into special units since the time of Francis I, replaced the last of these in 1831, when Louis-Philippe created the Foreign Legion, whose 5,600 members helped France conquer Algeria. Reorganized in 1884 into two *Régiments Étrangers* totaling about 8,000 men, with headquarters and stations in Algeria, and led by French and a few specially commissioned foreign officers, the legion fought in colonial wars in Tongking, Dahomey, Madagascar, Morocco, and Indochina. It also saw action in the Crimean and Franco-Prussian Wars, as well as World Wars I and II. In 1961 the legion took part in the "Generals' Revolt" against the government policy favoring Algerian independence. Its headquarters were subsequently moved to Corsica.

The Spanish Foreign Legion dates from 1911, when Spanish troops landed in Morocco for combined action with the French against uprisings. Because of opposition at home to colonial warfare, Col. Dámaso Berenguer formed the *Regulares*, Moorish regiments officered by Spaniards. Gen. Francisco Franco moved the legion to Spain upon the outbreak of the Spanish Civil War in 1936. MARTIN BLUMENSON

FOREIGN POLICY ASSOCIATION, nonprofit, voluntary organization devoted to educating the American public by providing information on international affairs, founded in 1918. Its activities include publishing and organizing communities for world affairs education. One of its notable publications is the bimonthly pamphlet, *Headline Series*. Headquarters of the association are in New York City.

FORESTS AND FORESTRY. A forest is a large area dominated by a dense growth of trees and underbrush. Within the forest complicated layers of vegetation are common from ground cover of mosses and low flowering plants through middle layers of bushes and secondary trees. Forest vegetation once occupied perhaps half the earth's land surface and supplied much of early man's food, shelter, and fuel. Today about one-third of the earth's land area is forested. The need for commercial commodities such as lumber and wood pulp for paper, rayon, and cellophane makes forests of ever-increasing importance. Forest land is unevenly distributed. Of the 10,500,000,000 acres of world forest nearly half is in tropical broadleaf types that are little used. Forests differ greatly in species, form, and in capability to grow timber useful to man. Climate, especially precipitation, is the major factor in determining the kind of forest and distribution.

Tropical rain forest, or selva, occurs under continuous heat and copious precipitation with no dry season. Plant growth is luxuriant. The trees are broadleaf with thin bark, and a great many species grow together with many having little commercial value. The forest appears evergreen because new leaves grow continually, and there is no dormant season when leaves are shed. Individual trees tend to vary in height, thus forming a dense canopy over the ground. Underbrush is not generally dense, but there are many ropelike plants and tropical orchids growing on branches. In clearings or along rivers where sunlight reaches the ground, dense tangles of underbrush and second-growth forest, known as jungle, develop. The tropical rain forest occurs in equatorial South America, especially the Amazon Basin, the east coast of Brazil, coastal Colombia, and portions of Caribbean Middle America; in Africa, notably the Congo with an extension westward in Liberia; and in the East Indies.

Monsoon forest is composed of broadleaf trees but is semideciduous because of a dry season. Teak is an important commercial tree of this type of forest. Bamboo is widespread. The principal areas are northeast India, Burma, Indochina, and eastern Indonesia.

Tropical thorn forest, or savanna wood land, is a transitional form of vegetation between humid tropics and the dry lands and occurs where the dry period is long. Usually trees are too far apart to form a canopy and the formation is more wood land than forest. Trees such as acacia and mimosa are usually deciduous, thick-barked, and often thorny. Chief areas of development include the area from northeastern Brazil to northern Argentina, northwest India and Pakistan, large areas surrounding the Congo selva, and northern Australia.

Mediterranean broadleaf scrub and forest is a drought-resistant vegetation found bordering the Mediterranean Sea, and in southern California, central Chile, southern Australia, and southern Africa. The trees do not shed their small, shiny, thick leaves. The dominant trees such as oak form an open wood land rather than a true forest, and there is considerable ground cover of grasses and low plants. Areas of mixed stunted trees, bush, woody shrubs, and bunch grasses have been designated in Europe as maquis, or *garigue*, and in California as chaparral. In general these areas are second growth and represent deterioration of the former vegetation.

Mature cedars rise majestically over the verdant ground cover near Black Oak Creek in the Mount Baker National Forest, in the state of Washington.　(U.S. FOREST SERVICE)

Tropical rain forest in the Amazon Basin.
(EMIL SCHULTHESS—BLACK STAR)

Tropical thorn and scrub in Kruger National Park, South Africa. (GEORGE ROGER—MAGNUM)

PRINCIPAL TYPES OF FORESTS

Coniferous growth near Mount Hood, Oreg. (EWING GALLOWAY)   Broadleaf monsoon forest in Bengal, India. (FPG)

Deciduous broadleaf forests occupy middle latitude areas having 30–60 in. precipitation and seasonal changes causing a dormant season and shedding of leaves. The trees develop protective bark, but leaves are thin and broad. Oak and hickory are the dominant species with various mixtures of walnut, beech, birch, maple, and conifer. Within the area of this type of forest, high mountain slopes, with colder environment, or sandy areas generally support coniferous trees. In contrast to the tropical rain forests, there are few climbing plants and fewer tree species growing together, but there is generally a well-developed understory vegetation. The main areas of broadleaf deciduous forests are eastern United States from southern New England westward beyond the Mississippi River to the prairies, Western Europe and into the Soviet Union, and eastern Asia. Because these areas are among the best agricultural lands, most of the original forest has been cleared for agriculture.

Coniferous forests composed chiefly of evergreen, needleleaved trees occupy middle- and high-latitude areas generally too cool and with too little moisture for the broadleaf trees. Their size and growth varies greatly depending upon the climate and local soil environment. Coniferous forests have supplied at least 80% of commercial forest commodities, partly because of their proximity to the population centers and because their wood is better

known and in many cases more easily worked than tropical species. A vast earth-girdling belt of spruce, fir, larch, and pine known as the taiga stretches from Alaska across Canada and from Scandinavia across the Soviet Union to the Pacific Ocean. Trees seldom are over a foot in diameter. On the poleward side, where forest merges with tundra, trees are stunted and grow very slowly. Within these forests swampy areas of sphagnum moss have developed and are known as muskeg.

The western coniferous forests of North America, extending along the coast from Alaska to northern California and inland on the mountain slopes to the Rockies, include some of the world's finest tree-growing environment. The Douglas fir forest of western Washington and Oregon covers only 5% of the United States commercial forest land, but supplies about 25% of the nation's lumber. Inland from the coast, Western forests are dominated by pine species. Coniferous Southern pine forests of the United States are dominated by loblolly, shortleaf, and slash pine, and extend from Virginia to Texas. Trees are smaller than in the Western forests, generally not over 2 ft. in diameter, but are fast-growing and account for about 40% of all timber harvest of the United States. Other coniferous forest areas include Western Europe, especially the slopes of the Alps and Carpathians and sandy coastal areas, as in France, Brazil, southern Chile and Australia.

Deciduous broadleaf forest in the midwestern United States.
(JOHN H. GERARD—NATIONAL AUDUBON SOCIETY)

Mediterranean broadleaf growth on the southern coast of France.
(FRENCH EMBASSY PRESS AND INFORMATION DIVISION)

Forest vegetation has multiple utility. It affords cover for wildlife, regulates precipitation-runoff, controls erosion and stream flow, and serves recreation. In the past forests were often destroyed by expanding settlement and by widespread fires. Today, however, forestry, the scientific management of forest lands, is making major contributions to improve forested areas and provide sustained yield harvests of timber.

J. GRANVILLE JENSEN, Oregon State University

Forestry

Forestry is the science of handling forest lands as a permanent and continuously productive resource. It involves the growth and orderly utilization of timber, the management of forests for watershed protection and regulation of stream flow, the regulation of livestock grazing on forest lands, and management of forest-inhabiting wildlife.

Silviculture. The science of forestry includes a number of specialized fields. That phase of forestry that deals with the growing of timber as a crop is known as silviculture. Its aims are the production of maximum yields of timber of good quality and adequate new growth of the most desirable species of trees following harvesting. Rapid growth of the most valuable species may be promoted through cultural measures such as thinning of overcrowded stands and removal of undesirable "weed" trees. Reproduction

may be secured by leaving adequate numbers of seed trees after harvesting, by replanting, or by selective harvesting of mature trees with the younger trees left for future cutting as they mature. The latter method is advocated by foresters for most types of forest growth in the United States. In some types, however, such as in old growth Douglas fir stands of the Pacific Northwest, clear-cutting in strips or patches may be practiced with uncut areas left around them to seed in the cutover land. In Europe it is frequently the practice to grow even-aged stands of trees, which are clear-cut when mature, and the area is replanted by hand.

Reforestation. Reforestation is the restoration of an area to forest, either by natural or artificial means. Under natural conditions, the seed scattered by forest trees, or vegetative reproduction by sprouting, produce successive generations of trees. Such natural reforestation is usually the cheapest way of obtaining the restocking of cutover land, and foresters encourage natural restocking whenever possible. As a result of destructive logging methods and fires, however, there are many areas that cannot come back to forest growth by natural means for decades or centuries. On such areas artificial reforestation is necessary if restoration of forest growth is to be obtained. The usual practice in such cases is to grow tree seedlings in nurseries and set out the young trees at the planting site after they have attained suitable size. This usually requires from one to five years' growth in the nurseries. Seed-sowing on the ground has been increasing in practice during the past several years. The use of this method has been made feasible through development of a chemical application that coats the seeds and repels birds and rodents that might eat them prior to germination.

Afforestation. Afforestation is the planting of a forest on land that has not previously borne trees. It may be undertaken to reclaim waste land, to control shifting sand dunes, to protect watersheds, or to provide shelter belts for the protection of fields or buildings from the wind.

Forest Protection. Protection of forests from fire is another specialized field of forestry work, particularly in the United States where weather factors and the types of forests are naturally conducive to high fire danger. Forest fire protection involves the development of fire-control techniques for various forest regions and types, the development of preventive measures, detection, communication and transportation systems, specialized equipment, and fire-fighting methods.

Another aspect of forest protection centers on forest entomology, which deals with the study and control of insects affecting forest trees. In the United States, pine bark beetles are among the most destructive forest insects, causing the loss of millions of dollars' worth of timber annually. Where infestations reach epidemic proportions, control by spraying or by felling infested trees is undertaken. Gypsy moths, tent caterpillars, spruce budworms, and pine-tip moths are other destructive forest insect pests. Forest pathology is concerned with tree diseases. One of the most serious is white pine blister rust, a fungus disease introduced to the United States from Europe. This disease has spread widely among white pines and related species in the Northeast, the Great Lakes states, and the Northwest. It can be controlled by the removal of currant

Jack pines being top-pruned in a nursery (*above*). When sufficiently grown the trees will be transplanted to areas needing reforestation.

Seedling pines being planted in an abandoned field. The tractor-drawn planting machine prepares the ground into which the trees are manually inserted by the occupant of the wire-enclosed planter.

Shortleaf pine seedlings being planted in a field gullied by erosion. The trees will prevent further erosion once they have become established (*right*).

All photos: U.S. Forest Service

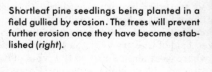

This open, sandy-soiled area has been planted with many red pine and jack pine seedlings to prevent loss of topsoil through wind erosion.

A stand of ponderosa pine in which mature trees have been cut in a planned lumbering operation (*above*).

Aerial view of an old-growth region of Douglas fir and western hemlock. Selected blocks of mature trees have been cut and roads have been constructed through the cut areas. The denuded blocks will be replanted and the lumbering operation shifted to other old-growth regions.

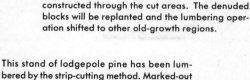

This stand of lodgepole pine has been lumbered by the strip-cutting method. Marked-out strips are cut and reforested in succession, allowing almost continuous lumbering.

and gooseberry bushes, the alternate hosts of the disease, in the vicinity of the pines. Only recently certain antibiotics have been found effective in controlling white pine blister rust on western white pine. These materials have been effectively applied as basal stem sprays, and aerial applications of these same materials to the foliage seems promising. Fungi responsible for the decay of the living tree and wood in use cause serious losses. They can best be kept in check by good silvicultural practices and by proper care in the use of wood.

Wood-utilization Research. Efficient utilization of wood and other forest products is also the concern of forestry. Research in this field seeks improved methods of harvesting, processing, and utilizing the products of the forest, which, in turn, help to prevent wastage of forest growth, enhance the value and utility of the products, and make more profitable the growing of timber according to scientific forestry principles as a permanent enterprise. At Madison, Wis., the U.S. Forest Service maintains a Forest Products Laboratory, the largest institution of its kind in the world. Research at this laboratory has resulted in many new and valuable products that have been derived from the forests.

Other specialized fields of forestry include forest mensuration, the determination of the volume of material in timber stands and the calculation of yields; planning and regulating recreational use of forests; and forest wildlife management, which seeks to develop and maintain forest environments suitable for the continued production of game animals and birds, fur bearers, and fish.

Forest management in accordance with sound principles of forestry has long been practiced in most of the countries of Europe. In the United States, however, destructive exploitation and liquidation has been the prevailing practice, and only in recent years has forestry gained much headway. American forestry at first developed mainly through governmental activity or governmental encouragement. The largest-scale practice of forestry in the United States has been on the federally administered national forests; but in recent years many progressive lumber companies and private owners of forest land have begun to apply scientific forestry in the management of their holdings.

Forests in the United States

As stated above, the forests in the United States, exclu-

273

U.S. Forest Service

Flying low over a forested region, a light plane sprays DDT to control the pine butterfly.

A forester applies a chemical spray in an experiment to devise new methods of tree disease control.

sive of Alaska and Hawaii, cover approximately 648,000,-000 acres, or about one-third of the total land surface, and of this, a total of 485,000,000 acres is classed as commercial forest land, producing or capable of producing timber of commercial value. The estimated total stand of saw timber in 1953 was 1,967,789,000,000 board feet. In 1909 it was estimated at 2,826,000,000,000 board feet. The total volume of standing saw timber declined almost 40% in about three decades, but the trend has been slightly upward since World War II. Three-fourths of the commercial forest area is east of the Great Plains, but more than two-thirds of the present saw timber is in the West.

The ownership of commercial forest land in the United States is as follows:

Federal government	98,874,000 acres
State, county, and municipal	27,216,000 "
Wood-using industries	62,382,000 "
Farm woodland	165,217,000 "
Other	130,651,000 "

Government forestry work began in 1876 with the appointment of a forestry agent to study general forest conditions in the United States. Later a Bureau of Forestry was created, and in 1905 the Forest Service was established in the Department of Agriculture. Most of the states now maintain state forestry departments, which administer state forest land and co-operate with the Forest Service in promoting good forestry practice. New York, Pennsylvania, Michigan, Minnesota, Oregon, and Washington are among the states having substantial areas of state-owned forest lands.

Forestry Schools. Courses in forestry are now given by about 40 colleges and universities in the United States. The usual curriculum covers four years, leading to the degree of Bachelor of Forestry or B.S. in Forestry. Several universities offer graduate work leading to advanced degrees in forestry; Yale, Harvard, and Duke universities maintain graduate schools of forestry.

The professional organization of foresters in the United States is the Society of American Foresters, with headquarters in Washington, D.C.

National Forests

Publicly administered forest areas in the United States, maintained for watershed protection, conservation of timber, and other forest values, are known as "national forests." The first national forest was established in Wyoming in 1891. Originally known as "forest reserves," the earlier national forests were set aside from public domain lands already under federal ownership, mostly in the western states. The Weeks Law of 1911 authorized the government to purchase land for national forest purposes and several national forests have been established in the East and South under this law.

In administering the national forests the U.S. Forest Service has as its first aim the protection of resources so that they will always be there to use, and at the same time to see to it that as many of the people as possible have an equal chance to use them.

The large amount of ripe timber within the national forests is sold at a fair price to the highest bidder. Anybody may purchase timber, but no one can obtain a monopoly of it or hold it for speculative purposes. The federal government is anxious to sell the mature timber on the forests because it is no longer growing at a profitable rate, and should give way to young trees and seedlings. Purchasers of national-forest timber may cut only those trees designated by forest officers, who supervise the cutting to insure that cutover areas will be left in the best condition for future growth.

In addition to administering the national forests, the U.S. Forest Service conducts a number of special investigations relating to the growth and management of forests and their utilization. It studies the characteristics and growth requirements of the principal species of trees in order to determine how different types of forests should be handled, and also the best methods of forest planting, both for the national forests and for other parts of the country.

Forest Rangers. In the national forests, administered by the U.S. Forest Service, the key man on the ground, responsible for the protection and management of the forest, is the forest ranger. The lone forest ranger riding adventurous trails on his faithful horse has been much romanticized in fiction. Actually, he is the hard-working manager of a district often embracing 100,000 acres or more, and spends much of his time in his headquarters office planning and directing protection and improvement work, supervising sales of timber, issuing livestock grazing permits, and arranging the recreational use of his forest district. Fire guards, lookout men, and planting and road maintenance crews work under the ranger's supervision. His ranger station may be located in a town of some size near the national forest, and in addition to office facilities usually includes warehouses, equipment repair shops, and perhaps bunkhouses for seasonal employees.

The ranger's work, however, is not without its adventures and hazards. He still travels by horse on inspections of back-country areas, although most of his travel now is by automobile or pick-up truck. In the national forests of Alaska the rangers travel mainly by chartered aircraft and water. They must know navigation and seamanship in addition to being expert woodsmen. Directing searches for lost persons, rescue work, law enforcement work against poachers or incendiaries—all may come within the ranger's field of duties. The work calls for technical forestry training, physical stamina, resourcefulness, and administrative ability. Ranger positions are filled by promotion of qualified junior foresters or other personnel in the Forest Service. Each national forest is controlled by a forest supervisor responsible for its administration and development. The national forest is divided into ranger districts, varying in size from 100,000 to 500,000 acres, with a ranger in charge of each.

Forest Fires

The most destructive forest fire on record in the United States occurred in Peshtigo, Wis., in 1871. The actual amount of property damage is unknown, but the toll of human life was 1,500 and 1,280,000 acres of timber were consumed. In recent years an average of 150,000 fires have burned over some 6,000,000 acres of United States forest land each year. Of late the fire patrol and lookout services of state and federal forestry agencies have proved of inestimable value and have been able to hold the vast majority of fires to under 10 acres.

Lightning causes many fires, but more than 90% of the fires that occur in the United States are man-caused—mostly the result of human carelessness. Among the chief causes are incendiarism, careless burning of brush and debris, and carelessly discarded cigarettes. In some sections, especially in the Southern states, the practice of annual woods-burning still continues, resulting in severe damage to timber stands. Conservation agencies continuously campaign against such careless habits or misguided practices.

The U.S. Forest Service and state forestry departments have developed efficient fire protection agencies. Lookout stations are maintained for prompt detection of fires. When a fire is reported, central dispatchers send patrolmen, or "smokechasers," to the blaze to effect prompt control. If a fire reaches large proportions, crews of fire fighters are mobilized, emergency communication and supply services are set up, and a battle is conducted

---

FORESTRY | CAREER GUIDE

Characteristics of the Field. About 50% of the professional foresters in the United States and Canada are employed by private industries, chiefly pulp, paper, logging, and lumbering concerns. A small but increasing number of foresters work as consultants to such companies. The second-largest area of employment in the United States is with the federal government, principally the Forest Service of the Department of Agriculture and to a lesser extent the Department of the Interior and other agencies. Other employers are state and local government and educational institutions.

The work of the professional forester is described in FORESTS AND FORESTRY. As in other professions there is a tendency to specialization. In addition to the management and protection of timberlands, forestry includes recreational use of woodlands; conservation of game animals, birds, fish, and other wildlife; and extension work — teaching scientific forest practices to farmers, loggers, and the public. A relatively new field is wood technology, the study of the properties of wood and the development of new and more efficient uses of wood. Research in many areas is a major concern of forestry.

As the section on forest rangers in the article FORESTS AND FORESTRY points out, much of a forester's work may be administrative and may be done in an office. However, a forester must be prepared for hard outdoor work — dangerous work in the case of fire fighting — and for assignment to isolated spots. Good eyesight, strong physique, and a willingness to live out-of-doors are essential. Beginning foresters should expect to spend extra time on fire fighting and other emergency duties, to travel, and to be transferred from one location to another. Experienced men can hope for long-term assignments to one post. Some of the places government foresters work are listed in FOREST SERVICE, UNITED STATES.

Qualifications and Training. The usual start toward a forestry career is a four-year course leading to a bachelor's degree. The course of study typically includes physical and biological science, engineering, economics, and humanities courses, in addition to special instruction in forestry. Summer camp or work experience is helpful. A few men enter forestry with training in such areas as botany, agronomy, engineering, or chemistry, but they are exceptions. Teaching and research positions in forestry require a master's degree, and a doctor's degree is advantageous. In 1960 about 20% of Canadian foresters had graduate degrees.

Foresters in U.S. government service are governed by Civil Service regulations. (See the Career Guide accompanying CIVIL SERVICE.)

Income. Beginning salaries for foresters are modest, falling in the same range as teachers' salaries. Men with the Ph.D. degree can start at a much higher rate than those with the B.A. or B.S. degree. Experienced foresters can expect substantial increases in their earnings. Salaries in U.S. government service are determined by Civil Service grades.

Prospects for Employment. The profession of forestry is expected to grow. Industry faces the need to find more effective ways of producing wood and to find new uses for it. Government agencies are expected to expand their programs of forest management and conservation. A rising trend in the number of forestry graduates has been noted, which may lead to competition for choice starting jobs. Very few women have entered forestry, and the prospects for women in this field continue to be poor.

Sources of Information. General suggestions on career planning are in VOCATIONAL GUIDANCE. Information on forestry can be obtained from the Society of American Foresters, Washington, D.C. (which accredits forestry schools), the U.S. Forest Service, and the Canadian Institute of Forestry, among others.

against the flames. Mechanized equipment, including portable pumps, tractor-drawn plows, and "brush-busters," has been used increasingly in recent years. Airplanes are used extensively for reconnaissance and to deliver supplies or even men (by parachute) in roadless areas.

Systematic protection against forest fires has progressed rapidly in the 20th century, and in 1960 only about 4% of the total forest land area in the United States still lacked organized protection. However, most of the total burn is on this 4% of unprotected acreage.

American Forest Practice

In the practice of forestry in America the general principles of management worked out in Europe through centuries of experience were adopted as rapidly as economic and other conditions permitted. For many reasons, however, European practices cannot be employed directly, but must be modified to suit American conditions. Managerial practices different from those used in Europe must be employed because of the highly developed and specialized methods and machinery of American lumbering; the great variety of tree species; the difficulties attendant on removing timber from remote areas; transportation facilities which make most places in the country much less dependent on the local supply than is the case abroad; the vast number of small holdings of forest land; and the high taxes on forest property. The fundamentals of American forest practice are protection from fire, insects, and diseases; conservative lumbering; and care of the young growth. American practice aims at securing a sustained yield of timber, with the rate of harvesting in balance with the rate of growth.

The American forester has to deal with many different species of trees, as well as a great variety of environmental conditions, and in a large measure is compelled to work out his own methods. Generally the method advocated to ensure the perpetuation of forests is the selection of large and defective trees and the inferior species for cutting. The young growth of preferred species is preserved during the logging operation, and sufficient large trees are left to restock the area or to furnish protection for the young growth.

Forestry has made great progress in America since the turn of the century. During that time it has been built up from almost nothing to a point where it is recognized as being of vital importance to the continued prosperity of the country. The technical equipment and training of the American forester have been brought to a very high standard; many of the essentials of American practice have been worked out; great advances have been made in the study of conditions peculiar to America; and intensive and specialized investigations have been made into problems of forest management and wood utilization. The investigative work of American foresters may soon rival in accomplishment the work which has been under way in Europe for several centuries. Since 1891, when the first forest land was dedicated by the government to the practice of forestry, a tremendous advance has been made in the forest policy of the nation. In the beginning the creation of the national forests met with much opposition, due chiefly to the ideas of speculation prevalent in the great timber regions of the West, and to the fear of local interests that public ownership of the forests would interfere with their plans. This opposition has not completely died away, and at times manifests itself strongly, but it no longer has much popular support.

For the United States the current saw timber growth nearly equals current drain; much forest land is now being handled with conscious regard to future timber growth; and destructive practices are diminishing. A further rise in the general level of forest practices will have to be achieved, however, to assure a continuous and never-failing supply of timber.

Consult Boerker, R. H. D., *Behold Our Green Mansions* (1945); Allen, S. W., *An Introduction to American Forestry* (2d ed., 1950); Shirley, H. L., *Forestry and Its Career Opportunities* (1952).

CLIFFORD D. OWSLEY, U.S. Forest Service
See also RECLAMATION.

FOREST SERVICE, UNITED STATES. The Forest Service is a bureau of the U.S. Department of Agriculture. Almost 200,000,000 acres of public lands are under its administration. This includes 155 national forests, 29 land-utilization projects, 13 experimental areas, and 18 national grassland areas located in 43 states and Puerto Rico.

The Forest Service is responsible for managing these lands under the multiple-use and sustained-yield principles. Each resource—timber, water, forage, wildlife, and recreation—is managed in co-ordination with the other uses so as to obtain maximum practical yield and use to the American public on a continuing basis.

Research is conducted by the Forest Service to increase knowledge and improve practices in forest, range, and watershed management and protection; in the utilization of forest products; and in forest economics. Co-operation is furnished the states and private-forest landowners in the protection of their properties against fire, insects, and diseases and in the promotion of better forest practices.

The offices of the Chief of the Forest Service and his staff are located in Washington, D.C. Regional offices are maintained at Missoula, Mont.; Denver, Colo.; Albuquerque, N. Mex.; Ogden, Utah; San Francisco, Calif.; Portland, Oreg.; Upper Darby, Pa.; Atlanta, Ga.; Milwaukee, Wis.; and Juneau, Alaska. Research activities are conducted at nine regional Forest and Range Experiment Stations and at a Forest Products Laboratory. Experiment Station headquarters are located in Columbus, Ohio; Ogden, Utah; St. Paul, Minn.; Upper Darby, Pa.; Portland, Oreg.; Berkeley, Calif.; Fort Collins, Colo.; Asheville, N.C.; and New Orleans, La. Forest Research Centers are maintained in Alaska and Puerto Rico. The Forest Products Laboratory is located in Madison, Wis.

CLIFFORD D. OWSLEY, U.S. Forest Service

FORGERY, in criminal law, the act of falsifying a document to defraud or deceive; or, with the same intent, circulating one known to be false. In popular usage forgery is a false signature. The law, however, goes beyond this narrow definition. It embraces all material alterations of a document, complete fabrications, manipulation of evidence so as to give a false impression, as well as the deliberate circulation of falsified documents.

FORGERY IN ART. Forgeries, which have been produced in the plastic arts, literature, and music, are works attributed to authors other than their true ones. They may be fake, intentionally created to deceive—and usually to defraud; old works that have been deliberately altered; or copies of works, studio productions, or the creations of a derivative artist, which were not originally meant to mislead. Forgery in the arts is often hard to prove. It has been the springboard for several sensational trials and for acrimonious exchanges between noted authorities, and it has tarnished respected names in art and literature.

Motivation for forgery is usually a desire for financial profit, although frequently it is psychological. In some instances the creators of forgeries set out to prove their competence as artists in the face of public apathy to their works. In other instances the creators of the works, who had derivative styles, were not at fault, but were taken advantage of by unscrupulous dealers who realized that their productions might be passed off as the valuable originals of recognized artists. The production of fakes usually follows the trend of the art market; hence, in a peak period, forgeries may be expected in every field of art from the most ancient to the most modern. The lifespan of a fake is generally about 30 years; a new generation can usually detect the fraudulent in the art produced in the preceding generation.

Famous Forgeries. Early in 1961 three heroic-size terra-cotta sculptures in New York's Metropolitan Museum of Art, formerly thought to be Etruscan antiquities, were shown to be modern enlargements, manufactured in Italy about 1914, of ancient models. Another notable forgery is the medieval frescoes perpetrated by Lothar Malskat in the Church of St. Mary at Lübeck in the late 1940's. These forgeries are especially vicious in that traces of genuine medieval frescoes, which had been discovered after the church was burned out following an air raid in 1942, were utterly destroyed by Malskat and replaced with his free fantasia in medieval style.

Even better known are the "Vermeers" produced by the Dutch painter Han van Meegeren, revealed in 1945. Van Meegeren, who created a so-called early period of Vermeer, painted his works on old canvas and only employed materials available in the 17th century. They were exposed as forgeries when Van Meegeren, who had sold works to the German Hermann Göring, confessed in order to avoid prosecution for collaborating with the Nazis. Earlier notable forgeries include the "Van Goghs" manufactured and sold by the German dealer Otto Wacker in the 1920's and the sculptures in many antique styles by the Italian Alceo Dossena.

Among the most scandalous literary forgeries are the pamphlets and other works privately printed by the English collector and bibliographer Thomas J. Wise in the late 19th and early 20th centuries. Also notable are those of James Macpherson, who in the late 18th century issued poems purportedly by the Irish bard Ossian.

In music the Mass composed by Révérend Père Émile Martin for the 2000th anniversary of the founding of Paris must count as a forgery, since it was presented at the Church of St. Denis in 1951 as *La messe du sacre des rois de France* (*Coronation Mass*), by Étienne Moulinié, an obscure 17th-century composer.

Consult Kurz, Otto, *Fakes: A Handbook for Collectors and Students* (1948).

ROBERT RIGGS KERR, *The Newark Museum*

FORGET-ME-NOT, common name for the more than 50 species of low-growing annual and perennial herbs of the genus *Myosotis*, in the borage family, Boraginaceae, native to northern Europe, Asia, and North America. The common garden forget-me-not, *M. scorpioides*, bears small blue flowers with yellow, pink, or white centers. This species is often planted in spring flower beds, sometimes with yellow tulips, offering a pleasant contrast of color. *M. alpestris*, a related species, is the floral emblem of Alaska. Forget-me-nots do well when planted close together and should be provided with partial shade and abundant moisture.

FORGING, process in which metals are formed into desired shapes by using compressive force. Forging, as an art, was an old process at the time of earliest recorded history. It probably came into existence coincidentally with the discovery of metals. The first forging machine undoubtedly consisted of two rocks, one used as an anvil and the other as a hammer. The principal early products were implements of war. Early forging power was completely human. However, in the 13th century water

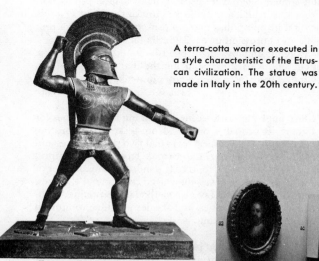

A terra-cotta warrior executed in a style characteristic of the Etruscan civilization. The statue was made in Italy in the 20th century.

A museum exhibition of types and methods of forgery. A fake "Vermeer" by Han van Meegeren is seen on the back wall.

1. The steel bar stock, heated to the plastic state in the forge furnace, is placed in the first impression (A) in the special steel alloy die block.

2. The first forging operation, known as edging and fulling, produces flat areas and bulges corresponding to the finished shape.

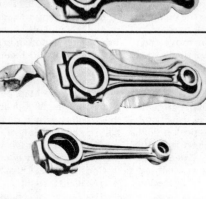

3. The billet is transferred to the third impression (B), the blocking die, where several hammer blows forge the stock into definite shape.

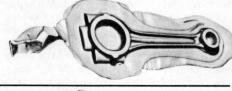

4. The blocked piece is moved to the second impression (C), the finishing die, and the still plastic metal is hammered to precise contours.

5. The end is clipped and the forging goes to the trim press, which uses special dies to remove all of the excess metal, or "flash."

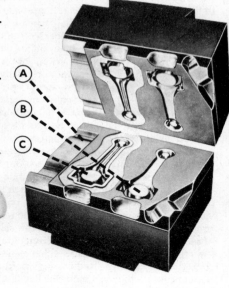

Drop Forging Association

power for lifting forging weights, from less than 100 lb. to nearly 1,000 lb., came into use. With the introduction of the steam engine early in the 18th century, followed by direct-acting piston hammers in about 1840, the size and production of forgings were greatly increased.

Until 1850 forging machines, with a flat stationary die and a vertically movable die, were incapable of duplicating items beyond the skill of the operator. Owing chiefly to the demand for identical gun parts during the Civil War, forging dies evolved from flat-faced types to the closed-contour type, in which the shape of the finished part is completely contained in the two closed dies. Until the 20th century, most forgings were used for building machinery. The introduction of the automobile increased the use for forgings, and today about two-thirds of forging production goes to the automotive industry. Forging hammers now weigh up to 50,000 lb. and forging presses exert thousands of tons of force.

Drop forging, as the name implies, consists of forming heated bars, or billets, of metal in either open- or closed-contour dies in which the force is applied by means of a falling weight (hammer or ram). Most drop-forging machines are of the gravity or steam drop-hammer type. Either type consists of a stationary anvil to which the bottom die is bolted, a frame which contains guides for the hammer, the ram which carries the movable top die, and a power source. The most commonly used gravity-type drop-forging machine is the board drop-hammer. In this machine the ram is fastened to hardwood boards which pass between rotating rolls to raise the hammer. The application of force is regulated by the weight of the hammer and the height from which it falls. Typical products of hammer forging are crankshafts, connecting rods, wrenches, gear blanks, and a variety of machine tool components.

Press-forging machines use dies similar to those of the drop-forging process but force usually is applied hydraulically with a slow, squeezing action. Press forging handles parts too large for drop forging, and because of the slower action, beneficial effects penetrate deeper into the metal. Large presses capable of exerting forces to 15,000 tons normally use flat, open-face dies, whereas small capacity presses may use closed dies.

Roll forging is used in the production of simple, continuous shapes including rails, rods, beams, and sheets. In this method the heated billet is passed between pairs of rolls, resulting in the change of the billet's shape to the configuration machined on the roll faces.

Upset forging, used in producing nails, bolts, screws, and similar headed items, is usually a high-production process in which a suitable amount of the billet extends beyond gripping dies and is upset, or headed, by a ram with an impression or cavity in its face.

Swaging employs high-speed hammers arranged in a circle, and is used for reducing the diameters of rods or cylinders, usually to form a taper or neck.

PAUL B. EATON, Purdue University

FORK, implement for eating or cooking that has tines for piercing. It probably derived from a skewer before the 12th century. The earliest forks had two straight tines and held meat for carving. Later forks, having curved tines, were used to convey food to the mouth. The number of tines and the style of handle varied throughout the ages. Engraving has been a favorite method of decoration. Modern forks have four tines, and are designed for comfort in handling as well as eating.

FORLANA, also called furlana, couple dance of Friuli, in northeast Italy. As in the *Ländler* of adjoining Austria, the man and woman waltz or skip in lilting 3/4 time. In Venice couples glide and whirl more impetuously to spirited

6/8-time melodies. Bach's orchestral Suite in C Major includes a forlana.

FORLÌ [fôr-lē'], capital of Forlì Province, in the district of Emilia-Romagna, northern Italy. Originally named Forum Livii, it lies on the ancient Aemilian Way. It is a prosperous agricultural market and processing center noted for wines, canned foods, and beet sugar. Notable buildings include the Church of San Mercuriale, a 13th-century palace, and a 14th-century citadel. Pop., 91,945.

FORM, philosophical expression given its most extensive technical development by Aristotle. Originally, Plato had called "form" that third thing which two men share, namely humanity. Aristotle, denying that humanity is something independent of the things which are human, said that humanity, the form shared, was the peculiar structure and powers of the individual, as distinct from the biological material structured. Thus, form and matter are correlative notions, somewhat like structure and what-is-structured. The marble of a statue is its matter, whereas, "its being a statue of Plato," for example, is its form. In a given object, what the object is made of, the material employed, is the matter; and the way that that material is ordered or structured is the form. (Francis Bacon said that form consists of those characteristics of a thing described in the laws governing it.) A given form, although it cannot be received in every kind of matter, is not always limited to one kind; for instance, you can have a desk of wood or metal, but not of sand.

Aristotle thought the hylomorphic (matter-form) theory explained how there could be change without annihilation. In a substantial change the form is lost and replaced by another, but the matter remains; thus one can suppose that a thing can be destroyed without being committed to the view that when paper is turned to ashes one thing is annihilated and another created. The matter in an object is the source of its limitations, whereas the form is the source of its actual powers.

JAMES F. ROSS, University of Michigan

FORMALDEHYDE [fôr-măl'də-hīd], CH_2O, pungent gas ordinarily available in a water solution of 37% strength. It is then called Formalin. Formaldehyde is a strong reducing agent and the simplest member of the class of compounds known as aldehydes. Three polymerized forms of formaldehyde exist and are known are paraformaldehyde, trioxane, and tetroxymethylene, all of which are reconverted back to formaldehyde on heating.

Formaldehyde is used as a starting material in the synthesis of Bakelite and many dyes, as a preserving fluid for anatomical specimens, and as an embalming fluid. It is soluble in water, ether, and alcohol. Reduction of formaldehyde yields wood alcohol (methanol) and oxidation yields formic acid, the simplest member of the class of organic acids, CH_2O_2. It is a toxic agent both in liquid and in vapor forms. Early symptoms of formaldehyde poisoning are irritating action on the membranes of the eyes and nose and also the skin. In case of undue exposure to formaldehyde gas the patient should be removed to fresh air, and a physician should be summoned.

WALTER COOK, University of Akron, Ohio

FORMALIN. See FORMALDEHYDE.

FORMALISM: In ethics, the doctrine that the basic principles of conduct, which determine one's duties or the moral worth of one's actions, are purely formal, and therefore independent of one's personal inclinations or circumstances. Kant, for example, maintained that the formal categorical imperative, governing all moral conduct, is that one should so act that he can will the maxim of his action to be a universal law for all men.

In aesthetics, the doctrine that the aesthetic merit of a work of art depends exclusively upon its abstract formal structure, and is completely independent of any representational function it may serve. Aesthetic formalism is most plausible as applied to music and abstract plastic art, but serious difficulties arise when it is applied to such art forms as drama and literature generally.

In mathematics, the doctrine that mathematics consists essentially of symbols and operations performed upon them independent of their meaning or content. It is the culmination of the tendency to develop systems of mathematics, especially geometry, independently of spatial intuitions which may mislead the mathematician as to what the necessary consequences of his axioms are.

Consult Bell, Clive, *Art* (1914); Wilder, R. L., *Introduction to the Foundations of Mathematics* (1952).

IRVING M. COPI, University of Michigan

FORMICA. See PLASTIC LAMINATES.

FORMIC ACID, also known as methanoic acid, HCOOH. Originally it was isolated from red ants. It is the strongest of the aliphatic acids and forms blisters on contact with the skin. Sodium formate, HCOONa, is prepared by the action of carbon monoxide on caustic soda at 200° C. (392° F.) and 10 atmospheres pressure. The acid is obtained by treatment of the salt with sulfuric acid. Formic acid is a powerful reducing agent capable of reducing mercury salts to metallic mercury. It is used in the dyeing and finishing of textiles, in the coagulation of rubber latex, and the removal of lime from hides in the leather industry.

FORMOSA, province of northern Argentina, lying in the Gran Chaco, and bounded on the north and east by Paraguay. Covering an area of 28,778 sq. mi., much of the province is sparsely settled, but there are cattle ranches in the west and petroleum fields in the north. The capital city is Formosa, near the eastern border. Pop., Formosa city, 16,505; province, 112,056.

FORMOSA. See TAIWAN.

FORMOSA STRAIT, arm of the Pacific Ocean, about 115 mi. wide, between Fukien Province on the southeast China mainland and Taiwan (Formosa) Island. It is the location of the Pescadores and links the East and South China seas. Its ports include Amoy on the mainland and Chilung (Keelung), Anping (Tainan's port), and Kaohsiung on Taiwan.

FORMS OF ADDRESS include the name and title of the addressee and, in written addresses, the directions for delivery on the envelope, and the salutation and the complimentary close within the letter. It is important to give all these parts completely and correctly not only to assure efficient handling and delivery of mail but also to make the proper impression on the reader.

In the address on the envelope, street name and house number, city, state, and country (if foreign) all must be written with care since incorrect or incomplete directions for delivery will almost certainly result in delayed delivery if not return to the sender. With the volume of mail they have to handle rapidly, postal employees often toss aside for later handling any piece of mail incompletely addressed. In cities that are divided into postal zones or sections (N.E., S.E., N.W., S.W.), even a missing zone number or section designation may cause delay. The standard form is a block form (all lines beginning at the left margin) with open punctuation (no marks at the ends of lines except periods after abbreviations):

Mrs. Herta A. Murphy
1125 Pacific Street, N.W.
Seattle 5, Washington

The inside address at the upper left of the letter is single spaced but the one on the envelope is double spaced unless it contains more than three lines.

In an early form—still correct but no longer widely used—each successive line is further indented; there is a comma at the end of each line except the last, which ends with a period. Also correct but rarely seen is an official form that begins with the salutation directly. In this form the inside address appears at the lower left corner of the letter.

Because the postal service will usually deliver the mail, ultimately, even with a bare minimum of directions, care in the other parts of addresses is perhaps even more important. Certainly almost everyone resents seeing his name misspelled or written in any form other than the one he normally uses (Jack, Jack H., Harwood, or J. Harwood Wilkerson instead of J. H. Wilkinson, for example). The correct way to write the name of a business firm or other organization is exactly the way the organization writes it. Special attention should be given to (1) whether *The* is used at the beginning, (2) whether *and* is spelled out or written as &, (3) whether *Company* or *Incorporated* is used and, if so, whether abbreviated, and (4) the handling of commas in a series of names.

Custom and courtesy demand that everyone addressed in writing be given some title. In the absence of special titles of respect or identification of position, the usual courtesy titles are *Mr.* (plural *Messrs.*) for men, *Miss* for unmarried women, and *Mrs.* (plural *Mmes.*) plus husband's name for married women and widows, or plus maiden name and former husband's surname for divorcees.

Letters addressed to businessmen in connection with their businesses should include their official titles—after a comma on the same line with the courtesy title and name or, if long, on the next line. When a person has earned a title of respect or position, he naturally expects to see it when he is addressed formally; and courtesy demands that a writer use the highest-ranking title which the addressee has earned.

The salutation, even more than the title, indicates the degree of formality and respect a writer assumes in addressing his reader. Hence it affects the reader's reactions by setting the tone of the communication. Although salutations to people vary with their special titles, the usual salutations that go with the standard courtesy titles are (in descending order of formality) *Sir* or *Madam*, *My dear Sir*, *Dear Sir*, *My dear Mr. Jones*, *Dear Mr. Jones*, *Dear Jones*, and *Dear John*. The invariable salutation for a corporation or other group is *Gentlemen* (*Ladies* or *Mesdames* if all are known to be women).

In business and official correspondence, the salutation is regularly followed by a colon. In familiar and social letters, the usual mark is the comma.

Like the salutation, the complimentary close indicates the degree of formality and respect existing in the relationship between writer and reader. Hence it needs to match the salutation. The key words, in descending order of formality, are *Respectfully*, *Truly*, *Sincerely*, and *Cordially*. *Respectfully* is used in addressing all high-ranking government, clerical, military, and academic officials considered the writer's superiors. *Truly* and *Sincerely* are the most frequently appropriate business forms, though *Cordially* is appropriate in letters to close business friends as well as in social letters. The use or omission of *Very* or *Yours* before or after the appropriate key word makes little difference, though some authorities insist that *Yours* should always be used. A comma usually follows the complimentary close, though some authorities say that open punctuation in the inside address calls for omission of that comma and of the colon after the salutation.

In the interest of efficiency of typing and consistency in tone, some business writers use a form that omits salutations and complimentary closes. This type of letter, sponsored by the National Office Management Association (NOMA) since the 1940's and known as the NOMA Simplified Letter, obviously reduces typing time. Although salutations and complimentary closes may be criticized as outmoded forms that are unrealistic and often inconsistent with the tone of the rest of the letter, tradition still prevails in the great majority of cases, as reflected in the preceding discussion.

C. W. WILKINSON, University of Florida
See also LETTER WRITING.

FORMULA, CHEMICAL, represents the exact atomic composition of a single molecule of a substance, embodying the idea that all the molecules of a compound are identical. It is written by grouping the symbols of the component elements in a prescribed order. Each symbol stands for a single atom; a small number following it, and dropped half below the line, indicates the actual number of atoms in the molecule. A number, preceding the formula and placed on the line, indicates the number of molecules being considered. Thus $3H_2SO_4$ means three molecules of sulfuric acid, each consisting of two atoms of hydrogen, one atom of sulfur, and four atoms of oxygen.

Formulas are determined in the following way. The unknown compound is analyzed to find the percentage by weight of each element in it. The percentages are divided by the respective atomic weights. The resulting figures will indicate the simple ratio of the elements. For example, in hydrogen peroxide the ratio of hydrogen to oxygen is $\frac{5.88\%}{1}$ to $\frac{94.12\%}{16}$, or 1 to 1. The empirical formula is therefore HO. The molecular weight, 34, is then determined by one or more of several methods. The molecular formula is therefore H_2O_2, and not HO, H_3O_3, or some other multiple. With electrovalent compounds the number of charges on each ion is also written in, thus $Ca^{++}(OH^-)_2$. The formulas for radicals are written in the same way, for they are considered to be separate particles.

On the whole, valence relationships can be worked out from most formulas. An inorganic formula lists the most metallic elements first and the least metallic last. Hydrogen is always the first element given. With organic compounds, isomers require that structural formulas be used. Formulas using dots for valence electrons are useful for instructional purposes. Without formulas, no chemical equation could be written, and chemistry could never have developed beyond qualitative descriptions.

Louis Vaczek, The New School for Social Research
See also Chemistry.

Nathan B. Forrest, brilliant Confederate cavalry leader. After a victory at Brices Cross Roads, Miss., in 1864, he is believed to have stated that the secret of his success was, "To git thar fustest with the mostest men." (THE BETTMANN ARCHIVE)

FORNAX, known also as the Furnace, a constellation of the Southern Hemisphere. It was named in the 18th century to represent faint stars near the southern end of the constellation Eridanus. Fornax contains within its boundaries the first elliptical galaxy to be recognized.

FORRES [fŏr'ĭs], Royal Burgh, largely residential, in Moray County, Scotland. One of the oldest towns in Scotland, it was the residence of early Scottish Kings and site of witch burnings. It is thought to be the scene of Macbeth's murder of Duncan, whose palace was here. Pop., 4,780.

FORREST, EDWIN (1806–72), noted American actor, born in Philadelphia. He had his first major success in his New York debut as Othello in 1826. He toured America and Europe in major tragic roles, including Lear, Macbeth, and Hamlet; and in commissioned plays by American authors. Two of his greatest parts, Spartacus and Metamora, resulted from prize competitions. Tempestuous on and off stage, he pursued a rivalry with the English actor William Charles Macready that culminated in the Astor Place riot in New York in 1849.

FORREST, NATHAN BEDFORD (1821–77), Confederate general in the U.S. Civil War. He was born in Bedford County, Tenn. and brought up in Mississippi. His father's death deprived him of formal schooling as he assumed responsibility for the support of his family. Forrest was first a farmer, then a cattle dealer, and later a slave trader and real-estate speculator. He finally became the wealthy owner of cotton plantations in Mississippi and Arkansas.

He enlisted in the Confederate army as a private but was commissioned a lieutenant colonel, when he raised and equipped a mounted battalion at his own expense. Forrest strenuously opposed surrendering Fort Donelson (Feb., 1862), and made good the escape of his small cavalry unit. He joined Gen. Albert S. Johnston's army and distinguished himself at Shiloh (Apr., 1862), where he was wounded. Forrest performed in outstanding fashion during Gen. Braxton Bragg's Kentucky campaign, and

later at Chickamauga. He was so dissatisfied with Bragg's failure to exploit the latter victory that he resigned his commission. He then accepted promotion to major general and fought in western Tennessee with relatively few troops. Forrest harassed the Union forces, destroying transportation, garrisons, and supply depots. He commanded the rear guard during the retreat from Nashville. In Feb., 1865, a lieutenant general, he campaigned between Decatur, Ala., and the Mississippi River. The virtual massacre of the Union garrison (many of the troops Negro soldiers) at Fort Pillow, about 40 mi. north of Memphis, on Apr. 12, 1864, was committed under his command. After the war Forrest was a businessman and was influential in the early activities of the Klu Klux Klan.

Martin Blumenson, formerly, Senior Historian,
Department of the Army

FORRESTAL [fôr'ĭs-tôl], **JAMES VINCENT** (1892–1949), American banker and public official, born in Beacon, N.Y. Forrestal graduated from Princeton and joined Dillon, Read and Company, a New York investment bank, as a bond salesman. After service as a naval aviator in World War I, he returned to Dillon, Read, of which he became president in 1937. Appointed administrative assistant to President Franklin D. Roosevelt and then (1940) undersecretary of the Navy, he later (1944) succeeded Frank Knox as Secretary of the Navy. After the creation of the National Military Establishment (1947), he took office as the first Secretary of Defense. Nervous exhaustion caused his resignation and suicide in 1949.

FORREST CITY, city of eastern Arkansas, and seat of St. Francis County. Forrest City is an agricultural trading center, and manufactures include hand trucks and clothing. Inc., 1873; pop., 12,521.

FORSSMANN, WERNER THEODOR (1904–   ), German physician who shared the Nobel Prize with André Cournand and Dickinson W. Richards in 1956 for his work on passing a tube into the heart. Forssmann used himself as a subject, introducing the tube through an artery at the elbow and pushing it upward until it reached the heart. This technique was later perfected by Cournand and Richards and was used to study heart function.

FORSTER, E(DWARD) M(ORGAN) (1879–1970), English novelist, short-story writer, and essayist. Born into the middle class, he was unhappy as a boarding-school day boy, but at Cambridge University he found a congenial environment. Early short stories and novels were followed by *A Room with a View* (1908), a novel in which Forster characteristically exposed members of the English middle class to an Italian milieu. *Howard's End* (1910) used two families to epitomize the contrast between a hard, bustling, outer life and a sensitive, contemplative, inner one, the task for both families being to "only connect" and balance these two attitudes toward life.

Stays in Egypt and India preceded *A Passage to India* (1924), Forster's masterpiece. This novel went beyond the conflicts among and between Indians and the British who ruled them, exploring different modes of apprehending truths of religion and the human spirit. Forster has since written no novels. Best known among his essays and criticism is *Aspects of the Novel* (1927).

Consult Trilling, Lionel, *E. M. Forster: A Critical Guidebook* (rev. ed., 1964).

JOSEPH L. BLOTNER, University of Virginia
See also ENGLISH LITERATURE.

FORSYTE SAGA, THE. *See* GALSWORTHY, JOHN.

FORSYTH [fôr'sĭth], **JOHN** (1780–1841), American statesman, born in Fredericksburg, Va. He graduated from Princeton and practiced law in Georgia. Forsyth served in the U.S. House of Representatives (1813–18) and U.S. Senate (1818–19). He first achieved national prominence as U.S. minister to Spain (1819–23), when he gained (1819) Spanish assent to the treaty ceding Florida to the United States. He again served in the U.S. House of Representatives (1823–27), was elected Governor of Georgia (1827), and U.S. Senator (1829). President Andrew Jackson appointed him Secretary of State in 1834, a position he retained under President Martin Van Buren until 1841. He competently dealt with such questions as the annexation of Texas and the controversy with Canada over the *Caroline* affair.

FORSYTHIA [fôr-sĭth'ē-ə], a genus of handsome, yellow-flowered, spring-blooming shrubs in the olive family, Oleaceae, native to southeastern Europe and Asia, and widely cultivated in North America. In addition to the natural species, improved cultural varieties are popular, especially varieties of the hybrid, *Forsythia intermedia*. Forsythias thrive in ordinary, well-drained soil and can be grown in full sunlight or partial shade. They are easily propagated by cuttings or division. During the winter cut branches may be placed in water indoors and will soon produce flowers.

FORT, PAUL (1872–1960), French poet. He was an active member of the symbolist movement; he admired Mallarmé and attended the Tuesday evening gatherings in Mallarmé's Paris apartment. His poetry, however, is not symbolist. His more than 50 volumes of poems deal with popular themes, legends, and mythology.

FORTALEZA [fôr-tə-lä'zə], sometimes called Ceará, a city on the eastern part of Brazil's north coast, near the mouth of the Ceará River in the state of Ceará and about 850 mi. southeast of the mouth of the Amazon River. Fortaleza is the capital and the chief seaport of the state, as well as one of the major port cities of Brazil. The town was founded by the Portuguese in 1609 as a fortress site to protect nearby sugar settlements from hostile Indians. The Dutch seized and held the town from 1637 to 1654 in an attempt to gain control of Portugal's rich sugar colonies in northeastern Brazil. When the Portuguese expelled the Dutch (1654) the town was named Villa do Forte da Assumpção. In 1810, Fortaleza became the capital of Ceará; it was raised to city status in 1823 and renamed Fortaleza da Nova Bragança. The hinterland of Fortaleza is composed largely of semiarid country that is subject to severe droughts and alternately to floods. When such disasters occur people from the back country temporarily flock into the city. Gathered products, along with commodities from irrigated and nonirrigated farms in the interior, are exported from Fortaleza, including castor beans and oil, oiticica oil, carnauba wax, cotton, coffee, sugar, rum, rice, cattle hides, and goat skins. Harbor facilities have been increased by new construction at Mucuripe Point, 5 mi. to the northeast. Today, Fortaleza is a modern city providing higher educational facilities and business opportunities. Pop. (greater city), 794,000.

PHYLLIS R. GRIESS, Pennsylvania State University

FORTAS, ABE (1910–   ), U.S. lawyer and Supreme Court justice. Born in Memphis, Tenn., the son of an immigrated British-Jewish cabinetmaker, Fortas helped earn his way through Southwestern College, Memphis (A.B., 1930), by playing the violin, an avocation he was to enjoy throughout his subsequent career. Named to the faculty of Yale Law School on graduation (1933), he taught there briefly until drawn to Washington, D.C. for a series of New Deal administrative posts, culminating in the undersecretaryship of the Interior (1942–46). He was a founding partner of a Washington, D.C. law firm, with clients ranging from major corporate accounts to nonpaying criminal defendants in such landmark civil liberties cases as *Durham* and *Gideon*. Another Fortas client was fellow-New Dealer Lyndon B. Johnson, who sought his services in 1948, when alleged irregularities threatened removal of Johnson's name from the Texas ballot for U.S. Senator. As President, Johnson appointed Fortas to the Supreme Court in 1965 and sought to elevate him to Chief Justice in 1968. Senate opposition thwarted the appointment. In 1969 disclosure of an earlier financial link with an industrialist since convicted of selling unregistered securities led Fortas to resign from the bench.

FRED RODELL, Yale Law School

FORT ATKINSON, city of southeastern Wisconsin, on the Rock River. Vegetable canning and the manufacture of dairy equipment and lighting fixtures are leading industries. Pop., 9,164.

FORT COLLINS, city of north-central Colorado, and seat of Larimer County. Nearby Laporte was settled earlier, while the Fort Collins townsite did not reach public notice until 1871, when members of an agricultural colony settled here and successfully made irrigation farming a profitable enterprise. An agricultural school erected in 1879 grew to the present Colorado State University. The city has a diversified industrial and agricultural economy. The Pioneer Museum houses trophies and weapons.

FORT-DE-FRANCE, capital of the Island of Martinique (Overseas Department of France), in the Lesser Antilles of the West Indies. The city has been Martinique's leading seaport and commercial center since the destruction of Saint-Pierre by the eruption of Mt. Pelée on May 8, 1902. It is on the deep and landlocked Bay of Fort-de-France on the west (leeward) side of the island, where it is protected from the trade-wind surf.

FORT DODGE, city of north-central Iowa and seat of Webster County. Settlement came with the establishment in 1850 of Fort Clarke, which was renamed in 1851 for the U.S. senator from Wisconsin, Henry Dodge. The military post was abandoned in 1853, and the town was platted and incorporated in the following year. The economy of Fort Dodge is now based on manufacturing and agribusiness.

FORTEN, JAMES (1766–1842), American Negro reformer. During the American Revolution he served in the Pennsylvania navy. He became a sailmaker in Philadelphia, and amassed a fortune of $100,000. Forten gave much of his time and wealth to such causes as temperance, peace, and woman's rights. An ardent foe of slavery, although born free himself, he was an influential figure in organizing the abolition movement.

FORT ERIE, town of southern Ontario, Canada, located on Lake Erie and on the Niagara River, opposite Buffalo, N.Y. The Peace Bridge here connects the city with Buffalo, and Fort Erie is an important port of entry. The city has various manufacturing plants. Originally settled by United Empire Loyalists, it became an important American strong point during the War of 1812.

FORT FRANCES, town of northern Ontario, Canada, on the Minnesota-Ontario border, at the west end of Rainy Lake. It was founded as a fur-trading post in 1731. There is still good hunting and canoeing in the area, but the main industry is dependent upon a large pulp and paper mill.

FORTH, FIRTH OF, estuary of the North Sea and an outlet for the Forth River in southeastern Scotland. About 48 mi (77 km) long, the Firth of Forth varies in width from 1½ mi (2.4 km) to 19 mi (31 km) at its mouth. The greatest depth, 200 ft (about 60 m), is found in the inner portions of the firth.

The Firth of Forth is spanned by two bridges: a cantilever bridge carrying railroad traffic, completed in 1889, and a suspension bridge carrying automobile traffic, completed in 1963. The suspension span of the latter bridge is 3,300 ft (1 005 m) long, and for a short time was the longest in Europe.

Nashville Chamber of Commerce
Crude but effective, Fort Nashborough, built in 1780 at Nashville, provided protection against attack. This is a replica.

FORTIFICATION, system of defenses to deter enemy attack and increase the fighting power and effective weapon action of defending troops. Fortifications range from complex, multiple, garrisoned fortresses, with every caliber of ordnance and elaborate subterranean communications chambers, down the command scale to earth trenches or foxholes defended by a few troops with hand weapons. The installations can be permanent or temporary, depending upon the military mission to be accomplished.

History of Fortification. Fortifications have been important throughout the history of man. Every civilization has used its ablest architects and engineers to design and build defenses. The earliest fortifications were little more than earth mounds topped with stone or earth barricades, but the science of permanent defense construction had achieved a standard plan by 5000 B.C. Fortifications constructed some 4,500 years ago by the Minoans, and subsequently by the Assyrians, Persians, Egyptians, Etruscans, Greeks, and Romans, remain visible today on the Aegean islands, on Cyprus, and on Malta. Delicate classical walls and colonnades stand in marked contrast to the ponderous battlements and towers of the Crusaders, Saracens, and Turks, and they are incongruous compared with the reinforced concrete shelters and airfields built by the Italians, Germans, and British during World War II.

Since the days of the Minoan Empire fortifications have had one characteristic in common: the wall, which forms the main defense perimeter of all forts. The number, height, thickness, and contour of walls changed as the art of fortification became more sophisticated. Through the centuries the perimeters of the walled city or fortress were expanded by adding escarpments, widening moats, reinforcing ramparts, and raising towers, until 13th-century feudal cities resembled masonry arsenals.

Military engineers of ancient and feudal times designed forts for combined military and civilian occupation, with the scope and purpose of the defenses dictated by civil authorities whose strategy was often at odds with that of military leaders. During the Renaissance and succeeding centuries, however, military technicians gained more authority, and military defenses began to emerge in the distinctive form known today. The standard military fort was a walled, rectangular structure, capped with a parapet,

283

CHARACTERISTICS OF PERMANENT FORTIFICATIONS

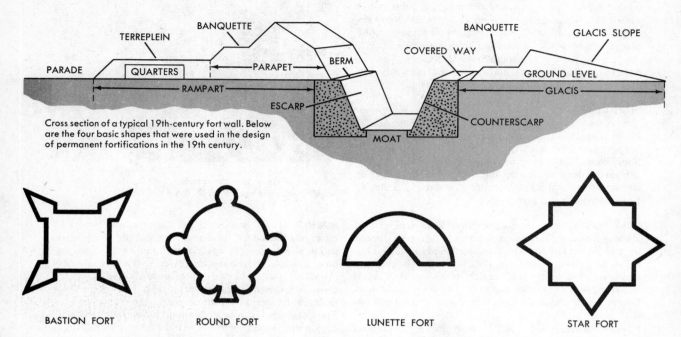

Cross section of a typical 19th-century fort wall. Below are the four basic shapes that were used in the design of permanent fortifications in the 19th century.

BASTION FORT　　　　**ROUND FORT**　　　　**LUNETTE FORT**　　　　**STAR FORT**

slotted with embrasures for weapons, entered through a single gate, and usually accommodating a battalion of troops. Conditions of the terrain, relative to expected enemy approach, determined its location. As invading armies increased their range of mobility and ordnance capacity,

the strength of the fort was increased with bastions, terrepleins, and moats.

The bastioned fortification, regimental size, was the hallmark of military power in the 19th century. It was variously called a bastion fort, star fort, round fort, or lu-

Castillo de San Marcos, started in 1672 in St. Augustine, Fla., withstood sieges and attacks up through the 19th century.

FIELD FORTIFICATIONS

Right, entrenched field fortification with communication trench under foreground camouflage. Below, sandbag revetment for vehicle or supply protection.

U.S. Air Force

U.S. Army Signal Corps

nette fort, as determined by its outline. All such forts had certain common characteristics. They included, on the exterior, a moat, a drawbridge, an escarp or face wall, a berm, and a parapet; sometimes they were topped with a rampart protecting the crenels or embrasures in the parapet. On the interior the parade was at ground level, with ramps rising to the terreplein, where cannon were mounted for firing through the parapet embrasures. Casemated guns were located under the terreplein. The projecting flanks of bastion and star forts permitted defenders the advantage of enfilade fire on attackers crossing the moat or scaling the walls.

Modern Permanent Fortifications. Missile sites, either for ground-to-air or intercontinental ballistic missiles, may properly be considered modern permanent fortifications. Their garrison complex includes reinforced concrete underground silos, launchers, elevators, and adjacent quarters, both administrative and domiciliary.

Classic fortifications like castles, walled cities, and bastioned forts are outmoded because of their vulnerability to modern artillery and nuclear missiles and to observation and destruction by aircraft, the impracticality of camouflaging them, and the immobility of troops and artillery garrisoned within them. German and French military engineers during World War II learned that deliberate permanent defenses with their concrete parapets, casemates, pillboxes, and escarpments were highly susceptible to encirclement, flank attack, or strategically planned frontal attack by mobile troops and artillery. Inception of jet aircraft and ballistic missiles and the use by mobile forces of nuclear surface-to-surface missiles place questionable value on the establishment of permanent surface fortifications. In modern warfare temporary, or field, fortifications have tactical value in mobile campaigns, and they can be redeployed or destroyed easily should enemy maneuvers necessitate such action.

Field Fortifications. Principal considerations in the establishment of field fortifications are (1) an unobstructed field of fire toward the enemy; (2) maximum concealment and protection for troops, vehicles, tanks, and artillery; (3) trenches supported by wire entanglements, tank traps, and other obstacles to attack; (4) lines of communication

such as roads, rivers, canals, bridges, telephone, radio, and landing fields for helicopters and light aircraft; and (5) the removal or obstruction of communication lines that may assist enemy attack. Consideration should be given to possible enemy air observation of field fortifications. Troops and ordnance should not be grouped so as to provide obvious targets for missiles, artillery, or aircraft. Ammunition supplies should be deployed over as wide an area as tactics will permit, and they should be provided with sandbag revetments. Command control between the various units should be maintained with radio and telephone systems. EDWARD J. REILLY

See also BLOCKHOUSE; CASEMATE; FORTRESS; SIEGE.

FORT KNOX, a permanent U.S. military post and the gold bullion depository of the U.S. Treasury, 30 mi (48 km) southwest of Louisville, Ky. The site served as a training camp during World War I and was made a permanent military post in 1932. At that time the name was changed from Camp Knox to Fort Knox.

The depository was built in 1936. The treasure house, 100 ft (30 m) square, is of bombproof construction. Its walls and roof have interlaced steel coils set in concrete with openings too small to admit a man's hand. Constant inspection of the vault is maintained. Mirrors and bright lights make every spot visible, and microphones are sensitive to slight sounds. During World War II many treasures of the U.S. government were safeguarded in the depository.

FORT LAUDERDALE [lô′dər-dāl], resort city of southeastern Florida, and seat of Broward County, located on the Atlantic Ocean and connected by canal with the Everglades and Lake Okeechobee. Scores of miles of inland waterways and an average elevation of 10 ft (3 m) give the city a Venetian look. It is famous as a yachting, fishing, and golf center, and is the trading center of a winter-vegetable and dairying region. Deepwater Port Everglades is located at the edge of the city. The site was settled around a fort built in 1837 during the Seminole Indian War. Its population grew rapidly after World War I.

FORT LEE, borough of northeastern New Jersey, and a suburban community, located at the western terminus of the George Washington Bridge. Photographic film processing is the principal industry. Fort Lee was the center of the motion-picture industry before World War I. Fort Lee Battle Monument marks the site of the original Fort Lee, a Revolutionary fort after which the town was named.

FORT MADISON, city of southeastern Iowa and a seat of Lee County, on the Mississippi River. It is a railroad division point and also has manufactures of fountain pens, paper, paints, safety equipment, and chemical products. The state penitentiary is here. Settled in 1808 as a frontier trading post, it was abandoned after being besieged by Indians in 1813. Resettled, 1833.

FORT MORGAN, city of northeastern Colorado and seat of Morgan County, on the South Platte River. The townsite was a way station for the overland stage express from Missouri and was on a route traversed by explorers and forty-niners. Sugar-beet processing has been a major industry here since 1906 and the city is also a supply center for an outstanding livestock-feeder region. It is headquarters for oil-and-gas concerns, and new industries, such as the manufacture of generators, have developed.

FORT MYERS, city of southwestern Florida, and seat of Lee County, on the Caloosahatchee River, 15 mi (24 km) from the Gulf of Mexico. It is the trading center of a winter-vegetable, citrus, and gladioli region. Thomas A. Edison built a botanical research center for tropical plants here.

FORT PAYNE, city of northeastern Alabama, and seat of DeKalb County. Hosiery mills and wood industries (lumber, prefabricated houses, and boats) dominate manufacturing.

FORT PIERCE, city of southeastern Florida, and seat of St. Lucie County, located on the Indian River. It is a citrus and winter-vegetable center, and a resort noted for fishing.

FORT ROSS, monument on the coast of northern California, 50 mi (80 km) north of San Francisco. On this site Russian fur traders founded a colony in 1812, containing a fortress. When the fur trade declined, it was expanded to provide for agriculture and stockraising, but with little success. This failure, poor relations with neighboring Spanish and later Mexican officials, and finally the Monroe Doctrine brought about sale of the colony to Capt. John A. Sutter (1803–80) in 1841. Its name comes from *Rusos* (Span., "Russians").

FORT ST. JOHN, town of British Columbia, Canada, near the Peace River, 40 mi (63 km) north-northwest of Dawson Creek. The name Fort St. John was given to a trading post created by the North West Company in 1805 and taken over by the Hudson's Bay Company in 1821. This post was destroyed by Indians in 1823 and rebuilt on a nearby site in 1860. The present town was established in 1925 on a hill just north of the Peace River. It is on the Alaska Highway.

FORT SCOTT, trade center of southeastern Kansas, and seat of Bourbon County. The city began as a settlement near the site of old Fort Scott (built, 1842) and was incorporated in 1860. It has diversified manufactures, chiefly the processing of agricultural products. Fort Scott Junior College and Fort Scott National Cemetery are located here.

FORT SMITH, administrative center of the southern region of the Mackenzie District of the Northwest Territories of Canada. It is situated on the Slave River close to the Alberta boundary, 60° N. lat. The Slave, emptying into Great Slave Lake, is part of the Mackenzie River drainage basin and part of the historic water route to the Arctic Ocean. The only unnavigable stretch in 1,700 mi (almost 2 750 km) is 23 mi (37 km) of rapids, at the foot of which Fort Smith was established in 1874. It was named after Donald A. Smith (later Lord Strathcona), a governor of the Hudson's Bay Company, and is still an important shipping center for this company.

Fort Smith has daily scheduled plane service from Edmonton. In the 1960's, it was linked with the Alberta highway system, and also with major communities in the Great Slave Lake area by a highway. Some 250 mi (400 km) of road radiate from Fort Smith into Wood Buffalo Park, the largest national park in Canada. Sanctuary for the only remaining herds of wood buffalo, it is also a summer nesting ground of the nearly extinct whooping cranes. The village has a government hospital and educational services for a large contributory area, as well as meteorological and radio services. JOHN E. ROBBINS

FORT SMITH, city of Arkansas, in Sebastian County, at the junction of the Arkansas and the Poteau rivers on the Oklahoma line. It is the second largest and most industrialized city in Arkansas. Natural-gas wells and coal mines in the county have attracted such industries as furniture, brick, scissors, and glass to the city. The surrounding rural area produces corn, livestock, and vegetables.

The original fort was established at a strategic position in the Arkansas Valley in 1817 as a small outpost to maintain peace between the Osage and Cherokee Indians. It was enlarged in 1841 and one of its first commanders was General Zachary Taylor. Prosperity came in 1848 when the fort and town became a supply depot and departure point for the Santa Fe route west. Judge Isaac C. Parker, the famous hanging judge, presided over the federal court here from 1875 until 1896. It enforced the law for the vast Indian Territory that lay just west of Fort Smith. Many of the West's most famous lawmen began their careers as marshals under Judge Parker. Inc. as a town, 1842; as a city, 1851. JAMES WOODRUFF

FORT THOMAS, city of northern Kentucky, on the Ohio River. It is an attractive residential community within the metropolitan group of cities opposite Cincinnati, Ohio. Balsa fishing floats, tool dies, and cut gems are produced here. A Veterans Administration Hospital Rehabilitation Center is on the site of Fort Thomas Army Post.

FORTUNATUS [fôr-chŏŏ-nā′təs], **VENANTIUS** (c.530–c.600), Latin poet. Born at Treviso, Italy, he was educated at Ravenna. After traveling to different Frankish courts, he settled in Poitiers, where he became Bishop in 599. He wrote poems flattering various Frankish nobles and is the author of the hymns "Vexilla Regis," a Good Friday hymn, and "Pange Lingua."

FORT VALLEY, city of south-central Georgia and seat of Peach County. It is the marketing and distribution center for the bulk of the state's peach production. The city was originally named Fox Valley in recognition of the numbers of foxes in the area. Fort Valley State College (established 1895) is here.

FORT WAYNE, city in northeastern Indiana and seat of Allen County. The city's main industries are in the fields of electronics, automotive equipment, food products, electric machinery, and hardware and tool manufacturing. The French built the first settlement on the present site of Fort Wayne in about 1680. It was established as Fort Miami in 1704 and was the site of many Indian battles. The British occupied it in 1760. Gen. Anthony Wayne erected Fort Wayne as a military post in 1794. It became a trading post in 1815 and was incorporated as a city in 1840. Its commercial development began in the 1850's when the railroads came. Concordia Senior College and Saint Francis College are located here, as well as a combined Indiana and Purdue Universities extension center.

Johnny Appleseed (John Chapman), the pioneer apple grower, is buried here. The city has a philharmonic orchestra, festival theater, and a ballet company. A children's zoo and a museum of natural history are also located in Fort Wayne. THEODORE R. SPEIGNER

FORT WORTH, city of north-central Texas and seat of Tarrant County, at the junction of the West and Clear forks of the Trinity River, 32 mi (51 km) west of Dallas. It is one of the nation's leading aircraft production centers, and also has important manufactures of boats, air conditioners, electronic and oilfield equipment, clothing, furniture, mobile homes, and candy. There are large stockyards and meat-processing plants and grain-storage and flour-milling facilities. The city is regional headquarters for a number of large insurance and financial firms. A major transportation center, it is served by the Dallas-Fort Worth Airport, Meacham Field, railroad trunk lines, and numerous bus and truck lines.

The city maintains more than 11,000 acres (4 400 ha) of park and recreation areas, and also has a botanic garden, museums, and a science center. The Fort Worth Symphony and the Fort Worth Opera Association are widely known. Texas Christian University (established 1873), Texas Wesleyan College (1890), Southwestern Baptist Theological Seminary (1908), and Tarrant County Junior College (1965) are situated in Fort Worth.

The site of the city was settled in 1843, and in 1849 a military post was established here to protect settlers against marauding Indians. The post was named for Gen. William Jenkins Worth, a hero of the Mexican War. After the Civil War it developed as a provisioning center on the Chisholm Trail. The town, with a population of about 500, was incorporated in 1873. The arrival of the Texas & Pacific railroad in 1877 placed the city in an advantageous position between the expanding western range lands and the eastern markets. Chronic water shortages caused by rapid expansion plagued Fort Worth, and in 1909 a large section of the city was destroyed by fire. Failure of the artesian water supply was blamed for the disaster and shortly thereafter Lake Worth, a reservoir, was constructed to impound the waters of the West Fork of the Trinity River. The discovery of oil in the area to the west of the city in 1917 further advanced the economic growth. CHARLES C. BAJZA

The Fort Worth Livestock Exchange serves as a reminder that the cattle industry built the city in the 19th century. The city's economic base today has been broadened, however, by manufacturing, finance, wholesale and retail sales and distribution, convention and visitor activities, agribusiness, and education.

Fort Worth Chamber of Commerce

FORTY FORT, residential borough of north-central Pennsylvania, near Wilkes-Barre. The town was named for 40 Connecticut settlers who built a fort on the bank of the Susquehanna River in 1772. During the American Revolution, it became the scene of the Wyoming Valley Massacre of 400 colonists (1778). The Forty Fort meetinghouse, built in 1807, was renovated in 1922.

FORTY-NINERS, in American history, the treasure hunters who poured into California during the gold rush of 1849. News of the gold strike at Sutter's Mill (near what is now Sacramento) in Jan., 1848, spread eastward that summer and gold fever began to infect men from every station in life. They booked passage for the dreary voyage around Cape Horn, dared the fever swamps of the Isthmus of Panamá, or attempted the grueling trip overland by covered wagon. All endured hardships and many fell victim to Indians, disease, or starvation on journeys lasting perhaps three months. The golden magnet drew men from all over the world, almost 50,000 in 1849, and San Francisco's streets swarmed with strange costumes and echoed to foreign tongues. San Francisco Bay became clogged with ships abandoned by their crews. A restless, brawling crowd, the forty-niners panned gold by day and gambled by night—a third of San Francisco's buildings were gambling saloons. Prices were high and few managed to keep the gold they found. Many returned home, some settled in California, and others pursued fortune in later strikes in Australia, Nevada, and the Klondike.

Consult Caughey, John W., *The California Gold Rush* (1976); Perkins, William, *Three Years in California, 1849–52* (1964); White, Stewart E., *The Story of California* (reprinted, 1975). ELISABETH MARGO

FORT YUKON, village of extreme northern Alaska, located 125 mi (200 km) by air northeast of Fairbanks on the Yukon River, and 1 mi (1.6 km) above the Arctic Circle. Fort Yukon was settled in 1847 by the Hudson's Bay Company as a fur-trading post and became the permanent residence for members of the Athabascan tribe. A mission and hospital, a modern school, and public health experiments in arctic village sanitation spurred the village progress. Summer temperatures reach as high as 100° F (38° C); the winter minimum is − 70° F (− 57°C).

FORUM [fo′rəm], the center of business and public life in ancient Roman cities. The term is derived from the Lat. *foras, foris,* words denoting any open space in front of a tomb, temple, or public building. In Rome the term came to be applied specifically to the flat, roughly rectangular area between the Palatine and Capitoline hills. This Forum Romanum served originally as both a marketplace and an area for the conduct of public business. Later it was devoted more to civic business and to religious observances. In early Republican times, gladiatorial contests were held in the Forum, with galleries for spectators atop the surrounding buildings. The various structures comprising the Forum Romanum were erected at different periods over the course of about 1,000 years. Naturally, several were replaced, repaired, or rebuilt. Buildings attributed to the Regal period (753–509 B.C.) include the Regia, originally the royal palace, later used

by the Pontifex Maximus, head of the Roman state religion; the sanctuary of Vesta, goddess who guarded the public hearth, and the adjacent House of the Vestals; the Curia, or Senate house; the fountain of the goddess Juturna; a number of small shops and booths called *tabernae;* and a public altar, associated by some with the tomb of Romulus. The Forum, like the Greek *agora,* was a place where people met to discuss the affairs of the commonwealth.

Republic. During the Republic (509–27 B.C.), the Forum was enhanced by the construction of magnificent temples, public buildings, and basilicas. The venerable temple of Saturn, built c.497 B.C., served for some time as a public treasury. The temple of Castor and Pollux, built c.484 B.C., of which only three columns remain standing, was a favorite meeting place for Romans and also housed the standard weights and measures. Part of the open space of the Forum was called the *Comitium,* the place where the assembly (*comitia*) met to consider legislation or other proposals. Speakers addressed the people from a raised platform, called the Rostra. As Rome became more commercially oriented after 200 B.C., the older stalls and shops were replaced by new ones, built under colonnades and next to basilicas, such as the Basilica Porcia (184 B.C.), the Basilica Aemilia (179 B.C.), the Sempronia (170 B.C.), Opimia (121 B.C.) and the Julia, erected by Julius Caesar in 46 B.C. Passing through the Forum was the Via Sacra, the Sacred Way, along which victorious generals marched in their triumphs up to the Capitoline hill. The first triumphal arch over this road was built by Fabius Maximus in 121 B.C. In 29 B.C. a temple to Divus Julius (the deified Julius Caesar) was constructed.

Imperial Rome. More additions were made in the imperial period. Augustus in 19 B.C. and Tiberius in 16 A.D. built arches, which marked off the eastern and western entrances to the Forum. The temple of Vespasian dates to 79–81, and the Arch of Titus (81 A.D.) still bears witness to that emperor's capture of Jerusalem. Later imperial monuments were a temple dedicated jointly to Venus and Roma (135 A.D.); the arch of Septimius Severus (203), which is still preserved; the temple of Romulus (307); and a basilica, begun by Maxentius, but completed by Constantine (306) and still used for outdoor concerts. The last monument was that of the Byzantine Emperor Phocis (608 A.D.).

As early as 46 B.C. the increase in the size of the city's population made the need for another forum apparent. In that year Julius Caesar built a new forum. Its chief building was a temple to Venus Genetrix, the goddess from whom Caesar claimed descent. The continuing expansion of Rome's population and the complexity of public affairs led to the construction of still other fora during the imperial period. Some were little more than monuments to the reign of an emperor. These fora continued to be built on a rectangular plan. In the imperial period, there were two classes of fora. One was the *fora veniala,* market and commercial centers. Examples are the *forum boaricum* (cattle) and the *forum olitorium* (vegetables). The *fora civilia* were devoted to civic and religious affairs. As a rule the imperial fora were not thoroughfares, but the Forum of Nerva (97 A.D.) had a vehicular street running through it. The extremely large Forum of Trajan

(1) The Colosseum, inaugurated by the Emperor Titus in 80 A.D.
(2) The temple of Antoninus and Faustina, built in 141 A.D.
(3) Honorary columns set up at the beginning of the 4th century A.D.
(FOTOTECA UNIONE)

(111–14) consisted of a triumphal arch, the Basilica Ulpia, libraries, and a tall column, still standing, whose carved surface depicts important events in Trajan's conquest of Dacia (modern Rumania). A temple in honor of Trajan was added to his forum by his successor, Hadrian.

Decline. From the beginning of the 4th century A.D., Rome began to lose her position as the hub of the Empire. With the selection of a succession of new capitals, first at Milan and then at Constantinople and Ravenna (4th century), large-scale building operations ceased. The sack of the city by Vandals and Goths in the 5th century accelerated the decay of the fora. Later they became quarries for builders of fortresses and for Renaissance architects. By the 18th century the Forum Romanum was 40 ft (12 m) below ground level. In 1870 Rodolfo Lanciani and Giacomo Boni began systematic excavations of the fora.

Consult Grant, Michael, *Roman Forum* (1970); Lanciani, Rodolfo, *Ruins and Excavations of Ancient Rome* (1897, reprinted 1968). GERALD E. KADISH

FORZA DEL DESTINO [fôr'tsä dĕl dĕs-tē'nō], **LA** (The Force of Destiny), opera in four acts by Giuseppe Verdi; libretto by Francesco Maria Piave, after a Spanish play *Don Alvaro o la fuorza de sino* by the Duke of Rivas; première, St. Petersburg, Nov. 10, 1862; first performance of revised version, La Scala, Milan, Feb. 20, 1869.

Leonora's father is accidentally shot to death when she and her lover Don Alvaro attempt to elope. Seeking vengeance, her brother Don Carlo finally duels with Alvaro in a monastery and is mortally wounded. Before he dies he stabs Leonora, who has sought refuge there.

The opera is the last one of Verdi's second creative period. The revision consists mainly in the addition of the very effective overture and the alteration of the conclusion of the opera with a superb terzetto (trio), whose gentle ending foreshadows the last scene of *Aida*. There are colorful choral numbers, such as those accompanying the procession, the tarantella in the army camp, the distribution of the soup in the monastery, and above all the magnificent scene when Leonora is received as a "brother" in the monastery. JOSEPH BRAUNSTEIN

FOSDICK, HARRY EMERSON (1878–1969), famous American preacher. Born in Buffalo and educated at Colgate, Union Theological Seminary, and Columbia, he rose to national prominence as a radio preacher, author of many influential books, seminary professor, and leading spokesman for Protestant liberalism. His efforts at stating religious faith so as to appeal to scientifically minded moderns aroused both admiration and opposition. He became pastor of the Riverside Church in New York, from which he retired in 1946.

FOSS, LUKAS, original surname Fuchs (1922–), composer and pianist, born in Berlin. He studied in the United States and held a Guggenheim Fellowship in 1945. His style is essentially lyrical, with romantic overtones, and shows a predilection for complex counterpoint. His works include a cantata *The Prairie* (1944), piano concertos, the *Symphony of Chorales* (1958), *Phorion* (1967), *Concert* (1967), and *Paradigm* (1970). From 1963 to 1970 he was musical director and conductor of the Buffalo Philharmonic Orchestra. He then became principal conductor and musical adviser for the Brooklyn Philharmonic Orchestra and the Jerusalem Symphony Orchestra.

FOSSA, long-tailed, short-legged carnivore, *Cryptoprocta ferox*, a catlike member of the civet family, found only in Madagascar. The fossa, about the size of a small puma, has short glossy-brown fur, small rounded ears, retractile claws, and well-developed cutting teeth. It is at home both on the ground and in trees, and is an active predator of birds and small mammals. The fossa is sometimes confused with the fanaloka, another member of the civet family found only in Madagascar. It is gray-brown, with four rows of black spots on each side.

FOSTER, JOHN WATSON (1836–1917), American diplomat, born in Pike County, Ind. He graduated (1855) from Indiana University and attended Harvard Law School. He served in the Union army during the Civil War and then edited (1865–69) the Evansville, Ind., *Daily Journal*. After becoming a leader in Republican state politics, he served as U.S. minister to Mexico (1873–80), Russia (1880–81), and Spain (1883–85). President Benjamin Harrison appointed him Secretary of State (1892–93). Foster represented the United States in the Bering Sea controversy over fur seals and at numerous arbitration conferences. Among other works, he wrote *A Century of American Diplomacy, 1776–1876* (1900).

FOSTER, STEPHEN COLLINS (1826–64), American composer, born in Lawrenceville, Pa. As a child he played the flute and was generally self-taught in the rudiments of music. He published his first song in his teens, and by 1850 already had a wide reputation as a writer of both the words and music of folklike American songs, with melodies which were simple and readily singable. Foster wrote almost 200 songs, many of which have become national favorites: *Oh, Susanna!* (1848), *Swanee River* (1851), *My Old Kentucky Home* (1853), *Jeanie With the Light Brown Hair* (1854), *Old Black Joe* (1860), and *Beautiful Dreamer* (1864), his last song.

Consult Howard, J. T., *Stephen Foster, America's Troubadour* (new ed., 1953).

FOSTER, WILLIAM ZEBULON (1881–1961), American Communist leader. He was born in Taunton, Mass., and reared in a Philadelphia slum. Self-educated, a seaman, and an itinerant worker, he was strongly influenced by Marxism and engaged in radical activities. He joined the Socialist party and later the Industrial Workers of the World. An ardent champion of industrial unionism, he led the national steel strike in 1919. He became a leader of the newly founded Communist party after 1919 and was the party's presidential candidate in 1924, 1928, and 1932. His maximum support, 102,991 votes, came in the depression year of 1932. Succeeded in 1930 by Earl Browder as the party's general secretary, Foster resumed his position in 1945 after Browder's expulsion on charges of revisionism. He was indicted in 1948 with 11 other Communist leaders on charges of conspiring to teach and advocate the overthrow of the government by force. But ill health prevented his standing trial, and he was obliged to withdraw from the party leadership for the same reason. He spent his last years in the Soviet Union.

JOHN DUNBAR, Editor and Writer

FOSTORIA, city of northwestern Ohio, 33 mi. south of Toledo. Located in an agricultural area, it is nonetheless an industrial city noted for its glassware. It was founded in 1854 by the merger of the villages of Risdon and Rome. Pop., 16,037.

FOUCAULT [foo-kō'], **JEAN BERNARD LÉON** (1819–68), French experimental physicist, credited with the invention of the gyroscope. Foucault was born and educated in Paris. He demonstrated the rotation of the earth on its axis in his pendulum experiment. Foucault measured the velocity of light in air by means of a rotating mirror, and was the first to show that light travels more slowly through water. One of the giants of French science, he also invented the Foucault prism and discovered the induced electric current called the eddy or Foucault current.

FOUCAULT PENDULUM. *See* PENDULUM.

FOUCHÉ [foo-shā'], **JOSEPH** (1759–1820), French revolutionist, political schemer, and police expert. He was a member of the Oratorian teaching order before 1789. Fouché championed the popular cause early in the Revolution, joining the Jacobin Club and winning election to the National Convention, where he voted for the King's execution. Despatched (1793) to subdue the antirepublican rebellions in the Vendée and at Lyons, he acted alternately with ferocity and restraint. Fouché, with Pierre Gaspard Chaumette, promoted the anti-Christian "Festival of Reason" (Nov. 10, 1793), mocking the religious Maximilien Robespierre, who later expelled him from the Jacobin Club (July 14, 1794). In retaliation, Fouché aided Robespierre's enemies in their coup of 9 Thermidor (July 27, 1794), which signaled the end of the Terror; he escaped arrest and was later amnestied. Appointed Minister of Police on July 20, 1799, he developed a remarkably efficient spy system and reorganized the criminal police along enduring lines. Fouché was a consummate opportunist—by skillful maneuvering he simultaneously served Napoleon I as Minister of Police and (after 1804) of the Interior and stayed in good standing with the monarchists. In 1809 Napoleon gave him the duchy of Otranto but later (1810) dismissed him. Ever agile, Fouché entered the service of Louis XVIII during the first Restoration, quickly rejoined Napoleon as Minister of Police during the Hundred Days, and within 24 hours after the Emperor's final abdication became President of the provisional government. During the second Restoration, he held the ambassadorship at Dresden briefly before retiring. He died in Trieste, an immensely wealthy man.

RALPH H. BOWEN, Northern Illinois University

FOUNDATION, in engineering, structural base that transfers a structure's weight safely to the underlying soil or rock. In a broader sense the foundation also includes the soil or rock beneath the structure. The type of foundation depends on the weight and character of the supported structure and on the characteristics of the underlying deposits of soil or rock. Foundations not designed or constructed properly can result in the structure's settling, resulting in serious and costly damage.

The simplest foundation is the spread foundation, or footing. It is built in areas where soil or rock can sustain the structure's weight. Basically, the footing foundation involves widening the base of the wall or column so that the pressure (load per unit area) does not exceed the allowable bearing pressure of the soil. In most cases a reinforced concrete slab is constructed beneath walls and columns. If the loads are very heavy, it is sometimes necessary to use a special type of spread foundation called a grillage. A grillage consists of layers of steel beams or rails imbedded in concrete. A more extreme form of spread foundations is a mat, or raft, foundation. It is a large heavily reinforced concrete slab called a mat, or raft, on which the entire structure rests.

If the soil capable of sustaining the loads is deep beneath the structure, it is sometimes possible to use a pier foundation of concrete columns extending down to the suitable soil or rock. If the depth is very great, piles which are long, slender structural members of wood, steel, or concrete, are used. They are driven deeply enough into the ground so that the structural load is safely transmitted to the underlying soil.

ARMAND J. SILVA, Worcester Polytechnic Institute
See also EXCAVATOR AND EXCAVATION.

FOUNDATIONS. The foundation in its broadest sense is an instrument for contributing private wealth to public purpose. Such foundations date from antiquity. They include provisions made by individuals or groups in ancient civilizations for recurring sacrificial feasts which benefited priests, wayfarers, and the poor; perpetuities set up by the Pharaohs of Egypt for religious purposes; Greek and Roman endowments; and the ecclesiastical and charitable trusts which sprang up by the hundreds in Tudor and Stuart England. Nearly 100,000 are now registered in England under the new Charities Act.

A few similar trusts were established in the United States in the 18th and 19th centuries. Benjamin Franklin's funds in Boston and Philadelphia, which still survive, were among the earliest. At the beginning of the 20th century the foundation idea began to take deep root in American soil but had a significant difference. Large endowments were set up, often in perpetuity as in England, but frequently with wide latitude in their uses. "To promote the well-being of mankind throughout the world," the purpose clause of the Rockefeller Foundation, was not unusual. Some funds limited to special purposes were set up: the James Dean Fund in Boston was established solely to supply Sunday newspapers to the men on the *Boston Light Vessel* and the Lollipop Foundation of America to provide these delicacies to children in hospitals, but today usually the larger foundations exercise great freedom. Their trustees spend less time in conserving money than in exploring new and enterprising ways of spending it. The usual purpose has become research, prevention, and discovery. The very word "foundation" has acquired connotations of freedom of action.

Andrew Carnegie was a chief advocate of such ideas, first in his *Gospel of Wealth* (published as *Wealth* in 1889) and in the foundations he himself established. Other early famous foundations include the Rockefeller Foundation, the General Education Board (a Rockefeller benefaction now dissolved, having spent all its funds), the Russell Sage Foundation, and the Milbank Memorial Fund. The Ford Foundation and several other present giants were established, strangely enough, in the economic depression decade of the 1930's.

By the middle 1940's a new wave of foundations began to sweep over the country, induced in part by high taxes resulting from World War II. Many of these were family-sponsored foundations, set up by living individuals, with both contributions and direction held closely within the family group. Another large class was the company-sponsored foundation, set up by a business corporation to receive substantial contributions in years of good profits (or especially high taxes) and to disburse these funds, through good years and bad. Both family- and company-sponsored foundations differed in one significant respect from the older, traditional type: they usually had no large initial corpus, but carried on their often substantial programs with moneys received currently.

Further to complicate the picture, foundations constantly arose that did not fit any of these categories; for example, community foundations that were amalgamations of many small funds, and two wholly tax-supported foundations, the National Science Foundation and the National Foundation on the Arts and Humanities. Some organizations devoted to fund-raising, propaganda, or subsidized research have assumed the name "foundation."

Therefore in a narrower sense, a foundation may be defined as a nongovernmental, nonprofit organization managed by its own trustees or directors, not soliciting funds from the general public, and established to maintain or aid social, educational, charitable, religious, or other activities serving the common welfare.

Foundations in the United States. Under this definition it is estimated that at the close of 1966 there were about 18,000 foundations in the United States. Their assets vary substantially with stock market levels, since many of the large foundations have heavy common stock investments. Total assets are estimated at about $20,300,000,000. Individual foundations vary in size from the gigantic Ford Foundation with assets of approximately $3,050,000,000 to one New York foundation that soberly reported to the government total assets of 26 cents.

A 1966 tabulation disclosed 237 foundations with assets of $10,000,000 or more. This relatively small group possessed about three-quarters of the total assets of the some 18,000 foundations in the United States. It is clear that it takes thousands of small foundations to equal the financial strength, and probably the social impact, of a single large one.

Flow of Funds. Programs supported by foundation grants are almost infinite in variety, but there is concentration in certain fields. Traditionally, grants have gone chiefly to health and education, with social welfare a close third. That design for giving has changed radically and is still changing. The accompanying chart shows disbursements in millions of dollars to principal fields. Total grants reported for the 17,303 foundations it represents were $1,244,000,000.

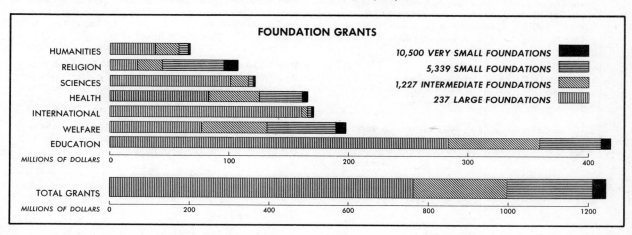

FOUNDATION GRANTS

HUMANITIES
RELIGION
SCIENCES
HEALTH
INTERNATIONAL
WELFARE
EDUCATION

10,500 VERY SMALL FOUNDATIONS
5,339 SMALL FOUNDATIONS
1,227 INTERMEDIATE FOUNDATIONS
237 LARGE FOUNDATIONS

MILLIONS OF DOLLARS 0   100   200   300   400

TOTAL GRANTS

MILLIONS OF DOLLARS 0   200   400   600   800   1000   1200

Assets at Market Value unless Otherwise Indicated

Avalon Foundation, New York, N.Y. (1940). Emphasis on civic and community programs, cultural projects, education, health, medicine, youth programs.

Assets $139,635,306

Bishop (Bernice P.) Estate, Honolulu, Hawaii (1884). Limited to educational programs in Hawaii.

Assets (ledger value) $131,914,769

Carnegie Corporation of New York, New York, N.Y. (1911). Training and research programs in higher education and international affairs, chiefly in colleges and universities.

Assets $289,136,000

Carnegie Institution of Washington, Washington, D.C. (1902). Primarily an operating organization, advancing research in astronomy, geophysics, physics, plant biology, embryology, and genetics.

Assets $112,801,703

Cleveland Foundation, Cleveland, Ohio (1914). The pioneer community trust, disbursing income of many funds to charitable and educational institutions in Ohio.

Assets $102,000,000

Commonwealth Fund, New York, N.Y. (1918). Primarily the improvement of medical education; fellowships to young potential leaders from abroad for travel and study in the United States.

Assets $146,928,366

Danforth Foundation, St. Louis, Mo. (1927). Grants "to strengthen the essential quality of education," with special concern for equal opportunities, and humane and religious values.

Assets $145,805,004

Duke Endowment, New York, N.Y. (1924). Grants chiefly to named educational and charitable institutions in North and South Carolina.

Assets $691,903,708

Fleischmann (Max C.) Foundation of Nevada, Reno, Nev. (1952). General giving emphasizing education, with prior consideration to institutions and areas favored by Major Fleischmann in his lifetime.

Assets $95,067,180

Ford Foundation, New York, N.Y. (1936). The vast programs of this foundation fall under four divisions: International Affairs, including training, research, and overseas development; Humanities and the Arts, the cultural life of the United States and other advanced countries; Education and Research, concerned with schools, colleges, individual scholars, especially in the social sciences; and National Affairs, including minorities, responsibilities of government and law, problems of urban and metropolitan development, and national resources.

Assets $3,050,421,739

Hartford (The John A.) Foundation, New York, N.Y. (1929). Emphasis on medical research, particularly the clinical aspects, in voluntary nonprofit hospitals.

Assets $341,991,844

Houston Endowment, Inc., Houston, Tex. (1937). Medical institutions, higher education including scholarships, welfare, hospitals, and religious activities.

Assets $168,000,000

Kellogg (W. K.) Foundation, Battle Creek, Mich. (1930). Grants made through divisions concerned with agriculture, dentistry, public affairs and education, hospitals, medicine and public health, nursing, and Latin America.

Assets $491,523,754

Kresge Foundation, Detroit, Mich. (1924). Grants emphasizing higher education, research, hospitals, youth agencies, the aged, and religion.

Assets $172,829,719

Lilly Endowment, Inc., Indianapolis, Ind. (1937). Major interests in education, religion, and community services, with concentration on philanthropic needs in Indiana.

Assets $319,502,940

Longwood Foundation, Wilmington, Del. (1937). Primarily maintenance of the Longwood Gardens, with minor amounts for education and local philanthropy.

Assets $251,000,000

Mellon (Richard King) Foundation, Pittsburgh, Pa. (1947). Grants primarily for education, health, and civic and cultural development, with preference for the Pittsburgh area.

Assets $121,969,748

Moody Foundation, Galveston, Tex. (1942). Support for health, science, education, and religion, limited to the state of Texas.

Assets $243,675,747

Mott (Charles Stewart) Foundation, Flint, Mich. (1926). Adult education, recreation, children's health services, particularly in Flint; also grants for other educational, health, and welfare programs.

Assets $424,118,660

Old Dominion Foundation, New York, N.Y. (1941). Support for liberal education, the arts, mental health, and conservation.

Assets $105,062,082

Pew Memorial Trust, Philadelphia, Pa. (1948). General giving, including education, social welfare, and health.

Assets $272,726,058

Rockefeller Brothers Fund, New York, N.Y. (1940). Grants, and on occasion its own programs, concerning international affairs, economic and social development, urban planning, health, welfare, religion, equal rights, conservation, population, and the visual and performing arts.

Assets $210,393,600

Rockefeller Foundation, New York, N.Y. (1913). Activities and grants throughout the world supporting biological and medical sciences, the social sciences, the humanities, and research and experimentation in agriculture.

Assets $854,201,490

Sloan (Alfred P.) Foundation, New York, N.Y. (1934). Supports research and education in economics, business management, physical science, certain aspects of medicine, and gives general aid to colleges and universities.

Assets $309,322,985

Waterman (Phoebe) Foundation, Philadelphia, Pa. (1945). Grants for hospitals, educational institutions, research, youth and welfare services, chiefly in Philadelphia.

Assets $133,943,225

In the reported year (usually 1964 or 1965) these foundations gave $418,000,000 to education, about one-third of their total grants. In all recent years education has been the favored foundation field, "placing within reach," to use Andrew Carnegie's colorful phrase, "the ladders upon which the aspiring can rise." Welfare was in second place, receiving $196,000,000. International activities, at $170,000,000, is a newcomer in heavy grant recipients, recording a sharp increase in concern with problems and opportunities beyond the boundaries of the United States. Health follows closely, with $167,000,000. Its drop from an earlier higher position may be largely due to vastly increased governmental expenditures in this area through medicare, medical research, and other large programs.

The sciences at $120,000,000 claim about one-tenth of foundation grant expenditures. Here the most radical recent changes have been among the branches of science. The life sciences, chiefly medical research, had long led. Then after Sputnik was launched by the Soviet Union in 1957, the physical sciences climbed to top position. In the mid-1960's they have sharply declined, doubtless due to vast governmental programs for space research. But it should be remembered that one of the earliest investigations of space, that of Robert H. Goddard, who in 1920 was proposing to explode gunpowder on the moon's surface, was financed by foundations (Smithsonian Institution and The Daniel and Florence Guggenheim Foundation), when funds were not elsewhere available for so venturesome a project.

Religion and the humanities are lowest in order of foundation preference, accounting for only $107,000,000 and $67,000,000 respectively. Religion is by no means a stepchild of philanthropy in general, receiving about half of all private benefactions; but foundations apparently assume that religious gifts are best made personally. The interest of foundations in the humanities appears to be steadily increasing.

Foundations continue to grow in number in the United States. About 1,500 new foundations are created each year. Most of these are small, and many of them do not survive; but it is also possible that among today's smaller foundations may be some that will grow to great size and significance.

Canadian Foundations. On a smaller scale a similar development of foundations has been taking place in Canada. Only a partial registry exists, but there are at least several hundred. The largest, the Canada Council, is not a private foundation. It was set up by the government with an initial capital of $100,000,000, half of which went as capital gifts to universities; the remainder is held as capital, with income (together with annual governmental appropriations) devoted to the humanities and the social sciences.

Of the private foundations the largest appear to be J. P. Bickell Foundation, limited to Ontario, with assets of $27,000,000; The Atkinson Charitable Foundation, also limited to Ontario, with assets of $14,312,890; and the Laidlaw Foundation, with assets of $8,648,100. Two substantial community trusts exist, Vancouver Foundation with assets of $9,319,020, and The Winnipeg Foundation, with assets of $6,871,106.

Consult Andrews, F. E., *Philanthropic Foundations* (1956) and (ed.) *Foundations: 20 Viewpoints* (1965); Fremont-Smith, M. R., *Foundations and Government* (1965); *Canadian Universities' Guide to Foundations*, ed. by Watson, W. R., and Winter, R. M. (1966); Nelson, R. L., *The Investment Policies of Foundations* (1967); Council on Foundations, *Community Foundations in the United States and Canada, 1965 Status* (1967); *The Foundation Directory* (3d ed.), ed. by Lewis, M. O. (1967).

F. EMERSON ANDREWS, President,
The Foundation Library Center

FOUNDING. *See* CASTING.

FOUNDRY PRACTICE, branch of metallurgy concerned with melting metals and solidifying them in a mold to obtain an object of desired shape and dimension. Foundries, with their multi-billion-dollar plant facilities, produce products for transportation, communication, construction, agriculture, power generation, and countless other fields.

The basic steps in foundry practice begin with pattern-making, constructing a wood or metal replica of the desired item. The core is then made of baked sand, which together with binders, produces voids in hollow castings. A mold, consisting of the sand in its container, pattern removed, and cores in place, then receives the molten metal, which is melted in a furnace then transferred to the mold by a ladle. After solidification is complete and the castings are removed from the mold, they are cleaned —to remove imperfections and imbedded sand—by tumbling, sand or shot blasting, or grinding.

Foundries can be classified according to the metals cast. Cast iron foundries produce gray, chilled, white, and malleable iron. Steel foundries work with the carbon steels and alloy steels. Nonferrous foundries produce items from aluminum and copper, and from alloys of magnesium, nickel, zinc, lead, tin, titanium, and cobalt.

The first copper casting was produced in Mesopotamia, about 4000 B.C. From that time on, metals have been cast into various shapes. Probably the first true foundry center originated in the days of the Shang Dynasty (1766–1122 B.C.). Later, Egypt, Greece, and Rome began casting chiefly ornamental items. England became noted, along with Belgium and later other European countries, for bell foundries. As the foundry practice became more general, the production of utilitarian objects promoted the growth of foundries into a major basic-forming industry. Massachusetts, in 1642, claimed the distinction of producing the first American casting, the famous Saugus pot. Now, because of their widespread use, castings are produced almost everywhere that manufacturing occurs.

PAUL B. EATON, Purdue University

See also CASTING.

FOUNDRY TYPE. *See* TYPE AND TYPESETTING.

FOUNTAIN, natural or artificial spring, jet, or flow of water that falls into a basin. A fountain may be designed for either a practical or decorative purpose or for a combination of both. The artistic development of fountains began

Fountain of Neptune in the gardens of Versailles, France. The palace is in the background.

French Embassy Press and Information Division

in ancient Greek cities, where water was brought through underground conduits to stone tanks. The people filled their jars with water flowing from bronze spouts of lionhead form. The basin itself was adorned with columns. The chief municipal springhouse, as in the Pirene Spring at Corinth, sometimes became an elaborate sunken court, with marble basins in front of underground reservoirs whose façades were decorated with columns and niches. The great aqueduct system of ancient Rome distributed water to many street fountains and also to the courtyards and gardens of private houses and villas. Charming examples, restored and again in use, appear in the excavated city of Pompeii and in Emperor Hadrian's Villa (125–35 A.D.), at Tivoli.

Although public fountains during the Middle Ages were primarily utilitarian, a few fine examples remain, especially in Italy. These are overshadowed, however, by hundreds of splendid Renaissance fountains, found not only in the great cities but even in small village plazas and modest villas. Leading sculptors and landscape architects collaborated in bringing fountain art to its climax in the great baroque age (17th–18th centuries). Magnificent Italian villas, like the Villa d'Este at Tivoli, with their terraced gardens and natural water sources, called forth amazing feats of decoration. In their fountains, in which the patterns of the water were used with sculpture, the theatrical trend of the baroque found full expression. The great master in this exuberant vein was Giovanni Lorenzo Bernini, who designed not only the superbly simple fountains in front of St. Peter's, but also others in Rome, such as the grotesque Fountain of the Four Rivers in the Piazza Navona and the famous Trevi Fountain. The latter is perhaps the most dramatic of all baroque examples.

In France the gardens of Versailles, designed by André Le Nôtre for Louis XIV, feature a vast system of fountains in landscaped terraces that are studded with sculptured nymphs and classic river gods. The water supply is raised 500 ft. from the Seine by a complex pumping system and distributed in spouting jets about the various sculptural groups.

In contrast with these, the fountains in Muslim lands are reduced to a trickle, the water lying in quiet reflecting pools and long, narrow channels, as in the gardens of the Taj Mahal at Agra, India. The Fountain of the Lions, in the Alhambra at Granada, Spain, is closer to the European type in its use of basins and sculpture.

Recent fountain development has appeared most strikingly at various world's fairs, where dramatically changing jets have been orchestrated with variously colored floodlights after nightfall.

EMERSON H. SWIFT, Columbia University

FOUNTAIN CITY, suburb about 5 mi. north of Knoxville, eastern Tennessee. Pop., 10,365.

FOUNTAIN HILL, borough of east-central Pennsylvania, on the Lehigh River between Allentown and Bethlehem. Fountain Hill is mainly residential, but there is some industry, notably the manufacture of clothing. Inc., 1893; pop., 5,384.

FOUNTAIN OF YOUTH, in American folklore, a mythical rejuvenating spring. The Central American Indians believed it lay in a north country called Bimini. It was one of the legends, like those concerning Cibola and El Dorado, that inspired daring explorations. Ponce de Léon, who discovered Florida in 1513, reputedly was seeking the fountain.

FOUQUÉ [fōō-kā'], FRIEDRICH HEINRICH KARL, BARON DE LA MOTTE- (1777–1843), German romantic writer. Born in Brandenburg of Huguenot ancestry, he received a military education. In his poetic works, he tried to blend Nordic legends with motifs from medieval French courtly literature. He is best known for his fairy tale *Undine*, 1811 (trans. by Edmund Gosse, 1932), the story of the love between a water nymph and a knight.

FOUQUET or FOUCQUET [fōō-kě'], JEAN (c.1416–c.1480), French painter. Influenced by both the Italian painting of Tuscany and the realism of the Van Eycks, he created a style that was to be the basis of 15th-century French art.

In Italy for a time, he executed a portrait of Pope Eugene IV. In France he worked for the court of Charles VII and was appointed court painter to Louis XI. Important surviving works include the Melun Diptych, one wing of which represents Agnès Sorel as the Madonna (now Antwerp) and the other Fouquet's contemporary Étienne Chevalier with St. Stephen (Staatlichen Museen, Berlin); a portrait of Charles VII (Louvre, Paris); a group of 40 miniatures from a book of hours (Chantilly, France); and miniatures illustrating a translation of *Antiquities of the Jews* by Josephus (Bibliothèque Nationale, Paris).

FOUQUET, NICOLAS (1615–80), French government official. He was a protégé of Jules Cardinal Mazarin, the Prime Minister, who appointed him to several important offices. He helped Mazarin suppress the Fronde and received as reward the lucrative post of superintendent of finances (1653). He accumulated a huge fortune dishonestly, and used his wealth to patronize artists and writers, and on living lavishly. His arrogance coupled with Jean Baptiste Colbert's ambition ruined him. After Colbert had reported shortages in Fouquet's accounts to Louis XIV, Fouquet was arrested by royal order (1661) and charged with embezzlement and, on a pretext, with threats to the security of the state. Tried by a special court (partly on forged evidence), he received (1664) a sentence of life imprisonment and confiscation of his property. He died a prisoner.

FOUR-COLOR PROBLEM. *See* TOPOLOGY.

FOURCROY [fōōr-krwä'], **ANTOINE FRANÇOIS, COMTE DE** (1755–1809), French chemist who helped develop modern chemical nomenclature. He studied medicine, but his great interest was chemistry, which he later taught, being one of the first to accept Lavoisier's theory. During the French Revolution he was active politically and participated in the founding of the modern French system of education.

FOUR-EYES. *See* ANABLEPS.

FOUR FREEDOMS, phrase used by President Franklin D. Roosevelt to describe Allied aims in World War II. In an address (Jan. 6, 1941) to Congress proposing the lend-lease program, the President declared four freedoms essential to the postwar world: freedom of speech and expression; freedom of religion; freedom from want, provided by international economic understandings; and freedom from fear, guaranteed by arms limitation. The substance of these aims was included in the Atlantic Charter (Aug., 1941).

4-H CLUBS, organization of U.S. youth clubs, whose aim is to give training in practical skills through real-life experiences to young people between the ages of 9 and 19. Its name may be gleaned from the organization's pledge: "I pledge my HEAD to clearer thinking, my HEART to greater loyalty, my HANDS to larger services, and my HEALTH to better living for my club, my community, and my country." Members may choose from

SOME 4-H CLUB ACTIVITIES

A youngster studies a potato beetle.

One girl teaches pie baking to another.

Examining ripe wheat in Arkansas.

A boy proudly shows his prize Angus.

An Arkansas boy checks tomato plants.

Elected officers conduct a club meeting in Illinois.

All photos—National 4-H Service Committee

some 100 different programs in agriculture, home economics, and community service. Character and good citizenship are long-range goals.

Originally a rural organization, 4-H clubs later spread to urban areas as well. The town member may raise small animals, grow plants in pots or backyard plots, or train in science, business, or leadership. Television stations in many states offer 4-H "action series" that teach by video tape presentations. Since the early 1900's, about 25,000,000 young people have participated in 4-H projects, with clubs scattered throughout the 50 states and Puerto Rico. Similar organizations are found around the world in some 70 countries on every continent.

FRANCES C. DICKSON, Federal Extension Service, USDA

FOUR HORSEMEN OF THE APOCALYPSE, THE, four colorful figures in the Book of Revelation (6:1–8), who symbolize the ravages of war: rider with bow on white horse —conquering invader (perhaps Parthians); rider with sword on red horse—civil war; rider with balance on black horse—famine; rider named Death on a dun horse—death. In 1916 Vicente Blasco Ibáñez published his famous war novel *Los cuatro jinetes del Apocalipsis* (*The Four Horsemen of the Apocalypse*, 1918), and in 1921 this was used as the basis of a very popular film, which starred Rudolph Valentino.

FOUR HUNDRED, term for the socially elite of New York City. The name originated when Mrs. William Astor, the recognized social queen of her era, found it necessary to shorten her guest list for a projected ball in 1892. She was advised by Ward McAllister, who reputedly said later at the Union League Club that there were "only about four hundred people in New York society." In the ensuing controversy, the phrase was widely publicized.

FOURIER [foo-ryā'], **FRANÇOIS MARIE CHARLES** (1772–1837), French utopian socialist. Reacting against his commercial background, Fourier developed a plan for a new society. The basic unit of the utopian community was the phalanx, a group of 1,620 people living in a common building or phalanstery. Work was to be divided among the inhabitants according to their abilities, the goal being a systematic agricultural society. Fourier made a number of converts to his scheme in France and the United States, where several unsuccessful attempts were made to establish Fourierist communities.

FOURIER, JEAN BAPTISTE JOSEPH (1768–1830), French mathematician and physicist who is especially noted for his contributions to the theory of heat. Fourier series, of the form, $\sum_{0}^{\infty} (a_n \cos n \alpha x + b_n \sin n \alpha x), n = 0$, are now a standard device in the study of partial differential equations with given boundary conditions. The study of the conditions under which a series of this form will converge has had important consequences in such branches of pure mathematics as integration and point set theory.

FOURNEAU [foor-nō'], **ERNEST FRANÇOIS AUGUSTE** (1872–1949), French physician, chemist, and pharmacologist. Chief of staff at the Pasteur Institute in Paris, Fourneau became well known for his investigations leading to the introduction of anesthetics (stovaine, 1903) and for drugs used in the treatment of tropical diseases, especially African sleeping sickness. His principal work on the chemical synthesis of drugs, *Organic Medicaments and Their Preparations* (1925), was translated into several languages.

FOURNIER [foor-nyā'], **ALAIN-,** pseudonym of Henri Fournier (1886–1914), French novelist. After abandoning plans for a career in the merchant marine, he attended a secondary school near Paris, hoping to enter the École Normale Supérieure. When he failed the entrance examinations he decided to become a journalist. His one completed novel, *Le Grand Meaulnes*, 1913 (*The Wanderer*, 1928), is a beautiful portrayal of the adolescent mind. He was killed in action in World War I, leaving several manuscripts which were published posthumously.

FOURNIER, PIERRE SIMON (1712–68), French typefounder and engraver. Born in Paris, Fournier studied painting as a youth, then turned to wood and steel engraving, and then to type design. His celebrated *Manuel typographique* (2 vols., 1764–66) consists of instructions for cutting and casting of types, together with numerous specimens of type faces, flowers, and ornaments.

FOUR O'CLOCK, perennial herb, *Mirabilis jalapa*, in the four o'clock family, Nyctaginaceae, native to tropical America. The plant is widely grown in North America and derives its common name from the fact that its flowers open only during the late afternoon. Four o'clock grows from 14 to 30 in. tall, has oval, smooth leaves, and bears bell-shaped, white, yellow or red flowers. It is easily grown from seed sown in ordinary soil.

FOURTEEN POINTS, U.S. President Woodrow Wilson's statement of American objectives in World War I. On Jan. 8, 1918, in an address to a joint session of Congress, Wilson listed the following war aims: (1) abolition of secret diplomacy; (2) freedom of the seas; (3) removal of economic barriers between nations; (4) reduction of armaments; (5) impartial adjustment of colonial claims; "restoration" of (6) Russia, (7) Belgium, (8) France; "readjustment" of frontiers for the peoples of (9) Italy, (10) Austria-Hungary, (11) the Balkans, and (12) the Turkish Empire; (13) independence for Poland; (14) "a general association of nations" to secure "mutual guarantees of political independence and territorial integrity to great and small states alike." George Creel, head of the U.S. Committee on Public Information, gave the Fourteen Points exceptionally wide circulation, stressing such phrases as "political independence," "democracy," and "peace without victory." The result was that Wilson's program came to represent the hopes of the world for a sane and just peace. In Oct., 1918, Germany sued for a peace based on the Fourteen Points. The Allies agreed, although Great Britain expressed reservations regarding freedom of the seas and France about reparations. At the Paris Peace Conference so many compromises were made that the Treaty of Versailles bore little resemblance to Wilson's original Fourteen Points.

Consult Link, A. S., *Wilson the Diplomatist* (1957).

DENNIS F. STRONG, Princeton University

FOURTH DIMENSION, fourth co-ordinate in a four-co-ordinate system. An event such as the flashing of a light signal at a given time and place could be specified by four co-ordinates: x, y, z, t, where $x, y,$ and z are the co-ordinates of the place and the fourth co-ordinate, t, tells the time of its occurrence. Interest in a fourth dimension has been aroused by descriptions of unusual phenomena in four-dimensional space, such as turning a sphere inside out without tearing it.

FOURTH ESTATE, term commonly applied to the public press. It is an extension of the use of "estate" to signify the three traditional social orders of feudal society—the lords spiritual, lords temporal, and commons—and formerly was applied to other groups, such as the army and the mob, until journalists claimed the title. Apparently Thomas Babington Macaulay was the first to use the term in its current sense (*Essays*, 1828), although Thomas Carlyle ascribed it, probably mistakenly, to Edmund Burke. Burke's remark, supposedly made about 1790 in reference to the reporters' gallery in the House of Commons, is not in his published works.

FOURTH OF JULY. *See* INDEPENDENCE DAY.

FOURTH REPUBLIC, in French history, regime established with the ratification of a new constitution in a national referendum in Oct., 1946, and terminated by a revolt of French settlers and army officers in Algeria in May, 1958. Like the Third Republic, the Fourth was characterized by a weak executive, multiplicity of parties, and chronic cabi-

net instability. It was a period, however, of rapid economic recovery.

FOUTA DJALLON [foo-tá' ja-lôn'], highland plateau of western Africa, in the Republic of Guinea. The Fouta Djallon consists of thick layers of sandstone, and gives rise to headwaters of the Niger and Senegal rivers. The highest areas are densely populated by the pastoral Fulani. The chief towns are Labé and Timbo, the latter on the Conakry-Kankan railroad, which crosses the highlands. Area, approx. 7,500 sq. mi.; average elevation, 3,000 ft.

FOVEAUX [fō'vō] **STRAIT,** strait in southern New Zealand, separating South Island from Stewart Island. It is noted for its fine oysters and for stormy weather. Width, about 21 mi.

FOWL, term applied to birds of the pheasant family, Phasianidae, particularly to jungle birds of the genus *Gallus* and their domesticated descendants. The pheasants, quail, partridges, peacocks, and jungle fowl that make up the family are characterized by strong legs, heavy bodies, and relatively small wings which suit them for running rather than flight. They are seed eaters, using their strong toes to scratch for food. The red jungle fowl, *Gallus gallus*, is the ancestor of all domesticated breeds of chickens. It is native to India, Burma, China, and the Malay Peninsula, and lives in thickets and woods, laying its eggs on the ground. Their eggs and meat have made them prized sources of food. Domestication must have taken place sometime prior to 1000 B.C., the date of the earliest rec-

SEVERAL KINDS OF FOWL

The red jungle fowl (*left*) inhabits the forests of southeast Asia. It is the probable ancestor of the domestic chicken.

R. Van Nostrand—National Audubon Society

The ring-necked pheasant (*below*), a native of Asia, has been introduced into North America and Europe.

Leonard Lee Rue III—National Audubon Society

Karl Maslowski—National Audubon Society

Anita Este—National Audubon Society

The male common peafowl, or peacock (*above*), may attain a length of 90 in. from tip of beak to the end of its splendid train of tail coverts.

The chukar partridge (*left*) is native to western Europe, where it is known as the red-legged partridge. It has been introduced into southwestern United States.

ords of cockfighting. The numerous breeds of domestic fowl have been bred for specific purposes: the Leghorn was developed in the Mediterranean region for egg production; the large (over 10 lb.) Brahma was bred in Asia for its meat. Other varieties were developed for all-purpose use. Included in the latter category are the popular Orpington and Sussex of English origin and the Plymouth Rock and Rhode Island Red, breeds developed in the United States.

CLARENCE J. HYLANDER, Author, *Feathers and Flight*
See also GUINEA FOWL; JUNGLE FOWL; PARTRIDGE; PEACOCK; PHEASANT; POULTRY; QUAIL.

FOWLER, SIR JOHN (1817–98), British civil engineer. He built the first railroad bridge over the Thames, the Pimlico, in 1860, and was the chief engineer of the world's first "subway" in London, the first section of which was opened in 1863. It was completed in 1884 and Fowler was knighted in 1885. In 1875 his principal assistant, Benjamin Baker, became his partner in a famous association that was later identified with two of the greatest engineering works of the ages, Firth Bridge and the first Aswan Dam.

FOWLIANG. *See* KINGTEHCHEN.

FOX, CHARLES JAMES (1749–1806), English politician. The third son of Henry, 1st Baron Holland, Fox studied at Eton and Oxford and began (1768) his political life as a supporter of the Duke of Grafton, then principal minister. Under Grafton's successor, Lord North, he became a lord of Admiralty (1770–72), and a lord of Treasury (1772–74). Going into opposition (1774), Fox violently assailed North's policy of coercion in America and later attacked the American war. After North's fall (1782), he served briefly as a Secretary of State, quarreling with the Earl of Shelburne, the other Secretary, over the American peace negotiations. When Shelburne became principal minister (1782), Fox went into opposition, and presently shocked the country by forming (1783) a short-lived coalition with North, his old enemy. Back in opposition Fox regained some of his popularity by taking a leading role in the prosecution of Warren Hastings (1788–95). But he lost it again because of his pronounced sympathy for the French Revolution, and his pacificism during the French wars. These views also cost him his friendship with Edmund Burke. Their break (1792) caused a major realignment of parties. The longevity of George III, who hated him, frustrated the political hopes Fox built upon his close friendship with the Prince of Wales. The Prince himself ultimately came to prefer Fox's foes. During his long opposition Fox became the advocate of social and political change, calling for Parliamentary reform, abolition of the slave trade, and removal of Catholic disabilities. Just before his death, he had a brief tenure as Foreign Secretary under Lord Grenville (1806). Fox had brilliance, talent, and charm, but expediency and lack of discipline robbed him of the greatness he might have achieved.

Consult Hobhouse, Christopher, *Fox* (1948).

J. JEAN HECHT, Stanford University

FOX, GEORGE (1624–91), founder of the Society of Friends, or Quakers. Born of humble parentage in the English Midlands, Fox was brought up under Puritan influences. In 1643, deeply troubled by the contrasts between Christian profession and Christian practice, he entered a three-year period of spiritual depression, struggle, and seeking. Peace came to him at last through mystical "openings" in which he came to the conviction that he knew God and Christ not through the Scriptures, but directly by revelation, or a divine Inner Light. Believing henceforth that true religion was primarily an inward matter, he sought to live the sanctified life, despising compromises with the world and its ways, and rejecting external religious forms, established churches, and paid ministries.

Fox began his public ministry in 1647, testifying boldly against many of the accepted religious and social practices of his time. He was frequently persecuted as a blasphemer and disturber of the peace. Many times he was imprisoned, suffering severely in loathsome jails. But he early attracted some ardent followers, and by the 1650's Quaker communities were being formed. Among those whom he won to Quaker beliefs was Margaret Fell of Swarthmore Hall, whom he later married (1669). In 1671–73, Fox led a mission to Barbados, Jamaica, and North America, there helping to stabilize the Quaker movement. He later journeyed to Holland and Germany.

Fox's mysticism was indirectly but clearly influenced by the Familists and by Jacob Boehme and his followers, and his spiritual insight not only gave a small but significant religious body its direction and depth, but also had influence far beyond Quakerism. Fox's formal education had been limited, but he was a courageous, prophetic, intense evangelist and spiritual leader.

Consult Jones, R. M., *George Fox, Seeker and Friend* (1930).

ROBERT T. HANDY, Union Theological Seminary

FOX, JOHN WILLIAM, JR. (1863–1919), American novelist, noted for his sentimental novels of the Kentucky mountains. Born in Stony Point, Ky., he lived for some years in the Cumberland Mountains, which served as the setting for most of his fiction. He wrote novelettes, such as *A Cumberland Vendetta* (1895) and *Hell fer Sartain* (1897), which are conventional melodramatic tales. He is best known for his tearful and sentimental novels *The Little Shepherd of Kingdom Come* (1903) and *The Trail of the Lonesome Pine* (1908).

FOX, SIR WILLIAM (1812–93), New Zealand statesman and Prime Minister (1856, 1861–62, 1869–72, 1873). Born in England, Fox studied at Oxford and read law before migrating (1842) to New Zealand. There he entered politics and joined in the struggle for self-government. As principal agent of the New Zealand Company (1848–51), spokesman for the Wellington Settlers' Constitutional Association, and newspaper editor, Fox had a thorough knowledge of local problems. Though the Colonial Office refused to receive him when he returned to Britain (1850) to lobby for self-government, he won wide support for the New Zealand Constitution Bill (1852). As Premier (1861–62), Fox worked with Governor George Grey to introduce a system of indirect government in Maori districts, but racial relations had already deteriorated too far to avert full-scale war. Prominent in the Domett and Whitaker ministries (1863–64), Fox vigorously defended the confiscation of Maori land against English charges that the policy was a scheme of self-aggrandizement. Until 1865, when Wellington replaced Auckland as the capital, Fox resisted centralization but then (1869–72) co-operated with Julius Vogel in carrying out a vast scheme of national development financed by foreign loans.

PETER J. COLEMAN, Washington University

FOX, name for several carnivorous mammals of the dog family, Canidae. Compared with other canines, the foxes have longer, bushier tails, larger ears, more pointed muzzles, and more slender bodies. The foxes have adapted to a wide variety of environments and are found in Arctic regions, in forested regions of the Northern and Southern Hemispheres, and in the plains and deserts of Africa.

A North American red fox. (LEONARD LEE RUE III—NATIONAL AUDUBON SOCIETY)

The foxes are alert and cunning. Chiefly nocturnal in habit, they do not hibernate. They eat many kinds of food, but especially small mammals and birds. The well-known North American red fox, *Vulpes fulva*, ranges over most of the United States and Canada. It is the size of a small, slender dog and has fur that is reddish above and white on the undersides, and black feet and legs. The red foxes have white-tipped tails. Color variations of the red fox are the cross, black, and silver foxes. All four types have been observed in the same litter. The silver fox is darkly pigmented, with a silvery appearance due to the white tips of many of its hairs. The kit fox, *V. velox*, smallest of the foxes, is found in the Great Plains. The American gray fox, *Urocyon cinereoargenteus*, found from New England to South America, frequently climbs trees and lives in hollow tree trunks. The Arctic fox, *V. lagopus*, often shows seasonal variation in the color of its pelt.

MARY M. TOWNES, North Carolina College at Durham

FOXBORO or FOXBOROUGH, residential town of southeastern Massachusetts, west of Brockton. Cannon and ammunition were cast here during the Revolutionary War. Settled, 1704; inc., 1778; pop., 14,218.

FOXE, JOHN (1516–87), author of the popular 16th-century book now known as Foxe's *Book of Martyrs* (referring to Protestant victims during Mary Tudor's reign in England, 1553–58). Exiled on the Continent during that time, he acquired strict Calvinist views and was later ordained in London as an Anglican clergyman.

FOXE BASIN, arm of the Atlantic Ocean, lying within Franklin District, Northwest Territories, Canada, between Melville Peninsula on the west and Baffin Island on the north and east. Southward, it is connected with Hudson Bay and Hudson Strait by Foxe Channel. It was explored by Luke Foxe in 1631. Length, 300 mi.; width, 200–250 mi.

FOXGLOVE, handsome biennial and perennial plant of the genus Digitalis, in the figwort family, Scrophulariaceae. Foxglove is native to Europe, North Africa, and Asia and is grown in North America. The plants are of erect growing habit and bear showy spikes of bell-shaped flowers that are usually purple, yellow, or white in color. The common foxglove, *D. purpurea*, is the most widely grown species and is raised from seed sown in ordinary garden soil of moderate moisture content. Digitalis, an extract prepared from the leaves of this species, is used medicinally.

FOXHOUND, member of the hound group of dogs named for its use as a trailer of foxes. Two varieties of the breed are recognized: the American foxhound and the English foxhound. The former is used primarily for night hunting; the latter for the open chase. The origin of the breed is not known but the type has changed little through the centuries. The foxhound is a streamlined dog with long ears, a high, sickle-shaped tail, deep chest, and mellow baritone bark. The dogs are of many colors but are usually black, tan, and white, or combinations of these colors. The breed has a keen sense of smell. Hunted in packs, foxhounds are a picture of liveliness, eagerness, and single intent.

FOXING, term applied to rusty stains on the pages of books. Caused by dampness and fungus growths, such stains appear most frequently in paper with high acid content or iron impurities. Well-ventilated book stacks and low humidity reduce the danger. Stains can be removed with a bleach, but the bleach may further harm the paper.

FOX POINT, city of southeastern Wisconsin, a residential suburb northeast of Milwaukee, on Lake Michigan. Pop., 7,939.

FOX RIVER, river in east-central Wisconsin, rising east of Portage. It flows west to within 1½ mi. of the Wisconsin River at Portage, where a canal connects the two streams, then generally northeast through Lake Winnebago into Green Bay. It forms, with the Wisconsin River, a continuous waterway from the Great Lakes to the Mississippi River. Louis Jolliet and Jacques Marquette in 1673 were the first Europeans to use the portage between the two rivers to reach the Mississippi; this route was later chosen by many explorers and traders. Length, 176 mi.

FOX TERRIER, one of the most popular of the terrier breeds of dog. Two varieties of fox terrier are known—the wire-haired, which has a bristly, coarse coat, and the smooth-haired, which has a flat, smooth coat. Fox terriers are predominantly white with markings of black or tan. They attain a shoulder height of about 15 in. and weigh 18 lb. Fox terriers are alert, curious, vivacious, and always interested in killing vermin and small burrowing game. The name of the breed is derived from its former use of chasing foxes from their burrows. The fox terrier of today is a faithful companion and an alert watchdog.

FOX TROT, American social dance originated in 1913 by Oscar Duryea. Originally two slow steps followed by four quick steps, in 4/4 time (♩ ♩ ♫ ♫), the form has undergone some modification by the substitution of a two-step (step-together step-pause) for the four quick steps.

FOXX, JAMES EMORY ("JIMMY") (1907–67), American baseball player, born in Sudlersville, Md. He played for Philadelphia (1925–35) and Boston (1936–42) of the American League, and Chicago (1942, 1944) and Philadelphia (1945) of the National League. He was primarily a first baseman, though he also performed as a catcher and third baseman. One of the most powerful right-handed batters in the sport's history, he hit 58 home runs in 1932 and 534 during his major-league career. He was elected to the National Baseball Hall of Fame in 1951.

FRACKVILLE, coal-mining borough of east-central Pennsylvania, north of Pottsville. Textiles are also manufactured here. The town is situated on the summit of Broad Mountain and occupies a very exposed terrain. Inc., 1876; pop., 5,445.

FRACTION, an expression of the form $\frac{a}{b}$ (or a/b, for typographical convenience), where a and b are numbers. The fraction a/b represents the number which, when multiplied by b, yields a: That is a/b represents the result of dividing a by b. In the fraction a/b, a is called the numerator and b is called the denominator. The denominator of a fraction cannot be zero.

Different fractions may represent the same number. If so, we say that the fractions are equivalent. Thus, 3/6 and 4/8 represent the same number. We indicate equivalence by the symbol "=". The rule for deciding whether two fractions are equivalent is: $a/b = c/d$ if, and only if, $ad = bc$. Neither b nor d may be zero.

In elementary arithmetic, the numerator and denominator of a fraction are whole numbers. In this case the number represented by the fraction is called a rational number.

To add (or subtract) fractions with the same denominator, we merely add (or subtract) the numerators and use the common denominator. Thus, $3/5 + 4/5 = 7/5$ and $4/7 - 2/7 = 2/7$. To add two fractions with different denominators, it is convenient to replace the fractions by equivalent fractions which have a common denominator and then use the rule of the preceding paragraph. Thus, to add 13/15 and 7/10, we may replace 13/15 by 130/150 and 7/10 by 105/150 and then add to obtain 235/150. Or we may replace 13/15 by 26/30 and 7/10 by 21/30 and obtain the sum 47/30, which is equivalent to 235/150. The formula for the sum of two fractions is $(a/b) + (c/d) = (ad + bc)/bd$. Similarly, $(a/b) - (c/d) = (ad - bc)/bd$. Thus, $8/17 - 7/15 = 120 - 119/255$, or 1/255. To multiply two fractions, we multiply the numerators to obtain the new numerator and the denominators to obtain the new denominator. Thus $3/8 \times 4/7 = 12/56$. In general $(a/b)(c/d) = ac/bd$. To divide one fraction by another, we invert (interchange the numerator and denominator) the divisor and multiply. Thus, $a/b \div c/d = a/b \times d/c = ad/bc$.

For each of the rules discussed, there is a valid principle of consistency. For addition, "if in a sum of fractions, each summand is replaced by an equivalent fraction, the sum will be replaced by an equivalent fraction." The important concepts here are that a fraction represents a number, and that a number has many different representations as fractions. The rules for adding (subtracting, and so on) fractions tell us how to operate with the representations, rather than with the numbers themselves. The principles of consistency tell us that we will end with a representation of the same number, no matter what representation we start with. Thus the distinction between the numbers and their representations is often disregarded.

If the numerator is smaller than the denominator, the fraction is called proper. Thus, 1/2, 3/8, and 3/6 are proper fractions. If the numerator is at least as large as the denominator, the fraction is called improper. Thus, 8/7 is an improper fraction. An expression of the form $3\frac{5}{8}$ is an abbreviation for $3/1 + 5/8$ and is called a mixed fraction.

If the denominator is 10, 100, or some other power of 10, the fraction is called a decimal fraction, or simply a decimal. When written, only the numerator appears, while the position of the "decimal point" indicates which power of ten is the denominator. Thus, $32/10 = 3.2$; $32/100 = .32$; $32/1000 = .032$; and so on.

A fraction whose numerator or denominator (or both) involves a fraction is called a complex fraction. Examples are $\frac{a/b}{c/d}$ and $\frac{a/b + c/d}{e}$. In a complex fraction, the restriction against zero denominators applies to all denominators.

Thus, in $\frac{e/f}{a/b + c/d}$ we must have $f \neq$ (not equal to) 0, $b \neq 0$, $d \neq 0$, and $\frac{a}{b} + \frac{c}{d} \neq 0$.

MICHAEL AISSEN, *Fordham University*
See also ARITHMETIC.

FRACTURES, disruptions of bone structure which most commonly result from accidents in which excessive stresses are applied to bones. The nature of the fracture depends upon the strength, direction, and location of the force applied to the bone, the condition of the bone, and the age of the patient. Every fracture damages the soft tissues of the body, producing injuries which may range from slight bruising to severe crushing and tearing. Such damage is especially serious when it involves nerves or major blood vessels.

Types. When the skin over a fracture remains unbroken, it is spoken of as a closed (or simple) fracture. If there is communication with the outside, or, as in the case of the skull, with one of the air-containing cavities of the nose or ear, the fracture is called an open (or compound) fracture. The opening may be produced by some object penetrating the skin from without, or by a sharp portion of the broken bone penetrating the skin from within. The presence of bleeding and tissue damage at the fracture site provides an ideal medium for the growth of bacteria. Every open fracture is contaminated to some degree, and should the patient's resistance be inadequate, or treatment delayed too long, a serious infection may develop. Persistent infection may prevent the fracture from healing.

When a force that normally could be well tolerated causes a bone to break, it does so because some process has reduced the strength of the bone. The bone may be weakened because of abnormal development, as in "brittle bone disease" (osteogenesis imperfecta); nutritional inadequacy, such as scurvy caused by lack of vitamin C; hormonal disturbances (such as hyperparathyroidism, where there is oversecretion of the parathyroid hormone); or in senile osteoporosis (a generalized decrease in the amount of bone substance). Tumors may also weaken the bone and cause pathologic fractures. These may have arisen in the bone (primary tumors) or, more commonly, spread to the bone from elsewhere in the body.

Diagnosis. Fractures alter the form of the affected part, preventing normal function and permitting motion where normally there is none. Bleeding from the broken blood vessels of the bone and surrounding tissue produces early and marked swelling. Pressure or movement at the fracture site stimulates the nerve endings, causing pain. The grating together of broken bone ends—crepitus—is proof of a fracture, but is a sign which should not be deliberately sought. In certain fractures in which the bone ends may be jammed together there will be little bleeding, moderate swelling, and no abnormal motion. The examination of an injured person suspected of having a fracture is not considered complete until good quality X rays are taken to confirm or rule out the presence of a break in the bone.

Treatment. Treatment begins with first-aid splinting. Splinting serves to prevent further bleeding, to relieve the pain, and to minimize further damage to adjacent soft tissues. All fractures should be splinted as soon as possible after they have occurred.

Medical treatment of a fracture aims to bring the two segments of the broken bone back into their normal alignment. This is usually spoken of as reduction and is best done as soon as possible, before too much swelling has occurred. Adequate anesthesia is essential to reduce the voluntary and involuntary muscle contractions which interfere with the surgeon's attempts to set the bone. Manipulation of the fracture is carried out carefully and deliberately to achieve reduction with the least additional injury to the tissues. After manipulation, further X rays are taken and if the position is satisfactory, it is maintained, usually by the application of a plaster cast to the injured limb. In certain cases, however, a plaster cast alone is not adequate and must be supplemented by other means. In some instances weights are used to maintain a constant pull on the limb so as to keep the bone fragments properly aligned: this is termed traction.

In still other situations, surgery is necessary. The bones are reduced under direct vision, and the position is main-

tained by plates, nails, screws, or other devices made of special nonreactive metal.

Although the physician brings the bone fragments back into a normal position, the body itself joins the two ends in a firm union. The specialized tissue which forms for this purpose is called callus. The external callus is produced by the bone-forming cells of the covering layer of bone; the internal callus is produced by the cells which line the marrow cavity. A collar of callus composed of some fibrous tissue, some cartilage, and some newly formed bone, grows from each end of the broken bone. The collars get larger and thicker and finally meet. This is the first stage in the healing process of the fracture. The callus eventually is converted completely into new bone, and usually at that time the splint, or cast, or other external support of the fracture can be removed. The final stage in the healing process consists of a reconstitution of the shaft of the bone, and a remodeling process which removes that portion of the callus which is no longer needed for strength.

Abnormally prolonged callus formation with a delayed conversion of callus to mature bone is usually referred to as a slow, or delayed, union. This term implies that if the treatment is continued the fracture will eventually heal. In some cases, where optimum conditions for healing are not present, the bone ends become united by fibrous tissue, which will not be converted to bone, no matter how long the fracture is immobilized. This is called nonunion, and requires such treatment as bone grafting.

Treatment cannot be considered complete until the patient has regained as nearly normal function of the injured part as can be expected from the type and severity of the injury. As soon as the degree of healing will permit the removal of whatever type of fixation has been applied, the patient is carefully instructed in the way in which to start using the injured limb again, to regain normal function of the muscles and joints. In some cases specific physical therapy may be helpful, but in the majority of instances functional restoration is best secured by active exercises, under the supervision of the doctor.

LeRoy C. Abbott, M.D. and Robert M. Jameson, M.D.

FRAGONARD [frà-gô-nàr], **JEAN HONORÉ** (1732–1806), French painter of the waning years of the French monarchy. Along with his predecessor Jean Antoine Watteau

"Outdoor Party at Rambouillet," by Jean Honoré Fragonard

Giraudon

"The Meeting" by Fragonard

The Frick Collection, 1938

and the somewhat older François Boucher, with whom he studied, Fragonard is the painter *par excellence* of the manners and mores of the court of Louis XVI. Although he also studied with Jean Baptiste Chardin, the light, frivolous style and subject matter of Boucher were most influential on his development. Fragonard won the *Prix de Rome* and worked in Italy from 1756 to 1761. In 1765 he was admitted to the French Academy by virtue of a large historical painting, done in the traditional "grand manner," but this type of painting was not typical of him. Rather, in keeping with the desires of his courtly patrons, among them Mme. du Barry, and in complete accord with the decadent atmosphere of the court, he concentrated on paintings of illicit meetings, amorous adventures, and idyllic pastoral scenes, all with scarcely veiled erotic overtones. Mythological and allegorical figures are ever-present and lend to his works an air of unreality and escapism so desired by the court circles.

Within this framework of limited and limiting subject matter, Fragonard's achievements are all the more remarkable. His strongest assets as an artist are his brilliant use of color and his superb draftsmanship. His paintings literally sparkle with strong, bright colors working harmoniously with subtle pastel tones, giving his works a coloristic richness that reflects the richness of the society which patronized him. Even more important to his work are his hundreds of drawings in sanguine and water-color wash. These amply demonstrate the artist's skill in quickly and economically capturing the quality of a landscape or a sitter's character in a portrait. Indeed, these superb drawings are as much collector's items as are any of Fragonard's paintings. Fragonard's drawings and paintings are admirably represented in the Louvre, Paris. The Wallace Collection, London, and the Frick Collection, New York, are exceptionally rich in Fragonard paintings.

STANLEY FERBER

FRAMINGHAM [frā'mǐng-hăm], residential and industrial suburb west of Boston, northeastern Massachusetts. Automobiles and paper goods are manufactured here. A state college established in 1839 at Lexington was moved to Framingham in 1853. Crispus Attucks (1723?–1770), leader of the Boston Massacre in 1770, was a resident.

FRANCE [frăNs], **ANATOLE,** pseudonym of Jacques Anatole Thibault (1844–1924), French writer. Initiated to literature by his father, a bookseller on the Quai Malaquais in Paris, he wrote some of his early books on his memories of childhood, notably *Le livre de mon ami*, 1885 (*My Friend's Book*, 1913).

France emulated to some degree the learned dilettantism of Ernest Renan, whom he admired. His skeptical attitude toward highly respected values and doctrines gave to much of his writing a tone of mockery and wit. In his novels he fused sympathy and irony with great skill and elegance. After the Dreyfus Affair, in which he espoused the cause of Alfred Dreyfus, he became a more polemical writer; in *L'affaire Crainquebille*, 1904, he denounced the forces of power and lent support to the meek in heart.

One of the most famous French writers in the first two decades of the 20th century, Anatole France was looked upon at the time as a stylist of classical clarity and perfection. Today his style seems artificial, but its finesse is still apparent. His most widely read book in English translation is *L'Île des Pingouins*, 1908 (*Penguin Island*, 1909), a social satire of wide scope. His *Thaïs* (1890) inspired Jules Massenet's opera of the same name. His most lasting work may well be the four volumes of *Histoire contemporaine* (1897–1901), in which his hero, Professor Bergeret, is the wise observer of small-town intrigues. Anatole France always used his knowledge of the world and his erudition as weapons against dogmatic ideas, both religious and secular. He was awarded the Nobel Prize for literature in 1921.

WALLACE FOWLIE

Portrait of Anatole France, by Pierre Calmettas

The Bettmann Archive

FRANCE

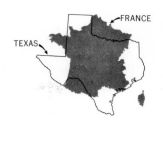

AREA	211,207 sq mi (547 026 km²)
ELEVATION	
Highest point (Mont Blanc)	15,781 ft (4 810 m)
Lowest point	Sea level
POPULATION	52,544,400
PRINCIPAL LANGUAGE	French
LIFE EXPECTANCY	69–76 years
PERCENTAGE OF LITERACY	Almost 100%
UNIT OF CURRENCY	Franc
NATIONAL ANTHEM	Marseillaise, words and music by Rouget de Lisle
CAPITAL	Paris
PRINCIPAL PRODUCTS	Automobiles, aircraft, steel, aluminum, refined petroleum, rubber, plastics, chemicals, textiles, wheat, barley, cheese, wine

Armando Curcio Editore SpA

The Eiffel Tower, symbol of Paris, capital of France.

FRANCE, republic of Western Europe. Almost rectangular, France has a coast line of 1,870 mi (3 000 km), with a shore line on both the Atlantic Ocean and the Mediterranean Sea. The territory of Metropolitan France includes the island of Corsica, and there are a number of overseas departments and territories.

The Land

Physical Features. France is a country of great topographical variety. It can be roughly divided by a line from southwest to northeast into a western and northern region of low-lying plain and plateau, and an eastern and southern region of hill and mountain. In the latter region is the highest mountain in western Europe, Mont Blanc (15,781 ft, or 9 810 m), on the Franco-Italian border.

The plains region extends from close to the Spanish border into Belgium, its northern part being occupied by the fertile Paris basin, the heart of France. The plain is interrupted by the shallow valleys of numerous rivers and also by low hills and a series of partly forested limestone and sandstone ridges, particularly conspicuous to the east of Paris. The older, harder rock base of the westerly peninsula of Brittany produces low rounded hills.

Aside from a strip of lowland along part of the Mediterranean shore, southern and eastern France is hilly or mountainous. A large part of this region consists of the Massif Central, an undulating plateau of old rock which rises steeply from the surrounding lowland, although its greatest heights reach only 6,000 ft (1 800 m). Toward the southeast the Massif rises to the Cévennes range, which then drops abruptly to the Rhône Valley and the Mediterranean coast. To the south the Massif Central is separated from the Pyrenees by a narrow depression, known as the Carcassonne Gap. This mighty range extends without a significant break for more than 260 mi (420 km), with many peaks over 10,000 ft (3 000 m). To the northeast the Massif Central is continued in the mountains of the Morvan, which in turn are linked with the Vosges. The deep and narrow valleys of the Rhône and Saône rivers separate the Massif Central and its related hills from the Jura Mountains and the Alps.

The Jura, stretching in a series of parallel ridges from the Rhine to the Rhône, are geologically related to the Alps, which extend from Lake Geneva (Lac Léman) southward to the Mediterranean, where they form the picturesque backdrop to the resorts of the French Riviera. The Alps present a formidable obstacle to international communication, partly overcome by a railroad tunnel through the mountains and the Mont Blanc highway tunnel. The most important passes are the Little St. Bernard and the Mont Cenis on the Franco-Italian border.

Rivers. Most French rivers rise in the Massif Central or its bordering hills and flow either northwest to the English Channel (La Manche) or west to the Bay of Biscay. The three major river systems are the Seine, Loire, and Garonne.

Armando Curcio Editore SpA

Mont Blanc, the highest peak in Europe, guards France's Alpine frontier with Italy.

The Seine and many of its tributaries rise in the Morvan and neighboring hills. The most important tributaries are the Yonne and the Marne. These rivers, and the Oise and the Aisne, which flow from the scarped country to the northeast of Paris, join the Seine in the vicinity of the city to form a navigable waterway, which enters the sea at Le Havre.

The Loire rises in the Massif Central, where it is joined by its chief tributary, the Allier. It flows westward across central France, between gentle, vine-clad, castle-crowned slopes, to Nantes and St.-Nazaire. In summer the Loire has very little water and is generally not navigable.

The Garonne rises in the Pyrenees, but receives its more important tributaries—the Tarn, Aveyron, and Lot —from the Massif Central. Below Bordeaux it is joined by the Dordogne and enters a long, broad estuary, known as the Gironde. In summer water levels here are even lower than those of the Loire.

The fourth major French river is the Rhône, which rises in the Swiss Alps, and flows southward to the plain of Provence, where its valley widens. The river enters the Mediterranean by a delta. Silt carried westward by the current forms a series of bars and lagoons along the coast toward the Spanish frontier. In summer the Rhône, fed by the melted Alpine snows, is a swift-flowing river, and it and its tributaries—with the exception of the quiet-flowing Saône—are not easily navigable.

A series of dams has been constructed across the Rhône to generate power, to provide irrigation, and to regulate the flow for navigation. The Rhône's longest tributary, the Saône, rises in the hills of eastern France, and the Isère and the Durance rise in the French Alps. Eastern France is drained to the Rhine; both the Meuse and the Moselle rise in France.

Climate. France spans the northwest European and Mediterranean climate zones. The proximity of the sea moderates the temperature of northern and western France, which has warm summers and mild winters and a well-distributed rainfall. At Brest the average temperature ranges from 45° F (7° C) in January to 65° F (18° C) in July and annual rainfall is about 32 in (81 cm). Toward the east, extremes of temperature are more marked; in Strasbourg, where summer days are hot and thundery, the January average is 30° F (−1° C). Toward the south, as the climate merges with that of the Mediterranean, summers become drier and hotter and winters warmer. Temperatures at Marseille average 44° F (7° C) in January and 72° F (22° C) in July. A characteristic of the south is the chill north wind known as the mistral. These climatic contrasts explain the concentration on grain and fodder crops in the north and on vines and fruit in the south.

Soils, Natural Vegetation, and Wildlife. The good lowland soils of France, partly formed by the deposit of loess, have encouraged extensive cultivation, although alluvial areas in the south need to be irrigated. Along the Atlantic coast are long stretches of wind-blown sand, known as the Landes, most of which are now planted with conifers. France has been inhabited too long for much of its natural vegetation or primitive wildlife to have survived. Originally, there was a forest cover of oak, beech, ash, and elm, with conifers on the higher ground. Toward the Mediterranean the forest cover gave place to drought-resistant shrubs. The olive trees and other species characteristic of the region have been planted by man. So, too, have the long avenues of poplars and other trees in northern and central France. On the hills of Brittany considerable stretches of heather-covered moorland still survive.

The varieties of animal life were formerly very numerous, and there are still many small field animals. But the

PHYSICAL REGIONS OF FRANCE

Elevations in feet:
Over 5000
2000 to 5000
500 to 2000
Under 500

0   50   100
Miles

France's Spanish frontier spans the heights of the Pyrenees. View is of the Abbey of St. Martin of Canigon, in the heart of the French Basque country.

Lucien Offenberg

wolf and the wild boar, once common as game in the forests, are now rare and, where they still occur, are protected.

Mineral Resources. France has extensive mineral deposits, especially of coal and iron ore. The largest coal fields are in the extreme north and in Lorraine, and there are numerous smaller coal fields in central France. Lorraine also contains the most important iron ore deposits in Europe, and there are also small quantities in Normandy, the Alps, and the Pyrenees. France possesses one of Europe's largest reserves of bauxite, which is named for Les Baux in Provence, though the deposits at this site are no longer important.

Consult Clout, Hugh D., *The Geography of Post-War France: A Social and Economic Approach* (1972); Dollfus, Jean, *France: Its Geography and Growth* (1972); Evans, E. Estyn, *France: An Introductory Geography* (1966); Fox, Edward W., *History in Geographic Perspective: The Other France* (1972); Pinchimel, Philippe, *France: A Geographical Survey* (1970).

NORMAN J. G. POUNDS

FRANCE **STUDY GUIDE**

France is not only part of Europe, but in a special sense is also part of world culture. This can be shown by the significance of French names to people of other lands and languages. Joan of Arc symbolizes religious and patriotic idealism, Napoleon military genius, Voltaire wit and satire, Descartes rationalism in modern philosophy. The Sorbonne is synonymous with scholarly study. The roster of great names is continued in this Study Guide, following an outline of the main article, FRANCE.

The Land. Physical features; climate, soils, natural vegetation, and wildlife; mineral resources.

The People. Ethnology; population and chief cities; the geopolitical role of France; language and regional characteristics; religion; artistic and intellectual life; education and science.

The Economy. Economic development; labor; agriculture; industry; foreign trade; the state and the economy; international co-operation.

Government. The structure of the government and the constitution of the Fifth Republic; political parties and elections; legal system and public administration.

History. Survey starting with ancient Gaul and continuing to the Fifth Republic.

Architecture. From Romanesque and Gothic to modern styles.

Art. From medieval to modern art.

Literature. Poetry and prose from their beginnings to 20th-century writing.

Music. From church music in the Middle Ages to the music of the 20th century.

Theater. From medieval religious drama to realistic and 20th-century works.

The scope of coverage of France may be shown by listing, under a number of headings, examples of the hundreds of pertinent articles in the Encyclopedia.

Cities, regions, rivers: PARIS, LIMOGES, MARSEILLE, NICE, LE HAVRE, VERDUN, TOULOUSE, PROVENCE, CORSICA, MARNE RIVER, RHONE RIVER.

History: GAUL; CELTS; FRANKS; VISIGOTHS; MIDDLE AGES; FEUDALISM; CRUSADES; ALBIGENSES; HUNDRED YEARS' WAR; HUGUENOTS; NANTES, EDICT OF; THIRTY YEARS' WAR; COLONIES, COLONIZATION, AND COLONIALISM; CANADA: *History;* SEVEN YEARS' WAR;

FRENCH AND INDIAN WARS; ESTATES GENERAL; FRENCH REVOLUTION; NAPOLEONIC WARS; VIENNA, CONGRESS OF; FRANCO-PRUSSIAN WAR; DREYFUS AFFAIR; WORLD WAR I; WORLD WAR II; ALGERIA; INDOCHINA; FIFTH REPUBLIC; FRENCH COMMUNITY; EUROPEAN COMMON MARKET.

Rulers, statesmen, and other public figures: MEROVINGIANS, CHARLEMAGNE, CAPET, LOUIS IX, CHARLES VII, HENRY IV, CATHERINE DE MEDICIS, RICHELIEU, LA SALLE, BOURBON, LOUIS XIII to LOUIS XVIII, Maximilien ROBESPIERRE, Charles Maurice de TALLEYRAND-PERIGORD, NAPOLEON I, Georges CLEMENCEAU, Ferdinand FOCH, Henri Philippe PETAIN, Charles DE GAULLE.

Language and literature: FRENCH, PROVENCAL LITERATURE, TROUBADOUR AND TROUVERE, François RABELAIS, François VILLON, Michel Eyquem de MONTAIGNE, Pierre de RONSARD, Victor HUGO, Gustave FLAUBERT, Emile ZOLA, Marcel PROUST, Albert CAMUS, André MAUROIS, and CANADA: *Canadian Literature (French).*

Philosophy and science: ACADEMIE FRANCAISE, Blaise PASCAL, René DESCARTES, VOLTAIRE, MONTESQUIEU, Denis DIDEROT (and ENCYCLOPEDIA), Antoine LAVOISIER, Louis PASTEUR, and PARIS, UNIVERSITY OF.

Theater: DRAMA, Pierre CORNEILLE, Jean Baptiste RACINE, MOLIERE, Alexandre DUMAS *fils,* André GIDE, Jean ANOUILH, and COMEDIE FRANCAISE, LA.

Music: GREGORIAN CHANT, Charles GOUNOD, Louis Hector BERLIOZ, Georges BIZET, Claude DEBUSSY, OPERA.

Religion: JOAN OF ARC; BERNARD OF CLAIRVAUX, ST.; VINCENT DE PAUL, ST.; BERNADETTE, ST.

Architecture: ROMANESQUE ART AND ARCHITECTURE; GOTHIC ARCHITECTURE; CATHEDRAL; CASTLE; CHATEAU; ARCHITECTURE, MODERN; and LE CORBUSIER.

Art: STAINED GLASS; RENAISSANCE ART; PAINTING, HISTORY OF (with color plates); IMPRESSIONISM; Jean Antoine WATTEAU; Eugène DELACROIX; Pierre Auguste RENOIR; Paul CEZANNE; Paul GAUGUIN; Claude MONET; Henri MATISSE.

Cuisine: FRENCH COOKERY, WINE, Anthelme BRILLAT-SAVARIN, Auguste ESCOFFIER.

Whether the reader's interest is in cooking, cathedrals, or the Carolingians he can find informative books through which to continue his study of France. Selected titles are listed at the ends of articles.

The People

Ethnology. France, because of its location, has over the centuries been accessible by sea and land to a variety of migrating peoples and has experienced a remarkable mingling of different ethnic elements. Marseille, the oldest city of France, was founded by the Greeks about 600 B.C., but they were soon succeeded by the Celts from Central Europe. The Celts invaded Gaul and gradually pushed the native Ligurians and Iberians down to the Mediterranean and across the Pyrenees to Spain.

The important ethnic contribution of the Celts was later profoundly modified, first by the Roman conquest and then by the Germanic invasions. Whereas the Roman conquest was of cultural rather than ethnic importance—there was no true implantation of Italian colonies —the Germanic hordes, chief among them the Franks, drove the Celts completely from certain regions of France. In the 9th century the Norsemen from Scandinavia, later known as Normans, established themselves in northern France. After the 10th century France experienced a long period without migrations. This ethnic stability made possible the unification of the country under a single authority, and also facilitated the growth of a single language.

It was not until the end of the 19th century that new foreign elements slightly modified the ethnic composition of France. Whereas in 1851 there were only 379,000 foreigners living in France, by 1881 this figure had risen to 1,000,000 and by 1931 to 2,891,000. As of 1970, there were about 2,700,000 foreign immigrants living in France.

Population and Chief Cities. There are indications that barbaric Gaul, which was larger than modern France, had between 4,000,000 and 7,000,000 inhabitants. The beneficial effects of the Pax Romana, which followed the Roman conquest, caused a rapid increase in population, and it is estimated that under the domination of Rome, Gaul had over 9,000,000 inhabitants. The population then grew steadily until the beginning of the Hundred Years' War (1337–1453), but the ravages of war, famines, and epidemics reduced the population from more than 20,000,000 to about 18,000,000. By the eve of the Revolution (1789), however, population had reached 26,000,000.

Until 1815 France was, with the exception of Russia, the most populous country of Europe, and at times this demographic superiority had important political consequences. A decline in the number of births during the 19th century, followed by the terrible losses of World War I, slowed demographic expansion to the point of creating a disturbing situation. The end of World War II brought a marked improvement, because the institution of a fairer social system, coupled to a comprehensive program of prenatal, maternity, and family allowances, made it possible for families to assume greater responsibilities. A moderate upswing in the population growth rate occurred in the 1960's, and the trend persisted into the next decade, although the norm continued to hover at two to three children per family.

France has a population density of about 249 persons per square mile (96 per km²) and, in common with other highly developed countries, is witnessing an exodus from rural areas to the towns and cities. About 70% of the population is classified as urban, and there are more than 30 cities with over 100,000 inhabitants. The largest city is Paris, capital of France and long one of the great cultural centers of the world. Other leading cities are the Mediterranean port of Marseille; Lyon, renowned for its silk; Toulouse and Bordeaux, both important commercial centers, while the latter has also given its name to the surrounding wine-growing region; and Nice, the famous resort on the Riviera.

The Geopolitical Role of France. France is an Atlantic, and therefore a Western, nation, and is naturally associated with countries like the United Kingdom, whose political and intellectual history has been almost constantly tied to that of France. But France is also Continental. If France is acknowledged a leader in the unification of Europe, it is because it is bound to the Continent by physical and spiritual ties. And finally France is Mediterranean. The first Phoenician and Greek colonists came from those shores, as did the Roman conquerors, who permanently influenced France's cultural, economic, and social life. Moreover, from its southern ports France has always been in contact with Asia, trying at one time to re-establish the empire of Christ through the Crusades; at another to protect the Christians of the Ottoman Empire, through the capitulations, or treaty rights, accorded to them by the Ottomans; and later to extend its political, economic, and cultural influence, through the construction of the Suez Canal.

The geographic location of France does not alone suffice to explain the country's formation and evolution. But if its unity is the result of slow assimilation, location also played a part in its destiny, for the country's political problems are largely due to its Atlantic, European, and Mediterranean location.

Language and Regional Characteristics. The paradox of diversity in unity can also be seen in the language of France. Although French, with a variety of dialects, is spoken throughout the country, local languages persist in certain regions, imparting to each a distinctive char-

In the center of old Paris: activity fills the bustling street market in the Rue Mouffetard.

Babout—Rapho

Attention to the creature comforts, as French as crepes suzette, is good business as well as good hospitality at this luxury restaurant in Antibes.

Sabine Weiss—Rapho Guillumette

acter. In the northeast of France Flemish is still widely spoken, and the peasants of the Pyrenees preserve the ancient language of the Basques, together with many of their traditional customs. In isolated districts along the rocky coast of Brittany, the fisherfolk converse in Breton and are as distinctive in their dress and character as the people of Auvergne, who are also of Celtic ancestry. In Provence, the oldest settled region of France, where the Roman influence is still apparent in architecture and institutions, the Romance tongue of Provençal survives.

Many of the regions of France were once powerful duchies, such as Aquitaine, Berry, Anjou, Normandy, Picardy, and Lorraine, or even, in the case of Burgundy, a kingdom that ruled extensive areas beyond the frontiers of modern France.

The names of other regions have become synonymous with their products, which delight wine-lovers and gourmets the world over: champagne, brandy from Armagnac and Cognac, the wines of Burgundy and Beaujolais, cheese from Brie, and the goose-liver pâté of Strasbourg in Alsace. The people of these many regions may vary in temperament and habits, but they are united in their awareness of the great cultural heritage of France. Although the somewhat taciturn northerner may seem a very different person from the loquacious inhabitant of the sunny Midi, both are as undeniably French as the contrasting scenery of the Alpine peaks of Savoy or Dauphiné and the orchards and châteaux of Touraine, "the garden of France." (*See* FRENCH.)

Religion. France is recognized as the "eldest daughter" of the Roman Catholic Church, a tradition which dates from the Middle Ages and accounts for the importance of religious problems to the French. Approximately 90% of the French population is formally baptized as Roman Catholic. There are some 800,000 Protestants and about 550,000 Jews, concentrated mainly in the large cities. The role of the Roman Catholic Church in France is, therefore, considerable. Prior to the French Revolution in 1789, the church, in addition to its religious functions, was responsible for keeping birth, marriage, and death certificates and for much education. It also exercised a significant economic influence through its financial assets. Although the church subsequently lost some of its functions, its varied institutions and associations enabled it to support its

spiritual efforts on the material level. There are five Roman Catholic universities, many colleges and primary schools, hospitals, homes for the poor and aged, newspapers, youth groups, and labor unions.

The history of France from the Middle Ages is a chronicle of the struggle of Kings and their ministers against the power of the church. In 1905 church and state were legally separated, and today the conflict, somewhat subdued, is limited to the field of primary and secondary education. A parallel conflict is that between faith and liberal thought —the great metaphysical drama of France. Thus this land produced Ste. Jeanne d'Arc, Ste. Thérèse de Lisieux, and St. Vincent de Paul as well as François Rabelais, Voltaire, and Denis Diderot.

Cultural Life. It is in the realm of culture that the greatness of France is generally acknowledged. Closely associated with the country's religious calling is its artistic and intellectual vocation. Art pervades French life and is a national attitude. The French, admiring particularly the example of classical antiquity, believe that their country and their life should be a work of art. There is a fundamental harmony in the great cathedrals of Chartres, Reims, Amiens, and Vézelay; in the châteaux and grounds of Versailles and of the Loire valley; and in such town squares as the beautiful Place Stanislas in Nancy. The history of French art has been dominated by the belief in the universality of art and by the search for beauty allied with truth; idealism must be accompanied by the highest technical skill. The artist is always also a craftsman. This is equally true of Nicolas Poussin in the 17th century; of the elegance of Jean Antoine Watteau in the 18th century; of the sometimes glacial perfection of Jean Auguste Ingres; of the impressionists like Claude Monet and Pierre Auguste Renoir; of the depth and density of Paul Cézanne, the father of contemporary art. Sculpture, too, has given France a great legacy in the stone, bronze, and clay works of Pierre Puget, Jean Antoine Houdon, Auguste Rodin, and Émile Bourdelle. (*See French Architecture; French Art.*)

It is sometimes said that music is not as highly developed in France as the other arts. Yet there has been a French musical tradition from the Gregorian chant and the chansons of the Middle Ages through François Couperin and Jean Baptiste Lully to Hector Berlioz, César

Franck, Georges Bizet, and Claude Debussy. (*See French Music.*)

The most significant form of artistic expression for the Frenchman is literature. In this field are united the artistic and intellectual vocations of France, the land of writers and philosophers. Of the dazzling procession of moralists and political writers, poets and novelists, only a few can be mentioned here. The prose of Rabelais and Michel de Montaigne in the 16th century was matched by the poetry of Pierre de Ronsard, whose chosen art form was to reach its heights with Arthur Rimbaud and Stéphane Mallarmé in the 19th century, and with Paul Claudel in the 20th century. The 17th century brought not only the philosophy of René Descartes and Blaise Pascal but also the great classical tragedies of Pierre Corneille and Jean Baptiste Racine, and the comedies of Molière. The Philosophes of the 18th century, in particular Montesquieu and Jean Jacques Rousseau, were followed a century later by Victor Hugo and others of the romantic school. Moral and political thought found its chief expression in the novel, from Honoré de Balzac and Stendhal to Gustave Flaubert and Émile Zola, and later to Marcel Proust and Albert Camus.

Since literature is a national affair it penetrates the press in all its forms; the most celebrated writers lend their talents to the major newspapers, which in turn devote important columns to the discussion of ideas and cultural problems of all kinds. The best-known French newspapers are *Le Monde*, *Le Figaro*, and *France-Soir*, all in Paris. There are numerous newspapers published throughout the provinces.

Education and Science. The outstanding position occupied by literature in France indicates the importance attached to education. Certainly any educational problem can violently excite French public opinion. All public education is secular and most of it is free, and official degrees and diplomas are granted by the state. The French government spends close to one fourth of its total public expenditure on education and is responsible for paying the salaries of the teachers and administrators of the public educational system, collectively known as the Université de France. Freedom of education enables private schools receiving state aid to exist alongside the public school system.

Schooling is compulsory between the ages of 6 and 16. The educational system includes noncompulsory preschool instruction for children aged 2 to 5, primary education for ages 6 to 11, secondary and technical education for pupils aged 11 to 18, and higher education, at a university or a specialized *grande école*, for those over 18. Secondary education consists of two cycles. At the age of 15, on completing the first, four-year cycle of study, the pupil is oriented toward the future course of study to which he seems best suited. At the completion of the second cycle he may, depending on his course of study, either take the *baccalauréat* in order to qualify for admission to the university, or receive some other nationally recognized degree.

The structure of the university was modified after the school reforms instituted in 1959 and again by a law of 1968, enacted in the wake of a student revolt. The first degree, the *licence*, is awarded after three years of study,

and the master's degree is gained after an additional year. The doctorate requires a minimum of three more years of study. The oldest French university is the University of Paris. Founded in 1253, its original college of arts and sciences, the Sorbonne, is world famous. The universities of Toulouse, Montpellier, Lille, and Grenoble are only slightly younger. A number of new universities, including those at Amiens, Nice, Orléans, and Rouen, were founded during the 1960's, raising the total number of French universities to 23. (See EDUCATION: *National Systems of Education.*)

In becoming the center of modern French scientific research, the university continues a tradition which goes back to the foundation of the Sorbonne and which after the French Revolution saw the creation of those unique French institutions, the *grandes écoles*, the best known of which are the École Polytechnique and the École Normale Supérieure.

The contribution of France to the progress of science and modern technology has been considerable. René Descartes discovered analytical geometry, and was followed by such outstanding figures as Antoine Laurent Lavoisier, the founder of modern chemistry; the physiologist Claude Bernard; and Louis Pasteur, who revolutionized medicine. The moral and social consequences of such scientific discoveries are a problem that occupies the minds of many modern scholars, philosophers, and writers in France.

Consult Ardagh, John, *The New French Revolution* (1969); Dupeux, Georges, *French Society 1789–1970*, tr. by Wait, Peter, (1976); Seignobos, Charles, *The Evolution of the French People* (1972); Thompson, I. B., *Modern France: Social and Economic Geography* (1971).

EDOUARD MOROT-SIR AND ROBERT BOUCHER

Breton women in traditional dress are the descendents of Celts, more closely allied in language and blood to the Welsh than to their neighbors in France.

Katherine Young

FRANCE

†Population of metropolitan area.
FRANCE: Total pop.—1975 prelim. census; metropolitan areas—1969 off. est.; other pops—1968 final census. **MONACO:** Total pop.—1968 final census.

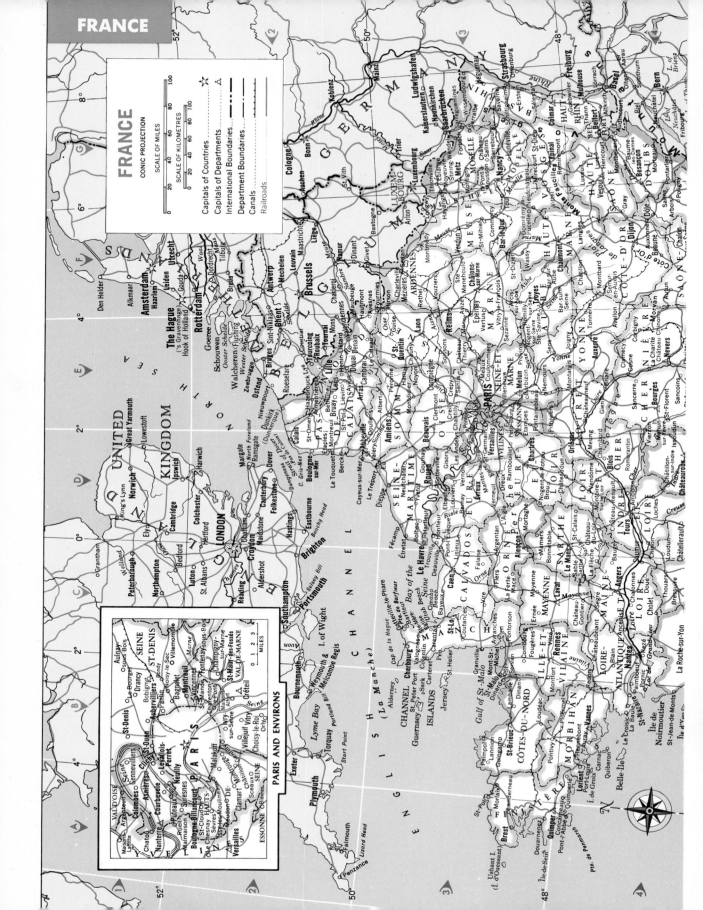

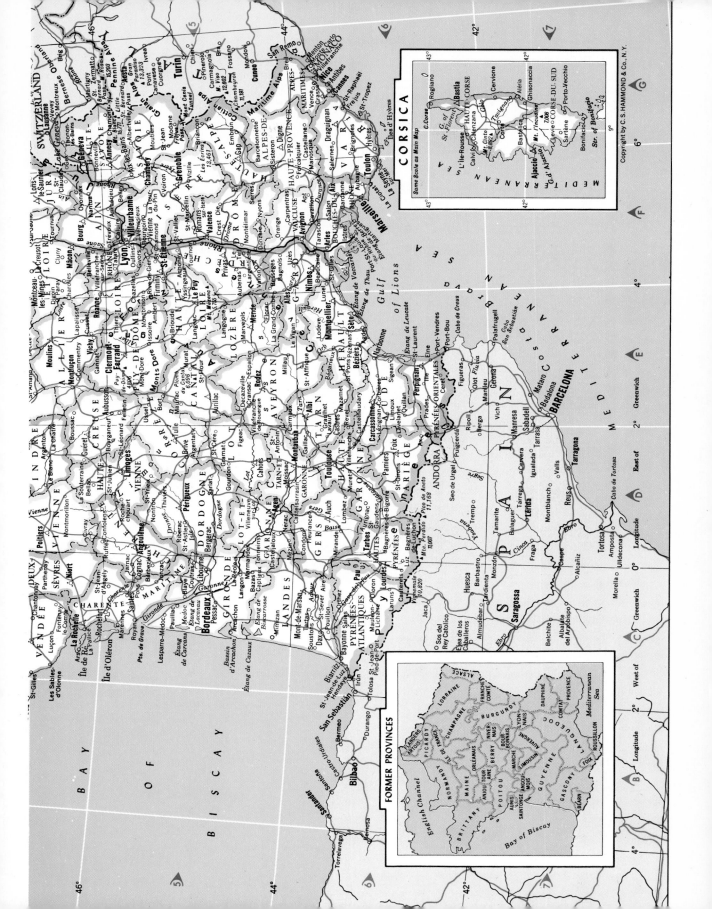

FRANCE: Map Index

Economy

France ranks among the most advanced industrial countries and has one of the world's highest per capita incomes. With only 96 persons to the square kilometer it is, compared to its neighbors, sparsely populated. Some 59% of the country is under cultivation, and agriculture retains considerable importance in the economy, including the export trade. In the mid-1970's agriculture still employed about 12% of the active population, compared with 39% in industry; the rapidly growing service sector accounted for most of the balance. France is the leading European producer of automobiles, and the rapid growth of the auto industry since World War II has been a key factor in business prosperity. Apart from hydroelectric power and some coal the country is short of energy sources and depends almost entirely on imports for petroleum and natural gas.

Regional Diversity. The highly concentrated urban population of the Paris region, of the industrial areas of the North and East, and around such centers as Lyons, Marseille, and Bordeaux contrasts with the vast amount of cultivated land, forest, woodland, and mountain making up rural France. Differences in climate and topography as well as the historical imprint of varied cultures—Germanic, Roman, and Celtic—promote considerable regional diversity despite the pressures of administrative centralization and the standardizing tendencies of modern industrial society.

The size of the agricultural sector ensures that France is self-sufficient in most of the basic food-stuffs except those requiring a tropical or semitropical climate. French wines are world famous for their quality, but a large quantity of ordinary table wine is produced and consumption per head is the highest in the world. The variety and quality of food products and varied regional cuisines provide the basis for France's gastronomic reputation. The traditional attention paid to the pleasures of life as well as the wealth of historic monuments, art treasures, and scenic and recreational attractions have made the country an international tourist center and contributed to foreign exchange earnings.

An assembly line in a Citröen factory. In the 1970's France was Europe's foremost producer of automobiles.

C.I.R.I.

Late Industrialization. Despite steady economic growth in the 19th and early 20th centuries, France was eclipsed by more powerful industrial rivals—first Britain, then Germany and the United States. Incomplete industrialization left intact a large peasantry as well as many small firms dependent on hand work. Population growth slowed almost to a standstill before 1914 and was hard hit by the heavy loss of life in the 1914–18 war. Although the destruction of that war, which fell heavily on some of the most advanced industrial districts, was repaired in the 1920's, no attempt was made to modernize the structure of the economy as a whole. The depression of the 1930's brought a sharp fall in production and no real recovery occurred before World War II. Economic stagnation contributed to France's rapid defeat by Nazi Germany in 1940. The northern half of the country was occupied and exploited for the German war effort, and occupation was extended to the whole country in November 1942.

Liberation of the country in 1944–45 resulted in considerable dislocation and serious damage to the transport system. Industry suffered from a long period of stagnation and a chronic shortage of raw materials. Food and consumer goods were scarce, and prices shot up. In the immediate postwar years the economy was sustained by foreign loans and aid. This aid was the starting point for recovery and a period of unprecedented economic growth.

Postwar Reconstruction. The shock of military defeat discredited prewar policies and those responsible for them. In government and business new men, less hidebound by tradition, came on the scene, desiring to restore France's greatness and overcome the effects of years of depression and decline. The postwar leaders felt that the state should play an interventionist role in economic life. They recognized the importance of modernizing the economy and building up the science-based industries. They were ready to learn new techniques of government and business management from the United States and other countries. A new government body, the *Commissariat Générale du Plan*, was set up under Jean Monnet in 1946 to initiate the reconversion and re-equipment of the economy. The first of a series of four- or five-year plans was launched.

After negotiating the first difficult postwar period, France's economy moved into a long phase of rapid growth and restructuring. This took place in a favorable international context: the restoration of world trade and renewed expansion. France's neighbors were undergoing a similar upsurge, and relations with them improved, as shown by the formation of the European Economic Community (the Common Market). By 1967–68 trade barriers between member countries had virtually disappeared and France's traditional protectionist policies had given way to liberalization.

From 1949, France experienced rapid but not altogether regular economic growth, with an annual average increase in net domestic product of about 5%. Basic to the growth was a high rate of investment, boosted by the support of the state and by foreign, particularly American, private capital. The inflow made possible a rapid expansion of science-based and mass production industries producing, especially, durable consumer goods, in which the

French market had been comparatively lacking before 1939. The plant and equipment in these industries incorporated highly productive technology in firms managed on modern lines. Labor productivity increased steadily, while the average workday and the number of hours worked per year were higher than prewar despite longer vacations. An upsurge in the birth rate occurred. Moreover, some 1,900,000 immigrant workers were absorbed into the work force, and about three quarters of a million French subjects were repatriated from Algeria after 1962.

Structural Reform. A major role in the transformation of the French economy from the mid-1950's was played by the "automobile sectoral complex"—the car industry itself together with petroleum, rubber, accessory, and servicing industries. The French took to four wheels as Americans had done 30 years earlier. Whereas fewer than 1,000,000 cars traveled French roads in 1954, some 13,500,000 were on the road by 1971.

Meanwhile a steady reduction of the labor force in agriculture was ongoing. Many of the small, inefficient peasant holdings disappeared. New, large farm units came into being. A substantial number of medium-sized farms remained, but for them the adjustment to market changes and price fluctuations was often burdensome and roused the peasants to anger. On the technical side, farm output grew enormously through increased use of fertilizers and a general adoption of the tractor and farm machinery.

Although France possesses a large, diversified industrial structure with some of the most modern plants in Europe, concentration has not gone as far as in some countries, and many small-scale firms remain. The old industrial areas based on coal and iron ore have declined. In their place new, high technology steel-making complexes have risen on the coast at Dunkirk and Fos (near Marseille) to take advantage of cheap, imported ores. The growth sectors in automobiles, engineering, chemicals, petroleum refining, electronics, and aerospace provide the basis for new industrial areas. The steel industry produces more than Britain but less than West Germany. France also has large deposits of bauxite and manufactures aluminum with hydro-electric power.

Capital Investment and Control. Much foreign capital went into building France's modern plant. The government tried to prevent foreign control of key firms when such control appeared contrary to the national interest, but it did finally permit the U.S.-owned General Electric Company to take over the only French-owned computer firm in 1964. The bulk of the automobile industry, however, remained under French control, and the largest firm, Renault, is state owned. The successful aerospace industry is partly under state control.

The state plays a prominent role in the economy through the ownership of key industries, holdings in others, and the operation of the economic plan. The government controls the Bank of France and some of the other banks, the main airline, and other transport facilities. Planning is of an "indicative" variety, the only kind possible where the main manufacturing industries are still privately owned and geared to market demand. The planners cannot tell the private firms what to invest, but can draw their representatives into discussion so that some coordination of intentions becomes possible. Public investment

O. J. Bottin—C.I.R.I.

Booming tourist development has transformed the Camargue from an estuarial bird sanctuary into a thriving resort.

and social expenditure can thus be taken into account, and the different investment plans of industries can be fitted together. The drawing up of the Plan by various joint consultation bodies operates as a kind of large-scale market research.

Government Planning. The aims and strategy of the Plan have varied over the years according to changes in the economic situation and the complexion of the government in power. Economic policy generally reflects current exigencies rather than Plan targets. Thus the Plan passed in July 1976 took into account rapid changes in economic prospects arising from a sharp rise in oil prices, continued inflationary pressure, and world recession. The plan aimed to increase exports while economizing on imports, especially of petroleum and raw materials, to di-

ECONOMIC RESOURCES OF FRANCE

Dairy products
Hogs
Potatoes
Poultry
Sugar beets
Wheat

Cattle and pasture
General farming
Wine

Aircraft
Al Aluminum
Automobiles
Cement
Chemicals
Machinery
Rubber
Steel
Textiles
Coal
Fe Iron ore
H·E Hydro-electric power
Petroleum and natural gas

versify sources of supply and build up stocks. Its target for growth was 5.5% per annum, and it envisaged the creation of new jobs to reduce the historically high level of unemployment, mainly by an expansion of the service sector.

Employment. France's industrial successes have depended to a large extent on the possession of a highly skilled labor force. The composition of that force has changed considerably under pressure of technological advance. Agriculture, mining, and other occupations based on manual labor have declined. Employment has fallen as well in older industries, such as textiles, clothing, and leather. Much unskilled factory and other work is done by immigrant workers, while French nationals have moved into more skilled jobs. The newer industries require a higher proportion of white collar workers than the old. The need for executive and supervisory grades has increased with changes in the business structure. Management techniques have been reshaped, mainly along American lines, stimulated since World War II by the presence of many branch plants of United States corporations. Merchandizing has witnessed an improvement in selling methods, extension of installment buying and increases of every type of advertising.

Traditional French entrepreneurship, much criticized in the past, has not entirely disappeared. A multitude of small and medium-size enterprises survives in some fields. Without doubt, however, the contemporary French business executive is a different sort from his counterpart of the 1930's. He conforms more closely to an international pattern. He is well paid, with an income more than six times that of the average worker. Income taxes are modest, and widespread evasion by professionals and the self-employed persists.

The expansion of the service sector, a marked feature of development in France, reflects rising incomes, changing tastes, and the high productivity of manufacturing and agriculture. Retail trading, notoriously inefficient and overmanned, has undergone extensive changes. While the small shopkeeper survives and every French town has numerous bars and cafes, competition from large concerns is increasing. Greater use of the automobile has seen a rapid rise of supermarkets with their vast parking lots. Most grocery stores have been converted to self-service.

Big stores in city centers have had to reorganize in the face of competition from suburban supermarkets and discount stores. Chain and department stores have gone into the supermarket business. Big shopping malls and multistory car parks have been built in city centers and in large housing complexes. While corner grocery stores have been closing, specialty shops, such as so-called "drugstores" and fashion shops, have sprung up to serve a clientele with more spending money, especially the young.

Problems. Rapid growth since the 1950's has left notable deficiencies and has not been accomplished without social costs. The housing shortage remains serious. Relaxation of wartime controls has caused increases in rentals, and new house prices are high. In the mid-1970's only 55% of French houses and flats had inside toilets, and only 48% had bathrooms. Although the new apartment blocks have modern facilities, many complaints are heard about their drabness and the psychological problems of living in them. Telephone facilities are similarly inadequate.

Growing affluence has enabled many French families to acquire a second residence. Emptied by migrations from the farm, some picturesque sites have been appropriated by affluent city dwellers seeking the calm of rural life— and often tennis courts and swimming pools. Whether such change gives declining areas the breath of life or hastens their decay depends on viewpoint. But indisputably part of the overhead of rapid modernization has been the destruction of old folkways and landscapes. Many Frenchmen now believe that more should be done to protect the environment, to save forests from destruction and preserve the scenic beauties and character of historic cities and villages.

Rapid economic growth and industrialization also have created social and political tensions. Expansion has entailed almost continuous inflation, benefitting some sectors of the population while harming others, often the defenseless or inarticulate. Many persons have had to migrate in search of jobs, often finding living conditions difficult. Educational facilities have lagged behind rapidly rising demand.

The 1970's saw the beginning of a new phase. International monetary confusion hurt the franc. Inflation raged. A fourfold increase in oil prices staggered a country dependent on imports. Recession in the other industrial countries damaged France's brilliant growth record. Investment fell; unemployment rose; government finances came under pressure; and in 1974 and 1976 balance of payments deficits appeared. Accordingly, a reassessment of economic prospects began.   Том Кемр

Government

The Structure of Government and the Constitution. France is a highly centralized unitary republic, divided into 94 metropolitan departments, the city of Paris, and four overseas departments. In each department a prefect, appointed by the minister of the interior, represents the national government and supervises departmental as well as local governmental affairs. The president of an elected general council functions as chief executive in each department. His powers, as well as those of mayors and municipal councils, are severely limited not only by restrictions on local right of taxation but also by the predominant role of the national administration.

The constitution of the French Fifth Republic was adopted on Sept. 28, 1958, by an overwhelming majority of French voters. In its preamble the constitution affirms its faithfulness to the principles of the French Revolution of 1789 and to the republican traditions that subsequently developed. The constitutional arrangements, however, mirror clearly the fact that the Fifth Republic came into being after the inefficiency of the preceding regime and the war in Algeria had brought Gen. Charles de Gaulle, the symbol of the Resistance in World War II, back to power as the first President. The new constitution, drafted according to De Gaulle's directives, reflects his views.

The apex of the new system is the president of the republic. Elected for seven years by direct popular vote (after the amendment of 1962), he has not only the traditional attributes of a head of state, but is also designated as guardian of the constitution. Thus he is empowered to arbitrate possible conflicts between different organs of the state and may submit bills of his choosing to a popular referendum. Although the constitution stipulates that the government, headed by a premier, shall determine and conduct the policy of the nation and shall have the administration and the armed forces at its disposal, in fact, political developments tended to make the president the sole source of all major decisions. This was true even before President de Gaulle used sweeping emergency powers following an attempted mutiny of French generals in Algeria. The constitution gives the president such powers, but states that the decision as to whether or not a crisis exists must be made in consultation with the constitutional council, the premier, and the president of the assemblies.

The constitution stipulates in great detail which matters are reserved for parliamentary legislation. On all other questions the cabinet legislates by ordinances. Moreover, parliament may authorize the government to take measures that are normally within the domain of parliament.

Parliament is composed of two chambers which share in the exercise of the limited lawmaking power vested in the legislature. The national assembly is elected for five years by direct suffrage. Senators, the members of the upper house, hold their seats for nine years, but one-third of them stand for election by an electoral college every three years. Like its predecessors, the Fifth Republic adheres to the rules of a parliamentary regime; government action requires the approval of a majority of the national assembly. But the rules governing the parliamentary right to censure the government tend to ensure the cabinet stability lacking in earlier regimes. The right of the president to dissolve parliament and to call for new elections contributes further to this stability.

An economic and social council, composed of appointed representatives of the major economic and cultural interests, advises both the executive and parliament on bills and problems of an economic or social character.

Under the constitution of 1958, France joined with those of its overseas territories which had accepted the constitution by referendum in the French Community, presided over and represented by the president of the French republic. An executive council, a community senate, and a court of arbitration are the organs of the French Community. All of the former French colonies in Africa, with the exception of Guinea, voted to join. The French Community retained its original form for only a little over a year, after which all of the former member states gradually obtained complete independence. Although their relationship to France and the community changed, they found it expedient to maintain some ties among themselves and to the French Republic.

Political Parties and Elections. Freedom of action is guaranteed by the constitution to all political parties which "respect the principles of national sovereignty and democracy." The traditional multiplicity of parties continued under the Fifth Republic. The electoral system, by which deputies to the national assembly are chosen by majority vote in single-member districts, usually after a runoff election, results in a marked disparity between the popular vote and the distribution of seats in parliament. In the early 1970's the Gaullist Union of Democrats for the Republic (UDR) was the strongest party numerically. The

Independent Republicans, a conservative breakaway group within the Gaullist coalition, showed increasing strength during those years. The Center for Democracy and Progress (CDP) joined the UDR and the Independent Republicans in a governing coalition. The political left is composed of the Communists, left-wing Radicals, and the Socialists, the latter corresponding to the social democratic parties in other European countries. Following a unity pact of 1972 the Communists and Socialists increased their support, winning a clear majority of the vote in the municipal elections of 1977.

Neither the UDR nor, with the exception of the extreme Left, any of the other French parties has the kind of national organization that is customary in other European democracies. When voting in parliament, only the UDR and the Communists abide by party discipline.

Legal System and Public Administration. The institution of judicial review of legislation is traditionally unknown in France. A constitutional council, an innovation of the constitution of 1958, may be consulted on the constitutionality of a law by the president, the premier, or the presidents of each of the two legislative houses. The council is not similar to a court of law; it functions mainly to delimit the respective spheres of parliament and the executive. It consists of nine members—three appointed by the president, three by the president of the national assembly, and three by the president of the senate—and former presidents of the Republic who serve ex officio.

French civil and criminal law is entirely codified. Prior to the Fourth Republic the ministry of justice was solely responsible for judicial appointments. The 1946 and 1958 constitutions provide for a high council of the judiciary, composed of government officials and members of parliament, which presents nominations for the highest judicial positions and advises on all others. For criminal as well as civil cases, the court of cassation in Paris is the supreme court of appeals.

Administrative law is very highly developed. The council of state, to which highly trained civil servants are permanently appointed by the government, interprets the rules of administrative law and advises the government on the legality of executive regulations, on administrative procedures, and frequently on the drafting of bills.

The French administrative apparatus is composed of different corps. Most prominent among them is the inspectorate of finance which, either directly or through the ministry of finance, controls the expenditures and the general management of many other governmental bureaus. The number of ministries is always large, but their organization varies from time to time.

With a few exceptions all taxes are levied nationally, with the government offering grants-in-aid to departments and municipalities. In comparison with other industrial nations, the French tax system is characterized by a high incidence of indirect, rather than direct, taxes.

Consult Blondel, Jean, and Godfrey, E. D., *Government of France* (4th ed., 1974); Duverger, Maurice, *The French Political System* (1975); Suleiman, E. N., *Politics, Power & Bureaucracy in France* (1974); Woodward, A. R., *French Economic Planning & Regional Development* (1977); Zysman, John, *Political Strategies for Industrial Order* (1977).

HENRY W. EHRMANN

Beneath the brooding gables of Quimper, Brittany, a narrow street leads to the Cathedral Saint-Corentin. The medieval overhangs derive from fortress design.

History

From Gaul to the Carolingians. The first major conquest of France was undertaken by the Gauls, Celtic invaders from the Danube Valley who penetrated to the Pyrenees in about the 6th century B.C. and subjugated earlier inhabitants, of whom little is known. The Gauls enjoyed no political unity, being divided into many half-savage tribes, and by 51 B.C. they had been conquered by the highly disciplined armies of Julius Caesar, despite a desperate and, for once, united stand under Vercingetorix in 52 B.C. Gaul remained Roman for five centuries, assimilating Roman culture and becoming a center of Roman civilization. Urban life developed, and a network of roads fanned out from Lyon. By the 4th century A.D., however, the disintegration of the Roman Empire had begun. The landed aristocracy evaded taxation and grew richer and more independent, while the small farmers became tenants; commerce and industry lagged. During the 5th century, in the wake of Visigoths and other invaders, the Germanic Franks were able to establish themselves along the lower Rhine and the Burgundians in the valleys of the Saône and the Rhône.

In 481 the Merovingian Dynasty was founded by the Frankish ruler Clovis, whose conversion to Christianity in 496 won him papal support against the Burgundians, who were completely merged with the Frankish empire in 613. Meanwhile, Clovis had defeated the Visigoths at Vouillé in 507, annexing much of southern France and establishing his capital at Paris. After the death of Clovis in 511, the Frankish empire was torn by the rivalry of his four sons, and was not reunited until 613. During the 7th century the mayors of the palace, or chief officers of the royal household, representing the aristocracy, emerged to take direction of government, and royal power went into serious decline. The family later known as the Carolingians

took hereditary control of the palace mayoralties, and under Charles Martel defeated the invading Muslims at Tours in 732. Charles's son, Pepin the Short, recognized as the first Carolingian King in 751, then went to the aid of the Papacy against the Lombards, who threatened to conquer all Italy. This Franco-Papal alliance reached a climax under Charlemagne, who was crowned Emperor in Rome in 800, an act which Constantinople regarded as a usurpation and which made definite the split between Eastern and Western Christianity. Charlemagne imposed Frankish rule upon the Lombards, Bavarians, and Saxons. If his Empire had become Roman in name, it was increasingly Franco-Germanic in fact. However, his son, Louis the Pious, was incompetent, and in 843 a family compact, the Treaty of Verdun, divided the Empire among Louis' three sons into three administrative units, which proved to be lasting national divisions. Lothair I, retaining the title Emperor, ruled Italy, Provence, and Burgundy. Louis the German kept the territories east of the Rhine, which became medieval Germany. And Charles (II) the Bald retained the western lands, which became medieval France. Royal power was by now very weak, and Northmen from Scandinavia were able to invade France, advancing up the rivers. The failure of Charles (III) the Fat to defend Paris against the Northmen in 886 doomed the Carolingian Dynasty, and in 911 the Northmen were granted the lower valley of the Seine as a fief. This Scandinavian colony, known as Normandy, quickly became French in speech and law. Meanwhile, the Carolingians were being challenged by the Counts of Paris for the throne, and in 987 Hugh Capet, a relative of the Count of Paris, was crowned and the new Capetian Dynasty founded.

Medieval France. The history of medieval France is the story of the monarchs' attempts to increase royal authority at the expense of the nobility, upon whom, however, they had to depend for military support. The crown was generally supported by the Church, which continually sought political unity within the Roman Empire. But as royal powers gradually increased, a second rivalry arose, since the Church resisted royal encroachment upon spiritual power. Finally, the revival of trade after 1100, and the rapid growth of towns, added new political and economic dimensions to the French scene.

The most serious threat to the Capetians arose from the successful invasion of England by William, Duke of Normandy, in 1066, and the subsequent conquest of Normandy itself in 1135 by Geoffrey, Count of Anjou, Maine, and Touraine, who had married Matilda, daughter of the English King, Henry I. A further setback occurred in 1152, when Eleanor, heiress of the Duke of Aquitaine and divorced wife of Louis VII, married the Duke of Normandy, thus putting him in possession of the western half of France. Two years later he became Henry II of England. The French crown was saved by the accession in 1180 of Philip II, a vigorous King who took advantage of internal difficulties in England to consolidate royal power in France. By 1214 the English were driven from nearly all their French lands, and under (St.) Louis IX, whose administration of justice and piety made him the ideal medieval King, the realm was further enlarged.

In 1243 a number of rebellious nobles were forced to recognize the King's authority. Political gains were accompanied by cultural progress in the 12th and 13th centuries: Gothic architecture reached its zenith, the University of Paris was chartered, and the French capital became the philosophical center of Europe. However, Pope Boniface VIII caused a surge of anticlerical feeling when, in 1296, he forbade secular governments to tax their clergy. Philip IV's financial retaliation against the Papacy brought a great defeat for spiritual power, while the Estates General was summoned by the King for the first time in 1302 to gain national support.

The Hundred Years' War. In the 14th century, that series of wars known as the Hundred Years' War threatened the recent gains of the French monarchy. A number of preliminary disagreements between England and France were followed in 1340 by Edward III of England proclaiming himself King of France. His claim to the throne through his mother, valid according to English law, had been nullified in France by the so-called Salic Law of 1322, which permitted the crown to pass only through the male line. Philip VI immediately deprived Edward of his French lands, notably Guienne, but suffered a heavy defeat at Crécy in 1346. Calais was taken the following year, and military disaster was compounded by the appearance in 1348 of the epidemic known as the Black Death, which drastically reduced the population and precipitated an economic and financial crisis.

The capture of John II at Poitiers in 1356 seemed to be the end of the French monarchy, but the Estates General, which had won control of the national revenue, proved unequal to the task of governing without a King. The accession of Charles V in 1364 brought a temporary recovery. He reformed the royal finances and the military establishment, and found an able commander in Bertrand Du Guesclin. By 1380 the English held only a few Atlantic and Channel ports. However, Charles VI was weak, and the Dukes of Burgundy, now allied with England, were increasingly strong. In 1415 Henry V of England defeated the French at Agincourt, and in 1428 the English began the siege of Orléans.

At this critical moment, however, the celebrated Jeanne d'Arc emerged to save the French monarchy. Allowed to lead an army to the relief of Orléans, she won a victory that proved to be the turning point in the struggle, and which imbued the French with new vigor. Their military revival led the Burgundians to make a separate peace in 1435, but further campaigns were necessary to expel the English from Normandy and Guienne. It then fell to Louis XI to smash the power of Burgundy; in 1477 he defeated the Burgundians at Nancy and annexed the duchy. France

was saved, and the power of the monarchy can be measured by the fact that Louis XI called the Estates General only once. Charles VIII, who succeeded Louis, acquired Brittany through his marriage to Anne, heiress of the duchy.

The Italian and Religious Wars. With the consolidation of their realm by the end of the 15th century, the Kings of France launched themselves into Italian affairs, taking advantage of Italian disunity to pursue claims to Naples and Milan. These Italian campaigns served to disturb the equanimity of the Habsburgs of Austria, whose territories surrounded France by 1519; they also hastened the introduction of Italian Renaissance culture into France. Meanwhile, in 1516, Francis I had concluded with the Papacy the favorable Concordat of Bologna, which gave him the right to nominate French bishops. A redivision of Habsburg lands in 1556 lessened the danger to France, and peace was finally concluded at Cateau-Cambrésis in 1559. Save for Calais, which was taken from the English in 1558, France won no territorial gains.

The second half of the 16th century saw the French involved in religious wars that had serious political implications. The French Calvinists, or Huguenots, were increasingly persecuted under Henry II, who favored religious orthodoxy in the interest of national unity. Henry's untimely death left the throne in weak hands, and the subsequent aristocratic reaction enabled the Huguenots to organize themselves under the leadership of the Bourbon Princes of Navarre, Protestant descendants of Louis IX. Francis II, little more than a child at his accession in 1559, was dominated by his mother, Catherine de Médicis. Striving to maintain royal authority, the Queen Mother played off one faction against another, sometimes supporting the Huguenots, and sometimes such ultra-Catholics as the powerful noble family of the Guises. Catherine remained dominant during the reign of her second son, Charles IX, and was still powerful in the time of her third son, Henry III.

A series of civil wars were fought between 1562 and the end of Henry's reign in 1589, the most infamous incident being the massacre of St. Bartholomew's Day (Aug. 24) in 1572, in which many Huguenot leaders were slaughtered. Since all Catherine's sons were childless, the crown passed in 1589 to Henry of Bourbon (King of Navarre), despite a last desperate attempt by the Guises to prevent this Protestant victory by intriguing with Philip II of Spain. As Henry IV, the new King broke the back of factionalism when, in 1593, he became a Roman Catholic. This shocked the Huguenots, but demonstrated Henry's recognition

The medieval fortified city of Carcassonne was magnificently restored by Viollet-le-Duc in the 19th century.

World Films Enterprise

that Catholicism was the religion of the vast majority of Frenchmen. By the Edict of Nantes (1598), however, he gave Protestants equal political rights with Catholics, and the right to fortify specified cities. One of the most popular French Kings, Henry IV restored a strong monarchy and gave the country peace.

Le Grand Siècle. In the 17th century the French crown reached its apex of absolute power. Louis XIII, while not a strong King, employed men whose aim was to centralize the nation. After the long disorders of the previous century, the people generally supported the royal policy, preferring absolutism to aristocratic anarchy. The powerful Cardinal Armand du Plessis, Duke of Richelieu, was noted for his harsh measures against the nobles who resisted this centralizing policy. He also destroyed the political power of the Huguenots, because he would not tolerate a state within the state; his foreign policy involved France in the Thirty Years' War against the Habsburgs. Richelieu, who must be considered the chief architect of French power in the 17th century, prepared the ground for Louis XIV.

As Louis XIV was only five at his accession in 1643, power was exercised by Cardinal Mazarin until his death in 1661. Under the Peace of Westphalia in 1648, after the Thirty Years' War, Mazarin gained for France the bishoprics of Metz, Toul, and Verdun, and the province of Alsace, excluding Strasbourg. However, increased taxation, necessary to complete the war, was made odious by the corruption in Mazarin's regime, and helped to bring on the last armed opposition to absolutist government, a confused revolution known as the *Fronde*. An attempt by the Parlement of Paris to establish a financial check upon the monarchy was followed by demands by the nobility for concessions from the crown. The possibility of a revival of anarchy frightened the middle classes and gave Mazarin the final victory. The *Fronde* made a deep impression upon the young King, contributing to his determination to tame the nobility.

Louis XIV inherited from Mazarin a staff of able administrators, notably Jean Baptiste Colbert, Controller General of Finance, and François de Louvois, Minister of War, and such outstanding generals as Henri, Vicomte de Turenne, the Prince de Condé, and Sebastien, Marquis de Vauban. Royal policy was concentrated upon the maintenance of domestic tranquillity through a rigid control of all political and religious opposition and upon the search for natural frontiers to offset Habsburg preponderance in Central Europe and Spain. In the process, the King made himself and France—he did not always distinguish between the two—both admired and feared. He established France as the center of European culture, his palace at Versailles being the architectural symbol of pomposity and pride. But his military power and his wars quickly revealed to the other European powers the need to unite against him. Thus, while the French won impressive victories during the latter half of the 17th century, territorial annexations were relatively small and the wars brought about the gradual impoverishment of the nation. At the Treaty of Nijmegen in 1678, Louis reached the height of his power. But by 1701 his intrigues for the partition of the Spanish Empire had led him into the War of the Spanish Succession. Aside from establishing the Bourbons on the Spanish throne, France gained nothing from the war, whereas the

English victory laid the ground for further successes against France in the 18th century and undermined the prestige of French absolutism.

The 18th Century. Louis XV was a minor at his accession in 1715, and a regency was established under the Duke of Orléans until 1723. Orléans made a futile attempt to restore nobles to high positions in government, which convinced the King of the necessity of continuing the absolutist policies of his great-grandfather. An honest attempt to solve the national debt was made by Orléans, but this resulted in a ruinous financial crash in 1720. Criticism of the monarchy subsequently increased, a more rational government being demanded in the name of "science and reason." The intelligentsia also criticized the government for its close alliance with the Church. Charles de Montesquieu, Voltaire, and the Encyclopedists led by Denis Diderot were most influential critics, despite official censorship.

During the 18th century the government gradually sank into deeper debt, being either unwilling or unable to reform the constitution to make efficient government possible. Even the military establishment was allowed to deteriorate, so that as a result of the critical Seven Years' War (1756–63), the French lost most of their colonial empire to the English. The decline continued under Louis XVI. The intervention in the American Revolution against Britain was doubly disastrous, for the expenses incurred were the final blow to the royal finances, and the American success inspired French reformers.

The Revolution. The Estates General had not been called since 1614, and the royal decision to summon that body in 1789 was a sure indication that absolutism had failed. While it is true that a century of criticism had bred a spirit of revolution, and that the country's long development had made France a patchwork of irregular administrative practices and anachronistic social and economic conditions, the fact is that a revolution started only when the government of the most prosperous country in Europe had become bankrupt. When the King asked the three estates—nobility, clergy, and commoners—to prepare their

HISTORICAL REGIONS OF FRANCE

lists of grievances for the convening of the Estates General, an enormous backlog of business became focused.

The estates were unanimous on one point: that France should henceforth be governed under a constitution that would limit the monarchy. After disagreeing over whether the three estates should sit separately or together in one hall, the commoners, on June 17, 1789, declared themselves to be the National Assembly and invited the first two estates to join. Though he disapproved this action, the King ultimately gave way, allowing the French Revolution to move a step to the left. Rumors that the King intended to dissolve the Assembly led to the raising of a National Guard. To obtain arms, a mob stormed the Bastille in Paris on July 14. This recourse to violence intimidated the King and set a precedent for settling constitutional deadlocks. Almost at once, some aristocrats began emigrating.

In its first momentous constitutional decisions the National Constituent Assembly, as it was now called, abolished titles, as well as feudal rights and privileges, those vestiges of the Middle Ages which had been cherished by the first two estates. There followed the Declaration of the Rights of Man, a statement of equality before the law for all men. When Louis hesitated to accept a suspensive, rather than an absolute royal, veto on legislation, he was removed from Versailles to Paris, where he was more subject to pressure. The seizure of ecclesiastical property forced the Papacy to condemn the Revolution and made it an international issue.

France was now a limited monarchy, but the new Legislative Assembly contained a large group of deputies who no longer had faith in Louis XVI and wanted a republic. The republican movement grew out of literary-political clubs, notably the Jacobins and the Cordeliers, which had existed since 1789. In 1791 Louis was suspended by the Constituent Assembly. The republican cause was enhanced by the Declaration of Pillnitz of 1791 in which the sovereigns of Prussia and Austria called for the return of Louis XVI to the French throne. This was widely interpreted in France as interference by the European powers in the Revolution. In September Louis swore to uphold the revised constitution. On Apr. 20, 1792, France declared war on Austria, but early defeats intensified the struggle within France between the Girondists, who wished to carry the ideals of the Revolution beyond the frontiers of France, and the Jacobins, whose leadership came from Paris. A National Convention was formed, and the Revolution entered its most radical phase. A republic was proclaimed, the monarchy was abolished, and Louis XVI, declared guilty of treason, was executed on Jan. 21, 1793.

The Jacobins, led by Georges Jacques Danton, Maximilien de Robespierre, Louis de Saint-Just, and Lazare Carnot, now exercised a dictatorship. Foreign invasion threatened from all sides, the Jacobins responded with emergency legislation, and the Reign of Terror began. Finally Robespierre himself was caught in the tide, and with his fall, the Revolution began its shift to the right. The Convention came to be dominated by moderate republicans, and in 1795 a new constitution was adopted, which placed executive power in a directory of five. The Directory, lasting for four years, seems the most confused period of the Revolution. Its leaders were usually self-seekers dedicated to maintaining themselves in office rather than pursuing political ideals, and the period is full of coups and countercoups, with the inevitable rise of military leaders.

Napoleon. In this way, Gen. Napoleon Bonaparte came to the fore, first as a defender of the government against riots, and later, in 1796, as the victorious commander in Italy against the Austrians. The political uncertainty was finally resolved by the coup of Nov. 9, 1799 (18th Brumaire), in which Napoleon overthrew the Directory and established the Consulate, with himself as First Consul. A new constitution provided a tricameral legislature, but in reality a military dictatorship had been founded.

Although Napoleon is best known for his military abilities, which enabled him to conquer much of Europe and maintain himself in power for 15 years, he should also be remembered as an administrator who established an efficient regime, many aspects of which survive in modern France. In fact, the Revolution and Napoleon completed the political centralization of France, the traditional role of the monarchy. Prefects appointed in each department were directly responsible to Paris, and a new tax system and a state-controlled system of public education were introduced. Relations with the Papacy were resumed by the Concordat of 1801, the government retaining the right to nominate Bishops and pay the clergy.

In 1802 Napoleon created a new order of knighthood, the Legion of Honor; and, after a national plebiscite, became First Consul for life. This was merely a step toward the restoration of the monarchy, which he accomplished in 1804. His action in crowning himself Emperor was again sanctioned by plebiscite, the traditional monarchical forms thus merging with the democratic principles of the Revolution. Through his conquests, Napoleon did much to launch the unification of Germany and Italy, for his destruction of the Holy Roman Empire in 1806 was followed by the creation of the Confederation of the Rhine, by which many small German states lost separate identity.

Napoleon reached the peak of his power in 1808. By then only Great Britain remained in the war against him, the Continental system inaugurated in 1806 having failed in its purpose to stop British goods reaching the Continent. Napoleon's decision to occupy Spain in 1808 proved to be a turning point. The Spanish were provoked into a general uprising, the French were unsuccessful against guerrilla warfare, and Napoleon's Continental enemies revived. The decision to invade Russia in 1812 suggests the deterioration both of Napoleon's position and his military judgment, and the winter retreat from Moscow became a disaster. Napoleon was never more brilliant, however, than in his defense of France in 1813 and 1814, but on Mar. 31, 1814, the Allies entered Paris. Napoleon abdicated on Apr. 11, the Allies granting him the title Emperor of Elba. The Bourbon monarchy was restored in the person of Louis XVIII, but a new constitution, the Charter of 1814, was unpopular with most political elements in France, and Napoleon was able to stage a return to power —the Hundred Days—in 1815. The Allies quickly united, and Napoleon was finally crushed at Waterloo and banished to the Island of St. Helena.

The Restoration and the July Monarchy. France has never ceased pulsating from the revolutionary upheaval.

Virtually every political party can trace its social philosophy to some period between 1789 and 1814. And the fact that France, in the course of a century and a half after 1815, had two monarchies, one empire, and four republics, suggests that even the form of its government is a lasting issue. The adjustment of legislative to executive power was especially difficult and often resulted in one branch of government seeking to overwhelm another, rather than striving for a proper division of powers. Louis XVIII, for instance, honestly attempted to govern constitutionally, but was plagued by disloyal elements in the Chamber. By 1820 the King was forced to seek an alliance with the extreme right-wing Ultras, or Absolutists. The political power of the large landowners was therefore considerably increased, guaranteeing the success of reactionary bills. Charles X, who was leader of the Ultras before his accession in 1824, even introduced laws restricting personal liberty and the freedom of the press. But when it became apparent that Charles really intended the establishment of personal rule, many members of Parliament, however reactionary, became alarmed. Further angered by the King's appointment of the Prince of Polignac as chief minister in 1829, they were little impressed by the successful conquest of Algeria a year later. Finally, on July 26, 1830, Charles issued royal ordinances designed to give himself absolute control of the government. The July Revolution, led by Adolphe Thiers, together with liberal monarchists and republicans, immediately broke out in Paris. Charles fled to Britain, and the liberal Duke of Orléans was elected constitutional monarch as Louis Philippe.

However, the July Monarchy, lasting 18 years, followed the pattern of the Restoration. Louis Philippe had by now lost much of his earlier radicalism, and pursued a policy of *laissez-faire*, which guaranteed low wages and wretched industrial conditions for the working classes. Labor agitation was met with force, notably the insurrections of 1834 in Paris and Lyon. Repressive laws in 1835 drove the opposition underground and gave impetus to the rising tide of socialism, especially that of Louis Blanc. Parliamentary majorities were maintained through electoral manipulation and corruption, giving parties hostile to the regime ample grounds to demand reforms. In 1846 a serious depression caused widespread misery and created revolutionary sentiments among the masses, who were mobilized by those who sought true parliamentary government. An insurrection in Paris on Feb. 22, 1848, led to the abdication of Louis Philippe and the establishment of the short-lived Second Republic (1848–52).

The Second Republic. The pattern of drift from liberalism toward conservatism was now repeated. The moderate republicans, led by Alphonse de Lamartine, recognized the conservative temper of the country and resisted the establishment of the socialist republic favored by the radical republicans, who were led by the socialist Louis Blanc. For a brief period the moderates appeased the radicals by establishing national workshops, which provided employment at government expense. But when elections for the constituent Assembly showed the antisocialist views of the nation, Blanc was dropped from the government and the workshops curtailed. This led to the Parisian insurrection known as the June Days (1848). These events contributed to the election of Louis Napoleon Bonaparte, the man of "Order," as the first President of the Second Republic.

This was, however, doomed from its start because of the substantial majority of royalists in Parliament. The Falloux Law of 1850, an education bill extending Roman Catholic influence in the public schools, was but one of many signs of reaction. When the Assembly refused to amend the constitution to allow the President to extend his term of office, Louis Napoleon engineered the *coup d'état* of Dec. 2, 1851, and dissolved the Assembly, a move overwhelmingly sanctioned by the French in a plebiscite. A year later, having already sharply reduced the legislative check upon the executive, Louis Napoleon became Emperor as Napoleon III, and was again approved by plebiscite.

The Second Empire. The Second Empire (1852–70) reversed the established political pattern by beginning as a dictatorship and ending as a parliamentary monarchy. Between 1852 and 1860 the authoritarian regime emphasized material progress, encouraging industrialization, building railways, and undertaking the controversial rebuilding of Paris as a modern, healthful city, the Emperor's personal project, directed by Baron Georges Haussmann. The successful but unpopular Crimean and Italian wars enhanced French prestige while revealing that Napoleon III favored national self-determination. After 1860, however, when parliamentary powers were legally increased, imperial prestige waned, and was further harmed by repeated defeats in foreign policy, the intervention in Mexico being the most notorious. Then, in 1867, the Prussian Chancellor, Otto von Bismarck, humiliated Napoleon III by frustrating his attempt to purchase Luxembourg and following this in 1870 by provoking a war over the Hohenzollern candidacy for the Spanish throne. The disastrous Franco-Prussian War gave the republicans a pretext for overthrowing a regime that nevertheless still enjoyed considerable popularity. The capture of Napoleon III, followed by a revolution in Paris on Sept. 4, 1870, came only a few months after the regime had apparently won a long lease on life by establishing a limited monarchy under the direction of the liberal Émile Ollivier.

The months immediately following the downfall of the Second Empire were among the most agonizing in French history. An emergency Government of National Defense was organized by the Parisian republicans to continue the hopeless war against Prussia, but soon Paris surrendered. The elections held under the armistice granted by Bismarck resulted in an overwhelmingly conservative vote, meaning that France was ready for even a harsh peace; and under the Treaty of Frankfurt in 1871 the country lost Alsace and part of Lorraine, as well as paying a heavy indemnity. The Parisians, outraged by the treaty, burst into insurrection, defying the new National Assembly and rallying to the municipal government of Paris, the Commune. Adolphe Thiers, who headed the national government, reduced the insurrection; but fighting was fierce, and a residue of bitterness divided radical Paris from the remainder of France for many years. Furthermore, the split within republican ranks, already evident in 1848, now became deeper, and made a monarchical restoration a possibility. Had the Legitimists and the Orléanists been able to agree on whether they would reign under the Tricolor or under the Bourbon lilies, the Count of Chambord might have become Henry V.

RULERS OF FRANCE

Merovingian Kings

Clovis to Childeric III	481–751

Carolingian Dynasty

Pepin the Short	751–68
Charlemagne or Charles the Great	768–814
Louis (I) the Pious	814–40
Charles the Bald	840–77
Louis II	877–79
Louis III } joint rulers	879–82
Carloman } joint rulers	879–84
Charles the Fat	884–87
Eudes or Odo, Count of Paris (of the Capetian Line)	888–98
Charles the Simple	893–923
Robert I (of the Capetian Line)	922–23
Raoul or Rudolf, Duke of Burgundy	923–36
Louis IV	936–54
Lothair	954–86
Louis V	986–87

Capetian Dynasty

Hugh Capet	987–96
Robert II	996–1031
Henry I	1031–60
Philip I	1060–1108
Louis VI	1108–37
Louis VII	1137–80
Philip II or Philip Augustus	1180–1223
Louis VIII	1223–26
Louis IX or St. Louis	1226–70
Philip III or Philip the Bold	1270–85
Philip IV or Philip the Fair	1285–1314
Louis X	1314–16
John I	1316
Philip V or Philip the Tall	1317–22
Charles IV	1322–28

House of Valois

Philip VI	1328–50
John II	1350–64
Charles V	1364–80
Charles VI	1380–1422
Charles VII	1422–61
Louis XI	1461–83
Charles VIII	1483–98
Louis XII	1498–1515
Francis I	1515–47
Henry II	1547–59
Francis II	1559–60
Charles IX	1560–74
Henry III	1574–89

House of Bourbon

Henry IV	1589–1610
Louis XIII	1610–43
Louis XIV	1643–1715
Louis XV	1715–74
Louis XVI	1774–92
Louis XVII (titular ruler only)	1793–95

The First Republic

National Convention	1792–95
The Directory	1795–99

The Consulate

	1799–1804

The First Empire

Napoleon I	1804–14; 1815

The Bourbon Restoration

Louis XVIII	1814–24
Charles X	1824–30

House of Orleans

Louis Philippe	1830–48

The Second Republic

Louis Napoleon, President	1848–52

The Second Empire

Napoleon III (Louis Napoleon)	1852–70

The Third Republic (Presidents)

Louis Adolphe Thiers	1871–73
Patrice de MacMahon	1873–79
Jules Grévy	1879–87
Sadi Carnot	1887–94
Jean Casimir-Périer	1894–95
Félix Faure	1895–99
Émile Loubet	1899–1906
Armand Fallières	1906–13
Raymond Poincaré	1913–20
Paul Deschanel	1920
Alexandre Millerand	1920–24
Gaston Doumergue	1924–31
Paul Doumer	1931–32
Albert Lebrun	1932–40

Vichy Government

Henri Philippe Pétain, Chief of the State	1940–44
Pierre Laval, Chief of Government	1942–44

Heads of the Provisional Government

Charles de Gaulle	1944–46
Felix Gouin	1946
Georges Bidault	1946
Léon Blum	1946–47

The Fourth Republic (Presidents)

Vincent Auriol	1947–54
René Coty	1954–58

The Fifth Republic (Presidents)

Charles de Gaulle	1959–69
Georges Pompidou	1969–74
Valery Giscard d'Estaing	1974–

The Third Republic. Between 1875, the date of the Third Republic's constitution, and 1900, the republic suffered numerous crises, in which the enemies of moderate republicanism combined to threaten its existence. In 1877 President MacMahon, an avowed royalist, dismissed a Premier who had the Chamber's confidence, but he was forced to resign two years later. The next challenge came from the Minister of War, Gen. Georges Boulanger. Originally sponsored by radical republicans anxious to force through democratic reforms, Boulanger, by 1886, had been adopted by the monarchists, who hoped for a restoration. The movement collapsed in 1889 when the radicals realized the danger and withdrew their support. More celebrated and more complicated was the Dreyfus Affair, which began in 1894 as a simple espionage case, but became a matter of injustice, finally dividing France into two camps eager to make political capital out of the affair. The reversal of the decision against Dreyfus in 1906 constituted a victory for republicanism and a defeat for those conservatives, monarchists, and nationalists who generally supported the army in the interest of national strength.

Colonialism was another issue dividing the republicans, for the moderates favored the recovery of a colonial empire as the economic basis for revenge against Germany, while the radicals opposed colonialism in principle, accusing the moderates of ignoring the proper goal, Alsace-Lorraine. A protectorate was established over Tunis in 1881, and at the end of the century France was securing British and Italian backing for French penetration of Morocco. France had already emerged from isolation in 1894 through the Dual Alliance with Russia, a marriage of convenience reached out of common fear of Germany; in 1904 the Entente Cordiale was concluded with Great Britain, and France's international position was further strengthened by weaning Italy away from the Triple Alliance with Germany and Austria.

World War I and Its Aftermath. When World War I broke out in 1914, the republic proved that it could provide great leadership and command the backing of the French. By 1917, however, after suffering great casualties and the long occupation of its industrial areas, France was clearly weakening. In that year of discouragement, Georges Clemenceau, who became both Prime Minister and Minister of War, ruthlessly organized the country's remaining resources for resistance. But when victory came in 1918, France had stood too long as the main barrier to German expansion, and the cost in blood and treasure left it little better off than a defeated nation. Great disenchantment followed upon the refusal of the United States to participate in the League of Nations and the realization that the United States appeared considerably more lenient on the question of German reparations than on the problem of the Inter-Allied war debt. Thus, French material recovery seemed jeopardized, and its security inadequately guaranteed; when, in the 1920's and 1930's, most European states degenerated into dictatorships, there were many in France who questioned the future of French democracy.

In fact, however, this pessimism was chiefly due to a collapse of morale. Since much of the material damage to France occurred in its most heavily populated and industrialized areas, the actual job of reconstruction represented a remarkable economic achievement. After the financial reforms of Premier Raymond Poincaré in 1926, France began enjoying real prosperity under sound government, and was virtually the last European country to feel the effects of the world-wide depression of the 1930's. In the aftermath of that economic collapse, however, the parliamentary system was endangered by the failure of the multiparty political structure to produce coalitions which could tackle the country's social and economic problems. The growth of communism on the left contrasted with neoroyalist and fascistic parties, such as the Action Française and the Croix de Feu, on the extreme right. The elections of 1932 brought the leftist parties to power, but their inability to co-operate brought a reaction in 1934, and a series of emergency cabinets containing men such as Pierre Laval, who were later suspiciously inactive in the face of Mussolini's and Hitler's aggressive activities. The national divisions deepened after the elections of 1936, which produced a leftist coalition government called the Popular Front, under the Socialist Léon Blum. He was not adequately supported by his Communist colleagues. His antifascist measures won him much criticism from the right; antirepublicanism and defeatism grew apace.

World War II and the Fourth Republic. War came in 1939, after many French attempts to avoid it through appeasement of the fascist dictators. Although much money had been spent on armaments, the French were only prepared to fight a defensive war. The Germans drove through the incomplete northern defenses in 1940, the vast French army was immobilized in a matter of weeks, and the Third Republic collapsed. Marshal Henri Philippe Pétain headed a new government, which signed an armistice on June 22, 1940, and established a new capital at Vichy. Gen. Charles de Gaulle refused to accept the armistice and formed a National Committee in London pledged to fight on. At Vichy, Pétain and Pierre Laval formed an authoritarian regime as puppets of Germany under the armistice terms.

After the liberation of Paris in 1944, De Gaulle established a provisional government which introduced nationalization of much basic industry and credit to hasten national recovery. When it became apparent that the newly elected constituent assembly was bent on establishing a republic with weak executive power, De Gaulle resigned. The Fourth Republic (1946–58) was not enthusiastically accepted, for it recalled the parliamentary chaos of the 1930's. The period saw a remarkable economic regeneration, but no political reorganization took place.

Lack of responsible leadership was most clearly felt in the conduct of foreign affairs. The army, having fought well in Indochina and North Africa, felt itself betrayed by politicians as France slowly abandoned its overseas territories. By 1958 many feared that Algeria, too, where civil war had been raging since 1954, would eventually be surrendered. A group of officers seized power in Algeria by a *coup d'état* in May, 1958, and called upon Gen. de Gaulle to re-establish political responsibility in Paris. The Assembly gave way, and empowered De Gaulle to prepare a constitution for the Fifth Republic.

The Fifth Republic. The new constitution, overwhelmingly ratified, increased executive power at the expense of Parliament, making De Gaulle, as President, closer to

Strasbourg, historically more German than French, was seized by Louis XIV in 1681.

World Films Enterprise

Napoleon III in power than any executive since 1870. De Gaulle immediately announced that he would support self-determination for Algeria. Rightists, in both France and Algeria felt betrayed, and their plots to overthrow De Gaulle culminated in a military insurrection in Algeria in 1961. The mutiny was quickly crushed, but fighting in Algeria continued for a year. Algeria was finally proclaimed independent on July 3, 1962.

De Gaulle also made overtures to the West German government for an end to Franco-German enmity, and the co-operation between the two countries gave Western Europe a significant voice in the power struggle between East and West. Some of De Gaulle's European partners, however, felt that his determination to make France a major power, evidenced by his decision to create an independent French nuclear force and by his repeated veto of Britain's bid to join the Common Market, ruled out the concept of a greater Europe. He caused further consternation in some quarters when he established diplomatic relations with Communist China in 1964 and, after his re-election in 1965, barred NATO from French soil. De Gaulle governed with supreme aplomb until April 28, 1969, when, having lost a referendum on proposed constitutional changes, he resigned. Georges Pompidou, a former Premier under De Gaulle, was elected to succeed him.

While adhering to Gaullist views, Pompidou showed much more flexibility than his predecessor. Thus, in 1971, France agreed to terms for Britain's entry into the Common Market. It was evident, however, that the Gaullist era was waning, and with Pompidou's death on April 2, 1974, it ended. A conservative, Valéry Giscard d'Estaing, was then elected President.

Consult Aron, Raymond, *France, the New Republic* (1960); Brogan, D. W., *The French Nation, 1814–1940* (repr., 1970); Guerard, Albert, *France; A Modern History* (rev. ed., 1969); Lewis, W. H., *The Splendid Century* (repr., 1971); Stewart, J. H., *A Documentary Survey of the French Revolution* (1951). ROGER L. WILLIAMS

FRENCH ARCHITECTURE

The architects of France began in the 11th century to develop a distinctive national style of architecture. It was first realized in Romanesque churches, in which vaulting in massive stone was gradually mastered. The semicircular arch and its derived forms of groined and tunnel vault served as essential elements both of structure and design. The Romanesque style gave rise to a rich variety of provincial modes, each typical of its own area. Provençal builders clung to ancient Roman and Byzantine models and those of Périgord. However, the Burgundian and, especially the Norman, architects were bolder and more progressive. Their vaults became more lofty, their structure more daring until there appeared in the famous Norman abbeys at Caen a massive form of rib vaulting that foreshadowed Gothic architecture.

Originating in the Île-de-France with Paris at its center, Gothic architecture became in the 12th century the first great creative style of northern Europe. Based on the functional use of rib vaulting combined with the pointed arch, the control of thrusts by flying buttresses, and the replacement of ponderous walls by stained-glass windows, the Gothic style culminated in the great 13th-century French cathedrals. From France it spread throughout Europe, dominating all forms of building until the Renaissance.

The Renaissance

French Renaissance architecture was a foreign importation fostered by Kings and nobles, who, on expeditions into Italy, had been vastly impressed by the building there. Resolving to introduce the Renaissance style into France, they employed many Italian artists and builders to remodel their old Gothic dwellings. A picturesque mingling of contrasting styles was thus achieved during the reign of the Valois Kings (ruled until 1589), when the feudal castle and château were overlaid with a fanciful sheathing of classical ornament, delicately carved on Gothic doorways, pinnacles, and chimneys. Charming châteaux of this early phase are Blois and Chambord in the Loire valley. The court of the Louvre Palace in Paris, by Pierre Lescot, and the now destroyed château at Anet for Diane de Poitiers by Philibert Delorme, both mid-16th century, are more obviously classic. The aristocratic elegance which characterizes these buildings is typical of all French Renaissance art, which not only was supported by the nobles but also lavishly subsidized by the King himself.

The 17th and 18th Centuries

No French architect before the Bourbon period had understood classic design, and during its earlier years an obvious baroque infusion had appeared at Paris, in the Place-des-Vosges and in the Luxembourg Palace by Salomon de Brosse. As the Louis XIV style arose, however, the understanding of classic design became fuller. It was typified in works of monumental dignity that approximated the finest 16th-century Italian compositions.

Sorbonne Church in Paris (begun, 1635), was built for Cardinal Richelieu by Jacques Lemercier in the style of Rome's famous Gesù Church. Lemercier, in collaboration with François Mansart, designed the Val-de-Grâce Church, also in Paris (mid-17th century); he also added a wing to the Louvre. François Mansart built the distinguished Château de Maisons near Paris and designed the Orléans Wing of the château of Blois, both works of the mid-17th century. The Louvre's magnificent east façade was designed by Claude Perrault; the Porte Saint-Denis, by François Blondel (1672); and the Place Vendôme (finished, 1698), and the Invalides Church (finished, 1706), now renowned as Napoleon's Tomb, by Jules Hardouin-Mansart. He collaborated in creating the resplendent palace at Versailles, where André Le Nôtre designed the famous gardens and Charles Le Brun devised sumptuous decorations.

Although French architecture of the 18th century retained much of its earlier pompous tone, it lost the stateliness of Louis XIV's reign and, in interior decoration, developed the dainty and fragile rococo style. Its most distinguished works are Jacques Ange Gabriel's Place de la Concorde (mid-18th century), the most beautiful vista in Paris, and his Petit Trianon at Versailles (begun, 1762),

Chambord, the largest of French Renaissance chateaux, was built as a hunting lodge for Francis I.

the elegant villa erected by Louis XV for his mistress Madame du Barry. Equally famous is Jacques Germain Soufflot's Paris Panthéon (begun, mid-18th century). A magnificent domed structure with a portico of Roman columns, it foreshadows the 19th-century revivalist styles and marks the end of French Renaissance architecture.

The 19th and 20th Centuries

The general character of architecture since 1800, in France as elsewhere, has been formed through a synthesis of retrospective and progressive tendencies. Architects had to deal with these factors, which interacted with great complexity, and had also to deal with the new problems in building created by modern civilization. Rapid and widely shared engineering and scientific advances at the same time provided novel materials and new structural methods, which served in themselves to eliminate national trends by substituting international movements. The latter, spreading with great speed throughout the civilized world, began with the revivalist styles of the 19th century and moved imperceptibly toward an unrestrained eclecticism. This last trend was eventually checked by the rigorous precepts of scientific functionalism.

French conservatism rendered largely indistinguishable the successive Roman and Greek revivalist modes, although, in Paris, the Vendôme Column, the Arch of Triumph (1806–36) by Jean François Chalgrin, and Napoleon's Temple of Glory, now the Madeleine Church —a building begun in the reign of Louis XV and redesigned by Barthélemy Vignon—are obviously Roman. The Empire style, Napoleon's favorite for interior decoration, used delicate Greek detail. The Gothic revival, flourishing for a century in England, was unimportant in France except for the enthusiasm it inspired in Eugène Emmanuel Viollet-le-Duc for restoring medieval structures. On the other hand eclecticism, which offered the architect complete freedom of choice among historical styles, motivated several conspicuous Parisian buildings of the latter part of the 19th century. The dazzling white marble church Sacré-Coeur-de-Montmartre was conceived in mingled Byzantine-Romanesque by Paul Abadie, and the famous Opéra (1861–74) was built by Charles Garnier in a sparkling adaptation of baroque.

Functionalism, the idea that architectural forms should express their function, grew out of 19th-century science with its innovations of structural iron and reinforced concrete. Henri Labrouste, in his Bibliothèque Sainte-Geneviève in Paris (finished, 1850), pioneered in using slender iron columns supporting metal vaults. Viollet-le-Duc, in many writings on functionalism, not only popularized its theories but advocated designs divorced from traditional styles, an ideal realized in the famous Eiffel Tower in Paris (completed, 1889). French architects in the 20th century have participated in the break with tradition. The Perret brothers, Auguste, Gustave, and Claude, inspired by cubism in painting and a freedom of design made possible by combining steel, concrete, and glass, produced such advanced structures as the Champs-Elysées Theater in Paris (1911–13), and the Notre-Dame Church at Le Raincy (1923–25). The most extreme phase of functionalism, which flourished from about 1920 to the outbreak of World War II in 1939, found its most persuasive advocate in the Swiss-born Le Corbusier, who coined the term "a machine for living" to describe his famous houses. Designed in severe geometrical forms, they nevertheless introduced new ways of enclosing space by guiding its flow, so that outdoor and indoor living were separated only by plate glass walls. In the postwar period, a reaction against geometrical severity and abstraction produced a more free and varied style known as organic architecture. Le Corbusier continued to lead the field, always seeking "to give architectural expression to a machine civilization."

Consult Fletcher, Banister, *A History of Architecture* (17th ed., 1961); Lavedan, Pierre, *French Architecture* (trans. 1956); Le Corbusier, *Towards a New Architecture* (repr. 1970).   EMERSON H. SWIFT

See also ARCHITECTURE; ARCHITECTURE, MODERN; BAROQUE ART AND ARCHITECTURE. CASTLE; CATHEDRAL: *Architecture*; CHÂTEAU.

FRENCH ART

A distinctively French art first emerged in the 11th century and evolved through many phases and variations in the succeeding periods. But despite these changes certain salient characteristics tended to persist. French art is usually clear and lucid, well defined in its aims, rarely excessive or fanciful, and often in healthy contact with its external environment.

The Middle Ages

During the Middle Ages, in France as elsewhere, art served a predominantly religious purpose and was subordinated to architecture. The Romanesque period of the 11th and 12th centuries witnessed the erection of many church buildings which were ornamented with sculpture. This sculpture was in low relief, protruding only slightly from the wall surface, and was concentrated in the areas around doorways and on the capitals atop columns. The subject matter illustrated scenes from the Bible and was intended to instruct the illiterate populace. The Last Judgment and scenes from the Apocalypse were popular subjects because they gave a graphic warning to the sinner and permitted the execution of the fanciful monsters which obsessed the imagination of this feudal era. As this was an art for a unified corporate society the artists remained anonymous, and traditional arrangements were almost invariably followed for a given subject. In a world seeking immutable transcendental truth originality was eschewed, and reference to the confusing multiplicity of external nature became irrelevant. Despite technical limitations this sculpture in relief was often vigorously animated and thoughtfully arranged to fill the assigned surface, the latter already testifying to the French predilection for clarity of design.

In its crowded two-dimensional composition and vivid coloring (now faded by time), Romanesque sculpture represented an effort to translate painting into stone. Because of the Christian prejudice against idols, sculpture had declined for several centuries and was only revived in this period of cultural renewal. There was, however, an ample tradition of painted representations, which the sculptors sought to imitate. Cycles of paintings were carried out on the walls and vaults of church interiors. The surviving examples exhibit strong colors and firm outlines arranged in decorative flat patterns that sought to make real the awesome hierarchy of heaven for the medieval worshiper below. Numerous manuscripts also contained illuminations of the textual content in a similar hieratic style.

During the late 12th century Romanesque style evolved into the more articulate and idealized Gothic. Whereas art had previously been scattered throughout France under monastic supervision, it was now concentrated in the rising municipalities in the north and principally adorned the great civic cathedrals. The sculpture spread over the entire façade and onto the large side portals. The subject matter, while still selected within the context of a religious system, became more varied and comprehensive; and the warning intent relaxed into optimistic affirmation of faith. Narrative scenes were carved in high relief, and long rows of prophets and apostles were cut in the round and then placed against the building. Co-ordinated with the structure rather than subordinated, the figures nonetheless gained in dignity and significance from this association with a larger entity. Although little effort was made to study nature in detail, the excessive elongations and jagged distortions of Romanesque art gave way to the more normal proportions and stance of the human body. This change resulted in a quieter, more humanized art, which aroused not fearful awe but feelings of respectful communion with the sacred personages.

The development of Gothic sculpture was one of the great contributions of French culture, and during the 13th century this art form spread throughout western Europe. Another outstanding achievement of northern France at this time was stained glass. The virtual disappearance of the wall in the Gothic cathedral entailed the abandonment of painting and its replacement by large expanses of glass. Realizing the intrinsic limitations of this medium, the French craftsmen fitted together within lead bands small pieces of lustrous red, blue, and yellow glass. They restricted painted additions to indications of facial features and other absolutely required details. Although varied religious scenes were represented, it was essentially the impalpable soft radiance of colored light that communicated the sense of spiritual presence. In the minor arts of small carved ivories, enameling, and metalwork France also assumed the lead during this brilliant period.

In the 14th century French art took on a mannered aspect that reflected aristocratic and courtly taste. Gracefulness and elaboration characterized much of the sculptural production, and prettiness replaced serene strength.

"Landscape with Orpheus and Euridice," painted about 1650 by the French neoclassicist Nicolas Poussin, foreshadowed the formal elegance and discipline of much later French painting.

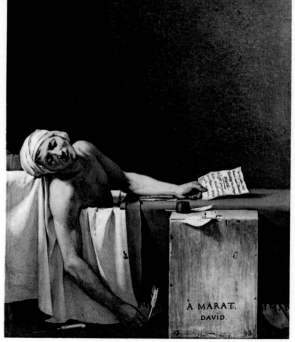

Jacques-Louis David's "The Death of Marat" (1793) signaled a sharp break with the mature rococo style of the monarchy.

The Renaissance

At the turn of the century several invasions of Italy by the armies of the revitalized monarchy revealed to the French the glories of the Renaissance. Early efforts to lure Italian artists to France began to be successful after 1530, and the court of Francis I and his successors at Fontainebleau became an important outpost of the new art in northern Europe. Several galleries and halls in the palace were decorated with cycles of mythological and allegorical paintings by Primaticcio and Il Rosso. Their French followers, still largely anonymous, produced easel pictures of similar subjects, and the nude, abhorred in the Middle Ages, became increasingly the central motive of this art which endeavored to exalt sensuous earthly life. Yet the Renaissance in France remained for some decades an imported fashion, limited largely to the court, without roots and only superficially understood. In the paintings of the School of Fontainebleau the figures were subordinated to the demands of surface design, and the artists executed variations on accepted models with little reference to observed nature. These procedures, common to medieval art, made the new importation more palatable to conservative French patrons. Surfaces were smooth, outlines precise, and color slightly cold. The paintings differed from comparable Italian work of the mid-16th century by the sometimes extreme figural distortions and by the greater attention to fastidious detail.

In sculpture the French artists, no longer anonymous, transcended the decorative artificiality of the Fontainebleau style. Jean Goujon's exquisite low reliefs of nymphs in clinging draperies captured the supple elegance of earlier Florentine work. For the first time a French artist began to comprehend the classical sense of the human body as a beautiful and free organism. The royal tombs by Germain Pilon were triumphal monuments to the heroic deeds of their illustrious occupants, testaments to Renaissance pride rather than to Christian piety. Yet the powerful figures of Pilon also retained much of the sturdy realism of one segment of the late medieval heritage. In less adulterated form this northern realism persisted in the countless portraits that proliferated in these years. The work of Jean and François Clouet, a father and son of Flemish origin, best exemplified this truthfulness to fact softened by French selectivity and polish. Thus the 16th century in French art was a period of transition: the displacement of medieval forms by imported Renaissance motives alongside the deepening subtilization of late medieval realism.

The Baroque and Rococo Eras

Torn apart by civil strife in the late 16th century France experienced a drastic cultural decline that was finally halted by the victory of Henry IV. But artistic revival was slow, and her painting remained pinched and provincial until the return of Simon Vouet from Italy in 1627 marked the beginning of a new epoch. This artist brought back an ample baroque style that was spacious and atmospheric, asymmetrical in design, and somewhat warm in color; idealized figures communicated easily comprehended emotions by means of conventional rhetorical gestures. This suave, Italianate baroque style, cleverly toned down for French consumption, was instantly suc-

Sculpture increasingly freed itself from the previous relationship to architecture and became an independent form. The courtly taste for charm and artificial stylization reached its peak in some manuscript illuminations of the early 15th century. In this secular art the elegant, richly clad figures of nobles were shown hunting or dining in a colorful splendor that reflected the last overripe manners of the doomed feudal aristocracy. This love of tasteful decorative elegance was a feature that was to recur in subsequent phases of French art.

Interwoven with this courtly style was a tendency toward sharp observation of actuality, perhaps influenced by Flemish artists working in Paris. Behind the fashion-plate figures of the nobles were depicted peasants plowing the fields or swimming in the rivers. In sculpture sharply individualized portraits began to appear. In the region of Burgundy an important new school of sculpture was characterized by monumental power and brutal expressiveness that were strongly at variance with the conventional desire for mincing beauty and reflected a more profound view of life.

The artistic development of France in the 15th century was greatly disrupted by the English invasions. Paris became less important, and once again artistic production was dispersed in various centers. As in the rest of Europe panel painting supplanted sculpture and illumination in importance, and some fine examples were created by French artists. But these paintings, reflecting diverse influences from the progressive schools of Flanders and Italy, lacked strong features in common that marked them as French. An exception was Jean Fouquet, who fused Flemish realism with Italian classicism and science to produce a balanced, restrained art that was indubitably French and that anticipated, tentatively, the subsequent viewpoint of the entire stream of French art.

cessful and was developed in various ways by a host of artists. Originally a product of the current religious revival, the style was also adapted for secular purposes. The paintings in this manner, although generally lacking in profundity, at their best were extremely handsome decoration and much more robust than the canvases of the previous century. Flourishing especially in Paris, this advanced art embodied the ideals and standards of the ruling classes.

At the same time the realistic strain in French art produced some of its most memorable works. Genre scenes depicting the life of the peasants and townspeople were executed for a middle-class clientele just as in contemporary Holland. However, such scenes in France were interpreted in a sober, grave manner that imparted to the quiet groups of humble people great dignity and an underlying sense of inward spiritual existence. Muted refined colors, stable composition, economy of detail, and a sensitivity to almost imperceptible nuances of attitude and gesture revealed the maturation of a distinctively French realism. A similar attitude was manifested in some religious paintings of the period, especially in the provinces. Interpreted in terms of contemporary life, religious scenes such as those of the Lorraine artist Georges de La Tour conveyed a depth of feeling made more poignant by an outer restraint that minimized gesture, movement, and detail. Shunning the standard devices of official religious painting, this art sought in the manner of early Gothic sculpture to deepen the devotional sensibility by revealing the immediate relevance of the Christian experience to the common human condition.

A third type of painting, traditionally considered the most French, took shape principally in the work of Nicolas Poussin and Claude Lorrain, expatriates who spent almost their entire lives in Rome. Poussin was the direct heir both of antiquity and the Italian Renaissance and the first French artist to comprehend completely the inner spirit as well as the outer forms of the Mediterranean classical tradition. Organizing a multitude of idealized figures into dense, rigidly ordered compositions and subordinating a judicious coloring to purity of line, he endeavored to reveal the permanent essence of things within a world view that was more Stoic than Christian. The logical discipline and uncompromising intellectualism of his profoundly thoughtful painting provided a lofty standard for subsequent artists and helped to ensure the continuing vitality of the French artistic tradition.

As a result of the absolutist policies of Louis XIV, artists after 1660 were organized into academies under state control. They were expected to produce for the royal palaces paintings and sculpture that extolled the power and glory of the King and to work in a common style whose principles were laid down by the academy. The artists gained in wealth and prestige but at the loss of the fertile individuality that had engendered the richly varied masterpieces of the previous period. Although Poussin was revered as the great model to be followed, the academic codification of dry rules and dogmas constituted a gross debasement of the earlier artist's probing thoughtfulness. Not philosophic depth but ostentatious propaganda characterized this eclectic state art. Despite an admixture of superficial classicism, it belonged essentially in the baroque tradition

of Vouet. Not surprisingly this school made its most distinguished contribution in the decorative arts, in tapestries, furniture, and bronzes, and it was at this time that French taste began to set the fashionable norm throughout Europe.

At the beginning of the 18th century the decline of royal power and the growing affluence of the upper middle classes brought about a relaxation of academic control. Art no longer had to convey a moral, political, or even religious message but was designed solely to delight the eye of a private patron. Genre subjects, although despised by the academy, multiplied; the lighter, more erotic scenes from mythology also enjoyed great popularity. Paintings became intimate in scale as well as subject and were characterized by sinuous asymmetrical arrangements of small interwoven forms further blended with atmospheric harmonies of soft pastel shades. The leader in the development of this rococo style was Antoine Watteau, whose deftly executed depictions of fashionably dressed people amusing themselves out-of-doors with music and conversation epitomized this sophisticated society. More conventionally decorative, the countless mythologies of François Boucher exemplified that fusion of unabashed hedonism and faultless taste which secured for France unchallenged artistic leadership. There also arose a great demand for portraits, many of them generalized and artificial, but others perceptive character studies that reflected the penetrating scepticism of the Enlightenment. The carefully observed domestic scenes of Chardin were likewise based on new empirical principles that stood in opposition to rococo conventions.

The 19th and 20th Centuries

With the French Revolution the rococo style became anathema and was replaced by neoclassicism, a revival of the unrelenting rationalism that is the counterweight to French hedonism. The paintings of Jacques Louis David,

Edgar Degas's technical mastery, as shown in "After the Bath, Woman Drying Her Foot," helped vindicate French impressionism.

Scala New York

the leader of this school, were statically composed, cold in color, tight in drawing, and archeologically pedantic in detail; their subjects from ancient history were intended as moral exhortations to the citizenry of the Republic and the Napoleonic empire. Once again art became an arm of the state and aesthetic appeal was subordinated to moral and political purposes.

After 1815 the impersonal discipline of neoclassicism was challenged by the romantics, especially by Eugène Delacroix. Inspired by Rubens rather than by Poussin, the paintings of Delacroix were tempestuous creations of color and movement that extolled an untrammeled individualism seeking intuitive expression of the seething forces of life. He often depicted historical scenes from the Middle Ages that involved conflict and intense emotion. The Near East, too, provided him with many scenes of the exotic, the exciting, and the unusual. His experiments in color and his assertion of the absolute freedom of the artist were of lasting significance.

Both these movements were strongly literary and increasingly remote from the scientific materialism that was radically altering the nature of French society. Although the work of Camille Corot and Honoré Daumier had drawn new vitality from a study of the external environment, it was the unflinching realism of the large paintings of Gustave Courbet that inaugurated a genuine artistic revolution after the abortive political one of 1848. Resolutely limiting himself to contemporary subject matter, chiefly of rural life, he tried to strip away all pretension from art and to show that direct reality alone had validity. This attitude was greatly subtilized by the Parisian painter Édouard Manet, who with typically French intellectual finesse shifted the emphasis from what is seen to how it is seen. In endeavoring to transpose only the retinal image Manet developed a new technique of thin washes of cool colors applied directly to the canvas, a procedure that contrasts with the thick paint and dark colors of Courbet. Yet this increasing concern for the technical problems of painting, the artistic counterpart of the growth of modern specialization, did not prevent Manet from investing his paintings with a static balanced composition of carefully co-ordinated parts. Fused with the new realism, this sensitive concern for integrated unity constituted an important renewal of French classicism.

After 1870 the impressionist school carried this analytic, realistic viewpoint still further. Painting in small intermingled strokes of pure pigment so as to lose nothing of the brilliance of external lighting, its artists ostensibly sought to portray only the irreducible essentials of vision, light, and color, but in so doing they also captured superbly the absolute freshness of nature. Their central doctrine was best exemplified in the brilliant landscapes of Claude Monet. Other members of the group diverged from these aims in various directions: Auguste Renoir used the new discoveries in color to evoke a voluptuous expression of human well-being, whereas Edgar Degas explored the exciting designs that arose from the chance relations of people and objects within the animated urban environment.

In 1885 a reaction set in against impressionism's relentless concentration on pure instantaneous vision, and many artists, the so-called postimpressionists, started to reintro-

duce such factors as composition, solidity, and subject significance. Georges Seurat tried to tidy up impressionism: to reduce its spontaneous brushwork to methodical application of dots, to work from rules of color rather than from observation, to draw up compositional schemes that would invariably produce certain emotional reactions. This typically French attempt to apply principles in art as precise as those in science would have resulted in a dry academic painting were it not for Seurat's sensitivity and wit.

Under the increasing influence of primitive art Paul Gauguin evolved a form of painting which consisted of the reduction of natural forms to their essential shapes and the rearrangement of these brightly colored, relatively flat shapes in a pattern at once decorative and emotionally evocative. Although his obsession with exotic peoples and places and with elemental emotional states represented a romantic resurgence, his effort to absorb the actual principles of primitive art went far beyond romanticism and foreshadowed a radical break in the Western cultural tradition. The abstract logic of Seurat and the tormented imagination of Gauguin both led to the abandonment of visual appearance as a condition of artistic endeavor.

Their contemporary, Paul Cézanne, outwardly less radical, wanted to balance the claims of nature against those of art. In his heroic attempt to co-ordinate the impressionist sense of visual immediacy with the traditional concern for solidity and space, he discarded modeling in light and dark as well as linear perspective; instead he fashioned mass and space entirely by means of carefully adjusted strokes of color. This brilliant enlargement of the impressionist technique was incorporated in compositions of a Poussinesque grandeur and permanence which transmitted to the art of the 20th century a revitalized sense of classical structure.

Inspired directly by Cézanne, the artists Pablo Picasso

Both cubism and surrealism underlie "The Jungle" (1943) of Wilfredo Lam, a French surrealist of Cuban extraction.

The Collection, Museum of Modern Art, New York, Inter-American Fund

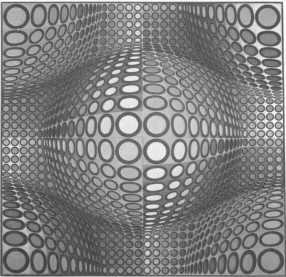

Photo Gallery Denise René

Victor Vasarely's constructivist "Cedull" (1971) epitomizes the internationalism of contemporary French art.

and binding order this cubist style represented one of the most original manifestations of the tradition of French classicism. The intellectual approach of early cubism was subsequently enriched in various ways ranging from the sensitive shape and color orchestrations of later Braque to the deliberately dry, mechanistic purism of Fernand Léger. Likewise the sensuous hedonistic aspect of French art reappeared afresh in the paintings of Henri Matisse. His striking color arrangements and bold patterns continued in the abstract style of the 20th century the optimistic materialism of the impressionist Renoir. Another modern French artist, André Breton, was one of the founders of surrealism, a movement which despite its avowed aim to utilize the emotional force of the unconscious often proceeded with an intellectual dispassion.

During the second half of the 19th century France had become the embattled citadel where a few courageous painters rejected the vapid anecdotal and sentimental art demanded by the new masses and their leaders. These artists forged a progressive art that reflected the swiftly changing values of an emerging industrialized world without sacrificing what was still vital in the traditions of the past. Because of its unique role as innovator and preserver, French art in the 20th century has served as the catalyst for artistic revivals in many countries. Paris has attracted vast numbers of foreign artists, and the French tradition has engendered and in part merged with the new international style in the arts.

Consult Blunt, Anthony, *Art and Architecture in France 1500 to 1700* (1973); Brownell, W. C., *French Art: Classic and Contemporary* (1972). NATHAN T. WHITMAN

and Georges Braque had developed by 1910 a highly analytic painting in which a few simple objects were so ruthlessly dissected in terms of their manifold minute planes that virtually all connection with visual reality had disappeared. In its relentless logicality, formal consistency,

FRENCH LITERATURE

French literature includes literature in modern French and in earlier forms of the language, such as Francien, which was the dialect of northern France. The term excludes medieval Latin literature and Provençal literature.

Poetry

The earliest literary works in French are in poetic form. French literature begins with the epic *chansons de geste*, sung by troubadours in the provincial courts centuries before the first one was written down, prior to 1080. The greatest of these is the *Chanson de Roland* (Song of Roland), which tells of the heroic death of Roland (nephew of Charlemagne) while fighting the Saracens. This is the finest example of many *chansons de geste* celebrating the genius and prowess of Charlemagne.

Out of these heroic works, which combined historical fact and legend, developed long verse romances mingling the great figures of the *chansons de geste* with imaginary characters. Details in the original epics were expanded, often to ludicrous proportions. Among the principal subjects were the Crusades and antiquity, for despite medieval ignorance of Greek and Roman literature, enough minor works were available so that the siege of Troy and the life of Alexander figured in these romances.

Far more significant and enduring are the Breton romances, which tell of Tristan, of Arthur and the Knights of the Round Table, of the search for the Holy Grail. The Tristan poems are the earliest love stories. The passion of

Tristan and Isolde is no longer treated as the mere physical desire of the *chansons de geste*, but as an eternal love, mingling sacrifice with devotion and ending in tragedy. The greatest author of Breton romances was Chrétien de Troyes, who wrote in the second half of the 12th century. Chrétien combines his poetic gift with psychological acuity and the ability to describe exactly. He creates suspense and interest through skillful composition.

The Breton romances were essentially noble in character. The same period saw the development of bourgeois narrative poems, the most famous among them being the *Roman de Renart* (Romance of Reynard the Fox), which presented an animal world whose inhabitants bore human characteristics, and the *fabliaux*, humorous verse tales of venal priests, gullible husbands, and errant wives. Bourgeois and aristocratic elements blend in the *Roman de la rose* (Romance of the Rose), composed in the 13th century in two parts by two different authors, Guillaume de Lorris and Jean de Meung. The first part, highly allegorical, relates the attempts of the hero to pluck the symbolic rose in the garden of love. The second part, by Jean de Meung, substitutes for the idealistic description of courtly love an erudite blend of philosophical, mythological, and scientific information, a kind of encyclopedia of medieval learning in which the rose and its eventual capture become incidental.

For several centuries narrative verse eclipsed lyrical poetry. The first medieval poet of magnitude was Rutebeuf, whose satirical and realistic poems present a vivid picture of his times. But despite the vigor and originality of poets like Eustache Deschamps (c.1345–c.1405) and Christine de Pisan (1364–c.1430), no poet of significance appeared before Charles d'Orléans (1391–1465), whose ballades and rondeaux have a subtle charm. D'Orléans is overshadowed, however, by his great contemporary François Villon (b.1431), the first modern poet and one of the greatest of all time. Villon left no tradition, and the sterility of poetry in the late 15th century is typified by the school of *grands rhétoriqueurs*, who made skill in versification their primary goal.

It was primarily against this group that the Pléiade poets, led by Pierre de Ronsard (1524–85), reacted. Clément Marot (c.1496–1544) had formed a link between the Middle Ages and the new poetic age. The Lyon poets, especially the subtle and hermetic Maurice Scève (c.1501–60), and Louise Labé (1524–66), author of intense love sonnets, were early champions of Italian literature. The Pléiade's manifesto, the *Défense et illustration de la langue française* (1549), by Joachim du Bellay (1522–60), proclaimed the group's resolute break with the recent past and advocated the literatures of antiquity and of Italy as the only models worthy of imitation. The Pléiade marks a specific turning point, beginning a classical tradition which remained unchallenged until the 19th century.

With the Wars of Religion, which demonstrated anew man's inability to control his destiny, skepticism began to color the prevailing admiration for antiquity as an infallible guide and source of truth. The influence of the Bible, earlier manifested in Marot's translations of the Psalms, appears at the end of the century in baroque poetry, which mingled religious and pagan imagery, and treated contemporary events and religious subjects with didactic zeal. Jean de Sponde (1557–95), Jean de La Ceppéde (1548–1622), and particularly Théodore Agrippa d'Aubigné (1552–1630), are baroque poets of lasting importance. In the early 17th century the baroque tradition

Arachne, from a French Renaissance illuminated manuscript, "Vie des femmes célèbres," in the Musée Dobrée, Nantes.

Giraudon

continued in the works of Marc Antoine de Saint-Amant (1594–1661), François Maynard (1582–1646), Tristan l'Hermite (1601–55), and Théophile de Viau (1596–1626), who successfully achieved an intimate lyricism in poems describing nature. In some cases their work verges on the burlesque, as in Saint-Amant's delightful *Moïse sauvé* (Moses Preserved), 1653.

François de Malherbe (1555–1628), a contemporary opponent of these poets, strove to codify and discipline poetry. His strict definitions of the language, form, and function of verse eventually triumphed, since the whole trend under Louis XIII and later under Louis XIV was toward the regulation and legislation of literature. The French Academy, chartered in 1636, had as a primary function the criticism of literary works. As a result, lyrical poetry began to disappear, and poets tended to confine themselves to occasional odes, satire, and verse paraphrases of religious writings. Even love poetry, while it did not vanish entirely, conformed to rules. The *précieux* poets, who frequented the salon of Mme. de Rambouillet, obeyed the codes established there; they wrote of love with grace and wit, but never with feeling. Personal lyricism survived in the *Fables* (1668–94) and *Contes* (Tales), 1664 and 1666, of Jean de la Fontaine (1621–95), but only incidentally. By the time Nicolas Boileau-Despréaux (1636–1711), in his *Art poétique* (1664), erected the precepts of Malherbe into law, lyric poetry was dead.

The 18th century did not lack verse and versifiers; it did lack poetry. Antoine Houdar de Lamotte (1672–1731) and Jean Baptiste Rousseau (1671–1741), to name only two poets of competence, wrote brilliant but empty odes. Voltaire (1694–1778) attempted the epic in *La Henriade* (1728), but with indifferent success. A new preoccupation with nature and landscape was palely reflected in *Les jardins* (Gardens), 1782, by Jacques Delille (1738–1813) and in an imitation by Jean François de Saint-Lambert (1716–1803) of James Thomson's *The Seasons*. But these attempts failed, largely because their authors approached nature from the intellectual viewpoint. Instead of describing landscapes, they drew up lists of nature's attributes. At the end of the century lyricism reappeared in the works of André de Chénier (1762–94), who reached back for inspiration to the Greek and Roman classics much as Ronsard had done. His poems express the range of his emotions: his joy before the spectacle of nature, his hatred for the terrorists of the Revolution.

The romantic poets—Victor Hugo (1802–85), Alphonse de Lamartine (1790–1869, Alfred de Vigny (1797–1863), Alfred de Musset (1810–57)—determined to reject classicism and to substitute for the outmoded and impoverished poetic language which even Chénier had been obliged to use, an idiom enriched by a vocabulary drawn from exotic, popular, and technical sources. In versification they threw off the constraints that had been imposed since Malherbe, seeking unusual rhymes, new rhythms, and new stanza forms. Their subject matter was almost invariably themselves. The romantic poet confronts the universe; his poem attempts to define his role therein. Such works as Lamartine's *Méditations* (1820) and Vigny's *Les destinées* (Destinies), 1846, seek a philosophy of life. But Hugo was the dominant force of romanticism. As a poet he is a figure of towering importance; he alone of the romantic poets attempted every innovation he preached. His early works, *Odes et ballades* (rev. and enlarged ed., 1828), *Les Orientales* (1829), and *Les feuilles d'automne* (Autumn Leaves), 1831, give proof of a mastery of his art acquired before that art was called upon to express the deeper philosophical preoccupations of which *Les contemplations* (1856) and *La légende des siècles* (The Legend of the Ages) 1859, 1877, and 1883, were the fruit. Hugo worked with equal power in every genre—in the theater, the novel, and poetry. But he was more than the genius of romanticism: he was a statesman and a political exile as well as a poet, and as such was a symbol of the artist responsible to society.

Inevitably there arose opponents of romantic poetry: Théophile Gautier (1811–72), in his concern for realistic detail and in his theories of "art for art's sake," prepared the ground for the Parnassians, who were determined to minimize the personal element. Charles Marie René Leconte de Lisle (1818–94), rejecting the romantic attachment for the Middle Ages, returned to Greek and Roman subjects, and sought a new exoticism in descriptions of the French West Indies. The *Trophées* (1893) of José Maria de Hérédia (1842–1905) are sonnets of gem-like brilliance.

But Charles Baudelaire (1821–67) dominated the latter half of the century. His Villonesque themes (death in its macabre and revolting aspects, the poet accursed) are by-products of decadent romanticism, but the perfection of his verse, his startling imagery and unusual rhythms, invest these themes with a unique poetic quality, with what Hugo called, in admiration, "a new shiver." Baudelaire's poems, often intensely personal, frequently centered upon a symbol: his albatross, sublime in flight but awkward on earth, is clearly the poet.

His followers pushed symbolism a step further, suppressing the symbol's obvious identity. Gérard de Nerval (1808–55), Tristan Corbière (1845–75), Paul Verlaine (1844–96), Arthur Rimbaud (1854–91), and above all Stéphane Mallarmé (1842–98) made symbolism the reigning poetic mode. Mallarmé's pronouncement that "to name a thing was to suppress much of its beauty, to suggest it is the ideal" set the tone for future poets. Modern poetry has, however, taken various directions, both in content and in form. Jules Laforgue (1860–87) brought to symbolism an irony which resulted from his use of popular language and his subtle perception of the contemporary world. Similarly, Guillaume Apollinaire (1880–1918), calling himself a "cubist" poet, found lyrical beauty in modern technology, in folklore, and even in battle scenes of World War I. For Apollinaire poetry was an "adventure" and the printed poem on the page was a form in itself.

The surrealists, chief among whom was André Breton (1896–1966), claimed the 19th-century Lautréamont as their ancestor and pushed disregard for form and meaning to extreme lengths. In general, free verse (unrhymed lines of unequal length) became the favored medium. Paul Claudel (1868–1955) introduced the *verset*, a free-verse stanza recalling Biblical rhythms. But classical forms persisted in the works of the sensitive Charles Péguy (1873–1914), and particularly in those of Paul Valéry (1871–1945). A modern disciple of Mallarmé, Valéry maintains in his *La jeune Parque* (The Young Goddess Fate), 1917, and *Charmes* (1922) the rigorous beauty of the alexandrine line.

The age of poetic schools now seems past. Poets like Paul Morand (1888–   ), Paul Éluard (1895–1952), and Pierre Reverdy (1889–1960) bear their own individual and distinctive qualities. Apollinaire's disciple Jean Cocteau (1891–1963) found a refuge in prose. A combination of symbolism and epic characterizes the works of Saint-John Perse (1887–1975). Modern poetry seems to have shut its doors to philosophy, although Marxism survives in the poems of Louis Aragon (1897–   ). Among the many contemporary French poets of genius are Francis Ponge (1899–   ), Henri Michaux (1899–   ), René Char (1907–   ), Raymond Queneau (1903–   ), and Yves Bennefoy (1923–   ).

Prose

In France it is frequently difficult to make a clear and precise distinction between prose literature and history, criticism, polemics, and philosophy. The works of medieval and Renaissance chroniclers, Geoffroi de Villehardouin (c.1160–c.1213), Jean de Joinville (1224?–1317), Jean Froissart (c.1337–c.1404), and Philippe de Comines (c.1447–c.1511), contributed greatly to the creation of French prose style, as did the ecclesiastical writings of John Calvin (1509–64). An outstanding characteristic of the French writer in general is his self-imposed mission to criticize and amend the society in which he lives. This tendency first began to be obvious in the humanistic writings of the Renaissance, and in particular in the *Essais* (1580–88) of Michel Eyquem de Montaigne (1533–92). Blaise Pascal (1623–62) wrote *Lettres provinciales* (1656–57), and *Pensées* (Thoughts), 1670, which, though polemical in nature, are among the masterpieces of French prose, as are the *Maximes* (1665) of François de la Rochefoucauld (1613–80). The letters of Marie de Rabutin-Chantal, Marquise de Sévigné (1626–96), stand far above the rest of the voluminous epistolary literature of the 17th century. Pulpit eloquence became literature in the sermons and funeral orations of Jacques Bénigne Bossuet (1627–1704).

Critical quarrels, which were to characterize the history of French literature, began with the Quarrel of the Ancients and Moderns, in which the followers of Greek and Roman literature were opposed by the modernists, who claimed the superiority of modern literature. This debate produced the exquisite *Digression sur les anciens et les modernes* (1688) of Bernard le Bovier de Fontenelle (1657–1757). The mordant *Les caractères* (Characters), 1688, of Jean de La Bruyère (1645–96) and *Les dialogues* of François de Salignac de la Mothe-Fénelon (1651–1715) forecast in style and thought the century of reason, when philosophical prose almost becomes the dominant genre. Charles de Secondat, Baron de la Brède et de Montesquieu (1689–1755), Voltaire, and the Encyclopedists Rousseau, Diderot, Jean Le Rond d'Alembert (1717–83), and Paul Henri Dietrich, Baron d'Holbach (1723–89), were thinkers first and men of letters second.

Literary critics in the 17th and 18th centuries, with the possible exception of Diderot, were exclusively concerned with the literary work and the rules that governed it. The romantic critics sought instead a synthesis of author, society, and literary work. After Mme. de Staël's

De l'Allemagne (Germany), 1813, the first work of romantic criticism, came the biographical approach of Charles Augustin Sainte-Beuve (1804–69), and the formula for the study of literature—"race, milieu, and moment"—of Hippolyte Taine (1828–93).

But in an age of synthesis, distinctions become almost pointless: Jules Michelet (1798–1874), the historian, is a great literary figure; Ernest Renan (1823–92), the philologist, the author of Vie de Jésus (Life of Jesus), 1863, is the 19th-century Montaigne: both are critics. Significantly, no 19th-century critic accurately judged his contemporaries. Since the end of the century, criticism has become not only the province of university men like Ferdinand Brunetiére (1849–1907), Gustave Lanson (1857–1934), and Émile Faguet (1847–1916), and of professionals like Francisque Sarcey (1827–99), Jules Lemaître (1853–1914), and Albert Thibaudet (1874–1936), but also of the writers themselves: Proust refuted Sainte-Beuve in his Contre Sainte-Beuve (Against Sainte-Beuve), 1954, and Valéry produced in his Variété (1924–44) critical works of high order. Gide, Mauriac, Romains, and Montherlant have written significant literary criticism. Since World War II, Sartre, in his remarkable essay "Qu'est-ce que la Littérature" (What is Literature?), has attempted to define the role and responsibilities of the writer in society.

The Novel. Although narrative poetry appeared very early, the novel in prose is the most recent of literary genres. Gargantua and Pantagruel (1533–52), the great work by François Rabelais (c.1490–1553) can scarcely be called a novel: it is unique, defying classification. One may date the French novel from L'Astrée (1607–27) by Honoré d'Urfé (1567–1625), in which shepherds and shepherdesses pursue love in a pastoral world that faithfully transcribes the social life of the time. Later writers of the novel preferred heroic themes: Madeleine de Scudéry (1607–1701), Marin le Roy de Gomberville (1600–74), Gauthier de Costes de la Calprenède (c.1610–63), although they located their stories in Rome, Mexico, and Gaul, only thinly disguised their descriptions of contemporary events, settings, and customs. Their interminable novels were supplanted by a masterpiece, the brief La Princesse de Clèves (1678), by Marie de la Vergne, Comtesse de la Fayette (1634–93). Her psychological novel drew its inspiration from the conflicts of dramatic tragedy. Coexisting with the pastoral and analytical novels were realistic or comic novels such as Francion (1623) and Le berger extravagant (The Extravagant Shepherd), 1627, both by Charles Sorel (1599–1674), Le roman comique (The Comic Novel), 1651, by Paul Scarron (1610–60), and Le roman bourgeois (The Bourgeois Novel), 1666, of Antoine Furetière (1619–88).

But the novel gained its greatest impetus in the 18th century. Gil Blas (4 vols., 1715–35), a picaresque novel by Alain René Lesage (1668–1747), was the first of the romans de moeurs (novels of customs). It combines action and adventure with realistic attention to detail. Pierre de Marivaux (1688–1763), a dramatist who was also a novelist, pushed realism even further, engaging his characters in a self-analysis which frequently tended to be moralistic. Passion as a central theme returned in Manon Lescaut, by the Abbé Antoine François Prévost d'Exiles (1697–1763), and as a weapon in the war between the sexes in Les liaisons dangereuses (Dangerous Acquaintances), 1782, by Choderlos de Laclos (1741–1803).

The century of ideas inevitably produced novels of ideas, the most remarkable of them being Voltaire's attack on the German philosopher Leibniz, Candide (1759). Denis Diderot (1713–84) wrote two short novels, Jacques le fataliste (1786) and La religieuse (The Nun), 1796, which are remarkable despite their untidy form. La nouvelle Héloïse (The New Héloïse), 1761, by Jean Jacques Rousseau (1712–78), is a novel of ideas, but it is much more than that: for the first time nature is not merely a setting, but plays a role in the development of character. One of the novel's themes, the rise of a hero of humble birth in an aristocratic society, was to inspire novelists in the following century.

From Rousseau descends the early romantic novel: Paul et Virginie (Paul and Virginia), 1787, by Bernardin de Saint-Pierre (1737–1814); the feminist novels of Madame de Staël (1766–1817); the exotic and autobiographical works (Atala, 1801; René, 1802) of François René, Vicomte de Chateaubriand (1768–1848)—all established the novel as a vehicle for the author's self-expression. The immense production of George Sand (1804–76) follows this pattern. Another territory claimed by romantic novelists was history: Hugo's Notre-Dame de Paris (The Hunchback of Notre Dame), 1831, Vigny's Cinq-Mars (1826), and the works of Alexandre Dumas père (1802–70) were reconstructions of bygone eras.

Historical elements abounded in the works of Stendhal (1783–1842), who disciplined Rousseauistic themes with precise description and analysis. La comédie humaine (The Human Comedy), by Honoré de Balzac (1799–1850), the work of 20 years (1829–50), reflects the transition from romanticism to realism. Gustave Flaubert (1821–80), who made objectivity his goal, whether in a novel of contemporary setting like Madame Bovary (1857), or in a historical novel (Salammbô, 1862) about the Carthaginians, set the novel firmly in the path of documentary realism.

Émile Zola (1840–1902), founder of naturalism, was a disciple not only of Flaubert and the brothers Edmond (1822–96) and Jules (1830–70) de Goncourt, but also of the critics Hippolyte Taine and Jules Michelet; in his Rougon-Macquart (1871–93) he added a scientific dimension to realism, claiming that his characters acted according to determined laws, chief among them heredity. Alphonse Daudet (1840–97) was a lesser naturalist, and of the Goncourts' works only Germinie Lacerteux (1865) retains historical importance. Guy de Maupassant (1850–93), Flaubert's disciple, is the master of the French short story. In the midst of the naturalistic period appeared the psychological novels of Paul Bourget (1852–1935), the exoticism of Pierre Loti (1850–1923), the neoclassicism of Anatole France (1844–1924).

Consult Brereton, Geoffrey, A Short History of French Literature (1955); Cazamian, L. F., History of French Literature (1955 ed.); Peyre, Henri, Historical and Critical Essays (1969).

JOHN C. LAPP

20th-Century French Novel. Roger Martin du Gard (1881–1950), Georges Duhamel (1884–1966), and Jules

Romains (1885–1972) continued the tradition of Émile Zola in their panoramic series of novels. Although there are many differences of ideology and technique, their work is essentially an adaptation of realism to the events of the 20th century. The novels of Henri Alain-Fournier (1886–1914) and Jean Giraudoux (1882–1944) can be seen as representative of the opposing tradition of symbolism, first introduced into the novel by J. K. Huysmans (1848–1907) in À Rebours, 1884 (Against the Grain, 1930).

André Gide (1869–1951) began his career with a series of short narrations that reflect the dominant influence of symbolism. But in L'Immoraliste, 1902 (The Immoralist, 1930) he inaugurated the long series of 20th-century confession novels, characterized by lack of inhibition and precision of psychological analysis. In Les Caves du Vatican, 1914 (Lafcadio's Adventures, 1925) he explored the possibility of totally unmotivated action, and with Les Faux-monnayeurs, 1925 (The Counterfeiters, 1927) he presented an ironic novel about the writing of a novel. His last work of fiction, Thésée, 1948 (Theseus, 1948), is a retelling of the Greek legend which represents a disguised form of personal confession.

If variety is the most striking quality of Gide's novels, Marcel Proust (1871–1922) can be considered the author of one book, À la Recherche du temps perdu, 1913–27 (Remembrance of Things Past, 1922–34). This monumental work is concerned with the relationship between art and experience. Although it contains an enormous cast of characters and can be read as a social history of the period before World War I, its focus is on the personal experience of the narrator and his finally successful attempt to transform that experience into art and thereby to triumph over time. So powerful and original are Proust's conception and his style, that this novel dominated the whole first half of the century and provided a standard of literary excellence and intellectual complexity that few could approach.

The novels of André Malraux (1901–   ), who has been an adventurer, a soldier, a politician, and an art historian as well as a novelist, attempt to come to grips with the 20th-century experiences of revolution and war. La Condition humaine, 1933 (Man's Fate, 1934), dealing with events in China in the 1920's, and L'Espoir, 1937 (Man's Hope, 1938), concerned with the first nine months of the Spanish Civil War, explore the complex interaction of individuals and historic events. Louis-Ferdinand Céline (1894–1961), whose later writings were marred by hysterical anti-Semitism, re-created the picaresque novel for the 20th century with Voyage au bout de la nuit, 1932 (Journey to the End of Night, 1934). It deals with the wanderings and violent experiences of a social outcast, told in a French that is unusually colloquial for a work of literature. Classical in style, but modern because of their subject—the experience of flight—the novels and autobiographical works of Antoine de Saint-Exupéry (1900–44) are combinations of adventure stories and philosophical speculation.

Novels with an explicitly Catholic point of view were written by François Mauriac (1885–1970) and Georges Bernanos (1888–1948). In Thérèse Desqueyroux, 1922 (Thérèse, 1947), Le Noeud de vipères, 1932 (Vipers' Tangle, 1933), and numerous other works, Maurice presents middle-class families in and around Bordeaux as protagonists in dramas of sin and salvation. Bernanos dealt in symbolic form with the problems of temptation and faith in Sous le soleil de Satan, 1926 (Under the Sun of Satan, 1949) and Journal d'un curé de campagne, 1936 (The Diary of a Country Priest, 1937).

One of the most important literary movements of the 20th century was surrealism, one of whose major principles was to find the strange and significant in the everyday. This was exemplified in Nadja, 1928 (Nadja, 1960) by the leader of the movement, André Breton (1896–1966), who was primarily a poet. Another poet, who began as a surrealist and later became a Communist, Louis Aragon (1897–   ), wrote a series of realistic novels in the 1930's and '40's. In 1965 he demonstrated his continuing vitality with a novel about the very modern theme of writing a novel, La mise à mort (The Death Blow). Julien Gracq (1909–   ) remains a disciple of surrealism. Raymond Queneau (1903–   ) shows some surrealist influence, but is essentially a comic novelist of great verve, who sometimes uses comedy to deal with complex philosophical problems.

If Proust was the dominant influence of the first part of the century, Jean-Paul Sartre (1905–   ) is the most significant figure in French literature after World War II. Together with Albert Camus (1913–60) and Simone de Beauvoir (1908–   ) he combined philosophic, political, and literary concerns to formulate the doctrine of existentialism. Sartre, a playwright and philosopher as well as a novelist, has in fact written no fiction since 1949. In La Nausée, 1938 (Nausea, 1949) he explored the problem of personal freedom from an intensely philosophic point of view. And in the unfinished tetralogy, Les Chemins de la liberté, 1945–49 (The Roads of Freedom, 1947–51), he dealt with the experience of occupied France in a style like that of John Dos Passos. Since then he has given up fiction for the writing of plays, philosophy, and political essays. Simone de Beauvoir has shared many of Sartre's interests, and in Les Mandarins, 1954 (The Mandarins, 1956) she presented a fictionalized account of the postwar experiences of French intellectuals.

Camus, who is usually considered together with Sartre, was much less concerned with explicitly philosophic problems. In L'Étranger, 1942 (The Stranger, 1946) he deals with the consciousness of a condemned man who feels estranged from the society in which he lives. La Peste, 1947 (The Plague, 1948) is an account of a plague in a North African city, which has been read as a metaphor of the German occupation of France. These two works, direct and classical in style, established Camus as one of the most important writers of his generation. La Chute, 1956 (The Fall, 1957), his last published novel, was a richly ironic monologue about the problem of guilt and indicated that Camus had not remained content with his earlier success.

In the mid-1950's there appeared a new "school" of novelists, even more loosely associated than the existentialists, known simply as "new novelists." Different as they are from one another, they share a common ambition to renew the form of the novel by dealing directly with immediate experience, without using conventional psychological categories. Alain Robbe-Grillet (1922–   ) seems primarily concerned with the accurate presentation of the physical circumstances of human action. Michel Butor (1926–) and Claude Simon (1913–) deal with the psychological complexity that lies behind the apparently simple everyday act, as well as with the difficulty of reconstructing the experience of reality. The subject of the novel has frequently become the impossibility of writing a novel.

Consult Peyre, Henri, *The Contemporary French Novel* (1955); Brée, Germaine, and Guiton, Margaret, *The French Novel from Gide to Camus* (1962); Ullmann, Stephen, *The Image in the Modern French Novel* (1963); Le Sage, Laurent, *The French New Novel* (1962); Frohock, W. M., *Style and Temper* (1967).

GEORGE A. HOLOCH, JR., Columbia University

FRENCH MUSIC

From the Middle Ages to the 20th century France has held a position of leadership in Western musical art. Some of its outstanding contributions have been the innovations in polyphony (part-music), the chansons of the troubadours and trouvères, impressionism of the 19th century, and "concrete music" of the 20th century.

The Middle Ages

France held a particularly vital position in the development of medieval religious music. A special branch of Christian chant, known as Gallican chant, was at first sung in French churches. However, in the 9th century the Carolingian sovereigns substituted Gregorian chant. This type of chant was subsequently developed and enlarged, first at the abbey of Jumièges, near Rouen, and then at the abbey of St. Martial, at Limoges, the latter being the most active musical center in France from the 10th to the 13th centuries. The chant developments consisted in the addition of certain alleluia and other sections called sequences and tropes.

Secular music also flourished at this time. Monophonic music (music for one voice) was in some cases set to Latin texts, but mainly it was set to poems in the vernacular. The latter type was best represented in the chansons of the troubadours (11th–13th centuries), poet-musicians from southern France, and the trouvères (12th–13th centuries), who transported this art to northern France. Almost 2,000 of these songs, which minstrels performed with instrumental accompaniment in the châteaux, survive to this day.

By the 13th century France was the most active center of Western polyphonic music (music for many voices). Particularly outstanding was the Notre Dame school of composition at the Cathedral of Paris, represented by the two successive chapel masters Léonin and especially Pérotin. The latter's four-voice *organa* (polyphonic compositions based on liturgical melodies) mark an important date in the evolution of polyphony. In the 14th century a new musical style (*Ars nova*), which encouraged more rhythmic freedom and variety, as well as expressiveness, had as its most famous exponent Guillaume de Machaut.

The Renaissance

In the 15th century the Hundred Years' War nearly paralyzed musical life in most of France. However, music continued to develop in Burgundy and in the city of Cambrai. The greatest composers of the epoch, Guillaume Dufay, Gilles Binchois, Johannes Ockeghem, Antoine Busnois, and Josquin des Prez, while speaking the French language, were for the most part of Flemish origin. They evolved a completely new style, characterized by a rich, full vocal texture and the most elaborate techniques of counterpoint. This style is customarily referred to as Franco-Flemish, a term reflecting the continued influence of French culture, even though France had lost the position of musical supremacy it held during the Middle Ages.

In the 16th century a new style, representing a typically national popular spirit, made its appearance in the Parisian chanson, with Clément Jannequin as its most important composer. In 1571 the poet Antoine de Baïf and the musician Thibaut de Courville founded l'Académie de Poésie et de Musique (Academy of Poetry and Music), the most original attempt of the French Renaissance to revive the union of poetry and music that had been realized in antiquity. Musicians like Claude Le Jeune and Jacques Mauduit composed music "measured as in ancient times" (with a long note to a long syllable and a short note to a short syllable). These compositions were performed every Sunday at the academy reunions and were significant in the development of French music. During the same century important music appeared for lute, flute, and various keyboard instruments. Published (1529–33) by Pierre Attaingnant, this music consisted of adaptations of chansons and motets (sacred choral works), most often those of Claudin de Sermisy.

The Baroque and Classical Eras

During the 17th century politics and music were closely connected, since Louis XIV exercised a veritable artistic dictatorship in favor of the classical style. The taste of the King and of the court became that of France, especially setting the vogue for small forms. As a result, the two most important secular musical forms evolved, *l'air de cour* (court air) and *le ballet de cour* (court ballet). These provided the favorite entertainment of the nobility, in which the King himself took part with his courtiers. French composers, rejecting the polyphonic complexities of the preceding era along with the boldness of the new Italian style, remained under the influence of measured music and the precious and limited expression of the court air, which later took on the name *l'air sérieux* (serious air). Distinct from this aristocratic style, *l'air à boire*, the drinking song of the middle classes, perpetuated the 16th-century Gallic spirit.

Under the influence of Jules Cardinal Mazarin, there was an influx of Italian musicians into France, and Italian opera, at first opposed, later became very popular. Surprisingly, it was an Italian, Jean Baptiste Lully, who led the opposition to the Italian style by composing operas which appeared as the most perfect expression of the French genius. After him, André Campra, André Cardinal Destouches, and above all Jean Philippe Rameau continued this operatic genre. In the final years of the reign of Louis XIV, a reaction against the classical spirit, in favor of Italian music, provoked the "War of the Buffoons" (in the form of published criticisms). The Encyclopedists sided with Italian opera, demanding the return to the simplicity which the philosopher Jean Jacques Rousseau was to illustrate in his light opera *Le devin du village* (The Village Soothsayer). But once again, a foreigner, Christoph Gluck, with his operas *Orfeo ed Euridice*, *Armide*, and others, was to accomplish the dramatic reform demanded by the Encyclopedists.

At variance with this movement of ideas, religious music developed along traditional lines, primarily producing a new genre, the concerted motet. This form was characteristic of the Versailles school, which realized the classical ideal in music extending through the reign of Louis XV. The group included the greatest composers, from Lully, Michel de Lalande, and Campra to François Couperin and Rameau.

In the field of instrumental music, the important composers were Denis Gaultier, who wrote for the lute; Jacques Champion de Chambonnières, who introduced a harpsichord style continued by Jean d'Anglebert, the Couperin family, and Rameau. The French organ style founded by Jean Titelouze was carried on by Louis Marchand and others. Instrumental ensemble music appeared in 1753 with the first symphonies of François Gossec. Musical life particularly flourished in Paris, where the first public concerts were organized: the Sacred Concerts in 1725 and the Amateur Concerts in 1769.

The 1789 Revolution transformed the style of music, which was no longer performed in churches or salons, but in public places and theaters. Gossec was the most active of the musicians who tried to create a new art for the times. His hymns, designed for national ceremonies, were adapted for the populace which participated in them. Meanwhile, light opera (*opéra comique*), appearing as a distinct form in the early 1700's, continued to be written, by André Grétry, Nicolas Dalayrac, Pierre Berton, and François Devienne. In 1795 the National Convention created a National Institute of Music, which later became the Paris Conservatory of Music.

The Romantic Era

In the 19th century foreign musicians such as Gasparo Spontini, Gioacchino Rossini, and Giacomo Meyerbeer achieved great success with their operas, the latter especially with his "grand" operatic style. Numerous French composers, such as Étienne Méhul, François Boieldieu, Daniel Auber, Jacques Halévy, and Charles Gounod, also composed operas. By contrast, religious and chamber music were in evident decline. Only Hector Berlioz brilliantly developed a symphonic style and with his *Symphonie Fantastique* (Fantastic Symphony) of 1830 introduced large orchestral works into France. In the last quarter of the century the majority of the public remained faithful to the lyric theater of Georges Bizet, Jules Massenet, Léo Delibes, and Édouard Lalo. In spite of this, an effort in favor of instrumental music was begun by Camille Saint-Saëns, who in 1871 founded the Société Nationale de Musique (National Society of Music) in order to perform chamber and orchestral works of living French composers. This endeavor was supplemented by César Franck, professor at the conservatory, who reintroduced a taste for

serious music in France. Among Franck's pupils was Vincent d'Indy, who perpetuated the teachings of his master at the Schola Cantorum of Paris from 1896 to 1931 and contributed to the rise of diverse talent. These included Emmanuel Chabrier, Paul Dukas, Ernest Chausson, Henri Duparc, and Gabriel Fauré. Moreover, the influence of Wagner was very decisive for the greater number of French musicians.

The 20th Century

At the turn of the century, in 1902, with his opera *Pelléas et Mélisande* Debussy introduced an impressionist aesthetic, which vigorously opposed Wagnerian art. This marked one of the most important dates in French music. Debussy's style was expanded by Ravel, who also produced an art more amenable to the French sensibility than that of the Wagner disciples. In 1918 a new generation of musicians, rejecting the refinements of impressionism and influenced by the revolutionary antiromantic theories of Jean Cocteau, formed a "Group of Six," of whom Darius Milhaud, Arthur Honegger, and Francis Poulenc are best known. In 1923 the "School of Arcueil" (a town near Paris) gathered around Erik Satie. This was the time when Stravinsky, living in Paris, dominated musical life and when everyone was excited by the new jazz rhythms (appearing earlier in the century as ragtime). Paris became an artistic center toward which young foreign composers moved and where in 1925 a "School of Paris" was formed (Conrad Beck, Marcel Mihalovici, Bohuslav Martinů, Prokofiev, and others). Later, in 1933, P. O. Ferroud founded The Triton, a chamber music society which made known the works of Schoenberg and the 12-tone school.

In protest against musical abstraction, the group Young France was organized in 1936 (Yves Baudrier, André Jolivet, Daniel Lesur, and Olivier Messiaen), and in 1947 a new youthful group, The Zodiac, appeared in turn as a reaction against both the neoromanticism of Young France and the strict 12-tone discipline. In spite of this, the latter technique attracted many of the most adept young composers, including Pierre Boulez, perhaps the most remarkable. Important, too, are the experiments in the domain of *musique concrète* (concrete music), the "organized noise" style related to electronic music and pursued since 1949 by Pierre Schaeffer and his associates. Finally, in recent years French musical life has shown increased vitality, reflected in the numerous festivals organized every year in such cities as Aix-en-Provence, Besançon, Bordeaux, Strasbourg, Prades, and Royan, this last city specializing in contemporary music.

Consult Locke, A. W., *Music and the Romantic Movement in France* (1920); Hill, E. B., *Modern French Music* (1924); Yates, F. A., *The French Academies of the Sixteenth Century* (1947); Cooper, Martin, *French Music: From the Death of Berlioz to the Death of Fauré* (1951); Lesure, François, *Musicians and Poets of the French Renaissance* (1955); Rostand, Claude, *French Music Today* (1957); *Chanson and Madrigal*, ed. by James Haar (1964).

NANIE BRIDGMAN, Département de la Musique,
Bibliothèque Nationale, Paris

See also ELECTRONIC MUSIC; IMPRESSIONISM, MUSICAL; OPERA; TROUBADOUR AND TROUVÉRE; and entries on individual composers.

Villagers gather about an open-air stage to watch the actors perform. The miniature is from a manuscript of the 15th century.
(LIBRAIRIE HACHETTE)

FRENCH THEATER

Since life in Europe during the Middle Ages revolved around the Church, it is not surprising that the French drama originated within the Christian ritual. A priest frequently delivered his sermon in dialogue to hold the attention of his flock. On festive occasions the Gospels were read by two or more priests to intensify the dramatic line. During certain phases of the Mass, liturgical hymns (tropes) were sung antiphonally; by the 9th century, parts were assigned to definite singers. In time, Latin gave way to French; themes were intensified; the play was severed from the Mass; finally, liturgical drama, performed in the area in front of the church, was initiated. And as the theater developed, three distinct types of drama evolved: the liturgical play, which later became the mystery play of the 14th and 15th centuries; the miracle play, based on the life of a saint; and the secular, comic play.

Production of Medieval Drama. A group of Parisian artisans and tradespeople, the Confrères de la Passion (Confraternity of the Passion), devoted Sundays and holidays (weekday performances were unknown until 1597) to performing mysteries, dramas dealing mainly with Biblical events but also with some secular material. When such a work was announced by the town crier either in Paris or elsewhere, festivities began with a parade through the streets. These plays were long, performances often requiring several days. Consequently they were divided into *journées* (days) rather than acts. Productions, sometimes requiring 500 performers and multiple settings, usually took place in a square or, as in Bourges, in an amphitheater.

Comic plays included the farce, a comic interlude between parts of a miracle play or other serious drama; the *sotie*, or political satire; and the *moralité*, or dramatized allegory. During the 13th century comedy was likely to be satirical in tone, and it flourished best in bourgeois centers. Two Parisian societies staged comedies: the *basoche*, a group of parliamentary or law-court clerks, and the *enfants sans souci*. The latter group, as *sots* ("fools"), paraded about in parti-colored costumes including hoods with long ears.

The Renaissance. During this period secular drama grew in popularity; religious drama declined. Plays of a secular character were for the most part no longer given out-of-doors to elevate or to entertain the masses. They were now performed for social groups: the nobility, the students, the bourgeois. As a result, theaters, castles, and schools soon replaced outdoor areas as the locales of performances.

The 16th century saw the discovery of classical antiquity. Translations of Sophocles and Euripides appeared in French. Seneca's concept of tragedy prevailed. Themes were borrowed from the works of the ancients, as in Étienne Jodelle's *Cléopâtre captive* (1552), the first French tragedy. Plays were now divided into acts; monologues, descriptions, and choruses came into fashion; action was simpler and more concentrated. However, these plays were still lyrical rather than dramatic, and their chief element was the dénouement. With *La mort de César* (1560), Jacques Grévin's tragedy on Julius Caesar, warmth, humanity, and idealism created a new atmosphere in the theater. Jean de la Taille championed the unities of time, place, and action, based on Aristotle's *Poetics* as interpreted by Julius Caesar Scaliger. In Robert Garnier's lyrical tragedies, including *Hippolyte* (1573), the characters come close to being flesh and blood. Not until the works of the prolific Alexandre Hardy, however, were choruses done away with. Action now unfolded before the eyes of the audience, and the development of the tragic climax was cumulative. The three unities were finally established early in the 17th century.

During the Renaissance and until Molière's time, comedy was for the most part an imitation of the *commedia dell'arte* and the comedies of antiquity. However, even at the hands of Jodelle, Grévin, Rémy Belleau, and Pierre de Larivey, comedy lacked originality, spontaneity, and the frolicsome nature of the farces so popular during the Middle Ages.

Corneille, Molière, and Racine. Though not lacking in talented playwrights—Jean de Rotrou, Pierre Du Ryer, Jean Mairet, Georges de Scudéry, Thomas Corneille, Philippe Quinault, Florent Dancourt, Paul Scarron—the 17th century became renowned for the birth of three geniuses: Pierre Corneille, Molière, and Jean Racine.

Corneille used the alexandrine to convey genuine poetic effects, and added concentration and conflict to the plot. Each of his plays had one great subject, one problem to solve, and called for a victory of the will and an appeal to reason over emotion and the heart. His major works are *Le Cid* (1636), *Horace* (1640), *Cinna* (1640), and *Polyeucte* (1642).

When Molière returned to Paris (1658) with his troupe after having toured the provinces for 13 years, he wrote and produced *Les précieuses ridicules* (*The Affected*

Young Ladies), 1659, a satire on the blue-stockings of his time. It revealed, as did Molière's subsequent works—*Dom Juan* (1665), *Le misanthrope* (1666), *Tartuffe* (1669), *Le bourgeois gentilhomme* (*The Would-be Gentleman*), 1670—a sharp sensibility, an acid sense of ridicule, and a great gift for penetrating into man's mind, down to his most laughable absurdities.

After Molière's death in 1673, a general deterioration of the three main Parisian theatrical companies ensued. The Marais troupe disbanded. Some of its actors joined the Hôtel de Bourgogne, and the rest affiliated with what was left of Molière's troupe. In 1680 Louis XIV merged the two remaining groups and decreed that one company of actors should suffice for the "amusement of the Court and the City." Thus, the Comédie Française was born.

Racine was the third of France's three great playwrights; with him, the classical theater reached its apogee. In his plays—*Andromaque* (1667), *Britannicus* (1669), *Phèdre* (1677)—the dramatic line was direct, forceful, and poetic; the plot was devoid of any extraneous incident. He wrote with a tragic passion of man's inevitable conflicts.

The 18th Century. The 18th century saw the decline of tragedy in spite of Voltaire's theatrical innovations. Voltaire, a neoclassicist who continued the tradition of Corneille and Racine, was also influenced by Shakespeare and Crébillon. His quasi-philosophical plays, such as *Oedipe* (1718), *Alzire* (1736), and *Mahomet* (1741), written in a "noble style," were perhaps monotonous and seldom spontaneous. Their interest, however, resided elsewhere: in the political, religious, and philosophical themes they treated.

Though the Molière tradition was continued in the comedies of Jean François Regnard and Alain René Lesage, only two 18th-century playwrights, Pierre Carlet de Chamblain de Marivaux and Pierre Augustin Caron de Beaumarchais, were outstanding.

Marivaux's works, including *Le jeu de l'amour et du hasard* (*The Game of Love and Chance*), 1730, and *Les fausses confidences* (False Disclosures), 1737, are a unique mixture of truth and artifice, gaiety and superficial emotion. He created comedies of intrigue in which love was the motivating force. Beaumarchais' comedies of social revolt and satire—*Le barbier de Séville* (1775), *Le mariage de Figaro* (1784)—were cleverly conceived, witty, and spirited. They gave birth to a new character in the French theater—the quick, resourceful, and gay Figaro.

19th-Century Romanticism. In the early 19th century a decisive influence made itself felt. This influence was due to the passionate interest of Mme. de Staël in the German stage; to Claude Fauriel's translation of the works of the Italian poet and novelist Alessandro Manzoni, which advocated the abolition of the three unities; to the Parisian tours of English actors (Edmund Kean and Charles Kemble); and, finally, to the rise of melodrama in the plays of Louis Sébastien Mercier and Guilbert de Pixerécourt. All these forces prepared the way for Victor Hugo's theatrical reforms and the victory of the romantic movement.

One of the writings that had great impact on the theater of his time was Hugo's *Préface de Cromwell* (1827), which advocated the mingling of the tragic and comic, the juxtaposition of the beautiful and ugly, the doing away with the unities, and the relaxing of the stringent alexandrine. It was around Hugo's *Hernani* (1830) that the critical battle between the moderns and the classicists was waged. Hugo won the day. However, his own plays, including *Marion Delorme* (1831) and *Ruy Blas* (1838), lacked solid construction, a sense of reality, and insight into humanity. Alexandre Dumas père, with his historical spectacles and his romantic flair for passionate histrionics, as seen in *Antony* (1831) and *La tour de Nesle* (The Tower of Nesle), 1832, proved to be even more of a purveyor of the shallow picturesque than Hugo. Alfred de Vigny dramatized the plight of the poet-martyr in society; his theater is characterized by symbolism and sharp character analysis. Alfred de Musset's 18 plays, which include *On ne badine pas avec l'amour* (*No Trifling with Love*), 1834, and *Un caprice* (*The Caprice*), 1847, were written to be read, not acted,

Louis XIII, his family, and court at a play in the 17th century. (LIBRAIRIE HACHETTE)

Victor Hugo's *Hernani* creates a furor at its opening in Paris. (GIRAUDON)

Jean Anouilh supervises a rehearsal in Paris of his play *Becket*.
(PARIS MATCH—PICTORIAL PARADE)

though many of them are still stageworthy. Most of Musset's plays deal with love, at times ethereal, frequently guilty, always unhappy.

Romantic drama, popular during the restoration and July monarchy, generally lacked a poised insight into humankind. It indulged in stage tricks, in declamatory feats. It was followed by an experimental realistic theater, the social comedy, and the thesis play. Émile Augier, waging a battle against the romantics, wrote political and social comedies. Dumas fils, author of *La dame aux camélias* (*Camille*), 1852, and *L'Étrangère* (*The Foreigner*), 1876, moralized, sentimentalized, sermonized, and was the virtual creator of the thesis play.

Rise of Realism. The realistic theater, the *comédie rosse*, began to make its mark late in the 19th century. Playwrights of this inclination took their cues from the realistic novelists who stressed down-to-earth characters, actualities—even when sordid—and social conflicts. They dealt with love in its social aspects (including adultery and divorce) and with conflicts and cleavages between classes and professions. Realism passed into naturalism, following the trend set by Zola and the Goncourts. Henry Becque and Octave Mirbeau employed sharp, concise techniques, satiric strokes, and close observation of detail. Eugène Brieux pressed for reform with clinical themes and a realistic style.

Certain producer-directors of this period set about reforming the theatrical arts. André Antoine, founder of the Théâtre Libre (1887), tried to infuse naturalness on to the stage in his productions of plays by Hauptmann and Ibsen. Paul Fort, reacting against such naturalism, opened the doors to his symbolistic theater, the Théâtre d'Art in 1890. Aurélien Lugné-Poe, an actor in Fort's group, founded the Théâtre de l'Oeuvre (1892). He sought to inject poetry and an aura of mystery onto the French stage. He is best known for his productions of *Pelléas et Mélisande* by Maurice Maeterlinck, and *Ubu Roi* (*King Ubu*) by Alfred Jarry.

The popular dramatists interested chiefly in psychologiual sleuthing and social conflicts caught the public's attention—Paul Hervieu, Georges de Porto-Riche, François de Curel, Henri Bataille, and Henry Bernstein. There also were lighthearted playwrights in this period when analysis of one sort or another was so much in demand. Eugène Labiche made Paris laugh for nearly 40 years. He was joined by Henri Meilhac and Ludovic Halévy; Victorien Sardou, who carried on the tradition of Scribe's "modern vaudeville" and was responsible for the trend toward the ''well-made'' play; and by Édouard Pailleron, Georges Courteline, Tristan Bernard, and Georges Feydeau. Among the neoromantic playwrights, Edmond Rostand, author of *Cyrano de Bergerac* (1897), was unique in combining lyricism with audacity.

The 20th Century. New faces and new ideas appeared in the 20th century. New conceptions of the theater were born, including radical interpretations of the classics.

Jacques Copeau, establishing the Théâtre du Vieux-Colombier (1913), introduced sober and simple acting techniques and a novel scenic architecture in each of his productions. Louis Jouvet and Charles Dullin, both of whom had worked with Copeau, opened their own theaters respectively, producing classical and modern works in a personal and highly artistic vein. Other directors created further innovations: Sacha Pitoeff, Gaston Baty, Jean-Louis Barrault, Jean Vilar. Leading innovators among the dramatists of this period were Paul Claudel, André Gide, Jean Cocteau, Jules Romains, Jean Giraudoux, Albert Camus, Jean-Paul Sartre, Henry de Montherlant, Armand Salacrou, and Jean Anouilh.

But the theater, like all the arts, must constantly renew itself or decay. Influenced by Antonin Artaud's conceptions of a "theater of cruelty," dramatists such as Jean Genêt, Eugene Ionesco, Samuel Beckett, Arthur Adamov, whose works are said to belong to "the theatre of the absurd," have returned to the theater its mythlike and mysterious nature. Each dramatist has brought his own strongly individual quality to his work: groping, trying to understand, and to relate to his human condition and to the turbulent times in which he is living.

Consult Lancaster, H. C., *A History of French Dramatic Literature in the Seventeenth Century* (9 vols., 1929–42), *French Tragedy 1715–1774* (1950), and *French Tragedy 1774–1792* (1953); Esslin, Martin, *The Theatre of the Absurd* (1961).

BETTINA L. KNAPP, Hunter College
See also COMÉDIE FRANÇAISE, LA; COMEDY; DRAMA; MEDIEVAL THEATER; MELODRAMA; TRAGEDY.

FRANCESCA, PIERO DELLA. *See* PIERO DELLA FRANCESCA.

FRANCESCATTI [*frăn-sĭs-kŏt′ē*], **ZINO** (1905–), French violinist, born in Marseille. He first studied with his father, a cellist, and made his first public appearance when only 5 years old. Five years later he successfully played the Beethoven Violin Concerto in public. In 1938 he made his United States debut with the New York Philharmonic and since then has given concerts throughout the world. He is firmly established as one of the outstanding contemporary concert violinists.

FRANCIS II (1768–1835), Holy Roman and Austrian Emperor. As Francis II, this Habsburg was the last of the Holy Roman Emperors, succeeding his father, Leopold II, in 1792, and resigning in compliance with Napoleon's dissolution of the Empire in 1806. As Francis I, he became the first Emperor of Austria in 1804, elevating himself to that status in emulation of Napoleon and in defiance of the law of the dying Holy Roman Empire. His military and political apprenticeship was served under the rationalist Emperor Joseph II, who formed rather a low opinion of his capacities. A sense of his own inferiority was heightened by the successive defeats inflicted by Napoleonic France. He emerged from this experience with an urgent fear of revolution, a passive attitude toward the world in general, a patient courage in adversity, a jealous grasp of his prerogatives, and a care for practical detail. He became a petty bureaucrat, neglecting policy and refusing to delegate authority, but himself working with loving persistence through enormous amounts of paper work. Only one exception did he permit himself: he delegated foreign affairs to his Chancellor, Klemens von Metternich, whose policy of international counterrevolution rendered him entirely trustworthy. The charge of domestic affairs the Emperor reserved to himself, evading even Metternich's pleas for conservative reform.

LEONARD KRIEGER, Yale University

FRANCIS I (1494–1547), King of France (1515–47), of the younger branch of the Orléans family. He succeeded his cousin, Louis XII, in 1515. At the beginning of his reign he revealed his driving ambition to recover the French position in Italy by launching an invasion. Victorious in the decisive battle of Marignano (Sept., 1515), he secured Milan and signed with the Pope the Concordat of Bologna, which settled the government of the French church until the Revolution. The succession (1516) of Charles I to the throne of Spain and his assumption (1519) of the Imperial title as Charles V intensified the struggle between France and the Habsburgs for the control of Italy. Francis was forced to adopt an aggressive posture because of the encirclement of France by lands in the control of the Habsburgs. The first of his prolonged wars with Charles V ended in disaster at Pavia (1525), where he was captured and taken prisoner to Madrid. By the Treaty of Madrid (1526) Francis promised to give up Burgundy as well as his Italian possessions. Francis later repudiated the treaty and the struggle resumed, occupying the remainder of his reign.

Francis' internal administration was distinguished by a reform of the treasury and an improvement in the financial administration. In contrast to Louis XI and Louis XII, who had to some extent depended on bourgeois advisers, Francis employed members of the old nobility, with disastrous effects on his military and diplomatic policy. Above all, the reign of Francis I is illustrious for the introduction into France of modes of art and thought of Renaissance Italy. Architecture was revolutionized, and Italian artists working at Fontainebleau created a school that became the dominant influence in the decorative arts in France throughout the remainder of the century. Rabelais and Marot, to name only two, were among the celebrated writers of the period. Scholarship flourished in such fig-

Alinari—Art Reference Bureau

Portrait of Francis I, by court painter Jean Clouet.

ures as Guillaume Budé. During this period, too, the Reformation came to France. The French reformer John Calvin dedicated (1536) the first edition of his *Institutes of the Christian Religion* to Francis I. Favorable to reform at first, Francis later persecuted the French Calvinists.

Despite foreign policy failures and financial exhaustion, the reign of Francis I must count as one of the most illustrious in French history. A vigorous, creative, and sensitive King, he left the stamp of his personality on every aspect of national life.

MYRON P. GILMORE, Harvard University

FRANCIS, JAMES BICHENO (1815–92), American hydraulic engineer and canal builder. Born in England, he was employed at an early age on harbor and canal work, and in 1833 emigrated to the United States. In 1846 Francis built a northern power canal near Lowell, Mass., providing a great floodgate which, although referred to as "Francis' Folly," saved the Lowell textile plants in the flood of 1852. Here also, using canal locks as measuring basins, he made classical experiments on the flow of water over dams. He recorded the results in *The Lowell Hydraulic Experiments* (1855), thus making a notable contribution. He also improved the Howd inward-and-downward flow type of water turbine, a standard American form, later known as the Francis turbine.

FRANCIS, SAM (1923–   ), American painter of the abstract expressionist school, born in San Mateo, Calif. His large canvases are covered with bright color that forms an over-all textural pattern, partially achieved by the dripping and running of the wet paint. Francis is represented at the Albright Art Gallery in Buffalo, N.Y., the Museum of Modern Art and the Guggenheim Museum in New York City, and other galleries.

FRANCISCAN FRIARS OF THE ATONEMENT, religious congregation devoted to preaching, missionary work, and the Catholic press. Founded in 1898 by Lewis Thomas Wattson as an Anglican order, the congregation was received into the Roman Catholic Church in 1909. It has been active in promoting the Octave of Prayer, Jan. 18 to Jan. 25, for the reunion of Christendom. The membership is about 300, with generalate at Graymoor in Garrison, N.Y.

JOHN A. HARDON, S.J., West Baden College

FRANCISCANS [frăn-sĭs′kənz], popular name of the men and women of the numerous religious orders who follow some form of the rule of St. Francis of Assisi—specifically: the first order of St. Francis, the mendicant Friars Minor; the second order, known as the Poor Clares; and the third order, divided into third order regulars and the tertiaries, known as Brothers and Sisters of Penance.

The first order of St. Francis was officially recognized by Pope Innocent III on Apr. 16, 1209, after about a year of unofficial existence. The rule of 1209 (the *Primitiva*) is not extant, but consisted of little more than some Gospel passages with comments by St. Francis. The order met yearly in a general chapter, and statutes were added from experience, and approved by the Holy See as circumstances dictated. Later Francis found that this rather simple organizational procedure was inadequate, so he wrote a detailed rule (*Regula prima*) in 1220. It proved to be too severe for the brethren, so was revised in 1223 (*Regula secunda*), and received papal approval on Nov. 29. The ideal of poverty, not only of the individual but even of the order itself, is set forth in this rule, and it was the source of controversy and division even while Francis lived. After his death, on Oct. 3, 1226, the difficulties of observance became even more pressing and eventually culminated in the division of the order.

St. Francis' final work, his *Testament*, repeated his teaching about absolute poverty and literal obedience to the rule and refusal of all privileges. It was thought by some to supersede the rule of 1223, since it was written in 1226. But Pope Gregory IX determined that the *Testament* did not have the force of law, in his bull *Quo elongati*, of Sept. 28, 1230. Yet some Franciscans still felt bound in conscience to follow the *Testament* rigorously. A compromise whereby third parties held goods for the order was put into practice, but was thought by many to make a fiction of absolute poverty. The general chapter of Metz, in 1254, found the order divided into those who wanted to return to the primitive ideals of St. Francis, called Spirituals, and those called Conventuals, who saw the necessity for the order becoming more clerical, in order to fulfill its obligations of preaching and missionary activity. This deep division within the order determined its subsequent history. In 1257 St. Bonaventure became master general. He accepted the duties thrust on the order by the needs of the church and endorsed the practice of engaging in intellectual pursuits, having larger monasteries, and preserving some privileges. Accused of laxity by the Spirituals, he drew up the Constitutions of Narbonne in 1260, which served as a model for future constitutions and aimed at insuring the unity of the order. The tensions between the Spirituals and Conventuals increased, but in 1317 Pope John XXII denied permission to separate, and on Dec. 8, 1322, he restored all property to the order, literally ending the ideal of absolute poverty and thus increasing the tension in the order. Those wishing for reform and a return to the original observance of the rule increased in number from 1367 on and were called Observants. Finally Pope Martin V, in the bull *Ad statum*, of Aug. 23, 1430, gave the Conventuals permission to hold property in common; and this ended all hope of a union of the order along lines of the original observance. A permanent division of the order was inevitable, especially since no masters general from 1443 to 1517 were Observants.

Under the auspices of Pope Leo X, a general chapter was called in 1517, in which all the reformed communities were unified under the Observants, henceforth called Order of Friars Minor (O.F.M.); and the other communities were joined under the Conventuals, henceforth called Order of Friars Minor Conventual (O.F.M. Conv.). In 1525 there was a split among the Observants, and the third part of the Franciscan first order came into existence, the order of Friars Minor Capuchin (O.F.M. Cap.), known simply as Capuchins.

Despite the long history of tension and division, it must be remembered that all the members of the three branches of the Franciscan first order are true sons of St. Francis, since each branch is the result of an unbroken continuity starting with their holy founder. The reason for all these divisions was not any real difference in the understanding of the ideals of St. Francis, but rather derived from the differences which arose when holy men had to make prudential judgments as to how practically to live this ideal in an ever changing world. The glorious contributions of each branch give glowing testimony to the validity of each such judgment.

The tertiaries of St. Francis, known officially as Brothers and Sisters of Penance, trace their existence back to St. Francis himself. They were established in 1221, and their rule consists of three chapters, which give in detail the manner of life and the works required of members, most of whom are laymen and laywomen living in the world. There are some 3,500,000 Franciscan tertiaries in the world.

Consult Huber, R. M., *A Documented History of the Franciscan Order* (1944).

RICHARD J. WESTLEY, Barat College
See also CAPUCHINS; POOR CLARES.

FRANCIS DE SALES [sālz], **ST.** (1567–1622), Roman Catholic missionary. Born at the Château de Sales in Savoy, he received his education in the arts and in law at Paris and Padua. Ordained in 1593, he began missionary work the next year in the strongly Protestant Chablis district south of Lake Geneva. His attractive personality and literary skill soon restored this area to Catholicism. In 1602 he became Bishop of Geneva. In 1610, with St. Jane Frances de Chantal, he founded the Order of the Visitation of Our Lady, a community of nuns. He was beatified in 1661, canonized in 1665, and in 1877, Pope Pius IX proclaimed St. Francis de Sales Doctor of the Church and patron saint of journalists. His feast day is January 29.

FRANCIS FERDINAND (1863–1914), Austrian Archduke whose assassination by a Serbian nationalist at Sarajevo, Bosnia, on June 28, 1914, touched off the crisis that led to World War I. Nephew of Emperor Francis Joseph and unofficially considered the Austrian Crown Prince, he was a passionate defender of dynastic prerogative. He opposed all groups he deemed a threat to the monarchy—German-Austrian liberals, Magyar aristocrats, Poles, and Czechs—and favored their enemies. His patronage of the Croats against the Magyars made him an obstacle to Serbian nationalists' plans to detach the Croats from the Habsburg Empire and join them to an enlarged Serbia.

FRANCIS JOSEPH (1830–1916), Austrian Emperor (1848–1916). He came to the throne in the midst of the Revolution of 1848 when his uncle, the weak-minded Emperor Ferdinand I, abdicated in his favor. He never forgot the threat to his throne, or the lesson taught him by his Minister President, Prince Felix von Schwarzenberg, on how to deal with it. The revolutionary Austrian National Assembly was removed from Vienna to Kremsier and then dissolved (Mar., 1849). To avoid popular protest, the Emperor immediately proclaimed his own constitution, which he at once suspended and ultimately canceled (Dec., 1851). He then adopted the policy, initiated by Schwarzenberg and continued by Minister of the Interior Alexander von Bach, of bureaucratic centralization at home and assertion of Austrian prestige abroad. The result was the alienation of Russia during the Crimean War (1854–56), Austrian isolation during her wars with France and Sardinia (1859) and with Prussia (1866), and domestic crises during the 1860's. Francis Joseph's solution was, in domestic affairs, creation (1867) of the Dual Monarchy, which assured the loyalty of the German-Austrians and Magyars to his dynasty, and, in foreign affairs, co-operation with Germany, which enabled him to counter Russian designs in the

Balkans. As the years went by, he clung all the more desperately to this system, amending it only in 1907 with the grant of universal suffrage to appease the discontented middle class.

Francis Joseph considered himself, and was generally considered to be, "the last monarch of the old school." Popularly associated with the gaiety, romance, and stability of old Vienna, he actually presided over the slow disintegration of the Habsburg state. He possessed the conscientiousness, the diligent attention to the details of government, and the stubborn addiction to dynastic prerogative that was so characteristic of the Habsburgs, but he added to these traits an unwonted admixture of flexibility. He was willing, therefore, to make tactical concessions that would leave the crown its exclusive direction of diplomacy and the army. Confident at first in his own power to achieve a solution along these lines, he was faced with the overlapping problems of democracy, socialism, and nationalism. He was oppressed also by personal tragedies, such as the execution (1867) of his brother Maximilian in Mexico, the suicide (1889) of his son Rudolph, and the assassination (1898) of his wife Elizabeth. His attitude changed to one of resignation, and he sought only to hang on during his own lifetime to a rule he knew to be doomed. The Balkan Wars of 1912–13 undermined the Habsburg position in southeastern Europe, and when Francis Joseph consented to a belligerent policy after the assassination (1914) of Archduke Francis Ferdinand at Sarajevo, it was with a fatalism that gave due recognition to the probability of a tragic outcome for his realm.

Consult Redlich, Joseph, *Emperor Francis Joseph of Austria* (1929).

LEONARD KRIEGER, Yale University

FRANCIS OF ASSISI, ST. (1182–1226), Christian mystic, and founder of the Franciscans. St. Francis is perhaps the most popular of the saints, and many maintain that he is the perfect disciple of Jesus Christ.

Early Life. Born in Assisi, in Umbria, the son of Peter and Pica Bernardone, he was baptized John the Baptist Bernardone, but his father, who was a Francophile, called him Francis. He was educated by the priests of the Church of St. George, where he learned Latin, having learned French at home. His father was a merchant and hoped that Francis would follow in his footsteps; but Francis dreamed of knighthood and the glories of the successful soldier and crusader. He was handsome, gay, gallant, and courteous, and was the most attractive of the wealthy young men of Assisi, delighting in fine clothes and display. In 1201 he took part in a war against Perugia, was captured and returned home after the treaty of Nov., 1202. Illness overtook him after his return, and he began to see the emptiness of his life of ease and pleasure, but after convalescing he returned to his former ways. In the spring of 1205, again seeking glory in arms, he joined Walter of Palearis, Chancellor of young Frederick II, in a war of succession. Before they reached Spoleto Francis heard a voice telling him to return to Assisi. A second illness befell him, and this time the change was permanent. Upon recovering, he sought to bring his proud nature into subjection by austere penances and by working with the poor and sick, even with lepers.

Emperor Francis Joseph of Austria.

Brown Brothers

After Conversion. One day in 1206, while praying before the crucifix in the dilapidated church of St. Damian, Francis heard a voice from the crucifix say: "Francis, do you not see that my house is falling to ruins? Go and repair it." Francis, taking the words literally, sold his horse and fine clothes, and began to beg stones to rebuild the building. He worked at this task off and on until 1208. His father was outraged and humiliated by these actions, and actually took Francis to court over the selling of his possessions. The case was tried eventually before the Bishop, and Francis returned what he could to his father, and then accepted God as his only true father.

Up to this time Francis had been living as a hermit, but on Feb. 24, 1208, he heard in the Gospel at Mass (Matt. 10:9) the call to penance and preaching. He abandoned the hermit's life, put on a rough tunic tied round him with a cord, and began to preach the teachings of Christ in the Gospels. Joined by two companions, he gave them as their rule three Gospel texts (Matt. 10:9, 20:21; and Luke 9:23). When his companions numbered 11, he wrote a rule, the lost *Primitiva*, which was simply a short commentary on the three scriptural texts. Then in 1209, he led his brethren to Rome to seek papal approval.

The Beginnings of Friars Minor. After Innocent III gave verbal approbation to the group on Apr. 16, 1209, they returned to Assisi, where they settled in huts at Rivotorto, near Portiuncula, and preached penance throughout central Italy. So the simple life began with very few formalities and with Francis as the model. Francis himself had no desire to found an order. He had turned from the cloistered security of the monasteries, and wished only to follow the Christ of the Gospels. But despite his hopes, the brotherhood could not help but take on the form of a monastic body. As the group grew, it was increasingly necessary to delegate authority; and once a year a Great Chapter was held at Portiuncula. In 1212 Francis encouraged St. Clare of Assisi to found the Poor Clares, and with her counsel decided that the brotherhood would take on missionary goals and not be merely a contemplative group. He himself was to attempt missionary journeys to Syria (1212) and to Morocco (1213); but illness forced him back each time. Finally, in 1219, he got to Egypt and preached before the Sultan, with little effect.

In his absence the brotherhood, due to its informal organization and the good-willed but erroneous innovations of those whom Francis had left in authority, faced a severe crisis. Francis returned to establish the brotherhood on a firm canonical basis. He now (1220) wrote a detailed rule: *Regula prima*, which proved too simple and severe, and which he then revised as *Regula secunda* or *Bullata*. (This rule received papal approval from Honorius III on Nov. 29, 1223.) At the chapter of 1220 Francis reproached his brothers for their innovations; but he eventually realized that he could no longer rule the brotherhood in a patriarchal way, and that a representative form of government was now necessary.

The Glorious End. Though still in indirect control, Francis retired, leaving the actual management of affairs to his Vicars. In 1221 Francis established the rule of the third order, or Brothers and Sisters of Penance; and in 1222 he commanded St. Anthony of Padua to teach the-

Alinari—Art Reference Bureau

"St. Francis' Sermon to the Birds," painted about 1300 by Giotto, is one of a series of frescoes of the saint's life in the basilica of St. Francis in Assisi, Italy.

ology in Italy and southern France. On Sept. 14, 1224, Francis experienced an ecstasy in which he received the stigmata from a fiery seraph, thus confirming him in the likeness of Christ. Physically exhausted by his extreme penances and the sufferings of the stigmata, he eventually became blind and had to be carried from place to place. He wrote his famous *Canticle of the Sun* in 1225–26, and his *Testament* in 1226. The former is the earliest masterpiece of the new Italian language, the latter his final teaching regarding absolute poverty, refusal of all privilege, and literal obedience to the rule. After a last visit to St. Clare and the city of Assisi, he died joyfully on Oct. 3, 1226. Due to the many miracles performed through his intercession, he was canonized by Pope Gregory IX on July 16, 1228; and in 1230 his body was transferred to the basilica of St. Francis in Assisi, where it remains.

Francis was a saint in the universal sense, for he is not limited to any particular age any more than is the Gospel he so literally followed. Thus, though Francis is the flower of medieval sanctity, he is not a medieval saint, but always remains an exemplar for any Christian who wishes to answer the invitation of Christ: "If thou wilt be perfect, go sell what thou hast and give to the poor and come follow me" (Matt. 19:21).

Consult Huber, R. M., O.F.M., *A Documented History of the Franciscan Order* (1944).

RICHARD J. WESTLEY, Barat College

FRANCIS OF PAOLA [pä'ō-lä], **ST.** (1419–1507), founder of a Roman Catholic congregation of monks called the Minims ("the least"). They followed a severe rule of perpetual abstinence, celibacy, and dire poverty. Born in Paola, Italy, he died in Plessis, France, and was canonized by Pope Leo X in 1519.

FRANCIS XAVIER, ST. *See* XAVIER, ST. FRANCIS.

FRANCIUM [frăn'sē-əm], radioactive alkali metal. It was reported detected in 1931 and named "virginium," but the report was not confirmed and is now believed to have been mistaken. In 1939 M. Perey detected the francium isotope, Fr²²³, as occurring naturally in small amounts among the breakdown products of uranium. She at first named it "actinium K" but eventually named it after her native land, France. Fr²²³ is the longest-lived francium isotope. It emits beta particles and has a half life of 21 minutes.

PROPERTIES	
Symbol	Fr
Atomic number	87
Atomic weight	223
Valence	1

FRANCK [frängk], **CÉSAR AUGUSTE** (1822–90), noted Belgian composer, born in Liège. He studied at the conservatories of Liège and Paris, and settled as an organist and piano teacher in Paris, where he was appointed professor of organ in the Conservatory in 1872.

Franck's enduring contributions include his famous Symphony in D Minor (1888), the symphonic poems *Les Éolides* (1876) and *Le chasseur maudit* (1882), the Symphonic Variations (1885) for piano and orchestra, the oratorio *Les Béatitudes* (1869–79), the well-known Piano Quintet (1879) and Violin and Piano Sonata (1886), a number of piano and organ pieces, and the perennial vocal favorite, *Panis angelicus*.

Unlike Wagner's continuous chromatic flow, Franck's chromaticism results mainly from temporary alterations of chords and contrapuntal lines that later resolve in familiar cadences. His use of thematic relationships between movements (cyclic form) influenced later composers such as Camille Saint-Saëns and Vincent d'Indy. Franck's organ style affected his compositions in other mediums, producing block changes in orchestration, enormous left-hand piano chords, and consistent interest in contrapuntal texture and devices such as the canon. His music occasionally suffers from a weak chromaticism and overuse of formulas such as the two-bar phrase and successive modulations (key changes) each a third higher.

Consult Demuth, Norman, *César Franck* (1949).

JAN LARUE

FRANCK, JAMES (1882–1964), German-born physicist who shared the 1925 Nobel Prize with Gustav Hertz "for their discovery of the laws governing the impact between an electron and an atom." Franck was Director of the Physics Institute at Göttingen, 1920–33. He later taught at Johns Hopkins, at California, and Chicago, and worked on the atomic bomb. Subsequently he worked on photosynthetic processes.

FRANCO [fräng'kō], **FRANCISCO** (1892–1975), Spanish dictator. Born in El Ferrol of an old naval family, he was educated at the Toledo Military Academy. Beginning in 1912 he saw service in Morocco, and in 1923 he became commander of the Spanish Foreign Legion. At 33 he was Spain's youngest general. Demoted under the republic, he served as chief of staff (1935) during the brief interregnum of the right. He was sent (1936) to the Canary Islands as military governor, a post which amounted to exile. From there he flew to Morocco to help direct the July, 1936, uprising against the republic. Crossing to Spain, he was named head of the nationalist government and generalissimo of the armed forces in September. In Apr., 1937, he became *Caudillo* (leader) of the Falangist party.

Victory in 1939 found Franco deeply indebted to Germany and Italy and committed in principle to creating a totalitarian state. He had already (Apr., 1939) joined the Anti-Comintern Pact. The outbreak of World War II greatly hampered economic reconstruction in his war-shattered country, thus compelling his declaration of strict neutrality. France's collapse and Italy's entry into the war changed neutrality to nonbelligerency (June, 1940), and Franco began to stake a claim in the spoils of Axis victory while avoiding active commitment beyond the dispatch of a Blue Division to the Russian front in 1941. The war ended with Spain again a "strict neutral" and her totalitarian regime rebaptized an organic democracy.

Spain's ostracism by the United Nations (1946) rallied Spanish opinion behind the *Caudillo*. In reviving (1942) a purely consultative Cortes (parliament), he had relinquished none of his power, and he consistently thwarted the Falangist party's ambition to identify itself with the state. By a Succession Act (1947) he declared Spain again a kingdom with himself as regent, to be succeeded eventually by a monarch sworn to uphold the fundamental principles of the regime. Spain was admitted to the United Nations in 1955. In 1969, Franco chose Prince Juan Carlos de Borbón as his successor, to become king and chief of state on his death. Juan Carlos was given temporary power during Franco's final illness, and became king on Nov. 22, 1975.

WILLIAM C. ATKINSON

FRANCONIA [fräng-kō'nē-ə] (Ger. **FRANKEN**), a long-extinct German duchy whose name now refers to a historic region in southern Germany on the Rhine. Created as a duchy in the 9th century and named for the Franks, a Germanic tribe, Franconia included the present-day Rhineland, Hesse, and part of Bavaria. Holy Roman Emperor Otto I dissolved and partitioned the duchy in 939.

FRANCO-PRUSSIAN WAR, conflict (1870–71) between Prussia, supported by other German states, and France. The war, which destroyed the Second Empire of Napoleon III, was the third and last by which the Prussian Premier, Otto von Bismarck, brought unity to a divided Germany.

Bismarck needed a war with France to frighten the South German states into joining the North German Confederation, a coalition of states organized by Prussia after the Austro-Prussian War of 1866. Napoleon III was determined to halt the process of German unification and, if possible, to inflict a defeat on Prussia that would reverse the decision of 1866. Between 1866 and 1870 Bismarck deliberately encouraged Franco-Prussian discord while he worked to isolate France from prospective allies. The generous terms that Bismarck gave Austria in 1866, together with Austrian outrage at Napoleon's role in Italian unifica-

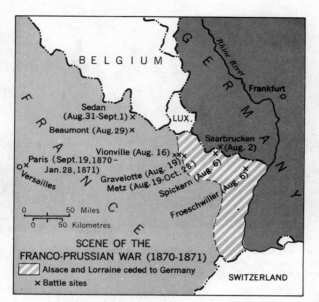

BELGIUM
GERMANY
Rhine River
Frankfurt
Sedan
(Aug.31-Sept.1) ×
Beaumont (Aug.29) ×
LUX.
Saarbrucken
×(Aug. 2)
Vionville (Aug. 16) ×××
Paris (Sept.19,1870 –
Jan.28,1871) ×
Gravelotte (Aug. 18) ×
Metz (Aug.19-Oct. 28)×
Spickern (Aug. 6)
Froeschwiller (Aug. 6)
Versailles
FRANCE
0   50 Miles
0   50 Kilometres
SWITZERLAND

SCENE OF THE
FRANCO-PRUSSIAN WAR (1870-1871)
▨ Alsace and Lorraine ceded to Germany
× Battle sites

tion, ensured Austrian neutrality. Italy was anti-French because French troops garrisoned Rome and prevented the fulfillment of Italian unification. Bismarck tacitly offered Russia a revision of the Black Sea clauses of the Treaty of Paris (1856), and his calculation that the British would remain neutral proved correct.

In 1868, in order to further embitter relations with France, Bismarck discreetly supported the candidacy of a Hohenzollern Prince to the vacant Spanish throne by bribing influential Spaniards. The throne was offered to the Prince in June, 1870. It was accepted but then declined when Napoleon III protested to King William I of Prussia. Overly confident, Napoleon then demanded assurances through his ambassador that no Hohenzollern would ever again seek the Spanish throne. The King, on a vacation in Ems, refused (July 12) and sent a telegram to Bismarck describing the interview. The adroit Premier abridged this famous Ems dispatch to make it seem that the King had insulted the French ambassador. He released it to the press, and, as he had hoped, French public opinion was wildly inflamed. On July 19, 1870, France declared war on Prussia, and Bismarck was thus able to lead a united Germany into the fight.

Helmuth von Moltke, the Prussian chief of staff, conducted a brilliant campaign. Between Aug. 4 and Sept. 1 the main French armies were defeated, Napoleon was captured, and the Second Empire collapsed. A provisional government fought on, but with dwindling chances of gaining even a stalemate. Paris, besieged on Sept. 19, was the last point of resistance to fall (Jan. 28, 1871). On Jan. 18 the German Empire was proclaimed in Versailles, and Bismarck, now imperial Chancellor, dictated the peace terms that were signed in Frankfurt-am-Main (May 10). France was forced to cede Alsace and part of Lorraine, to pay an indemnity of 5 billion gold francs, and to support an army of occupation. The war removed France from its position of dominance in Europe, held for some two centuries, and Germany supplanted it.

Consult Howard, Michael, *The Franco-Prussian War* (1961).

JOHN G. SPERLING, Northern Illinois University

FRANGIPANI [frăn-jĭ-păn'ē], common name for about 50 species of flowering shrubs and trees of the genus *Plumeria*, in the dogbane family, Apocynaceae, native to tropical America. *P. rubra*, the frangipani of Mexico and the West Indies, is often called "red jasmine" because of its fragrant scarlet blossoms. Other species have flowers of white, yellow, pink, or rose. Frangipani is grown outdoors in California, Florida, Hawaii, and other regions with a warm climate. It is propagated by cuttings.

FRANK, ANNE. *See* DIARY OF ANNE FRANK, THE.

FRANK, ILYA M. (1908–   ), Soviet physicist who shared the 1958 Nobel Prize with P. A. Cerenkov and I. Y. Tamm, for the discovery and interpretation of the phenomenon called the Cerenkov effect. Discovered in the 1930's, it is an important tool in the study of cosmic rays and atomic particles. A corresponding member of the Academy of Sciences of the U.S.S.R., Frank is professor of physics at Moscow University and has done work on gamma rays and neutrons.
See also CERENKOV RADIATION.

FRANKEL, ZACHARIAS (1801–75), pioneer of the scientific study of Judaism. He was Chief Rabbi of Dresden (1836–54) and became first president of the Breslau Rabbinical Seminary in 1854. Combining religious with secular learning, Frankel was one of the founders of the conservative trend in modern Judaism.

FRANKENSTEIN [frăngk'ən-stǐn], **OR THE MODERN PROMETHEUS,** English novel (1818) by Mary Shelley. Victor Frankenstein, a Swiss scientist, imparts life to a construction of human remains. The resulting creature is powerful, but it is loathed by all who see it, so that it comes to hate its creator and kills Frankenstein's brother, bride, and best friend. Frankenstein, who searches for the monster in order to kill it, finally dies himself. In common usage, the word "Frankenstein" has come to mean a creation which destroys its creator.

FRANKENTHAL [frăng'kən-täl], city of western Federal Republic of Germany (West Germany). A modern industrial center, it has heavy industries but is especially noted for its costly porcelain. Frankenthal flourished as the capital of the Rhineland-Palatinate in the reign (1733–77) of Elector Charles Theodore. The porcelain manufactory, founded in 1755, was abandoned about 1800 but since World War II has been re-established. Pop., 33,949.

FRANKFORT, city of central Indiana and seat of Clinton County. It is a trade and distributing center for a grain and livestock farming region, and has railway shops. Foundry products, porcelain and enamelware, clothing, and fertilizer are manufactured here. Laid out, 1830; pop., 14,956.

FRANKFORT, city and state capital of Kentucky, and seat of Franklin County. The city, a port on the Kentucky River, near its picturesque gorge, is located in the center of the famous Bluegrass region, noted for its tobacco and thoroughbred horses. Frankfort has four famous bourbon

Above, the tower of the 14th-century Cathedral of St. Bartholomew rises above Main River at Frankfurt. (BIRNBACK PUBLISHING SERVICE) **Left,** Eschenheim Tower, one of Frankfurt's remaining medieval landmarks. (JUPP FALKE—BILDARCHIV)

distilleries, open for public tours. Products manufactured in the city are shoes, clothing, electric and machine parts, wood products, and concrete. In addition to its river transportation, Frankfort is served by the Capital City Airport, four major U.S. highways, and two railways.

The state capitol is one of the most impressive structures of its kind. It was constructed in 1909 of Indiana Bedford limestone and Vermont marble, with ornamentation in granite and marble from Georgia, Tennessee, and Italy. The Kentucky Historical Society houses a museum in the Old Capitol (1827–30), a notable example of Greek revival architecture. Liberty Hall, designed by Thomas Jefferson and constructed in 1796, is of historical interest. Daniel Boone was buried in Frankfort, and a monument marks his grave. Kentucky State College is here.

The site of Frankfort was first visited in 1751 by the explorer Christopher Gist. The city derives its name from Stephen Frank, a frontiersman who was killed by Indians in 1780, and the river ford he used ("Frank's ford"). Frankfort was made Kentucky's capital in 1792, when the state was admitted to the Union. Inc. as city, 1792; pop., 21,902.

J. R. SCHWENDEMAN, University of Kentucky

FRANKFURT AM MAIN [frängk'foort äm mīn'] (Eng. **FRANKFORT ON THE MAIN**), city in the center of the Federal Republic of Germany (West Germany), on the right bank of the Main River, 25 mi. above its junction with the Rhine. Of great historic importance, Frankfurt is one of Germany's oldest cities; it was a Roman settlement in the 1st century A.D. and later passed to the Franks, hence its name meaning "ford of the Franks." Charlemagne spent his winters at Frankfurt, and beginning in the 14th century the Emperors of the Holy Roman Empire were elected here. From 1562 to 1792 the Emperors were also crowned in Frankfurt. It became a free city in 1219. Thereafter Frankfurt developed into one of the richest and most powerful cities in the world, the city in which, for example, the great Rothschild international banking house originated. It was the meeting place of the Diet of the German Confederation from 1816 to 1866, and in 1848–49 was the scene of the National Assembly, which attempted unsuc-

cessfully to unify Germany. It became part of the Prussian province of Hesse-Nassau in 1866 and five years later the treaty ending the Franco-Prussian War was signed here.

Much of the former Gothic architecture of the old district between the center of the city and the river was heavily damaged during World War II and has been replaced by modern buildings. Some buildings have been restored, however, including the Gothic Cathedral of St. Bartholomew in red sandstone (1315–53), in which the Emperors were crowned; the Römer, a late medieval Town Hall; the Fahrtor and the Rent Tower, built in 1219; the Romanesque St. Leonard's Church, with its three naves; the 13th-century Church of St. Nicholas; and the imperial court room and ruins of the chapel of Emperor Frederick I (Barbarossa). Near the present center of the business district is the Eschenheim Tower (1426), the only remaining vestige of the town's inner fortifications. The house where the poet Johann Wolfgang von Goethe was born was restored by international subscription after World War II and is now a national monument. The city was occupied by American forces after 1945, and although it suffered much damage during World War II, industrial recovery was rapid. Manufactures now include cigarettes and cigars, women's clothing, machinery, chemicals, and electric apparatus. It is also a printing and publishing center; the daily newspaper the *Frankfurter Allgemeine Zeitung* is internationally known. Frankfurt is the headquarters of the Bank of the German Länder and of the central district bank of Hesse. It is a major transportation center; main lines from northern Europe to the Mediterranean intersect those from Paris to eastern Europe, and the city has an international airport. Pop., 683,081.

ALICE F. A. MUTTON, University of London

FRANKFURT AN DER ODER [än der ō'der], city in the German Democratic Republic (East Germany), lying on the west bank of the Oder River, 50 mi. east of Berlin. Today it is the capital of the *Bezirk* (district) of the same name. The city was founded by settlers from western Germany in the 14th century and became a leading commerical city and member of the Hanseatic League. In the 19th century it was linked by canal with Berlin and the Elbe. The city was heavily damaged toward the end of World War II but has been largely rebuilt. Notable buildings include late medieval churches and the city hall. Frankfurt has a number of industries: mechanical engineering, textiles, and processing of leather, wood and foodstuffs. Twelve miles south is the postwar iron and steel center, Eisenhüttenstadt. Frankfurt's eastern suburb is today the Polish city of Słubice. Frankfurt's population is smaller than in 1939. Pop., 56,356.

NORMAN J. G. POUNDS, Indiana University

FRANKFURTER [frăngk'fərtər], **FELIX** (1882–1965), Justice of the U.S. Supreme Court. Born of Jewish parents in Vienna, he came to the United States at the age of 12. A graduate of the College of the City of New York and Harvard Law School, he served with Henry L. Stimson in the U.S. District Attorney's office and in the War Department. He returned in 1914 to Harvard as a professor of law. With one interruption, for government service in World War I, he remained at Harvard until 1939. Frankfurter was an inspiring teacher, an outstanding scholar, and a crusader for legal and social reform. He became the nation's outstanding student of the Supreme Court, and his appointment as an Associate Justice by President Franklin D. Roosevelt in 1939 was widely acclaimed.

Frankfurter frequently refused to lend his judicial support to causes in which, as an individual, he firmly believed. It was his conviction that judicial restraint was required in order that policy determinations remain with the branches of government responsible to public opinion. It is important nevertheless, not to overemphasize his differences with his more "activist" colleagues. He played an important part in the dramatic growth of constitutional protection against racial discrimination and unfair criminal procedures as well as in the extension of powers of the federal and state governments to regulate for the public interest. Frankfurter retired from the Court in 1962, because of ill health.

ALBERT ROSENTHAL, Columbia University, School of Law

FRANKINCENSE [frăngk'in-sĕns], fragrant, clear-yellow resin obtained from trees of the genus *Boswellia*, found in Africa and Asia. Frankincense has been valued since Biblical times as an ingredient of incense used in religious ceremonies. It is also used in perfumes and fumigating powders. The chief source of the resin is *B. carteri*, a tree native to southern Arabia and eastern Africa.

FRANKLIN, BENJAMIN (1706–90), American printer, writer, scientist, and statesman. He was born in Boston, the youngest son of Josiah Franklin, a chandler, and his second wife, Abiah Folger. Conditions at home interrupted Ben's formal schooling at the age of ten, and after several restless years he was apprenticed to his brother James, a printer. While learning the trade, he continued his education by reading as widely as he could. When James founded the *New England Courant* (1721), Ben gained valuable experience in journalism. But, growing restless under his brother's tutelage, he left home at 17 to seek his fortune.

Philadelphia Printer and Citizen. In the fall of 1723 Franklin arrived in Philadelphia, where for the next six years, save for a trip to England, he worked for various printers. In 1729 he bought out a former employer and began publishing the *Pennsylvania Gazette*, which became his main source of livelihood for the next 20 years. Aided by government printing contracts and his appointment in 1737 as Philadelphia's postmaster, the young printer's business prospered. Franklin's most successful undertaking was *Poor Richard's Almanack*, first appearing in 1734, which soon sold 10,000 copies a year. In both the *Almanack* and the *Gazette*, as well as in frequent essays, he emphasized the importance of temperance, industry, and frugality for those who would make the most of their opportunities. The one virtue he himself found impossible to attain was chastity, a problem partially solved by his common-law marriage in 1730 to Deborah Read Rogers, whose first husband had deserted her. Deborah took Ben's admittedly illegitimate son William into the household and bore Franklin two other children.

Franklin quickly became a leader among the lively young citizens of Philadelphia. In 1727 he founded the Junto, a club to promote philosophical discussion that eventually led to the founding (1744) of the American Philosophical Society. The Library Company, which he helped establish in 1731, was the prototype for private circulating libraries throughout the colonies. Franklin published numerous pamphlets on public issues, including his *Proposals Relating to the Education of Youth in Pennsylvania* (1743), in which he urged the establishment of the academy that eventually grew into the University of Pennsylvania.

Scientist and Public Servant. By 1748 Franklin had amassed enough wealth from his printing interests to retire from active business. For many years he had been

Left, printing press used by Benjamin Franklin in 1722. (SY SEIDMAN) **Below,** Franklin testifies on the Stamp Act before the House of Commons in 1766. (THE BETTMANN ARCHIVE)

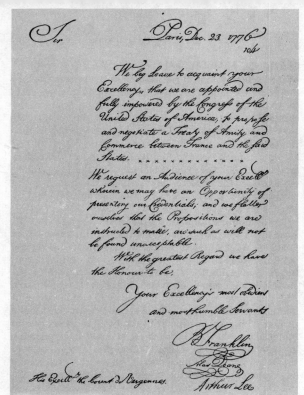

Franklin signed the congressional letter of Dec. 23, 1776, to France that concerned the "Treaty of Amity and Commerce."

Portrait of Franklin by Charles Willson Peale (1741–1827).

fascinated by science. Largely ignorant at first of earlier European discoveries, Franklin continually experimented to prove theories that he had hypothesized from observations. The results of his study of the Leyden jar, confirming his revolutionary single-fluid theory of electricity, were published (1751) in England, and his reputation as a scientist became international. Seeking to prove his conviction, shared by many others, that lightning was electricity and that its charges could be drawn off by a pointed iron rod, he conducted a famous experiment with a kite during a thunderstorm, probably in June, 1752. His success led to the development of the lightning rod, soon adopted throughout America.

Franklin turned other findings into practical use, such as his Pennsylvania fireplace and his studies of the Gulf Stream. But he never lost his primary interest in discovering by experimentation the scientific theory behind the phenomena he observed. During the 1750's came wide recognition of his achievements, election to the Royal Society of London, honorary degrees, and letters from European scientists.

Franklin began still another career after retiring from business—public service. This he considered the obligation of every successful citizen. Even before election to the Pennsylvania assembly in 1751, he had aroused Philadelphians to the need for intercolonial unity during King George's War by his pamphlet *Plain Truth* (1747). His study of demography, which he wrote in 1751 under the title *Observations Concerning the Increase of Mankind*, showed that only westward expansion could accommodate the rapidly increasing population of the colonies. He advocated a union among the colonies to protect the advancing frontier from French and Indian attacks. When the Albany Congress was summoned in 1754 to arrange a new Indian treaty, delegate Franklin brought with him a plan proposing an intercolonial council to handle Indian affairs, common defense, and western policy. But none of the commissioners at Albany approved of surrendering so much power to a higher authority, and Franklin's Plan of Union was rejected. When Indians attacked along the Pennsylvania frontier the following year, Franklin did what he could to improve defenses, finding wagons and supplies for Gen. Edward Braddock's ill-fated expedition and helping to build a stockade in the wilderness.

Franklin's emergence during these years as leader of the antiproprietary faction in Pennsylvania took him to England in 1757, where he gained recognition of the Assembly's right to tax the estate of the Penn family. While in England at the close of the Seven Years' War he argued that Great Britain should retain Canada rather than Guadaloupe. He believed that only in this way could America, the frontier of the British Empire he loved so well, prosper and expand. Returning to the colonies in 1762, he resumed his duties as a deputy postmaster general, a post he had held since 1753, and under his direction the colonies soon enjoyed excellent service. But in 1764 the antiproprietary Assembly once more sent him to England.

Patriot and Statesman. This time the Revolutionary crisis kept Franklin in London for over a decade. No sooner had he arrived than Parliament passed the Stamp Act. Franklin heartily disapproved of the legislation, but when he learned of the riots in America he was deeply chagrined. It was largely his persuasive testimony before the House of Commons, however, that brought about repeal in the spring of 1766. Franklin opposed the Stamp Act as internal taxation, but with the passage of the Townshend duties in 1767 he declared that Parliament had no right to levy external taxes on the colonies either. He argued that the colonies owed allegiance only to the King and hoped that they could achieve the freedom of dominion status within the Empire. Even after the Boston Tea Party Franklin still hoped for reconciliation. But passage of the Coercive Acts (1774) convinced him that war was virtually inevitable.

Upon his return to Philadelphia in the spring of 1775, Franklin became a delegate to the Continental Congress, where he worked quietly for measures promoting independence. As a member of a five-man committee he helped draft the Declaration of Independence, which Congress adopted in July, 1776. He then turned to the task of strengthening the union of former colonies, only to be disappointed in the weak Articles of Confederation.

With independence declared but not won, Franklin sailed for France in late 1776 to gain support for the American cause. He became a national hero in France, and from his headquarters in Passy a deluge of propaganda poured forth. When news of the American victory at Saratoga arrived in Dec., 1777, he played on the French fears of a reconciliation between the colonies and Great Britain. Louis XVI joined the war against the British the following spring, thus assuring American independence.

Franklin stayed on in Paris as American minister. After the British surrender at Yorktown opened the way to negotiations in 1782, he served as one of the peace commissioners along with John Adams and John Jay. When Jay suspected a Franco-Spanish plot to deprive the Americans of territory west of the Alleghenies, Franklin agreed to ignore Congressional instructions and the terms of the French alliance by signing a secret agreement with Great Britain. By shrewd diplomacy, American independence was recognized and the Mississippi boundary guaranteed.

Franklin returned to Philadelphia and a hero's welcome in Sept., 1785. Though nearly 80 and afflicted with the gout and a kidney stone, he was soon called to the presidency of the Pennsylvania Executive Council, an office he held for three years. He sat in the Federal Constitutional Convention (1787) and proposed the crucial compromise between large and small states. He gave his consent to the final version of the Constitution, although not without reservations. His last years were spent supporting various worthy causes by letters and essays.

With the exception of two or three Presidents, probably no American has been more loved by his countrymen than Benjamin Franklin. The warmth of the man pervades his *Autobiography* and is especially revealed in his personal correspondence. Always appreciative of beautiful women, many of whom found him charming, he remained a devoted husband to his "plain Joan," Deborah. Equally at ease with chiefs of state and journeyman printers, he proved to more than one astounded European that not all colonials were utter bumpkins. Within him was the best that colonial America had to offer—self-reliance, inquisitiveness, an optimistic view of his own and his nation's future, and a respect for other men, no matter what their stations. In a real sense, Franklin was the first American, for his life personified the rise of a disunited people to the stature and responsibilities of nationhood.

Consult Van Doren, Carl, *Benjamin Franklin* (1956); *The Papers of Benjamin Franklin*, Vol. I (1959), II (1960), III, IV (1961); V (1962), VI (1963), ed. by L. W. Labaree and others.

BENJAMIN W. LABAREE, Harvard University

FRANKLIN, FREDERIC (1914–), British dancer, born in Liverpool, England. In 1935 he joined the Markova-Dolin Company and in 1938 the Ballet Russe de Monte Carlo as premier danseur. He established himself as a popular favorite in such ballets as *Coppélia, Gaîté Parisienne*, and *Rodeo*. Chiefly famed as a character dancer, he has also excelled in classical ballet.

FRANKLIN, SIR JOHN (1786–1847), British naval officer and pioneer Arctic explorer. Following a brief Arctic voyage (1818) as commanding officer of the *Trent*, Franklin received command of an expedition (1819–22) that reached York Factory on Hudson Bay in Aug., 1819. The expedition proceeded overland to Great Slave Lake, and north to the mouth of the Coppermine River (1821). Franklin then turned east and surveyed 500 mi. of Arctic coastline. His second overland expedition (1825–27) wintered at Great Bear Lake, advanced to the mouth of the Mackenzie River, and conducted coastal surveys as far west as 149°27′, and east to the mouth of the Coppermine. These two expeditions mapped nearly 2,000 mi. of the North American Arctic coast line.

National Portrait Gallery

"The Arctic Council. Planning a Search for Sir John Franklin," by Stephen Pearce (1851). Franklin's portrait hangs on the wall (*left*).

In May, 1845, Franklin set out with two ships, *Erebus* and *Terror*, and 129 officers and men, to search for the Northwest Passage. The vessels cleared Lancaster Sound north of Baffin Island, penetrated Wellington Channel to 77° N., then wintered at Beechey Island. Continuing his search in 1846, Franklin successfully navigated Peel and Franklin straits. But on Sept. 12, 1846, both *Erebus* and *Terror* were trapped by pack ice in McClintock Channel between King William Island and Victoria Island. During the months that followed many of the party weakened and died, Franklin himself perishing June 11, 1847. The survivors did not abandon the ships until Apr. 22, 1848, and they, too, perished while attempting to reach Boothia Peninsula. Six years passed before John Rae found the first traces of the missing expedition. In 1859, Sir Francis Leopold McClintock discovered some of the skeletons and the records that provided a history of the expedition and its fate.

Consult Copper, P. F., *Island of the Lost* (1961).

HAROLD P. GILMOUR, Polar Explorer

FRANKLIN, JOHN HOPE (1915–), U.S. Negro historian and educator. Born in Rentiesville, Okla., he received his undergraduate degree from Fisk University, and his Ph.D. in history from Harvard University. Franklin taught at a number of universities including Fisk, North Carolina, and Brooklyn College, and was appointed chairman of the history department of the University of Chicago in 1967. He has written a number of books on the history of the Negro in the United States. *From Slavery to Freedom: A History of the American Negroes* (rev. ed., 1960) is a comprehensive survey of the field, and is considered an important contribution to U.S. historical writing.

FRANKLIN, WILLIAM (1731–1813), American colonial Governor, son of Benjamin Franklin, born in Philadelphia. He served in the French and Indian War and was comptroller (1754–56) of the general post office in Philadelphia. When his father went to England in 1757 as agent for Pennsylvania and New Jersey, the younger Franklin accompanied him. He studied law and was admitted to the English bar. In 1763 he was appointed royal Governor of New Jersey. During the American Revolution he actively supported Great Britain, and consequently was estranged from his father. Arrested and imprisoned (1776), he was released on exchange in 1778. He went to England and remained there on a British pension despite reconciliation with his father.

FRANKLIN, unincorporated village of western Idaho, a suburb just west of Boise. Pop., 7,222.

FRANKLIN, city of central Indiana, and seat of Johnson County. A trading center, primarily for an agricultural area, it also produces automobile parts. Franklin College (estab., 1834), a Baptist coeducational institution, is located here. Laid out, 1822; pop., 11,477.

FRANKLIN, city of southern Kentucky and seat of Simpson County, 20 mi. south of Bowling Green, near the Tennessee border. It is a trading center for a tobacco and grain region. Pop., 6,553.

FRANKLIN, city of south-central Louisiana, and seat of St. Mary Parish. Its industries are based on agricultural products, chiefly sugar cane, and on petroleum from nearby fields. Inc., 1830; pop., 9,325.

FRANKLIN, town of southeastern Massachusetts, north of Providence, R.I. Horace Mann (1796–1859), the noted educator, was born here. Settled, 1660; inc., 1778; pop., 17,830.

FRANKLIN, city of central New Hampshire on the Merrimack River. It has paper mills and is also a trade center for agricultural goods of the surrounding area. Daniel Webster was born here. Settled, 1764; inc. as city, 1895; pop., 7,292.

FRANKLIN, city of southwestern Ohio, on the Miami River. It has manufactures of varied paper products, felt, and plastics. It was founded in 1796 by Gen. William Schenck. Inc., 1814; pop., 10,075.

FRANKLIN, industrial city of north-central Pennsylvania, and seat of Venango County. Oil was discovered here in 1860. Franklin's chief industries are associated with petroleum and natural gas. The city is built on the site of an Indian village and of early French, British, and American forts. Inc. as city, 1868; pop., 8,629.

FRANKLIN, city of central Tennessee, and seat of Williamson County, located on the Harpeth River. It is the center of a general farming and phosphate-mining area. Industries include the manufacture of ranges, heaters, and work clothing. A famous Civil War battle in which Union forces, under Gen. John McA. Schofield, defeated Confederate forces, was fought in Franklin on Nov. 30, 1864. Battleground Academy is located there. Inc. as village, 1799; pop., 9,497.

FRANKLIN, town in southeastern Virginia, on the Blackwater River, about 38 mi. southwest of Portsmouth. It is in a peanut-growing area and mills lumber and paper. Pop., 6,880.

FRANKLIN, city of southeastern Wisconsin, a residential suburb of Milwaukee. Pop., 12,247.

FRANKLIN, STATE OF, in American history, a short-lived state (1784–88) formed by the people of frontier Tennessee in the troubled times following the American Revolution. The frontiersmen, fearing that they would be left without government when North Carolina ceded its western holdings to the United States in 1784, met at Jonesboro (Aug., 1784) to draft a petition to Congress asking for immediate statehood. North Carolina was so alarmed at this show of independence that it rescinded its act of cession. Thus the Tennesseans who met in a second convention to frame their constitution were divided into two groups: one under Col. John Tipton favored continued loyalty to North Carolina, the other under John Sevier favored separate statehood.

The Sevier faction possessed a majority and adopted a temporary constitution for the state of Franklin which Congress refused to recognize. Nevertheless the same group drafted (Nov., 1785) a permanent constitution.

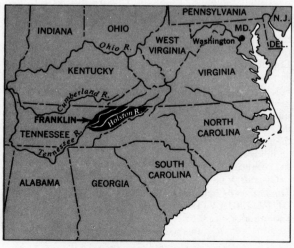

STATE OF FRANKLIN

– – – – – – – – – Present-day state boundaries

The President's Room in the Franklin D. Roosevelt Library.
(FRANKLIN D. ROOSEVELT LIBRARY, HYDE PARK, N.Y.)

North Carolina tried to suppress the rebellion by promising pardons and tax benefits to all accepting its authority. This accentuated the conflict between the rival factions within Franklin and the Sevier forces were defeated (Feb., 1788) in a brief battle. The separatist movement died out, and North Carolina again ceded (1789) its western lands to Congress. This territory later became (1796) the state of Tennessee.

Consult Williams, S. C., *History of the Lost State of Franklin* (1933).

RAY A. BILLINGTON, Northwestern University

FRANKLIN DISTRICT, northernmost district of Canada's Northwest Territories. Its 549,253-sq.-mi. area (including 7,500 sq. mi. of fresh-water surface) embraces the islands of the Canadian Arctic Archipelago, the islands in Hudson Strait, and two mainland peninsulas—Boothia and Melville. The name commemorates the expedition led by Sir John Franklin (1845–47) which disappeared seeking the Northwest Passage, causing search and exploration of the archipelago.

FRANKLIN D. ROOSEVELT LAKE, lake impounded by the Grand Coulee Dam on the Columbia River in northeastern Washington and extending almost to the Canadian border. It is part of the Columbia River basin power generation, flood control, and irrigation project. It is also an important recreational center. Area, 185 sq. mi.; length, 151 mi.

FRANKLIN D. ROOSEVELT LIBRARY, Hyde Park, N.Y. contains the personal and public papers of Franklin Delano Roosevelt, many of his books and other printed items relating to him, and materials dealing with his special interests (U.S. Navy; Dutchess County, N.Y. history). His own collection was augmented by extensive contributions from his widow Eleanor Roosevelt and from con-

temporaries and associates to form an enormous collection of source material for the study of 20th century American politics. The library building was completed in 1940 and made available to scholars in 1941. The former Roosevelt home adjoins the library and is a National Historic Site.

FRANKLIN INSTITUTE OF THE STATE OF PENNSYLVANIA, founded in Philadelphia in 1824, conducts fundamental and applied research in the physical sciences and biochemistry. It houses an extensive science library, a museum, and Fels Planetarium, and awards the coveted Franklin Medal to outstanding workers in the physical sciences. The *Journal of the Franklin Institute* has been published since 1826.

FRANKLIN PARK, residential suburb west of Chicago. Pipe, wire, and cement blocks are manufactured here. Inc., 1892; pop., 20,497.

FRANKLIN SQUARE, residential village of southeastern New York, on western Long Island, near Queens Borough of New York City. Pop.

FRANKS, leading confederacy of west Germanic tribes, first mentioned in 241 A.D., including the western Chauci, the Ampsivarii and Chamavi (later forming the Salian Franks), the Bructeri, Sugambri, Chattuarii (later the

FRANKS OF THE EIGHTH CENTURY

Male attire of the 8th century included a long-sleeved tunic and cross gartering. Women's tunics were sometimes trimmed with fur.

Ripuarian Franks), and Chatti. The Franks began their successful offensive against Rome in 253. The Salians were permanently settled in the region occupied by the modern Flemish and Dutch Netherlands by 410, and the Ripuarians and Chatti in the Rhineland, Hesse, and northern Bavaria by c.450. Frankish traditions and idiom are preserved there. Further expansion of the Salians under King Clovis (reigned 481–511), of the Merovingian Dynasty, led to the conquest of the northern Franks after the battle of Soissons (486), of the Alamanni after Zülpich (496), and of the Visigoths after Vouillé (507).

The Ripuarian kings were eliminated by Clovis through foul play. Later extensive Salian settlement as far south as the Seine and Ripuarian settlement in Lorraine are archeologically verified. In both areas Frankish idiom was preserved after c.900 only in place and personal names. The Franks were Christianized after 496. After adding Thuringia (528) and the Burgundian lands (534), the Frankish kingdom dominated western Europe, halting the Arab advance at Poitiers in 732. Under Charlemagne (q.v.) the remaining Germanic kingdoms were incorporated. Subdivided by the Treaty of Verdun (843), the Carolingian Empire split into France and Germany. The Franks gave their name to France and to Franconia, in Germany.

KARL W. BUTZER, University of Wisconsin

FRANZ [fränts], **ROBERT** (1815–92), German composer, born in Halle. He devoted almost all his creative gifts to the writing of songs, of which he left close to 260. Among the German lieder composers of the romantic period, Franz has long been accorded an enviable, if minor, position. There is nothing of Schubert's drama and variety, or Schumann's lyricism and imagination in his music. His best works, of which *Die Widmung*, *Schlummerlied*, and *Die Lotosblume* are fair examples, reveal a style too dependent on the short phrase and lacking the power of extended development. His response to words is genuinely quick and sensitive and his accompaniments always unobtrusively graceful, but his constant use of the strophic (stanza) form and the restrictive choice of literary material too often make for a monotony of tone and blandness of temper.

Consult Einstein, Alfred, *Music in the Romantic Era* (1947).

ALBERT WEISSER, Brooklyn College

FRANZ JOSEF [fränts jō'zəf] **LAND,** archipelago in the Arctic Ocean north of Novaya Zemlya, and part of Archangel Oblast, R.S.F.S.R., Soviet Union. This group of some 85 islands, discovered by an Austrian expedition in 1873, is 90% covered by permanent ice. There are observation stations on some of the islands. The archipelago reportedly contains large deposits of low-grade lignite coal. Area, approx. 8,000 sq. mi.

FRASCH [fräsh], **HERMAN** (1851–1914), American industrial chemist who invented the Frasch process for mining sulfur. Born in Germany, he went to the United States at 16 and became interested in petroleum products. As technical consultant for the Standard Oil Company and in his own plant in Canada, he developed many improve-

International News

Peter Fraser, Prime Minister of New Zealand from 1940–1949.

ments in petroleum refining. In 1891 he patented his revolutionary process for pumping melted pure sulfur out of deposits.

FRASCH PROCESS, method of extracting sulfur from its underground deposits. A boring is made to the deposit and concentric pipes are sunk to it. Superheated water is forced down through the outer pipes and air down through the central pipe. The sulfur is melted and is forced up through an intermediate pipe to the surface. The sulfur thus obtained is 99.5% pure and for most commercial purposes requires no further treatment.

FRASER [frā'zər], **PETER** (1884–1950), New Zealand statesman, Prime Minister (1940–49). Fraser was a leading figure in the development of the Welfare State in New Zealand. Attracted by New Zealand's reputation for social and economic experimentation, he emigrated from England in 1910. He was active at first as a laborer and a union organizer, and he helped found (1916) the New Zealand Labour party which gave the labor movement a political instead of an industrial bent. Jailed during World War I for opposing conscription of men without conscription of wealth, he entered Parliament in 1918, served as party secretary (1919–35), and in 1935 joined Michael Joseph Savage's Labour Ministry. Fraser's administration of the education and health departments was outstanding. In 1938 he played a major role in the establishment of a full social security system, including a publicly financed national health service. When Savage died (1940), Fraser became Prime Minister and held office for nine years. Though he never enjoyed the public affection won by Savage, Fraser eventually gained considerable, if sometimes grudging, respect because of his courageous wartime leadership.

New Zealanders were equally slow to appreciate his statesmanship in the United Nations, particularly as a spokesman for small nations at the San Francisco Conference (1945). He also made important contributions to U.N. social and trusteeship policies at the 1946 and 1948 meetings. In British Commonwealth affairs, he negotiated the Australian-New Zealand Agreement (1944) providing for collaboration on matters of mutual interest and showed statesmanship in negotiations over Irish and Indian relations at meetings of Commonwealth Prime Ministers. Fraser's inability to gain the unstinting admiration of New Zealanders may have arisen from an overreliance on his great talents as a parliamentary tactician and politician. Though his government effectively mobilized national resources during the war, and later carried through generous veterans' and welfare programs, the Labour party became exhausted, the trade union movement restive, and the public dissatisfied with prolonged rationing and economic controls. Abolition (1945) of the country quota, a system favoring rural areas in legislative representation, and strong support from Maori voters, who were grateful for the welfare system inaugurated in 1935, strengthened the Labour party temporarily. But while Fraser won a great personal victory in 1949, when the voters backed compulsory military training, the issue disrupted the labor movement and helped to bring Sidney George Holland's National party to power (Dec., 1949).

Consult Thorn, James, *Peter Fraser* (1952).

PETER J. COLEMAN, Washington University

FRASER, SIMON (1776–1862), Canadian fur trader and explorer. Born in Vermont of Loyalist parents who moved to Canada (1784), Fraser joined the North West Company in 1792 and became a partner in 1801. He directed (1805-8) the extension of the company's posts west over the Rocky Mountains to forestall the Hudson's Bay Company, founding Forts McLeod, St. James, Fraser, and George in the interior of present-day British Columbia. In 1808 he descended the river bearing his name to its mouth, an extremely hazardous journey. After service in Athabasca he was transferred (1811) to Red River at the time that rivalry between North West Company traders and the Earl of Selkirk's colonists flared into violence. Charged with complicity in the Seven Oaks massacre (1816), Fraser won acquittal. He retired in 1820 and died poor.

Consult The Letters and Journals of Simon Fraser, 1806-8, ed. by W. K. Lamb (1960).

W. J. ECCLES, University of Toronto

FRASER, city of southeastern Michigan, a residential suburb situated northeast of Detroit. Inc., 1956; pop., 11,868.

FRASER RIVER, in British Columbia, rises in the Rocky Mountains some 300 mi. north of the U.S. border and follows a course of about 900 mi., roughly S-shaped, to the Pacific Ocean at Vancouver. With its numerous important tributaries, including the Thompson, Nechako, and Chilcotin, it drains 91,000 sq. mi., of mainly mountainous area. Descent of the main and contributing streams, often precipitous, makes them the potential source of 6,000,000 hp. of energy. The lower part of the valley, including the delta islands, is an important farm-

ing area. Higher up, the Fraser and its contributing streams provide important spawning grounds for salmon, and fish ladders are provided at power dams. Both transcontinental rail lines and the Trans-Canada Highway follow the Fraser along much of its course through the mountains, often along narrow and precipitous canyons.

The river is named after Simon Fraser, who, in 1808, explored its upper reaches. Its inland valley was the scene of the Cariboo gold rush in 1858 and ensuing years.

Consult Hutchison, Bruce, *The Fraser* (1950).

JOHN E. ROBBINS, President, Brandon University

FRATERNITIES AND SORORITIES. In American colleges, student social organizations known as fraternities evolved from the literary clubs of the 18th and 19th centuries, which were founded for the advancement of literature and promotion of friendship and social intercourse. The year 1776 saw the birth of both the United States of America and Phi Beta Kappa, the first American society bearing a Greek-letter name. A large number of such societies appeared after this modest beginning. College social organizations for men are called fraternities. Sororities, organizations for women patterned after fraternities, were established in the 1850's. Phi Beta Kappa has become entirely an honor society, whereas contemporary fraternities and sororities concentrate on social activities and student extracurricular affairs.

After the Civil War fraternities and sororities began to build and to buy houses in which their members could live. In this manner these societies became a physical part of the American college campus and today are the most important social centers for their members at the colleges where they are established.

Since the 1930's fraternities have abolished many objectionable practices and as a result have become a more positive influence in college and university life. Besides promoting school spirit among undergraduates and school loyalty among alumni, fraternities have sponsored charitable projects and intellectual discussions within their groups, furnished campus housing for students which otherwise might not have been available, and worked with the school administrators to provide the students with a more rounded educational experience. To help defray some of the expense associated with group living, many fraternity members wait on tables or perform similar household tasks.

Many educators have recognized these groups as a means of maintaining and teaching the American way of life to students, thus preparing them to be better citizens after graduation. Acknowledging the fact that fraternities are an adjunct of the educational system, many schools have promoted the fraternity way of life by providing financial assistance and guidance in connection with housing projects and undergraduate activities. Some school administrations have made their aid contingent upon the fraternities and sororities abolishing any discriminatory practices they may have.

The modern concept of "fraternity" is different from what it was in the 1930's. Fraternities provide a proving laboratory in human relations and serve to develop leadership within their ranks. Each year many new chapters are

The Phi Beta Kappa key, symbol of the oldest American Greek-letter society. Above, front and back view of the key designed in 1776, the year the fraternity was founded. Right, present-day Phi Beta Kappa key shows little change.

formed on campuses where other fraternity chapters are already established, and more schools which have never had fraternities are seeking the establishment of chapters on their campuses to further over-all student programs. In 1961 there were 229 national societies, 11,626 campus chapters, and a total membership of 5,366,299 men and women.

Most chapters today are affiliated with a national organization of their own fraternity, and most of the national organizations have formed organizations of fraternities to make the fraternity relationship of greater value to the student. Among them are the National Interfraternity Conference, the National Panhellenic Council, the Professional Interfraternity Conference, and the Professional Panhellenic Association.

ROBERT E. JEPSON, President,
College Fraternity Editors' Association
See also PHI BETA KAPPA.

FRAUD, a willful misrepresentation made in order to induce another who relies upon it to part with something valuable or to surrender some legal right. The misrepresentation must be a statement of fact rather than one of opinion, value, law, or intention, and the reliance must be reasonable.

A fraudulent statement need not necessarily be made expressly. Silence and action, which do in fact misrepresent the truth, can be the basis for liability much the same as the most explicit statement. Furthermore statements of value, opinion, intention, or law may be the basis for legal action if it is fair to infer that the assertions are representations of an existing state of mind, falsely reflected by the statement.

In the criminal field fraud is punished under laws which prohibit the obtaining of property by false pretenses and which forbid larceny by trick. One of the great issues in criminal law has been whether a "false promise," that is, a promise made without the intention to keep it, should be a crime. Many have feared that it would punish those who

were merely unable to carry out their contracts. "Business affairs," one court has said, "would be materially encumbered by the ever present threat that a debtor might be subject to criminal penalties if the prosecutor and the jury were of the view that at the time of the borrowing he was mentally a cheat." The dissenting opinion thought the fears were overdrawn and that "no particular danger to honest men" distinguished this crime from others.

Fraud is also a ground for rescinding a contract or annulling a marriage. Whenever a legal arrangement is consensual, it may be undone if consent has been obtained by a lie. There are legislative enactments called statutes of fraud under which certain types of contracts cannot be enforced in a court of law unless there is a written memorandum of the arrangement signed by the party who is charged with the breach of the agreement.

MONRAD G. PAULSEN, Columbia University
School of Law

FRAUNCES TAVERN [frôn'sĭs], historic building in New York City. A four-story structure at the corner of Broad and Pearl streets, it is designed in the Georgian style with square proportions and a hipped roof. It was erected in 1719 as a family mansion by the French Huguenot Étienne de Lancey. Purchased by Samuel Fraunces, it was operated (1762–85) as the Queen's Head Tavern. The Sons of Liberty met there before the American Revolution, and on Dec. 4, 1783, George Washington bade his officers farewell in the Long Room. Since 1904 it has been the local headquarters of the Sons of the Revolution. Open to the public, the building houses a restaurant, a museum, an art gallery, and a library.

FRAUNHOFER [froun'hō-fər], JOSEPH VON (1787–1826), German physicist and astronomer who investigated the dark lines in the solar spectrum, later designated the Fraunhofer Lines. Born in Straubing, Bavaria, Fraunhofer became highly skilled in working optical glass and joined the optical institute near Munich in 1806. Here he constructed the famous refractor for the Dorpat (Tartu) Observatory in Estonia, and other optical instruments and lenses of the highest quality. Fraunhofer rediscovered the dark lines in the solar spectrum parallel to the spectrometer slit (first noticed by W. H. Wollaston in 1802), measured their relative distances, and designated the principal lines by letters of the alphabet from A to G. He also studied the spectra of the moon, planets, and stars.

FRAUNHOFER LINES, thousands of dark lines in the continuous spectrum of the sun, named for Joseph von Fraunhofer who studied them in 1814. The wave lengths of the Fraunhofer lines correspond to the bright lines emitted by gases when they are excited into radiation. The presence of these lines in the solar spectrum indicates that the sun consists of hydrogen, calcium, iron, sodium, and other familiar elements. Helium was discovered through studies of the spectrum of the sun before the gas was found on earth.

Fraunhofer lines are formed in the apparent surface layer of the sun, the opaque white gas called the photosphere. Much of the hydrogen in the photosphere is in the form of negative ions (atoms that have captured extra electrons). Light of all wave lengths is generated continuously in the core of the sun, but atoms and ions of hydrogen, helium, and other elements composing the solar gas repeatedly absorb their characteristic wave lengths and reradiate them in all directions. This reradiated energy is heavily absorbed by negative hydrogen, which reradiates it at random wave lengths. The result is that the characteristic wave lengths of the elements are largely subtracted from the continuous bright spectrum, leaving the relatively dark Fraunhofer lines at these wave lengths.

JOSEPH H. RUSH, National Center
for Atmospheric Research

See also SPECTROSCOPY.

FRAZER [frā′zər], **SIR JAMES GEORGE** (1854–1941), British anthropologist. Though he studied law and was also an able classical scholar, his main contribution lay in the collection and synthesis of data on world religion and folklore. He became famous for his work *The Golden Bough; A Study in Magic and Religion*, first published in two volumes in 1890, later in 12 volumes (1907–15) and in 13 volumes (3d ed., rev. and enlarged, 1958). A one-volume abridgment by Frazer was issued in 1922, and a one-volume abridgment by T. H. Gaster was published in 1959.

The Golden Bough is a comparative analysis of ritual and mythology from ancient times onward, drawing on folklore, history, and 19th-century anthropological reports on primitive peoples. Frazer introduced the concepts of imitative and sympathetic magic to the study of religion. His writings became major points of reference for the intellectuals of Europe and America. Sigmund Freud's use of anthropological material, for example, stemmed from Frazer's writings. Much of Frazer's theory has been rejected, but his books remain literary classics. His many publications include *Totemism and Exogamy* (1910) and *Folk-lore in the Old Testament* (1918).

MARIO J. A. BICK, Columbia University

FRÉCHETTE [frā-shĕt′], **LOUIS HONORÉ** (1839–1908), French-Canadian poet, born in Levis, Quebec. Throughout his life he was active in politics and in journalism. He published four essays, three plays, and many books of poetry, including *Mes loisirs* (My Leisure), 1863; *La voix d'un exilé* (The Voice of an Exile), 1867; and his best-known work, *La légende d'un peuple* (The Legend of a People), 1887. Several of his volumes of poetry received prizes from the French Academy.

FRECKLES, also called ephelides, are small pigmented spots that occur on the face, neck, shoulders, and hands. Freckles may disappear during the winter months and grow darker during the summer. They usually do not appear before the age of six and are most common in blonds and redheads. The tendency to develop freckles seems to be inherited.

FREDERIC, HAROLD (1856–98), American novelist. A newspaperman in his native Utica and in London, he turned to fiction, creating realistic pictures of small-town and farm life in upstate New York. *The Copperhead* (1893) records intolerance during the Civil War, and his best work, *The Damnation of Theron Ware* (1896), traces a young clergyman's decline from orthodoxy. Doggedly realistic and based on deeply felt convictions, his novels, perhaps because of a journalist's haste, are uneven in quality.

FREDERICK I or FREDERICK BARBAROSSA (1123?–1190), Holy Roman Emperor (1155–90). One of the most admired medieval rulers renowned for chivalry and justice, Frederick devoted much of his reign to a struggle with the Papacy for the domination of Italy. The son of Frederick Hohenstaufen, Duke of Swabia, he accompanied his uncle, the German king Conrad III, on the disastrous Second Crusade (1147–48). He won the King's confidence and became (1152) his successor. By making great concessions to the nobles, Frederick maintained order in Germany. His major ambition was to rule Italy and to secure the independence of the Empire from the Papacy. To achieve this, he led five great military expeditions to Italy.

Frederick first crossed the Alps in 1154 allegedly to support Pope Adrian IV, who had been exiled by the rebellious Romans. He put down the revolt and was crowned Emperor by the Pope (1155). He returned to Germany without further assisting Adrian. The Pope, now allied with Frederick's enemies, declared to the Diet of Besançon (1157) that the Empire was a papal fief. Frederick rejected the claim and invaded Italy (1158). He took Brescia and Milan and at the celebrated Diet of Roncaglia laid claim to all imperial rights in Italy. He also asserted his sovereignty over the cities of Lombardy. This attempt to reimpose feudalism upon the virtually independent Italian cities provoked a series of revolts encouraged by the Pope. Frederick invaded Italy a third time, overpowering and burning Milan (1162). Many other towns submitted, but he failed to conquer Sicily. Frederick now set up an antipope in opposition to the new Pope, Alexander III, who

Frederick I and his sons, a miniature (c.1180).
The Bettman Archive

excommunicated him. On a fourth expedition (1166) he captured Rome, but pestilence in his army forced him to abandon plans to subjugate Sicily. In 1167 the Italian communes formed the Lombard League, and Frederick retreated to Germany. A fifth campaign led to his complete defeat by the Italian communes at Legnano (1176).

Both sides were exhausted; Frederick concluded peace first with Alexander III (1176), and then with the Lombard towns (1183). After returning to Germany, he secured the downfall of the powerful Duke of Saxony and Bavaria, Henry the Lion. At the Diet of Nuremberg (1186), Frederick promulgated laws reinforcing the prohibition of private wars (first proclaimed in 1158). Although he brought disaster to Italy, the Emperor fostered prosperity in Germany by pursuing a policy of domestic peace and by colonizing Slavic lands in east Germany. In 1188 Frederick joined the Third Crusade and set out on the land route to the Holy Land. He drowned while crossing a river in Asia Minor.

The handsome Emperor, with flowing blond hair and red beard, was idolized by the peasants, whom he constantly protected. According to German legend, he is not dead and will return when the country needs him.

Consult Deeds of Frederick Barbarossa, ed. by C. C. Mierow (1953).

Istvan Deak, Columbia University

FREDERICK II (1194–1250), Holy Roman Emperor and King of the *Regno* (southern Italy and Sicily) and of the

A miniature of Frederick II from his book on falconry.

The Bettmann Archive

Latin Kingdom of Jerusalem. Frederick's youth was unsettled. The deaths of his father Emperor Henry VI Hohenstaufen (1197) and of his mother Constance (1198) left him with claims to a brilliant inheritance (the *Regno*, Hohenstaufen lands in Germany, preferential consideration for election to the imperial crown) but with little actual resources. He grew up as a ward of the Pope in the cosmopolitan atmosphere of the Sicilian-Norman court, and acquired a lifelong predilection for Sicily, its warmth and almost oriental way of life, and a corresponding aversion to the lands of his German ancestors.

Starting with virtually nothing, Frederick was able between 1210 and 1220 to gain papal support, a French alliance, and finally (1220) coronation at Rome as Holy Roman Emperor. The costs, however, were high: Frederick assured the Pope that the Empire and the *Regno* would not be permanently united, and in 1220 he granted to the ecclesiastical Princes of Germany virtual sovereignty. Nevertheless, Pope Gregory IX grew suspicious of his intentions, and in 1227 excommunicated him when he proved reluctant to leave Italy on a Crusade. In 1228 the still-excommunicated Frederick set forth on the so-called Sixth Crusade, winning temporary possession of Jerusalem from the Muslims by skillful diplomacy. He returned to Italy to claim another diplomatic victory in the peace with the Pope concluded at San Germano (1230).

Frederick now began to pursue more openly what seems to have been the aim of his life: the creation of a Mediterranean empire founded upon a unified Italy, and including Latin Palestine and perhaps Byzantium. In 1231, to win German support in the anticipated struggle in Italy, he extended to lay Princes in Germany the generous concessions already made to ecclesiastical rulers. He then proceeded to pacify and reorganize the *Regno*. In 1231, as part of that reorganization, he issued the Constitutions of Melfi. The Constitutions, drawing heavily upon Roman law principles, strongly affirmed the crown's authority, and are often considered an early example of truly modern legislation.

Meanwhile, opposition to Frederick was growing. His son Henry openly revolted against him (1234). The north Italian towns, fearful of his growing power, revived the Lombard League that had defeated his grandfather Frederick Barbarossa. In 1237 Frederick defeated the League at Cortenuova, but in 1239 Pope Gregory joined his enemies and again excommunicated him. During the last decade of his reign Frederick waged a bitter battle of words and swords against an alliance of the Papacy and the towns. Pope Innocent IV, whose elevation Frederick had favored, proved to be a more confirmed enemy than Gregory. At a council in Lyons (1245), Innocent formally deposed Frederick. In northern Italy, Parma revolted, and Frederick's long siege of the city ended in failure (1248). Frederick remained a power in Italy, but when he died no one could continue his work.

Frederick possessed one of the most brilliant personalities of the 13th century. He was remarkably tolerant of Jews and Muslims (but not of Christian heretics), and followed Muslim custom in keeping a harem. He was reputed to be a skeptic and a rationalist, given to conducting quasi-scientific experiments. (He had heard, for example, that a baby who heard no spoken language

Statue of Frederick II, known as Frederick the Great, by Johann G. Schadow.

Frederick II playing the flute at Sans Souci palace, by Adolf von Menzel (1815–1905).

would grow up naturally speaking Hebrew, the language of Eden, and tried to find out if this was true.) He welcomed scholars and translators to his court, founded a university at Naples, and patronized poets who produced, in imitation of the troubadours, the first lyric poetry in the Italian language. He himself wrote a book on falconry, read and on occasion criticized Aristotle. The Constitutions of Melfi attest to his skill as a statesman, and he many times proved himself an able diplomat. Still, his dream of building a Mediterranean empire based on a unified Italy had some reckless aspects. To achieve that dream, he abandoned almost all imperial authority within the German states. The failure of the medieval Empire in Germany, as well as a certain new ruthlessness in politics, must be reckoned as his legacy.

Consult Einstein, D. G., *Emperor Frederick II* (1949); Andrewes, Patience, *Frederick II of Hohenstaufen* (1970).

DAVID HERLIHY

FREDERICK III (1831–88), German Emperor (1888). The son of Emperor William I, he married (1858) a daughter of Queen Victoria of England. He took an active part in Prussia's wars against Denmark (1864), Austria (1866), and France (1870–71). He had little opportunity to participate in imperial politics, although he was regent for some months in 1878 when his father was recovering from an assassination attempt. His brief reign of 99 days (Mar.–June, 1888), cut short by a fatal cancer of the throat, showed promise of inaugurating a liberal regime.

FREDERICK IX (1899–1972), King of Denmark (1947–72). The son of Christian X, he was early attracted to the sea, chose a career in the navy, and eventually rose to the rank of rear admiral. During the Nazi occupation he supported the underground resistance movement, and frequently acted for his father in dealings with the German forces. He acceded to the throne in 1947. Because he had no male heirs, the Danish law of succession was changed in 1953 to allow the crown to pass in the female line, too. King Frederick was an accomplished musician who particularly enjoyed conducting.

FREDERICK II or FREDERICK THE GREAT (1712–86), King of Prussia. This most famous son of the Hohenzollern Dynasty excelled as statesman, administrator, and military commander, but he also wrote in the fields of poetry, politics, and philosophy, and played and composed respectable music for the flute. His life reveals a conflict between the feeling for power inherent in his heritage and position, and the dedication to spirit, freedom, and human welfare that he felt as artist and philosopher.

The latter side dominated Frederick's early years and led him, as Crown Prince, into bitter conflicts with his stern, pious, uncultured father, Frederick William I. Raised under the gentle, Francophil influence of his mother, Sophia Dorothea of Hanover, Frederick rejected his father's regimen of severely practical training for war and administration. In 1730 he concocted plans to escape with his friend Hans Hermann von Katte, but they were discovered and Frederick had to endure both the beheading of Katte and his own imprisonment in the fortress of Küstrin. Though Frederick finally submitted to his father, he managed to build a private life that suited his own tastes. He dutifully married Elizabeth Christina of Brunswick but did not live with her. Instead, he established (1736–40) a little court at Castle Rheinsberg, where he studied, wrote, and worked himself into the Enlightenment's idealistic "republic of letters." Frederick's chief works of this preparatory period reflected his dual life. In his *Considerations on the Present Condition of the States of Europe* he insisted on the necessity of a third great Continental power as a counterpoise to the weight of France and Austria, while in his *Anti-Machiavelli* he rejected political amorality in favor of the doctrine of the prince who was "the first servant of his people."

During the first period (1740–56) of his reign Frederick alternated the two motifs of his career. In 1740, on the death of Austria's Charles VI, he began the War of the Austrian Succession by seizing Silesia. He asserted but hardly believed old Hohenzollern legal claims to this Habsburg territory, admitting that his real motives were glory and the extension of Prussian power. After the Peace of Dresden (1745) had ratified the conquest, Frederick

357

governed for 11 peaceful years as "the philosopher of Sans-Souci," devoting himself to cultural contacts, especially with the French writer Voltaire, and to welfare measures for Prussia.

From the outbreak of the Seven Years' War (1756) until his death, Frederick followed the dictates of harsh necessity and subordinated everything to the needs of the state. Fearful of revived Austrian power, he allied himself (Jan., 1756) with Great Britain. This forestalled the threatened Anglo-Austro-Russian lineup against him, but produced the "diplomatic revolution" which aligned France with Austria and Russia. When Frederick launched a preventive attack upon Austria's ally, Saxony, he started a conflict that almost destroyed him. Despite English assistance with subsidies and an army led by Prince Ferdinand of Brunswick, Frederick could not begin to match the forces marshalled against him. He won signal victories at Rossbach and Leuthen (1757), but after the Austro-Russian triumph at Kunersdorf (1759) he lived in imminent danger of ruin. He was saved only by his own desperate courage, the disunity of his foes, and the accession to the Russian throne (1762) of his mentally defective admirer, Tsar Peter III.

Frederick emerged from the war territorially unscathed and with a heroic repute in Germany, but he had become a hardened, skeptical ruler, trusting only in himself and in precepts that sacrificed personal inclinations and morality to the state. In 1772 he engineered the cynical first partition of Poland, which brought him West Prussia and cemented an alliance with Russia that remained the cornerstone of Prussian policy for over a century. In 1778–79 and again in 1785 Frederick frustrated Austria's plans to acquire Bavaria, and took advantage of the latter crisis to form a League of Princes (Fürstenbund), in which he manipulated German patriotism for Prussian ends. Although he never lost his interest in art and philosophy, Frederick in his domestic rule showed an increasing preoccupation with rationalism as an instrument of state power. He kept his father's absolutist institutions and wove them into a unified system held together by his own intelligence, force, and indefatigable labors. Frederick cared little for the shibboleths of legitimacy, religion, aristocracy, regulated economy, and justice, but used them all —and himself—as tools of the state. So doing he created a progressive bureaucracy that in time modernized Prussia from above.

Consult Gaxotte, Pierre, *Frederick the Great* (1942); Gooch, G. P., *Frederick the Great, the Ruler, the Writer, the Man* (1947); Reiners, Ludwig, *Frederick the Great* (1960).

LEONARD KRIEGER, Yale University

FREDERICK, city of northwestern Maryland, and seat of Frederick County. It is an important agricultural and dairying center, and has many points of historic interest. Gen. Jubal Early of the Confederate army levied a ransom of $200,000 on the city in 1864. The home of Roger Brooke Taney contains the table on which Chief Justice Taney wrote the Dred Scott decision.

The Mount Olivet Cemetery contains the graves of Barbara Frietchie, Francis Scott Key, and Thomas Johnson (1732–1819), the first Governor of Maryland. Hood

College (estab., 1893) and the Maryland School for the Deaf are both located in Frederick. Inc., 1786; pop., 23,641.

FREDERICK, city of southwestern Oklahoma, and seat of Tillman County. It is a wheat- and cotton-marketing center and has several small industries. There is some oil production in the vicinity. Pop., 6,132.

FREDERICKSBURG, city of northeastern Virginia on the Rappahannock River, between Richmond and Washington, D.C. It is a trading and shipping center in an agricultural region. The world's largest cellophane manufacturing plant is located here. Fredericksburg was the home of George Washington until he moved to Mount Vernon. The law office of James Monroe, the Hugh Mercer Apothecary Shop, and Kenmore, the home of Betty Washington Lewis, sister of George Washington, are tourist attractions. Mary Washington College (estab. 1908), now the women's College of the University of Virginia, is located here. The townsite was laid out in 1727 and named for Frederick, Prince of Wales, father of George III. Fredericksburg was the site of several major battles during the Civil War. The Fredericksburg and Spotsylvania County Battlefields Memorial is located in and around the city. Inc. 1781; inc. as city, 1879; pop., 14,450.

THEODORE R. SPEIGNER, North Carolina College at Durham

FREDERICKSBURG, BATTLE OF, engagement of the U.S. Civil War at Fredericksburg, Va., Dec. 10–15, 1862. Gen. Ambrose E. Burnside replaced Gen. George B. McClellan in command of the Army of the Potomac on Nov. 7, and two days later proposed to threaten Gen. Robert E. Lee's communications with Richmond. Lee's Army of Northern Virginia, with about 78,000 men, after retiring from Antietam, moved to the heights overlooking Fredericksburg. Burnside, with 120,000 men, began sending troops across the river just below Fredericksburg during the night of Dec. 10, under the mistaken impression that Lee was concentrated at Port Royal. Lee offered no resistance at the river.

On Dec. 13, the Union forces attacked. Repeated Union charges that morning were repulsed with heavy casualties. Burnside ordered Gen. Joseph Hooker to storm Marye's Heights. Hooker concluded that further assault would be useless, but was unable to convince Burnside. Late in the afternoon, after a heavy artillery preparation, Hooker's men attacked, but to no avail. Burnside wished to renew the offensive on Dec. 14, but was dissuaded, and after a day of artillery exchanges, withdrew. Union casualties totalled about 12,000, Confederate losses about 5,000. Disappointed, President Abraham Lincoln removed Burnside from command of the Army of the Potomac in Jan., 1863, and replaced him with Hooker.

MARTIN BLUMENSON, formerly, Senior Historian, Department of the Army

FREDERICK WILLIAM III (1770–1840), King of Prussia (1797–1840). A simple, earnest, well-meaning, but unimaginative and indecisive monarch, he began his reign by ending the influence of favorites and clerical reactionaries that had featured the regime of his father, Frederick William II. Until 1806 he stimulated the production of reform commissions and proposals of all kinds but could not resolve to act on any save for some alleviation of the peasants' lot on the royal domains. In foreign policy Frederick William kept Prussia in an uneasy neutrality between Napoleonic France and the allied powers until, in 1806, for the sake of Hanover, he permitted himself to drift first into co-operation with the French against Britain and then, without allies, into war against France. After crushing military defeats in 1806 and 1807, Frederick William appointed reformers to leading posts in his government. He accepted their administrative, economic, social, and educational reforms but rejected both their plans for a Prussian constitution and for a national war against Napoleon. In 1813 he shifted from co-operation with the French to alliance with Russia, after the tide of war had turned in favor of the coalition, and during the War of Liberation he promised a constitution. With the defeat of Napoleon, however, Frederick William followed the conservative line laid down by the Austrian Chancellor, Prince Klemens von Metternich, and for the duration of his reign opposed the rising liberal and national movements in Germany.

LEONARD KRIEGER, Yale University

FREDERICK WILLIAM IV (1795–1861), King of Prussia (1840–61). A cultured, high-spirited, and imaginative prince, he was handicapped by a vacillating character, romantic illusions, and a stubborn belief in the traditions of divine right. His succession to the throne of his plodding and conservative father, Frederick William III, aroused liberal expectations which seemed confirmed by an immediate amnesty for political prisoners and a relaxation of the censorship. By 1843, however, these measures were reversed and the King's fundamental desire for a patriarchal monarchy began to emerge.

When the revolutionary movement of 1848 spread into Prussia, Frederick William pursued an uncertain course, caught between his paternalism on the one hand and his absolutism on the other. At first he yielded to the revolution and liberalized his government, but in November he expelled the popularly elected Prussian National Assembly from Berlin, and in December he imposed a conservative constitution of his own. Because of its revolutionary origin, he rejected (1849) the crown of a united Germany offered by a national parliament meeting at Frankfurt. He sponsored instead a plan for a constitutional Germany under his leadership created by agreement among the German rulers. When the opposition of Austria and Russia forced Frederick William to drop his scheme in the humiliating Prusso-Austrian Agreement of Olmütz (1850), his policies became increasingly reactionary. In 1857 mental illness forced him to retire from affairs of state.

LEONARD KRIEGER, Yale University

FREDERICK WILLIAM (1620–88), Elector of Brandenburg (1640–88), known as the "Great Elector." He was the first in a succession of able Hohenzollern rulers who expanded scattered dynastic holdings around the electorate of Brandenburg into the powerful state of Prussia. He was educated at Leyden in the Netherlands, where he was exposed to a Calvinist environment in which piety, the commercial spirit, and aggressive politics were all combined. This experience helped set him apart from other German princes, whose exclusive concern for the preservation of the existing order imposed narrow limits upon their achievements. The Thirty Years' War, which ravaged Germany after his accession in 1640, impressed upon him the necessity of a large standing army, secure tax revenues, and a unified administration. By the Peace of Westphalia (1648), he acquired East Pomerania and other territory. His domestic reforms laid the basis of future Prussian military power. Frederick William, though a progressive ruler in many respects, saw himself as a defender of Protestantism and as patriarch of his people.

LEONARD KRIEGER, Yale University

FREDERICTON, capital city of New Brunswick, Canada, located on the banks of the St. John River. It is a trade center in the heart of a prosperous fruit-growing and lumbering region. Boot and shoe manufacturing is the city's primary industry. Fredericton is the governmental and cultural center of New Brunswick and headquarters of the New Brunswick Military Area.

The city was built on the site of a former Indian village and French mission station. It was made capital of New Brunswick in 1785, shortly after the loyalist immigration insured the area's growth. The establishment of an Anglican episcopal see led to the city's incorporation in 1848.

The city is noted for its scenic natural surroundings, its stately buildings, and the charm of its elm-lined streets. The Lord Beaverbrook Art Gallery, on the south bank of the St. John River, was presented to New Brunswick by Lord Beaverbrook, a native of the province. Opened in 1959, the gallery contains a fine collection of British, French, and Canadian paintings. Government House, a massive example of colonial architecture constructed in 1828, now serves as a barracks for the Royal Canadian Mounted Police. Christchurch Cathedral is one of the finest examples of church architecture in Canada.

The University of New Brunswick, one of Canada's first universities, is located on a hill to the south of the city. Its arts building is the oldest college building in Canada. Among its former students are Sir Charles George Douglas Roberts and William Bliss Carman, founders of the first authentic school of Canadian poetry.

The headquarters of Camp Cagetown, one of the largest military training centers in Canada, is at Oromocto, 12 mi. south of the city. Pop. 19,683.

WILLIAM STEWART MACNUTT,
University of New Brunswick

FREDERIKSTED [frĕd′rĭk-stĕd], one of the two ports (with Christiansted) on St. Croix Island in the Virgin Islands of the United States, in the West Indies. Frederiksted is located on the southern part of the island's west coast. Its harbor is shallow; lighters must be used to load and unload ships standing offshore. Crude sugar and alcohol are its main exports. The quaint Danish colonial town is a tourist attraction. It became a U.S. possession when Denmark sold the present American Virgin Islands to the United States in 1917. Pop., 2,177.

FREDONIA [frĭ-dōn′yə], resort village of extreme western New York, near Lake Erie. Fredonia processes vegetables and fruits, especially grapes, from the surrounding area. The village is believed to be the first U.S. community to employ natural gas for street lighting. Inc., 1829; pop., 10,326.

FREDONIAN [frĭ-dō′nē-ən] **REBELLION,** abortive uprising (1826) of Texans against Mexican rule. An American, Haden Edwards, contracted to settle families on a land grant already partly occupied. When he attempted to oust established settlers, Mexico annulled his contract. In retaliation his brother Benjamin and a few insurgents proclaimed the Republic of Fredonia in Nacogdoches. Support was lacking, however, and the revolt collapsed. But Mexico was alarmed and tightened her control over Texas, thus hastening the Texas revolution.

FREE ASSOCIATION, the process in which a patient undergoing psychoanalysis speaks any and all thoughts which come to his mind, without attempting to conceal those which he might feel to be embarrassing or unimportant. The analyst uses this technique to attempt to understand the unconscious drives which underlie the patient's behavior. The process was originated by Sigmund Freud and constituted the basic tool with which he developed his theories of human behavior.

The literary style known as "stream of consciousness" is an attempt to utilize free association for the purposes of artistic creation.
See also FREUD, SIGMUND; PSYCHOANALYSIS.

FREE CITY, politically independent municipality, generally owing no formal allegiance to a larger political entity. The free city has its roots in the Greek city-states and the Italian and German cities of the Middle Ages. These cities functioned as miniature nations, conducting their own foreign and trade relations as well as local governmental duties within their own territories. Frequently, they joined together in economic and political alliances—such as the Hanseatic League of north German cities and the Rhenish League of south German cities, but each free city retained its sovereignty. These leagues helped pave the way for Italian and German unification in the 19th century, and the free cities eventually relinquished their political independence for the advantages of union. In modern times, the term "free city" is used to designate cities over which there is international dispute. The most important examples are Danzig (Gdańsk), Tangier, and Trieste.

Danzig was internationalized under Article 102 of the Treaty of Versailles and put under the protection of the League of Nations. It was a port connected to Poland by a corridor running through German territory. Danzig was occupied by Germany in 1939 and reverted to Poland after the war.

Tangier was given international status after the Agadir incident in 1911–12, when France, Spain, and Great Britain agreed to create an international zone on Africa's northwest coast near Gibralter. The Spanish seized control in 1940, but Tangier was restored to international status after World War II. It is now part of Morocco.

Trieste, a port at the northern end of the Adriatic, was contested by Italy and Yugoslavia after World War II. It was accorded international status and was occupied by the Allied forces. It was awarded to Italy in 1954.

No free city, in the true sense of the word, exists in the world today. In 1947 a U.N. resolution provided for the internationalization of Jerusalem, but the Arab-Israel war which broke out immediately afterward left the city divided between Israel and Jordan. Since 1958 the Soviet Union has proposed that Berlin be established as a free city within the German Democratic Republic (East Germany) but this proposal has been rejected by the Western powers.

WAYNE WILCOX, Columbia University

FREEDMEN'S BUREAU, in American history, a government agency (1865–69) intended to furnish assistance and protection to Southern Negroes after the Civil War. It functioned well under chaotic conditions, directing vast stores of relief to the needy of both races, improving labor relations, administering justice, and developing Negro educational facilities. But its prestige suffered in the North and was irreparably damaged in the South by corrupt practices, especially those connected with insuring Republican control of the Negro vote. These excesses stiffened resistance to Negro suffrage and encouraged secret terrorist organizations such as the Ku Klux Klan.

The bureau was established under the War Department and was supposed to exist for one year after the war. It was strengthened and its life extended, however, in 1866 over President Andrew Johnson's veto. Directed by Oliver O. Howard, the "Christian general," it functioned through ten districts, each under an assistant commissioner. With its sweeping authority—the "control of all subjects relating to refugees and freedmen"—it became the strongest single instrument of Reconstruction. In four years the bureau distributed 21,000,000 rations, founded 100 hospitals, aided 500,000 patients, and established for Negroes more than 4,000 schools and 3 universities. Though it could not fulfill the Negro's dream of forty acres and a mule, it did lease farms to thousands. The bureau completed its principal work in 1869, but its educational activities were extended to 1872 and its soldiers' bounty payments to 1874. Its total expenditure of about $20,000,000, almost half of it in bounties, was more than offset by Southern tax collections.

FREEDOM. *See* ACADEMIC FREEDOM; ASSEMBLY, FREEDOM OF; CIVIL RIGHTS AND LIBERTIES; LIBERTY; PRESS, FREEDOM OF THE; SPEECH, FREEDOM OF.

FREE ENTERPRISE SYSTEM. *See* ECONOMIC SYSTEMS.

FREE FRENCH, those Frenchmen who, after the fall of France in 1940, continued the war against Germany under the leadership of Gen. Charles de Gaulle. According to the Free French and De Gaulle, France had "lost a battle, not the war." A provisional French National Committee was set up in London by De Gaulle, who denounced the Vichy government as illegal. A Vichy court, in turn, tried De Gaulle *in absentia* and condemned him to death for treason. Although a number of African colonies adhered immediately to the Free French movement, it gained strength slowly, until it became apparent that Britain was not going to be defeated and that German measures in France were growing increasingly harsh. In 1941, the French National Committee included various political parties and resistance groups. After the invasion of North Africa, the French National Committee was expanded to form, in 1943, the French Committee of National Liberation, at first under the copresidency of De Gaulle and Gen. Henri Honoré Giraud. After a struggle for power with Giraud, De Gaulle emerged as the sole president. Shortly before the Allied invasion of France in 1944, the Committee of National Liberation took the name of Provisional Government of the French Republic. The enthusiastic reception accorded to de Gaulle by the French people brought belated official Allied recognition of the government in Oct., 1944. After the surrender of Germany, the provisional government proceeded to establish the Fourth Republic.

CHARLES E. FREEDEMAN, Wisconsin State College

FREEHOLD, borough of eastern New Jersey, and seat of Monmouth County. It is the center of a prosperous truck-farming area. The principal industries are the manufacture of rugs, food products, and glass. The battle of Monmouth was fought nearby on June 28, 1778. During this battle one of America's most famous heroines, Molly Pitcher, reputedly took her husband's place in combat. Noted historical buildings and sites here include St. Peter's Episcopal Church (1683) and Old Tennent Church (1715), with its adjoining cemetery. The town, originally called Topanemus, was named Monmouth Court House in 1715, and renamed Freehold in 1869. Inc. as a borough, 1919; pop., 10,545.

FREELAND, coal-mining borough of east-central Pennsylvania. The town was founded in 1868, and named Freeland because the land in the town was open to public purchase and not owned by the mining companies. Inc., 1876; pop., 4,784.

FREE LIBRARY OF PHILADELPHIA, chartered in 1891 and opened in 1894. In the early 1960's it comprised the central library, 38 branches, the Mercantile Library, and three bookmobiles; its holdings included 1,914,359 bound volumes. Its library for the blind circulates more material to blind persons than any other library in the world. The library's Edwin A. Fleisher Music Collection and rare-book department are other noteworthy components.

FREEMAN, DOUGLAS SOUTHALL (1886–1953), American journalist and historian, born in Lynchburg, Va. He was educated at Richmond College (A.B., 1904) and Johns Hopkins (Ph.D., 1908). Freeman was a journalist most of his adult life, editing the Richmond *News Leader* from 1915 to 1949. He was also a productive writer in the field of American history. His four-volume *R. E. Lee* (1934–35) won a Pulitzer Prize in 1934. It was followed by *Lee's Lieutenants* (3 vols., 1942–44) and *George Washington* (6 vols., 1948–54).

FREEMAN, LAWRENCE ("BUD") (1906–   ), American jazz musician, born in Chicago. This distinctive and influential tenor saxophonist was associated, during the early 1920's, with the "Austin High School Gang" in that city. Subsequently he played with Red Nichols, Ben Pollack, Joe Haymes, Gene Kardos, Ray Noble, Tommy Dorsey, Benny Goodman, and others, and led various groups in Chicago and Dixieland styles.

FREEMAN, MARY ELEANOR WILKINS (1852–1930), American author. Born in Randolph, Mass., she lived in New England, the region about which she wrote, until at the age of 49 she married and moved to New Jersey. One of the best of the regional writers, she specialized in tales of frustrated rural people living in a decaying social structure. The best of her work is to be found in two early collections of short stories, *A Humble Romance* (1887) and *A New England Nun* (1891). Later works of greater length were much less successful, but in 1918 she returned to what she did best in *Edgewater People*.
See also REGIONALISM.

FREEMAN, WALTER (1895–   ), American neurologist and neurosurgeon best known for his work in introducing prefrontal lobotomy into the United States. In this procedure a portion of the cerebrum is detached from the lower brain to treat certain mental disorders. Freeman's best-known works are *Neuropathology* (1933) and *Psychosurgery* (with J. W. Watts, 1942).
See also LOBOTOMY.

FREEMAN-THOMAS, FREEMAN. *See* WILLINGDON, FREEMAN FREEMAN-THOMAS, 1ST MARQUESS OF.

FREEPORT, city of northwestern Illinois, and seat of Stephenson County, located on the Pecatonica River. It is a trade, transportation, and distribution center for a dairy-

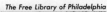
The Free Library of Philadelphia

The Free Library of Philadelphia, on Logan Square.

ing and general farming district. The manufacture of cheese is the leading industry, and farm machinery, patent medicines, auto and truck bodies, hardware, batteries, toys, and engines are also produced. The second Lincoln-Douglas debate was held here Aug. 27, 1858. Settled, 1835; inc., 1855; pop., 27,736.

FREEPORT, residential and resort village of southeastern New York, on the south shore of Long Island. Freeport has sport fishing and some light industries. Settled, c.1650; inc., 1892; pop., 40,374.

FREEPORT, city of southern Texas, a shipping port situated on the Gulf of Mexico, about 40 mi. southwest of Galveston. Magnesium extraction, from sea water, is an important industry. Velasco, the port through which the early Texas colonists debarked, has been included within the limits of Freeport since 1957. Inc. as city, 1947; pop., 11,997.

FREE PORT, a port, or zone within one, where customs duties are not collected on all entering goods. In extreme cases there are no duties. Generally, duty collection is only deferred until articles enter the country. But they may never enter and instead be shipped out, even after processing, without customs formalities. Leghorn, Italy, apparently was the first free port (1547); eventually, there were dozens. New York has had a free-port zone since 1937, New Orleans since 1946.

FREE RADICAL, in chemistry, group of carbon atoms that participates as a unit in a variety of reactions without decomposing. The group has no ionic charge but has a free valence electron on a terminal carbon atom, which can form a covalent bond with other free radicals, functional groups, or atoms. Such persistent clusters of carbon atoms are the basis of all homologous series, without which it would be impossible to categorize and name hundreds of thousands of organic reactions.

A free radical affects the properties of any group to which it becomes attached. Its inherent nature is derived from the homologous series, to which the radical belongs. For example, all aldehydes have the formula RCHO in which R— is any free radical. The—CHO aldehyde ending determines the reactions of the compound; yet its properties depend very much on the R—. Inorganic operations, such as nitration, are also categorized by the particular kind of R— used. In general, the ending -yl is used to designate a free radical.

Free radicals exist independently only for fractions of a second, between couplings, and therefore they cannot be studied apart from their formation products, yet organic chemistry is comprehensible only in terms of free radicals. The most dramatic work with free radicals has been in the field of synthetic fibers, plastics, pharmaceuticals, and, in biochemistry, with the protein molecule.

LOUIS VACZEK, The New School for Social Research

FREE-SOIL PARTY, American political party. It was formed in 1847–48 largely to oppose the extension of slavery into the territory newly annexed from Mexico. A national convention was held (Aug., 1848) in which "Barnburners" (radical New York Democrats), antislavery Whigs and former members of the Liberty party combined with land reformers to nominate Martin Van Buren the Free-Soil presidential candidate. With a platform prohibiting the extension of slavery, providing for free homesteads, and advocating a tariff for revenue only, Van Buren polled 291,263 votes. By drawing off Democratic strength, the Free-Soilers gave New York state to the Whigs and Zachary Taylor became president. The Barnburners returned to the Democratic party, and in the campaign of 1852 the Free-Soil candidate, John P. Hale, did poorly. In 1854 the party merged with the Republicans.

FREETOWN, largest city and capital of the Republic of Sierra Leone, western Africa. The city is on the hilly, wooded, humid Sierra Leone Peninsula adjacent to the Rokel River estuary. It is the country's chief port and terminus of the main railroad. There is a small fishing industry, and palm oil, leather, and gold are produced in the area. Fourah Bay College (estab., 1827) is here and an airport is nearby. Freetown was founded in the 1760's for the settlement of freed slaves. Pop., about 86,000.

FREE WILL, understood philosophically, is the power of the individual agent to determine his choice (of action or inaction) by and of himself. Free will may also be defined negatively as "uncaused choice," where "uncaused" is understood to mean that no force or power external to the chooser is operative in determining his choice.

The affirmation and denial of free will constitute one of the most important and persistent controversies in the history of Western thought. The issue is important, because metaphysics, theology, ethics, jurisprudence, and psychology all meet here.

The free will question first became important during the early formulation of Christian theology. The doctrine that Christ, the Son of God, came to earth to save man from sin seemed to suggest man's need of external aid; yet sin implied his moral responsibility, hence his freedom. Moreover, divine omnipotence and omniscience appeared incompatible with human freedom of will. St. Augustine (354–430) and John Calvin (1509–64) tried to reconcile these divergent elements by their doctrine of predestination: In Adam the whole human race was (negatively) free to choose good or evil. Adam's choice of evil corrupted all men, rendering them justly subject to eternal damnation. But God's inscrutable act of grace has elected certain souls to the acceptance of the Gospel (positive free will) and the eternal salvation following therefrom.

Since the Renaissance the remarkable progress of the physical and biological sciences has presented the free-will problem in a new light, showing will as only one aspect of the human spirit. Scientific thought, moral decision, and artistic creation all seem to many thinkers essentially meaningless, if viewed scientifically as only a series of causally determined events.

The case for negative freedom of will (freedom from causal determinism) is weak. Many have claimed that without such freedom moral judgments on human decisions would be absurd, since the moral "ought" is incompatible with the scientific "must" and "cannot." The obvious reply is that a decision which does not spring from the agent's own character is not a decision for which he is morally responsible. And the appeal to Werner Heisenberg's physical Principle of Indeterminacy in support of free will has been generally discredited as a misguided attempt to exalt a scientific predicament into a human prerogative.

A case for positive freedom of will (freedom through causal determinism) is to be found in the pantheism of Benedict Spinoza (1632–77). Here God is the unitary, self-sufficient, self-explanatory Whole of Reality from which all existent details follow with a rigorous necessity, both causal and logical. Determinism pervades the universe; there is no arbitrary freedom of uncaused choice, divine or human. The essential nature of every finite being, including man, is a striving to preserve and increase its power (freedom). Power consists of causes, and a cause is what explains, what necessitates its effect. So to have insight is to have freedom. The more men understand the necessary dependence of all things on God, the more their minds expand toward the mind of God, as they grow in power and freedom. In this process men are united rather than separated, since knowledge (from which power and freedom spring) is a co-operative rather than a competitive good. Free will is the affirmation of a Reality absorbed into one's own mind through the very necessities pervading it.

Consult Cranston, M. W., *Freedom: A New Analysis* (1953).

Stephen A. Emery, University of North Carolina

FREEZER. *See* Food Freezer Plant; Food Freezing, Home; Refrigeration.

FREEZING POINT, temperature at which a substance changes from the liquid state into the solid state. The freezing point of most substances varies with pressure and is normally measured at one atmosphere. Some amorphous substances, such as glass, do not have a definite freezing point and gradually harden over a wide temperature range as they are cooled. In some cases it is possible to cool a liquid below the freezing point if none of the solid is present. This is called supercooling; the liquid is in an unstable state and will solidify quickly on the addition of a small amount of solid. For pure substances the temperature at which the substance changes from a solid to a liquid, called the melting point, is the same as the freezing point.

The freezing points of some of the pure substances are easily measured and are readily reproducible, and are therefore used as fixed temperature points on the temperature scale. For instance, water freezes at 0° C. (32° F.), which defines 0° C.; zinc freezes at 320.9° C. (624.2° F.), and copper freezes at 1,083° C. (1,981.4° F.). For those substances which expand on freezing, such as water, an increase in pressure lowers the freezing point. Thus the pressure of an ice skate on the ice melts the ice under the blade, and the skater slides on a layer of water in a groove.

The freezing point of a solution, consisting of a solvent and a solute, depends on the concentration of the solute. As the concentration of the solute is increased, the freezing point is lowered, a property often used in the laboratory to determine the molecular weight of the solute. This behavior of solutions is also used in refrigeration, as the freezing point of a salt solution, for example, is lower than that of water. The salt spread on icy roads dissolves, and lowers the freezing point of the mixture.

W. D. Whitehead, University of Virginia

See also Cryogenics.

FREGE [frā'gə], **FRIEDRICH LUDWIG GOTTLOB** (1848–1925), German mathematician noted for works on the logical foundations of arithmetical concepts. Frege defined the cardinal number of any class as the class of all equivalent classes. From this definition Frege derived the properties of numbers as given in ordinary arithmetic.

FREIBERG [frī'bûrg], city of southern German Democratic Republic (East Germany), in the district of Karl-Marx-Stadt (Chemnitz), on the Münzbach near its confluence with the Mulde River, southwest of Dresden. Situated on the northern slopes of the Erzgebirge, Freiberg is the center of a mining district. Principal manufactures are iron goods, woolen goods, gold and silver articles, and sugar. Freiberg is the seat of Bergakademie, a famous mining academy, founded in 1765. Abraham Gottlob Werner (1750–1817) and Alexander von Humboldt (1769–1859) studied at the academy and Werner later taught there. The town was founded by Margrave Otto the Rich between 1185 and 1190, after silver had been found in the area. The most interesting buildings are the 12th-century cathedral, later rebuilt and restored, and the 15th-century Rathaus (town hall). Pop., 46,567.

FREIBURG IM BREISGAU, commonly known as **FREIBURG,** the main city of the Black Forest (Schwarzwald) in south Baden, Federal Republic of Germany (West Germany), in the part of the Rhine plain called the Breisgau. It lies in an amphitheater of hills partly covered with vineyards, where the Dreisam River emerges from the Himmelreich in the Black Forest. Streams which have flowed through the streets since the 13th century and the surviving medieval streets and façades add a distinctive charm to Freiburg. The old town is dominated by the splendid Gothic cathedral, the spire of which rises to over 350 ft. The cathedral windows date in part from the 13th and 14th centuries. In the cathedral square are the Renaissance Kaufhaus (1532), the Wenzingerhaus, which houses the academy of music, and the Bishop's palace. In the Town Hall square are a Franciscan church with ancient cloisters and a memorial to Bertold of Zähringen, who founded the city in 1118. Other buildings of historic interest are the Basler Hof, the Haus zum Walfisch (the municipal savings bank), the St. Martin's medieval town gate, and the now restored Schwabentor. There are a number of museums, one of which contains an interesting Black Forest exhibition. The city is the seat of a university founded in the 15th century, but whose main building dates from about 1900. Its schools of medicine and science are world famous. Freiburg is on one of the main routes from England and Scandinavia to Switzerland and Italy. Industries include printing and publishing, textiles (synthetic fibers), pharmaceuticals and furniture. Pop., 145,016.

Alice F. A. Mutton, University of London

BRIDGE WING

HEAVY LIFT BOOM

BRIDGE

WINCHES

KING POSTS

CARGO BOOMS

New York Shipbuilders Corp.

The freighter SS *Export Ambassador*. Freighters handle cargo by means of booms secured to masts or shorter king posts. Heavy lift booms move very heavy cargo. The cables that lead from the booms to pick up cargo are controlled by power winches.

FREIGHTER, the general "dry cargo" merchant ship, propelled by steam or diesel engines. Freighters are distinct from oil tankers or bulk carriers with cargoes of ore or grain. Freighters transport manufactured goods, raw materials, foodstuffs, machinery, and all types of crated and boxed goods.

Freighters constitute the largest class of merchant ship. They have a gross tonnage ranging from 6,000 to 24,000 tons, and speeds from 10 to 21 knots. The bridge and engines are usually amidships; some new freighters have machinery aft. In the U.S. Merchant Marine, freighters are customarily propelled by steam turbines. Freighters of other nations include steamers, but large diesel engines are more popular. Freighters may carry up to 12 passengers. Although popular conception regards them as weatherbeaten "tramp ships," most are fine vessels owned by long-established companies and are operated on fixed schedules.

Loading and unloading of cargo is usually done by the ship's winches, with intricate cargo gear rigged on masts and cargo booms. Efforts are being made to devise faster ways of handling cargo, as time spent in port is both expensive and unproductive.

During the 1940–60 period American freighters were the Liberty and Victory ships and the U.S. Maritime Commission C-1, C-2, C-3, and Mariner classes. Speeds range from the 10 knots of the Liberty ships to the 21 knots of the Mariners.

Typical of the new U.S. freighters is the *Export Ambassador*, launched in 1960. Built at a cost of $12,000,000, she is 492½ ft. long, cruises at 18½ knots, and has a crew of 54. There are accommodations for 12 passengers. Steam turbines developing 13,750 maximum horsepower drive the single-screw vessel. The capacity is 10,210 tons deadweight. Cargo-handling gear includes hydraulically operated hatch covers over six cargo holds, Ebel rig cargo gear, atmospheric control in cargo holds, and capacity to carry refrigerated cargo.

CAPT. L. S. McCREADY, USMS, U.S. Merchant
Marine Academy, Kings Point, N.Y.

See also MERCHANT SHIPPING.

FREISCHÜTZ, DER, opera in three acts by Carl Maria von Weber, libretto by Johann Friedrich Kind; first performance, June 18, 1821, Berlin. A Bohemian forester Max, in order to win the head ranger's daughter Agatha in a marksmanship contest, is persuaded to use magic bullets cast under the spell of the Evil One. When Agatha is almost struck by the seventh bullet, Max confesses and is forgiven.

From this typically German tale of the supernatural, Weber created what is generally considered the first German romantic opera whose influence persisted throughout the 19th century. Weber's special genius is revealed in his descriptive use of the orchestra to invoke the varying moods of natural landscape. His aria forms are often akin to the intimate German lied of sentiment and piety. Melodic inflections are often of a strongly popular flavor, especially in the choruses, and his harmonic style is marked by a dramatic use of unconventional modulations.

WILLIAM KIMMEL, Hunter College

FREITAL [frī′täl], town of southern German Democratic Republic (East Germany), in the district of Dresden, located on the Weisseritz River, southwest of Dresden, within that city's metropolitan region. It is connected with Dresden by a streetcar line. Nearby coal mines are the basis of some industrial establishments. Principal manufactures include machinery, leather, and optical instruments. Freital has a commercial school and a museum. Pop., 38,639.

FRELINGHUYSEN [frē′lĭng-hī-zən], **FREDERICK THEODORE** (1817–85), American statesman, born in Millstone, N.J. He graduated from Rutgers College (1836), studied law, and was admitted to the bar (1839). He served as attorney general of New Jersey (1861–66) and U.S. Senator (1866–69; 1871–77). In the Senate he strongly supported the Reconstruction program of the Radical Republicans and was a leading figure in the movement to impeach President Andrew Johnson. Frelinghuysen returned to private law practice (1877–81) until appointed Secretary of State by President Chester A. Arthur. In that office (1881–85) he successfully negotiated for canal rights across Nicaragua (1884), but the treaty was later withdrawn by President Grover Cleveland and never ratified. He was a strong supporter of trade with Latin America and sought to strengthen it with reciprocity treaties.

FRELINGHUYSEN, THEODORE (1787–1862), American statesman. Born in Millstone, N.J., he graduated (1804) from Princeton and established a brilliant reputation as a lawyer. He was New Jersey attorney general (1817–29) and U.S. Senator (1829–35). In 1844 he was the Whig party's candidate for Vice President. Chancellor of New York University (1839–50) and president of Rutgers College (1850–62), he was also associated with many religious and charitable organizations.

FREMANTLE, port of Australia, on the southwest coast of Western Australia. It lies at the mouth of the Swan River, 12 mi. southwest of Perth. Fremantle serves as the port for Perth and is the chief port of Western Australia. Major exports are wool, meat, wheat, gold, and refined petroleum products. Crude petroleum and various manufactured goods account for the bulk of imports. Pop., 24,343.

FRÉMONT [frē′mŏnt], **JOHN CHARLES** (1813–90), U.S. explorer, first Republican candidate for the presidency, and Civil War general. Frémont was born in Savannah, Ga., the son of a French emigré. After an early nomadic existence he graduated from the College of Charleston. The great oportunity for his career came in 1838 when he joined Joseph N. Nicollet's government-financed expedition of the Minnesota country. Under the exacting French scientist, Frémont received invaluable training in mathematics, surveying, mapping, and botanical and geological observation. By 1842 he was ready for his own command. His position had undoubtedly been enhanced by marriage to Jessie Benton, daughter of influential U.S. Senator Thomas Hart Benton.

On his first expedition Frémont made a reconnaissance of the western plains to the South Pass crossing of the Continental Divide, explored the Wind River chain, and scaled its second highest peak. His second expedition took him to Fort Vancouver in the Oregon country. He then turned south, and in midwinter crossed the Sierra Nevadas to Sutter's Fort on the Sacramento River. After both expeditions Frémont, with the aid of Jessie, wrote official reports. They were published by Congress and widely read and he became known as the "Pathfinder."

In 1845 he was sent with some 60 men to make further explorations of the Great Basin and California. Here he became involved in the Mexican War. As Commodore Robert F. Stockton's appointee as civil governor in California, Frémont became drawn into the quarrel between Stockton and Gen. Stephen Watts Kearny as to the chief command. Eventually forced to recognize Kearny's authority, Frémont was ordered home and court-martialed in Washington. He was saved from dismissal by President James K. Polk, but resigned, embittered, and equipped an unsuccessful private expedition to seek a railroad pass along the 38th parallel. Frémont served a brief term as U.S. senator from California (1850–51) and invested heavily in his California gold-bearing

John C. Frémont, frontier explorer. (THE BETTMANN ARCHIVE)

property, the Mariposa. In 1853 he made his fifth and last expedition into the West, again seeking a railroad pass.

In 1856 the newly formed Republican party nominated Frémont for the presidency, but he was defeated by James Buchanan. Nominated again in 1864 by the radical wing of the party, he withdrew before the election.

The Civil War brought a major generalship, the command of the Western Department, with headquarters at St. Louis, and severe criticism, especially of his emancipation proclamation for Missouri.

Resigning from the army in 1864, Frémont entered business but was unable to attain any financial success. In 1878 he was appointed governor of Arizona Territory. He resigned in 1883 to turn his attention to southwestern mining and land schemes. A few months before his death in New York, Congress authorized the president to appoint Frémont a major general in the army.

Consult Nevins, Allan, *Frémont: Pathmarker of the West* (1939).

MARY LEE SPENCE, Assistant Editor,
John C. Frémont Papers, University of Illinois

FREMONT, city of western California, on San Francisco Bay. It was incorporated in 1956 when five former residential townships consolidated in an effort to control rezoning. Pop., 100,869.

FREMONT, city of east-central Nebraska, and seat of Dodge County, on the Platte River. It is a marketing center for an agricultural area, and is known as the hybrid-seed-corn center of Nebraska. The city has poultry, dairy, and soybean processing plants, and meatpacking industries. Midland College (estab., 1887) and Central Lutheran Theological Seminary are here. The city was named in honor of Gen. John C. Frémont, the Western explorer. Inc., 1871; pop., 22,962.

FREMONT, city of northwestern Ohio and seat of Sandusky County, situated on the Sandusky River in an important agricultural area. Refined beet sugar, cutlery, automobile parts, electric goods, rubber tile, and clothing are manufactured. The home and burial ground of President Rutherford B. Hayes are located in Fremont. Pop., 18,490.

FREMSTAD [frĕm′städ], **OLIVE** (1871–1951), dramatic soprano, born in Stockholm. She went to Minnesota at an early age where she studied the piano and violin. In 1890 she traveled to New York to study singing, going on in 1892 to study in Germany with Lilli Lehmann. Although she was most famous as a soprano, Fremstad made her debut in 1895 as a contralto singing Azucena in *Il Trovatore*. Even later in soprano parts her voice was most beautiful in the middle and lower registers.

Fremstad made her American debut in 1903 at the Metropolitan Opera as Sieglinde in Wagner's *Die Walküre*. She achieved her greatest success in such Wagnerian roles as Kundry, Venus, and Isolde. Her rich and powerful voice was enhanced by her statuesque beauty and the intensity which she brought to her interpretations. Unfortunately the few recordings Fremstad made give little indication of the extraordinary quality of her voice. After singing 12 seasons at the Metropolitan to 1914, she devoted herself to occasional concert performances, finally settling into a secluded retirement. The main character of Willa Cather's *Song of the Lark* (1915) is modeled on Fremstad.

SUSAN THIEMANN, Music Division, New York Public Library

FRENCH, DANIEL CHESTER (1850–1931), American sculptor, born in Exeter, N.H. An outstanding figure among American sculptors of his period, he produced statues distinguished for their plastic beauty and grace. His notable works include "The Minute Man," executed in 1873 for the town of Concord, Mass., and the statue of Lincoln in the Lincoln Memorial, Washington, D.C.

FRENCH, SIR GEORGE ARTHUR (1841–1921), British soldier and Canadian police officer, born in Ireland. Trained at Sandhurst and Woolwich, England, he received an artillery commission in 1860 and served in Canada, India, and Australia. As first commissioner (1873–76) of the famous North West Mounted Police (later Royal Canadian Mounted Police), he helped achieve the traditional efficiency and discipline of that famous force.

FRENCH, JOHN DENTON PINKSTONE, 1ST EARL OF YPRES (1852–1925), British soldier. He participated in the Nile expedition in the Sudan (1884–85) and commanded a cavalry division with distinction during the Boer War (1899–1902). He became chief of the Imperial General Staff in 1912 and a field marshal in 1913. He took command of the British Expeditionary Force at the beginning of World War I and moved it to France "with unprecedented efficiency." After the battles of Mons and the Marne (Aug.–Sept., 1914), he shifted his troops to Flanders, where he fought in the Ypres area in October and November. A dispute with Lord Kitchener, the war minister, and the continuing stalemate and heavy losses prompted his resignation in Dec., 1915. He was com-

mander in chief in the United Kingdom until May, 1918, and then served as Lord Lieutenant of Ireland until 1921.

MARTIN BLUMENSON, Senior Historian, Department of the Army

FRENCH, Romance language spoken in France, in western Switzerland, in southern Belgium, in French possessions (former and current) in Africa and Asia, in Haiti, and in the province of Quebec, Canada. In the European homeland there are three major groups of dialects: (1) Northern, or *langue d'oïl* (Norman, Picard, Walloon, Angevin, Champenois, Saintongeais, Poitevin, Bourguignon), (2) Southern, or *langue d'oc* (Limousin, Auvergnat, Gascon, Provençal), (3) Franco-Provençal (upper Rhône valley and western Switzerland).

After Caesar's conquest (58–51 B.C.) of France (then called Gaul), Latin superseded various Celtic (Gaulish) tongues. Gaul became one of the richest and most important provinces of the Roman Empire. Hence it was thoroughly Latinized in culture and language, the Celtic idioms leaving but scanty traces in the vocabulary and sound system of Gaulish Latin.

The modern French dialects, which are derived from Latin, most likely continue ancient local variations of Latin. They have maintained themselves only as patois in oral currency, and are considered substandard in relation to the standard literary language. In the Middle Ages, however, a number of dialects, notably Norman, Picard, and Provençal, had literatures. Provençal, thanks mainly to the writings of the troubadours, developed an interregional literary language. But history favored the north, and in particular the Île-de-France. Paris became the capital of France in the 12th century, the residence of the royal court, and the intellectual and artistic center of the country. Hence Parisian French (Francien) attained preeminence over all other dialects. With national unity continuing uninterrupted, and Paris remaining the capital, Parisian standard speech was never again challenged.

In the development from Latin, the French dialects show a number of changes in common, and some common to all Romance languages. But many changes are peculiar to each of the dialects, owing to the history—both linguistic and non-linguistic—of each dialect area, to the variety of linguistic substrata, and to the linguistic superstrata which modified Gaulish Latin in the early Middle Ages. Among the last are the idioms of Germanic tribes which, crossing the Rhine into Gaul in the 5th century, established themselves more or less permanently. The most important of these tribes were the Visigoths, who settled in the southwest and in Spain; the Burgundians, who occupied the east and southeast, and after whom Burgundy is named; the Normans, who lived along the Channel and who, crossing to England in 1066, introduced there all those words of Romance origin which now form about half of the English lexicon; and the Franks, who originally held the northeast of Gaul and eventually dominated all the rest, giving the country and the language their name: *France* and *français*.

In the evolution of the language, the Germanic contribution extends mainly to the vocabulary. Some scholars also think that the diphthongization of Latin vowels in certain positions is due to German influence. Other changes ($u > \ddot{u}, p > b, k > g, t > d$) are, according to some, due to the Celtic substratum.

The earliest document in Old French is the *Oaths of Strasbourg* (842), a treaty among Charlemagne's grandsons; it was followed by various poems. Old French literature reaches a culmination in the *Chanson de Roland* (Song of Roland), 11th century.

Thanks to the cultural and political prestige which France enjoyed, especially in the 17th, 18th, and 19th centuries, French became the language of international diplomacy and society. But this linguistic eminence is not actually due to any alleged greater clarity or logic inherent in the language. Such virtues reside in no language, but rather in the user, language being merely his vehicle. But Frenchmen have concerned themselves greatly with the proper and pleasing use of French, an endeavor which was reflected in the foundation of the French Academy (1635) and in the emphasis on language study in the schools.

Consult Ewert, Alfred, *The French Language* (rev. ed., 1948).

Ernst Pulgram, University of Michigan
See also Romance Languages.

FRENCH ACADEMY. *See* Académie Française.

FRENCH AND INDIAN WARS (1689–1763), four colonial wars between Great Britain and France for control of North America. In America the separate wars were called King William's War (1689–97), Queen Anne's War (1702–13), King George's War (1744–48), and the French and Indian War (1754–63), but they were only parts of a general struggle for power and empire among Great Britain, France, Spain, Holland, Portugal, and Austria. The European phases of these wars are usually known,

respectively, as the War of the League of Augsburg, the War of the Spanish Succession, the War of the Austrian Succession, and the Seven Years' War. The term "French and Indian" is derived from the support given the French by the Indian tribes of Canada, Maine, and the Ohio Valley, although the six-nation Iroquois confederation usually gave the British valuable assistance. The chief prizes in dispute were Lake Champlain and the land and commerce of the Mohawk and Ohio valleys.

King William's War was marked by French and Indian massacres of settlers in Schenectady, Salmon Falls, and Casco Bay in 1690. The British and colonists under Sir William Phips retaliated by capturing (May 11, 1690) Port Royal, Acadia. The Treaty of Ryswick (1697) restored all North American conquests, but there were several adjustments in Europe and India among the European powers.

Queen Anne's War began in North America when the British destroyed (1702) St. Augustine in Spanish Florida. Two years later the French and Indians wiped out the settlers in Deerfield, Mass. A British colonial force of 4,000, led by Francis Nicholson, took Port Royal and Acadia in 1710, but elaborate military preparations for the conquest of Canada collapsed. Nevertheless, the warfare weakened France, and in the Treaty of Utrecht (1713) she lost Newfoundland, Acadia (renamed Nova Scotia), and Hudson Bay to Britain.

After 30 years of relative peace between England and France, warfare again broke out in the 1740's. During King George's War, William Pepperell led (1745) New England volunteers to victory at Louisbourg, which had been France's strongest fortress in America. The English frontier settlements again suffered from raids while the British fleet defeated the French in the Caribbean and

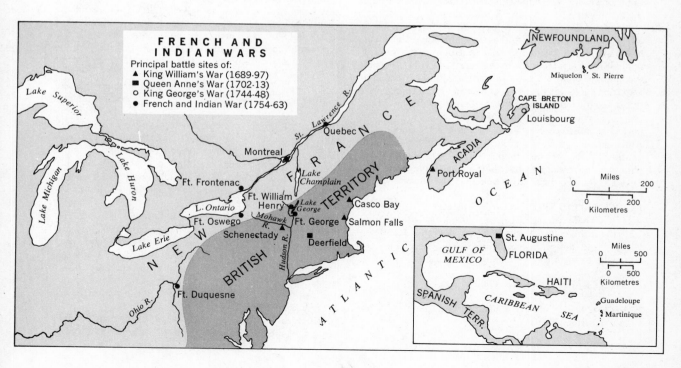

FRENCH AND INDIAN WARS

Principal battle sites of:
▲ King William's War (1689-97)
■ Queen Anne's War (1702-13)
○ King George's War (1744-48)
● French and Indian War (1754-63)

captured Fort Louis in Haiti. The Treaty of Aix-la-Chapelle (1748), however, restored all conquests.

Frontier massacres on both sides had so inflamed Anglo-French relations that despite the formal peace armed hostilities continued in Nova Scotia, the Ohio Valley, and the Cherokee country to the south. In June, 1755, these skirmishes became large-scale warfare, and historians generally mark that date as the commencement of the French and Indian War. The colonists fought for control over the Ohio River Valley, which linked French possessions in Canada and the Mississippi Valley, but once the war had begun the British attempted to take possession of Canada. A three-pronged campaign was directed by the British commander in chief, Gen. Edward Braddock. Personally leading the attack on the French at Fort Duquesne, Braddock was killed when his forces were ambushed. Only the campaign against the French in the Lake George region showed any success. War was formally declared between Britain and France in May, 1756. The French, under Gen. Louis Joseph Montcalm, took the initiative and captured Fort Oswego and Fort George from the English in 1756 and the newly built Fort William Henry at the southern end of Lake George a year later. But before long the tide turned. Louisbourg, Fort Frontenac, and Fort Duquesne (renamed Fort Pitt) fell to the British in 1758. On Sept. 18, 1759, the key French city of Quebec surrendered, five days after both commanding generals, Montcalm and James Wolfe had been killed in the Battle of the Plains of Abraham. A year later Montreal capitulated, and the British conquest of Canada was complete.

The Treaty of Paris (1763) formally concluded the French humiliation, and Great Britain emerged the dominant imperial power of the world. France ceded to Britain all claim to Acadia, Canada, Cape Breton, and that part of Louisiana east of the Mississippi. Britain restored to France the islands of St. Pierre and Miquelon off the south coast of Newfoundland and Guadeloupe, Martinique, and a few other islands in the West Indies. In many ways, the Treaty of Paris doomed British imperial control over the 13 original colonies, for, freed from the fear of French invasion, the colonies could do without British military protection. The treaty also left France embittered and eager for retribution against Britain. The American Revolution gave it that opportunity. The end of the war also brought a period of moral consciousness of the slavery issue to the American colonists. They faced, for the first time, the contradictions between their position as colonists struggling for new freedoms and their role as slave owners.

RICHARD M. ABRAMS, University of California

FRENCH BROAD RIVER, river in western North Carolina and eastern Tennessee. It rises in the Blue Ridge Mountains in southwestern North Carolina, flows north and west through the mountains, and joins the Holston River near Knoxville to form the Tennessee River. Length, 204 mi.

FRENCH CAMEROONS. *See* CAMEROUN.

FRENCH-CANADIAN LITERATURE. *See* CANADA: *Canadian Literature (French).*

FRENCH CANADIANS. *See* CANADA: *People;* QUEBEC.

FRENCH COMMUNITY, association of the French Republic and six other sovereign states, formerly French overseas territories—that is, territories lying outside Europe that until 1958 had been tied to the French Republic either as colonies or by arrangements providing for various degrees of self-government. The French Republic consists of: (a) Metropolitan (that is, European) France; (b) Overseas Departments (Martinique, Guadeloupe, Réunion, and Guiana); and (c) Overseas Territories (French Polynesia, New Caledonia, French Somaliland, Comoro Islands, St. Pierre and Miquelon, Southern and Antarctic Territories, and Wallis and Futuna Islands). The other six members of the French Community—all independent African states—include the Central African Republic, Republic of Chad, Republic of the Congo (Brazzaville), Republic of Gabon, Malagasy Republic, and Republic of Senegal.

Formation. The creation of the French Community in 1958 marked the second major effort since the end of World War II to reform the structure of the former French empire in view of altered circumstances. The first reform was the creation of the French Union, set up by the 1946 constitution of the Fourth French Republic. That constitution considerably altered the governmental framework of the Third Republic (1871–1940) but provided for continuing close ties between France and its overseas possessions. The Fourth Republic, however, failed to maintain the "union": in 1954 France lost Indochina (Laos, Cambodia, and Vietnam) in Southeast Asia; in 1956 the French protectorates over Morocco and Tunisia came to an end; and after 1954 war raged in Algeria. Unable either to suppress or to come to terms with the Muslim rebellion in Algeria, and beset by numerous other problems, the parliamentary Fourth Republic gave way in 1958 to the more authoritarian Fifth Republic. In a referendum on the new constitution, President Charles de Gaulle offered all French Overseas Territories four choices: to retain their status as Overseas Territories; to become Overseas Departments; to become autonomous member states of the new French Community; or to sever all ties with France and become completely independent.

Only a single territory, Guinea, voted for independence. Twelve other overseas territories, with a combined area and population many times those of Guinea, voted to become autonomous republics within the French Community: Madagascar, Sudan (Mali), Upper Volta, Ivory Coast, Niger, Senegal, Dahomey, Mauritania, Chad, Central Africa, (French) Congo, and Gabon. Six—St. Pierre and Miquelon, the Comoro Islands, Wallis and Futuna Islands, French Somaliland, Polynesia, and New Caledonia—chose to remain overseas territories.

President De Gaulle's answer to Guinea's 97% vote for independence was swift: all French administrative and other personnel, including teachers and physicians, were withdrawn, as well as all French technical and economic assistance. But after Guinea was accorded membership in the United Nations, France recognized its independence and approved Guinea's continued participation in the French franc bloc.

Structure. The provisions of the 1958 constitution went into effect for the twelve territories that had voted to stay within the French Community. They were to "administer themselves and manage their own affairs democratically and freely," with the proviso that all citizens—irrespective of race, origin, or religion—were to be equal before the law and "have the same duties," so that there would be, for example, no special legislation or discrimination against white minorities. Since, however, those republics were to be not independent but autonomous, the following matters were reserved to the French Community: foreign policy, defense, currency, common economic and financial policy, and policy on strategic raw materials. Furthermore, except when specific agreements provided differently, the Community (and not the autonomous republics) was empowered to handle "the supervision of the law-courts, higher education, the general organization of external transportation and transportation within the Community, as well as telecommunications." The 1958 constitution also recognized "only one (common) citizenship in the Community." In short, the first French Community scheme offered a great deal of political, economic, military, and cultural co-operation among the member states.

The important matters not left to the autonomous republics were vested in the following organs:

The Presidency of the Community, an office to be held by the President of France.

The Executive Council of the French Community, composed of the President (chairman), the French Premier, the heads of government of the autonomous republics, and those French Ministers (Cabinet members) responsible for the common affairs of the community (the Foreign Minister, Defense Minister, Finance Minister, and so forth).

The Senate of the Community, consisting of the members of the French Parliament and the legislatures of the African republics. The Senate of the Community was to hold two sessions annually; each was to last one month at the most.

The Court of Arbitration, appointed by the President, to decide on litigations occurring among member states of the Community.

Evolution. The 1958 constitution specifically opened the door to "other states," which did not participate in the 1958 referendum, to join the French Community at a later time. Evidently, this invitation was addressed to the moderates among the Algerian nationalists, and such states as Morocco, Tunisia, Laos, Cambodia, and (South) Vietnam. Hopes that these states would join the Community were not fulfilled. On the contrary, by 1960 the trend toward independence had become so strong in the autonomous republics that the 1958 constitution had to be amended on May 18, 1960, to permit them, after gaining independence, to continue membership in the French Community. Led by the Malagasy Republic (the new name of the island of Madagascar, off the east coast of Africa) and the short-lived Mali Federation (Mali and Senegal), all twelve of the former autonomous republics became independent during 1960, but only six of them chose to retain their membership in the French Community. The functions of the community in those six independent countries have since then been largely limited to the spheres of economic aid and defense.

By the end of 1961 all of the original twelve republics had become members of the United Nations. In this respect, the situation within the French Community is, therefore, not very different from that prevailing among the members of the (British) Commonwealth of Nations. In fact, the ties of some of the former autonomous republics with France are stronger than those of some former dominions or colonies with Great Britain. Linguistically and culturally, the ties of the member states with France are very close, and even those of the original twelve that are not formal members continue cultural and economic co-operation. A further, albeit indirect, important link between France and its former colonial and otherwise dependent territories that are now sovereign states is provided by their association with the European Economic Community, of which France is a leading member.

JOHN H. E. FRIED, New York University

See also FRANCE.

FRENCH CONGO. *See* CONGO, REPUBLIC OF THE (BRAZZAVILLE).

FRENCH COOKERY. The happy marriage of the land and the people of France has produced a national cuisine which is perhaps the world's finest. The fruits of the land are abundant and its products diverse. Yet it is by no mere chance that the French have succeeded in fulfilling the promise of their harvests. With frugality, ingenuity, and instinctive taste, they have evolved dishes both distinctive in flavor and individual in character.

Modern French cookery can be said to date back to the medieval monasteries. At a time when all of Europe was gripped in turbulence, the monasteries—Benedictine and Cistercian—preserved the methods of preparing fine foods and wines. A glance at the map of France also suggests another source of influence. Its neighbor countries—Germany, Switzerland, Italy, and Spain in particular—have lent many a national recipe to the border regions of France. Almost invariably, however, the French have applied their own Gallic touch to the immigrant dish, making of it a unique creation.

France is a land of regional cookery. The central and northern part of the country, marked roughly by Calais to the north, Bordeaux to the west, and Grenoble to the east, contains fertile grazing lands. Thus this area bases its cooking on butter as the principal fat. To the south, where the hardy olive tree flourishes and the climate is too dry for profitable grazing, the principal cooking fat is olive oil. North and northeastward, where the pig thrives, pork fat is used predominantly, though both here and in certain parts of the south goose fat is also of prime importance. A variety of dishes characteristic of a particular valley, peninsula, or even town may be found within any of these three broad areas.

The food of Alsace and less particularly that of Lorraine, in the northeastern corner of France, reveals the historic ties of this region to Germany. Although the land is relatively fertile, the people of Alsace-Lorraine have provided the economical pig and goose from Germany for a rich, substantial diet—sausages of all kinds, sauerkraut (*choucroute*), goose, and *pâté de foie gras*, a delicate meat paste made from the enlarged livers (up to 4 lb.) of specially fattened geese.

Another area which defers to both pig and goose is that

south and east of Bordeaux along the Pyrenees to the Mediterranean. This relatively remote region can boast of exceptional food and good eating. Here, in a productive land, the Toulouse goose is king by preference. From the Languedoc, west of the Rhône River, comes the *cassoulet,* a meat and white bean stew; and from the region of the Garonne, the finest of truffles.

In the northeastern districts, such as Normandy, cheese (Camembert, Neufchâtel, Pont l'Evêque, and fresh cream cheese), butter, and cream are important products of the rich pasturelands. The extensive orchards of the region provide a bountiful harvest of apples and the channel coast a rewarding variety of sea food. Apples find their way into many a Norman dish and are also used in the making of cider or the potent Calvados. Among this region's many dishes are *poulet à la Vallée d'Auge,* chicken cooked in butter, cider, and cream with onions; *sole normande,* sole in a sauce of butter, cream, and egg yolks garnished with seafood and mushrooms; and *tripe à la mode de Caen,* a slow-cooked tripe casserole.

In the arid region southeast of the Rhône, in Provence, olive oil and, less often, pork or goose fat are used. And as one travels along the Mediterranean shore, the cooking more closely resembles that of Italy. Here we find a wide choice of sea food, which makes possible the famous bouillabaisse of Marseilles, a sumptuous fish chowder spiced with saffron. Garlic asserts itself in many of the regional dishes. Also of importance are anchovies, dried codfish, onions, and tomatoes.

These are but three examples of the extremes in regional cookery within the broad scope of French cuisine. Of equal importance are the foods and dishes of Brittany, hearty and simple; the good eating of the Bordeaux country, where the food is either cosmopolitan in preparation or robust in its simplicity; the varied fare of Burgundy, reflecting the wealth of the land; and the superb cuisine of the Loire Valley north to Paris.

French cookery may also be divided by yet another means that both transcends and embraces regional boundaries. Thus the cuisine of the country may be identified as *la haute cuisine, la cuisine bourgeoise, la cuisine régionale,* and *la cuisine improvisée.* Translated, this breakdown of Gallic cooking means professional chef's cooking, home cooking, regional cooking, and "off the cuff," or improvised, cooking.

To write of French cookery without mention of wine would be akin to omitting the eggs from a *soufflé.* Wine is not only a national industry for the French but a part of life. It is not only a welcome—if not necessary—adjunct to the meal, but often an ingredient of the dish. The northern plains of the country lack the climate for growing the grape, and, with the exception of Normandy, their food suffers. The two most famous French wine regions are Bordeaux and Burgundy. Also well known beyond the borders of France are the fresh white Alsatian wines and the wines of Champagne, the Côte du Rhône, and the Loire Valley.

Consult Chamberlain, Samuel, *Bouquet de France* (rev. ed., 1958); Root, Waverly, *The Food of France* (1958).

NARCISSA CHAMBERLAIN, Coauthor, *The Flavor of France*
See also BRILLAT-SAVARIN, ANTHELME; CARÊME, MARIE ANTOINE; ESCOFFIER, AUGUSTE; WINE.

FRENCH EQUATORIAL AFRICA was a federated administrative unit created by France in 1910, consisting of four territories—Gabon, Middle Congo, Ubangi-Shari (now Central African Republic), and Chad. These colonies had been acquired piecemeal by France during the 19th century. After federation the governors of each territory were made responsible to a governor-general in Brazzaville. Guided by their belief in assimilation, the French made little effort to duplicate the British policy of indirect rule. The area was the poorest in French Africa, largely because of its difficult climate and lack of communications. Having assumed title to all the land, the French government portioned out vast tracts on a concession basis to large monopolistic companies. Human and natural resources were depleted and the French government took 15% of the profits. A ten-year development plan initiated in 1947 repaired some of the damage. It was in Brazzaville, the capital of French Equatorial Africa, that, in 1944, Black Africa's constitutional advance began. The French decision to reject the federal plan of development led in 1958 to the establishment of self-governing states. Each of the four territories achieved full independence in 1960.

RICHARD P. STEVENS, Lincoln University
See also CENTRAL AFRICAN REPUBLIC; CHAD; CONGO, REPUBLIC OF THE (BRAZZAVILLE); GABON.

FRENCH GUIANA. *See* GUIANA, FRENCH.

FRENCH HORN, brass wind instrument (aerophone), with a conical tube wound in a circle and ending in a bell-shaped opening. Its mouthpiece is funnel-shaped. The modern horn has three rotary valves, and although pitched in F can play complete scales in any key, unlike the old valveless horn of the 17th and 18th centuries. Today the horn is highly valued by composers as an important instrument of the orchestra, particularly because of its contributions to orchestral color and climax. The instrument has been part of the orchestra since the early 18th century. Mozart wrote concertos for horn and orchestra, as did Richard Strauss, more than a century later.

FRENCH INDOCHINA, officially **INDOCHINE,** former French colony on the Indochina peninsula. *See* CAMBODIA; INDOCHINA; LAOS; VIETNAM.

FRENCH LICK, town of southern Indiana. French Lick was a French trading post during colonial times. The town is well known for its mineral springs and is a popular health resort. Pop., 2,059.

FRENCHMAN FLAT, desert basin 40 mi. northwest of Las Vegas, Nev., used as an atomic testing ground. It is a part of the Las Vegas Bombing and Gunnery Range, and is closed to the public.

FRENCH POLYNESIA, island dependencies in the southeast Pacific Ocean, formerly called French Settlements in Oceania. They include the Society, Austral, Tuamotu, Gambier, and Marquesas islands. The colony is administered by a governor and an elected assembly, sitting at Papeete, Tahiti. Area, 1,544 sq. mi.; pop., 73,201.
See also OCEANIA.

H. Roger-Viollet

The Estates General, composed of representatives of the three estates—clergy, nobles, and commoners—was convened at Versailles on May 5, 1789, in an attempt to remedy France's difficult financial situation.

FRENCH REVOLUTION, the most significant of the revolutions in France. It overthrew (1789–99) the absolute monarchy of Louis XVI and gave expression to liberal and democratic aspirations foreshadowed by the Enlightenment. It led to many permanent legal and administrative reforms, modernized the government of France, and greatly stimulated the development of nationalism in Europe. It gave rise to lasting social and ideological divisions—monarchists versus republicans, Right versus Left, clericals versus anticlericals, economic laissez faire versus state intervention—which have since played a major part in French and European politics. The doctrines of socialism and communism were anticipated to some extent in the programs of the most radical revolutionary groups, and the seeds of fascism appear in the ideas and attitudes of the counterrevolution.

Causes. Among the social and economic causes of the revolution, two were of major importance: the hunger of the peasantry for land free of feudal encumbrances, and the desire of the urban middle classes for legal and civic equality and an end to aristocratic privilege. Popular discontent reached a high pitch in the spring of 1789 because of extensive unemployment, crop failures, food shortages, and attempts by landlords to increase their manorial dues and rents in order to keep pace with rapidly rising prices. The royal family, especially the frivolous and tactless Austrian-born Queen, Marie Antoinette, was unpopular. The government was on the verge of bankruptcy as a result of extravagance and mis-

management of the public finances. To secure new revenues and eliminate the tax exemptions enjoyed by the clergy and nobility a meeting of the Estates General—the first since 1614—was called, and representatives of the three estates (clergy, nobles, and commoners) assembled at Versailles early in May, 1789.

The Moderate Phase of the Revolution. King Louis XVI had hoped for the support of the Third Estate, the elected representatives of the common people of the entire nation, and he therefore gave them 600 seats—a number equal to that of the other two estates combined. During the election campaign, freedom of the press was granted. Journalists and pamphleteers like the Abbé Sieyès published inflammatory writings and thereby created a mood of determination among the commoners. When the latter proved too independent for the King's purpose, he ordered the three estates to sit separately and to vote "by order" rather than "by head." Thus the Third Estate would have been placed in a permanent minority of one to two.

Under the leadership of the Comte de Mirabeau, an aristocrat elected as a commoner, the Third Estate defied the King and declared itself a sovereign National Assembly with power to change the constitution. When royal officials then locked the members out of their usual meeting place on June 20, 1789, they convened in a nearby tennis court and swore an oath not to disband until they had given France a constitution. They were soon joined by many sympathetic nobles and lesser clergy from the other two estates. On June 26 the King was obliged to accept this arrangement. But the influence of the Queen and of Louis's two reactionary brothers led him to surround Paris with troops, giving rise to widespread rumors that he intended to disperse the Assembly by force.

Alarmed by these military moves, the people of the poorer quarters in the eastern part of the city joined with the disaffected French Guards regiment on July 14 to storm and capture the feebly defended Bastille, a fortress prison that had formerly housed political offenders and had come to be a symbol of tyranny. The Bastille also contained large stores of gunpowder needed by the popular forces.

After the fall of the Bastille the King could no longer intimidate the capital city, for he dared not risk the loss of life it would cost to subdue Paris by military action. He had no choice but to give in to the Assembly's demands and to accept the formation of a National Guard under the command of the Marquis de Lafayette consisting of armed citizens sworn to defend the National Assembly. The Revolution was now secure against the possibility of counterrevolution from the throne. The Assembly proceeded to enact a far-reaching series of reforms, the most important of which were later incorporated in the first of the revolutionary constitutions (1791). As a preamble, the Assembly drafted the Declaration of the Rights of Man and of the Citizen, which established equality of civil rights and obligations, equality before the

The Fogg Art Museum—Art Reference Bureau

The Tennis Court Oath of June 20, 1789, depicted in a study by Jacques Louis David, court painter who supported the Revolutionary cause. When Louis XVI locked out the Third Estate, or commoners, from their regular assembly place, they met on an indoor tennis court and vowed to remain until they had a constitution for France.

The fall of the Bastille on July 14, 1789. Rebelling against royal authority, the Paris populace attacked the Bastille, a fortress prison that had become a symbol of the tyranny of the crown.

Bulloz—Art Reference Bureau

law, and equal access to public careers for all men. Before this document was completed the Assembly heard with alarm news of widespread peasant uprisings, the "Great Fear." To calm these disorders, the Assembly on the night of Aug. 4–5, 1789, decreed the abolition of the feudal system and most other forms of local and special privilege. In October a crowd of lower-class Parisian housewives marched 12 mi. in the rain to Versailles to beg the King to reduce the price of bread. Criminal elements had infiltrated the ranks of the demonstrators, and in the dead of the night they invaded the royal apartments and threatened the Queen and her children. The following day the mob brought the royal family back to Paris as virtual hostages and lodged them in the palace of the Tuileries under guard.

From Monarchy to Republic. Until the outbreak of war between France and the leading monarchical powers of Europe in Apr., 1792, the Revolution remained essentially a moderate reform movement. Leaders such as Mirabeau, Lafayette, and Sieyès sought guarantees for civil and individual liberties under a limited constitutional monarchy. Personal and property rights were firmly established, and economic affairs—including profiteering, unemployment, and steady inflation—were allowed to take their "natural" course. The church was deprived of its vast landholdings, the value of this property being assigned to pay the royal debt which the Revolution had inherited. In exchange the nation assumed the obligation to pay the salaries of the clergy. Priests were required to swear allegiance to the new constitution, however, and many refused on grounds of conscience. These dissenters from the "civil constitution of the clergy" eventually comprised about half the parish priests of France. They were expelled from their pulpits, while those who took the oath were excommunicated by the Pope. This growing religious conflict troubled Louis XVI and made it impossible for him to assume in good faith the role of constitutional monarch assigned him by the Assembly. The new constitution embodied the principle of the separation of powers and gave the crown only a suspensive veto over acts of the legislative assembly.

Many idealists and persons of strong democratic leanings, particularly the leaders of the lower classes in Paris, were outraged by the heavy property qualifications placed on voting and office-holding and became active in various radical political clubs like the Cordeliers or the more important Jacobin Society. However, moderate members of the Girondist faction (so-called because many were from this region of France) retained the support of the Assembly and controlled the government. Although the Girondists favored a liberal republic, they had little sympathy for the poorer classes and were eventually displaced by the more popular and more ruthless Jacobins. Led at first by Georges Danton and Jean Paul Marat, later by Maximilien Robespierre and Louis de Saint-Just, the Jacobins gained rapidly in influence after Apr., 1792, when the Girondist Cabinet, in the hope of compromising the King, provoked a war with Austria, Prussia, and Great Britain. Owing partly to the emigration of many experienced military officers belonging to the aristocracy, the nation was woefully unprepared for war.

Invaded by a Prussian army under the Duke of Brunswick in the summer of 1792, France seemed to face certain defeat and possible dismemberment. The King, who had attempted to flee the country with his family a year earlier, was popularly suspected, and with good reason, of collaborating with the enemy. On Aug. 10, frightened by Brunswick's manifesto threatening to raze the city of Paris if any of the royal family were harmed, a huge mob, led by Danton and the Jacobin-dominated municipal government, invaded the Tuileries, massacred the Swiss guards, and forced Louis XVI and his family to take refuge in the adjoining hall of the Legislative Assembly. The Assembly voted at once to suspend the King from his executive functions, to dissolve itself, and to arrange for the election, by universal manhood suffrage, of a National Convention that would make a new constitution. Until the meeting of this body six weeks later, France was led by Danton and his followers in the Insurrectionary Commune of Paris. Calling for "Audacity, more audacity and still more audacity!" Danton rallied the "nation in arms" and inspired such an effective war effort that the enemy was turned back in the Battle of Valmy on Sept. 20. Soon afterward Brunswick withdrew from French territory.

Meeting on the day following the victory of Valmy, the National Convention proclaimed the abolition of the monarchy and later tried and condemned Louis XVI and Marie Antoinette to death despite the efforts of the Girondins to save their lives. Louis XVI was beheaded

Bulloz—H. Roger-Viollet

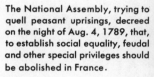

The National Assembly, trying to quell peasant uprisings, decreed on the night of Aug. 4, 1789, that, to establish social equality, feudal and other special privileges should be abolished in France.

by the newly invented guillotine in Jan., 1793. To break the hold of "reactionary" traditions, the Convention established a Revolutionary calendar that began its Year I on Sept. 22, 1792; introduced the new metric system of weights and measures; and confirmed the substitution of "naturally defined" departments in place of the old provinces.

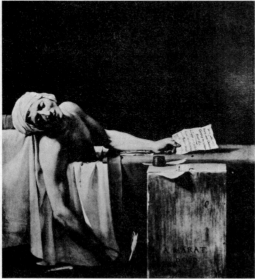

"Marat Assassinated" (1793), by Jacques Louis David. The Revolutionary figure was killed in his bath.

Bruckmann—Art Reference Bureau

Bulloz—H. Roger-Viollet

Above, Marie Antoinette as a prisoner of the Revolutionaries, drawn by David. The unpopular French Queen was guillotined on Oct. 16, 1793.

In addition, the codification of the laws was begun; free and compulsory public education was instituted, at least in principle; and a brief attempt was made to substitute the worship of Reason for Christian church services. But on the whole, the Convention opposed extreme projects such as the abolition of Christianity and upheld freedom of conscience. Through economic measures like the Law of the Maximum, a partially successful effort was made to control rising prices, but huge public expenditures for defense were financed by the printing of *assignats*, and the steady depreciation of this paper currency could not be checked.

Jacobin Rule. To exercise the executive power, a system of committees was established by the Convention. These bodies were placed under the supreme control of the Committee on General Security (for police affairs) and of the more famous Committee of Public Safety, which was in theory responsible to the Convention, but in practice ruled with full authority during the period of the Jacobin dictatorship (June, 1793–July, 1794). After the assassination of Marat by the royalist fanatic Charlotte Corday and the execution of Danton for corruption and correspondence with the enemy, Robespierre rose to unchallenged leadership of the Jacobin political machine.

Robespierre's authority rested on brilliant oratory, personal honesty, austere patriotism, and incorruptible revolutionary zeal. He gained lower-class support by his measures to control inflation and profiteering, by his effort to allot public lands to poor peasants, and by other attempts at social and economic reform. He had to cope with the foreign war, which was again going badly, and with a full-scale civil war in the western provinces of

Below, the execution of Robespierre and his collaborators.

Brittany and the Vendée. The domestic conflict was led by reactionary nobles, *émigrés*, and the recalcitrant clergy, and it was financed and supplied by the hostile monarchical coalition—chiefly Great Britain. To surmount these crises, Robespierre instituted rigid centralization of government and severe limitations upon civil liberties. A Revolutionary Tribunal was created to mete out summary justice to spies, traitors, and other "enemies of the people."

Reasonable judicial safeguards were maintained at first, but in the spring of 1794 the number of victims multiplied rapidly and the Terror began to strike at the Jacobins themselves. When Robespierre made the mistake of denouncing "public enemies" within the National Convention—without giving their names—he sealed his own doom. The frightened members voted to outlaw him and his close colleagues.

The Conservative Republic. Under the leadership of Jean Tallien, the Jacobins were overthrown and "Thermidorean Reaction" (July 27, 1794; the 9th Thermidor by the Revolutionary calendar) established the moderates in power. Robespierre and his collaborators died on the guillotine the next day, and many prominent Jacobins lost their lives in the "white terror" that followed. The new leaders of the Convention abolished the Revolutionary Tribunal and the extraordinary committees, together with much of the price-control legislation and other social measures of the Jacobin period. Political prisoners were granted amnesty and many exiled priests and nobles were allowed to return. The political climate became more relaxed and more hospitable to official corruption.

The Convention established a new executive in the form of a five-man Directory and provided for new legislative bodies; but a popular uprising was provoked by the Convention's attempt to force the re-election of two-thirds of its own members to the new assemblies. On this occasion a young officer of artillery, Napoleon Bonaparte, fired his famous "whiff of grapeshot" to break up a Parisian mob and save the day for the entrenched politicians.

The Directory's rule was weak, venal, and unpopular. Only the veteran armies of the Republic were still motivated by Jacobin zeal. Led by able young commanders, they occupied much foreign territory which the Directory stripped of valuable booty and works of art under the pretext of protecting newly liberated sister-republics from a return of their tyrants. In 1799, however, the threat of bankruptcy and economic collapse brought an electoral triumph for the resurgent Jacobins. The moneyed interests were frightened because the Jacobin program included a levy on capital, and the conservative Directors sought a military dictator. After two other generals had disappointed the conspirators, Bonaparte was chosen to be the "man on horseback." In the narrowly successful *coup d'état* of 18 Brumaire (Nov. 9, 1799), he used troops to disperse the elected representatives of the people and made himself supreme under the title First Consul.

Consult Gershoy, Leo, *French Revolution and Napoleon* (1933); Brinton, Crane, *Decade of Revolution, 1789–1799* (1935); Thompson, J. M., *French Revolution* (5th ed., 1955).

RALPH H. BOWEN, Northern Illinois University
See also FRENCH REVOLUTIONARY WARS; NAPOLEON I.

FRENCH REVOLUTIONARY CALENDAR, calendar introduced during the Jacobin phase of the French Revolution. The National Convention decided soon after the abolition of the monarchy (Sept. 21, 1792) that public documents should be dated "from the first year of the Republic," but a definite plan for a calendar, founded on the decimal system, was not adopted until Oct. 5, 1793. The scheme remained in effect until discontinued by Napoleon in 1806. The year was to begin at midnight on the day of the autumnal equinox at Paris (Sept. 22), and consisted of 12 equal months of 30 days each, followed by five (six in leap-year) "complementary days" to be celebrated as national holidays. Each month had three weeks of 10 days each, and each week had one day of rest. Months were given new "natural" names designed to suggest the weather or seasonal activity normal for that time of year, as the following table indicates:

AUTUMN

Vendémiaire (vintage)	September 22–October 21
Brumaire (fog)	October 22–November 20
Frimaire (frost)	November 21–December 20

WINTER

Nivôse (snow)	December 21–January 19
Pluviôse (rain)	January 20–February 18
Ventôse (wind)	February 19–March 20

SPRING

Germinal (seeds)	March 21–April 19
Floréal (blossoms)	April 20–May 19
Prairial (meadows)	May 20–June 18

SUMMER

Messidor (harvest)	June 19–July 18
Thermidor (heat)	July 19–August 17
Fructidor (fruit)	August 18–September 16

RALPH H. BOWEN, Northern Illinois University

FRENCH REVOLUTIONARY WARS, conflicts (1792–1802) in which the French, fighting against two successive coalitions of monarchical powers, sought to defend their new regime and to export their revolutionary principles. They changed the nature of modern warfare by developing new tactics based on the rapid movement of large masses of men, the substitution of patriotic enthusiasm for rigid discipline, the establishment of a democratic officer corps, and the subordination of civilian life to the war effort.

Early in 1792 the Austrian Emperor Francis II was under strong pressure from German Princes and French *émigrés* to intervene on behalf of the French royal family. The French, however, were the first to declare war (Apr. 20). The government, then under Girondist domination, had deliberately precipitated hostilities in order to bring about the downfall of King Louis XVI. Appealing to neighboring peoples to overthrow their "tyrants," the French deployed three armies along their eastern frontier. But many officers had emigrated, discipline had become lax, and the supply system was disorganized. The French were, consequently, forced to retreat toward

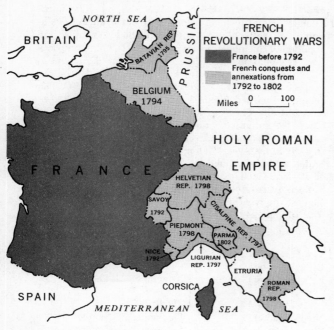

FRENCH
REVOLUTIONARY WARS

France before 1792

French conquests and
annexations from
1792 to 1802

Miles   0   100

ther reverses in midsummer, a *levée en masse* (conscription) of the able-bodied male population was proclaimed. The tide turned in the autumn, and the French again crossed the Rhine.

In December a plan proposed by Napoleon Bonaparte, until then an obscure artillery officer, led to the recapture of Toulon from the British. Further French victories followed in 1794, and the Austrians were forced to evacuate Belgium. By the beginning of 1795 Gen. Charles Pichegru had overrun the Netherlands, which became the Batavian Republic. Prussia and several German states made peace by the Treaty of Basel (Apr. 5, 1795), thus neutralizing northern Germany and leaving the left bank of the Rhine under French control.

In 1796–97 three French armies set out to bring the Austrian Emperor to terms. Gens. Jean Jourdan and Jean Moreau were defeated in southern Germany, but Bonaparte's brilliant campaigns in northern Italy and Austria forced the Habsburgs to recognize French conquests in Belgium, Germany, and Italy (Treaty of Campo Formio, Oct. 17, 1797). In Feb., 1798, the French occupied Rome, taking Pope Pius VI prisoner and establishing the Roman Republic. In April, Switzerland was conquered and renamed the Helvetian Republic.

Bonaparte was now a national hero. Fearing his political ambitions, the Directory was glad to authorize a strike at Britain's Indian Empire through the Near East. Bonaparte sailed from Toulon (May 19, 1798) with an army of 35,000. Capturing Malta, he landed in Egypt, took Alexandria and Cairo, but lost his fleet when it was surprised and sunk by a British fleet under Adm. Horatio Nelson in the Battle of the Nile, Aug. 1, 1798. A year later Bonaparte abandoned his army and hastened back to France when the Directory's collapse appeared imminent.

The Second Coalition. Meanwhile Tsar Paul I of Russia who, as Grand Master of the Knights of Malta, had been outraged by the seizure of that island, concluded an alliance with Britain. The Second Coalition, later joined by Spain, Austria, Sardinia, and Naples, was thus formed against France. Hostilities began in Italy. After some reverses, the French regained control, only to be expelled by Russian Gen. Aleksandr Suvorov in the spring and summer of 1799. Disgusted with their Austrian allies, the Russians then withdrew from the war.

Having seized power by the *coup d'état* of 18 Brumaire (Nov. 9, 1799), Napoleon renewed the war against Austria. He gained a decisive strategic surprise by crossing the Alps (May, 1800) with 40,000 men. Milan was taken immediately and, by the narrowly won battle of Marengo (June 14), Italy was quickly recovered. After Moreau's sweeping victory at Hohenlinden (Dec. 3), Austria yielded to virtually all French demands in the Treaty of Lunéville (Feb. 9, 1801). The Holy Roman Empire practically ceased to exist, and the terms of Campo Formio were confirmed. All hostilities ended with the Treaty of Amiens between France and Britain (Mar. 27, 1802) which recognized all the French conquests. This peace violated Britain's traditional policy of maintaining a balance of power on the Continent, however, and was destined to be short-lived.

RALPH H. BOWEN, Northern Illinois University
See also FRENCH REVOLUTION; NAPOLEON I; NAPOLEONIC WARS.

Paris. The Duke of Brunswick, the Prussian commander of the invading forces, issued a threatening manifesto (July 25), news of which precipitated the storming of the Tuileries palace in Paris (August) and the overthrow of the monarchy.

Under the leadership of Georges Danton, the insurrectionary Commune of Paris acted as a provisional government. A volunteer army was organized and the civilian population was mobilized. On Sept. 20, in a confused engagement consisting mainly of an artillery exchange, the French halted the enemy advance at Valmy. Sickness and lack of supplies then caused Brunswick to withdraw. Valmy had little military significance, but it greatly improved the morale of the revolutionary forces. In late September, Gen. Adam Custine's army crossed the Rhine into Germany while another force occupied Nice and Savoy. A third army under Gen. Charles Dumouriez overran Belgium.

The First Coalition. Following the execution of Louis XVI (Jan. 21, 1793), Britain, the Netherlands, and Spain entered the war, joining Austria, Prussia, and Sardinia to form the First Coalition against France. Aid was given by these powers to the royalist rebels in western France who had taken up arms to oppose conscription. France annexed Belgium (Feb. 1, 1793), but Brussels was lost in March when Dumouriez was defeated by the Austrians. The beaten general defected to the enemy, gravely compromising his Girondist friends and hastening their fall.

Supreme direction of the war was then assumed by the Jacobin-dominated Committee of Public Safety, with Lazare Carnot in charge of military affairs. Discipline, training, and supply were rapidly improved; able young officers were promoted to high commands; defeated generals were punished as traitors; and "representatives on mission," clothed with full powers, were sent to exercise political vigilance over field commanders. After some fur-

FRENCH SOMALILAND. *See* SOMALILAND, FRENCH.

FRENCH UNION. *See* FRENCH COMMUNITY.

FRENCH WEST AFRICA, federated colonial administrative unit officially created by France in 1904, covering 1,789,182 sq. mi. of African territory with an estimated population of 17,167,000. It comprised eight territories, now all independent states: Dahomey, Guinea, Ivory Coast, Mauritania, Niger, Senegal, Sudan (now Mali), and Upper Volta. The federal government was headed by a Governor-General and the Grand Council at Dakar (now the capital of Senegal), while each of the territories had a Lieutenant-Governor and a territorial assembly.

After World War II, the eight territories were each given representation in the French Parliament in Paris. The federation was dissolved in 1958 when, under the Fifth French Republic, seven of the eight territories became autonomous republics within the French Community (q.v.) and Guinea decided in favor of independence. *See also:*

DAHOMEY	MAURITANIA
GUINEA	NIGER
IVORY COAST	SENEGAL
MALI	UPPER VOLTA

FRENEAU [fra-nō'], **PHILIP MORIN** (1752–1832), American poet and editor, born in New York and educated at Princeton University. In 1772 he began publishing poetry, continuing to do so in an ardently patriotic vein during the American Revolution. Following service as privateer, militiaman, and militant propagandist, he became a verse-writing sea captain after the war. During the 1790's he edited partisan Jeffersonian newspapers, notably the *National Gazette* (1791–93). His poetry, when not vitriolic in satire, celebrated common things and common people, thus anticipating English romantic literary trends. Five collections appeared during his lifetime; a modern edition in three volumes is *Poems of Philip Freneau* (ed. by F. L. Pattee, 1902–7).

FREON [frē'ŏn], registered trade name for the series of fluorinated derivatives of short-chain hydrocarbons. The most commonly used is Freon 12, dichlorodifluoromethane, CCl_2F_2, boiling point, $-29.8°$ C. ($-21.6°$ F.). Its principal uses are as cooling gases in refrigerating and air conditioning systems, and as aerosol propellants in pressure spray-containers. Freons are nontoxic at ordinary temperatures and are nonflammable.

FREQUENCY, in physics, the number of complete oscillations per second of a vibrating body. For example, an alternating current may have a frequency of 60 cycles per second. Radio waves can have frequencies of one megacycle (1,000,000 complete oscillations) per second. Frequency may also be expressed as vibrations per second. Velocity (v), frequency (f), and wave length (L) are related by the formula $v = f \times L$.

FRESCO [frĕs'kō], technique of painting on wet plaster; also, a painting produced by using this method. The colors, mixed with water, are applied to a wet lime plaster sur-face, and as the plaster dries, it encases the color within the crystalline surface. The pigments thus form a permanent chemical bond with the wall. The amount of plaster applied to the wall at any one time is limited to the area which the artist can paint before it dries.

The permanence of fresco led to its widespread use in Byzantine art. It became extremely popular in the Renaissance, and was practiced by most of the leading artists of the time. In the 20th century it has been revived as an important technique by such Mexican artists as Diego Rivera and José Clemente Orozco.

FRESCOBALDI [frās-kō-bäl'dē], **GIROLAMO** (1583–1643), famous Italian composer and organist, born in Ferrara. He was organist at St. Peter's in Rome (1608–28; 1634–43), where his performances were attended by tens of thousands. He has been called "the father of keyboard music" and is responsible for many of the earliest idiomatic compositions for keyboard instruments. These pieces include toccatas, *ricercari*, and *canzoni* for organ. His style was marked by dramatic intensity and dissonant, chromatic harmonies in advance of his time. Johann Sebastian Bach was so impressed with Frescobaldi's compositions that in 1714 he copied out the latter's *Fiori musicali* (Musical Flowers) for his own study and use.

Consult Apel, Willi, "Neapolitan Links Between Cabezón and Frescobaldi," *The Music Quarterly* (Oct., 1938).

FRESNAY [frā-nā'], **PIERRE,** professional name of Pierre Laudenbach (1897–   ), French actor. His long career on the French stage included service with the Comédie Française (1915–26). Fresnay is best known to U.S. audiences for roles in the French films *Marius* (1932), *Fanny* (1932), *César* (1933), *La Grande Illusion* (1937), and *Monsieur Vincent* (1947).

FRESNEL [frā-nĕl'], **AUGUSTIN JEAN** (1788–1827), French lighting pioneer, engineer, and inventor. Although an engineer by profession he is best known for his studies on the diffraction of light and the Fresnel system of lenses, which revolutionized the lighting of lighthouses. Called to Paris in 1819 to serve on a commission on lighthouses, he devised a series of concentric glass rings or lenses in echelon as a substitute for the earlier parabolic reflectors. Appointed in 1821 examiner in physics at the École Polytechnique, he became secretary of the commission of lighthouses in 1824 and was named engineer in chief of *ponts et chaussées* in 1825.

FRESNILLO DE GONZÁLEZ ECHEVERRÍA [frāz-nē'yō #hä gôn-sä'läs ā-chā-vĕr-rē'ä], mining city of central Zacatecas, Mexico. Fresnillo is one of Mexico's oldest mining districts and its Proaño silver mine is among the country's most productive bonanzas. Lead, zinc, mercury, copper, and gold also are mined, and there are foundries and a mining school. Pop., 29,908.

FRESNO [frĕz'nō], city of central California, and seat of Fresno County, in the agricultural San Joaquin Valley, about midway between San Francisco and Los Angeles. With annual rainfall less than 10 in. and with summer temperatures exceeding 80° F., Fresno is surrounded by rich, flat farmland, heavily irrigated from deep wells and supplemental water from the nearby King's River and Pine Flat Reservoir. Although field crops, primarily cotton, provide the largest revenue, Fresno is best known for its sun-dried fruits, especially grapes, peaches, and figs. The county's grape crops alone, largest in the United States, occupy over 150,000 acres. The city has several wineries and claims to be the dessert-wine capital of the United States. Additional food products are turkeys and cottonseed oil. Diversified industries include the manufacture of work-clothing, rugs, pumps, truck bodies, and aircraft equipment. With the state's two main cities equally distant, Fresno developed excellent shopping, hotels, restaurants, parks, and educational facilities. Fresno State College (estab., 1911) and Fresno City College (estab., 1910) are here. The city is the gateway to Kings Canyon and Sequoia national parks. Pop., 165,972; urb. area 413,053.

ADOLF STONE, *Long Beach City College*

FREUD [*froid*], **ANNA** (1895–   ), psychoanalyst, the youngest child of Sigmund Freud and the only one to follow in his footsteps. She was educated in the schools of Vienna, her home city. She became her father's secretary and studied psychoanalysis with him. In 1923 she began specializing in the psychoanalysis of children—a specialty neglected since Sigmund Freud's successful analysis of a five-year-old boy in 1908. She accompanied her father to London in 1938 and has lived there since. After serving as co-director of the Hampstead War Nurseries for Homeless Children, she became head of the Hampstead Child-Therapy Clinic where she continued to practice child analysis. *Ego and the Mechanisms of Defense* and other writings have enlarged the horizons of general psychoanalysis.

FREUD, SIGMUND (1856–1939), Austrian physician widely known as the founder of psychoanalysis. Freud entered the medical school of the University of Vienna in 1873 with the intention of preparing himself for a career in science. In medical school he studied with the eminent physiologist Ernst von Brücke, from whom he learned to regard the living person as a dynamic system to which the

Sigmund Freud, founder of psychoanalysis.

The Bettmann Archive

laws of chemistry and physics apply. During his eight years in medical school and for several years following graduation, Freud engaged in original research on the nervous system. His investigations were well thought of and he was rapidly making a name for himself in science. Anti-Semitism in Austrian universities and the practical necessity of supporting a family, however, led Freud to choose private practice over an academic career.

Because of his scientific interest in the nervous system, Freud specialized in the treatment of nervous disorders. In order to improve his skill as a practitioner he studied in Paris during the winter of 1885–86 with the leading French psychiatrist Jean Charcot, who used hypnosis for the treatment of hysteria.

Freud's work in psychoanalysis grew out of his association with another Viennese physician, Joseph Breuer, who had devised a new method for treating hysterical patients. This method consisted of hypnotizing the patient and having him express the suppressed emotions which were associated with the origin of the hysterical symptoms. Freud and Breuer collaborated on a book, *Studies in Hysteria* (1895), which discussed their use of this method.

Shortly after this work appeared, Freud and Breuer dissolved their association, because Breuer was unwilling to accept Freud's hypothesis that sexual conflicts were the cause of hysteria. Freud abandoned hypnotism, which had proved inapplicable to many patients, and substituted the method of free association, in which the patient was encouraged to allow his ideas to flow in an unrestricted stream and to speak his thoughts as they came. This method enabled Freud to explore the unconscious mind and to develop a theory of human behavior. The early results of his investigations were set forth in his book *The Interpretation of Dreams* (1900), in which he dealt with the psychological mechanisms underlying dreams.

This book and other writings which appeared during the first decade of the 20th century brought his work to the attention of other psychiatrists. Alfred Adler of Vienna and Carl Jung of Zurich joined with Freud and helped to promote psychoanalysis as a method of treating patients, as a theory of abnormal behavior, and as a system of psychology. Freud and Jung traveled together to the United States in 1909 to give lectures at Clark University in Worcester, Mass. The International Psychoanalytic Association was founded in 1910 to advance psychoanalysis throughout the world. Jung was its first president.

Dissension broke out among the three men; Adler, in 1911, and Jung, in 1914, broke with Freud and started their own schools of psychoanalysis. Under the leadership of Freud, however, the movement prospered. New recruits were attracted and institutes for the training of psychoanalysts were established in many cities. Freud had been named professor in the University of Vienna in 1902, but his chief work consisted of treating patients and expanding and revising his views.

In spite of a heavy practice which occupied his days, Freud was a prodigious writer. His complete psychological writings are published in an English edition of 24 volumes. Among his best-known books, in addition to *The Interpretation of Dreams*, are *The Psychopathology of Everyday Life* (1901), which explains the unconscious significance of forgetting, mistakes, and accidents; *Three Essays on the*

Theory of Sexuality (1905), which traces the development of the sex impulse and its aberrations; *Jokes and Their Relation to the Unconscious* (1905); *Introductory Lectures on Psychoanalysis* (1916–17); *Beyond the Pleasure Principle* (1920), which postulates the existence in man of a death instinct as well as a life instinct; *The Future of an Illusion* (1927), which is a psychoanalytic study of religion; *Civilization and Its Discontents* (1930), in which he examines the reasons for modern man's unhappiness, and *New Introductory Lectures on Psychoanalysis* (1933). His style of writing is lively and lucid and reflects his highly developed sense of humor and his broad knowledge of literature. He was awarded the Goethe Prize in 1930.

In contrast to his scientific life, in which his ideas were violently opposed by many other scientists and during which many of his followers broke with him, Freud's domestic life was quiet and uneventful. He was married to Martha Bernays in 1886 and they had six children. Only one of his children, Anna, became a psychoanalyst. The Freud family lived in a flat at 19 Bergstrasse, Vienna, for 47 years. Freud had his consulting rooms in the same building. Freud's main interest outside of his family and work was archeology, and he made numerous trips to Italy in pursuit of this interest.

In 1923 the first signs of cancer in his upper jaw and palate were detected and during the rest of his life Freud suffered from the progressive ravages of the disease, for which he underwent 33 operations. Although he was preoccupied by the thought of death, he continued to write and to see patients to the very end of his life.

Freud died in exile in London. In 1938, after the Nazi take-over in Austria, he realized his dangerous position (the Nazis had banned and burned his books). Although his home was searched and later seized, and his daughter and son interrogated by the Gestapo, Freud and his family were finally allowed to leave Austria in safety, aided by the efforts of Princess Marie Bonaparte, William Bullitt, American ambassador to France, and others.

Freud's impact upon psychiatry and psychology has been enormous. He emphasized the powerful unconscious and irrational forces which motivate and shape man's behavior and developed a pessimistic image of man as a more or less helpless victim of these forces. The influence of his ideas extends into the domains of art, literature, politics, economics, sociology, religion, anthropology, and philosophy. Probably no other man has so profoundly affected the intellectual currents of the 20th century.

Consult Jones, Ernest, *The Life and Work of Sigmund Freud* (1961).

CALVIN S. HALL, Author, *A Primer of Freudian Psychology*

See also PSYCHOANALYSIS; PSYCHOTHERAPY.

FREY [frā] **or FREYR** (Old Norse, "Lord"), Norse god. Son of Njord and ruler of Alfheim, Frey controlled the weather, crops, peace, and prosperity. His ship, *Skidbladnir*, sailed over land and sea and could be folded like a handkerchief; his chariot was drawn by a boar with golden bristles, a fertility symbol. From Odin's hall, Hlidskjalf, Frey saw, fell in love with, and married the giantess Gerda. Frey was worshiped throughout Scandinavia, especially in Sweden. The *Yngling*, the ancient Kings of Norway and Sweden,

claimed descent from him. In Iceland horses were dedicated to him.

See also MYTHOLOGY, NORSE.

FREYA or FREYJA [frā'ə] (Old Norse, "Lady"), Norse goddess. Sister of Frey, she was goddess of love and fertility. When deserted by her husband Od ("Soul"), she shed golden tears. With Odin, Freya shared the right of choosing fallen heroes, whom she took to her abode, Folkvang. Her chariot was drawn by two cats. She possessed the magnificent ornament called Necklace of the Brisings, which was stolen by Loki, who was compelled to return it by Heimdall. Like her father and brother, Freya was extensively worshiped in Scandinavia.

See also MYTHOLOGY, NORSE.

FREYBERG [frī'bûrg], **BERNARD CYRIL FREYBERG, 1ST BARON** (1889–1963), New Zealand soldier. After serving with great distinction with the New Zealand forces in World War I, especially at Gallipoli (Victoria Cross, 1916), Freyberg held various commissions in the British army in England until the outbreak of World War II, when he became commander of the 2d New Zealand Expeditionary Force. Under his command the New Zealand Division served in Greece and in the North African campaign, including the battle of El Alamein (1942), until its successful conclusion in Tunisia (1943). Freyberg also led the division in the Italian campaign (1943–45). From 1946 to 1952 he was Governor-General of New Zealand. In 1953 he became Lieutenant Governor of Windsor Castle.

FREYRE [frā'rē], **RICARDO JAIMES** (1868–1933), Bolivian writer and diplomat. He served at various times as Minister of Foreign Affairs, Minister of Education, and as Ambassador to the United States and other countries. A playwright, historian, poet, and author of *Los sueños son vida* (Dreams Are Life), 1917, he was also influential as a founder of the modernist literary movement. His study of versification (1912) is the first work of this kind in Spanish.

FRIA [frī'ə], city in the Republic of Guinea, 96 mi. by rail from the port and capital of Conakry. Fria is an entirely new city, completed in 1960, to house a community with industries based on bauxite mining and aluminum production. The aluminum plant, at completion, was the 3d-largest, and one of the most modern, in the world. Pop., approx. 35,000.

FRIAR [frī'ər], generic name used to designate members of religious orders who are not monks or hermits. Unlike monks, who are not usually engaged in apostolic labors, whose vows of poverty do not prevent the corporate owning of property, and whose stability comes from being attached to a single house, or monastery, the friars have an active ministry in the world. Their poverty includes—or originally included—renunciation of even corporate possession, and their stability comes from obedience to a common superior and membership in a common order. Unlike hermits, they live a common life, but move from house to house as their superiors dictate, and are actively engaged in some external ministry. The term was used from the 13th century on especially to designate the members of the mendicant orders. Dominicans, Augustinians, Franciscans, Carmelites, and Jesuits are all, technically, friars.

RICHARD J. WESTLEY, Barat College of the
Sacred Heart

FRIAR LANDS, properties, including very large estates, owned by different orders of the Roman Catholic Church in the Philippines. Their accumulation through the years provided a source of income for the church's religious and educational activities. Objections arose to the amount of agricultural wealth in the friars' hands and to their activities as landlords. In 1903 Governor William Howard Taft, at a cost of approximately $7,240,000, negotiated for the purchase of about 410,000 acres of the friar lands, including some of the choicest property in the Philippines. These lands were resold to private purchasers (primarily former tenants) usually on terms of easy payments.

FRIARS CLUB, American theatrical organization founded in 1904. It is a social club whose rules specify that three-fourths of its membership must be engaged in the entertainment field. Its headquarters are in New York. A similar club with the same name, based in Beverly Hills, Calif., was part of the other club until 1962, when they became independent.

FRIAR TUCK, leading member of Robin Hood's band of merry men. A fat and jolly figure and a fighter of considerable prowess, he appears in many stories about Robin Hood and also in Walter Scott's *Ivanhoe.*

FRIARY. *See* MONASTERY.

FRIBOURG [frē'boor], canton in western Switzerland, stretching from the Lake of Neuchâtel on the west to the outer ranges of the Bernese Alps on the east. Its chief river, the Sarine (Ger. Saane), runs north-south through the canton, traversing the cantonal capital of Fribourg. The Sarine Valley, with its fertile terraces and forested gorges, is the most populated zone in the canton. Cattle, timber, and cheese (particularly from the Gruyère region) are the chief produce. The only industries are the production of chocolate, paper, and watches. The population of Fribourg is largely French-speaking and Roman Catholic. Area, 645 sq. mi.; pop., 158,695.

FRIBOURG, city and capital of the Swiss canton of the same name, located on the winding Sarine River in the Swiss Mittelland. A high portion of the city is located on the cliffs, and the low portion along the river. Fribourg was founded in 1178 and became part of the Swiss Confederation in 1481. Sections of the city date back to the time when weaving and blacksmith guilds ruled the city. The bilingual (French-German) International Catholic University was founded in 1889. Three-fourths of the city's inhabitants speak French and most are Roman Catholic. Pop., 32,583.

FRICK, FORD CHRISTOPHER (1894–   ), American baseball executive, born in Wawaka, Ind. He was a sports writer for the New York *Journal,* 1921–34, and a radio-news commentator, 1930–34. From 1934 to 1951 he was president of the National League of Professional Baseball Clubs. In 1951 he became national commissioner of baseball. During Frick's reign as commissioner each of the major leagues expanded to the West coast and became a 10-team organization.

FRICK, HENRY CLAY (1849–1919), American industrialist. Born on a farm in Westmoreland County, Pa., he worked as a clerk and a bookkeeper before helping to organize (1871) Frick and Company, coke operators. A millionaire at 30, he merged his interests with those of steel magnate Andrew Carnegie. In 1889 Frick became chairman of Carnegie's firm, which was reorganized as the Carnegie Steel Company three years later. He was largely responsible for a vast expansion of the company's holdings. His uncompromising antiunion policies during the Homestead, Pa., steel strike (1892) helped precipitate violence, and he narrowly escaped assassination. Differences with Carnegie caused him to resign in 1899, and in 1901 he helped organize the United States Steel Corporation. He bequeathed his New York mansion, an art collection, and $15,000,000 for a public museum.

FRICTION, in physics, force of opposition developed at the surface of contact when one body is moved in contact with another body. Being a surface force and therefore tangential, it is unlike a pressure force which is perpendicular to the surface. When two surfaces are rubbed together, the ever-present surface irregularities, which sometimes are only microscopic in size, constitute obstructions which must be overcome. Thus, force is required to slide one body over another one, even at constant speed, whereas, ordinarily, force is associated with a change of motion in overcoming inertia.

If, initially, the two bodies in question are at rest with respect to each other, more force is required to overcome friction to start the motion than is required to maintain constant relative motion once it is started. Thus, two kinds of friction are recognized, static and kinetic, the latter being the smaller. Moreover, there are two kinds of kinetic friction, sliding and rolling, of which rolling is the smaller. Thus, ball or roller bearings are used wherever possible to minimize mechanical friction between the moving parts of machinery. Where sliding friction must be tolerated, it is minimized by the use of a lubricant, such as oil or graphite, which fills the microscopic pores of the contact surfaces and thereby makes them smooth.

Although the details of the friction mechanism are not completely understood, a general law of friction is recognized. This law states that the force of friction between two bodies divided by the perpendicular force pressing them together is constant for a given pair of substances, independent of the contact area. This constant is known as the coefficient of friction between the two substances. It is static or kinetic as the case may be, the latter always being the smaller of the two. Whereas, the static coefficient of steel on steel may be 0.15 in contrast to a kinetic coefficient of 0.10, leather on polished wood may display coefficients of 0.50 and 0.40 respectively. In the case of rubber on concrete, there is some 30% difference in the values of the coefficient, depending upon whether the surfaces are dry or wet. This explains the well-known loss of traction of

THERE ARE TWO TYPES OF FRICTION

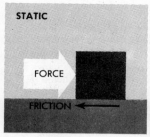

STATIC

The force of friction occurs in a direction opposite to motion. Static friction resists initial motion.

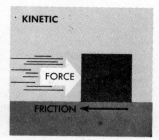

KINETIC

Kinetic friction is a force that resists the force of a body already in motion.

TWO TYPES OF KINETIC FRICTION

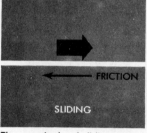

SLIDING

The magnitude of sliding friction depends on the nature of the surfaces in contact.

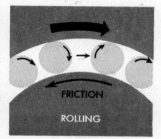

ROLLING

Ball bearings between the surfaces provide rolling friction, the lesser of the two frictional forces.

automobile tires on wet pavements. Since, however, the static coefficient is always greater than the kinetic coefficient, a car whose wheels simply spin on slippery ice when the power is applied rapidly will often creep to a start if the power is applied very slowly. Although the law of friction indicates that the force of friction is independent of the contact area of the sliding surfaces in question, this does not appear to hold for extremely small surface areas.

From the point of view of energy, friction forces are dissipative forces, that is, mechanical energy associated with friction forces is not conserved, but is dissipated in the form of heat. It was through the generation of heat by friction that the mechanical equivalence of heat was first established.

CLARENCE E. BENNETT, University of Maine

FRIDAY, the sixth day of the week. The name comes from the Norse Frigg, goddess of married love and housewifery. Frigg parallels the Roman Venus, for whom the day was named in the Roman week, *dies Veneris.* Friday has long been associated with bad fortune, probably deriving from Christ's crucifixion. Catholics observe it as a day of abstinence.

FRIDESWIDE [frĭ′də-swē-də], **ST.** (died c.735), probably a Mercian Princess who founded a convent in or near Oxford. In 1180 her shrine was erected in St. Frideswide's priory, Oxford, and she was recognized as patron saint of the city and university. The priory was suppressed by Cardinal Wolsey in 1525 and replaced by Cardinal College (now Christ Church). Frideswide's shrine was plundered in 1538 by Henry VIII.

FRIDLEY, village of eastern Minnesota, a residential and industrial suburb north of Minneapolis. Inc., 1949; pop., 29,233.

FRIDTHJÓFS SAGA, fictitious 14th-century Icelandic saga. Fridthjóf, a dauntless Norwegian yeoman, was supposed to have lived in the 8th century. The romantic story of his adventures inspired the Swedish poem, *Frithiofs Saga,* written by Esaias Tegnér in 1825.
See also TEGNÉR, ESAIAS.

FRIEDRICHSHAFEN [frē′drĭks-hä-fən], city of southern Federal Republic of Germany (West Germany), on the shore of Lake Constance. A center of tourism, it has ferry connections with Switzerland. It was formerly the site of Germany's chief Zeppelin yards and of the Maybach Motor Works, both of which were primary bombing targets in World War II. The 17th-century castle served as the summer residence of the Dukes of Württemberg, and there is also a baroque monastery church. The Municipal Lake Constance Museum houses a Zeppelin exhibition. Pop., 32,083.

FRIENDS, SOCIETY OF, commonly called Quakers (q.v.), the most significant of the new religious movements arising on Puritan soil during the period of the civil wars in England. The founder was George Fox, who came to an illuminating conviction that every man receives from God a divine Inner Light, which if followed can lead to spiritual truth. Fox began his stormy public ministry in 1647 and soon attracted a few followers. The Friends believed that the Scriptures were a true Word of God, but that revelation was not confined to them. They rejected the Calvinistic concept of man's total depravity, insisting that there is a seed of God in every soul. The central principle of the Quaker movement was belief in the inwardly present and creative work of God's Spirit operating in man. Emphasizing the inward nature of religion, the Friends reacted against outward ceremonies. They did not observe the sacraments, objected to established churches and professional ministries, and refused to take oaths or use "artificial" titles. They put great stress on economy and simplicity. They believed that war was unlawful for Christians. Rigorous and intense, they grew by accession from various other Puritan and separatist bodies. The first Quaker community was gathered in Preston Patrick in northern England by 1652.

The new faith was soon carried by enthusiastic adherents throughout the British Isles, to the Continent, and to America (1656). The movement met with persecution during the Cromwellian and Restoration periods; thousands were imprisoned, and in Massachusetts four were hanged. Tendencies toward extravagance in the society caused an internal system of discipline and order to be worked out in the 1660's. Monthly meetings were instituted to watch over the life and conduct of Friends in local areas, and quarterly and yearly meetings, culminating in the London yearly meeting, provided some over-all coherence for the society. The stabilization of the movement was greatly aided by the work of "public Friends," or traveling Quaker "ministers," who journeyed from meeting to meeting and from continent to continent. An able theological apologist for the movement was Robert Barclay (1648–90), who wrote *An Apology for the True Christian Divinity* (1678).

The colonies of Rhode Island, New Jersey, and especially Pennsylvania, which was founded by an eminent convert to Quakerism, provided refuges in which the Friends could flourish in peace. The Toleration Act of 1689 brought freedom of worship and relief from the more pressing disabilities. By 1700 there were about 50,000 Friends in the British Isles and 40,000 more in North America.

Quaker life of the 18th century was marked by the growth of mystical quietism in religious thought and practice and by the flowering of a notable humanitarian spirit. A distinctive Quaker culture developed during that century, especially in America. Following a tradition of opposition to slavery, they established the first U.S. antislavery society in 1775, and were important members of Abolitionist societies and the Underground Railroad.

In the 19th century the Quakers were torn by tension and declined somewhat in influence. In general, the conflict was between "evangelical" Quakers, who put considerable stress on correct doctrine, and "mystical" Quakers, whose theological views were somewhat liberal in tone. In England only small schisms resulted from the tension, but in the United States the society divided into two main parts, an evangelical wing influenced by an English Quaker, Joseph John Gurney, and a liberal wing following Elias Hicks, a Long Islander. Other schisms followed the major split. Some Quakers adopted the pastoral system and became more like the traditional denominations.

The 20th century has seen both a renewed interest in social questions on the part of the Friends and the development of forces making for Quaker unity. These are illustrated in the forming of the American Friends Service Committee with the support of many Quaker bodies during World War I. Under the chairmanship of Rufus Jones, the Quaker witness against war was continued, and a ministry of service was extended to victims of war and disaster. An All-Friends Conference was held in London in 1920, and in 1937 the Friends World Committee for Consultation, representing 45 Quaker groups in 24 countries, was organized. Many Quaker bodies participate in world, national, and local councils of churches.

Consult Bacon, Margaret H., *The Quiet Rebels: The Story of the Quakers in America* (1969); Braithwaite, William C., *The Beginnings of Quakerism* (2d ed., 1955); Brinton, Howard H., *Friends for Three Hundred Years* (1965); Taylor, Richard K., *Friends and the Racial Crisis* (1970); Trueblood, D. Elton, *The People Called Quakers* (1962).

ROBERT T. HANDY

FRIENDS SERVICE COMMITTEE, AMERICAN (AFSC), nonprofit, nonsectarian agency doing relief, rehabilitation, and reconciliation work in the United States and other countries. It was founded in 1917 in Philadelphia by members of the Religious Society of Friends (Quakers) to provide conscientious objectors with constructive alternatives to military service. In 1947 the AFSC was corecipient, with the Friends Service Council, England, of the Nobel Peace Prize. The committee functions in five areas: inter-national service, international affairs, youth services, peace education, and community relations. National headquarters are at Philadelphia. GRACE PERKINSON

FRIESLAND [frēz'lənd], Netherlands province including the West Frisian Islands of Ameland, Vlieland, Shiermonnikoog, and Terschelling. The mainland is bounded on the southwest by the Northeast Polder, on the west by the Ijesselmeer (Zuider Zee), and on the north by the North Sea. North and west, it is well-canalized. The low-lying polders provide pastures for horses and the native Frisian-Holstein dairy cattle. Lakes cross the central part of the province while much of the south is heath and fenland. Leeuwarden is the capital and principal cattle market, Harlingen the main port. The language, in which there is considerable literature, is Frisian, different from Dutch. Area, 1,249 sq. mi. (3,235 sq. km.).

FRIGATE BIRD, name for 5 species of tropical water birds of the genus *Fregata* in the frigate bird family, Fregatidae. Also called man-of-war birds for their habit of robbing the fish that other birds have caught, frigate birds occur on tropical seacoasts throughout the world. The birds have long, slender bodies, a forked, swallowlike tail, a long, hooked beak, and a wingspread of up to 6 ft. Frigate birds are dark-blue or greenish-black in color. The males have a scarlet throat pouch which they inflate during the breeding season. Common species are *F. magnificens*, found throughout the New World tropics, and *F. minor*, native to the South Pacific and Indian Ocean regions.

FRIGG or FRIGGA (Old Norse, "Woman," "Wife"), chief Norse goddess. Wife of Odin and mother of Balder, she was known to all Germanic tribes, but apparently not worshiped by them. Frigg had traits in common with her rival Jord and was sometimes confused with Freya. Through Frigg's identification with Venus, her name survives in Friday, a translation of *dies Veneris*. Although notoriously sensual and unfaithful, she was the protectress of married life, the symbol of which was the keys at her belt.

FRILLED LIZARD, large, tree-dwelling lizard, *Chlamydosaurus kingi*, in the Old World lizard family, Agamidae, native to Australia and New Guinea. Frilled lizards grow to a length of about 30 in. (76 cm.) and have two remarkable features—a large, loose piece of skin at either side of the neck which can be erected to form an umbrellalike collar 10 in. (25 cm.) across; and the ability to run on their hind legs, after gathering speed on all fours.

FRIML [frĭm'əl] **RUDOLF** (1879–1972), operetta composer. Born in Prague, Czechoslovakia, he settled in the United States in 1906. He ranks with Victor Herbert and Sigmund Romberg for quantity and quality of successes in the field of light opera. His best-remembered works are *The Firefly* (1912), *High Jinks* (1913), *Katinka* (1915), *Rose Marie* (1924), and *The Vagabond King* (1925). An amazingly fast writer with a musical shorthand style, he reputedly wrote *The Song of the Vagabonds* in 15 minutes. A first-rate pianist, he appeared in recitals over a five-year period as accompanist for the violinist Jan Kubelík. He also wrote compositions for piano, violin, and cello.

FRINGE TREE, large shrub or small tree of the genus *Chionanthus*, in the olive family, Oleaceae. The two species, *C. retusus*, native to China, and *C. virginicus*, native to eastern and southern United States, bear a profusion of delicate white flowers with four narrow, fringelike petals, in May or June. Fringe trees also have handsome dark-green foliage that turns yellow in the fall. They are used in landscaping and are easily grown in open, light soil.

FRISCH, FRANK FRANCIS (1898–1973), American baseball player and manager, one of the greatest second basemen, as indicated by his early election (1947) to baseball's Hall of Fame. Known as the Fordham Flash, he went from the Fordham campus to the New York Giants in 1919 to begin a 19-year playing career—eight with the Giants, 11 with the St. Louis Cardinals. He had a .316 lifetime batting average (hitting both left- and right-handed) and was a fiery baserunner. As a playing manager, Frisch imparted his rough-and-tumble style to the Cardinals of 1934, the Gashouse Gang, and they won a world championship. His managerial career served the Cardinals (1933–38), Pittsburgh Pirates (1940–46), and Chicago Cubs (1949–51).

FRISCH, MAX (1911–   ), German Swiss novelist and playwright. Born in Zurich, he studied architecture there, having previously abandoned a promising career in journalism. Frisch returned to writing—novels and plays—as a Swiss soldier in World War II and thereafter continued to write while pursuing a successful career in architecture in Zurich. Following publication of *Stiller*, 1954 (*I'm Not Stiller*, 1958), a psychological novel of one man's struggle for self-realization, he quit architecture to write full time. There followed, among many other works, *Homo Faber* 1957 (trans., 1960), a novel of the private anguish of technological man, and *Herr Biedermann und die Brandstifter*, 1958 (*The Firebugs*, 1963), an allegorical play about bourgeois susceptibility to fascist violence. His later plays include *Andorra*, 1961 (trans., 1962), and *Wilhelm Tell für die Schule*, 1971 (*William Tell, School Edition*).

FRISCH, OTTO ROBERT (1904–   ), Austrian-born physicist and professor at Cambridge University. In 1939 Frisch and Lise Meitner, his aunt, interpreted the recently conducted Hahn-Strassmann experiments (in which a uranium nucleus broke into two approximately equal parts after collision with a neutron) to be what they termed "nuclear fission," and predicted that large amounts of energy were released in this fission. These predictions were experimentally confirmed shortly thereafter and led to the development of the atomic bomb.

FRISCH, RAGNAR (1895–1973), Norwegian economist. In 1969 he and Jan Tinbergen of the Netherlands were named joint winners of the first Nobel Prize in economic science for their work in developing econometrics, the mathematical expression of economic hypotheses. Born in Oslo, Frisch was educated at Oslo University, where he subsequently taught economics and statistics and was director of the university's Economic Institute until his retirement from both posts in 1965. He was one of the founders of the international Econometrics Society in 1931. Frisch's contribution to the development of econometrics began in the 1930's, when he first applied his pioneering method to analyzing market conditions and economic growth. Interned by the Nazis in World War II, he subsequently advised several countries on economic planning.

FRISIAN [frĭzh'ən], member of the Western branch of the Germanic subfamily of the Indo-European family of languages. The other West Germanic languages are English, Dutch, Low German, and High German; of these, Frisian is most akin to English.

Frisian is spoken by about 300,000 people in the province of Friesland in the Netherlands. It is also spoken in Germany in the Saterland in Oldenburg and on the coast and some offshore islands of Schleswig. These three areas represent the dialect division into West Frisian, East Frisian, and North Frisian, respectively. The latter two are threatened by the steady advance of Low German. The modern literary language is based on West Frisian. It began in the 17th century and was established in its present form in the 19th century in a vigorous renaissance of Frisian in the Netherlands. Courses in Frisian have been offered by Dutch universities. An earlier stage of Frisian is called Old Frisian; its texts, the earliest of which dates from the 13th century, are from East and West Frisian areas.

HERBERT PENZL

FRISIAN ISLANDS, chain of islands in the North Sea, extending along the coasts of and belonging to The Netherlands, Germany, and Denmark, and located from 3 to 20 mi (5 to 32 km) offshore. They were once a part of the shoreline and were broken into islands by storms; marine erosion has caused their area to decrease slowly. Cattle grazing and fishing provide economic support, and in the summer tourism is important.

FRISIANS, west Germanic people, originally from Denmark, who settled in coastal areas between the Rhine and Ems in Roman times. Their economy was based on fishing, stock raising, and farming in the marshlands, where they inaugurated drainage and dike building. Under Roman control from 12 B.C. to 28 A.D., they were temporarily reconquered in 47 A.D. They expanded southward to the Scheldt after 400 A.D., eastward to the Weser by 700, and to western Schleswig by c.900. Some probably joined the Anglo-Saxons in the settlement of Britain. The whole area was incorporated into the Frankish kingdoms and Christianized in the 8th century. East Frisia regained autonomy after 911 as the Duchy of Friesland. Politically disintegrated after the 11th century, the western and middle Frisians were absorbed by Holland and the See of Utrecht in the 13th century.

FRITILLARY [frĭt'ə-lĕr-ē], name for several species of butterflies in the family *Nymphalidae*, found in many parts of the world. Fritillaries are orange or brownish in color, usually marked with silvery, yellow, or dark-brown spots. Common species include *Speyeria idalia*, the regal fritillary, *S. cybele*, the great spangled fritillary, and *Boloria toddi*, the meadow fritillary. Fritillaries are usually found in meadows; their caterpillar larvae feed on flowers.

FROBISHER [frŏ′bĭsh-ər], **SIR MARTIN** (1535?–1594), English mariner and explorer. Commissioned (1576) by Queen Elizabeth I to find a Northwest Passage to the Orient, he excited Europe for a time with the news of straits he discovered west of Greenland and by his claim to have found gold in the northwestern islands. Frobisher's next two voyages (1577–78) were concerned more with digging gold than with seeking a Northwest Passage, and the revelation of the worthlessness of the ore ended his explorations. His reputation suffered, but in 1585 he gained fresh renown as a member of Sir Francis Drake's expedition to the West Indies. He won a knighthood for his part in the defeat of the Spanish Armada in 1588.

FRÖDING [frö′dĭng], **GUSTAF** (1860–1911), Swedish lyric poet. He made his literary debut with *Guitarr och dragharmonika* (Guitar and Concertina), 1891. Due to its folklike quality, it was an immediate success; the poet's reputation was enhanced by *Nya dikter* (New Poems), 1894. In the next few years he published three more volumes of poetry. Fröding's mental health, always weak, broke down completely in 1898. Although his productive period spanned only seven years, Fröding was one of the greatest modern Swedish poets, combining unusual mastery of language and form with deep humanitarian feeling, droll humor, and sometimes almost prophetic vision. His first two volumes of poems were translated as *Guitar and Concertina* (1925).

FROEBEL [frö′bəl], **FRIEDRICH WILHELM AUGUST** (1782–1852), German educator, originator of the kindergarten. His childhood in Thuringia was lonely and neglected, and he received little education until he was ten. At the age of 15 he was apprenticed to a forester, and experiences in the forest influenced him to study the natural sciences. After a brief period at the University of Jena he was variously employed in clerical work, farming, and surveying. While studying architecture at Frankfurt am Main, he was invited to teach at a model school there. For two years (1807–9) he was affiliated with the school of Johann Pestalozzi at Yverdon, Switzerland. Then followed further study, besides service in the Prussian army during the Napoleonic Wars. From 1817 to 1831 he conducted a boys' school at Keilhau in Germany. He then returned to Switzerland, where he established several schools and trained women elementary school teachers.

During this period Froebel concluded that children needed careful training in the preschool years, a neglected area in organized education. Returning to Germany, he established the first kindergarten ("children's garden"), at Blankenburg, in 1837. Thereafter he devoted his energies to founding kindergartens and training kindergarten teachers. He suffered a blow in 1851, the year before his death, when the Prussia government, suspecting him of socialism, forbade the establishment of schools based on his teachings.

Through Froebel many of the ideas of Pestalozzi and of Jean Jacques Rousseau were applied to the education of young children. He believed that education should start with very young children and that the unifying purpose of education should be full development of the physical, mental, and spiritual natures of children. True development, he believed, came freely from within the individual and was not imposed from outside. Froebel emphasized the use of play, the study of nature, and the importance of the family.

ROBERT D. HARTMAN, University of Illinois
See also KINDERGARTEN.

FROG, name for many species of smooth-skinned amphibians of order Salientia, and referring especially to those of family Ranidae, the true frogs. Frogs of this family are found in all parts of the world except South America and the Antipodes. The chorus or tree frogs of family Hylidae are especially common in the American tropics. Frogs are adapted for living both on land and in the water. Because their thin, unprotected skin must be kept moist, frogs are restricted to damp terrestrial habitats, usually near fresh water, in which they can lay their eggs. Frogs are rarely found in arid regions, and reach their maximum abundance in warm, swampy lowlands. The family Ranidae includes over 200 species, among them the edible frog, *Rana esculenta*, of Europe, the common North American bullfrog, *R. catesbiana*, and the pickerel frog, *R. palustris*, of eastern North America. Frogs range in size from the tiny cricket and chorus frogs which are about ¾ in. long, to the bullfrogs, up to 6 in. long.

The body of a frog is squat and clumsy, and consists of head and trunk but no neck or tail. A large mouth extends from one side of the head to the other. The tongue of a frog is attached to the forward portion of the floor of the mouth and can be thrown outward to capture insects. Small teeth located along the edges of the upper jaw and on the palate are used for holding food but are inadequate for chewing. A pair of nostrils, which can be closed by valvelike flaps of skin, opens into the mouth cavity, making it possible for the frog to breathe without opening its mouth. A pair of bulging, periscopelike eyes enables the frog to see even when the rest of its body is submerged. Because the sense organs have to function both under water and on land, a transparent eyelid, or nictitating membrane, keeps the eyeball moist on land. Special muscles can rotate the eyeballs so that even when motionless, a frog can look in all directions for food and enemies. The eye of a frog functions like a fixed-focus camera, since it has no adjustment for distance. Behind and below the eyes is a pair of unprotected eardrums, the tympanic membranes, with which the frog receives sound waves. A frog's skin possesses numerous glands whose mucous secretion coats the body with slime, useful in escaping captors. Special chromatophores (pigmented cells) in the skin contain black, brown, red, or yellow pigments which are responsible for the frog's effective camouflage.

A frog has two pairs of unequal-sized limbs. The stocky, weak forelegs, which terminate in 4 clawless toes, are used chiefly for grasping food and for breaking the shock of landing after a jump. The large hindlegs are powered by strong muscles which produce the frog's characteristic leaping gait. Each hind foot terminates in 5 webbed toes used in swimming. Frogs are able to breathe both on land and in the water. On land, air is taken in through the nostrils and forced into a pair of thin-walled lungs.

Hugh Spencer—National Audubon Society

The green frog inhabits ponds and swamps in eastern North America.

In another method of land breathing, the frog gulps air in through its mouth: gaseous exchange occurs through the mucous membranes of the mouth cavity. A frog can also breathe through its skin surface. This method of respiration is employed in the water and especially makes possible respiration while the frog stays under water or when the frog hibernates. The larynx of a frog has two vocal cords, whose tension is controlled by special muscles. Air expelled from the lungs makes the cords vibrate, producing the varied sounds from the deep "jug-o-rum" of the bullfrog to the bell-like notes of the spring peeper. Male frogs have a special vocal sac in the throat which can be inflated like a balloon to act as a resonator and increase the volume of sound.

Reproduction in frogs takes place in early spring when the females release eggs in the water, where they are immediately fertilized by the sperm released by the males. The eggs, while still in the jelly in which they were laid, hatch into small, fishlike tadpoles. The tadpoles swim by lateral movements of their long tail, and breathe through feathery external gills. A round, suckerlike mouth is used for attachment to underwater plants, and to scrape off bits of plant food. Within a few weeks, the tadpole undergoes several transformations: the external gills disappear; tiny hindlegs appear at the base of the body; and the forelegs begin to develop beneath the operculum, a fold of skin on the underside of the body. Later the forelegs push their way to the exterior of the operculum, and the tadpole acquires the four limbs typical of a frog. The tadpole, now greatly increased in size, spends more and more time near the surface of the water, gulping air as the gills are replaced by lungs. The tail shrinks in size and is completely resorbed; the mouth broadens; the muscles in the hindlegs strengthen; and soon the frog begins its life on land. Metamorphosis in some species is completed by mid-

summer; in other species the metamorphosis may take as long as two years.

CLARENCE J. HYLANDER, Author,
Adventures With Reptiles

See also:

BULLFROG	SPRING PEEPER
LEOPARD FROG	TADPOLE
MARSUPIAL FROG	TOAD
PICKEREL FROG	TREE FROG

FROG HOPPER, common name for insects of the family Cercopidae, found in many parts of the world. Frog hoppers are small and inconspicuously colored with squat, flattened bodies. They are named for their preference of hopping about from plant to plant and are also called spittlebugs because of the frothy material the females secrete to cover eggs laid on stems and twigs. Frog hoppers of the genus *Philaenus* are common throughout North America; some species are pests, injuring various cultivated grasses and garden plants.

FROGMOUTH, common name for 12 species of very large-mouthed insect-eating birds in the family Podargidae, native to the Australian region. Frogmouths are large, rather sluggish birds, and spend most of the daylight hours sleeping in the trees.

FRÖHLICH'S [frō′lĭ-KHs] **SYNDROME,** rare glandular disorder characterized by obesity, with fat deposits in the upper arms, legs, back, and chest, and by small sex organs. Although seen in adolescents of both sexes, it is more common in boys. The disease is caused by a tumor or inflammation of the pituitary gland, which lies on the undersurface of the brain, or of the adjacent region of the brain, the hypothalamus. Disturbances also appear in other endocrine glands, particularly in the sex glands. When a tumor is responsible, the condition can be treated by X-ray therapy or surgery. Hormones are given to correct the deficiencies in hormone production.
See also ENDOCRINE GLANDS.

FROHMAN [frō′mən], **CHARLES** (1860–1915), American theatrical manager and producer, born in Sandusky, Ohio. His first successful independent production in New York was Bronson Howard's *Shenandoah* in 1889. In 1893 he opened the Empire Theater in that city and maintained an outstanding company including John Drew, Maude Adams, and Ethel Barrymore. He also controlled many other U.S. and London theaters and pioneered in introducing U.S. playwrights and actors in London, and the works of European dramatists, including Sir James M. Barrie, to America. His brother, DANIEL FROHMAN (1851–1940), was also a noted theatrical manager in New York.

FROISSART [frwả-sảr′], **JEAN** (c.1337–1410?), French chronicler. He went to England in 1361 and was presented to Queen Philippa, who appointed him one of her secretaries. Soon he was recognized as the court chronicler. When the Queen died in 1369, he returned to France, and under the patronage of several nobles he continued to record the events of his time. Battles, tournaments, and court affairs interested Froissart, not social or political development. Since he relied on oral testimony rather than archives (which were available), his *Chronicles*, though distorted and incomplete, convey a sense of immediacy. For all their deficiencies, they are useful as contemporary accounts of the 14th century and as an index to the medieval mind.

Consult Shears, F. S., *Froissart* (1930).

FROMM, ERICH (1900–   ), psychoanalyst. Born in Frankfurt, Germany, he took his Ph.D. at Heidelberg and later studied at the University of Munich and at Berlin's Psychoanalytic Institute. He lectured at Bennington College from 1941 to 1950 and was a professor in the National University of Mexico after 1951 and concurrently a professor at Michigan State University after 1957. One of the better-known revisers of Freudian psychology, he developed the concept that many neuroses result from the insecurity created by the increased freedom of choice in complex modern society, as opposed to the rigid, but secure, conditions of earlier times. Among his published works are *Escape From Freedom* (1941), *The Forgotten Language* (1951), and *The Art of Loving* (1956).

FRONDE [frônd], in French history, a rebellion (1648–53) of the French administrative and military nobility against the royal government represented by Jules Cardinal Mazarin, chief minister of the queen mother and regent, Anne of Austria, during the minority of Louis XIV. (The name means "sling" and was used derisively by contemporaries to indicate the frivolous character of the movement, particularly in its later stages, by comparing it with the activities of mischievous children.) Civil war broke out (Aug., 1648) when the citizens of Paris threw up barricades in protest against the arrest of a leader of the opposition to Mazarin in the Parlement, the highest court in the kingdom. The deeper issues underlying the conflict were the magistracy's resistance to increasing royal absolutism and centralization. Mazarin's predecessor, Cardinal Richelieu, had overridden their opposition, but Mazarin, a foreigner notorious for lining his own pockets and those of his relations, was more vulnerable by reason of his unpopularity. Parlement demanded the abolition of the royal intendants and recognition of its claim to grant or withhold approval of new laws, especially those concerning finance.

Because French participation in the Thirty Years' War had emptied the treasury, Mazarin and the queen mother held out as long as possible against these demands, but were forced to give in when two powerful princes, the Duc d'Orléans and the popular general Condé, as well as the Coadjutor of Paris, Paul de Gondi (later Cardinal de Retz), intervened as mediators. The "parlementary Fronde" was followed by the "Princes' Fronde" led by Condé, whose vanity had been wounded by real or fancied slights at court. He was abetted by his brother, the Prince de Conti, by Gondi, and by a party of disgruntled noble intriguers which included the Prince d'Elbeuf, the Ducs de Belfort and de Bouillon, the future Duc de la Rochefoucauld, the Duc and Duchesse de Longueville, and the Duchesse de Montpensier ("La Grande Mademoiselle"). These malcontents were joined by the Parlement of Paris and several provincial parlements.

Condé himself at first remained loyal to the crown and blockaded Paris—which had again risen in rebellion—against a relieving army. Hunger finally forced Parlement to accept the compromise peace of Rueil (Mar. 11, 1649), which limited new taxation and granted a general amnesty. But in Jan., 1650, Mazarin provoked a new Fronde by imprisoning Condé, Conti, and Longueville. Opposition was so violent that Mazarin had to release them (Feb., 1651) and flee into exile in Germany; he continued, however, to control policy through advice and instructions sent to the queen mother, who had removed the King from Paris. Condé negotiated for aid from Spain, with whom France was then at war, and threatened Paris with an army raised in the south. The Vicomte de Turenne ably commanded a loyal army but failed to prevent Condé from entering Paris and then escaping again when Parlement refused its support. The Duchesse de Montpensier covered Condé's retreat by firing her own cannon from the Bastille. Meanwhile Gondi was weaned from the rebel cause by the grant of a Cardinal's hat, and Mazarin returned to power, profiting from a reaction in favor of the royal cause.

Consult Doolin, P. R., *The Fronde* (1935).

RALPH H. BOWEN, Northern Illinois University

FRONDIZI [frŏn-dē′zē], **ARTURO** (1908–   ), Argentine politician of Italian immigrant parentage. Trained in the law, he entered politics and served as a parliamentary deputy. He became a leading Radical (moderate) party opponent of the Juan Perón regime. In 1951 he ran for Vice President on the Radical ticket but was defeated by the Peronista candidate. During the provisional presidency of Gen. Pedro Aramburu the Radical party split, and Frondizi became the leader of the Intransigent Radicals and their successful presidential candidate (1958). His administration was beset with many political and economic difficulties. In 1962 he was forcibly removed from office and held captive by the military. José María Guido replaced him as President.

FRONT, in meteorology, boundary between two air masses of different temperature and density. Usually fronts are marked by characteristic weather features. The term is used somewhat ambiguously to include three related phenomena, which should be distinguished: (1) A frontal zone is the relatively narrow transition layer between the different air masses. Within this zone the temperature and density change rapidly. (2) A frontal surface is the side of the frontal zone next to the warmer of the two air masses. (3) A surface front is the line along which a frontal surface intersects the earth's surface. The first two definitions are technical, and the third indicates the ordinary usage of the word. In this article the surface front in the Northern Hemisphere will be discussed, except as otherwise noted.

The term "front" was introduced into meteorology by the Scandinavian "air mass and frontal analysis" school in the years following 1918. This group demonstrated that the weather elements in an extratropical cyclone, or large, migratory low-pressure area, are distributed discontinuously, rather than continuously as had been formerly supposed. They gave the name "front" to the zones or lines of discontinuity, and they devised a model

Fig. 1 MAP VIEW OF A MATURE EXTRATROPICAL CYCLONE

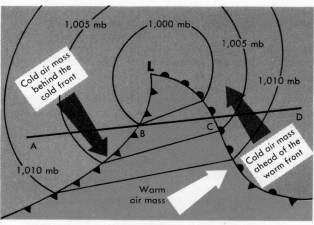

ABCD is the line along which the cross section is taken in Fig. 2.
Arrows show general wind flow in warm and cold masses.

L Low-pressure center

—— Isobar, or line of equal
barometric pressure, in millibars (mb)

▲▲▲ Cold front
●●● Warm front
▲▼▲▼ Stationary front

Fig. 2 SIDE VIEW OF THE CYCLONE SHOWN IN FIG. 1

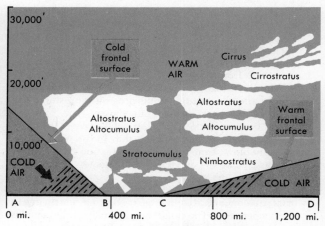

Typical cloud forms and precipitation are indicated.
White arrows show upward motion of warm air
mass at both fronts. Dark arrow shows motion of
cold air forcing warm air upward at cold front.

B Surface cold front   C Surface warm front   B-C Warm sector

of the frontal structure of an extratropical cyclone that proved sufficiently realistic to provide a fresh basis for practical forecasting. Simultaneously, the "polar front" was identified as the boundary between polar and tropical air masses, introducing a new approach to the study of the general circulation of the atmosphere. Subsequent meteorological experience, along with the development of methods of upper-air observation, has both extended the air mass and frontal discoveries and modified them from their original forms. It is now recognized that a front in nature may depart considerably from the model, but that the concept itself is quite valid.

According to the Scandinavian school, the polar front extends around the Northern Hemisphere, not continuously, but in segments where the wind field tends to bring together polar and tropical air masses. By a process not yet completely understood, a low-pressure center and a cyclonic (counterclockwise) wind circulation may develop at the meeting point of two contrasting air masses. A ripple forms at this point on the front, and a wave, or frontal, cyclone originates. It passes through the mature state (Fig. 1) to the occluded state (Fig. 3), and eventually to dissolution.

In the mature extratropical cyclone two kinds of fronts are involved. A warm front marks the line where the

warmer air mass is advancing against the colder one and gliding up over it. Along a cold front the colder air mass is replacing the warmer air, which is forced aloft. Fig. 2 shows these interactions by a vertical cross section along the line ABCD in Fig. 1. When all the warm air has been forced aloft and the cold front has overtaken the warm front near the center of the low, an occluded front results, as shown in Fig. 3.

All fronts have a temperature and density discontinuity, and they occur in a trough in the pressure field. Thus, the passage of a front is ordinarily marked by a dip in barometric pressure and by a rise or fall in temperature. Each of the two main kinds of fronts presents a distinct set of weather features. As shown in Fig. 2, the slope of a warm front is much less than that of a cold front. The warm-front slope is of the order of a vertical rise of 1 mi. in a horizontal distance of 250 mi. compared to 1 mi. in 50 mi. for a cold front. The warm front aloft, in other words, extends several hundred miles ahead of its surface position. It is up this sloping surface that the warm air rises over the colder surface air. As the warm air rises, it is cooled and its water vapor content condenses to form clouds. The warm-front cloud system therefore forms in a wedge, with the vertical thickness greatest near the surface front. The wedge gradually rises and becomes thinner

OCCLUDED FRONT IN THE FINAL STAGE OF AN EXTRATROPICAL CYCLONE

Fig. 3A MAP VIEW

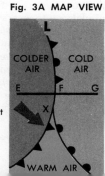

▲▲▲ Cold front
●●● Warm front
▲●▲ Occluded front

L Low-pressure center

The cold front, wedged under the warm front between the center of the low (L) and the point X, has forced the warm front aloft. The warm front is said to be occluded in this area, and X is the point of occlusion.

Fig. 3B SIDE VIEW ALONG LINE EFG

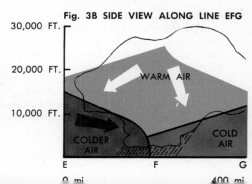

in advance of the surface front. The highest clouds and the advance guard of the warm front are the wispy cirrus clouds. Next comes the denser cirrostratus sheet. Lower and nearer the surface front come altostratus and altocumulus clouds. In the vicinity of the surface front is the thick, rain- or snow-bearing nimbostratus layer, usually with low fractostratus, or scud, clouds beneath it, and sometimes frontal fog.

With the passage of the warm front the cloudiness decreases and the steady frontal precipitation stops. The warm air, however, may contain shower-type clouds, so complete clearing does not always take place. But there is a temperature increase and a shift in the wind, which typically blows from an easterly direction in the colder air mass, while the air in the warm sector flows from a southerly quadrant.

The cloudiness and precipitation associated with a cold front are concentrated in a narrower belt, partly due to the steeper slope. The clouds are generally of the cumulus type, sometimes developing into cumulonimbus, or thunderstorm, clouds, which bring heavy showers and strong wind squalls. At the rear of a cold front the barometric pressure rises, the wind shifts to northerly, and temperature and humidity fall. Skies may or may not clear abruptly, depending upon the nature of the cold air mass.

The foregoing refers to active fronts; both warm and cold fronts may be inactive and cause little change in weather. An occluded front may behave as either a warm or cold front, depending upon the relative temperatures of the cold air masses separated by the front. All fronts may become stationary, showing practically no movement. In addition to the polar front in the Northern Hemisphere, other fronts are found in various other parts of the atmospheric circulation. Examples are the arctic front between arctic air and less cold polar air, and the comparable antarctic front.

Consult Miller, A. A., and Parry, M., *Everyday Meteorology* (1959).

JAMES K. McGUIRE, U.S. Weather Bureau
See also AIR MASS; ATMOSPHERE; CLOUDS; METEOROLOGY.

FRONTENAC [frŏn′tə-năk], **LOUIS DE BUADE, COMTE DE PALLUAU ET DE** (1620–98), French colonial administrator, twice Governor of New France (1672–82, 1689–98). Although involved in continual quarrels with other officials as well as with the Jesuits in Canada, the remarkable if controversial Frontenac accomplished much during his administrations. He encouraged the explorations of Daniel Duluth, Louis Jolliet, Sieur de La Salle, and Jacques Marquette; he dealt effectively and justly with the Indians; he established posts and forts—such as Fort Frontenac (Kingston) on Lake Ontario—in the newly claimed French territories. Frontenac had served in the French army, rising to the rank of brigadier general, before going to Canada. His vigorous policies in New France, especially with regard to the fur trade, alienated the merchant class and consequently the Sovereign Council. Louis XIV, supporting the council, reduced the Governor's powers and then recalled him in 1682, only to reinstate him in 1689 when his successors proved in-

effectual. Frontenac launched campaigns against the Iroquois, who were eventually subdued, and the British during this phase of the French and Indian Wars. In 1690, in his greatest victory, he repulsed William Phips's attack on Quebec. Frontenac died in Quebec; his body reposes in the crypt of the cathedral.

Consult Parkman, Francis, *Count Frontenac and New France Under Louis XIV* (1877); Eccles, W. J., *Frontenac, the Courtier Governor* (1959).

MONSIGNOR ARTHUR MAHEUX, Laval University

FRONTIER IN AMERICAN HISTORY. During the three centuries when the continental United States was being settled, the edge of the country's occupied area moved steadily westward. This frontier played an important role in shaping the distinctive characteristics of the people of the United States and their institutions. A frontier existed from the early 17th century, when Englishmen first landed on the Atlantic coast, to 1890, when the director of the census announced that an unbroken line no longer separated the settled and unsettled portions of the country. During that entire period men and women constantly moved westward to begin life anew and to re-create civilization from primitive beginnings.

The Frontier Cycle. Those attracted to the frontier by cheap land and a thirst for adventure moved in a series of well-defined waves. First into the wilderness were hunters and fur traders, seeking wealth in the form of beaver and otter pelts or deer and buffalo skins. They made little impression on nature, for most succumbed to the savage ways of the Indians who were their constant companions. Behind them, when conditions warranted, came the gold and silver miners, moving far ahead of the settled areas whenever mineral wealth was found. They were followed by ranchers whose constant quest was for unfenced lands where their cattle could roam freely. A "cowman's frontier" existed on the fringes of the Massachusetts Bay Colony in the 1630's and amidst the "peavine marches" of backwoods Virginia in the 1640's, just as it did on the Great Plains of the Far West in the 1870's and 1880's. All these pioneer types were intent upon utilizing rather than subduing nature's rawness. Most were nomads who planned to move on as soon as the surface wealth was skimmed away. Hence they did little toward fostering the birth of civilization in the region through which they passed.

This was not the case with those who followed them in the ever-repeated frontier cycle. The "squatters" who next invaded the lands over which trappers and cattlemen had hurried were usually propertyless small farmers who lacked the capital and energy to subdue the wilderness, but who dreamed of acquiring wealth as the West matured. Few realized this ambition, for they exhausted their energy by clearing away a few trees, building a rough cabin, and planting their first crops. As indolence overtook them, they reverted to hunting as the principal means of supporting their ever-growing families, yet they played an important role in the frontier process by locating good land and absorbing the initial attacks of the Indians they displaced. When neighbors began to appear, they were ready to sell their "improvements" and move on. The newcomers were normally "equipped farmers"

A glorified view of the colony of Savannah, from a pamphlet printed in London in 1733 and designed to lure settlers to Georgia. The colony is shown with a strong fort for protection against Indians, who are, however, pictured as eager to help the colonists.

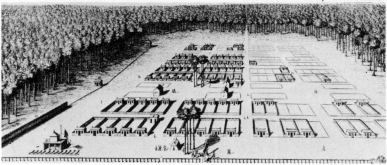

Savannah as the colonists actually saw it in 1734 (*right*). It was a good deal less prosperous than its enthusiastic Board of Trustees had made it seem in the pamphlet that contained the picture above. The fort was not nearly as strong as they had suggested.

with both capital and ambition, who came to stay and grow up with the country. They built substantial homes, cleared the forests or broke the prairie sod, and gradually increased farm production until surpluses were available. The marketing of these surpluses required roads to link the new settlements with the East. Flour millers and distillers, bankers and merchants, and lawyers and newspaper editors were also needed for their export and sale. As these pioneer businessmen concentrated at strategic points, villages emerged to signal the passing of the frontier and the emergence of a new civilization. By this time the whole process was beginning anew farther west.

The Early Pioneers. Before migration settled into this well-defined pattern, Europeans had to learn the techniques of frontiering. Their education began with the first English settlements in Jamestown, Plymouth, and Boston. Suffering was intense among these pioneers, for they were so poorly equipped to utilize nature's riches that they starved to death amid plenty. Slowly they learned from the Indians which native plants could be grown, and which animals to hunt. Imported artifacts were also adapted to frontier needs. Stubby guns were lengthened into the efficient "Kentucky rifles" that would bring down game and provide protection against redskinned foes. Clumsy axes were refashioned into amazingly efficient tools. Experimentation also taught the budding frontiersmen the techniques needed to subsist in a new country; they learned to "girdle" trees, to use a "jump plow" to prepare the soil for planting, to plant several crops of corn before wheat or barley was sown. From Swedish settlers the pioneers learned how to build snug log cabins that would provide protection against cold weather and savage foes; from German newcomers they adopted the large "Palatine barns" that afforded domestic animals shelter against winter's blasts. Trial and error also taught them that they must move and settle in groups. Needed community tasks were performed through co-op-

erative effort at "cabin raisings," "logrollings," and "cornhusking bees." Within a few generations the leather-clad woodsmen, who roamed the forests with all the assurance of their Indian foes, were fully equipped to carry the frontier westward to the Pacific.

The settlers advanced in a series of well-defined thrusts. During the first three-quarters of the 17th century, the coastal lowlands bordering the Atlantic Ocean were occupied. Small farms pushed slowly westward across the southern tidewater region and advanced up the river bottoms of New England. By 1670 the assault on the hilly upland known as the "Old West" had begun. To this less hospitable land, formed of the Appalachian foothills and mountain valleys, came younger sons of Eastern farmers, former indentured servants, and farmers whose soil was losing its fertility through repeated plantings. They were joined in the Old West by two migratory streams from abroad, one of Germans from the Rhenish Palatinate, the other of Scotch-Irish from Ulster. Driven from their homelands by persecution and hard times, these newcomers were attracted to Pennsylvania, whose kindly Governors welcomed all arrivals. Their quest for cheap land led them first to the interior of that colony (where descendants of the Palatines remain today as the Pennsylvania Dutch) and then southward along the great valley of the Appalachians. By the 1750's, their cabins extended through the Shenandoah Valley of Virginia into the Carolina back country, and the settlers on the extreme outer edge of the migration were ready to push through the mountain gaps into the Mississippi valley.

For a time this next advance was halted by the French and Indian War (1754–63) and by Pontiac's Rebellion (1763–64), but with peace the westward-flowing tide moved again. It flowed in four streams, each governed by the desirability of the lands ahead and the availability of transportation routes. One stream was directed to Fort Pitt on the forks of the Ohio River, another to the

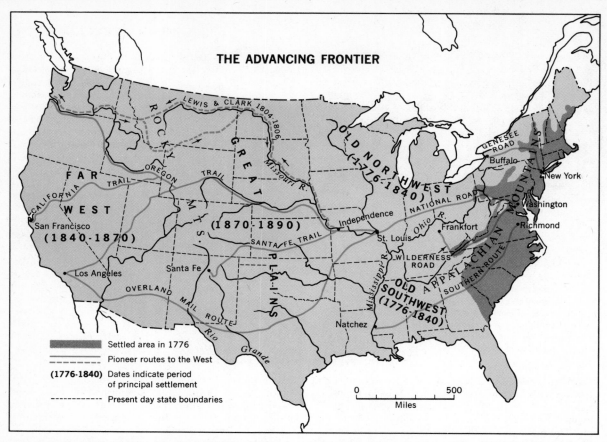

THE ADVANCING FRONTIER

FAR WEST (1840-1870)

(1870-1890)

OLD NORTHWEST (1776-1840)

OLD SOUTHWEST (1776-1840)

Settled area in 1776
Pioneer routes to the West
(1776-1840) Dates indicate period of principal settlement
- - - - - - Present day state boundaries

0   500
Miles

river bottoms of the region that later became West Virginia, a third to the bluegrass country of Kentucky, and a fourth to the valleys of the Holston and Watauga rivers in eastern Tennessee. Scarcely had they established their outposts when the Indian warfare accompanying the American Revolution (1776–83) drove them back, but so strong was the expansionist urge that the westward movement began anew after 1778–79 when the campaigns of George Rogers Clark temporarily subdued the Western Indians. By 1783 some 25,000 persons lived in Kentucky, the settlements about Fort Pitt were pushing down the

Ohio River, and not only eastern Tennessee but the distant Nashville basin was being occupied.

The Old Northwest and the Old Southwest. Migration was slowed again while the new government of the United States struggled with a number of diplomatic problems affecting the West and sought to evolve a national Western policy. The latter task proved easy, for the monumental ordinances of 1785 and 1787 increased the attractiveness of the frontier by establishing an orderly procedure for the survey and sale of land and by providing eventual political equality for all entering the

New York Public Library

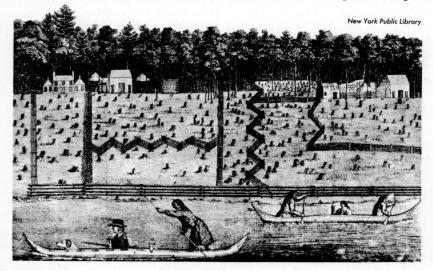

"Plan of an American New Cleared Farm," from Patrick Campbell's *Travels in the Interior Inhabited Parts of North America* (1793), printed in Edinburgh, Scotland. This view of a New Brunswick farm was intended to depict American farming methods for the benefit of Europeans.

public domain. The diplomatic problems were more difficult, but they too were gradually solved as Jay's Treaty (1794) ended British meddling in the Old Northwest and Pinckney's Treaty (1795) with Spain assured pioneers an outlet for their surpluses and an end to Indian uprisings in the Old Southwest. With the gates to the Mississippi Valley opened by these maneuvers, migration mounted steadily until it was again checked by the threat of new Indian troubles on the eve of the War of 1812. During those years western New York was occupied by New Englanders, Kentucky and Tennessee were so heavily settled that they became states in 1792 and 1796, and the conquest of the Old Northwest began. Ohio became a state in 1803, and by 1812 wilderness clearings bordered the north bank of the Ohio River as far as the Illinois country.

During the War of 1812 the decisive battles of the Thames (1813) and Horseshoe Bend (1814) so broke the spirit of the Indians of the Old Northwest and Old Southwest that they had no heart for further resistance. Population was free to move westward to the Mississippi and beyond with no further interruption save the brief Black Hawk War of 1832. The result was a "great migration" that jammed every road and trail leading to the West. The newcomers moved in two streams, one directed northward toward the Lake Plains fringing the Great Lakes, the other southward to the Gulf Plains of western Georgia, Alabama, and Mississippi. Between 1815 and 1830 most of the pioneers entering the Lake Plains came from the upland regions of the South to fill southern Indiana and Illinois. After 1830, Yankees, New Yorkers, and Germans flooded into the northern halves of those states and pushed on into Michigan and Wisconsin. Newcomers into the Gulf Plains, on the other hand, came almost entirely from the Southeast, where the multiplication of cotton-growing plantations displaced countless small farmers. In their new homes they turned as rapidly as possible to the production of cotton, transforming that land into an area of plantations and slavery, a pattern of society that contrasted sharply with the small farms, diversified agriculture, and democracy characteristic of the region north of the Ohio River. By 1840 both the Lake Plains and

the Gulf Plains had been largely occupied, while settlement had crossed the Mississippi to bring statehood to Louisiana (1812), Missouri (1821), Arkansas (1836), and (in 1846) Iowa.

The Far West. Long before this time more venturesome pioneers were probing the secrets of the vast hinterland acquired from France in the Louisiana Purchase of 1803. Their reports were usually discouraging. Some explorers, such as Meriwether Lewis and William Clark, brought back news of plentiful fur-bearing animals in the Rocky Mountains. Others, such as Stephen H. Long, reported the whole West to be a "great American desert" unsuitable for white habitation. Fur trappers were quick to seize the opportunity opened by Lewis and Clark; between the 1820's and the 1840's several hundred "mountain men" lived in the Far West, trapping beaver ruthlessly and renewing their contacts with civilization only when they gathered to meet the annual caravan from St. Louis. By the middle 1840's, when the extermination of the beaver ended the fur trade, they had explored every nook and cranny of the West and were ready to serve as guides for the homeseekers already turning their footsteps toward the Pacific.

The mecca of these advance pioneers was the lush valleys of Oregon and California where, they believed, land could be had for the taking. Starting in 1841, when the first sizable caravan began its wearisome journey at Independence, Mo., the Oregon and California trails were crowded with settlers, all bound for the Willamette Valley of Oregon or the Sacramento and San Joaquin valleys of California. By 1846, the 5,000 Americans who had reached the Oregon country could make their weight felt in the diplomatic negotiations between England and the United States that ended with the Pacific Northwest firmly in American hands. The 1,000 pioneers clustered in the lower Sacramento Valley engineered the Bear Flag Revolt that helped win California's independence from Mexico. This minor rebellion merged into the larger war between Mexico and the United States which ended in 1848 with the cession of all the Southwest to the United States.

Despite these remarkable feats, the pioneers of the Far

Bruff's Camp, a way station for migrants headed for the California gold fields, was sketched in 1849 by Joseph Goldsborough Bruff. Many immigrants left their wagons and cattle here and continued on foot.

Henry E. Huntington Library and Art Gallery

"Hand Cart Pioneers" by C. C. A. Christensen. The idea of handcart migration originated with Mormon leaders who urged this less costly method of travel on their poorer brethren. Between 1856 and 1860, 10 handcart companies, comprising 3,000 people, crossed the plains to Utah.

Utah State Historical Society

West remained few in number until the chance discovery of gold on the western slopes of California's Sierra Nevada mountains touched off the rush of the forty-niners. Few of the 100,000 would-be miners who reached the gold fields "struck it rich," but most of those who failed settled down to become farmers or merchants, endowing California with such a large population that it became a state in 1850. Others, incurably infected with the prospecting fever, fanned out to seek their fortunes in the mountains and deserts of the Far West. While most died in poverty, a fortunate few made "strikes" that attracted a rush of settlers, some to the Apache-ridden deserts of Arizona, others to the fabulous riches of Nevada's Comstock Lode, still others to the clear streams of Idaho and Montana. As capital flowed in to finance the exploitation of subsurface wealth and farmers appeared to capitalize on the high prices that could be charged miners, permanent communities gradually evolved. Congress recognized this growth by carving all the Far West into states or territories by the 1870's.

The Great Plains. By this time the conquest of America's last frontier—the Great Plains—was under way. This giant grassland, stretching from the tier of states bordering the Mississippi to the Rockies, could be utilized only by devising an economic enterprise suitable to its distinctive characteristics or by employing man-made devices to subdue its hostile environment. The first pioneers to exploit the plains—the cattlemen—employed the former approach. Beginning in the 1860's, herds of longhorns were driven northward from Texas, some to be shipped to Eastern markets on the railroads that were creeping across the continent, others to be used to stock the northern range. Within two decades the entire region had been converted into a single pasture where herds roamed freely and grass was king. The days of the cattle kingdom were numbered. Pressing upon it from the east were small farmers whose advance was made possible by the products of Eastern industrialists. They

came with a whole arsenal of equipment: barbed-wire fences to guard their fields from cattle, windmills and well-drilling machines to allow the use of subsurface water, railroads to bring in fuel and materials and to carry out bulky crops, efficient farm machinery that would allow one man to till the large acreage needed to support a family in that semiarid land. In the largest migration in the history of the frontier, the Great Plains was overrun by farmers between 1870 and 1890. When that migration had run its course, the West was occupied and the expansion of the American people had become a part of history.

Influence of the Frontier. The passing of the frontier did not mean the end of the frontier's influence on the American people or their institutions. The recurring "beginning

Colorado ranch in the 1860's. Colorado was well settled by this time. Gold discoveries had brought many thousands into the state.

Brown Brothers

over again" in successive Wests, repeated in thousands of pioneer communities over a span of three centuries, had gradually altered the nature of both the people and the society. In each of those communities the impact of the distinctive environment, the accident of separate evolution, and the contributions of persons from differing backgrounds who mingled to create the new social order had served as ingredients in the creation of a civilization that was based on older orders, but that had been slightly changed. An Americanization of men and institutions had taken place.

Many features of life and thought that are today considered the most uniquely American can be traced in part to the influence of the frontier. Americans are a mobile people, moving often, with little attachment to place; their pioneer ancestors similarly showed little permanent loyalty to any locality as they drifted westward in search of new opportunity. They are an inventive people, ready to experiment constantly and to accept innovation as normal; frontiersmen were forced to improvise constantly to meet the problems of Western living for which precedent had no answers. Americans are a wasteful people and have built their economy on the concept of planned obsolescence; their forebears learned this trait among natural resources of such plenty that their exhaustion seemed impossible. They are a materialistic people, emphasizing practical values and inclined to be scornful of the artist or intellectual; the pioneers similarly had little interest in aesthetic standards or speculative thought in a world where material tasks were all-important. Finally, the people of the United States, like their pioneer ancestors, have always looked askance at governmental interference in their economic activities, feeling that individual enterprise should be unrestrained in a land of plenty. The traits that visitors from overseas most frequently isolate as peculiarly American—mobility, inventiveness, wastefulness, materialism, and individualism—are all inheritances from the frontier experience.

So are certain social attitudes basic in today's thought. A lack of rigid class divisions and a corresponding social mobility that allows any man to attain his true level in society are so accepted in the United States today that sociologists refer to stratification rather than classes and stress the "open-endedness" of each division. This attitude, although traceable in part to the opportunities stemming from industrialization, is a heritage of pioneer days, when cheap frontier land allowed each individual to attain a place in society based on his skill and intelligence rather than on hereditary status. In pioneer communities a division soon occurred between the "better sort" and the "common folk," but all frontiersmen knew that society was sufficiently fluid to allow anyone to move from one segment of society to the other. This insistence on the natural equality of man, accompanied by a refusal to accept servant status for even the least gifted, has persisted down to the present.

An abiding faith in democracy as the only acceptable governmental system has also persisted. Democratic theory and practice were, of course, well developed in Europe before their transfer to America, but both were deepened by the frontier experience of the people. In the West the leveling influence of the poverty that had

driven men from their homes, the lack of any prior leadership structure to perpetuate aristocratic practices, and the need to solve local problems by local governing bodies accentuated the pioneers' belief that self-rule was the God-given right of Americans. This deep-rooted belief in democracy, for themselves and all others in the world, is still part of the creed of the nation's citizens.

That these values and characteristics stemmed entirely from the frontier or that the frontier alone was responsible for the distinctive traits and institutions of the United States is, of course, not true. American civilization is a product of a variety of forces, past and present: the European heritage, the continuing impact of other societies throughout the world, the flow of immigration from abroad, the rapidity of industrialization and urbanization, and a host of additional factors. Among these, however, none has been more important than the frontier.

Consult Turner, F. J., *The Frontier in American History* (1920); Billington, R. A., *Westward Expansion: A History of the American Frontier* (2d ed., 1960).

RAY A. BILLINGTON, Northwestern University

FRONTO [frŏn'tō], **MARCUS CORNELIUS** (fl. 2d century A.D.), Roman orator and beloved tutor of Marcus Aurelius. Fronto left behind him ten books of lettters to his imperial pupil and patron, with a few from Marcus Aurelius to Fronto, over half of which were recovered in 1815. They deal largely with personal affairs, are wordy, and of small historical value. Fronto's speeches have not survived. He tried unsuccessfully to revitalize the Latin language.

FRONT RANGE, easternmost range of the Rocky Mountains in Colorado, extending from the north fork of the Cache la Poudre River to the Arkansas River. Some geographers include ranges farther north and south in the Front Range. It has numerous high peaks, including Grays (14,274 ft.), Pikes (14,110 ft.), and Longs (14,255 ft.). Rocky Mountain National Park is within the range. Principal passes are Berthoud (11,314 ft.) and Loveland (11,992 ft.). Length, about 200 mi.

FRONT ROYAL, city of northern Virginia, and seat of Warren County, in an agricultural region. A large rayon factory is here. Skyline Caverns is nearby. Inc., 1788; pop., 8,211.

FROST, ROBERT (1874–1963), American poet, born in San Francisco. He was named Robert Lee by his father, who had wished to serve in the Confederate army, but he discarded his middle name as a writer. The father, an erratic newspaperman and politician, died in 1885 of tuberculosis and his widow and their two children returned east to Lawrence, Mass., where Frost completed high school. He studied for a term at Dartmouth in 1892 and then was a mill hand until he and Elinor White, a former schoolmate, began teaching in a private school founded by his mother. They were married in 1895. Supported by his grandfather, Frost undertook to earn a degree at Harvard but quit in his sophomore year (1899) to live on a farm in Derry, N.H., and to teach.

Because he had written verse since high school, which

The American poet Robert Frost.

appeared occasionally in periodicals like the *Independent*, the Frosts decided to stake all on his future as a poet. In 1912 they sold their farm and sailed for England, where his first volume, *A Boy's Will* (1913), was published and where he found a partisan in Ezra Pound. *A Boy's Will* was imitative of Emerson, Lowell, Longfellow, and Housman, but with *North of Boston* (1914) Frost produced a poetry uniquely his own, terse, paradoxical, fresh, and invigorating as October weather. When he returned to America (1915), he found that his fame had preceded him, and he was in great demand as a lecturer and teacher. Volume after volume of verse came from his pen in the next four decades and he was four times awarded the Pulitzer Prize. Most of his poems deal with life in rural New England and reflect the old-fashioned individualism of that region. Among his best-known poems are "Mending Wall," "The Black Cottage," "Home Burial," "The Road Not Taken," "Stopping by Woods on a Snowy Evening," "Fire and Ice," "Two Tramps in Mud Time," and "To a Thinker." He was poetry consultant to the Library of Congress (1958–61).

Consult Brower, Reuben A., *Poetry of Robert Frost: Constellations of Intention* (1963); Cook, Reginald L., *Robert Frost: A Living Voice* (1974); Frost, Lesley, *New Hampshire's Child: Derry Journals of Lesley Frost* (1969); Sergeant, Elizabeth S., *Robert Frost: The Trial of Existence* (1960).   Oscar Cargill

FROST, ice crystals formed on objects by the deposition of water vapor from the air when the temperature of the objects is below freezing. This direct change from vapor to solid is called sublimation. On clear nights the earth loses heat by radiation; the cool ground may then cool the air, increasing its relative humidity. If saturation is reached at a subfreezing temperature, frost (also called hoarfrost) may form on plants, fences, and other exposed objects. The term "frost" is also used to designate a temperature condition damaging to plant life; there need not be visible ice crystals. A killing frost is one that kills plants.

When frosts are caused by radiation to the night sky, the temperature is lowest at the earth's surface and increases upward. To warm the lower air layers and prevent frost, fruit growers often use small, oil-burning orchard heaters spaced on the ground among the trees. Also used are large fans that mix the various layers of air in order to raise the temperature at plant level. Low-growing plants may be insulated against frost by flooding them with water.   Louis J. Battan

FROSTBITE, freezing and destruction of the tissues, which usually occurs at temperatures below 10° F., but may develop at higher temperatures (around 23° F.) if the part is damp and subjected to high winds.

Improper clothing, poor circulation, and general body weakness predispose to frostbite. There may be no warning symptoms, or a sharp pricking sensation. The involved skin appears yellowish-white and is numb or hard. Freezing of the superficial parts may result in local redness and blistering. In severe cases large blebs, ulceration, and gangrene occur.

Prevention. Warm, dry clothing should be worn. Exposure to cold should be brief if possible. The arms and legs should be periodically exercised and smoking should be avoided before and during exposure. Exposed skin should be covered with grease.

Treatment. The frozen tissues should be warmed as rapidly as possible. If nothing else is available, the bare hand should be placed over the part. When possible the part should be placed in warm water until thawed and then be exposed to warm room air. The skin should not be rubbed with snow.

After recovery the affected area may be especially sensitive to cold and liable to repeated frostbite.

Robert Brown, M.D.

FROSTBURG, town of western Maryland, 10 mi (16 km) west of Cumberland. It is a trading center for a nearby coal-mining area; its industries manufacture tiles and firebricks. Scenically attractive, Frostburg is a popular resort area and the home of Frostburg State College (established, 1902). The town was founded about 1812 and incorporated in 1870.

FRUCTOSE [*frŭk'tōs*], also known as levulose and fruit sugar, is a simple sugar (a monosaccharide) which is widely distributed in nature, being found in fruit juices, vegetables, the nectar of flowers, the sap of green leaves, honey, plant stalks, human blood plasma, and human seminal plasma (where it serves as the major food for the spermatozoa). When combined with glucose, it forms the disaccharide sucrose, or ordinary table sugar. Solutions of fructose have the property of remaining sirupy, and because of this and its sweet taste, fructose is of importance in the candy and jelly industries.

FRUIT. In a popular sense the word "fruit" is only applied to sweet, pulpy, plant foods. Botanically a fruit is the ripened, seed-containing ovary of any angiosperm, or flowering plant. Therefore, nuts, many vegetables, and the ripened pods of roses, poppies, and other flowers are actually fruits. A fruit is the final result of plant reproduction, and begins its development after the ovules, or eggs, within the ovary have been fertilized by pollen. A fertilized ovule becomes a seed; thus the number of seeds in a fruit corresponds to the number of ovules.

There are many different kinds of fruits, classified by the number of ovaries that contribute to their formation, the structure of the fruit, and the parts of the flower—other than ovary—that share in fruit development. Simple fruits are those that arise from a single ovary. Several kinds of simple fruits are recognized. A dry fruit is formed

DIFFERENT KINDS OF FRUITS

SIMPLE FRUITS

A fruit is the matured ovary (seed-containing portion) of a plant. A simple fruit is one that consists of a single ripened ovary.

FLESHY FRUITS

The wall (pericarp) of a ripening ovary usually thickens and forms three layers: the outermost exocarp; the middle mesocarp; and the inner endocarp. In fleshy fruits, such as the drupe, the mesocarp thickens greatly to form the fleshy, edible portion of the fruit.

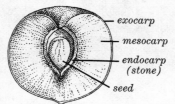

- exocarp
- mesocarp
- endocarp (stone)
- seed

The Peach — A Drupe

DRY FRUITS

In dry fruits the pericarp becomes dry and hard at maturity. Many dry fruits develop from a columnar structure, the pistil, located at the flower's center. The pistil consists of units called carpels, in the base of which are the ovaries. Atop the pistil is the pollen-catching stigma. The capsule is a dry fruit formed from several fused carpels.

- stigma
- carpel

The Poppy Fruit — A Capsule

ACCESSORY FRUITS

In accessory fruits, flower structures other than the ovary form most of the fruit. The edible part of the strawberry consists of a fleshy receptacle. The actual fruits are the tiny, seedlike achenes, each of which is a single-seeded dry fruit.

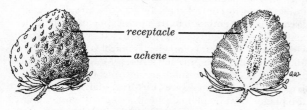

- receptacle
- achene

The Strawberry — An Accessory Fruit

when the ovary wall matures into a dry, often brittle covering for the seed or seeds within. A dry fruit that splits open when it is fully mature is called a dehiscent fruit. Dry, dehiscent fruits typically contain many seeds, as in the soybean and mustard and the seed capsules of larkspur, columbine, and peony. A dry fruit that does not split open upon maturity is called an indehiscent fruit, and typically contains only one or two seeds. Sunflower, dandelion, corn, wheat, rice, elm, maple, carrot, and chestnut fruits are examples of dry, indehiscent fruits.

A second type of simple fruit is the fleshy fruit which is formed when the ovary wall becomes soft and juicy during its development. Two types of simple, fleshy fruits are recognized. When the entire ovary wall becomes soft and pulpy at maturity the resulting fruit is called a berry. Tomatoes, bananas, cucumbers, oranges, and watermelons are berries. If, while it is maturing, the ovary wall becomes differentiated into three distinct layers—a thin outer skin; a thick, fleshy central layer; and a hard, stony interior

layer—the resulting fruit is called drupe. The olive, plum, cherry, peach, and almond are drupes.

Fruits not formed from a single ovary (as are simple fruits) may be aggregate or multiple fruits. An aggregate fruit, such as a raspberry or blackberry, is formed from several ripened ovaries, clustered together in a single receptacle. A multiple fruit, such as the mulberry, fig, or pineapple, results from the fusion of the ripened ovaries of several different flowers.

Some fruits are formed from plant parts in addition to the ovary and are called accessory fruits. The strawberry is an accessory fruit in which the actual fruits are the tiny, hard seeds which are embedded in a fleshy receptacle. Apples and pears are special types of accessory fruits called pomes. In a pome, the core or inedible portion is the true fruit. The surrounding flesh represents an enlargement of the receptacle.

CLARENCE J. HYLANDER, Author, *The World of Plant Life*
See also FLOWER; FRUIT GROWING; SEED.

FRUIT BAT, name for several species of mostly large bats of suborder Megachiroptera, native to Africa, southern Asia, Australia, and the American tropics. The larger individuals, such as *Pteropus* of Australia and *Eidolon* of Africa, are destructive to cultivated fruits. Since these bats are gregarious and visit orchards in large numbers, the loss of fruit may be substantial. Smaller fruit-eating bats of the American tropics have modified tongues for licking out the soft pulp or juices of fruits. The molar teeth of these vegetarians are flat-crowned.

FRUIT FLY. *See* DROSOPHILA.

FRUIT GROWING. Fruit forms an important part of the diet of people in all parts of the world except in the coldest arctic areas. Fruits are valuable nutritionally because of their high vitamin, pectin, and mineral content, as well as for the bulk they provide.

Botanically, the ripened seed and surrounding tissue of any seed-bearing plant is termed a fruit. In common and horticultural usage, however, a fruit is an edible fleshy tissue surrounding or bearing seeds. The term "fruit" is generally applied only to the sweet, fleshy, edible, seed-bearing organs borne on plants that are long-lived.

Certain fruits can be grown only in tropical climates where temperatures are always well above freezing. The most important of these tropical fruits are bananas, pineapples, mangoes, and papayas, although many other kinds are also grown. Certain other fruits are adapted to somewhat cooler conditions and will endure slight exposure to freezing. These subtropical fruits include oranges, lemons, grapefruit, dates, and avocados. Tropical and subtropical fruits are produced on evergreen plants—plants that retain their foliage throughout the year.

A second major group of fruits includes those that thrive in temperate climates: apples, grapes, pears, peaches, plums, apricots, cherries, and most of the berries are the best known. With the exception of some of the berries, temperate climate fruit trees shed their leaves in winter. The Temperate Zone fruits vary in hardiness. Nearly all will withstand temperatures down to 0° F. in midwinter; many will withstand temperatures of −20° F.

FRUIT GROWING

Pruning branches of an apple tree.

Roche

Philip Gendreau

Disking breaks up the soil between rows of fruit trees.

Philip Gendreau

Spraying controls pests and diseases in a fruit orchard.

without injury; and the hardiest will withstand temperatures down to −40° F.

Fruit plants for commercial production are almost always propagated vegetatively, because seed-grown plants do not reproduce true to the parent type. A tree grown from the seed of Delicious apple, for example, may produce fruit very unlike that of the parent tree in size, shape, flavor, and other characteristics. The grower who wants an orchard that will produce uniform fruits must therefore obtain trees that have been propagated from some vegetative part of the parent plant. This may be accomplished by budding or grafting, as is done with most tree fruits; by growing the new plants from cuttings, as is commonly done with grapes; or by divisions of the crown, commonly done with bananas.

Soils and Site for Fruit Culture. Fruits may be grown on a wide range of soils. Most kinds thrive best on soils that are well drained, moderately deep, and near neutral in reaction—neither acid nor alkaline. Medium-textured soils are preferred.

Particularly in the Temperate Zone, fruit trees should be planted in regions where there is a minimum danger of spring frost. Crops are often lost when spring freezes occur after the plants have started growth and particularly when the blossoms have opened. Temperatures down to 25° F. during the spring will kill most of the blossoms so that no fruit will be produced during the year. Elevated sites for commercial orchards are the most suitable. Locations adjacent to large lakes are often favorable.

To produce well, fruiting plants must be kept growing vigorously. This generally requires the use of commercial fertilizers. The best fertilizer to use and the amount applied varies according to the soil condition in a particular area. Nitrogen-containing fertilizers are almost universally necessary for favorable growth of fruit plants. Under many growing conditions, putting a mulch of organic materials, such as grass or straw, about fruit plants is helpful to growth.

Water Requirement. Most fruit plants require ample soil moisture for satisfactory growth and production. In temperate climates an annual minimum rainfall of about 30 in., most of it during the growing season, is needed. If less than this amount occurs naturally, artificial irrigation of the plantings is necessary. Many of the best fruit districts are located in low-rainfall areas with water supplied by irrigation. In such districts fungus and bacterial diseases are less likely to cause severe damage than in humid, high-rainfall areas.

Pest Control. Nearly all fruit plants are subject to attack by diseases and insects. Diseases may be caused by parasitic fungi, by bacteria, or by viruses. Chemical fungicides are available to control most fungus diseases. Bacterial diseases are not common in fruit plants but are difficult to control when they do occur. No cure is known for a plant with a virus. The best commercial control is to be sure the stock planted is free of plant viruses. Many commercial producers of fruit plant stock are now making every effort to insure that their stocks are virus-free. Many insect pests also plague fruiting plants, and spraying with insecticide chemicals is a necessary part of successful fruit culture. To control insects and diseases in commercial fruit plantings may require spraying with insecticides and fungicides ten or more times per year with some crops.

Harvesting and Utilization. Practically all fruit crops are hand picked, and require a large labor force during the harvest. After harvest the crop may go to market directly for use as fresh fruit; it may be placed in cold storage for a later fresh market; or it may be canned, frozen, or dried. Most tropical and subtropical fruits are not suited for long storage. Temperate Zone fruits, on the other hand, particularly some varieties of apples, pears, and grapes, may be held from 6 to 9 months in cold storage. Processing plants take a great portion of the fruit crop. Large quantities of apples, pears, peaches, apricots, cherries, pineapples, and berries are canned or frozen; the juices of citrus fruits are also extensively frozen or canned. Through storage or processing, many fruits that were formerly seasonal products are now available throughout the year.

JOHN R. MAGNESS, Editor, *Proceedings of the American Society for Horticultural Science*

FRUMENTIUS [froo-měn'shē-əs], **ST.** (c.300–c.380), evangelizer and first head of the Church in Ethiopia, or Abyssinia. He received the title of Abba Salamah after his death. From Tyre, he was captured as a boy and enslaved in Ethiopia. When he was freed, he reported to Athanasius about his life and work there, and after being ordained a Bishop, returned to Ethiopia.

FRUNZE [froon'zyə], **MIKHAIL VASILIEVICH** (1885–1925), Soviet military figure. Associated with the Communist party from 1904, Frunze was one of the outstanding commanders of the Red Army in the civil war. He clashed with Trotsky, Commissar for Military and Naval affairs, on matters of military theory. Frunze maintained that there should be a particular proletarian method of war and debated the issue with Trotsky at the Eleventh Congress of the Communist party in 1922. He worked out and administered the reform of the Red army in 1924–25, succeeding Trotsky as Commissar in 1925. He died under controversial circumstances while undergoing an abdominal operation which had been ordered by the Politburo.

FRUNZE, city of the Soviet Union, and the capital of the Kirgiz S.S.R. It is located near the Chu River in Soviet Central Asia, 300 mi. northeast of Tashkent. Frunze is an important administrative, commercial, and industrial node serving a rich, partially irrigated hinterland. Its basic industries are the production of machine tools and agricultural equipment, metal fabrication, and the spinning of cotton yarn. There are numerous food-processing plants as well as establishments manufacturing shoes, clothing, and construction materials. Power for these industries is supplied by a nearby hydroelectric station. Frunze, named in 1925 for Gen. Mikhail V. Frunze, who was born here, was founded (1873) as a fortress and originally called Pishpek. The building of the Turkestan-Siberian Railroad, a branch of which reached Frunze in 1924, was a major stimulus to its industrial development, for it linked the region with western Siberia. The city was rebuilt as it expanded; among its cultural assets are a civic center and several theaters. The post-World War II period witnessed a spectacular growth of population, linked to the expansion of heavy industry and the inauguration of cotton textile production. Pop., 217,000.

ALLAN L. RODGERS,
The Pennsylvania State University

FRUSTRATION AND AGGRESSION. Frustration is normally considered to exist for an individual when temporary or semipermanent interference gets between him and a goal. Such interference may arise from within the person (for example, moral conflict), or from his physical or social environment (for example, from a competitor or some physical barrier). Thus frustration is a response, emotional in nature, that is presumed to be made by a person when his motivated behavior is interfered with; whether or not frustration does arise is best determined from his subsequent behavior. Aggression is often taken as evidence of frustration when the conditions of interference are apparent.

In scientific psychology the following would be acceptable as a definition of frustration: that it exists when interference with a person's ongoing behavior leads to aggression. Unfortunately, however, aggressive acts themselves are often considered sufficient evidence of frustration, particularly when no other obvious explanation is available. When this is done, frustration becomes simply "that which induces aggression," and in this role the term serves no useful purpose.

Aggression, then, which is characterized by forceful or harmful acts, or both, against a person or object, is often taken as a sign of frustration. Juvenile delinquency, when seen as aggression against society, is commonly thought to result from frustration, and efforts are made to identify sources of frustration in the juvenile's environment. It should be noted, however, that the frustration-aggression dependency is merely a hypothesis and that aggression might reasonably arise in the absence of interference with ongoing behavior. Thus, for example, Sigmund Freud saw aggressive behavior as an indicator of a death wish that he imputed to all people. Also, at least in some animals, aggression seems to be occasioned by what more suitably might be called fear. Some young people become delinquent even though they seem to be facing no frustrations more serious than those endured by nondelinquent children.

LAWRENCE R. BOULTER, University of Illinois

FRY, CHRISTOPHER (1907–   ), English dramatist. Several short religious works in verse and *A Phoenix Too Frequent* (1946) preceded his first commercial success, *The Lady's Not for Burning* (1948). Later plays, also in verse, include *Venus Observed* (1950), *A Sleep of Prisoners* (1950), and *The Dark Is Light Enough* (1954). His dramatic verse, often described as "Elizabethan," is paradoxical, witty, and mannered; his treatments are imaginative and romantic. His plays on religious themes include *The Firstborn* (1948) and *Thor, with Angels* (1948). His adaptations from Jean Anouilh include *Ring Round the Moon* (1950) and *The Lark* (1955); from Jean Giraudoux, *Tiger at the Gates* (1955).

FRY, ELIZABETH (1780–1845), English Quaker. Though mother of a large family, in 1813 she began to devote much attention to the plight of female prisoners at Newgate in London and became renowned as a prison reformer in England and on the Continent.

FRY, ROGER ELIOT (1866–1934), English art critic. As a painter, he was noted for his design and technique. In his writings he championed the unrecognized modern artists, particularly Paul Cézanne and other French painters. A perceptive biography of Fry by Virginia Woolf was published in 1940.

FRYING. *See* COOKERY.

FUCA [foo'kə], **JUAN DE,** real name Apostolos Valerianos (fl.1588–96), Greek navigator. While in the service of Spain, he claimed to have sailed up the northwest coast of Mexico into a broad inlet between present-day Vancouver Island and Washington State. In 1787 Capt. C. W. Barkley of the British navy entered this strait and named it Juan de Fuca Strait.

FUCHSIA [fū′shə], genus of shrubs or small trees in the evening primrose family, Onagraceae. The approximately 100 species are found in Central and South America and New Zealand, and are widely grown in California and other warm regions. *Fuchsia magellanica*, the species most often grown in North America, bears showy clusters of red, purple, blue, or white flowers. Some varieties of this species are hardy in cool climates. Fuchsia may be grown from seed, but the varieties named are usually propagated by cuttings.

FUCHU, city of Honshu, Japan, and suburb of Tokyo. It manufactures silk and is the site of the Tokyo race course, where the Japanese Derby is held. Okunitama Shrine is an important tourist attraction. Pop., 40,691.

FUEL, material possessing energy that can be converted into heat or work. For example, food is fuel for the body, natural gas is fuel for a cooking range, gasoline is fuel for an automobile engine, the uranium-235 isotope is fuel for an atomic reactor, and liquid hydrogen is fuel for a rocket engine. However, the most important fuels are the conventional ones that are burned with oxygen from the air to give useful heat or power. These are the fossil fuels—coal, petroleum, and natural gas—the principal sources of energy.

The amount of fuel used per person per year in a country is one of the best indicators of its wealth. The United States has the highest per capita consumption of fuel of any country in the world, followed closely by other industrialized countries such as Canada, Great Britain, the Scandinavian nations, and West Germany. Japan has a per capita consumption of about one-tenth of that of the United States, whereas India has about one-thirtieth. The rise of industrial power in Soviet Russia can be observed in the steady rise of coal production from about 30,000,000 tons per year in 1925 to over 500,000,000 tons per year in the early 1960's.

From Wood to Petroleum. Historically, the first fuel was wood, which is still an important fuel in many underdeveloped countries. (Vegetable fuels are still important in some underdeveloped countries. For example, the fuel used in India in 1960 was equivalent to nearly 100,000,000 tons of coal, but most of this energy was in the form of cow manure and wood.) In Great Britain, Germany, and the United States the industrial revolution of the 18th and 19th centuries led to the large-scale use of coal. Toward the end of the 19th century coal overtook wood as the most widely used fuel in the world. Although it is still the most important world fuel, it is followed closely by petroleum.

In the United States, which enjoys large reserves of coal, petroleum, and natural gas, petroleum is the most important fuel. It is followed by natural gas, which has been used increasingly since the 1920's, until it now supplies slightly more of the country's fuel needs than coal. In 1960 35% of the energy used in the United States was supplied by petroleum (300,000,000 tons), 30% by natural gas (12 trillion cu. ft.), 29% by coal (400,000,000 tons), 2% from wood and farm wastes, and the remaining 4% by hydroelectric power. The value of the raw fuels produced per year in the United States is over $10,000,000,000 but the value of these fuels when delivered to the consumer is several times greater due to refining, transportation, and distribution costs.

Origin of Fossil Fuels. When wood decays under water, chemical changes occur and peat is formed. In past geological eras beds of peaty material were laid down from semitropical forests. Sedimentation and volcanic upheavals overlaid these beds with many hundreds of feet of rock. The high pressures from the weight of the rock plus the heat within the earth's crust led to compaction and gradual chemical change of the decayed wood into coal. Oxygen and hydrogen were lost and the remaining material became relatively richer in carbon. Different types of coal range all the way from coals which are somewhat like compacted peat to anthracites (hard coals), which contain mainly carbon. The deeper and older the coal bed, the more changed is the coal dug up now. Most coal beds were laid down about 70 to 250 million years ago.

Petroleum was formed by a similar decomposition of marine organisms and it is found in porous rocks or sands capped by impermeable rock. The impermeable rock traps the oil which would otherwise be driven to the surface by displacement by water, which is heavier than the oil.

Natural gas originates from gases dissolved in the petroleum. In many cases the natural gas gradually seeped away from the trapped oil and collected in more impermeable traps of its own.

Typical chemical compositions of coal, petroleum, and natural gas are given in the table below.

TYPICAL CHEMICAL COMPOSITION OF FUELS

CONSTITUENT	Weight of Constituent (%)			
	SOFT COAL	HARD COAL	CRUDE PETROLEUM	NATURAL GAS
CARBON	75	82	85	75
HYDROGEN	5	2.5	12.5	23
OXYGEN	9	5	.5	
NITROGEN	1	1		2
SULFUR	1	.5	1	
MOISTURE	3	3	1	
ASH	6	6		

Combustion. Coal, oil, and natural gas are burned with the oxygen in the air to provide heat. This heat may be used directly for cooking, melting steel, roasting cement ores, or numerous other applications. It may be used to produce steam for steam turbines and electric power or it may be used to expand hot gases driving a piston, as in the internal combustion and diesel engines. In any case, the amount of heat produced when a pound of fuel is burned is a measure of the value of the fuel. The carbon in a fuel burns to carbon dioxide, the hydrogen burns to water, sulfur burns to sulfur dioxide, and the nitrogen in the air remains unchanged. The chemical energy of combustion heats up these combustion products and a hot flame is produced. It should be noted that there is a highest possible temperature which a fuel flame can reach since if we put in more fuel to give more energy, we also have an equivalent extra amount of combustion products to be heated. This is why ordinary flames will not melt some ma-

FUEL

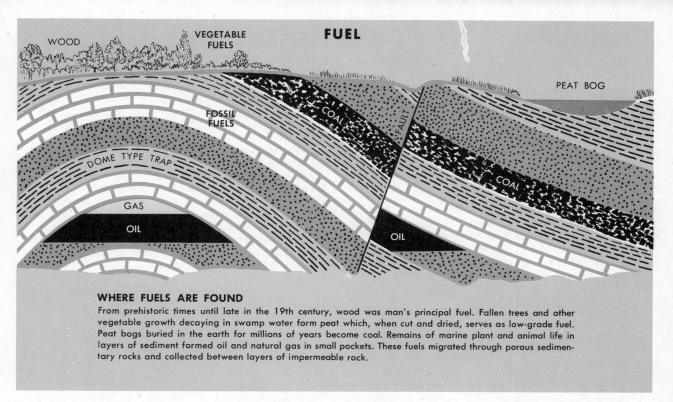

WHERE FUELS ARE FOUND

From prehistoric times until late in the 19th century, wood was man's principal fuel. Fallen trees and other vegetable growth decaying in swamp water form peat which, when cut and dried, serves as low-grade fuel. Peat bogs buried in the earth for millions of years become coal. Remains of marine plant and animal life in layers of sediment formed oil and natural gas in small pockets. These fuels migrated through porous sedimentary rocks and collected between layers of impermeable rock.

terials such as rocks or carbon; the flames simply cannot get hot enough to reach the melting temperature of the materials.

If a flame is cooled before all the chemical reactions are finished, or if not enough air is used, then we get droplets of tar and bits of unburned carbon, which are smoke. Combustion equipment should be designed and used so that the maximum fuel energy is converted into useful heat while only a trace of smoke is produced.

Fuels in the Home. Electricity is, of course, available in all modern houses but the home owner usually has a choice of fuels for cooking, water heating, and home heating. The two main considerations in the choice are convenience and cost. Electricity and gas are the most convenient fuels, but electricity is often considerably more expensive than the other fuels for home heating. In areas where natural gas is relatively cheap it is common to find all three heating loads fueled by gas. Where gas is more expensive, cooking and water heating may be done by gas or electricity and home heating by oil or coal. Coal is nearly always the cheapest fuel for central heating, but it requires daily ash removal and disposal and a large storage space. For these reasons, coal has lost much of its home-heating market to oil. Similarly, natural gas home heating has offered severe competition to oil even when gas is more expensive, since it costs less to install, requires no storage space, and needs virtually no attention. Public utilities and local heating engineers will usually give free estimates of the size of furnace needed and the yearly fuel cost for a specified fuel. The home owner must then make his choice of fuel by balancing installation cost, fuel cost, and convenience.

Fuel Safety. No fuel is completely safe. As a precaution everybody, including children, should be familiar with the odors accompanying gas. If a warning odor is detected in or near the house, all flames and electric appliances should be turned off and the fuel supplier notified immediately. Cooking ranges, whether they be gas or electric, should have controls, preferably at the back, out of the reach of children. Chimneys should be kept in good condition and there must be enough suction from the chimney to prevent smoke from leaking out of the furnace into the basement. This is especially important with coal since coal gases sometimes contain large amounts of poisonous carbon monoxide. Coal dust should never be thrown into a red-hot fire since this may cause an explosion. Oil burners should be checked regularly to see that they are not dripping oil.

Fuels in Industry. About half of the total fuel usage of the United States is for home use or for transport (transport fuels include gasoline for automobiles and fuel oil for locomotives and ships). The other half is used for industrial heating and power. The electric power utilities, which produce electricity for the home as well as industry, use almost one-fifth of the total fuel burned. Some large central power stations burn 1,000,000 tons of coal a year each. Much coal is also treated to produce coke, which is used in iron and steel manufacture. Large quantities of fuel are used in the manufacture of cement, glass, bricks, ceramics, and nearly all metals. Cheap electricity from hydroelectric power systems is particularly important in the manufacture of aluminum. In industries where fuel cost is an appreciable fraction of the production cost, constant research is being carried out to increase the efficiency of fuel usage and lower the total price paid for fuel.

Future Fuels. For some time it has been realized that the ever-increasing world use of coal, oil, and gas will eventually use up all of these fossil fuels stored in the earth. When this will occur will depend on how rapidly world population grows and how rapidly the underdeveloped nations become industralized. Reasonable estimates state that fossil fuels will have to be replaced with other major energy sources within 50 to 150 years' time. Therefore electricity from atomic energy is going to be of greater and greater importance in the years ahead.

Consult Brame, J. S. S., and King, J. G., *Fuel* (1955); Thirring, Hans, *Energy for Man* (1958).

LEONARD G. AUSTIN,
Pennsylvania State University

See also ATOMIC POWER; COAL; ELECTRIC POWER; HYDROELECTRIC POWER; NATURAL GAS; PETROLEUM.

FUEL CELL, a device which generates low voltage dc electric current by a reaction between two chemicals continuously supplied to the cell. Its three basic parts are the annode chamber, cathode chamber, and electrolyte solution. Sir William Grove designed the first fuel cell in 1839 with hydrogen fuel at the positive terminal and oxygen at the negative terminal. Sulfuric acid served as the electrolyte, the solution in which the electrochemical reaction took place.

The electrolysis of water as demonstrated in the basic study of chemistry, provides an example of the reverse fuel cell operation. In an electrolysis reaction a dc electric current is passed through water made conductive by the addition of a small amount of acid or chemical salt. The current decomposes the water into hydrogen and oxygen, which bubble up about the electrodes. The fuel cell combines hydrogen and oxygen in the presence of the electrolyte, producing electric current and, as a by-product, water.

The main difference between a fuel cell and an ordinary dry cell (flashlight battery) or storage cell (auto battery) is that in the fuel cell, the fuel is continuously supplied and not limited by the amount supplied at manufacture or which can be stored by charging. The advantages of a fuel cell over other energy sources are its large energy output per pound of weight and its reliability and long life. Some of the disadvantages are the high cost of pure hydrogen and oxygen, and the necessity for storage and supply of these fuels. Other less expensive fuels have been considered but are less efficient and may produce waste products which limit cell life. A promising compromise is the use of air rather than oxygen, and common fuels, such as coal or kerosene, which are first converted to hydrogen by a preliminary chemical reaction.

Fuel cells have been used in space vehicles and experimental electric automobiles because of their high power and low weight. The water which is generally considered as a by-product in a fuel cell reaction can be used to supplement the water supply on a long duration space mission. Their reliability and long life have made fuel cells valuable for use in remote communication relay stations.

MARTIN L. SHOOMAN,
Polytechnic Institute of Brooklyn

See also POWER PLANT.

FUEL-INJECTION SYSTEM, for diesel or gasoline engine, measures the correct amount of fuel required by the engine and injects this amount in a spray pattern at the proper time and place in the engine cycle.

In a diesel engine, fuel is injected directly into the cylinder toward the end of the compression stroke. Because of the high compression ratio, the air within the cylinder is so hot that the injected fuel ignites very shortly after it enters the cylinder and a spark plug is not needed. A fuel-injection pressure of several thousand lb. per square inch is not uncommon and small piston-type pumps usually are used to produce the required pressure.

In a gasoline engine, a fuel-injection system can replace the carburetor. The fuel is sprayed directly into the engine cylinders as in the diesel engine, or it may be sprayed into the intake manifold. A spark is then used to ignite the fuel-air mixture in the cylinder. The fuel is injected during the air intake stroke, as this allows time for the mixing of fuel with air to form the proper combustion mixture. Because the fuel is not pumped into the cylinder against full compression pressure, as it is in the diesel system, much lower pressures are needed—less than 100 lb. per square inch is sufficient.

WILLARD L. ROGERS, University of Arizona

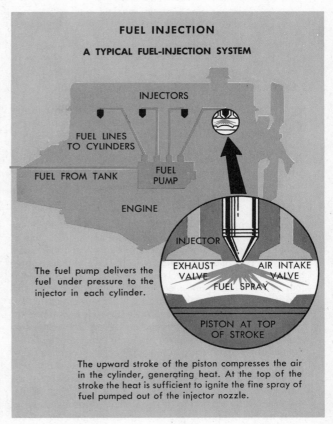

FUEL INJECTION

A TYPICAL FUEL-INJECTION SYSTEM

INJECTORS

FUEL LINES TO CYLINDERS

FUEL FROM TANK

FUEL PUMP

ENGINE

The fuel pump delivers the fuel under pressure to the injector in each cylinder.

INJECTOR

EXHAUST VALVE

AIR INTAKE VALVE

FUEL SPRAY

PISTON AT TOP OF STROKE

The upward stroke of the piston compresses the air in the cylinder, generating heat. At the top of the stroke the heat is sufficient to ignite the fine spray of fuel pumped out of the injector nozzle.

FUGGER [fŏŏg'ər], German family of merchant princes during the Renaissance. The family may be traced to JOHANN FUGGER, a weaver, who lived near Augsburg in the 14th century. His descendants built up the family fortune by trading and banking. Under JAKOB FUGGER (1459–1525), called "the Rich," family wealth increased markedly through the acquisition of silver mines in the Tyrol and copper mines in Hungary, and through trading monopolies. Large sums were loaned to Holy Roman Emperor

Maximilian I, and in 1519 Jakob financed the election of Charles V as Emperor. Under RAIMUND FUGGER (1489–1535) and ANTON FUGGER (1493–1560), the family fortune and power reached a peak. With the help of the Emperor, the family extended its operations to the New World. At this time, the total wealth of the Fuggers was estimated at 63,000,000 gold florins. Their power gradually declined when the Habsburg emperors and kings of Spain were unable to redeem their enormous debts to the family. The Fuggers were great art patrons and collectors of valuable manuscripts. Letters addressed to the family by Fugger agents are important historical sources.

Consult Ehrenberg, Richard, *Capital and Finance in the Age of the Renaissance* (1928).

ISTVAN DEAK, Columbia University

FUGITIVES, THE, group of poets and critics who published *The Fugitive*, a little magazine which appeared bimonthly (1922–25) in Nashville, Tenn. The group consisted chiefly of Vanderbilt University students and young faculty members, and the magazine largely published their own poetry and criticism. It produced a distinctive modern poetry and a vigorous criticism. Members of the group who went on to achieve honor as critics, poets, and novelists included Allen Tate, Donald Davidson, John Crowe Ransom, and Robert Penn Warren. Because four "Fugitives" were later leaders in Southern agrarianism, the group is often and improperly linked with agrarianism.

FUGITIVE SLAVE LAWS, in American history, acts of Congress passed in 1793 and 1850 providing for the return of escaped slaves. The North not only ignored the 1793 law, but developed the Underground Railroad to help fugitives reach Canada in violation of it. As part of the Compromise of 1850, a stronger law was passed enjoining the public to co-operate in enforcement measures and requiring that captured runaways be brought before a federal court without the usual constitutional safeguards. The law aroused bitter opposition in the North. Most Northern states passed personal liberty laws in defiance, and the Fugitive Slave Law was finally repealed by Congress on June 28, 1864.

See also SLAVERY IN THE UNITED STATES.

FUGUE [*fūg*], musical form in which a principal subject, or theme, is developed in a contrapuntal texture of two or more independent melodies ("voices"). The fugue is the most systematic and highly developed of the contrapuntal forms of music.

In general terms the formal design of a fugue consists first of an exposition, which introduces the principal subject in each of the voice parts successively. These initial statements are made alternately at the tonic and dominant (the two harmonic centers of gravity that define a key). The exposition is followed by a development, in which the subject is led through a series of related keys, appearing now in one voice, now in another (always in new contrapuntal contexts), and undergoing various modifications of shape and character. The successive statements of the subject in the development are generally separated by modulating episodes of lighter texture; here motives from the subject are combined in continually changing patterns of

contrapuntal imitation. The final statement of the subject at the tonic re-establishes the principal key of the fugue.

The term *fuga*, literally "flight" (of one voice after another), appeared as early as the 14th century and continued thereafter to refer to an imitative contrapuntal style. However, the systematic development of a specifically fugal form and style did not take place until the second half of the 17th century, reaching its culmination in the works of J. S. Bach, the undisputed master of fugue. In the great organ fugues, those of *The Well-tempered Clavier* and of *The Art of Fugue*, and in the great choral fugues of the cantatas, motets, and masses, Bach virtually exhausted the possibilities of fugue as a compositional procedure.

After the Baroque the fugal principle fell into relative disfavor as composers turned their constructive imagination to the possibilities of the sonata form. Nevertheless, both Haydn and Mozart occasionally returned to fugal forms, especially in their choral works. In his late quartets and the *Missa Solemnis* Beethoven produced fugues of great breadth and dramatic power.

The purely musical architecture of fugue found little favor with the lyrical temperament of romantic composers and was ill suited to the programmatic realism of later 19th-century music. The neoclassic movement of the 20th century, however, with its aversion to both the subjective emotionality and the descriptive realism of the romantics, and with its zeal for pure, abstract (absolute) music, found in the fugue an ideal vehicle for pure speculation in tones. In the works of Max Reger, Ferruccio Busoni, and especially Paul Hindemith it achieved its greatest redevelopment.

The term *fugato* refers to those fugal expositions of themes that occur as sections of larger movements. It is one of the many means of developing thematic material.

Consult Oldroyd, George, *The Technique and Spirit of Fugue: An Historical Study* (1948); Dickinson, A. E. F., *Bach's Fugal Works* (1956); Adrio, Adam, *The Fugue* (1961).

WILLIAM KIMMEL, Hunter College

See also BACH, JOHANN SEBASTIAN; CANON; COUNTERPOINT; HARMONY; POLYPHONY.

FUGUE, in psychiatry, an episode of abnormal behavior marked by aimless wandering and possibly confusion, agitation, and amnesia. The fugue is considered to be a form of dissociation—the tendency to detach portions of the mental life from the main stream of the personality. It usually develops from a desire to escape from an intolerable situation. In short fugues the patient may be highly emotional and disoriented. In long fugues he may travel far from his normal surroundings, and appear normal in all respects. Upon emerging from the fugue the patient may have amnesia for the period of the fugue or for his entire past life.

FUJI, MOUNT, also called Fujiyama, the highest mountain of Japan (elev., 12,389 ft.), located about 70 mi. west-southwest of Tokyo. Mount Fuji is a dormant volcano of Tertiary origin; it last erupted in 1707. A number of resorts are situated at its base, which measures 65 mi. in circumference. As a sacred mountain of Shintoism, it is a place of pilgrimage. Until 1868 no woman was allowed to make the ascent to its peak. Snow-capped and standing alone, it is a favorite subject of Japanese artists. The area is now a part of Fuji-Hakone National Park.

FUJINOMIYA [foo-je-nō-mī-yä], city of Shizuoka Prefecture, Honshu, Japan. It is the starting point for one of the climbing routes for Mount Fuji, and the site of a 16th-century shrine. Pop., 79,645.

FUJISAWA [foo-jē-sä-wä], city of Kanagawa Prefecture, southern Honshu, Japan. A resort center with bathing beaches on Sagami Bay, it is near beautiful Enoshima Island. Fujisawa is the site of an ancient and historic Buddhist temple. Pop., 124,601.

FUJIWARA [foo-jē-wä-rä] **CLAN,** the first aristocratic family of Japan. It is second in importance to the imperial house and can trace its origin to the beginning of the nation. Its prominence in Japanese history dates back to Nakatomi no Kamatari, who rendered invaluable service to the ruling house by helping to initiate and launch the Reforms of Taika in 645 A.D. He removed the Soga family, which posed a great threat to the security of the imperial family, and in gratitude Emperor Tenchi conferred on Kamatari the family name of Fujiwara. Intimate relations thus established with the ruling house were strengthened further by marital ties begun under Kamatari's son, Fuhito. The fortunes and power of the clan continued to grow until they reached their zenith under Michinaga in the first half of the 11th century. The peak of Fujiwara supremacy was insured by having five daughters become imperial consorts, and by the clan's monopoly of power, its members holding important positions at court. The imperial house was controlled, manipulated, and completely overshadowed by the clan. In the late 11th century its power declined as local magnates in the outlying areas acquired military power and began to challenge it. Fujiwara authority finally was destroyed by feudalism in the late 12th century.

CHITOSHI YANAGA, Yale University

FUKIEN [foo-kyěn'], coastal province of southeast China, across the Taiwan Strait from the island of Taiwan (Formosa), bounded on the north by Chekiang, the west by Kiangsi, and the southwest by Kwangtung. The surface of the province is quite hilly and mountainous, dominated by the Wuyi range which runs along the western border. Level land is limited to small coastal delta plains and a few valleys. The indented coast line offers sites for good natural harbors. The major rivers, the Min and the Chiulung Chiang, all drain eastward from the western highland toward the sea. Fukien has a subtropical climate, almost frost-free throughout the year, and the typhoons of late summer are often hazardous.

The major agricultural subsistence products are rice, corn, peanuts, rape seed, tobacco, and sugar cane. The tea of Fukien, Wuyi tea, is an important product as well as being world famous. Fishing and lumber industries also contribute to the economy of the province. Coal, iron of high quality, alum, copper, and salt are major mineral products. Fukien is also well known for its lacquer-work industry. The province is administratively divided into five

shih ("municipalities"), five chuan-ch'ü ("special districts"), and 62 hsien ("counties"). The principal cities are Foochow, the capital, and Amoy, the chief industrial city and port. Area, 47,529 sq. mi.; pop., 13,143,000.

CHARLES Y. HU, University of Maryland

FUKUI [foo-koo-ē], city of Honshu, Japan, and capital of Fukui Prefecture. An ancient and well-known silk textile center producing a special, thin silk, habutae, Fukui also produces rayon, processes food, and manufactures soy sauce. In 1948 the city suffered a severe earthquake and has been largely rebuilt as a modern city. Pop., 149,823.

FUKUOKA [foo-koo-ō-kä], capital of Fukuoka Prefecture, Kyushu, Japan. It is the second-largest city of Kyushu and an important commercial, administrative, cultural, and political center. Located on the island's west coast, it is part of a twin city area divided into two sections by the Naka River, with Hakata on the east bank and Fukuoka on the west. Formerly a castle town, Fukuoka is the administrative and business center, while Hakata is the shopping and amusement center. Although Fukuoka is not primarily an industrial city, it does produce expensive silks and cottons, chemicals, machinery, and the world-famous Hakata dolls. The city is the site of Kyushu University and other institutions of higher learning.

Fukuoka figured prominently in early contacts between the Asian mainland and Japan. The Mongols attempted two invasions of Japan during the 13th century in this area. After successfully repelling the first invasion in 1274, the Japanese built a 10-ft.-high wall along the coast. When the Mongols launched their second attack in 1281 they were unable to get over the wall and a typhoon finally destroyed their fleet. A monument commemorating this event can be seen in East Park, and relics are preserved in the Hakozaki Hachiman Shrine. Pop., 647,122.

ROBERT B. HALL, JR., University of Rochester

FUKUSHIMA [foo-koo-shē-mä], city of Honshu, Japan, and capital of Fukushima Prefecture. It is a major commercial center of northeastern Japan, manufacturing machinery and textiles. The surrounding area specializes in the production of vegetables and fruits. Pop., 138,961.

FUKUYAMA [foo-koo-yä-mä], city of Hiroshima Prefecture, Honshu, Japan. A port on the Ashida River, it manufactures textiles, machine tools, chemicals, rubber goods, and reed matting. The ruins of the 17th-century Fukuyama Castle make this an important historic site of the Inland Sea area. Pop., 140,603.

FUKUZAWA [foo-koo-zä-wä], **YUKICHI** (1834–1901), Japanese educator and publicist, and founder of Keio Gijuku, originally a school for Dutch studies in Edo that eventually became Keio University. In 1860 Fukuzawa was a member of the Japanese mission sent to Washington to exchange ratifications of the commercial treaty negotiated by Townsend Harris in 1858. He visited the West three times and was profoundly influenced by English utilitarianism. In order to disseminate Western ideas and methods, he founded the newspaper Jiji Shimpo, and his prodigious writings made him the leading publicist of his time. His works made the nation aware of the urgency to modernize itself in order to cope with the new era of progress already established in the West.

Consult Backer, C., *Japanese Enlightenment* (1964); Fukuzawa, Yukichi, *Autobiography*, tr. by E. Kiyook (1966).

FULANI [foo-lä'nē], western Sudanic peoples, numbering more than 5,000,000 persons, living in widely scattered groups. Some are nomadic cattle herders, organized in small independent bands led by headmen. Others are sedentary farming peoples, living in larger groups traditionally characterized by continuous warfare, a class society ranging from royalty to slaves, and cities that were important governmental, craft, and trade centers. Whereas nomadic Fulani are both pagan and Muslim, the settled groups are heavily Islamized.
See also AFRICA: *African Peoples* (MAP).

FULBERT [fül-bâr'], **ST.** (c.960–1028), Bishop of Chartres. Born in Italy. He was educated in a cathedral school and later became chancellor of the school in Chartres. In 1006 he became Bishop, and through his efforts Chartres became one of the most famous schools of Europe. He taught that the intellect is the discusser and judge of universals, not their institutor. He rebuilt the Cathedral of Chartres after the fire of 1020.

FULBRIGHT, JAMES WILLIAM (1905–), U.S. Senator, born in Sumner, Mo. He was educated at the University of Arkansas and became a Rhodes scholar at Oxford. He received (1934) an LL.B. at George Washington University and served as a Department of Justice attorney until he became a professor of law (1936) at the University of Arkansas, and then its president (1939). He was elected a Democratic member of the House of Representatives in 1942. There and in the Senate, beginning in 1945, he was a liberal internationalist, noted especially for the Fulbright Act (1946). A delegate to the U.N. General Assembly (1954), he became chairman of the Senate Foreign Relations Committee in 1959. A persistent critic of U.S. foreign policy in the 1960's, he led the Senate opposition to U.S. military involvement in Indochina during both the Johnson and Nixon administrations. He was defeated for reelection in the 1974 primary.

FULBRIGHT FELLOWSHIPS. Under Public Law 584, 79th Congress (Fulbright Act, 1946), U.S. citizens may receive grants to lecture or study abroad. To qualify, an applicant must be a citizen, have a bachelor's degree or its equivalent, and know the language of the country in which he wants to study. Scholastic and personal achievement, value of the proposed project, and veteran's status influence selection. The Board of Foreign Scholarships, appointed by the President, must approve all grants. Awards are made in the currency of the country in which the work will be done, and they cover round-trip transportation, tuition, maintenance, and other costs. Grants are usually for one academic year. Grants are also provided for scholars from other lands who wish to carry on teaching or research in the United States.

ROBERT D. HARTMAN
See also EDUCATION: *International Exchange Programs.*

FULCRUM. *See* LEVER.

FULDA [fool'dä], town of southern central Federal Republic of Germany (West Germany), 53 mi (85 km) northeast of Frankfurt am Main. The 18th-century baroque cathedral occupies the site of the Benedictine Abbey of Fulda, founded in 744 by St. Sturmius, a disciple of St. Boniface. In 968 the Abbot of Fulda was made the Primate of all Benedictine abbeys in Germany and France. The abbey became a famous center of learning, and because St. Boniface was buried there, a center of devotion and pilgrimage. In 1802 the abbey was secularized and the monks dispersed. The city is now the site of a U.S. Army post and has light manufacturing.

FULLER, ALFRED CARL (1885–1973), American merchant, born in Welsford, Nova Scotia. Fuller began (1903) working at odd jobs in Boston, Mass. After he had bought brushes at wholesale and sold them at retail door-to-door, he became convinced of the potential in home sales and founded (1906) the Fuller Brush Company. It grew into a multimillion dollar concern that, at his death, had about 25,000 salesmen calling door-to-door in Canada, the United States, and Mexico.

FULLER, (SARAH) MARGARET (1810–50), American writer and social reformer. Born in Cambridgeport, Mass., and educated at home, she became a prodigy of learning. She assisted Bronson Alcott in educational experiments, conducted cultural "conversations," edited America's first little magazine, the *Dial* (1840–42), and was literary editor of Horace Greeley's New York *Tribune* (1844–46). Her *Woman in the Nineteenth Century* (1845) was the first mature consideration of feminism and her *Papers on Literature and Art* (1846) the first volume of distinguished literary criticism in the United States. While she was European correspondent of the *Tribune*, she composed papers (posthumously collected) and married Giovanni Angelo, Marquis Ossoli. She was drowned on her return trip to America when her ship was wrecked off the Long Island coast. Her *Memoirs* (1852) were prepared by Emerson and other literary friends.

FULLER, MELVILLE WESTON (1833–1910), American jurist. Born in Augusta, Maine, Fuller graduated from Bowdoin College (1853), studied law for one year at Harvard, and then moved to Chicago. There he became a prominent attorney and Democratic politician. When Morrison R. Waite died in 1888, President Grover Cleveland appointed Fuller Chief Justice of the United States. In that post (1888–1910), Fuller followed the strictest interpretation of the Constitution, strongly opposed federal power over state governments, and supported traditional civil liberties. Fuller also served (1900–10) on the Permanent Court of Arbitration at the Hague.
Consult King, W. L., *Melville Weston Fuller* (1950).

FULLER, RICHARD BUCKMINSTER (1895–), American engineer, architect, and inventor, born in Milton, Mass. Fuller in 1927 invented the Dymaxion house, whose hexagonal glass-enclosed living quarters on the second floor were suspended from the top of a central tripod that also provided means of access to that area. This highly original idea has not been generally accepted. Other inventions of Fuller are the three-wheeled Dymaxion car, a distortion-free map, and the geodesic dome (q.v.). The last has excited great interest among contemporary builders.

FULLER'S EARTH, earthy or clayey material that removes coloring agents from oils and fats during filtration. The term is applied to any industrially useful bleaching clay or silt without regard to its mineralogical and chemical composition. In England the term is used also as a geologic name for certain beds of clay.

FULLERTON, city of southern California, a residential suburb 20 mi. southeast of Los Angeles. Inc., 1904; pop., 85,826.

FULTON, ROBERT (1765–1815), American inventor, engineer, and artist. Throughout his lifetime Fulton's mechanical and artistic talents blended harmoniously to make a remarkably creative man. He was a successful portrait painter and inventor of many time-and labor-saving machines. He is best known for the *Clermont,* the first commercially successful steamboat.

Fulton was born on a farm in Lancaster County, Pa. and brought up by his widowed mother. Although he was not much of a student, his artistic and inventive talents were evident at an early age. To help support his family, he drew original designs for ornamenting rifles sold in the village arsenal during the Revolutionary War.

At 17, Fulton went to Philadelphia to pursue a career in art. He apprenticed himself to a jeweler, while making a name for himself as a portrait painter. Among his patrons was Benjamin Franklin, who advised him to study in England, and gave him a letter of introduction to Benjamin West, one of the most prominent American painters of the time. At 21, Fulton went abroad, where he remained for the next 20 years. He was personable,

The Bettmann Archive

A self-portrait of Robert Fulton beneath a copy of plans used in the construction of his steamboat which in 1803 was navigated on the Seine River in France.

Brown Brothers

handsome, and talented, and had no difficulty supporting himself as an artist, but his restless interest in invention continued. By 1793 Fulton decided to devote his full attention to invention, while painting only for enjoyment.

Foremost in his mind were ways in which travel could be facilitated. At this time, virtually all inland water transportation went one way—downstream. Man-made canals were one solution. Fulton invented a machine for cutting the hard stone needed for canal piers and locks, and machines for making the ropes by which canalboats were pulled. He also devised a system of inclined planes to replace locks, a dredging cart, a system of cast-iron bridges and aqueducts, and many types of canalboats.

During the wars that accompanied the French Revolution, Fulton, now in England, turned his attention to submarine warfare with torpedoes and underwater mines. His experimental submarines were able to surface and dive. While displaying one of his underwater boats in France, he successfully blew up a test craft in the Seine River. Neither Napoleon, nor the British Admiralty, to whom Fulton offered his submarines, were sufficiently impressed to grant him funds for further experiment.

In 1802 Fulton turned all his great energy to designing a steamboat. Most Americans whom he consulted were skeptical. The heavy steam engines of the day were considered practical only for driving water pumps in mines. Yet, as early as 1786, John Fitch had operated a steamboat on the Delaware River, though his enterprise failed for lack of funds. Fulton's first experiments were made in France. A boat launched in Paris in 1803 sank under the tremendous weight of its engine's iron.

Fulton then joined in a partnership with Robert Livingston, an American scientist appointed minister to France. Fulton supplied the ideas and Livingston the badly needed money. In the hope of future profits, Livingston arranged for a monopoly over the operation of all future steamboats in New York State. Such monopoly contracts were often granted by state legislatures of the day to encourage the undertaking of expensive and risky ventures. Fulton and Livingston returned to the United States in 1806. Conservative Americans laughed at Fulton, calling his proposed steamboat "Fulton's Folly." The laughter stopped when Fulton's *Clermont* made a spectacular trip under steam power up the Hudson River from New York City to Albany. Further improvements soon made the boat reliable enough to provide regular passenger service on the Hudson. Within four years, a steamboat had been constructed at Pittsburgh, Pa., capable of steaming down the Ohio and Mississippi rivers and back.

Fulton's courage and genius were directly responsible for the great "age of the steamboat" that contributed so much to opening the American West. Fulton continued to direct the construction of many of the boats himself, experimenting with ferryboats, torpedo boats, and a steam gunboat. The gunboat was intended for the defense of New York harbor during the War of 1812. Fulton's enterprises brought him great wealth, and not until nine years after his death did the United States end the Livingston steamboat monopoly in New York, in a decision by which "navigation was made free."

CHARLES AND LINDA FORCEY,
State University of N.Y. at Binghamton

FULTON, city of central Missouri, and seat of Callaway County. It is a trade center for an agricultural region. William Woods College and Westminster College are in the city. Fulton, founded in 1825, was named after the American inventor of the steamboat, Robert Fulton. Pop., 12,248.

FULTON, city of north-central New York, on the Oswego River and the New York State Barge Canal. Fulton manufactures include felt, paper products, frozen vegetables, and asphalt roofing. Inc. as village, 1835; as city, 1902; pop., 14,003.

FUMAROLE [fū'mə-rōl], opening where hot gases (fumes) issue from the earth. Fumaroles are found near active volcanoes and in areas of recent volcanism. The gases, from cooling igneous rock within the earth, include steam, hydrogen sulfide, oxides of sulfur and carbon, and hydrochloric and hydrofluoric acid. Deposits of sulfur, sodium and potassium chlorides, and various metals and metallic minerals form around the openings. Solfataras are fumaroles at which sulfurous gases predominate, mofettes those that mainly emit carbon dioxide. Sulfur has been mined from solfataras in Italy, New Zealand, and Mexico. *See also* GEYSER; VOLCANO.

FUMIGATION. *See* EXTERMINATION, HOUSEHOLD PEST.

FUMITORY [fū'mə-tôr-ē], common name for an annual plant, *Fumaria officinalis*, in the Fumariaceae, or fumitory family, native to Europe. The plants grow to a height of from 2 to 3 ft., have finely divided, fernlike leaves, and bear loose clusters of small, crimson-tipped purple flowers. Extracts of fumitory plants were once highly regarded as a remedy for scurvy and other ailments. Fumitory is propagated from seed and does well in ordinary garden soil.

FUNABASHI [foo-nä-bäsh-ē], city of Chiba Prefecture, Honshu, Japan, just east of Tokyo. It is a major fish-marketing center and manufactures wood products and other light consumer goods. It is also a resort area with race tracks, amusement centers, and hot springs. Pop., 135,038.

FUNAN [foo'nan], **KINGDOM OF,** first important kingdom in Southeast Asia. It existed for approximately 500 years, beginning in the middle of the 1st century A.D. The center of the kingdom was in the delta and lower reaches of the Mekong River, an area now divided between South Vietnam and Cambodia. During the 2d and 3d centuries Funan developed into an extensive empire, controlling most of modern Thailand and receiving tribute from a number of petty rulers in the Malay Peninsula. In the 6th century the vassal kingdom of Chen-la, located on the upper reaches of the Mekong, revolted against Funanese rule and, by the 7th century, converted Funan into a vassal state. From this succesful Chen-la revolt the Khmer empire and modern Cambodia developed.

According to Chinese accounts, Funan was founded by a refugee Indian prince, who married a local princess and conquered the inhabitants. True or not, it was an early center of Indian cultural influence, with Buddhism as the dominant religion and the whole pattern of government and society modeled upon Hindu examples. Funan, as did its successor states, paid tribute to China when it had to and carried on an extensive trade throughout its existence. The basis of its power, however, rested on an intensive system of irrigation agriculture.

ROBERT C. BONE, Florida State University

FUNCHAL [foon-shäl'], principal city of the Madeira Islands, located on the south coast of the largest island, Madeira. It is the third-largest city of Portugal, an important port of call for ships operating between Africa and Europe and North America, and a submarine-cable station. It exports famous Madeira wines, fruit, fish, and wickerwork. There is a late 15th-century cathedral here, but the city is best known for its beautiful hillside location and mild climate. Pop., 37,035.

FUNCTION, in mathematics, relation among variables. If two variables, x and y, are related by any means so that to each value of one a value of the other is determined, then the two values are said to be functionally related, and the second is said to be a function of the first. Functions originate in geometry; for example, the area of a circle is a function of the radius ($A = \pi r^2$); in algebra, an equation such as $3x - y = 2$ expresses a functional relation between x and y; and in physical science, the distance a body falls is a function of the time ($d = 16t^2$). If more than two variables are involved, one of them may be a function of the other two. Thus the area of a rectangle is a function of the length and the breadth.

The concept of a function is central in many branches of mathematics. The discoveries of men such as Galileo, Copernicus, and Kepler drew attention to relations among physical variables. The analytic geometry of Descartes furnished a graphic means of representing such relations, and the calculus of Newton contributed a powerful method of studying them. Applied mathematics is largely concerned with the study of functions that scientific investigations bring to light.

Functions are expressed by equations, graphs, tables of corresponding values, and verbal sentences. That y is a function of x is expressed by the symbolic equation $y = f(x)$. In this notation x is called the independent variable, f symbolizes the relationship, and y is often called the dependent variable although it may be a constant. For example, if $y = 2x^2$, then $f(x) = 2x^2$, f symbolizing the operations of squaring and multiplying by 2. If the independent variable, x, is assigned the value of 1, then $f(1) = 2 \cdot 1^2 = 2$.

HOLLIS R. COOLEY, New York University

FUNCTIONAL PSYCHOLOGY, school of psychology frequently considered to have been founded by John Dewey, though its development was actually the work of others as well, both before and after Dewey's first writing. It stressed the utility or function of mental activity and thus the adaptive nature of behavior. A functionalist was concerned with mental processes rather than with structure or content of the mind; he sought to explain the "why" of observed behavioral phenomena.

Historically, functionalism was a forerunner of behaviorism. It also provided an appropriate climate for Edward

L. Thorndike's law of effect, the principle that learning can be explained in terms of the effect of actions—those reactions that produce satisfying states are learned readily, whereas those that produce displeasing states are learned slowly or not at all. Functionalism was itself significantly influenced by evolutionary theory. In contemporary psychology such a school is no longer readily discernible; an interest in the "why" of behavior exists beyond the bounds of any school, and points of view in psychology differ largely on issues not specifically raised by functionalism.

LAWRENCE R. BOULTER, University of Illinois
See also BEHAVIORISM.

FUNDAMENTALISM, conservative Protestant theological movement based on belief in the verbal infallibility of the Bible. It developed in America in the late 19th century as a reaction against the theory of evolution and the historical study of the Bible (the Higher Criticism). Two of its outstanding leaders were William Jennings Bryan (1860–1925), a major figure in the attempt to prevent evolution from being taught in the public schools, and John Gresham Machen (1881–1937), of Princeton Theological Seminary, a rigorous opponent of Higher Criticism. The essential doctrines of the movement, in addition to Biblical infallibility, are the deity of Christ, the Virgin Birth, the Substitutionary Atonement, the bodily resurrection of believers, and the Second Coming of Christ. Fundamentalists hold these doctrines to be fundamental to Christian belief.

FUNDAMENTAL ORDERS OF CONNECTICUT, the frame of government adopted (Jan. 24, 1639) by the towns of Hartford, Windsor, and Wethersfield. It served as Connecticut's fundamental law for almost 200 years. Reflecting the social and political views of its chief authors, Thomas Hooker, Roger Ludlow, and John Haynes, the Fundamental Orders represents the first written codification of basic law in America. The Orders served the dual purpose of setting up a government separate from that of Massachusetts while expressing the desire of the Connecticut settlers for a defensive confederation with other New Englanders. Because the Orders explicitly established the principle of government by consent, some historians regard it as the first democratic constitution, in contrast, particularly, to the more oligarchic government of Massachusetts.

Indeed, Hooker and other leaders of the Connecticut settlements apparently did object to many governmental practices of the Bay Colony. Among these were the re-election of the same men each year as provincial assistants (Governor's councilors); the deliberate limitation of church membership (and therefore of those eligible to participate in government) to a minority of the population; and the absence of written law, permitting the magistrates extensive powers. Hooker regarded the government of Massachusetts as rule by men rather than by law. The Fundamental Orders purported to correct these defects. It provided for a Governor, assistants, and a legislature, or General Court, elected by the "inhabitants." No man could serve as Governor or assistant for two consecutive years, and neither the Governor nor the assistants had veto power over the General Court. The legislature could be adjourned only by a majority vote of all the members rather than by the Governor, as in Massachusetts. Actually, however, the Connecticut government differed little from that of Massachusetts. Both governments established Congregationalism as the official religion, and supported it by taxes; after 1642, moreover, heresy in Connecticut was punishable by death.

The authorities interpreted "inhabitants" to mean "freemen," and although there was no formal religious requirement for freemen, the legislature admitted to that status only church members. Moreover, the limited electorate chose the same men as Governor and assistants every alternate year, and within a few years after the Orders passed, assistants were allowed to veto legislation. Nevertheless, the Fundamental Orders did give emphasis to the principle of government by law and by consent.

RICHARD M. ABRAMS, University of California

FUNDY [fŭn'dē], **BAY OF,** an arm of the Atlantic Ocean, almost separating Nova Scotia from New Brunswick. About 50 mi. wide at its mouth, it narrows to the northeast and forks at Cape Chignecto. It probably originated as a river valley which was later submerged by the sea. Steep cliffs, some over 300 ft. high, wall the bay at Blomidon, Sharp, D'Or, Chignecto, and Enragé capes, and at Owl Head. In marked contrast are the Tantramar Marshes. The tidal fluctuation is great. On July 16–17, 1916, tidal ranges of over 53 ft. were measured at Burntcoat Head. On several rivers, notably the Petitcodiac, the rising tide advances as a wave, or bore. Near its mouth the St. John River flows through a gorge where the normal seaward rush of water is reversed by the rising tide. At Passamaquoddy Bay, Chignecto Bay, and Minas Basin the tides could be harnessed for power. The water is cold, causing frequent summer fogs, but St. John, a major Canadian east-coast port, remains ice-free all year.

JOHN E. WELSTED, Brandon University
See also NOVA SCOTIA (physical map).

At high tide the waters of the Bay of Fundy reverse the flow of the St. John River at Saint John, forming the Reversing Falls.
(NEW BRUNSWICK TRAVEL BUREAU)

FUNDY NATIONAL PARK, recreational area of New Brunswick, Canada. It is located on the Bay of Fundy, between Saint John and Moncton, and has diversified recreational facilities, including a heated salt-water swimming pool. Estab., 1948; opened, 1950; area, 80 sq. mi.

FUNERAL RITUALS AND CUSTOMS. All peoples have some conventional method or methods of disposing of the dead, usually one or more of the following: burial in single or mass graves in the earth; interment in mounds or tombs; burial at sea; exposure of the body on a scaffold out of the reach of animals (often with a later earth burial of the bones, called secondary burial); exposure to vultures; cremation; preservation of the body by mummification. Earth burial and cremation are most common in the modern world.

Funeral rites are associated with belief in spiritual beings and life after death. The purpose of the rites may be to honor the dead. Almost universally, the manner of burial varies with the wealth or social status of the deceased and for royal persons, great leaders, and chiefs receiving high honors. One barrow erected for a chief in prehistoric Britain, for example, was 300 ft. long. Another purpose of funeral procedures is to provide the dead with equipment considered to be needed in the other world. This has ranged from stone tools and weapons to food, treasure, chariots, horses, a whole ship (in the case of Viking chiefs), and retainers sacrificed at the grave. Various rites have been used to protect the living against ghosts of the departed, and one reason for honoring the dead person is to appease his spirit. Because ghosts are believed to try to return to the place of death, some peoples abandon a dwelling in which a death has occurred. The Eskimos remove a corpse through a hole made in the dwelling and later filled in, since the ghost is expected to try to come back by the way the body was taken out. If the body were taken out through the door, the ghost might return through the door.

Some customs observed in the United States, such as wearing black and going in procession to the funeral, were brought from England, where they survived from the Roman occupation of Britain. Mourning customs such as wailing or chanting dirges are found among both primitive and civilized peoples. Many religions have special rituals for funerals, and some have special prayers for the dead. Erecting a marker for a grave is not a universal custom but has been a common practice in the Western world and has been reported among Eskimos and other North American Indian groups, the Ainu of Japan, and some tribes of Southeast Asia.

WILSON D. WALLIS, Annhurst College

See also EXORCISM; MUMMIFICATION; RITES OF PASSAGE.

FUNGICIDES [fŭn'jə-sīdz], term for chemical compounds that destroy fungi or inhibit their growth. Fungicides that kill fungi are called eradicants; those that inhibit growth are called protectants. In common usage the term fungicide also includes compounds that are toxic to bacteria—bactericides.

Kinds of Fungicides

Sulfur Compounds. Until about 1940 the chief fungicides used in the control of plant diseases were compounds of copper and sulfur. "Pest-averting sulfur" was mentioned as long ago as 850 B.C. by Homer, making sulfur the longest-used fungicide. Sulfur was recommended specifically for powdery mildew in 1824. Lime-sulfur, a solution of calcium polysulfides, first tried as an eradicant spray for peach leaf curl in 1888, is still used as a dormant spray and occasionally as a summer protectant. As a protectant, however, sulfur is usually prepared as a wettable powder or as a dust with particles fine enough to pass through a 325-mesh screen. Sulfur effectively controls powdery mildews, rusts, apple scab, brown rot of stone fruits, rose black spot, and other plant diseases. It is compatible with most insecticides but should not be used shortly before or after oil sprays have been applied. It has a tendency to burn foliage in hot weather, above 85° F.

Copper Compounds. Copper, first mentioned in 1761 for the treatment of wheat seed, came into wide use after 1882 when the French botanist Alexis Millardet (1838–1902) reported that bordeaux mixture controlled downy mildew. This accidental discovery, which marked the real beginning of modern plant disease control, was made when it was noted that a poisonous-looking mixture of copper sulfate and lime, applied to grapes growing near the highway to Bordeaux, France, to discourage thieves, kept the vines free from disease. So-called fixed coppers are now available, somewhat more stable and less toxic to plants than bordeaux mixture. Copper sprays control many blights, leaf spots, and powdery as well as downy mildews. They cannot be used with lime-sulfur fungicides and are of questionable value when used with some organic compounds. Copper sprays may also injure sensitive plants if applied in cool, cloudy, or rainy weather.

Mercury Compounds. Mercury compounds function chiefly as eradicants. Mercuric chloride is used for the treatment of soil, seed, tubers, and with mercurous chloride (calomel) for brown patch and other turf diseases. Phenyl mercuries are used as early season eradicant sprays for apple scab and sycamore anthracnose.

Dinitro compounds are sometimes used as ground sprays to eradicate the apple scab fungus in overwintering leaves. Formaldehyde, perhaps the oldest organic fungicide, is strictly an eradicant and must not be used around living plants. It is used to treat soil for seed flats in order to prevent damping-off.

Synthetic Organic Fungicides. Synthetic organic fungicides are being used increasingly as protectant sprays and are rapidly replacing sulfur and copper fungicides. Most of them have been given coined names to replace their complex chemical names. The dithiocarbamates, first patented in 1934, include ferbam, a black iron compound used as a spray or dust for apple rust, grape black rot, anthracnoses, and downy but not powdery mildews; maneb, a manganese salt, effective for many vegetable diseases, rose black spot, and other leaf spots; zineb, a zinc salt used to control potato and tomato blight, azalea and camellia flower blights, snapdragon rust, and many other plant diseases; nabam, a liquid that forms a zinc salt on a plant when used with zinc sulfate; and ziram, another zinc spray or dust used chiefly in the control of vegetable diseases.

Thiram, a disulfide, is widely used as a seed protectant

(marketed as Arasan) and as a turf fungicide (marketed as Tersan). Chloranil, a benzoquinone, is a popular seed protectant and is sold under the name Spergon; dichlone, a naphthoquinone, is used for protectant spraying. One of the safest fungicides (for man) is captan, a phthalimide. It is widely used in disease control of fruits, vegetables, ornamentals, turf, and seed and bulb treatment. Captan does not control powdery mildews, but its analog, phaltan, is effective against them.

Karathane, a dinitro compound, is a specific in the control of powdery mildews. Glyodin, a liquid acetate that leaves no visible residue, is useful for cherry leaf spot and certain other diseases of fruit trees, and for rose black spot. Dodine, another acetate, is recommended for apple scab and is effective for rose black spot. Dodine is, however, somewhat toxic to plants. Dyrene is used to control fungus diseases of potatoes and tomatoes but is considered unsafe for ornamentals.

Antibiotic Fungicides. Antibiotics are substances produced by bacteria and fungi and are being increasingly used as fungicides. Streptomycin is an effective protectant spray for bacterial leaf spots, fire blight, and for downy mildews. Terramycin has proved useful for bacterial spot of peach. Cycloheximide (actidione in various formulations) is used for powdery mildews, certain leaf spots, for inhibiting spore development on cedar-rust galls, and for treating blister-rust cankers on pine.

Soil Fungicides. Pentachloronitrobenzene (marketed as PCNB or Terraclor) is a soil fungicide that is safe to use around living plants. It is used as a dust or liquid to control clubroot and diseases, such as azalea and camellia flower blights and crown rot, that start from sclerotia in the soil. Fumigants that are primarily insecticides or nematocides are sometimes used as soil fungicides. These include carbon bisulfide for mushroom root rots and chloropicrin, a tear gas, used to control various soil fungi.

How Fungicides Are Used

The equipment used to apply fungicides varies from small atomizers and pressurized bombs to large power sprayers that pump 20 or more gallons per minute; and from small plastic squeeze dusters to large power dusters. For home gardeners, midget rotary dusters and spray attachments for the garden hose are easy to use and relatively efficient. Also available for home gardeners, and marketed under innumerable trade names, are combination pesticides, which are compounded of one or more insecticides combined with one or more fungicides. According to law the label must list the amounts of all active ingredients and give the specific uses of the mixture, together with directions for proper dosage and precautions necessary for the safety of the user and the eventual consumer of the plant products. The manufacturer's instructions should be carefully studied before any commercial fungicide is used.

Consult Hough, W. S., and Mason, A. F., *Spraying, Dusting, and Fumigating of Plants* (1951); Frear, D. E. H., *Chemistry of Pesticides* (1955); Horsfall, J. G., *Principles of Fungicidal Action* (1956); *Pesticide Handbook*, ed. by D. E. H. Frear (rev. annually).

CYNTHIA WESTCOTT, Author, *Plant Disease Handbook*
See also PLANT DISEASES; SPRAYING.

FUNGUS [fŭng′gəs]. The word "fungus" is literally the Latin for mushroom. It is used to describe a member of the Fungi, a group of nongreen plants that lack true leaves, stems, and roots and do not produce flowers or seeds. The majority of fungi consist of microscopically small filaments called hyphae (sing., hypha). These filaments form the spreading, cottony mass (the mycelium) in addition to forming the well-defined structure of the mushroom, puffball, toadstool, and bracket fungus. The bacteria and slime molds, which in some ways resemble these true fungi, are thought by most botanists to be only distantly related to them.

The History and Importance of Fungi

Because the activities and many of the important structures of the fungi are difficult to observe without special techniques, especially skillful use of the microscope, and because the conspicuous fruiting bodies of the fungi appear very rapidly, many legends and superstitions have been associated with this group of organisms. Early botanists, prior to the invention and extensive use of the microscope, sometimes described fungi as the aborted fetuses of plants. A fungus growing on a tree was often thought to be a product of the tree rather than an organism with its own life cycle. Fungus growths on diseased plants were considered as symptoms of the disease rather than causes of it. The truffle, a fungus that grows underground, was once thought to be formed where lightning had struck the soil.

Felice Fontana (1730–1805), an Italian scientist, demonstrated in 1767 that rust on cereal grain plants was not the result of scorching caused by the focusing of solar rays by droplets of water on the leaves of the plants, but was instead caused by the attack of a microscopic plant—a fungus. Although the work of Fontana was overlooked for many years, new methods and concepts in the study of microorganisms in the 19th century gradually led to the replacement of mysticism and gross error by a rational approach to the fungi. In 1801 the Dutch botanist Christiaan Persoon (1762–1836) published the first comprehensive and reliable classification of fungi. In the mid-19th century the French botanists Louis and Charles Tulasne published magnificently illustrated works on the structures and life cycles of fungi. In 1864–66 the German botanist Anton De Bary (1831–88) produced a study of the physiology and structure of microorganisms which revolutionized many of the then current concepts of the nature of the fungi. The works of these and other investigators not only produced studies which are themselves classics but also stimulated the activity of many others.

The importance of fungi to humans is greatly underestimated by those who are not thoroughly acquainted with them. Leavened bread, alcoholic beverages, many cheeses, and many organic chemicals and antibiotics depend on the activities of fungi. The decay of organic debris in the soil and the destructive rotting of fabric, food, and leather are often partially or wholly the result of fungus action. Most of the known plant diseases and some animal diseases are caused by fungi. Mushrooms as flavorful additions to the diet are widely appreciated. Some mushrooms are of considerable interest as sources of drugs which cause hallucinations and related mental aberrations. Geneticists and biochemists have utilized fungi extensively as adaptable, cheap, and easily grown laboratory "tools."

Compared to other groups of living organisms, the fungi are more abundant and more widespread. However, no comprehensive studies on the distribution of fungi have been made. The available data indicate that species of fungi tend to be more widely distributed than are species of higher plants.

The Physiology of Fungi

Fungi contain no chlorophyll and therefore do not carry out the basic food-producing process, photosynthesis, characteristic of green plants. Food materials for the fungi must come from outside organic sources, that is, from the living or dead tissues of other organisms.

The hypha is not only the basic unit of structure of the fungi, it is the basic food-getting device. When hyphae permeate the tissues of another organism, the food materials which they encounter are generally in the form of molecules too large to pass through the hyphal walls. The hyphal cells secrete digestive enzymes which dissolve these foods and enable their absorption by the fungus. The action of these secretions is a partial cause of the injury to or decay of the invaded tissue.

Fungi that obtain food from living plants and animals are parasites and disease-causers. Those that obtain their food from dead organic matter are saprophytes, or saprobes, and cause rot or decay. Some fungi are highly restricted in the sources from which they can obtain food; for example, certain fungi grow only on a single portion of the wing of a single species of beetle. Other fungi can utilize a wide variety of organic sources for food.

The Life Cycle of Fungi. Reproduction in the fungi is both sexual and asexual. In sexual reproduction two hyphae come together and their nuclei fuse. When fusion of two nuclei takes place, the result is a single nucleus containing twice the amount of hereditary materials (a diploid number of chromosomes) present in either of the two nuclei prior to fusion. This double nucleus occupies only a brief period of the life cycle. Nuclei with the single (a haploid number of chromosomes) rather than the double amount of hereditary material are present during most of the life cycle of fungi. The reverse of this situation is true of most animals and the higher plants.

The diploid nucleus soon divides in such a way that the products of nuclear division again have a haploid number of chromosomes. Subsequently the spore, the characteristic reproductive structure of the fungi, is formed. Spores are formed in several ways and are enclosed in many different kinds of fruiting bodies prior to their release. When the fruiting body, such as the cap of a mushroom, is mature, the spores, each consisting of a single, tiny cell, are released in enormous numbers and are blown about by the wind. The great majority of such spores eventually die. Those few that land on a suitable source of nutrition may begin to form new hyphae that can grow and branch and, perhaps with the hyphae of other spores of the same species, form a new mycelium. There is no embryo in a fungus spore as there is in the seeds of higher plants.

All fungi can reproduce asexually. This may be simply

CLASS PHYCOMYCETES (Algalike Fungi)

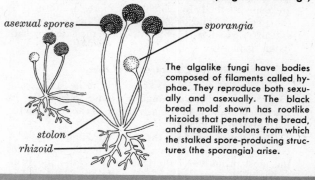

asexual spores — sporangia

stolon

rhizoid

The algalike fungi have bodies composed of filaments called hyphae. They reproduce both sexually and asexually. The black bread mold shown has rootlike rhizoids that penetrate the bread, and threadlike stolons from which the stalked spore-producing structures (the sporangia) arise.

CLASS ASCOMYCETES (Sac Fungi)

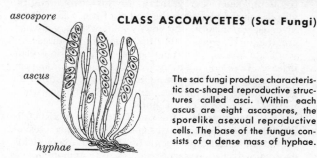

ascospore

ascus

hyphae

The sac fungi produce characteristic sac-shaped reproductive structures called asci. Within each ascus are eight ascospores, the sporelike asexual reproductive cells. The base of the fungus consists of a dense mass of hyphae.

CLASS BASIDIOMYCETES (Basidium Fungi)

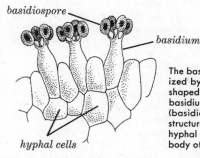

basidiospore

basidium

hyphal cells

The basidium fungi are characterized by the possession of a club-shaped reproductive structure, the basidium, on which four spores (basidiospores) develop. These structures arise from the mass of hyphal cells that form the main body of the fungus.

CLASS DEUTEROMYCETES (Imperfect Fungi)

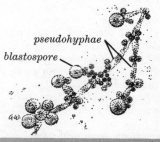

pseudohyphae

blastospore

The imperfect fungi are characterized by the fact that they have never been observed to reproduce sexually. The fungus shown produces asexual reproductive structures called blastospores. Its body mass is composed of filamentous pseudohyphae.

a breaking up of the mycelium with each fragment continuing growth and changes in form. Some fungi form spores asexually, that is, without fusion taking place. There are many methods by which such spores are formed. In some cases the ends of branch hyphae become rounded and are released and blown away, or in the case of aquatic fungi, swim away.

The Classification of Fungi

Mycologists, specialists in the study of the fungi, recognize four classes of true fungi, or Eumycophyta. The distinction is based mainly on structure of the reproductive parts and on life cycles.

Class Phycomycetes—The Algalike Fungi. This class consists of about 1,500 species including the water molds, the most primitive of the true fungi. Water molds are saprophytes or parasites of water plants and fish and are frequently seen as gray, fuzzy growths surrounding the gills or injured places on the bodies of fish. Class Phycomycetes also includes the downy mildews, among which are the molds responsible for damping-off disease of seedlings, late blight of potatoes, and other serious plant diseases. Common bread mold and its allies are also members of this class. The distinguishing characteristic of the algalike fungi is the possession of tubular hyphae which usually lack cross walls, or septa.

Class Ascomycetes—The Sac Fungi. From 25,000 to 30,000 species belong to this class. The ascomycetes are important as causative agents of disease in many plants, especially fruits; as severe though uncommon human pathogens; as producers of the drug ergot; and as flavoring agents in some cheeses. A few ascomycetes, particularly the morel and the truffle, are edible mushrooms. Yeast, the fungus which is probably of greatest importance to humans, is an ascomycete. The vast baking and alcoholic fermentation industries are dependent upon this fungus. *Penicillium*, although sometimes classed with the imperfect fungi, is a sac fungus well known as the producer of the earliest antibiotic drug, penicillin. Members of this class have hyphae which are septate, that is, divided into cells, each of which has a single nucleus. The sexually produced spores of ascomycetes are contained within club-shaped asci, or sacs.

Class Basidiomycetes—The Basidium Fungi. From 20,000 to 30,000 different fungi belong to this class. Among them are the well-known gill fungi, including the cultivated mushroom, the highly poisonous amanitas, most of the common wild toadstools and mushrooms, the puffballs, and the bracket and other pore fungi.

The basidiomycetes are mostly saprophytes and live on dead organic material such as wood, forest litter, dung, and the like. The decay process in these materials probably results largely from basidiomycete activity. Some members of this class live in conjunction with the roots of higher plants in a mutually advantageous relationship. Others are parasites on forest trees and garden crops, and two groups of this class, the rusts and the smuts of grains, are the most destructive of plant pathogens.

No special sex organs are produced by the basidiomycetes. The hyphae are septate and have one nucleus in each cell during one growth phase and two nuclei during another growth phase. The sexually produced spores are borne on short projections extending from the club-shaped basidium, the characteristic reproductive structure of basidiomycetes.

Class Deuteromycetes—The Imperfect Fungi. The 15,000 to 20,000 species in this class form the most heterogeneous group of the fungi. Deuteromycetes are fungi that either do not reproduce sexually or whose sexual reproduction has never been observed. When sexual reproduction of one of the species is observed, it is often reclassified and placed in the class and family indicated by its reproductive characteristics. For example, the genus *Penicillium* was at one time placed in the class of the imperfect fungi; however, since this fungus was observed to produce asci (the characteristic reproductive structures of sac fungi) under some conditions, it is therefore frequently classified among the sac fungi under the genus name *Eurotium*.

A number of plant diseases and diseases of stored fruits and vegetables are caused by imperfect fungi. Some deuteromycetes are human parasites and cause various skin diseases, such as athlete's foot, ringworm, and barber's itch, as well as respiratory diseases.

Consult Krieger, L. C., *The Mushroom Handbook* (1936); Thomas, W. S., *Fieldbook of Common Mushrooms* (1936); Wolf, F. A. and F. T., *The Fungi* (1947); Alexopoulos, C. J., *Introductory Mycology* (1952); Fuller, H. J., and Tippo, Oswald, *College Botany* (rev. ed., 1954).

LAWRENCE KAPLAN, Roosevelt University

See also:

AMANITA	MOREL
BEEFSTEAK FUNGUS	MUSHROOM
BOLETUS	MYCORRHIZA
BRACKET FUNGI	OYSTER MUSHROOM
BREAD MOLD	PARASOL MUSHROOM
CHANTERELLE	PUFFBALL
DESTROYING ANGEL	SLIME MOLDS
FAIRY RING	STINKHORN
FLY AGARIC OR FLY	TRUFFLE
AMANITA	WATER MOLD
INKY CAP	YEAST
LICHEN	

FUNK, CASIMIR (1884–1967), naturalized Polish-American biochemist who pioneered in the study of vitamins. He isolated a substance from rice polishings which effectively prevented beriberi. He named this substance "vitamine." It is now known as vitamin B_1, or thiamine. Following this discovery, Funk was invited to English, American, and Polish research institutes and universities. From 1928 to 1935 he owned a private pharmaceutical firm near Paris, which he gave up to become research consultant of the U.S. Vitamin Corporation of New York.

FUNK, ISAAC KAUFFMAN (1839–1912), American publisher, editor, and lexicographer, born in Clifton, Ohio. In 1877, with Adam Willis Wagnalls, he founded the publishing firm that in 1891 became Funk and Wagnalls Co. In 1890 Funk was founder and editor of *The Literary Digest*. He also was editor of *A Standard Dictionary of the English Language* (1890–93).

FUNSTON, FREDERICK (1865–1917), American Army officer. A Kansas farm boy, then botanist, then soldier of fortune, Funston fought for the Cuban rebels in 1896. Joining the U.S. Army in the war with Spain, he commanded a regiment in the Pacific but saw no action. He advanced to brigadier general on his outstanding record in the Philippine Insurrection (1899), and won a transfer (1901) to the regular army when, through a ruse, he captured the Filipino leader, Emilio Aguinaldo. As commander of the Department of California, he restored order (1906) after the San Francisco earthquake. He later led troops used in the Goldfield mining strike (1907–8). When the United States intervened (1914) in politically turbulent Mexico, Funston governed Vera Cruz. Promoted to major general, he held the border command while Gen. John Pershing pursued the insurrectionist, Pancho Villa, in Mexico.

FUR. The term "fur" is derived from the Old French words *forre* ("sheath") and *vair* ("red squirrel"). Fur may be defined as the skin of animals with the hair covering so preserved and prepared as to remain wearable without undue shedding. Fur may be used for an entire garment, as a garment lining, or for trimming purposes. The use of fur since ancient times has been established from the earliest records of mankind. Originally, fur was used for warmth-giving garments, for ceremonial purposes, as a mark of rank and distinction, and also as a covering for helmets and shields. In this last use, fur was preferred to smooth leather because a combination of various colors, especially of squirrel, lent itself to a variety of designs, resulting in the symbolic heraldic shields used by the nobility.

History. The Chinese have used furs for thousands of years. Their methods for preparing the skins have remained unchanged for centuries. The Assyrians, Greeks, and Romans made lavish use of furs. Herodotus mentions the practice, and the mythical hero Hercules used the skin of the Nemean lion as a garment. The legend of the Golden Fleece may well have been about an early fur-gathering expedition. Much earlier proof of the use of fur, however, appears in pictorial representations and preserved artifacts found in the caves of the Pyrenees between France and Spain. The cave dwellers of the Reindeer Age, following the last glacial period on the European continent, employed needles, fur scrapers, and other tools fashioned from reindeer bones to prepare and sew fur garments.

The use of fur in the early Middle Ages became so widespread that royal edicts were issued, forbidding its wear by the people. Fur thus became a mark of rank. To this day, royal coronation robes are made from or trimmed with ermine. Art galleries abound in portraits of men and women of the nobility and of official position wearing garments richly embellished with fur. During the Stuart period furs fell into disuse in England.

When Prince Rupert and his "honourable company of gentleman adventurers" founded the Hudson's Bay Company in northern Canada in 1670, British fur trading began to develop on a large scale. However, this merely followed upon French exploration and fur trading which began in Canada in the 16th century and continued in lively competition with the British trade for several centuries. The principal fur was beaver, then used chiefly for felt hats.

Early in the 19th century American fur-trading companies developed and expanded. Chief among these was the American Fur Company, controlled by John Jacob Astor of New York. The ever-widening activities of the fur companies played a vital role in opening vast regions of the Western Frontier of America.

Fur Trade. The principal fur-producing nations are the United States, the Soviet Union, Canada, Norway, Sweden, Denmark, Finland, and, to a lesser degree, China, Japan, Australia, New Zealand, Great Britain, France, Poland, southern and eastern Africa, Brazil, Argentina, Peru and Bolivia.

The principal United States furs are Alaska fur seal, beaver, chinchilla, fox, mink, muskrat, nutria, raccoon, and skunk. Canada raises beaver, chinchilla, fisher, fitch, fox, lynx, marten, mink, muskrat, white weasel, and wolf. From Soviet areas come broadtail, ermine, fox, kolinsky, lynx, marten, mink, muskrat, Persian lamb, sable, and squirrel. China supplies kidskin, caracul lamb, Asiatic mink, and dog. South America furnishes guanaco, jaguar, river otter, spotted cat, vicuna, and lamb (for processing into Lammoire). Eastern Africa is noted for leopard, southwestern Africa for Persian lamb. Australia and New Zealand furnish rabbit and sheepskin (for mouton-processed lamb). Europe raises fox, marmot, baum and stone marten, mink, mole, and squirrel.

The terms "prime" and "unprime," applied to fur, refer to the period of year in which the skin has been taken. Those taken before or after the winter are unprime and are not as lasting or substantial as those taken in the colder season, when the animal has a thick undercoat of short hairs. This terminology does not apply to skins from the tropics.

Originally, all furs were taken either by hunting or trapping. The trapping of skins from small fur bearers such as muskrat, mink, and skunk was for many years a profitable occupation of United States and Canadian farm and town boys. In Louisiana, muskrat and nutria trapping still is a substantial industry and large quantities of these skins are taken annually.

If it were not for fur conservation instituted by many governments, certain fur-bearing animals would have been long extinct. Pelagic sealing near the Pribilof Islands caused a steady shrinkage of the seal herds until a four-nation agreement was signed between the United States, Canada, Russia, and Japan, imposing strict controls on sealing. Similar controls are applied in the United States and Canada to beaver trapping.

Fur Farming. One reason for the United States' superiority in fur production is its long lead in ranch or farm breeding of furs. By far the chief fur farmed in the United States is mink; the annual crop amounts to about 6 million animals. Scientific breeding not only has curbed diseases and irregular nutrition to which the animals were subjected but, in the case of mink, has brought about the development of mutations in a vast range of colors from pure white to nearly black. Some of the more significant color phases are standard ranch (dark brown), pastel (medium brown), taupe, beige, silver-blue, and sapphire. Breeder associations keep members informed of constant improvements in technique as well as market developments. A growing industry is that of chinchilla farming,

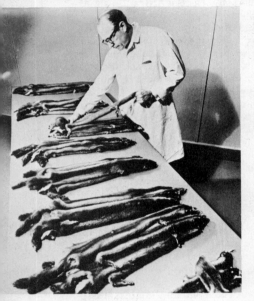

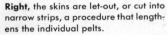

Above, at a fur auction, buyers bid for skins that have been graded into lots according to quality.
(FUR INFORMATION & FASHION COUNCIL)

MAKING A FUR COAT

Left, an expert grader groups skins into matched bundles.

Right, the skins are let-out, or cut into narrow strips, a procedure that lengthens the individual pelts.

while the ranching of fox and nutria is advancing into the mutation stage.

Marketing. As the fur trade has progressed from trapping of wild animals to raising fur bearers, so has the system of trading companies and collection agents gradually disappeared. In their place are highly organized marketing systems in which breeder associations ship members' pelts to auction houses on a co-operative basis. The crop year begins on Dec. 1, when pelt shipments start. In the case of mink, auctions are held at least once a month from December through June, and then periodically until the entire crop has been sold. Skin merchants and fur garment manufacturers purchase their supplies at auctions in New York, Minneapolis, Seattle, London, Oslo, Stockholm, Copenhagen, Helsinki, Leningrad, Leipzig, Winnipeg, Montreal, Edmonton, and Vancouver. Furs are shipped raw, in bales, to the auction company, where they are assorted and graded into lots according to color, texture, size, and quality. In the United States skins are auctioned either raw or dressed, while elsewhere they are sold only raw. Millions of dollars' worth of merchandise may be sold at a single day's auction. The closeness of the international markets is such that buyers often travel from country to country just for the sales. It is stated that even as the auctioneer's hammer descends in Stockholm, the price has already been transmitted to the New York market.

Processing. Skins purchased raw are sent to a dressing firm for cleaning and tanning, then, unless they are to be used in the natural colors, to a dyer. The art of fur dyeing is thousands of years old. The first commercially used fur dyes were mainly vegetable compounds. In the 17th century logwood and brazilwood came into use, followed by tannins, aniline, and oxidation colors and, finally, acid and other nonoxidizing dyes that are now in general use.

Important advances in methods of applying dyes have been made in recent years. Techniques used include immersion in vats and stenciling and tipping with a feather or brush. Although new dyes have been developed to withstand extremely long exposure without fading, some of the ancient dyes still are used for such furs as Persian lamb, broadtail, and fox. The modern dressing and dyeing processes defy comparison to primitive ways, but in principle many of the present-day mechanized processing methods are basically the same as those formerly performed by hand.

Manufacture. When skins return from dressing, dyeing, or both, they are ready to be made into garments. A large trade in skins exists in all principal cities where the furrier may buy pelts in assorted bundles ready for manufacturing. It has been the historic function of the skin merchant to assort the skins into bundles according to the needs of his individual customers. The sorting is done according to the quality and type of garment planned.

The manufacture of fur garments is still basically a hand craft. Skins require individual handling and, in effect,

After letting-out, the strips are sewn together, forming an elongated, supple skin.

Wetted skins are tacked to a board and dried in the exact shapes they will have in a coat.

every garment is almost entirely handmade. The manufacturer does this on a wholesale basis, usually specializing in a particular fur or garment. His distribution is chiefly through department and specialty stores. On the other hand, the retail furrier engages in what is primarily a custom business, making a garment to the customer's order.

Most retail establishments, including departments of large stores and custom furriers, combine the sale of ready-made garments with custom order work. They also offer such services as cleaning, repair, remodeling, and storage. The handling of fur storage has become a large part of almost every fur establishment's business.

Fur Labels and Names. The Fur Products Labeling Act of 1952 was designed to protect the American consumer by prohibiting any fur advertising that was misleading or contained false claims, including those relating to comparative prices. These regulations, and also regulations in force in other countries, further require that the true fur name appear in advertising as well as in garment hangtags. For example, Hudson seal is not true seal, but sheared and dyed muskrat, and therefore must be labeled "black-dyed sheared muskrat"; lapin is the French word for the fur that must be labeled rabbit.

The principal furs used by the fur industry are Alaska fur seal, American broadtail (Lammoire), badger, bassarisk (American ringtail), burunduki, beaver, Russian broadtail, caracul, cony (rabbit), ermine, fisher, fitch, fox, Indian lamb, jaguar, Japanese mink (weasel), kidskin, kolinsky, leopard, leopard cat, lynx, lynx cat, marmot, marten, mink, mole, monkey, mouton-processed lamb, muskrat, nutria, ocelot, opossum, otter, Persian lamb, pony, raccoon, sable, skunk, spotted cat, spotted skunk (wrongly called civet cat), squirrel, wallaby, weasel, wolf, wolverine, and wombat (koala).

Consult Bachrach, Max, *Fur* (rev. ed., 1946); Samet, Arthur, *Pictorial Encyclopedia of Furs* (rev. ed., 1950).

SANDY PARKER, Fur Editor, *The Women's Wear Daily*
See also FUR TRADE IN NORTH AMERICA.

FURFURAL [*fûr′fe-răl*], C_4H_3OCHO, known also as furfuraldehyde and fural, a colorless liquid of pleasant odor, important to organic synthesis and petroleum refining. First made in 1840 by distillation of bran, it is now made from farm wastes such as corncobs and straw. Preparation of furfural depends on removing the elements of water from certain plant sugars to give molecules having the furfural-ring structure. Furfural is an excellent gum solvent for purifying lubricating oil. It is also used to remove butadiene from a mixture of other gases so it can be used for synthetic rubber, and is important in the making of hexamethylenediamine, an ingredient of nylon.

FURIES, Roman name for the female spirits whom the Greeks called Erinyes or Eumenides (q.v.). The Roman term emphasizes the passion with which they pursued transgressors.

FURLONG, unit of length, theoretically the side of a square containing 10 acres. One furlong = ⅛ mi. = 40 rods = 220 yd. = 660 ft. = 201.17 meters. Its most common present-day usage is in the measurement of distance in horse racing.

FURNACE, enclosure designed for safe, convenient, and efficient burning of fuel for the production of usable heat. The heat is most commonly transferred to air or water, for the area-heating of buildings; to hot water for domestic or industrial use; or to steam for heating or power. The term "furnace" is also applied to enclosures in which heat is to be generated by means other than combustion, such as electricity (electric-arc furnace), or the sun's heat (solar furnace).

The more familiar combustion furnace consists of a steel or brick enclosure and two inlets—an air inlet to provide oxygen for combustion and a fuel inlet where gas or oil may be fed to the burner. (Coal and other solid fuels must be manually fed onto a grate.) There must also be an exit or escape outlet where the hot gases transfer their heat energy to the boiler or other heat exchanger. From the heat exchanger, the gases travel through the flue and up the chimney.

In its operation, the furnace receives air and fuel, and gives off hot gas (heat is the useful product) and ash. The need for putting in coal (stoking) and removing ash is eliminated in many modern furnaces by the use of fuel oil or gas. The liquid or gaseous fuel enters the furnace under pressure, through a jet, and burns immediately, as in the familiar gas stove.

Progress of the air, from its original entry to its exit at the flue, is called the draft system, and determines the rate of combustion. The draft system must assure enough air to attain complete combustion. The usual system of moving air through the furnace is the "natural draft," in which a tall chimney induces draft by convection. The column of hot gas in the chimney is lighter than the outside air; hence it rises, pulling fresh air into the furnace behind it. For very high rates of combustion, a "mechanical draft" is generated by blowers, either on the intake side ("forced draft"), or at the exit flue ("induced draft"). "Balanced draft" is a combination of natural and mechanical draft.

Furnaces are required in the smelting of ores and in the later melting and alloying of metals. For example, the blast furnace is a forced-draft furnace for the smelting of iron ore and the open hearth furnace is used in making steel.

Electric furnaces use the heating effect of an electric current, and have the advantages of high temperatures, accurate control, quick heating, and the absence of contaminating gases.

The solar furnace is a new laboratory instrument in which radiation from the sun is focused on a sample to be tested. It shares with the electric furnace the advantages of high temperature and lack of contamination, and also makes it possible to heat the sample in open air.

MAURICE BARRANGON, The American Society of
Mechanical Engineers

See also BLAST FURNACE; CUPOLA FURNACE; ELECTRO-METALLURGY; OPEN-HEARTH PROCESS; REGENERATIVE FURNACE.

FURNACE, BLAST. *See* BLAST FURNACE.

FURNITURE, movable equipment for domestic or public interiors. It is designed for personal use (beds, chairs, tables), or for storage (chests, cabinets). Usually of wood, furniture is also manufactured of metal and other materials, some of which make it suitable for outdoor use as well. From primitive forms furnished by nature—tree trunks for sitting, hollow trees for storage, forked branches for supports—the various articles of furniture have evolved in nonnomadic civilizations to accommodate stationary living habits and needs for comfort.

Antiquity

Present knowledge of early furniture is restricted by the perishable materials used and by the absence of pictorial representations up to the time of the Assyrians and Egyptians. Stone reliefs from the palaces of the former show ornate thrones, chairs, and tables with lion's legs. The Egyptians left not only extensive documentation in reliefs and wall paintings, but also actual pieces of furniture, preserved in tomb chambers by the dry climate. Simple low stools with plaited fiber seats seem to have been in common use, along with a prototype of the x-legged folding stool. Low couches, chairs, and armchairs were set on carved ox legs or lion's legs, their backs and sides decorated with carving that was painted in vivid colors. Small chests with hinged covers also were carved and painted.

Many of these basic forms reappear in Greek furniture, known mostly from vase paintings and funerary steles (stone slabs used as gravestones). Couches were higher and footstools were used to reach them. Small circular tables on lion's legs served as portable dining tables. The heavy, ornate chair called *thronos* was reserved for ceremonial use. Ordinary chairs were rather slender; one typical form had gracefully outward-curving legs and back posts.

In Rome, too, a lighter style developed side by side with a more monumental one. Carved in marble or cast in bronze, lion's legs, surmounted by heads and sometimes winged, formed supports for a variety of stands and tables, or, back to back, formed slabs, a pair of which carried a rectangular table top. Tripods, pedestal tables, and candelabra with squat animal legs were other typical pieces of Roman furniture, many of which have been found in the ruins of Pompeii and Herculaneum. Wood furniture was often veneered with precious exotic woods or with ivory and bone plaques, or inlaid with colored glass.

The Medieval Era

Late Roman and Byzantine chairs and chests retained much of this ornamentation, as is shown in medieval mosaics and illuminated manuscripts. In contrast to these ornamented pieces, ordinary domestic furniture was crude and utilitarian, with simple stools and benches serving for sitting, and chests for storage. Toward the end of the 12th century, with the diversification of society and an increasing urbanization, domestic as well as church furniture began to adapt itself to special purposes. In the monasteries, writing pulpits and lecterns were evolved; church choirs were equipped with elaborately wrought stalls and screens; and church vestiaries were furnished with chests and cupboards to hold vestments and liturgical vessels.

For their domestic interiors, both the nobility and the growing class of wealthy burghers demanded increasing variety and refinement. Chairs were still rare and reserved for the head of the family or the honored guest, but cushioned benches with high backs and armrests provided reasonable comfort. Cupboards and cabinets to hold the growing household possessions came into use, and *dressoirs*, buffets, and credenzas permitted the display of treasured pieces. Although rather heavy and angular in shape, Gothic furniture was finely carved in linen-fold design or with motifs borrowed from Gothic architecture: ogee tracery, trefoils and quatrefoils, pierced galleries, and crockets. Painting on furniture was rarely employed except in Italy, where it appeared mainly on the *cassone* (chest), along with carving and plaster relief.

The Renaissance

Spreading from Italy during the 15th and 16th centuries, the Renaissance brought a renewed interest in harmonious proportions and in classical motifs like columns, pilasters, pediments, lion's legs, and moldings. The long rectangular table with carved slab supports was revived, as were folding chairs with x-hinged legs. Straight chairs and armchairs upholstered in velvet or leather were more commonly used, and their vogue spread over the whole Continent and to England. Cupboards and tables often rested on baluster-shaped legs joined with stretchers, the horizontal pieces used to strengthen the construction. French, Flemish, and Burgundian cabinetmakers excelled in sculptural carving, whereas the Dutch showed a preference for heavy paneling, used mainly in the *kas*, a large cupboard on ball feet. Design books, published by famous architects and designers like the French Jacques Androuet du Cerceau and the Dutch Jan de Vries, contributed to the spread of Renaissance forms, which began to permeate the English Gothic style toward the middle of the 16th century. The stiff straight lines of the Tudor style yielded to voluminous carved decoration, and turned (carved on a lathe) or spiral legs appeared on chairs.

The Baroque Period. The taste for the ornate found its supreme expression in the style of Louis XIV at the court in Versailles. Lavish gilt carving, incorporating scrolls and balusters as well as plant forms and classical elements, was used on legs and stretchers, and table tops and bureau fronts were decorated with marquetry of exotic woods. A special technique of inlaying tortoise shell panels with brass strips was evolved by André Charles Boulle. Gilt bronze mounts contributed to the splendor of these ornate pieces, the total effect of which was surpassed only by tables, candelabra, and capacious planters, or receptacles for flowerpots, made entirely of silver.

Such luxury and refined craftsmanship did not fail to impress the exiled English monarch and upon his restoration to the throne in 1660, Charles II influenced English furniture styles in this direction. The magnificent country mansions built during this time, as well as a general refinement in manners and living conditions, demanded more elegant furnishings, for which Flemish and French artists like Daniel Marot provided designs. Ornately carved high-backed chairs, chests of drawers, cabinets and tables on scroll and turned legs were made in walnut instead of the oak that had long been used for English furniture. Veneers and marquetry of burl walnut and other materials were employed for surface decoration, often with ivory inlay. Increased contacts with the Far East brought in the vogue of Oriental lacquer work, soon supplemented by Western japanning in *chinoiserie* designs. The latter was used in abundance on cabinets and similar pieces.

The 18th Century

With the beginning of the 18th century and the reign of Queen Anne in England, richly carved heavy furniture was gradually replaced by new designs emphasizing personal comfort instead of pompous grandeur. Chair backs had vertical splats (the wooden members running between the seat rail and top rail) that conformed to the curve of the human back. Upholstered wing chairs, armchairs, and settees provided softer seating. Chair legs adopted the organic animal form in the cabriole leg with its modified s-curve. Marquetry displaced carving, which disappeared almost entirely until its revival in the 1730's by William Kent. Cabinets appeared in many variations: with or without drawers, as chest-on-chest, writing cabinet, or secretary. Small tables served the new fashion of tea drinking and the growing taste for gambling.

France did not adopt this relatively simple taste but did shed some of the more ponderous forms and elaborate carvings, following the death of Louis XIV in 1715. During the period of the régence the cabriole leg replaced the baluster, or columnar leg. As in England, stretchers continued to be employed until the inherent structural strength of the cabriole leg was recognized. This was finally emphasized in the continuous curve of leg and seat, that is, the top of the leg joined the seat rail in a curve that continued in the bottom line. With the vogue of literary salons and intimate gatherings, furniture of the mid-18th century produced a whole array of smaller, more graceful furniture pieces, ranging from the *poudreuse* to the escritoire and from console to corner cabinet, while the bulging three-drawer chest remained in fashion. This style of the reign of Louis XV, characterized by rococo scrollwork in marquetry, lacquer, gilt bronze, and carving, was created by designers like Juste Aurèle Meissonnier and cabinetmakers like Charles Cressent, Gilles Joubert, and Jean François Oeben, the last already heralding in his late works the simpler style of Louis XVI.

The Classical Revival. The excavations at Herculaneum and other Italian sites around the middle of the 18th century once more brought classical forms to the attention of designers. The asymmetrically scrolled, bulging forms of the rococo were replaced by rectilinear furniture with straight, fluted legs, geometric marquetry, and bronze mounts with classical motifs. Porcelain plaques from Sèvres, then at the peak of its production, were used for inlay or small table tops. Some of the foremost cabinetmakers in Paris between 1760 and 1790 were of German descent, like Jean Henri Riesener, David Roentgen, and Adam Weisweiler, who all worked for the Court.

The Directoire style, which followed the French Revolution, exaggerated delicacy of proportion and favored fragile little chairs and tables, still with the classical ornamentation of urns, swags, and garlands. This style spread the vogue of furniture painted in pale colors that had begun in the preceding decades.

FURNITURE THROUGH THE AGES

Egyptian boxwood and acacia chair (c.1500 B.C.) from Thebes.

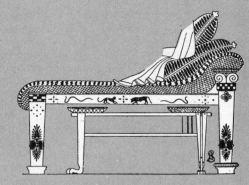

Ancient Greek couch and a low table with a relatively simple construction.

Ancient Roman marble stool with lion leg and human head motif.

Gothic English oak cupboard (c.1475) with cutout woodwork and a single door.

Renaissance Italian walnut chest (16th century) with a carving of the triumphal procession of Bacchus.

English canopied oak bed (late 16th century) with inlay of walnut, ebony, and ash bole and elaborate decorative carving.

English Restoration walnut chest (c.1660–1685), with embellishment of intricate wood inlay and with twist-turned legs.

Carved Louis XIV armchair upholstered in Beauvais tapestry.

Satinwood commode of the Louis XV period, with locking drawers, ormolu mounts, and a marble top.

Louis XVI side chair employing classical revival forms, such as fluted legs.

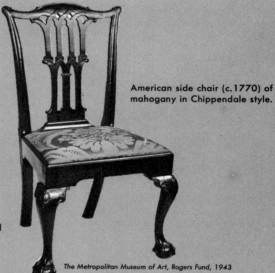

American side chair (c. 1770) of mahogany in Chippendale style.

English Adam-style harewood desk (c. 1770) inlaid with rosewood, boxwood, and ebony.

American mahogany desk topped by carved figures (c. 1760).

French Napoleonic chair of painted and gilded wood (c. 1803).

Modern shelf and cabinet unit of oiled walnut and aluminum, and twin-cushioned stools.

While continuing the emulation of classical prototypes, the Empire style created by Napoleon's designers in the first decade of the 19th century differed from its immediate neoclassic predecessors. The forms were heavier and plain mahogany was relieved only by gilding or gilt bronze mounts in the form of anthemions, victories, griffons, and lion's feet. In modified variations, reduced to less heroic forms and incorporating floral motifs as well, the basic forms of this style persisted into the time of Louis Philippe in the 1830's, although maple and other light-colored woods were preferred. Austria produced its own version of this style, known as the Biedermeier.

The Georgian Era of England. The middle decades of 18th-century England were dominated by the inexhaustible fund of ideas in Thomas Chippendale's book of designs for furniture "in the Most Fashionable Taste," encompassing gracefully scrolled rococo and *chinoiserie* forms as well as Gothic tracery and Chinese latticework. An important innovation was the claw-and-ball foot, suggested by the Chinese dragon clutching the mystic jewel in his talon. Mahogany was most commonly used for such carved furniture, until toward the end of the century imports of satinwood and other light woods from India and the East Indian islands displaced it.

By this time the classical revival had taken hold of English furniture design, too, and Robert Adam perfected a delicate linear style. Most of its urn, swag, and husk decoration was borrowed from antiquity. The design books published by George Hepplewhite and Thomas Sheraton in the last two decades of the century brought on the vogue for satinwood or light mahogany veneer, often painted, in elegant shield-back chairs, slender tables, and cabinets on finely tapered legs.

In the early 19th century the Regency style reacted against the simple linear grace of this furniture with a profusion of exuberant decoration, both carved and gilded, with *mascarons* and swags, and generally heavier forms.

The United States. In the beginning of their settlement, the American colonies did not provide the leisure or the means for anything but the simple necessities of life, and furniture was kept to unadorned utilitarian forms, mainly in pine. By the early 18th century however, urban centers on the Eastern Seaboard were sufficiently well established to indulge in the luxury of fine furniture, and English styles were followed rather closely. A great deal of furniture was imported, but the available pattern books inspired many New York and Philadelphia cabinetmakers to elegant variations of Chippendale and other designs. A few regional types were also evolved, among them the block-front desks and cabinets of the Newport, R.I., cabinetmakers John Goddard and John Townsend.

Because of the American Revolution and the break with England, the Adam style never got a foothold in the United States. Hepplewhite and Sheraton designs, however, enjoyed popularity into 19th century, as did the French Directoire and Empire designs, brought in by immigrants like the cabinetmaker Charles Honoré Lannuier. Responding to this inspiration, Duncan Phyfe of New York in his early career built graceful chairs with curving legs reminiscent of Greek chairs, or with fluted legs, lyre backs, and turned arm supports. From the middle of the 1820's his pieces became more ponderous and were often set on lion's feet. Mahogany continued to be the favorite material, until the Victorian predilection for rosewood made it look old-fashioned.

19th and 20th Centuries

From the third decade of the 19th century a series of rapidly changing style revivals followed each other, with Augustus Pugin of England as the foremost representative of Neo-Gothic design. In New York, John Henry Belter developed a personal method that utilized richly carved laminated rosewood variations on rococo forms. These are perhaps the most striking embodiments of the mid-Victorian style.

Rapid technical developments during the 19th century made possible the industrialization of the manufacture of furniture, and a profusion of cheap ornamentation was easily applied to cover up deficiencies in construction. In protest against the imitative, overdecorated products of the machine, William Morris of England advocated a return to handmade, simple furniture, and Charles Lock Eastlake proclaimed unpretentiousness and fitness in form the chief criteria of quality.

About the turn of the century the European *art nouveau* movement gave furniture a new, sinuous, almost organic form, represented in the works of the Belgian Henry van de Velde and the French architect Hector Guimard, among others. But after World War I a reaction set in against these decorative forms.

The new concept declared the functional soundness of furniture to be the paramount concern of the designer. In the 1920's Le Corbusier in France, and Ludwig Mies van der Rohe and the Bauhaus workshop in Germany began experimenting with tubular steel and canvas combinations, stripping their designs of all but the necessary structural components. Perhaps the ultimate point in this direction was reached in the "butterfly" sling chair of metal rods and canvas by the Argentine designers Antonio Bonet, Juan Kurchan, and Jorge Ferrari-Hardoy in 1938. New man-made materials prompted further departures from conventional forms in the United States in the 1940's and 1950's, with molded plywood and plastic shells of chairs by Charles Eames and Eero Saarinen, perhaps inspired by the molded plywood-sheet furniture of the Finnish architect Alvar Aalto.

Case furniture, too, underwent a change toward the functional and unadorned, mainly through the designs of Paul McCobb and George Nelson. Most of these designs are intended for mass production, but have influenced custom-made furniture as well. There are, however, such personal expressions of dissent as the opulent curvilinear chairs and sofas of Vladimir Kagan. Good craftsmanship and simple form have brought Scandinavian design of the mid-century to the fore. Best represented perhaps by the Danes Hans Wegner and Finn Juhl, it exercises a considerable influence on contemporary furniture.

Consult Schmitz, Hermann, *Encyclopedia of Furniture* (1957); Reeves, David, *Furniture; An Explanatory History* (rev. ed., 1959); Boger, L. A., *Complete Guide to Furniture Styles* (1959).

HEDY BACKLIN, The Cooper Union Museum for the Arts of Decoration

See also INTERIOR DECORATION AND DESIGN.

"A Fur Train from the Far North" by Frederic Remington. Fur trappers played an important role in American history as explorers and trail blazers.

The Bettmann Archive

FÜRSTENFELDBRUCK, town of the Federal Republic of Germany, some 15 mi (25 km) west of Munich in the *Land* of Bavaria, on the Amper River. It is a swimming resort and tourist center. The monastery church, built between 1716 and 1741, is a magnificent example of south German baroque architecture, and there are several attractive medieval merchants' houses.

FÜRTH, industrial suburb northwest of Nuremberg, Federal Republic of Germany (West Germany), at the confluence of the Regnitz and Pagnitz rivers. It was settled in the 10th century, and possession of the town was long disputed among Bamberg, Nuremberg, and the Margraves of Ansbach. From the 17th century until German dictator Adolf Hitler's rise to power, Fürth had one of the largest Jewish populations in Germany. The synagogue, built in 1616, and the Jewish cemetery were destroyed in 1938. Widespread damage was inflicted during World War II, but after 1945 recovery was rapid and many new industries were formed. The city is especially noted for production of radio and television sets, tape recorders, and furniture and for a number of light industries.

FUR TRADE IN NORTH AMERICA. The fur trade played a decisive role in the development of the North American continent. It was the principal avenue of contact between the native Indian population and the white man. It provided a major stimulus for exploration, a necessary forerunner to expansion and settlement. It contributed much to the economic growth of the country north of the Ohio River, and especially north of the St. Lawrence and Great Lakes region. It was a dominant factor in shaping the history of Canada, and it became a point of contest that led to wars and conquest.

The French led the way in the exploitation of the fur trade. When Samuel de Champlain made his initial voyage to the St. Lawrence in 1603, he stopped at the trading station at Tadoussac. Returning to France, he published his first book, *Des Sauvages*, which included comments on the fur riches of the region he had visited. His second voyage had one primary objective: the establishment of a fur-trading post.

By 1763, when New France was ceded to Great Britain under the terms of the Treaty of Paris, the French had built a fur-trade empire. They had penetrated south to the Gulf of Mexico, west to the Rocky Mountains, north to the Arctic Circle.

Recognizing the immense value of the trade, the British moved to end the French monopoly. On May 2, 1670, the crown chartered an English syndicate in Hudson Bay. That charter stands as a landmark in fur-trade history: it was the birth of the still-thriving Hudson's Bay Company.

With the independence of the United States, Great Britain's control of the fur trade was sharply challenged by the new nation. Indeed, British control of the region northwest of the Ohio after 1783 was a sore point in U.S.-British diplomatic relations—and the fur harvest of the area was a primary factor. After the settlement of the issue by Jay's Treaty (1795), the United States pushed westward. The heralds of America's westward expansion were fur traders who, by 1840, had earned the name "mountain men." Following the pattern used by both the French and the British, corporations were formed as the essential ingredient of the trade. Noteworthy among such concerns were John Jacob Astor's American Fur Company and his short-lived Pacific Fur Company. More important for American movement west of the Mississippi was the work of William H. Ashley and his successors, Jedediah Strong Smith and William Sublette, and later the Rocky Mountain Fur Company.

Although by the 1840's, the fur trade of North America had ceased to play a dominant part in exploration, settlement, and territorial acquisition, the economic aspects of the trade still contribute to the prosperity of Canada and Alaska.

Consult Innis, H. A., *The Fur Trade in Canada* (1956); Phillips, P. C., and Smurr, J. W., *The Fur Trade* (2 vols., 1961; repr., 1967). DOYCE B. NUNIS, JR.

FURTSEVA [fŏŏr′tsə-və], **YEKATERINA ALEKSEYEVNA** (1909–74), the first woman elected to the Secretariat and Presidium of the Central Committee of the Soviet Communist party. She served in the Komsomol (the Communist youth organization) until 1937 and was secretary of the Frunze District of Moscow (1942–50). When Nikita S. Khrushchev became head of the Moscow party organization, Furtseva was named second secretary (1950) and in 1952 was elected to the Central Committee. Appointed U.S.S.R. Minister of Culture in 1960, she lost her position on the party Presidium in 1961.

HOW A FUSE WORKS

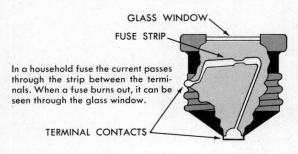

GLASS WINDOW

FUSE STRIP

In a household fuse the current passes through the strip between the terminals. When a fuse burns out, it can be seen through the glass window.

TERMINAL CONTACTS

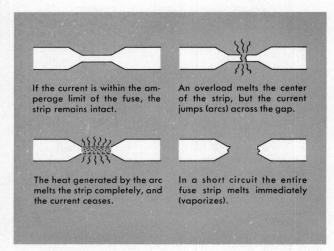

If the current is within the amperage limit of the fuse, the strip remains intact.

An overload melts the center of the strip, but the current jumps (arcs) across the gap.

The heat generated by the arc melts the strip completely, and the current ceases.

In a short circuit the entire fuse strip melts immediately (vaporizes).

FURTWÄNGLER [foŏrt'vĕng-lər], **WILHELM** (1886–1954), German conductor. After studies in Munich, Furtwängler conducted in several small opera houses. In 1919 he became the conductor of the Tonkünstler Orchestra in Vienna and the musical director of the Berlin State Opera. He was appointed conductor of the Staatskapelle, Berlin, in 1920 and conductor of the Berlin Philharmonic in 1922. From 1922 to 1928 he also conducted the Gewandhaus Orchestra of Leipzig. He appeared with the New York Philharmonic in 1925, 1926, and 1927.

In 1934 Furtwängler resigned all his posts, protesting the Nazi government's anti-Semetic policies. Later, he made a partial peace and conducted the Berlin Philharmonic during World War II. In 1946 he was cleared of pro-Nazi charges. Still, hostile public opinion prevented engagements in America, although he was well received in England and France.

Furtwängler's conducting was noted for its eloquence, combining technical virtuosity with impassioned interpretation. He composed two symphonies, a piano concerto, a *Te Deum*, and several chamber works.

BENJAMIN PATTERSON, Music Division, N.Y. Public Library

FURUNCLE. *See* BOILS.

FURZE [fûrz], spiny shrub, *Ulex europaeus*, in the pea family, Leguminosae, originally found in Europe but now naturalized in North America. The plants grow to a height of from 2 to 3 ft. and have scalelike leaves. The younger stems and spines are green, producing an "evergreen" effect throughout the year. The flowers, which appear in profusion from early spring through fall, are fragrant, yellow, and pea-shaped. Furze is generally propagated from seed, although a double-flowered variety is grown from cuttings. Furze thrives in sunny locations and does best when planted in slightly acid, sandy soil.

FUSE, city of Osaka Prefecture, Honshu, Japan, near Osaka. It is an important center in the expanding industrial belt of Osaka, producing heavy metal products, celluloid, sewing machines, drugs, chemicals, rubber goods, and light metal products. Pop., 212,754.

FUSE, ELECTRIC, an electric safety device that acts as a circuit breaker (q.v.) when electric current exceeds the specified amperage. Most household fuses consist of a wire or strip of metal having a relatively low melting point. When a current, passing through the wire, exceeds a critical value, it heats the wire until it melts, breaking the connection. Most household fuses are self-destroying and must be replaced after burnout. Large, heavy-duty fuses are renewable; new meltable strips may be inserted to replace the damaged ones.

Fuses are available in many current-ratings from two milliamperes, used to protect sensitive d.c. meters, to several hundred amperes, for heavy electric power service. They are manufactured principally in screw-type (plug), pigtail, and cartridge-type. Special types include slow-burning, fast-acting, and time-delay fuses.

In the home, fuses range from 15 to 30 amp. depending upon the type of circuitry installed. Standard fuses have capacities of 15 amp. for lighting; 20 amp. for small appliances like toasters and irons; and 30 amp. for large appliances like electric dryers.

RUFUS P. TURNER, Author, *Basic Electricity*

FUSE, EXPLOSIVE, device for igniting an explosive charge. It consists of a cord impregnated with combustible material or of a flexible fabric tube filled with combustible material. The time between lighting the fuse and the ignition of the charge is controlled by cutting the fuse to the proper length. Fuses are used to explode blasting and demolition charges and in certain munitions. The earliest fuses, used by the Chinese after their invention of gunpowder about 1200 A.D., probably were much like those used today to ignite firecrackers.

See also DETONATOR; EXPLOSIVES; FUZE.

FUSELAGE [fū'sə-lĭj, fū'sə-läzh], the streamlined structure of an airplane that houses the crew, passengers, cargo, mail, and baggage. It supports flying and control equipment and, sometimes, the engine and landing gear.

The two principal types of fuselage are the truss-frame and the monocoque. The truss-frame fuselage usually has a welded-tubing framework, called a truss, which is covered with fabric. The truss is sometimes strengthened by diagonal wires or rods. A monocoque fuselage is a metal shell that bears a part, or all, of the stresses arising in the fuselage. To reinforce the shell and to prevent heavy loads from wrinkling the metal skin, which is necessarily thin, the monocoque fuselage is reinforced with upright, stiffening rings along its length. Another type, the semimonocoque, is reinforced by longitudinal ribs, called stringers or longerons, in addition to the rings. A third type of monocoque, the reinforced shell, is strengthened with additional stress-bearing ribs. Small aircraft are usually of the truss-frame design, whereas passenger and military aircraft are of monocoque construction or one of its modifications.

On large passenger aircraft, the fuselage may contain seating arrangements for as many as 200 passengers. On all scheduled airlines it houses galleys for meal service and lavatories. Aft and lower sections of a fuselage are usually reserved for mail, cargo, and baggage. Modern fuselages are air-conditioned and pressurized so that interior air pressure at any altitude is the same as that at low altitudes.

L. L. DOTY, *Aviation Week*

See also AIRCRAFT STRUCTURE; AIRPLANE.

FUSELI [fū′zə-lē], **HENRY**, original name Johann Heinrich Füssli (1741–1825), Swiss-born painter who worked mostly in England. His characteristic style, which combined the macabre with the erotic, resulted in works of a highly imaginative quality. Fuseli's peculiar individuality is perhaps best seen in his numerous drawings and sketches. Among his important oil paintings is "The Nightmare" (Collection Paul Ganz, Basle).

FUSEL OIL. *See* AMYL ALCOHOL.

FUSHUN [foo′shoon′], city of northeastern China, in Liaoning Province, adjacent to Mukden on the east. Since 1907 it has been the center of one of China's largest coal-mining operations. The accessible coal beds lie at the surface in the west and dip gently eastward, overlain by thick beds of oil shale. The Fushun mine is one of the largest open-pit coal beds in the world. The reserves of both coal and oil shale are enormous, though much of the coal is not of coking quality. In 1931 the Japanese began development of an industrial complex at Fushun, installing a thermal power plant, a shale-oil reduction plant, an aluminum-processing plant, and other industrial units. The Communists have added to the complex, installing blast furnaces, steel mills, fabricating plants, machine shops, chemical factories, and by-product plants. Pop., 678,600.

FUSIBILITY, property that a metal or alloy has of melting. It is usually expressed in terms of a temperature reading at the melting point. Some alloys of metals have much lower melting points than those of the individual metals composing the alloy. For example, lead, bismuth, and tin separately melt near or above 200° C. (392° F.) but when they are mixed in the right proportion to form an alloy, the alloy melts at a little above 100° C. (212° F.). The fusibility of metals and alloys is made use of in automatic sprinklers and in fuses.

FUSIN [foo′sin′], city in western Liaoning Province, northeastern China. Coal mining began in the early 1930's, and the completion of a railroad in 1937 furthered development. Coal is mined by open-cut methods from seams nearly 200-ft. thick. Though the coal is not of cok-ing quality, the mines are becoming one of China's chief coal sources. Pop., 188,600.

FUSION, in physics, process by which a substance changes from a solid to a liquid. For pure substances this change takes place at a definite temperature, and all of the substance melts at that temperature, called the melting point. For amorphous substances, such as glass, fusion takes place gradually over a wide range of temperature, and the glass softens and becomes plastic as the temperature is raised. Some alloys are amorphous and gradually soften, whereas others such as Wood's metal have a definite melting point that is lower than that of any of the component metals.

For most substances there is a change of volume during the process. On fusion of a pure substance that has a crystalline structure, the atomic or molecular arrangement changes from an orderly array to random motion in the liquid state, without a change in temperature. This change or arrangement requires additional energy, which is called the latent heat of fusion.

W. D. WHITEHEAD, University of Virginia

FUSION, HEAT OF. *See* HEAT OF FUSION.

FUSION, NUCLEAR. *See* THERMONUCLEAR REACTION.

FUST [foost] or **FAUST** [foust], **JOHANN** (d.1466), German printer and partner of Gutenberg. A citizen of Mainz, Fust financed Gutenberg's invention of printing from movable type and eventually acquired the business, entering into partnership with his son-in-law, Peter Schoeffer. Together Fust and Schoeffer produced the first book to be printed in color, the *Psalter* (1457), and the first dated Bible (1462).

FUTURE FARMERS OF AMERICA, a national organization whose membership consists of young men who are studying agriculture in public high schools. The Future Farmers of America was founded in 1928 and incorporated the farm youth groups that had arisen with the passage of the National Vocational Education Act of 1917. The organization consists of local (high school) chapters and state associations whose aim is to promote farming education and to develop good citizenship. Supervised farming projects, livestock-raising, contests, field trips, and social and athletic events are some of the activities engaged in by the nearly 400,000 members. The Future Farmers of America holds an annual convention in Kansas City, Mo., and publishes the bimonthly *Future Farmer Magazine*.

FUTURE HOMEMAKERS OF AMERICA, a national organization of students studying home economics in junior and senior high schools. Founded in 1945, it is an incorporated, nonprofit organization supported by annual membership dues. Affiliations are open to all secondary schools, both public and private, which provide instruction in home economics. Total membership in the early 1960's was over 500,000 in nearly 10,500 chapters throughout the United States, Puerto Rico, and the Virgin Islands.

The motto of the FHA is "Toward New Horizons." To guide their activities toward the over-all goal of helping individuals improve personal, family, and community living, FHA'ers adopt national projects for three-year periods. Each year the members elect 12 youth officers to help promote the national work program and to plan and preside over the annual national meetings.

The national magazine of FHA is *Teen Times*. Cosponsors of the organization are the Home Economics Education Branch of the Office of Education and the American Home Economics Association. National headquarters are in the Office of Education, Department of Health, Education, and Welfare, Washington 25, D.C.

RUTHANNA RUSSEL, Future Homemakers of America

FUTURE INTEREST, in law, refers to a right in property which entitles the owner to the possession or enjoyment of that property at some future time. The term is used in contrast to present interest, which gives the owner present, possessory rights. Future interests may be created by deed or will and are useful in planning the distribution of estates. For example, a father may make a will leaving his property to his wife for life and the remainder to his children equally. On his death, the wife receives a life estate—a present interest, entitling her to possession and hence to rents and profits during her lifetime—and the children have a vested remainder—a future interest, entitling them to no possessory rights until the death of their mother. The children's future interest is, however, a specific right in the property, and they are certain to receive it at some indefinite time in the future. It is more than a mere expectancy, since it is a presently owned "thing" with only the right to possession postponed. The wife cannot defeat the future interest by selling or willing the property to someone else.

Another example of future interest would be where an owner leases his land to a tenant for 20 years. The tenant now has a present leasehold estate, with full rights of possession under the terms of the lease. The owner, who prior to the lease had a fee simple absolute (the highest ownership right allowed by the law), now has a reversion, a future interest which entitles him to possession again at the expiration of the lease.

Future interests are traditionally classified as remainders, reversions, possibilities of reverter, powers of termination, and executory interests, all of which are highly technical rights in property.

The law of future interests originated in feudal England and developed principally as a device to keep real property in the hands of the landed aristocracy. Today, it may also apply to personal property and forms an important part of the law of trusts, enabling many forms of split ownership with tax-saving consequences.

Consult Simes, L. M., *Future Interests* (1951).

JOHN EDWARD CRIBBET, University of Illinois
School of Law

FUTURISM, the name given to an early 20th-century Italian art movement, encompassing painting, sculpture, and literature. The official birthdate of the movement was 1909 when the poet Filippo Tommaso Marinetti published the "Foundation and Manifesto of Futurism" in the Paris newspaper, *Le Figaro*.

The movement, influenced by the formal experiments of the Cubist painters, emphasized the dynamic, industrial nature of 20th-century society. The artists thus utilized the fragmented forms of the Cubists to convey a sense of movement and power. Visually, they created paintings which show an object in motion by depicting a series of overlapping forms, each repeating the other with slight variation. The effect is similar to a series of still photos of a moving object. In sculpture the problem was more difficult to solve. Perhaps the most successful solution was found by the sculptor Umberto Boccioni, whose "Flight of Forms in Space" (The Museum of Modern Art, N.Y.) shows a succession of abstract, overlapping solid forms, somewhat streamlined to suggest movement.

In addition to Marinetti and Boccioni, other Futurist artists were Gino Severini, Luigi Russolo, Carlo Carrà, and Giacomo Balla. The Futurists brought a stronger, more dramatic sense of color to their works than did the Cubists. Although already declining as a movement after World War I, the real end of Futurism came when the artists of the movement split over support of Mussolini's Italian Fascism in the 1920's.

STANLEY FERBER, State University of N.Y. at Binghamton

FUX [fŏoks], **JOHANN JOSEPH** (c.1660–1741), Austrian composer and conductor. He was famous in his country at a time when Italian musicians traditionally held all important posts there. Born in Hirtenfeld in Styria, he came to Vienna after the victory over the Turks, which inaugurated Austria's most glorious epoch in music. Fux became Imperial Composer in 1698 and in 1715 First Imperial Conductor. He is best known for his famous theoretical work on counterpoint *Gradus ad Parnassum* (1725), which was soon translated into Italian, German, French, and English. His greatness as a composer of operas, oratorios, and Masses, however, was rediscovered in the middle of the 20th century, and an edition of his collected works was begun in 1959. Fux is one of the key figures in the formation of the Viennese preclassical school, and his influence is evident even in Haydn.

EGON WELLESZ, Oxford University

FUZE, electrical, chemical, or mechanical device used to initiate a detonation under desired conditions. The effectiveness of fragmentation bombs and grenades is determined by the fuzes with which they are armed. Short delay fuzes are used mainly for low-altitude raids by large bomber formations to permit planes to clear a target area before the explosion. Delayed action fuzes function a fraction of a second to hours or even days after impact. Mechanical time fuzes are accurately adjusted clockwork mechanisms, which start running when a bomb is released or a missile launched, exploding the charge at a preset time. During World War II a large family of devices called V.T., or proximity fuzes, were developed, which detonated charges when activated by external influence other than contact. Each consists of a minute radio-transmitting and receiving oscillator, an amplifier, an electrical firing circuit, and a series of electrical and mechanical safety devices. The fuze is designed and set to detonate when its shell, bomb, or rocket comes within lethal range of the target.

MARTIN BLUMENSON, formerly, Senior Historian,
Department of the Army

See also DETONATOR; EXPLOSIVES; FUSE, EXPLOSIVE.

G

1	2	3	4	5	6	7
⬠	No Phoenician form	⌐	G	g	Ʒ	℔

8	9	10	11	12	13	14	15	16
𝒢	g	G	g	G	G	g	G	g

The letter G was introduced into the Latin alphabet to represent the sound made by a hard C. In the Latin alphabet it was put in the place of the Greek *zeta* (Z), not used in Latin. Some of its historical forms are shown in the top row. They are hieroglyph 1, Greek 3, Roman (Trajan) 4, Irish uncial 5, Caroline 6, and Gutenberg blackletter 7. Common forms of the letter G as it appears today are illustrated in the bottom row. These forms are handwritten cursive capital 8, handwritten lowercase 9, roman capital 10, roman lowercase 11, roman small capital 12, italic capital 13, italic lowercase 14, sans serif capital 15, and sans serif lowercase 16.

G, seventh letter of the English and Latin alphabets. In the latter it replaced the Greek Z, which did not exist in purely Latin words. It had been invented by adding a small diacritic to C, the third letter, in order to differentiate between *k* and *g*, a distinction which the Etruscan intermediary between Greek and Latin had discarded. The place of Z was vacant, and the resemblance between G and some varieties of Z, though distant, made the two signs not incompatible. Actually C and G are confused in Latin inscriptions of all ages, especially in Gaul and Germany.

The symbol *g* has two values in modern English spelling: (1) a palatal stopped consonant as in go, grant, wagon, dog, and league; (2) a palatal spirant consonant, as in gentle, *George*. The latter sound also appears in ri*dg*e and *j*am. Final *ng* (as in ki*ng*) is a single consonant, but the medial form between vowels (a*ng*er, fi*ng*er) is *ng* plus *g*.

JOSHUA WHATMOUGH

GABBRO [găb′rō], dark, coarse-grained igneous rock mainly composed of the minerals pyroxene and plagioclase. Olivine is a major constituent of many gabbro bodies, and with increasing olivine content the rock is transitional to peridotite. Gabbro has the same composition as basalt, but it is more coarsely crystalline, having cooled slowly deep in the earth. Gabbro is common in many parts of the world, usually in large, tabular masses. *See also* BASALT; PERIDOTITE; ROCKS.

GABÈS, GULF OF, inlet of the Mediterranean Sea indenting the east coast of Tunisia. The Gulf of Gabès is protected by the Isle of Djerba and the Kerkennah Islands. Gabès, the chief seaport of southern Tunisia, is situated on the Gulf.

GABIN [gȧ-băN′], **JEAN,** professional name of Jean-Alexis Montcorgé (1904–76), noted French film actor. He became widely known to U.S. audiences through leading roles, ranging from romantic to character parts, in such films as *Pépé le Moko* (1937), *La grande illusion* (1937), *Le jour se lève* (*Daybreak*), 1939, *Le cas du Docteur Laurent* (*The Case of Dr. Laurent*), 1956, and *L'Affaire Dominici* (1973).

GABLE, CLARK (1901–60), U.S. actor who played in more than 65 motion pictures and became known as "The King" for his masculine bearing and vigorous manner. Born William Clark Gable in Cadiz, Ohio, he became a touring actor in 1920 and gained his first Hollywood leading role, opposite Joan Crawford, in *Dance, Fools, Dance* in 1931. He made *A Free Soul* (1931) memorable by slapping Norma Shearer in the face. *It Happened One Night* (1934) revealed his flair for comedy, won him an Academy award, and brought stardom. His most famous role was that of Rhett Butler in *Gone With The Wind* (1939). During World War II Gable rose from private to major in the Air Force. His last picture, *The Misfits*, in which he played an aging cowboy, was released posthumously in 1961.

Clark Gable

UPI

GABO [gä′bō], **NAUM** (1890–1977), Russian-born abstract sculptor. With his brother Antoine Pevsner he was a central figure in the Russian movement called constructivism. His works, made of metal, glass, celluloid, nylon, and other materials, include small pieces and monumental architectural sculptures, such as the "Construction in Space" (1955–57) in front of Marcel Breuer's Bijenkorf Building in Rotterdam. Gabo emigrated to the United States in 1946.

GABON

AREA	103,346 sq mi (267 667 km²)
ELEVATION	
Highest point (Mount Iboundji)	5,165 ft (1 574 m)
Lowest point	Sea level
POPULATION (1977)	550,000
PRINCIPAL LANGUAGES	French; tribal languages
UNIT OF CURRENCY	Franc CFA (Communauté française d'Afrique)
NATIONAL ANTHEM	La Concorde (The Concord), words and music by Georges Damas
CAPITAL	Libreville
PRINCIPAL PRODUCTS	Cocoa; okoumé wood, plywood, veneer; manganese, iron ore, uranium, gold, diamonds, potassium, crude petroleum

GABON [gȧ-bôN], an independent republic on the west coast of Africa, astride the equator. Formerly one of the four colonies comprising French Equatorial Africa, Gabon is bordered on the west by the Atlantic Ocean, on the north by Equatorial Guinea and the Republic of Cameroun, and on the east and south by the Republic of the Congo. The official name is République gabonaise.

The Land. The deeply indented coastline gives way to coastal lowlands between 18 and 125 mi (about 30 to 200 km) deep. Fringing the lowlands is a precipitous escarpment that rises as high as 2,000 ft (610 m) in places. Behind this escarpment is a series of plateaus covering the northern and eastern sections of the country. In the central region are several mountainous areas, the highest peak being Mount Iboundji (5,165 ft or 1 574 m). The river systems of Gabon have cut deep valleys in the plateaus and through the coast escarpment. The entire country forms the basin of the Ogooué (Ogowe) River, which has two major tributaries, the N'Gounié and the Ivindo. Both of these afford entry by water into the interior.

The climate of Gabon is hot and humid the year round and there is little seasonal temperature change. The year is marked by two rainy seasons, October to mid-December and mid-January to May. Rainfall is very heavy along the coast, and the entire country is covered by heavy rain forests.

The People. The average density of population is very low, but the concentration is very uneven. Many areas of the interior are completely uninhabited. Virtually all of the republic's people are Africans. There are nearly 40 ethnic groups, the major ones being the Fang (who invaded from the north only a century or so ago), the Bakota, the Omiené, and the Eshira. In the interior are scattered groups of Pygmies.

Most of the people live in isolated villages, and there are only two major centers, Libreville, the capital, and Port-Gentil. Lambaréné in the interior is known for its hospital, established and run, until his death in 1965, by Dr. Albert Schweitzer. The people are predominantly animists, although mission work has resulted in a substantial number of Christians. There are several African languages spoken, but French is taught in the schools and is the official language. Gabon's educational system is very good and primary school facilities are sufficient to accommodate most of the school children.

Economy. The currency of Gabon is the same as that of the other former French colonies in West Africa, the franc CFA. Gabon's economy, one of the most prosperous in that part of Africa, is undergoing great changes. While the relative value of timber (mainly okoumé wood, renowned for its excellence as plywood) has decreased due to intensified exploitation of the country's mineral wealth, scientific cutting and reforestation methods are likely to produce still higher output. Gabon is one of the largest producers in the western world of manganese ore, extracted mainly at Moanda, in the southeast. Petroleum production is rapidly expanding and there is an oil refinery

INDEX TO GABON GENERAL REFERENCE MAP
Total Population 550,000

Total—1977 est.; Libreville, Port-Gentil, Franceville—1973 est.; others—1970 est.)

GABON

SCALE OF MILES
0 50 100 150
KILOMETRES
0 50 100 150

© C. S. HAMMOND & Co., Maplewood, N. J.

Long. 14° East of Greenwich 16°

at Port-Gentil. Uranium ore and gold are mined in considerable quantities; diamonds and potassium are also found. The deposits of iron ore at Mekambo, in the northeast, are considered to be one of the world's richest.

Because of the difficulty in clearing land, agriculture is largely confined to production of locally consumed foods, although a few thousand tons of cocoa are exported annually. Plywood and veneer are manufactured at mills near Port-Gentil. Gabon's further development depends to a large extent on expanding the internal transportation system. Libreville and Port-Gentil are the major ports. An internal air network carries both freight and passengers.

History. Gabon proclaimed its independence on Aug. 17, 1960, but remained a member of the French Community. The constitution adopted on Feb. 21, 1961, provides for a legislative assembly elected by universal suffrage. The president, who is head of the state, is also the prime minister. He exercises executive power and is responsible for the civil service. President Léon Mba was ousted in a *coup d'état* on Feb. 17, 1964, but was reinstated three days later, after French troops, airlifted to the capital, had overpowered the insurgents.

Gabon became a member of the United Nations on Sept. 20, 1960, and joined in a customs union with Chad, the Central African Republic, and the Congo. This agreement also covers economic cooperation and the establishment of common government services among the four states. In 1967, after the death of President Léon Mba, Albert Bongo took office, maintaining tight control over all government agencies. The development of Gabon's first railroad, begun in 1970, helped exploit the country's mineral resources.

Consult Patterson, K. David, *The Northern Gabon Coast to 1875* (1975); Weinstein, Brian, *Gabon: Nation-Building on the Ogooué* (1967).   L. GRAY COWAN

Libreville, the capital, is the largest community in Gabon, where most people live in isolated villages. The French set up a fort, trading post, and mission on the site in 1843; six years later, a group of freed African slaves settled here.

A-A-A Photo—Freelance Photographers Guild

GABOON VIPER, a highly poisonous snake, *Bitis gabonica*, of the viper family, Viperidae, native to Africa. The gaboon viper is a stout-bodied snake, grows to a length of less than 4 ft (1.2 m), and has fangs over 1 inch (2.5 cm) long with which it can inject large amounts of lethal venom. The snake's body is marked in buff, brown, and purple. Its broad, wedge-shaped head terminates in a blunt snout which is surmounted, in some individuals, by a forked horn.

GABORIAU [gȧ-bô-ryō'] **ÉMILE** (1835–73), French author of detective novels. The originator of the detective novel in France, he was the creator of Monsieur Lecoq, who in the use of his acute intelligence foreshadowed Sherlock Holmes. Gaboriau's novels, sometimes compared to the detective stories of Edgar Allan Poe, are marked by dramatic realism, rigorous logic, and the skillful development of character and plot. Among his extremely popular books were *L'affaire Lerouge*, 1866 (*The Widow Lerouge*, 1891); *Le crime d'Orcival*, 1867 (*The Mystery of Orcival*, 1883); *Le dossier no. 113*, 1867 (*File no. 113*, 1883).

GABRIEL [gā'brē-ĕl], the archangel who is the messenger of divine comfort. He helped Daniel interpret visions (Dan. 8:15f.; 9:21f.) and announced the coming birth of John the Baptist to Zacharias and the coming of Jesus Christ to the Virgin Mary (Luke 1:11, 26). His feast is March 24.

GABRIEL [gȧ-brē-el'], **JACQUES ANGE** (1698–1782), French architect, born in Paris. He assisted his father, Jacques Jules Gabriel, who was royal architect to Louis XV, succeeding him in this post in 1742. His designs are characterized by exquisite refinement of proportion and by an almost classic restraint in the handling of architectural forms. His masterpieces are the Petit Trianon and the palaces on the Place de la Concorde in Paris. He also worked on Versailles, for which he designed the theater.

GABRIELI [gä-brē-â'lē], **ANDREA** (c.1520–1586), noted Italian composer. Born in Venice, he was organist there at the famed St. Mark's Cathedral. Best known of his works are the *Sacrae Cantiones* (Sacred Songs), 1565. Chordal textures, brilliant sonorities, and the use of *cori spezzati* (divided choirs) characterized Gabrieli's choral style. His keyboard music placed new emphasis on the structural coherence of the *canzona*, the *ricercare*, and the *fantasia*.

Gabrieli's nephew Giovanni Gabrieli (c. 1557–1612), was also a leading composer of the Venetian school of composition. His style is distinguished by its contrast of textures and sonorities and of large and small groups within a single work, anticipating the *concertato* style of the later Baroque. His *Sacrae Symphoniae* (1597) demonstrates the first use of dynamic markings (forte, piano, and so on) and of precise instrumentation.

GABRILOWITSCH [gä-brĭ-lô'vich], **OSSIP SOLOMONOVICH** (1878–1936), noted pianist and conductor. Born in St. Petersburg, he studied piano there at the Conservatory (1888–94) and in Vienna. Beginning his career in Berlin in 1896, he made successful tours in Germany, Austria,

Russia, France, and England. His American debut in 1900 was followed by several tours of the United States. In 1909 he married Clara Clemens, singer and daughter of Mark Twain, and appeared with her in joint recitals. Settling in the United States, he turned to conducting and from 1918 until his death was conductor of the Detroit Symphony Orchestra.

GAD (Heb., "good fortune"), an Israelite tribe settled in the central region of Palestine, east of the River Jordan. It claimed as its tribal ancestor a son of Jacob (Gen. 30:11).

GADARENE DEMONIAC, a madman living in the tombs near the Sea of Galilee in a region belonging to the city of Gadara, from whom Jesus is reported to have cast out a legion of demons (Mark 5:1–20).

GADDI [găd′dē], **TADDEO** (c.1300–c.1366), Florentine painter, according to tradition a pupil of Giotto. He painted during the transitional period between the Gothic and Renaissance eras. His style was influenced by Giotto, but he introduced more movement in the compositions and showed greater interest in realistic detail. A number of his works have survived, the most important being the frescoes in the Baroncelli Chapel of the Church of Santa Croce in Florence.

GADES, ancient Phoenician name for Cádiz (q.v.).

GADFLY, name for several species of flies of the genus *Chrysops* in the horsefly family, Tabanidae, found in many parts of the world. Gadflies are dark-colored and usually have yellow markings. They commonly inhabit wooded regions and lay their eggs in damp places. Male gadflies are harmless and feed mainly on plant juices; the females inflict painful bites with their piercing-sucking mouth parts. Gadflies are a special nuisance to wild and domestic animals, and one species, *G. discalis*, transmits the bacteria that cause tularemia from rodents to man.

GADOLIN, JOHANN (1760–1852), Finnish chemist who made extensive studies of the rare earth elements. He studied in Finland and at Uppsala, Sweden, with Torbern Bergman, traveled widely, and later returned to Finland. He investigated the mineral gadolinite (named for him) found at Ytterby, near Stockholm, and isolated the oxide yttria from it. A large number of rare earth oxides were later isolated from this substance.

GADOLINIUM [găd-ə-lĭn′ē-əm], chemical element and metal of the lanthanide series, discovered in 1880 by J. C. G. de Marignac. It is one of the few elements to

PROPERTIES

Symbol	Gd
Atomic number	64
Atomic weight	157.25
Density	7.95
Valence	3

show strong magnetic properties, and its salts have therefore been used to obtain temperatures close to absolute zero.

GADSDEN [gădz′dən], **JAMES** (1788–1858), American diplomat and railroad promoter. He was born in Charleston, S.C., and graduated from Yale in 1806. He served in the War of 1812 and in the campaign against the Seminole Indians under Gen. Andrew Jackson. Leaving the army (1821), he moved to Florida and was appointed commissioner to settle the Seminoles on reservations. In the 1840's Gadsden became interested in railroad promotion and worked actively to consolidate the small lines of the South. He hoped to extend the system to the Pacific coast, thereby avoiding the South's economic dependence on the North. His plan necessitated the purchase of border territory from Mexico. Appointed minister to that country (1853) through the efforts of his friend Secretary of War Jefferson Davis, he negotiated the Gadsden Purchase. He was recalled in 1856 and died before his railroad project could be realized.

JAMES P. SHENTON, Columbia University

GADSDEN, city of northeastern Alabama, and seat of Etowah County. Founded in 1840 on the Coosa River, it was originally a trade center. The minerals of the region attracted metals manufacturers, and Gadsden became Alabama's second industrial center. Manufactures are dominated by iron and steel products, but include over 100 other items, such as rubber tires and tubes, foundry products, and farm machinery. The city was named for the statesman James Gadsden. Inc. 1871; pop., 53,928; surb. area, 67,706.

GADSDEN PURCHASE, territory acquired (1853) from Mexico by the United States. The purchase agreement, negotiated by James Gadsden, the U.S. minister to Mexico, was intended to provide a southern route for a railroad to the Pacific coast. The treaty was narrowly ratified by the Senate in 1854. An area of 45,535 sq. mi. was purchased for a sum of $10,000,000. It now forms the extreme southern section of Arizona and New Mexico.

GADSKI [găt′skē], **JOHANNA EMILIA AGNES** (1872–1932), noted German dramatic soprano, born in Anclam. She made her debut at 17 at the Kroll Opera, Berlin, and by 1894 was at the Berlin Staatsoper. A year later she sang with the Damrosch Opera Company in New York as Elsa in *Lohengrin*. Between 1898 and 1917 she sang as leading dramatic soprano at the Metropolitan Opera, specializing in the Italian and German repertoire. She was still singing well up to the time of her death in Berlin.

GADWALL, large duck, *Anas strepera*, of the family Anatidae, found throughout the Northern Hemisphere. Gadwalls reach a length of about 20 in., have a wingspread of up to 3 ft., and weigh about 2 lb. Males are grayish with chestnut wing markings, a white underside, and black tail markings. Females are a mottled brown color and have a yellow bill. Gadwalls are found near marshy areas and along pond and stream banks. Like most ducks they are herbivorous and eat pondweed and grasses.

GAEA [jē′ə] **or GE** [jē], in Greek mythology, goddess of earth, the first being born from Chaos. Without a mate she bore Uranus (sky) and Pontus (sea). By Uranus she bore the Titans, Cyclopes, Hecatonchires, Erinyes, and Giants. She helped her son Cronus overthrow Uranus, and prophesied Cronus' overthrow by Zeus.

GAELIC LANGUAGES or GOIDELIC LANGUAGES. *See* CELTIC LANGUAGES.

GAELIC LITERATURES. *See* IRISH LITERATURE; ANCIENT; MANX LANGUAGE AND LITERATURE; SCOTTISH GAELIC LITERATURE.

GAFFNEY, city of northern South Carolina and seat of Cherokee County, in the upper Piedmont. Textiles and clothing are the principal manufactures. Limestone College (estab., 1845) is the oldest women's college in South Carolina. Cowpens National Battlefield site is 12 mi. northwest. Inc., 1875; pop., 13,253.

GAFSA, largest town in Tunisia's phosphate mining area. Because of discoveries of prehistoric artifacts nearby, its ancient name Capsa was given to the Capsian paleolithic culture of North Africa and southern Europe. During the North African campaign of World War II it was the location of early battles between Americans and Germans. Pop., 24,345.

GÁG [gäg], **WANDA** (1893–1946), American artist and author of children's books, born in New Ulm, Minn. Her picture books, while strikingly original in style and execution, are reminiscent of European folk art. *Millions of Cats* (1928) has become a modern classic for young children. In *Tales from Grimm* (1936) she edited and illustrated her own translations from the German. Her woodcuts, etchings, and lithographs brought recognition in art circles.

GAGAKU (Jap., "elegant music"), ceremonial court and temple music of Japan, introduced from China and elsewhere in the 8th century A.D. A dance performance of *Gagaku* is called *Bugaku.* The dance movements are not theatrical, for the ceremonial motivation is kept intact. There are three basic divisions of *Gagaku* music and dance. *Togaku,* which forms the largest part of the repertory, includes elements from China, India, and Central Asia. Music modes taken from Korea and Manchuria are called *Komagaku.* Masked dances (*hashiri-mai*) are a part of both repertories. A third type, which includes vocal music, is called *utamono.*
See also JAPAN: *Japanese Music.*

GAGARIN [gə-gä′rĭn], **YURI ALEKSEYEVICH** (1934–68), Soviet astronaut who made the first earth-orbiting flight into space. A colonel in the Soviet air force, Gagarin graduated from air cadet school in 1957. On Apr. 12, 1961, he was sent aloft in the 10,460-lb. space craft *Vostok I,* and made a single orbit of the earth, a distance of some 25,000 mi., in about 108 minutes, including ascent and descent. Gagarin was killed in a jet plane crash while on a training mission.
See also SPACE EXPLORATION.

GAGE, THOMAS (1721–87), British general and colonial Governor. He joined the British army as a youth and fought against the French in Flanders (1747–48) during the War of the Austrian Succession. Transferred to North America, he served in the French and Indian War (1755–63). Under Gen. Edward Braddock he took part in the disastrous expedition to Fort Duquesne, and he fought in the unsuccessful siege of Fort Ticonderoga under Gen. James Abercrombie. He was briefly (1760) military governor of Montreal after participating in its capture. Promoted to major general in 1761, he succeeded Gen. Jeffrey Amherst as the commander of all British forces in North America (1763–72).

His policy was one of patience in dealing with the increasingly violent resistance of the colonies to British imperial policy. Becoming Governor of Massachusetts in 1774, he was confronted with a critical situation. He attempted to confiscate colonial military stores, and his order sending troops to Concord (Apr. 18, 1775) to seize an arms cache precipitated the first battle of the American Revolution. Following the British losses at Bunker Hill on June 17, for which he was severely criticized at home, he resigned and returned to England.

ROBERT MIDDLEKAUFF, Yale University

GAGE, instrument used for measuring properties such as thickness, temperature, pressure, electric resistance, velocity, time, surface roughness, or radioactivity. The term "gage" customarily refers to mechanical measuring devices; the term "instrument" to electric and other measuring devices. Gages are often used to establish standards; for example, thickness of sheet metal, diameter of wire, or pressure and temperature of a liquid.

When gages are used to measure, errors of various types occur. These errors have been classified as those inherent in the type of gage, those due to the method by which the gage is used, and those made by the observer. The type of gage required for measuring a physical property, such as temperature, varies according to the amount of accuracy desired. An ordinary mercury-filled glass thermometer would be satisfactory for measuring temperature from $-35°$ F. to $+750°$ F. with an accuracy of $\pm 2°$. An electric-resistance thermometer would be required if an accuracy on the order of .005° F. between $-400°$ F. and $+2,000°$ F. were required.

Statistical techniques are often utilized when accounting for residual errors that may accrue during measurement. Probability analysis is applied after several data are taken.

The accuracy of gages is improved when the measurements are differences rather than absolute values. For instance, the manometer utilizes the difference in liquid level as a pressure-differential measuring device. Gonogo gages, which are widely used in manufacturing inspection processes, measure differences in size.

Several types of gages, each utilizing a different scientific principle, are often used for measuring the same quantity. One means of measurement is then used as a check on another. Measurements of time may be accomplished by clocks, by radar signals, or radioactive decay. Gages which measure speed might include the tachometer, the stroboscope, or a stop watch.

SEVERAL TYPES OF GAGES

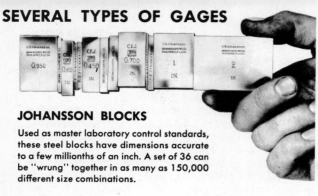

JOHANSSON BLOCKS

Used as master laboratory control standards, these steel blocks have dimensions accurate to a few millionths of an inch. A set of 36 can be "wrung" together in as many as 150,000 different size combinations.

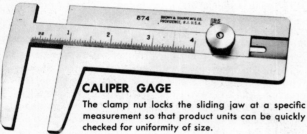

CALIPER GAGE

The clamp nut locks the sliding jaw at a specific measurement so that product units can be quickly checked for uniformity of size.

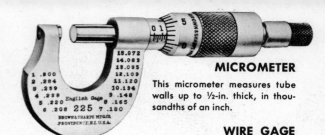

MICROMETER

This micrometer measures tube walls up to 1/2-in. thick, in thousandths of an inch.

WIRE GAGE

The number of the smallest slot the wire slips through is taken as the wire size in terms of the gage standard used. (BROWNE & SHARPE MFG. CO.)

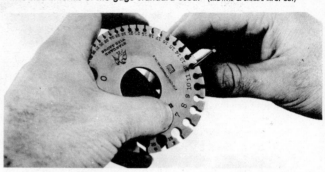

The use of gages for maintaining the accuracy of similar parts has made interchangeable manufacture possible. In the machine tool field, for example, gages are usually classified as working, inspection, and reference. Working gages are those used by the workmen in the assembly or manufacture of a product. Inspection gages are used by inspectors to check the product during various stages of manufacture. Reference gages are used for periodic checks of the inspection gages to make sure that standards of manufacturing accuracy have not been changed.

Many machine shops, in order to establish a precision linear measurement, use gage blocks. These blocks, often referred to as Johansson blocks, are small hardened steel blocks of a given thickness, held to a tolerance of a few millionths of an inch.

DONALD N. ZWIEP, Worcester Polytechnic Institute

See also:

ANEMOMETER	PRESSURE GAGE
FLOW METER	SPEEDOMETER
GAS METER	TACHOMETER
PEDOMETER	WATER METER

GAGLIANO [gä-lyä′nō], family of famous violin makers working in Naples, Italy, from the 17th to 19th centuries. The founder of the dynasty was ALESSANDRO (worked c.1695–1725), whose instruments, many of which are of fine quality, are distinguished by a reddish varnish. His sons NICOLA and GENNARO followed the designs of Antonio Stradivari more closely than their father, as did FERDINANDO and GIUSEPPE, the sons of Nicolà. The instruments of the third generation were not generally comparable to the work of the earlier Gagliani. Altogether, more than 20 of the family followed the craft, but the later workmanship was generally inferior.

GAINES'S MILL, BATTLE OF. *See* PENINSULA CAMPAIGN.

GAINESVILLE, city of north-central Florida, and seat of Alachua County. The city is the trading center of a forestry and agricultural region. Industries include processing of treated-wood products and tung oil, and electronics. The University of Florida (estab., 1853) and Florida State Museum are located here. Settled, 1854; inc., 1869; pop., 64,510.

GAINESVILLE, city of northeastern Georgia, and seat of Hall County, on Lake Sidney Lanier, one of the state's recreational areas. It is a leading poultry-processing center, and has highly diverse industries, the most important being the production of textiles and furniture. Brenau College for Women (estab., 1878) is here. Inc., 1821; pop., 15,459.

GAINESVILLE, city of northern Texas and seat of Cooke County, located on the Red River. The principal industries include flour milling, cotton-seed processing, and petroleum refining. Pop., 13,830.

GAINSBOROUGH, THOMAS (1727–88), one of the most noted English painters of the 18th century. Although most famous for portraits of his contemporaries, Gainsborough's landscapes are also of great merit. The youngest son of a wool merchant from Suffolk, Gainsborough went to London at the age of 15 as the apprentice of a silversmith. While learning the silversmith's trade he met a painter and drawing teacher, Hubert Gravelot. He worked with Gravelot and also studied with Francis Hayman, one of the most popular painters of the day. Gainsborough set himself up as a practicing artist in his native Suffolk in 1745, specializing in portrait painting. By 1760 he had established himself at Bath, the favorite 18th-century resort of well-to-do Englishmen. Here he gained a certain reputation, which led to commissions for portraits by some of the most prominent people in English society. Among his famous sitters were the theater personalities David Garrick, Mrs. Siddons, and Richard Sheridan, as well as the lawyer Sir William Blackstone, and Samuel Johnson, the litterateur. By 1774 Gainsborough was settled in London and included among his patrons King George III and his family.

Gainsborough characterized himself as something of a "wild goose." Although one of the founders of the Royal Academy in 1768, he had broken with it by 1784. Ostensibly a dispute arose over the hanging of his pictures at an exhibition, but more likely this break with the Academy was the result of differences in approach to art. His free use of color and fresh, almost spontaneous brushwork and his delight in painting landscapes from nature were all inimical to the stolid, official style of the Academy. In his late landscapes especially, Gainsborough achieves a lightness and directness of approach which anticipates many of the visual achievements of the late 19th-century Impressionist painters. Similarly, his portraits display an incisiveness quite contrary to the flattering portraits of some of his contemporaries. But throughout all of his work his fine draughtsmanship, love of the texture and quality of paint, and the freedom with which he handles his medium are outstanding.

His most famous, popular portrait is "The Blue Boy" (Huntington Library and Art Gallery, San Marino, Calif.). Among his best portraits are "The Artist's Daughters" and "Mrs. Siddons," both in the National Gallery, London. "The Watering Place," also in the National Gallery, is notable among his landscapes.

STANLEY FERBER,
State University of N.Y. at Binghamton

GAINSBOROUGH, urban district and inland port of west Lincolnshire, England, on the Trent River. Industries include farming and flour milling and, since 1950, the manufacture of corsets and underwear. The town was the model for St. Ogg's in George Eliot's *Mill on the*

Thomas Gainsborough's portrait of the great actress Mrs. Siddons (1785; National Gallery, London). (ART REFERENCE BUREAU)

Floss. John Robinson, a Pilgrim Father, was born here. Pop., 17,276.

GAINZA PAZ [hīn'sä päs'], **ALBERTO** (1899–   ), Argentine newspaper publisher. He was born into a prominent newspaper family, his grandfather having founded *La Prensa* of Buenos Aires in 1869. The paper came to be recognized as one of the world's greatest, and Gainza Paz had active charge of it by 1939. Because it opposed the military regime which seized power in 1943, it was subjected to many reprisals in the years following. *La Prensa* was finally forced to suspend publication in 1951, and the paper was turned over to labor unions to become a pro-government organ. Gainza Paz regained control of *La Prensa* after the fall of Juan Perón in 1955.

GAIRDNER [gârd'nər], **LAKE,** saline lake of south-central Australia, in the state of South Australia. It occupies the bottom of a basin of interior drainage north of the Gawler Ranges. Area, 1,600 sq. mi.

GAISERIC. *See* GENSERIC OR GAISERIC.

GAITSKELL [gāt'skəl], **HUGH TODD NAYLOR** (1906–63), British statesman and leader of the Labour party. Educated at Oxford, he taught economics at London University, joined the civil service in 1939, and entered Parliament in 1945. In 1947 he became minister of fuel and power in the government of Clement Attlee and in 1950 became chancellor of the exchequer. After Labour left office in 1951, Gaitskell led the conservative wing of the party in a bitter struggle against the leader of the left, Aneurin Bevan. In 1955 Attlee retired and Gaitskell became party leader. Despite his skillful campaigning, Labour was defeated in 1959. Gaitskell then fought with some success to convince the party to stop advocating the extensive nationalization of industry. He favored cooperation with the United States in foreign policy and, despite a determined campaign by the Labour left for unilateral disarmament, he favored Britain's keeping nuclear weapons. By the time of his sudden death, Gaitskell had converted the Labour party, still officially socialist, to the more moderate policies of the mixed economy and the welfare state.

MELVIN SHEFFTZ, State University of N.Y. at Binghamton

GAIUS CAESAR, real name of Caligula (q.v.).

GALAGO. *See* BUSH BABY.

GALAHAD, son of Elaine and Lancelot. Galahad was the perfect knight, who in late versions of the Arthurian legend achieved the Holy Grail. *See* GRAIL, HOLY.

GALÁPAGOS ISLANDS, group of 13 large and many small islands belonging to Ecuador, lying 650 mi. from its coast, in the Pacific. Known officially as El Archipielago de Colón (Columbus), they are governed by Ecuador's Ministry of National Defense. Although the group is on the equator its climate is temperate, cooled by the Humboldt Current.

A Spaniard, Tomas de Berlanga, discovered the Galápagos in 1535 but they were not permanently settled until

Ecuador claimed them in 1832. The English naturalist Charles Darwin visited them on his voyage in the *Beagle* in 1835. He was intrigued by the unusual wildlife: four-eyed fish, flightless cormorants, a finch that uses a stick as a tool to obtain food, and unique sunflower trees. Of particular interest were the giant tortoises (many over 300 lbs.) which live for 400 years—the world's longest-living animals. *Galápago* is Spanish for tortoise. The chief town is Puerto Baquerizo. The people earn their living mainly from fishing and farming. Pop., 1,900.

MELVIN MORRIS, N.Y. State University College at New Paltz

GALAPAGOS TORTOISE. *See* GIANT TORTOISE.

GALATEA [găl-ə-tē'ə], in Greek mythology, a water nymph, daughter of Nereus and Doris, who loved the handsome youth Acis. She was loved by the ugly Cyclops Polyphemus, who killed Acis, leaving Galatea inconsolable. Galatea is also the name of an ivory statue created by the sculptor Pygmalion that came to life as a result of his prayers to Aphrodite.

GALAŢI [gä-läts'], city of eastern Rumania, in Galaţi Region, situated on the left bank of the Danube between the mouths of Prut and Siret rivers, near the border of the U.S.S.R. A major naval base and transportation center, Galaţi has many ship- and dockyards, and in and around its Bădălan district new industries have been developed. Among its historical and architectural features are the monument of the Union of the Principalities, by Rafael Romanelli; the Precista Church (17th century); and the Sfântu Gheorghe Church (1665).

The first written records of the town date from the 17th century. First under Turkish control, Galaţi became the headquarters of General Potemkin, a protégé of Catherine II of Russia, during the later 18th century. Pop., 95,646.

GALATIA [gə-lā'shə], ancient district of central Asia Minor comprising parts of Cappadocia and Phrygia. It took its name from the Gauls, or Galatians, a Celtic people brought into Asia Minor as mercenaries by Nicomedes I of Bithynia in 278 B.C. The Galatians proved hard to control, indulging in plundering raids against the cities of the coast, from which they exacted tribute. By the mid-3d century they inhabited the territory between Bithynia and Pontus on the north and Pamphylia on the south, forming a buffer state between the Seleucid power of the interior and the kingdoms of the coast. They continued to make raids, exact tribute, and expand, until checked by a severe defeat at the hands of Attalus I of Pergamum c.230, and again by a Roman army under Manlius Vulso in 189. The Galatians consisted of three tribes: Tolistobogii in the district of Pessinus, Tectosages around Ancyra, and Trocmi at Tavium. The Galatians helped Pompey in the Mithridatic wars and were rewarded by an increase of territory. In 25 B.C. Galatia became a province of the Roman Empire. A Celtic language was still spoken in this area in the 4th century A.D.

RODNEY S. YOUNG, University Museum, University of Pennsylvania

GALATIANS, EPISTLE TO THE, a letter from St. Paul to the inhabitants of the cities in Asia Minor who were evangelized by him on his first missionary journey. St. Paul writes passionately against the Judaizers, who were urging Gentile converts to accept circumcision and the Jewish Law. The Law, he retorts, has served its time; now that Christ has come, salvation depends on faith in him. But freedom does not mean license; the Christian must reflect Christ's spirit in his conduct.

This epistle defines Christianity as being the true Israel, not just one sect of Judaism. It also contains important autobiographic material about St. Paul's conversion and his relations with the older apostles, particularly St. Peter and St. James.

Some scholars date Galatians 49 A.D., before the Council of Jerusalem, to ease certain discrepancies with Acts. But a comparison with the style and content of other epistles suggests a date near 54 A.D.

G. M. STYLER, Cambridge University

GALAX [gā'lăks], city of southwestern Virginia near the North Carolina boundary. It is a manufacturing center for furniture and textiles. The Annual Old Fiddlers' Convention held here each August is a popular folk-music festival. Fincastle Resolutions, a local document similar to the Declaration of Independence, was adopted Jan. 20, 1775, at the nearby settlement of Lead Mines. Inc., 1906; pop., 6,278.

GALAXY [găl'ək-sē], huge system of stars in gravitational association with each other, and usually well removed in space from similar systems. Most galaxies are disk shaped, but a substantial number are elliptical or nearly spherical. The band of stars that we call the Milky Way is formed by the disk-shaped galaxy to which our sun belongs. The center of the Milky Way galaxy lies be-

Galaxies have different shapes. Many are elliptical as in A. Most are disk-shaped, and have a spiral structure as in B and C. Less common is the irregular galaxy D, which has no particular shape. (YERKES OBSERVATORY)

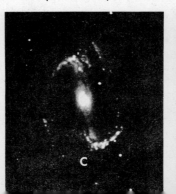
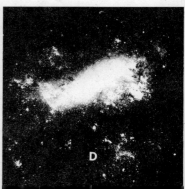

A   B   C   D

yond the constellation Sagittarius. Many stars and clouds of cosmic dust block the galactic center from view with optical telescopes, but radio telescopes are able to "see" even beyond the center.

The Milky Way galaxy contains some 10 billion stars, most of which lie within a region about 80,000 light-years wide and 20,000 light-years thick. The Milky Way was long thought to be the largest galaxy, but revised distance concepts have revealed that many other galaxies are larger. Our sun is in the outer regions of the galaxy, about 26,500 light-years from the galactic center.

Because of the obscuring effect of stars and cosmic clouds, external galaxies (those other than the Milky Way, formerly called Island Universes) are best observed when we look out of the sides of our galaxy, away from the Milky Way. One external galaxy is faintly visible in the Northern Hemisphere in the constellation Andromeda. Two relatively nearby galaxies are conspicuous in the Southern Hemisphere. These are the Magellanic Clouds, noted by Ferdinand Magellan during his pioneer voyages of the early 16th century. Thousands of other galaxies have been studied with large telescopes throughout the world.

Most disk-shaped galaxies have a spiral structure, with long arms composed of stars and cosmic clouds spiraling outward from the galactic center in the plane of the disk. The galaxies rotate generally about an axis through the center and perpendicular to the plane of the disk, and in a direction such that the spiraling arms are trailing. Rotation periods are of the order of a half-billion years. Studies with radio telescopes have shown that our own galaxy is of the spiral type.

Unlike stars, external galaxies present a definite surface of finite size to the astronomer's scrutiny. Their outlines, however, are often hazy and indefinite, and early astronomers classified them as nebulae. This name is still sometimes used in the term extragalactic nebulae, synonymous with external galaxy. Their identification as galaxies, however, clearly distinguishes them from the galactic nebulae, which are amorphous clouds of gas and dust within our own galaxy.

Galaxies tend to occur in clusters rather than being sprinkled uniformly through space. Most galactic clusters contain about 200 members.

External galaxies are systematically speeding away from us at ever-increasing speeds, leading to the concept of an expanding universe. This motion is revealed by the "red shift," the shifting of their spectral lines toward the red end of the spectrum. This phenomenon, a Doppler effect caused by the receding light sources, is one of the most striking and puzzling problems of galactic research.
R. GRANT ATHAY

GALBA [găl′bə], **SERVIUS SULPICIUS** (3 B.C.–69 A.D.), Roman Emperor (68–69). While governor of Spanish Tarraconensis, Galba joined Vindex's revolt against the Emperor Nero, and after the deaths of both Vindex and Nero was proclaimed Emperor by the Praetorian Guard. His reign was marked by avarice, severity, and favoritism. His choice of Piso Licanianus as his successor proved fatal: Otho, eager himself for the succession, bribed the Praetorian Guard to assassinate Galba.

GALBRAITH, JOHN KENNETH (1908–   ), Canadian-born U.S. economist, who has won world acclaim for his iconoclastic writings. He was graduated from the University of Toronto and continued his studies at the University of California, Berkeley. He has held high governmental positions and taught economics at Harvard.

Galbraith, a prolific writer, has given eloquent expression to heterodox views concerning the organization of the economic system. He differs from orthodox economists in many ways. He rejects the orthodox model of an economy organized by beneficent competition; stresses the role of power, especially as exerted by mastodonic business firms; and believes that quality of life rather than volume of production should be the measure of economic achievement. He holds that consumers' demand for goods is largely created through advertising by mammoth companies and does not often originate spontaneously out of human wants, as postulated by the neoclassical economist. Although not warmly accepted by orthodox scholars, Galbraith is grudgingly admired by many of them for his original insights and brilliance.

Galbraith has also achieved fame outside the realm of economics. He is a versatile essayist, amusing, satirical, elegant. He was wartime price administrator, 1941–43, and U.S. ambassador to India 1961–63—and some of his writings lampoon the U.S. State Department. He has written on East Indian art and has given us charming memoirs of his early life in Canada. His most important books are *Economics and the Public Purpose* (1973), *The New Industrial State* (1967) and *The Affluent Society* (1958).)
JOHN S. GAMBS

GALEN [gā′lən], Lat. name Claudius Galenus (c.150–c.200), "the prince of physicians," revered as the supreme medical authority until the 16th century. Born in Pergamum in Asia Minor and educated at Pergamum, Smyrna, and Alexandría, he served as personal physician to three Roman Emperors. He wrote more than 500 books, including a dictionary of five volumes. Galen made extensive anatomical and physiological investigations, and although his contributions were significant, his authority was such that his erroneous concepts stifled medical progress for centuries.

GALENA [gə-lē′nə], a city of extreme northwestern Illinois, and seat of Jo Daviess County. It is a minor agricultural trade center and has some diversified manufacturing, including dairy products, gloves, stoves, and thermometers. Galena was once the largest city of northern Illinois and a principal mining center.

Galena mined and smelted lead and zinc from the early 18th century until after the Civil War. The city was named after the local lead sulfide ore. During the 1840's and 1850's, its shipments of lead, zinc, and grain made it the principal port on the upper Mississippi River. Its mines declined in importance after 1865, and the town, though well preserved, has steadily lost population. Tourists are attracted to its old buildings, including the Market House, the first courthouse, and two homes of Ulysses S. Grant: his original home and Memorial House, presented to him by the city after the Civil War. There is also a museum of history and art.
JEROME D. FELLMAN

GALENA, lead sulfide mineral, PbS. It is found in cubic crystals or granular masses. It is heavy and gray, with a bright, metallic luster. Common throughout the world, galena is the principal ore of lead. About 2,500,000 tons are mined annually, mostly from the United States, the U.S.S.R., Australia, Mexico, Germany, and Canada.

PROPERTIES: *Crystal System,* Isometric; *Hardness* (Mohs' Scale), 2½; *Density,* 7.6.
See also CRYSTALLOGRAPHY; LEAD; MINERALOGY.

GALENA PARK, city of southeastern Texas, located just east of Houston. It has oil refineries and chemical, gypsum, and steel plants. Pop., 10,479.

GALERIUS VALERIUS MAXIMIANUS [gə-lēr-əs və-lēr′ē-əs măk-sĭm-ē-ā′nəs], **GAIUS,** Roman Emperor (reigned 305–11). After serving in the army under Diocletian, Galerius was made Caesar in the East (293). As such he was chiefly concerned with the defense of the Danube and Persian frontiers. He instigated Diocletian's persecution of the Christians (303). When Diocletian abdicated (305), Galerius became Augustus in the East, nominally second to Constantius I in the West, but actually superior to him. Galerius refused to accept Maxentius as successor to Constantius in the West (306) and succeeded in having Severus appointed. An illness prompted Galerius to issue an edict of partial toleration to the Christians in 309.

GALESBURG, city of western Illinois, and seat of Knox County. Its economy is based on agriculture, mining, manufacturing, and transportation. Nearby areas produce grains, and coal, clay, sand, and gravel. Galesburg contains major railroad shops and yards. It has foundries; manufactures refrigeration equipment, steel products, bricks, and clothing; and processes agricultural goods. Knox College and Galesburg State Research Hospital are here.

The community was founded as Knox College Town in 1836 and was the site of a Lincoln-Douglas debate in 1858. It was a station on the Underground Railroad before the Civil War. The birthplace of poet Carl Sandburg is preserved here. Pop., 36,290.

GALICIA [gə-lĭsh′ə], historic region northeast of the Carpathian Mountains, now divided between Poland and the Soviet Union. A rich agricultural region, western Galicia became medieval Poland's political and cultural heartland when the Polish capital was moved to Cracow in the 14th century. Its natural resources and vast mineral deposits made western Galicia an industrial center.

Long disputed between Poland and Hungary, Galicia was acquired by Poland in 1372. The San River became the dividing line between the Polish Roman Catholic population in the west, and the Ukrainians belonging to the Uniat denomination in the east.

Following the first partition of Poland (1772), Galicia was acquired by Austria; it was restored to Poland in 1919. After World War II the Soviet Union claimed eastern Galicia. The postwar Polish-Soviet border treaty (1945) yielded most of eastern Galicia, including the city of Lvov, to the Soviet Union, which incorporated it into the Ukrainian S.S.R.

DRAGOŠ D. KOSTICH, New School for Social Research

GALICIA, former kingdom of northwestern Spain corresponding to modern provinces of La Coruña, Pontevedra, Lugo, and Orense. It is characterized by mountainous terrain, heavy rainfall, and a rocky coast line indented by the estuaries (*rías*) of numerous swift-flowing rivers. The harbors of El Ferrol, La Coruña, and Vigo are among the best in Spain. Agriculture and fishing, the chief industries, are inadequate to support the population, and emigration has traditionally been heavy. Area, 11,254 sq. mi.

GALILEE [găl′ə-lē], hilly region of northern Palestine, west of the Jordan rift, extending from Lake Hule southward 35 mi. almost to Scythopolis. Jesus of Nazareth lived his youth there, and as an adult preached around Capernaum at the north end of the Sea of Galilee.

GALILEE, SEA OF, also Lake Tiberias or Kinneret, freshwater lake in northern Israel, formed mainly by the Jordan River as it widens in its flow through a basin. The lake, 696 ft. below sea level, is 13 mi. long and 8 mi. wide, with an area of 64 sq. mi. Its maximum depth is 200 ft. It is encompassed by mountains, the most notable of which is Mount Hermon in Lebanon to the north. On the southern shore is the village of Deganya, founded in 1909 as the first collective settlement in Palestine. On the western shore is Ein Gev, where Israel's annual music festival is held.

The Sea of Galilee often appears in the Old Testament as the Sea of Chinnereth, or Chinneroth, and in the New Testament as the Sea of Tiberias and the Lake of Gennesaret. At the shore town of Capernaum are the ruins of the synagogue where Jesus preached. Other ancient lakeside towns associated with Jesus are Chorazin, Magdala, Gadara, Tabgha, and Tiberias. At Tabgha, where the Feeding of Five Thousand is believed to have occurred, is the Church of the Multiplication of the Loaves, which has a mosaic depicting the miracle.

YAAKOV MORRIS, Consul of Israel in New York City

Shores of the Sea of Galilee, Israel.

Birnback Publishing Service

GALILEO [găl-ə-lā′ō] (1564–1642), Italian scientist, founder of modern physics and of telescopic astronomy, and champion of freedom in scientific research. He was born in Pisa on February 15, 1564; his father, Vincenzio Galilei, was an able musician and author of distinguished works on music theory. Galileo, as he is generally called,

Portrait of Galileo, the founder of modern physics, by Sustermans.

received his early schooling from Augustinian monks at Vallombrosa, near Florence. He studied medicine at the University of Pisa from 1581 to 1585, but was obliged to stop short of a degree because of poverty. About 1583 Galileo's interests had turned to mathematics, and his continued studies in that field won him a professorship at Pisa in 1589.

Careful observations of the pendulum, of floating bodies, and of motion had convinced him that physical problems should be dealt with mathematically, in opposition to the prevailing physics of Aristotle. It is said that at Pisa Galileo publicly demonstrated an error in Aristotle's conclusions by dropping weights from the Leaning Tower. His antagonism toward traditional philosophy placed him in sharp conflict with the older professors. In 1592 he left Pisa to take the chair of mathematics at the University of Padua, where he also gave private lectures and composed works on mechanics, fortification, and cosmology.

In 1597 he began manufacturing for sale his proportional compass, a mathematical instrument of great practical utility. Shortly after 1600 he invented a primitive thermometer and a device utilizing the pendulum for timing of the pulse. In 1604 Galileo discovered the mathematical law governing freely falling bodies, though his conception of uniform acceleration was still defective. In July, 1609, Galileo heard rumors of the invention of the telescope in the Netherlands and devised a superior instrument which he promptly applied to astronomical observations. Early in 1610 he published his discoveries concerning the mountains of the moon, the nature of nebulae and the Milky Way, and the existence of four satellites of Jupiter. This book excited wide interest and enabled Galileo to secure appointment at Florence as court mathematician to Cosimo (II) de' Medici. Soon afterward he announced his discovery of the phases of Venus, a strong argument against the Ptolemaic system, and some observations of Saturn's shape.

In 1611 he visited Rome, where he was made a member of the pioneer scientific academy known as the Lincei. Upon his return to Florence he composed a book on hydrostatics which aroused violent opposition from several professors, and in 1613 the Lincei published his book on sunspots. In this work Galileo refuted the views of a Jesuit scientist and openly supported the Copernican

theory, which he had privately accepted for many years. Attacked by the clergy for maintaining that the earth moved, Galileo next wrote a spirited letter in defense of free scientific research, which his enemies copied and forwarded to the Inquisition at Rome. In 1615 Galileo countered by expanding and circulating this letter. In December he went personally to Rome to argue against prohibition of the Copernican theory. Early in 1616, however, a commission appointed by Pope Paul V ruled adversely. Galileo's previous books were not banned, but he was told to abandon the idea that the earth moved.

For some time Galileo concentrated on practical applications of science and perfected a compound microscope. Following the appearance of three comets in 1618, however, he had entered into controversy with a Jesuit mathematician over the nature of such bodies, and in 1623 published an exposition of his scientific philosophy under the auspices of the Lincei. Heartened by the election that year of his friend Maffeo Cardinal Barberini as Pope Urban VIII, Galileo decided to write his famed *Dialogue Concerning the Two Chief World Systems*, which he published in 1632. On various grounds this book was found to be in violation of the instructions given to him in 1616, and he was summoned to Rome for trial by the Inquisition. In June, 1633, the book was prohibited, Galileo was forced to abjure, and was sentenced to indefinite imprisonment. This sentence was not harshly enforced, but for the rest of his life Galileo remained under direct custody of officers of the Inquisition, first at Siena and later at his own dwelling at Arcetri, near France. Resuming and perfecting his investigations of the laws of motion, mechanics, and strength of materials, Galileo then composed his crowning scientific work, the *Discourses and Mathematical Demonstration Concerning Two New Sciences*, published at Leyden in 1638. Though now completely blind, he continued to dictate scientific letters and even to design a pendulum clock. Galileo died in January, 1642.

Galileo was of average stature, robust build, florid complexion, and had reddish hair. He is said to have been easily moved to anger, and as quickly restored to good humor. Galileo's musical, literary, and artistic talents nearly equaled his scientific genius. He wrote most of his books in Italian, caring less for the opinions of scholars abroad than for the education of his countrymen. During much of his life Galileo was subject to severe arthritic afflictions and a painful double hernia, being frequently bedridden. He enjoyed the loyal and devoted friendship of many scholars, noblemen, and churchmen, and suffered the implacable enmity of others. Brilliant students inspired by his enthusiasm ably carried on the scientific revolution which Galileo did so much to begin. Among his pupils are to be numbered such celebrated scientists and mathematicians as Benedetto Castelli, Evangelista Torricelli, Bonaventura Cavalieri, and Vincenzio Viviani.

Consult *Dialogues Concerning Two New Sciences*, trans. by Henry Crew and Alfonso de Salvio (1914); *Dialogue Concerning the Two Chief World Systems*, ed. by Stillman Drake (1953); Santillana, Giorgio de, *The Crime of Galileo* (1955); *On Motion and on Mechanics*, ed. by I. E. Drabkin and Stillman Drake (1960).

STILLMAN DRAKE, Author,
Discoveries and Opinions of Galileo

GALION [găl′yən], city of north-central Ohio, about 55 mi. north of Columbus. Manufactures include telephone equipment, road-construction machinery, steel bodies for trucks, burial vaults, and clothing. Settled, 1831; inc., 1840; pop., 13,123.

GALL [gôl], **ST.** (c.550–645), Irish missionary. His early life in Ireland is unknown. He first emerges as one of 12 companions of St. Columbanus on his missionary journey from Bangor to Leuxeuil. When the group fled from Burgundy to Italy, St. Gall, being ill, was left at Lake Constance. An ardent fisherman, he adopted the solitary life and resided and was buried in a cell near the Steinach River. The celebrated monastery of St. Gall, a leading European center of literature and the arts, was subsequently erected over his remains.

GALL (c.1840–94), Sioux Indian chief. As subordinate to Sitting Bull, he distinguished himself in the battle of Little Big Horn (1876) and fled with his chief to Canada. Returning to the United States in 1881, he surrendered and settled down as a farmer on the Standing Rock Reservation in the Dakotas. There he urged Indian education and supported the U.S. government in its efforts to divide the Sioux reservation and obtain certain land cessions. In later years he was a judge of the court of Indian affairs at Standing Rock.

GALL [gäl], **FRANZ JOSEPH** (1758–1828), German physician, pioneer in brain studies and founder of the pseudoscience of phrenology. Gall correctly pointed out that gray matter is the active part of the brain in which nerve impulses originate, while white matter is connecting material. He also believed that specific areas of the brain control specific body movements. Modern neurologists can now map the brain and pinpoint the part which controls finger movements, for example, thus proving Gall's idea correct. Gall felt that the shape of the brain, and thus the shape of the skull, had to do with mental capacity, emotional qualities, and character. By touching the skull, he believed, one could deduce the relative amount of the characteristic located directly underneath. This was the beginning of the pseudoscience of phrenology, in which a man's character may be analyzed by feeling the bumps on his head. While his views were not accepted by the medical profession, they gained wide favor with the general public. After his death, Gall's disciples exaggerated his "science" to almost total nonsense. As a result, the stigma of quack in now attached to Gall, and his valuable work tends to be forgotten.

E. CARWILE LeROY, M.D.

GALLA PLACIDIA [găl′ə plə-sĭd′ē-ə] (388–450), Western Roman Empress, daughter of Theodosius I. Taken prisoner by the Visigoths, she married Ataulphus in 414, but after his death returned to the imperial court. In 417 she married Constantius who in 421 became co-Emperor with her brother Honorius. After the death of Constantius she quarreled with Honorius, and retired to Constantinople, where she ruled for 25 years as Regent for her son, Valentinian III. Her tomb at Ravenna, adorned with famous mosaics and sculptured sarcophagi, is preserved.

GALLATIN [găl′ə-tĭn], **ALBERT** (1761–1849), American statesman and diplomat. He was born in Geneva, Switzerland, and emigrated to the United States in 1780. In 1784 he settled in Fayette County, Pa. Relatively unsuccessful as a farmer and land dealer, he rose quickly in politics. Gallatin was an active Antifederalist and a democratic spokesman at the state constitutional convention (1789–90). He made his mark in the state legislature (1790–92) as a proponent of social reform and an expert in public finance. Elected (1793) to the U.S. Senate as a Republican, he was unseated by Federalists the next year on a technicality regarding the length of his citizenship. In the House of Representatives (1795–1801) he demonstrated an unexcelled grasp of complex fiscal questions.

Gallatin served as Secretary of the Treasury under Presidents Thomas Jefferson and James Madison, and in both administrations he was an influential figure. His principal objective was to reduce the public debt by economy of expenditure, specific appropriations, and strict accountability. The progress made was frustrated by increased expenses, in particular for the Louisiana Purchase. He departed from strict Jeffersonian principles in advocating the Bank of the United States and the use of federal funds for internal improvements. He found the problem of financing the War of 1812 overwhelming and received a leave of absence to become commissioner to Russia in a fruitless effort to secure mediation of the conflict (1813). Joining the American peace commissioners, he played a major role in negotiating several important features of the Treaty of Ghent with Great Britain (1814). Declining to return to his position in the Treasury, he served as minister to France (1816–23) and as minister to Great Britain (1826–27).

Still vigorous in old age, he lived in New York City and became a bank president and businessman, an occasional polemicist and orator, and a sponsor of cultural projects. He was president of the University of the City of New York, the New York Historical Society, and the American Ethnological Society. For the latter he wrote monographs on the American Indian which earned him a reputation as the "father of American ethnology." Contemporaries recognized Gallatin for his intellect, poise, integrity, and selflessness. Historians rank his achievements in fiscal

Albert Gallatin, by Rembrandt Peale (1778–1860). (INDEPENDENCE NATIONAL HISTORICAL PARK COLLECTION)

policy and diplomacy on a par with those of Alexander Hamilton and John Quincy Adams.

Consult Walters, Raymond, *Albert Gallatin, Jeffersonian Financier and Diplomat* (1957; repr., 1969).

ALFRED YOUNG

GALLATIN, city and Burley-tobacco market of north-central Tennessee, and seat of Sumner County. The center of an agricultural and livestock-producing area, it processes agricultural products and manufactures tobacco and shoes. It is the site of a Tennessee Valley Authority steam electric plant. Founded in 1802, it was named for Albert Gallatin, Secretary of the Treasury under President Thomas Jefferson and President James Madison. Inc., 1815; pop., 13,271.

GALL BLADDER AND GALLSTONES. The gall bladder is a pear-shaped sac attached to the under-surface of the liver. Its function is to store bile—the greenish-yellow liver secretion which contains both waste products and substances important in the digestion and absorption of fats. The gall bladder receives bile from the liver and discharges it into the small intestine via the common duct.

GALL BLADDER AND BILE DUCTS

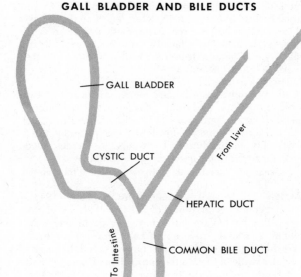

Gallstones, or biliary calculi, are concretions, consisting principally of cholesterol, calcium, and bile salts, which are formed in the gall bladder. The number and size vary from one large stone completely filling the gall bladder to hundreds of stones no larger than small pebbles. The stones result from the precipitation of cholesterol and other components of the bile fluid while the bile is stored in the gall bladder. Factors which are thought to contribute to the formation of the stones include a sluggishness of bile flow from the gall bladder, a relative increase in the cholesterol content in the bladder, excessive bile pigment formation and inflammation and infection of the bladder. In some cases gallstones taken from patients who have previously had typhoid fever have been shown to contain live typhoid germs.

Gallstones may develop in pregnancy as a consequence of the slowing of bile flow and an increased cholesterol content in the blood. It has been estimated that approximately 20% to 30% of women over 40 who have borne children have gallstones. Diabetics and obese persons also develop gallstones more frequently than others. There has been speculation that a diet rich in cholesterol may predispose to gallstone formation. The comparative rarity of gallstones among Orientals supports this view.

Many individuals with gallstones have no symptoms. When symptoms do appear they vary with the location of the stone. Stones in the gall bladder may produce dull sensations of discomfort, especially after eating fried foods. Attacks are apt to follow a heavy meal. Stones lodged in any of the ducts which conduct the bile from the liver and gall bladder to the intestine may cause biliary colic—attacks of severe pain in the right upper quarter of the abdomen. The pain radiates to below the right shoulder blade. Stones lodged in the cystic duct cause the bladder to become distended and sometimes infected. Stones lodged in the common duct, through which bile enters the intestine, often cause jaundice, a yellowish tinting of the skin and eyes resulting from the presence of excess bile pigments in the blood.

Diagnosis of gallstones may be made through X rays; calcium-containing stones appear as opaque ring-shaped areas in regular X-ray plates; noncalcium-containing stones appear as negative shadows on X-ray plates made after the patient is given a dye which concentrates in the gall bladder. Patients suffering from gallstones are advised to avoid fatty or fried foods, pork, and gas-producing foods. Surgical removal of the gall bladder (cholecystectomy) may be necessary in many cases. This operation leaves intact the duct which conducts bile from the liver to the intestine.

IRVING SOLOMON, M.D.

GALLE [*gäl*], seaport of southwest Ceylon. Its small but well-protected natural harbor was long an important port of call for vessels plying between the Red Sea and the Far East. Some believe that it was the Biblical Tarshish; in any case Arab geographers of the 14th century certainly knew it. The harbor retained its importance until the construction (1885) of the artificial harbor of Colombo. Today it serves mainly Ceylonese coastal shipping and the local trade of the southern part of the island. In 1507 the Portuguese occupied Galle and through their far-flung mercantile activities greatly increased its wealth. The Dutch, who succeeded the Portuguese in 1643, built a great fort, which is well preserved. The populations speak Singhalese, the principal language of Ceylon.

GALLEGOS [*gä-yē′gōs*], **RÓMULO** (1884–1969), Venezuelan novelist and statesman, born in Caracas. After holding several positions under the Gómez dictatorship, he finally broke with the government and in 1931 went into exile. In 1936 he returned to Venezuela as Minister of Education. In 1948 he became the first democratically elected President in the history of the country, but was overthrown the same year by a military coup. His novels are considered some of the best examples of Spanish-American realism. His most famous is *Doña Bárbara*

(1929; trans., 1931). Other novels are *Cantaclaro* (1931); *Canaima* (1935); and *Sobre la misma tierra* (On the Same Ground), 1943.

GALLEON [găl′yən], large, seagoing vessel prevalent during the 16th and 17th centuries. Ranging from under 100 to more than 1,000 tons, the galleons of the English and Spanish were square-sterned, bulky, heavily superstructured ships carrying projecting forecastles and four masts. The hull curved sharply upward at bow and stern with no continuous deck. The riggings varied, usually being a combination of square and lateen rigs. While speedy, the galleon had to be handled judiciously because of her top-heaviness. Primarily ships of war, galleons were also used as cargo carriers by the Spanish.

GALLFLY or GALL GNAT, name for the tiny, mosquitolike flies of family Cecidomyidae, found in many parts of the world. Gallflies are plant and animal pests. The chrysanthemum gallfly, *Diarthronomyia hypogaea*, produces galls on chrysanthemums and related garden flowers. Other species feed on decaying organic matter.

GALLIC RITE, liturgy peculiar to northern Italy, France, Spain, the British Isles, and Germany from the 4th century until sometime between the 8th and the 12th centuries, when it was generally superseded by the Roman rite. The origin of the Gallic rite is disputed, but some scholars believe that it is a Latin adaptation of the ancient Greek liturgy, because of similarity in such details as the preparation of the bread and wine at the beginning of Mass and the procession at the offertory, and that the Eastern influence was exerted especially through Auxentius, a 4th-century Bishop of Milan. The use of the Gallic rite continued in Gaul until the 8th century, in Scotland and Spain until the 11th, in England and Ireland until the 12th. Two varieties of Gallic rite are still in use: the Ambrosian in Milan and the Mozarabic in a few parishes in Toledo.

FREDERICK P. MANION, S.J., Xavier University, Cincinnati

GALLI-CURCI [gäl′lē-koor′chē], **AMELITA** (1882–1963), Italian coloratura soprano, born in Milan. She was self-taught as a singer and made her debut as Gilda in *Rigoletto* at the Costanzi, Rome, in 1909. A tour of Italy and South America followed. She first sang in the United States at the Auditorium, Chicago, 1916, as Gilda and created a furor. Her Metropolitan Opera debut was made in 1920 as Violetta in *La Traviata*, and she remained there through the 1930 season, when illness hastened the end of her career. Following Tetrazzini, she is among the finest Italian coloratura sopranos of the 20th century. Her vocal prime, however, lasted only about a dozen years.

GALLIC WARS, famous campaigns in Gaul waged by Julius Caesar against Gallic and Germanic tribes from 58 to 51 B.C. As proconsul (governor) of Transalpine Gaul, Caesar undertook the conquest of the region in order to end the threat from the restive tribes north of the Roman-held territory (Provence). In 58 B.C. he defeated the Helvetii at Bibracte, halting their attempt to penetrate southern Gaul. In the same year, Caesar defeated the German chief and drove him and his people back across

SCENE OF THE GALLIC WARS

The Roman Republic about 57 B.C.

Caesar's conquests

the Rhine. With the defeat of the Belgae (57 B.C.) and the Aquitanians and Veneti (56 B.C.), Caesar had placed practically all Gaul under Roman control. In 55 B.C. Caesar crossed over to Britain, returning there the following year with a larger force. After another German campaign, the Romans were faced by a general revolt of the Gallic tribes. Caesar defeated the leader of this revolt, the Arvernian Vercingetorix, at Alesia in 52 B.C. By 51 B.C. all Gaul was pacified.

Caesar's campaigns extended Roman rule from the Pyrenees to the Rhine and from the Atlantic to the Mediterranean. They also provided Caesar with an opportunity to train an army personally loyal to its commander, thus ensuring his political future. The campaigns are described by Caesar in his *Commentaries on the Gallic War*.

GERALD E. KADISH, State University of N.Y. at Binghamton

GALLIENI [gȧ-lyä-nē′], **JOSEPH SIMON** (1849–1916), French general. A graduate of St. Cyr, veteran of the Franco-Prussian War, and conqueror of Madagascar, Gallieni, as military governor of Paris after the outbreak of World War I, is credited with having saved the capital in the first battle of the Marne (Sept., 1914). He dispatched two infantry regiments to the front in taxicabs, buses, and trucks—the first movement of troops to a battlefield by motor transport in military history. He was Minister of War (1915–16).

GALLIENUS [găl-ē-ē′nəs], **PUBLIUS LICINIUS VALERIANUS EGNATIUS** (218–68), Roman Emperor (253–68). Born into a distinguished family, and well educated, he was co-Emperor with his father Valerian until the Persians captured the latter in 260. Gallienus seems to have displayed energy, loyalty, and intelligence in the struggle to preserve a rapidly disintegrating empire. However, the miseries of inflation, indiscipline, plague, the growth of powerful states in the East, and barbarian pressure from the north, produced devastating effects in his reign, for which he unfairly received the blame and was assassinated. His wife Salonina was the patroness of the philosopher Plotinus.

GALLINACEOUS [găl-ə-nā'shəs] **BIRDS,** name for the heavily built, chickenlike birds of order Galliformes. The birds have strongly clawed toes adapted for scratching and wings poorly suited for flight. The order includes seven families, many of them of considerable economic importance as food or game birds. Quail, pheasant, partridge, and fowl make up the family Phasianidae; turkeys are in the family Meleagrididae; guinea fowl comprise the family Numididae; grouse and ptarmigan are included in the family Tetraonidae; guans and curassows are in the family Cracidae. Unusual species are found in two families: the mound birds of Australia are in the family Megapodiidae, and the hoatzin of South America is the sole member of family Opisthocomidae.

See also:

CHACHALACA	PARTRIDGE
CURASSOW	PEACOCK
FOWL	PHEASANT
GROUSE	PTARMIGAN
GUAN	QUAIL
GUINEA FOWL	TURKEY
HOATZIN	

GALLINULE [găl'ə-nūl], name for several species of long-legged birds of the genus *Porphyrio* in the rail family, Rallidae. Gallinules occur in North and South America and in Europe and are commonly found in marshy areas or near lakes. The purple gallinule, *P. porphyrio*, grows to a length of 19 in., is dark blue-purple in color, and has red eyes and legs. It is found in warmer parts of the New World and in the Mediterranean region. Other species are Allen's gallinule, *P. alleni*, and the green-backed gallinule, *P. madagascariensis*, both native to southern Europe and Africa.

GALLIO, JUNIUS, a brother of Seneca who became proconsul of Achaea in 51–52 A.D. At Corinth, Paul was haled before Gallio, by Jewish opponents (Acts 18:12–17), probably in the spring of 52.

GALLIPOLI. *See* GELIBOLU OR GALLIPOLI.

GALLIPOLIS [găl-ə-pə-lēs], city of southern Ohio and seat of Gallia County, on the Ohio River. Settled in 1790 by French immigrants, it was Ohio's third settlement. Inc., 1808; pop., 7,490.

GALLITZIN [gə-lĭt'sĭn], **DEMETRIUS AUGUSTINE** (1770–1840), Catholic missionary in the American West. Born in The Hague, the Netherlands, where his father was the Russian ambassador, he received an excellent education in Europe before taking an American "grand tour" that brought him to Baltimore in 1792. There he was so impressed with the needs of the struggling Catholic Church that he determined to devote his life to its work. Gallitzin was ordained in 1795, the first priest to receive full theological training in the United States. Four years later, having renounced seminary life for a missionary career, he began building a small mission settlement called Loretto in the heart of the Allegheny Mountains. There he labored for the rest of his life, spending his family patrimony to support his religious colony.

GALLIUM [găl'ē-əm], chemical element and metal resembling aluminum in its chemical properties. It has an unusually low melting point for a metal and an extremely high boiling point. This wide range over which gallium is liquid makes it useful as a filling for high temperature thermometers. The existence and properties of gallium were predicted in 1869 by D. I. Mendeleyev, who called the element eka-aluminum. The discovery of gallium in 1875 by Lecoq de Boisbaudran, who named it after Gallia, the Latin name for France, bore out the prediction in every detail and silenced most of the objections to Mendeleyev's periodic chart of the elements. Gallium is a rare metal, and is obtained commercially from zinc ores, in which it occurs in small quantities.

PROPERTIES	
Symbol	Ga
Atomic number	31
Atomic weight	69.72
Valence	2, 3
Density	
Solid	5.904 g./cc.
Liquid	6.095 g./cc.
Melting point	29.78° C. (85.6° F.)
Boiling point	1,983° C. (3,601.4° F.)

ISAAC ASIMOV, Boston University

GALLON, unit of capacity used to measure liquids. The common standard in the United States is the Winchester, or wine, gallon of 231 cu. in., equivalent to 3.785329 liters. In England and Canada the imperial gallon of 277.42 cu. in. is in general use.

See also WEIGHTS AND MEASURES.

GALLORETTE, American race horse, foaled in 1942. She won 21 of 72 races in which she competed in the 1940's, often defeating male horses. Her earnings totaled $445,535. In 1956 the American Trainers' Association named her the best female horse in U.S. turf history.

GALLOWAY, JOSEPH (c.1731–1803), American Loyalist. He was born in West River, Md., and achieved prominence and wealth in Philadelphia as a lawyer, businessman, and land speculator. A Pennsylvania assemblyman (1756–64; 1765–76), he was elected speaker of the assembly (1766–75) and became a member of the first Continental Congress (1774). His chief contribution to the Congress was a plan—later rejected—for a colonial legislature with a veto over acts of Parliament. He supported Britain during the Revolution and became civil administrator of Philadelphia under Gen. Sir William Howe. When the city was captured by Continental forces (1778), he went to England and became the spokesman of the American Loyalists. His holdings in America were confiscated after the war, and his request (1793) to return to Pennsylvania was denied.

GALLOWS. *See* CAPITAL PUNISHMENT; HANGING.

GALLS, a term describing local swellings of plant tissues due to stimulation by insects, bacteria (as in crown gall), fungi (as in cedar-apple rust), viruses, or physiologic factors within the plant itself. Species of the fungus *Exobasidium* cause leaf galls of camellia, azalea, rhododendron, and blueberry. Species of *Synchytrium* cause leaf galls of many flowering plants and also cause potato wart, a disease that has been limited by quarantine and is now almost eradicated. Black knot of plum and cherry trees, due to the fungus *Dibotryon morbosum*, appears as a dark, elongated enlargement on twigs. The main control measure for galls is the removal and disposal of infected plant parts. *See also* CEDAR-APPLE RUST; CROWN GALL; PLANT DISEASES.

GALLUP [găl'əp], **GEORGE HORACE** (1901–), American statistician and public opinion pollster. Born in Jefferson, Iowa, he was educated at the state university, where he received his Ph.D. in 1928. After teaching journalism for several years, he founded the American Institute of Public Opinion in 1935 and the Audience Research Institute in 1939, which conduct the Gallup polls for measuring public opinion on various issues.

GALLUP, trading town of western New Mexico and seat of McKinley County. Gallup is the major supply center for the extensive Navajo and Zuñi reservations northwestward in Arizona, New Mexico, and Utah. Among articles traded here are wool, Navajo rugs, and Navajo and Zuñi silver jewelry. The town's Inter-Tribal Indian Ceremonial, held each August, is a program of dances and exhibits in which Indians of many North American tribes participate. Inc., 1891; pop., 14,596.

GALLUP POLL. *See* POLL, PUBLIC OPINION.

GALLUS [găl'əs], **GAIUS VIBIUS TREBONIANUS** (c.207–253), Roman Emperor (251–53). As a successful governor of Lower Moesia (249–51) during the Gothic invasion, Gallus appeared to the soldiers a suitable replacement when the Emperor Decius died in battle. But Gallus made a shameful treaty with the Goths which brought no peace, and after more than a year of disaster his soldiers murdered him.

GALOIS [gà-lwà'], **ÉVARISTE** (1811–32), French mathematician who applied the theory of substitution groups to the question of the reducibility of algebraic equations. He was killed in a duel at the age of 20. On the eve of the duel he wrote out a memorandum of his important mathematical discoveries; but the ideas and exposition were so unconventional and so poorly organized that it was only in 1846 that they were published. The basic concept of Galois is the unification of algebra through the theory of groups. He showed that the reducibility of an equation depends upon the transformation group of the roots. In the 1870's the importance of Galois's ideas came to be appreciated as the result of applications of group theory made by M. Camille Jordan, Felix Klein, and M. S. Lie. The papers of Galois were published again, in German translation as *Abhandlungen über die algebraische Auflösung der Gleichungen* (1889).

GALSWORTHY [gôlz'wûr-thē], **JOHN** (1867–1933), English novelist and playwright. He studied law, but never practiced. His first books appeared under the pen name of John Sinjohn. The novels which made his reputation include *The Man of Property* (1906), *The Country House* (1907), *Fraternity* (1909), and *The Patrician* (1911). In all these works he examined critically the psychology of the property-owning classes. His observations gained poignance from personal experience: the situation of Soames and Irene Forsyte in *The Man of Property* parallels that of the novelist and his cousin, Ada, whom he married after her divorce from her first husband. In 1922 *The Man of Property* was combined with two sequels—*In Chancery* (1920) and *To Let* (1921)—and a couple of short sketches to form *The Forsyte Saga*, the work by which Galsworthy's repute as a novelist must stand or fall.

Galsworthy's work for the stage, in which he attacked social evils, began in 1906 with *The Silver Box*. Among his successes were *Strife* (1909), *Justice* (1910, leading role created by John Barrymore), *The Skin Game* (1920), and *Loyalties* (1922). In 1932 he was awarded the Nobel Prize for literature.

DeLancey Ferguson, Brooklyn College

GALT [gôlt], **SIR ALEXANDER TILLOCH** (1817–93), Canadian businessman, cabinet minister, and diplomat. He was born in London, England, the son of John Galt, the novelist. Alexander moved permanently to Lower Canada in 1835 as clerk of the British American Land Company. He became its secretary in 1843; commissioner in 1844.

Actively involved in railroad financing and construction, he entered provincial politics in 1849 as an independent liberal. By 1857 Galt had joined the Liberal-Conservative coalition. In 1858 he was appointed inspector-general (minister of finance) in the Cartier-Macdonald administration, a post he held until 1862. One of the earliest and most influential supporters of a federal union for British North America, Galt served for several months in 1867 as Canada's first minister of finance. Knighted in 1870, he spent his last years out of political office, advocating greater diplomatic autonomy for Canada. From 1880–83 Sir Alexander served as Canada's first high commissioner to Great Britain.

John M. Bumsted, McMaster University, Ontario

GALT, city of southern Ontario, located on the Grand River, 20 mi. west of Lake Ontario. It has been a manufacturing center since its founding in 1817. Industries produce flour, iron products, textiles, and shoes. Inc., 1915; pop., 27,830.

GALTON, SIR FRANCIS (1822–1911), English scientist. Known as a brilliant person from childhood, he made contributions in meteorology, natural history, psychology, statistics, criminology, anthropology, genetics, and eugenics. His *Meteorographica* (1863) was a pioneer attempt to chart weather. His development of the composite portrait and his demonstration of the characteristics of fingerprints were major advances in scientific criminal identification. In psychology his studies included color blindness, instincts, and criminality. He is best known for his classic studies of genius and heredity, which led him to found the eugenics movement in 1905. He advocated encouraging those considered most highly endowed to produce more children and discouraging the less fit from having children. His eugenic theories have been challenged for failing to distinguish between inherited and environmental factors in genius. Galton's books include *Inquiries into Human Faculty and Its Development* (1883), *Natural Inheritance* (1889), *Finger Prints* (1892), *Hereditary Genius: An Enquiry into Its Laws and Consequences* (2d ed., 1892), and *Essays in Eugenics* (1909).

MARIO J. A. BICK, Columbia University

GALVANI [gäl-vä′nē], **LUIGI or ALOISIO** (1737–98), Italian physician-physiologist whose name is given to galvanism, or electricity produced by chemical action. He observed that whenever he touched a frog's leg with a metallic instrument at the same time that an assistant drew a spark from an electrostatic machine the frog's leg twitched. He assumed that the frog contained "animal electricity"; however, this theory was later proved wrong by Alessandro Volta.

GALVANIZING, the process in which steel is coated with zinc to improve corrosion resistance. This is accomplished by either dipping the steel in molten zinc (hot-dip method) or by electroplating (electrogalvanizing). Of the two, the hot-dip method is more widely used. Steel wire or strip is passed through molten zinc, and a layer of zinc adheres to the surface.

The actual corrosion resistance of zinc to water is greater than steel; therefore, it will corrode at a slower rate. However, once the zinc is perforated, it will sacrificially corrode in preference to the steel because of galvanic corrosion. Galvanic corrosion occurs when two dissimilar metals are in contact with each other in the presence of an electrolyte. Under such conditions, a current will flow between both metals. One of the metals will corrode at an accelerated rate while the other will not suffer attack. With galvanized steel, zinc will corrode in preference to the steel.

ADOLPH LENA,
Allegheny Ludlum Steel Corporation

GALVANOMETER [găl-və-nŏm′ə-tər], instrument for detecting and measuring small electric current. The D'Arsonval type of galvanometer is the most common; it consists of a coil suspended in a magnetic field by a light gold or phosphor bronze strip. The magnetic field is produced by a permanent magnet which also acts as the instrument's housing. The suspension provides one contact to the moving coil, and a spiral strip at the bottom makes the second connection. Current through the coil causes rotation through an angle proportional to the current. In a special type, a light beam reflected from a mirror mounted on the coil indicates the magnitude of deflection. *See also* AMMETER.

GALVESTON [găl′vəs-tən], city of eastern Texas and seat of Galveston County, located on the eastern portion of Galveston Island on the Gulf of Mexico. It is a major deepwater port and large volumes of cotton, crude sulfur, grain, and raw sugar are exported, and tea, coffee, and ores are imported. Approximately 90 steamship lines maintain connections between the city and world ports. Numerous barge lines serve the port through the Intracoastal Canal, handling large quantities of iron and steel products, grain, and sulfur. Two giant causeways connect the city with the mainland.

It is also a major manufacturing and processing center. The principal industries are petroleum refining, chemical manufacture, shipbuilding and repair, machine shops, nail and wire manufactures, grain storage, textiles, brewing, and meat packing. A large fishing fleet adds to the city's economy. Adjacent Pelican Island is being developed as an industrial and residential suburb.

Galveston is a popular convention and recreation center. The medical branch of the University of Texas is here. Cultural facilities include civic and county symphony orchestras and community theater groups.

The island and the city are named for Count Bernardo de Galvez, governor general of the Spanish possessions in America, whose troops temporarily occupied the island in 1777. The city was founded and laid out in 1836 by Col. Michael B. Manard, a Canadian civil engineer, and in the same year it was the temporary capital of the Re-

Fairchild Aerial Surveys

Wharves line the 1,200-ft.-wide Galveston channel, leading from the Gulf of Mexico to a well-protected harbor on the north side of Galveston Island.

439

public of Texas. The early settlement served as a trading post. During the Civil War, Galveston was an important supply port of the Confederacy, although it was occupied by Union forces for brief periods. A disastrous hurricane and tidal wave struck the city in 1900 and took 5,000 lives. Shortly thereafter, a sea wall 17 ft. high and 7½ mi. long with a thickness of 16 ft. at its base, was constructed to protect the city. Inc., 1839; pop., 61,809; urb. area 69,812.

CHARLES C. BAJZA, Texas College of Arts and Industries

GALVESTON BAY, inlet of the Gulf of Mexico, on the northeast Texas coast, separated from the gulf by the Bolivar Peninsula and Galveston Island. The principal arms are West, San Jacinto, Trinity, and East bays. It serves a major industrial area and has deep-water channels to Galveston, Texas City, and Houston (via Houston Ship Channel). Length, 35 mi.; max. width, 19 mi.

GALWAY [gôl'wā], county in Connacht Province, western Ireland. Between Lough (lake) Corrib and Galway's fiords, the ancient metamorphic peaks of Connemara overhang the granitic, lake-studded heaths of Iar Connaught. A mile-wide coastal strip supports most of the Connemara population, who live meagerly by working sand, seaweed, and manure into peaty barrens, on farms of 10 acres or less. In the eastern two-thirds of the county, drained by the Shanon and the Suck, thin glacial drift surmounts unfolded limestone. Outcrops of this, high enough to be dry, have produced in this portion of Galway the only Irish lowland where sheep outnumber cattle. Toward the south, cattle are fattened for market on the lusher boglands, while oats, hogs, poultry, and potatoes flourish north of the Aughty range. In districts distant from the larger rivers, shallow depressions supplement local stream water supplies when the water table is high. Salmon fishing, marble quarrying, and woolen and linen handicraft provide additional employment. Galway city is the principal emigrant and general passenger seaport in the "congested" west of Ireland. Area, 2,292 sq. mi.; pop., 155,553.

JOHN J. HOOKER, The Catholic University of America

GALWAY, municipal borough on the west coast of Ireland, capital of County Galway. On Galway Bay at the mouth of Lough (lake) Corrib, it has a fine harbor and important fisheries. Exports include agricultural produce, marble, and wool. Fish net, furniture, textiles, fertilizers, flour, chemicals, and machinery are manufactured. Galway was an Anglo-Saxon outpost in medieval Connacht. It became a center of trade with Spain, the influence of which is seen in Spanish-styled buildings. Its University College (1849) is a constituent unit of the National University of Ireland. Pop., 21,989.

GAMA [gä'mə], **JOSÉ BASÍLIO DA** (1740–95), Brazilian poet, born in Minas Gerais. Accused of being a partisan of the Jesuits in their controversy with the Marquis of Pombal, he cleared himself of the charge when he published *O Uruguay* in 1769. It is a blank verse epic of considerable beauty dealing with the war of the Spanish and Portuguese against the Jesuit missions in Paraguay.

GAMA, VASCO DA (c.1460–1524), Portuguese explorer. In 1497, nine years after Bartholomeu Dias had rounded Africa's Cape of Good Hope, King Manuel of Portugal selected Da Gama to realize Prince Henry the Navigator's dream of a sea route to India. Unlike Christopher Columbus, who had an original idea and hunted hard for someone to back it, Da Gama was selected—for reasons which are not clear—to carry out a long-standing policy.

He sailed from Lisbon in July, 1497, with four ships. Instead of hugging the African coast as the earlier Portuguese had done, he struck out boldly almost across the South Atlantic before turning southeast for South Africa. He was out of sight of land for 3,800 mi., as compared with 2,600 for Columbus. He made his landfall about 100 mi. north of Good Hope, which he rounded on Nov. 22, 1497. Gales led his crews to mutiny, as Dias's had done in those waters, but he overcame them and proceeded up the east coast of Africa. At Quelimane, Mozambique, and Mombasa, he encountered hostility from the Arabs, but at Malindi he was given a highly experienced pilot for crossing the Indian Ocean.

On May 20, 1498, he reached Calicut (Kozhikode) on the Malabar Coast of western India. The local ruler, influenced by Arab traders who saw a grave threat to their long-established commerce up through the Persian Gulf or Red Sea, put continued obstacles in his way and, finally, gravely threatened the Portuguese ashore. Da Gama managed to escape (Aug., 1498) with a cargo of spices. Returning by way of Malindi, he rounded Good Hope on Mar. 20, 1499, and reached Lisbon that September in battered condition, two months after another of his ships. Portugal, on the threshold of its brilliant but exhausting career in the East, celebrated with wild enthusiasm.

Twice again, Da Gama sailed to India. In Feb., 1502, after the voyage of Pedro Cabral, he was sent out as Admiral of India with 15 ships. In reprisal for Calicut's wip-

Vasco da Gama, Portuguese explorer who made the first sea voyage from Europe around the southern tip of Africa to India in 1497–98.
(THE BETTMANN ARCHIVE)

ing out a trading post left by Cabral, he bombarded the city with shocking cruelty. He then set up other trading posts at Cochin and Cannanore, and returned to Lisbon (Sept., 1503) with a rich cargo. In 1524, after abuses had crept into the Portuguese administration in India, Da Gama went out on a third voyage, this time as viceroy, but died in Cochin before the year was out.

Consult Hart, H. H., *Sea Road to the Indies* (1950); Hamilton, G. M. H. L., *In the Wake of Da Gama* (1951).

ROBERT G. ALBION, Harvard University

GAMAGORI, city of Aichi Prefecture, Honshu, Japan, southeast of Nagoya. It is a seaside resort on Atsumi Bay and a fishing center which also produces cotton textiles and optical goods and processes foodstuffs. Pop., 55,926.

GAMBETTA [găm-bĕt′ə], **LÉON** (1838–82), French statesman. A lawyer and an outspoken critic of the Second Empire, Gambetta sat in Parliament in 1869 as an Opposition deputy from Marseilles. After the overthrow of the regime in 1870, he became Minister of the Interior in the Government of National Defense. He was a zealous advocate of all-out resistance to Prussia, and vainly proposed the evacuation of Paris in favor of a stand in the south. Later he left the besieged city by balloon, going to Tours to direct the organization of a relief army, but the inexplicable surrender of Marshal Achille Bazaine at Metz rendered his work useless.

After the armistice, he won election to the National Assembly at Bordeaux but resigned in protest when the Assembly accepted the treaty surrendering Alsace-Lorraine to Germany. Of the loss of Alsace he later said, "Let us think of it always, but never speak of it." Soon back in politics, he fought to make France a republic. When the royalists threatened the republic in 1877, Gambetta challenged President Marie MacMahon either to submit to the will of the republican majority or resign. When that resignation came (1879), Gambetta could have had the presidency, but preferred to become president of the Chamber of Deputies. In 1881 he agreed to become prime minister, but his strong personality made him feared, and the cabinet fell after 66 days. He died of an accidental gunshot wound.

ROGER L. WILLIAMS, Antioch College

THE GAMBIA

AREA	4,003 sq. mi.
ELEVATION	Sea level and slightly higher
POPULATION	315,486
LANGUAGES	English, Mandingo, Wolfo, tribal languages
UNIT OF CURRENCY	West African pound
CAPITAL	Bathurst
PRINCIPAL PRODUCTS	Peanuts, rice

GAMBIA [găm′bē-ə], officially **THE GAMBIA,** an independent country in the Commonwealth of Nations, situated on the bulge of West Africa. A strip of land 7 to 20 mi. wide along the lower Gambia River, it extends inland 200 mi. from the Atlantic Ocean. Bathurst (pop., 27,809), chief city and capital, is on the island of St. Mary at the mouth of the Gambia River, a fine natural harbor. The river is navigable by ocean-going vessels for 150 mi. upstream.

The Land. The entire territory is low-lying, rising to no more than 120 ft. above sea level in the interior. Mangroves border the lower Gambia River, forming solid banks of vegetation often 100 ft. high. Behind are swamps and river flats, submerged during the wet season. Farther back, sandhills and rolling plateaus appear, covered with coarse grasses and occasional shrubs and clumps of trees. From June to October the climate is hot and wet, and from November to April cooler and dry. Annual rainfall varies from 30 to 55 in. Temperatures vary from 60° F. to 110° F.

The People. Most of the population lives in rural areas. The principal ethnic groups are Mandingo (40%), Fula (13%), Wolof (12%), and Jola and Serahuli (7% each). There are about 400 Europeans (chiefly English), and a few hundred Syrians, Lebanese, and Mauritanians. Islam is the principal religion, followed by animism. There are a few thousand African Christians. English is the official language.

Economy. Gambia is naturally situated to handle the overseas trade of a large hinterland. Except for the Gambia River, the nation's chief artery, Gambia is poor in natural resources. Some subsistence crops are raised—

Working the rice fields in the tidal lands along the Gambia River.
(MONKMEYER)

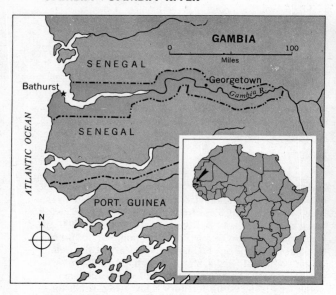

Students at a secondary school in Bathurst, capital of Gambia.
(MONKMEYER)

chiefly grain, sorghum, and rice—but not enough to feed the inhabitants. Although a strong effort is being made to diversify agriculture, nearly all suitable land is still planted with peanuts grown for export. Peanuts normally account for about 95% of total annual exports by value. Other exports are palm kernels, hides, dried mollusks, and beeswax. Local industries are limited to peanut-oil refining, cotton weaving, garment making, soft-drink bottling, and fishing. There are no known minerals of value, although some ilmenite has been mined along the coast. Leading imports are cotton cloth, foodstuffs, and hardware from the United Kingdom, Japan, India, and Burma. The Gambia has a chronic balance-of-trade deficit, which is made up by annual grants-in-aid from the United Kingdom. It also provides important developmental assistance.

Government. Gambia achieved full independence on Feb. 18, 1965, as a constitutional monarchy within the Commonwealth of Nations. Queen Elizabeth II is represented by a governor-general. He appoints the prime minister. The Parliament consists of 32 elected members chosen by universal adult suffrage, 4 chiefs' representative members elected by the chiefs in assembly, and 2 members without vote appointed by the governor-general after consultation with the prime minister.

There are three political parties in Gambia: the governing Progressive People's Party, the United Party (UP), and the leftist Gambian Congress Party.

Education. Besides a number of primary and a few secondary schools there are technical and teacher-training institutions. Students go abroad, chiefly to Britain, for higher education.

History. Portuguese visited Gambia in 1455 and some 50 years later were trading in the lower river area. They were interested chiefly in slaves and gold. Then, in 1588, English merchants acquired exclusive trading rights on the river. Thereafter, England and France struggled for control of the area until 1783, when Gambia was yielded to Britain. Though slave trading was abolished by Britain in 1807, the slave traders in Gambia resisted stubbornly. In 1816 the British established Bathurst as a military post.

In the ensuing years Bathurst sometimes was under the jurisdiction of the government of Sierra Leone, but in 1843 it was made a separate colony. Gambia and Sierra Leone were again united in 1866 but since 1888 Gambia has been a separate entity. After 1816 the British acquired additional territory upriver. The present borders were established in 1889. Slavery was finally abolished in 1906.

During World War II Gambia contributed soldiers for the Allied campaign in Burma and served as an airstop and port of call for Allied naval convoys. President Roosevelt stopped overnight at Bathurst en route both to and from the Casablanca Conference. This was the first visit to Africa by an American president in office. After World War II the pace of constitutional advance quickened, and full internal self-government was achieved in late 1963.

Foreign Relations. Though Gambia is formally nonaligned, it has close and friendly relations with the United Kingdom, Senegal, and other African Commonwealth states. It is a member of the Organization of African Unity (OAU) and of the United Nations. Gambia cooperates with Senegal for defense and foreign affairs.

Consult Woolf, B. S., *Gambia: The Story of the Groundnut Colony* (1952); Gailey, H. A., *A History of the Gambia* (1965).

RICHARD P. STEVENS, Lincoln University

GAMBIA FEVER, a disease of cattle and other domestic animals, caused by infection with a trypanosome. Common to central Africa, it is carried by tsetse flies and other biting flies, and causes fever and swelling.

GAMBIA POD, fruit of an African acacia, usually *A. nilotica*, used as a source of tannin for tanning and dyeing.

GAMBIA RIVER, navigable river of western Africa, with most of its length in Gambia, which is bisected by the river. It rises in the Fouta Djallon Plateau of Senegal and flows about 460 mi. to the Atlantic Ocean. The Gambia estuary extends 93 mi. from Bathurst to Elephant Island. Ships of 13-ft. draft reach Kuntaur, 150 mi. above.

Bathurst; those up to 6½-ft. draft reach Fatoto, 288 mi. from Bathurst. No shipping reaches Senegal.

GAMBLING, wagering money or other valuables on the result of a sporting event or game of chance. Evidence indicates that gambling has been universal throughout history. The ancient Greeks and Romans played games of chance involving dice; lotteries (bets on numbers drawn by lot) were used by Roman Emperors to raise revenue. The Roman historian Tacitus records that the Germanic tribesmen gambled heavily, often staking their lives on a throw of the dice.

Most European countries have attempted to curb gambling by law or to abolish it entirely. Germany suppressed gambling casinos in 1873. In France, the operation of gambling houses was forbidden after Jan. 1, 1838, but the prohibition was later modified. Monte Carlo, in the Mediterranean principality of Monaco, is the leading European gambling resort; but state lotteries are legal in several countries and constitute an important source of revenue. In 1960 Great Britain passed the Betting and Gaming Act legalizing off-track betting at shops operated by licensed gambling brokers or bookmakers. Previously, betting had been legal only if done on track or by telephone on a credit basis so that no cash settlements were made until after the race. Since 1947 the British government has taxed all bets at dog and horse races and prizes awarded in football pools.

In Canada, pari-mutuel wagers on horse races are legal, but off-track betting is prohibited. Under specific conditions, the operation of games of chance is permissible in legitimate social clubs and in places used by religious or charitable institutions. The operation of lotteries and the possession of slot machines are illegal. Raffles may be held but are subject to strict regulations.

The U.S. federal government has no laws prohibiting gambling; regulation is left to state and local governments. Off-track betting through bookmakers, or bookies, is illegal in all states except Nevada, but pari-mutuel betting on horse races is permitted in 25 states. Since 1931 gambling in establishments having roulette wheels, slot machines, and card and dice games has been legal in Nevada; 12 states permit bingo, a game of chance played with numbered cards, if the games are properly licensed by local authorities.

A widespread form of illegal gambling is the so-called numbers racket, in which bets are placed on the appearance of three-digit numbers in the daily balance of clearinghouse totals or racing pari-mutuels. In numbers the amount bet and the chances of winning are small, but the odds paid are large.

The lucrative returns from illegal gambling enterprises, such as betting on amateur and professional sports events, make them attractive to organized crime; gambling interests are protected through collusion between corrupt police and politicians and criminal syndicates. In illegal gambling there is much "fixing" of the results of events to deprive the bettor of his chances, and bookmakers establish two sets of odds so that they profit, whatever the result.

In 1951 the Senate Crime Investigating Committee headed by Senator Estes Kefauver revealed the extent to which official corruption facilitates and promotes organized criminal activities in gambling. On the basis of evidence obtained at hearings, the committee estimated that $20,000,000,000 a year changed hands in illegal gambling. The committee's report opposed legalized gambling and urged the imposition of more severe controls over gamblers and their financial affairs. Laws were passed requiring gamblers to register with the Internal Revenue Bureau, to pay a base tax of $50 a year and subsequently to remit as tax 10% of their gross receipts. All attempts to legalize gambling as a means of eliminating corruption and increasing revenues have thus far proved unsuccessful.

JOSEPH S. ROUCEK, University of Bridgeport
See also BANKING GAMES; DICE GAMES; DOG: *Dog Racing*; HORSE: *Horse Racing*; POKER.

GAMELAN [gŭm'ə-län], orchestra of varied size, instrumentation, and quality native to Java and Bali. A complete *gamelan sapangkon* in the princely residences of central Java consists of two sets of instruments, one tuned to the five-tone *slendro* system and the other to the seven-tone *pelog.* Most of the instruments—gong chimes, metal slabs, and xylophones, among others—are made of any one of three different grades of bronze or brass; in the villages the keys may be made of iron or bamboo. In both Java and Bali different types of *gamelan* are appropriate for different functions. Venerated for their great age and beauty of sound, such *gamelan* often bear proper names; for example, the two holy *gamelan sekati* are known as *Kangjeng Kjai Guntur Madu* ("Venerable Sir Downpour of Honey") and *Kangjeng Kjai Naga Ilaga* ("Venerable Sir Snake in the Battle"). These two *gamelan* are said to be more than 400 years old.

In Java a male chorus and female soloists are considered part of the *gamelan,* and the total ensemble is led by the rebab, a two-stringed bowed lute. A type of zither and a flute are also part of the ensemble. In Bali vocal music is not a part of *gamelan* performance; the rebab is rarely used in the large *gamelan* (although it is a principal instrument in the small and ancient ensemble known as *gamelan gambuh*); there are no zithers; and the flute, when used, is not particularly prominent except in *gamelan gambuh.* The use of hard wooden *panggul* in the Balinese *gamelan* produces a very brilliant ensemble. Characteristically, a single drummer is used in the Javanese *gamelan,* and a pair of drummers are used in the Balinese.

MANTLE HOOD, University of California,
Los Angeles

GAMELIN [găm-lăn'], **MAURICE GUSTAVE** (1872–1958), French army officer. Born in Paris, Gamelin graduated (1893) from the St. Cyr Military School. He fought in World War I, and suppressed (1925) the Druse uprising in Syria. As chief of the general staff (1931–35), he followed a defensive military strategy, relying on the Maginot Line for protection against the threat of German invasion. He later served as army inspector general (1935–39) and Allied commander in chief early in World War II. After his defeat by the Germans (1940) Gamelin spent the war as a prisoner.

Spirits run high during a game of bronco tag. The three children grouped in the foreground make up one bronco—head, middle, and tail. To avoid being tagged by the chaser, the runner puts his arms around the third child.

George J. Adams

GAMES, CHILDREN'S.

Games for the child of preschool and elementary school age take many forms, ranging from "playing house" to highly skilled athletic contests between two teams. In all cases, games and contests represent planned efforts by parents, teachers, recreation leaders, and children themselves, and are designed to encourage the child in enjoying, and provide means for achieving, the greatest benefits from his innate desire for physical activity.

Active games and contests are the most widely accepted forms of play for children 5 to 12 years of age. Although most play activities, such as creative movement, musical play, dance, dramatic play, and arts and crafts, can be organized into games, the young child prefers active, vigorous, yet simple movement patterns. The child's attempt to explore big movement, the excitement of the chase, the opportunity to excel, and the pleasure of group participation all add to the appeal of active physical play.

Active games have the common ingredients of strategy, deception, and decision making as necessary elements for successful participation. Such a classification includes tag games, chasing and fleeing activities, modified combat games, minor lead-up games of the athletic type, and modified individual and dual sports and games. Contests and relays, usually included in any discussion of children's games, provide simple comparisons of the abilities of individuals or groups and do not involve the strategy or decision making inherent in games as defined in this article.

Active Games

Tag and Chasing-Fleeing Games. These involve flight and a chase ending in escape or capture. Many of the games are simple group activities requiring individual thought and action; others encourage group cooperation.

Hindu Tag, simple tag involving individual action. Children scatter throughout a designated play area. One player is "it" and is free to run throughout the area and tag anyone who is not in Hindu position; that is, on his knees with his forehead on the floor. When a player is tagged while out of position, he becomes "it" and attempts to tag another player. If players stay in Hindu position too long, the one who is "it" may stand back several feet and count to three; then any player in that position must stand and run or he becomes "it." The object is to avoid becoming "it."

Bronco Tag, cooperative tag involving small group action. Children are in groups of three with one designated the head, another the middle, and the third the tail of a horse, or bronco. The middle and tail players of each horse place their arms around the waist of the player in front. Another player is the runner and a second player the chaser. To avoid being tagged by the chaser, the runner tries to put his arms around the waist of the child representing the tail of any bronco. If the runner succeeds before he is tagged, the head of the bronco becomes the new runner and the game continues. If the runner is caught, he and the chaser reverse roles. The broncos are free to move and twist around to avoid helping the runner.

What Time Is It, Old Witch? This is a mass chasing and fleeing game. Within a sizable area a large circle or square is drawn to represent the witch's den. A larger area is designated 50 ft (15 m), or more away as the children's home. One player is "it" (witch) and goes to her den. Another plays mother or daddy and gathers all players in the children's home. As a group they move to the witch's den, where the children taunt the witch while mother asks, "What time is it, old witch?" If the witch makes any reply except "Midnight," the children continue to play about the den. When the children move in close, the witch finally says, "Midnight," the signal for the children to run home to safety. The witch attempts

444

to catch them. Those players caught become the witch's helpers and aid in catching children when the procedure is repeated.

Combative Games. With young children these games are modified on an individual or small-team basis and should not be considered games leading up to the generally recognized combative activities of fencing, wrestling, and boxing. Minor combative activities appeal to the individual competitive spirit of the boy of 10 to 12 years of age, and continue to have such appeal after he reaches the teens.

Rooster Fight. Standing on a tumbling mat or soft surface, two contestants face each other. Each holds his left foot up and to the rear with his left hand gripping the ankle firmly. The right arm is pressed firmly to the side of the body and the fist is clenched to help keep the arm close to the body. On signal the opponents hop forward and try to upset each other by pushing, so that one must put his left foot down to regain balance. The winner is the boy who remains balanced on his right foot longer than his opponent.

Lead-up Games. These are popular with children 8 to 12, and serve as transitional activities that stress the fundamental skills and strategies found in seasonal sports and team games such as baseball, basketball, football, hockey, soccer, and volleyball. The more highly developed lead-up games, even when appropriate to the skills, age, and understanding of children, are not always suitable for neighborhood or home play because of their demand for special equipment, extensive areas, and large numbers of participants. The following examples encourage the practice of basic skills involved in ball handling; little special equipment is needed by the groups of varying size that participate.

Ten Catches, elementary ball handling and passing skills in basketball. The group is divided into two teams of equal size. Teammates are given distinguishable markings (sashes, skirts, or similar clothing). At a given signal one team member, in possession of a basketball, begins by passing it to a teammate. As each pass in a series is completed successfully, the number of passes is counted aloud. A team is declared the winner when it has completed 10 passes. Counting stops whenever a member of the opposing team intercepts the ball or the ball touches the ground. When a team intercepts the ball, it begins its own series.

Spud, basic throwing skills involving attention and decision making. Players form a circle with one player in the center. Center player tosses a volleyball or light playground ball in the air while calling the name or number of another player. The player called catches or retrieves the ball while all others scatter for safety. As soon as the player has gained possession of the ball, he shouts, "Spud," a command for all players to stop where they are. Without moving, he throws the ball in an attempt to hit any player below the waist. Players may twist and dodge to avoid the throw as long as one foot stays on the ground. If the thrower misses, one "spud" is scored against him. He resumes play by tossing the ball in the circle and calling the name of another player. If the player who throws the ball succeeds in hitting his target, either by throwing the ball on the fly or on the bounce,

a "spud" is scored against the player hit. That player can pick up the ball immediately, call "spud" as a signal to stop the players' motion, and try to hit another player. This continues until the thrower misses his mark. If scores are kept, a player charged with three "spuds" leaves the game, and may reenter only when another player is eliminated. (In order to keep all children participating, a player may perform a stunt to gain reinstatement.)

Schlag Ball, kicking skills and baseball strategy. A marker 2 ft (61 cm) square is designated home base, and a post is placed 40 ft (12 m) in front of it. Players are divided into teams. One team scatters in the field and the other team is "in bats." One player of the defensive team stands behind home base. The first "batter" punts a soccer or playground ball (he may not kick the ball as it rests on the ground) and then attempts to score a run by running around the post in the field and returning home. The defensive team, stationed in the field, retrieves the ball and tries to put the runner out by hitting him with the ball or throwing the ball to the player at home base before the runner returns. No player may run with the ball, and a fielder may hold the ball only five seconds before passing it to a teammate. A run is scored for the team "in bats" if the ball is held longer. The ball may not be passed between the same two players more than twice in succession. A kicker is out if he: (1) fails to punt the ball on the third attempt; (2) if the ball is caught on the fly; (3) if he is hit by the ball while running; (4) if the ball is held by an opponent at home base before he returns. The teams change sides after three outs have been made. The winner is the team scoring the greatest number of runs during a specified number of innings.

Modified Individual and Dual Sports and Games. Many children in their 10th, 11th, and 12th years are ready for these activities, including handball, shuffleboard, paddle tennis, modified horseshoes, table tennis, and box hockey. These games should be encouraged; they are relatively easy to learn, have lasting recreational value, and provide early opportunities to practice courtesies and etiquette appropriate to competition.

Contests and Relays. These events challenge the skill, form, and speed of an individual performer. Group contests include relays; mass competition in which all compete at once, as in tug of war; and group competition in which individuals compete separately but score points in a team effort, as in a track and field meet. Most appropriate for the young child are the relays in which groups are formed of equal size, with each child participating as an individual. Such relays include running events, obstacle events, animal imitations, stunts, and tandem and riding events. Relays can develop group consciousness among children and provide opportunity for joint effort in achievement of a common goal. Contests are held in any of the fundamental physical movements such as running, jumping, climbing, kicking, throwing, and striking.

Turk Stand, individual contest. The child sits on the floor in a cross-legged position with arms folded across the chest. He attempts to rise to a standing position without changing positions of arms or legs. If successful, he tries to sit in the same manner.

Count the Turns, group contest. Each child takes his or her turn with a jump rope that has handles. Holding both feet together, the child turns the rope and then hops as it passes beneath his feet. The child recording the greatest number of turns in 50 seconds is the winner. A variation of this involves standing on one foot and hopping as the rope passes under it. The winner is the child recording the greatest number of turns in 30 seconds.

Skipping Relay, group effort involving individual participation. Establish starting and turning lines about 50 ft (15 m) apart. Arrange players in two files with the first players toeing the starting line. On signal the first players skip forward, touch the turning line, turn, and skip back to the starting position. They touch the hands of the second players as a signal for them to begin, and the first contestants go to the end of their respective files. The race continues until the last contestants return to the starting line. The team finishing first is the winner.

Wheelbarrow Relay, a cooperative effort. This tandem event requires one player to place his hands on the floor and stretch his legs to the rear. His partner stands between his legs, lifts them to waist level, and holds them firmly while the partners move from the starting line toward the turning line as a "wheelbarrow." At the turning line they reverse positions and return to the starting line to touch the next pair of contestants.

Games suitable for indoor use or for occasions when less active play is desired include modified stunts and novelty events, quizzes and puzzles, magic tricks, table games, dramatic and musical games, and social games. The wise parent will find these activities helpful for the inevitable rainy days.

Consult Brandreth, Gyles, *Games for Trains, Planes, and Rainy Days* (1975); Brewster, Paul G., *Children's Games and Rhymes* (1976); Nelson, Esther L., *Movement Games for Children of All Ages* (1975); Withers, Carl, *A Treasury of Games* (1976).   HALLY B. W. POINDEXTER

GAMES, CLASSICAL. The earliest athletic games in Greece were connected with the funeral rites of heroes. Homer gives the first detailed account of such contests in the *Iliad* when he describes the matches in chariot racing, boxing, wrestling, foot racing, discus throwing, spear casting, archery, and armored combat enjoyed by the princely warriors after Patroclus' funeral at Troy. Physical fitness then, as in most periods of Greek history, was a prerequisite for survival in battle.

Early in the 1st millennium B.C. the more settled conditions in cities permitted the establishment of athletic festivals in honor of some god at regular intervals and in fixed locations. The Olympic games were so established very early and remained the most celebrated throughout antiquity. The other great Panhellenic festivals (Pythian, Nemean, Isthmian) likewise included games similar to those described by Homer. At first, entrants were probably self-trained, but by the 7th century B.C., years of formal training lay behind each. Gymnastic exercises and sports with well-formulated rules early became as regular a part of Greek education as reading and music. In Sparta they were compulsory, state financed, and ruthless; in Athens, optional, but customary. There, in special schools (palaestrae) children practiced carefully graded exercises under the teacher, who owned the establishment, and later, if they desired, went for more in-

tensive study to an ex-athlete tutor who prepared them for the festival games. Much ancient pottery still exists which portrays athletes using jumping weights (*halteres*), discuses, boxing thongs for hands, pick-axes, oil flasks, strigils (scrapers), punching bags, and cold-shower arrangements. Under such a system, Greece from 540–440 B.C. reached her highest point of athletic excellence.

Traditionally, Rome held its first games (Ludi) in the reign of Romulus, but its athletic program was restricted to one event: horse racing. Later, Ludi assumed a greater importance when they were held regularly in the Circus Maximus at a fixed annual date, and after chariot races, farces, gladiatorial contests, beast hunts, and other novelties calculated to amuse were introduced from Etruria. From beginning to end these Ludi Magni or Ludi Romani were always spectacles, Romans seldom competing except in equestrian events or occasionally in foot races. In 186 B.C. Greek actors and athletes were introduced. In time the number of Ludi increased, often serving to celebrate military triumphs. Though the Romans as individuals appreciated the value of exercise like running, swimming, riding, hunting, wrestling, and boxing, they never seem to have cared to train themselves professionally for competition. The general impact of the excesses and bestiality of the Ludi under the Roman Empire upon the Roman character was the reverse of the noble, unifying influence of Greek festivals on Greece during the days of its independence.

RACHEL S. ROBINSON

GAME THEORY is concerned with the logical and mathematical analysis of rational decision in situations involving conflicts of interest among decision-makers. Games of strategy (chess, bridge, tic-tac-toe) present situations of this sort.

Zero-Sum Games. Most games of strategy are too complex to yield to game-theoretic methods of analysis, but the principles of game theory can be illustrated by simple patterns of decision situations. The simplest situations are those involving only two decision-makers, or players, and the simplest of these are so-called zero-sum games, in which whatever one player wins the other loses. A game of this sort can be represented by a game matrix:

	C_1		C_2		C_3	
R_1		3		−18		20
	−3		18		−20	
R_2		1		−5		−2
	−1		5		2	
R_3		2		4		−15
	−2		−4		15	

The first player's alternatives of choice, called strategies, are the horizontal rows (R_1, R_2, R_3); those of the second are the vertical columns (C_1, C_2, C_3). A simultaneous choice of row and column by the two players determines the outcome of the game, and with it a payoff to each of the players, as shown. The number at lower left in each box is the payoff to the first player; that at upper right, to the second.

The matrix shows that Row can be assured of not losing more than one unit and that Column can be assured of winning at least one. This outcome, shown in Row 2, Column 1, is arrived at by applying the *maximin principle:* each player chooses a strategy that contains the maximum of the minima of the payoffs associated with each choice.

In the example shown, each player has a "best pure strategy," that is, a choice that guarantees for him the best possible outcome in the face of an opposing "rational" player. In some games there is no "best" pure strategy. Each player can maximize his statistically expected payoff only by "mixing" strategies, assigning a certain probability to each of his own possible choices. "Bluffing" in a poker game is essentially an application of the mixed strategy principle.

In 1928 the mathematician John von Neumann showed that in every two-person zero-sum game, each player has a best strategy, either pure or mixed, based on the maximin principle. However, the maximin principle does not take into account that the interests of the players may not be diametrically opposed and that, in games with more than two players, coalitions may form that can yield to their members more than they can get if every person plays individually. The analysis of these situations is beset with intricate difficulties.

Business, Diplomacy, and War. There has been considerable speculation about the possibility of applying game theory to the search for rational decisions in situations of actual conflict, as, for example, competitive business, diplomacy, and war. Such applications meet with three kinds of difficulties.

1—Real conflict situations can seldom be formulated with sufficient precision to warrant translation into a game model.

2—The assumption of "rationality" implies complete knowledge of the situation and calculating prowess not ordinarily available to real-life decision-makers.

3—Except in conflicts resembling two-person zero-sum games, the very concept of "rationality" becomes ambivalent. What may be individually rational may not be collectively rational (as in a decision to launch or not to launch a preventive war; to try or not to try to undersell competitors, and so on).

A Clarifying Role. For these reasons, the principal value of game theory, as it relates to theories of conflict, is in a clarifying rather than in a prescribing role. Given a set of decision-makers, the alternatives open to each, the utilities they assign to the outcomes, and the possibility of forming coalitions, game theory makes clear the relations (often of immense complexity) among the several interdependent interests. Except in the simplest case of a two-person zero-sum game, the theory is not usable to prescribe a "best" decision. It can, however, bring into focus aspects of the situation that may not occur to players pursuing their individual interests.   ANATOL RAPOPORT

GAMETOPHYTE [gă-mē′tō-fĭt], the sexual generation in the life cycle of many plants, during which male and female reproductive cells, or gametes, are formed. The gametophyte is the green, dominant generation in the

life cycle of mosses and liverworts.
See also REPRODUCTION: *Reproduction in Plants.*

GAMMA GLOBULIN [găm′ə glŏb′yə-lĭn], a group of proteins, in the blood plasma, that includes most of the antibodies used by the body to fight bacterial and viral diseases. Gamma globulin extracted from the blood of any donor may be used to prevent or modify the course of measles, hepatitis, and poliomyelitis. To protect against chicken pox, German measles, or mumps, gamma globulin from convalescent donors is used, since their blood contains the necessary high concentration of antibodies for their specific disease. An injection of gamma globulin provides protection for about four weeks.

Individuals suffering from agammaglobulinemia, a rare congenital deficiency of gamma globulin, are subject to frequent infections and require periodic injections of gamma globulin for protection.
See also ANTIBODIES AND ANTIGENS; IMMUNITY.

GAMMA RAY (γ-ray), most penetrating of the radiations composing the electromagnetic spectrum. Gamma rays were discovered as one of the radiations emitted by radioactive substances. They have a wave length of less than 10^{-9} cm and a quantum energy greater than 100,000 electron volts. Gamma rays of greater quantum energy than those emitted in radioactive decay can be produced by making a beam of fast electrons strike a metal target. If its quantum energy is greater than 1.1 Mev, a gamma ray may disappear when it passes near an atomic nucleus; a pair of electrons, one positive and one negative, is created in its stead. This "materialization" of gamma rays was the first observed example of the creation of antimatter. Gamma rays, produced in the radioactive decay of radioisotopes such as cobalt-60, are used in medicine, for the treatment of tumors, and in metallurgy for detecting flaws in heavy metal castings.
                                        CECIL FRANK POWELL

GAMMER GURTON'S NEEDLE, English comedy (c.1553) of uncertain authorship, but believed to be by William Stevenson. A farce involving the frantic search for Gammer Gurton's lost mending needle, it is one of the earliest known comedies in English drama. In dealing with contemporary village life, it combines the structure of classical Latin drama with colloquial dialogue and realistic characterization.

GAN-DAN, Lamaist monastery located about 25 mi (40 km) southeast of Lhasa in Tibet. It was founded in 1409 by the great reformer Tsong-k'a-pa, whose throne is reserved here for the sect's best scholar, the "Enthroned of Gan-Dan." Although its congregation of lamas is the smallest of the triumvirate (Dre-Pung, Se-Ra, and Gan-Dan), it still is acknowledged as the main source of the Yellow Hat Sect. Claimed as affiliated institutions by Gan-Dan are the two famous academies for occultist studies in Lhasa.

GANDER, town of eastern Newfoundland, Canada, about 50 mi (80 km) east of Grand Falls. It is the site of a major airport, important for transatlantic flights.

GANDHI [gän'de], **INDIRA** (1917–   ), third prime minister of India (1966–77) and the only child of Jawaharlal Nehru, first prime minister. Through her father and grandfather, Motilal Nehru, who was also an important leader of the Indian nationalist movement, she was identified from childhood with politics.

Early Life. After attending a number of schools in India and England, she entered Somerville College, Oxford, in 1938, but she did not take a degree. She had joined the Indian National Congress in 1938 and was imprisoned in 1942 for her political activities. She was married in 1942 to Feroze Gandhi (no relation of Mohandas K. Gandhi), a journalist and politician, who died in 1960. They had two sons, Rajiv and Sanjay.

After India became independent in 1947, Mrs. Gandhi served as her father's hostess and his political confidant. A member of many important committees of the Congress party, she became its president in 1959. After Nehru's death in 1964, the new prime minister, Lal Bahadur Shastri, appointed her minister of information and broadcasting.

Presidency. When Shastri died in 1966, the Congress leaders elected Mrs. Gandhi prime minister, partly because of the great prestige of the Nehru name and partly because they thought she would be amenable to their control. A series of economic and political crises involving food supplies and the nationalization of the banks brought her into conflict with the older leaders, and in 1969 a split took place in the Congress. Her chief opponent, Morarji Desai, resigned from the Cabinet to lead the opposition group. Mrs. Gandhi showed herself to be a skillful and, according to many observers, a ruthless, political tactician, and in the 1971 elections she made a successful appeal to the masses with her promise to rid India of its poverty.

Indira Gandhi, third Prime Minister of the Republic of India.

Dennis Brack—Black Star

Her standing was increased by the successful war in 1971 against Pakistan in support of the people of Bangladesh.

During this period Mrs. Gandhi had signed a treaty of friendship with the U.S.S.R., and relations between India and the United States became strained. Within India, bad harvests, inflation, and a general worsening of the economic situation led to strong criticism of Mrs. Gandhi and her advisers.

In 1975, she was found guilty of a technical violation of the election laws. Her opponents, under the leadership of Jayaprakash Narayan, one of the most famous of the old nationalists, demanded her resignation and called for a nationwide strike. On June 25, without warning, Mrs. Gandhi had the president of India declare a state of emergency that gave her sweeping powers. Fundamental legal rights were suspended, the press was censored, opposition leaders—including Desai and Narayan—were imprisoned without trial, and elections were postponed. Mrs. Gandhi argued that threats to national security demanded authoritarian rule. Social and economic conditions, she said, required that order and discipline be imposed for the good of the people. The apparent acceptance of the changes imposed during the emergency led Mrs. Gandhi to hold elections in March 1977. She campaigned with great vigor, but the opposition united against her. Particular animosity was shown to her son Sanjay, who had played a dominant role in politics during the emergency, especially in the controversial sterilization program, which had been aimed at curbing the high birth rate. The Congress suffered a crushing defeat, and both Mrs. Gandhi and Sanjay lost their own seats in Parliament. She immediately resigned as prime minister, and a new government was formed by her old rival, Morarji Desai.

AINSLIE T. EMBREE

GANDHI [gän'dē], **MOHANDAS KARAMCHAND** (1869–1948), preeminent nationalist leader of India, and saintly world figure known everywhere by his informal title of Mahatma ("Great Soul"). Born in the small princely state of Porbandar on the Kathiawar Peninsula of western India, Gandhi came from an orthodox *vaishya* (merchant) caste family. His father, as chief minister of Porbandar, provided Gandhi with a disciplined elementary education and arranged for his marriage at the age of 13. Kasturba, his wife, who bore Gandhi four sons, died in 1944.

Gandhi went to London when he was 18 for legal training and was called to the bar at the Inner Temple in 1891. His life in England included time spent on intensive reading of the *Bhagavad-Gita*, the New Testament, and other religious texts, as well as close study of the social philosophies of Leo Tolstoy, John Ruskin, and Henry David Thoreau—all of whose influences are to be seen in his own personal and political creeds.

Upon returning to India he practiced law for a time in Bombay, but in 1893 he went to South Africa to join an Indian law firm. Although he conducted a successful professional business there, the racial discriminations to which Indians and colored South Africans were subjected so disturbed Gandhi that he relinquished most of his legal practice and devoted himself to the cause of securing social, civil, and political rights for the Indian community in South Africa. Suffering arrest and bodily assault on several occasions, Gandhi nevertheless perfected techniques for nonviolent resistance to South African repressive measures which he called *Satyagraha*, literally, "holding fast to truth."

He was a persistent and effective foe of British and Boer policies which segregated white and nonwhite communities in South Africa. But during times of national conflict, such as the Boer War of 1899–1902, the Zulu Rebellion of 1906, and the early phase of World War I, Gandhi helped organize and recruit personnel for British ambulance corps units. In 1914, after years of bitter dispute, Gen. Jan Christiaan Smuts of the Union of South Africa signed an amicable agreement with Gandhi removing some of the restrictions on the Indian community. It was a matter of deep regret to Gandhi in later years that the 1914 pact proved to have little lasting benefit. But the resistance techniques of *Satyagraha*, developed in South Africa, were to provide Gandhi with a dramatic and persuasive political and moral method for reducing the effectiveness of British power in India.

Gandhi returned to India in 1915. His mentor, Gopal Krishna Gokhale of Bombay, a leader of the moderate forces in the All-India National Congress, drew Gandhi into politics. Gandhi did not immediately make his influence felt, despite his celebrated South African reputation. He proved to be a poor speaker when compared with senior colleagues, and his ideas on nonviolence appeared defeatist to the more radical members of the Congress.

At his *ashram* (religious retreat) established near Ahmadabad, and in talks and articles, Gandhi advocated *swaraj* ("self-rule," or "home rule"). Deeply concerned by disturbances in the Punjab, by the massacre at Jalianwalla Bagh, and by the passage of the Rowlatt Acts in 1919 which ordered severe penalties for sedition, Gandhi persuaded the Congress to undertake a campaign of civil disobedience in protest against the government on a mass basis. Members of the Congress were ordered to give up governmental appointments and titles, to form national schools, to boycott British goods, to use Indian-made articles exclusively, and to participate in disciplined, nonviolent demonstrations. Although the movement was remarkably nonviolent, considering the numbers involved, some violence did occur. Gandhi called off the mass campaign when he learned of violence in the town of Chauri Chaura instigated by a group of Congress resistors. Gandhi was arrested in 1922 and sentenced to six years' imprisonment, but was released in 1924 following an operation. In the same year he was elected president of the Congress. He was imprisoned often in the years that followed.

Until his death Gandhi remained the undisputed leader of the Indian nationalist movement. He led the India-wide boycott of the Sir John Simon Commission in 1927—a mission sent to India to determine the next stage for constitutional advance. He also led the famous march to Dandi in 1930 for the purpose of making salt from the sea in defiance of the government's tax on salt. He attended the second Round Table Conference in London in 1931. When the London conference failed to move

Mohandas Karamchand Gandhi, Indian nationalist leader.

India rapidly toward self-rule, he returned to India and organized a new civil disobedience campaign. During World War II he encouraged non-cooperation with the Allied forces because freedom was not guaranteed for India. Gandhi similarly rejected the constitutional solutions, first offered by Sir Stafford Cripps in 1942, and later by Lord Wavell, as inadequate, partial measures.

Concurrently with his fight for independence, Gandhi also fought for the betterment of the status of noncaste Hindus (untouchables), whom he called *Harijans* ("children of God"), and worked for closer relations between the Hindus and the many minorities of India, especially the Muslims. But he was unable to quell the rising tide of the Pakistan movement. In 1946 riots between Hindus and Muslims broke out first in Calcutta, and then spread throughout India. Gandhi spent his last months in sorrow; even though India became free on Aug. 15, 1947, it was partitioned, and Pakistan was founded as a separate state.

From the 1930's Gandhi shared leadership with a selected group of nationalists whom he especially encouraged and advised, such as Vallabhbhai Patel, Maulana Abul Kalam Azad, and Jawaharlal Nehru. Gandhi had the authority to control Congress policy with a dictator's hand, but he sought consensus in his dealings with colleagues by means of discussion and persuasion in the interests of truth—as he saw it. Gandhi's political activity was intimately tied to his exploration of ultimate truth, which to him was a religious experience. "The little voice within," his moral appraisal of right action, gave him a conviction of correctness of interpretation in debate that to others often appeared to be unshakeable resistance to any point of view other than Gandhi's own.

The full measure of Gandhi's political greatness may lie

in the leaders of eminence he left behind to guide the Republic of India in its years of nation building. More likely, he will be remembered for his saintly qualities that transcend the political moment and attach Gandhi to the ancient spiritual heritage of his country.

Mahatma Gandhi was shot to death on Jan. 30, 1948, in Birla House, New Delhi, by an extremist Hindu who blamed Gandhi for the partition of India. He died with the words "Ram! Ram!"—an invocation to God—on his lips.

Consult Bondurant, Joan V., *Conquest of Violence: The Gandhian Philosophy of Conflict* (1965); Brown, Judith M., *Gandhi and Civil Disobedience* (1977); Fischer, Louis, *Gandhi* (1962); Gandhi, M. K., *The Story of My Experiments With Truth* (reprinted); Pyarelal, *Mahatma Gandhi* (2 vols., 1965).   RICHARD L. PARK

GANG, group of persons acting in common, generally for criminal purposes. It is also a special term designating youthful groups whose members are intensely loyal to each other and whose behavior and attitudes are strongly exclusive and even hostile to outsiders, whether adults or other adolescents. Ordinarily regarded as a separate entity characterized by antisocial and delinquent practices, the gang illustrates a universal tendency of adolescents to

Hindu pilgrims at Varanasi bathing in the Ganges, undisturbed by the bustle of the ghats.

FPG

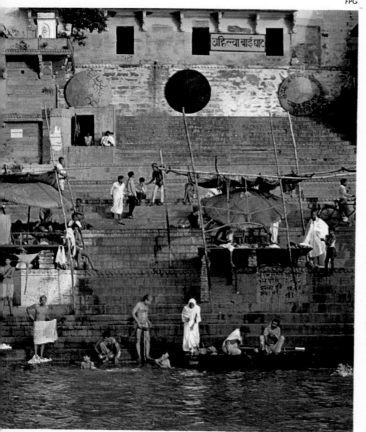

form closely knit groups.

The typical boys' gang, largely an urban phenomenon, identifies itself closely with a few city blocks, regarded as its territory. This is the so-called "turf," which the gang defends against the real or imagined inroads of outsiders. Each new group in urban slums produces its own gangs, similar but distinguished by ethnic and racial differences.

The romanticized names designating the group and its leadership express the adolescent's sense of adventure and bravado, as well as his imaginative effort to rise above the surroundings. Thus, such names as the Gaylords, the Chaplains, and other colorful epithets, describe the groups, and the leaders hold such honorifics as Overlord, King, and President. A significant aspect of the development of boys' gangs since the end of World War II has been the tendency toward an apparently formal organization, with acknowledged leadership and membership responsibilities. The growth of urban gangs has been accompanied by the formation of affiliated groups of those too young for membership and of loosely associated groups of girl affiliates, or "Debs."

Social agencies, accepting the principle that, for slum youths, these gangs satisfy a natural and deeply implanted need, have attempted to work with them through "detached street workers." These workers are trained in social work procedures, which they employ in attempting to divert gang activity into constructive channels. They meet and work with the gang largely in its own milieu—the local candy store, gymnasium, or pool hall—to overcome initial resistance to their acceptance by the gang boy.

Consult Bloch, Herbert A., and Niederhoffer, Arthur, *The Gang: A Study in Adolescent Behavior* (repr., 1976); Cartwright, Desmond S., and others, eds., *Gang Delinquency* (1975); Cloward, Richard A., and Ohlin, Lloyd E., *Delinquency and Opportunity: A Theory of Delinquent Gangs* (1960); Thrasher, Frederick M., *The Gang: A Study of 1,313 Gangs in Chicago* (1963).   HERBERT A. BLOCH

GANGES [găn'jēz] **RIVER** of northern India, known as the great holy river. It rises on the southern slopes of the Himalayas and, penetrating the mountains, flows southwest and emerges onto its extensive delta at Hardwar, where the Upper Ganges Canal irrigation system begins. It then flows southeast to Allahabad where it receives its great tributary river, the Jumna, and finally into the Meghna estuary of the Bay of Bengal.

The total length of the main stream of the Ganges is about 1,540 mi (2 478 km); with its longest affluent, it is 1,680 mi (2 704 km) long. The Upper Ganges extends from its source to Allahabad, and since the region receives rainfall (approximately 25 to 40 inches, or 40 to 80 cm) only during the hot summer-monsoon season, irrigation is necessary. Principal crops include wheat, barley, and cotton. The natural fall of the Upper Ganges Canal (146 ft, or 44 m), broken into a number of smaller falls of 8 to 12 ft (about 3 to 4 m), each, has been utilized to operate small hydroelectric plants. The major cities of this region are Hardwar, Farrukhabad, Kanpur, and Allahabad.

The Middle Ganges extends from Allahabad east to West Bengal. Rain averages 40–70 inches (100–170 cm) and late summer floods are common. Rice, wheat, barley, and oilseed are grown. The major cities along this section of the river are Varanasi (Benares), Mirzapur, Patna, and Ghazipur.

The Lower Ganges is that part of the river that lies in West and East Bengal. This region may receive up to 150 inches (about 3.8 m) of rain per year, and floods, shifting bars, and shifting river courses are common. Rice, jute, and sugar cane are the principal crops. Calcutta, the largest city of the Ganges basin and of India, is located on the Hooghly tributary of the Lower Ganges. The channel is navigable to ocean-going vessels to this point, 90 mi (143 km) above the Bay of Bengal; beyond Calcuttta carriage is by native craft. Other cities in the Ganges region include Howrah, New Delhi, and Agra.   FREDERICK HUNG

GANGRENE [găng′grēn], death of body tissue caused by inadequate blood supply. The most common and well-known type of gangrene is associated with arteriosclerosis obliterans. This type of arteriosclerosis is seen most frequently in elderly people (especially diabetics) and causes gangrene by a slow and gradual obliteration of the blood supply. Substances are deposited in the arterial walls, causing the opening to narrow until the blood flow is insufficient to supply the needs of the tissues. The legs are usually affected; the area involved may include a large portion of the foot or be limited to the toes. Tissue death of this type is called "dry gangrene," because the skin becomes dry as parchment. The term "wet gangrene" is usually used when a gangrenous part becomes infected.

Gangrene may also be caused by other conditions that decrease blood supply. Mechanical obstruction to blood flow may be the result of freezing or an arterial embolus. An embolus is a blood clot that forms in one portion of the circulatory system and is carried away by the blood stream until it becomes wedged in an artery in another part of the body. An embolus may obstruct an artery in a limb, causing sudden severe pain, coldness, paralysis, and absence of pulse. The tissues of the affected portion eventually die.

Gangrene may occur in the intestinal tract when a portion of the bowel loses its blood supply either from infection, embolus, or by twisting upon itself—a condition known as a volvulus.

The term "gas gangrene" is applied to an infection caused by bacteria of the Clostridium group. These organisms grow only in the absence of air and produce bubbles of gas that distend the tissues. They may contaminate wounds and frequently produce infections following criminal abortions. Gas gangrene is almost always fatal if not treated.   JEROME D. WAYE, M.D.

GANNET [găn′ĭt], large sea bird, *Sula bassana*, of the family Sulidae. Gannets occur along coastal areas of northern North America and Europe and winter in southern United States, Mexico, and western Africa. They grow to a length of 3 ft (91 cm), have a wingspread of 6 ft, and are white with black wingtips. Gannets are frequently sighted far out at sea and are excellent swimmers and divers. They feed on fish and often make spectacular power dives into the water while searching for food.

GANNETT PEAK, high peak in west-central Wyoming, 55 mi (89 km) northwest of Lander. On the crest of the Wind River Range, in the Middle Rocky Mountains, Gannet Peak forms part of the Continental Divide and is the highest point in Wyoming. Its elevation is 13,795 ft (4 202 m).

GANOID FISH, a term applied to certain ancient bony fishes and also to primitive ray-finned fishes that have ganoid scales. A ganoid scale is a heavy, shiny scale composed of three layers, the top layer covered by enamel. Living fishes with this type of scale include the African bichirs of family Polypteridae, the sturgeons of family Acipenseridae, and the gars of family Lepisosteidae.

GANYMEDE [găn′ə-mēd], in Greek mythology, a Trojan Prince, son of Tros, or Laomedon. Attracted by his extraordinary beauty, Zeus took on eagle form, swooped down upon him as he tended flocks on Mount Ida, and carried him off to Olympus to become cupbearer of the gods. Zeus gave divine horses to Ganymede's father in recompense.

GANZ [gănz], **RUDOLPH** (1877–1972), conductor and pianist, born in Zürich. He made his debut as a pianist in Berlin (1899) and subsequently toured extensively in Europe, Canada, and the United States. He conducted the St. Louis Symphony Orchestra (1921–27) and the New York Philharmonic Young People's Concerts (1938–49). He was also director of the Chicago Musical College (1929–54).

GAPON [gə-pôn′], **GEORGI APOLLONOVICH** (1870–1906), Russian Orthodox priest in St. Petersburg. He cooperated with the police in the organization of workers' clubs designed to act as a moderating influence on the workers. When he led an orderly street procession carrying a petition to the Tsar's palace on Jan. 9, 1905, frightened guards opened fire and killed well over 100 persons. After this "Bloody Sunday," he openly condemned the authorities, was unfrocked, and joined the Socialist Revolutionary party. The latter, with evidence that "Father Gapon" had again communicated with the police, instigated his assassination.

GARAMOND [găr′ə-mŏnd], **CLAUDE** (d.1561), French type designer. A student of Geofroy Tory and one of the most important typographers of the 16th century, Garamond produced beautiful, legible type faces used by Estienne, Elzevir, Plantin, Bodoni, and other printers. Among his better-known type faces are the cursive Greek letters called *Grecs du roi*, produced (c.1542) on the order of Francis I of France; and the *Canon* and *Petit Roman* faces. His italic and roman types helped to bring an end to the use of the gothic letter.

GARBO [gär′bō], **GRETA**, professional name of Greta Lovisa Gustaffson (1905–   ), Swedish-born film actress. Having first attracted notice in the Swedish silent film *The Story of Gösta Berling* (1924), she went to the United States in 1925 and became perhaps the most celebrated motion-picture actress of all time, a provocative, enigmatic embodiment of feminine beauty and mystery. *Flesh and the Devil* (1927) was her best-known silent film; among

Armand Duval and Marguerite of Dumas' *La dame aux camélias* were portrayed in a 1936 film by Robert Taylor and Greta Garbo.

her notable talking pictures were *Anna Christie* (1930), *Anna Karenina* (1935), *Camille* (1936), and the comedy *Ninotchka* (1939). Miss Garbo, who became famous for her withdrawn, aloof off-screen personality, retired after *Two-Faced Woman* (1941).

GARCÍA [gär-sē'ä] **(ÍÑIGUEZ), CALIXTO** (1836–98), Cuban revolutionary leader. García helped organize the Ten Years' War against Spain (1868–78) and became commander in chief of Cuban forces, but was captured and taken to Spain. After returning to Cuba (1879), he was again arrested and kept in Spain for 15 years. He went back in 1895 and commanded forces in eastern Cuba in the final revolt against Spain. Cubans remember him as one of a trio of military heroes that included Máximo Gómez and Antonio Maceo. Americans remember him as the Garcia of Elbert Hubbard's celebrated essay, *A Message to Garcia*.

GARCÍA, CARLOS POLISTICO (1896–1971), 4th President of the Republic of the Philippines, born in Bohol and educated at Silliman University and the Philippine Law School. From 1914 to 1917, he taught school, but in 1925 became involved in politics as a representative of the 3d District of Bohol in the lower house of the Philippine Congress. He remained in the House of Representatives until 1931, and two years later was elected Governor of his province. His term as a national Senator (1941–53) included his achieving the position of minority floor leader (1946–51). During World War II, he led the guerillas in the southern Philippines. As a stalwart of the Nacionalista party, he was selected in 1953 to be Ramón Magsaysay's running mate. Elected Vice President of the Philippines for the 1953–57 term of office, he also served as Foreign Secretary from 1954 until Mar. 17, 1957, when he assumed the presidency upon the death of President Magsaysay. In his role of Foreign Secretary, he was closely identified with the reparations agreement with Japan, the "Asia for the Asians" program, and the Southeast Asia Treaty Organization. His re-election to the presidency in Nov., 1957, led to a term of office marred by political scandals and frequent evidences of graft and corruption. The standards of political service deteriorated and the processes of democracy were badly abused.

President García took great satisfaction in the economic achievements of his administration: the increase of agricultural and industrial production, the achievement of a favorable balance of international trade, and the insistence upon more economic nationalism to cope with perennial problems of poverty and austerity. In foreign affairs he continued to co-operate with the United States and the anti-Communist bloc, while pressing for more generous American treatment of the Philippines in matters of aid, claims, and military bases. He also worked hard to improve economic and cultural relations with his friendly Asian neighbors. In the Nov., 1961, presidential election, García was defeated by Diosdado Macapagal, a Liberal party candidate who had been Vice President. García was considered a well-read man and won recognition as a poet in his native dialect, Visayan.　　　　CLAUDE A. BUSS

GARCÍA MORENO [mō-rā'nō], **GABRIEL** (1821–75), Ecuadorian dictator. García Moreno studied law and theology and for some years taught in the University of Quito, which he also served as rector. A stanch conservative (he was a son-in-law of Juan José Flores) and devoted Catholic, he overthrew the incumbent regime in 1860 and twice served as President (1861–65; 1869–75). His religious fervor colored his rule, and Ecuador became virtually a theocracy during that decade and a half. The climax came in 1873 with his solemn dedication of the republic to "the Sacred Heart of Jesus." García Moreno purged the church of unworthy priests and brought in Jesuits and others from Europe. Aside from his preoccupation with religion, he contributed much to Ecuadorian economic and cultural advance, but sharply curtailed civil rights within the country. García Moreno died at the hands of assassins.

GARCILASO DE LA VEGA [gär-thē-lä'so thä lä vä'gä] (1501?–1536), poet and gentleman of the Spanish Renaissance whose life combined the practice both of arms and letters. He is one of Spain's great poets despite his small output—principally 35 sonnets, five odes, three eclogues. More than any other, he was responsible for adapting the Italian metrical forms to the peculiar requirements of the rhythms of the Castilian dialect.

GARDA [gär'dä], **LAKE,** lake in East Lombardy, northern Italy. It covers an area of 143 sq. mi. and is about 32 mi. long and from 2 to 10 mi. wide. The Sarca River flows into the lake on the north and the Mincio emanates from the south portion. The lake, Italy's largest, was known as Lacus Benacus to the ancient Romans.

GARDEN, MARY (1874–1967), soprano, born in Aberdeen, Scotland. She went to America as a child and started vocal study in 1893. Garden made her debut at the Opera-Comique in Paris in 1900 when the leading soprano became ill during a performance of Charpentier's *Louise.* In 1902 Debussy selected her to create the role of Mélisande in *Pelléas et Mélisande.* Her American debut was in *Thaïs* at the Manhattan Opera House (1907). Later she was chiefly associated with the Chicago Opera, including one disastrous season as director (1921–22).

Although her voice was itself never outstanding, Mary Garden was capable of singing a wide variety of parts from a coloratura Ophelia to a sultry Carmen. She was best known for her vibrant personality and her extraordinary acting ability. She concentrated almost exclusively on the French repertoire, preferring to sing even Italian and German roles in French. After 1930 she appeared only occasionally and in 1939 she returned to Scotland.

Consult Garden, Mary, and Biancolli, Louis, *Mary Garden's Story* (1951).

Susan Thiemann, Music Division, New York Library

GARDEN. *See* Gardens and Gardening.

GARDENA, industrial suburb of Los Angeles, Calif. Formerly a truck-gardening center, it now has aircraft and electronics industries. It is 10 mi. south of Los Angeles. Inc., 1930; pop., 41,021.

GARDEN CITY, city of southeastern Georgia, a residential suburb situated just northwest of Savannah. Inc., 1941; pop., 5,790.

GARDEN CITY, trade center of southwestern Kansas, and seat of Finney County. Diversified industries include food processing and petroleum refining. Garden City Junior College and an extension center of the University of Kansas are located here. Pop., 14,790.

GARDEN CITY, residential suburb about 10 mi. west of Detroit, Mich. Pop., 41,864.

GARDEN CITY, village of southeastern New York, on Long Island. Garden City was one of the first planned residential communities in the country. Publishing is its largest industry. Adelphi College is located here. Founded, c.1869; inc., 1919; pop., 25,373.

GARDEN GROVE, city of southern California, 15 mi. east of Long Beach. Orange groves and strawberry gardens vie with light industries and commuter residences for space in this congested area. Inc., 1956; pop., 122,524.

Gardenia blossoms stand out against glossy green leaves. (ROCHE)

GARDENIA [gär-dēn'yə], a genus of ornamental trees and shrubs in the madder family, Rubiaceae, native to subtropical regions of China, Japan, and Africa. The solitary white, or infrequently yellow, flowers of gardenias are showy, highly fragrant, and have velvety petals. Of the more than 50 species the best-known is *Gardenia jasminoides,* sometimes called Cape jasmine. Many horticultural varieties of this species have been developed and are in great demand as cut flowers for use in corsages, or for seasonal gifts as potted plants. In the warmer regions of North America, particularly in southern United States, gardenias are used extensively in outdoor landscape plantings. In cooler regions gardenias are popular as house plants. However, to bring them into bloom successfully they should be grown in a clear glass greenhouse and exposed to as much sunlight and humidity as possible. The great differences in day and night temperatures in the home generally cause flower buds to form prematurely and to drop off before full bloom is reached. Gardenias are propagated from hardwood or softwood cuttings and grow best in moderately acid soil. The plants should be exposed to an evenly maintained temperature of about 65° F.

Walter Singer, New York Botanical Garden

GARDEN OF THE GODS, city park of Colorado Springs, Colo., and a favorite tourist attraction. Its principal features are massive, exposed vertical strata of red rocks, the product of differential erosion. They provide a striking foreground for 14,110-ft. Pikes Peak. Area, 1.2 sq. mi.

GARDEN REACH, city in West Bengal, India, on the Hooghly River 4 mi. southwest of Calcutta. Its docks handle the bulk of Calcutta's trade. In 1757 its fort was seized by Robert Clive en route to recapture Calcutta. Subsequently it became a residential city. Pop., 109,160.

GARDENS AND GARDENING. A garden may be formally defined as an enclosed area, adjacent to a dwelling, where flowers, fruits, and vegetables are grown. Thus, a garden is a special part of one's land set aside. The amount of land available and the terrain determine to a certain extent the type of garden that can be established in a given location.

The History of Gardening

Gardening is not a new pastime. Since man's earliest recorded history, flower and garden lovers have experimented with gardens large and small, and with specialized plantings featuring color, scent, or many varieties of the same plant. The ancient Babylonians, Egyptians, Persians, Greeks, and Romans made use of and cultivated many trees, shrubs, flowers, fruits, and herbs that nature supplied them. The Hanging Gardens of Babylon, one of the seven wonders of the ancient world, were built (in tiers) to assuage the homesickness of the wife of a King of Babylon who longed for the hills of her native country. Another King of Babylon had a herb garden of 70 different species, most of them cultivated for their fragrance. In the Old Testament are found instructions for the planting and care of fig and olive trees. In ancient Greece arbors were constructed on which to grow grapes. Garden patterns were created with small and large beds, fountains, and arbors. Romans strewed the floors of palaces with rose petals, imported from Egypt, for their entertainments and celebrations. With this ancient heritage it is not surprising that modern man strives to create bigger and better, more stylized, and more specialized gardens. Most of the ancient peoples renowned for their gardening lived in warm and tropical climates and had slave labor. It has been up to modern man to make equally exciting gardens in the temperate and cooler zones of the earth with a minimum of labor. As with the peoples of ancient times so it is with modern man a challenge to make the best use of the area, soil, and flowers at his command.

Kinds of Gardens

No matter what type of garden is planned, soil, fertilizers, light, and temperature are important. There are plants that need lime, and those that will not grow in a limey soil; there are plants that need a great deal of leaf-mold and moisture; there are plants that will grow in the shade, and those that will grow only when the sun reaches them; there are many plants that grow well in a cool atmosphere, and others that require a temperate or even tropical climate. All of these factors must be considered before one can plan a successful garden.

Among the many kinds of gardens are the small suburban garden, the larger country garden, the city back-yard, the terrace, and the penthouse garden. There are also special gardens which are usually part of a larger garden, park, or botanic garden and consist of a particular group of plants such as roses, herbs, or collections of native wild flowers.

Suburban and Country Gardens. The small suburban garden is usually planned to include some flowering plants that bloom throughout the growing season, and also a tree or two and some flowering shrubs. The larger country garden may be much the same but might also include a rose garden or a herb garden, and if in a wooded area, a

DIFFERENT KINDS OF GARDENS

Water Garden. A small, artificial pool planted with water lilies and water hyacinths and surrounded by weathered rocks.

Roche

wild-flower garden. A great deal depends upon the gardener; men often prefer to plant roses or dahlias, and will often give up most of the garden to the plant of their choice.

City Gardens. The city garden is a problem as it often gets little or no sun and has poor drainage conditions and little air circulation. Plants for these gardens must be chosen for their ability to grow under city conditions, and in the usual back yard it is unwise even to think of a lawn. Trees, shrubs, and other plants are often better grown in containers or raised beds so that the drainage can be regulated. In a few cases, where the gardens of a whole block have been opened up and high fences removed, a wider variety of trees and shrubs can be grown successfully.

Terrace and Penthouse Gardens. The roof or terrace garden poses problems opposite to those encountered in city-yard gardening. There often seems to be too much air, too much wind, and in many cases exposure to full sun all day. However, in this type of garden many annuals and some trees and shrubs will flourish. California privet (*Ligustrum ovalifolium*) does well in exposed positions and is often used as a windbreak for other plants. Trees that will grow on a terrace are willows, crab apples, wisteria vines, climbing roses, and other deciduous flowering shrubs. Spring-flowering bulbs and even vegetables, in-

Dry Wall Garden. Candytufts, sedums, and pinks cascade from crevices in a rock wall, accented by clumps of daffodils.

City Back Yard. A flagstone-paved area is surrounded by beds of pine, broad-leaved evergreens, and other city-hardy plants.

Gottscho–Schleisner

Gottscho–Schleisner

Gottscho–Schleisner

Herb Garden. A variety of herbs grow in neat beds separated by brick walks. A sundial is the focal point of the garden.

cluding tomatoes, can be grown successfully in a roof garden. Some very beautiful penthouse gardens are in existence complete with lawns and fountains.

Special Gardens. One of the most popular types of special garden is the rose garden. Although roses are often planted with other shrubs or flowers, they really look better and are more easily taken care of if planted by themselves. A rose garden should be located in areas where the plants will be exposed to at least 6 hours of sun daily, and where air circulation is good. The soil must be well drained and have an abundance of well-rotted manure dug into it. (Peat moss with dried manure in a half-and-half mixture may be substituted.) If the soil is heavy, sand should also be added. The ground for a rose garden should be dug to a depth of at least 15 in. The hybrid tea roses are among the hardiest and most popular plants in a rose garden and have large and usually fragrant flowers. Floribunda roses are shrublike plants, not often fragrant but colorful and easy to care for. Climbing roses may be grown on a trellis against the house, or on a post, pergola, or fence. Roses produce their best bloom during June and then again in the autumn, but with the extensive hybridizing that has been done, many flower all summer, but not as profusely during very hot weather. Watering is important if the climate is very dry, and a regular pesticide

spraying schedule keeps the plants healthy. Rose bushes should be fertilized in early spring and again in July. In cool climates it is better not to apply fertilizer after July because this encourages too much soft growth before the winter. Many new varieties of roses are developed each season and it is advisable to consult rose catalogs to see what is available. Some people prefer to specialize only in old-fashioned roses and these are often difficult to find.

Herb gardens are quite popular and are often small parts of the garden proper rather than separate plantings. Herb gardens are sometimes enclosed and arranged in a formal design. Here are collected the many herbs used in cooking, medicine, and perfume. The past histories of many lands and peoples include mention of herb gardens. Through the ages gardening has been intimately connected with the plants used in cookery and medicine. There are nurseries that specialize in supplying the plants and seeds of herbs and currently great interest is being shown in making collections of herbs used by the American Indians, as well as the herbs of other countries.

The wild-flower garden is of special interest to those people who have a woodland or partly shady garden, for many of the most interesting native plants of eastern North America grow best under these conditions. There are many plants that thrive in sunny fields. Gardeners

455

who have open, grassy areas on their property would save themselves considerable effort if they introduced native plants into much of this area and just kept for lawn the immediate land around the house. The effect is charming as well as laborsaving, for the grass where wild flowers are grown needs cutting only once a season, just like a hay-field. There are nurseries where native plants are sold, and unless they are already growing on the property, purchase from nurseries may be the only way of obtaining certain species since it is forbidden to collect many native plants from the wild. A wild-flower garden is an interesting hobby and if the situation is suitable can be combined with any garden as long as the setting is naturalistic—with woodland, stream, or meadow.

The Care of Gardens

Plant requirements have to be considered when thinking of a garden, especially the soil. In certain areas the soil is very sandy and dries out quickly, but even so, some plants will grow and thrive under these conditions. Most of the plants that are usually grown in gardens, however, need better treatment. Sandy soil, for example, can be improved by adding peat moss, humus, and manure. Some soil is heavy and clayey and holds moisture better than a sandy soil but is hard to cultivate. Heavy soil can be improved by the addition of peat moss, humus of any kind, and sand, all well worked into the soil.

Most plants grown in gardens are not native to the area in which they are being grown. Their soil requirements are generally different from the soil in which they are to be planted and fertilizers must be used to compensate for the difference. The soil should be analyzed when planning a garden to see what is necessary for the particular plants selected. Most plants will grow in a neutral soil, but some may need a more acid soil and others a more alkaline one.

Many different kinds and strengths of fertilizers are available: there are organic and inorganic commercial fertilizers, all of which are required by law to have their formula indicated on the bag or box. The chief plant requirements are nitrogen, phosphorus, and potash and these can be acquired separately. Plants need nitrogen for the growth of stem and leaves, and because it is quickly used up, nitrogen has to be replaced constantly. On the other hand, too much nitrogen will encourage too much leaf growth and no flowers. Nitrogen may be given to the plants through dried blood, fish meal, dried sewage sludge, nitrate of soda, nitrate of potash, sulfate of ammonia, urea, and other sources. Phosphorus helps in maturing the plants and ripening the wood, thus making them flower (an immature plant seldom produces flowers). Phosphorus is available as basic slag, raw bone meal, steamed bone meal, and superphosphate. Potash is available as kainite, muriate of potash, sulfate of potash, and wood ash. The latter must be kept dry until used.

Most commercial fertilizers contain all three essential plant nutrients, mixed in varying degrees of strength, and should be chosen accordingly. If an acid fertilizer is wanted for rhododendrons, for example, then sulfate of ammonia should be used. For the average garden, different combinations of ready-mixed fertilizers are best suited and should be selected according to requirements of particular plants. Most of the inorganic fertilizers are quick-

acting and help to give the plants a boost in the spring. Organic fertilizers are slower acting but longer lasting, and most soils can use both. Many other elements in the soil are necessary to plant growth, and occasionally these have to be provided. In some mixed fertilizers this has been done. All fertilizers, however, are useless without water to release the elements and dissolve them for plant use.

Water, light, and air are necessary for all plant life. Some plants require little water and others grow in water, but the great majority need just the necessary amount of moisture that will release the elements in the soil, and will also make up for moisture loss due to transpiration from the leaves. Water requirements differ with climatic conditions and in different types of plants. In nature, plants adjust themselves to their environment but in gardens, many different plants are grown together and it is necessary to provide for the change of conditions. Water must be used in sufficient quantity to reach the roots to be of use, but must not be provided in such quantity that the soil becomes waterlogged.

A regular spraying schedule will help to keep plant pests and diseases under control. Watering is important in dry weather, but mulching the ground with peat moss, buckwheat hulls, sawdust, or any material available is a great help in conserving moisture and keeping weeds down. Fertilizing should be done in the spring, on shrubs and perennials, and on the annual beds as soon as the plants are established. A later dose of fertilizer on the flower beds will keep plants growing through the season. Too much fertilizer can be more harmful than too little: the same thing applies to spray. Package directions should always be carefully read and followed. Trees should be fertilized in spring and late autumn.

Planning the Garden

When planning a garden much depends on the size of the garden wanted or the land available, and where it is located. The garden should be planned in relation to the house so that the general view from windows or patio is pleasing. A city yard could have a point of interest at the end of the yard facing the house: this could be a small wall fountain with shrubs on either side. Flagstone or gravel (in lieu of a lawn) with some planting on either side, possibly featuring bulbs for early spring bloom, would make a satisfactory planting. If the yard is sunny, annuals can be planted for summer bloom.

In the larger garden, where city conditions do not have to be considered, a lawn is generally required and much time and energy is spent on it. The lawn is a natural and beautiful setting for the house and flower beds if it is well kept, but time and effort must be spent to keep it looking in first-rate condition.

Under trees where it is difficult to keep grass growing, or on narrow strips on each side of a driveway, it is sometimes better to plant a ground cover such as ivy, pachysandra, or vinca. For woodland sections, with a good leafmold soil, the choice of ground cover is almost unlimited; ferns, epimediums in variety, lily-of-the-valley, and many other plants are available to suit different growing conditions.

The garden owner who is lucky enough to have trees does not have to worry about shade, but starting a garden

GARDENS

From the start of history, man has made some gardens solely for his pleasure. From a patch of color outside his hut to green oases in modern cities, he has grown plants only for their beauty.

RIGHT, *Paley Park, a miniature garden in congested New York City. The trees and waterfall ensure year-round pleasure.* (JACQUES JANGOUX)

BELOW, *painting of an Egyptian garden, from about 1250 B.C., reproduced from the tomb of a sculptor, Apuy, at Thebes.* (METROPOLITAN MUSEUM OF ART)

ABOVE, *red begonias and silver dusty miller border summer flowers in a U.S. home garden.* (MAX TATCH—SHOSTAL)

LEFT, *English cottage garden. Ivy climbs the house, snapdragon and marigold bloom in foreground.* (MACINTOSH—FPG)

BELOW, *Colonial garden in restored Williamsburg, Va. Tulips and pansies circle the elm tree, day lilies hug its base.* (SHOSTAL)

Wisteria partly covers the elaborate trellis of a showplace garden, Dumbarton Oaks, Washington, D.C. For display, the chrysanthemums were plunged in already in bloom.
(SHOSTAL)

Red and gold coleus, white periwinkle, and golden amaranth iresine, all annuals, form a triple border between wall and lawn in this formal sunken garden. Scarlet sage lines the far wall.
(SHOSTAL)

A Canadian flower border of annuals and perennials. White sweet alyssum borders petunias, French marigolds, and scarlet sage. Veronica and nicotiana bloom in the background.
(SHOSTAL)

Plate 3

Placement of rocks, sand, and gravel is as important as the mosses and hedges in this temple garden in Japan. (MANLEY PHOTO)

A variety of different plants creates formal patterns in Knot Garden, Hampton Court Palace, England. (WHITELY—PHOTO RESEARCHERS)

Plate 4

ABOVE, *Dutch bulb growers display their new varieties of spring flowers at the Keukenhof open-air show at Lisse, Holland. The bulbs were planted in the preceding fall.* (LAVINE—MONKMEYER)

RIGHT, *ageratum and sheared boxwood edge geometric flower beds of red and white begonias and golden iresine in a castle garden at Angers, France.* (ELMER SCHNEIWIND—RAPHO GUILLUMETTE)

Spring flowers in the formal Maude Moore Latham Memorial Garden, Tryon Palace Restoration, New Bern, N.C. (SHOSTAL)

ABOVE, *a variety of native and exotic shrubs and trees in an Oregon garden.* (RAY ATKESON)　　LEFT, *a cactus garden in Arizona. Indigenous plants include the century plant (foreground), prickly pear (left), and saguaro (center).* (DARWIN VAN CAMPEN)

Bluets, phlox, columbine, and barrenwort grace a superb rock garden in a New Jersey woodland setting. (GOTTSCHO-SCHLEISNER)

ABOVE, *informal spring garden in a shady woodland setting, northeastern U.S. Scarlet and white azaleas predominate.*
(GOTTSCHO-SCHLEISNER)

LEFT, *stone wall rock garden used in a terraced garden landscape. Yellow candytuft contrasts with red tulips and mountain pink.*
(MONKMEYER)

Herb garden at the New York Botanic Garden. Mixed herbs, chives, and giant flowering onion are included.
(GOTTSCHO-SCHLEISNER)

Plate 7

A lush combination of terraced fountains and ancient trees, the garden of Villa D'Este in Tivoli, near Rome. (PEARL KORN—DPI)

Konigsschloss Linderhof garden, Bavarian Alps, a typical small imitation of the gardens at Versailles, France. (DPI)

(GOTTSCHO—SCHLEISNER)

Spaciousness and privacy have been achieved through thoughtful landscaping in this city garden. The plan of the garden is shown to the right and its contents are identified in the chart below.

A WELL-PLANNED GARDEN

KEY TO THE GARDEN PLAN

1. Hardy ferns
2. Caladiums (not winter hardy)
3. Bamboo (hardy species)
4. Rhododendrons
5. English ivy
6. Petunias (planted annually)
7. Violets
8. Wax begonias (not winter hardy)
9. Azaleas
10. Andromeda
11. Japanese holly
12. Astilbe
13. Iris
14. Plantain-lily
15. Grass
16. Flowering crab
17. Ailanthus
18. Dogwood
19. Hawthorne
20. Geraniums (not winter hardy)

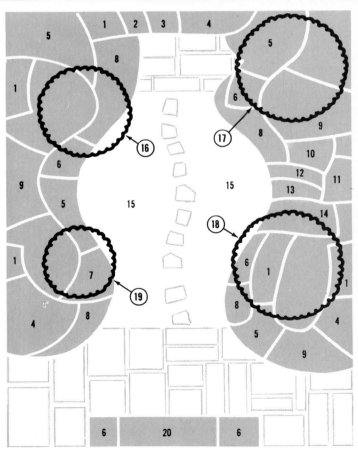

in an open space with no shade trees presents many difficulties. Some shade is usually needed near the house, but care must be taken to select trees that do not have a long root run that might interfere with the foundations of the house. On the other hand, quick-growing trees are wanted. Pin oak (*Quercus palustris*) is a good, quick-growing shade tree, and it turns a pleasing color in the autumn. The crab apples are good small trees: *Malus floribunda* is one of the best small crab apple trees for shade; *M. sargentii* is the smallest of the crab apples and makes a nice shrubby background with vivid pink flowers in the spring. All of the maples are quick-growing trees and are valuable for shade; but because of extensive root systems they should not be planted near the house or the drainage system. Sorrel tree or sour-wood (*Oxydendrum arboreum*) is an attractive and unusual small shade tree. Visits to nurseries will provide an idea of what trees are available and suited for planting in a given area. Deciduous trees and shrubs are usually planted in autumn or early spring. Evergreens should be planted in spring or in August or September. The hole in which the tree or shrub is to go should be twice the size of the root or ball as it comes from the nursery, so that a layer of well-prepared soil can go in the bottom and be filled in around the roots. All newly planted trees and shrubs must be kept well-watered in dry weather for at least the first year or two.

When planning flower beds, location is of prime consideration. Small beds scattered about a lawn produce a spotty effect. Borders give a more restful appearance and may be planted according to the amount of time the owner has for care of the garden. A border may be planted with flowering shrubs carefully chosen from catalogs to get a long blooming season; this type of border needs little care. Perennial plants that make attractive borders include candytuft (*Iberis sempervirens*), coral bells (*Heuchera*), perennial phlox (*Phlox divaricata*) for edging, iris, peonies, hemerocallis, delphiniums, Shasta daisy, and tall summer phlox (*Phlox paniculata*). All of these perennials come in a wide range of color and flowering season to last through the summer. They make a handsome border but need care to keep in good condition. A border may also be planted entirely of annuals. These may be put in as soon as the ground has warmed up in the spring. Petunias, snapdragons, salvia, asters, and stocks are best set out as plants.

The many different spring-flowering bulbs begin the show of spring color in the garden: snowdrops planted in a shady place come first, followed by yellow, blue, and white crocus. Later, narcissus, or daffodils, of many varieties appear, followed by tulips in all colors. Daffodils grow well when planted beneath shade trees, where they come up year after year. Tulips are better in a more formal planting, as are hyacinths. Ideally, fresh bulbs should be planted each autumn for a good display. Bulb catalogs come out each autumn and these should be consulted for variety, height, and color.

Consult Wyman, Donald, *Shrubs and Vines for American Gardens* (1949); Everett, T. H., *American Gardener's Book of Bulbs* (1954); Bush-Brown, Louise and James, *America's Garden Book* (1958); Graf, A. B., *Exotica* (1959); Klaber, D.O., *Rock Garden Plants* (1959); Rockwell, F.

F., and Grayson, E. C., *Complete Book of Bulbs* (1959); Wyman, Donald, *Trees for American Gardens* (1959); *Encyclopedia of Gardening*, ed. by Norman Taylor (4th ed. rev., 1961).

ALYS SUTCLIFFE, Brooklyn Botanic Garden

See also:

COLD FRAME	LAWN
COMPOST	PLANT DISEASES
FERTILIZER	ROCK GARDEN
FRUIT GROWING	ROOF GARDEN
FUNGICIDES	VEGETABLE GARDEN
HERBARIUM	WEEDS AND WEED
HOTBED	CONTROL

GARDINER, CHARLES ("CHUCK") (1904–34), hockey player, born in Edinburgh, Scotland. He was reared in Canada and became one of the outstanding goal tenders in the history of hockey. He played for the Chicago Black Hawks of the National Hockey League from 1928 through 1934 and led his team to victory in the Stanley Cup championship competition in his final year. He was named to the league all-star team in 1931, 1932, and 1934, and won the Vezina Trophy, awarded to the leading goal tender, in 1932 and 1934. Gardiner is a member of the National Hockey Hall of Fame.

GARDINER, STEPHEN (1493?–1555), English Roman Catholic Bishop. A graduate of Cambridge, Gardiner entered public life in Cardinal Wolsey's service, and in 1528 went to Rome on behalf of Henry VIII's suit for annulment. His conduct in this affair won him Henry's favor and the bishopric of Winchester (1531). In 1535 Gardiner wrote *On True Obedience* to justify Henry's break with Rome, but in doctrine he always adhered to the Catholic faith. Because of this, Cranmer and the regents deprived him during Edward VI's reign and had him imprisoned from 1548 to 1553. Queen Mary, on her accession, restored him and appointed him Lord Chancellor.

GARDINER, city of central Maine, on the Kennebec River, 8 mi. south of Augusta. It has paper mills and light manufacturing industries. Edward Arlington Robinson grew up here and it is the "Tilbury Town" of his poems. Settled, 1754; inc. as city, 1850; pop, 6,742.

GARDNER, ERLE STANLEY (1889–1970), American lawyer and writer of detective fiction. His 80 novels about the lawyer-detective Perry Mason, beginning with *The Case of the Velvet Claws* (1932) and *The Case of the Sulky Girl* (1933), constitute one of the most celebrated series in the history of crime fiction, and have frequently been adapted for motion pictures and television. Gardner's novels usually conclude with a courtroom scene in which Mason reveals the solution of the crime. They owe their chief interest to the author's encyclopedic knowledge of criminological procedure.

GARDNER, industrial city of central Massachusetts, west of Fitchburg. It is noted for the manufacture of chairs. Settled, 1764; inc. as town, 1785; as city, 1921; pop., 19,513.

SHOT DOWN.

President Garfield Dangerously Wounded.

AN ASSASSIN'S WORK.

Fired at Entering the Railroad Depot at Washington.

THE SERIOUS HIP WOUND.

Carried in an Ambulance to the White House.

CHEERFUL IN THE FACE OF DEATH.

Grave Symptoms Succeeded by a More Hopeful Condition.

A STRONG MAN'S STRUGGLE

Arrest and Imprisonment of the Criminal.

CHARLES 'JULES GUITEAU.

SCENE OF THE ASSASSINATION.

Map of Washington Showing Location of the Baltimore and Potomac Railroad Depot.

New York Historical Society

President Garfield, inaugurated in March, 1881,
was assassinated four months later.

Library of Congress

Library of Congress

Lucretia Rudolph Garfield

JAMES A. GARFIELD

20th PRESIDENT OF THE
UNITED STATES

1881

GARFIELD, JAMES ABRAM (1831–81), 20th President of the United States (1881). Born in Cuyahoga County, Ohio, he spent a "log-cabin" childhood of poverty and hardship. As a youth he worked as a farmer, a carpenter, and a canal boatman. After much sacrifice, he was able to complete his education at Williams College (1856). From 1856 to 1861 he taught ancient languages and literature at Hiram Institute (now Hiram College), Ohio, also serving for a time as principal. In addition, he became a lay preacher for the Disciples of Christ.

Garfield was admitted to the bar in 1859 and, in the same year, running as a Republican on an antislavery platform, he was elected to the state senate. He volunteered for the Union army after the outbreak of the Civil War and eventually rose to the rank of major general. He fought in the battles of Shiloh and Chickamauga, and his military reputation made him a popular figure in Ohio. While still in service he was elected to the House of Representatives (1863) and resigned his commission. A faithful party man, he supported the administration of Abraham Lincoln and the Reconstruction program of the Republican Radicals. He was a "hard-money" man, upholding monetary deflation and rejecting greenbacks, or paper money, as financially unsound. His only departure from Republican orthodoxy was his lukewarm attitude toward a high protective tariff. He was re-elected eight times, and though respected as an orator and parliamentarian, he demonstrated little initiative. Twice during his Congressional career he was touched by conflict-of-interest scandals, but his constituents paid little heed.

Garfield played a conspicuous role in the disputed election of 1876 between Rutherford B. Hayes and Samuel J. Tilden. He helped to frame compromise legislation that settled the contest, and as a member of the electoral commission, he consistently voted for Hayes. When James G. Blaine became a Senator in 1876, Garfield replaced him as leader of the Republican minority in the House. Early in 1880 the Ohio legislature elected him to the U.S. Senate, an office he was never to fill. As the Milwaukee *Sentinel* commented at the time, he was "exceptionally clean for a man who has been engaged for twenty years in active politics." At the Republican convention in Chicago during the summer he was the campaign manager of presidential hopeful John Sherman. But none of the leading favorites could gain a majority, and on the 35th ballot, 20 Wisconsin votes shifted to Garfield as a compromise candidate. On the next roll call the delegates stampeded to his support, and he was unanimously nominated. The "Stalwart" faction, led by Senator Roscoe Conkling, never forgave him for blocking their candidate, former President Ulysses S. Grant. In an attempt to mend the party split, one of Conkling's associates, Chester A. Arthur, was chosen as Garfield's running mate. The Democratic candidate, Winfield S. Hancock, was defeated in the election by 214 electoral votes to 155, although the popular vote was very close.

As President, Garfield was immediately confronted with questions of patronage. A man of integrity and distrustful of political machines, he passed over the Stalwarts in his more important appointments. The lucrative post of Collector of the Port of New York was conferred upon a rabid anti-Conkling Republican, and Conkling's major political rival, Senator Blaine, became Secretary of State.

Garfield's interest in prosecuting the "Star Routes" postal frauds, in which the government had paid exorbitant rates for mail contracts, gave promise of a reform administration. But on July 2, 1881, he was shot in the Washington railroad station by Charles J. Guiteau, a Chicago lawyer and a disappointed office seeker. As he fired, the assassin is said to have shouted, "I am a Stalwart and Arthur is President now." Garfield succumbed to his wounds the following Sept. 19. Lucretia Rudolph Garfield, whom he married in 1858, and five children survived him. Friends of the dead President raised a generous sum for their support.

Garfield's tragic death silenced hostile critics and gave rise to many laudatory biographies. The brevity of his term of office, however, prevents any judgment of his administration. Civil service legislation was a direct result of the agitation that followed his assassination.

Consult Smith, T. C., *Life and Letters of James Abram Garfield* (1925).

JAMES P. SHENTON, Columbia University

GARFIELD, industrial city of northeastern New Jersey, on the east bank of the Passaic River. The manufacture of clothing, textiles, and paper products are leading industries. The city was named in honor of President James A. Garfield. Founded, 1881; inc. as a city, 1917; pop., 30,722.

GARFIELD HEIGHTS, residential and industrial suburb southeast of Cleveland, Ohio. It has heavy industries. Inc., 1932; pop., 41,417.

GARFISH or GAR PIKE, name for the six species of large, primitive, fresh-water fishes of genus *Lepisosteus* that comprise the family Lepisosteidae. Garfishes occur from the eastern United States south into Central America, and in Cuba. They are predaceous fishes and have elongated jaws similar to those of the pike and pickerel. The long-nosed gar, *L. osseus*, has the longest jaws of all species of garfish. The alligator gar, *L. spatula*, is the largest gar and reaches a weight of over 100 lb. Gars feed primarily on other fishes, but ducks and muskrats have also been found in the stomachs of alligator gars.

GARGANO, MOUNT (anc. *Garganus Mons*), mountainous peninsula in Foggia Province on the east coast of southern Italy, extending about 25 mi. into the Adriatic Sea. It consists of an isolated, irregular plateau of limestone rock called karst that rises to a maximum height of 3,465 ft. (Mount Calvo). Its dry and rugged surface provides grazing for sheep. Olives and grapes grow on the slopes, and bees are raised, much as in ancient times. Bauxite and marble are quarried. Area, 778 sq. mi.

GARGANTUA AND PANTAGRUEL. *See* RABELAIS, FRANÇOIS.

GARIBALDI [găr-ə-bôl'dē], **GIUSEPPE** (1807–82), Italian patriot and soldier. A sailor by trade, Garibaldi became a follower of the republican revolutionary, Giuseppe Mazzini, joining the Young Italy society in 1833. The failure of a republican plot in which he was involved forced Garibaldi to flee to South America, where he fought in the Rio Grande do Sul revolt against Brazil (1836–42) and the Uruguayan civil war (1842–46). His courage and exploits in guerrilla warfare made him famous.

Returning to Italy, he led volunteers to the aid of King Charles Albert of Sardinia in the war against Austria (1848), declaring to the surprise of his republican friends that he was "not republican, but rather, Italian." Garibaldi's declaration symbolized the decline of republicanism and the rise of the House of Savoy to the leadership of the movement for Italian unification. After Austria defeated Sardinia, Garibaldi vainly battled to save Mazzini's short-lived Roman Republic. He escaped in a

Brown Brothers

Giuseppe Garibaldi, Italian hero and nationalist leader.

spectacular retreat across central Italy, pursued by troops of France, Austria, Spain, and Naples. Exiled, Garibaldi later returned (1854), supported Camillo Cavour and King Victor Emmanuel II of Sardinia, and took part (1859) in the war against Austria.

In 1860 came the most brilliant military feat of his career: leading 1,000 volunteers, the Red Shirts, he conquered the Kingdom of the Two Sicilies. He voluntarily handed his conquests to Victor Emmanuel, who became (1861) ruler of the newly proclaimed Kingdom of Italy. Victor Emmanuel, fearing a foreign invasion on behalf of the Pope, sent troops (1862) to prevent Garibaldi's forces from taking Rome. After leading his Red Shirt volunteers to victories in the Austro-Prussian War (1866), Garibaldi tried again to take Rome, but was defeated by French and papal forces (1867). Again a volunteer (1870), he won his last battle during the Franco-Prussian War when, at Dijon, his Red Shirts gave France its only victory of the war. More than any other man the symbol of the *risorgimento*, Garibaldi remains a hero of Italians everywhere.

Consult Trevelyan, G. M., *Garibaldi and the Making of Italy* (1948); Mack Smith, D., *Garibaldi* (1956).

ARMAND PATRUCCO, Queens College, New York

GARIBALDI PROVINCIAL PARK, wilderness area of British Columbia, Canada, including mountainous sections which bar access from one section of the park to another. The northern section is reached from Garibaldi on the Pacific Great Eastern Railway, the southern section from Squamish on Howe Sound. Camping, climbing, skiing, and similar activities are possible amidst magnificent lake and mountain scenery. Estab., 1920; area, 957 sq. mi.

GARIGLIANO RIVER. *See* LIRI RIVER.

GARLAND, HAMLIN (1860–1940), American author, born on a farm near West Salem, Wis. As his family moved westward to Iowa and then to South Dakota, he shared in their unending struggle to extract a livelihood from the soil. His realistic stories about the Midwest include *Main-Travelled Roads* (1891) and *Other Main-Travelled Roads* (1910). In *Crumbling Idols* (1894) he called for a new kind of fiction which would honestly explore all aspects of life. *A Son of the Middle Border* (1917), the best known of his autobiographical works, was followed by *A Daughter of the Middle Border* (1921), which won a Pulitzer Prize, and *A Pioneer Mother* (1922).

GARLAND, suburb northeast of Dallas, Tex. The principal industries include the manufacture of precision and electronic instruments, light aircraft, and paints. Pop., 81,437.

GARLIC, bulb-bearing perennial plant, *Allium sativum,* in the lily family, Liliaceae, native to southern Europe and widely cultivated in many other parts of the world. Garlic plants, which are closely related to the onion, grow to a height of up to 1 ft. and have very narrow, sword-shaped leaves. During early summer a rounded cluster of small, purplish flowers appears. This cluster ripens into the characteristic garlic head, composed of several separable parts called cloves. When the cloves are fully mature, in late summer or early autumn, they are gathered and used as a culinary herb. Garlic is cultivated in much the same manner as onion. In the spring the cloves are set out, 4 to 6 in. apart, in ordinary garden soil. Garlic thrives under a wide variety of soil and climate conditions and does best if the soil is not too rich.

Burton Berinsky—ILGWU Justice

Paper patterns are used in cutting the garments.

GARMENT INDUSTRY. The garment industry until the middle of the 18th century centered largely on the home. Skins, leather, and rough homespun cloth were the chief materials used in the making of garments. The home worker had little more than the spinning wheel and hand loom as mechanical aids. Then starting with John Kay's flying shuttle (1733) came a revolutionary series of inventions. James Hargreaves' spinning jenny (1764), Samuel Crompton's spinning mule (1799), and Edmund Cartwright's power loom (1785) all contributed to the forward rush of textile technology. In America, the establishment of the first cotton mill by Samuel Slater and the invention of the cotton gin by Eli Whitney (both in 1793) lowered textile cloth costs. Finishing clothing, however, remained a manual process.

The ready-made garment industry began about 1830 with the manufacture of army uniforms in France and sailors' "slop" clothes near Boston. But it did not gain real headway until Elias Howe invented the sewing machine (patented 1846).

For years after the entry of the sewing machine, there were no regular facilities for mass production. Fabrics were cut at a central supply point and "farmed out" to local seamstresses on a piece-work basis. After 1880 the "sweatshop" system for finishing clothes became dominant. Dozens of workers were crowded into ill-ventilated, poorly lighted rooms where they labored 72 to 84 hours a week for wages ranging from three to five dollars. In protest, the workers founded the United Garment Workers of America (1891), predecessor of the Amalgamated Clothing Workers (1914) and the International Ladies' Garment Workers' Union (1900). These protest efforts,

and revulsion over the death of 146 workers in the Triangle Shirtwaist Fire (1911), led to the elimination of the sweatshop and the development of the modern clothing factory.

The end of the sweatshop system and the adoption of a modern approach to textile operations brought a number of benefits: scientific pattern construction, laborsaving machinery, effective factory arrangement, division of labor, economies arising from mass purchase and fabrication of material, and standardization of styles.

Unlike other modern mass production industries, the garment industry does not need much capital, nor does it need to worry about the rapid advance of technology that tends to make machine products quickly obsolete. Moreover, the average garment factory still employs less than 100 persons. Machinery is inexpensive and movable, and many operations are still done by hand. The assembly line method used to turn out huge quantities of identical products in giant plants would be far from ideal in an industry whose customers lay stress on individuality as well as style. Garment manufacturers have therefore found small-scale production safer than large-scale production, yet just as profitable.

Garment manufacturing begins with the shrinking of the fabric (wool, cotton, linen, silk, synthetic, or blends), either by steam or water treatment. After drying, the fabric goes to the manufacturer of ready-made clothing.

Factory-made garments can never be exclusive. Hundreds come from the same pattern. The "pattern cutters," after stretching out the material in layers, put the pattern pieces on the material, as close together as possible in order to avoid waste. They next rub powdered

Specialized Tasks of Garment Workers

The hands of a grader (*above*) are employed in adapting a basic pattern for various sizes. The cutter (*right*) uses a power tool as he follows a pattern tracing to cut through many thicknesses of cloth, producing numerous identical pieces at once.

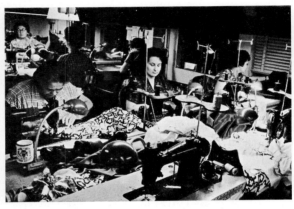

The pinner positions cloth for sewing by machine operators.

Operators stitch pinned parts together as garments near completion and send them to the finishers. (ALL PHOTOS BURTON BERINSKY—ILGWU JUSTICE)

The finisher in a hand-sewing operation adds the last touches.

chalk through perforations in the patterns to make a white line on the top layer of cloth and, following the chalk outline of the pattern, cut the material. Depending on the thickness of the material and the number of times it has been folded, cutting machines can cut many pieces of cloth at one time. Fabrics for better clothing undergo less folding than work-clothes fabrics.

After the pieces have been cut, they are sorted, numbered, and tied in bunches containing the necessary buttons and trimmings. The bundles move on to workers called "operators," who sew the pieces together into garments and send them to "finishers." The finishers, expert craftsmen, do all stitching, buttonhole work, and other work visible on the outside of a garment. They then pass the completed garments to "pressers" who iron out wrinkles and press seams flat. Finally, the "examiner" gives the finished clothes a thorough inspection to see that they meet rigid requirements of size and workmanship. Only then do garments go to the shipping room for wrapping and shipment to stores.

From a handful of scattered, inefficient factories in the 19th century, the garment industry has developed into one of America's largest industries in terms of value of output. The industry employs about 950,000 persons

who earn over $2,500,000,000 yearly. Approximately 7% of the total national income (5.6% of all expenditures) is spent on clothing, with more than 80% of the spending done by women.

Factories producing women's wear make up the largest part of the industry. Over 20,000 specialize in dresses, skirts, suits, coats, and other women's and children's apparel. Another 5,500 plants produce men's and boys' apparel. The largest concentration of garment factories is in the middle Atlantic region, especially New York City. Illinois (Chicago) and Ohio have many plants. California (Los Angeles) is foremost on the west coast.

Whatever their source, today's ready-made clothes are generally of good quality and cost less than made-to-order garments. They fit nearly all sizes and shapes, and offer great variety in color, fabric, and design.

RALPH REUTER, Assistant Educational Director, International Ladies' Garment Workers' Union

See also DOMESTIC SYSTEM; FASHION; INTERNATIONAL LADIES' GARMENT WORKERS' UNION (ILGWU).

GARMISCH-PARTENKIRCHEN [*gär′mĭsh pär-tən-kir′*KHən], health resort and winter-sports center at the foot of the Bavarian Alps, Federal Republic of Germany (West Germany). It was the site of the Winter Olympics in 1936, and the town was a favorite resort of German dictator Adolf Hitler and his Nazi leaders. Today it has a large number of hospitals and sanatoria, especially for respiratory, heart, and lung diseases.

GARNEAU [gàr-nō'], **FRANÇOIS XAVIER** (1809–66), Canadian historian, born and educated in Quebec. Garneau became a notary in 1830. Sailing for Europe in 1831, he found a position in London as secretary to the Canadian assembly's English agent, Denis-Benjamin Viger. After meeting influential people and gaining insights into French-Canadian affairs, Garneau returned to Quebec in 1833. There he resumed his notary practice, contributed verse to *Le Canadien*, and initiated two short-lived publications, *L'Abeille* in 1883–34 and *L'Institut* in 1841. Influenced by the works of François Guizot and Augustin Thierry, Garneau began his study of Canadian history in 1836, publishing accounts of battles in *Le Canadien*. Because of references to former *Patriotes*, now officials of the Canadian government, he was asked to withdraw an account of his early trip to Europe, *Voyages en Angleterre et en France* from publication. His chief work is *Histoire du Canada depuis sa découverte jusqu'a nos jours* (4 vols., 1845–52). ERNEST C. GIORDANI

GARNER, ERROLL (1921–77), American jazz pianist, born in Pittsburgh, whose highly romantic, extremely rhythmic, and firmly melodic playing made him a favorite of both jazz and popular music audiences from the late 1940's until his death. A self-taught pianist, he was rejected by the local Musician's Union in Pittsburgh because he could not read music. He then moved to New York, where he built his reputation as a soloist with a style that mixed a tremendously driving beat with elements of Earl Hines's playing, the French impressionists, and Hollywood film scoring.

GARNER, JOHN NANCE (1868–1967), Vice President of the United States (1933–41). Born near Detroit, Tex., Garner studied law, practiced at Uvalde, Tex., and developed wide business interests. A conservative Democrat, he sat in the U.S. House of Representatives from 1903 to 1933 and was Speaker in the 72d Congress (1931–33). In the 1932 Democratic convention, "Cactus Jack" was chosen as a compromise vice presidential candidate to run with Franklin D. Roosevelt. After 1936 he became increasingly disenchanted with New Deal policies. He broke with FDR on the third-term issue and retired.

GARNET, HENRY HIGHLAND (1815–82), U.S. Negro clergyman and Abolitionist. Born a slave in New Market, Md., he escaped with his family to Pennsylvania when he was 10. Garnet was educated at Oneida Institute, Whitestone, N.Y., and held a number of Presbyterian ministries including one for a white congregation in Troy, N.Y. He was employed as a speaker by the American Anti-Slavery Society and was considered one of the leading Negro Abolitionists. After a speech at the 1843 convention of the society in which he advocated violence to overthrow slavery, his influence declined. He served as the U.S. minister to Liberia for two months before his death.

GARNET [gär'nĭt] **MINERALS,** group of silicate minerals with the general formula $X_3Y_2Si_3O_{12}$. X may be calcium (Ca), magnesium (Mg), iron (Fe), or manganese (Mn), and Y may be aluminum (Al), iron, or chromium (Cr). Garnet commonly occurs in well-developed crystals such as dodecahedrons (12-sided forms), and it is also found as coarse to fine granular masses. The color is variable, but most specimens are dark red or reddish brown. Garnet is typically a constituent of metamorphic rocks, although it has been found in some igneous rocks and as a detrital mineral in sands and sandstones.

On the basis of chemical composition the garnet minerals are grouped into several species. Almandite ($Fe_3Al_2Si_3O_{12}$), one of the common garnets, is generally red or reddish brown. Pyrope ($Mg_3Al_2Si_3O_{12}$), less common than most other garnets, is red to almost black. Spessartite ($Mn_3Al_2Si_3O_{12}$) is orange to dark red or brown. Grossularite ($Ca_3Al_2Si_3O_{12}$) is white if pure, otherwise yellow, pink, green, or brown. Andradite ($Ca_3Fe_2Si_3O_{12}$) is yellow, greenish yellow, greenish brown, or black. Uvarovite ($Ca_3Cr_2Si_3O_{12}$) is characteristically emerald green.

Garnet is used as an abrasive; for this purpose the crystals are crushed to provide the garnet "sand" used to make sandpaper. Several thousand tons of crushed garnet are produced annually from mines on Gore Mountain near North Creek, N.Y. Transparent, unflawed garnet is cut into attractive and relatively inexpensive gems. Cinnamon stone is a variety of grossularite. When it is cabochon-cut, precious garnet is called carbuncle. Demantoid is a brilliant green gem variety of andradite.

Properties: *Crystal System,* Isometric; *Hardness* (Mohs' Scale), 7–7½; *Density,* 3.6–4.3, depending on the composition. BRIAN MASON

See also CRYSTALLOGRAPHY; GEM; MINERALOGY.

GARNISHMENT, in law, method by which creditors may attach and obtain a defaulting debtor's property which is in the possession of a third person. It may sometimes be loosely called attachment. Garnishment is a statutory remedy and may be utilized during or after a lawsuit to satisfy a judgment in favor of the creditor. It may also be used at the commencement of a suit to obtain jurisdiction over a nonresident debtor who has property in the possession of another within the court's jurisdiction. One's wages may be garnished to the extent permitted by statute.

GARONNE [gà-rôn'] **RIVER** of southwestern France, rising just across the Spanish border in the central Pyrenees and flowing northwest 402 mi (647 km) to the Bay of Biscay. It receives a number of small tributaries from the Pyrenees together with rivers from the Central Massif of France. Below Bordeaux it widens into a large estuary, known as the Gironde. Near the head of the Gironde it receives the Dordogne River, its largest tributary. The Garonne has an irregular flow but is navigable for seagoing vessels to Bordeaux, after which it parallels the Garonne Lateral Canal to Toulouse.

GARRICK, DAVID (1717–79), English actor, one of the outstanding players in the history of the stage. He had his first success in London in 1741, as Richard III, one

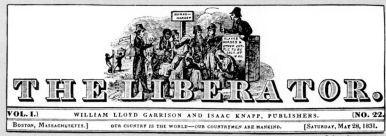

William Lloyd Garrison and the masthead of his abolitionist newspaper.

Culver Pictures, Inc.

of his many Shakespearean roles. In 1742 he moved to Drury Lane, where he ruled, as actor and co-manager (from 1747), until his retirement in 1776. Garrick was equally skilled in tragic and comic parts, among which his most famous were Lear, Hamlet, Macbeth, and Bayes in *The Rehearsal*. He was among the first to abandon the formal elocutionary style for more naturalistic acting characterized by freshness, ease, and intensity. His reforms also included pioneering work in stage lighting concealed from the audience, and elimination of the audience from the stage. He also wrote a number of plays and adapted others for his excellent company.

GARRISON, EDWARD H. ("SNAPPER") (1868–1930), American jockey, born in New Haven, Conn. He was the highest-paid jockey of the 1880's and 1890's and retired in 1897 to become a trainer and racing official.

GARRISON, WILLIAM LLOYD (1805–79), American abolitionist. Born in Newburyport, Mass., Garrison worked there for seven years (1818–25) as an apprentice printer and anonymous journalist. He later edited and printed newspapers in Newburyport, Boston, and Bennington, Vt., before accepting (1829) an offer to join Benjamin Lundy in publishing *The Genius of Universal Emancipation* in Baltimore.

Jailed (1830) for a libelous accusation of slave trading, he left Lundy after his release and returned to Boston, where (Jan. 1, 1831) he published the first issue of the *Liberator*. In it he promised to be "as harsh as truth, and as uncompromising as justice." The leading article ended with a ringing call to battle: "I am in earnest—I will not equivocate—I will not excuse—I will not retreat a single inch—and *I will be heard*." Although its circulation never exceeded 3,000, the *Liberator* and its editor gained world fame when Southern editors began to reprint Garrison's violent denunciations of slavery and slaveholders in order to answer the charges. Garrison also helped to organize the American Anti-Slavery Society (1833) and later served as its president (1843–65).

Garrison was a man of strong emotions for whom unpopular causes had an almost hypnotic appeal. He reduced problems to simple questions of right and wrong. For him slavery was a sin; those who maintained it were sinners; and anyone who urged moderation or compromise deserved denunciation. His philosophy of nonresistance led him to eschew all direct political action, even voting. He came to advocate disunion, with the slogan "No Union with Slaveholders," and denounced the Con-

stitution as "a Covenant with Death and an Agreement with Hell," because it allowed slavery. He opposed the Civil War until the Emancipation Proclamation was issued (1863), but later appreciated Lincoln. With the adoption of the Thirteenth Amendmant in 1865, he discontinued the *Liberator* and resigned as president of the American Anti-Slavery Society.

Interpretations vary concerning Garrison's role. To some he was the unquestioned leader of the movement to abolish slavery. More recent investigations suggest that his excesses may have made more difficult the work of those who sought more conciliatory means for ending slavery. He continued as an advocate of Negro rights, denouncing the Union government for wartime treatment of freed Negroes, and urging the acceptance of Negro troops into the Union army.

Consult Korngold, Ralph, *Two Friends of Man* (1950); Nye, R. B., *William Lloyd Garrison and the Humanitarian Reformers* (1955).

HERBERT WISBEY, JR., Keuka College

GARROS [gȧ-rôs'], **ROLAND** (1888–1918), French pilot who pioneered in combat flying. He mounted an automatic rifle before his cockpit and fired it through the propeller which he fitted with deflecting armor. The plane was captured by the Germans in World War I and Anthony H. G. Fokker improved the device. Before the war Garros had set high-altitude records: 12,828 ft. in 1911 and 18,405 ft. in 1912, and made the first trans-Mediterranean flight in 1913. He died in combat.

GARSHIN [gär'shĭn], **VSEVOLOD MIKHAILOVICH** (1855–88), Russian short-story writer. A member of the nobility, he studied at the St. Petersburg Mining Institute, but failed to graduate. His first and best story, "Four Days" (1877), describes a wounded Russian soldier's experience during four days on the battlefield beside the body of a dead Turk. In "The Red Flower" (1883), he wrote of a madman for whom the red poppy symbolizes evil. Long subject to fits of melancholia. Garshin committed suicide. His 20 stories were greatly instrumental in popularizing the short story in Russia. His work was translated in *The Signal and Other Stories* (1912).

GARTER SNAKE, name for the most common type of snake in North America. Garter snakes, genus *Thamnophis*, family Colubridae, are harmless snakes 1 to 4 ft. long and about an inch in diameter when mature. The color pattern varies but is mainly green with three narrow lighter stripes running the length of the body and tail. Because of this coloration they are sometimes called ribbon snakes. The best-known garter snake is *T. sirtalis*, which is found throughout the entire United States, in Southern Canada, and in Mexico.

Garter snakes are found in all types of habitats, including swamps, grassy meadows, and along the roadside, but are seen most often near the borders of streams. They capture and eat frogs, toads, fish, and shrews. In turn, garter snakes are preyed upon by the blacksnake, copperhead, and many reptile-consuming birds and mammals.

The young develop inside the mother's body and are born alive, sometimes as many as 30 at one time. The young snakes feed on earthworms.

MARY M. TOWNES, North Carolina College at Durham

GARVEY, MARCUS MOZIAH (1887–1940), American Negro leader. Born in Jamaica, British West Indies, he had a fragmentary education and at 14 was apprenticed to a printer in Kingston. He became skilled at his trade, and in 1910 he began to publish a newspaper, *Garvey's Watchman*, and to engage in other part-time ventures in journalism. In 1912 he went to London, hoping to learn more about the condition of Negroes in other parts of the British Empire. He was associated in the publication of the *African Times and Orient Express*, an experience that awakened his interest in his ancestral homeland. Meanwhile, a copy of Booker T. Washington's *Up from Slavery* turned his attention toward the Negro in the United States. In 1914 he returned to Jamaica and founded an association to foster Negro nationalism. He extended his activities to the United States in 1916. His Universal Negro Improvement Association (UNIA), using the slogan "Africa for the Africans" and appealing to racial pride, became the first U.S. Negro organization since Reconstruction to obtain a mass following. Garvey's organization was opposed by the more moderate Negro groups. The UNIA is considered a forerunner of present-day U.S. Negro separatist groups such as the Black Muslims. Garvey's career was abruptly ended when he was convicted of fraud and misappropriation of funds. He was imprisoned (1925–27) and later deported.

ARNA BONTEMPS, Fisk University

GARWOOD, industrial borough of northeastern New Jersey, 6 mi. southwest of Elizabeth. Machine tools, foundry products, metal goods, hardware, plastics, and cleaning compounds are produced in its many factories. Inc., 1903; pop., 5,260.

GARY, ELBERT HENRY (1846–1927), American industrialist, born near Wheaton, Ill. He graduated (1868) from Union College of Law in Chicago, and practiced law in Wheaton, where he became mayor and then county judge. An expert on corporate law, he was responsible for organizing the American Steel and Wire Company (1898) and the United States Steel Corporation (1901). As board chairman of the latter, he sponsored a stock ownership program for employees and planned the steel town of Gary, Ind. His antiunion policy helped to precipitate the steel strike of 1919 which, though unsuccessful, led to reduced working hours.

GARY, ROMAIN (1914–   ), French novelist. Born in Russia, he spent his boyhood in Vilnius and Warsaw, finally emigrating to France with his mother. He entered the French diplomatic service in 1945 and eventually became an ambassador, in fulfillment of his ambitious mother's high hopes for him. His novels include *Le grand vestiaire*, 1949 (*The Company of Men*, 1950); *Les racines du ciel*, 1956 (*The Roots of Heaven*, 1958); *Lady L. . . .* (in English, 1958); the autobiographical *La promesse de l'aube*, 1959 (*Promise at Dawn*, 1961); *Le mangeur d'étoiles*, 1960 (*The Talent Scout*, 1961); and *The Ski Bum* (in English, 1965); as well as a volume of short stories *Gloire à nos illustres pionniers*, 1962 (*The Hissing Tales*, 1964).

GARY, city of northwestern Indiana, at the southern tip of Lake Michigan, about 30 mi. southeast of Chicago. It is part of the greater Chicago metropolitan area. Gary owes its early development to the United States Steel Corporation, which in 1906 selected what was almost a wilderness as the site for the establishment of its chief works. Built on an artificial harbor, it was for many years the largest steel manufacturing plant in the world. The city was named after Elbert H. Gary, who was instrumental in bringing the industry to the area. Notable products besides steel are cement, made from furnace slag, and glass. The so-called Gary Plan was a pioneer educational development. Indiana University has an extension center here. Pop., 175,415.

GAS. Matter ordinarily is in one of three phases, solid, liquid, or gaseous. The characteristic of the gaseous phase is that any individual atom or molecule may move freely to any part of the accessible volume. In the case of the atmosphere, any atom or molecule may move upward from the top layer into space but will travel in a trajectory under gravity and will almost always fall back into the atmosphere at some distant point.

Air is a typical gas and is a mixture of roughly 80% molecular nitrogen, 19% molecular oxygen, just under 1% atomic argon, and small traces of other gases. Other substances which are in the gaseous phase at standard temperature (0° C., or 32° F.) and pressure (760 mm. mercury) include neon, krypton, xenon, chlorine, fluorine, and a large number of hydrocarbons. At lower temperatures these substances enter the liquid phase, and at still lower temperatures (and sometimes at higher pressures) the solid phase. The transition phase between liquid and gas is called a vapor, familiar examples of which are water vapor and gasoline vapor.

The concept of a gas is fairly broad, air being a typical example. It is, however, also customary to speak of an electron gas, such as exists in the atmosphere of the sun, or of a gas of neutrons diffusing about in an atomic reactor. Usually a gas is limited in extent by the container in which it finds itself, but some gases such as neutrons will pass through most solids. The volume occupied by a gas may be altered, this process being called expansion or compression.

Three quantities determine the state of a gas: its volume, its pressure, and its temperature. The volume is determined by the geometrical shape of the container, the pressure is determined by the average momentum trans-

THE BEHAVIOR OF GASES
IN EACH CASE, THE WEIGHT OF GAS IS THE SAME

LARGE VOLUME

LOW PRESSURE

SMALL VOLUME
HIGH PRESSURE

LARGE VOLUME

HIGH
TEMPERATURE

GAS CONDENSES TO A
LIQUID AT LOW TEMPERATURE

In a large container, the bombardment of the restraining walls by the fast-moving gas molecules is spread out over a large area. As the volume decreases, smaller and smaller areas are subjected to the same bombardment and pressure exerted by the gas increases.

Kinetic energy of molecules varies with temperature. At high temperatures the molecules move faster and the gas increases in volume and pressure. At low temperatures they move so slowly they are enmeshed by intermolecular attraction and the gas becomes a liquid.

ferred per unit time to the walls of the container by the atoms or molecules bouncing off a unit area, and the temperature is proportional to the average kinetic energy of the individual atoms, some individuals of which move slightly faster and others slower than the average. Pressure, temperature, and volume are therefore interrelated, their relationships being expressed by the gas laws.

If the walls of the container are removed, and if there is no other force such as gravity present to limit expansion, the individual atoms of the gas will in general diffuse away from one another. The pressure of the gas then drops, approaching zero, as the volume occupied by the gas expands toward infinity. The limiting case is a perfect vacuum, a volume in which there are no atoms or molecules at all. In the opposite direction, if a gas is compressed, its pressure and temperature rise.

If a gas is cooled, so that the gas becomes cooler and denser, eventually the atoms will start sticking together, and the gas will liquefy. For example, ordinary air will become a liquid at about − 185° C. (−301° F.), and the other common gases likewise become liquid, each at its characteristic liquefaction temperature. The converse of this process is boiling, in which process the liquid is heated until it becomes a gas.

Occasionally there is no liquid phase, and a gas can go directly into the solid phase or vice versa. This process is called sublimation. For example, iodine and dry ice, or solid carbon dioxide, sublime at room temperature.

SERGE A. KORFF, New York University
See also BOYLE'S LAW; CHARLES' LAW; KINETIC THEORY OF GASES.

GAS, ILLUMINATING. See COAL GAS.

GAS, MANUFACTURE OF, process in which heat is applied to solid or liquid fuels, like coal or oil, to produce combustible gas. Beginning with experiments in the early 19th century, the manufacture of gas grew into a giant industry. Tremendous quantities of manufactured gas were used to illuminate streets, places of business, and homes. Since the invention of the electric light in 1879, this usage is now almost nonexistent. Manufactured gas

has been used extensively as a fuel for cooking and heating. Fifty years ago a local gasworks could be found near almost any sizable city. In recent times, particularly in the United States, natural gas has replaced manufactured gas until today the manufactured gas industry has shrunk to a small fraction of its former size.

C. R. HARTE, American Oil Company
See also BOTTLED GAS; COAL GAS; NATURAL GAS.

GAS, NATURAL. See NATURAL GAS.

GAS, POISON. See CHEMICAL WARFARE.

GASCOIGNE [găs′koin], **GEORGE** (c.1539–1577), pioneer English poet, dramatist, and fiction writer. After studying at Trinity College, Cambridge, and at Gray's Inn, he became a soldier and fought against the Spaniards in Holland. His works include *The Supposes* (1566), the first prose comedy in English; *Certain Notes of Instruction* (c.1575), the first treatise on poetry in the language; *The Adventures of Master F. J.* (1573), one of the earliest works of English psychological fiction; and *Posies* (1575), which includes perhaps the best English lyrics of the early Elizabethan period.

GASCONY [găs′kə-nē], region and former province of southwest France. It is bordered in the west by the Bay of Biscay; the Pyrenees form its border with Spain in the south. It is drained by the Garonne and Gironde rivers, which form the northern and eastern boundaries. Auch is the historic capital, and other towns are Biarritz, Dax, Bayonne, Luchon, Lourdes, and Tarbes. Gascons, like D'Artagnan in Dumas' *Three Musketeers*, are supposed to be characteristically brave and flamboyant.

GASHERBRUM. See KARAKORAM.

GASKELL [găs′kəl], **ELIZABETH CLEGHORN STEVENSON** (1810–65), English novelist. The wife of a Unitarian minister, she frequently undertook visits of charity into working-class homes, the impressions from which she successfully converted into fiction. Thus, in *Mary Barton*

(1848), unrivaled among novels of the time, she painted a movingly sympathetic picture of Manchester's cotton-mill workers. Less passionate is *North and South* (1855), contrasting the industrial north with the landed south. Her later novels include her finest ones, *Sylvia's Lovers* (1863), *Cousin Phillis* (1864), and *Wives and Daughters* (1866). The latter, her masterpiece, subjects different parental relationships and different kinds of children to a subtle and vivid moral analysis. *Cranfield* (1853) is more a series of provincial sketches than a novel. Mrs. Gaskell also wrote a celebrated *Life of Charlotte Brontë* (1857).

Consult Pollard, Arthur, *Mrs. Gaskell* (1965).

CLAIRE SPRAGUE, Brooklyn College

GAS MASK, device to protect the eyes and lungs from toxic gases, germs, and radioactive dust. It consists of a facepiece, usually of rubber, and eyepieces of plastic or glass. It fastens to the head with straps. Air is breathed into the common military mask through a canister containing activated charcoal, which adsorbs gases. A filter removes air-borne particles. Rebreathing masks contain chemicals that change exhaled carbon dioxide and water vapor into oxygen. Other masks use air supplied from a tank carried by the wearer. These masks are used when the surrounding air is heavily contaminated or deficient in oxygen, as happens in certain industrial operations.

GAS METER, instrument which measures the volume of flowing gas. The common type has a casing divided by a rigid diaphragm into two chambers. Sliding valves alternately admit gas from the supply pipe to the two chambers. As the gas enters one of the chambers, a flexible diaphragm moves to admit a known volume. The valves then allow the gas to flow into the discharge pipe, while admitting supply gas to the other chamber. Thus, each side delivers a known volume of gas per cycle. The valve motion actuates dials calibrated in cubic feet. There are

READING A GAS METER

Gas meter dials are read left to right. The small dial is used only for testing. When a pointer is between two numbers, the reader records the lower number. Top row of dials reads 2-6-1-3. Subsequent reading, shown on bottom row, is 2-6-5-0. Then 2650 — 2613 = 37 units (of 100 cu. ft. each), or 3,700 cu. ft. of gas used.

also types of gas meters which indicate the rate of flow of gas as well as total quantity passed.

GASOLINE, liquid fuel mixture of hydrocarbons. It has a boiling range, vapor pressure, and octane number that provide satisfactory operation of a spark-ignition engine. Gasoline is produced in refineries by one of several methods. Fractional distillation of crude oil is the oldest and simplest method; however, it does not produce the high-performance gasoline needed by many of today's engines. Cracking, a thermal or catalytic decomposition of organic compounds, converts the gasoline produced by fractional distillation into a more refined product. Chemically, gasoline can contain more than 120 individual hydrocarbons, depending on the crude oil.

While modern gasoline is synthetic in the sense that its components are produced by a variety of chemical processes, a true synthetic gasoline can be produced by either the Bergius or the Fischer-Tropsch process. The former converts coal to liquid hydrocarbons by catalytic hydrogenation under high pressure. The latter converts methane to carbon monoxide and hydrogen which are recombined catalytically into liquid hydrocarbons. Both processes have been used in Germany; however, they are costly and produce an inferior grade of gasoline. There is little likelihood that these processes will assume any substantial industrial importance in the foreseeable future. Vast deposits of oil-bearing shale which can produce a light crude oil exist in the United States. Similarly, deposits of tar sands such as those along the Athabasca River in Canada are available as a source of petroleum. It is generally believed that these latter sources will be commercialized prior to synthetic sources.

Requirements. In order to fulfill its function as a motor fuel, commercial gasoline must be manufactured in such a way as to (1) burn without knock under varying loads and speeds, (2) vaporize sufficiently in cold weather to permit easy engine starting, (3) avoid excessive vaporization with consequent vapor lock in hot weather, (4) eliminate high-boiling compounds which tend to form carbon deposits in the engine, (5) not oxidize in storage, and (6) minimize spark-plug fouling and carburetor icing.

Octane number (an indication of the relative ability of gasoline to resist knock during combustion) is the most important quality factor of gasoline If the octane number is too low, knock and engine malfunction occur. If the octane number is too high, the money paid for the extra fuel quality is wasted. Since automobile engines vary widely in octane requirement, several grades of gasoline are marketed, the main difference being octane number. There is little difference between the energy delivered by the various grades of different brands of gasoline. If the car will operate without knock, the mileage recorded with different gasolines will be substantially the same.

History. The automobile provided the first market for the volatile by-product of the illuminating oil industry, gasoline. Gasoline technology has been linked to the evolution of the motorcar ever since. In 1904 the average crude oil yielded approximately 10% of its volume as gasoline, a figure which contrasts with modern refinery yields of about 43%. Early technical advances in crude-oil refining were concerned primarily with increasing the yield of

FOUR SYSTEMS ESSENTIAL TO THE GASOLINE ENGINE

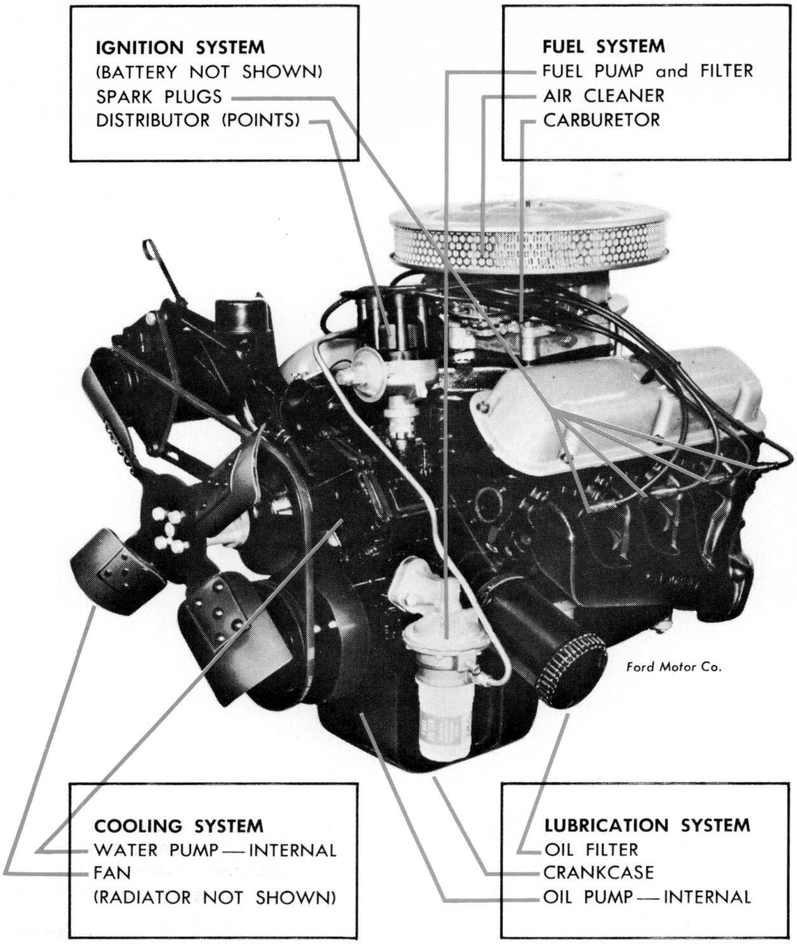

IGNITION SYSTEM
Pulses of electricity from the battery are delivered to each spark plug alternately by the distributor. Electric sparks across the narrow gap between the electrodes on the spark plugs ignite the fuel mixture.

FUEL SYSTEM
The fuel pump delivers gasoline to the carburetor, where it is vaporized and mixed with air. The carburetor feeds this mixture through the intake manifold and valves to the combustion chambers of the cylinders.

COOLING SYSTEM
In a water-cooled engine water is pumped into channels surrounding the cylinders, where it absorbs heat. The hot water is then circulated through the radiator, cooled by the fan, and returned to the engine.

LUBRICATION SYSTEM
Oil is forced by the oil pump from the crankcase to all moving parts in the engine. It reduces friction between the metal surfaces, helps cool the engine, and carries away dirt, which is removed by filter.

IGNITION SYSTEM
(BATTERY NOT SHOWN)
SPARK PLUGS
DISTRIBUTOR (POINTS)

FUEL SYSTEM
FUEL PUMP and FILTER
AIR CLEANER
CARBURETOR

Ford Motor Co.

COOLING SYSTEM
WATER PUMP — INTERNAL
FAN
(RADIATOR NOT SHOWN)

LUBRICATION SYSTEM
OIL FILTER
CRANKCASE
OIL PUMP — INTERNAL

gasoline at the expense of the heavier and less salable portions of the crude.

In 1913 the first thermal cracking units were placed in operation to convert gas oil to gasoline. A second major innovation, thermal re-forming, occured in 1930. This was a form of mild cracking especially adapted to the conversion of high-boiling gasoline and kerosene to gasoline. Re-forming not only increased gasoline yield but also improved octane number and volatility. Both cracking and re-forming reduced the knocking tendency of gasoline; therefore the automotive industry could increase the efficiency of its engines through increased compression ratio. In this same period tetraethyl lead was introduced as an antiknock additive to assist the refiner in providing efficient fuels. In 1936 octane numbers received another boost with the advent of fixed-bed catalytic cracking of gas oils. Catalytic polymerization of olefins from refinery gases also added volume and octane numbers in the late 1930's. During World War II, manufacture of high-octane gasoline components reached unprecedented volumes. In 1945 aviation gasoline of 100 octane number was produced at the rate of about 500,000 barrels a day. High volumes of high-quality gasoline were made possible by newly developed processes—fluid catalytic cracking, moving-bed catalytic cracking, and catalytic alkylation.

Following World War II, the automotive industry was quick to take advantage of the petroleum industry's high-quality gasoline potential with the development of new high-compression engines. The most important postwar refining development was catalytic re-forming. In this process, low-octane naphthas and gasolines are converted to high-octane-number fuels by dehydrogenation and isomerization. The total motor fuel production in the United States approximates 60 billion gallons a year with a substantial reserve refining capacity.

W. Nelson Axe, Phillips Petroleum Company
See also Cracking, Petroleum; Fuel.

GASOLINE ENGINE. Primarily because it is a small-package unit, the gasoline engine has resulted in a technological revolution. It has a large power output in comparison to its weight. Its cost of manufacture has been so drastically reduced that ownership by many has become possible. Automobiles are powered by gasoline engines; they were used in the first propeller-driven airplanes; today, smaller gasoline engines power boats and such household machinery as lawn mowers. Still others are used in many varieties of farm equipment.

This engine is technically described as an internal-combustion, reciprocating engine. The phrase "internal-combustion" means that the fuel is burned inside the engine. The place where it is burned is the combustion

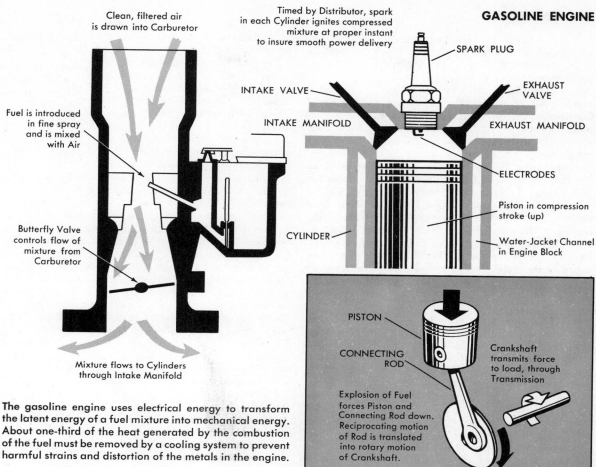

Clean, filtered air is drawn into Carburetor

Timed by Distributor, spark in each Cylinder ignites compressed mixture at proper instant to insure smooth power delivery

SPARK PLUG

INTAKE VALVE

EXHAUST VALVE

INTAKE MANIFOLD

EXHAUST MANIFOLD

Fuel is introduced in fine spray and is mixed with Air

ELECTRODES

Piston in compression stroke (up)

Butterfly Valve controls flow of mixture from Carburetor

CYLINDER

Water-Jacket Channel in Engine Block

Mixture flows to Cylinders through Intake Manifold

PISTON

CONNECTING ROD

Crankshaft transmits force to load, through Transmission

Explosion of Fuel forces Piston and Connecting Rod down. Reciprocating motion of Rod is translated into rotary motion of Crankshaft.

The gasoline engine uses electrical energy to transform the latent energy of a fuel mixture into mechanical energy. About one-third of the heat generated by the combustion of the fuel must be removed by a cooling system to prevent harmful strains and distortion of the metals in the engine.

chamber above the piston. The burning, or combustion, of fuel causes the piston to move inside a cylinder in what is called a reciprocating motion from one extreme end to another. As it does this, the up-and-down motion is converted into rotary motion by a rod connected from the piston to a shaft, called the crankshaft. Gasoline engines can be classed as four-stroke or two-stroke, depending on how many strokes are needed to complete a cycle.

History. Like all internal-combustion engines, the gasoline engine is relatively new. The first known gasoline engine was built in 1857 by Barsanti and Matteucci. The fuel in the piston chamber was ignited by gunpowder. The heavy piston then moved up in its cylinder and on its return downward, engaged a toothed wheel, or ratchet, which caused a shaft to turn in rotary motion.

The next serious attempt to construct a gasoline engine was made by Étienne Lenoir in 1860. In Lenoir's engine the piston moved halfway up a cylinder and drew in a mixture of gas and air. After the mixture was ignited, resulting hot gases expanded and pushed the piston into the second half of its stroke. Unlike today's gasoline engines, Lenoir's engine did not compress the gas-air mixture before ignition and had low efficiency. In 1862 Beau de Rochas, a Frenchman, developed the theory of a more efficient engine. Then Nikolaus Otto, a German, developed the same theory and in 1876 built an engine that was

the forerunner of modern gasoline engines. Otto's engine was a four-stroke cycle engine. In 1878 Sir Dugald Clerk of Glasgow built and exhibited the first two-stroke cycle gasoline engine. Another major advance in engine design came when Gottlieb Daimler of Germany developed the gasoline engine to a point where higher speeds giving more power to smaller-size engines were possible.

Four-Stroke Cycle Engine. To describe the operating cycle of the gasoline engine, it must first be understood that the piston moves back and forth in the cylinder from an extreme upper point to an extreme lower point. As it moves in reciprocating motion between these two points, other things happen: fuel and air enter the chamber, are compressed, burned, and then forced out. The action occurs in four strokes of the piston: intake, compression, power, and exhaust.

Intake Stroke. In the intake stroke, the fuel and air mixture is drawn into the cylinder. The mixture is made up of air and partially vaporized gasoline which enter through an inlet valve. At the end of the intake stroke the piston reaches a lower extreme point. As it begins its return upward stroke, the inlet valve closes, leaving the fuel mixture trapped in the cylinder.

Compression Stroke. In the compression stroke, the piston's upward motion pressurizes the fuel mixture. (In an automobile engine that is idling and therefore requires

469

only minimum fueling, this pressure may be 50 lb. per square inch. At full throttle opening, when the engine is going at full speed, and maximum fuel is being used, the pressure may be 200 lb. per square inch.

In the process of compression, a temperature rise of as much as 500° F. or 600° F. causes more vaporization of the gasoline. As the compression stroke is nearly completed, most of the gasoline in the fuel mixture has been vaporized. Combustion will be poor in the presence of liquid gasoline.

Power Stroke. The power stroke begins at the end of the compression stroke, when the piston is at its upper extreme point. At this time (or even earlier in high speed engines) the fuel is ignited by a spark plug. The combustion results in the release of a large quantity of heat as the fuel-air mixture is changed into hot gases that exert increasingly higher pressures. The rising pressures exert a force on the piston that pushes it down in the power stroke. At the end of the power stroke, the piston is moved to the extreme lower end. Then an exhaust valve on the cylinder opens so that the burned fuel gases can be released.

Exhaust Stroke. Some gases remain after the exhaust valve is opened and the pressure in the cylinder becomes closer to that of normal atmosphere. Most of the remaining gases are swept or forced out of the cylinder by the piston as it returns upward in the exhaust stroke. As the piston nears this upper point, the exhaust valve closes. Then the inlet valve opens and the cycle begins again with the intake stroke.

During the four-stroke cycle there are two complete revolutions of the crankshaft. The turning crankshaft eventually drives the wheels of an automobile. The inlet and exhaust valves, which open and close only once each cycle, are actuated by a camshaft which moves only one complete turn for two turns of the crankshaft.

Two-Stroke Cycle Engine. Although the four-stroke cycle engine described above is highly developed, it is sometimes too complex and too costly for light power applications, for example, an outboard motor or a power lawn mower. Therefore, the two-stroke cycle engine is used. In its simplest form it has no valves for inlet and exhaust and hence requires no camshaft. Its cylinder design and lubrication system are much simpler.

The two-stroke cycle engine has ports for the fuel inlet. On the downward stroke the fuel-air mixture, which has been already compressed, enters the chamber and pushes out the spent gases from the previous cycle. The pressure may be caused by compressing the fuel-air by the underside of the piston or may be caused by a blower. As the piston starts upward in a compression stroke the inlet ports are closed off and the fuel mixture compressed more. Near the end of the stroke a spark plug ignites the charge. The resulting high-pressure gases push the piston down on the expansion stroke. As it nears the bottom position, the exhaust ports are uncovered and some of the spent gases released. There are only two strokes—compression and power.

In comparison to the four-stroke engine, the two-stroke is less efficient. Some of the power is needed to compress the mixture or to drive the blower that pressurizes the fuel-air mixture and forces it into the cylinder. Also since for a short time both the intake and exhaust ports are both open there is apt to be less usable fuel in the cylinder than there would be in a four-stroke cycle engine.

Fuel. The fuel used in a gasoline engine is made expressly to give special qualities for efficient operation. It must resist detonation, which causes engine knock, and must also cause the engine to warm up rapidly when it is being started. It should not form vapor while in the fuel line, since this interferes with or stops an even flow of gasoline, and it should not leave gum and varnish deposits. The chemical composition of the gasoline is varied to suit climatic conditions in different geographical areas.

The gasoline fuel and air are mixed in the carburetor in proportions that will give the finely atomized droplets necessary for good combustion. The strength of the mixture is determined by the load and speed requirements of the engine. The total quantity of the mixture sent to the engine is determined by the amount of engine power the driver wants as he presses his foot on the gas pedal. The fuel mixture is partially vaporized in the intake manifold, then further vaporized during the intake stroke. The latter is due to the heat in the normally hot cylinder wall and the mixing of the fresh charge with residual hot gases from the previous cycle plus the work done by the piston during compression. A spark plug ignites the mixture of air and gasoline vapor in the cylinder. The exact time when the spark is fired (spark timing) varies with the speed and load of the engine. However, it generally occurs in the period just before the compression stroke finishes at inner dead center.

Ping or Knock. The familiar sharp pinging sound heard when an automobile engine using an unsuitable low-octane gasoline is making an uphill climb on a hot day is caused by a detonation that occurs too early. It happens when there is ignition of the unburned mixture upstream of the flame front advancing from the spark plug. This causes pressure waves within the mixture that, in turn, cause the cylinder block to vibrate. The cause of this sudden self-ignition of the unburned mixture of end gases is the relatively long time they spend at high temperature and pressure. Gasolines that resist self-ignition are called high-octane-number fuels. (Octane number is based on an arbitrary scale which indicates the degree of resistance to early detonation.) Gasoline engines that require high-octane gasoline detonate more and have higher compression ratios.

Cylinder Head. The part of the engine above the cylinder and piston arrangement is called the cylinder head. It is designed with several things in mind. Among these are the reduction of the possibility of predetonation by placing the spark plug nearer the exhaust; the improvement of the engine's "breathing" capacity by drawing in the maximum desired amount of fuel mixture; the reduction of heat losses in the cooling water jacket; and keeping the end gases cool during the combustion period.

PHILLIP S. MYERS, *University of Wisconsin*

See also :

GASOMETRY [găs-ŏm'ə-trē] **or GAS ANALYSIS,** analysis of a mixture of gases by measurement of the volumes of each of the components. This is done by removing each component in turn from the mixture by suitable chemical reaction and measuring the remaining gas volume. Since the volume of a gas depends on the temperature and pressure, a gas burette is used. It is surrounded by a liquid jacket kept at constant temperature, and it is connected by a flexible tube to a leveling bulb so that the gas pressure inside the burette can be made equal to the atmospheric pressure.

For example, if a flue gas is to be analyzed for carbon dioxide, oxygen, carbon monoxide, and nitrogen, a measured volume, usually 100 cc., of sample is bubbled successively through potassium hydroxide to remove carbon dioxide, through pyrogallol to remove oxygen, and through cuprous chloride to remove carbon monoxide. The decrease in gas volume after each absorption is a direct measure of the percentage by volume in the sample of the component absorbed.

Other components are measured by extensions of the above scheme. Hydrogen, for example, would be left with nitrogen at the end of the sequence. By adding excess oxygen, igniting the mixture to form water, and absorbing the remaining oxygen, the hydrogen is removed and is thereby measured.

H. A. LAITINEN, University of Illinois

GASPÉ [găs-pā'], **PHILIPPE AUBERT DE** (1786–1871), author of one of the first novels published in French Canada. His historical romance—*Les Anciens Canadiens,* 1863 (*The Canadians of Old,* 1864)—still ranks as a classic of Canadian literature. At the age of 79, De Gaspé wrote his *Mémoires* (1866), a valuable book of reminiscences for historians of the period immediately following the conquest of Canada.

GASPÉ PENINSULA, peninsula extending into the Gulf of St. Lawrence between the St. Lawrence River estuary and Chaleur Bay, southeastern Quebec, Canada. The interior, the heart of which comprises Gaspesian Provincial Park, is mostly rugged and densely forested; there are many lakes and rivers. The highest parts comprise an extension of the Appalachian Highlands, the Shickshock Mountains, culminating in Mount Jacques Cartier (4,160 ft.). The population, mostly French-speaking, is composed of people of French-Canadian, Acadian, Scotch, Irish, and English descent. Only the shore is inhabited. Principal economic activities are fishing, lumbering, pulp milling, and tourism. An important copper-mining district centers around Murdochville, east of the park. Increasing numbers of tourists have visited the area since completion (1928) of the 550-mi. belt highway (Perron Boulevard) that encircles the peninsula. Scenery, salmon fishing, hunting, and Old-World type villages and customs form the principal tourist attractions. Chief towns are New Carlisle, Chandler, Percé, Gaspé, and Matane. A railroad extends to Gaspé from the south and to Matane from the west. Jacques Cartier, who took possession of Canada for France, landed on the Gaspé in 1534. Length, 150 mi.; width, 60–90 mi.

PHYLLIS R. GRIESS, Pennsylvania State University

GASSER, HERBERT SPENCER (1888–1963), American physiologist and pharmacologist who shared the Nobel Prize with Joseph Erlanger in 1944 for their work *The Electrical Signs of Nervous Activity.* After receiving his medical degree from Johns Hopkins in 1915, he taught at Washington University, St. Louis, and the Medical College at Cornell. From 1935 to 1953 he was director of the Rockefeller Institute for Medical Research.

GASTONIA [găs-tō'nē-ə], town of southern piedmont North Carolina, and seat of Gaston County in a textile-manufacturing area. Mill settlements surround the 62 textile plants here. A strike and trial at Gastonia in 1929 marked the first major conflict between capital and labor in North Carolina. Pop., 47,142.

GASTRECTOMY [găs-trĕk'tə-mē], operation involving the complete or partial (subtotal) removal of the stomach. After a section of the stomach is removed the remaining portion is connected with the small bowel. The majority of partial gastrectomies are performed for ulcers which have resisted medical therapy or which have been complicated by hemorrhages, obstruction, or perforation. Most total gastrectomies are performed in cases of stomach cancer. In most instances the body adjusts well to partial gastrectomy. When the stomach is completely removed, malnutrition, digestive disturbances, and anemia may result. *See also* DIGESTION.

GASTRIC JUICE, secretions given off by the stomach glands during the process of digestion. The principal constituents are hydrochloric acid and the enzyme pepsin, which breaks down the proteins found in meat, eggs, milk, and other foods into simpler substances. *See also* DIGESTION.

GASTRIC ULCER. *See* ULCERS.

GASTROENTERITIS, illness of the gastrointestinal tract. In the United States it is primarily an acute illness characterized by watery diarrhea, abdominal cramps, nausea, and vomiting. Dietary indiscretions, excess alcohol, and psychological stress can cause these symptoms, but many cases are caused by viruses. The most important are the entero viruses, which produce an illness that begins with loss of appetite and nausea. Vomiting occurs on the first day and is followed by abdominal pain and diarrhea. Some individuals have mild headache and fever up to 101° F. The illness lasts 3 to 4 days. Viral gastroenteritis occurs mostly in the summer and fall, but one form occurs in the winter.

Gastroenteritis caused by bacteria or protozoa can usually be distinguished from the viral forms. Staphylococcal food poisoning occurs 1 to 6 hours after eating contaminated food. Vomiting and retching are most severe, without diarrhea. An outbreak of salmonella gastroenteritis, often associated with fever and a raised white blood-cell count, is sometimes confused with a viral illness. There is no specific treatment for viral gastroenteritis, except replacement of fluids. Bacterial forms must be treated with an appropriate antibacterial agent.

HAROLD NEU, M.D.

GASTROINTESTINAL INTUBATION, a procedure in which a tube is passed either through the nose or mouth into the stomach or small bowel. The tubes are constructed of a flexible material so that they may be passed easily and exist in a variety of sizes and shapes in order to accomplish specific functions, such as removal of stomach or bowel contents in cases of poisoning, to obtain material for analysis, or to relieve distention. Occasionally patients are fed through tubes.

GASTROINTESTINAL ("GI") SERIES, an X-ray examination of the digestive tract. The structures of the tract are made visible by administering a suspension of barium sulfate in water. This material blocks passage of the X rays, so that the stomach and intestines appear opaque on X-ray film. A series of X-ray exposures may be made as the barium sulfate passes along the digestive tract. A barium enema is used to investigate the lower parts of the digestive tract.

GASTROPOD [găs'trə-pŏd], snails, slugs, whelks, and other mollusks, belonging to the class Gastropoda. Since they have only a single shell, they are sometimes called univalves. Most gastropods have a spiral shell into which they can withdraw completely, but some have only a tiny shell, and a few have none at all. Though most are marine, some are found in fresh water as well as on land. They move about on one large, muscular foot, which often secretes slime on the path it travels. They usually have a definite head with tentacles, eyes, and a mouth equipped with a radula, or rasping tongue. A snail moving along the front of an aquarium can be seen to scrape off the algae with its radula. The oyster drill *Urosalpinx* uses its radula to drill holes through oyster shells in order to eat the meat inside.

Land snails and slugs are largely planteaters, sometimes becoming serious pests. The African land snail *Achatina fulica* causes damage in Hawaii and other islands to which it was introduced. The auger snails and cone snails of the South Pacific, whose beautiful shells are sought by collectors, possess radulas equipped with poisonous barbs. The many species of nudibranchs, a kind of sea slug, have no shells at all, but some have feathery appendages and lovely colors. Many species of gastropods are edible, including abalone, periwinkles, whelks, conchs, and snails.

BARBARA NEILL, American Museum of Natural History
See also ABALONE; CONCH; COWRIE; MOLLUSK; SHELLS AND SHELL COLLECTING; SLUG; SNAIL.

GASTROTRICHA [găs-trŏt'rĭ-kə], name of a class of microscopic animals in phylum Aschelminthes, commonly found in the bottom debris of still, fresh and salt water. Gastrotrichs have elongated bodies and glide along by moving hairlike cilia located on the underside of their bodies. They often have a forked tail provided with cement glands for anchorage to solid objects. Gastrotrichs feed on algae. Common genera include *Chaetonotus* and *Lepidodermella*, both found in fresh water, and *Neodasys*, a salt-water gastrotrich.

GAS TURBINE, engine which develops a high-energy stream of partially burned fuel used either for thrust or to power a rotary shaft. The most widespread application for gas turbines is for aircraft propulsion; however, they are also widely used for industrial applications. All gas turbines require four major components, to continually handle the stream of air: the compressor, the combustor, the engine turbine, and an energy converter. The first three work together to generate the stream of high-energy gas, which is characterized by high pressure and temperature. The function of the energy converter is to obtain useful power from this available energy, and its type depends on the power need.

Air enters the turbine through the compressor, where it is pressurized. Compressors of the rotary type are used because they are suited to the gas turbine's need for a large air flow in a steady stream. A rotary compressor consists of alternating sets of rotating and stationary vanes, or blades, with aerodynamic shapes. These are called rotors and stators. As the rotor turns, its blades pump air into a smaller volume between the adjacent stator blades, with a corresponding rise in pressure. This air then flows into a combustor, where fuel is added and the mixture ignited. Combustors are usually of double-wall construction, the air flowing through holes in the inner wall, or liner, to the combustion area for mixing and burning. Leaving the combustor, the hot gases are accelerated through stationary blades, called the turbine nozzle diaphragm, which direct the flow against rotating turbine blades or buckets to provide energy for driving the compressor, which is directly connected by a shaft to the turbine. When shaft power is desired to drive a propeller, pump, generator, or other load, an additional turbine section is added. This power turbine is connected by appropriate transmission and gearing to the load which it drives.

History. Attempts to develop gas turbines were unsuccessful at first because of extensive energy losses in compressors and turbines. However, a by-product of one of the early attempts to develop a gas turbine was the Eugene Houdry process (British patent awarded in Feb., 1933). Houdry (1892–1962) developed a machine to supply high-pressure air for industrial cooling purposes to allow a more compact and less expensive heat exchanger than would have been possible with the use of low-pressure air. A compressor supplies high pressure air, after the addition of heat. This air is expanded through the turbine to drive the compressor but without any additional shaft power output.

During World War I Sanford A. Moss (1872–1946) developed the turbosupercharger as a by-product of another unsuccessful attempt at building a gas turbine engine. Moss supplied a reciprocating engine with high-pressure air from a compressor. The compressor was driven by a turbine which was powered by the hot exhaust gas from the reciprocating engine. Use of a turbosupercharger maintains the power level of reciprocating engines at high altitudes. Turbosuperchargers developed by Moss were extensively used on bombers and fighters during World War II.

By the mid-1930's understanding of turbine and compressor aerodynamics had increased to the point where it had become feasible to develop a gas turbine power plant. Developments of gas turbines for propulsion of aircraft

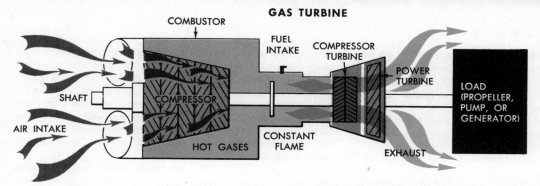

GAS TURBINE

COMBUSTOR

FUEL INTAKE

COMPRESSOR TURBINE

POWER TURBINE

LOAD (PROPELLER, PUMP, OR GENERATOR)

SHAFT

COMPRESSOR

AIR INTAKE

HOT GASES

CONSTANT FLAME

EXHAUST

Air is forced into the compressor where alternating rows of rotating and stationary vanes progressively reduce its volume, with a corresponding increase in pressure. A mixture of the compressed air and fuel is burned with a constant flame in the combustor. The rapidly expanding hot gases are directed first against the turbine that drives the compressor, then the power turbine. These are connected to different shafts. The gases exhaust through the power turbine.

were started in secret during this period because of their possible military use. The gas turbine was expected to be substantially more compact and would therefore generate less drag on an airplane than a reciprocating engine. At low-flight speeds, early turbojets were lower in efficiency than reciprocating engines, but they did permit a breakthrough in the streamlining of airplanes for higher speeds. The world's first turbojet-propelled flight was made on Oct. 14, 1939, by Germany's Heinkel Airplane Company. In a similar, but independent, development in England by Sir Frank Whittle (1907–   ), a jet-powered flight was made on May 15, 1941. In the United States the work of Moss was combined with that of Sir Frank Whittle when the General Electric Company was asked to produce and develop further the Whittle engine. The first American-built jet engine was flown on Oct. 2, 1942. After 1945 most aircraft engine manufacturers concentrated their research and development work on aircraft gas turbines. The first American engine had a rated output of only 1,250 lb. of thrust. By 1944 the thrust had been increased to over 4,000 lb. By 1960 engines were delivering thrusts of 20,000 lb. and higher. Refinements in gas turbines have made them more efficient and have also increased their capacity. The gas turbine has developed from a pure jet, or reaction engine, into an entire line of individual engine types. When equipped with a jet nozzle, it is termed a turbojet. When using an additional compressor, called a fan, the gas turbine becomes a turbofan, the fan air traveling partially or completely around the main air stream depending on the fan location. When the engine is used to rotate a propeller, it is called a turboprop, and when the engine rotates a shaft for other purposes, it is usually called a turboshaft. The rapid growth of applications of the gas turbine in industrial fields is attributed to its inherent advantages; it can use either gas, liquid, or powdered fuels; it is comparatively compact, lightweight, and requires little maintenance; it does not require an extended warm-up time to deliver normal power and efficiency.

C. G. DIBBLE, General Electric Company

GATES, HORATIO (1728?–1806), American general in the Revolution. Born in Maldon, Essex, England, Gates became a lieutenant in the British Army and served (1749) in Nova Scotia. Promoted to captain (1755), he joined Gen. Edward Braddock and was wounded at Fort Duquesne. After other colonial assignments, he left the army (1765) and resided in England until 1772, when at

George Washington's suggestion he settled in Berkeley County, Va. (now W. Va.).

In 1775 he joined the Revolutionary movement and as adjutant general of the Continental Army participated in the siege of Boston with Gen. Washington. Gates became a major general in 1776, and the following year commanded the northern army in the decisive victory at Saratoga. Acclaimed a hero, Gates was appointed president of the board of war and became implicated in the Conway Cabal to give him Washington's post as commander in chief. Though the plan failed and Washington averted a rupture, Gates retired to his plantation.

In 1780 he received command of the southern army, but after his overwhelming defeat (Aug. 16, 1780) at the Battle of Camden he gave way to Gen. Nathanael Greene. Though ordered by Congress to investigate the debacle, Greene never held the inquiry, and Gates was permitted (1782) to join Washington at Newburgh, N.Y. In 1783, he returned home where he remained until 1790 when he emancipated his slaves and moved to New York.

CLARENCE L. VER STEEG, Northwestern University

GATES, JOHN WARNE (1855–1911), American financier and promoter, born near Chicago. He became a barbed-wire salesman, later entered the manufacturing end of the business, and organized the American Steel and Wire Company (1898). A colorful speculator, he was nicknamed "Bet-A-Million" Gates. After besting J. P. Morgan in a railroad transaction, Gates was maneuvered by Morgan into Wall Street investments that considerably reduced Gates's fortune. He then became a successful oil promoter in Texas.

GATES, SIR THOMAS (d. 1621), American colonial Governor. He served with Sir Francis Drake in the Caribbean (1585–86). On the expedition's return trip Drake stopped at Roanoke Island off Cape Hatteras and rescued the survivors of Sir Walter Raleigh's first colonial experiment. The experience interested Gates in colonization, and in 1606 he invested in the Virginia Company, a corporation chartered by the King which founded Jamestown in 1607. On June 8, 1609, he sailed for Virginia as second in command to Lord De La Warr. Gates' vessel, however, was shipwrecked in the Bermudas, and it took 10 months to outfit new boats. (The story of the adventure, as related by William Strachey, one of the passengers, is said to have inspired Shakespeare's *Tem-*

pest.) When he arrived at Jamestown Gates found the colonists in such desperate straits that he ordered the colony abandoned. As the colonists were in the process of embarking, De La Warr arrived with supplies and new settlers. Gates then sailed to England for fresh supplies and returned in Aug., 1611, with his family to assume the governorship. In 1614 he returned to England. His plans for new expeditions never materialized.

RICHARD M. ABRAMS, University of California

GATINEAU [găt'ə-nō], industrial town of Quebec, Canada, located at the confluence of the Ottawa and Gatineau rivers near Ottawa. Inc., 1946; pop., 13,022.

GATINEAU RIVER, river in southwestern Quebec Province, Canada. It rises in a cluster of lakes in the Laurentian Mountains and flows south through Baskatong Lake and Reservoir to the Ottawa River at Hull. Mercier Dam on the Gatineau, where the river leaves Baskatong Lake, stores water for hydroelectricity. Length, 230 mi.

GATLING GUN. *See* MACHINE GUN.

GATOOMA, city in Salisbury Province of Southern Rhodesia. Gatooma is an agricultural and cotton-milling center with an experimental cotton research station. Northeast 5 mi. is the town of Eiffel Flats, the center of the richest gold-mining area in Southern Rhodesia. Pop. (including Eiffel Flats), 9,901.

GATT. *See* GENERAL AGREEMENT ON TARIFFS AND TRADE (GATT).

GATTI-CASAZZA [gät'tē-kä-zät'tsä], **GIULIO** (1869–1940), Italian impresario. Born in Udine, he spent most of his youth in Ferrara, where in 1893 he succeeded his father as director of the Municipal Theater. This position led to his appointment as director of La Scala at Milan in 1898. After 10 highly successful years there, he left in 1908 to become general director of the Metropolitan Opera, where he remained until his retirement in 1935. Under his efficient leadership, both artistic and financial gains were made; works by American composers were performed, and the Metropolitan became the scene of many world premières of works by foreign composers.

GATUN LAKE, man-made lake on the Isthmus of Panama, within the Canal Zone, 85 ft. above sea level. It forms a part of the Panama Canal route. Area, 163 sq. mi.

GAUCHO [gou'chō], the cowboy of the South American pampas. In the 18th century he was commonly an outcast from lower-class rural society. He was usually of mixed Spanish and Indian blood, sometimes of Spanish and Negro descent. A bold nomad, skilled as a rider and bola thrower, he subsisted largely by raising cattle and horses. He was gradually accepted in the economy of the frontier. Later, as a warrior for independence from Spain or a supporter of some revolutionary *caudillo*, he achieved greater social recognition. When cattle raising became a major industry, the Gaucho's independent way of life virtually ended, and he was customarily employed as a kind

of feudal retainer on the great cattle estates. The wave of late 19th-century immigration from Europe furnished the pampas with new agricultural workers and completed the Gaucho's eclipse as a distinct Latin-American type. He survives in the picturesque attire—wide-brimmed hat, bright shirt and scarf, baggy trousers and high boots—worn by contemporary ranch hands and as a folk hero in the literature, art, songs, and dances of Argentina, Uruguay, and Paraguay.

HARRY BERNSTEIN, Brooklyn College

GAUCHO LITERATURE, school of writing in Uruguay and Argentina representing an outgrowth of the popular songs and tales current among the mestizo inhabitants of the pampas. The subsequent works have tended to look upon the Gaucho as the symbol of Argentine and Uruguayan nationality. In frank imitation of the narrative oral poetry of the Gaucho himself are the parody *Fausto* (1870) by Estanislao del Campo and the quasi epic *Martín Fierro* (1872) by José Hernández, which is easily the most famous and typical of such works. In later years numerous novels appeared with a Gaucho theme. Some of these are folkloric in intent, such as those of Roberto J. Payró and Javier de Viana, while others look back in nostalgia. The best-known Gaucho novel, *Don Segundo Sombra* (1926), by Ricardo Güiraldes, is of the latter type. Eduardo Acevedo Díaz of Uruguay and Benito Lynch of Argentina also wrote in this vein. In English, some of the works of W. H. Hudson can be considered within this movement.

GREGORY RABASSA, Columbia University

GAUDÍ [gou-dē'], **ANTONIO** (1852–1926), Spanish architect, sculptor, and artisan. Gaudí began his career as an inventive revivalist, creating original forms later to be recognized as constituents of the not-yet-developed *art nouveau* style. For him this style became the basis not only of ornament but of structure as well. His later buildings, using shapes derived from mathematical calculations of tensions, natural topography, plant life, and the sea, employed various art forms: sculpture, wrought iron, calligraphy, and tiles (whole and broken). Gaudí's most famous works are in Barcelona: the Milá Apartment House (1905–10), the Güell Park (1900–14), and the Church of the Sacred Family (Iglesia de la Sagrada Familia), begun in 1884 and still being built.

Consult Collins, G. R., *Antonio Gaudí* (1960).

GAUGAMELA [gô-gə-mē'lə], village in ancient Assyria where Alexander the Great defeated the hosts of Darius III in 331 B.C., and thus brought to an end the Persian Empire.

GAUGUIN [gō-găN'], **(EUGÈNE HENRI) PAUL** (1848–1903), French painter, born in Paris. He has become a symbol of the romantic artist because he gave up a successful banking career (in 1883) and abandoned his wife and children in order to be a painter. Gauguin's early work was influenced by the impressionists, with whom he exhibited in 1886. He was in Pont Aven in Brittany in that year and again in 1888. During the latter stay he became associated with Émile Bernard and a group of

The Metropolitan Museum of Art, Bequest of Samuel A. Lewisohn, 1951

Christ and Mary are represented in a Polynesian setting in Gauguin's "We Greet Thee, Mary."

GAUHATI [gou-hä'tē], city on the Brahmaputra River, Assam State, India, capital of Kamrup District. Gauhati was the capital of the Hindu Kingdom of Kamarupa and, in the 18th century, the capital of the Ahom Kingdom. Ceded to Great Britain in 1826, it was the administrative center for Assam until 1874. The temple at Kamakhya, 2 mi. southwest, is a Hindu pilgrimage site. Gauhati University (1948) is the affiliating university for Assam. Pop., 43,615.

GAUL [gôl] (Lat. **GALLIA**), ancient Roman name designating two areas: Cisalpine Gaul, the area in northern Italy between the Apennines and the Alps; and Transalpine Gaul, the area between the Alps, Pyrenees, Atlantic, and Rhine, corresponding roughly to modern France.

Cisalpine Gaul was inhabited by Ligurians, Veneti, and others in prehistoric times, but in the 5th century B.C. Celts crossed the Alps, seized the fertile Po Valley, and inflicted severe defeats even upon Rome. Rome, however, began conquering these Celts before 222 B.C. and by 191 B.C. had subjugated them. Acquiring many south Italian settlers, Cisalpine Gaul became very populous, productive, and prosperous. In 42 B.C. it was incorporated into Italy.

Transalpine Gaul was Gallia par excellence. Its unidentified prehistoric peoples have left impressive memorials—Paleolithic cave art and Neolithic dolmens and menhirs. Iron-using Celts appeared c.900 B.C., and by 500 B.C. controlled virtually all Transalpine Gaul except Greek Massilia (Marseille). Tombs at Vix and elsewhere confirm Julius Caesar's picture of a wealthy ruling caste in the quarreling Gallic tribes.

To safeguard communications with its Spanish provinces, Rome annexed southern Gaul and made it a province (whence Provence) c.121 B.C. Julius Caesar's campaigns (58–51 B.C.) won central and northern Gaul for Rome. Under Augustus, Gaul was divided into six provinces: Narbonensis (the heavily urbanized south, whose cities today exhibit numerous Roman monuments and still bear their ancient names); Lugdunensis, Aqui-

other young painters, whom he greatly influenced. During this period Gauguin was instrumental in the formation of synthetism, a style of painting characterized by stylized drawing and patterns of strongly outlined areas of flat color. A series of Breton peasant and landscape scenes and such notable canvases as "The Yellow Christ" (Albright Art Gallery, Buffalo, N.Y.) and "Jacob Wrestling with the Angel" (National Gallery of Scotland, Edinburgh) date from this time.

Gauguin went to Tahiti in 1891, came back to Paris in 1893, and returned to Tahiti in 1895. In 1900 he settled in the Marquesas Islands, where he died in poverty. On these South Seas islands he created luminous paintings that depict native subjects but whose spirit is sophisticated and European. His style wavered between surface pattern and sculptured relief, and was at its best when the former was employed with bright flowerful coloring, as in "We Greet Thee, Mary" (Metropolitan Museum of Art, New York). Other outstanding canvases are "The Day of the God" (Chicago Art Institute), "Nevermore" (Courtauld Institute, London), and "From Where do we Come? What are we? Where are we Going?" (Museum of Fine Arts, Boston).

In addition to his paintings, Gauguin produced numerous prints, drawings, and sculptures. His works, which had a powerful influence on the subsequent development of modern painting, are found in the Louvre in Paris, the Museum of Modern Art in New York, and many other galleries. He was the author and illustrator of the autobiographic novel *Noa Noa*, based on his first stay in Tahiti.

Consult Goldwater, Robert, *Gauguin* (1958).

ALBERT ELSEN, Indiana University

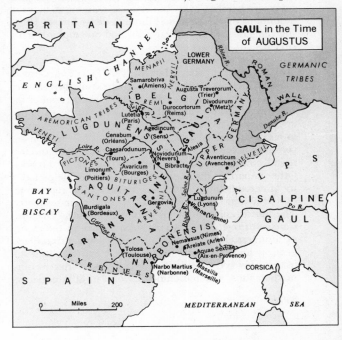

GAUL in the Time of AUGUSTUS

tania, and Belgica (the relatively unurbanized "Three Gauls," where today's cities bear the names of Gallic tribes, not Gallic towns); and Upper and Lower Germany (military zones along the Rhine). In the 1st and 2d centuries A.D. Romanization, despite occasional revolts, was rapid, and Gaul achieved great prosperity. Because of its magnificent rivers and fertile soil, agriculture and stock raising flourished, and its industries—especially pottery—burgeoned. In the 3d century, Gaul, already partly Christianized, suffered severely from invasion, separatism, and the brigandage of the Bagaudae. Order, however, was reestablished, and in the Late Empire, Latin literature, moribund elsewhere, still flourished in Gaul—for example, Ausonius, Paulinus of Nola, and Apollinaris Sidonius. In the 5th century Roman garrisons withdrew, and although Gaul retained its Latin character, Germanic invaders, notably the Franks under Clovis (c.486), consolidated independent kingdoms there. Thereafter Gaul became France.

Consult Chilver, G. E. F., *Cisalpine Gaul* (1941); Brogan, O. P. F., *Roman Gaul* (1953).

E. T. SALMON, McMaster University, Hamilton, Ontario

GAULISH or GALLIC, member of the Celtic subgroup of the Indo-European family of languages. It was spoken during Roman times in what is now France, Belgium, the Rhineland, and northern Italy; these areas formed a part of the vast portion of Europe once overrun by the Celtic tribes. Gaulish was closely similar to Brythonic, the Celtic language of Britain whose surviving descendant is Welsh. Since only a small number of inscriptions have been preserved, our knowledge of the structure of Gaulish is scant. It has been supplemented through careful study of names of places and of persons, like Vercingetorix, whom Caesar and other ancient authors mention.

GAUNT, JOHN OF. See JOHN OF GAUNT.

GAUR [gour] or **SELADANG** [sā-lä′däng], wild forest ox, *Bos gaurus*, found from Assam to Malaysia. Its coat is a uniform blackish-brown, and the legs and great sweeping horns are white. Gaurs are sociable, roaming in herds of a dozen or more individuals through dense forests. Hunting the gaur requires great skill, and no trophy is more prized.

GAUSS [gous], **CARL FRIEDRICH** (1777–1855), German mathematician and one of the greatest mathematicians of all times. His doctoral dissertation was a proof of the fundamental theorem of algebra. Many of his early discoveries were never published, but were simply recorded in his diary. Before he was 21, he had discovered the criterion for constructibility of regular polygons and had found how to construct a regular polygon of 17 sides. Other important discoveries include the double periodicity of certain elliptic functions, the graphical representation of complex numbers, and non-Euclidean geometry. The most significant of his publications is the *Disquisitiones arithmeticae* (1801), a masterpiece in the theory of numbers. His later years were devoted primarily to geodesy and terrestrial magnetism, electricity, and statistics. However, he continued his discoveries in pure mathematics, which included a work in differential geometry in which the idea of "Gaussian curvature" is developed.

GAUTAMA. See BUDDHA.

GAUTIER [gō-tyā′], **THÉOPHILE** (1811–72), French poet and novelist. At first a romantic, he was famous for his role in the 1830 so-called battle of Hernani (q.v.), which assured the triumph of the romantic drama over the criticisms of the classicists. A defender of "art for art's sake," he was later a precursor of the Parnassians. In the famous preface to his novel *Mademoiselle de Maupin* (1835) he denounces the utilitarian motive which sullies the purity of art. Supporting himself through journalism from 1836 on, Gautier escaped this routine existence through travel and the composition of exquisitely chiseled poems. *Émaux et camées* (Enamels and Cameos), 1852, his masterpiece, reflects an essentially plastic concept of formal beauty and exalts beauty for its own sake.

GAVIAL [gā′vē-əl], name for several species of slender-snouted crocodilians in family Gavialidae, found in India and the Malay Peninsula. The Indian gavial, *Gavialis gangeticus*, one of the largest living reptiles, reaches a length of over 21 ft. It feeds on fish and is seldom hostile to man. The Malayan gavial or false gavial, *Tomistoma schlegeli*, grows to a length of 15 ft.

GÄVLE [yâv′lə], city of Sweden, a seaport and industrial center situated on the Gulf of Bothnia about 100 mi. north-northwest of Stockholm. It is the chief port of entry for Norrland, the vast region which comprises the northern two-thirds of the country. Diversified industries include saw-milling, food-processing, and the manufacture of chemical pulp, tobacco products, and woolen textiles. The origins of the city date from the 14th century. Pop., 54,618.

GAVOTTE [gə-vŏt′], originally a French peasant dance of Dauphiné, the natives of which were called "Gavots." Danced in 2/4 or 4/4 time, the gavotte was introduced at the court of Louis XIV. At first a lively dance with kissing and jumping, it later became more formal. It was also a movement in baroque instrumental dance suites.

GAWAIN [gä′wĭn], nephew of King Arthur, son of Loth and Anna. He is the hero in the 14th-century Arthurian romance *Sir Gawain and the Green Knight*.

GAWLER, city of Australia, in South Australia, on the Para River 25 mi. northeast of Adelaide. It is a trade and processing center for a region of wheat and general farming. Pop., 5,639.

GAY, JOHN (1685–1732), English poet and dramatist. He went from the grammar school of his native Barnstaple to an apprenticeship to a London silk mercer (c.1702–6), and then to a career as a writer. His first published piece was the poem *Wine* (1708), a Miltonic imitation. He became friends with Pope and his circle, served in a number of minor public offices, and had the good fortune to come under the patronage of the Duke and Duchess of Queensberry. His bent for parody and satire found expression in the delightful *Shepherd's Week* (1714), *Trivia, or the Art of Walking the Streets of London* (1716), and in his masterpiece, the ballad opera *The Beggar's Opera* (1728). His songs and fables are also of a high order.

Consult Irving, W. H., *John Gay: Favorite of the Wits* (1940).

GAYA [gə-yä'], city on a Ganges tributary in Bihar State, India, capital of Gaya District. The city, sacred to both Hindus and Buddhists since ancient times, has a Vishnuite temple where Hindu pilgrims come to hold rituals for their dead. Seven mi. south is Buddh Gaya where, under the famous Bo tree, Buddha received his enlightenment. The site is marked by a temple. Sixteen mi. north is Barabar Hill, on the peak of which is a Hindu temple. There also is an Ashokan cave with inscriptions and carvings. Pop., 151,105.

GAY-LUSSAC [gȧ-lü-sȧk'], **JOSEPH LOUIS** (1778–1850), French chemist who discovered the law of combining volumes, which helped to establish the distinction between atoms and molecules. After a formal education he became an assistant to C. L. Berthollet and then, successively, professor of chemistry at the École Polytechnique, of physics at the Sorbonne, and again of chemistry at the Jardin des Plantes. He studied many industrial problems and in 1804 made a balloon ascent to carry out scientific observations. His studies on gases showed that they combined in definite ratios by volume and that they expanded with heat, as previously noted by Jacques A. Charles. He isolated iodine, and in his studies on prussic acid he proposed the concept of organic radicals which was important in later chemical theory. He was elected to the French Academy in 1806.

GAY-LUSSAC'S LAW. *See* CHARLES' LAW; COMBINING VOLUMES, LAW OF.

GAZA [gä'zə], principal city of the so-called Gaza Strip, located on the coastal plain of southern Palestine, northwest of the Negev and 3 mi. east of the Mediterranean. Before the 1947–49 Israel-Arab hostilities, Gaza was a road junction and commercial center of southwest Palestine. The city and its environs produce orchard fruits, olives, and dates, as well as handicraft. Interesting features of the city include its 13th-century market, the Great Mosque built on the foundation of a Knights Templars' church, the Tomb of Samson, and the Tomb of Hashim, great-grandfather of Mohammed.

Gaza is mentioned in ancient Egyptian and cuneiform documents as an important city on the trade route from Egypt on the south, through central Palestine to the Tigris-Euphrates Valley on the northeast. In the 16th–12th centuries B.C. it was the residence of Egyptian governors. Mentioned often in the Bible, it was named as one of the five principal Philistine cities and the scene of Samson's destruction of the Philistine temple. At different times it belonged to Israel, Assyria, Babylonia, Egypt, and Persia. In 332 B.C. Alexander the Great sacked it, and it became a Hellenistic center. During the Hasmonean (Maccabean) and Herodian dynasties it was a Jewish stronghold, but

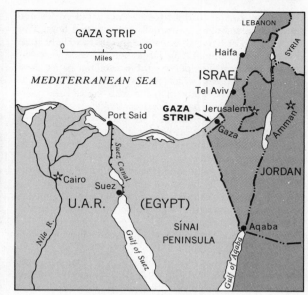

eventually it capitulated to the influx of Christianity. In 634 A.D. Gaza was captured by the Muslims, but during the Crusades the Knights Templars refortified it. In 1517 it was seized by the Turks; in 1799 it fell to Napoleon. The Turks surrendered the city to the British on Nov. 2, 1917. Under the British Mandate of Palestine, it was the government seat of the Gaza Territory. Egyptian-controlled since 1949, it has been twice captured (1956; 1967) by Israel. Pop., about 35,000.

YAAKOV MORRIS, Consul of Israel in New York City

GAZA STRIP, a splinter of territory 25 mi. long and 4 to 5 mi. wide, located between the Sinai Peninsula and Israel at the southeastern end of the Mediterranean. The strip came into being on Feb. 24, 1949, under an Egyptian-Israel armistice agreement. Successive governments of Egypt proclaimed the strip held in trust for the Palestine Arabs, and the greater part of its population of 330,000 is made up of Arab refugees from Palestine. Since only half of the 50,000 acres is cultivable, the swollen population, cut off from the Egyptian and Israel economies, became wards of the international community. The United Nations Relief and Works Agency for Palestine Refugees in the Near East provided food, clothing, shelter, and social services. Egyptian-mounted guerrilla raids from Gaza in 1955–56 deep within Israel contributed to the Sinai War during which Israel occupied the strip. The U.N. Emergency Force administered the area immediately after Israel's withdrawal (Mar. 7, 1957), but the U.A.R. later resumed control. Israel recaptured the strip during the Arab-Israel war of June, 1967.

J. C. HUREWITZ, Columbia University

See also ISRAEL.

GAZELLE [gĕ-zĕl'], name for several species of antelopes of the genus *Gazella*, which contains the greatest number of antelope species. The gazelles are slender, small, graceful, and delicate, with large, soft, shiny eyes. They are the most widely distributed of the antelope family, with more than 30 species found throughout Africa and southern Asia. Both sexes usually have ringed horns that are S-shaped or lyre-shaped. Some species have light spots over the body, and all have large, pointed ears. Very few species reach a shoulder height exceeding 30 in. Best known is *G. dorcas*, which grows about 2 ft. high at its shoulders, and is sandy in color with white undersides and a broad brown band along each side. Its face has a dark triangular space formed by white stripes on each side. The lyrate horns are longer in the male than in the female. The dorcas gazelle is found in Asia Minor, Arabia, and in northern Africa.

Gazelles often roam open plains and deserts in large herds. They are herbivorous and frequently group with other antelopes, giraffes, and zebras. Very swift runners, some species leap high while running, giving the impression of skimming the ground.

MARY M. TOWNES, North Carolina College at Durham

GAZETTEER [găz-ə-tēr'], dictionary of places, giving names and descriptive information in alphabetical order. Such works date from the 6th century; however, the first to bear the name was Lawrence Echard's *The Gazetteer's or, Newsman's Interpreter: Being a Geographical Index* (1703). Gazetteers may be regional, national, or international in scope, and range from simple pronouncing geographical dictionaries to those giving basic social, economic, and geographical data. Often an index to an atlas or encyclopedia serves as a gazetteer. Old gazetteers frequently provide valuable historical information.

GAZIANTEP [gä-zē-än-těp'], city of southeastern Turkey and capital of the province of Gaziantep. Pistachio nuts, tobacco, wheat, barley, and rice are grown in the vicinity, and olive trees are abundant. Weaving, skin tanning, and coppersmith work are the major crafts, and there are two spinning mills. Gaziantep (*gazi*, "hero," added to its earlier name Antep) is famous for its defense against invaders from the time of the Crusaders until the French occupation of Syria, when the city withstood a six-month siege (1920–21). The old fortress of Gaziantep is an outstanding landmark. Pop., 125,498.

GDANSK [gə-dänsk'] (Ger. **DANZIG**), industrial city and port of Poland, lying on the Motlawa River, one of the branches by which the Vistula (Wisła) River discharges into the Baltic Sea. The city is 4 mi. from the sea, but the river is navigable for ships of medium size. Gdańsk is primarily a port and shipbuilding city. Ships tie up at the quays along the Motlawa River. Downstream from the city are shipbuilding yards. Other industries are primarily those associated with a port, such as the processing of imported foods.

Gdańsk, mentioned in historical records of the 10th century, later became one of the most important cities of the Hanseatic League. During the Middle Ages it belonged in turn to the Teutonic Knights, whose fortress of Marienburg lay only 30 mi. away, and to Poland. In 1793, at the second partition of Poland, Gdańsk was absorbed by Prussia. Its very great prosperity during the Middle Ages and early modern times had been based on the trade that it carried on with its Polish hinterland.

A view of tall, gabled houses in the old section of Gdańsk.
(POLISH EMBASSY, WASHINGTON, D.C.)

Gdańsk was especially important in the grain and timber trades, exporting the wheat and lumber brought down the Vistula by boat. Though inhabited almost wholly by people of German speech and culture, Gdańsk's prosperity was bound up with that of the rest of Poland, and its citizens resisted incorporation into Prussia.

The re-establishment of the Polish state in 1918 raised the question of the future of Gdańsk. Its port was considered essential to Poland, but as an almost exclusively German city, it could not easily be incorporated into Poland. The solution was to create the Free City of Danzig, in customs union with Poland but politically independent and self-governing. In the course of Poland's war with the Soviet Union in 1920, some of the citizens of Gdańsk had adopted an anti-Polish attitude and had hindered the flow of munitions to the Polish army. This led to the Polish government's reluctance to rely exclusively on the port of Gdańsk for its seaborne commerce, and the neighboring port of Gdynia was founded. The growth of Gdynia did some harm to Gdańsk and helped to increase the anti-Polish feelings of its citizens and to strengthen the National Socialist movement. At the end of World War II most of the German population either fled or was driven out, and the city itself was incorporated into Poland. A single harbor authority has since been established for the ports of Gdynia and Gdańsk, and, with the increasing specialization in their port activities, competition between them has been eliminated.

Before World War II Gdańsk was one of the most attractive of German cities. Much of the old city dated from the later Middle Ages and Renaissance, and included exceptionally fine examples of North German Gothic architecture, executed in brick, and of early domestic architecture. The 14th-century Church of St. Mary and the 16th-century town hall were outstanding among the ancient buildings of the city. In 1945 the city was more than half destroyed during the advance of the Soviet forces. Since then much of the city has been rebuilt, and the best of the ancient buildings have been restored to their former appearance. Pop., 286,500.

NORMAN J. G. POUNDS, Indiana University

GDYNIA, industrial city and port of Poland, lying on the coast of the Baltic Sea, 12 mi. northwest of Gdańsk. Until 1920 it was a small fishing village. In that year the Polish government decided to create a port here rather than rely exclusively on Gdańsk (Danzig), which had the status of a free city. The port grew rapidly, due in part to the excavation of dock basins in the soft coastal deposits; and in part to the construction of a large breakwater and the building of jetties. Gdynia concentrated on the handling of bulk cargoes, especially the export of coal and the import of iron ore. In tonnage handled, Gdynia came to exceed Gdańsk, and the large German population of Gdańsk viewed its rival's growth with hostility. Gdynia was severely damaged in the German attack of 1939, but has since been rebuilt. Since 1948 the two ports have been jointly controlled by a single port authority. Gdynia has a fishing industry, and the preparation and processing of fish constitute one of its industries. Gdynia has become a passenger port from which it is possible to sail to New York, but its chief role remains the handling of bulk cargoes. Pop., 147,800.

NORMAN J. G. POUNDS, Indiana University

GE. *See* GAEA *or* GE.

GEARS AND GEARING. Gears are mechanical devices for transmitting motion from one rotating body to another. In this sense gears perform functions similar to belt and chain drives. The advantage of gears, however, is that the motion is transmitted without slip between contacting surfaces because of the successive engagement of uniformly spaced teeth.

Gears are used extensively in machinery, but the automobile is the most familiar example. Here, the gears transmit the power available at the engine into the turning power for the driving wheels. When the driver puts the car "in gear" he establishes a certain power ratio, ranging from high to low. When he puts it out of gear, that is, when the gears are not meshed, no power is transmitted from the engine to the wheels.

The gear derives its rotating motion from the fact that it is mounted on a shaft or axle that turns. Typical body shapes on which the gear teeth are cut are the cylinder and the cone. The sizes and shapes of the gear teeth have been standardized and can be found in handbooks dealing with machinery.

One way to classify gears is by the position of the shafts on which they turn. Spur gears are used on parallel shafts. Bevel gears are used on intersecting shafts; their toothed surfaces are slanted at an angle (a cone shape) that permits the two shafts to join. Worm gears are used when one shaft crosses above or beneath another without intersecting it. The worm gear teeth resemble screw threads. The gear that meshes with it may be a modified spur gear. Two or more gears in an operating unit comprise a gear train.

Internal gears have their teeth on the inside surface so that a smaller gear can rotate inside. The principal ad-

TYPES OF GEARS

Boston Gear Works

SPUR GEAR

Boston Gear Works

BEVEL GEAR

Boston Gear Works

WORM GEAR

Boston Gear Works

INTERNAL GEAR

The spur gear transmits motion between parallel shafts, the bevel between intersecting shafts, and the worm between shafts that are at right angles but do not intersect. The internal gear is a modified spur gear that does not reverse the direction of the motion as do ordinary spur gears. The planetary gear elements rotate independently of the cage that holds them together. Usually the unit is meshed between other gears, one in the center and one or more on the outside.

William Smith, Inc.

PLANETARY GEAR

vantages of an internal gear system include the compactness of the drive, less relative sliding between teeth, and increased length of contact between meshing teeth. Internal gears are usually more expensive to manufacture than other types of gears.

A planetary gear train consists of an outer ring gear that revolves around one or more inner gears that are also revolving. An example is the automatic transmission gearing used in automobiles. Planetary gear trains often form a part of another gear train and can be used to give large speed-reductions.

A pair of gears in direct contact with each other results in a reversal of direction of the rotational motion. If it is necessary to have the motion proceed in one direction, then an intermediate gear, called an idler, is used. The effect of the idler is to cause the driven gear to rotate in the same direction as the driving gear. The simpler gears have one gear for each shaft; a compound gear has two or more gears fastened to the same shaft. When two gears are in mesh, the smaller gear is called the pinion. A gear ratio is the ratio of the number of teeth on the gear to the number of teeth on the pinion.

Gearing in a machine provides a pulling power. A smaller gear driving a larger gear increases the pulling power but lowers gear speed. A multiplying gear increases gear speed but reduces pulling power. It uses a driving gear larger than a smaller gear or pinion. In an automobile, this is the high gear used for smooth, level, high-speed driving which requires less power than does climbing a hill.

Gear Manufacture. Gears are manufactured by either casting or machining processes. In casting, the accuracy of the tooth profile is limited. Gears made this way are used in low-speed operations. In machining, the gear profiles are cut by power tools, then heat-treated to increase the strength of the gear teeth. Additional finishing brings the tooth to its final, accurately shaped form to compensate for the slight inaccuracies after heat-treating.

The strength of the gear lies in the load-carrying ability of the gear teeth, which must be carefully formed. A gear tooth can be considered as a cantilever beam with the full load applied at the tip of the tooth. It is assumed that gear performance will be satisfactory if the beam strength of the gear tooth is slightly greater than the load on the tip.

DONALD ZWIEP, Worcester Polytechnic Institute

GEBER [jē′bər], Latin form of the name Jabir ibn Hayyan, a noted Arab alchemist of the 8th century. His influential books, which were the first clear metallurgical treatises, transmitted to European alchemists the theory that metals were composed of mercury and sulfur and described the preparation of mineral acids, the purification of salts, and the separation and properties of metals. They remained standard alchemistic texts for centuries.

GECKO [gĕk′ō], common name for about 300 species of small lizards that comprise the family Gekkonidae. Geckos are found in warm regions throughout the world. Many species have adhesive pads on their feet that enable them to crawl on smooth surfaces. Some species are able to pro-

duce sounds similar to the chirps of frogs. Geckos are most often found in desert regions, but some live in rocky or wooded areas. The banded gecko, *Coleonyx variegatus*, is marked by alternating bands of brown and dull yellow and is white on the undersurface. It inhabits the deserts of southwestern United States and Mexico. The Turkish gecko, *Hemidactylus turcicus*, originally found in the Mediterranean region, Africa, and India, has been introduced to the West Indies and southern Florida.

GEDDES [gĕd′ēz], **NORMAN BEL** (1893–1958), American theatrical and industrial designer, born in Adrian, Mich. Beginning in 1916, he designed scenery and costumes for more than 200 stage productions, notably *The Miracle* (1924); and *Hamlet* (1931) and *Dead End* (1935), which he produced. He also pioneered in arena staging. Like his theatrical work, his industrial designs were marked by imagination, boldness, and great variety. His models for furniture, airplane interiors, highways, and metropolitan buildings did much to popularize modern streamlining.

GEDDES [gĕd′ĭs], **SIR PATRICK** (1854–1932), Scottish sociologist and town planner. Trained as a biologist, he was deeply interested in the influence of environment upon life. In 1919 he taught sociology and civics at the University of Bombay. Returning to Scotland, he established University Hall in Edinburgh, which served as his laboratory for sociological observations and stimulated his interest in the reconstruction of the city. Active in city planning in both Great Britain and Europe, Geddes wrote extensively on the subject.

GEELONG [jē-lông′], port city of southeastern Australia, situated on Corio Bay 45 mi. southwest of Melbourne. It is the trade center for a rich agricultural area and has an important wool market. Diversified industries include automobile assembly and the manufacture of woolen goods, rope, cement, machinery, and petroleum products. Several seaside resorts are located nearby. Pop., 20,034; metropolitan area, 91,790.

GE'EZ. *See* ETHIOPIC LANGUAGES.

GEHENNA [gĭ-hĕn′ə] (Heb. GE-HINNOM, "Valley of Hinnom"), name of a valley south and southwest of Jerusalem, in early days, a place of human sacrifice—particularly to Moloch. Jeremiah doomed it as "valley of slaughter"; whence the Rabbinic and New Testament use of "Gehenna" as a place of torment and punishment.

GEHRIG [gĕr′ĭg], **HENRY LOUIS ("LOU")** (1903–41), American baseball player, born in New York. He played first base (1923–39) for New York of the American League. He was a left-handed batter who compiled a lifetime batting average of .340 and hit 493 home runs. He and "Babe" Ruth comprised the most formidable pair of hitters on a single club in the history of the sport. Gehrig won the nickname "Iron Horse" by setting a major-league record for consecutive games played—2,130 from 1925 to 1939. His career was ended when he contracted amyotrophic lateral sclerosis, which eventually proved fatal. He was elected to the National Baseball Hall of Fame in 1939.

GEIGER [gī′gər], **ABRAHAM** (1810–74), German-Jewish theologian and a founder of the modern science of Judaism. Rabbi in Wiesbaden, Breslau (later Wrocław), and Berlin, he published extensively, stressing the evolutionary character of Judaism, thus becoming one of the first theoreticians of the Jewish reform movement.

GEIGER, HANS (1882–1947), German physicist and a leading investigator in atomic theory, cosmic rays, and radioactivity. He devised many types of counters, the best known of which is the Geiger (or Geiger-Müller) counter for detecting and measuring radioactivity. He was assistant to Rutherford at the University of Manchester and later a professor at Kiel, Tübingen, and Berlin technical universities.

GEIGER COUNTER, a device that registers the passage of radiation through it, operating as a quasi-stable gas-discharge tube. It was first developed by Ernest Rutherford and Hans Geiger in England about 1911 and further developed about 1927 by Geiger and Müller; it is sometimes called a Geiger-Müller counter. It is widely used as a detecting device for nuclear radiation.

Essentially, a Geiger counter consists of two electrodes in a gas, across which a potential is applied. The potential is just below that needed to sustain a glow-discharge, but when a charged ionizing particle passes between the electrodes a momentary discharge is produced. Usually the electrodes consist of a cylinder and a central wire along its axis, and usually the gas is argon or neon to which some "quenching gas," such as alcohol vapor, methane, or butane, at one- or two-tenths of an atmosphere pressure

HOW A GEIGER COUNTER WORKS

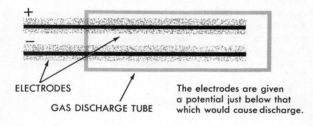

ELECTRODES

GAS DISCHARGE TUBE

The electrodes are given a potential just below that which would cause discharge.

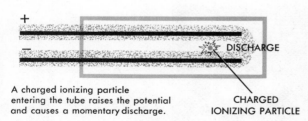

DISCHARGE

A charged ionizing particle entering the tube raises the potential and causes a momentary discharge.

CHARGED IONIZING PARTICLE

The discharge must be transferred to a visible or audible reading to be of any value. Some methods are:

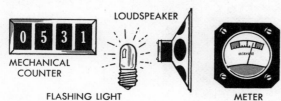

0 5 3 1

MECHANICAL COUNTER

LOUDSPEAKER

FLASHING LIGHT

METER

is added to help terminate the discharge. However, both the geometrical arrangement of the electrodes and the kind and amount of gas may be varied over large ranges depending on observational and engineering convenience. Sometimes the discharge termination is accomplished by an electronic circuit called a "quenching circuit." The voltage required in most counters is between 1,000 and 2,000 volts, and depends on the size of the electrodes and the kind and pressure of the gas. The impulse observed when the counter discharges may be as much as many volts in amplitude, and rises rapidly to its maximum value in a few microseconds, followed by a slower recovery lasting 100 or 200 microseconds. Such counters will therefore in general be able to count up to perhaps 10,000 counts per second, but become paralyzed at faster rates.

The impulses may be recorded and made to operate mechanical registers, to flash lights, or to make a "plop" on a telephone receiver or loudspeaker. The output of the counter is therefore usually connected to an electronic circuit to perform whatever recording may be desired. Counters can be built to be especially sensitive to alpha particles, beta particles, neutrons, X rays, or other entities in nuclear or electron physics.

Consult Korff, S. A., *Electron and Nuclear Counters* (2d ed., 1947).

Serge A. Korff, New York University
See also Ionization Chamber.

GEIKIE [gē′kē], **SIR ARCHIBALD** (1835–1924), British geologist noted for his studies of volcanic rocks and of erosion and for his accomplishments as director of the Geological Survey of Great Britain. He entered the Geological Survey in 1855 and mapped the geology of Scotland until 1869. He directed the Survey's Scottish division after 1867 and concurrently, starting in 1871, was professor of geology at the University of Edinburgh for 11 years. Geikie was director-general of the survey from 1882 to 1901. His *Textbook of Geology*, published in 1882, was widely used in Britain and America. He was knighted in 1891, later received the Order of Merit, and was made Knight Commander of the Bath. He was elected to office in several learned societies, and he was president of the Royal Society from 1908 to 1913.

GEISEL [gī′zəl], **THEODOR SEUSS**, real name of "Dr. Seuss" (1904–   ), author and illustrator of children's books, who was born and raised in Springfield, Mass. He worked in sculpture, painted murals, and wrote motion picture scripts, winning two Academy Awards. In *The 500 Hats of Bartholomew Cubbins* (1938) and other picture books, the hilarious and imaginative verse-stories are matched with absurdly inventive illustrations. *The Cat in the Hat* (1957) demonstrates that a piece of literature can be created even within the strait jacket of a "controlled" vocabulary.

GEISHA [gā′shə], Japanese term meaning "accomplished person." It refers particularly to Japanese professional female entertainers whose talents include singing, dancing, and making conversation. Some of the famous geisha of the past were versatile in their accomplishments, and wrote belles-lettres, especially poetry. The profession originated at the beginning of the 18th century, if not earlier. Tokugawa society placed women in a subordinate position to men and prohibited them from enjoying any social freedom. Marriage was undertaken for the purpose of perpetuating the family. Men who desired romance and social intercourse found it outside the home, usually in amusement quarters where daughters of impoverished parents had been sold as indentured servants. The geisha, notable for her beauty and talents, held a recognized status. She often met her patrons by appointment and demanded a period of courting according to a code of etiquette. Wealthy merchants who pursued these women frequently bought the freedom of their favorites, establishing them as mistresses or even as legal wives. These geishas, possessing beauty and accomplishments, have not infrequently captured the hearts of great statesmen such as Prince Hirobumi Ito, Count Munemitsu Mutsu, and Takayoshi Kido.

CHITOSHI YANAGA, Yale University

GEISSLER [gĭs′lər] **TUBE,** evacuated glass tube with anode and cathode electrodes sealed at opposite ends, and containing a small amount of a selected gas. When high voltage from a transformer or induction coil is applied to the electrodes, the gas glows, emitting light of a color characteristic of the gas in the tube. The tube, named for its inventor, Heinrich Geissler (1814–79), may be considered the forerunner of the X-ray, fluorescent, and glow-discharge tubes.

GEL. *See* COLLOIDS.

GELA [jä′lä], ancient Greek and modern Italian city on the south coast of Sicily. Ancient Gela was colonized by Cretans and Rhodians under Antiphemus about 689 B.C., and was itself the founder of nearby Acragas (Agrigentum) in 582. In the late 6th and early 5th centuries it was the most important city in Sicily, prospering under the tyrants Cleander (505–498), Hippocrates (498–491), and Gelon, who came to control Syracuse in 485. The great Athenian tragedian Aeschylus died in Gela in 456.

Joining Syracuse against Athens in the Peloponnesian War, Gela was then attacked and destroyed by the Carthaginians in 405. In the 4th century Timoleon attempted to restore the city, but after the slaughter of 4,000 Geloans by Agathocles of Syracuse (312) the population eventually moved to the new city of Phintias (modern Licata) in 280.

Modern Gela was founded as Terranova di Sicilia by Frederick II in 1230. The Allies landed at Gela in 1943 in the invasion of Sicily. Pop., 43,235.

JOHN H. YOUNG, Johns Hopkins University

GELASIUS I [jĭ-lā′shē-əs], **ST.** (d.496), Pope (492–496). It is not certain whether he was born in Rome or North Africa. As Pope he upheld the primacy of the Roman See against Constantinople, insisted on the use of both bread and wine in communion, and established the rule of holding ordinations at the Ember Seasons.

GELATIN [jĕl′ə-tĭn], protein obtained from the collagen extracted from the skin, white connective tissue, and bones (not hoofs and horns) of animals. The collagen is heated in solution with a small amount of acid, dried in a cool atmosphere, and ground to the desired granular size. In solution, gelatin produces a heat-reversible clear gel. When placed in cold water, it swells due to water absorption, then dissolves readily when heated.

Gelatin is used mainly in flavored desserts or custards but also in canned soups and meat and bakery products. Pharmaceutical uses include the manufacture of hard and soft elastic capsules, pill coatings, pastilles, and emulsions. It is the basic ingredient in the manufacture of silver-sensitized photographic film emulsions and other graphic arts reproduction processes.

GELDERLAND [gĕl′dər-lănd] **or GUELDERLAND,** province of east-central Netherlands bordered on the northwest by Lake Ijssel (Ijsselmeer) and on the east by Germany. The province is drained by the Maas, Ijssel, Lower Rhine, and Waal rivers, the last two enclosing the Betuwe district, a rich dairy and farming area. In the north, near Lake Ijssel

Netherlands Information Service

Farmers threshing and sacking grain in Gelderland, the Netherlands.

is the Veluwe district, a range of low glacial hills covered by heather and scrubby woods. Part of this district has been made a national park which contains the Kröller-Müller Museum famous for its collection of paintings by Vincent van Gogh. Arnhem, the provincial capital, and Nijmegen were damaged by heavy fighting during World War II. Near Apeldoorn is a royal summer palace. Area, 1,965 sq. mi.; pop., 1,205,044.

GELIBOLU [gě-lē-bō-lōō'] **or GALLIPOLI** [gă-lĭp'ō-lĭ] (anc. *Callipolis*), town of European Turkey, in the province of Çanakkale, located at the northern end of the Strait of Dardanelles near the neck of the Gallipoli Peninsula. Gelibolu is connected to the other parts of Turkey by highways and a steamer service. A daily ferry service between Eceabat, 20 mi. south of Gelibolu, and Çanakkale links Europe to Asia. The town is noted for its sardine and sponge fisheries, and large grapes are exported. The town has been inhabited since the early Hellenistic period. It was the first place in Europe taken by the Ottoman Turks (1354). Because of its strategic location, it has been the scene of many military events, of which the most notable was the Gallipoli Campaign of World War I. On Apr. 24, 1915, in order to gain control of the Dardanelles and capture Constantinople (İstanbul), Allied troops landed on the Gallipoli Peninsula. The first expedition failed because of the stubborn resistance of the Turks led by Mustafa Kemal, later known as Atatürk, and the German commander, Gen. Liman von Sanders. The second landing of Aug., 1915, also failed after a fierce fight, and on Jan. 9, 1916, the Allied forces were compelled to withdraw. Pop., 12,956.

INCI PIRINCCIOGLU, University of İstanbul

GELIGNITE. *See* DYNAMITES.

GÉLINAS [zhā'lĭ-nä], **GRATIEN** (1909–), Canadian actor, born in St. Tite, Quebec. He first gained fame in 1936 through stage and radio appearances as Fridolin, a vaudeville character of his own creation that has been likened to a French-Canadian Charlie Chaplin. He also wrote and starred in the comedy *Ti-Coq* (Little Rooster), 1949; acted at the Stratford Shakespearean Festival of Canada in the 1950's; and in 1957 became founder-director of Le Théâtre de la Comédie Canadienne, Montreal.

GELLÉE, CLAUDE. *See* LORRAIN, CLAUDE.

GELON [jē'lŏn] **or GELO** [jēlō] (c.540–478 B.C.), Tyrant of Syracuse in Sicily. Cavalry commander in his native Gela, Gelon usurped supreme power there c.491 B.C., and by supporting certain aristocractic exiles gained control of Syracuse in 485 B.C. He was instrumental in repelling the Carthaginian attack on Himera, which tradition says occurred on the same day as Salamis. Two years later Gelon died, at the zenith of his power and prestige, and was succeeded by his brother Hiero I.

GELSENKIRCHEN [gěl-zən-kĭr'кнən], city in the west of the Federal Republic of Germany (West Germany) on the Emscher River, about 17 mi. west of Dortmund. A center of the vast Ruhr industrial area, Gelsenkirchen is the lead-

ing coal-mining center of Europe and the second-largest inland port in West Germany. It also has important iron, steel, chemical, and clothing industries. The city covers a wide area and now includes the formerly independent towns of Buer and Horst. Gelsenkirchen was a major bombing target during World War II, and nearly half the city has since been rebuilt. Pop., 382,689.

GEM, precious or semiprecious stone cut and polished. Apart from ecclesiastical metalwork, the main use of gems has been for personal adornment. For many centuries in Europe they were also thought to possess protective and other magical powers. The gems were either engraved in intaglio or in relief (to form cameos) or cut to improve their powers of reflecting light.

Until the middle of the 15th century gems were usually cabochon-cut. The top of the stone was rounded without facets by means of rubbing and polishing; the base was either convex, concave, or flat. This partly explains why the diamond ranked only third in order of value; the lapidary's craft was not sufficiently developed to bring out the best in the stone. The ruby, which was rare because of the limited trade with the Orient, ranked first; the emerald, diamond, and sapphire followed.

During the 16th century gems were table-cut or faceted haphazardly, while diamonds were cut to a pyramidal shape (point cut). The table cut was produced by removing the upper point of the pyramid shape, the top facet being the table. The stones were usually set in a *pavé*, or boxlike, setting, the sides of the setting being pushed down over the stones to hold them in place. Open settings were of two types: in one the bottom of the rim of the mount was cut away; in the other, the stone was fixed in a setting of tiny claws that held onto the facets on the crown, or upper part.

As the Renaissance jeweler was limited to simple cuts, he resorted to the use of foils, or thin leaves of shiny metal, placed under the stones to improve their color and sparkle. In the 16th century it was often the irregularity of a pearl or gem that made it desirable for a design. Oddly shaped pearls, for example, were mounted as the bodies of monsters and animals. In the 17th century, however, came the rose cut, a hemisphere generally of 24 facets with a flat base. At the end of the century the Venetian Vincenti Peruzzi invented the brilliant cut, normally with 33 facets on the crown and 25 on the pavilion, or lower section, of the stone. These two cuts established the diamond as the premier stone and rendered the use of a foil backing unnecessary.

REVEL ODDY, Royal Scottish Museum

See also JEWELRY.

GEM, SYNTHETIC, manufactured substance that corresponds in composition and crystal structure to natural gem minerals. Rubies and sapphires were the first gems to be synthesized. In nature they are varieties of the mineral corundum (Al_2O_3), which is readily available at low cost. The commercial synthesis is a flame-fusion process (the Verneuil process), whereby aluminum oxide powder mixed with a small amount of coloring agent (chromium oxide for ruby, iron and titanium oxide for sapphire) is fed into an inverted oxyhydrogen blowpipe flame. The material melts

SYNTHETIC GEM FURNACE

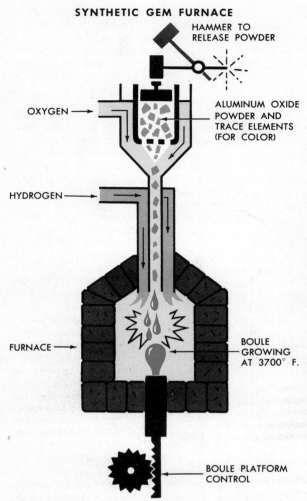

HAMMER TO RELEASE POWDER

OXYGEN

ALUMINUM OXIDE POWDER AND TRACE ELEMENTS (FOR COLOR)

HYDROGEN

FURNACE

BOULE GROWING AT 3700° F.

BOULE PLATFORM CONTROL

Furnace used to produce rubies and star sapphires synthetically. Powder, fused by heat, accumulates as a boule (ball). After cooling, the boule may be cut into several gems.

and collects on a rod or spindle placed beneath the flame, where it crystallizes as a carrot-shaped boule. Synthetic spinel is manufactured in a similar way. Emeralds are made synthetically by a different process, the details of which have not been made public. Diamonds were synthesized by the General Electric Company in 1955, but these are not of gem quality. A recent synthetic is rutile, marketed under the name "titania."

BRIAN H. MASON, American Museum of Natural History
See also CORUNDUM; DIAMOND; EMERALD; RUBY; RUTILE; SAPPHIRE; SPINEL.

GEMARA, part of the Talmud (q.v.), a commentary on and supplement to the other part, the Mishnah.

GEMINI. *See* CASTOR AND POLLUX.

GEMINI [jĕm′ə-nī] **or THE TWINS,** a winter constellation of the Northern Hemisphere, and the 3d sign of the zodiac. The brighter stars in Gemini form an oblong figure, the southern part of which is in the Milky Way. At the northern end are its two brightest stars, Castor and Pollux, which represent the twin brothers of Helen of Troy in Greek mythology. The summer solstice, where the sun is farthest north in its apparent path around the earth, is in Gemini.

See also CONSTELLATION; SOLSTICE; ZODIAC.

GEMINI

GEMINIANI [jā-mē-nyä′nē], **FRANCESCO** (1687–1762), Italian violinist and writer. A pupil of Corelli and Alessandro Scarlatti, he received great acclaim in London as a violinist. His important treatise *The Art of Playing on the Violin* (London, 1730; several enlarged editions later), the earliest-known violin method, preserved Corelli's principles of violin technique.

GEMISTUS PLETHO [jǐ-mǐs′təs plē′thō], **GEORGIUS** (c.1355–1452), Byzantine humanist and philosopher. After having been a professor in Greece, he represented the Eastern Orthodox Church (1438–39) at the Council of Ferrara-Florence, which did so much to bring a knowledge of the Greek language and Greek scholarship to the West. After the council he remained in Florence as professor at the Platonic Academy founded by Cosimo de' Medici at his suggestion, where he taught Neoplatonic philosophy. In addition to philosophical and philological works, he wrote an important geographical treatise and played a significant part in the transmission of the Greek learning which inspired the Western Renaissance.

GLANVILLE DOWNEY, Dumbarton Oaks
See also BYZANTINE LITERATURE.

GEMSBOK [gĕmz′bŏk], large antelope, *Oryx gazella*, native to the deserts of southwestern Africa. Gemsboks are light reddish-gray in color, with a white head marked

A gemsbok in the Kalahari National Park, Botswana.
(SOUTH AFRICAN TOURIST CORPORATION)

with black, and have black thighs and a tufted black tail. They grow to a shoulder height of 4 ft., and both sexes have straight, ringed horns up to 4 ft. in length. Gemsboks are not as fleet-footed as some antelopes, and if overtaken will use their horns as weapons.

See also ANTELOPE.

GENDARME [zhäɴ-därm'], member of the uniformed French national police. Militarily organized and answerable to the minister of armed forces, the gendarmerie's major purpose is to relieve the national army of any internal police duties. While its official mission is "to safeguard public order and the enforcement of the laws," serves as much in routine policing of rural areas as in the suppression of civil disturbances.

Gendarme officers and men are recruited from former professional soldiers. They are stationed in squads of five to seven men. Within each local district the squads form a section, the sections of each *département* (analogous to an American county) a company, and the companies of the *départements* making up a military region form a legion commanded by a colonel or lieutenant colonel. The *Garde républicaine*, mounted and picturesquely uniformed, is an elite unit within the gendarmerie. Concentrated chiefly in Paris, it serves as special escort for dignitaries and reinforces the regular gendarmerie.

The term "gendarme," man at arms, successively designated the lowest rung of knightly warriors, mounted, heavily armored shock troops, and various constabulary formations of the old regime. The present organization of the national gendarmerie, which has been widely copied in other countries, derives from laws passed between 1790 and 1802. The gendarmerie must be distinguished from the *Sureté*, French equivalent of the U.S. Federal Bureau of Investigation, and from the municipal police, which are under the minister of the interior.

PETER AMANN, State University of N.Y. at Binghamton

GENDER [jĕn'dər], property of nouns and pronouns designating whether they are masculine (*man, he, him*), feminine (*woman, she, her*), or neuter (*table, it, its*). Some English nouns have special forms to indicate gender (*lion, lioness; hero, heroine*). Although the problem of gender is rather complicated in some languages, in English it is fairly simple, the major requirement being that pronouns agree in gender with the nouns to which they refer (as, for example, in: The *tree* lost *its* leaves. The *saleswoman* ate *her* lunch.)

GENE [jēn]. Gregor Johann Mendel, an Austrian monk, first described the gene in his investigations on peas in 1865, although the term "gene" was not used until 1909. Genes are the fundamental units of heredity. They are located along the chromosomes in the cells of living it serves as much in routine policing of rural areas as in particular chromosome. Through the genes of the sperm and egg the potentialities for growth and development are transmitted to new organisms. Genes permit certain enzymes to be formed, and the enzymes in turn permit specific chemical reactions to take place which ultimately determine specific patterns of growth and development. Genes can also reproduce themselves. These unique characteristics make the genes important objects of study in investigations on the nature of living material.

The great majority of present evidence indicates that genes are composed of deoxyribonucleic acid (DNA), although some protein must also be present in order for the genes to function. Approximately 1 time in 100,000 a gene, through a change in its chemical structure, will produce a new hereditary trait. Such a spontaneous change is called a mutation. Genes mutate more often under irradiation or in the presence of certain chemicals.

THOMAS H. RODERICK, Roscoe B. Jackson Memorial Laboratory

GENEINA, town in Darfur Province, western Sudan, near the Chad border, 200 mi. west of El-Fasher. It is a market center and frontier post on the main route from Khartoum to Fort-Lamy. Pop., 11,817.

GENEALOGY, the study of human pedigrees. It is an old science that has become more exacting with the passing centuries, as by degrees genealogists have been brought to confine themselves to the limits of the verifiable. Much nonsense has been published concerning royal and noble ancestries of American, British, and Continental families. The Hungarian House of Esterházy, for instance, once claimed that it was directly descended from the grandfather of Adam, the first man. Almost equally fabulous pedigrees, tracing to Irish, Scottish, and Welsh kings, and from them to Biblical characters and Greek mythological figures, have been perpetrated on the gullible public.

GENEALOGICAL CHART

Chart shows that Franklin Delano Roosevelt, Gen. Douglas MacArthur, and Sir Winston Churchill are distant cousins. Only the family lines that clarify their common ancestry are indicated.

Francis Cooke and wife, Hester, went to Plymouth, Mass., on the *Mayflower* in 1620.

Richard Warren and wife, Elizabeth, went to Plymouth, Mass., on the *Mayflower* in 1620.

SON, JOHN COOKE ——— married (m.) ——— DAUGHTER, SARAH WARREN

── 2 DAUGHTERS ──

ESTHER COOKE
m. THOMAS TABER

ELIZABETH COOKE
m. DANIEL WILLCOX

Thomas Pope and wife, Anne, established by 1633, in Plymouth, Mass.

Enoch Hunt and wife, established by 1637, in Weymouth, Mass.

Joseph Farnsworth and wife, Elizabeth, established by 1635, in Dorchester, Mass.

ESTHER TABER
m. SAMUEL PERRY

DANIEL WILLCOX (2)
m. HANNAH

2 DAUGHTERS
REBECCA   MARY

EBENEZER PERRY
m. ABIGAIL

DANIEL WILLCOX (3)
m. SARAH

GREAT-GRANDCHILDREN
LEMUEL POPE
HANNAH POPE

GREAT-GRANDCHILDREN
ELIZABETH HUNT
SAMUEL HUNT

married

DR. SAMUEL PERRY
m. SUSANNAH

WILLIAM WILLCOX
m. DOROTHY

MERCY POPE
m. CALEB CHURCH

DAUGHTER
DEBORAH HUNT

GRANDSON
JOSEPH BELCHER

married

DEBORAH
PERRY

JOSEPH CHURCH

married

GREAT-GRANDDAUGHTER
SARAH

WILLIAM
WILLCOX (2)

married

DEBORAH CHURCH
m. CAPT. WARREN DELANO

GRANDDAUGHTER
CLARISSA WILLCOX
m. AMBROSE HALL

WARREN DELANO
m. CATHERINE LYMAN

GREAT-GREAT-GRANDDAUGHTER
AURELIA BELCHER
m. JUDGE ARTHUR MacARTHUR

CLARISSA HALL
m. L. W. JEROME

SARAH DELANO
m. JAMES ROOSEVELT

LT. GEN. ARTHUR MacARTHUR
m. MARY PINKNEY HARDY

JENNIE JEROME
m. LORD CHURCHILL

── 7TH COUSINS ONCE REMOVED ──

6TH COUSINS
ONCE REMOVED

8TH COUSINS

Franklin D. Roosevelt Library
FRANKLIN DELANO ROOSEVELT

U. S. Army—Cushing
GEN. DOUGLAS MacARTHUR

SIR WINSTON CHURCHILL

486

There are also claims of descent from the Ptolemies of Egypt and from Romans of 200 B.C. Happily, such claims have been exposed and are no longer being made by any who can truly claim to be genealogists.

Family names were unknown prior to 1050 A.D. Thus genealogical research for periods before that time is impractical. Even by 1300 family names were used only by the higher ranks of nobility. In England it was not until the 16th century that records were kept of any but the most powerful noble families, and even in those cases it was usually only the descents of oldest sons that were recorded, as the law of primogeniture emphasized such descent. Younger sons, daughters, and even wives were neglected. The great subsidy (1523–24) of Henry VIII, the "Domesday Book of the Middle Classes," together with the beginning of parish registers in 1538 made genealogical research among the middle classes feasible.

The value of genealogical study lies largely in its contributions to history. It is also of value to the science of eugenics, which must depend considerably on genealogical research for its data. Critical genealogical research is necessary in the probate of some estates, especially trust estates, when the beneficiary dies without near relatives. Many lawyers are unfamiliar with the best methods and sources to established distant next of kin. Much genealogical research is done in applications for membership in patriotic and hereditary societies. Interest in most of these societies began around 1890, and since that time there has been a vast improvement in the nature of proofs acceptable to establish eligibility. At first no proof at all was demanded, the societies accepting claims which often, though perhaps not intentionally, were inaccurate, and the lineage sometimes obviously impossible. In the last two decades, however, the pendulum has swung perhaps too far the other way, some societies demanding proof that even courts of law do not require.

There is very little—if any—absolute proof in genealogy. No class of records has been found invariably correct. Vital records of towns or health departments, though generally accepted as proof, contain many errors due to misspelling, misreading of handwriting, and misinformation, sometimes intentional, furnished to clerks for recording. Wills cannot be depended upon in every instance to establish true relationships, since testators often used to refer to sons-in-law as sons, stepchildren and adopted children as the testators' children, and nephews and nieces as cousins. Bible records are not always reliable. In many instances the data was entered long after the event and hence may not be accurate; occasionally dates have been purposely changed for personal reasons. Church records are sometimes in error, too, particularly in the spelling of names. Tombstone inscriptions are frequently misread because of weathering of dates, and cases have been known of intentional juggling. Family traditions, passed on from generation to generation in good faith but often with embellishment, cannot be relied upon, although they may contain some truth.

When there exist no records at all of birth, marriage, and death, or of family relationships, the genealogist must use his critical faculties in sorting and evaluating circumstantial evidence. It is this ability together with knowledge of what records are to be found and where to find them that distinguishes a good genealogist from a poor one. Fellows of the American Society of Genealogists, the number being limited to 50, are recognized in the United States, England, and on the Continent as competent amateur and professional genealogists.

Consult Jacobus, D. L., *Genealogy as a Pastime and Profession* (1930); Doan, G. H., *Searching for Your Ancestors* (3d ed., 1960); American Society of Genealogists, *Genealogical Research—Methods and Sources* (1961).

H. MINOT PITMAN, F.A.S.G.

See also HERALDRY.

GENERAL ACCOUNTING OFFICE (GAO), an agency of the U.S. Congress which serves as a watchdog over the expenditures of the public money. The GAO is headed by the Comptroller General of the United States, who is appointed by the President with the advice and consent of the Senate. He serves for a term of 15 years and since he does not report to the President, he is not a member of the executive branch of the government. This is to make sure that he is neither a political appointee nor personally interested in the spending operations of the government. The GAO audits all government accounts and exercises final authority on expenditures. It may disallow expenditures which, in its judgment, are not compatible with appropriation acts of the Congress.

GENERAL AGREEMENT ON TARIFFS AND TRADE (GATT), international trade agreement which sought to encourage free trade and lower tariff rates. GATT was negotiated in 1947 by a Preparatory Committee established by the Economic and Social Council of the United Nations. The instrument includes over 120 bilateral trade agreements covering some 60,000 items. Immediately after World War II the United States requested that a specialized agency, the International Trade Organization (ITO), be created by the United Nations in order to pursue the goal of free trade and common tariff policies. The plan's adoption was inhibited by the dollar shortage, which was acute at the time. Free trade would have accentuated the balance of payments problem and might have interfered with the reconstruction of the economy of Europe.

ITO was discussed and modified in meetings in London, Geneva, and Havana, but was finally rejected by all nations including the United States. GATT, on the other hand, as a less stringent system, did establish a basis for reciprocal reductions of tariff barriers. The United States accepted GATT by executive agreement in 1947.

The functions of GATT are administered by a secretariat under the direction of an executive secretary, with headquarters in Geneva. Parties to the agreement, now numbering about 60, meet frequently to discuss international trade policies, especially tariff concessions. One of the organization's most important duties has been to oversee the development of the European Economic Community and to insure that the goal of unrestricted trade was not hampered by the new customs unions.

WAYNE WILCOX, Columbia University

GENERAL DYNAMICS CORPORATION, a major manufacturer of complex aerospace, marine, electronic, nuclear, and related systems. Among the leading products of General Dynamics are military aircraft, turboprop planes for commercial use, nuclear submarines, nuclear reactors, space vehicles, surface ships, weapons systems, guided missiles, communication networks, coal products, refractory materials, and metalworking equipment.

Between 1957 and 1967 the company developed the world's first all-weather interceptor, first supersonic bomber, fastest airliner, and the highly sophisticated F-111A variable sweepwing aircraft. Manufacturing plants, shipyards, mines, quarries, and research operations owned by General Dynamics are located in 30 states of the United States, as well as in Canada and in several other countries, with the home office in New York City. There are almost 100,000 employees. The parent company was the Electric Boat Company, but the name was changed to General Dynamics Corporation in 1952.

STANLEY A. ARBINGAST, The University of Texas

GENERAL ELECTRIC COMPANY, one of the world's largest manufacturers of electric products. The company arose from a merger (1892) of the Edison General Electric and the Thomson-Houston Electric companies. During its early years General Electric concentrated in the fields of power, lighting, and electric railways. It has since become highly diversified, with some 250,000 employees in more than 160 U.S. and Canadian plants. Subsidiaries do business in a score of other countries.

General Electric's products fall into four broad classifications: (1) consumer goods—radio and television receivers and electric housewares such as ranges, refrigerators, washing machines, and other appliances; (2) heavy capital goods—turbine generators, motors, transformers, switchgear, and atomic power plants; (3) industrial machines and materials—electronic systems, meters and instruments, plastics, and special metals; and (4) equipment for national defense—items for use in radar, flight propulsion, and missiles.

Research has characterized the company's history. In 1900 General Electric opened the first industrial laboratory devoted to pure research. The number of G.E. laboratories in the United States and Canada now totals more than 100. Among the prominent inventors and scientists associated with the company have been Thomas Edison, Charles Steinmetz, and Irving Langmuir. General Electric played an important part in the development of electric locomotives and ship motors, X-ray tubes, electric refrigeration, fluorescent lighting, air conditioning, synthetic diamonds, and jet aircraft engines. Its radio station, WGY Schenectady, pioneered in U.S. radio and television broadcasting. Its executive offices are in New York City.

IAN H. WILSON, General Electric Company

GENERAL FOODS CORPORATION, processor and marketer of several hundred packaged-grocery products. General Foods sells its items under a wide variety of brand names, including Baker's, Birds Eye, Gaines, Jell-O, Kool-Aid, Log Cabin, Maxwell House, Post, and Swans Down. In the United States, the corporation operates more than 60 plants, plus grain elevators, laboratories, and sales and distribution centers. There are subsidiaries in Canada, Europe, South Africa, South America, the Philippines, and Japan. The present corporation came into being in 1929 as the result of a series of mergers undertaken by the Postum Cereal Company (founded 1895).

GENERALIZATION, process of going from one or more specific ideas to a general concept that encompasses them, or from one or more specific propositions to a more general proposition that implies them. Sometimes the product of this process is itself called a generalization. The generalization of ideas is studied in psychology, and of propositions, in logic, especially inductive logic and statistical theory, whose central concern is to discover techniques of generalization whose conclusions will have maximum probability of being true.

GENERAL MOTORS CORPORATION, manufacturer of cars, trucks, buses, automobile parts, diesel engines, locomotives, construction equipment, aircraft parts, prop-jet engines, military electronic equipment, and household appliances. The corporation consists of 37 semiautonomous divisions and the General Motors Overseas Operations Division. It has 129 plants in the United States, five in Canada, and various operations in 19 other countries. (It makes the Vauxhall car in England, and the Opel in Germany.) General Motors is the result of an amalgamation, by W. C. Durant in 1908, of the Oldsmobile, Cadillac, Buick, and Oakland companies. Chevrolet became part of GM in 1918.

GENERAL SERVICES ADMINISTRATION (GSA), an agency of the U.S. government charged with procuring, supplying, and maintaining real and personal property for executive agencies, disposing of domestic surplus property, and keeping the permanently valuable noncurrent government records. The GSA was established in 1949 by amalgamation of several lesser agencies. It includes the Bureau of Federal Supply, Defense Materials Service, Public Buildings Service, and the National Archives. The administrator is appointed by the President, with the advice and consent of the Senate, and is assisted by a staff of experts in the fields of maintenance and procurement.

GENERAL STAFF, group of officers who advise and assist a major military commander. The staff developed as armies grew in size and complexity. Staff members have authority only in the commander's name. They are planners who work out the basis for a commander's decision and the means of implementing it.

King Gustavus Adolphus of Sweden organized rudimentary staffs, and Louis XIV of France continued the practice. The Prussians were the first to use the term (1809) to designate officers assisting the commander of the entire army. In 1880 the French founded the École de Guerre to train staff officers. The British created a modern staff early in this century. The United States established the Command and General Staff College in 1902 and organized a general staff in 1903.

The general staff usually deals with personnel, intelligence, training, plans, operations, and logistics. In the United States it assists commanders at division, corps, army, and higher levels.

MARTIN BLUMENSON, Senior Historian,
Department of the Army

GENERATOR, ELECTRIC, a device which converts mechanical energy into electrical energy. In the broader sense, an electric generator is considered to be any source of electricity. However, the commonly accepted definition of an electric generator is a driven, rotating machine that supplies alternating or direct current electricity.

Generators may be large steam turbine–driven machines used to supply electric power systems. Or they may be wind-driven generators supplying electricity to charge farm storage batteries, or attached to an automobile engine to charge the battery, and power the heater, lights, radio, and ignition system.

There are two basic types of electric generators: direct current (d.c.) and alternating current (a.c.). The output of a d.c. generator is a current that flows in only one direction. These generators were once the prime source of power in commercial electric power systems; however, because it was not economical to transmit d.c. power over long distances, this type of generator has been replaced by a.c. generators for most power system service. At present, d.c. generators are used mainly for charging automobile, aircraft, and marine engine batteries and for special applications such as supplying the d.c. power for the field of an a.c. generator and for industrial and railway use.

Output current of an a.c. generator reverses periodically. The standard alternating current supplied in the United States is 60-cycle, that is, the reversal occurs 60 times per second. Most other power systems supply 50-cycle alternating current. Reversals of current depend upon the speed of the generator and its number of poles.

Large a.c. generators supply power to commercial power systems for home and industrial use. Alternators, smaller special a.c. generators, are finding wider use in automobile and outboard motor applications. In an alternator, the a.c. output is rectified to supply the direct current needed for battery charging. Alternators are more desirable for this type of service because they supply higher current at lower rotational speeds.

Power output of both d.c. and a.c. generators may range from less than a watt to thousands of kilowatts. For example, the maximum output of an automobile generator is about 60 watts. Huge steam turbine–driven alternators have been designed to supply power over 300,000 kw.

Voltage output of either an a.c. or d.c. generator depends upon the load which it was designed to supply. Direct current generators must supply a voltage equal to or higher than that required by their loads, since direct current cannot be transformed to higher voltages, but can be reduced with suitable resistance in the circuit. Alternating current, however, may be generated at low voltages and raised to higher voltages by means of transformers. High voltages are more economical for long-distance power transmission. The high voltage can also be stepped down by means of transformers for home and industrial use. Alternating current generation is almost universally used in power systems throughout the world.

Principles of Electric Power Generation. Electric generators produce electricity in terms of current, voltage, and power. Current, measured in amperes, is the flow of electricity through the wires. It is often compared to the flow of water through a pipe. For example, heavy industrial loads on a water system require much more water flow through the pipes than do a few residential customers. Likewise, high horsepower motors connected to an electric generator demand more current flow than a few light-appliance loads. Current flow in an electric system also depends upon the voltage output of the generator.

Voltage is the pressure in the system which maintains the current flow, just as water pressure in a water system maintains the required flow of water. Low-voltage motors of the same horsepower rating as high-voltage motors demand proportionately greater current. For example, a 12-volt motor rated at the same horsepower as a 120-volt motor requires 10 times the amount of current from the system. This can be explained by the formula for power, which is the product of voltage and current. Thus, generators of various voltage outputs connected to equal loads are required to supply the same amount of power, but at different currents.

In 1831 Michael Faraday discovered that a current could be induced in a wire if the wire was moved through a magnetic field, the direction of current flow depending upon the direction in which the wire is moved through the field. This is the basic principle used in all electric generators to produce electricity.

The *magnetic field* is created by magnetic poles, which may be electromagnets or permanent magnets. In most generators these magnetic poles form the stationary part of the generator, called the *stator*. Where the magnetic field is created by an electromagnet, the coil wound around the magnetic core is called the *field*, or *field winding*. The rotating part of the generator, called the *rotor* or *armature*, is mounted within the magnetic field and carries the conductors in which current is induced. The amount of current induced depends upon the strength of the magnetic field and the speed with which the conductors pass through the magnetic lines of force.

To understand the operating principle of a generator, assume that the conductors on the rotor are only a single loop of wire. As the loop of wire is rotated in the magnetic field, current is induced which reverses at each half revolution. When the conductors of the loop are parallel to the magnetic field between the north and south poles, maximum current is induced, which flows in a certain direction. When the loop reaches a point at right angles to the lines of force of the magnetic field, no current flows at that instant. As the loop continues its rotation and reaches the point where it is again parallel to the magnetic field, the conductors of the loop have reversed positions and are passing between the poles in a direction opposite from that previously. Therefore maximum current is induced in the opposite direction. As the loop rotates then, current alternates periodically from positive to negative polarity. This is an elementary a.c. generator.

To connect the loop to a circuit and use the electricity thus generated, the ends of the loop are connected to rings called *slip rings*. Slip rings are fixed to the rotor shaft and rotate with the rotor. Carbon or graphite brushes contact the rings and take off the current.

Output of a d.c. generator is always of the same polarity. Therefore, to take off current which does not reverse polarity, the slip rings are replaced with a split ring, called a *commutator*. Each half of the ring is connected to one end of the loop. Then, as the rotor turns, the brushes are

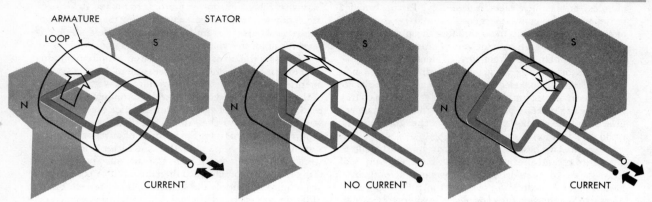

Current is generated when a loop of wire in the armature cuts through the magnetic field. It is at a maximum when the loop is parallel to the magnetic lines of force.

When the rotating loop is at right angles to the magnetic field, the wire slips between the lines of force. No current flows in the loop for a fraction of a second.

As the rotation continues, the halves of the loop reverse position with respect to the stator (stationary magnets) so the current flow is reversed with respect to the loop.

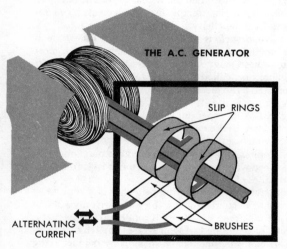

THE BASIC DIFFERENCE BETWEEN A.C. AND D.C. GENERATORS IS THE MANNER IN WHICH CURRENT IS REMOVED FROM THE ARMATURE.

Each half of the loop is connected to a slip ring that rotates with the armature. Each slip ring is in contact with a brush that alternately draws off current or serves to complete the circuit.

One loop end is connected to each half of the split-ring commutator. As the loop rotates, the commutator halves change brush contacts so the drawn-off current flows in one direction only.

arranged to switch the conductors when the loop is at right angles to the magnetic field. The commutator reverses the connection of the loop to the outside circuit each time the current is about to reverse. The current rises from zero to maximum, drops to zero, then rises to maximum in the same polarity. Practical d.c. generators have many windings and many commutator segments so that the current never drops to zero. However, it always flows in the same direction.

Practical D.C. Generators. Direct current generators may be classified as bipolar, multipolar, series, shunt, compound, self-excited, and separately excited.

Bipolar machines contain only two poles, similar to the elementary generator. Multipole machines, however, are most common because of their greater capacity for their physical size; poles of multipole machines are always in multiples of two.

Series-wound generators have their field coils con-

nected in series with the generator output. With an increase in load, current flow through the field coils increases, thus increasing the magnetic field between the poles. With a constant rotational speed, the generated voltage increases with an increase in load. To take full advantage of series-wound generators, the wire size of the field coils must be large. This requirement limits the usefulness of a series-wound generator. Series-wound generators are self-excited since the output of the generator produces its own field current.

Shunt-wound d.c. generators have their field coils connected in parallel, or across the output terminals. An increase in load causes the current through the field coils to drop, thus decreasing the magnetic field between the poles. Output voltage drops with an increase in load. Shunt field coils can be wound with small-diameter wire and can be designed to produce a strong magnetic field with small field currents. If the field coils are connected directly to the generator output terminals, the shunt-wound generator is self-excited. But the excitation voltage may be supplied from a storage battery or a separate d.c. source. Then the generator is classed as separately excited.

Most d.c. generators are compound-wound. That is, they are a combination of series- and shunt-wound generators to take advantage of the best features of both types of construction and to provide a constant voltage output with changes in load.

A small amount of magnetism is always present in the iron pole cores; therefore, when a generator is started, a small amount of current is always generated. In a self-excited generator, just enough current is supplied to the field to begin generating electricity. As the output voltage increases, the magnetic field strength increases, which in turn brings the output voltage up to its operating value. The output voltage is limited by the internal resistance of the machine.

The stationary field structure of a d.c. generator contains rectangular magnetic poles supported by a cast-iron yoke. The poles are made of steel laminations and the field coils are wound around the poles. The core of the rotor is made of laminations of sheet steel. Laminated construction prevents currents from being induced in the rotor core rather than the copper conductors. Rotors are notched to receive the coil windings, so that the resulting surface of the rotor is smooth. Several forms of rotor windings are used in practice, but basically, all the types of windings consist of a series of loops connected to individual commutator segments.

The commutator is made of copper bars arranged in a ring around the rotor shaft. They are insulated from each other by small pieces of sheet mica. Commutator brushes, mounted in holders, are usually made of carbon or graphite; springs hold them in tight contact against the commutator. Where extremely high currents are carried, the brushes are made of copper.

Heat in generators is caused by the heating of conductors carrying current and by the friction of the brushes and the commutator. Some of this heat is dissipated by the metal parts of the generator. The remainder of the heat is removed by blowing air through the machine. This is usually accomplished by mounting fan blades on one end of the rotor shaft.

Practical A.C. Generators. Alternating current generators, or alternators, are very similar in construction to d.c. generators. They consist of a stationary field and a rotating armature. But they are simpler in that they do not require a commutator. The current generated by an alternator is not switched to maintain the same polarity, as in the d.c. generator.

Alternating current generators can differ from d.c. generators in another respect. The functions of the stator and armature can be reversed. Because the armature windings carry higher currents than the field coils, it is more desirable to have the slip rings and brushes handle the lighter currents supplied to the field. Therefore, the field coils are made to rotate and the armature coils are made the stationary part of the machine.

Because the field coils of alternators require d.c. excitation, the alternator cannot be self-exciting. However, it is possible to rectify a small portion of the output of a small machine and use the resulting direct current to excite the field windings. Alternators such as those used in automobiles and outboard marine engines utilize permanent magnets to provide the necessary magnetic field. Generally the field coils of large commercial alternators are energized from separate d.c. generators. Usually these generators, called exciters, are connected directly to the shaft of the large alternator.

Stators of alternators are constructed of laminated steel, as in the d.c. generator. Coil windings are placed in slots in the stator. Many types of windings are used in alternator construction, depending upon the application of the machine. Basically, however, the windings consist of many single loops connected in series.

Rotors are made in two ways. One method of construction is that using steel laminations. Laminated rotors are used in slow-speed alternators. The other method of construction employs a solid steel rotor, which is used in high-speed machines. Both types of rotors provide slots in which the field coils are wound.

Alternating current generators are classified into two types: *single-phase* and *polyphase*. A single-phase machine produces one voltage at a time from its set of armature coils. A polyphase machine has more than one set of armature coils and produces many equal voltages at the same time. The maximum and minimum points of the various voltages occur at different times. The most common polyphase system is three-phase—three separate voltages generated from three like sets of coils, and the generator contains three slip rings. Three-phase power is generated for high-power applications.

Alternating current generators are designed to run at closely controlled speeds. Most power systems in the United States are operated at a frequency of 60 cycles per second. At the generator a conductor passes a magnetic pole in the machine each one-sixtieth of a second. A bipole alternator must rotate 60 times per second and a four-pole alternator must rotate at 30 revolutions per second to maintain that frequency.

Electric clocks, for example, depend upon power-line frequency for their accuracy. Many industrial processes are controlled by motors synchronized with the power line. In a power plant where many generators are supplying power to the system, all are synchronized and are running at exactly the same speed.

Cooling problems in a.c. generators are much the same as those in d.c. generators. Forced-air and water cooling are employed to dissipate heat. In very large machines, hydrogen gas is used as a coolant. These machines are sealed in gastight enclosures.

Small Generating Plants. For farm, ranch, or home use where publicly distributed power is not available, a small power plant is necessary. It may be a gasoline engine–driven generator, a generator driven by water power, or a windmill. For this type of service, the power is usually supplied by storage batteries. The generator maintains the batteries at full charge. Gasoline engine–driven a.c. generators are not economical for operating small loads and water-driven or wind-driven alternators are not practical because of the variations inherent in water and wind supply.

Capacity for a small generator to supply power for the

average home should be about 5 kw. Generating plants with a capacity of about 2 kw. or less are driven by a one- or two-cylinder air-cooled engine. Generators are sometimes equipped with a series winding which is used for cranking the engine to start the plant.

Special Types of Generators. *Amplidyne* generators are classed as rotating regulators. They are used to control or regulate the voltage or current output of large d.c. generators. Changes in the load current or voltage of the large generator is translated into changes in the amplidyne field current. Response of the amplidyne to load changes is very fast. Effectively, an amplidyne generator amplifies the small voltage which, in turn, controls the field of the large generator. The amplidyne is used as the exciter of the d.c. generator.

The *electrostatic*, or *Van de Graaff*, generator is capable of developing up to 10 million volts. It is used primarily for production of X rays of high penetrating power and for operation of discharge tubes. Electrostatic generators are used extensively in nuclear research work. A recent form of electrostatic generator uses a rapidly moving endless belt within a sealed metal container. A charge is induced on the belt at one point of its travel and is removed from the belt at the opposite end of its travel. The top of the metal container becomes negatively charged with respect to ground, and is used as the negative terminal.

High-frequency alternators capable of generating alternating current at frequencies up to 100,000 cycles per second (cps) are used in the metalworking industry for induction heating of metals. These alternators are characterized by their many poles and high rotational speeds. Common frequencies used in induction heating are 480, 960, 3,000 and 9,600 cps. Choice of frequency depends upon the application. Power output of this type of high-frequency alternator depends upon the size of the induction furnace. It may be as high as 100 kw.

Magnetos, or permanent magnet alternators, are small a.c. generators whose field is supplied by permanent magnets. In telephone apparatus, they are hand-cranked to supply bell ringing current. When cranked normally, the telephone magneto is designed to supply about 75 volts at a frequency of about 10 to 15 cps. Another form of magneto is used to supply ignition voltage in aircraft engines and in some high performance automobiles.

A generator is also called a dynamo, or dynamoelectric machine, when it converts mechanical energy into electrical energy. A dynamo may be called a motor if it converts electrical to mechanical energy.

LAURENCE SHERGALIS, Associate Editor, *Electronics*
See also BATTERY, ELECTRIC; ELECTRIC POWER; FARADAY, MICHAEL; MOTOR, ELECTRIC.

GENESEE RIVER [jĕn′ə-sē], river in western New York. It rises in the Allegheny Plateau in north-central Pennsylvania and flows north to Lake Ontario at Rochester, N.Y. Part of its gorge (350–600 ft. deep) and three waterfalls are in Letchworth State Park (13,350 acres). Falls at Rochester supply hydroelectricity. Length, 158 mi.

GENESEO [jĕn-ə-sē′ō], city of northwestern Illinois, 20 mi. east of Moline. Geneseo is an agricultural trade center, and bituminous coal mining and general farming are carried on nearby. Settled in the 1830's; inc., 1855; pop., 5,840.

GENESIS [jĕn′ə-sĭs], first book of the Old Testament. It is so called after its title in the Septuagint, the ancient Greek version, because in its opening chapters it deals with the origin of things. Many Old Testament scholars hold that the book is a compilation of material from three major sources, together with separate traditions in chaps. 14 and 49. Genesis is divided into two main parts: (1) primeval history (chaps. 1–11), telling of the creation of man, the introduction of sin through disobedience to God, the tragic consequences of this in human history, the judgment of God in the Flood, the sin of the Tower of Babel and the disunity of the nations; (2) patriarchal history (chaps. 12–50), which tells of the divine purpose of salvation for all nations through God's choice of Abraham, the promise of his family becoming a nation·and possessing the land of Palestine, the story of Isaac and Jacob, and of Jacob's sons. The tribes of Israel, in whom the promises were fulfilled, are regarded as descendants of Jacob. The tradition of Israel's stay in Egypt is traced back to Joseph.

RONALD E. CLEMENTS, University of Edinburgh

GENÊT [zhə-nĕ′], **EDMOND CHARLES** (1763–1834), French diplomat. Born into a family of exceptional court connections, Genêt was a child prodigy who followed his father into diplomatic service at the age of 17. When the French Revolution broke out in 1789, Genêt was in Russia, where he became *chargé d'affaires*. His shabby treatment at Russian hands helped convert the erstwhile royal protegé into a convinced democrat. Soon after his expulsion from Russia in 1792, Genêt was sent as minister plenipotentiary to the United States, with instructions to further French war efforts against Britain and Spain. To the dismay of President George Washington, Genêt proceeded to outfit several French privateers to prey on British commerce. Declared unacceptable by the U.S. government, Genêt tried to promote expeditions against Spanish Florida and Louisiana until the arrival of his replacement in Feb., 1794. Because of unsettled conditions in France, Genêt was permitted to remain in the United States, where he became a gentleman farmer.

PETER AMANN, State University of N.Y. at Binghamton

GENÊT, JEAN (1909–   ), French dramatist and novelist. He is best known for a series of plays dealing on a psychological plane with aspects of human evil; non-naturalistic in style, they are notable for their frankness and powerful imagery. They include *Les Bonnes*, 1948 (*The Maids*, 1955); *Haute surveillance*, 1949 (*Deathwatch*, 1958); *Le Balcon*, 1956 (*The Balcony*, 1957); and *Les Nègres*, 1957 (*The Blacks*, 1961). His other writings include the novel *Le miracle de la rose* (1946) and the autobiographical *Journal d'un voleur* (Diary of a Thief), 1949.

GENET [jĕn′ĭt], a small carnivore of genus *Genetta* in the civet family, Viverridae. Genets are found in Europe, Africa, and Asia. They have short, grayish or yellowish fur, spotted with brown or black, and a long, ringed tail, and are about the size of a domestic cat. They are easily tamed and make excellent ratters.

GENETICS [jə-nĕt′ĭks], the science of heredity. The primary concern of genetics is the transmission of hereditary units from generation to generation and the expression of these hereditary units during the development of the organism. The fact that heredity exists has been known for hundreds of years. The rules by which heredity operates were first discovered and published by the Austrian monk Gregor Mendel in 1866. Unfortunately, the scientists of that time failed to appreciate the extraordinary significance of Mendel's lucid experiments, and it was not until 1900 that Mendel's laws were rediscovered independently by Karl Correns, Hugo De Vries, and Erich Tschermak. Six years later the English biologist William Bateson coined the word "genetics" (from Greek, "to generate").

Early Genetic Investigations

The early genetic investigations were carried out not for their own sake but to serve as confirmatory evidence for the theory of evolution. The major weakness of Charles Darwin's concept of the origin of species was his ignorance of the rules of heredity, which were unknown when his great treatise was published in 1859. It it not surprising that two of the early American geneticists, William E. Castle and Thomas Hunt Morgan, were embryologists intent on demonstrating the truths of evolution as reconstructed during the development of an organism.

There was also an early burst of activity in human genetics. Interest in eugenics (the science that deals with the improvement of human heredity) was widespread and it, like evolution, lacked the essential knowledge of the principles of heredity. The first demonstration of a human trait that behaved according to the Mendelian rules was provided in 1903 by William C. Farabee and William E. Castle, who showed that albinism in three generations of a Negro family behaved as a Mendelian recessive. A much more significant paper by Archibald Garrod appeared in 1908 but was generally neglected. He suggested that four human metabolic disorders—albinism, alkaptonuria, cystinuria, and pentosuria—were genetic and were present at birth. The baby was assumed either to lack an enzyme necessary for normal metabolism, or the enzyme was present and blocked in its activities. Since then many more diseases have been found to result from genetic inborn errors of metabolism. Years later, the Nobel Prize winners George Beadle and Joshua Lederberg utilized Garrod's concept in demonstrating the direct control of enzymes and metabolism by specific genetic units (genes) in the mold *Neurospora* and in bacteria.

Mendel's studies with peas grown in a monastery garden established the first principles of genetics, but peas were not the best organisms for genetic research. Studies on poultry, mice, and man confirmed the essential truths of Mendel's laws, but these subjects were also not the ideal material for the explosive growth of genetic research that was to come. The creature that was to revolutionize biology was introduced by Professor William Ernest Castle to the genetics laboratory. He utilized some very small flies, now known as *Drosophila melanogaster*, raising them first on grapes and then on bananas. A paper by Castle and several of his students brought *Drosophila* to the attention of Professor Thomas Hunt Morgan at Columbia University. Morgan and his students could not

have possibly imagined the fame that this then insignificant insect would bring to them. For it was through *Drosophila* that the structure of genetics was established.

The first of Morgan's classic papers, which appeared in 1910, was entitled, "Sex Limited Inheritance in *Drosophila.*" The behavior of many traits in plants and animals according to Mendel's rules had been reported, but this time the trait involved was linked (not limited as Morgan stated) to the determination of the sex of the particular fruit fly. The new trait was white eye color as contrasted with the usual red eye color. It had been shown previously that in other insects sex was determined by the presence of specific chromosomes, the easily observable bodies in each cell nucleus which contain the hereditary units, or genes. The first miracle of *Drosophila* was that all of its genes were contained on only four pairs of chromosomes. One of the four pairs carries genes that affect the usual wing and eye colors and in addition determine the sex of the developing fly. This pair of chromosomes determines sex by altering the balance of the genetic make-up of the animal. Nature's device for doing this is remarkable for its simplicity. During evolution the pair of sex chromosomes has become visibly different with respect to the size of each of the two members of the chromosome pair. One member is long and contains genes of the usual kinds and is called the X chromosome. Its partner, if it is proper to call it a partner, is very short and does not have anything corresponding to the genes in the part of the X chromosome which extends beyond it. Thus, much of the X chromosome has no possible gene mates for most of its length. The short, genetically deficient chromosome is known as the Y chromosome.

The female fruit fly, *Drosophila*, has two X chromosomes. In each cell of the male there is only one X and one nonmatching Y chromosome with relatively few functions. It is the balance of two X chromosomes against the other three pairs of chromosomes which causes development of the egg to proceed toward femaleness. If there is only one X chromosome, and the very different Y chromosome, balanced against the other three pairs of chromosomes, it is easy to see that the chemical interactions would be somewhat different, and in this case the egg develops into a male.

Genes located on the X chromosome, such as Morgan's gene for white eyes, will have no mate in males because of the lack of anything on the Y chromosome to mate with. Consequently, the ratios of red- to white-eyed offspring will be different depending upon whether the father or the mother has the white eyes. Thus, the development of both sex and eye color is dependent upon whether the embryo has two X chromosomes or only one X, and whether each X chromosome has a gene for white or for red eye color upon it. The correlation between the determination of the sex and the color of the eye of the fly is predictable, and this association is termed sex-linkage.

Many other genes at other loci on the X chromosome were soon found. They resulted from new mutations, that is, chemical changes of the material along the X chromosome so that eyes, wings, bristles, or other parts of the body were different from the "wild" type flies. These changes were hereditary and appeared in the offspring in the predictable Mendelian ratios.

One of the truly amazing discoveries of science was made in the early years of genetics. It was found that the two X chromosomes, as well as the other three pairs, called autosomes (any chromosome other than a sex chromosome), not only came into physical contact with each other, but the chromosome pairing was precise, each gene pairing with its similar partner all up and down the length of the chromosome. Each pair of chromosomes is coiled about itself during the gene pairing, and at a few points along the length there may be sufficient torsion produced so that both chromosomes break and the four broken ends will then rejoin. If they rejoin in the same order as before breaking, no genetic change will be observed. However, if the two chromosomes swap partners, the new genetic order which results may be observable. This partner-swapping is known as crossing over. It is detectable when different mutant genes, such as those for white eye and miniature wings, enter the cross together on the same X chromosome and come out separately, the white eye gene on one X chromosome and the gene for miniature wings on the other X chromosome. Sometimes the two X chromosomes will not cross over between the genes for white eye and miniature wings,

WHAT IS INHERITED?

The shape and height of the body, the color and texture of the hair, and virtually every other physical characteristic is controlled by heredity.

WHAT DOES EACH PARENT CONTRIBUTE?

The child receives half of his hereditary potential from each parent.

WHY DOES THE CHILD INHERIT A PARTICULAR TRAIT FROM ONE PARENT?

BROWN EYES   BROWN EYES   BLUE EYES

WHY DO CHILDREN SOMETIMES HAVE TRAITS THAT NEITHER PARENT HAS?

BROWN EYES   BLUE EYES   BROWN EYES

WHY ARE BROTHERS AND SISTERS DIFFERENT?

BROWN EYES   BROWN EYES   BLUE EYES   BROWN EYES

SOME FACTS ABOUT HEREDITY

INHERITANCE IS TRANSMITTED BY GENES

THE BODY	THE CELL	THE CHROMOSOME	THE GENE
	NUCLEUS 	NUCLEUS CHROMOSOMES	 GENE FOR EYE COLOR
The body contains billions of cells which are organized into tissues and organs.	Each cell contains a central structure (the nucleus), which controls reproduction.	The reproductive material is contained in the chromosomes.	A hypothetical chromosome showing the gene which controls eye color.

THE CHILD RECEIVES TWO COMPLETE SETS OF CHROMOSOMES.

The heredity contribution is wrapped in specialized reproductive cells called gametes.

FATHER'S GAMETE (SPERM)    MOTHER'S GAMETE (EGG)

 EYE COLOR GENE FROM MOTHER
EYE COLOR GENE FROM FATHER

Body cells of child contain matching chromosomes.

Cells contain two genes for each trait.

GENES MAY BE DOMINANT OR RECESSIVE

Father's gamete contains brown-eye gene.

Mother's gamete contains blue-eye gene.

Cells of child contain both genes: Brown-eye gene is dominant— therefore child has brown eyes. Blue-eye gene is recessive.

RECESSIVE GENES CAN BE EXPRESSED.

FATHER

Here, the cells of both parents contain a dominant brown-eye gene and a recessive blue-eye gene. The blue-eye gene may appear in the gametes of both parents.

MOTHER

BROWN EYES

BROWN EYES

GAMETE

GAMETE

The union of these gametes produces a child with two blue-eye genes— the child is therefore blue-eyed.

EACH CHILD RECEIVES A UNIQUE COMBINATION OF GENES FROM THE PARENTS.

FATHER'S GAMETES

Both parents produce many different kinds of gametes from their chromosomes, just as any two hands drawn from a deck of cards are different.

MOTHER'S GAMETES

BROWN EYES

The differences between the children thus result from different combinations of genes.

BLUE EYES

and the resulting chromosomes will be like the parental chromosomes and called noncrossovers.

It should be clear from the above discussion that the genes for white eye color and miniature wings are associated, or linked, with each other because they are found to be located on the X chromosome. This last fact means that both white eye and miniature wings are also sex-linked as well as being linked with each other. (Sex-linked means that the gene for the particular trait is located on the sex chromosome.)

The Principles of Genetics

At the end of the first decade of *Drosophila* genetics, or about 1920, the major principles of transmission of the hereditary units had been well established. The four general principles are listed below.

The Principle of Segregation. In the offspring of a hybrid individual there is a separation and redistribution of all the unit characters which were in the hybrid. (A hybrid individual is one that differs in one or more heritable characters from its two parent organisms.) When two different varieties of a particular gene pair are present in a hybrid, each maintains its chemical and physical identity and segregates out cleanly without contamination in subsequent generations.

The Principle of Independent Assortment. When two pairs of genes are studied simultaneously, it is found that the two pairs segregate, or assort, completely independently of each other, if the two pairs of genes are not on the same pair of chromosomes.

The Principle of Linkage. If two pairs of genes are located on the same pair of chromosomes, they remain linked to each other during subsequent generations except when chromosomal crossing over separates them. The physical location of two pairs of genes on one pair of chromosomes prevents their independent assortment, as would be expected according to the second principle of independent assortment.

The Principle of the Linear Order of the Genes. The genes are arranged on the chromosomes in a linear order. The distances between the genes can be determined from the amount of crossing over which occurs between them.

The first two principles of heredity were discovered by Mendel and the second two by Morgan and his students. In order to study genetics at all there must be differences between the organisms that are to be crossed. Mendel crossed tall with dwarf peas. No matter how he did it, "tall" pollen with "dwarf" egg cells, or vice versa, the mixed, or hybrid, offspring of the first generation were all tall. The dwarf character had disappeared in the first filial generation (F_1). Plants of this generation were self-fertilized and produced plants of the second filial generation (F_2). Mendel counted 787 tall plants and 277 dwarfs, a ratio of 3 to 1. This second generation 3 to 1 ratio is the most famous of all genetic ratios, but there are also many other important Mendelian ratios. The fact that the dwarf plants reappeared in pure, unaltered form in the second generation proves that the gene for the dwarf trait passed through the first generation plants without being changed. The genes are independent units. The dwarf gene was "recessive" to the tall gene in the first generation hybrid. In the second generation one-fourth of the plants had both

genes of the dwarf type and so had no alternative but to be dwarf in stature. The "tall" gene was completely efficient in the first generation hybrid, producing by itself enough growth substance to give a normal tall plant, and therefore was considered to be "dominant" to the partner dwarf gene in the hybrid.

The fact that crossing over between genes on the same pair of chromosomes occurs prevents their being inseparably linked. The greater the distance between two genes on a chromosome, the more often they will cross over and become separate. This permits the distances between genes on a chromosome to be plotted, and a chromosome map can be constructed. There are hundreds of pairs of genes known in *Drosophila* and since it is also known that there are only four pairs of chromosomes, only four linkage maps of all these genes should result. This was found to be the case. Corn has 10 pairs of chromosomes and 10 linkage groups. Man has 23 pairs of chromosomes, but because of the widespread lack of support for human genetics, hardly anything is known about the human linkage groups.

The principles of genetics apply to all forms of life. They are so remarkably simple and straightforward that any high school student can confirm them with ease. The student can raise *Drosophila* in his home, confirm the crossover percentages obtained by Morgan, and construct a map of the locations of the genes which will agree with those published in the textbooks of genetics.

Salivary Gland Chromosomes

Geneticists used to dream of an organism as useful genetically as *Drosophila* but which also possessed large chromosomes that could be studied easily under the microscope. In 1933 such desired giant chromosomes were found, and miraculously enough they were discovered in the species where they were most wanted—in *Drosophila melanogaster*. The important cells containing the giant chromosomes are in the maggots of *Drosophila*, not in the adults. The giant chromosomes are in the cells of the salivary glands and are from 100 to 200 times longer and from 1,000 to 2,000 times greater in volume than the salivary gland chromosomes of the adult flies. The extraordinary phenomenon of the salivary chromosomes results from the continuous longitudinal division of the chromosomes without the usual separation, and without cell division. They continue to grow and divide but remain in place instead of being pulled away from each other. This process of chromosome enlargement without cell division is called endomitosis. The second miracle of *Drosophila* had occurred.

Geneticists worked day and night utilizing the giant salivary gland chromosomes to test genetic theories. It was possible to locate the position of each gene on the salivary chromosomes because of their striking banded structure. A direct comparison could then be made between the positions of the genes of the chromosome map constructed from crossing over data, and their positions as determined by microscopic observation of the giant chromosomes. The linear order of the genes is identical for both methods, a convincing proof of the principle of linear order of the genes.

The discovery of the salivary chromosomes permitted

numerous exciting advances, one of which was the study of the precise genetic differences between the chromosomes of different species of *Drosophila*. Some *Drosophila* species can be crossed, and the salivary chromosomes of the hybrid larvae are a tangled and disorderly mass of chromosomes instead of the neatly paired chromosomes found in a fly of either of the parent species. The American geneticist Theodosius Dobzhansky, and others, have made a band-by-band analysis of the differences in the chromosomes in the hybrids from *D. pseudoobscura* crossed with *D. persimilis*. It was found that some bands (or genes) present in the chromosomes of one of the parent species were absent in the other parent. Most obvious were the rearrangements of large segments of the chromosomes. A block of genes located on the first chromosome in one parent would be found attached to a different pair of chromosomes in the other parent. When genes are moved from their normal position on one pair of chromosomes to another pair of chromosomes a translocation has occurred. If a block of genes is broken out of a chromosome, inverted 180° and replaced, the changed order of these genes is known as an inversion. A set of genes may be repeated in tandem on the chromosome and is then referred to as a duplication. Study of these chromosomal aberrations which varied from one species to the next provided great insight into incipient speciation and information as to how evolution proceeds through the ages.

Evolution and Speciation

The cycle is now complete. Genetics was at first of interest because it might contribute something to the theory of evolution. Today, evolution is a major subdivision of genetics. This shift resulted from the understanding that evolution is fundamentally the genetic change which occurs as a result of mutation, with natural selection determining which genes of one generation will survive through the subsequent generation. Natural selection is inefficient and its genetic screening is very coarse-meshed, but it is the most important factor in the survival or extinction of a species. The survival of a species depends upon its successful adaptation to the available environments encountered over millions of years. The phrase "survival of the fittest" merely means that those individuals who become the ancestors of the most descendants are reproductively the fittest. The fitness has no necessary relationship to athletic ability or intelligence. One of the evolutionary "fittest" of the animals is the oyster; not much can be said for its intelligence.

Large genetic changes may have occurred in the formation of some species, but generally evolution has depended upon change at the level of the gene. Some plant species have resulted from polyploidy, the duplication in the cell of complete sets of chromosomes. Inversions and translocations have also played their part in speciation. However, the fundamental genetic changes have been the appearance of gene mutations which permitted the organism to adapt itself to the environment more successfully than its ancestors. The new gene mutations with selective advantages work with the rest of the genes in the organism in order to produce their beneficial effects and cannot be considered separately from them. However, the new mutant must gradually replace its less

desirable partner in the population. Mathematical models for this dynamic process of substitution of the more advantageous mutant for the established, less effective gene have been constructed. The mathematical description of speciation has been primarily the product of Professor Sewall Wright and Sir Ronald Fisher.

Evolution is always progressive in that, by definition, it implies genetic change, even though the genetic changes may result in extinction of the species. Successful evolution depends upon three aspects of population dynamics.

1. Gene mutations should occur at moderate rates. Very high rates would result in an array of freaks.

2. Moderate inbreeding is necessary to fix the successful genotype (the genetic constitution of an organism). Too much inbreeding would reduce the necessary genetic variability which is needed to prevent extinction when the environment changes.

3. There must be moderate natural selection. Too severe selection would eliminate genetic variability when the environment changes.

Thus, the species depends upon moderation in the many factors that produce it if it is to survive.

Practical Genetics

It is probably true that domestic plants and animals have been improved more by the breeder during the last 50 years than in the previous 5,000 years. The super-abundance of agricultural products in the United States is due in good measure to genetically improved strains. The continuing failures to meet agricultural quotas in the Soviet Union are certainly due in part to the rejection of Mendelian genetics on political grounds. Genetic improvements have resulted in better yielding strains with genetic resistance to diseases, economy in nutrition, and specialized strains for cold and dry climates. The desired strains can be obtained most effectively by the utilization of the Mendelian principles of genetics. It is somewhat difficult to apply the Mendelian rules to economic traits, such as milk production or yield of oats, because many pairs of genes are involved with these physiological characteristics. The more pairs of genes involved, the more complicated the genetic ratios become. Nonetheless, the Mendelian principles still hold and rapid genetic progress can be made.

One of the most brilliant accomplishments of practical genetics has been the development of hybrid corn. This was not an accidental discovery but the result of theoretical genetic considerations. A number of strains of maize were inbred for several generations. These inbred strains were inferior products, but a few of them, which were selected for combining ability, gave extremely uniform, vigorous, high yielding hybrids when crossed. The valuable hybrid vigor which resulted from the crosses of the inbred strains depended upon the masking of deleterious genes (which are unavoidably present in all strains) by advantageous genes in the strains with which they are crossed. It is also likely that some pairs of genes give beneficial reactions called "over-dominance" when the partner genes (alleles) are slightly different chemically. During the decade from 1930 to 1940, corn yields in the United States were raised from 22 bushels an acre to 33 or more bushels an acre in areas where hybrid corn had been introduced. This agricultural revolution paid millions of dollars of profits to the farmer for no extra work. Similar exploitation of the principle of hybrid vigor (heterosis) has been successful with hogs, chickens, and many other useful species of plants and animals. Further gains are to be expected.

Counseling in human genetics is a very practical application of the Mendelian rules. Parents who have produced a child with a gross mental or physical defect are always upset by this misfortune and wish to know what the chances are of a repetition of the calamity at each subsequent pregnancy. Any trait that behaves as a simple, clear-cut Mendelian recessive can be expected to affect one-quarter of the offspring subsequent to the affected child. It is also possible to predict with reasonable accuracy the expectation of a repetition of a trait with complicated genetic and environmental causes in the same way insurance companies determine life insurance premiums. The risk of repetition of a complicated genetic trait is called an empiric risk, which means that it is the average expectation of a repetition of the trait subsequent to an affected child. The risk figure for harelip and cleft palate is in the neighborhood of 5% to 10% among babies born subsequent to the affected child. The risk figure is higher if one or both of the parents, as well as a child, have been affected. It is not necessary to settle upon a precise percentage as the parents will usually be concerned only with the general magnitude of the possible risk.

One of the most exciting scientific breakthroughs has been the development of human cytogenetics. If human cells are grown in tissue culture and then treated with colchicine (a plant alkaloid), each member of the 23 pairs of chromosomes becomes distinct. By the use of this new technique it was shown that the common type of mental retardation known as Mongolism is due to the presence of an extra member of the 21st pair of chromosomes in each cell of the affected child. The presence of an extra or third member of a particular pair of chromosomes is well known in laboratory organisms and it is no surprise to find a trisomic, as it is called, in man. In fact, since the classic example of Mongolism, several different anomalies in man have been found to be due to the trisomic condition for other specific chromosome pairs. The third member of a particular pair of chromosomes results most frequently from what is known as nondisjunction. In the formation of the egg (or sperm) each pair of chromosomes in the cell of the ovary (or testis) must separate so that the egg or sperm will have only one member of each pair of chromosomes. This process of reducing the chromosomes from pairs to single members is called meiosis. The fertilization of the egg by the sperm then restores the usual cell picture of two members of each of the 23 pairs of chromosomes. If meiosis is faulty, in that the egg fails to lose one member of each pair of chromosomes, and one chromosome gets left in the egg, we have nondisjunction. When the chromosome that is left behind is of the 21st pair, the entrance of the sperm will bring the total chromosomes of this pair up to three, and Mongolism results.

The practical advances in plant and animal genetics have raised the standard of living very significantly, but the practical side of human genetics (eugenics) has been grossly neglected. Adequate support for applied human genetics will not come about until it becomes a universally accepted fact that the Mendelian laws apply to man as well as to corn. The eugenic approach depends upon the willingness of the present generation to make sacrifices in personal desires in order to benefit future generations.

Biochemical Genetics

The earliest genetic investigations were devoted to the study of such edible subjects as peas, poultry, rabbits, and larger mammals. Some work was done on insects, and by coincidence *Drosophila* turned out to be superb genetic material. However, it was many years before geneticists really selected organisms for experimentation solely because of their advantages for research in theoretical genetics. It was discovered that microorganisms were the best genetic material, partly because of their rapid reproduction. A mold, Neurospora, and certain bacteria and viruses, all multiply at such amazingly rapid rates and are simple enough in structure so that the path between the gene and the trait it influences is short. Use of such microorganisms has permitted examination of the way in which the gene regulates the most fundamental growth processes. The work of George Wells Beadle, Edward Tatum, Joshua Lederberg, and others brought about the final union between biochemistry and genetics.

Mutations can be readily produced by exposing bacteria and the mold *Neurospora* to X rays. In the bacterium *Escherichia coli* mutations were obtained, each of which prevented the synthesis of important constituents of protoplasm, such as various amino acids. One mutant gene was observed to block the synthesis of thiamin, another methionine, and another biotin. Still another mutant gene results in the inability to ferment lactose, and resistance to virus infection by the bacterium was similarly provided by the usual process of gene mutation. It has been possible to work out the linkage relationships of these genes and others in the bacterium *E. coli*.

An interesting example of biochemical genetics may be observed in *Neurospora*. All living things require the amino acid tryptophan as a part of their protoplasm. *Neurospora* can live on a medium which does not include this amino acid because the mold can produce it from other compounds which are present in the medium on which it is grown. It does this through the action of a particular enzyme which it produces. This enzyme is capable of combining the amino acid serine with indole to produce tryptophan. The enzyme is tryptophan synthetase and can be extracted from *Neurospora*. A mutant form of *Neurospora* was found which cannot synthesize tryptophan. Consequently, tryptophan must be added to the food if the mutant mold is to grow. The mutant gene has somehow altered the enzyme so that it cannot function.

Many traits in molds and man have been found to depend upon the rather direct effects of genes on enzymes. Once the precise way by which the genes control enzymes is discovered, a great deal more will be known about the essential qualities of life itself.

The Nature of the Gene

Study of microorganisms has focused attention on the

nature of the gene and has contributed much of the information about the finer details of the structure of the gene. Some strains of bacterial viruses have been utilized for this work. Mutants in the T4 strain of virus (one of a group of viruses that attack bacteria) are easily isolated, and their recombinations can be detected, even in extremely low frequency, by a selective technique. When two mutants are crossed, one expects that some "wild" type organisms will be obtained as a result of the recombination of the genetic material after crossing over has taken place. The reciprocal recombinant, containing both mutational alternations, also occurs. The results of crosses involving a group of mutants can be plotted on a diagram where each mutant is represented by a point, thus giving a chromosome map. Virus T4, which parasitizes *E. coli*, has been mapped and behaves as a single chromosome.

The rapid reproduction of the virus and the techniques available allow the study of extremely short map distances and, in fact, even the subdivision of the gene itself. Indeed, it is now feasible to "resolve" the detailed structure of the gene down to the molecular level.

The genes are thought to be arranged in precise linear order on the chromosome, but they should not be thought of as beads on a string because there is no insulation between any two neighboring genes. The differentiation along the chromosome results from the variation of the atoms in a continuing giant chemical molecule which makes up the core of the chromosome. The essential genetic material is deoxyribonucleic acid (DNA) which extends from one end of the chromosome to the other. The variations in the structure of the DNA molecule provide the opportunity for the differences observed from one species to the next. If the configuration at one point is altered by irradiation, or some other mutant-producing agent, the organism will be different from its ancestors because of the chemical (structural) change.

It is fortunate that a well-established hypothesis is available as to the structure of the all-important DNA molecule. This is known as the Watson-Crick model, named for the biochemists who proposed the configuration in 1953. The DNA molecule consists of repeating units of smaller molecules called nucleotides, each of which contains phosphate and deoxyribose (a 5-carbon sugar), plus one of four bases—adenine, thymine, guanine, and cytosine. The phosphate and deoxyribose are linked in two chains which are coiled around a common axis to form a double helix. The two chains are joined together by hydrogen bonds connecting the nucleotide bases. (*See* Nucleic Acids). The distance from the axis of the helix to the phosphorus atoms (of the phosphates) on the outside is ten angstrom units. The unique feature of the molecule depends upon the arrangement of the bases. These are arranged perpendicular to the axis and are joined together by the hydrogen in specific pairs. Adenine always pairs with thymine, and guanine pairs with cytosine. The order of the bases within a pair varies, but the pairing must be that just given.

The linearity of the DNA structure, which can be visualized as a double spiral staircase, and the nondetermined sequence of bases fit the genetic requirements for a molecule that determines hereditary characteristics, since the genetic information can be contained in the sequence of bases which forms a linear code. It has been determined that a specific sequence of three nucleotide bases in the DNA molecule encodes for each of the approximately 20 amino acids which form the chief components of proteins. Perhaps, then, a mutation represents a mistake in the duplication of the order of the bases.

The isolation of a single gene, the one that directs the metabolism of sugar in the bacterium *E. coli*, was achieved in 1969, and in 1970 scientists accomplished the first complete chemical synthesis of a gene. This gene, 77 nucleotide pairs long, specifies the synthesis of alanine transfer RNA in yeast.

New Mutations

There is more than ample evidence that the genetic material which is transmitted from generation to generation is DNA. It is true that heredity also functions through the transmission of cytoplasmic particles (called kappa particles) in paramecia and plastids in plants. Cytoplasmic, or maternal, inheritance is intriguing but does not give promise of being of great importance in explaining the grand scale of evolutionary change.

The building blocks of evolution are the genes. New combinations of genes can produce infinite variation, but changes or mutations in the genes are the ultimate source of new variations. The specific chemical to be changed is therefore some part of a DNA molecule. In the late 1800's the German biologist August Weismann pointed out that heredity is transmitted through the germ plasm, which is well insulated against trivial environmental fluctuations. Biologists were generally unsuccessful in demonstrating the production of mutations by environmental agents, but this was due to poor techniques and not to the failure of mutations to appear. This impasse was removed by the American geneticist Hermann Muller, who devised a brilliant breeding plan for *Drosophila* which demonstrated the linear relationship between the number of mutations produced and the amount of irradiation used on the flies. This clever proof that mutations were produced by an environmental agent such as X rays earned the 1946 Nobel Prize in physiology for Professor Muller. Since that time other ionizing irradiations, various chemicals, and even heat shocks have proved to be mutagenic agents.

Muller's discovery was not only of the greatest theoretical importance, but also of immense practical importance. With irradiation, new strains of Penicillium were obtained which gave much greater yields of penicillin and thus cut the cost of the drug many-fold. Other examples of useful mutations are produced almost daily. However, the great majority of mutations which deviate from the "wild" type are harmful to the organism and are eliminated by natural selection. The rare mutation that proves to be of greater adaptive value than the "wild" type gene will spread throughout the population and will itself then become the "wild" type.

Genetic Engineering

Eugenics is the application of our knowledge of human genetics to social affairs. Numerous other terms such as euthenics and environmental engineering have been employed to indicate a manipulation of the environment in order to permit more advantageous expression of the genetic makeup, or genotype. Genetic engineering is the application of basic principles of molecular and cellular biology to the prevention of disease. Genetic engineering includes not only the manipulation of the genotype by technical means but also the replacement of proteins, vitamins, enzymes, and other substances which are abnormal in quality or quantity because of the person's heredity. Genetic counseling would often be undertaken before genetic engineering techniques were initiated.

A few of the specific therapies employed at present to correct genetic defects include the transfusion of the hemophiliac with normal blood plasma, the administration of insulin to the diabetic, and the withholding of phenylalanine-containing foods from the baby with phenylketonuria. Other techniques involve enzyme replacement in the treatment of cystic fibrosis and transfusions of Rh-immune globulin to prevent erythroblastosis—a disease which results in red-blood cell destruction—in children of high-risk mothers. The development of amniocentesis, a technique for sampling human amniotic fluid (the fluid that surrounds the fetus), permits the detection of gross chromosomal abnormalities and enzyme deficiencies as well as viral infections of the embryo in the uterus.

Speculative developments in genetic engineering include genetic surgery and clonal reproduction. Genetic surgery would involve the introduction of "normal" chromosome material in order to replace or neutralize the deleterious gene. Genetic surgery is not possible in man at present. Clonal reproduction could become a practical technique within a few years. This technique involves the propagation of cells from an individual in such a manner as to produce numerous other genetically identical persons. Fortunately, society still has time to decide if, and in what circumstances, this technique should be used.

Speculation as to how genetic engineering will develop is highly exciting but rather uncertain because the direction and results of future research defy prediction.

Consult Castle, W. E., *Note on Mr. Farabee's Observations on Heredity of Albinism in Man* (1903); Garrod, A. E., *Inborn Errors of Metabolism* (1909); Morgan, T. H., *Sex Limited Inheritance in Drosophila* (1910); Srb, A. M., and others, *General Genetics* (1965); Sonneborn, T. M. (ed.), *The Control of Human Heredity and Evolution* (1965); Carter, C. O., *An ABC of Medical Genetics* (1969).

SHELDON C. REED, Director, Dight Institute for
Human Genetics, University of Minnesota
See also CELL; CHROMOSOME; EVOLUTION; GENE; LIFE; MUTATION.

GENEVA (Fr. **GENEVE**), city of southwestern Switzerland, located on the western end of Lake Geneva, where the Rhône River emerges from the lake. The river, spanned by eight bridges, bisects the heart of the city, placing the old town on the left bank, and the modern, residential community on the right. To the south can be seen a distant view of Mont Blanc, and along the shores of the lake are luxurious resorts. Toward the west is the Jura mountain range, and on the south and east, Mont Salva. Long, narrow, winding streets lined with 17th- and 18th-century houses characterize the old town and small attractive shops are scattered throughout. On the highest point of the

Seen from across the Mont Blanc Bridge, the towers of the 13th-century Cathedral of St. Pierre rise over the old section of Geneva on the left bank of the Rhône River. (ASSOCIATION DES INTÉRÊTS DE GENÈVE)

old town stands the 13th-century Cathedral of St. Pierre. Promenades, sidewalk cafes, and landscaped parks add to the city's beauty.

More important than Geneva's scenic wonders, however, is its international significance. The activities of the International Red Cross have been centered in Geneva since 1864. From 1920 Geneva was the headquarters of the League of Nations, and since 1946 the buildings occupied by the League have been used as the European headquarters of the United Nations. The World Health Organization, the International Labor Office, and the European Organization for Nuclear Research, organized in 1952, are also here. Watchmaking has been the city's principal industry since 1587, but there are also important manufactures of jewelry, gold and silverware, electric machinery, precision instruments, chocolate, and furniture. The city is an international financial center and has a large airport at suburban Cointrin.

The University of Geneva, founded by John Calvin in 1559 as the Academy of Geneva, is especially famous for its schools of medicine and theology. The city also has academies of art and music, a museum of art and natural history, and botanical and zoological gardens.

The site of the city was settled in ancient times and was first recorded under the name Geneva by Julius Caesar in 58 A.D. It belonged to the kingdom of Burgundy in the 5th century and later passed to the Holy Roman Empire. During the 12th century it was ruled by its Bishops, and in the 13th century the city attained the right of municipal government. Its citizens accepted the Reformation, as preached by John Calvin and Guillaume Farel, in 1536 and it became the center of Protestantism. Napoleonic armies entered Switzerland in 1798 and Geneva was annexed to France. The Congress of Vienna (1814) restored the city's independence, and it became the capital of the newly created canton of Geneva. In 1815 the city joined the Swiss Confederation. Geneva became an influential cultural center during the 18th century; the French philosopher Voltaire was a frequent visitor and Jean Jacques Rousseau was born here. The Geneva Convention (1864) provided for an international agreement designed to lessen the needless suffering of soldiers in war. The agreement was revised and improved by another convention in 1906. After World War I Geneva, for two decades, was the focus of hopes for peace as the world followed the deliberations of the League of Nations. Geneva was the site of the "Summit Conference" of 1955, with the heads of state of Great Britain, France, the Soviet Union, and the United States participating. Pop., 176,183.

ROY MILLWARD, The University, Leicester, England

GENEVA, city of northeastern Illinois and seat of Kane County, located in the Fox River Valley. Foundry products, auto parts, steel kitchen equipment, and timers and switches are manufactured, and the city is also an agricultural center. Settled in the early 1830's; inc., 1887; pop., 9,115.

GENEVA, city of west-central New York, in the Finger Lakes region, at the north end of Seneca Lake. The city manufactures canning machinery, radiators, and optical equipment, and is the seat of the Colleges of the Seneca and a state agricultural experiment station. Settled, 1788; inc. as village, 1812; as city, 1898; pop., 16,793.

GENEVA, city of northeastern Ohio, southwest of Ashtabula. Manufactures include building hardware, plywood containers, forgings, and sports equipment. Founded, 1805; inc., 1866; pop., 6,449.

GENEVA, LAKE (Fr. **LAC LÉMAN**), lake in southwestern Switzerland and eastern France. The largest lake in central Europe, covering an area of 225 sq. mi., it is 45 mi. long and from 1½ to 9 mi. wide. Lake Geneva is formed by the Rhône River, which flows into it on the east and leaves the lake at the city of Geneva at the west end. The lake is divided into two parts, Grand Lac and Petit Lac, by the strait of Promenthoux. Important towns along the lake besides Geneva are Nyon, Lausanne, and Vevey in Switzerland, and Thonon-les-Bains in France.

GENEVA, UNIVERSITY OF, Swiss institution founded by John Calvin in 1559 as the Schola Genevensis, a seminary for instruction in theology and pedagogy. It was established as a university in 1873, and a medical faculty was added in 1876. Its school of dentistry (1882) was the first in Europe. The university has faculties of sciences, arts, economics and social sciences, law, medicine (including dentistry), Protestant theology, and 40 specialized institutes. Emphasizing its international character are its school for interpreters (1940) and its affiliated Graduate Institute of International Studies. It is the largest of the six Swiss universities. Annual student enrollment in 1961 totalled about 4,300 (3,650 full-time and 650 part-time). The proportion of students from other countries (almost 60%, chiefly from Germany, France, Italy, and the United States) is probably the highest found in any university in the world. The many international organizations having headquarters in Geneva are doubtless a contributing factor.

GENGHIS KHAN [jĕng'gĭs kän'], also known as Jenghiz, Jinghis, Chinghiz, Chingis, or Chinggis, original name Temujin (1155?–1227), famous Mongol conqueror. In the words of Rashid al-Din, 13th-14th-century Persian historian: ". . . Genghis Khan was sovereign seigneur of the conjunction of the planets, autocrat of land and time; all Mongolian clans, related and otherwise, have become his slaves and servants." Genghis organized an empire as well as invincible armies; promulgated a legal code, the *jasagh*, known also in its Turkish form, *yasa*; and struck terror

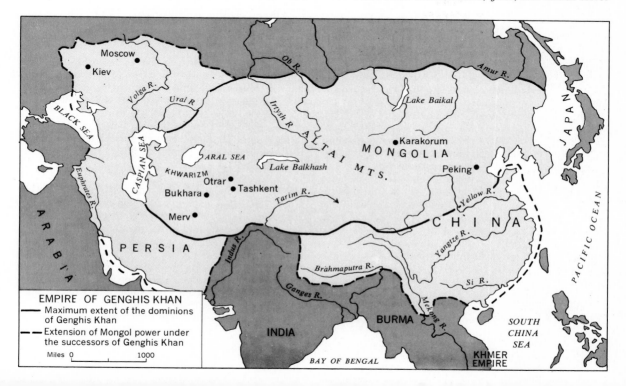

EMPIRE OF GENGHIS KHAN
— Maximum extent of the dominions of Genghis Khan
- - - Extension of Mongol power under the successors of Genghis Khan
Miles 0   1000

into the world of the 13th century. His famed tolerance and wisdom, and—considering the standards of his day—his fair treatment of enemies, won him wide respect.

Genghis Khan's clan, the Borjigid, suffered defeat at the hands of a Tatar tribe, and the young Temujin possessed little power or promise of reasserting the clan's authority. But through adversity and allegedly with the assistance of his forceful mother, he gradually reconstituted his own tribe and defeated others. In 1202 he took revenge on the Tatars, who had defeated the Mongols and poisoned his father. In 1209 Genghis sent his eldest son, Juchi, or Juji, against the Oirats (Western Mongols) and the Kirgiz, and his best general, Subotai, fought in the Altai Mountains in Central Asia. Juchi, along with another son of Genghis, Jagatai, then invaded north China. All this, however, still fitted the old pattern of Central Asian relations, which were traditionally marked by nomadic expansion on settled lands, followed by a withdrawal of the nomads.

An event in 1218 sparked Genghis Khan's latent military genius: the Khwarizm Shah, who was Turkic and Muslim master of Turkestan, Afghanistan, and Persia, massacred Mongolian merchants and envoys at Otrar (near Tashkent), even though these particular Mongols themselves professed the Muslim faith. In revenge, Genghis Khan in 1219 personally led a Mongolian army of 70,000, supported by some 130,000 allies, to Bukhara, which he besieged in 1220. For a time Genghis remained at Bukhara, then returned to Mongolia in 1225. Meanwhile the army divided: part, under Subotai, crossed the Amu Darya in pursuit of the Shah of Khwarizm and continued into the Caucasus and south Russian steppes, laying the foundation of empire. But Genghis himself died in 1227 in north China, in what later became Kansu Province; his remains were carried back to Khalkha Mongolia.

In 1229 the *khuriltai*, or congress of Princes, met to choose Genghis' son Ogodai as his successor. At the *khuriltai*, Batu, the son of Genghis' eldest son, Juchi, received the *ulus*, or territory, of western Turkestan and southern Siberia. Jagatai received eastern Turkestan; Ogodai, the Altai–Lake Balkhash area. The fourth son, Tului, inherited his father's "home"—the valleys of the Kerulen, Onon, and Tula Gol rivers. Until 1259, when Tului's son, Mangu, died, the empire remained united and accepted central direction, but after that was divided and split.

Many stories surround the romantic figure of Genghis Khan. Legend claims he came into the world with clotted blood in his hand, while eagles circled above, screaming, "Genghis! Genghis!" His banner was hung with nine white horsetails since he reputedly possessed only nine horses before his rise to power. Genghis' death, allegedly in Ejen Khoro in Inner Mongolia (Kansu Province), led to the later development of a "Genghis Khan cult" in that area, and his supposed relics and remains have been guarded there for centuries. Recently the People's Republic of China erected a Genghis Khan mausoleum in Ejen Khoro. It seems quite definite, however, that Genghis Khan's body was in fact returned to Mongolia and buried in a secret place in the area of the Onon and Kerulen rivers, in northeastern Khalkha Mongolia.

Most later political movements in Mongolia, even in the 20th century, claimed to represent actual or symbolic rebirths of Genghis Khan, the reconstitution of the glorious empire of old.

Consult Lamb, Harold, *Genghis Khan, the Emperor of All Men* (1927); Vladimirtsov, Boris, *The Life of Chingis-Khan* (1930); Martin, H. D., *The Rise of Chingis Khan and His Conquest of North China* (1950).

ROBERT A. RUPEN, University of North Carolina
See also MONGOLS.

GENIE. *See* JINNI OR GENIE.

GENIUS [jēn'yəs], in ancient Roman religion, a protective spirit that attached itself to a man, corporation, community, or place. The name, meaning "begetter," indicates that originally the genius was a family spirit, active at each birth and marriage of a member. The classical Romans believed that every man had his individual genius, born with and always protecting him, like the Greek personal daemon or the guardian angel, and every woman had a personal Juno. A man took oath on his genius. Later the genius was identified with the Manes, or the spirits of the dead. Under the Empire the Emperor's genius (*Genius Augusti*) became a powerful deity, ruling all genii as Caesar ruled all men, and received offerings of food, drink, and incense, as did lesser genii also.

GENIUS, an individual with extraordinary creative talent in some area of intellectual or artistic ability. Geniuses are difficult to define statistically or in terms of psychological tests. In general they are individuals who with respect to any esteemed ability fall, when ranked according to some order of merit, among the topmost minute per cent of the population—perhaps 1 in 10,000. Persons with intelligence quotients over 140 have sometimes been classified as near genius, but this is a misappropriation of the ordinary use of the term "genius." Even an I.Q. of 160 does not proclaim a genius; the classification depends on what factors go with the superior intellectual ability.
See also EDUCATION: *Education of Exceptional Children;* INTELLIGENCE.

GENJI MONOGATARI [gĕn-jē mō-nō-gä-tä-rē] (*The Tale of Genji*), greatest work of Japanese prose fiction, written by Lady Murasaki Shikibu probably in the early 11th century. A long and discursive narrative of life at the feudal court of the Emperor of Japan, it features the amorous intrigues of Prince Genji. The work both in length and in literary merit far surpasses earlier and later examples of the genre. An English translation by Arthur Waley appeared in 1935.

GENOA [jĕn'ō-ə] (Ital. **GENOVA**), city on the Gulf of Genoa, the major seaport of Italy and gateway to the Italian Riviera. Italy's fifth-largest city, it is the capital of the Province of Genoa and of the region of Liguria. Genoa and Marseilles, France, are the two major Mediterranean ports of Europe. Genoa's economic life is contingent on the activity of its port, the outlet for northern Italy and much of central Europe. Rice, wine, silk, olive oil, soap, marble, and automobiles are important exports; coal, wheat, oil, hides, chemicals, machinery, and iron are the chief imports. During World War II much of the old port

A modern ocean liner at Genoa. The port, badly damaged during World War II, has been rebuilt.

was destroyed; but, in 1954, its rebuilding was completed and the port was handling more traffic than ever before. Iron, steel, and cement works, as well as other industrial plants, grain silos, oil refineries, and shipyards line the port area. Genoa is also a financial and banking center.

The city is a maze of narrow, winding, and sloping streets, on one of which Christopher Columbus was born. It is a mixture of old and new: skyscrapers rise in the middle of the city dominating the old buildings. Among the palaces are the Ducal Palace, once residence of the doges and now a courthouse, and the 16th-century Doria Palace. The Reale, Rosso, and Bianco palaces are art galleries, and the municipal Tursi Palace contains Nicolò Paganini's violin and letters of Columbus besides art treasures. Among the many churches are San Donato and the 12th-century Cathedral of San Lorenzo with its striking black and white marble façade. The Cemetery of Staglieno has some of the most impressive monuments in the world. Genoa's university was founded in the 13th century.

Genoa's history dates to before the founding of Rome. At the end of the 3d century B.C., it became a Roman *municipium*. By the 11th century A.D. it had become a republic embarking on great maritime expansion. With the end of the Crusades Genoa's naval and colonial power had reached its peak. The Genoese empire extended to Constantinople, the Greek Archipelago, North Africa, and Spain. The city, however, was in the throes of constant internal strife among ambitious families. Outside powers were finally summoned and Genoa passed to Milan and then to France. In 1528, the Genoese hero Andrea Doria finally drove out the French and re-established the republic, but Genoa's maritime power was declining. Turkey had conquered Constantinople, and much Mediterranean trade had shifted to the Atlantic. In 1797, it was occupied by Napoleon and incorporated into Liguria; in 1805 it was annexed to France. When, in 1815, the Congress of Vienna made Genoa part of the Kingdom of Sardinia, there followed several unsuccessful uprisings, among the leaders of which was the republican Giuseppe Mazzini. In 1861, Genoa joined the Kingdom of Italy. Under dictator Benito Mussolini, the Genoese were mostly anti-Fascist. Later underground movements against the Nazis culminated in a rebellion forcing the Germans to surrender (Apr., 1945). The Republic of Italy later conferred the highest military medal upon the entire city. Pop., 784,194.

ANNA CROGNALE HANSEN, Italian Institute of
Culture, New York

GENOCIDE [jĕn'ə-sĭd], decimation or extermination of a racial, ethnic, religious, or nationality group by a more powerful co-occupant of a territory. The most carefully premeditated and deliberate instance of this type of "population policy" was the attempt by Nazi Germany to exterminate the Jews before and during World War II.

The term "genocide" was first used by Raphael Lemkin, the Polish-American jurist, in his work *Axis Rule in Occupied Europe* (1944), based on a collection of documents relating to Axis atrocities in Europe during World War II.

On Dec. 11, 1946, the U.N. General Assembly declared genocide an international crime and Lemkin was appointed to the committee which drafted the Genocide Convention. The actual *Convention on the Punishment of the Crime of Genocide*, which was adopted Dec. 9, 1948, and became effective Jan. 12, 1951, declared genocide a crime under international law. The contracting parties undertook to pass necessary legislation, complete with sanctions against genocide, to make the offense punishable in national courts and to classify the crime so that extradition was possible for those accused in foreign countries. The convention defined genocide as "any of the following acts committed with intent to destroy in whole or in part, a national, ethnical, racial, or religious group as such." The important words are "intent" and "destroy"; no action, however destructive, is considered genocide unless it is deliberate.

The punishable acts of genocide enumerated in Article II of the convention include killing members of the group; causing serious bodily or mental harm to members of the group; deliberately inflicting on the group conditions of life calculated to bring about its physical destruction in whole or in part; imposing measures intended to prevent births within the group, such as sterilization, separation of spouses, and prohibitions against marriage; and forcibly transferring children from the group.

The objective of the U.N. convention is to embody in international law the moral principle that intergroup differences based on race, religion, political beliefs, or culture should be resolved by mutual accommodation or assimilation.

No changes have been made in the convention since 1951. By the early 1960's, 64 states, including the Soviet Union but not the United States, had ratified the convention. Although genocide is punishable under international law, there is no specific code of offenses or any qualified body authorized to enforce it, so that the convention is limited by national applications and interpretations.

Consult Drost, P. N., *The Crime of the State* (1959).

DONALD J. BOGUE, University of Chicago

GENRE PAINTING [zhän'rə], painting whose subject matter consists of realistic, commonplace scenes and objects from everyday life. A French term first used with reference to 18th-century painting, the style actually had culminated a century earlier in Holland in the works of Vermeer, Hals, Steen, and others. In France it was exemplified by Chardin. Genre has remained popular with artists down to modern times, for example, in the work of the American realist painters who worked in New York City early in this century.

GENS [*jĕnz*], in ancient Rome, a clan or group of families supposedly descended from a common ancestor, particularly old landowning families who from early days shared cult ceremonies (*sacra gentilicia*). Members of the same gens had a common burial place, and, under the Republic, in the absence of direct male relatives, they inherited on intestacy. In Roman nomenclature the *nomen gentilicium*, or the common name borne by all members of the gens, came in second place in a man's name, for example, Julius in the name of Gaius Julius Caesar. Freedmen received the family's *nomen gentilicium* and perhaps the right to participate in certain religious rites, but they did not become part of the gens.

GENSERIC [*gĕn'sə-rĭk*] **or GAISERIC** [*gī'zə-rĭk*] (d.477), King of the Vandals (reigned 428–77). The ablest of the German leaders of the time, Genseric led his people from Spain to Africa (429) on the invitation of the Roman general Bonifacius. When he had become established in Africa, Genseric defeated Bonifacius, and in 439 captured Carthage. He developed Vandal maritime power, made an alliance with Attila in 450, and by 455 was supreme in Africa, Sardinia, and Corsica. By 476 he had conquered Sicily. When the Empress Eudoxia appealed to him for help against the Emperor Maximus, he sailed for Rome and sacked the city for 14 days with the "vandalism" which has become proverbial (455). After Genseric's death the power of the Vandals declined.

GENTIAN [*jĕn'shən*], name for about 400 species of annual, biennial, and perennial herbs of the genus *Gentiana* in the gentian family, Gentianaceae. Native to Europe, Asia, and North America, gentians are chiefly found in cool, moist habitats, especially in mountainous regions. The plants bear showy flowers, usually blue in color, but some species have white, red, yellow, or purple blossoms. Among the more popular species are *G. crinita*, the fringed gentian, native to North America; *G. andrewsii*, the closed or bottle gentian, also native to North America and especially easy to grow in cool, moist habitats; and *G. tibetica*, a yellow-flowering species native to the Himalayas. Gentians are propagated by seeds, cuttings, or division. Most species thrive in very moist soil. Gentians make excellent rock garden or wild-flower garden plants, and some species are well suited to border plantings.

GENTILE [*jän-tē'lā*], **GIOVANNI** (1875–1944), Italian philosopher and educator. Born at Castelvetrano, he studied at the University of Pisa and first became known as the student and associate of Benedetto Croce. He taught philosophy at the University of Rome, and with Croce edited *La Critica*, a journal of philosophical and literary criticism, until 1922. Then, associating himself with the Mussolini regime, he became one of the foremost exponents of the philosophy of fascism. As Minister of Education in the Fascist government (1922–24) he initiated wholesale reforms in the Italian educational system, and became president of the Supreme Council of Education (1926–28). He was planner and editor of the *Enciclopedia Italiana* from 1925 to 1943, when he became president of the Italian Academy. In Apr., 1944, he was killed by anti-Fascist partisans. Gentile's philosophy greatly emphasized the all-powerful, totalitarian state, in whose interest the individual might well be sacrificed. His philosophical views were largely embodied in the development of the Fascist Corporate State, which he helped to create.

CARL COHEN, University of Michigan

GENTILE DA FABRIANO [*dä fä-brē-ä'nō*] (c.1370–c.1427), Italian painter, one of the founders of the Umbrian school. A practitioner of the so-called International Style, the type of painting that was widespread in the late Gothic era, Gentile delighted in splendor and rich ornamentation, though his coloring shows refinement and subtlety. His most famous work is "The Adoration of the Magi," in the Uffizi in Florence. Many of his panel paintings have survived and are in collections in Europe and America. He exerted a strong influence on later painters, especially Pisanello.

GENTILES [*jĕn'tīlz*], word in the Bible usually meaning "non-Jews," though the Greek word it translates can equally well mean "nations." Some Old Testament prophets recognized that God is God not just of Jews, but of all people (Isa. 42:6; 56:7). Nevertheless, Jewish exclusiveness persisted. Even Jesus, while proclaiming a gospel for all the world (Matt. 28:19; Acts 1:8), seems sometimes to have favored Jews over Gentiles (Matt. 6:32; 10:5f.; 15:24; 20:19,25). Among Jesus' followers, Paul was one of the earliest to assert that Gentiles might come into the Church on an equal footing with Jewish Christians. Among Mormons, the term is used to designate non-Mormons.

GENUS. See ANIMAL: *Classification of Animals*.

GEOCHEMISTRY [*jē-ō-kĕm'ĭs-trē*], application of the principles and techniques of chemistry to the solution of geological problems. The science is divided into several branches, according to the materials studied.

Lithogeochemistry deals with the chemistry of the rocks that constitute the solid part of the earth. Essentially, it is the chemistry of the earth's crust, because only crustal rocks have been available for study. Only recently have men attempted to obtain samples from the mantle—the layer occurring immediately beneath the crust. Lithogeochemistry seeks to determine the composition and abundance of the various kinds of rocks and minerals and to explain their origin. The average composition of the earth's crust is given in the accompanying table.

Element	% by Weight
Oxygen	46.60
Silicon	27.72
Aluminum	8.13
Iron	5.00
Calcium	3.63
Sodium	2.83
Potassium	2.59
Magnesium	2.09
All others	1.41
Total	100.00

Hydrogeochemistry is concerned primarily with the waters of the earth—the rivers, lakes, and oceans, and the subsurface water in the pores of rocks and soil. It also includes the study of the role of water in the formation, alteration, and erosion of rocks and minerals. To this extent hydrogeochemistry coincides with lithogeochemistry.

Atmogeochemistry deals with the composition of the atmosphere and its changes with locality and time. The atmosphere is an important agent in the weathering and erosion of rocks and minerals, and studies of the chemistry of the air necessarily overlap lithogeochemistry.

Biogeochemistry, or organic geochemistry, is the study of life processes as they affect the earth. Many important geological deposits, such as limestone, petroleum and natural gas, coal, sulfur, some sedimentary iron ores, and some silica deposits (diatomaceous earth) are formed largely or entirely by the action of living organisms. In order to explain and understand the formation of such deposits, it is necessary to understand the chemical behavior of the organisms involved.

Cosmochemistry attempts to determine the composition of extraterrestrial bodies such as comets, planets, the moon, the sun, and other stars. It also analyzes the composition of meteorites, which fall to earth from space. Though not strictly a part of geochemistry, cosmochemistry relates to it in two important ways: (1) The more that is known about the composition of the universe, the better chance there is to formulate a correct theory concerning the formation of the earth. (2) The study of meteorites is a help in understanding the earth's interior, since meteorites are thought to be analogous to layers deep in the earth. Information about the earth's core is obtained from nickel-iron meteorites, and stony meteorites provide data on the mantle.

Applications. When the term was first coined by the German chemist Friedrich Schönbein in 1838, geochemistry involved little more than an attempt to determine by analytical chemistry the abundance and distribution of chemical elements in the earth's crust. Gradually the science grew to include methods and principles of physical, organic, and crystal chemistry, each contributing to our understanding of the distribution of elements in nature. More recently geochemistry has helped to solve many problems, such as the origin of mineral deposits and the age of the earth. For example, the temperature of formation of a zinc deposit is indicated by the amount of iron in zinc sulfide; and the age of a uranium mineral can be computed from the amount of lead it contains.

Geochemical prospecting locates deposits of metals by studying distribution patterns of compounds of the metals in rocks, soils, water, and plants. Similar techniques are employed in searching for petroleum and natural gas. Geochemistry is also helpful in metallurgical problems, especially the locating and recovery of rare elements. Increasingly it contributes to the solution of nutritional problems. For example, geochemical studies demonstrated that a cattle disease in the western United States, attributed to excess alkali, was actually caused by selenium in soil overlying certain geological formations. Similarly, the causes of deficient plant nutrition are discovered by geochemical studies of soils and of the rocks from which the soils are formed.

EARL INGERSON

See also ATMOSPHERE; CHEMISTRY; EARTH; GEOLOGY; HYDROLOGY; METEOROLOGY; MINERALOGY; PETROLOGY; ROCKS.

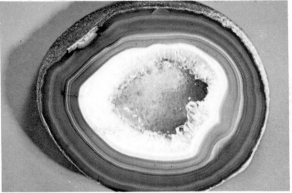
Katherine H. Jensen

Geode of onyx-banded agate

GEODE [jē′ōd], hollow body of rock partly filled with mineral crystals, usually quartz, growing inward from the walls. Geodes are nearly spherical, and they may be more than a foot in diameter. Most have walls of chalcedony, a microcrystalline quartz mineral, although some consist entirely of calcite. Usually they occur in limestone.

GEODESIC [jē-ə-dĕs′ĭk], in mathematics, curve of shortest length connecting two points of a surface and lying wholly on the surface; for example, an arc of a great circle joining two points of the surface of a sphere. On a surface of revolution, the meridians are geodesics; when a straight line lies on a curved surface such as a cone, the line is a geodesic for the surface. In Einstein's geometry of space-time, the path of each planet is a geodesic.

GEODESIC DOME, structural framework (or space frame) in the shape of a dome or sphere. It is formed from short, straight struts fastened into a gridwork of triangular geometric shapes and their combinations (tetrahedrons, or 4-faced shapes, and icosahedrons or 20-faced shapes). These frames may be covered with a lightweight surfacing material (aluminum, plastic, canvas) to make a building that is strong, lightweight, low in cost, and speedily erected. They have been used for banks, factories, amusement and civic centers, and for military installations.

The geodesic dome was developed by the American designer-inventor R. Buckminster Fuller, who received U.S. patents on the geodesic system in 1954.

GEODESY [jē-ŏd′ə-sē], science concerned with the size and shape of the earth. The shape of the earth is approximately that of an oblate spheroid (a flattened sphere). This is because of the earth's rotation which leads to a slight bulging at the equator and corresponding flattening at the poles. The theoretical sea-level surface, however, deviates somewhat from the shape of a spheroid. This theoretical surface is called the geoid. It coincides approximately with mean sea level, or with the extension of sea level under land areas. The geoid is everywhere perpendicular to the pull of gravity.

The geoid deviates from a mathematical spheroid because the direction of the force of gravity at any point is influenced not only by the over-all form of the earth, but by variations in topography and by the irregular distribution of mass below the earth's surface. For example, a plumb line (which indicates the direction of gravity) that is set up near a mountain is attracted by the mass of the mountain. Similarly, a plumb line set up near a large valley may be deflected slightly away from the depression. The geoid, therefore, undulates slightly from place to place.

Geodetic surveying requires the use of a smooth mathematical surface, or datum, from which elevations can be computed. This surface should match the geoid as closely as possible. In 1924 the International Union of Geodesy and Geophysics adopted such a reference surface, called the international ellipsoid, for use in geodetic computations. In areas where the geoid deviates significantly from the reference ellipsoid, the amount of deviation may be computed from careful measurements of the force and direction of gravity. The international ellipsoid has an equatorial diameter of 12 756.78 km (7,921.96 mi) and a polar diameter of 12 713.82 km (7,895.28 mi). The difference is 42.95 km, or 26.68 mi.

Measuring the Earth. The earliest successful attempt to measure the size of the earth was made by the Greek astronomer Eratosthenes in the 3d century B.C. Assuming the earth to be spherical, Eratosthenes computed the difference in latitude between Alexandria and Syene (Aswan), Egypt, by noting the difference in the direction of the sun's midday rays at each city during the summer solstice, when the sun is directly overhead at Syene. By measuring the distance between the two cities he was able to convert a degree of latitude to a unit of distance. This enabled him to compute the earth's circumference by multiplying the unit distance by 360, the number of degrees in a full circle. Although the exact value of his distance units is not known, his result is estimated to have been correct to within 20%.

In measuring distances and computing the size of the earth, contemporary geodesists use triangulation. Their measurements are supplemented by star observations and radio time signals to check exact latitude and longitude. Elevations are determined with the help of such instruments as spirit levels, working inland from base stations near the sea.

Consult Bomford, Guy, *Geodesy* (1971); Ewing, C. E., and Mitchell, M. M., *Introduction to Geodesy* (1970); Heiskanen, Weikko, and Moritz, H., *Physical Geodesy* (1969); Veis, G., ed., *Use of Artificial Satellites for Geodesy* (1963).   K. E. BULLEN
See also GEOPHYSICS; GRAVITY; ISOSTASY; SEA LEVEL; SURVEYING.

GEOFFREY OF MONMOUTH

GEOFFREY OF MONMOUTH [jĕf′rē; mŏn′məth] (c.1100–1154), English writer and historian. His works, written in Latin, are the *Prophecies of Merlin* (c.1135), the *Life of Merlin* (1148–51), and most important, the *History of the Kings of Britain*, which purported to be a chronicle of the Kings of Britain from the legendary Brutus to Cadwallader, King of Wessex. Based largely on Nennius, Welsh genealogies, and Geoffrey's imagination, the *History*, translated first into Anglo-Norman and later into English, was the source for the medieval Arthurian legends, in which much of Arthur's prestige was derived from Geoffrey's account of his victories. Since the *History* also included the story of Lear, it had immense later literary influence.

GEOGRAPHY [jē-ŏg′rə-fē], the study and interpretation of the distribution of phenomena on the face of the earth. Geography has also been defined as the study of the earth's surface and of man's relationship to his environment. The phenomena examined may be physical, such as climates, landforms, and soils; or human (cultural), such as religions, population densities, and transportation routes. Since the types of such phenomena are numberless, geography is preferably defined in terms of this concept of distribution rather than of content.

Any feature of the earth's surface that has unequal distribution is subject to geographic study. In order adequately to understand, explain, and describe any one topic—the distribution of population in a given region, for example—it is usually necessary to study other topics as well. For this reason geography is a subject for interrelations and associations of a high order. The ultimate in geographic competence is the ability to integrate numerous facts in such a way as to describe meaningfully the true nature of the area under study (regional geography). The area with which the geographer deals may range from the entire world to small areas of topographic scale.

Geography employs maps to a greater degree than does any other field of study.

Development. The concept of the earth as a sphere is most often credited to the Greek philosopher Aristotle. He determined this by using a combination of philosophical reasoning and direct astronomical observation. His theory was supported by Eratosthenes of Alexandria (c.276–c.194 B.C.), who employed a geometric procedure to ascertain a close approximation of the circumference of the earth.

Ptolemy (fl.2d century A.D.), another Alexandrian, also made significant contributions to mathematical geography, but unfortunately many of his calculations were in error. He did, however, construct a map of the world that, considering the information available at the time, displayed remarkable accuracy. He also established a hierarchy of area study, ranging from the general study of large areas (chorography) to the detailed study of small areas (topography).

The Roman geographer Strabo was an outstanding describer of classical lands and peoples. He realized the disadvantage of describing the earth in terms of political divisions and substituted instead more real and lasting regional divisions based on natural boundaries such as mountain and drainage systems.

The development of geography as an academic subject was retarded, as were other divisions of knowledge, during the Middle Ages. This period, however, did witness certain developments in commerce and exploration. Trading interest in the Mediterranean lands was sustained. The so-called Portolan charts were produced by the mercantile states of this inland sea to facilitate navigation. Constructed by compass triangulation, these charts are almost as accurate as present-day charts of the Mediterranean. The writings of Marco Polo helped the few 14th-century cartographers who mapped parts of Asia.

During the 15th century, Ptolemy's maps were rediscovered, and the most serious cartographic errors of the Middle Ages were corrected. The great age of exploration soon followed, and maps of the world were speedily

To the layman, "geography" suggests the study of countries, cities, rivers, and mountains, but the term actually includes much more. Not only do geographers study all of the features of the earth's surface, but they are also concerned with how these phenomena affect man and how man adapts himself to them.

The article on these pages traces the history of geographic studies from the time of Aristotle to the 20th century and then surveys American contributions to geography. The article also discusses three major divisions of geographic study.

Systematic, or Topical, Studies. These include the following:

Physical geography, which is concerned with landforms, soils, water, and climates.

Biogeography, which deals with the distribution of plants and animals, and medical geography.

Cultural, or human, geography, which includes such fields as population and settlement geography, economic geography, political geography, historical geography, and military geography.

Regional Studies. Regional geography is the study of areas in which certain related phenomena appear.

Cartography. Map projections; types of maps.

A number of articles elsewhere in this Encyclopedia shed light on the work of the geographer. Of outstanding interest is MAP, which discusses cartography more thoroughly than is possible in the main article on geography. The treatment of maps includes scales, projections —cylindrical, conic, and azimuthal—and the history of maps, which provides details of the history of geography.

The relation of geography to other fields can be exemplified by referring to the article GEOMORPHOLOGY, which deals with the branch of geology that studies landforms. Geomorphology is closely related to physical geography, but there are important distinctions. The geologist, for one thing, goes beyond the scope of geography in that he studies the origins of mountains, volcanoes, basins, and other features. Biogeography is closely linked with the biological science described in ECOLOGY.

The application of geographic knowledge to problems of national strategy is the subject of GEOPOLITICS.

---

improved. In rapid succession the Portuguese, Spanish, French, and British sought out the new lands. The German cartographer Martin Waldseemüller constructed a map in 1507 that clearly indicated North and South America. The circumnavigation of the globe (1522) by the expedition of the Spaniard Ferdinand Magellan confirmed the roundness of the earth.

This event coincided with the birth of modern map making. Gerhardus Mercator in the 16th century constructed a wide array of maps and globes based on accurate astronomical and earth measurements, as well as on information from explorers. His activity represented just one step in the evolution of accurate and detailed mapping, recording, and cataloging of phenomena on the earth's surface.

The rebirth of geography as an academic study occurred in the middle of the 17th century. In 1650, *Geographia Generalis*, written by a German, Bernhardus Varenius, was published; it established the concepts of systematic, or topical, and regional geography. This work considered the distribution of a number of topics over the earth's surface and attempted to interrelate their

cause and effect. Unfortunately Varenius died before producing his work on "special geography" that was to consist of the regional description of different areas of the world.

Immanuel Kant, the 18th-century German philosopher, developed the systematic classification of physical phenomena employed by Varenius and incorporated the material into a lecture course on physical geography at the University of Königsberg. Kant realized that the classification and study of distributions over the surface of the earth could also be applied to human as well as to physical topics. This encouraged the development of systematic (topical) geography.

Classical Period. The classical period in geography began in the first half of the 19th century, primarily as a result of the contributions of Alexander von Humboldt and Karl Ritter. They were both German geographers resident in Berlin, yet neither was trained as a professional geographer. Humboldt was in government service the greater part of his life, but he spent the period from 1799 to 1804 on a scientific expedition to tropical America and in 1829 traveled widely in central Asia. On the

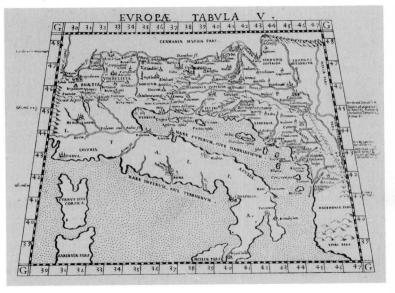

Map of part of Europe from the works of Ptolemy, printed in Italy in 1561. After the rediscovery of Ptolemy's geographic works in the early 15th century, numerous editions with contemporary maps added were printed in Europe and had a great influence on European geographic thought.

Argosy Gallery

Two eminent geographers. Left, Gerhardus Mercator (1512–94), and William Morris Davis (1850–1934).

basis of his travels and studies he wrote his best-known work, *Kosmos* (5 vols., 1845–62). Humboldt's fame rests on his ability to gather, classify, and synthesize facts. His approach emphasized topical rather than regional distinctions, and he tended to stress physical geography.

Ritter's emphasis was on regional organization, and he seemed to have little interest in topical studies as such. Although his primary concern was with human rather than physical geography, he did draw heavily upon the works of Humboldt. Ritter's major work, *Erdkunde*, was first published in two volumes in 1817 and 1818. Although it was designed to be a regional description of the world, it dealt primarily with Asia and part of Africa.

Humboldt and Ritter both died in 1859, and the next few decades in Germany were characterized by various deviations from Ritter's emphasis on regional and human geography. Possibly as a result of the tremendous advances being made in the natural sciences, geographers of this period felt the need to make geography more scientific and precise. The result was a strong trend toward physical systematic geography.

Although not all studies were restricted to physical geography, most were based on the idea that physical factors fundamentally determined man's behavior. Friedrich Ratzel, a German geographer, published his work, *Anthropogeographie*, in two volumes (1882, 1891). The first volume implied that the physical environment definitely limited man's social and economic activities. The second volume presented a much more humanistic approach—that is, that man's activities are determined by his attitudes, objectives, and technical abilities, and the physical environment is but a stage on which he operates. The early publication of his first volume assured its wide circulation, and this seed of environmental determinism quickly spread to the New World.

At the same time, however, Élisée Reclus, who during his student days attended some of Ritter's lectures in Berlin, carried the regional humanistic method to France and perpetuated it in his 19-volume *Géographie Universelle*. Paul Vidal de la Blache, another French geographer, is credited with elevating regional descriptive geography to its zenith and with being a stalwart supporter of the humanistic approach. He initiated a new

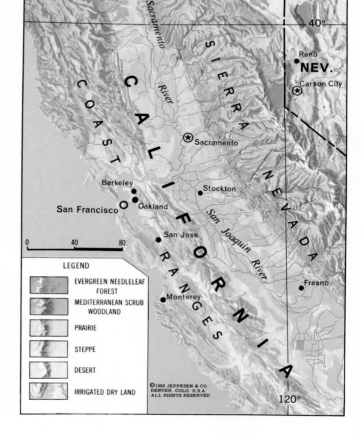

The map is the primary tool of the geographer and is used for plotting, studying, and interpreting the variety of distributions of phenomena with which he deals. On this and the facing page are three maps of the same landscape, each designed to reveal a different aspect of the physical characteristics of the area or some aspect of man's use of it.

Géographie Universelle series that attained world renown. His most famous student, Jean Brunhes, wrote a classic and widely read work entitled *La Géographie Humaine* (1910). In Germany, during this period, the regional and human approach was revived and nurtured by Alfred Hettner.

American Geographers. Since early in the 20th century, American geographers have played an active role in the development of modern geography, and the field has emerged gradually but steadily as a recognized branch of learning in the United States.

The Association of American Geographers was formed in 1904. William Morris Davis, its first president, was a geomorphologist who claimed to be a geographer rather than a geologist. This claim, from an astute and recognized scholar, helped to place geography in a strong position in American universities.

At this time the emphasis was on physical geography and in particular on geomorphology, the study of the formation of landforms and their distribution and significance to man. It is not surprising that geography was, for many years, regarded as an offshoot of geology. To this day a significant number of geography departments in colleges in the United States are combined with geology departments.

Divergence from this initial physical trend occurred in the writings of such turn-of-the-century scholars as Ellen Churchill Semple, who was influenced by the anthropogeographic works of Ratzel. Since the 1920's there has been an increasing emphasis on human geography.

Physical geography is not neglected, but it is now regarded as the base for understanding human adjustment on the earth's surface.

The transition from physical to human emphasis in American geography was much influenced by the regional descriptive methodology of the French, for example, Reclus, Vidal de la Blache, and Brunhes. Although in the mid-20th century the humanistic approach has been retained, a greater emphasis on topical, rather than regional, studies has become evident.

Defining the Field. When geography was regarded as primarily a physical science there was no great concern as to what the field comprised. But as the emphasis shifted and the variety of subjects considered by geographers increased, it became evident that some kind of definition was needed. This was provided by Nevin Fenneman in an article entitled "The Circumference of Geography" (1919). He maintained that geography drew upon the basic factors of many fields and combined them in such a way as to form a distinctive field of its own. This explanation proved too indefinite.

There were no further serious attempts to define the field until Richard Hartshorne completed *The Nature of Geography* in 1939. His approach to the problem was distinctly historical. He looked back to the theories of the past, particularly to those of the Germans, and especially of Humboldt, Ritter, and Hettner. He assumed that geography had already been defined by historical precedent. His most important point was that the content of the field could not be determined since it was

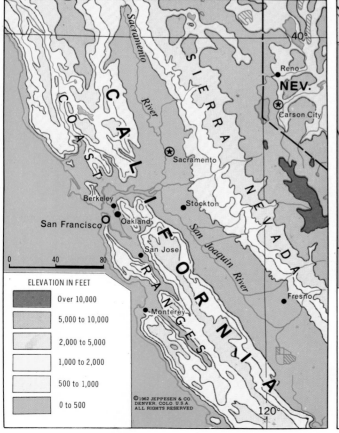

ELEVATION IN FEET

Over 10,000

5,000 to 10,000

2,000 to 5,000

1,000 to 2,000

500 to 1,000

0 to 500

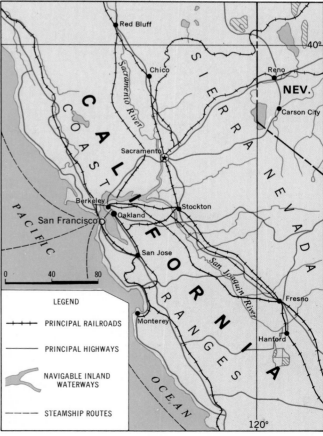

LEGEND

PRINCIPAL RAILROADS

PRINCIPAL HIGHWAYS

NAVIGABLE INLAND WATERWAYS

STEAMSHIP ROUTES

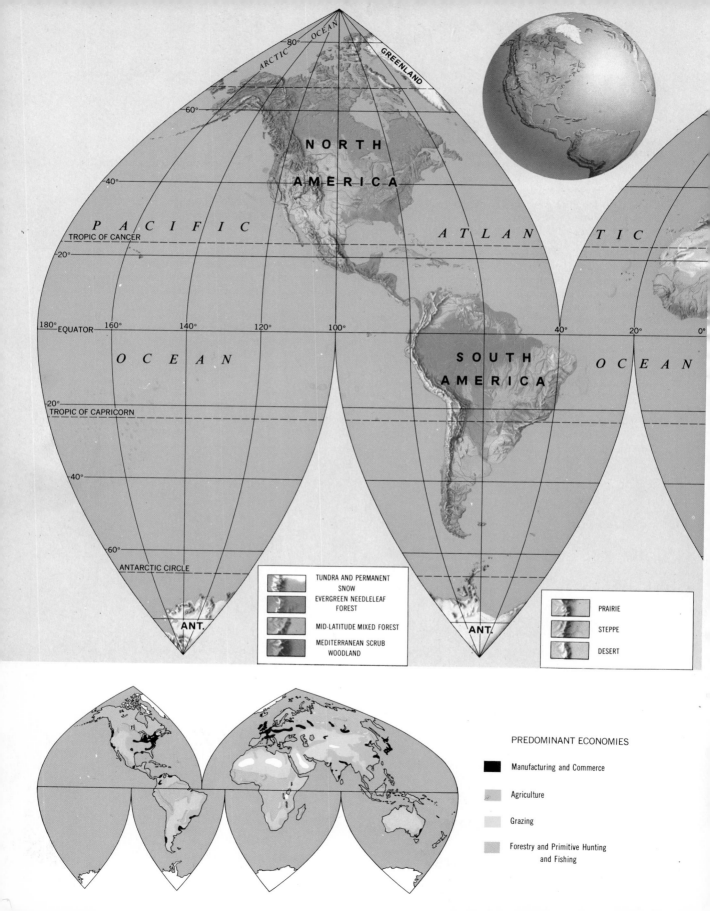

ARCTIC OCEAN

80°

GREENLAND

60°

NORTH

AMERICA

40°

P A C I F I C

A T L A N T I C

TROPIC OF CANCER

20°

180° EQUATOR   160°   140°   120°   100°   40°   20°   0°

O C E A N

SOUTH

AMERICA   O C E A N

-20° TROPIC OF CAPRICORN

-40°

-60°

ANTARCTIC CIRCLE

ANT.   ANT.

	TUNDRA AND PERMANENT SNOW
	EVERGREEN NEEDLELEAF FOREST
	MID-LATITUDE MIXED FOREST
	MEDITERRANEAN SCRUB WOODLAND

	PRAIRIE
	STEPPE
	DESERT

PREDOMINANT ECONOMIES

Manufacturing and Commerce

Agriculture

Grazing

Forestry and Primitive Hunting and Fishing

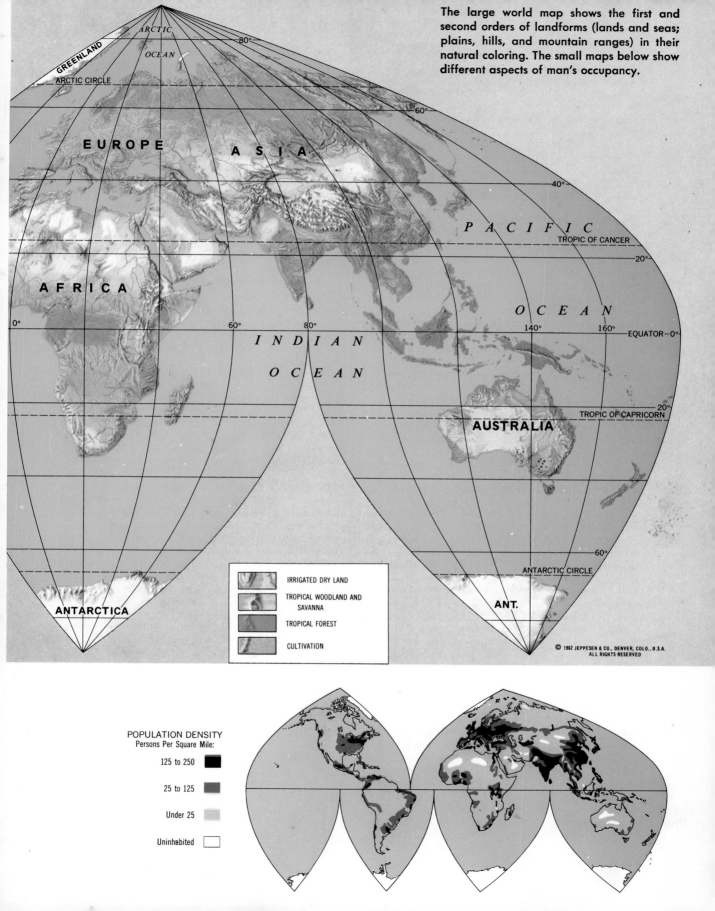

The large world map shows the first and second orders of landforms (lands and seas; plains, hills, and mountain ranges) in their natural coloring. The small maps below show different aspects of man's occupancy.

ARCTIC OCEAN

GREENLAND

ARCTIC CIRCLE

80°

60°

EUROPE

ASIA

40°

PACIFIC

TROPIC OF CANCER

20°

AFRICA

0°

60°

80°

140°

160°

O C E A N

EQUATOR—0°

INDIAN

OCEAN

20°

TROPIC OF CAPRICORN

AUSTRALIA

60°

ANTARCTIC CIRCLE

ANTARCTICA

ANT.

IRRIGATED DRY LAND

TROPICAL WOODLAND AND SAVANNA

TROPICAL FOREST

CULTIVATION

© 1962 JEPPESEN & CO., DENVER, COLO., U.S.A.
ALL RIGHTS RESERVED

POPULATION DENSITY
Persons Per Square Mile:

125 to 250

25 to 125

Under 25

Uninhabited

too inclusive. Geography must be defined, therefore, in terms of a concept—the region. This meant that geographers should concentrate on the analysis of areas, or regions, of the world. He maintained that geographers were best equipped to associate meaningfully the variety of phenomena composing areas into understandable and significant descriptions.

Although Hartshorne has acquired a large following among professional geographers, some geographers do not accept the regional concept. This group, which has gained prominence, contends that the most productive approach to geography is systematic, or topical, rather than regional.

Significantly, however, both the topicalists and the regionalists agree that the primary instrument of geography is the map. Both approaches utilize the map to a greater degree than does any other field to show the distribution of phenomena on the earth. Agreement on this point has led modern geographers to define geography as the study and interpretation of distributions of phenomena on the earth.

The distributions studied and the interpretations made may include either physical topics such as climate, soils, and landforms, or human (cultural) topics such as transportation routes, agricultural types, death rates, ethnic groups, or innumerable other topics. Depending on the degree of detail, these distributions may be plotted and interpreted on a world-wide basis or in a region, or area, of less than world scale. One or several topics may be considered at the same time depending on the objectives of the particular study and on the degree of comprehension of the analyzer. Thus it becomes apparent that topical and regional geography complement one another rather than work at cross purposes.

Environmentalism Versus Humanism. Superimposed on the attempts to define geography has been the contest between the environmentalists and the possibilists, or humanists. It is not surprising that as human geography emerged from the earlier "physical science" phase it had a strong environmentalist bent. That is, man's activities were interpreted in the light of the limitations placed upon him by his physical environment.

Ellen Churchill Semple was instrumental in transplanting the environmentalism of Ratzel to the United States. Her major works, which unduly emphasized the physical environment as it limited and influenced man's activities, were widely read in America and absorbed by laymen and professionals alike. The environmentalist cause was further supported by such scholars as Ellsworth Huntington and Griffith Taylor. The result was a deterministic mold in American geography that held until the 1940's, when a shift from environmentalism to humanism occurred.

The most aggressive spokesman for possibilism, Preston E. James, contended that the significance to man of the physical features of the land is determined by the culture, or way of living, of the people. Hence, any change in attitudes, objectives, or technical abilities of a people inhabiting an area requires a re-evaluation of the significance of the land. According to James, the physical environment is, for the most part, passive, and what man can do with it is largely determined by man himself.

Quantity and Quality in Geography. Another trend among professional geographers is an emphasis on quantitative and statistical data. Part of this stems naturally from the greater availability of more and improved quantitative data. Superimposed on this is an apparent attempt to make the field more exact and "scientific." The more traditional quarters of geography have criticized the statisticians, stating that the statistical approach implies a degree of objectivity that may be more apparent than real and also that such an approach tends to eclipse the descriptive artistry that is such an important part of the field.

It seems evident that quantification, if properly employed, need not operate to the detriment of professional geography. Statistical techniques are best regarded as providing just one more available instrument for geographic studies.

Main Divisions of Geographic Study

There are three main divisions of geographic study. The first two—systematic, or topical, studies and regional studies—are simply different approaches to the same end. Cartography is the third main area of geographic endeavor because the map is the primary instrument of geography.

Systematic, or Topical, Studies. It has been said that modern geography begins with the knowledge provided by the systematic sciences. Nonetheless, in many instances, the distributional approach to geography provides original insights that may be adopted as integral parts of these systematic studies. Systematic studies by geographers have thus been incorporated into such fields as meteorology, geology, economics, medicine, and urban planning.

The possible topics for geographic study are infinite in number: virtually any phenomenon that has unequal distribution on the face of the earth is subject to the geographic approach. Traditionally, geographers have restricted their efforts to a certain set of physical and human topics, but the last decade has witnessed a much wider range in subject interest. A well-known inventory of the field, *American Geography: Inventory and Prospect* (1954), lists more than a score of broad areas of topical interest. No one geographer can become expert in all topical areas or, for that matter, in the application of even one topical field to the entire world. For this reason most geographers focus upon one topic and one region. As their expertness in their chosen subjects develops, their knowledge of other topics and other areas will naturally increase as well.

Physical Geography. American geography began essentially as a physical science. Published papers were dominantly, but not exclusively, concerned with studies in geomorphology. This trend was led by such masters as W. M. Davis, Wallace W. Atwood, and Rollin D. Salisbury. In more recent times other physical topics such as climates, soils, and hydrography have come under close scrutiny. The absolute importance of physical geography is greater now than ever before, but its relative importance has declined due to the large number of younger geographers who have developed an interest in human, or cultural, geography.

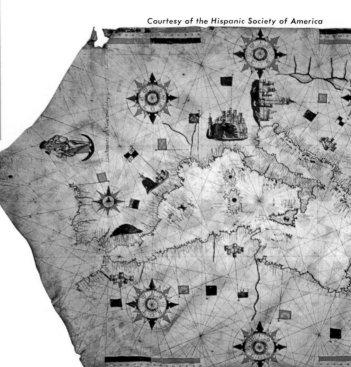

Courtesy of the American Museum of Natural History

MAPS AS AN AID TO COMMERCE AND EXPLORATION

A primitive pilot chart prepared by islanders of the Pacific Ocean. The curved palm spines show prevailing wave fronts, the straight spines indicate sailing courses, and the shells locate islands.

Courtesy of the Hispanic Society of America

A 16th-century portolan chart. Such charts were the earliest seafarers' maps that achieved wide distribution. The radial lines show compass directions from many different locations. These lines enabled mariners for the first time to set accurate sailing courses far out of sight of land, with fair expectation of reaching their destinations without losing time skirting the shores.

A portion of an accurate, modern air navigation chart.

Courtesy of the U.S. Coast and Geodetic Survey

Biogeography. Biogeography involves the study of the distribution of plant and animal organisms. Some aspects of biogeography overlap with physical geography, and other aspects are closely related to human geography.

Biogeography is often subdivided into plant geography (closely allied to plant ecology) and animal geography (zoogeography). Such scholars as A. W. Küchler have made significant contributions to plant geography, but so far geographers have contributed little to zoogeography.

Medical geography can best be considered in conjunction with biogeography since it deals with the effect of organisms, as well as of the physical environment, on man's physiological condition. Meaningful subjects for study in medical geography thus include the distribution and intensity of both communicable and noncommunicable diseases as they affect health and mortality. Important contributions in this area have been made by Jacques May of the American Geographical Society.

Cultural, or Human, Geography. Cultural geography focuses on the study and interpretation of the distribution of man and his works on the earth's surface. Some of the broad topical fields considered in this category include the following:

Population and Settlement Geography. The mapping and analysis of the unequal distribution of people on the surface of the earth is of prime concern to geography. This is the first element that must be ascertained before the geographer can determine the adequate sustaining capacity of any area. The interpretation of present world population pressures depends upon an accurate regional analysis of the relationship between population numbers, the resource base, and the attitudes, objectives, and technical abilities of societies.

Subdivisions of population geography may also include the mapping and interpretation of such factors as racial types and ethnic groups. Societal attitudes and culture forms such as religions and languages are also subject to this type of investigation.

People usually depend on building structures and other material facilities of various types both for residential purposes and to assist their economies. The essential study of the distribution and arrangement of such structures is considered under the term "settlement geography." A highly specialized subdivision of this field is urban geography, which concerns itself with the distribution and arrangement of structures and other facilities in urban areas. Urban geographers are important adjuncts of urban planning boards.

Economic Geography. Any part of geography that focuses its attention on the distribution of those phenomena reflecting man's means of gaining a livelihood is considered economic geography. This naturally involves a wide array of topical considerations including such factors as transportation, manufacturing, agriculture, mineral production, and resources.

Economic distributions are closely tied to population densities and physical geography. In other words, economic geography is ultimately concerned with the entire spectrum of man-land relationships. For this reason some geographers consider economic geography as the primary focus of geographic endeavor.

Political Geography. One of the most obvious cultural distributions on the face of the earth is that of areas of political authority. The accurate mapping of such areas is, in itself, a major problem, since political authority is dynamic through time. New political authorities emerge, others are absorbed, and boundaries are subject to change.

Although the boundaries of political authorities are usually not visible on the landscape they are, nonetheless, extremely important human concepts. In many cases, for example, boundaries abruptly separate different economies, social structures, and governments.

The political geographer is concerned with the effect of a variety of physical and cultural distributions on the emergence, development, and manifestations of areas of political authority, ranging from entire nations to rural or urban areas.

Geopolitics is sometimes incorrectly considered as a synonym for political geography. Originally envisioned as primarily a field of academic enquiry, geopolitics developed, however, as an applied field employing the techniques and concepts of a variety of studies to formulate strategic policy in international relations.

Historical Geography. Historical geography concerns itself with the study and interpretation of the distributions of phenomena in the historical past, thus representing a chronological sequence of distributional changes. A sequence of maps portraying chronologically the westward migration of peoples in the United States from 1800 to 1900, for example, would represent a simple illustration of historical geography. The meaningfulness of such maps, however, would depend upon their interpretation in the light of the variety of geographic (distributional) factors operating in conjunction with the population migration. This exemplifies what historical geography strives to do.

Studies in historical geography facilitate our understanding of contemporary distributions, too. The work of Ralph Brown well illustrates this point; see, for example, *Mirror for Americans* (1968).

Historical geography is a difficult field of endeavor because of the relative paucity of and inconsistency in documentary materials for ascertaining past distributions of phenomena. It should not be confused with geographical history, which involves the interpretation of historical events in the light of the significance of environmental factors on those events.

Military Geography. The study and interpretation of distributions of phenomena for the express purpose of ascertaining military strategy and tactics comes under the heading of military geography.

Although the military geographer may be interested in a wide array of physical and cultural distributions, the purpose of his interest is militarily oriented. Work in this area can be best accomplished by persons having both military and geographic training.

Regional Studies. Many geographers feel that the study of areas or regions of the world constitutes the core of the field. The approach is still distributional, but the regional geographer is less inclined to limit the variety of subject matter with which he deals.

The extent and limits of a given region will vary depending upon the objectives and criteria employed in any particular study. Regions of political authority, for

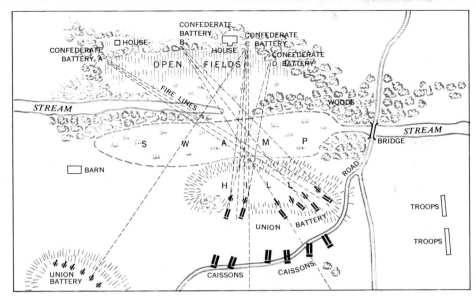

Dotted lines on a military map used in the Civil War indicate the paths of Confederate artillery fire. This skirmish between Confederate troops and the First Maryland Light Artillery occurred at New Bridge, Va., on June 5, 1862.

example, are easily recognized and may be regarded as regions defined on the basis of a single criterion. Consequent analysis of such areas, however, indicates that political boundaries are often inadequate indicators of meaningful regions simply because the functional behavior of such regions frequently transcends these boundaries. For this reason advanced works in regional geography often employ a variety of criteria, rather than just one, to define areas of study.

There is still lack of agreement among geographers as to whether the topical or the regional offers the better approach. It is evident, however, that both approaches are interdependent.

Cartography. Whether geographers are systematically or regionally oriented, they generally agree that the interest in a real differentiation is the unifying element of the field. For this reason the map is the primary tool of geography.

One area of cartography of interest to geographers deals with map projections, that is, the globe or parts thereof projected on a flat surface. The geographer must retain a long-established interest in the perfection of old, and the development of new projections in order to satisfy his special and changing needs. The best type of projection depends upon the particular topic or area under study and the scale at which the work is being done. Geographers who have contributed significantly to map projection development include J. Paul Goode, Vernon Finch, and O. M. Miller.

Surface relief is one of the primary physical elements affecting man's adjustment on the earth's surface. Thus cartographic representation of landforms is of prime concern to the geographer. If relief is to be shown on a flat surface, it must be accomplished by a method that will give a three-dimensional perspective. A variety of methods are employed; some of these have resulted from the

Characteristics of the Field. In most professions some degree of specialization is necessary, and in many professions there is a trend toward narrower and narrower specialization. Within the broad field of geology, for example, there are specialists in mineralogy; and within the field of mineralogy there are experts who focus on gemology, the study of precious stones. Geographers usually specialize in one of the main divisions of their field discussed in the article on these pages. Their work has an unusual characteristic, however. Although a geographer is a specialist in his own profession, he cannot focus his studies as narrowly as can the expert on gems or the horticulturist who devotes his studies to one kind of vegetable. He must often use a comprehensive approach to his problems, drawing on the work of specialists in many other fields—geology, meteorology, biology, economics, and demography, for example.

The majority of geographers are employed by universities and colleges. State and local governments also employ geographers, for example, on regional and city-planning commissions. Private enterprises, such as map and textbook publishers and market research companies, require the services of geographers. Some professionals in the field, particularly in universities, have the title geographer. Others work under such designations as cartographer, intelligence specialist, regional analyst, community planner, or market analyst.

Qualifications and Training. Geographic research may require field work under conditions much like those experienced by some geologists and engineers. For some positions, physical stamina plus willingness to travel extensively may be essential.

The undergraduate education of a geographer typically includes such courses as physical geography, economic geography, political geography, regional studies, and cartography, as well as mathematics, geology, biology, economics, political science, and foreign languages. Graduate degrees are usually necessary for more responsible positions.

Income. Starting salaries for geographers in government posts tend to range below those for engineers, chemists, and some other scientists. In teaching, salaries are determined by the scale of individual colleges. Professors often add to their income by writing and consulting.

Prospects for Employment. The field is expected to grow at a moderate rate. Since geography is a relatively small profession, competition for desirable posts may be keen.

efforts of such geographers as W. M. Davis, Armin K. Lobeck, and Erwin Raisz. Ways of showing topographic relief continues to be a challenging field of enquiry for geographers.

The greatest effort in geographic cartography, however, is concerned with methods of portraying the unequal distribution of phenomena in two dimensions (planimetric maps). Since the phenomena with which geographers deal are numberless, this phase of geography is a constant challenge, and the best methods of qualitative and quantitative portrayal must be individually suited to the particular study.

There are individuals in geography who concentrate their efforts on cartographic improvement, but every geographer must be, to some extent, his own cartographer. He must develop a good sense of cartographic representation before he can effectively portray, and thus interpret, his distributional information.

Consult Estall, Peter, *Modern Geography of the United States* (1972); Jeffries, William W., ed., *Geography and National Power* (4th ed., 1967); Lock, C. Muriel, *Geography: A Reference Handbook* (rev. 3rd ed., 1976); Minshull, Roger, *The Changing Nature of Geography* (1970); Stanford, Q. H. and Moran, Warren, *Geography: A Study of Its Elements* (1969); Taaffe, E. J., ed., *Geography* (1970).

MALCOLM A. MURRAY

GEOLOGICAL SOCIETY OF AMERICA, professional organization of geologists and teachers of geology. It was founded in 1888 to promote the science of geology and support geological research. The GSA has a membership of about 8,000. The organization's headquarters are located in Boulder, Colo. Its publications include *Memoirs*, *Special Papers*, the monthly *Bibliography and Index of Geology Exclusive of North America*, and a monthly *Bulletin*.

GEOLOGICAL SURVEY, UNITED STATES. The Geological Survey was established by law in 1879 to provide for "the classification of the public lands and the examination of the geological structure, mineral resources, and products of the national domain." In 1888 Congress added topographic mapping and chemical and physical researches to the investigations and studies to be undertaken by the survey. The work of this Department of the Interior agency has included classification of lands available for irrigation, gauging streams and determining the water supply of the nation, and the publication, sale, and distribution of maps, bulletins, water-supply papers, professional papers, and other documents related to geological matters. It gives engineering supervision to federal power permits and enforces regulations applied to private oil, gas, and mining permits or contracts on federal lands. Its other services range from collecting royalties from private companies under contract to the federal government to ensuring the safety and welfare of workmen employed by companies which develop the national domain. The survey is also involved in marine research, in lunar and planetary studies, and in investigations of earthquake and volcanic phenomena in an effort to develop methods of prediction.

STUART GERRY BROWN

Hétier—Atlas Photo

The Giant's Causeway, a curious accumulation of basaltic columns on a promontory along the northern coast of Northern Ireland, fascinates geologists. The columns, which are up to 20 ft (6 m) tall, are of volcanic origin.

GEOLOGY [jē-ŏl′ə-jē], science of the earth. It encompasses both the study of present physical features and the unraveling of the history of the earth from the time of its inception. A geologist applies the basic sciences—chemistry, physics, and biology—to the study of the earth. He identifies minerals, which are natural chemical compounds; he studies the chemical and physical properties of rocks; and he investigates physical processes of the earth, including earthquakes, volcanoes, and the effects of wind and rain upon the land. He applies biology to the study of fossils, which are the remains of organisms that lived in the past. He investigates the oceans and mountains and seeks to explain their origin and distribution. And he helps to locate deposits of valuable raw materials, including ores of metals, deposits of coal and oil, and underground supplies of water and building stone. Most geologists specialize in a specific branch of the science. Major subdivisions are briefly described below.

Mineralogy. Rocks are composed of minerals; therefore study of the solid part of the earth begins with mineralogy, the identification and investigation of natural compounds and native elements. Fortunately the common rock-forming minerals and the major ore minerals are not numerous, and many of them have distinctive physical properties, such as the color of gold, the hardness of diamond, the taste of rock salt, the cleavage (splitting) of mica, and the crystal form of quartz. Even the beginner experiences little difficulty in recognizing many minerals. But elaborate study is often required to

A characteristic of 20th-century science is the great degree of overlapping and interconnecting of fields. This is well illustrated by geology, which draws on physics, chemistry, and other sciences in studying the earth. The scope of geology is evident in the article on these pages, which covers the following topics.

Major Branches of Geology. Mineralogy, petrology, geochemistry, structural geology, geophysics, geomorphology, paleontology, stratigraphy, economic geology.

Geologic History of the Earth. The beginnings — theories of the origin of the solar system. The Precambrian interval. The Paleozoic Era: time of early life. The Mesozoic Era: age of dinosaurs. The Cenozoic Era: arrival of modern life. (See the Geologic Time Scale for subdivisions.)

History of Geology as a Science. Roots in ancient times; theories developed in the 17th and 18th centuries: Neptunism and uniformitarianism; contributions of Lamarck, Cuvier, Lyell, and others; geology in America.

Current and Future Trends. Extent of geologic investigation of the earth; the enunciation of the theory of plate tectonics; its growing acceptance and the confirmation of continental drift; use of new techniques developed in physics, chemistry, and electronic engineering.

Careers in Geology. Principal fields of opportunity.

The extent of coverage of geology in other articles can be shown by listing entries pertinent to the major divisions of the science. These include MINERALOGY and treatment of a related topic, CRYSTALLOGRAPHY; PETROLOGY and ROCKS; GEOCHEMISTRY; GEOPHYSICS, often treated as a separate field and including topics such as those covered in GEODESY, SEISMOGRAPH, and EARTHQUAKE; VOLCANO; GEOMORPHOLOGY and the allied entries PHYSIOGRAPHY, DIASTROPHISM, WEATHERING, EROSION, GEOSYNCLINE, MOUNTAINS AND MOUNTAIN RANGES, GLACIERS AND GLACIATION, GLACIAL DEPOSITS, HYDROLOGY; OCEANOGRAPHY; PALEONTOLOGY (some contributions are noted in EVOLUTION). Another important earth science is treated in METEOROLOGY.

The geologic history of the earth is further discussed in EARTH, which also summarizes data on the shape, size, and physical structure of the planet. The origin of the solar system and its relations to its surroundings are discussed in SOLAR SYSTEM, UNIVERSE, and COSMOLOGY. The geologic eras and subdivisions are treated in individual entries and there is an additional entry ICE AGES.

The reader interested in the history of scientific geology can turn to articles on once-prominent theories: NEPTUNISM, PLUTONISM, and CATASTROPHISM. Additional information is in biographic entries on such men as Baron CUVIER, Jean Baptiste LAMARCK, Sir Charles LYELL, John Wesley POWELL, and James Dwight DANA. A major event in the history of geology and other sciences is recorded in INTERNATIONAL GEOPHYSICAL YEAR. Useful background for reading about the development and characteristics of any science is presented in SCIENTIFIC METHOD and SCIENTIFIC RESEARCH.

As many articles point out, information about the earth is growing as scientists refine their methods of research. To keep abreast of developments, the reader may consult authoritative books and periodicals, available in most libraries. Major advances and discoveries in the field of geology are recorded in such sources as the annual supplement to this Encyclopedia.

distinguish minerals with similar physical properties and to identify uncommon minerals and those in small particles. Most silicate minerals are distinguished readily by measuring their optical properties with a polarizing microscope. Sulfides and native metals yield diagnostic products upon treatment with simple chemical reagents and upon exposure to heat with the blowpipe. X rays are used to investigate the internal arrangement of atoms in minerals and to identify minute mineral particles, such as the clay minerals. A related field essential to the study of minerals is crystallography, the science of crystal forms. An example of applied mineralogy is gemology, the identification and study of gem stones.

Petrology. The study of the properties, classification, and origin of rocks is called petrology. Rocks are divided genetically into three major groups: igneous (solidified from melted rock), sedimentary (made of particles deposited by water, wind, or ice), and metamorphic (altered from other rocks by pressure and heat within the earth). The rocks in each group are named according to the minerals they contain and the textural relations of the minerals. The part of petrology that involves describing and classifying rocks is called petrography; much of this work is done with the aid of a petrographic (polarizing) microscope. The study of the origin of rocks is called petrogenesis. In recent years laboratory equipment has been designed to reproduce rock-forming conditions that exist within the earth, even to producing the great pressures necessary to synthesize diamonds. The study of the orientation of mineral grains in rocks is called petrofabrics; and the subdivisions of petrology dealing with sedimentary rocks are known collectively as sedimentology.

Geochemistry. In geochemistry the study of the chemistry of the earth is extended beyond the traditional limits of mineralogy and petrology. The distribution of elements in the earth, the fractionation of isotopes by natural processes, and the thermodynamics of chemical reactions in rocks are investigated by geochemists. Of particularly great interest has been the investigation of radioactive isotopes and the determination of the age of minerals and rocks in which they occur.

Structural Geology. Structural geology deals chiefly with the shape and distribution of bodies of rock and with their physical behavior as they are deformed by folding and crushing. Mountain ranges are produced by the gradual movement and collision of large segments of the earth's crust. Earthquakes are caused by such movements as rocks break and slip past each other along fractures, or faults. Nearly all parts of the earth's surface have undergone such fracturing in the past. Although the deformation of solid rock in the earth is almost immeasurably slow in some regions and spasmodic in others, it is nevertheless constantly occurring. Changes of almost unbelievable magnitude have occurred through the immensity of time since the earth was formed. Sediments laid down as flat layers on the floor of the sea 15 million years

GEOLOGIC TIME SCALE

Eon / Era	Period				Epoch	Age*	Main Characteristics in North America
PHANEROZOIC EON — Cenozoic Era / 63 million years	Neogene	Quaternary			Recent	.01	Postglacial changes / Advent of man
					Pleistocene	2.5	Flowering plants dominant / Great ice age
		Tertiary			Pliocene	7	Formation of coastal ranges in western North America; the Alps in Europe
					Miocene	25	
	Paleogene				Oligocene	36	First monkeys
					Eocene	58	First placental mammals / Extensive volcanic activity in western U.S.
					Paleocene	63	Formation of Rocky Mts. and Andes Mts.
Mesozoic Era / 167 million years	**Cretaceous**					135	Early folding of Rocky Mts. / Dinosaurs become extinct / Flowering plants first abundant
	Jurassic					180	Beginning of Sierra Nevada uplift / First birds
	Triassic					230	Volcanic activity in New England, Pa., N. J. / Appearance of dinosaurs / First primitive mammals
Paleozoic Era / 370 million years	**Permian**					280	Folding to form Appalachian Mts. / Extensive glaciation / Rise of reptiles
	Pennsylvanian					325	Two periods known as Carboniferous from extensive coal-forming swamps of large nonflowering plants
	Mississippian					345	
	Devonian					405	Acadian Mts. / Abundant fishes
	Silurian					425	Caledonian Mts. / Rise of land plants; first amphibians
	Ordovician					500	Taconic Mts. / First known fishes
	Cambrian					600	First abundant invertebrates

*Age in millions of years from the present.

CRYPTOZOIC EON (Precambrian)

Total time span 4 billion to 5 billion years
Oldest evidence of glaciation. Extensive volcanic activity. Great movement of existing rocks. Scanty record of primitive plants and animals. Algae fairly common.

ago now rise at weirdly tilted angles in the highest peaks of the Alps and Himalayas.

Structural geologists are concerned with the framework, or tectonics, of the earth. They record on geologic maps and cross sections the position of folds and faults and the size and distribution of bodies of rock. In the laboratory they study the strength and behavior of earth materials under different conditions of pressure and temperature. It is especially significant that all rocks deform and flow like highly viscous liquids when stresses are applied for a long enough time, and that some crystalline solids, such as ice, rock salt, gypsum, and even marble, flow readily in the solid state if they are subjected to enough pressure.

Geophysics. Geophysics, defined broadly, is the study of the physical properties of all parts of the earth, including the atmosphere, the oceans, and the inaccessible interior. Electrical and magnetic properties of the earth, heat transfer, and the propagation of various kinds of waves through air, water, and rock are the special concern of the geophysicist. Seismology, the study of earthquakes, is a basic part of geophysics, for most of our knowledge of the internal structure of the earth has been deduced from the effect of earthquake waves on internal layers of different densities. The petroleum industry applies seismic methods to determine the arrangement of buried layers of rock by setting off explosive charges and recording the resultant waves as they are reflected and refracted back to the surface.

Careful measurements of the force of gravity at the earth's surface yield information about the specific gravity and distribution of underlying rocks, as well as about the effects of earth tides on elevation, latitude, and the shape of the earth. Magnetic measurements disclose variations in the earth's magnetic field, and magnetic surveys are useful in locating deposits of iron ore and other magnetic materials.

Geomorphology. Geomorphology, or physiography, is the study of the surface forms of the earth and the processes that produce them. The dominant processes are weathering and erosion. Weathering involves the solution and slow disintegration of rocks by rain water, by alternate freezing and thawing, and by other agents. Erosion is the wearing away of the land by wind, water, and glacial ice, which remove soil and rock fragments and transport them to new sites of deposition. Although erosion seems slow in its attack upon mountains and plateaus, it is a continuous and effective process. Often man unwittingly and carelessly speeds erosion to disastrous proportions in some areas by overgrazing, forest removal, and farming. Rivers annually transport millions of tons of soil and stones to ocean basins. Within a short time, relative to the age of the earth, all the land above sea level would be eroded away if it were not for internal processes that renew the land by lifting new mountain ranges and building new volcanoes.

Modern investigations of the topography of the ocean floors are giving us a new appreciation of the landscapes of three quarters of the surface of the earth, where gigantic mountain ranges and great plains are hidden from our view. This is part of the broad subject matter of oceanography, in which geology, biology, and other sciences are applied to investigation of the oceans. Another branch of physiography, called glaciology, is the study of glaciers and the land forms for which they are responsible.

Paleontology. Ancient animal and plant remains preserved in rocks have long aroused man's curiosity and stirred controversy regarding the origin and history of the earth. The paleontologist collects and classifies these fossils. As nearly as possible his methods are the same as those used by biologists in classifying living species. The paleontologist is handicapped by the incompleteness of his material, however, for soft tissues are rarely preserved when an organism dies. Nevertheless the comparison of fossil bones, teeth, shells, leaf impressions, and other remains with similar parts of living animals and plants has enabled paleontologists to reconstruct past faunas and floras with surprising completeness.

Paleontology has documented the concept of evolution; new species have arisen by modification of older forms. Many forms of life evolved, spread widely over the earth, then became extinct as more successful types displaced them. Certain species lived so short a time, compared with the age of the earth, that all rocks containing remains of one of these species may be considered to be of approximately the same age. Rocks containing more primitive species of the same genus may be considered older, and those with more advanced forms, younger. Fossils must be used cautiously as a measure of relative age, for some species have persisted for a remarkably long time. Others have spread over the earth exceedingly slowly or have persisted in some areas long after becoming extinct elsewhere.

Micropaleontology, the study of minute fossils, and palynology, the study of fossil pollen and spores, are especially useful in the petroleum industry, for minute rock fragments are the only materials recovered during routine drilling through buried layers of rock.

Stratigraphy. Stratigraphy is the investigation of the chronologic order in which layers of rock were deposited, including the recognition of gaps in the record produced either by nondeposition or by the erosion of layers that once were present. It involves the comparison of rock sequences in widely separated areas; therefore it requires criteria for determining contemporaneity of strata. The approximate contemporaneity of sedimentary rock layers in different areas can generally be established by the presence of identical or similar fossils.

Stratigraphy is the key to geologic history. Events and environmental conditions are deciphered insofar as possible from the incomplete records preserved in the rocks at various localities. Then the records are correlated and a composite geologic history is synthesized.

Economic Geology. Economic geology includes those parts of the science that can be applied to the discovery and investigation of valuable mineral deposits. Some economic geologists specialize in metallic ores, studying ore minerals, the origin of the deposits, exploration and mining methods, and economics of the mining industry. Others work especially with deposits of nonmetals such as clay, limestone, asbestos, coal, and sulfur. Most economic geologists are employed by the petroleum industry. They are trained especially in stratigraphy, structural geology, and sedimentary petrology.

Geologic History of the Earth

The Beginnings. How did our planet come into being? And when? We know that it is one of nine planets whirling around the sun and spinning like tops on their own axes. The planets and the sun seem to be related in physical behavior and composition, and it is likely that they had a common origin. Other stars in our galaxy may have families of planets, too, and their origin is probably similar. Many theories to account for the solar system have been propounded, but no one theory is yet completely acceptable. The most probable hypothesis suggests that the sun and planets condensed simultaneously from a whirling lens of gases and dust. The dust eventually collected to form the planets or fell to the center of the system to comprise in large part the mass of the sun.

According to this theory of solar system formation the earth grew to its present size by accretion of solid particles attracted by the force of gravity as it traveled around the sun. Nevertheless the internal structure of the earth could hardly have been attained except in a partially or wholly liquid state. Hence the earth is assumed to have passed through such a state, and even now part of the earth's core behaves with earthquake waves as a liquid and is apparently still molten. The heat necessary to melt the earth was probably provided by impact energy of the accreting particles, by compression as the mass increased, and by radioactivity of the original material. As the interior heated, heavy metals sank to the center of the sphere, much as metals gather at the bottom of a furnace during the smelting of ores. Around this the greater volume of silicon-oxygen compounds gathered in a vast shell, called the mantle, which extends from the metallic core almost to the surface of the earth and which has solidified to rock that is assumed to be made chiefly of magnesium-iron silicates. The skinlike, outermost layer of the earth, called the crust, is made of the rocks that we see at the surface. It is separated from the underlying mantle by a distinct boundary, the Mohorovicic discontinuity (commonly called the Moho), along which earthquake waves are strongly refracted.

From careful examination of the earth's crustal rocks, geologists have worked out a fairly detailed time scale, or geologic calendar, based chiefly on the evolution of life as recorded in the progression of fossils. Four major divisions of geologic time have been recognized. The oldest, longest, and least known is called the Precambrian interval. Second is the Paleozoic Era, the era of ancient life. Third is the Mesozoic Era, or the time of middle life forms. Youngest is the Cenozoic Era, the age of recent life. Each era is divided into periods and the periods into epochs.

Many minerals in igneous rocks and a few in sedimentary deposits contain radioactive elements that disintegrate at a uniform rate. The disintegration yields other elements that are retained in quantities proportional to the age of the original minerals. After chemical analysis, therefore, the age of many rocks can be computed with relative accuracy. With the use of such age determinations, approximate dates in years have been placed with some confidence on the geologic calendar, which had been worked out earlier by stratigraphers and paleontologists.

The age of the universe and of our solar system is placed at approximately 5 billion years by estimates based on several lines of reasoning and by measurements of the ratios of radioactive isotopes and their decay products in meteorites. The most ancient rocks on earth for which satisfactory measurements of radiogenic isotope ratios have been made are about 4 billion years old.

The Precambrian Interval. The oldest rocks containing abundant fossils were deposited approximately 600 million years ago during the Cambrian Period, the first part of the Paleozoic Era. The long part of earth history prior to this time is called the Precambrian interval. It spans at least five sixths of the age of the earth. We can deduce, from examining the remnants of deeply eroded, ancient mountain ranges, that during these early stages of earth history primitive continents came into existence as thick accumulations of the lighter crustal rocks, chiefly granite and allied igneous rocks. Between these lay basins floored by thinner sheets of heavier crustal rocks similar to the basalt found in many oceanic islands today. Water later accumulated to fill the ocean basins, and the earth took on a more familiar appearance.

If the earth formed by accretion in a cosmic dust cloud, the primitive atmosphere probably contained little or no free oxygen. It may have contained considerable carbon dioxide, water vapor, nitrogen, and even methane and ammonia. In such an atmosphere the synthesis of more complex hydrocarbons, amino acids, sugars, and similar complex compounds could occur easily under the influence of electrical discharges, ultraviolet radiation, and heat. One theory of the origin of life proposes that the first living material arose spontaneously in this environment. Some of the earlier life forms were probably similar to primitive plant-like organisms that exist today, such as certain single-celled bacteria or multi-celled blue-green algae. The remains of such primitive organisms are reasonably common in Precambrian sedimentary rocks, but more complex shell-bearing animal fossils are absent throughout the long Precambrian record. The first appearance of such fossils marks the beginning of the Paleozoic Era.

The Paleozoic Era: Time of Early Life. The earliest abundant fossilized hard parts of animals are those in Cambrian rocks. The most abundant and characteristic Cambrian fossils are forms of arthropods called tribolites, which lived in great numbers in the seas that extended far

American Museum of Natural History

Trilobite fossil embedded in rock. Trilobites were invertebrate sea animals that lived during the Paleozoic Era.

inland across portions of the deeply eroded continents. From Cambrian time onward marine sedimentary rocks are mostly fossil-bearing, and the relative ages of different deposits can be determined by comparison of the fossil faunas.

During late Cambrian and early Ordovician time noteworthy deposits of limestone and dolomite were precipitated from warm, shallow ocean waters on submerged parts of the continents. In North America a wide trough extended northeastward where the Appalachian Mountains are now, and another was located in the Rocky Mountain region. Similar great troughs, called geosynclines, were developed within and at the margins of other continents. Each of these geosynclinal belts sank progressively as it received sediments that accumulated to much greater thickness than on other more stable parts of the sea floor. At times during the early Paleozoic Era sea water spread across as much as three-quarters of the present land area of the world. Before the end of Paleozoic time sedimentary deposits in the geosynclinal troughs had accumulated in some cases to depths of several miles.

Trilobites continued to be abundant in Ordovician seas, and a great variety of other marine invertebrates flourished. Brachiopods were the most abundant shellfish, and sponges, corals, and floating graptolites were common. The first fishes had appeared, but they were small and primitive, and their remains are scarce. Land plants had also appeared, but they too were probably small, primitive, and not abundant.

During Silurian time the oceans receded somewhat, and by the close of the period rugged mountains of the Caledonian range were lifted up from the sea floor in northwestern Europe. During the subsequent Devonian Period land sediments accumulated in areas near the Caledonian mountains; in England they are represented by the Old Red Sandstone. In New York thick deltaic deposits were laid down, and in most of North America thin layers of shale and limestone were deposited. Shallow seas remained over much of the land during the Mississippian Period, but by Pennsylvanian time the land had emerged and great swamps occupied the position of former seas in the mid-continent region of North America and in parts of Europe. Vegetation flourished in the swamps, and layers of woody material were buried to later become extensive coal beds. In Europe the Pennsylvanian and Mississippian periods are grouped together as the Carboniferous Period.

During Pennsylvanian time many new mountain chains began to emerge from old geosynclinal troughs. These included the Hercynian ranges of Europe, the Appalachian and related ranges in North America, and several great mountain ranges in the Southern Hemisphere. Pennsylvanian and Permian glacial deposits are found at many places in Australia, India, Africa, and South America, and some of the fossil land plants and animals in these are quite similar. This evidence, combined with additional geophysical data, suggests that during Late Paleozoic time all the great southern land masses were joined together as one continent, to which the name Gondwana is given. The continents stood generally well above sea level during Permian time, but several land areas subsided

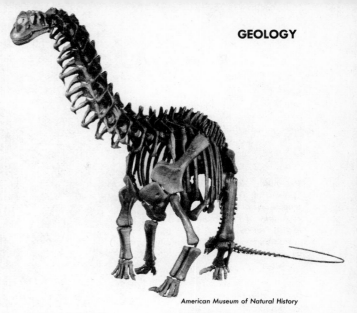

American Museum of Natural History

Model skeleton of a brontosaurus, a plant-eating dinosaur that inhabited shallow lagoons and lakes during the Mesozoic Era.

locally to form great inland basins. In the southwestern part of the United States, in Germany, and at a few other places the evaporation of marine water in restricted basins produced thick rock-salt deposits that are accompanied by valuable potassium salts.

New forms of life evolved rapidly both on the land and in the sea during late Paleozoic time, and at the end of the Paleozoic Era many kinds of organisms, including trilobites, disappeared from the earth. Trees and seed-bearing plants spread over the land, and amphibious animals emerged from the sea to live on the land vegetation. Reptiles had evolved before the end of Paleozoic time, but their great development was yet to come. Insects flourished on the land and in the air, and some attained great size.

During the Mesozoic Era the large Late Paleozoic continent of Gondwana was gradually broken apart by continuous crustal movements. These movements ultimately led to the configuration of separated continents that exists on the earth today.

The Mesozoic Era: Age of Dinosaurs. Sediments of the Triassic Period, the first part of the Mesozoic Era, include great sheets of red shale and sandstone, mostly deposited on land rather than in the sea. They were deposited near the great Paleozoic mountain ranges in a relatively arid and probably cool climate. Not until the Jurassic Period did the sea again begin to encroach very far onto the land. During the Cretaceous Period, the last and longest part of the Mesozoic Era, the continents were largely submerged as they had been in early Paleozoic time, and marine sediments were again deposited over them. Near the end of the Cretaceous Period there was great crustal unrest that ultimately resulted in the upheaval of some of the highest mountains of the present time, including the Rocky Mountains and the Andes. But much of this mountain building continued intermittently through the following era.

The dominant animals throughout the Mesozoic Era were reptiles, and the most spectacular of these were the

The north wall of the Grand Canyon of the Colorado River reveals one of the most significant exposures of Precambrian (Cryptozoic) rocks. Here, the tilted Precambrian formation is overlain by horizontal Lower Cambrian sandstone.

dinosaurs. Huge species evolved as masters of the land, others returned to the seas from which their amphibious ancestors had come, and some even took to the air. Mammals and birds put in their first appearance, but neither group was important until the following era. Cone-bearing trees became common on the land, although cycads and ferns were still abundant, and by late Cretaceous time the angiosperms, or true flowering plants, appeared and began their diversification into ancestral strains of the common trees and flowers of the modern world. The most characteristic Mesozoic marine invertebrates were ammonites, relatives of the present nautilus; but other forms, including arthropods, were plentiful and diverse. Strangely, both the ammonites and the great reptiles became extinct at the close of the Mesozoic Era.

The Cenozoic Era: Arrival of Modern Life. The most recent 60 million years of the earth's history, including the present, is classified as the Cenozoic Era. It is divided by American geologists into the Tertiary and Quaternary periods and by many European geologists into different periods called the Paleogene and Neogene. The Tertiary Period was a time of high-standing continents and continued mountain growth, which culminated after the middle of the period in the formation of the great Alpine and Himalayan ranges. Inland seas were generally small; in North America the Mississippi embayment and the coastal plains were flooded. Vast land areas adjoining the Pacific Ocean were covered by lava flows, and volcanoes are still concentrated today in the Pacific "circle of fire." The Tertiary Period was followed by the Quaternary, which began with the Pleistocene Epoch, or the Ice Ages. The climate of the world turned generally colder and large icecaps formed in both polar regions and spread until ice covered a quarter of the land. The continental ice sheets caused profound changes in living things. Plants and animals moved toward the equator, adapted to colder conditions, or perished.

During the Tertiary Period mammals became the dominant land animals and, like the Mesozoic reptiles, some evolved into large and grotesque beasts, while others turned to the sea to become ancestors of modern whales,

seals, and porpoises. Most of the giant mammals became extinct before the Ice Ages, but those that remained were generally well adapted to variable and cooler climates. One of the most successful survivors of the glacial advances was early man, who devised new ways to keep warm and obtain food under adverse conditions.

About 10 to 15 thousand years have elapsed since the retreat of the last great ice sheet. This interval, sometimes considered part of the Pleistocene Epoch, is called Recent time. There were four major glacial advances, and it is possible that we live in a fourth interglacial period and that ice will again cover great portions of the land. Recent time has seen man's gradual domination of the rest of the animal kingdom. Man has begun to control his environment, which is an evolutionary development of special biological significance: for the first time a living species has the power to determine its destiny.

History of Geology as a Science

Geology is a comparatively young science, although its roots go back to ancient times. Many early Greek and Roman scholars doubted the supernatural causes then accepted for earthquakes and volcanic eruptions, and they recognized that fossil shells found in the high mountains were the remains of animals that lived in the sea. The early Christian Era was marked by regression in part, for logical explanations of many geologic phenomena seemed to conflict with the Bible. Fossil sea shells in mountain sites, for example, were attributed to the great flood.

In the 17th century a Danish doctor, Nicolaus Steno, published the first reasonable interpretation of sedimentary rocks and the fossils they contain, and he compiled the first geologic history of an area. He also made remarkably keen observations in the field of crystallography. Soon after this the French scientist René Descartes and a German, Baron Gottfried von Leibniz, put forth revolutionary ideas on the origin of the earth, suggesting that it cooled from a gaseous mass to the liquid state and then hardened on the outside to form a solid crust over a hot, molten interior.

TWO BILLION YEARS OF GEOLOGY

The Grand Canyon of Arizona reveals a unique cross section of rocks dating from the time life appeared in the ancient seas. Its geologic evolution is illustrated below.

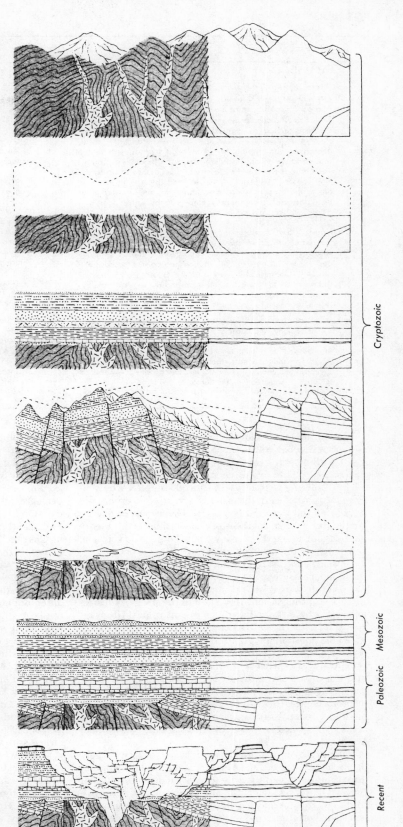

A rugged terrain composed of highly metamorphosed rock (schist), into which molten granitic rock had been intruded, marks the original landscape of the region.

These rocks, subjected for centuries to the various forces of erosion, were worn down to a flat, rather featureless plain and covered by the sea.

Late Precambrian sedimentary and volcanic rocks accumulated under the ancient sea to a thickness of more than 12,000 feet.

Intense forces buckled the earth and caused great blocks of the earth's crust to move upward and become tilted, forming rugged fault-block mountains.

Extensive erosion soon wore down the great mountains. At the beginning of the Cambrian Period, all that remained were low hills of tilted, late Precambrian strata rising above the generally featureless surface.

Gradually marine waters covered the schists and the late Precambrian rocks. During the Permian Period sedimentary rocks were deposited that document fluctuating marine and fresh-water environments. More recent rocks, deposited during Mesozoic and Cenozoic time, have been mostly eroded from this area.

Finally, in recent times, perhaps 5 million years ago, the Colorado River began to flow in its present course over a great plain. A gentle, steady rising of the land caused the river to run more swiftly, cutting a deeper and deeper valley. Today, the river is cutting into the ancient metamorphic rocks of the inner gorge.

Characteristics of the Field. Ways of earning a living in geology are numerous and varied, and most geologists specialize in a particular branch of the science. Engineering geologists, for example, are concerned with problems connected with the construction of highways, tunnels, dams, and similar structures. A relative newcomer to the field is the astrogeologist, who applies his knowledge of the earth to the interpretation of data gathered from the moon and planets. The occupations may be classified in a number of ways, the most basic being academic, favored by geologists who are primarily concerned with adding to our knowledge of the earth and are generally employed by universities and other institutions, and economic.

About 75% of all geologists are employed by private industry, and come in the latter category. Most work for the petroleum and natural gas industry, others for mining and construction companies and public utilities. Various departments of government employ geologists, for example, the U.S. Geological Survey and the Geological Survey of Canada. State agencies offer opportunities for employment, as do schools. A few geologists work for nonprofit organizations and museums.

Qualifications and Training. Graduate education is a necessity for a career in geology. The bachelor's degree seldom suffices for entry to the profession; for high-level research and administrative positions as well as college teaching positions the doctorate is required. The undergraduate studies such subjects as physical geology, historical geology, paleontology, and geophysics as well as the physical sciences, mathematics, and related subjects. The graduate student concentrates on a special branch of geology.

Geology is a science, and the person contemplating a career in it should have an aptitude for science in general. Also, since geologists often spend time in the field, he should have physical stamina and enjoy outdoor activities. Administrators, laboratory researchers, and some geologists work primarily indoors, however.

An ability to work as part of a team contributes to success in the profession, as does skill in preparing reports.

Outlook for Employment. The prospects for geologists who have advanced degrees is regarded as favorable, and the number of positions is expected to grow moderately. For the beginner with only a bachelor's degree, however, the competition will be keen. Demand for geologists fluctuates from year to year in petroleum and mineral extraction; however, openings also develop in such areas as land use and reclamation, highway and other large construction programs, and in establishing computer systems handling geologic information.

Income. Positions in industry generally pay better than those in government. Teaching pays less than either, but teachers commonly supplement their income with consulting work and writing.

Sources of Information. The reader should consult the Geology Study Guide for other articles that pertain to geology. General suggestions on career planning are in the article VOCATIONAL GUIDANCE. Details of geology as a profession may be obtained from the American Geological Institute and the American Geophysical Union, both in Washington, D.C., and from the Geological Association of Canada, in Toronto, Ontario.

One of the most influential of the early geologists was the great teacher Abraham Werner, who taught during the late 18th century at the Mining Academy at Freiberg, Saxony. He made extensive studies of the minerals and rocks of mining regions and inspired students who subsequently advanced the science greatly. Werner also advocated the so-called Neptunist Theory, an erroneous simplification of geologic history. According to this theory all rocks, including those that we now know to be volcanic, were precipitated from one great, world-wide ocean.

In sharp contrast to Werner's Neptunist teachings was the concept known as uniformitarianism advanced by James Hutton of Scotland. As summarized by the statement that "the present is the key to the past," Hutton's argument held that all geologic events in past times resulted from processes that are still active. Hutton recognized the continuous cycle of the erosion of rock from the land, transport of weathered material to the sea where it is deposited, eventual consolidation of the sediment, and uplift of the resulting rocks to form land again. Hutton's explanations were not all valid, but he led the way toward discrediting the theories of Neptunism and the rejection of most concepts of catastrophism, the theory that the earth's history involved a series of world-wide catastrophic events.

Paleontology was established as a science largely through the work of Lamarck in France, and his work on invertebrates paved the way for the theory of evolution. Baron Georges Cuvier, an anatomist, made extensive studies of ancient and recent animals, laying the groundwork for vertebrate paleontology. Also in France early

stratigraphic studies in the Paris Basin by Alexandre Brongniart were destined to influence American stratigraphers for many years, although the mapping and studies by William Smith in England are better known as pioneer work in stratigraphy. One of the greatest geologists of the 19th century was Sir Charles Lyell, who extended the stratigraphic and paleontologic studies of Smith and amplified the principles of Hutton. A friend of Charles Darwin, Lyell was profoundly influenced by Darwin's theory of evolution. Lyell's book, *Principles of Geology*, was a widely read and influential volume that remains a classic in geologic writing.

In America geology developed more slowly and in a different pattern, for much of the country was unexplored until the second half of the 19th century. The early governmental surveys, particularly in Pennsylvania, New York, and Massachusetts, made the first comprehensive geologic studies, from about 1830 to 1840. After the Civil War the geology of the Western states was investigated by Ferdinand Hayden, who explored vast areas of the Rocky Mountains and the Great Basin; by Clarence King, who conducted the geological survey of the 40th parallel and organized the U.S. Geological Survey; and by John Wesley Powell, who became director of the survey and who explored the Grand Canyon.

Many prominent American geologists have been teachers in colleges. The dominant figure among them near the end of the last century was James Dwight Dana at Yale, whose textbook of geology strongly influenced the science for years. He also organized and cataloged the field of mineralogy, and his books, in revised form, are standard references and texts today. William Morris Davis at Harvard established most of the modern concepts of physiography during the early years of the 20th century, and one of his colleagues, R. A. Daly, made significant advances in structural and theoretical geology. Waldemar Lindgren at the Massachusetts Institute of Technology established the leading classification of mineral deposits, and A. W. Grabau at Columbia developed systematic concepts in sedimentary petrology and stratigraphy. N. L. Bowen placed igneous petrology on a firm physicochemical basis through intensive laboratory studies. Other outstanding geologists too numerous to mention have continued to advance the science of geology at an ever accelerating pace.

Current and Future Trends

During the past 100 years a large portion of the land surface of the earth has been mapped geologically, and the geologic history of most areas is known at least in broad outline. Some regions, such as Great Britain, are now being remapped and restudied in great detail and with more refined techniques. Other regions have barely been investigated, but in the countries that are undergoing rapid economic development and industrialization, especially the U.S.S.R. and China, high priority is given to geologic mapping as a means of discovering additional mineral raw materials. Aerial photography has greatly simplified and refined the preparation of topographic maps, and geologists can now reach remote and difficult terrain rapidly by airplane, helicopter, and modern land vehicles. The search for oil has led to a three-dimensional investigation of the outermost layers of the earth, and efforts are being made to penetrate to significantly greater depths as well as to explore the submerged continental margins. In addition, an active program of exploratory drilling in the deep oceans has yielded important new clues to the origin and history of the ocean basins.

Recent advances in physics, chemistry, and electronic engineering have also provided new techniques and new instruments for investigation of the earth, and they have spurred development of the hybrid sciences of geochemistry and geophysics. Isotope analysis permits determinations of the age of nonfossiliferous rocks; rapid X-ray studies identify mineral grains too small to be seen; and new high-pressure furnaces duplicate conditions deep in the earth for the synthesis of minerals and rocks. These and similar advances have caused the development of a new kind of geology, which may be termed experimental geology. The science is moving into the laboratory as never before, and this is bringing about a shift of emphasis from descriptive and qualitative work to more exacting quantitative research into geologic processes.

Plate Tectonics. Among the most significant geologic advances of recent years has been the discovery, first suggested as a hypothesis in the 1950's and then confirmed in the late 1960's, that the earth's outer skin is divided into several large moving plates. Along certain margins of these plates new crustal rocks are being continuously created by upwelling lavas, while on opposing margins crustal rocks are destroyed as they plunge downward beneath adjacent plates. This discovery of what has come to be called "plate tectonics" has led to dramatic new insights into the origin of such seemingly diverse geologic phenomena as earthquakes, igneous rocks, and mountain ranges. This discovery has also confirmed the old but previously controversial suggestion that the continents move or "drift" into differing configurations over long intervals of geologic time. It is now clear that such movements occur as continents are passively rafted about by motions of the much more extensive crustal plates which underlie them.

Explorations in Space. A second series of important discoveries relating to the earth's geology has come from recent explorations of its nearest neighbors in space, particularly the moon and Mars. Radiometric dating and other analyses of lunar rocks have provided many clues to the origin and early history of the earth, while detailed surface photographs of Mars have revealed it to be far more earth-like than is the relatively lifeless, cratered crust of the moon.

Consult Calder, Nigel, *The Restless Earth* (1972); Dott, R. H., Jr., and Batten, R. L., *Evolution of the Earth* (1976); Leet, L. D., and Judson, S., *Physical Geology* (4th ed., 1971); McAlester, A. Lee, *The Earth: An Introduction to the Geological and Geophysical Sciences* (1973); Shimer, John A., *This Changing Earth* (1969).

STEPHEN E. AND PATRICIA S. CLABAUGH
Revised and updated by A. LEE MCALESTER
National Aeronautics and Space Administration

Harrison H. Schmitt, civilian astronaut who had obtained a doctorate in geology from Harvard University, collected rock samples and set up an array of scientific instruments on the moon after the Apollo 17 landing there in 1972. Apollo commander Eugene A. Cernan photographed Schmitt working near a huge boulder. The front portion of the lunar roving vehicle is visible at the left.

GEOMETRIC PROGRESSION, sequence of numbers, each successive pair having the same ratio: $a, ar, ar^2, ar^3, \ldots,$ where a is the first term and r the common ratio. If there are n terms, the last, or n^{th}, term is ar^{n-1}. For example, in the geometric progression $1, 2, 4, 8, \ldots, a = 1, r = 2,$ and the nth term is equal to $1 \cdot 2^{n-1}$. If there are 10 terms, the last term is $1 \cdot 2^9 = 512$. The sum of n terms is $S = a \dfrac{(r^n - 1)}{r - 1}$, or $a\dfrac{(1 - r^n)}{1 - r}$. Many qualities vary geometrically: the growth of money at compound interest, the growth of a population, and the decay of chemical elements by radioactivity.

See also ARITHMETIC PROGRESSION.

GEOMETRY, a branch of mathematics concerned with the analysis of spatial relationships. In its early stages, geometry developed as an empirical science, and as such became quite advanced. Between the 6th and 3d centuries B.C., a decisive change of attitude toward geometry occurred among Greek philosophers, which transformed it into a deductive science. The multitude of individual facts and techniques were woven into a pattern in which, from a few statements, all the rest could be deduced logically.

Euclid (c.300 B.C.) in his *Elements* provided a superb organization of the known material in geometry and arithmetic. The arithmetic, or number theory, was couched in geometric language. The style of the *Elements* set a standard for rigorous reasoning, which lasted until the 18th century. When Sir Isaac Newton wrote his great work *Principles of Natural Philosophy,* he used the format which Euclid initiated. In the 3d century B.C., the theory and application of geometry were extended, largely through the efforts of Archimedes and Apollonius.

Analytic Geometry. Usually attributed to René Descartes (1637), the basic ideas of analytic geometry were already implicit in the work of Apollonius. The basic idea is the representation of points by sets of numbers, in terms of which geometric statements and algebraic statements can be translated into each other. In the simplest version of plane analytic geometry, a point has two co-ordinates which represent the distance from the point to a pair of perpendicular lines, called co-ordinate axes. The algebraic signs of the co-ordinates tell on which side of the axes the point lies. Let P, Q, and R be points with co-ordinates (x,y), and (u,v), and (w,z), respectively. Then x and y are called the abscissa and ordinate of P, respectively. The distance between P and Q is given by $\sqrt{(x - u)^2 + (y - v)^2}$. P, Q, and R are collinear if and only if $uz + wy + xv = uy + wv + xz$. The midpoint of the segment PQ has co-ordinates $\left(\dfrac{x + u}{2}, \dfrac{y + v}{2}\right)$.

For each straight line there are constants a, b, and c (determined up to proportionality), where a and b are not both zero, such that the point (x,y) lies on the line if and only if $ax + by + c = 0$. The set of points on one side of the line is characterized by $ax + by + c > 0$, and the points on the other side by $ax + by + c < 0$. The distance between the point (u,v) and the line $ax + by + c = 0$ is given by $\left|\dfrac{au + bv + c}{\sqrt{a^2 + b^2}}\right|$. The lines $ax + by + c = 0$ and $a'x + b'y + c' = 0$ are parallel if $ab' = a'b$, and perpendicular if $aa' + bb' = 0$.

The examples given are a small sample of the way geometric information can be expressed in algebraic language.

In solid geometry, points are represented by number triples. Planes are described by equations of the form $ax + by + cz + d = 0$.

There are many extensions and variations of co-ordinates. Those described above are called rectangular Cartesian co-ordinates, after Descartes. On the surface of a sphere, latitude and longitude are co-ordinates.

In another direction, other number systems can be used for co-ordinates. In such cases algebraic differences between the number systems are reflected in different "geometrical" theories. In still another direction, the algebraic transition from two to three dimensions is so mild, that we can easily continue the process and construct n-dimensional geometries in which "points" are n-tuples of numbers. Such geometries are extremely useful in the analysis of various physical systems. They are usually studied under the name of "linear algebra." These ideas have been extended to the study of infinite dimensional spaces, crucial in the study of quantum mechanics.

Differential Geometry. Analytic geometry stimulated the development of the calculus. In turn, the methods of the calculus were applied to the study of geometry, and the result was differential geometry. The subject was put on a rigorous foundation (in the two-dimensional case) by Carl F. Gauss and in a more general setting by Georg Riemann. In the last two decades great strides have been made in differential geometry, using methods borrowed from algebraic topology.

Projective Geometry began in an attempt to analyze the principles of perspective drawing in the 15th century. The idea of deriving new figures from old ones by projection is very ancient, and the Greek mathematicians defined the conic sections in that manner. In order to treat separate cases more uniformly, Gérard Desargues (1639) introduced the technical device of a "line at infinity," each of whose "points" corresponded to a family of parallel lines. In this extended plane, after suitable definitions, it turns out that there are no parallel lines. What is remarkable is that no one saw the relevance to non-Euclidean geometry for another two centuries. The absence of parallel lines is largely responsible for the Principle of Duality in plane projective geometry. This asserts that if in a theorem of plane projective geometry, the words "line" and "point" are interchanged, and if collinearity of points and concurrency of lines is interchanged, the resulting statement will also be a valid theorem. This provided a mechanism for deriving new theorems from old.

As projective geometry developed it borrowed the methods of analytic geometry. In projective plane geometry a point is represented by a triple of numbers (a,b,c), not all zero. Further, any two proportional triples describe the same point. Lines are also represented by triples. Thus, $[r,s,t]$ represents a line, provided that not all three are zero. As with points, proportional triples represent the same line. A point (x,y,z) lies on the line $[u,v,w]$ if and only if $ux + vy + wz = 0$. It is important to note that the condition (whether or not $ux + vy + wz = 0$) remains unchanged, when either the point or line co-ordinates (or both) are multiplied by a nonzero proportionality factor. This property of the relation is called homogeneity, and for this reason, the co-ordinates used in projective geometry are called homogeneous co-ordinates. Another property of the relation is the symmetrical way in which the point and line co-ordinates are treated. This illustrates the principle of duality.

Projective geometry can also be studied in spaces of more than two dimensions. In such spaces the principle of duality becomes more complex. The "duals" of k-dimensional elements in n-dimensional projective geometry are $(n - k + l)$-dimensional elements.

Although it was originally conceived as a special branch of traditional geometry, projective geometry was finally recognized as an independent discipline which could be placed on its own axiomatic basis. By the latter half of the 19th century it was realized that both Euclidean and non-Euclidean geometry could be obtained from projective geometry by suitable specialization. In 1872, at Erlangen, Germany, Felix Klein pointed out that in each of the known geometries, a particular group of transformations was the underlying object of study. Using this point of view he even classified the infant discipline, point-set topology, as a special geometry. This view of geometry prevailed for a half century and, while no longer dominant, is still influential. The introduction of group theory was a much more profound merger of algebra and geometry than the use of co-ordinates and is a good example of the unity of mathematics. Finite geometries were introduced as a pedagogical device to illustrate the axiomatic method. Recently they have been studied in their own right and have found applications.

Algebraic geometry is an extension of projective geometry and is being actively studied, both with co-ordinates from arbitrary number systems and in a more abstract co-ordinate free manner.

Consult Eves, Howard, *A Survey of Geometry* (1963).

MICHAEL AISSEN, Fordham University

GEOMETRY, ANALYTIC. *See* ANALYTIC GEOMETRY.

GEOMETRY, DESCRIPTIVE. *See* DESCRIPTIVE GEOMETRY.

GEOMETRY, EVERYDAY USES OF. The name "geometry" itself came from a use and application (Gr., *ge*, "earth" and *metrein*, "to measure"). Geometrical methods were used by the ancient Egyptians in measuring land and were developed by the ancient Greeks into a science. Geometry is one of the most useful of the sciences, and almost every man-made object is shaped and proportioned by use of geometrical principles. The areas of all surfaces such as floors, rugs, and land are determined by methods of plane geometry, and the capacities (volumes) of all vessels and containers by the methods of solid geometry.

Examples. If the width *a* and the length *b* of a tele-

vision screen are 12 in. and 16 in., respectively, and *c* is the diagonal, then $c^2 = a^2 + b^2 = 12^2 + 16^2 = 144 + 256 = 400$ and $c = \sqrt{400} = 20$ in., the dimension used in stating the size of the screen. The same formula holds for any right triangle.

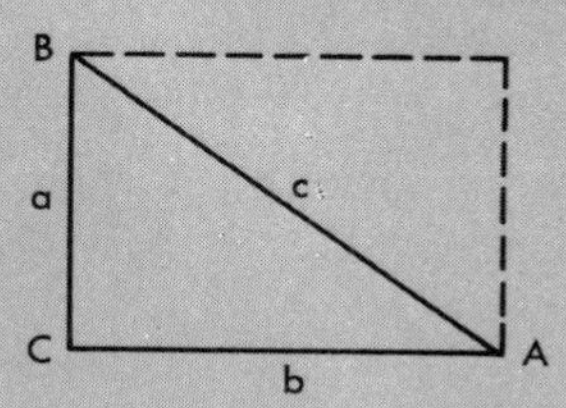

A lamp shade forming a frustum of a cone of small (top) diameter *d*, large (bottom) diameter *D*, slant height *s*, vertical height *h* has a curved surface area (on which the amount of material to make or cover it depends) of $A = 1.571 s(D + d)$. The volume (capacity) of a pail of the same form is $V = 0.2618 h(D^2 + Dd + d^2)$. If dimensions are in inches or feet, *A* is in square and *V* in cubic inches or feet, respectively.

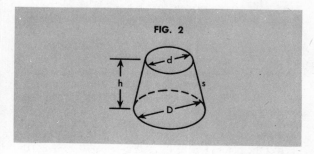

FIG. 2

To measure a distance *AB* to an inaccessible point (such as across a lake) or through a large obstacle, set up a vertical stake or rod *AC* at *A*, with a crosspiece *CE* fastened to it at *C* by a single nail or screw. Adjust the crosspiece by pivoting on *C* until it is sighted (aimed) directly at *B*. Then turn the rod *AC* while it remains vertical, without changing the setting of the crosspiece *CE*, and sight along the inclined crosspiece to *D*, the point where the line of sight meets the level ground. Then $AD = AB$ gives the distance.

To measure an inaccessible height *H*, measure on level ground the length of the shadow *L* cast by *H*; then immediately (before the shadow changes) set up a vertical rod of known length *h* and measure the length *l* of its shadow. Then $H = (Lh) \div l$ is the height.

To measure a height *BC* when there is no shadow, hold a draftsman's plastic 45° right triangle or one cut from cardboard so that one short side *EF* of the triangle is horizontal and the other short side *FG* is vertical and place one eye at *E*. Sight along the long edge *EG* toward the top of the height *C* and move toward or away from *B* on level ground until the line of sight *EG* passes through the top *C* when you are standing at *A*. Then measure the distance *AB* and add it to the height *AE* of the eye from the ground. Then, $AB + AE = BC$, the height of *C* from the ground.

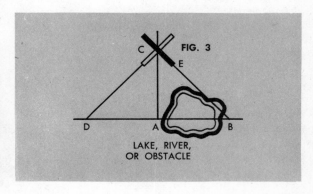

FIG. 1

FIG. 3

LAKE, RIVER, OR OBSTACLE

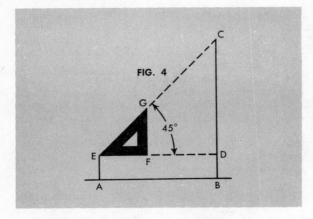

FIG. 4

45°

To divide a given line *AB* into any number of equal parts without a divided ruler or measuring rule, draw another line *AC* of convenient but indefinite length from one end *A* of the given line in any convenient position. On *AC* lay off from *A* the required number of parts, of any convenient length, all equal, and mark the dividing parts 1, 2, 3, 4, ... Join the last point so reached to *B* by a straight line, and draw lines parallel to this joining line through each of the points 1, 2, 3, 4, ... These parallels divide the given line *AB* into the required number of equal parts.

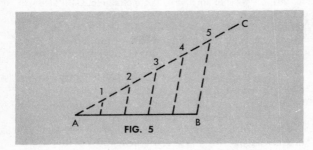

FIG. 5

From a point *T* high above the earth at a height $ET = h$ measured in miles or fraction of a mile (as the top *T* of a tall building or a mountain *ET*, or an airplane at the height *h*), a point *P* on the earth can be seen at a distance $TP = d = 89 \sqrt{h}$ mi. away from *T*. (Of course the distance or the weather or obstacles may affect the clearness of the view, but the earth is exposed to view to this distance *d* in every direction from *T*.) Thus the Empire State Building in New York is about 1,320 ft., or ¼ mi., high ex-

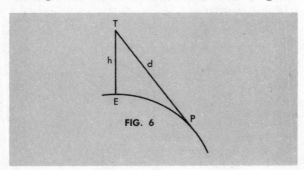

FIG. 6

clusive of the radio (television) tower on the top, and the earth is exposed to view for a distance $d = 89 \sqrt{¼} = 89 \times ½ = 44½$ or nearly 45 mi. from the top of the building in every direction.

JAMES E. THOMPSON, Pratt Institute

GEOMETRY, NON–EUCLIDEAN. In Euclid's *Elements*, the postulates were taken to be self-evident truths, an idealized version of actual physical space. This philosophical point of view was maintained for 2,000 years. Because the theorems were deduced logically from the postulates, they too bore the stamp of absolute truth.

Of the postulates, the most complicated and least intuitive was the Fifth: "If a straight line falling on two straight lines makes the interior angles on the same side together less than two right angles, the two straight lines, if produced indefinitely, meet on that side on which the angles are together less than two right angles."

One of the consequences of the first four postulates is that "If a point *P* and a line *L* are not incident, then there is at least one line through *P* parallel to *L*." If the Fifth postulate is also assumed, it can be shown that "there is exactly one line through *P* parallel to *L*." This last statement is called Playfair's Postulate, or the Parallel Postulate. It is equivalent to the Fifth postulate, if the first four postulates are assumed. There were many attempts, starting with Euclid, to prove the Fifth postulate from the first four postulates. Some more recent attempts were made by Giovanni Saccheri (1733), Johann Lambert (1766), and Adrien Legendre (1823).

An intellectual revolution occurred during the first half of the 19th century, when independently, Nikolai Lobachevsky, Farkas Bolyai, and Karl Gauss became convinced that there is nothing illogical in assuming the first four postulates, but replacing the Fifth postulate by "There is more than one parallel to *L* through *P*, if *P* is not on *L*." Their conviction was based on the fact that each had been able to derive an extensive collection of theorems, without arriving at a contradiction. They were unable to prove that no contradictions could arise, as more and more theorems were proved. This was done later by several mathematicians including Felix Klein and Henri Poincaré. They proved that "if Euclidean geometry is free from contradiction, then Lobachevskian geometry is also free from contradiction." Their method involved construction of a model for Lobachevskian geometry. Here, the new "points," "lines," "distance," and other elements were defined in terms of Euclidean geometry in such a way that the non-Euclidean postulates were Euclidean theorems.

In the Poincaré model, the "points" are points inside a fixed circle. The "lines" were circular arcs, cutting the circle at right angles, or diameters of the circle. The "angle" between two "lines" which intersect is the Euclidean angle between their tangents.

In 1854 Georg Riemann pointed out the distinction between a line being unbounded and a line being of infinite length. Using this, he constructed a consistent geometry in which there were no parallel lines. This also violated Euclid's second axiom, which states that a line segment can be extended indefinitely. Extensions of Riemannian geometry to higher dimensions were made by Riemann, Hermann Minkowski, and others. The mathematical formulation of relativity theory as developed by Einstein is one of the most prominent applications of non-Euclidean geometry to the natural sciences.

The theorems of non-Euclidean geometry are often interesting variants of familiar ones in Euclidean geometry. For example, the sum of the angles of a triangle is less than 180° in Lobachevskian geometry and greater than 180° in Riemannian geometry. The discovery of non-Euclidean geometry stimulated an intensive examination of the foundations of mathematics. Among the products of this activity were several reformulations of Euclidean geometry on a more complete axiomatic basis.

MICHAEL AISSEN, Fordham University

GEOMETRY, PROJECTIVE. *See* PROJECTIVE GEOMETRY.

GEOMORPHOLOGY [jē-ō-môr-fŏl′ə-jē], branch of geology concerned with the study of landscape features—their description, classification, origin, and significance. For purposes of analysis the landscape is divided into features called landforms, each of which has certain distinctive characteristics. Examples include volcanoes, dunes, deltas, terraces, and various kinds of mountains, ridges, hills, and valleys. Each landform is studied from the standpoint of origin and evolution, using the long-established principle that the present is a key to the past, that is, that all existing landforms were created by physical processes like those still at work on the earth. Thus, from observations of earthquakes and active volcanoes, of rivers in flood, of storm-driven waves and currents of the sea, and of other natural processes, complemented by laboratory experiments and by inductive and deductive logic, it is possible to discover how landforms have been produced.

In general, landforms fall into two major classes: those formed primarily by the earth's internal forces and those produced primarily by surface forces and processes. The first includes volcanoes and the various mountains, scarps, troughs, and basins formed by the bending or breaking of the earth's crust. The second group includes all the erosional and depositional features fashioned by running water, glacial ice, wind, waves and currents, and underground water, all of which work toward progressive modification and obliteration of landforms of the first group. The surface processes, in general, proceed through a definite sequence known as the erosion cycle. For each stage of the various processes the resulting landforms have distinctive characteristics that are related also to bedrock geology and structure and to other elements of present and past environment, such as climate.

Application of the foregoing principles to the particular assemblage of landforms in any given region, with due consideration of their complications and interrelations, provides a basis for description and classification of the terrain, for interpretation of certain aspects of bedrock geology and of recent geologic history, and for the most effective approach to many practical problems in engineering, land use, and development of natural resources.

Consult Thornbury, W. D., *Principles of Geomorphology* (1954).

H. T. U. SMITH, University of Massachusetts
See also EROSION; GEOLOGY; PHYSIOGRAPHY.

GEOPHYSICS [jē-ō-fiz′ĭks], study of the physical properties and structure of the earth. The scope of geophysics extends from the center of the earth to the surface and on to the outermost regions of the atmosphere. Certain studies of the moon, sun, and other planets are also considered geophysical because the information gained relates to the properties of the earth.

Divisions. Geophysics can be divided into several branches, each of which is a major science in itself. Geodesy is concerned with the over-all size and shape of the earth, and includes studies of the force of gravity. Tectonics, or structural geology, deals with the earth's structural features and their causes. Seismology is the study of earthquakes and the information they reveal concerning elastic and other properties of the earth. Volcanology is concerned with volcanic processes and their causes and effects. Physical oceanography is the science of ocean currents and waves, and the structure and configuration of ocean basins. Hydrology deals with the behavior of water on the earth's surface, including lakes and rivers. Glaciology is concerned with glaciers and glacial phenomena. Meteorology is the study of the earth's atmosphere, especially with regard to weather analysis and prediction.

In addition to these specific fields, geophysics includes studies of terrestrial heat, electricity, and magnetism. Geophysicists study the ionosphere to obtain information about such phenomena as auroras, airglow, and cosmic rays. The radioactive dating of rock formations, too, is part of geophysics.

None of the branches of geophysics is completely independent of the others. Many overlap and are closely interrelated. For example, studies of the earth's interior make use of observations of such widely different phenomena as earthquakes and details of the moon's motion, as well as laboratory experiments on the effects of pressure and temperature on rocks. Waves from nuclear explosions give information on the structure of both the earth's interior and the atmosphere. Investigations of the earth's magnetic field involve the understanding of electric currents in the earth's core, as well as the behavior of particles in the ionosphere. Some aspects of oceanography and glaciology are closely linked with meteorology. The gravitational attraction of the moon and sun causes tides not only in the oceans, but in the solid earth (bodily tides) and in the atmosphere. Questions of the solidity and elasticity of material within the earth are linked to studies of seismology, radioactivity, and terrestrial heat.

In spite of the complex interrelations between divisions of their science, geophysicists can be broadly divided into two groups. One group is concerned primarily with the earth from the surface downward; the other is concerned primarily with the atmosphere. Of those who study the atmosphere, meteorologists are interested mostly in the lower 20 miles, where 99% of the atmosphere's mass is concentrated and where all of our weather occurs. Geophysicists are closely related to astrophysicists, who include the entire universe in their field of study.

Geophysical Exploration. Geophysical instruments and techniques are widely used to determine characteristics of rocks in the outermost layers of the earth's crust, with the aim of locating ore deposits, mapping structures in layered rocks that may contain oil or natural gas, or determining the configuration of bedrock beneath the surface. The depth to bedrock is especially important where dams are to be built or where roads are to be cut through hilly country.

The methods and instruments used in geophysical exploration depend on the kind of information desired. Many mineral deposits and structural features can be found by the variations that they cause in the earth's magnetic and gravitational fields. Instruments called magnetometers and gravimeters, or gravity meters, are used to detect these variations. Some mineral deposits generate a minute electric potential with regard to surrounding rocks. This difference in electric potential can be detected with sensitive instruments. Sometimes a current is applied to the rocks, and their resistivity is measured. This provides an indication of the minerals present or of the fluid content of pores in the rock. The natural radioactivity of many rocks and minerals may also be used in geophysical exploration. Instruments such as Geiger counters readily detect deposits of uranium-bearing minerals or other radioactive ores used in atomic-energy research.

In seismic prospecting for oil and natural gas, vibrations are induced in the earth, either by explosives or by a vibrating apparatus. The vibrations, or waves, are reflected from or refracted through subsurface rock layers and then detected by a portable seismograph. Interpretation of the seismograph record provides a picture of underground structures where oil or gas may be trapped. Similar techniques are used to determine depth to bedrock for engineering purposes.

Consult The Planet Earth, ed. by D. R. Bates (1957);

The Planet Earth, ed. by staff of *Scientific American* magazine (1957); Jeffreys, Sir Harold, *The Earth* (4th ed., 1959).

K. E. BULLEN, University of Sydney, Australia

See also:

ATMOSPHERE   HYDROLOGY
EARTH   METEOROLOGY
GEODESY   OCEANOGRAPHY
GLACIERS AND   VOLCANO
  GLACIATION

GEOPOLITICS [jē-ō-pŏl′ə-tĭks], the study of the relationship between land and sea areas and politics for the purpose of serving foreign policy. It differs from political geography in that it is concerned with the evaluation of geographical conditions, boundaries, the distribution of people, and similar factors in the light of the requirements of the state. Rudolf Kjellén (1864–1922), a Swedish writer and disciple of the German geographer Friedrich Ratzel (1844–1904), is known as the father of geopolitics. Kjellén conceived of states not so much as legal entities but as powers that must be considered geographically.

Two broad schools of geopolitics have been dominant: the sea power approach, in which emphasis is placed on the control of the waterways of the world; and the land power or "heartland" theory, in which certain land masses become vital. The sea power concept is identified with U.S. Adm. Alfred Thayer Mahan (1840–1914), who interpreted world history largely as a continuing struggle for control of the seas. Drawing upon military, naval, and economic history, he argued that the nation that controls the seas would control the world. The heartland theory is as-

GEOPHYSICISTS AT WORK

Authenticated News

Oceanographer prepares to lower a magnetometer overboard. The device, towed by the ship, measures the earth's magnetic field.

Birnback Publishing Service

Radar antenna measuring height and structure of a thunderstorm. A radarscope records the impulses echoing from the clouds.

Authenticated News

Scientists plant explosives deep in the Arctic ice. Seismograms of such explosions indicate the nature of underlying strata.

sociated with Sir Halford Mackinder (1869–1947), the well-known Scottish geographer. He contended that the land mass from the Volga to the Yangtze and from the Himalayas to the Arctic Ocean dominated the world geographically and could do so politically. This heartland, or "pivotal area," which is entirely continental, is surrounded by an inner or marginal crescent, which is part continental and part oceanic, and by an outer or insular crescent, which is largely oceanic. Within the heartland, eastern Europe is the critical area. Sir Halford summarized this concept in these words: "Who rules eastern Europe commands the Heartland; Who rules the Heartland commands the World Island [Eurasia-Africa]; Who rules the World Island commands the World."

Nicholas J. Spyckman (1893–1943), a writer on international politics, questioned the validity of the heartland thesis and considered the inner crescent, or rimland, which occupies the intermediate region between the heartland and the marginal seas, as more significant than the heartland. He stated that Sir Halford's dictum should be reworded as follows: "Who controls the Rimland rules Eurasia; Who rules Eurasia controls the destinies of the world." In the hands of Karl Haushofer (1869–1946) and his disciples, geopolitics was used as an ideological weapon in the service of the national aspirations of Nazi Germany. During World War II, Sir Halford redefined the heartland but in the main reaffirmed the principles he had espoused. It is well to note, however, that none of these theories take into account factors that have become increasingly significant, such as air power, outer space developments, and the greater emphasis placed on the polar regions.

GUENTER WEISSBERG, Columbia University

GEORGE, ST., 4th century Christian martyr and patron saint of England. He probably suffered martyrdom at Lydda in Palestine before 303 A.D. Little is known of him; but his cult became widespread after the 6th century. The tradition which describes him as a dragon slayer started in the 12th century and became popular from its appearance in the "Golden Legend" (13th century). It was not until the 14th century that he became the patron saint of England. His feast day is April 23.

GEORGE I (1660–1727), King of Great Britain and Ireland (1714–27). A complex man whose unattractive character combined such diverse traits as obstinacy, bravery, sensuality, and dullness, George I successfully established the Hanoverian Dynasty upon the British throne. He was the son of Ernst August, Elector of Brunswick-Lüneburg, commonly called Hanover, and Sophia, daughter of Frederick, Count Palatine, and Elizabeth, daughter of James I of England. As a young man he served in the imperial army. He married (1682) his cousin Sophia Dorothea of Celle, whom he later divorced and imprisoned (1694) because of her intrigue with Count Königsmark, a Swedish adventurer. He succeeded his father as Elector (1698) and subsequently joined the Grand Alliance against Louis XIV (1701), personally commanding the imperial army on the Upper Rhine (1707–9).

On the death of Queen Anne (1714), he ascended the British throne as provided by the Act of Settlement (1701). Unpopular from the first because of his brusque manner, ignorance of the language, and preoccupation with Hanover, which he frequently visited, he nevertheless won the loyalty of his new subjects, admirably adapting himself to their constitutional government, although he disliked it intensely. He entrusted the conduct of affairs entirely to the Whigs, Sir Robert Walpole serving as principal minister during half of his reign (1721–27). Believing that his son, the Prince of Wales, sought to undermine his position, he quarreled violently with him and banished him from court (1717). The Prince thereupon set up a rival court at Leicester House, around which rallied the opposition Whig coteries. The allegiance of all political groups thus became firmly attached to the dynasty, which was solidly grounded when George I died.

Consult Plumb, J. H., *The First Four Georges* (1957).

J. JEAN HECHT, Stanford University

GEORGE II (1683–1760), King of Great Britain and Ireland (1727–60). A conscientious, industrious, methodical man, who, lacking self-confidence, leaned heavily on others for advice, George II perfectly filled the role of constitutional monarch. He was the only son of George I and Sophia Dorothea. He married (1705) his cousin Caroline of Ansbach, a clever, learned woman, whom he loved more than his mistresses, Lady Suffolk and Lady Yarmouth, and who exerted over him a considerable and salutary influence until her death (1737). A soldier by preference, he served with distinction under the Duke of Marlborough at Oudenarde (1708). When his father ascended the British throne (1714), he accompanied him to England. But a few years later, they quarreled violently, the Prince setting up a rival court at Leicester House, which became the center of the opposition.

After he succeeded his father (1727), he was generally expected to choose his principal minister from that group; but Queen Caroline persuaded him to retain Sir Robert Walpole. His relations with his son Frederick, Prince of Wales, were similar to those that had existed between himself and his father, Leicester House again serving as the center of the opposition (1737–51). Never greatly liked because of his quarrels with his father and his son, and his partiality for Hanover, he grew more unpopular during the War of the Austrian Succession, when he was thought to have subordinated British to Hanoverian interests. But he was momentarily acclaimed for leading the army to victory at Dettingen (1743), the last time a British King commanded in person. After Walpole's downfall (1742), his principal ministers, Henry Pelham (1743–54) and the Duke of Newcastle (1754–56), proved to be competent men. During his last years, popular clamor obliged him to entrust the conduct of affairs to William Pitt (1757–60), whose anti-Hanoverian utterances had earlier angered him.

Consult Plumb, J. H., *The First Four Georges* (1957).

J. JEAN HECHT, Stanford University

GEORGE III (1738–1820), King of Great Britain and Ireland (1760–1820). Mistaking obstinacy for firmness, rigidity for rectitude, and prejudices for principles, George III dealt ineptly with the difficult constitutional and imperial problems that confronted him during his long reign. The son of Frederick, Prince of Wales, and the grandson of George II, he was carefully reared by his mother, Augusta of Saxe-Gotha, who sought to inculcate a strong hatred of his grandfather and his grandfather's ministers. He became deeply attached to her chief advisor, the Earl of Bute, whom he made his political mentor, and later his principal minister (1762–63).

When he ascended the throne (1760), he was assisted by Bute in reversing the war policy of his grandfather's ministers (1763), and in securing their replacement (1761–63), which, since he desired no constitutional changes, was the only substantial innovation that he sought to introduce. Shortly after becoming King, he married (1760) Charlotte of Mecklenburg-Strelitz, an unattractive but fecund woman to whom he was a faithful and devoted husband. His marriage reduced his dependence on Bute, who faded from the scene (1766), leaving him to solve alone the problem of ministerial instability that plagued the early years of his reign (1760–70). He at last found the answer in Lord North, who both shared his views and could maintain a Parliamentary majority. Together they asserted the rights of Parliament against the American colonies (1770–82).

When the debacle of the American Revolution overthrew North (1782), there ensued another period of ministerial instability, during which the Marquess of Rockingham, the Earl of Shelburne, and Charles James Fox, all loathed by the King, succeeded each other as principal minister (1782–83). Ultimately, the younger William Pitt rescued the King, providing a stable administration for 18 years (1783–1801). At the same time the Prince of Wales set himself up as the patron of the opposition, making Carlton House its center. When the King went temporarily mad a few years later, Fox tried to secure for the Prince full regal powers (1788), but incurred only hatred for his pains.

From this point the King grew in popularity, to which his moral private life, his interest in science and agricul-

ture, the ill behavior of the Prince and his other undutiful sons, the lingering effects of his madness, all contributed. Soon, too, the French Revolution illuminated his virtues. From the time that Pitt resigned rather than press upon him the cause of Catholic Emancipation (1801), the King was carefully shielded and played a less active part in affairs. The manic-depressive affliction that had struck him twice before (1765, 1788), however, attacked him again (1804); and during his last years (1811–20) he was permanently mad.

Consult Watson, J. S., *The Reign of George III* (1960).

J. JEAN HECHT, Stanford University

GEORGE IV (1762–1830), King of Great Britain and Ireland (1820–30). Self-indulgent, unrestrained, and extravagant, George IV lived a profligate and disorderly life that disgusted the public and lowered the prestige of the throne. He was the eldest son of George III and Charlotte. Although strictly raised, he early became addicted to drinking and gambling. Like previous Hanoverian Princes of Wales, he quarreled continually with his father, making Carlton House the center of the opposition and taking Charles James Fox as his principal advisor. Having fallen in love with Maria Anne Fitzherbert, a Roman Catholic, he secretly married her (1785), although their union was neither valid nor legal. To obtain the payment of his debts, he later married Caroline of Brunswick (1795). But after the birth (1796) of their daughter, Princess Charlotte, they separated, the Queen eventually going abroad to live (1814).

When George III went permanently mad, the Prince of Wales was made Regent (1811), and then given full regal powers (1812). Contrary to expectations, he abandoned his old friends, the Foxites, retaining his Tory ministers whose views he shared. The vast sums that he expended on collecting art and on architectural projects such as the Brighton Pavilion and Windsor Lodge greatly embittered the economically distressed, and an attempt was made to assassinate him (1817). When he finally succeeded his father (1820), the Queen returned from abroad to assert her rights. The King countered by instituting divorce proceedings. But the outcry against him was so great—all disaffected elements uniting to support the Queen—that the proceedings had to be terminated. This unpopularity was accompanied by a decline in regal power.

Consult Fulford, Roger, *George IV* (1949).

J. JEAN HECHT, Stanford University

GEORGE V (1865–1936), King of Great Britain and Ireland (1910–36). At the age of 12 he entered the Royal Navy as a cadet and remained an active seaman until 1892, when his older brother, Albert Victor, Duke of Clarence and heir to the throne, died. The following year George married Princess Victoria Mary (1867–1953), daughter of the Duke of Teck. Upon the succession of his father, Edward VII, to the throne, George began to take on more state duties and made several trips outside of England. In 1901 he and the Princess went to Australia to open the first Commonwealth Parliament there. Later that year he was created Prince of Wales. In 1910 he became King and was crowned the following year. The reign, except for brief periods, was troubled and tumultuous.

George III, from the studio of Allan Ramsay, about 1767.
National Portrait Gallery

George V, King of Great Britain (reigned 1910–36).

George VI ascended the British throne upon the abdication of his brother, Edward VIII.

Shortly after his accession, the King had to deal with the Liberal party's insistence that the powers of the House of Lords be reduced. This was accomplished by the passage of the Parliament Bill of 1911. Labor unrest, suffragette agitation, and near revolution in Ireland made the first years of George V's reign exceedingly difficult.

Then came World War I, during which almost 1,000,-000 Britons lost their lives and several times that number were wounded. During the war the King renounced all of his German titles and officially changed the name of the royal house from Saxe-Coburg-Gotha to Windsor. In the early 1920's troubles in Ireland over the question of home rule gave the King particular concern. George V's choice of Stanley Baldwin over Lord Curzon to be Prime Minister, on Bonar Law's retirement in 1922, was an important exercise of royal power. The King sought to lessen the class feeling that the General Strike and mass unemployment generated in the 1920's and early 1930's. A strong conservative, he maintained a deep interest in the Empire, and while he did not entirely welcome the new status of the crown in the Commonwealth of Nations as created by the Statute of Westminster in 1931, he respected the changes. In 1935, when he celebrated his Silver Jubilee, there was an outpouring of popular affection for him and Queen Mary, and his death the following year was deeply mourned.

Consult Nicolson, H. G., *King George the Fifth* (1953).

STEPHEN GRAUBARD, Harvard University

GEORGE VI (1895–1952), King of Great Britain and Northern Ireland (1936–52). As the second son of George V, he had never expected to ascend the throne and had prepared for a career in the navy. He was educated at Osborne and Dartmouth naval college. After service in World War I, he studied at Cambridge and in 1920 was created Duke of York. In 1923 he married Lady Elizabeth Bowes-Lyon of Scotland. His service in the navy and his quiet life as Duke of York scarcely prepared him for

the heavy responsibilities that suddenly descended on him when his brother, Edward VIII, abdicated. Shy, retiring, and plagued by a speech impediment, he had none of the public talents that had made Edward so popular as Prince of Wales.

The first years of his reign were far from tranquil. This was the period when the great depression was coming to an end and when Prime Minister Neville Chamberlain sought to appease Nazi Germany. In the late spring of 1939, the King and Queen visited Canada and the United States and became acquainted with the American President Franklin Roosevelt. The friendship proved important during the dark days of World War II. The King's relations with the wartime Prime Minister, Winston Churchill, were exceedingly cordial, and the King did much to help in rallying the country to support wholeheartedly the government's war plans.

After the war, when the Labour party governed, George VI saw fundamental changes made in the Commonwealth. The two self-governing states of India and Pakistan were created in 1947; the King was no longer Emperor of that vast subcontinent. The same year the royal family made a successful trip to South Africa.

The marriage (1947) of his elder daughter, Elizabeth, to Lt. Philip Mountbatten gave the King great pleasure, as did the arrival of the first of his grandchildren. In the last years of his reign the King suffered from many illnesses.

Consult Wheeler-Bennett, John, *King George VI, His Life and Reign* (1958).

STEPHEN GRAUBARD, Harvard University

GEORGE, HENRY (1839–97), American economist. Born and raised in Philadelphia, he received little formal education. In 1857 he migrated to San Francisco and became a printer. Unable to support his family by writing, editing, and other jobs, he began to ponder the paradox of widespread poverty in a country of such vast natural wealth, and he studied the works of the leading economists to find the answer. Unsatisfied, he worked out his own theory, first published as a pamphlet, *Our Land and Land Policy* (1871), and later developed into *Progress and Poverty* (1879).

George blamed the unequal distribution of wealth on

private ownership of land, which he felt should be common property. Since landowners did nothing to increase land values—the result of population growth and the greater productivity of society—this "unearned increment" should be taken for public use. A single tax on land values, George argued, would pay the necessary expenses of government and at the same time effect a more equal distribution of wealth. *Progress and Poverty* attracted world-wide attention; it was translated into many languages and sold millions of copies.

In 1880 George moved to New York and spent the rest of his life writing and lecturing. In 1886 he ran as an independent candidate for mayor of New York. He lost but polled a heavy vote. His ideas are disseminated by the Henry George School of Social Science, founded (1932) in New York City, and by similar schools in England, Denmark, Australia, New Zealand, Spain, and Formosa. His economic theories have influenced tax policies in many countries.

Consult Barker, C. A., *Henry George* (1955).

HERBERT A. Q. WISBEY, JR., Keuka College

GEORGE [gā-ôr′gə], **STEFAN** (1868–1933), German poet whose authoritarian personality and precise poetic diction influenced a generation. Circles of disciples formed around him in the various cities in which he lived. In his journal, *Blätter für die Kunst* (Pages for Art), 1892–1919, as well as in his poetry, he propounded his idea of the mission of an elite to ennoble German culture. He followed French symbolism in his early work and stressed perfection of form. Opposing a materialistic world and a realistic and naturalistic literature, George advocated classicism, humanism, and austerity as means toward a national rebirth. He left Germany when the Nazis came to power, but ironically he was acclaimed the national poet after his death. A representative selection of George's poetry appeared in English translation as *Poems* (1943).

GEORGE, WALTER FRANKLIN (1878–1957), U.S. Senator (1922–57). Born near Preston, Ga., and educated at Mercer University, he practiced law in Vienna, Ga., and was a state supreme court justice (1917–22). As chief Democratic senatorial opponent of President Franklin Roosevelt's plan to "pack" the Supreme Court, George was the object (1938) of a "purge" attempt by Roosevelt. In the first administration of President Dwight D. Eisenhower, he promoted bipartisanship in foreign policy as chairman (1955–57) of the Foreign Relations Committee. Having declined (1956) the nomination for re-election, he accepted appointment as special representative to the North Atlantic Treaty Organization.

GEORGE, LAKE, lake in northeastern New York, in the southeastern foothills of the Adirondack Mountains. It drains north to Lake Champlain. Beautiful scenery and historic sites make it a favored resort area. The region was a battleground during the French and Indian and Revolutionary wars, and contains ruins of Fort George in Lake George Battleground Park and restored Fort William Henry. Principal towns are Lake George on the south and Bolton Landing, chief resort center, on the west. Length, 33 mi.; width, 1–3 mi.

GEORGETOWN, seaport, largest city, and capital of Guyana, situated at the mouth of the Demerara River on the Atlantic coast. Georgetown exports sugar cane, rice, and tropical fruits grown on the surrounding plains and also products brought there by rail, such as timber, bauxite, gold, and diamonds. Georgetown is a railroad center and also has an airport. The climate is characterized by an average temperature of about 80° F. and two rainy seasons, April to August, and November to January. Georgetown was founded by the British in 1781 and later held by the Dutch, who named it Stabroek. Recovered by the British in 1803, it was named Georgetown in honor of George III. Pop., about 160,000.

GEORGETOWN, farming town of southern Ontario, Canada, 29 mi. west of Toronto. Sandstone is quarried here, and there is some manufacturing. Inc., 1921; pop., 10,298.

GEORGE TOWN, deep-water port and capital of the state of Penang, northwestern Federation of Malaysia. Commonly called Penang, the city is on Penang Island 4 mi. across the Penang Channel from Butterworth and Prai on the Malay Peninsula. Noted for tin smelting, George Town is the second largest city and leading port in Malaysia, exporting tin, specialty foodstuffs (pepper, tapioca, spices), copra, and rubber. As a low-duty port it has an important entrepot trade. George Town, the first English outpost in Malaya, was founded in 1786 by the (British) East India Company to defend its Indian possessions and to secure the strategic Strait of Malacca. In 1829 it became a part of the Straits Settlements, which, in turn, received crown colony status in 1867. The population is over 70% Chinese; Indians and Malaysians constitute most of the remainder. Site of the first school in Malaya (1816), the city now has a teacher training college and a federal dental school. Pop., approx. 300,000.

RICHARD F. HOUGH, San Francisco State College

GEORGETOWN, section of Washington, D.C., at the confluence of the Potomac River and Rock Creek. Settled in the 17th century, Georgetown was independent until 1878 when it was annexed to Washington. Dumbarton Oaks, an estate in Georgetown, was the location of the 1944 meeting that initiated the plan to form the United Nations. Georgetown University is the oldest Roman Catholic institute in the United States.

GEORGETOWN, city of northern Kentucky, and seat of Scott County, 12 mi. north of Lexington. It is a marketing center for the bluegrass region. Georgetown College (estab., 1829) is here. Pop., 8,629.

GEORGETOWN, city of eastern South Carolina and seat of Georgetown County, on navigable Winyah Bay, about 15 mi. from the Atlantic. It has a large paper mill and is a yachting center. Founded, 1734; Inc., as a city, 1892; pop., 10,449.

GEORGETOWN, city of central Texas and seat of Williamson County, in a ranching and dairying area. Southwestern University (estab., 1840), a Methodist institution, is here. Pop., 6,395.

GEORGIA

Capitol at Atlanta

Live oak

Brown thrasher

Cherokee rose

CAPITAL	Atlanta
ADMITTED TO UNION	1788
ORDER OF ADMISSION	4th
POPULATION	
1970 (15th in Union)	4,589,575
1960 (16th in Union)	3,943,116
AREA	58,876 sq mi (152 489 km²)
Land	58,073 sq mi (150 409 km²)
Inland water	803 sq mi (2 080 km²)
ELEVATION	
At highest point (Brasstown Bald Mountain)	
	4,784 ft (1 472 m)

At lowest point (Atlantic Ocean)	Sea level
POPULAR NAMES	The Peach State
	The Empire State of the South
MOTTO	Wisdom, Justice, and Moderation
FLOWER	Cherokee rose
TREE	Live oak
BIRD	Brown thrasher
SONG	Georgia

REPRESENTATION IN U.S. CONGRESS	
Senate	2
House	10

GEORGIA [jor′jə], coastal Southern state of the United States and one of the 13 original states. It is the largest state east of the Mississippi River. At its greatest length Georgia extends about 315 mi (507 km) from its mountainous northern border to the flatlands in the south. From west to east its maximum breadth is 250 mi (402 km). Georgia has 100 mi (161 km) of coastline, with numerous offshore islands, sand beaches, marshlands, and major ocean port facilities at Savannah and Brunswick.

Physical Geography

Five distinct physiographic regions are represented within Georgia: the Coastal Plain, the Piedmont Province, the Blue Ridge Province, the Valley and Ridge Province of the Appalachian Valley, and the Appalachian or Cumberland Plateau. These fall within two natural divisions that extend into other states: the Coastal Plain is part of the Atlantic Plain and the remaining four provinces belong to the Appalachian Highlands.

Surface Features. The southern half of Georgia is in the Coastal Plain. The topography varies primarily from flat to rolling, and the elevations range from sea level at the Atlantic Ocean to 500 ft (152 m) along the border with the Piedmont Province at the Fall Line. (The Fall Line is formed where the higher terrain of the rocky Piedmont suddenly descends to the lower, softer Coastal Plain, producing rapids and falls in the rivers. It runs across Georgia from Augusta to Columbus.)

Cypresses in Okefenokee Swamp, one of the largest U.S. swamps.

Rivers and Lakes. Although there are a few small rivers in extreme northern Georgia which drain north and northwest to the Tennessee River, the state's major rivers flow southeast to the Atlantic Ocean, or south and southwest to the Gulf of Mexico. Those emptying into the Atlantic include the Savannah River (which forms part of the Georgia–South Carolina boundary), the Ogeechee, the Altamaha (which is formed by the Oconee and the Ocmulgee), the Satilla, and the St. Marys (which forms part of the Georgia–Florida boundary). Those that drain into the Gulf of Mexico include the Alapaha and Suwannee, the Ochlockonee, the Flint, and the Chattahoochee (which forms part of the Georgia-Alabama border).

Georgia's larger lakes are artificial. Noteworthy among these are Clark Hill Reservoir (shared with South Carolina), Lake Sidney Lanier, Allatoona Lake, and Lake Sinclair. Among springs in the state, Warm Springs is a well-known center for the treatment of paralytic patients. Its nonprofit foundation was created by President Franklin D. Roosevelt, who spent much time as a patient there. Radium Springs, near Albany, is the largest Georgia spring. In southeastern Georgia is Okefenokee Swamp, one of the United States' largest swamp areas.

Climate. Georgia has a mild climate year round. In the mountainous Blue Ridge region of the northeast, average temperatures range from 40° F (4° C) in January to 78° F (26° C) in July. In the southern Coastal Plain, average temperatures range from 53° F (12° C) in January to 82° F (28° C) in July. Temperatures in other areas of the state range between these extremes. The annual rainfall in the state averages 48 in. (122 cm). The growing season is about 179 days in northern Georgia's mountainous areas, and is 270 days or more in south Georgia. Springtime tornadoes and autumn hurricanes occasionally cause extensive damage.

Soils. Georgia has eight chief soil areas which run generally across the state, extending from southwest to northeast in irregular bands, or belts. Beginning in the extreme southeastern section and proceeding northwestward, the soil areas are those of the lower, middle, and upper Coastal Plain and the Sand Hill, Piedmont, Blue Ridge, Valley-and-Ridge and Cumberland Plateau provinces.

The Coastal Plain and Sand Hill provinces were once an ocean floor. The soils are primarily sands and sandy loams with some red clay loams occurring in the upper Coastal Plain. The soils are of moderate to high fertility. The Piedmont Plateau soils are sandy loam and clay loam of moderate fertility. The Blue Ridge and Cumberland

The northern half of Georgia is divided among four regions of the Appalachian Highlands. Approximately one-third of the state north of the Fall Line is in the Piedmont Upland, or Piedmont Plateau, section of the Piedmont Province. This region of Georgia ranges in elevation from about 500 ft (152 m) along the Fall Line to 1,500 ft (456 m) at points near the Appalachian regions to the north. There are some small mountains in the section, including Kennesaw, Pine, and Stone.

The extreme northeastern sector of the state is in the Blue Ridge Province of the Appalachian Highlands. This mountainous area exhibits numerous peaks of more than 4,000 ft (1 219 m), including Georgia's highest, Brasstown Bald Mountain, at 4,784 ft (1 472 m).

Most of the upper northwestern sector of the state is within the Valley and Ridge Province of the Appalachian Highlands. Parallel ridges rising to 1,000 ft (305 m) above the valley floor traverse the province in a north-south direction.

A relatively small area in the extreme northwestern corner of the state is in the Cumberland Plateau section of the Appalachians. With elevations ranging from about 1,700 to 2,000 ft (518-610 m), the section includes Sand and Lookout mountains and the valley between them.

Open kaolin mine, at Hephzibah. The power shovel at left is at the level of the clay vein.

Plateau soils are residual and of high fertility. The Valley-and-Ridge soils include limestone of high fertility, shale of fair fertility, and sand of low fertility.

Mineral Resources. Some 40 minerals are found in Georgia. The most valuable are clays, stone (granite and marble), sand and gravel, iron ore, mica, and coal. The clays, including kaolin and fuller's earth, occur mainly in a belt extending across the central part of the state. Granite and famous Georgia marble are found in the northern sections, particularly around Atlanta and near Elberton in the northeast. Stone Mountain, just east of Atlanta, contains an extensive body of exposed granite. The principal deposits of coal and iron ore lie within northwestern Georgia, and mica is found in both northwestern and northeastern sections of the state. Other minerals which are found within the state include bentonite, chromite, copper, corundum, halloysite, ilmenite, monazite, olivine, rutile, sillimanite, tripoli, vermiculite, and zircon.

Natural Vegetation. Because of the range of climate and soils in Georgia, there is great variety in the natural vegetation. Almost two-thirds of the area of the state is forested, and there are 163 species of trees.

In the Coastal Plain of southern Georgia and in the

(EWING GALLOWAY)

Workers in the marble quarry at Tate. The marble blocks, weighing up to 150,000 lb., are cut by machine and raised by steam derricks.

STUDY GUIDE

An efficient way to begin the study of Georgia is to examine the maps accompanying this article. They make it easy to follow the discussion, besides giving a great deal of information about the state. Mountain ranges, rivers, and other major features on the physical map are treated in separate articles, as are cities, larger towns, and important sites shown on the general reference map. Examples of related articles follow, grouped under the major headings that divide the main article.

Physical Geography. The geographical setting for the state is described in NORTH AMERICA and in SOUTHERN STATES. Surface features receive individual attention in such articles as APPALACHIAN HIGHLANDS, BLUE RIDGE MOUNTAINS, OKEFENOKEE SWAMP, CHATTAHOOCHEE RIVER, SUWANNEE RIVER, SAVANNAH RIVER, and SEA ISLANDS. Details on vegetation and wildlife may be found, for example, in PINE, LIVE OAK, and OPOSSUM.

Economy. The resources and industries of Georgia may be studied further in a number of articles. The economy of the region is described in SOUTHERN STATES. CLAY, GRANITE, and MARBLE treat important mineral resources of the state. Other articles containing information pertinent to the state's economy are FISHERIES, FORESTS AND FORESTRY, POULTRY, NAVAL STORES, and LUMBER AND LUMBERING. Georgia benefits from many of the activities of the TENNESSEE VALLEY AUTHORITY (TVA).

People. Additional information on how and where Georgians live is contained in city articles, such as ATLANTA, SAVANNAH, COLUMBUS, AUGUSTA, and MACON. Statistics on institutions of higher education are in the Universities and Colleges table, Vol. 20. Aspects of Georgia life are suggested by the list entitled Places of Interest. PULASKI, FORT is one of the Civil War monuments. Other parks and monuments are treated in NATIONAL PARK SYSTEM, UNITED STATES.

Government. Some of the problems with which Georgia's gov-

ernors and legislature have contended are discussed in SOIL CONSERVATION, in NATURAL RESOURCES, CONSERVATION OF, and in LABOR LAWS.

History. The history section of the article UNITED STATES provides the background for the history of Georgia. Details can be filled in from many other articles. Indians of the region are described in INDIAN TRIBES, NORTH AMERICAN and in CHEROKEE and CREEK. Hernando DE SOTO explored the region for Spain. Later James OGLETHORPE founded a colony for England. Conditions in early Georgia are discussed in COLONIAL PERIOD IN U.S. HISTORY. Participation in the war for independence is covered in AMERICAN REVOLUTION. An important legal and political issue is treated in YAZOO LAND CONTROVERSY. Georgia became a stanch advocate of STATES' RIGHTS and was one of the CONFEDERATE STATES OF AMERICA. Besides being a major supply and transportation area during the Civil War, the state was the scene of the ATLANTA CAMPAIGN and other events described in CIVIL WAR, AMERICAN. Postwar conditions are covered in RECONSTRUCTION.

One of the best ways to survey the history of the state, as well as its contributions to national and world culture, is to read biographic entries on the great men and women who have been associated with the state. This does not apply only to figures such as Button GWINNETT, Alexander Hamilton STEPHENS, Robert TOOMBS, William Gibbs McADOO, William Joseph HARDEE, and (David) Dean RUSK. It also applies to writers such as Joel Chandler HARRIS, Erskine CALDWELL, Margaret MITCHELL, Sidney LANIER, Conrad P. AIKEN, and Flannery O'CONNOR.

Basic statistics on agriculture, industry, population, education, and other features of the state are included in the Profile and in the body of the text. The growth and development of the state year by year can be followed in the annual supplement to this Encyclopedia and in sources available in the library. The library, moreover, can provide books that give extended treatment of Georgia history and the lives and contributions of important Georgians.

GEORGIA

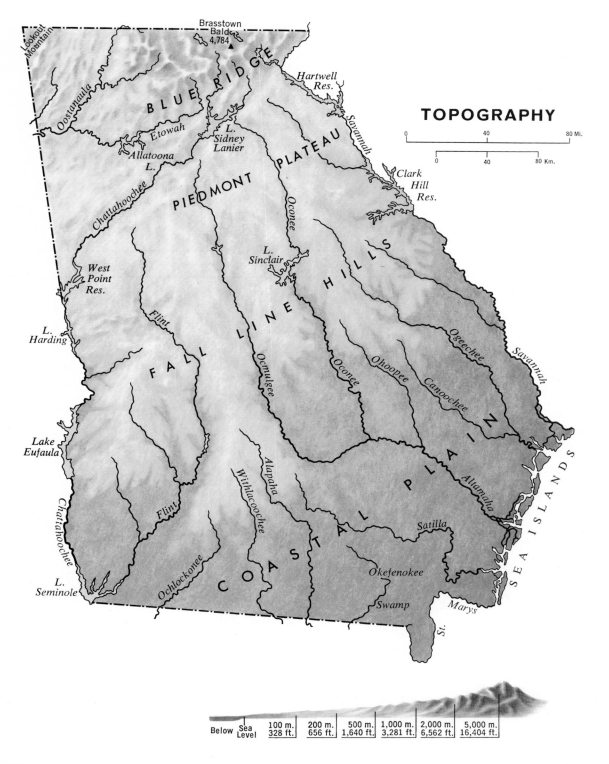

TOPOGRAPHY

Lookout Mountain

BLUE RIDGE

Brasstown Bald 4,784

Hartwell Res.

Oostanaula

Etowah

L. Sidney Lanier

PLATEAU

Savannah

Clark Hill Res.

Allatoona L.

PIEDMONT

Chattahoochee

Oconee

West Point Res.

L. Sinclair

FALL LINE HILLS

Flint

L. Harding

Ocmulgee

Oconee

Ohoopee

Ogeechee

Savannah

Canoochee

Lake Eufaula

Alapaha

Withlacoochee

Altamaha

Chattahoochee

Flint

Satilla

SEA ISLANDS

L. Seminole

Ochlockonee

COASTAL PLAIN

Okefenokee

Swamp

Marys

St.

		0	40	80 Mi.
		0	40	80 Km.

Below Sea Level	100 m. 328 ft.	200 m. 656 ft.	500 m. 1,640 ft.	1,000 m. 3,281 ft.	2,000 m. 6,562 ft.	5,000 m. 16,404 ft.

AGRICULTURE AND FORESTRY IN GEORGIA

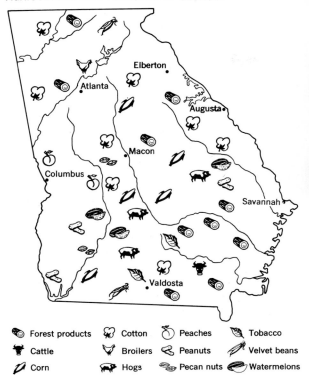

Elberton

Atlanta

Augusta

Macon

Columbus

Savannah

Valdosta

Forest products	Cotton	Peaches	Tobacco
Cattle	Broilers	Peanuts	Velvet beans
Corn	Hogs	Pecan nuts	Watermelons

J. C. Allen and Son

Modern hog farm near College Park.

turkeys are well distributed throughout the Coastal Plain; the Piedmont and the Blue Ridge have smaller populations. Ruffed grouse are found primarily in the Blue Ridge. Other game birds, including duck, geese, doves, woodcock, marsh hen, rail, and coot, are found in fewer numbers.

Fish found in the cold-water lakes and streams of the mountainous sections of the state include pike, small-mouthed black bass, and brook and brown trout. Muskellunge are found in Blue Ridge Lake and the Toccoa River. Largemouthed black bass, bream, perch, catfish, pickerel, and crappie are found in the lakes and streams

highland forests of northwestern Georgia pines predominate. Cypresses, palmettos, live oaks (the state tree), red maples, bays, magnolias, and canes are native to the lake, stream, and coastal-island areas. In the Piedmont section, across north-central Georgia, there are forests of pines, beech, sycamore, oaks, walnuts, hickory, and gum. The fertile Blue Ridge section of the northeastern part of the state presents the greatest variety of vegetation. Trees found in this area include ash, beech, birch, cherry, hickory, locust, oaks, walnut, basswood, buckeye, butternut, poplar, hemlock, and white pine.

Shrubby growth such as laurel and rhododendron are profuse in mountainous areas. Grasses, honeysuckle, Cherokee rose (the state flower), dogwood, redbud, chinaberry, crab apple, and mimosa are found throughout the state.

Wildlife. Georgia has a wide variety of animals, birds, and fish. There are over 40 species of mammals within the state. Rabbits, opossums, squirrels, muskrats, raccoons, and foxes are common to most sections, and deer are also widespread. Bears are found not only in the mountainous Blue Ridge but in the Coastal Plain, which also has beaver, otter, and mink.

Some 350 species of birds are found in Georgia. The most common song birds are the blue jay, brown thrasher (the state bird), cardinal, catbird, mockingbird, robin, thrush, towhee, and wren. Other birds found throughout the state include the crow and several varieties of birds of prey. By far the most important game bird is the quail, widely distributed throughout the state, with heavy concentrations in the Coastal Plain and the Piedmont. Wild

MANUFACTURING AND MINING IN GEORGIA

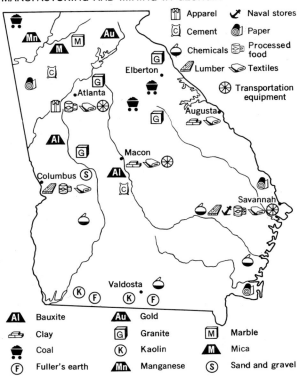

Apparel		Naval stores	
Cement		Paper	
Chemicals		Processed food	
Lumber		Textiles	
		Transportation equipment	

Elberton

Atlanta

Augusta

Macon

Columbus

Savannah

Valdosta

Al Bauxite		Au Gold			
Clay		G Granite		M Marble	
Coal		K Kaolin		M Mica	
F Fuller's earth		Mn Manganese		S Sand and gravel	

535

Visitors pause to admire ruins of old mansions on wild, lush Cumberland Island. Most of the island, which is off Georgia's coast, has been designated a national seashore. (NATIONAL PARK SERVICE)

of all sections. Record-making largemouthed bass and chain pickerel have been caught in Georgia.

Saltwater fish found in Georgia's coastal waters include the shad, red snapper, grouper, mackerel, bluefish, flounder, and sea, or channel, bass. Shrimp, crab, and oysters are the principal shellfish.

Among the state's reptiles, the largest are alligators, found in protected coastal areas. The diamondback terrapin is also found along the coast; the sea turtle, in coastal waters. The four poisonous snakes native to the United States are resident in Georgia—the rattlesnake, the copperhead, the moccasin, and the coral snake.

Okefenokee Swamp (GEORGIA DEPARTMENT OF INDUSTRY AND TRADE)

Economy

Manufacturing. Since the end of World War II manufacturing has replaced agriculture as Georgia's most important economic activity. In order of magnitude, leading sources of employment are manufacturing, trade, agriculture, government, services (including motels and hotels, laundry, cleaning, and miscellaneous business services), transportation and public utilities, and construction. Manufacturing accounts for approximately one third of all the employment in Georgia.

Georgia ranks first among the southeastern states in the manufacture of transportation equipment and in wholesale trade, second in the making of apparel and the processing of food, and third in the production of furniture and lumber. The textile industry is Georgia's oldest and largest. Other ranking industries are those making pulp paper and chemicals. Georgia leads all states in the nation in the production of paper and board and tufted textile products.

Atlanta and Savannah are chief centers of industry, although there are factories located throughout the state. Major textile manufacturing cities are Augusta, Columbus, and Macon.

Agriculture. Historically, agriculture has been of great importance to the state. As early as 1735 the first agricultural experiment station in colonial America was introduced at Savannah, and in 1874 Georgia established the nation's first state department of agriculture. The eight major soil regions and the long growing season make possible the cultivation of a wide diversity of farm products.

Although the number of people employed in agriculture in Georgia has decreased, income from agriculture

GEORGIA

COUNTIES

Appling, 12,726 H 7
Atkinson, 5,879 G 8
Bacon, 8,233 G 7
Baker, 3,875 D 8
Baldwin, 34,240 F 4
Banks, 6,833 E 2
Barrow, 16,859 E 2
Bartow, 32,663 C 2
Ben Hill, 13,171 F 7
Berrien, 11,556 F 8
Bibb, 143,418 E 5
Bleckley, 10,291 F 6
Brantley, 5,940 J 8
Brooks, 13,743 E 9
Bryan, 6,539 K 6
Bulloch, 31,585 J 6
Burke, 18,255 J 4
Butts, 10,560 E 4
Calhoun, 6,606 C 7
Camden, 11,334 J 9
Candler, 6,412 H 6
Carroll, 45,404 B 3
Catoosa, 28,271 B 1
Charlton, 5,680 H 9
Chatham, 187, 816 K 6
Chattahoochee, 25,813 C 6
Chattooga, 20,541 B 1
Cherokee, 31,059 D 2
Clarke, 65,177 F 3
Clay, 3,636 B 7
Clayton, 98,043 D 3
Clinch, 6,405 G 9
Cobb, 196,793 C 3
Coffee, 22,828 G 8
Colquitt, 32,298 E 8
Columbia, 22,327 H 3
Cook, 12,129 F 8
Coweta, 32,310 C 4
Crawford, 5,748 E 5
Crisp, 18,087 E 7
Dade, 9,910 A 1
Dawson, 3,639 D 2
Decatur, 22,310 C 9
De Kalb, 415,387 D 3
Dodge, 15,658 F 6
Dooly, 10,404 E 6
Dougherty, 89,639 D 7
Douglas, 28,659 C 3
Early, 12,682 C 8
Echols, 1,924 G 9
Effingham, 13,632 K 6
Elbert, 17,262 G 2
Emanuel, 18,357 H 5
Evans, 7,290 J 6
Fannin, 13,357 D 1
Fayette, 11,364 C 4
Floyd, 73,742 B 2
Forsyth, 16,928 D 2
Franklin, 12,784 F 2
Fulton, 607,592 D 3
Gilmer, 8,956 D 1
Glascock, 2,280 G 4
Glynn, 50,528 J 8
Gordon, 23,570 C 2
Grady, 17,826 D 9
Greene, 10,212 F 3
Gwinnett, 72,349 D 2
Habersham, 20,691 E 1
Hall, 59,405 E 2
Hancock, 9,019 G 4
Haralson, 15,927 B 3
Harris, 11,520 C 5
Hart, 15,814 G 2
Heard, 5,354 B 4
Henry, 23,724 D 4
Houston, 62,924 E 6
Irwin, 8,036 F 7
Jackson, 21,093 E 2
Jasper, 5,760 E 4
Jeff Davis, 9,425 G 7
Jefferson, 17,174 H 4
Jenkins, 8,332 J 5
Johnson, 7,727 G 5
Jones, 12,218 E 5
Lamar, 10,688 D 4
Lanier, 5,031 F 8
Laurens, 32,738 G 6
Lee, 7,044 D 7
Liberty, 17,569 J 7
Lincoln, 5,895 H 3
Long, 3,746 J 7
Lowndes, 55,112 F 9
Lumpkin, 8,728 D 1
Macon, 12,933 D 6
Madison, 13,517 F 2
Marion, 5,099 C 6
McDuffie, 15,276 H 4
McIntosh, 7,371 K 7
Meriwether, 19,461 C 4
Miller, 6,424 C 8
Mitchell, 18,956 D 8
Monroe, 10,991 E 4
Montgomery, 6,099 G 6
Morgan, 9,904 F 3
Murray, 12,986 C 1
Muscogee, 167,377 C 6
Newton, 26,282 E 3
Oconee, 7,915 F 3
Oglethorpe, 7,598 F 3
Paulding, 17,520 C 3
Peach, 15,990 E 5
Pickens, 9,620 D 2
Pierce, 9,281 H 8
Pike, 7,316 D 4
Polk, 29,656 B 3
Pulaski, 8,066 E 6
Putnam, 8,394 F 4
Quitman, 2,180 B 7
Rabun, 8,327 F 1
Randolph, 8,734 C 7
Richmond, 162,437 H 4
Rockdale, 18,152 D 3
Schley, 3,097 D 6
Screven, 12,591 J 5
Seminole, 7,059 C 9
Spalding, 39,514 D 4
Stephens, 20,331 F 1
Stewart, 6,511 C 6
Sumter, 26,931 D 6
Talbot, 6,625 C 5
Taliaferro, 2,423 G 3
Tattnall, 16,557 J 6
Taylor, 7,865 D 5
Telfair, 11,394 G 7
Terrell, 11,416 D 7
Thomas, 34,562 E 9
Tift, 27,288 E 7
Toombs, 19,151 H 6
Towns, 4,565 E 1
Treutlen, 5,647 G 6
Troup, 44,466 B 4
Turner, 8,790 E 7
Twiggs, 8,222 F 5
Union, 6,811 E 1
Upson, 23,505 D 5
Walker, 50,691 B 1
Walton, 23,404 E 3
Ware, 33,525 H 8
Warren, 6,669 G 4
Washington, 17,480 G 4
Wayne, 17,858 J 7
Webster, 2,362 C 6
Wheeler, 4,596 G 6
White, 7,742 E 1
Whitfield, 55,108 B 1
Wilcox, 6,998 F 7
Wilkes, 10,184 G 3
Wilkinson, 9,393 F 5
Worth, 14,770 E 8

CITIES and TOWNS

Abbeville⊙, 781 F 7
Acworth, 3,929 C 2
Adairsville, 1,676 C 2
Adel⊙, 4,972 F 8
Adrian, 705 G 5
Ailey, 487 G 6
Alamo⊙, 833 G 6
Alapaha, 633 F 8
Albany⊙, 72,623 D 7
Albany, ‡89,639 D 7
Aldora, 322 D 4
Alexander, 200 J 4
Allenhurst, 230 J 7
Allentown, 295 F 5
Alma⊙, 3,756 G 7
Almon, 400 E 3
Alpharetta, 2,455 D 2
Alto, 372 E 2
Alto Park, 2,963 B 2
Ambrose, 253 G 7
Americus⊙, 16,091 D 6
Andersonville, 274 D 6
Apalachee, 150 E 3
Appling⊙, 212 H 3
Arabi, 305 E 7
Aragon, 850 B 2
Arcade, 229 E 2
Arco, 6,009 J 8
Argyle, 206 G 8
Arlington, 1,698 C 8
Armuchee, 600 B 2
Ashburn⊙, 4,209 E 7
Ashland, 350 F 2
Athens⊙, 44,342 F 3
Atlanta (cap.)⊙, 497,421 D 3
Atlanta, ‡1,390,164 D 3
Attapulgus, 513 D 9
Auburn, 361 E 2
Augusta⊙, 59,864 J 4
Augusta, ‡253,460 J 4
Austell, 2,632 C 3
Avalon, 204 F 1
Avans, 150 A 1
Avera, 217 G 4
Avondale Estates, 1,735 D 3
Axson, 250 G 8
Baconton, 710 D 8
Bainbridge⊙, 10,887 C 9
Baldwin, 772 E 2
Ball Ground, 617 D 2
Barnesville⊙, 4,935 D 4
Barnett, 125 G 3
Barney, 150 E 8
Barretts, 275 F 8
Bartow, 333 G 5
Barwick, 432 E 9
Baxley⊙, 3,503 H 7
Beachton, 200 D 9
Bellville, 234 H 6
Bemiss, 325 F 9
Berkeley Lake■, 219 D 3
Berlin, 422 E 8
Berryton, 200 B 2
Bethlehem, 304 E 3
Bibb City, 812 B 5
Bishop, 235 F 3
Blackshear⊙, 2,624 H 8
Blaine, 130 C 1
Blairsville⊙, 491 E 1
Blakely⊙, 5,267 C 8
Blitchton, 256 J 6
Bloomingdale, 1,588 K 6
Blue Ridge⊙, 1,602 D 1
Blythe, 333 H 4
Bogart, 667 E 3
Boneville, 150 G 4
Boston, 1,443 E 9
Bostwick, 289 E 3
Bowdon, 1,753 B 3
Bowdon Junction, 200 B 3
Bowersville, 301 G 2
Bowman, 724 G 2
Box Springs, 600 C 5
Bradley, 125 E 4
Braselton, 386 E 2
Bremen, 3,484 B 3
Bridgeboro, 250 E 8
Brinson, 231 C 9
Bristol, 150 H 8
Bronwood, 500 D 7
Brookfield, 860 F 8
Brooklet, 683 J 6
Brooks, 172 D 4
Broxton, 957 G 7
Brunswick⊙, 19,585 K 8
Buchanan⊙, 800 B 3
Buckhead, 177 F 3
Buena Vista⊙, 1,486 C 6
Buford, 4,640 D 2
Bullard, 230 F 5
Butler⊙, 1,589 D 5
Byromville, 419 E 6
Byron, 1,368 E 5
Cadwell, 354 G 6
Cairo⊙, 8,061 D 9
Calhoun⊙, 4,748 C 1
Calvary, 500 D 9
Camak, 224 G 4
Camilla⊙, 4,987 D 8
Campania, 150 H 4
Canon, 709 F 2
Canton⊙, 3,654 C 2
Carbondale, 300 B 1
Carl, 234 E 3
Carlton, 294 F 2
Carnesville⊙, 510 F 2
Carrollton⊙, 13,520 C 3
Cartecay, 250 D 1
Cartersville⊙, 9,929 C 2
Cassville, 350 C 2
Cataula, 500 C 5
Cave Spring, 1,305 B 2
Cecil, 265 F 8
Cedar Springs, 200 C 8
Cedartown⊙, 9,253 B 2
Center, 213 F 2
Centerville, 1,725 E 5
Centralhatchee, 186 B 4
Chalybeate Springs, 266 C 5
Chamblee, 9,127 D 3
Chatsworth⊙, 2,706 C 1
Chauncey, 308 F 6
Cherrylog, 155 D 1
Chester, 409 F 6
Chickamauga, 1,842 B 1
Choestoe, 215 E 1
Chula, 300 E 7
Cisco, 175 C 1
Clarkesville⊙, 1,294 F 1
Clarkston, 3,127 D 3
Claxton⊙, 2,669 J 6
Clayton⊙, 1,569 F 1
Clem, 350 B 3
Clermont, 290 E 2
Cleveland⊙, 1,353 E 1
Climax, 275 D 9
Clinchfield, 180 E 6
Cloudland, 150 A 1
Clyattville, 500 F 9
Clyo, 300 K 6
Cobb, 125 E 7
Cobbtown, 321 H 6
Cochran⊙, 5,161 F 6
Cogdell, 150 G 8
Cohutta, 393 C 1
Colbert, 532 F 2
Coleman, 168 C 7
Colesburg, 150 J 9
College Park, 18,203 C 3
Collins, 574 H 6
Colquitt⊙, 2,026 C 8
Columbus⊙, 155,028 C 6
Columbus, ‡238,584 C 6
Comer, 828 F 2
Commerce, 3,702 E 2
Concord, 312 D 4
Conyers⊙, 4,890 D 3
Coolidge, 717 E 8
Coosa, 600 B 2
Cordele⊙, 10,733 E 7
Cornelia, 3,014 E 1
Covington⊙, 10,267 E 3
Crandall, 200 C 1
Crawford, 624 F 3
Crawfordville⊙, 735 G 3
Crest, 200 D 5
Crosland, 158 E 8
Crystal Springs, 500 B 2
Culloden, 272 D 5
Cumming⊙, 2,031 D 2
Cusseta⊙, 1,251 C 6
Cuthbert⊙, 3,972 C 7
Dacula, 782 E 3
Dahlonega⊙, 2,658 D 1
Daisy, 150 J 6
Dallas⊙, 2,133 C 3
Dalton⊙, 18,872 C 1
Damascus, 272 C 8
Danielsville⊙, 378 F 2
Danville, 515 F 5
Darien⊙, 1,826 K 8
Dasher, 452 F 9
Davisboro, 476 G 5
Dawson⊙, 5,383 D 7
Dawsonville⊙, 288 D 2
Dearing, 555 H 4
Decatur⊙, 21,943 D 3
Deenwood, 3,015 H 8
Demorest, 1,070 F 1
Denton, 244 G 7
De Soto, 321 D 7
Dewy Rose, 180 G 2
Dexter, 438 G 6
Dial, 150 D 1
Dillard, 186 F 1
Dixie, 200 E 9
Dock Junction (Arco), 6,009 J 8
Doerun, 1,157 E 8
Donalsonville⊙, 2,907 C 8
Doraville, 9,157 D 3
Double Branches, 175 H 3
Douglas⊙, 10,195 G 7
Douglasville⊙, 5,472 C 3
Dover, 200 J 5
Draketown, 150 B 3
Dry Branch, 700 F 5
Dublin⊙, 15,143 G 5
Dudley, 423 F 5
Duluth, 1,810 D 2
Du Pont, 252 G 9
Durand, 192 C 5
Eastanollee, 365 F 1
East Dublin, 1,986 G 5
East Ellijay, 488 C 1
East Griffin■, 1,479 D 4
East Juliette, 163 E 4
Eastman⊙, 5,416 F 6
East Newnan, 1,634 C 4
East Point, 39,315 C 3
Eastville, 135 E 3
Eatonton⊙, 4,125 F 4
Eden, 300 K 6
Edison, 1,210 C 7
Elberta, 500 E 5
Elberton⊙, 6,438 G 2
Eldorendo, 131 C 8
Elizabeth, 950 C 2
Elko, 450 E 6
Ellabell, 400 K 6
Ellaville⊙, 1,391 D 6
Ellenton, 337 E 8
Ellerslie, 615 C 5
Ellijay⊙, 1,326 C 1
Emerson, 813 C 2
Empire, 325 F 6
Enigma, 505 F 8
Ephesus, 212 B 4
Epworth, 300 D 1
Esom Hill, 200 B 3
Eton, 286 C 1
Eulonia, 500 K 7
Evans, 1,500 H 3
Everett, 300 J 8
Experiment, 2,256 D 4
Fairburn, 3,143 C 3
Fairmount, 623 C 2
Fargo, 800 G 9
Fayetteville⊙, 2,160 C 4
Felton, 300 B 3
Fender, 150 E 8
Fitzgerald⊙, 8,187 F 7
Fleming, 175 K 7
Flemington, 265 K 7
Flintstone, 150 B 1
Flippen, 600 D 3
Flovilla, 289 E 4
Flowery Branch, 779 E 2
Folkston⊙, 2,112 H 9
Forest Park, 19,994 D 3
Forsyth⊙, 3,736 E 4
Fort Gaines⊙, 1,255 C 7
Fort Oglethorpe, 3,869 B 1
Fort Valley⊙, 9,251 E 5
Fowlstown, 400 D 9
Franklin⊙, 749 B 4
Franklin Springs, 501 F 2
Fry, 300 D 1
Funston, 293 E 8
Gabbettville, 150 B 5
Gainesville⊙, 15,459 E 2
Gainesville Cotton Mills■, 2,060 E 2
Garden City, 5,790 K 6
Gardi, 125 J 7
Garfield, 214 H 5
Gay, 200 C 4
Geneva, 250 C 5
Georgetown⊙, 860 B 7
Gibson⊙, 701 G 4
Girard, 241 J 4
Glennville, 2,965 J 7
Glenwood, 670 G 6
Godfrey, 150 F 4
Good Hope, 202 E 3
Gordon, 2,553 F 5
Gough, 300 H 4
Gracewood, 1,200 H 4
Graham, 125 H 7
Grantville, 1,128 C 4
Gray⊙, 2,014 F 4
Grayson, 366 E 3
Greensboro⊙, 2,583 F 3
Greenville⊙, 1,085 C 4
Greggs, 250 F 8
Gresston, 200 F 6
Griffin⊙, 22,734 D 4
Grovania, 300 E 6
Grovetown, 3,169 H 4
Guyton, 742 K 6
Habersham, 225 F 1
Haddock, 600 F 4
Hagan, 572 J 6
Hahira, 1,326 F 9
Hamilton⊙, 357 C 5
Hampton, 1,551 D 4
Hapeville, 9,567 D 3
Haralson, 162 C 4
Hardwick, 14,047 F 4
Harlem, 1,540 H 4
Harrison, 329 G 5
Hartsfield, 175 E 8
Hartwell⊙, 4,865 G 2
Hawkinsville⊙, 4,077 E 6
Hazlehurst⊙, 4,065 G 7
Helen, 252 E 1
Helena, 1,230 G 6
Hephzibah, 987 H 4
Hiawassee⊙, 415 E 1
Higgston, 175 G 6
Hillsboro, 250 E 4
Hilltonia, 294 J 5
Hilton, 172 C 8
Hinesville⊙, 4,115 J 7
Hinsonton, 200 D 8
Hiram, 441 C 3

⊙ County seat. ‡ Population of metropolitan area. ■ Name not shown on map.

All figures available from 1970 final census are supplemented by local official estimates.

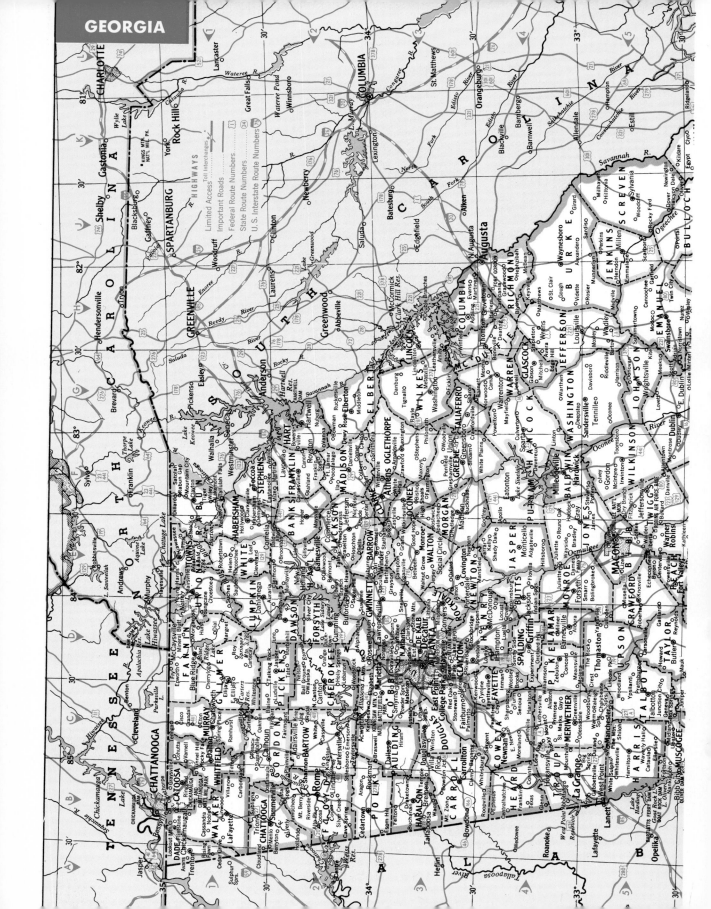

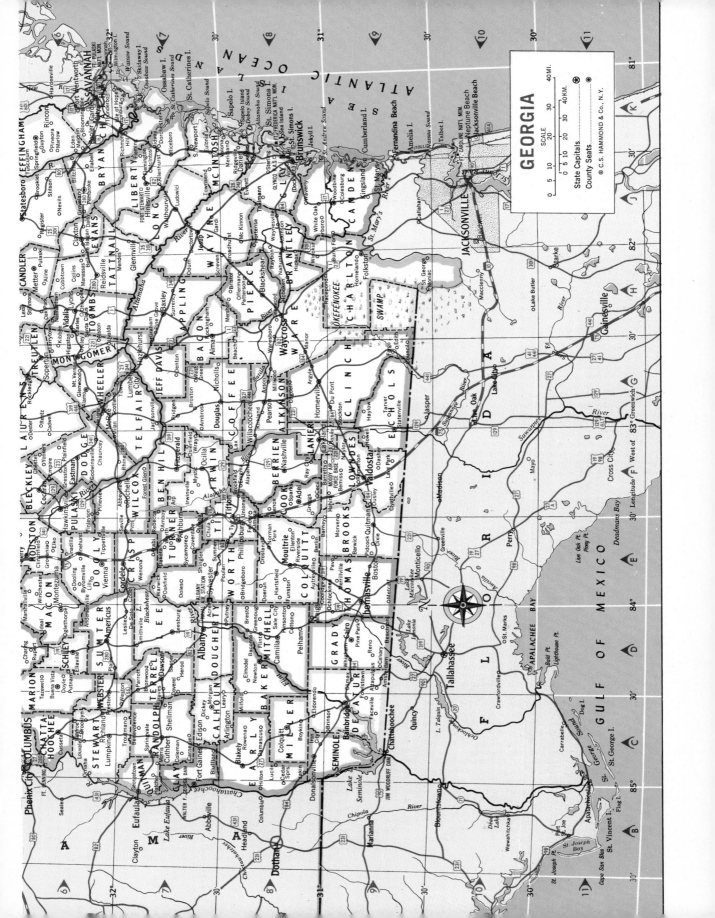

GEORGIA

Gum distillery in Georgia, world's largest naval stores producer.
(GEORGIA FORESTRY COMMISSION)

Cotton mill in Georgia, where textiles are the leading manufacture.
(PHILIP GENDREAU)

has increased sharply. Principal crops are peanuts, pimento peppers, tobacco, corn, cotton, and soybeans. Livestock, particularly cattle and hogs; poultry, eggs, and dairy products are important sources of farm income, contributing more than 60% of the total.

In the value of agricultural exports Georgia ranks seventeenth among the states. The six commodities that return the largest share of the total income from agricultural exports are tobacco, cotton, feed grain, nuts, soybeans, and poultry products. In exports, Georgia ranks second among the states in nuts and poultry products, third in tobacco, and ninth in cotton.

The trend in Georgia is toward fewer but larger farms. Approximately 30,000 acres of farmland are under irrigation. The increase in mechanization is illustrated by the fact that the number of tractors in use on Georgia's farms has quadrupled since the end of World War II. Concurrently, there has been a steady decrease in tenant farming in favor of owner-operated or manager-operated farms.

Fisheries. Georgia's fisheries are largely concentrated along the state's 100-mile (161-km) Atlantic coastline. Shrimp, oysters, crab, shad, and terrapin are the principal sources of income.

Forestry and Forest Products. Georgia's forests cover some 25,000,000 acres and are one of its major resources. The state ranks second in the nation in the net annual growth of saw timber and produces more than half the world's supply of naval stores, particularly gum turpentine and rosin. Pulpwood makes up about 65% of the total processed value, saw logs some 25%, and naval stores about 1%.

Georgia farms have about 12,100,000 acres (4,897,000 ha) of commercial forest, and wood-using industries own a third as much.

Fur Industry. The fur industry is based on such animals as muskrat, opossum, mink, and raccoon. There are few full-time commercial trappers; instead, trapping is carried on as a sideline to farm activities.

Aerial view of the Lockheed plant and parking lot at Marietta. A producer of large cargo planes, it is one of the biggest manufacturing facilities in the South.
(GEORGIA DEPARTMENT OF COMMERCE)

Riverfront and skyline of Savannah, viewed from the Savannah River. The domed city hall is visible to the right.

Tall buildings mark the commercial heart of Atlanta, Georgia's largest city. At right is Peachtree Street, the main thoroughfare.

Mineral Production. The more than 25 minerals mined commercially in Georgia annually exceed $200,000,000 in value, about 80% of which comes from clay and stone. Sand and gravel and iron ore are also important. Georgia is the country's leading producer of marble, crushed granite, and kaolin, a white clay used in ceramics and as filler and coating for white paper. The state is the second-largest producer of zirconium and fuller's earth; it ranks third in the production of scrap mica and bauxite, and fourth in barite and titanium concentrates. In addition, Georgia has deposits of talc, soapstone, feldspar, and gold.

Power. Power plants in Georgia have an installed capacity of about 4,000,000 kw., with generating and transmitting facilities supplied by the Georgia Power Company, the Tennessee Valley Authority, the Savannah Electric and Power Company, and the Crisp County Power Commission. Most of the state's power is produced by steam plants located near the centers of greatest demand. Since the mid-1960's an increasing amount of power is supplied by hydroelectric plants which have been developed on the Altamaha, Apalachicola, Savannah, and Chattahoochee Rivers. By the 1970's as much

as a quarter of the state's hydroelectric potential had been developed. Coal remains a significant source of power, although in some areas it has been replaced by fuel oils and natural gas, which are of growing importance throughout the state as sources of power.

Transportation and Communication. Georgia has an excellent transportation network. The Atlanta airport is the state's focal point for multiple airlines that provide regional, national, and international service. Atlanta is the South's largest rail center. From this center radiates a state-wide network of approximately 6,000 mi (9 656 km) of main-line and branch-line track. More than 100 scheduled motor carriers, plus some 400 irregular carriers domiciled in the state, serve Georgia and the nation.

The conventional highway system and the limited-access interstate system in Georgia link all major centers of population. These connect with an extensive network of improved country roads.

Georgia has deep-water ocean ports at Savannah and Brunswick, each with berthing facilities for large vessels. The construction of dams and locks on many of the rivers has provided the state with some 600 mi (966 km) of inland waterways. There are inland port facilities at Bainbridge, in southwestern Georgia; Columbus, on the Chattahoochee River; and at Augusta, 220 mi (354 km) up the Savannah River.

The *Georgia Gazette,* published in Savannah in 1763, was Georgia's first newspaper. Georgia has some 30 daily newspapers, reaching a total of almost 1,000,000 subscribers. One of the best-known newspapers in the country, the Atlanta *Constitution,* espouses the progressive philosophy of the "New South." There are more than 200 radio stations and about 20 television stations, of which 10 are educational outlets.

Savannah waterfront at night. The city, located on the Savannah River 17 mi above its mouth on the Atlantic Ocean, has a good harbor. It is a port of entry and an important shipping center.

People

In 1970 the population of the state was 4,589,575, representing an increase of 16.4% over 1960, when the population was 3,943,116.

Population Distribution. Georgia's population became predominantly urban for the first time during the 1960's. The urban section has since expanded to approximately 60% of the total.

Chief Cities. Atlanta, the state capital, is the largest city, with about 500,000 people. Columbus, Macon, and Savannah all have more than 100,000. Other sizable cities are Albany, Augusta, Athens, East Point, Warner Robins, Valdosta, and Rome.

Population Composition. Almost three-quarters of the state's population is white; most of the rest is black. The nonwhite population has been slowly decreasing since 1930. The foreign-born population in Georgia is small and has been for several decades.

Religion. Approximately 80% of the population of Georgia are members of churches, with Protestants composing the largest religious group. Baptists make up by far the largest Protestant group in Georgia, followed by the Methodists, Presbyterians, Disciples of Christ, and Episcopalians. The Roman Catholic faith has a sizable following and there is a significant number of Jews, especially in Atlanta. Virtually all other religious bodies have representation in the state.

The earliest Christian religious activity in the area that is now Georgia was the establishment of Roman Catholic missions by Spanish priests in the late 1500's along the Atlantic coast line.

In 1733 Christ Church was organized in Savannah by the Rev. Henry Herbert, a member of the Church of England, who had come over on the ship *Anne* with James Edward Oglethorpe and his company. It was here in 1736–37 that the Rev. John Wesley (then of the Church of England, later the founder of Methodism) preached and founded his Sunday School. In 1735 Scottish colonists brought Presbyterianism with them, and within a half-century the denomination was firmly established in Georgia.

In 1772 the Baptists founded a church near Appling, and the denomination grew rapidly throughout the area. The Methodist Church was firmly established in Georgia by 1788; the Roman Catholic Church, by about 1800.

Education. Although there was some provision for schools in colonial days and in the first years of statehood, Georgia had no comprehensive public school system financed by public taxes before the Civil War. After the war the constitution of 1868 provided for public education, free to all children, and the first public school law was enacted in 1870. The constitution of 1877, while providing for the education of all children through the elementary grades, specifically omitted state aid for high school education; as a result, private academies were established. This limitation on public education was not removed until 1912. The first legislation to compel school attendance was enacted in 1916, and today children between the ages of 7 and 16 are required to attend school regularly. Vocational rehabilitation programs were initiated as early as 1920, and Georgia now maintains vocational and trade schools, an academy for the blind, and schools for the deaf and for mental defectives. Per pupil expenditure for public elementary and secondary education has increased sharply during the last decade.

The state has shown an increasing trend toward peaceful and voluntary desegregation of its educational facilities. Some landmarks of the 1960's were the 1961 voluntary desegregation of the Atlanta public school system and the end of segregation at the Georgia Institute of Technology. In 1962 segregation was abolished in the public school systems of Savannah and Athens. By the end of the 1960's massive integration was accomplished pursuant to a federal court order. In Georgia, however, as elsewhere in the nation, de facto segregation continued into the next decade.

Among the accredited universities and senior colleges that are state-supported are the University of Georgia (Athens), which is composed of 13 schools and colleges, the Georgia Institute of Technology (Atlanta), and the Medical College of Georgia (Augusta). Private institutions include Emory University (Atlanta), Berry College (Mount Berry), and Agnes Scott College (Decatur). There are more than 20 two-year colleges, of which about half are privately supported. Among the well-known predominantly Negro colleges are Morehouse College and Atlanta University.

Georgia Institute of Technology

Philip Gendreau

Above, president's home, University of Georgia, Athens.

Left, the nuclear research center of the Georgia Institute of Technology, in Atlanta.

Philip Gendreau

Young Men's Library, Augusta, housed in a Tudor-style building erected in 1802 for the Academy of Richmond County.

Libraries and Museums. Georgia has more than 100 public libraries—state, regional, county, and municipal—many of which support extensive bookmobile services. The public library system is augmented by numerous college and university libraries. The most outstanding of these is the University of Georgia Library (Athens), rich in material on Georgia and Confederate history. Other important libraries are the Atlanta Public Library, housing an excellent collection of books, prints, and recordings, and the Asa Griggs Candler Library (Emory University, Atlanta), which owns large collections of Methodist church history and Southern economic history. The

Victorian house, surrounded by trees and shrubs, Madison.

Philip Gendreau

Georgia Department of Commerce

The former Savannah Cotton Exchange is now an office building. Savannah, Georgia's oldest city, has many antebellum homes that are historical attractions.

Library for the Blind (Atlanta) offers numerous volumes in braille. The Georgia Historical Society operates a library in Savannah and publishes a quarterly review. The Washington Memorial Library (Macon) houses manuscripts and first editions of Sidney Lanier's poetry.

Noteworthy museums include the High Museum of Art (Atlanta); The Telfair Academy of Arts and Sciences (Savannah); the Fernbank Science Center (Atlanta); and the Columbus Museum of Arts and Crafts. Several of Georgia's universities house museums. In addition, the Little White House and the Franklin D. Roosevelt Museum at Warm Springs are open to the public.

Cultural Life and Recreation. Some of the outstanding features of the cultural life of Georgia are reflected in its architecture, arts, and literature. There are fine examples of Georgian, Federal, Greek revival, and Gothic revival styles of architecture in the state's older cities and towns, while modern skyscrapers rise in present-day centers of trade and commerce. Interest in the arts is revealed by the large number of local music groups, drama groups, art schools, museums, and galleries throughout the state. Many Georgia artists have achieved national recognition. The writings of Joel Chandler Harris, Sidney Lanier, Margaret Mitchell, Flannery O'Connor, and Erskine Caldwell are internationally known.

Recreational facilities in Georgia are numerous. There are more than 40 state parks and two national forests, offering a variety of facilities. The Okefenokee Swamp National Wildlife Refuge is only one of 20 fish and wildlife reserves in the state. The Atlantic coast is lined with beaches and resorts. Georgia's important role in the Civil War is highlighted by many monuments and historical

The State Capitol in Atlanta was built in 1889.

The State Seal of Georgia

The soldier with drawn sword standing beneath a pillared arch inscribed "Constitution" represents Georgia's military forces, committed to defend that constitution. The three columns symbolize the three branches of government (legislative, judicial, and executive) which, in reality, form the supportive structures that sustain the constitution. The three banners that drape the pillars are inscribed with the words "Wisdom," "Justice," and "Moderation," noted as the state's basic principles in the official salute to its flag.

sites, particularly the Stone Mountain Monument near Atlanta. Impressive mounds mark prehistoric Indian sites and are reminders of the importance of the American Indians in Georgia's history.

Many entertainments and festivals take place in Georgia throughout the year. Georgia Day is observed as a state-wide holiday on February 12. The annual Masters Golf Tournament, played at the golf club in Augusta, is the best known sports event.

Government

Georgia's present constitution, its eighth since 1777, was adopted in 1945. Officers of state government include the governor, who is elected for a four-year term and cannot succeed himself; the lieutenant governor, who is elected for four years and holds the position of president of the senate; the secretary of state, comptroller general, attorney general, state treasurer, commissioner of agriculture, commissioner of labor, superintendent of schools, and the five members of the public service commission, all of whom are elected for terms of four years.

The state legislature consists of a Senate having 56 senators elected for two-year terms and a House of Representatives having 195 members also elected for two-year terms. It meets annually for a 40-day session beginning in January.

The judges of the seven-member state supreme court and the nine-member court of appeals are all elected for six-year terms. The governor, with the approval of the Senate, appoints judges to serve on the county courts and a few city courts.

Georgia was the first state to set the minimum voting age for its citizens at 18 years. There are no other requirements for voting.

Georgia has 159 counties, more than any other state in the nation except Texas. Each Georgia county has its own local government. The central governing authority of the county is usually a board of commissioners.

Health, Welfare, and Corrections. Hospitals and hospital services have greatly improved since the Hill-Burton Program was initiated in the state in 1947. Many hospitals with old and inadequate facilities have been replaced by modern hospitals. The number of public health centers and auxiliary health centers in Georgia meeting acceptable standards has increased fivefold since 1947.

Georgia's board of public welfare, established in 1919, cooperates with federal and local governments in various programs, including old-age and public assistance, child welfare services, and aid to the blind. The child welfare service program maintains 32 child-care institutions through private and local funds. Almshouses are provided in many counties. Institutions maintained by the state include a mental hospital, a training school for mental defectives, and three training schools for juvenile delinquents.

Responsibility for the state penal system rests with the five-member state board of corrections. The board carries out such duties as assigning convicted persons to the institution best suited for the individual and the state, approving or abolishing county work camps, and providing programs for prisoner rehabilitation. An efficient parole system is maintained by the three-member state board of pardons and parole.

Labor Legislation. Labor legislation in Georgia includes "right-to-work" laws. A state Employment Security Law taxes employers (of four or more persons) in order to provide partial income to workers during periods of unemployment. Coverage under Georgia's Workmen's Compensation Act is optional. Other legislation of significance requires safe working conditions for employees and prohibits employment of persons under 16 years of age in industrial plants.

Stone Mountain
Stone Mountain Park

Toccoa Falls
Philip Gendreau

Old Market House
Carolyn Carter—Photo Researchers

Fort Pulaski National Monument
Carolyn Carter—Monkmeyer

GEORGIA PLACES OF INTEREST

AMICALOLA FALLS, Dawsonville. Georgia's highest falls, the several cascades having a total drop of 729 ft (222 m).

ANDERSONVILLE NATIONAL CEMETERY, Andersonville. Burial ground with graves of Union soldiers and prisoners, near site of the Andersonville Confederate military prison.

CYCLORAMA, in Grant Park, Atlanta. Gigantic circular painting, some 50 ft high and about 400 ft in circumference (about 15 m by 122 m), depicting the Civil War Battle of Atlanta.

FORT FREDERICA NATIONAL MONUMENT, St. Simons Island. English fortification, built 1736–48, under leadership of James E. Oglethorpe.

FORT PULASKI NATIONAL MONUMENT, Cockspur and Mc-Queens islands, east of Savannah. Fortification with moat and drawbridges, built 1829–47 on site of earlier forts.

GEORGIA STATE CAPITOL, Atlanta. Designed to resemble the national capitol, completed in 1889. Dome gilded with gold from Dahlonega.

GEORGIA WARM SPRINGS FOUNDATION, Warm Springs. Health center using naturally warm spring waters for after-treatment of paralytic patients.

LIBERTY HALL, Crawfordville. Home of Alexander H. Stephens, Vice President of the Confederacy.

LITTLE WHITE HOUSE, Warm Springs. The Georgia home of President Franklin D. Roosevelt, now a memorial.

MIDWAY CHURCH, Midway. Built in 1792, one of the oldest churches in the United States.

OCMULGEE NATIONAL MONUMENT, adjoining Macon. Prehistoric Indian mounds and villages. Outstanding archeological exhibits.

OLD MARKET HOUSE (or Old Slave Market), Louisville. Slave market built of oak in 1758.

SIDNEY LANIER HOUSE, Macon. Birthplace (1842) of Sidney Lanier, best known for his poems "The Song of the Chattahoochee" and "The Marshes of Glynn."

STONE MOUNTAIN, six mi east of Atlanta. The largest exposed body of granite in the world. Unfinished Confederate memorial carved on one face.

TALLULAH GORGE, extreme northeastern Georgia. Scenic gorge of great depth. Accessible by trail.

TOCCOA FALLS, Toccoa. With a drop of 186 ft (57 m) over a precipice, one of the most beautiful falls in the state.

TYBEE LIGHTHOUSE, Savannah Beach. Earliest lighthouse on the south Atlantic coast, first used for this purpose in 1791. Site originally occupied by a tower completed in 1736.

WREN'S NEST, Atlanta. The preserved home and furnishings of Joel Chandler Harris, author of the Uncle Remus stories.

Conservation, Planning, and Development. The preservation and development of natural resources is the responsibility of several state agencies, including the forestry commission, the game and fish commission, the soil conservation commission, and the water resources commission. Wildlife preserves in the state include Okefenokee National Wildlife Refuge, Blackbeard Island Migratory Bird Refuge, Wolf Island Wildlife Refuge, South Sapelo Island Refuge, Piedmont and Tybee Wildlife refuges and four game preserves within the Chattahoochee National Forest. State economic development, state planning, and community planning assistance to local governments are the responsibility of the Georgia department of commerce.

History

Prehistoric Mound Builders were the earliest known inhabitants of the area which is now the state of Georgia. By 1540 when De Soto and his company passed through the region, they found it inhabited by tribes of Creek and Cherokee Indians. Permanent settlement by white men was not to take place for almost two centuries, but in 1562 Jean Ribault, the French explorer, visited the coast. Three years later Pedro Menéndez de Avilés was sent by Philip II to establish Spain's claim to the area; and he was soon followed by Spanish priests who established short-lived missions among the Indians.

Colony. Georgia was founded as a haven for persecuted Protestant sects and for the poor, as well as to serve as a buffer area to shield South Carolina from possible attack by the Spanish in Florida and the French in Louisiana. Thus, in 1732, the British granted a charter to a group of trustees for the establishment of "the Colony of Georgia in America." The new colony, the last of the original 13, was named for King George II of Great Britain. In February 1733, Gen. James Edward Oglethorpe landed with about 120 colonists in what is now Savannah and there established the first settlement in the new colony. Among the early colonists, in addition to Englishmen, Scottish Highlanders, Welsh, and Irish, there were Jews and European Protestants, including Moravians, Swiss, Germans, Italians, and Portuguese.

In 1742 Oglethorpe and a small force defeated the Spanish in the Battle of Bloody Marsh, St. Simons Island. The following year, the government was changed from military to civil status, and Oglethorpe left Georgia permanently.

The trustees of Georgia early established a ban on slaves and rum in the colony, and set about promoting the growth of mulberry trees for silkworms, grapes, and hemp (needed in the production of commodities which England could secure only through foreign trade). When these efforts were not successful, partly because of inadequate labor, the prohibition on importation of slaves into the colony was removed (1749).

In 1753 Georgia became a royal province, the colony's trustees having relinquished their charter (1752). During the next two decades under the rule of royal governors, there was considerable economic progress. In 1773 Britain was ceded 2,100,000 acres in Georgia by the Creek and Cherokee Indians. During the pre-Revolution period, loyalist sentiments were strong in Georgia. But in 1775 Georgia delegates were sent to the Second Continental Congress, and in 1776 they voted for independence. In 1777 a constitutional convention in Savannah ratified the first state constitution. During the Revolutionary War Savannah was captured by the British in 1778; Augusta, in 1779. Georgia ratified the U.S. Constitution on Jan. 2, 1788, the fourth state to do so.

State. In the early post-Revolution period Georgia's position was strongly national, and the state supported efforts to strengthen the central government. However, decisions by the U.S. Supreme Court and acts of Congress in subsequent years which asserted the sovereignty of the federal government over the individual state led to the development of a strong states' rights sentiment in Georgia.

Between 1830 and 1860 the economy of Georgia, based on cotton and the slave plantation, grew phenomenally.

The Bettmann Archive

Union Gen. James B. McPherson, on the rearing horse, was mortally wounded in the July 22, 1864 encounter depicted in "Battle of Atlanta," a contemporary print. Though experiencing heavy casualties, Confederate Gen. J. B. Hood held the beseiged city until Sept. 1. Union Gen. W. T. Sherman entered a shattered Atlanta on Sept. 2, and from there he later mounted his "march to the sea," a swath 60 mi (97 km) wide that devastated the South.

IMPORTANT DATES IN GEORGIA HISTORY

1540	De Soto marched from Florida through part of Georgia.
1733	Oglethorpe and his company settled and organized a community at Savannah, the first in Great Britain's Colony of Georgia in America.
1742	Oglethorpe and a small force defeated the Spanish in the Battle of Bloody Marsh.
1753	Georgia became a royal province.
1775	Georgia sent delegates to the Second Continental Congress.
1777	The constitutional convention in Savannah ratified Georgia's first state constitution.
1788	Georgia ratified the U.S. Constitution.
1861	Georgia seceded from the Union.
1870	Georgia readmitted to the Union.
1877	A new state constitution was adopted.
1943	Legal voting age lowered to 18.
1945	Present state constitution adopted.
1956	A new state flag adopted.
1961	Racial integration initiated at the University of Georgia, Georgia Institute of Technology, and in the Atlanta public schools.
1969	The U.S. Department of Justice ordered Georgia to create a racially balanced school system.

FAMOUS GEORGIA FIGURES

Conrad Potter Aiken (1889–1973), poet.

Martha McChesney Berry (1866–1942), educator, founder of Berry schools.

James Earl ("Jimmy") Carter, Jr. (1924–   ), President of the United States (1977–   ).

Erskine Preston Caldwell (1903–   ), author whose novels include *Tobacco Road*.

John Brown Gordon (1832–1904), Confederate army officer, U.S. Senator (1873–80, 1891–97), Georgia Governor (1886–90).

Button Gwinnett (1735–77), signer of Declaration of Independence, Georgia president (1777).

Joel Chandler Harris (1848–1908), author of works about "Uncle Remus."

Robert ("Bobby") Tyre Jones, Jr. (1902–71), golf player.

Martin Luther King Jr. (1929–68), civil rights leader and recipient of the Nobel Prize for Peace (1964).

Sidney Lanier (1842–81), poet.

Crawford Willamson Long (1815–78), surgeon, possibly the first to use ether as anesthetic.

Juliette Gordon Low (1860–1927), founder of the Girl Scouts of America (1912–13).

Carson McCullers (1917–67), prizewinning novelist and playwright, author of *Member of the Wedding*.

Margaret Mitchell (1900–49), author of *Gone with the Wind*.

James Edward Oglethorpe (1696–1785), English founder of Georgia colony.

Richard B. Russell (1897–1971), U.S. Senator.

Alexander Hamilton Stephens (1812–83), vice president of Confederacy (1861–65), Georgia Governor (1883).

Robert Augustus Toombs (1810–85), U.S. Senator (1853–61), stanch supporter of Confederacy.

Walter Francis White (1893–1955), author, officer in National Association for the Advancement of Colored People.

With this growth came a small but influential, wealthy aristocratic society which dominated state activity and played a major role in the political life of the nation. After several years of increasing political tensions between North and South, on Jan. 19, 1861, Georgia seceded from the Union, and with other Southern states formed the Confederate States of America. The latter days of the Civil War brought heavy fighting and great destruction to the state. In September, 1864, Atlanta was captured by Gen. William T. Sherman, who destroyed the city and began his ruinous march to the sea.

The post-Civil War brought the difficult years of Reconstruction. Georgia experienced two periods under military rule and was not readmitted to the Union until July 15, 1870. A new state constitution was adopted in 1877, and there followed a period of industrial promotion. Discontent ran high among the farmers as taxes rose and overproduction caused cotton prices to fall. Farm groups enthusiastically supported reform programs of the Farmers Alliance and became powerful politically.

At the turn of the century Georgia was still attempting to overcome the long-reaching effects of the Civil War. The state was gradually becoming more industrial, and faced new economic, social, and political problems.

World War I saw more than 93,000 Georgia men serving with the U.S. armed forces, and in the years following the war Georgia shared in the nation's prosperity. The 1929 crash and subsequent depression of the 1930's brought serious problems of unemployment and relief to the state as to the rest of the nation. With World War II came new industries which resulted in greatly increased employment and production.

Since World War II Georgia history has been marked by social and economic progress. The trend toward an urban-industrial society and economy is distinct. By mid-century manufacturing had surpassed agriculture as the leading employer in the state, and the U.S. population census of 1960 was the first in which the state's urban population exceeded its rural population. In 1961 the first Negro students entered the University of Georgia. Since that time a pattern of voluntary desegregation, particularly in urban areas, has been exhibited by Georgia in response to the federal government's desegregation rulings. Nevertheless, racial strife has sometimes broken out in violence, and so-called "white backlash" has been felt.

In 1968 delegates to the Democratic National Convention agreed to allow a biracial slate of delegates headed by Georgia's representative, Julian Bond, to cast half of the state's votes.

Consult American Guide Series, *Georgia, A Guide to Its Towns and Countryside* (rev. ed., 1954); Bonner, James C., *Georgia* (1965) and *Georgia's Last Frontier* (1971); Coleman, Kenneth, *Georgia History in Outline* (1960) and *Colonial Georgia* (1976); Meadows, John C., *Modern Georgia* (rev. ed., 1954); University of Georgia, *Georgia Statistical Abstract* (annually).   JOHN C. MEADOWS

GEORGIA, STRAIT OF, channel between the mainland of British Columbia and Vancouver Island, southwestern Canada. It forms part of the Inside Passage to Alaska, and is an important fishing area. The city of Vancouver is on its east shore. Length, 150 mi.; width, 20–40 mi.

GEORGIAN, member of the southern branch of the Caucasian family of languages. The most important of the Caucasian languages, Georgian is spoken by approximately 2,000,000 inhabitants of central and eastern Georgia; it is the official language of the Georgian S.S.R. As in other Caucasian languages, the verb in Georgian is highly complex, with a great number of forms to express a variety of grammatical relations. Georgian was a literary language at least as early as the 5th century B.C., and it is the only one of the Caucasian languages which functions as a modern literary language.

GEORGIAN BAY, inlet on the northeast coast of Lake Huron, southeastern Ontario, Canada. It is partly separated from the lake by Manitoulin Island and the Bruce (Saugeen) Peninsula, and connected with Lake Ontario by the Severn River, Lake Simcoe, and the Trent Canal. Georgian Bay Islands National Park (5.37 sq. mi.) comprises several islands in the bay. The shore of the bay is largely a resort area. Georgian Bay was visited by Étienne Brulé, probably in 1612, and was the first part of the Great Lakes seen by European explorers. Length, 120 mi.; width, 65 mi.

GEORGIAN BAY ISLANDS NATIONAL PARK, area reserved for public use in Ontario, Canada. The park comprises several wooded islands in the Georgian Bay region. Beausoleil Island (2,700 acres), in the southeastern part of the bay, contains park headquarters and camp grounds. Flowerpot Island, 100 mi. to the northwest, is noted for its rock pillars resembling flowerpots. Estab., 1929; area, 5.37 sq. mi.

GEORGIAN SOVIET SOCIALIST REPUBLIC, one of the 15 union republics of the U.S.S.R. Situated immediately to the south of the Caucasus Range, the Georgian S.S.R. has an area of 27,000 sq. mi., of which total 3,300 sq. mi. are taken up by the Abkhazian A.S.S.R., 1,000 by the Adzharian A.S.S.R., and 1,500 by the South Ossetian Autonomous Oblast. The population of the Georgian S.S.R. is about 3,978,000. It borders to the west on the Black Sea; to the southwest, on Turkey; to the South, on the Armenian S.S.R.; to the southeast, on the Azerbaidzhan S.S.R.

Land and Natural Resources. The climate and landscape of Georgia are varied. The coastal area and the Rioni valley in western Georgia are favored by mild, frostless winters and hot, damp summers. Vegetation is subtropical and profuse, including valuable timber on the hill slopes. Rivers descend rapidly from the mountains, forming marshes and alluvial deposits in the lowlands. Snow-capped peaks rise abruptly from these humid valleys, with Alpine pastures and rocky hill country running up to snow level. A more continental climate prevails in eastern Georgia, shut off by the Suram Range from the damp Black Sea basin. Fertile valleys alternate with windswept

plateaus. The main rivers are the Kura (Mtkvari), which flows through the capital, Tbilisi (Tiflis), toward the Caspian Sea; the Rioni, which passes through Kutaisi, chief city of western Georgia, and empties into the Black Sea at Poti; the Aragvi, which joins the Kura at the ancient cathedral town of Mtskheta; and the Alazani, which waters the vineyards and orchards of Kakheti Province in eastern Georgia.

The Georgian S.S.R. makes a large contribution to the Soviet economy. The Black Sea area produces tea, citrus fruits, tobacco; mulberry trees cover a large area. Maize, wheat, and barley are grown, though grain also has to be imported from south Russia. Cattle rearing is one of the chief occupations in the mountains. Kakheti is internationally famous for its wines—white, red, and champagne type—and there is a flourishing brandy industry.

From 1870 onward, with the building of the Transcaucasian railway and the massive development of the Baku oil fields in neighboring Azerbaidzhan, modern industry in Georgia has made rapid strides. Coal is mined at Tkvarcheli and Tkibuli in western Georgia. Hydroelectric power stations now harness the rivers Kura, Rioni, Khrami, and

© C. S. HAMMOND & Co., Maplewood, N. J.

INDEX TO GEORGIAN S.S.R. GENERAL REFERENCE MAP
Total Population 3,978,000

others, providing electricity for railways, city lighting, and industry. Two pipelines—one carrying kerosene and the other petroleum—run from Baku on the Caspian to Batumi, an important refinery center on the Black Sea.

The manganese mines at Chiatura provide over half of the Soviet Union's entire supply. The vast Rustavi steel plant near Tbilisi has been functioning since 1950 and supplies Caucasian industry with pig iron, coke, steel tubes, and other products. There are engineering works at Tbilisi, and chemical and fertilizer factories at Kutaisi. Silk spinning and weaving, and manufacture of woolen goods are carried on in many centers.

People and Culture. The Georgians, who call themselves "Kartvelebi" and their land "Sakartvelo," stand apart from all other known ethnic and linguistic groups. The beginnings of settled life in Georgia can be traced back to the Stone Age, and the present-day Georgian nation is probably the result of a fusion in remote antiquity of local, aboriginal inhabitants with immigrant tribes from Asia Minor. The Georgians have been Christians since the 4th century A.D., though the Laz and Adzharians were forced by the Turks to adopt Islam. Today, the Georgian Church is under strict Communist control and its influence curtailed.

Over the centuries the Georgian language split into three branches: standard Georgian, Svan (spoken in mountainous western Georgia), and Mingrelo-Laz. The Georgian alphabet, which has no affinity with the Slavonic one, was devised in the 5th century A.D. The population of the Georgian S.S.R. includes many national minorities and immigrant communities, such as Ossetes, Abkhaz, Armenians, Tatars, and Russians.

History. The kingdom of Colchis, the present-day Mingrelia, appears in the annals of Assyria and Urartu, and in the Greek myth of Jason, the Argonauts, and the Golden Fleece. Greek settlers colonized Georgia's Black Sea shores, while an independent kingdom grew up in Iberia, as the eastern region of Georgia was called in classical times. In 65 B.C. Pompey conquered Georgia for Rome, and later the country was an area of conflict between the Byzantine Emperors and the Sassanian Kings of Persia. Christianity was introduced by St. Nino, about 330 A.D.

The Arabs overran the Caucasus in the 7th century, but the Georgian monarchy was restored by King Bagrat III (reigned 980–1014). King David the Builder (reigned 1089–1125) and Queen Tamar (reigned 1184–1213) defeated the Seljuk Turks and helped the cause of the Crusaders. Architecture, the fine arts, philosophy, poetry, and historical writing reached their high point during this period, while feudal institutions and the cult of chivalry flourished.

The Mongol invasions from 1236 onward brought ruin. A national revival occurred under Erekle II (reigned 1744–98), who signed a treaty with Catherine the Great of Russia. Nevertheless, Tsar Alexander I declared Georgia annexed in 1801. Following the 1917 Revolution, Georgia regained its independence under the Social Democratic President Noe (Noah) Zhordania. The Georgian Republic was recognized by the principal powers, including Soviet Russia. In 1921 Joseph Stalin, himself a Georgian, led the Red Army in an onslaught on Georgia. Mass purges of patriots, intellectuals, and the clergy were intensified after the abortive uprising of 1924 and during the terror of 1936. Georgian agriculture was collectivized, and industrialization on the Soviet model was introduced. Education has made rapid progress; Georgia now has an Academy of Sciences, a university, and many schools, museums, and other learned institutions, staffed by scholars enjoying world reputations in their fields.

Consult Allen, W. E. D., *A History of the Georgian People* (1932); Kazemzadeh, Firuz, *The Struggle for Transcaucasia* (1951); Lang, D. M., *The Last Years of the Georgian Monarchy* (1957).

DAVID M. LANG, University of London
See also CAUCASUS; UNION OF SOVIET SOCIALIST REPUBLICS.

GEORGIAN STYLE, in architecture is named from the English kings and lasted from 1715 to 1760 or later. Led by the Earl of Burlington, this dignified and restrained style was based on the books of the Italian architect Andrea Palladio. Under Burlington's patronage Colin Campbell published the *Vitruvius Brittanicus*, and compendium of the best English buildings, as measured by Palladian standards.

Prior Park, Bath (1734), by John Wood is typical of the larger Georgian mansions. Secondary blocks of buildings are linked to the main unit by quadrants. A pedimented portico accents the entrance. The interiors were panelled and had plaster ceilings. Classical or Italianate

Hero's Square in Tbilisi. The round building, on the right, is the Tbilisi State Circus, used for various kinds of entertainment. At left are offices and apartment houses. (SOVFOTO)

The Church of St. Martin's in the Fields is in London. The architect James Gibbs formed the classic portico and the steeple into a unified design of great dignity.
(ILLUSTRATION RESEARCH SERVICE)

The upper staircase hall from **The Vyne** in Hampshire dates from the mid-18th century. (LOUIS FROHMAN)

Prior Park at Bath by John Wood. This great Georgian mansion has such classically inspired features as columns with Corinthian capitals and a portico with a pediment.
(NATIONAL MONUMENTS RECORD)

motives, such as acanthus scrolls, adorn the panels or fireplaces. These were occasionally varied by fanciful themes borrowed from the contemporary French rococo style, the Chinese, or the Gothic. Such playful details do not alter the basic Palladian character. James Gibbs designed the Church of St. Martin's in the Fields, London (1721–26). Its portico is typically Georgian, but, unlike his contemporaries, Gibbs preserved the freedom of Sir Christopher Wren in the fine steeple. While Sir William Chambers continued the Georgian style until the end of the 18th century, its domestic interiors were largely superseded by the Adam style after 1760.

Consult Summerson, John, *Architecture in Britain, 1530–1830* (1963). EVERARD M. UPJOHN

GEOSYNCLINE [jē-ō-sĭn'klīn], regional trough or basin, generally elongated and slowly subsiding, in which sediments are deposited. In most such basins 30,000 to 50,000 ft (9 000 to 15 000 m) of sediments have accumulated during millions of years.

Geosynclines commonly occur as two parallel belts along continental margins. Sediments in the near-shore belt come from the continent; they are mostly clay, silt, sand, lime muds, and reef-building materials. The offshore belt contains submarine lava flows and materials from offshore volcanic islands, as well as sediments from the continent.

Accumulation of the sediments generally takes place in shallow seas and on the adjacent coastal plains. This is inferred from shallow-water fossils found in the sediments and from the presence of mud cracks, ripple marks, and other depositional features. However, some geosynclinal deposits contain evidence suggestive of deep-water conditions at the time of depositions. In order for great thicknesses of material to accumulate in shallow waters, the geosyncline must subside as sediments are deposited.

The mechanisms that account for the subsidence of geosynclines have been debated for many years. Many geosynclines presumably form in response to the downwarping (the formation of a broad geological downfold) associated with tectonic plate boundaries at continental margins. Sediment aprons accumulate on the continental shelf, slope, and rise during plate divergence. This sediment wedge is then deformed and pushed upward when two plates converge.

Movement of the plates and the associated development of the geosynclinal troughs are presumed to be a response to lateral flow of subcrustal material. The process of subsidence may be aided to some degree by the weight of the accumulating sediments.

Inherent in some definitions of a geosyncline is the concept of the structure's deformational phase—folding, faulting, and uplift. Folded mountain ranges thus represent a late stage in the development of a geosyncline. Many mountain ranges, such as the Appalachians in eastern North America, were derived from ancient geosynclines.

The Gulf of Mexico is a currently developing geosyncline. Deep oil wells in the region show that more than 35,000 ft (10,000 m) of sediments have been deposited there during the last 60 million years.

ROBERT E. BOYER

See also CONTINENTAL DRIFT.

GEOTHERMAL GRADIENT, rate of increase of the earth's temperature with depth. Commonly it is about 1° F (.56° C) for each 55 ft (16.8 m) in the earth's outer crust, where the main source of heat is the radioactive disintegration of uranium, thorium, and potassium. Although the gradient lessens deep in the earth, temperatures increase to a maximum probably between 4,500° F and 10,000° F (2 500–5 600 C) at the center.

GEOTHERMAL ENERGY, the natural energy of steam obtained from the earth, used primarily for the production of electric power. Geothermal power was first used to provide electric power in Larderello, Italy, after World

Pacific Gas and Electric Company

Steam from deep within the earth rises in plumes at The Geysers, Calif., where a power plant captures the steam energy and transforms it into electrical energy.

War I, and is now a source of power in New Zealand, the United States, and other countries. In Iceland natural steam has long been used to heat homes and greenhouses.

The earth's crust is about 20 mi (32 km) thick, but, in its shrinking and shifting, cracks are formed that let superheated molten magma work up nearer the surface. Steam is formed by the water in the magma itself, and it passes up through fissures in the rock strata of the crust until it breaks through in steady spouts called fumeroles. These are tapped by pipelines, and the steam pressure is used to generate electricity. Testing equipment is installed at the wellhead to check steam pressure, volume, corrosive quality, and water content.

GEOTROPISM [jē-ŏt'rə-pĭz-əm], the movement of a plant in response to the stimulus of the earth's gravitational field. Positive geotropism (movement toward the gravitational field) is seen when a plant root is placed horizontally; it will bend downward, seeking to attain a vertical position. The stem of a plant will frequently exhibit a negative geotropism (movement away from the gravitational field). If placed horizontally, it will bend upward from the horizontal position.
See also PLANT RESPONSES.

GERA [gā'rä], town of central German Democratic Republic (East Germany), and seat of the district of Gera, located on the White Elster River, southwest of Leipzig. After having been an imperial residence for many centuries, it turned into an industrial base in the 19th century. Industries include the manufacture of texiles, machinery, musical instruments, and furniture. A botanical garden, a museum, a theater, and a weaving school are located here. Gera was first mentioned in 955 and became a town in 1237. It was the seat of the Princes of Reuss after 1563. A severe fire destroyed most of Gera in 1780, and only a few buildings from earlier periods remain.

GERALDTON, port city of Australia, on the west coast of Western Australia about 240 mi (386 km) north of Perth. Geraldton is a winter resort, fishing port, and trade center for an agricultural region.

GERANIUM, herbaceous perennial, with some annual plants native to most temperate regions, including the United States. Geranium, or cranesbill, is in the Geraniaceae family which has 12 genera. The familiar house and garden plants known as geraniums are in the genus *Pelargonium.*

Geraniums range in height from 4 inches to 2½ ft (10 to 76 cm). The leaves are usually deeply cut and some are almost fernlike. The flowers are white or shades of purple, red, blue, and pink. Cranesbill, the common name of geranium, comes from the seed capsules which resemble the bill of a crane (Gr. *geranos,* "crane").

There are nearly 200 species of geranium. Low-growing species are suited to the rock garden, taller ones do well in flower borders and the wild garden. They prefer slight shade and well-drained soil. All the species flower in the summer, with a long blooming period. Nearly all the species are hardy, needing little care. They are easily propagated from seed and by division.

Pelargonium, the geranium of florists and the popular garden and house plant, is tender, and shrubby or herbaceous. The shrubby kinds grow wild in South Africa, and the herbaceous kinds are native to Asia Minor and Syria. The name Pelargonium is derived from the Gr. *perlargos,* "stork," because the shape of the fruit resembles a stork's beak. Zonal pelargoniums are horticultural varieties hybridized for years from the best species. They include most of the geraniums used in bedding and in window boxes. Ivy-leafed geraniums have a trailing habit and are used in hanging baskets. Regal pelargoniums, or Martha Washington, are often called show geraniums. The flowers are large and rich and the whole plant is large and showy. Scented-leafed pelargoniums include several species and varieties. There is wide variety in leaf formation, leaves are strongly scented when crushed, but the flowers are often small. Scented geraniums are grown chiefly for their fragrant foliage. There are about five species of succulent pelargoniums, with thick stems.

ALYS SUTCLIFFE

See also PELARGONIUM.

GERARD [jə-rärd′], **JAMES WATSON** (1867–1951), American lawyer and diplomat. Gerard was born in Geneseo, N.Y., educated at Columbia, and in 1892 admitted to the New York bar. The next 15 years he spent as counsel for several corporations. In 1907 Gerard was elected to the New York State Supreme Court; but he resigned in 1913 to accept appointment by President Woodrow Wilson as U.S. ambassador to Germany. Gerard remained in Germany until diplomatic relations were severed, in Feb., 1917, and skillfully handled matters relating to treatment of prisoners, conduct of submarine warfare, and the Allied blockade. Gerard soon left the diplomatic service, but maintained an interest in foreign affairs. He was an advocate of membership in the League of Nations following World War I and fought ardently for American intervention in the late 1930's.

GÉRICAULT [zhā-rē-kō′], **JEAN LOUIS ANDRÉ THÉODORE** (1791–1824), French painter. His canvases, such as "Raft of the Medusa" (1819; Louvre, Paris), were influential in the development of Delacroix and the romantic

Roche

The common cranesbill, *Geranium maculatum,* a wild species

school. His last works, however, tended to be less dramatic. Many, painted from direct experience, reflected his sympathy for suffering humanity. Géricault's portraits of the insane, done from 1821 to 1824, are among the most perceptive psychological studies in art.

GERM, a primitive cell from which an adult living individual develops. The term has become popularly associated with microorganisms, particularly bacteria, and is commonly used as a synonym for "microorganism." *See* BACTERIA; GERM THEORY; MICROBIOLOGY.

GERMAIN [jûr′mən], **GEORGE SACKVILLE, 1ST VISCOUNT SACKVILLE** (1716–85), English soldier and politician. Although court-martialed for disobeying orders at the battle of Minden (1759) and thereafter universally vilified, he was gradually able, under George III, to rehabilitate himself. Securing minor office at first (1765), he then became (1775) Secretary of State for the Colonies, which entailed directing (1775–82) the prosecution of the American Revolution.

GERMAN [jûr′mən], member of the West Germanic branch of the Germanic subgroup of the Indo-European family of languages. It is the official language of West and East Germany, and one of the official languages of Luxembourg and Switzerland. Elsewhere, German is spoken in Alsace in France, in South Tyrol in Italy, in Rumania, and in Hungary. It is also spoken by German immigrants and their descendants in the United States, Canada, Australia, Brazil, and a number of other South American countries.

German is divided into many dialects. The basic division is into Low German (*Niederdeutsch, Plattdeutsch*) and High German (*Hochdeutsch*). Low German, spoken in the north, is divided into the Low Franconian and Low Saxon groups of dialects; High German, spoken in the central and southern regions, into the Middle German (*Mittel-deutsch*) and Upper German (*Oberdeutsch*) groups of dialects. The literary language that became the standard German literary language developed in the 16th century in the eastern Middle German area, where speakers of Middle and Upper German dialects (High German) had settled. Luther adopted this type of German for his translation of the Bible. Its popularity in Low German areas contributed to the failure of Low German to develop its own modern standard literary language. Dialects are still widely used in German-speaking territory, but in urban areas a compromise with the standard language is usually heard (*Umgangssprache*). In Switzerland local dialects are exclusively used in everyday speech, even by educated people. In Alsace some dialect speakers are not familiar with the standard language.

The Low Franconian dialects of the Netherlands developed in the 16th century their own standard literary language, Dutch. Yiddish, written in the Hebrew alphabet, in the Middle High German period (1100–1350) developed, essentially from High German dialects, as the language of German Jews. The so-called Pennsylvania Dutch is essentially a Middle German dialect.

The history of High German is usually divided into three periods. The earliest one is called Old High German (750–1100). Old High German shows the result of the so-called High German consonant shift by which it diverged from all other West Germanic languages, including Low German. The shift specially involved the proto-Germanic consonants *p, t, k, d*. This shift is revealed by comparing words in modern English, in which the original consonants are preserved, with words in modern German, which had the same origin: modern English o*p*en, modern German o*ff*en; modern English wa*t*er, modern German Wa*ss*er; modern English ma*k*e, modern German ma*ch*en; modern English ti*d*e, modern German Zei*t*. In the Middle High German period (1100–1350) there was a tendency toward a unified literary language which can be observed in the knightly poets' avoidance of dialectal and regional terms. But the dialects are again strongly reflected in texts from the beginning of the New High German period (1350 to the present). The East Middle German type of German, as found in the 16th-century language of the Upper Saxon electoral chancery and in Luther's writings, was not immediately accepted in the south and southwest. Its victory and general acceptance were only assured through its adoption by the writers of the classical period of German literature in the 18th century. It was only at the turn of the 20th century that a spoken standard developed beside the written literary standard. At that time a type of pronunciation slightly favoring the north was adopted for the German stage (*Bühnenaussprache*) on the recommendation of German language and theater specialists. This stage standard was later recommended for schools and universities as the standard pronunciation (*Hochsprache*).

The history of German shows the constant influence of foreign languages. Its first emergence as a written language was in translations from Latin in the Old High German period. Not until the 13th century was German used along with Latin as the language of documents and legal writing. The influence of Latin on German vocabulary and syntax has been great. French loan words came into German particularly in the medieval, courtly period and from the late 16th century on. English words have been borrowed since the 18th century. The period after World War II brought a flood of new loan words. Also, during the Allied occupation the special German Gothic print (*Fraktur*) and script were largely abandoned. Abandonment of the capitalization of nouns has been under consideration.

The oldest stage of Low German is called Old Saxon, which was contemporaneous with Old High German. Middle Low German developed a flourishing written commercial language, particularly in the period of the Hansa (14th and 15th centuries). In the modern period Low German was gradually replaced by High German as the language of city chanceries and of literature. Partly as a result of post-World War II population shifts, the Low German dialects are receding in industrial and urban areas.

Consult Wright, Joseph, *Historical German Grammar* (1907); Curme, G. O., *A Grammar of the German Language* (2d rev. ed., 1952); Priebsch, Robert, and Collinson, W. E., *The German Language* (4th rev. ed., 1958).

HERBERT PENZL, University of Michigan
See also GERMANIC LANGUAGES.

GERMAN-AMERICAN BUND, in American history, a pro-Nazi organization established in 1936 under the leadership of Fritz Kuhn. It grew out of a group called the Friends of the New Germany. The membership was composed largely of persons of German origin or descent who sympathized with the regime of the Nazi dictator Adolf Hitler and attempted to promote American support for it. It was charged that the organization received financial support from Germany. Testifying before a Congressional committee in 1939, Kuhn claimed that the bund had 71 branches, 23 of them in New York, with 20,000 members in 19 states, but these figures were probably exaggerated. After Kuhn was imprisoned for mishandling bund records and funds in 1939, he was succeeded by Gerhard Wilhelm Kunze, but the membership of the organization drastically declined. With American entrance into World War II the bund and its weekly organ, *Weckruf und Beobachter*, were suppressed and several members and leaders were imprisoned.

FRANK FREIDEL, Harvard University

GERMAN COOKERY. Hearty and satisfying are the two words which best describe German cookery. Its variety is all but infinite, for each region of Germany boasts its own variations and specialties.

No other country makes such diverse use of veal and pork, from roasts and chops to sausages and pies. No other native cookery depends as much on time and preparation for meats pickled, corned, and marinated.

Cabbage is the staple vegetable and red cabbage the ruling favorite. Sauerkraut and cabbage slaw are well known; but cabbage is truly Germanic when slowly simmered in a host of heavily seasoned juices, featuring apples and onions, or ham bones and chicken fat.

Noodles, potato dumplings, and dark breads are among

the popular starches found on every German table, and puddings are far and away the most popular dessert.

These dishes may be considered the mainstays of German cookery. Also important are the heavy but not rich sauces, soups, and sour creams and stuffings, and the fruits and berries of the seasons.

Sea food and game dishes, while not usually associated with German cuisine, are also prepared in great variety and have earned the respect of international gourmets.

Wiener Schnitzel, featuring veal cutlets, and *Sauerbraten*, with round steak as its base, have long ruled as the favorite German dishes in America, and it would be unthinkable not to find them listed on the menu of a German-American restaurant. Oddly, they are not popular dishes in their native land.

The excellence of German beer is well known to all, but German wines—wonderfully fresh and light in body—are not yet fully appreciated away from the homeland.

JAN MITCHELL, Author, *Lüchow's German Cookbook*

GERMANIC [jər-măn'ĭk] **LANGUAGES** (formerly called Teutonic languages), subgroup of the Indo-European language family. Germanic languages are usually divided into East Germanic, North Germanic, and West Germanic languages. The most important East Germanic language was Gothic, which is now extinct; no living languages belong to this sub-branch. North Germanic languages now spoken are Icelandic, Norwegian, Faroese, Danish, and Swedish. The West Germanic languages are English, Frisian, Dutch-Flemish, Low German, and High German. Afrikaans developed from Dutch; Yiddish from High German.

The features shared by all these languages have been investigated in detail; a common ancestral language, referred to as Proto-Germanic (formerly Primitive Germanic), has been reconstructed by comparative linguists. The differences between the Germanic languages and the other Indo-European languages have also been carefully studied. Rasmus Rask and others before him noticed that Germanic voiceless fricatives correspond to voiceless stops in other Indo-European languages: Gothic *f*adar, Latin *p*ater, Sanskrit pitā ("father"), and Old English *h*orn, Latin *c*ornu ("horn"); and that Germanic voiceless stops correspond to voiced stops in many Indo-European languages: Gothic *t*aihun, Latin *d*ecem, Greek *d*eka ("ten"). These and other correspondences were explained by Jacob Grimm as due to a sound-shift which differentiated Germanic from Indo-European; the name "Grimm's Law" is the usual designation in English-speaking countries of his explanation. Additional facts about these consonantal correspondences were brought to light by Karl Verner and described in his so-called "Verner's Law."

In Proto-Germanic the position of the Indo-European loud stress became restricted to the stem syllable; this led to many changes of the vowels and diphthongs in the inflectional endings. But the innovations in Germanic were not confined to the phonology (consonant and vowel systems). Among striking morphological innovations in Germanic were (1) the development of two sets of adjectival endings, the "weak" and the "strong" endings, which are still preserved in Modern German: der klein*e* Mann ("the little man"), klein*er* Mann ("little man"); (2) the development of two types of past tense formation, again called "weak" and "strong" by Grimm, which is still reflected in the existence of both the dental suffix of the regular verb and the vowel alternation of the irregular verb in Modern English. The oldest Germanic forms attested are names in the writings of Latin and Greek authors. The first extant texts are runic inscriptions of about the 3d century A.D. The earliest sizable Germanic text is Ulfilas' Gothic Bible translation of the 4th century A.D.

Consult Prokosch, Eduard, *A Comparative Germanic Grammar* (1939).

HERBERT PENZL, University of Michigan

GERMANICUS CAESAR [jər-măn'ĭ-kəs sē'zər] (15 B.C.–19 A.D.), Roman general, son of Drusus Germanicus (Augustus' stepson) and maternal grandson of Mark Antony. In 4 A.D., when Augustus adopted his stepson Tiberius, the latter was compelled to adopt his nephew Germanicus, whose father had died in 9 B.C. Germanicus married Augustus' granddaughter, Agrippina the Elder, who bore him nine children, including the future Emperor Caligula. Germanicus was also the brother of the Emperor Claudius and the grandfather of Nero. At Tiberius' accession in 14 A.D., Germanicus, now heir apparent, ended a mutiny among the legions on the Rhine and led them on two inconclusive campaigns into Germany. Recalled by Tiberius, he celebrated a spectacular triumph in 17 A.D. The emperor sent Germanicus on a diplomatic mission to the East (18 A.D.). He went to Egypt without the necessary imperial permission and accomplished his mission, but quarreled bitterly with Piso, whom Tiberius had assigned to give aid and advice to Germanicus. When Germanicus died in 19 A.D., many thought that Piso had poisoned him, perhaps at the Emperor's instigation. Piso committed suicide before his trial.

GERALD E. KADISH, State University of N.Y. at Binghamton

GERMANIUM [jər-mā'nē-əm], a chemical element and metalloid, or semimetal, similar to carbon and silicon in its chemical properties. It was one of the three elements, the existence and properties of which were predicted by D. I. Mendeleyev, in 1871, as a result of his development of the periodic table. Its discovery in 1886 by C. A. Winkler, who named it for his native land, Germany, bore out the prediction.

Before World War II germanium had only minor uses. Thus, germanium dioxide, GeO_2, was added to glass to increase the ability of glass to bend a beam of light, that is, to increase its refractive index. In the 1940's it was discovered that germanium containing minute quantities of

PROPERTIES

Symbol	Ge
Atomic number	32
Atomic weight	72.59
Valence	4
Density	5.35 g./cc.
Melting point	958.5° C. (1,757.3° F.)
Boiling point	2,700° C. (4,892° F.)

impurities such as arsenic or boron conducts electricity by means of the drifting of excess electrons or of "holes" representing sites where electrons are deficient. Bits of such germanium can be arranged in such a way that an electrical current can be rectified, or carried in only one direction, and amplified or increased in strength, without distortion. Such devices are called transistors.

For use in transistors, germanium should be purified to the point where only one atom out of billions is anything but germanium, and the impurities such as arsenic added to the germanium must be equally pure.

ISAAC ASIMOV

GERMAN MEASLES, also called rubella, is a contagious disease of childhood which is characterized by a skin rash and by swelling of the lymph nodes. Although the illness usually has little effect on the health of the patient, it may cause severe damage to the unborn child when it occurs in pregnant women.

The illness begins approximately three weeks after exposure, with moderate fever and possibly mild sore throat, sneezing, and coughing. On the same day a rash may appear on the face and neck, later spreading to the trunk and extremities. The rash may resemble that of measles or scarlet fever. It usually disappears within three days. A common sign of German measles is tenderness and swelling of the lymph glands behind the ear and in the back of the neck. The disease tends to be more severe in adults than in children. Complications may involve the joints or brain, but are not frequent.

If a woman contracts German measles in the first three months of pregnancy, there is a great risk of her baby being born with one or more serious abnormalities. It is generally agreed that a pregnant woman should be protected from exposure to the illness. A German measles vaccine was licensed for use in the United States in 1969 and a large-scale vaccination program was undertaken in the hope that mass immunization of schoolgirls would reduce the risk of contracting the disease when, at a later age, they may become pregnant. The vaccine must not be administered to women who are pregnant or who may become pregnant within two months of its administration. A susceptible pregnant woman exposed to German measles may require a protective injection of gamma globulin.

HARRY WEINER, M.D.

GERMAN-RUSSIAN PACT, also known as the Nazi-Soviet Pact, nonaggression treaty signed (Aug. 23, 1939) in Moscow by German Foreign Minister Joachim von Ribbentrop and Soviet Commissar of Foreign Affairs Vyacheslav Molotov. It secured the benevolent neutrality of the Soviet Union in Germany's approaching attack on Poland. The agreement astonished the Western powers, for Nazi Germany and Communist Russia had previously been confirmed enemies. A secret protocol (Sept. 28, 1939) partitioned Poland between the two powers and placed Finland and the Baltic states of Latvia, Lithuania, and Estonia, in addition to the Rumanian territory of Bessarabia, within the Soviet sphere of influence. The treaty remained in force until it was abruptly terminated by the German invasion of the Soviet Union that began on June 22, 1941.

GERMAN SILVER, also called nickel silver, an alloy of copper, nickel, and zinc. The material is so named because the white to silver-blue-white color of the alloy is very similar to that of silver alloys. German silver is corrosion resistant to water and the atmosphere, as well as to many organic products. It finds application in fasteners, decorative trim, optical parts, name plates, zippers, costume jewelry, and other objects. The alloy can be soft soldered, silver brazed, and welded, making it a very useful material for many applications where good appearance and ease of fabrication are necessary.

GERMANTOWN, BATTLE OF, engagement (Oct. 4, 1777) in the American Revolution during the campaign for Philadelphia. After defeating the Americans at Brandywine and occupying Philadelphia (Sept. 27, 1777), Gen. Sir William Howe established his main force of British and Hessians a few miles north of the city at Germantown, Pa. There Gen. George Washington confidently launched a predawn attack with four American columns. The right wing under Gen. John Sullivan was delayed by British forces barricaded in the stone house of Chief Justice Benjamin Chew. Gen. Nathanael Greene's left wing became confused in the heavy fog; one of its regiments was captured, and one column fired on another by mistake. British reinforcements under Lord Cornwallis hastened Washington's withdrawal. The Americans lost a total of 673 men in this engagement and the British lost 535.

GERMANUS, ST. [jər-mā′nəs] (c.378–448), Bishop of Auxerre. A Roman advocate, he ruled part of Gaul before his consecration (418). Going to Britain in 429, he eradicated Pelagianism, and in 432 consecrated his former pupil St. Patrick, Bishop of Ireland.

GERMAN VOLGA REPUBLIC was the first of four Autonomous Republics dissolved by the Soviet Government during World War II. It was founded by German emigrants in the mid-18th century and by 1914 had a population of over 500,000 and covered nearly 10,000 sq mi (25 900 km²) on both sides of the Volga around Samara and Saratov. In 1916 the Tsarist regime ordered the resettlement of the Volga Germans in Siberia, but the Bolshevik government annulled the decree in 1917. In 1918 the Volga German Autonomous Area was formed and on Jan. 6, 1924, an Autonomous Socialist Republic was created. By 1939 the republic had 400,000 ethnic Germans in a population of 605,000 and official 1939 sources praised the republic as a "leader in collectivization (86%) and mechanization of agriculture." Charging the population with disloyalty during the German military advance, the measure of Aug. 28, 1941, ordered the dissolution of the republic, the resettlement of the Volga Germans in Siberia, and the division of the territory between the Stalingrad (later Volgograd) and Saratov oblasts. Unlike the Tsarist decree, the 1941 order was immediately and vigorously implemented with considerable loss of life. Widely scattered in Siberia and Kazakhstan, the Volga Germans have not been rehabilitated or permitted to return to their former homes.

HERBERT RITVO

Germany

Neuschwanstein Castle looms above the mountainous, forested terrain of Bavaria, a state in West Germany. Ludwig II of Bavaria commissioned the castle in the 19th century.

Carl Purcell

GERMANY, a country of central and western Europe, with a coast line on the North and Baltic seas. The boundaries and extent of Germany have changed greatly over the centuries. After World War II the country's area was about 50% smaller than it had been up to World War I. In 1919 Alsace-Lorraine was ceded to France, small areas to Belgium and Denmark, and extensive territory to Poland. After World War II a larger area was occupied by Poland and small sectors by Belgium and the Netherlands, and what remained was occupied by American, British, French, and Soviet forces. This partition into zones of occupation was regarded as only a temporary expedient, but by 1949 the political division between western and eastern Germany had become absolute. The three western zones merged to form the Federal Republic of Germany (West Germany), while the eastern, Soviet, zone became the Democratic Republic of Germany (East Germany), whose sovereignty, however, was not recognized by the Federal Republic until 1970, when West Germany formally acknowledged the separateness of East Germany and accepted the Oder-Neisse as Poland's western border. Berlin, lying within the Democratic Republic, remained under quadripartite occupation.

NORMAN J. C. POUNDS

The People

Ethnology. Like other European peoples, the Germans are a mixture of several ethnic strains. Their land, lacking clearly defined geographical boundaries, has been subjected to repeated invasions over the centuries, and each group of conquerors has contributed to the national stock. But if Germany is a melting pot no less than the United States, the diverse elements are more difficult to identify. The west is generally Celtic and Latin in character, re-flecting the centuries of close association with the Roman Empire. The population of the central region is largely Celtic and Teutonic, while in the east Teutonic and Slavic influences are particularly strong. Yet these generalizations are at best only half-truths. They do not account for the Syrians and North Africans who settled along the Rhine and Danube in the days when Rome ruled the ancient world. Lithuanians once predominated in most of Prussia, until they were subjugated and assimilated by Teutonic invaders from the west of the Vistula. Many French Protestants expelled from their country in the late 17th century made their way to Brandenburg. The descendants of the prehistoric inhabitants who were overwhelmed by the Indo-Europeans can probably still be found in remote mountain villages. Hence Nazi theories of "racial purity" of the country were without any basis in fact, though they perhaps served to encourage a chauvinist pride.

By the end of the 19th century the Germans had become the largest single national group in Europe except for the Russians, and in 1939 their capital, Berlin, was the third-largest city in Europe. It remained the largest city of Germany after the political division of the country in 1949, followed by the historic centers of Hamburg, Munich, and Cologne, and the industrial cities of Essen and Düsseldorf, all in West Germany. The largest cities of East Germany are Leipzig and Dresden.

Language and Literature. German belongs to the West Germanic branch of the Germanic subgroup of Indo-European languages and is spoken in a variety of dialects as well as in the standard High German form. A literature in the vernacular can be said to have originated during the later Middle Ages; although there are sagas and epics of an earlier age, they interest the scholar rather than the

"Germany" means a region of Europe with a history dating from Roman times. After centuries of disunity Germany emerged in the 19th century as a world power and in the 20th century was the focus of two world wars. Following World War II, Germany was divided into Communist-occupied and Allied-occupied zones. After 1949 there were two German states. The article on these pages covers the history and culture of Germany as a region and at the same time gives individual descriptions of the West and East German states. The article is organized in the following manner.

The People. Ethnology; characteristics of the people as expressed in literature, philosophy, music, and art.

History. Roman times to Charlemagne; the Holy Roman Empire from the 10th to the 15th centuries; the age of the Reformation; religious wars; absolutism and the French Revolution; growth of liberalism; Bismarck and unification; the German Empire through World War I; the Weimar Republic; the Third Reich; Germany defeated and divided as a result of World War II.

Federal Republic of Germany (West Germany). The land, the people, the economy, government, history.

Democratic Republic of Germany (East Germany). The land, the people, the economy, government, history.

German Art and Architecture. Middle Ages, the Renaissance, the post-Renaissance period.

German Literature. Old High German Literature, c.750-1050; Middle High German Literature, c.1050-1350; 1350-1700; 18th century; romanticism; realism; naturalism; expressionism; mid-century.

German Music. The Middle Ages, the Renaissance, the baroque era, classic era, romantic era, and modern era.

German Theater. Strolling players, the classical theater, the 19th century.

Hundreds of additional articles deal with Germany and the German people and their works. The scope of coverage may be shown by citing representative articles in a number of areas. The reader who is interested in geography may consult EUROPE for a survey of the continent in which Germany is located. Features of Germany are described in the articles on major waterways, RHINE RIVER and DANUBE RIVER. Regions—for example, RHINELAND, SAAR, RUHR, SAXONY, and BAVARIA—are treated individually, and the same is true of great German cities such as AUGSBURG, BERLIN, BONN, BREMEN, COLOGNE, FRANKFURT AM MAIN, LEIPZIG, MUNICH, and STUTTGART.

The long history of Germany, involving many changes in government and many shifts of boundaries, can be studied in entries such as the following (listed in rough chronologic order): FRANKS; CHARLEMAGNE; HOLY ROMAN EMPIRE; HOHENSTAUFEN; TEUTONIC KNIGHTS; HABSBURG; REFORMATION; AUGSBURG, PEACE OF; THIRTY YEARS' WAR; WESTPHALIA, PEACE OF; PRUSSIA; HOHENZOLLERN; FREDERICK II OR FREDERICK THE GREAT; NAPOLEONIC WARS; VIENNA, CONGRESS OF; REVOLUTIONS OF 1848; BISMARCK; FRANCO-PRUSSIAN WAR; WILLIAM II; WORLD WAR I; WEIMAR REPUBLIC; NATIONAL SOCIALISM OR NAZISM; DICTATORSHIP; HITLER, ADOLF; GENOCIDE; AXIS POWERS; MUNICH TREATY; WORLD WAR II; ATLANTIC, BATTLE OF; BRITAIN, BATTLE OF; and WAR CRIMES.

Germany's situation as a divided country and a frontier zone in the cold war is underscored in such articles as POTSDAM CONFERENCE, BERLIN, BERLIN AIRLIFT; in the modern history sections of UNITED STATES and UNION OF SOVIET SOCIALIST REPUBLICS; and in biographies of such figures as Konrad ADENAUER, Ludwig ERHARD, and Willy BRANDT. COMMUNISM provides background for study of the East German state.

Only a few German leaders have been named thus far. The roster could be expanded, for example, by listing military men in addition to the military and political experts Frederick II and Bismarck. Gebhard von BLUCHER, Karl von CLAUSEWITZ, Baron von STEUBEN, Count Helmuth von MOLTKE, Paul von HINDENBURG, Alfred von TIRPITZ, and Erwin ROMMEL have helped make Germany famous in the history of warfare. Hermann GOERING, Joseph Paul GOEBBELS, and Heinrich HIMMLER became notorious for their leadership of the Nazis during the World War II period.

Interesting aspects of German economic history are found in three articles dealing with co-operative ventures at different periods: HANSEATIC LEAGUE, ZOLLVEREIN, and EUROPEAN COMMON MARKET.

Germans have made outstanding contributions in philosophy, science, the arts, and letters. Great names in theology include the Roman Catholic scholars THOMAS A KEMPIS and ALBERTUS MAGNUS and the Protestant Martin LUTHER. For secular German philosophy the reader may refer to the entries on such thinkers as Gottfried Wilhelm von LEIBNIZ, Immanuel KANT, Johann Gottlieb FICHTE, G. W. F. HEGEL and Arthur SCHOPENHAUER.

The range of German contributions in science can be shown by naming leaders in a number of fields: Johannes KEPLER in astronomy; G. D. FAHRENHEIT, Hermann von HELMHOLTZ, Wilhelm ROENTGEN, Heinrich R. HERTZ, and Max PLANCK in physics (see also the general article PHYSICS); Baron von LIEBIG in chemistry; Robert KOCH in medicine; Wilhelm WUNDT in psychology; Baron Alexander von HUMBOLDT in earth sciences; Heinrich SCHLIEMANN in archeology.

Germans are also known as technicians and inventors. Notable examples are Johann GUTENBERG, pioneer printer, and such men of the industrial age as Gottlieb DAIMLER and Rudolf DIESEL (see also AUTOMOBILE and INVENTION). German technical and industrial proficiency is exemplified in the record of the KRUPP family, producers of steel and munitions. In the 20th century Wernher von BRAUN and others took a leading role in the new technology described in ROCKET.

In the peaceful arts German contributions can be noted in such entries as GOTHIC ART; GOTHIC ARCHITECTURE; ARCHITECTURE, MODERN; and PAINTING, HISTORY OF. Famous individual artists include Matthias GRUNEWALD, Albrecht DURER, and Hans HOLBEIN the Younger.

The roster of great German musicians is longer. Outstanding names include Johann Sebastian BACH (and other members of his family), George Frederick HANDEL, Franz Joseph HAYDN, Wolfgang Amadeus MOZART (see also CLASSIC ERA, MUSIC OF THE); Ludwig van BEETHOVEN, Franz SCHUBERT, Johannes BRAHMS, Carl Maria von WEBER, Richard WAGNER, and Richard STRAUSS. Also pertinent are ROMANTIC ERA, MUSIC OF THE; OPERA; LOHENGRIN; and similar entries. The modern era is represented by Arnold SCHOENBERG, Kurt WEILL, and others.

German literature boasts such names as WALTHER VON DER VOGELWEIDE, Heinrich von KLEIST, Johann Wolfgang von GOETHE, and Johann Christolph Friedrich von SCHILLER. Moderns include the novelist Thomas MANN and the playwrights Gerhart HAUPTMANN and Bertolt BRECHT. The German language is discussed in GERMAN, with further details in GERMANIC LANGUAGES and INDO-EUROPEAN LANGUAGES.

International developments involving the status of Berlin and of all of Germany can be followed in periodicals and such references as the annual supplement to this Encyclopedia. Many sources can be found in the school or public library.

general reader. But the poetry of the Minnesinger and the Meistersinger from the 12th to the 15th centuries still retains its charm, and the subsequent age of humanism produced the lyrics of Ulrich von Hutten and the polemical writings of Martin Luther. The religious wars that followed exhausted the artistic vitality of central Europe for nearly 200 years. Toward the end of the 18th century, however, a literary renaissance heralded the golden age of belles-lettres in Germany, led by Johann Wolfgang von Goethe. Among his great contemporaries were the dramatists Friedrich von Schiller and Gotthold Ephraim Lessing and the poets Novalis and Friedrich Hölderlin. There followed after 1815 an era of prose, respectable but not outstanding. The novels of Gustav Freytag and the plays of Gerhart Hauptmann portray the industrialized world of the 19th century. Military defeat and economic collapse after 1914 inspired a literature of social protest to which Arnold Zweig and Erich Maria Remarque made important contributions. The greatest German literary figure of the first half of the 20th century was Thomas Mann, whose novels won him international acclaim.

Philosophy. The Germans are particularly proud of their contribution to philosophy, and sometimes describe their country as "the land of thinkers and poets." German thought is distinguished by its search for spiritual meaning beyond the realms of sensory experience or scientific truth. During the Middle Ages, Albertus Magnus and Thomas à Kempis enriched Catholic theology; Martin Luther and Philipp Melanchthon helped inspire the Protestant Reformation. Even after the Thirty Years' War, when the Holy Roman Empire reached its political nadir, the fame of Gottfried Wilhelm von Leibniz rivaled that of Sir Isaac Newton and Baruch Spinoza. In the 18th century Germany established an indisputable claim to primacy in philosophy. The school of idealism founded by the publication in 1781 of Immanuel Kant's *Critique of Pure Reason* bred such thinkers as Johann Gottlieb Fichte, Friedrich von Schelling, and Friedrich Schleiermacher. Its most famous member, however, was G. W. F. Hegel, whose writings greatly influenced the development of socialism. Toward the end of the 19th century Friedrich Nietzsche launched his devastating attack upon middle-class beliefs and ideals. After World War I Martin Heidegger and Karl Jaspers helped to lay the foundations of existentialism.

Music and Art. Germany has also gained a reputation as the land of classical music. The same age which produced Goethe and Schiller listened for the first time to Ludwig van Beethoven, successor in time, if not in spirit, to Johann Sebastian Bach. The musical inspiration of the country proved inexhaustible. Whereas the German creative genius has found its consummate expression in musical composition, its accomplishment in other art forms has also been impressive. The Gothic cathedral of Cologne and the baroque palace of Würzburg are regarded as genuine triumphs of architecture. The great age of painting in Germany was the 15th and 16th centuries. Albrecht Dürer was a genius fully the equal of his Italian contemporaries. Works of Hans Holbein the Younger are magnificent achievements of portraiture, and many others expressed the spiritual brilliance of the Renaissance, among them the painters Lucas Cranach and Matthias Grünewald and the sculptors Peter Vischer and Veit Stoss. After the Ref-ormation the graphic arts declined, but there was a significant revival in the 20th century, when George Grosz and Käthe Kollwitz, in particular, won international fame for their drawings and paintings of social criticism.

History

From ancient times until Germany emerged as a political state in the course of the Middle Ages, it was composed of three distinct regions and cultures. Latin Germany, the area along the left bank of the Rhine, was conquered by the Romans in the 1st century B.C. Reminders of Roman rule can still be found in the ancient ruins of many Rhenish towns and in the famous Rhine and Moselle wines, which were first produced when the land was under the protection of the imperial eagle. There are even those who maintain that the gaiety and charm of the Rhineland are part of the country's Latin heritage. More important historically was Teutonic Germany, the region lying roughly between the Rhine and the Elbe rivers, which was the home of the Germanic tribes never subdued by Roman military might. Indeed, as the empire gradually declined, Germans began to enter its borders in growing numbers, sometimes as mercenaries in the imperial armies, sometimes as ruthless invaders.

Following the Roman state's disintegration, a vast Germanic empire arose between the 5th and 9th centuries, extending over much of western and central Europe. The third major component of the emerging nation was Slavic Germany, the land stretching from the Elbe eastward to the Oder, Vistula, and Memel rivers. The Germanization of this territory was the result of a long period of peaceful settlement as well as military conquest between the 12th and 14th centuries. The prevalence of Slavic names and the stubborn survival of Slavic dialects in this part of Germany recall the days before the Teutonic invaders began their long eastward march.

The Franks, a Germanic tribe from the Rhine Valley, initiated the process by which these diverse political and cultural elements became a nation. Their ruler Clovis during his reign (481–511) acquired most of Gaul and consolidated his hold on western Germany. His conversion to Christianity, moreover, foreshadowed the involvement of German rulers in papal affairs which was to be so important throughout the Middle Ages. The greatest successor to Clovis was Charlemagne, who subjugated and Christianized the tribes along the Elbe, until his empire included most of modern France and Germany. In recognition of his position as the most powerful ruler in western Europe, Pope Leo III crowned Charlemagne Roman Emperor in 800, a curious combination of the German monarchy with the Roman emperorship that endured almost continually for 1,000 years. The immediate effects of the coronation, however, were negligible. Within 30 years after the death of Charlemagne his empire had fallen apart, most of it being divided into two states, east and west of the Rhine, the forerunners of Germany and France. The hard-won imperial title fell into disuse by the end of the 9th century, and the Carolingian Dynasty weakened and decayed. Finally, the German line ended in 911 with the death of Louis the Child.

The Empire from the 10th to the 15th Centuries. The magnates of the various German duchies now began to

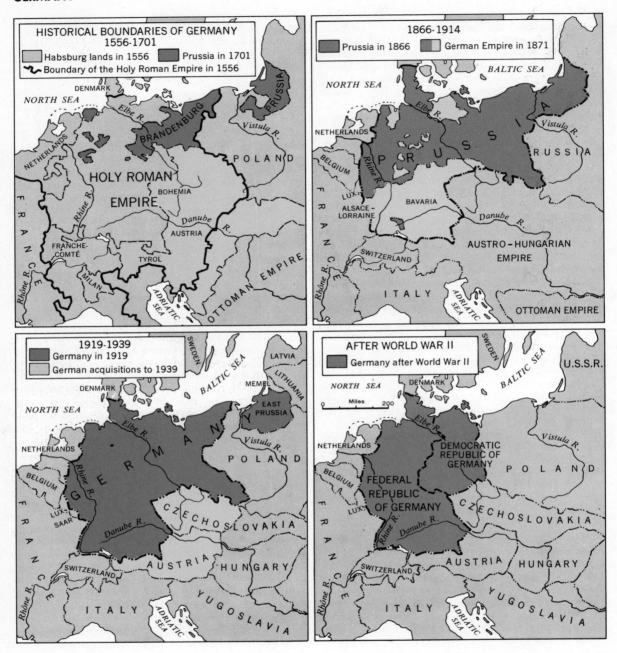

choose a ruler from among themselves. In 962 Otto I of the Saxon Dynasty revived the imperial title, and by the late 12th century the Holy Roman Empire included the Low Countries, eastern France, and northern Italy in addition to Germany. During the three centuries between the coronation of Otto I and the death of Frederick II in 1250, Germany became the most powerful state in Europe. Although other monarchs were trying without much success to assert their authority over the feudal nobility, the Holy Roman Emperor won recognition as the first prince of Christendom. Not only was his realm the most

extensive, but he was generally able to enforce obedience among the great landed aristocrats, upon whom the medieval system of government depended. Most important of all, the Emperors exercised power in spiritual as well as secular affairs, claiming the right to protect, strengthen, and guide the church. Time and again the ruler of Germany would cross the Alps and enter Italy to decide ecclesiastical disputes, to depose a pontiff, to chastise prominent churchmen, to dictate papal policy.

Yet the Holy Roman Emperors were pursuing an impossible goal. The future belonged to the German national state, not to some splendid vision of a universal empire such as that which the Caesars had once ruled. The Emperors of Germany, pursuing the will-o'-the-wisp of imperial hegemony, neglected the vital interests of the nation. While they were wasting their energies in futile attempts to subjugate the Papacy, the landed nobility of Germany gained strength. Ultimately the Emperors were defeated in their Italian ventures, at the same time losing ground in the complicated political struggle in Germany. They left to ambitious aristocrats and enterprising prelates the task of eastward expansion into Slavic lands; they played only a minor role in the growth of cities and the spread of commerce. By 1254, when the Hohenstaufen Dynasty came to an end, they had lost the game.

After an interregnum of almost 20 years, Rudolph of Habsburg was elected Emperor in 1273, but he and his successors had few illusions about the extent of their power. They gladly abandoned the contest with the Papacy, while only halfheartedly opposing the rising tide of feudal separatism. The political decline of Germany had begun, characterized in the first place by the growing decentralization of authority. The magnates of the empire, leading churchmen as well as temporal lords, gradually assumed many of the functions of government formerly exercised by the imperial court. Even after the 15th century, when it became customary to choose only Habsburgs for the emperorship, the decline of royal power continued.

To be sure, there were attempts from time to time to halt the political disintegration of Germany. In 1495, for example, the Diet of Worms prohibited private warfare and established a supreme court to deal with domestic disputes. The Diet of Cologne 17 years later tried to improve the administration and defense of the country by creating 10 administrative districts, each of which was to be responsible for the maintenance of law and order within its boundaries. It was all in vain. No acceptable compromise between the historic prerogatives of the throne and the growing ambition of the Princes could be found.

Political indecisiveness, moreover, led inevitably to military weakness. Throughout the 14th century German colonization in eastern Europe was losing vigor, and in 1410 a combined Polish and Lithuanian army crushed the Teutonic Knights who had established themselves in Prussia. Before long a bold and energetic monarchy in France was ready to embark upon a policy of expansion toward the Rhine.

The Age of the Reformation. The Reformation intensified political disunity in Germany. The religious revolt had a profound effect throughout western and central Europe, but only in the empire did it end in a stalemate, without a definite majority for either the old church or the new. National solidarity was threatened by the fact that, unlike in England and the Netherlands, France and Spain, Protestants and Roman Catholics remained evenly balanced. Perhaps still more important, they were so intermingled that no clear line of demarcation between them could be drawn. There can be no doubt that these differences in religion aggravated differences in politics. By the 16th century it was probably too late to halt the decline of imperial authority; moreover, the Reformation did much to hasten the process. While the Habsburgs remained loyal to Rome, many territorial princes asserted their independ-

Bibliothèque Protestante, Paris—Editorial Photocolor Archives

Portrait of Martin Luther, German Protestant reformer, attributed to Lucas Cranach, who also ran a printshop. It was on Cranach's press that Luther printed his revolutionary pamphlets.

ence by embracing Protestantism. The struggle between centralist and separatist forces was now expressed in theological as well as political terms.

The contention of some German historians that it was disunity which brought on the economic decline of central Europe is debatable. It may even be that the relaxation of imperial authority actually encouraged initiative among the well-to-do burghers. Certainly the political disorganization of the 14th century did nothing to prevent the rise of the Hanseatic League, an association of free towns formed for purposes of commerce and defense. For about 200 years it dominated the economy of the areas of the Baltic and the North seas. Similarly, such south German cities as Augsburg, Nuremberg, Ulm, and Regensburg flourished at a time when political reformers were vainly trying to check the debilitation of the imperial government. Strategically located along important trade routes, they grew rich on the traffic between the Mediterranean and the north. Their great banking houses even determined royal policy, for without loans the Emperor was unable to support his armies and enforce his will. The 15th and 16th centuries were also a period of remarkable cultural accomplishment. It was the age of German humanism, when a rich literature of social and religious criticism developed alongside the poetry of the Meistersinger. The art of painting reached a level of creativity which the nation never surpassed. In short, the life of the spirit and the

Dana Brown—FPG

Lübeck, chief Baltic port of West Germany, has been an important center of commerce since the 13th century.

vigor of the economy seemed immune to the vagaries of politics. Only when the great voyages of exploration had shifted the vital routes of commerce westward to the Atlantic did the financial decline of Germany begin, followed by the exhaustion of artistic vitality.

Religious Wars. The adverse effects of political disunity, religious division, and economic decay were soon aggravated by civil war. The coming of the Reformation coincided with the reign of an Emperor whose resources were so vast that he could seriously plan to restore his office to its former glory. Charles V was the ruler not only of Germany, but of Spain, the Low Countries, much of Italy, and most of the New World. A devout Catholic, he wanted above all to restore the old faith and the old imperial au-

The destruction and plunder of a village during the Thirty Years' War (1618–48) is depicted in an engraving by Jacques Callot.

The Bettmann Archive

thority in central Europe. Wars against the French and the Turks forced him to postpone his design for almost 30 years, but in 1546 he finally opened his campaign against the members of the Schmalkaldic League, whom he considered heretics as well as rebels. After a long period of indecisive fighting, the Emperor was forced in the Peace of Augsburg of 1555 to recognize the right of the Princes to introduce Lutheranism into their lands. Yet neither side was satisfied with the settlement, and in 1618 another internecine struggle began. The Thirty Years' War was an unmitigated disaster. The domestic quarrel soon became an international conflict, with Danish, Swedish, French, Spanish, and Italian troops fighting on German soil, plundering, ravaging, burning, killing. When the Treaty of Westphalia finally ended hostilities in 1648, the country was a shambles. Political power was now divided among hundreds of territorial units of varying size and strength; the religious schism became permanent, the economy was prostrated, the population diminished. A hundred years later Voltaire could still quip that the Holy Roman Empire was "neither holy, nor Roman, nor an empire."

Absolutism and the French Revolution. The Treaty of Westphalia was followed by a century and a half of absolutism in central Europe. Since the significance of the imperial office had become almost entirely symbolic, sovereign authority passed into the hands of local Princes, who maintained armies, concluded treaties, promulgated laws, levied taxes, and asserted their self-interest. Germany became a nation of countless principalities, some large, most small, all assiduously imitating the example of Louis XIV of France. Each ruler tried to transform his palace into a Versailles, adopted French speech and manners, suppressed aristocratic liberties and representative assemblies, introduced the economic practices of mercantilism, and fought in Europe's complicated dynastic wars. Political disunity invited foreign attack, and France succeeded in acquiring important territories along the Rhine and the Moselle. However, the armies and the wealth of Austria were able to restrain the ambitions of the Bourbons and prevent the complete partition of the Holy Roman Empire. In the course of the 18th century the Emperors in Vienna were challenged by another rival, the Hohenzollerns, who succeeded in making Prussia the greatest power in northern Germany. By 1789 Austro-Prussian rivalry had become a major factor in the politics of Europe.

The coming of the French Revolution destroyed the old order. The spirit of liberalism and nationalism moved east across the Rhine and began to spread among the educated classes of Germany. During the 18th century the subjects of the gingerbread princelings had been expected to pay their taxes and leave affairs of state to their betters. Now the doctrines of liberty, equality, and fraternity introduced by the invading armies of republican France brought about the collapse of one German state after another. By 1794 the French had taken the Rhineland. In 1806 Austria decided to proclaim the dissolution of the 1,000-year-old Holy Roman Empire, and a year later Prussia was forced to sign a humiliating peace, surrendering almost half of its territory and population. Napoleon was now the arbiter of Germany. He ended the independence of nearly all of the small territorial units, and formed most of the remaining principalities into the Confederation of the Rhine under his own direction. For about seven years these individual states of central Europe were satellites of the French empire. Yet it was during this period of political humiliation that an important reform movement developed, which sought to establish parliamentary government and a united national state to replace the dead empire. In 1813 the patriotic War of Liberation broke out against the Napoleonic regime, and the following year the statesmen of Europe met in Vienna to reconstruct the Continent and decide the future of Germany.

Growth of Liberalism. The hopes of the patriots were disappointed. The rulers of central Europe had accepted the reform movement only as long as it assisted them in the struggle against foreign domination. Once Napoleon fell, they no longer wished to sacrifice their prerogatives for the sake of constitutional government and a united nation. Their interests were brilliantly defended by the Chief Minister of Austria, Prince Klemens von Metternich, who dominated the Congress of Vienna. A loose association of 39 lands known as the German Confederation was established, but almost all functions of government were left to the member states. In theory, the confederation had authority to introduce a representative government and economic unity. In fact, it became a stronghold of reaction and particularism. There is no evidence that the masses of central Europe, impoverished and ignorant, had strong convictions about political organization, but middle-class parliamentarians openly voiced their dissatisfaction, and their number gradually increased as the industrial revolution made itself felt in Germany. The growing discontent was expressed in the Revolution of 1848, when the liberal opposition finally managed to achieve power. A parliament met in Frankfurt am Main to prepare the constitution for a new federal union, but by the time it completed its work, the opportunity for reform had passed. The conservatives gradually regained their courage, while the lower classes were more interested in economic changes than in representative government. In 1850 the German Confederation was restored, and many of the revolutionary leaders faced the choice of exile or imprisonment. The only significant

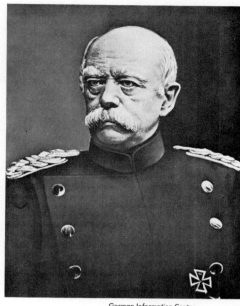

Otto von Bismarck unified Germany by "blood and iron" in the 19th century.

German Information Center

national achievement of the first half of the 19th century was the formation of the Zollverein, a customs union established under Prussian auspices and embracing most of the German states.

Bismarck. When political unification finally came, it was the work not of liberal reformers, but of a conservative genius whose purpose was to maintain the power of the aristocracy against increasing influence of the middle-class. Otto von Bismarck became Prime Minister of Prussia in 1862, at a time of bitter disagreement between Parliament and the crown. For four years he defied legislative disapproval, confident that the opposition would capitulate if he could offer it something that it valued more than liberalism: national unification. He pursued his objective with consummate skill, convinced that "the

Emperor William II (center) confers with Field Marshal Paul von Hindenburg and Gen. Erich Ludendorff during World War I.

Interfoto—Archiv

Soldiers and their families accepted the emperor's description of a "joyous" war as the army mobilized in 1914.

René Dazy

United Press International

In Vienna, on Mar. 12, 1938, Adolf Hitler announces the surprise annexation of Austria to the German Third Reich.

great questions of the time are not decided by speeches, and majority resolutions . . . but by iron and blood."

First he persuaded the Austrians in 1864 to join him in a brief and successful war against Denmark for the duchies of Schleswig and Holstein. Two years later the recent allies fought each other over the spoils of their common victory. The outcome was a decisive victory for Prussia, which was now free to unite the states north of the Main River in the North German Confederation. The liberals, intoxicated by success, sacrificed their principles and made peace with Bismarck. When in 1870 he goaded Napoleon III of France into a declaration of war, the south as well as the north was swept by patriotic fervor. On Jan. 18, 1871, while German guns besieged a starving Paris, William of Hohenzollern was proclaimed German Emperor.

The German Empire. The empire which Bismarck had created lasted 47 years. It was essentially a semi-autocracy. Although the legislature was chosen by manhood suffrage, it had little effective control over state policy. A growing demand for responsible government culminated in the election of 1912, when the opposition Social Democrats were returned as the largest single party. Political discontent would probably have been even greater but for the remarkable industrial growth of the nation. Between the Franco-Prussian War and World War I, Germany became the first industrial power of the Continent. Iron from Lorraine, coal from the Ruhr, chemicals from Prussian Saxony, precision instruments from Thuringia contributed to the support of a swiftly growing population by winning important markets abroad. Equally significant was the international respect which the great victories of the wars of unification had won for the German military. For nearly half a century the Hohenzollern empire was the most powerful state in Europe. But it lacked wisdom and moderation. As long as Bismarck remained in office, he used his extraordinary gifts as a diplomat to safeguard the dominant position of his country. But after the new Emperor, William II, dismissed the Iron Chancellor in 1890, the position of the government began to deteriorate. Saber

rattling in Berlin combined with ill-advised policies of imperialistic expansion and naval construction drove Russia and Britain into the arms of France. Germany found itself opposed by all the powers except Austria, whose support was probably more of a liability than an asset. When World War I broke out in 1914, central Europe became a besieged fortress, capable of determined resistance, but in the long run doomed to defeat.

The Weimar Republic. The military disaster of 1918 spelled the end of the German Empire. A bloodless revolution replaced the monarchy with a democratic republic. But the new order which was established by a National Assembly meeting in Weimar faced impossible odds. Born amid the bitterness arising out of a lost war, it was expected to find solutions to the problems which the previous regime had left behind. On one side were the Communists, who hoped that central Europe would follow the example of Soviet Russia. On the other were the reactionaries, who insisted that liberalism was to blame for defeat in the war. The victor powers did little to support democracy in Germany, and indeed the punitive Treaty of Versailles which they imposed on the Weimar Republic helped to strengthen its enemies. The result of domestic chaos and foreign hostility was a disastrous inflation which impoverished a good part of the middle class. There was an ephemeral economic recovery during the middle 1920's, but the world depression at the end of the decade doomed whatever chance of survival the republic might still have had. For about three years the supporters of democracy struggled desperately against the combined opposition of the right and the left. But the catastrophic collapse of business and the spread of unemployment caused more and more people to see salvation in a totalitarian regime. Finally, on Jan. 30, 1933, the senile President Paul von Hindenburg appointed as Chancellor the leader of the National Socialist party, Adolf Hitler.

The Third Reich. National Socialism had arisen out of the chaos and despair of the postwar period. It preached authoritarianism, racism, militarism, and a tub-thumping nationalism. Once in power, it dealt ruthlessly with every form of opposition. All expressions of political independence through parties, churches, schools, books, newspapers, or journals were silenced. Obedience to the will of the Führer became the supreme virtue. Close regulation of the economy was achieved by the elimination of independent labor unions and their replacement with new organizations of employers and employees subservient to the government. Democrats as well as Marxists were harassed and persecuted. But the most brutal treatment was reserved for the Jews. They became the major victims of a system of concentration camps instituted to imprison or kill opponents of the government. It resulted in the eventual extermination of the majority of the Jewish population of Germany. Most Germans, however, accepted the new regime gladly, for it seemed to offer them political and economic security. The Communist uprising which many had feared no longer threatened, and the problem of unemployment was solved by a program of public works and rapid rearmament. National pride, moreover, rejoiced in the impressive diplomatic successes which the government achieved with its policy of threats and extortions. But eventually Hitler overplayed his hand. Convinced that nothing could withstand the might of his armies, he plunged into a world war in 1939 from which the country emerged six years later exhausted, demoralized and partitioned. (*See* NATIONAL SOCIALISM OR NAZISM.)

Germany Defeated and Divided. No nation in modern history had suffered such a catastrophic defeat. Germany in the spring of 1945 was helpless, a land without a government or an army. The victorious Allies, after establishing zones of occupation, ordered the demilitarization of the country, the elimination of former Nazis from public life, and the trial of Hitler's close collaborators. Political reconstruction, however, was hampered by the economic collapse which had come with unconditional surrender. Hunger and privation stalked the ruined streets of once flourishing cities. As the United States and the Soviet Union became involved in the cold war, however, each began to seek support among the Germans. The Soviet Union gradually abandoned all claims to reparations in the region under its control, while the American, British, and French authorities introduced a drastic currency reform in their occupation zones. Together with American aid derived from the Marshall Plan, the currency reform soon produced a remarkable economic recovery. In 1949 the division of the country assumed definitive form. The western territories formed the Federal Republic of Germany, a democratic and capitalistic state largely modeled on the Weimar Republic. In the east the Russians assigned most of the territory east of the Oder River to Poland, while the rest of the area that they occupied became the German Democratic Republic, governed in accordance with the principles of communism. There were now two Germanys, each with a different orientation. (*See* GERMANY: *Democratic Republic of Germany; Federal Republic of Germany.*)

The result of this division was a strong movement for reunion. Both West and East Germany were agreed that a united country was desirable; the question was how to achieve it. Middle-of-the-road West German politicians insisted that since their government was the only one chosen in democratic elections, they alone represented the will of the German people. Reunification should be accomplished by a free vote of all Germans, east and west. The East German Communist leaders, on the other hand, realizing that they would probably be defeated in such a vote, main-

German Information Center

Nuremberg in ruins in 1945. The city has since been rebuilt.

tained that reunification must be brought about by direct negotiations between the two states of Germany. Because direct negotiations would represent a tacit admission by the West that East Germany was a sovereign state, Western leaders were long reluctant to open a dialogue with the East. No mutually satisfactory compromise was possible, and the division of Germany thus came to reflect the division of Europe and the world during the cold war. When a more realistic attitude was finally adopted by the two states' recognition of each other's sovereignty (1972) and establishment of diplomatic relations (1974), it only seemed to underline the fact that Germany was permanently divided into two states of opposing political ideologies.

Consult Delmer, D. S., *Weimar Germany: Democracy on Trial* (1973); Hamerow, Theodore S., *The Social Foundations of German Unification, 1858–1871* (2 vols., 1969–72); Pinson, K. S., *Modern Germany, Its History and Civilization* (2d ed., 1966); Speer, Albert, *Inside the Third Reich* (1970); Taylor, A. J. P., *The Course of German History* (rev. ed., 1962).

THEODORE S. HAMEROW

MODERN GERMAN HEADS OF STATE

HOUSE OF HOHENZOLLERN
Kings of Prussia

Frederick I	1701–13
Frederick William I	1713–40
Frederick II the Great	1740–86
Frederick William II	1786–97
Frederick William III	1797–1840
Frederick William IV	1840–61
William I	1861–71
	(crowned Emperor of Germany)

Emperors of Germany

William I	1871–88
Frederick III	1888
	(died after 99 days)
William II (Kaiser Wilhelm)	1888–1918

The Weimar Republic

Friedrich Ebert	1919–25
Paul von Hindenburg	1925–34

The Third Reich

Adolf Hitler	1934–45

Allied Military Government 1945–49

Federal Republic of Germany (West Germany)

Theodor Heuss, President	1949–59
Heinrich Lübke, President	1959–69
Gustav Heinemann, President	1969–74
Walter Scheel, President	1974–

Democratic Republic of Germany (East Germany)

Wilhelm Pieck, President	1949–60
Walter Ulbricht, Chairman of the Council of State	1960–73
Willi Stoph, Chairman of the Council of State	1973–

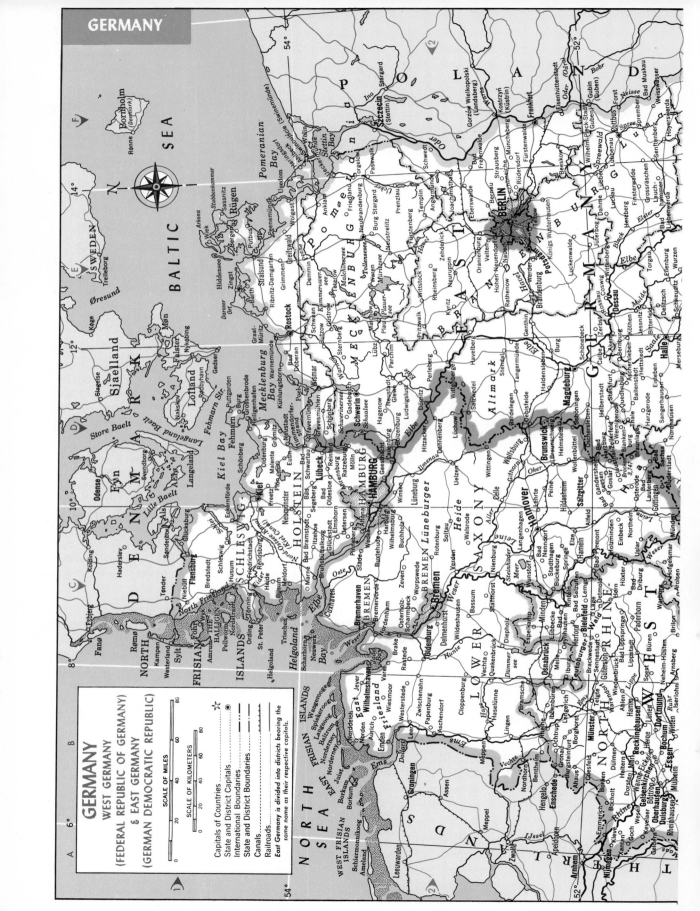

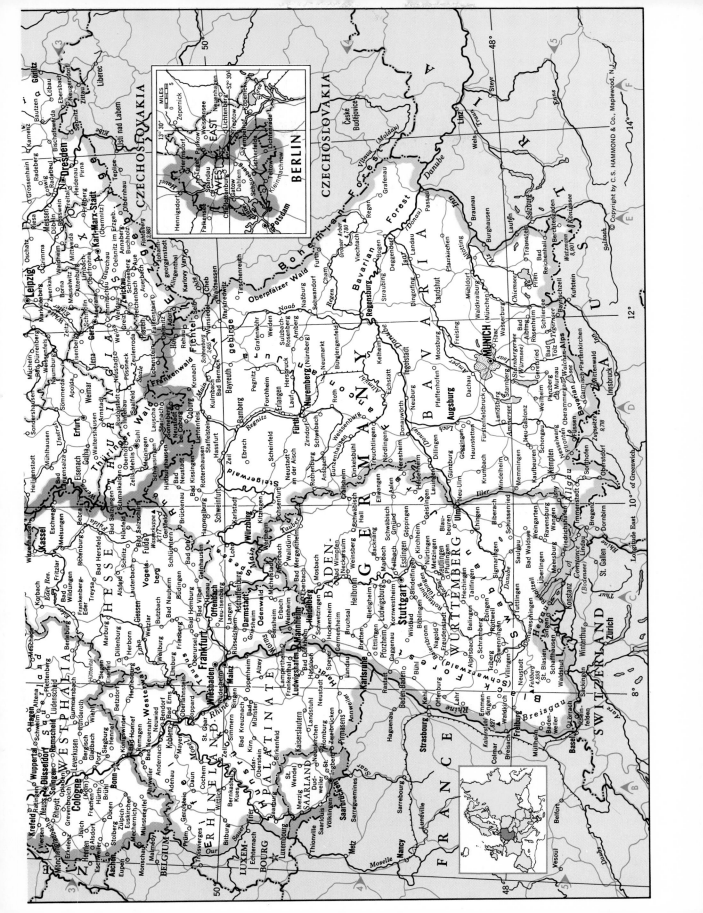

GERMANY

EAST GERMANY

DISTRICTS

Berlin (East), 1,084,000 ....F 4
Cottbus, 839,133 ....F 3
Dresden, 1,887,739 ....E 3
Erfurt, 1,249,540 ....D 3
Frankfurt, 660,666 ....F 2
Gera, 735,175 ....D 3
Halle, 1,932,733 ....E 3
Karl-Marx-Stadt, 2,082,927 ....E 3
Leipzig, 1,510,773 ....E 3
Magdeburg, 1,323,644 ....D 2
Neubrandenburg, 633,209 ....E 2
Potsdam, 1,127,498 ....E 2
Rostock, 842,743 ....D 1
Schwerin, 594,786 ....D 2
Suhl, 549,398 ....D 3

CITIES and TOWNS

Aken, 12,126 ....D 3
Altenburg, 47,462 ....E 3
Angermünde, 12,200 ....E 2
Anklam, 19,436 ....E 2
Annaberg-Buchholz, 28,663 ....E 3
Apolda, 29,735 ....D 3
Arnstadt, 27,674 ....D 3
Aschersleben, 36,777 ....D 3
Aue, 31,723 ....E 3
Auerbach, 19,673 ....E 3
Bad Doberan, 13,197 ....D 1
Bad Dürrenberg, 16,500 ....D 3
Bad Langensalza, 16,952 ....D 3
Bad Salzungen, 12,722 ....C 3
Barth, 12,688 ....E 1
Bautzen, 44,041 ....F 3
Berlin (East) (capital), 1,084,000 ....F 4
Bernau, 14,078 ....E 2
Bernburg, 45,885 ....D 3
Bitterfeld, 30,916 ....E 3
Blankenburg, 19,595 ....D 3
Borna, 20,669 ....E 3
Brandenburg, 90,753 ....E 2
Burg, 29,906 ....D 2
Calbe, 16,464 ....D 3
Chemnitz (Karl-Marx-Stadt), 295,443 ....D 3
Coswig, 18,600 ....E 3
Cottbus, 75,541 ....F 3
Crimmitschau, 30,752 ....E 3
Delitzsch, 23,480 ....E 3
Demmin, 16,755 ....E 2
Dessau, 95,682 ....E 3
Döbeln, 28,430 ....E 3
Dresden, 499,848 ....E 3
Eberswalde, 33,680 ....E 2
Eilenburg, 21,366 ....E 3
Eisenach, 50,234 ....D 3
Eisenberg, 13,858 ....D 3
Eisenhüttenstadt, 38,138 ....F 2
Eisleben, 32,402 ....D 3
Erfurt, 193,745 ....D 3
Falkensee, 29,884 ....E 3
Falkenstein, 15,269 ....E 3
Finsterwalde, 22,441 ....E 3
Forst, 29,823 ....F 3
Frankfurt-an-der-Oder, 58,866 ....F 2
Freiberg, 49,122 ....E 3
Freital, 42,675 ....E 3
Fürstenwalde, 30,527 ....F 2
Gardelegen, 13,218 ....D 2
Genthin, 15,619 ....E 2
Gera, 109,989 ....E 3
Glauchau, 33,103 ....E 3
Görlitz, 88,632 ....F 3
Gotha, 57,692 ....D 3
Greifswald, 47,402 ....E 1
Greiz, 39,313 ....E 3
Grimma, 16,509 ....E 3
Grimmen, 12,943 ....E 1
Grossenhain, 19,848 ....E 3
Grossräschen, 12,737 ....E 3
Guben (Wilhelm-Pieck-Stadt), 26,586 ....F 3
Güstrow, 38,185 ....E 2
Halberstadt, 46,071 ....D 3
Haldensleben, 20,547 ....D 2
Halle, 263,928 ....D 3
Heidenau, 20,161 ....E 3
Heiligenstadt, 12,627 ....D 3
Hennigsdorf, 21,398 ....E 3
Hettstedt, 19,218 ....D 3
Hoyerswerda, 43,922 ....F 3
Ilmenau, 19,852 ....D 3
Jena, 85,032 ....D 3
Johanngeorgenstadt, 10,801 ....E 3
Jüterbog, 14,416 ....E 3
Kamenz, 16,236 ....F 3
Karl-Marx-Stadt, 295,443 ....E 3
Kleinmachnow, 13,919 ....E 4
Klingenthal, 14,748 ....E 3
Köpenick, 52,294 ....F 4
Köthen, 38,154 ....E 3
Kottbus (Cottbus), 75,541 ....F 3
Lauchhammer, 28,680 ....E 3
Leipzig, 590,291 ....E 3
Lichtenberg, 62,841 ....F 4
Limbach-Oberfrohna, 26,053 ....E 3
Löbau, 17,068 ....F 3
Lübben, 12,742 ....E 3
Lübbenau, 16,976 ....F 3
Luckenwalde, 29,282 ....E 2
Ludwigslust, 11,512 ....D 2
Magdeburg, 268,269 ....D 2
Markkleeberg, 21,854 ....E 3
Meerane, 24,262 ....E 3
Meiningen, 25,025 ....D 3
Meissen, 47,166 ....E 3
Merseburg, 55,562 ....D 3
Mittweida, 20,440 ....E 3
Mühlhausen, 46,155 ....D 3
Nauen, 12,017 ....E 2
Naumburg, 37,990 ....D 3
Neubrandenburg, 38,740 ....E 2
Neuenhagen, 13,116 ....F 4
Neugersdorf, 11,889 ....F 3
Neuruppin, 22,424 ....E 2
Neustrelitz, 27,624 ....E 2
Nordhausen, 42,279 ....D 3
Oelsnitz, 15,954 ....E 3
Oelsnitz im Erzgebirge, 18,377 ..E 3
Olbernhau, 14,240 ....E 3
Oranienburg, 20,401 ....E 2
Oschatz, 15,582 ....E 3
Oschersleben, 18,078 ....D 2
Pankow, 68,785 ....F 3
Parchim, 19,226 ....D 2
Pasewalk, 14,086 ....F 2
Perleberg, 13,707 ....D 2
Pirna, 42,562 ....E 3
Plauen, 81,739 ....E 3
Pössneck, 19,468 ....D 3
Potsdam, 110,671 ....E 2
Prenzlau, 20,276 ....F 2
Quedlinburg, 30,840 ....D 3
Radeberg, 17,410 ....E 3
Radebeul, 41,437 ....E 3
Rathenow, 28,979 ....E 2
Reichenbach, 29,372 ....E 3
Ribnitz-Damgarten, 15,301 ....E 1
Riesa, 43,322 ....E 3
Rosslau, 16,256 ....E 3
Rosswein, 10,649 ....E 3
Rostock, 190,275 ....E 1
Rüdersdorf, 11,837 ....E 2
Rudolstadt, 30,433 ....D 3
Saalfeld, 32,145 ....D 3
Salzwedel, 19,534 ....D 2
Sangerhausen, 29,373 ....D 3
Sassnitz, 13,253 ....E 1
Schkeuditz, 17,131 ....E 3
Schmalkalden, 14,569 ....D 3
Schmölln, 13,992 ....E 3
Schneeberg, 21,225 ....E 3
Schönebeck, 44,551 ....D 2
Schwedt, 23,359 ....F 2
Schwerin, 92,356 ....D 2
Sebnitz, 14,655 ....F 3
Senftenberg, 24,532 ....F 3
Sömmerda, 16,061 ....D 3
Sondershausen, 22,456 ....D 3
Sonneberg, 29,804 ....D 3
Spremberg, 23,367 ....F 3
Stassfurt, 25,622 ....D 3
Stendal, 36,193 ....D 2
Stralsund, 68,925 ....E 1
Strausberg, 17,985 ....F 2
Suhl, 28,698 ....D 3
Tangermünde, 12,992 ....D 2
Teltow, 13,735 ....E 4
Templin, 11,203 ....E 2
Teterow, 11,039 ....E 2
Thale, 17,273 ....D 3
Torgau, 20,941 ....E 3
Torgelow, 13,584 ....F 2
Treptow, 22,302 ....F 4
Ueckermünde, 11,614 ....F 2
Zwickau, 127,688 ....E 3
Waltershausen, 14,250 ....D 3
Waren, 20,008 ....E 2
Weida, 11,950 ....E 3
Weimar, 64,300 ....D 3
Weissenfels, 47,704 ....D 3
Weissensee, 50,691 ....F 3
Weisswasser, 16,016 ....F 3
Werdau, 23,783 ....E 3
Wernigerode, 32,579 ....D 3
Wilhelm-Pieck-Stadt, 26,586 ......F 3
Wismar, 55,235 ....D 2
Wittenberg, 46,816 ....E 3
Wittenberge, 32,621 ....D 2
Wolgast, 14,955 ....E 1
Wurzen, 24,349 ....E 3
Zehdenick, 12,306 ....E 2
Zeitz, 46,393 ....E 3
Zella-Mehlis, 17,121 ....D 3
Zerbst, 19,527 ....E 3
Zeulenroda, 18,534 ....D 3
Zittau, 43,259 ....F 3
Zwickau, 127,688 ....E 3

OTHER FEATURES

Altmark (reg.), 288,928 ....D 2
Arkona (cape) ....E 1
Baltic (sea) ....F 1
Black Elster (riv.) ....E 3
Brandenburg (reg.), 3,726,413....E 2
Brocken (mt.) ....D 3
Darsser Ort (point) ....E 1
Elbe (riv.) ....D 2
Elster (riv.) ....E 3
Erzgebirge (Ore) (mts.) ....E 3
Fichtelberg (mt.) ....E 3
Havel (riv.) ....E 2
Kummerowersee (lake) ....E 2
Lusatia (reg.) ....F 3
Malchinersee (lake) ....E 2
Mecklenburg (reg.), 1,226,685....E 2
Mecklenburg (bay) ....D 1
Mulde (riv.) ....E 3
Müritzee (lake) ....E 2
Neisse (riv.) ....F 3
Oder (riv.) ....F 2
Ore (Erzgebirge) (mts.) ....E 3
Penne (riv.) ....E 2
Plauersee (lake) ....E 2
Pomerania (region), 711,075 .....E 2
Pomeranian (bay) ....F 1
Rhön (mts.) ....D 3
Rügen (isl.), 92,348 ....E 1
Saale (riv.) ....D 3
Saxony (region), 5,318,661 ....E 3
Schaalsee (lake) ....D 2
Schwerinersee (lake) ....D 2
Spree (riv.) ....F 3
Spreewald (forest) ....F 3
Stettin (bay) ....F 2
Stubbenkammer (point) ....E 1
Thüringer Wald (forest) ....D 3
Thuringia (Thüringen) (reg.), 2,017,924 ....D 3
Tollensee (lake) ....E 2
Ücker (riv.) ....E 2
Unstrut (riv.) ....D 3
Usedom (isl.) ....F 1
Warnow (riv.) ....D 2
Werra (riv.) ....D 3
White Elster (riv.) ....E 3

WEST GERMANY

STATES

Baden-Württemberg, 8,909,700 ..C 4
Bavaria, 10,568,900 ....D 4
Berlin (West) (free city), 2,134,256 ....E 4
Bremen, 755,977 ....C 2
Hamburg, 1,817,122 ....D 2
Hesse, 5,422,600 ....C 3
Lower Saxony, 7,100,400 ....C 2
North Rhine-Westphalia, 17,129,800 ....B 3
Rhineland-Palatinate, 3,671,300..B 4
Saarland, 1,127,400 ....B 4
Schleswig-Holstein, 2,557,200 ....C 1

CITIES and TOWNS

Aachen, 177,642 ....B 3
Aalen, 35,102 ....D 4
Ahlen, 50,411 ....B 3
Ahrensburg, 25,829 ....D 2
Alfeld, 13,726 ....C 2
Alsdorf, 31,726 ....B 3
Altena, 31,164 ....B 3
Altona ....C 2
Alzey, 12,749 ....C 4
Amberg, 42,141 ....E 4
Andernach, 22,367 ....B 3
Ansbach, 30,083 ....D 4
Arnsberg, 22,577 ....C 3
Aschaffenburg, 56,236 ....C 4
Augsburg, 214,376 ....D 4
Aurich, 12,299 ....B 2
Backnang, 28,086 ....C 4
Bad Dürkheim, 15,792 ....C 4
Baden-Baden, 38,852 ....C 4
Bad Harzburg, 11,356 ....D 3
Bad Hersfeld, 23,494 ....C 3
Bad Homburg vor der Höhe, 41,236 ....C 3
Bad Honnef am Rhein, 20,649 .....B 3
Bad Kissingen, 12,672 ....D 3
Bad Kreuznach, 42,707 ....B 4
Bad Mergentheim, 12,552 ....D 4
Bad Nauheim, 15,222 ....C 3
Bad Oeynhausen, 14,127 ....C 2
Bad Oldesloe, 18,915 ....D 2
Bad Pyrmont, 16,527 ....C 2
Bad Reichenhall, 14,894 ....E 5
Bad Salzuflen, 49,030 ....C 2
Bad Schwartau, 16,909 ....D 2
Bad Segeberg, 12,494 ....D 2
Bad Tölz, 12,468 ....D 5
Bad Vilbel, 18,315 ....C 3
Bad Wildungen, 12,189 ....C 3
Balingen, 13,693 ....C 4
Bamberg, 68,713 ....D 4
Bayreuth, 63,387 ....D 4
Bendorf, 14,361 ....B 3
Bensheim, 27,495 ....C 4
Berchtesgaden, 4,074 ....E 5
Bergisch Gladbach, 50,095 ....B 3
Berlin (West), 2,134,256 ....E 4
Biberach an der Riss, 25,597......C 4
Bielefeld, 169,347 ....C 2
Bietigheim, 22,488 ....C 4
Bingen, 24,452 ....B 4
Böblingen, 36,644 ....C 4
Bocholt, 48,134 ....B 3
Bochum, 346,886 ....B 3
Bonn (cap.), 299,376 ....B 3
Borghorst, 17,072 ....B 2
Borken, 30,614 ....B 3
Bottrop, 108,161 ....B 3
Brackwede, 40,254 ....C 3
Brake, 19,388 ....C 2
Braunschweig (Brunswick), 225,168 ....D 2
Bremen, 607,184 ....C 2
Bremerhaven, 148,793 ....C 2
Brilon, 15,301 ....C 3
Bruchsal, 27,103 ....C 4
Brühl, 41,782 ....B 3
Brunswick, 225,168 ....D 2
Bückeburg, 13,396 ....C 2
Burghausen, 16,630 ....E 4
Burgsteinfurt, 12,554 ....B 2
Buxtehude, 23,140 ....C 2
Celle, 56,335 ....D 2
Charlottenburg ....F 4
Clausthal-Zellerfeld, 15,744 ....D 3
Cloppenburg, 18,162 ....B 2
Coburg, 41,369 ....D 3
Coesfeld, 26,565 ....B 3
Cologne, 866,308 ....B 3
Crailsheim, 16,687 ....D 4
Cuxhaven, 45,218 ....C 2
Dachau, 33,093 ....D 4
Darmstadt, 141,075 ....C 4
Deggendorf, 18,601 ....E 4
Delmenhorst, 63,685 ....C 2
Detmold, 64,473 ....C 3
Diepholz, 11,639 ....C 2
Dillenburg, 10,236 ....C 3
Dillingen an der Donau, 11,606..D 4
Dingolfing, 10,747 ....E 4
Donaueschingen, 11,643 ....C 5
Donauwörth, 11,266 ....D 4
Dorsten, 39,393 ....B 3
Dortmund, 648,883 ....B 3
Duderstadt, 10,421 ....D 3
Dudweiler, 30,078 ....B 4
Duisburg, 457,891 ....B 3
Dülmen, 21,094 ....B 3
Düren, 54,867 ....B 3
Düsseldorf, 680,806 ....B 3
Eberbach, 14,369 ....C 4
Ebingen, 22,004 ....C 4
Eckernförde, 21,971 ....D 1
Ehingen, 12,957 ....C 4
Einbeck, 18,618 ....C 3
Eiserfeld, 22,490 ....B 1
Ellwangen, 13,128 ....D 4
Elmshorn, 41,353 ....C 2
Emden, 48,313 ....B 2
Emmendingen, 15,986 ....B 4
Emmerich, 24,512 ....B 3
Erkelenz, 12,275 ....B 3
Erlangen, 85,727 ....D 4
Eschwege, 22,219 ....D 3
Eschweiler, 39,622 ....B 3
Espelkamp, 12,309 ....C 2
Essen, 704,769 ....B 3
Esslingen am Neckar, 86,497 ......C 4

EAST GERMANY: Total pop.—1970 off. est.; cap.—1969 off. est.; cities (over 100,000)—1968 off. est.; other pops—1966 off. est.
WEST GERMANY: Total, states & cities (over 10,000)—1970 off. est.; other pops—1967 off. est.

FEDERAL REPUBLIC OF GERMANY

WEST GERMANY

OREGON

AREA	95,985 sq mi (248 599 km²)
ELEVATION	
Highest point (Zugspitze)	9,721 ft (2 963 m)
Lowest point	Sea level
POPULATION (excluding West Berlin)	62,000,000
PRINCIPAL LANGUAGE	German
LIFE EXPECTANCY	68–74 years
PERCENTAGE OF LITERACY	Almost 100%
UNIT OF CURRENCY	Deutsche mark
NATIONAL ANTHEM	*Deutschlandlied* (*Song of Germany*), words by Hoffman von Fallersleben, music by Franz Joseph Haydn
CAPITAL	Bonn
PRINCIPAL PRODUCTS	Potatoes, rye, sugar beets, wheat; coal, iron ore; automobiles, chemicals, electric equipment, steel products, textiles

The Federal Republic of Germany, also known as West Germany, is a republic of west-central Europe constituted in 1949 as a result of the political division of Germany. Occupying more than two thirds of the total area of Germany, the Federal Republic extends from Austria in the south to Denmark in the north.

The Land

Physical Features and Climate. The Alps form a wall-like barrier along the country's southern boundary, rising to 9,721 ft (2 963 m) in the Zugspitze, the highest peak in West Germany. In the southwest the mountain range ends where the Rhine River enters Lake Constance (Boden See). The rolling plateau of the Alpine foreland region stretches northward from the Alps to the Danube River and is grooved by the valleys of the many small rivers that flow from the Alps. The Danube, which rises in the Black Forest (Schwarzwald) of southwest Germany, carries this

drainage eastward. Separating the Danube and the Rhine valleys, the steep, forested, and picturesque slopes of the Black Forest form a link with the plateau region of central Germany, which extends northward in a landscape of asymmetric limestone ridges and intervening valleys. Rainfall is high in this region, and the climate is cool in summer and cold and snowy in winter. Many of the upper slopes are forested, but the valleys are warmer, more sheltered, and better suited to agriculture. The southern part of the central plateau region is drained westward to the Rhine by the Main and Neckar rivers and their tributaries. The Rhine itself here occupies a broad, flat plain, noted for the cultivation of grapes and other fruits, for winters are mild and summers warm. Farther north, approaching Cologne, the Rhine flows in a narrow gorge that constitutes one of the most picturesque areas of West Germany. The plateau west of the Rhine is divided into the Eifel and the Hunsrück regions by the similarly incised valley of the Moselle River. In the north the plateaus slope gently through a fertile, loess-covered region to the extensive northern plain. Much of this region is covered with glacial deposits and consists of sandy heaths, notably the Lüneburg Heath, with a dry, sterile soil, generally forested; plains of damp and heavy clay, frequently left under grass; and partly or wholly reclaimed marshland bordering the coast and river estuaries. The principal rivers of northwest Germany are the Ems, Weser, and Elbe, all of which have wide, navigable estuaries that have encouraged the growth of ports at considerable distances inland, notably Bremen and Hamburg. Offshore is a fringe of low, sandy islands.

Natural Resources. With some exceptions the soils of West Germany are not noted for their fertility. By way of compensation, however, the country has the richest reserves of coal in western Europe. Hard coal is found principally in the Ruhr district on the northern rim of the central uplands, and lignite is located in the Rhineland. West Germany also has important deposits of iron ore, chiefly in the Ruhr, and lesser quantities of lead and zinc in the hills of the Eifel. The southeast yields most of the salt from which the country's important production of potash is derived. There are scattered deposits of oil in the northern plain, in the states of Saxony and Schleswig-Holstein, and the same region produces large quantities of peat.

Norman J. G. Pounds

The People

Population and Principal Cities. The population of the Federal Republic of Germany grew from less than 48,000,000 in 1950 to some 62,000,000 in 1975. This increase had several causes: excess of births over deaths; addition of the Saarland, with a population of about 1,000,000, in 1957; the presence of some 4,000,000 foreign workers; and not least the fact that the number of persons moving from East to West Germany was much larger than of those migrating in the other direction, until the "Berlin Wall," built by the eastern regime in 1961, terminated this exodus.

With three fourths of its population living in cities, the Federal Republic is one of the most highly urbanized and industrialized countries of the world. The busy international port of Hamburg is the largest city, followed by

Heidelberg, an ancient castle and university town, occupies a scenic site on the Neckar River.

Munich, the historic capital of Bavaria. The most populous state is North Rhine-Westphalia, which contains the heart of German industry, the Ruhr valley, and several large cities—Cologne, Essen, Düsseldorf, and Dortmund. Frankfurt am Main can be considered the country's main commercial and financial center. West Germany is the only major European nation which lacks an historic, metropolitan capital. Bonn has grown since it became the seat of the federal government and legislature, but it is still relatively small.

Religion. Religious freedom, including the right to hold and to profess nonreligious views, is guaranteed by the Basic Law. About 96% of the population adheres to Christian denominations. Somewhat under one half belongs to the Roman Catholic church, which has its main strength in the Rhineland and Bavaria; the remainder are Protestants, belonging mainly to the Lutheran, Reformed, and United churches. After World War II, while maintaining their different theological creeds, Protestants in both Germanys allied themselves under the name of Evangelical Church in Germany (Evangelische Kirche in Deutschland, EKD). Then in 1969 the East German churches established their own Evangelical Church in the Democratic German Republic. The Roman Catholic Church is divided in West Germany into five provinces, with five archbishoprics and 16 bishoprics. Jews now number only about 24,000 in West Germany and 6,000 in West Berlin. Their 70 communities have a Central Council of the Jews in (West) Germany (Zentralrat der Juden in Deutschland) located in Düsseldorf.

Education. True to German tradition, education at all levels is controlled by the state. The state (Länder) governments regulate all aspects of the school system; all instructors are public employees. The local community, therefore, has no direct influence on its schools. There are very few private schools (about one out of every 300), but certain areas have denominational public schools. Religious instruction is obligatory in all public schools, but attendance of those classes by the individual pupil is at the discretion of his parents or guardian. School attendance is compulsory from the age of 6 to between 14 and 18, depending on state legislation. At age 10 or 11, most children proceed from elementary school to general secondary public schools, which in turn qualify them for vocational schools. Only those who go from elementary school to the more scholarly medium-level schools (the best known of this type is the Gymnasium) qualify for senior colleges and university-level institutions. A major reform, proposed in 1973, would gradually replace the entire elementary and intermediate school system with a new comprehensive school (Gesamtschule). The reform, going to the core of the traditional German system, is controversial. All public elementary and secondary schools, and in some states also the "medium-level" schools, are free. Nu-

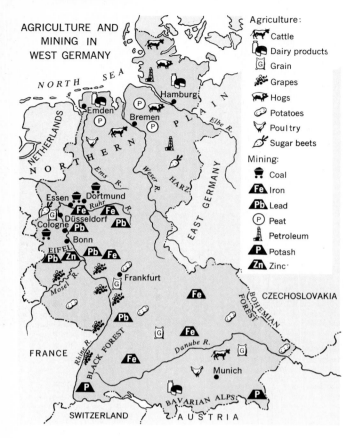

AGRICULTURE AND MINING IN WEST GERMANY

Agriculture:
- Cattle
- Dairy products
- G Grain
- Grapes
- Hogs
- Potatoes
- Poultry
- Sugar beets

Mining:
- Coal
- Fe Iron
- Pb Lead
- P Peat
- Petroleum
- P Potash
- Zn Zinc

The Economy

Economic Conditions and Policies. When Germany surrendered in 1945, much of the country lay in ruins. A few years later, the recovery and growth of the West German economy had become conspicuous. By the 1950's living standards in West Germany were among Europe's highest. An essential factor was massive American aid and investment that facilitated a rapid build-up of new plants; they worked at capacity, first for reconstruction and then for a continual expansion of the economy. However, the Western European recession of the early 1970's affected the Federal Republic; production levels fell, the purchasing power of the deutsche mark decreased by 26% between 1970 and 1975, and unemployment for the first time passed the 1,000,000 figure. While it was generally agreed that a changed world economy asked for new adaptations, and the Federal Republic showed some welfare state features, it continued to adhere to a capitalistic, free-market economy.

Industry. Industry is the most important sector of the country's economy, which has again become dominated by giant corporations. The decartelization policy officially demanded by the Western powers after the war was never carried out. Of the world's ten largest industrial corporations, half are German. In order of gross national product West Germany ranks fourth in the world. Her most important products include heavy and light machinery, automobiles and other vehicles, chemicals, aircraft, computers and data-processing equipment, armaments, precision instruments, and textiles.

Agriculture, Forestry, and Fishing. Although not self-sufficient in food production, West Germany has intensive agriculture, significant forest and fishing industries, and important vineyards. Agricultural income is derived mainly from animal products, of which poultry, hogs, and cattle are the largest categories. The principal crops are wheat, rye, barley, potatoes, and sugar beets. Forests cover more than 28% of all used land; nearly half of this is owned by the state. The number of persons fully employed in agriculture, forestry, and fishing is steadily decreasing mainly because of progressing mechanization and a trend

merous adult education centers offer lectures, courses, laboratory facilities, and the like, without demanding formal academic qualifications.

All of West Germany's 23 universities are generously financed by the federal budget. The oldest of these is Heidelberg, founded in 1386, two years before the university of Cologne. Others, such as Göttingen, Munich, Freiburg, and Tübingen, also have international reputation. There are eight technical colleges and many specialized academies. Almost one fourth of the student body of institutions of higher learnings is women. Students' dueling fraternities, forbidden by the Allied occupation authorities after World War II because of their militaristic tendencies in the past, are again active at many universities.

Cultural Life. Much of the literature of West Germany—nonfiction as well as the fiction of such internationally known novelists as Heinrich Böll, Günther Grass, Uwe Johnson, and Hans Hellmut Kirst—has been dedicated to searching inquiries into the reasons for the negative aspects of Germany's recent past, although tendencies to deny, or even to justify, these aspects have not been absent. At the same time, there has emerged a strong interest in foreign, especially American, fiction, plays, films, and way of life. The performing arts generally maintain a high standard, and the numerous theaters and concert halls, opera houses, and cultural festivals, including the famous Richard Wagner festival at Bayreuth, are subsidized by public funds.

The National Theater in Mannheim, designed by Gerhard Weber. Public funds are used to subsidize numerous cultural undertakings in West Germany.

to larger agricultural holdings.

Labor and Social Legislation. Trade unions and employers' associations play an important role in West Germany. The German Trade Union Federation (Deutscher Gewerkschaftsbund, DGB), comprising 16 unions, was reestablished in 1949; total membership is over 6,500,000. Politically, the DGB has close ties with the Social Democratic party. Among other employee organizations, the Christian Trade Union movement, though relatively small, is the mot influential. It supported the DGB in its struggle to introduce "co-determination." One main feature of this system of management-labor cooperation is that the boards of directors of all corporations above a certain size must include representatives of the employees.

West Germany has a highly-developed social security system, which covers most of the population. This includes obligatory health insurance (dating from 1883) providing free medical and hospital services, old-age pensions pegged to the cost of living index, allowances for surviving dependents, and monthly children's allowances. Non-employed and self-employed persons can, since 1972, join the (old-age) pension insurance scheme.

Communications and Transportation. According to German tradition, most branches of transport and public utilities, including postal, telegraph, and telephone service, are publicly owned and operated, as are postal savings banks and postal bus lines. About 17,900 mi (28 800 km) of federal railroads provide one of the densest networks in Europe. A spectacular growth in motor vehicle and air traffic has required extensive building of roads and airfields. There is a good network of canals, although the Rhine River carries the bulk of water-borne traffic. Hamburg handles nearly half of all freight passing through West German ports. Bremen, Emden, and Lübeck are also important. The government-owned international airline, Lufthansa, carries more than 10,000,000 passengers each year.

West Germany's three television and seven radio stations are operated by public, non-profit corporations, and the government, political parties, and cultural and other interested groups have a voice in the programing. As is common in Europe, the public has to pay television and radio user fees.

Foreign Trade. West Germany ranks second, after the United States, in world trade. But it depends much more than does the United States on imports, especially of raw materials, foodstuffs, and oil. Thus, because of its dependence on foreign markets and imports, West Germany was rather hard hit by the economic disruptions that followed the devaluation of the U.S. dollar and the oil crisis in the first half of the 1970's.

The country exports primarily heavy and light machinery, chemicals, motor and other vehicles, metal goods, and electric equipment. Its main trading partners, making up about one half of its foreign trade, are its fellow nations of the European Economic Community (EEC), and most notably France and the Netherlands. The United States and Italy each supply some 8% of West Germany's imports, and take some 9% of its exports. West Germany's trade with the USSR, East Germany, and other eastern European countries exceeds that of any other western

FPG

The Volkswagen factory at Wolfsburg contributes significantly to West Germany's exports.

European state. It also cultivates trade with third world countries and China.

The Federal Republic is second only to the United States—and would like to become the leader—in the nuclear industry. Toward this end it has sought to export to third world nations both nuclear reactors and uranium enriching and reprocessing facilities. Because it fears the spread of the capacity to make nuclear weapons, the United States has strongly opposed this commerce, whether by West Germany or any other state.

Government

The governmental system of the Federal Republic of Germany rests on the Basic Law, promulgated from Bonn on May 23, 1949, which united the British, French, and United States occupation zones of post-Hitler Germany into a new country. In the same year, the Soviet zone became the German Democratic Republic.

The Basic Law. The Basic Law defines the Federal Republic of Germany as a "democratic and social federative state." (The term "social" here means "concerned with social justice".) The states composing the federation may make and amend their own constitutions as long as these are "republican, democratic, and social." Federal law, however, supersedes the laws of the individual states.

The Basic Law contains an elaborate catalog of political and social rights and includes strong precautions against communism and a resurgence of fascism. Also noteworthy are the compromises about property (Art. 14). Property is guaranteed and may be expropriated only in the interest of the "public weal" and with just compensation.

With some exceptions, amendments to the Basic Law require only a two-thirds majority in both houses of the

Armando Curcio Editore SpA

The Bonn Cathedral, built from the 11th to the 13th centuries, stands in the central part of the West German capital.

federal legislature, but no action by the legislatures of the states. The most far-reaching amendments, together known as the "emergency constitution," were adopted in 1968. They apply in two types of emergencies: threats from outside the country or from a "state of internal tension," the existence of which can be declared at any time, but by the Bundestag only. Both emergencies permit intervention by extraordinary police, federal border guards, and the armed forces.

Structure of Government. The federal legislature consists of two houses. The more powerful is the lower house (Bundestag), whose 496 members are popularly elected for four-year terms by citizens of 21 years or more. The Bundestag also seats 22 nonvoting members from West Berlin, which is not part of West Germany. The upper house (Bundesrat) is composed of 41 delegates (three to five from each state, depending on its population), who are not popularly elected, but appointed by the state governments and subject to the latters' instructions. Enactments of the Bundestag which affect certain rights and interests of the states require approval by the Bundesrat in order to become law. Legislation on such matters as foreign affairs, monetary matters, railroads, and postal and telecommunication services is exclusively in federal hands. In other fields, the states may legislate "as long and insofar as the federation does not do so." Such concurrent legislation extends to civil, criminal, and administrative law, public welfare, labor, and economic law, and certain other topics. In practice, the trend has been toward centralization, since the federal legislature has tended to deal with many of these matters. In fields where the federation possesses neither exclusive nor concurrent legislative powers, only the states may legislate.

The president of the Federal Republic is elected by a special federal assembly convening exclusively for this purpose every five years and consisting of all members of the Bundestag, plus an equal number of delegates from among the Länder parliaments. Immediate reelection is permitted only once. The position of the federal president is, purposely, less strong than it was in the Weimar Republic. He formally nominates the federal chancellor, appoints and dismisses ministers (members of the cabinet) on the chancellor's proposal, and formally promulgates federal laws.

The most powerful office is that of the federal chancellor, or prime minister, who determines general policy. He is elected by a simple majority of the Bundestag. That body can also vote him out of office, but only if it simultaneously elects a successor by a majority of all its members. The chancellor's position is further strengthened by his right to request the federal president to dissolve the Bundestag if it fails, upon request, to give him a vote of confidence.

State and Local Government. A major new feature of Germany (both West and East) after World War II was the dissolution of Prussia which, between the foundation of the German Reich in 1871 and the downfall of the Hitler regime in 1945, was by far the largest and most important German state. The boundaries and even the names of some other West German states were also changed after the war. In addition to the two Hanseatic city-states of Bremen and Hamburg, and re-acquired Saarland, the states forming the Federal Republic are Baden-Württemberg, Bavaria, Hesse, Lower Saxony, North Rhine-Westphalia, Rhineland-Palatinate, and Schleswig-Holstein. Except for Bavaria, which has a two-chamber legislature, each state has a unicameral legislature. The state government is headed by a minister president, who appoints his cabinet. Each state is divided into a number of districts, counties, and communes, all of which have considerable responsibility for local affairs.

Political Parties. Of the three parties that have been significant in West Germany, the strongest until 1972 was the middle-of-the-road Christian-Democratic Union (Christlich-Demokratische Union, CDU) which together with its more conservative Bavarian branch, the Christian-Social Union (Christlich-Soziale Union, CSU) is known as CDU/CSU. The other mass party, the moderately left-of-center Social-Democratic Party (Sozialdemokratische Partei Deutschlands, SPD) gradually increased its strength, until the 1972 elections brought it more seats in the Bundestag than the CDU/CSU. The third, much smaller, moderately right-wing Free Democratic Party (Freie Demokratische Partei, FDP) has exercised more influence than its showing at the polls indicated, because both the CDU/CSU and the SPD have required its votes to muster a majority in the Bundestag.

The complicated federal electoral system of modified proportional representation deliberately favors large parties. For example, a party must obtain at least 5% of the total federal vote or elect at least three candidates in individual constituencies in order to win a seat in the Bundestag. The Communist Party was dissolved by the federal constitutional court in 1956. After being permitted to reconstitute itself in 1968, it was unable to reach the "5% vote or 3 candidates" quota in the 1972 and 1976

The Alps add excitement to placid Bavaria, the largest and the most agricultural state of West Germany.

elections, making West Germany the only parliamentary country in Western Europe without Communist deputies in the legislature.

Under Allied and West German rules an openly neo-Nazi party could not be formed. But a party calling itself National-Democratic (Nationaldemokratische Partei Deutschlands), with an evident Nazi flavor and an appeal especially to ex-members of Hitler's armed and police forces, was created in 1964; it quickly obtained representation in state and municipal legislatures. This caused concern, especially in countries which had experienced the cruelties of Nazi occupation during World War II. Gradually, the NDP declined. However, veterans' organizations which keep German military tradition alive through public memorial meetings and parades continue to be active.

Legal System. Justice is administered partly by federal and partly by state courts. Judges are appointed but are independent. In serious criminal cases the professional judge is assisted by lay assessors. The death penalty was abolished shortly after the war. A thorough law reform, started in 1969 with such measures as a prison reform and the abolition of the traditional discrimination in civil law against persons born out of wedlock, has made slow progress.

The Federal Supreme Court acts as court of last appeal in important civil and criminal cases. The Federal Constitutional Court, in Karlsruhe, exercises judicial review over the constitutionality of federal and state laws, and can dissolve (outlaw) political parties which it finds to pursue anticonstitutional ends. Because of the specialization of the court system, there are several other "su-

preme" courts. Thus, above the labor courts, which handle labor-management and trade union litigations, is the Federal Labor Court. Disputes about social insurance matters can be brought before specially designated social (insurance) courts and from there taken to the top Federal Social (Insurance) Court, located in Kassel. Many types of decisions by the authorities can be contested before administrative courts, and their decisions can be appealed through higher administrative courts all the way to the Federal Administrative Court, which sits in West Berlin. Similarly, important tax litigation can go through the lower fiscal courts to the top Federal Fiscal Court in Munich.

Much controversy has surrounded the question of the treatment of persons who committed atrocities in the Nazi era but who were able to hide or even to obtain important positions in the federal republic. Efforts to bring such persons to justice before the courts did not start in earnest until almost half a generation after the war. Following the trial in Jerusalem of Adolf Eichmann in 1961, a central federal agency was created to search for suspects, witnesses, and evidence. The largest German war-crimes trial, and, in fact, the largest trial ever held before a German court, was the "Auschwitz trial" between December, 1963 and August, 1965 in Frankfort am Main. It required 5½ years of preparation and heard 248 survivors of the death camp testify against the 20 defendants.

Defense. Measured by the size of its armed forces and defense expenditures, West Germany is Europe's biggest military power, except only the Soviet Union. Although the nuclear warheads located in West Germany have re-

Ships from the North Sea dock at Bremen, on the Weser River.

Armando Curcio Editore SpA

mained under strict American control, West German personnel have since 1957 received training in nuclear warfare in the United States.

The armed forces of the Federal Republic (Bundeswehr) are integrated into the North Atlantic Treaty Organization (NATO) system. Hence, the West German army, air force, and navy, while serving under their own officers, are under ultimate NATO command. Normally, the Bundeswehr is under the command of the federal defense minister; declaration of a state of emergency would transfer command to the federal chancellor, who heads the Federal Security Council. West Germany has a fully developed armaments industry, but is pledged not to produce nuclear, biological, or chemical weapons.

Outside the NATO system West Germany maintains a force called Bundesgrenzschutz (border guard). It is, like the police, under the authority of the Minister of the Interior. The Länder have their own regular and emergency, or standby (Bereitschaftspolizei) police. In case of need all can be put under federal command.

Public Finance and Monetary Matters. The republic's economic growth was accompanied by balanced budgets, greater revenue and expenditure, strengthening of the currency, enlarged savings, and increased investments at home and abroad. The country bears one of the heaviest burdens of taxation in the Western world. The main items of public expenditure are for social purposes, including education, and for defense and economic promotion. In 1952, the republic agreed to pay in installments $1,000,000,000, mainly in goods, to Israel as some compensation for the loss of Jewish life and property under the Nazi regime. The last of these installments was made in 1966. Soon thereafter the last installments were also paid to American creditors for debts still stemming from the 1920's and 1930's, as settled in a 1953 agreement with Bonn.

History

Toward Sovereignty. After Germany's unconditional surrender (May, 1945), no German government existed. The principal wartime Allies decided, and reconfirmed at the Potsdam conference in Aug., 1945, that Germany was to be provisionally administered by them. Until the conclusion of a peace treaty (then soon expected) the country was divided into four occupation zones—American, British, French, and Soviet—but matters affecting Germany as a whole were to be handled by an Allied Control Council (ACC) comprising the four zone commanders. Berlin, located in the Soviet zone, was itself divided into four zones, although matters affecting Berlin as a whole were to be regulated by a joint, four-power military headquarters. By Jan. 1, 1947, however, the U.S. and British zones were merged for economic reasons into a "Bizone," and in the spring of 1949 the French zone was added, for the same reasons, to form a "Trizone."

Even by 1948, East-West tensions had caused a breakdown of the four-power ACC. On June 1, 1948, the Western powers authorized the Germans in their zones to draft a constitution. The Soviet Union made strenuous efforts to prevent the formation of a separate West German state. One aspect of those efforts was the blocking of ground traffic through the Soviet zone into West Berlin that resulted in the Berlin Airlift (q.v.). In the summer of 1949, however, the Basic Law of the Federal Republic was ratified by the state diets, whose establishment the Western powers had previously permitted. Subsequently, the first free German elections since 1933, held on Aug. 14, 1949, resulted in a majority for the CDU/CSU. The party's leader, Konrad Adenauer (1876–1967), became the first chancellor of the republic.

The Federal Republic officially came into being on Sept. 21, 1949. In 1951–52 many countries, including the United States, Britain, and France, terminated the state of war with West Germany (although a formal peace treaty has never been concluded). The Soviet Union followed suit in 1955. As of May 5, 1955, the three Western powers renounced their remaining occupation rights. The Federal Republic of Germany thus became a sovereign nation, and simultaneously a NATO member.

The Cold War and West German Rearmament. From the moment of its creation in 1949 the Federal Republic, together with its counterpart to the east, the Democratic Republic of Germany, stood at the center of the cold war. Acceptance of West Germany as a military partner within NATO reversed altogether the decision of the Potsdam conference that Germany was to be "completely disarmed and demilitarized." The policy also contradicted Adenauer's declaration, upon becoming chancellor, that he was "once and for all against rearmament of the Federal Republic and thus also against formation of a new German Wehrmacht."

Western efforts to bind the Federal Republic ever more closely to the West and at the same time to loosen the Soviet Union's grip on East Germany were countered by Soviet endeavors to undermine West Germany's integration into NATO. As it grew in political and military strength, West Germany became an increasingly active participant in this contest, siding resolutely with the West and particularly with the United States. The road to this alignment, however, was not entirely smooth. West Germans agreed that it was desirable to regain sovereignty but were strongly divided over the price, namely, military participation in NATO and continued division of their country. The opposition, composed of the SPD, trade unions, churchmen, university youth, and women's organizations, as well as other groups, argued that remilitarization would delay, perhaps indefinitely, the reunification of West and East Germany, and made strenuous efforts to prevent West Germany's entry into NATO. The demand by several states for a popular referendum on the issue was rejected. One of the strongest protests took the form of a convention in Frankfurt's historic St. Paul's Cathedral (modeled after the 1848 convention in the same cathedral, which tried to establish a democratic German republic). It issued a manifesto urging Allied agreement on reunification rather than the formation of military blocs. Further stormy public and parliamentary debates attended the introduction of military conscription in 1956.

As NATO relied increasingly on nuclear strategy, the question of training West German troops for nuclear warfare deeply agitated German public opinion, as such warfare would first of all destroy both Germanys. In 1957, 18 West German atomic scientists issued a warning against nuclear armaments and vowed never to work for military purposes. In the same spirit, the Evangelical pastor Martin Niemöller declared that it could become a civic duty to commit treason in order to prevent atomic war. The 1958 SPD congress demanded withdrawal of all foreign troops from East and West Germany and abolition of military conscription. Soon, however, West Germany advocated plans that would give it "a finger on the nuclear trigger," and, in fact, demanded the right to acquire or produce nuclear weapons of its own. Such plans became impossible when, after long hesitation, West Germany ratified the Nuclear Non-Proliferation Treaty (effective Mar. 5, 1970).

West Germany's European Policies. Europe's history has been darkened by frequent enmity and wars between Germany and France. One bright aspect of the post-World War II era has been the establishment of friendly German-French relations. This spirit helped solve the old problem of the mineral-rich, highly industrialized border region of the Saarland. In 1956 a plebiscite there led to its reunion with West Germany. Although a defeat for France, this outcome lost much of its economic significance due to the existence of the supranational European Coal and Steel Community (ECSC). West Germany has strongly supported the political as well as the economic integration of Western Europe by playing a leading role in the European Economic Community. It also belongs to the Organization for Economic Cooperation and Development (OECD).

On the other hand, West Germany's relations with Eastern Europe and especially East Germany were long cold and, indeed, often hostile. Coldness was caused by several factors. The Bonn government claimed to represent all of Germany. It steadfastly refused to grant equal status to East Germany, but continued to call it "Soviet Occupation Zone." Contacts with East German authorities were kept to a minimum to avoid any semblance of recognition. Moreover, Bonn refused to acknowledge the Oder-Neisse line as the East German border with Poland. Instead, its official maps showed the German frontiers as they had been in 1937. In fact, claims to some territories occupied by Hitler, particularly the so-called Sudeten area of Czechoslovakia, were sometimes endorsed by government spokesmen. In its effort to isolate East Germany from the world scene, the Federal Republic severed relations with any country, except the USSR, that formally recognized the Democratic Republic.

These attitudes began very slowly to thaw in Dec., 1966. After an almost 18-year rule by governments either formed alone or dominated by the CDU/CSU (until 1963 under Chancellor Adenauer, then under Chancellor Erhard), a "grand coalition" was formed by the CDU/CSU (with Kurt Georg Kiesinger as chancellor) and the not much less strong SPD (with Willy Brandt as Vice-Chancellor). Their program called for the use of cautious flexibility, without changing the essentials of the Adenauer era.

Accommodation with Eastern Europe. The true break with the policy of confrontation came when, after SPD election gains in 1969, the "Grand Coalition" was replaced by a SPD/FDP government, with Brandt as chancellor and the CDU/CSU in opposition for the first time. Brandt embarked on a new "Ostpolitik" (Eastern policy), one of accommodation with Eastern Europe. It was based on the proposition that his country, in its own interest, had finally to accept the realities, since there was no chance to alter the actual situation except by a catastrophic war. The first steps of the resulting overall settlement were the pacts made with the Soviet Union (Aug. 13, 1970) and Poland (Dec. 7, 1970), in which West Germany formally recognized the separateness of East Germany, and East Germany's Oder-Neisse frontier with Poland. A comprehensive Basic Treaty with East Germany (Dec. 21, 1972) recognized each part's independence and sovereignty but envisaged various forms of cooperation through all-German institutions. The theoretical question of unification was not mentioned. Although West German parliamentary opposition, especially to the Basic Pact with East Germany, was unexpectedly strong, the Bundestag eventually ratified the pact.

The breakthrough opened the way for both Germanys to be admitted to the United Nations in 1973. West Germany's estrangement from the smaller Eastern states was also ended by the establishment, after December, 1973, of diplomatic relations with them. The treaty with Czechoslovakia also finally declared null and void the notorious Munich Pact of 1938, which gave Hitler the so-called Sudeten region of Czechoslovakia.

The West German federal elections of October, 1976 somewhat weakened the Social Democrats but strengthened their partners in governing, the Free Democrats. Helmut Schmidt (SPD), who had replaced Brandt as chancellor in 1974, continued in office.

Consult Chapman, Colin and Crossland, Norman, *Modern West Germany* (1973); Nelson, Walter H., *Germany Rearmed* (1971); Prittie, Terrence, *Willy Brandt: Portrait of a Statesman* (1974); Ryder, A. J., *Twentieth-Century Germany* (1976); Schalk, Adolph, *The Germans* (1971); Schmidt, Helmut, *The Balance of Power* (1971).

JOHN H. E. FRIED

DEMOCRATIC REPUBLIC OF GERMANY

EAST GERMANY

OHIO

AREA	47,767 sq mi (108 178 km²), excluding Berlin
ELEVATION	
Highest point (Fichtelberg)	3,983 ft (1 214 m)
Lowest point	Sea level
POPULATION	Approx. 17,000,000
PRINCIPAL LANGUAGE	German
LIFE EXPECTANCY	67 years
PERCENTAGE OF LITERACY	Almost 100%
UNIT OF CURRENCY	Deutsche mark
NATIONAL ANTHEM	*Nationalhymne*
	words by J. R. Becher, music by Hanns Eisler
CAPITAL	East Berlin
PRINCIPAL PRODUCTS	Barley, potatoes, rye, sugar beets, wheat; coal, copper, iron, lignite, potash; chemical products, electric equipment, steel products

The Democratic Republic of Germany, known also as East Germany, is a "people's republic" constituted in 1949 as a result of the political division of Germany. The Democratic Republic comprises rather less than one third of the total area of post-World War II Germany.

The Land

Physical Features. The Democratic Republic lies mostly in the northern plain of Germany, but extends south to embrace some of the hills and plateaus of central Germany. Along its southern border lie the hills of the Thuringian Forest (Thüringerwald) and the higher Erzgebirge, which include East Germany's highest peak, the Fichtelberg. The Harz mountains extend into East Germany from the west. Most of the rivers of East Germany drain into the Elbe, which flows mainly from southeast to northwest and is joined from the southwest by the Saale and from the east by the Havel. The Havel, with its tributary the Spree, drains the Berlin region. The river valleys tend to be wide, flat, and rather damp. Between them rise areas of heath land formed by the accumulation of sand and gravel. Such areas, notably the Fläming Heath, south of Berlin, are largely forested. In the north, the uneven deposit of boulder clay during the retreat of the ice sheet

created a damp, lake-studded, and well-wooded region known as the Baltic Uplands or Heights.

Climate, Soils, and Natural Resources. The climate of East Germany is more severe than that of the Federal Republic of Germany (West Germany). In particular, winters are colder. Ice becomes a hazard on the rivers, and tender crops cannot be grown. The best soils and the most productive agricultural area lie between the Baltic Uplands in the north and the hills of the south. Natural conditions elsewhere, however, are unfavorable to farming, and East Germany is not predominantly agricultural. The country's most valuable mineral resource is lignite, found over a wide area between Leipzig and Magdeburg, as well as farther east. Bituminous coal occurs in small quantities in the south, and there are uranium in the Erzgebirge and some iron ore in the Thuringian Forest. Copper is found in the Harz mountains, and farther north, at Stassfurt, are important potash deposits.   NORMAN J. G. POUNDS

The People

Population and Principal Cities. The Democratic Republic of Germany is one of the few countries in the world to experience decreased population. This was caused mainly by migration to West Germany from 1947 to 1964. During the Berlin crisis of 1961 the exodus of East Germans achieved panic proportions until, in August of that year, the East German government sealed off the principal escape route by erecting a wall which divided the city of Berlin. The exodus was not only politically harmful to the East German regime, but also drained the country of many professionals and skilled workers, thus disrupting the operation of plants, hospitals, public services, and so forth. Since 1964, however, the population has been slowly increasing; by the mid-1970's it was almost 17,000,000.

Berlin, the capital of Germany from 1871 to 1945, lies well inside East Germany. The city's unique situation is further complicated because ever since the end of World War II it has been divided into four sectors—American, British, French, and Soviet—with troops of each of those four powers stationed in their respective sectors. The three Western sectors do not form part of either East or West Germany. They are under a separate municipal government, run by Germans and variously linked to West Germany, but still formally under American, British, and French "occupation" authority.

East Germany's Soviet-backed claim that East Berlin (originally the Soviet sector) forms an integral part of East Germany is not accepted by the Western powers. Actually, East Berlin is the capital of the Democratic Republic and the seat of its government.

Apart from Berlin with its special status, East Germany's five principal cities are Leipzig, Dresden, Karl Marx-Stadt (formerly Chemnitz), Halle, and Magdeburg. Also important is the historic Hanseatic city of Rostock, site of the oldest university in northern Germany, founded 1419. Rostock port, East Germany's main outlet to the ocean, has been modernized, decreasing the country's dependence on the West German ports, especially Hamburg.

Religion. Over 80% of the people are Protestants, predominantly Evangelical (Lutheran). Although the country

Dresden ranks as one of the five principal cities of East Germany, in addition to East Berlin, the capital. Dresden has long been known as a cultural center. The Elbe River and a railroad network make the city a transportation and commercial center as well.

Interfoto MTI—FPG

is no longer divided into states, the Evangelical Church has maintained its historic organization by state churches (Landeskirchen). There are also "Evangelical Free" churches. The Roman Catholic Church, adhered to by 12% of the population, has two dioceses (Berlin, administered by a cardinal-archbishop, and Meissen) and four bishoprics. The few thousand Jews who returned to East Germany after World War II form eight communities, united in the Federation of Jewish Communities, located at Dresden. Destroyed synagogues were reconstructed with public funds, and new ones built at Magdeburg, Erfurt, and Karl-Marx-Stadt. Freedom of conscience and belief, which includes religious worship, is reiterated in the 1968–74 constitution.

The religious communities are financed partly by the government and partly by their adherents. They also derive income from landed property which was excluded from the post-war sequestration of large estates and from the transformation into farm cooperatives.

Education. Education, tuition-free on all levels, emphasizes "polytechnic instruction" (mathematics, physics, and other natural sciences), humanistic character formation in the service of socialist-democratic progress ("development of the whole personality"), and various combinations of theoretical with practical training. Compulsory school attendance, starting at 6, has gradually been extended to age 18. The traditional German secondary school system, which enabled only a minority of students to enter institutions of higher learning, was, after some experimentation, replaced by a "uniform higher school." It stresses polytechnic instruction but still permits spe-

cialization in the humanities. Graduates qualify to enter universities and other similar institutions. Attendance of professional schools at the graduate level is also encouraged. Students and apprentices who combine work and study receive pay for the time they attend school.

An "all-embracing socialist education" system was near enough to completion in 1975 that 82% of all preschool children were in nurseries, day-care centers, or kindergartens, and the number of full-time university-level students had passed the 100,000-mark. The scheme aims at a constantly updated technology and the development of a socialist economy according to a new, partly decentralized system of planning and management.

Cultural Life. The East German regime continued the social transformation started by the Soviet military government. The previously dominant position of the East Prussian Junkers, the landed gentry long identified with Prussian militarism, was destroyed through expropriation of their estates. Nationalization of industrial and other large-scale enterprises further altered the social structure. Many upper-middle-class and middle-class persons, even if offered relatively important positions in the nationalized sector, preferred to leave the country. On the other hand, the regime has, with high salaries and civic honors, favored scientists and other intellectuals. As East Germany gained in prosperity and self-assurance, insistence on ideological conformity in literature and the arts abated. The famous works of German and world literature are popularized and as widely consumed as in West Germany. Among the older writers representative of the post-1945 East German mind are Johannes R. Becher,

MINING AND AGRICULTURE IN EAST GERMANY

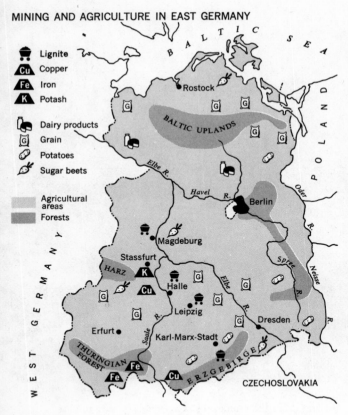

Heinrich Mann, Theodor Plivier, Anna Seghers, Erich Weinert, and Arnold Zweig. Younger, and less known abroad, are Bruno Apitz, Otto Gotsche, Stefan Heym, Dieter Noll, and Wolfgang Schreyer, the most-read East German author of adventure and detective books.

Theaters, operas, concerts, dramatic and musical festivals, and the like are richly subsidized. The internationally famous theater of playwright Bertolt Brecht (1898–1956) continues to receive acclaim for the work of his successors. Systematic efforts are made to render the performing arts accessible to all groups of the population, especially the young. The same is true of a variety of sports activities.

The Economy

Economic Conditions and Policies. World War II left enormous damages in East Germany, but they were no worse than in West Germany. Yet, East Germany suffered several special handicaps. It is a much smaller region and has always been a poorer one, lacking in raw materials and fertile soil. The territory produced merely 27% of Germany's prewar gross national product. As the only part of defeated Germany accessible to the Soviets, it had to deliver heavy reparations to the U.S.S.R. during the first eight postwar years; reparations from West Germany were stopped much earlier. Whereas the West German economy was strengthened by large-scale Western, especially U.S., aid and investments, Soviet assistance to East Germany came much later and on a much smaller scale.

The socialization of the economy and the changes in the social structure caused many dislocations, stimulating the mass exodus of key personnel and skilled workers. As a consequence, living standards rose much more slowly than in West Germany. However, they improved remarkably during the 1960's and were almost equal with West Germany's by the 1970's.

The East German family of four spent more for food, but paid lower rent. Various industrial products were dearer, but staples like milk, bread, and meat were cheaper in East Germany. Neither East nor West German had any direct expenses for such services as socialized medicine or education of his children. The problem of a rising unemployment did not affect East Germany. With two exceptions the overall living standard of the average German in both countries was not too different: by 1975 East Germany still had proportionately fewer passenger cars and it had not overcome the World War II legacy of scarce housing.

East Germany's planned economy is increasingly interrelated with the planning of the Soviet Union and the other Eastern European nations. This coordination, including such large-scale enterprises as the united electric power grid system, is done mainly through the Council for Mutual Economic Assistance (COMECON) to which all the Soviet bloc countries belong.

By the mid-1970's nationally-owned and cooperative enterprises accounted for 95% of East Germany's gross national product. All significant industrial enterprises are publicly owned; privately owned businesses account for only about 3% of the GNP. Each nationally-owned enterprise is a separate economic entity, with a budget of its own. All are run by government-appointed managers who are assisted by trade union-controlled boards, but who are responsible for fulfilling the production quotas set by the economic plan. Since the planning is done increasingly through modern techniques, including systems analysis, and since scientific methods are encouraged, outside observers believe that the managers and technicians have gradually gained in influence over the political bureaucracy.

Industry. After a slow start East Germany's industrial output rose spectacularly, especially in machines and electrical goods, textiles, precision instruments, and optical goods. After 1970 the country ranked fifth among industrial nations in Europe, and ninth or tenth in the world. Insistent effort at modernization has led to reforms that include the use of elements of capitalist cost accounting and management. The republic is still the world's largest producer of lignite, mining over 250,000,000 metric tons annually. Other minerals mined include bituminous coal, uranium, copper ore, and potash.

Agriculture. East Germany's main crops are potatoes, sugar beets, rye, wheat, and barley. Livestock includes pigs, beef and dairy cattle, sheep, and poultry. The country has experienced great difficulties in this part of the economy, as have other countries with a planned economy. The initial measures, namely, the sequestration of the estates of the Junkers, war criminals, and leading Nazis, and the distribution of some 7,600,000 acres (3 078 000 ha) among landless agricultural workers and

Ostman

Broad vistas add to the attractiveness of the Alexanderplatz, a main thoroughfare of East Berlin, the seat of the East German government. Smaller and poorer than West Germany, East Germany has been struggling to raise living standards.

victims of Nazism, proved highly popular. But the productivity of the resulting multitude of new smallholders' farms was so low that a second land reform—collectivization—became necessary, even though it was strongly resisted by many who had profited from the first reform. By 1953, about one fourth of the arable land had been pooled, mainly into cooperatives, but some also into large-scale state farms. Then, political unrest slowed down the process.

The big drive for collectivization started in 1960. Since 1963, when the process was declared complete, less than 10% of the agricultural land has been held by small private farmers. Official policy pursues these aims: to build collectivization in the countryside, which means not only collectivization and mechanization of agriculture on a large scale, but also improvement of the social, educational, and cultural standards of the rural population; and to increase the productivity of the private market sector, which specializes in cattle-raising and dairying.

Labor and Social Legislation. Some 7,800,000 workers and other employees, or three quarters of all men and women between 16 and 65, are members of the fifteen trade unions, which together form the very powerful Free Trade Unions' Association (Freier Deutscher Gewerkschaftsbund, FDGB). The FDGB identifies completely with the dominant Socialist Unity Party (SED). The East German constitution requires all governmental or-

gans and all managers to cooperate with the trade unions. Even the Council of Ministers is legally bound to consult with them, and in practice needs their consent on all matters affecting the working population. More than one eighth of the seats in the legislature is guaranteed to the FDGB. The trade unions participate in the determination of wages, working conditions, and output standards for the nationalized enterprises and negotiate collective agreements with the managements of private firms. They foster higher productivity through wage inducements, "socialist competition," public display of photographs of especially meritorious employees, and the like. They supervise the application of safety regulations and other labor laws. Above all, they administer the entire social insurance system, which covers the vast majority of the population, including the professions, artists, students above a certain age, and all independent entrepreneurs, such as craftsmen and shopkeepers. The social insurance system provides free medical care, free hospitalization, and cash payments in case of sickness and accident, maternity and unemployment benefits, old-age, disability, and survivors' pensions.

Communication and Transportation. As before, the mail, telephone, and telegraph services are government operated. The German Democratic State Broadcasting Committee shapes the radio and television programs. The transportation system includes some 32,000 mi

(51 500 km) of roads, 12,000 mi (19 300 km) of state railways, and 1,600 mi (2 575 km) of navigable inland waterways. The urban and overland bus network grew from some 66,000 to 92,000 mi (106 200 to 148 000 km) between 1965 and 1975. The single, government-run airline, Interluft, was carrying 1,000,000 passengers annually by 1974, principally on international flights.

Foreign Trade. From the beginning of the republic, the main trade partner has been the Soviet Union. This trade has greatly increased over the years, but not so much as did East Germany's total foreign trade. Hence, the Soviet share, previously amounting to one half or more, by 1975 constituted a little less than one third of East Germany's total exports and imports. Another third went to and derived from other COMECON countries, especially Czechoslovakia and Poland. Between 1965 and 1975, trade with West Germany and West Berlin almost tripled, and that with the United States increased eightfold. Trade with Asian and African nations also grew significantly; East Germany provides them with considerable credits and growing numbers of technical experts and other assistance for economic development. Exports are mainly machinery, industrial equipment, vehicles, electrical and chemical products, precision instruments, and fuels, minerals, and metals. Imports include industrial goods, high-grade coal, metal and other raw materials, and foodstuffs.

Government

Constitution. The republic's first constitution of Oct. 7, 1949, which still preserved the federal system and two-chamber legislature of the Weimar Republic, was replaced by the "socialist" constitution of April 6, 1968. That, in turn, was thoroughly amended as of Oct. 7, 1974. It starts with such declarations as "the human person stands in the center of all efforts of the socialist society"; "exploitation of man by man is forever abolished"; "from each according to his abilities, to each according to his performance." Its elaborate bill of rights links a wide range of individual rights with social responsibilities: "each citizen has the right to a job and free choice of job according to the needs of society and personal qualifications"; "everybody, regardless of sex and age, is entitled to equal pay for equal performance"; "the guaranteed right to work implies the duty to work" because "socially useful activity is an honorable duty of every citizen capable of work." To keep water and air clean, and to protect the beauty of the fatherland's landscape concerns not only the authorities but also every citizen. The abuse of science to the destruction of peace, international understanding, and human life and dignity is forbidden.

Structure of the Government. The republic's first and only president was the veteran Communist leader Wilhelm Pieck. After his death in 1960 the one-man presidency was abolished and replaced by a 23-member Council of State (Staatsrat) which soon overshadowed the Council of Ministers (cabinet). Both of these top bodies are elected by the legislature. For over a decade, the Council of State was chaired by Walter Ulbricht, an old-time Communist leader who became East Germany's dominant political figure. Since the early 1970's the power of the council has decreased. Although still formally authorized to issue decrees with the force of law, and to

declare the existence of a defense emergency with potentially far-reaching consequences, it is in essence a collective head of state.

In the legislature (Volkskammer) the predominance of one party is assured. The 500 members are elected every five years by secret, direct, and equal vote of all citizens over 18. But votes can be cast only for or against the single slate of the National Front. That slate is formed by pre-election arrangements between the political parties and the four mass organizations of the trade unions (FDGB), of women, of young people, and of "cultural workers," to each of which a specified number of Volkskammer seats is guaranteed. A certain degree of choice among potential candidates and issues exists because broad public participation in the caucuses is actively solicited, and the number of candidates exceeds the number of seats to be filled. Yet the common slate always contains a majority of members of the leading party.

In 1952, the states (Länder) of Saxony, Saxony-Anhalt, Thuringia, Bradenburg, and Mecklenburg, originally composing the Democratic Republic, were abolished. Instead, the country was divided into 15 districts (Bezirke), each with a governing council and district legislature, or diet. Thus, the second chamber of the central legislature, the Chamber of the States (Länderkammer), which possessed very limited powers to begin with, became obsolete.

Political Parties. Some areas of East Germany, including East Berlin, were Communist strongholds until Hitler abolished the party in 1933. After the end of the Hitler regime, the Soviet military government licensed the Communist and Social Democratic parties, and two middleclass parties, the Christian Democratic Union and the Liberal Democratic party. In the early elections, the Communists fared less well than the Social Democrats, although their combined votes assured comfortable majorities. In 1946, fearing that the Socialists, if left uncontrolled, might become as anti-communist in the Soviet zone as most of them were in the Western zones, the Soviet pressured them to merge with the Communists into a single new party, the Socialist Unity Party of Germany (Sozialistische Einheitspartei Deutschlands, SED). Some of the top SED leaders were old-time Social Democrats. In fact, one of them, Otto Grotewohl, was prime minister of East Germany from 1949 until his death in 1964. But on the whole the Communists control the SED and, through it, the Democratic Republic of Germany.

The Christian Democrats and the Liberal Democrats have continued to exist, and two other parties were formed after the establishment of the republic: The National Democratic Party, to attract ex-officers and former rank-and-file Nazis, and the Democratic Farmers' Party. These four parties have their own organizations, platforms, and even some newspapers, but they accept the essential philosophy of the regime and the SED. Rather than being in opposition, they give a wider base to the regime.

The constitution entitles the strongest party (SED) to designate the prime minister; it also entitles any other party with at least 40 seats in the Volkskammer to be proportionately represented in the cabinet. As all elections since the beginning have brought just over 50 seats

The simplicity of Leipzig's new opera house contrasts sharply with the ornate splendor of an old fountain.

German Information Center

to each of the four smaller parties, they have been represented in the government throughout. Willy Stoph became the prime minister in 1964.

Legal System. The gradual creation of an all-embracing "socialist legal system" for East Germany was completed in 1976 with the creation of a new Civil Code. It defines the property which may be owned, exchanged, bequeathed, and inherited. It simplifies the law, and underpins such premises as employment security, consumer protection, and low rents. The Family Code, in force since 1965, seeks to strengthen the family as the basic unit of society and is very protective of minors. It allows divorce only if a court decides that the marriage has irretrievably broken down, whereupon no guilt is attributed to either spouse. Abortion is legal if performed in a public health center. A new Criminal Code, in effect since 1967, emphasizes prevention rather than punishment of crime, but permits politically expedient interpretations in the case of crimes against national security. Incitement to war or to race hatred is punishable.

The administration of justice combines German traditions (strong bench, absence of common law and of adversary system, assessors rather than juries) with socialist reforms which emphasize decreased formality and popular participation in decision making, as, for example, neighborhood committees to deal quickly and inexpensively with everyday disputes. Most cases still going to courts, including major criminal cases, are handled by district courts. Each of their panels consists of a presiding judge and two lay assessors who have equal voting rights with the judge. The university-trained judges, government-appointees for life, have been gradually replaced with less formally trained "people's judges," many of them women, who are popularly elected. Supreme court judges are elected by the Volkskammer for 5-year terms.

Defense. Just as the Soviet Union would have preferred to forego the creation of an East German republic if it could have prevented the creation of a West German republic, so would the Soviets have preferred not to rearm the East Germans if they could have prevented West Germany's rearmament and NATO affiliation. Therefore, the signal for East Germany to create a "national people's army" and a defense ministry came as late as 1956. Even

after East Germany joined the Warsaw Pact (the Soviet bloc's counteralliance to NATO), the Soviet Union seemed reluctant to have the country rearm. The East German law requiring compulsory military service for male citizens between 18 and 26 dates only from 1962. Service in the German People's Police and in the "mobile police" are recognized alternatives. Great care has been taken to entrust command positions in the National People's Army only to officers with a proven antifascist record.

Under arrangements similar to those of NATO, the East German armed forces are integrated into the Warsaw Pact combined command, and the Soviet troops, since 1955, have been stationed in East Germany not as occupiers, but as allies. But while in West Germany the foreign NATO forces are not limited to the most powerful NATO partner, no forces of other Warsaw Pact nations are stationed in East Germany. Outside the Warsaw Pact system, there exists a government-supported "Workers' militia," open to all sectors of the population. It is a decentralized paramilitary volunteer force which trains in off-duty time and is primarily to protect factories and important installations. In an emergency is could be incorporated into the defense forces.

Public Finance. The East German budget has usually been in balance. One East German mark equals one West German mark. Both are named deutsch mark, but they are separate currencies, with different bank notes and coins. By western standards East German taxes are very low, but comparisons are difficult to make because of the disparities in the two economic systems.

History

Creation of a Separate East Germany. In Dec., 1947, the Socialist Unity party, with Soviet backing, convened in East Berlin a huge "German People's Congress for Unity and a Just Peace" to discuss German reunification. It was composed of delegates of political parties, trade unions, and youth, women's, veterans', and religious organizations, including 650 participants from the three Western zones. The second session of the congress, held in Mar., 1948, when many signs already pointed to the creation of a separate West Germany, adopted a draft for an all-German constitution and demanded a popular referendum on

Protest against Soviet occupation became so great that short-lived strikes and riots flared up in East Berlin on June 17, 1953. Left: Two youths stone a Soviet tank. Right: East Berliners march before the Brandenberg Gate.

reunification of all four zones, including Berlin, on the basis of that draft. The proposal was rejected by the Western Allies, but in the Soviet zone and in East Berlin the draft constitution, somewhat altered as a result of a deliberately fostered public discussion, was accepted by the voters, with 66.1% in favor and 33.9% against. Later on, both West and East Germany claimed that their respective constitution was made in a more democratic fashion than that of the other side. Actually, both were influenced by the respective occupation powers. The Länder legislators of the three western zones who together drafted the West German Basic Law at least had an indirect popular mandate which the East German People's Congress lacked. On the other hand, only the East German constitution was approved by a popular referendum.

The Republic. After its creation in 1949, the German Democratic Republic depended on the Soviet Union's political and, in 1953, overt military support. Its government lacked popular support. The country was internationally isolated and was continuously snubbed by its larger half brother, West Germany. In spite of these and other disadvantages, it achieved economic growth which enabled the regime to relax some of the political pressure. The grimmest period was the period of Stalinist terror.

After Stalin's death in Mar., 1953, unrest became so great that the SED, although Stalinist in its leadership, promised various reforms. These included amnesties for political offenders, relaxation of pressure on workers and farmers, and production of more consumer goods. Party leaders were publicly denounced for mismanagement. The concessions, however, proved insufficient. Sparked by a demonstration on June 16 of Berlin building workers against a 10% output increase without a wage increase, strikes and riots spread through the country on the following day. The workers, Communists included, demanded higher wages, lower prices, more freedom, free elections, and the abolition of the political police. Taken by surprise, the government promised further reforms; but when the disorders continued, the Soviet military authorities declared a state of emergency and fired on demonstrators who had defied the prohibition of public rallies.

Nevertheless, the disorders led to reforms within East Germany and to Soviet concessions. The remaining $2,537,000,000 reparations claims were canceled, East German industrial enterprises taken over by the Soviets after the war were returned, and occupation costs were limited to 5% of East Germany's national income. The U.S.S.R. also contributed 300,000,000 rubles' worth of food and raw materials and granted a credit of 485,000,000 rubles. After West Germany had been declared a sovereign republic by a treaty with the three Western Allies on May 5, 1955, the U.S.S.R. concluded a treaty with the East German republic on Sept. 20, 1955, granting sovereignty, ending occupation and the obligation to pay occupation costs, and declaring East Germany free to decide all questions of domestic and foreign policy, including its relations with West Germany. This was unacceptable to the Western allies, which rather than deal with East Germany continued to hold the Soviet Union responsible for all matters concerning East Germany and Berlin.

Relations between the two Germanys remained bad until 1967, when the first signs appeared of a possible dialogue. The Basic Treaty of Dec. 21, 1972 normalized relations between them. With the major exception of the United States, East Germany had established diplomatic relations with almost all nations by the mid-1970's.

Consult Gati, Charles, ed., *The International Politics of Eastern Europe* (1976); Kiss, T., ed., *The Market of Socialist Economic Integration* (1975); Starrels, John M. and Mallinckrodt, Anita M., *Politics in the German Democratic Republic* (1975).   JOHN H. E. FRIED

GERMAN ART AND ARCHITECTURE

The primary characteristics of German art are an exaggeration of general European styles and a tendency toward caricature. It emphasizes emotional qualities, rather than formal or intellectual ones.

Middle Ages

The earliest works of German art that have been discovered are ornaments and jewelry of the period from the mid-4th century to the time of Charlemagne. These are characterized by polychromy, an emphasis upon dynamic line, and the introduction of stylized animal forms. More sophisticated works date from the reign of Charlemagne and the Ottonian period (800 to mid-11th century). Practically no monumental painting or sculpture has survived from these centuries, but a number of gospels and psalters with miniatures and some ivory sculptures are preserved. The most important monument of the period, however, is architectural, the royal cathedral at Aachen, one of the most important circular buildings in Europe. Longitudinal churches also survive from this era, the abbey church at Gernrode and St. Michael's at Hildesheim. These have an apse at each end, double-ended churches being a German architectural feature.

Among the greatest of all German buildings are the cathedrals of the Romanesque era (mid-11th through mid-13th centuries), the vaulted basilicas of Speyer, Mainz, and Worms. In these structures the weight of the vaulting is supported by unadorned piers that alternate with attached colonnades. These churches retained the German double-ended naves. There appears to have been in Germany an aversion to architectural sculpture. The greatest sculptural monuments of the Ottonian era were the bronze doors at Hildesheim, installed in 1015. The portal and choir screen of the Cathedral of Bamberg are perhaps the most important Romanesque sculptures to have survived.

The Gothic era was ushered into Germany from France in the 13th century. In architecture particularly, the French Gothic style was completely dominant, as the still unfinished Cathedral of Cologne testifies. In north Germany, especially in Lübeck, a lack of suitable stone resulted in a brick Gothic architecture, a local German manifestation. The most important monuments of early German Gothic sculpture are the group of statues representing the Visitation and a figure of a mounted rider, both in the Cathedral of Bamberg, and a great series of sculptured figures in the Cathedral of Naumberg. These works, which are not only outstanding monuments of German art but are among the finest Gothic sculpture produced anywhere, represent a summation of the ideals of aristocratic chivalry. Gothic painting of the 14th century was influenced by the powerful, emotional art from Bohemia, although an elaborate and delicate interpretation of the courtly international style which had spread throughout Europe, was found in west Germany.

The late Gothic period (c.1430–c.1500) was one of immense production in Germany. There was much activity in the creation of civil architecture and in the development of the town hall, or *Rathaus*. Emphasis in church building was upon twisting and turning tracery, func-tional architectural forms being covered by the maze of vigorous lines. The major monument of the period was the great, single-towered Cathedral of Ulm. The late German Gothic sculptors resisted Renaissance influences, rejecting the clarity of form, the precise perspective, and the anatomical interests of Italian artists. The greatest sculptors of the period were Tilman Riemenschneider (c.1468–1531) of Würzburg, who created dreamy, idealized figures in wood and in stone, and Veit Stoss (c.1447–1533), who worked in Nuremberg and in Cracow, Poland. The latter's writhing, twisting figures with voluminous, intricate, and deeply undercut drapery mark the epitome of the Late Gothic in Germany. Italian restraint and harmony only occasionally appeared, as in the work of Pieter Vischer of Nuremberg (c.1460–1529).

In Late Gothic painting some artists, such as Stephan Lochner (d.1451) of Cologne, continued the conservative tradition of the international style, but others were strongly influenced by the art of Flanders. The elimination of the distinction between the human and the divine and the creation of solid monumental figures, in conjunction with an interest in textures and particularized details, is found in the work of Conrad Witz (c.1400–47), who was active in the upper Rhine region and in Switzerland, and in the painting of Michael Pacher (c.1435–1498) in south Germany. The emotionalism of the sculptor Stoss has its counterpart in the painting of the middle Rhine artist Matthias Grünewald, whose Isenheim altarpiece, now in the Museum in Colmar, is probably the greatest of all German paintings.

The Renaissance

Grünewald was active at the end of the 15th and the early 16th century, which was the great period of German painting. Most of the other painters of the era combine German medievalism and emotionalism with new influences from the Italian Renaissance. This is true of Albrecht Dürer of Nuremberg, who traveled in Italy and introduced a new monumentality into German painting and, even more, into the graphic arts of the woodcut and engraving. These were highly developed in Germany at this time by Dürer, Martin Schöngauer, and others. Other major German painters of the period were Hans Burgkmair (1473–1531), who visited Italy a number of times, Hans Baldung-Grien (c.1480–1545), who worked in Nuremberg with Dürer, and Albrecht Altdorfer (c.1480–1538), the leading painter of the Danube valley and the first German artist to interest himself in landscape.

Two other great artists of the period were Lucas Cranach the Elder and Hans Holbein the Younger. Cranach created highly decorative, often sensual paintings that won him the post of court painter to Frederick the Wise of Saxony. He executed both religious and mythological pictures and was also a fine portraitist. In the latter field, however, the greatest German artist of all was Holbein. Holbein, the most cosmopolitan of all German painters, best assimilated the ideals of the Renaissance. Although he painted in Germany, his greatest work was done in England at the time of Henry VIII, and it was he who introduced the great portrait tradition to English art.

The Post-Renaissance Period

The great era of German art came to an end with the cataclysmic destruction of the Thirty Years' War (1618–48). Only a century later did new momentum develop, particularly in the architectural work of the brothers Cosmas Damian Asam (1686–1739) and Egid Quirin Asam (1692–1750) in Munich, and in the residence for the Archbishop in Würzburg, built by Johann Balthasar Neumann (1687–1753).

In 19th-century architecture the neoclassic revival was strong; the major monuments are the works of Karl Friedrich Schinkel (1781–1841) in Berlin and Leo von Klenze (1784–1864) in Munich. As in the other countries of Europe and America, a series of revivals of past styles—for example, the Gothic—dominated throughout the century. In the 20th century, however, the geometric and functional work of such modern architects as Peter Behrens (1868–1940) and Walter Gropius appeared. The

GERMAN ART AND ARCHITECTURE

Frick Collection

Sir Thomas More (1527) by Hans Holbein the Younger.

Marburg—Art Reference Bureau

Mounted rider in the Cathedral of Bamberg.

Nave of Ulm Cathedral, a Late Gothic masterpiece.

Marburg—Art Reference Bureau

Resurrection panel from the Isenheim altarpiece (c.1515) by Matthias Grünewald.

"Kneeling Woman" (1911), by Wilhelm Lehmbruck.

Collection, The Museum of Modern Art, New York—
Mrs. John D. Rockefeller, Jr., Fund

Bruckmann—Art Reference Bureau

latter founded in 1919 in Weimar the highly influential school of architecture and design, the Bauhaus (q.v.). Its philosophy is the basis of the current International Style of architecture, examples of which are being built all over the world.

The 17th and 18th centuries were barren periods in Germany for the arts of painting and sculpture. In the early 19th century a group of painters and writers, known as the Nazarenes, tried to effect a return to religion through art. They included Peter von Cornelius (1783–1867) and Johann Friedrich Overbeck (1789–1869), who based their painting upon that of the Italian Primitives. More imaginative was the haunting, romantic art of Caspar David Friedrich (1774–1840) and later of Arnold Böcklin (1827–1901). French Realism found its counterpart in the brilliant work of the draftsman Adolph von Menzel (1815–1905) and in the peasant scenes of Wilhelm Leibl (1844–1900). A more vigorous style of painting was practiced by Max Liebermann (1847–1935), whose art recalls that of Édouard Manet in France. Liebermann was one of the founders of the *Berliner Sezession*, the movement that introduced French impressionist and postimpressionist art to Germany.

In the early 20th century expressionism (q.v.) blossomed in Germany. The *Brücke* (Bridge) movement of Dresden and Berlin gathered together such painters and graphic artists as Ernst Ludwig Kirchner, Erich Heckel, Max Pechstein, Karl Schmidt-Rottluff, and Emil Nolde. These painters created pictures of brilliant, harsh color contrasts, sharp angular forms, and expressively distorted figures. The *Blaue Reiter* (Blue Rider) in Munich was a decorative, coloristic movement which included such artists as Franz Marc and the two Russian *émigrés* Wassily Kandinsky and Alexi von Jawlensky. In the field of sculpture Wilhelm Lehmbruck and Ernst Barlach more consciously combined medieval sources with a contemporary style. In addition, there were other painters and sculptors who practiced an independent form of expressionism. Some of these, like George Grosz and Ernst Barlach, went to America with the proscription against modern, expressionist art under Hitler. In recent years abstraction has been in Germany, as throughout the world, the dominant force in the arts of painting and sculpture.

Consult Schmidt-Degener, Henri, *The German School*, Vol. 5: *Teach Yourself the History of Painting* (1956); Haftmann, Werner and others, *German Art of the 20th Century* (1957); Brion, Marcel, *German Painting* (1959).

WILLIAM H. GERDTS, The Newark Museum

GERMAN LITERATURE

The earliest Germanic literary document, the Gothic Bible translation by Bishop Ulfilas (311–83), is partially preserved in the *Codex argenteus* in Uppsala, Sweden.

Old High German Literature, c.750–1050. Several incantations, notably the *Merseburger Zauberspruche* (Merseburg Charms) and the *Hildebrandslied* (Lay of Hildebrand), c.800, are the only surviving examples of pagan mythological and heroic poetry. The remaining documents in Old High German, products of monasteries, are predominantly Christian; the 9th-century *Evangelienbuch* (Book of the Gospels) of Otfrid von Weissenburg and the *Heiland* (Saviour), author unknown, are Gospel paraphrases. Alliteration is preserved in the *Wessobrunn Creation and Prayer* (c.780) and the apocalyptic *Muspilli* (World Destruction), c.830. The *Ludwigslied* (Lay of Ludwig), 881, extolling the victory of King Louis III over the Normans at Saucourt in 881, employs assonance. An extensive scholarly literature survives, including translations of Tatian's *Gospel Harmony* and Isidore's *De fide catholica* (Concerning the Catholic Faith), both c.800, as well as classical and scriptural translations by the linguist Notker Labeo (d.1022) of St. Gall.

Under the Carolingian and Ottonian Emperors (c.900–1050), classical influence became so strong that Latin practically supplanted German as the literary language. The principal works surviving from this period are *Waltharius manu fortis* (Walter of the Strong Hand), c.930, written by Ekkehard I of St. Gall and based on Germanic heroic legend, and *Ruodlieb* (c.1030), the first novel of romantic adventure, which anticipated the courtly epic. The nun Hroswitha von Gandersheim (died c.1002) composed pious playlets. *Ecbasis captivi* (Flight of the Captive), c.940, was the oldest satirical beast epic. Old High German literature ended with vernacular religious poems reflecting the ascetic Cluniac reforms.

Middle High German Literature, c.1050–1350. During the 12th century literature passed from the clergy to the lower nobility, who represented the new secular culture dominating the period. Through the Crusades, German knights made contact with the cultures of France and the Near East. Transitional works include *Spielmannsepen* (minstrel epics), fabulous tales of bridal abductions and adventurous voyages to the Orient. Most significant among these are *König Rother* (c.1150), the hero of which is the Lombard King Rothari (d.650), and *Herzog Ernst* (Duke Ernst), c.1170, a mixture of Swabian history and legend. The first translations of French epics are the *Alexanderlied* (Lay of Alexander), c.1120, of Lamprecht and the *Rolandslied* (Lay of Roland) of Konrad der Pfaffe (died c.1131).

The herald of the first Golden Age (1180–1221) was the romancer and Minnesinger, Heinrich von Veldeke (fl.1184). The classicist among the great epic writers was Hartmann von Aue (died c.1215), whose two adaptations of French Arthurian court epics embody the virtue of moderation. The work of Wolfram von Eschenbach (died c.1220) emphasized religious and ethical themes; his *Parzival* (Parsifal), a verse epic, described the spiritual quest for the Holy Grail. The *Tristan und Isolde* (c.1210) of Gottfried von Strassburg is considered the greatest love story of the Middle Ages.

Related in spirit to the court epic is the *Minnesang*, or love song, which drew inspiration from the Latin verse of the Goliards, or wandering scholars, and from the French troubadours. Of the 160 known Minnesingers, or minstrels, the most individual and best known is Walther von der Vogelweide (fl.1227). This period also saw the emergence of the heroic epic dealing with such Germanic heroes as Siegfried and Dietrich von Bern. The greatest of these are the *Nibelungenlied* (Lay of the Nibelungs) and *Gudrun*. The decline of chivalry, realistically depicted in the satirical epic *Meier Helmbrecht* (Farmer Helmbrecht) by Wernher der Gärtner, is reflected in the exaggerations of Ulrich von Lichtenstein in his autobiographical *Frauendienst* (Chivalry). The transition from *Minnesang*, or courtly song of the chivalrous minstrel, to *Meistergesang*, or master song, written by middle-class craftsmen according to strict rules, is represented by the work of Heinrich von Meissen (1250–1318). Noteworthy didactic and satirical poems were written by Thomasin von Zirclaere (fl.1215), Der Stricker (fl.1240), Freidank (fl.1230), and Hugo von Trimberg (fl.1300). The greatest masters of German prose were the preacher Berthold von Regensburg (d.1272) and the mystic Meister Eckhart (d. c.1327).

PAUL SCHACH, University of Nebraska

1350–1700. During this period, which fell between peaks of productivity, strong forces lay dormant; they would have been capable of producing new literary masterpieces, but the Protestant Reformation distracted men's minds.

These years showed literary potentialities in the Germans which were revealed in the works of the mystics Heinrich Suso (c.1295–1366) and Johannes Tauler (1300?–1361); in the Low German version of the story of *Reinke de Vos* (Reynard the Fox), which was based on earlier beast fables in other languages but was characteristically German; in the manifestations of the creative impulse celebrated centuries later in Wagner's *Die Meistersinger*—the religious lyric, the folk song, and the Shrovetide comedies of Hans Sachs and others; and in the one great novel of the period, *Simplicissimus* (1669), by Hans Jakob Christoffel von Grimmelshausen (c.1622–76), which presented unforgettable pictures of the Thirty Years' War. Finally, there was one of the supreme achievements of Western letters, Luther's translation of the Bible (completed 1534), which virtually created the New High German language and had an influence on German literature comparable to that of the King James Bible on English literature.

18th Century. At the end of the 17th century German literature lacked a single outstanding figure in drama, fiction, or poetry. The chief reason for this situation, not paralleled elsewhere, was the destruction of life and property during the Thirty Years' War; fought on German soil, this war is reliably estimated to have reduced the German population by two-thirds. It is understandable that all the energies of the people were needed to repair the damage and to rebuild the framework of a normal existence; the surprising thing is the rapidity with which this was accomplished.

The first step in the literary revival was undertaken in poetry by Friedrich Gottlieb Klopstock (1724–1803). In 1748 Klopstock published the first three cantos of *Der Messias* (The Messiah), an idyllic epic poem in dactylic hexameters (introduced thereby into German literature) which retold the passion and death of Jesus Christ. Modern German literature dates from that event. *Der Messias* (completed in 20 cantos, 1773) was not Klopstock's only signal contribution to German literature. Discarding the "mere jingling" of rhyme, he wrote so-called odes remarkable for their poetic content and diction, which set a standard for later poets and mark the beginning of what was called a century later vers libre, or free verse.

Klopstock's poetry was emotionally charged, and emotionalism was an important aspect of a literary movement which, unique at that time in Western literature, was to lead to German romanticism. This movement, which the Germans later called *Sturm und Drang* (Storm and Stress) after the play (1776) by Friedrich Maximilian von Klinger (1752–1831), revealed in the German soul the 18th-century turbulence which in France became a political upheaval. The movement brought out such masterpieces as Johann Wolfgang von Goethe's *Die Leiden des jungen*

Title page, first edition of Martin Luther's translation of the Old Testament (Wittenberg, 1534).

Culver Pictures, Inc.

A 17th-century title page of the story of Reynard the Fox.

New York Public Library

Werthers (The Sufferings of Young Werther), 1774, the first German work to achieve international acclaim, and Friedrich Schiller's *Die Räuber* (Robbers), 1781, which glorified open defiance of the law.

The movement which those rebels opposed is generally known as rationalism, usually called the Enlightenment by the Germans. It is closely related to what followed the *Sturm und Drang* movement, a form of classicism which had been authoritatively fostered by J. J. Winckelmann (1717–68). He coined the often-quoted characterization of classical art, especially architecture and sculpture, as "noble simplicity and quiet grandeur." In the closing years of the 18th century, when Goethe and Schiller had become classicists, they presented the German people with unsurpassed masterpieces of profound content and polished form, such as Goethe's *Iphigenie auf Tauris* (Iphigenia in Tauris), 1787, *Torquato Tasso* (1789) and *Hermann und Dorothea* (1797), and Schiller's *Die Götter Griechenlands* (The Gods of Greece), 1788, and *Die Braut von Messina* (The Bride of Messina), 1803.

The energy and vitality of the German mind were shown in the 18th century in the work of many writers. Johann Gottfried von Herder (1744–1803) was less significant for his works than for the effect of his ideas. Against strong opposition he established the concept that folk literature is genuine poetry; he proved the close kinship between a nation's character and its literature. Not the least of his achievements was molding the mind of the young Goethe and directing him toward the heights of poetic creation. Gotthold Ephraim Lessing (1729–81) rescued German drama from the sterile shackles of French classicism, and in both his criticism and his plays inaugurated the development of a native German theater. Christoph Martin Wieland (1733–1813) showed by example that German verse could be both melodious (*Oberon*, 1780) and witty (*Musarion*, 1768), and in his humorous story *Die Abderiten* (The Republic of Fools), 1774, and his serious *Die Geschichte des Agathon* (The History of Agathon), 1766, he produced the first modern novels in German. The latter is a worthy precursor of the many novels of development—such as Goethe's *Wilhelm Meister* and Gottfried Keller's *Der grüne Heinrich* (Green Henry)—which Germany has produced. Goethe's *Urfaust*, the brilliant play of c.1774 that is an early version of *Faust*, preserves as no other single work does the drive and sweep of that age. To this day the *Urfaust* is perhaps the most powerful and affecting drama in the entire range of German literature.

Romanticism. At the beginning of the 19th century Germany was politically dominated by the Napoleonic tyranny, philosophically emerging from the rationalism of the preceding age, and in literature thoroughly committed to what is called the romantic movement. German romanticism, however, has its own peculiar character. As in other lands, it stressed imagination rather than reality, and it was radically opposed to what it called the classical spirit. Special features of German romanticism were its stress upon music, as in the work of E. T. A. Hoffmann (1776–1822); its frequent fragmentariness and formlessness, resulting from an undisciplined drive for self-expression; and its markedly escapist character, making it revert to the Middle Ages or seek the world of fancy and fable. A romantic impulse made the Grimm brothers collect and publish (1812, 1815) the body of folk tales which have become the possession of the world. From a similar prompting sprang the collection of poems called *Des Knaben Wunderhorn* (The Youth's Cornucopia), 1806–8, which has continued to influence German lyric poetry. A romantic inspiration underlay the great musical settings of lyrics by Schubert, Schumann, and others, creating so distinctive a song type that the German word *Lied* (song) is today a technical term among singers.

Germans are basically—some would say incurably—romantic, and German romantic literature is very rich. First and foremost among the romantic writers were the lyric poets, since most romantic writing is lyric in temper and tone: Adelbert von Chamisso (1781–1838), Joseph von Eichendorff (1788–1857), Heinrich Heine (1797–1856), Friedrich Hölderlin (1770–1843), Novalis (1772–1801), and Ludwig Uhland (1787–1862). There were excellent tellers of tales: Friedrich de la Motte-Fouqué (1777–1843), whose masterpiece was *Undine* (1811); E. T. A. Hoffmann, who is popularized in Offenbach's *The Tales of Hoffmann;* Heinrich von Kleist (1777–1811), author of the masterly *novella, Michael Kohlhaas* (1808); Jean Paul Richter (1763–1825), the only master of the full-bodied novel in this group; and Ludwig Tieck (1773–1853), whose fanciful inventions can still be read with pleasure. Lastly, there was only one truly great dramatist, Heinrich von Kleist; for the tension implicit within the dramatic form was not wholly consonant with the romantic spirit.

Reaching over into the romantic period, only partially a participant in it and yet inseparable from it, there was the towering figure of Goethe, noteworthy because of the extraordinary range and perfection of his work and because of its inescapable presence in all the literature that followed his own lifetime. It must suffice to refer to that work of his which like no other stands for all of German literature as the Germans' gift to the world: the two-part dramatic poem *Faust*, which occupied his mind for more than 60 years and which, by his own will, was published in its entirety only after his death in 1832. In this work, as in no other single literary creation except Dante's *Divine Comedy*, what is involved is the life of man and the meaning of the universe.

Realism. In its decline German romanticism seemed to succumb to its very opposite: the realism which dominated the central portion of the 19th century was as different as possible from the fanciful and sometimes fantastic creations of the romantic temper. Romanticism was not well suited to the happenings of the everyday world: the revolutionary disturbances of 1830 and 1848, the industrial revolution, the beginnings of rapid transportation and mass communication. It was natural that the novel, hitherto not very prominent in German letters, should begin to assume great importance, along with its sister form, the *novella*, in which the Germans have been particularly successful. The rise of German fiction was brought about by men of great ability: Willibald Alexis (1798–1871), the "Sir Walter Scott" of Germany; Gustav Freytag (1816–95), master of the novel of manners; Jeremias Gotthelf (1797–1854), unsurpassed in his depiction of Swiss village life; Gottfried Keller (1819–90), best known for his humor-

Birthplace of Friedrich von Schiller (1759–1805) in Marbach (left).

The Bettmann Archive
Woodcut portrait of the poet Rainer Maria Rilke, by Emil Orlik.

Fred Stein—Alfred Knopf, Inc.
Thomas Mann, winner of the Nobel Prize for literature in 1929.

ous *novelle;* Conrad Ferdinand Meyer (1825–98), who needed to be temporally and physically remote from his subject for ease in writing; Wilhelm Raabe (1831–1910), whose humor resembled that of Dickens; and Theodor Storm (1817–88), whose *Immensee* (1852), a story of lost love, must have been read by millions of students in American schools. The new realistic approach was seen in the dramas of Georg Büchner (1813–37) and C. D. Grabbe (1801–36), both of whom have had something of a resurrection in the 20th century; Franz Grillparzer (1791–1872), an Austrian of genuine genius and great versatility; Friedrich Hebbel (1813–63), considered by some critics to be unsurpassed in the intensity of his tragic effects; and Otto Ludwig (1813–65), author of two memorable plays. In the lyric, commonly a fertile field in German letters, the following were important: Annette von Droste-Hülshoff (1797–1848), often compared to Emily Dickinson; Nikolaus Lenau (1802–50), poet of melancholy and gloom; C. F. Meyer, polished and powerful; Eduard Mörike (1804–75), spontaneous and melodious, admirably set to music by Hugo Wolf; August von Platen-Hallermünde (1796–1835), an obstinate defender of classical form; Friedrich Rückert (1788–1866), who introduced Oriental forms and motifs into German poetry; and Theodor Storm, a born singer.

German romanticism was almost wholly an internal affair. But prior to it, and again after it, German literature received important stimuli from other lands. In the 18th century Germans had looked in two·directions for formal and factual material: to France for classical drama and fiction; to England for a sober realism of middle-class drama, the sentimentality of Ossian, the grandeur of Milton, and the overwhelming universality of Shakespeare. The influences which came to German letters in the 19th century were again twofold: the English contributed basic forms and patterns to the German novelists of the realistic school; and the naturalism of Ibsen, the Russians, and Zola gave vital force to both the novel and the drama late in the century.

Naturalism. Novelists remained dominant at least in number. It must suffice to name Ludwig Anzengruber

(1839–89), who drew striking pictures of Austrian village life; Theodor Fontane (1819–98), unsurpassed in his representation of every aspect of Berlin life; Gustav Frenssen (1863–1945), whose *Jörn Uhl* (1901) outwitted the critics; Paul von Heyse (1830–1914), winner of a Nobel Prize for his brilliant stories; Ricarda Huch (1864–1947), remembered most for her *Erinnerungen von Ludolf Ursleu dem Jüngeren* (Recollections of Ludolf Ursleu the Younger), 1893; Heinrich Mann (1871–1950), a savage critic of the contemporary scene, as in *Der Untertan* (The Patrioteer), 1918; Thomas Mann (1875–1955), of whose immense output perhaps *Buddenbrooks* (1901) is the masterpiece; Hermann Sudermann (1857–1928), whose *Frau Sorge* (1887) comes close to the stature of a classic; and Clara Viebig (1860–1952), a novelist of wide range and great power. More sensational than the naturalistic novel in the response it aroused was naturalistic drama. Here Anzengruber was again prominent, both for serious plays and delightful comedies. Gerhart Hauptmann (1862–1946), still regarded as the leading exponent of naturalistic drama, inaugurated the trend in his *Vor Sonnenaufgang* (Before Dawn), 1889. Hermann Sudermann, a master of stage effect and a box office favorite, failed to hold his place as a serious contender for high honors. Frank Wedekind (1864–1918), whose interest in sex was almost an obsession, made of *Frühlings Erwachen* (The Awakening of Spring), 1891, an eloquent plea for the frankness which Sigmund Freud battled for on a different ground. Naturalism is as alien to the lyric as it is congenial to fiction, and the poetry of this era is comparatively meager: Richard Dehmel (1863–1920) sang of sex as vigorously as Wedekind dramatized it; Arno Holz (1863–1929) with all his ability went astray into mannerism; Detlev von Liliencron (1844–1909) achieved some notable successes in the special vein of impressionism; only the poet-philosopher Friedrich Nietzsche (1844–1900) reached the highest peak of poetic achievement.

Action and reaction tend to go together in literature as elsewhere, and it was to be expected that the drabness of extreme naturalism would yield to something like its opposite. In Germany a school of neoromanticism, stressing beauty and music and the appeal of art, found adherents in Hauptmann and Sudermann. Almost wholly neoromantic, at this time, were the important poets Stefan George (1868–1933) and Hugo von Hofmannsthal (1874–1929); the latter produced superior dramas as well. Less easily defined is the poetry of Rainer Maria Rilke (1875–1926), one of the greatest lyricists of the 20th century, but much of his work is romantic in spirit.

Expressionism. A violent break in the continuity of German literature was caused by World War I, which was largely responsible for the development of a type of writing called expressionism. It was opposed to naturalism in insisting that what was important was not externals but the visions in the poet's soul. Concurrently, the insensate slaughter of the war caused a revulsion of the utmost intensity, along with an ecstatic cult of love as a counter to the hate which was destroying the world. Though short-lived, German expressionism was astonishingly vital, and its most characteristic documents showed the extravagance which readily develops under outrageous pressure. It can be observed in the plays of Georg Kaiser (1878–1945) and Ernst Toller (1893–1939); in the lyric poems of Ernst Stadler (1883–1914) and Franz Werfel (1890–1945); and in the fiction of Gottfried Benn (1886–1956), Max Brod (1884–   ), Alfred Döblin (1878–1957), Kasimir Edschmid (1890–   ), Franz Kafka (1883–1924), and Jakob Wassermann (1873–1934).

New Objectivity. Expressionism, probably the most violent eruption German letters had ever experienced, was followed by one of the soberest periods of realism, frequently called the New Objectivity. What came to the fore was reportage like *Im Western nichts Neues* (All Quiet on the Western Front), 1929, by Erich Maria Remarque (1898–   ); *Krieg* (War), 1928, by Ludwig Renn (1889–   ); *Kleiner Mann was nun?* (Little Man, What Now?), 1932, by Hans Fallada (1893–1947); *Fabian* (1931) by Erich Kästner; and *Die vierzig Tag des Musa Dagh* (The Forty Days of Musa Dagh), 1933, by Franz Werfel.

BAYARD QUINCY MORGAN, Stanford University

Since World War II. Violently broken traditions have long been the fate of German literature, but the National Socialist regime, which blighted the years from 1933 to 1945, produced a split in German culture that may well be permanent. Today, there is a new vigorous West German literature and a far less impressive East German literature, but no "unified" literature has developed.

The most serious figures in West German literature, best represented by Heinrich Böll (1917–   ), Günter Grass (1927–   ), and Uwe Johnson (1934–   ), are preoccupied with the hideous crimes and guilt of the Nazi past, the side effects of the German economic miracle, and the continuing dismemberment of Germany.

Heinrich Böll, the first important writer to emerge from the ruins of Hitler's *Reich*, has, since 1949, honestly recorded the causes and aftermath of Germany's greatest catastrophe. In novels like *Billiards at Half-Past Nine* (1959) and *The Clown* (1963), he mercilessly probed the conscience, values, and imperfections of his countrymen. If his style has been traditional, his indictment of an ephemeral, philistine society has been exceptional.

Günter Grass, using oblique, surrealistic techniques, created an international best seller with his *The Tin Drum* (1959), the garish fictional autobiography of Oskar Matzerath, a mad dwarf. Grotesque, anarchic, skillfully detailed, the novel recaptures the atmosphere of the Hitler years in episodes of richness, vigor, and absurd humor. *Dog Years* (1963), Grass's second major novel, deals with the final years of Nazi power by treating the fate of Prinz, Hitler's missing black police dog. Mock metaphysics, fierce satire, and marvelous buffoonery are fused into a narrative that startles and compels.

Uwe Johnson's chief theme is Germany's central problem, the political division into two artificial and hostile states. In novels like *Speculations About Jakob* (1959) and *Two Views* (1965), Johnson sensitively explores the relationships between East and West Germany. Since both states, in his view, are bleak, banal, empty, Johnson cannot be accused of writing propaganda for either side.

The state of writing in East Germany is much less fortunate, because literature there has been specifically formed by the Communist party dictatorship. Most contemporary writers of East Germany are spiritually rooted, if rooted at all, in the German proletarian school that began in 1927 with the publication of *Linkskurve*. This famous Communist periodical attracted figures like Bertolt Brecht (1898–1956), Johannes Becher (1891–1958), and Ludwig Renn (1889–   ), all of whom gained their greatest fame and influence after World War II in East Germany. Their young Marxist-oriented heirs deal almost exclusively, however, with ideological criticism and self-criticism which is unfathomable to non-Marxist readers. Among others, Johannes Bobrowski (1917–1965) and Manfred Bieler (1934–   ) are certainly exceptions to this rule, but much of their work remains untranslated. A cultural reconciliation between East and West Germany seems unlikely for many years to come.

Consult Bithell, Jethro, *Modern German Literature* (1959); Martini, Fritz, *History of German Literature* (1962); Moore, H. T., *Twentieth-Century German Literature* (1967).

EDWARD M. POTOKER, The City College of New York

GERMAN MUSIC

German music may be defined as music composed by and written for German-speaking communities of widely differing political allegiances and cultural traditions. Such communities belong to the population of central Europe and include Germans, Austrians, German-Swiss, Alsatians, Sudeten-Germans, and other ethnic groups outside the political framework of Germany.

After a late start German music assumed significance for surrounding communities and countries only at the time of the Reformation (early 16th century). It remained under the domination of Italian and French concepts of style until well into the 18th century, when its supremacy became international with the Mannheim symphonists, the precursors of Viennese classicism. German music continued to hold sway over Europe and the Western world in unbroken tradition from the late 18th century to the deaths of Richard Strauss (1949) and Arnold Schoenberg (1951), that is, for nearly 200 years. At present, it has dropped to comparative insignificance, partly as a result of its cultural disintegration under the Hitler regime.

The Middle Ages

German music first became apparent in the Middle Ages with the emergence of liturgical hymns (those with special refrains, called *Kyrieleis*, 10th century; hymns for Easter, such as *Christ ist erstanden*, c.1350; for Christmas, *Gelobet seist Du Jesu Christ*, c.1370; for Whitsun, *Nun bitten wir den heiligen Christ*). In the secular area the German contribution to monophonic (single-voiced) music proved to be considerable in the *Minnesang*, or song of the Minnesinger (12th–14th centuries), a highly imaginative offshoot of the French troubadour and trouvère movement. Great chivalric poets, such as Walther von der Vogelweide, Wolfram von Eschenbach, Gottfried von Strassburg, and the commoner Neidhart von Reuenthal, created lyrical melodies of great beauty (such as Walther's *Palestine Song*, probably for the Crusade of 1228). Late German Minnesingers, such as Hermann, the Monk of Salzburg; Oswald von Wolkenstein; and Heinrich Loufenberg, began to write polyphonic (many-voiced) songs. These found urban continuation through the Meistersinger guilds, which lingered on until the 19th century; however, their importance for the preservation of singing culture in Germany expired with their greatest figure, Hans Sachs (1494–1576).

The Renaissance

Earliest monuments of polyphonic music did not appear until about 1450. Two famous fundamental collections are Conrad Paumann's (d.1473) *Fundamentum organisandi* and the *Lochamer Liederbuch* (c.1452). The former, the work of a prominent blind organist, indicates the German preference for the organ and its characteristic style. The latter contains a collection of beautiful German folk tunes (*Ich fahr' dahin*, *Der Wald hat sich entlaubet*, and others).

The first group of German composers linked by a common concept of style emerged from the court chapel of Holy Roman Emperor Maximilian I (reigned 1493–1519), with Heinrich Isaac, Ludwig Senfl, and Paul Hofhaimer as the most prominent personalities. Creating a collection of Schubertian lyricism and universality of expression, Senfl (c.1490–c.1556), a Swiss, was the greatest exponent of the German *Tenorlied* (tenor song) with the main melody in the tenor, with instrumental accompaniment, and set to his own texts. He also completed Isaac's *Choralis Constantinus* (published in Nuremberg, 1550–55), the greatest collection of liturgical music for the proper of the Mass. Heinrich Finck (1445–1527) and Thomas Stoltzer (c.1480–1526) carried the German brand of Franco-Flemish polyphony to Poland and Hungary, where they served as court conductors for many years.

All these Germans cultivated the polyphonic *Tenorlied*, an important offshoot of the Franco-Flemish chanson, as well as music for the Roman liturgy. However, those born around 1490 and later (Senfl, Arnold von Bruck, Sixtus Dietrich, and Kaspar Othmayr) strongly sympathized with Luther's reform movement, even though still acknowledging the church of Rome. This younger generation of composers occasionally wrote music for both churches. Luther himself was a trained musician who composed some of the most beautiful German community hymns, or chorales, partly based on liturgical melodies of the Roman church, partly incorporating folk tune elements. At least 20 melodies are his own. In three theoretical publications Luther regulated the function of music in the Protestant service for centuries to come.

From then on the majority of German composers created music determined by the treasure store of Protestant hymnals, which appeared mainly between 1524 and 1736. The next 100 years marked the development of the unaccompanied chorale motet and the motet on scriptural proverbs, in which the south Tyrolean Leonhard Lechner (c.1553–1606) and Johann Eccard (1553–1611) excelled. The greatest chorale-inspired composer, however, was Michael Praetorius of Wolfenbüttel (1571–1621), who in his *Musae Sioniae* (1605–11) published 1,244 pieces in which 537 chorale melodies were utilized.

The Baroque Era

The *a cappella* (unaccompanied) motet was superseded in the 17th century by the *geistliches Konzert* (sacred concerto), which combined voices and instruments. Its greatest exponents were the three great "S's": Heinrich Schütz (1585–1672), Johann Hermann Schein (1586–1630), and Samuel Scheidt (1587–1654). All three were deeply influenced by Monteverdi, by Italian *basso continuo* (improvisation on a bass line), and by monody (solo song style). Schein wrote German madrigals and chorale settings in a *concerto grosso* style and in his *Banchetto musicale* (1617) presented an early example of the instrumental dance suite. Scheidt became most prominent as father of the German chorale prelude for organ. Schütz, the greatest individual figure of German music before Johann Sebastian Bach, brought German Passion composition to a tremendous climax. He replaced the archaic motet Passion by an oratorio Passion (such as *The Seven Words of Christ on the Cross*, c.1645) in which he used voices and instruments and applied the Italian *basso continuo* technique. The "sacred concerto" and the oratorio Passion became the cantata and Passion cantata at the end of the 17th century, when nonscriptural texts led to the inclusion of semioperatic arias and ariosos.

The German organ tradition had previously been established about 1530 by the colorist school (emphasizing melodic ornamentation) of Arnolt Schlick and others. It gained momentum in the North and South German schools of keyboard music throughout the 17th century (J. J. Froberger, Georg Boehm, Franz Tunder, and his son-in-law Dietrich Buxtehude). This organ tradition finally culminated in the artistry of Johann Sebastian Bach (1685–1750).

The same musical tradition became the artistic subsoil for George Frederick Handel (1685–1759). However, in joining the Hamburg Goosemarket Opera House (the earliest operatic nerve center of Germany) around 1704, he became involved in opera and oratorio in the Italian style. His 50-odd operas were forgotten by the time the last one was produced, but he remains a living force as creator of the modern oratorio and as master of the presymphonic *concerto grosso*. Furthermore, Handel's Venice- and London-born Italian opera (in the tradition of Alessandro Scarlatti and Agostino Steffani); his Corelli- and Lully-inspired *concerti grossi* Op. 3 and Op. 6; and his Chandos anthems, as well as his English oratorios, make him the first musical cosmopolitan of his epoch whose cultural allegiance cannot be limited to any single country.

Similarly, Bach, the German cantor of St. Thomas's School in Leipzig, created his finest instrumental music (four suites for orchestra, six Brandenburg Concertos, the four volumes of *Clavierübung*, and so on) as a disciple of François Couperin and the French harpsichord tradition and as an admirer of Antonio Vivaldi and his three-movement concerto form. Bach, whose "theatrical" Passion cantatas of 1723 and 1729, 200-odd church cantatas, and approximately 50 secular cantatas were of provincial and transitory fame throughout his lifetime, was remembered by his own century only as a master of the organ and as a contrapuntal specialist.

Both Bach and Handel, with Johann Mattheson (1681–1764), G. P. Telemann (1681–1767), Christoph Graupner (1683–1760), J. J. Fux (1660–1741), and a host of smaller masters, represent the glorious sunset of the Baroque, with its emphasis on *basso continuo* and a heavy, polyphonic style in trio sonata, cantata, opera, and organ piece. Their aesthetic tenets were in 1736 already under heavy attack by Johann Adolf Scheibe, whose *Critische Musicus* (1737–40), the first prominent German music periodical, set a new standard of style concepts. This was supported by the more scholarly Lorenz Mizler and his Society for Musical Sciences (Sozietät der musikalischen Wissenschaften, founded 1738), which made the first attempt to systematize musicological activity in Germany. Italian opera, firmly entrenched in German operatic centers, such as Vienna, Dresden, Brunswick, and Stuttgart, since the days of Monteverdi, continued to dominate German operatic life for the greater part of the 18th century, with Johann Adolf Hasse (1699–1783) as the leading figure.

The German Singspiel, the first indigenous trend in opera since the expiration (c.1738) of the Hamburg Goosemarket Opera, began as an offshoot of English ballad opera. This form inspired J. A. Hiller (1728–1804) and J. C. Standfuss (d.1756) first to make adaptations of English works with German text, later to produce original creations. The naïve realism of the latter paved the way for the comic operas of Mozart and later composers.

The Classical Era

Christoph Willibald Gluck (1714–87), born on the border of Bavaria and Bohemia, but a convinced exponent of Germanic culture, began in the Neapolitan tradition. He later absorbed features of Handel's operas, French *opéra comique* (comic opera), and the pomp and circumstance of Lully and Rameau's French operatic tradition. His Viennese opera reform, launched in 1762 with *Orfeo ed Euridice*, was based on Italian librettos by Ranieri di Calzabigi. Opera was thereby stripped of its virtuosic garnish and courtly extravagances and reduced to the "pure human," a reform reminiscent of Monteverdi's aesthetic principles.

The foundations of the classical sonata and symphony were laid by three more or less contemporary schools of musical thought, exemplified by (1) the works of Carl Philipp Emanuel Bach (1714–88), J. S. Bach's second son (such as the Prussian and Württemberg piano sonatas of 1742 and 1744); (2) the school of Viennese symphonists (G. M. Monn, J. C. H. Mann, G. C. H. Wagenseil); and (3) the Mannheim symphonists, led by the Bohemians Johann Stamitz, Anton Filtz, Ignaz Holzbauer, and others. Stamitz's symphonic form became the model for the Viennese classics, which also absorbed the new keyboard style of C. P. E. Bach and his pianistic teaching. Franz Joseph Haydn (1732–1809) and Wolfgang Amadeus Mozart (1756–91), both Austrians from the border provinces of Burgenland and Salzburg, were linked by bonds of mutual friendship and esteem, and their works were cross-fertilized by each other's achievements. They are equally great in instrumental music and church music and opera. Haydn's 77 string quartets and 104 symphonies are climaxed in Mozart's mature string quartets and string quintets, as well as in his divine symphonic triptych of 1788.

With his two oratorios *The Creation* and *The Seasons*, Haydn represented the sum total of a century of oratorio development, harnessing Handelian choral grandeur to the symphonic orchestra of the Viennese tradition. Mozart's 20-odd operas take their cue from Italian *opera seria* (serious opera) and *opera buffa* (comic opera), but also from Gluck's "reform" operas. His most glorious achievements are three Italian *buffa* on texts by Lorenzo da Ponte, *Le nozze di Figaro*, *Don Giovanni*, and *Così fan tutte*. His second Singspiel, *The Magic Flute*, anticipates 19th-century German romantic opera, with its contrasting elements of mystery and local Viennese comedy.

The Romantic Era

The Rhinelander Ludwig van Beethoven (1770–1827) and the Viennese-born Sudeten German Franz Schubert (1797–1828) were also exact contemporaries. But their personal link was tenuous, and their approach to music in general, widely divergent. Beethoven developed into a composer of sonatas and symphonies after having started as a pianist of genius, not unlike Mozart before him. Beethoven's nine symphonies, more than 32 piano sonatas, and 17 string quartets not only summed up Haydn's and Mozart's achievements, but created the matrices of modern musical thought. His Choral (9th) Symphony (1818–23) and its companion piece, the *Missa Solemnis* (1823), became the basis for Richard Wagner's new idiom of corresponding motives. Beethoven's last string quartets, with the number of movements increased to seven, anticipated Gustav Mahler's (1860–1911) symphonic form at the beginning of the 20th century. Beethoven's only opera, *Fidelio*, formed a bridge from the Singspiel of Mozart to the through-composed opera (opera without spoken dialogue) of Carl Maria von Weber (1786–1826).

Weber was the creator of a specifically German style in his national part songs (*Leyer und Schwerdt*, 1814), as well as in his spooky Singspiel *Der Freischütz* (1821). In his first through-composed opera *Euryanthe* (1823) he anticipated the German romantic opera of the *Lohengrin* type. What Weber achieved in opera was matched by Schubert's unparalleled creation of the German lied for voice and piano. In this respect Schubert is the climax of a century of North and South German lied tradition, started by C. P. E. Bach and Friedrich Reichardt, and reaching an eloquent level in the ballads of Johann Zumsteeg (1760–1802). In his instrumental music Schubert is the equal of Beethoven, expanding lyrically where the older master is bent on dramatic concentration.

German music after the deaths of Beethoven, Schubert, and Weber branched out into several starkly contrasted schools: (1) A school of romantic classicists that was headed by Felix Mendelssohn (1809–47) and Robert Schumann (1810–56); it recaptured something of Beethoven's complexity in the work of Johannes Brahms (1833–97). (2) A school of new German composers of strongly progressive and programmatic (literary and scenic) tendencies that was headed by Franz Liszt (1811–86), who was equally great as a creator of a new piano style and as a pioneer of the large-scale symphonic poem. This school culminated in a glorious genius, Richard Wagner (1813–83), and also in two Austrians, exponents of the post-Beethovenian symphony and the post-Schubertian lied, Anton Bruckner (1824–96) and Hugo Wolf (1860–1903).

Wagner's music drama grew as much out of Gluck and Mozart as out of Parisian grand opera. *Lohengrin* (1846–48), the last great romantic opera, was followed by the four music dramas of the tetralogy, *Der Ring des Nibelungen* (1848–74); *Die Meistersinger* (1862–67) and *Tristan und Isolde* (1857–59) served as colossal "interludes" and established Wagner's mature style in the direction of historic comedy and Arthurian legendary drama. Wagner's "total work of art," or *Gesamtkunstwerk*, materialized in the creation of the Bayreuth Festival Opera House, for which *Parsifal* (1877–82) was especially written. Although Wagner in his youth had to contend with many gifted German opera composers (Albert Lortzing, 1801–51; Heinrich Marschner, 1795–1861; and Otto Nicolai, 1810–49; among others), German opera seemed precariously balanced at the end of his life, with only minor talents appearing, such as Peter Cornelius (d. 1874) and Hermann Götz (d. 1876). Wagner's successors were three composers of remarkable talent, Engelbert Humperdinck (1854–1921, composer of *Hänsel und Gretel*; Hans Pfitzner (1869–1949); and Richard Strauss (1864–1949). Strauss's *Salome* (1905) and *Elektra* (1908) and Pfitzner's *Palestrina* (1917) are the glorious sunset of Wagnerian style. Max Reger (1873–1916), specializing in organ music, continued the retrogressive tendencies of Brahms.

Since the early 1880's musicology became an acknowledged academic discipline with its own public organ *Vierteljahrschrift für Musikwissenschaft* (Musicological Quarterly), edited by its founders Friedrich Chrysander,

Hermann Kretzschmar, and Guido Adler. Its remarkable achievements are recorded in the collections of the *Denkmäler* (Monument) series, begun by Guido Adler in 1892. It was between approximately 1850 and 1900 that the first critical complete editions of Bach, Handel, Schütz, Beethoven, Mozart, and Schubert were issued and published. Publishers such as Breitkopf and Härtel, C. F. Peters, B. Schott's Sons, Bote and Bock, Eulenburg, and, since 1901, Universal Edition, Vienna, have done much to disseminate the gospel of German music all through the world. It was in the later 19th and early 20th century that German conductors and performers became world figures. Among the former were Hans von Bülow (1830–94), Arthur Nikisch (1855–1922), Gustav Mahler, Richard Strauss, and Wilhelm Furtwängler (1886–1954). Among the latter were the venerable figure of Franz Liszt and his great pupils, Eugen D'Albert and Emil von Sauer, and the violinist Joseph Joachim (1831–1907).

The Modern Era

A great change came over German music in the songs and symphonies of Gustav Mahler, in the piano music and operas of the progressive and yet neoclassical Austro-Italian Ferruccio Busoni (1866–1924), and in the atonal and later dodecaphonic (12-tone) music of the Viennese Arnold Schoenberg (1874–1951). The latter's Austrian disciples Alban Berg (1885–1935) and Anton von Webern (1883–1945) paved the way for the electronic and constructional experiments of the youngest generation.

The brilliant achievements of German musical scholarship were cut short by the political revolution in 1933, which drove the cream of German scholars into exile, besides exiling leading composers of the young generation such as Paul Hindemith (1895–1963) and the near-genius Kurt Weill (1900–50), whose *Dreigroschenoper* (*Three-Penny Opera*) and *Aufstieg und Fall der Stadt Mahagonny* (*Rise and Fall of the City of Mahagonny*) re-echo through the scores of his imitators (Rudolf Wagner-Régeny and Carl Orff).

German music after 1945 has produced two figures of considerable stature: the opera and ballet composer Hans Werner Henze and the controversial Karlheinz Stockhausen, whose Cologne-based experiments in electronic music have found international acclaim. Nevertheless, the days of Germany's musical supremacy are over for the present.

Consult Lang, P. H., *Music in Western Civilization* (1941); Geiringer, Karl, *The Bach Family* (1954); Helm, E. E., *Music at the Court of Frederick the Great* (1960).

HANS F. REDLICH, University of Manchester

GERMAN THEATER

The theater in Germany, as in most of the other European countries, had its origin in the Middle Ages. Its beginnings were closely linked with the church festivals, when Biblical scenes were performed in churches, first in Latin and later in the vernacular. Presently, these performances moved outside the church, and were interspersed with farcical elements.

The Reformation provided a fresh impulse. By that time theatrical activities were mainly in the hands of the civic

guilds—above all, in Nuremberg. There Hans Sachs (1494–1576), a cobbler, wrote a large number of plays of every type, among them the popular *Fastnachtsspiele* (Shrovetide plays), rich in robust humor. At the same time the scholastic Latin play was cultivated by the Humanists and later by the Jesuits, especially in schools.

Strolling Players. From the end of the 16th century, English players toured Germany, performing works of Shakespeare and other Elizabethan dramatists in vulgarized forms. Their example was followed by German actors who presented so-called *Haupt- und Staatsaktionen*, crude, historical cloak-and-dagger plays, and popular farces. Owing to the devastating effects of the Thirty Years' War (1618–48), the low estate of German drama continued well into the 18th century. One of the most influential touring companies was that of Caroline Neuber (1697–1760), of Leipzig, who co-operated with the critic Johann Christoph Gottsched in raising the standards of the acting profession. It was from one of these touring companies that the first eminent German actor, Konrad Ekhof (1720–78), emerged.

The Classical Theater. It was not until the second half of the 18th century that the first regular theaters were founded. The earliest was the short-lived national theater in Hamburg (1767–69), which won fame through the active support of Gotthold Ephraim Lessing. A later, more successful venture was the national theater in Mannheim, founded in 1779, under the directorship of Wolfgang von Dalberg, who made theatrical history by producing the early plays of Friedrich von Schiller, from *Die Räuber* (The Robbers), 1781, to *Don Carlos* (1787). But the most frequent type was the court theater, subsidized by a reigning Prince—above all, the Burgtheater in Vienna, founded in 1776 by the Emperor Joseph II on the model of the Comédie Française; it has remained one of the leading German-speaking playhouses to this day.

The establishment of permanent theaters was accompanied by the rise of German drama to its supreme height. The first of the great classics was Lessing, with his *Minna von Barnhelm* (1767); *Emilia Galotti* (1772); and *Nathan der Weise* (Nathan the Wise), 1779. Through his theoretical writings Lessing directed German taste from the French classics to English drama and in particular to Shakespeare. His inspiration was followed by the movement known as *Sturm und Drang* (Storm and Stress), represented by a group of young playwrights including Jakob Michael Reinhold Lenz, Friedrich Maximilian von Klinger, and Heinrich Leopold Wagner. From their midst came the two greatest German dramatists, Johann Wolfgang von Goethe and Friedrich von Schiller. The early plays of this pair were still under the spell of the rebellious *Sturm und Drang*; in their maturity, however, they produced that series of classical plays which is the glory of German drama. Goethe's contributions are *Iphigenie auf Tauris* (Iphigenia in Tauris), 1787; *Torquato Tasso* (1790); and *Faust* (1808, 1832). Schiller wrote historical dramas ranging from *Wallenstein* (1798) to *Wilhelm Tell* (1804). Both took an active interest in the living stage, Goethe by directing the Weimar court theater from 1791 to 1817. Their work was supported by such outstanding actors as Friedrich Ludwig Schröder, August Wilhelm Iffland, and Ludwig Devrient. Along with the classical dramas of Goethe and Schiller, the theaters presented popular comedies and sentimental domestic plays, provided by such prolific writers as August Friedrich Ferdinand von Kotzebue and Iffland.

The 19th Century. During the 19th century theatrical life was cultivated primarily by the court theaters of various German Princes. This decentralization has remained characteristic of the German theater to the present time. The seeds sown by Goethe and Schiller and indirectly by

Scene from a 1962 production in Dresden of *Rise and Fall of the City of Mahagonny* (1930), by Bertolt Brecht and Kurt Weill. (EASTFOTO)

Shakespeare bore fruit in a line of dramatists whose status was fully recognized only after their deaths—Heinrich von Kleist, Christian Dietrich Grabbe, Georg Büchner, Friedrich Hebbel, and the Austrian Franz Grillparzer.

In Vienna, the imperial capital, theatrical life flourished in two distinct forms. The Burgtheater, under the directorships of men like Josef Schreyvogel, Heinrich Laube, and Franz Dingelstedt, presented the classical drama of all nations, and other stages offered popular local dialect plays, in particular those of Ferdinand Raimund and Johann Nestroy.

An important event was the opening in 1876 of Richard Wagner's Festival Theater in Bayreuth. Not only did this provide a home for an important annual festival, it also initiated a new form of building, one that discarded the traditional structure of boxes and tiers and substituted a fanlike arrangement of seats.

Another fresh impulse came from the court theater of the Duke of Saxe-Meiningen, where an exquisite ensemble was formed to present classical plays in a realistic historical style. By extensive tours throughout Europe between 1874 and 1890, this troupe developed ensemble acting to new high levels and prepared the way for the modern realistic theater.

The literary revolution known as naturalism, however, was initiated by a private enterprise, the Freie Bühne, a theater club founded in Berlin in 1889, whose productions included the first plays of Gerhart Hauptmann, from *Vor Sonnenaufgang*, 1889 (*Before Dawn*, 1909) to *Die Weber*, 1892 (*The Weavers*, 1899). Its leader, Otto Brahm, became the director of the influential Deutsches Theater, Berlin, in 1894, and thus introduced the new drama to the regular stage. Meanwhile, private theaters had sprung up in many cities, gradually taking the initiative from the somewhat stagnating court theaters. The Freie Volks-bühne, an organization designed to bring drama to the working classes, was formed in Berlin in 1890; it opened its own theater in 1915, and after 1918 spread throughout Germany, attaining nearly 500,000 members.

The 20th Century. In 1905 Max Reinhardt took over the Deutsches Theater, making it, through his brilliant productions, the leading playhouse in Germany. After World War I, he extended his activities to Austria and founded, together with the Viennese dramatist Hugo von Hofmannsthal, the Salzburg Festival, which still takes place every summer.

After the revolution of 1918, the court theaters were turned into state and municipal playhouses. Their lavish subsidies have made the theater in Germany more independent of commercial considerations than elsewhere. At the same time, the literary movement known as expressionism changed the face of the stage. Of the playwrights who led this movement, Georg Kaiser and Ernst Toller were the most prominent. Their revolutionary plays demanded a nonrealistic, highly emotive style of acting and production. Among the new directors, the most influential was Erwin Piscator, who introduced film and loudspeaker to support the stage action. Thus the German theater of the 1920's set the pace for the contemporary stages of the world.

These developments were cut short by the rise of Hitler in 1933. During the 12 years of Nazi rule the theater lacked any real vitality, owing to the emigration of most of the leading authors and producers.

In 1945 theatrical life reached a low point from which it was slow to recover. With the loss of Berlin as its capital, the theater became more than ever decentralized. The political division of the country had a deep effect. In the East the theater became an instrument of Communist propaganda; in the West it resumed contact with the outside world and embarked on an impressive rebuilding program. Nevertheless, the most notable theatrical event of the postwar period was the foundation in 1949 of Bertolt Brecht's Berliner Ensemble in East Berlin, devoted primarily to the production of his own plays.

After a long period of stagnation, a new generation of playwrights emerged about 1960. It turned its attention to the recent German past, the Nazi crimes, and the question of German guilt. Of these young playwrights, Rolf Hochhuth and Peter Weiss have been most prominent. Hochhuth is the author of the controversial play *Der Stellvertreter*, 1961 (*The Deputy*). Weiss, who lives in Sweden, has won wide acclaim for *Die Verfolgung und Ermordung Jean Paul Marats*, 1964 (*The Persecution and Assassination of Marat as Performed by the Inmates of the Asylum of Charenton under the Direction of the Marquis de Sade*), and *Die Ermittlung*, 1965 (*The Investigation*), a condensed presentation of the Auschwitz trial.

Consult Freedley, George, and Reeves, J. A., *A History of the Theatre* (1941); Nicoll, Allardyce, *World Drama from Aeschylus to Anouilh* (1949); Bruford, W. H., *Theatre, Drama and Audience in Goethe's Germany* (1950); Garten, H. F., *Modern German Drama* (1959).

H. F. GARTEN, Author, *Modern German Drama*
See also DRAMA; EPIC THEATER; articles on German dramatists and directors.

GERMICIDE [jûr′mə-sīd], agent that kills bacteria. The term commonly refers to chemical agents. Certain germicides, such as phenol, act to destroy the structural organization of the bacterial cell. Others, such as merthiolate, interfere with metabolism of bacteria. Germicides are used principally to disinfect sickrooms and to sterilize surgical instruments.
See also ANTISEPTICS.

GERMINATION [jûr-mə-nā′shən], a botanical term that describes the sprouting of seeds, usually after a resting period following their formation. Seeds are said to have germinated when the root appears, but the process is not completed until the seedling has produced leaves and become independent of the food stored in the seed.

Steps in Germination. When temperature and other conditions are favorable, a seed absorbs water, if moisture is available, and often swells visibly. The seed coat then becomes permeable to oxygen and eventually breaks. Enzymes that digest the food stored in the seed are activated within the embryo. The food then becomes available for energy and the building of cell walls and new protoplasm. Respiration, which is at a low level in the resting seed, becomes very rapid as evidenced by the production of heat and carbon dioxide during germination. Early embryo growth is generally by cell enlargement without cell division (which occurs later), and results first in the development of a root that grows downward to anchor the seedling and to absorb water and minerals. Later a stem grows upward, and leaves appear and develop to the point where they begin to photosynthesize. The stems and roots grow by cell divisions in a region at their tips. While certain of these cells retain their ability to divide, other daughter cells elongate to form a region back of the stem and root tips to add to the growth. The germinating embryo consists of one or more seed leaves, or cotyledons, which are attached to a short, thick, stemlike axis, the hypocotyl, and a bud, or plumule, containing several undeveloped foliage leaves attached just above the cotyledons. The root develops from the lower end of the hypocotyl. Some seeds, for example, the seeds of legumes, have all the stored food in the cotyledons; others have an external tissue for stored food called the endosperm.

Types of Germination. Stem growth is generally of two types. In the first type, which is characteristic of most dicotyledons and the onions, the hypocotyl elongates and pulls the cotyledons out of the ground; then the plumule grows. In the second type, characteristic of grasses and some dicotyledons, such as peas and oaks, only the plumule elongates so that the cotyledons remain underground within the seed.

EDWIN A. PHILLIPS, Pomona College
See also GROWTH: *Growth in Plants.*

GERMISTON [jûr′mĭs-tən], industrial city in the Witwatersrand area of Transvaal, Republic of South Africa, 9 mi. east of Johannesburg. Located in the world's largest gold-production area, Germiston is also the hub of South Africa's national railroad system. More than 700 trains enter and leave the city each day, and there are extensive railroad repair shops here. One of South Africa's largest generating stations is situated near Germiston Lake and

GERMINATION

A seed consists of a tiny, undeveloped plant (embryo), surrounded by stored food (endosperm), the whole enclosed by a protective coat (testa). Under favorable conditions the seed coat cracks and the seed sprouts, or germinates.

DICOTYLEDONS

The embryos of dicotyledons contain two seed leaves (cotyledons), which grow laterally from an elongated axis. The epicotyl, which becomes the stem of the plant, is the portion of the axis above the cotyledons' point of attachment. The portion below (hypocotyl) develops first and becomes the plant's primary root.

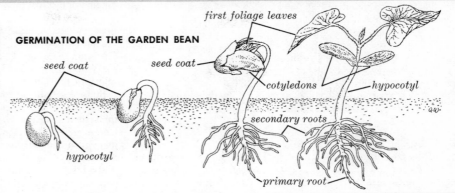

GERMINATION OF THE GARDEN BEAN

first foliage leaves
seed coat
seed coat
cotyledons
hypocotyl
secondary roots
hypocotyl
primary root

MONOCOTYLEDONS

The embryos of monocotyledons contain one seed leaf (cotyledon), attached to an elongated axis. The cotyledon absorbs stored food but does not emerge from the seed coat. The hypocotyl develops first, becoming the roots of the plant. The epicotyl pushes above ground and becomes the shoot, on which the leaves later develop.

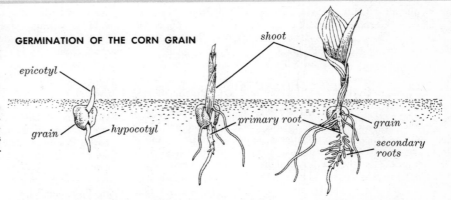

GERMINATION OF THE CORN GRAIN

shoot
epicotyl
grain
hypocotyl
primary root
grain
secondary roots

supplies electricity and compressed air to the city. The Rand Refinery, located here, is the world's largest gold-refining plant; about 55% of the world's gold is refined and exported from Germiston. Other important industries include the manufacture of explosives, concrete and steel pipes, chemicals, agricultural implements, starch, glucose, and clothing. Inc. as city, 1950; pop., 204,605.

GERM THEORY, the theory that certain diseases are caused by specific microbes. The theory was suggested long before the discovery of bacteria, but did not receive general acceptance until 200 years after the discovery of these microorganisms. In the early part of the 19th century convincing evidence was offered that certain plant diseases, such as the potato blight, were caused by fungi.

In 1876 Robert Koch demonstrated that the disease called anthrax is caused by a specific bacterium, *Bacillus anthracis.* Koch established a set of criteria for assigning a specific organism as the cause of a specific disease. Known as Koch's postulates, these state that (1) the suspected organism must always be found in natural cases of the disease; (2) the organism must be isolated in pure culture; (3) when introduced into a susceptible animal, the organism must produce the typical disease symptoms; (4) the presence of the organism must be demonstrated in the diseased tissues of the artificially inoculated animal by

growing a pure culture of the organism from these tissues.

The germ theory of disease is generally accepted in the scientific world today.

MICHAEL DOUDOROFF, Department of Bacteriology, University of California

See also MICROBIOLOGY.

GERONA [*hā-rō'nä*], city of northeastern Spain and capital of the province of Gerona, on the Ter and Oñar rivers. A communications and trade center, it produces cotton cloth, paper, and cork products. It is surrounded by ancient fortifications and has a Gothic cathedral of the 14th and 15th centuries. Pop., 24,831.

GERONIMO [*jə-rŏn'ə-mō*] (c.1829–1909), Chiricahua Apache prophet and chief. He was living quietly on a Chiricahua reservation near the Arizona–Mexico border when, in 1876, the Mexican government complained of Indian depredations in Sonora. To placate the Mexicans, the U.S. government moved the Chiricahuas to another reservation farther inland, whereupon Geronimo and some of the younger chiefs fled to Mexico. Returning to New Mexico, he was arrested, and resumed living in peaceful discontent on the San Carlos reservation in Arizona. In 1882 he led a raiding party into Sonora but surrendered when surrounded in the Sierra Madre

Geronimo (c.1829–1909), the Apache Indian leader.
(CULVER PICTURES, INC.)

by troops under Gen. George H. Crook. Two years later Geronimo started another reign of terror in the American Southwest and in the northern Mexican states of Sonora and Chihuahua, with U.S. troops in frenzied but vain pursuit. Finally, in Aug., 1886, Gen. Nelson Miles captured Geronimo and his entire ragged band of about 340 men. The group was deported to Florida, then Alabama, and finally to Fort Sill, Okla.

JOE B. FRANTZ, University of Texas

GERRY [gĕr′ē], **ELBRIDGE** (1744–1814), American statesman. Born to a prominent mercantile family in Marblehead, Mass., he graduated (1762) from Harvard College and joined his father in business. He was elected (1772) representative to the General Court, where he became a disciple of Samuel Adams. Although disillusioned with public life when a hospital he had built for smallpox patients was destroyed by a mob, Gerry was persuaded by Adams to participate in the pre-Revolutionary agitation against Great Britain. He aided Bostonians suffering under the Boston Port Bill and served (1774–76) in the first Provincial Congress and its Committee of Safety. He also helped to finance and to equip the Continental army and became a member of the Continental Congress.

After the war, Gerry prospered as a merchant and bought a confiscated Loyalist estate in Cambridge. Although interested in the expansion of commerce, he opposed centralizing the government in order to promote it. He was the largest holder of public securities among the delegates to the Federal Constitutional Convention (1787), but he refused to sign the Constitution. Once it was ratified, however, he supported the document and represented Massachusetts in Congress. There he followed an erratic policy: he sought a Bill of Rights, but opposed immediate amendment of the Constitution.

In 1797, as a peace commissioner to France with John Marshall and C. C. Pinckney, he became involved in the X Y Z affair. Despite damage to his prestige, he retained sufficient influence as a Republican to become the Governor of Massachusetts. In his first term (1810), the Republicans continued Federalist policies, but in his second term (1811), they made sweeping removals from office, bitterly attacked the Federalists, and redistricted the state to their advantage—a stratagem then and thereafter called a "gerrymander." Nevertheless, Gerry was defeated for the governorship in 1812. He was, however, elected Vice President of the United States in the same year.

ROBERT MIDDLEKAUFF, Yale University

GERRYMANDER, a term describing the establishment of an electoral district, created to give some group a political advantage within a governing body. The name was first used to characterize an odd-shaped legislative district created in Massachusetts in 1812, with the support of Governor Elbridge Gerry. A member of the opposition party said it looked "like a salamander." Another replied, "Better call it a Gerrymander."

State legislatures, working with their governors, are primary practitioners of gerrymandering. They determine their own districts and those of members of the U.S. House of Representatives. They also generally define the manner in which the legislative districts of their municipal governments will be drawn. Gerrymandering is accomplished by establishing geographical electoral districts, with the voting strength of the opposition party overconcentrated in a few districts to minimize the number of seats it can win, or conversely, to draw districts that will dilute the voting power of the rival party. Since the 1962 U.S. Supreme Court decision, *Baker* v. *Carr*, courts have enforced the principle that legislative districts must be as nearly equal in population as possible.

GEORGE GOODWIN, JR., University of Massachusetts
See also APPORTIONMENT, LEGISLATIVE.

GERSHWIN, GEORGE (1898–1937), American composer, born in Brooklyn, N.Y. Gershwin studied piano with Charles Hambitzer and theory and harmony with Edward Kilenyi. Later in life he studied composition with Henry Cowell and Joseph Schillinger. In 1919 Gershwin composed his first musical comedy score (*La, La Lucille*). The song "Swanee," also from 1919, became his first great success.

During the 1920's and '30's, Gershwin produced a series of musicals which established him as one of the most talented and successful composers in the field. His first concert work, *Rhapsody in Blue* (1924), was followed by the *Piano Concerto in F* (1925), *Three Preludes* for piano (1926), and *An American in Paris* (1928). His opera *Porgy and Bess* was produced in 1935. The most important characteristic of these works is the use of popular music idioms, such as jazz rhythms and melodies reminiscent of Negro blues. The successful employment of these idioms within the framework of classical forms could be regarded as Gershwin's chief contribution to American music.

Consult Ewen, David, *A Journey to Greatness: The Life and Music of George Gershwin* (1956).

RICHARD JACKSON, Music Division, N.Y. Public Library

GERSHWIN, IRA (1896–   ), American lyricist, born in New York City. He won fame as a writer for his brother, George Gershwin. Their first published song was *Waiting for the Sun to Come Out* (1920). Among their musicals were *Lady, Be Good!* (1924), *Funny Face* (1927), *Strike Up the Band* (1930), *Girl Crazy* (1930), *Of Thee I Sing* (1931), and *Porgy and Bess* (1935). Ira Gershwin also collaborated with other composers.

GERSON [zhĕr-sôn], **JEAN LE CHARLIER DE** (1363–1429), philosopher, theologian, and mystic. Made Chancellor of Notre Dame in 1395, he espoused the conciliar theory at the Council of Constance in 1415, which stressed the spiritual supremacy of the whole church in general council. Gerson sought a place in the general council for doctors of theology and canon law, as well as for laymen, to end restriction of participation to the hierarchy. In 1418–19 he wrote a work *On the Consolation of Theology*, patterned after Boethius. He gives the essentials of his doctrine in a work entitled *Mystical Theology*.

GERTRUDE OF NIVELLES [nĕ-vĕl′], **ST.** (631–59), patroness of travelers. Daughter of Pepin of Landen and St. Itta, she became abbess of the convent at Nivelles, endowed by her mother. Weakened by austerities, she died young, but was venerated almost immediately, and became one of the most popular medieval saints.

GERTRUDE THE GREAT, ST. (1256–c.1302), Christian mystic. She entered the Cistercian convent at Helfta, Thuringia, in 1261. After a vision in 1281 or 1282, she gave up profane studies and entered more vigorously into the spiritual life. She is noted for her miracles and prophecies, and for two works: her autobiographical *Herald of Divine Love* and her *Exercises of St. Gertrude*. She is patron saint of the West Indies. Her feast is Nov. 16.

GERYON [jē′rē-ən], in Greek mythology, a triple-bodied or three-headed monster who lived in the far west by the River Oceanus. He owned large herds of cattle; Hercules drove these off as his 10th labor, killing Geryon and his two-headed dog.

GESELL [gə-zĕl′], **ARNOLD LUCIUS** (1880–1961), American psychologist and pediatrician. He joined the Yale faculty in 1911, establishing the clinic later known as the Yale Clinic of Child Development. Director of this clinic from 1911 to 1948, he also studied medicine (receiving his M.D. degree in 1915) and was professor of child hygiene from 1915 to 1948. After 1950 he was a consultant to the Gesell Institute of Child Development. He is noted for studies of the growth and development of children. His books, written in collaboration with Frances Ilg and others, include *Infant and Child in the Culture of Today* (1943), *How a Baby Grows* (1945), *The Child from Five to Ten* (1946), *Vision: Its Development in Infant and Child* (1949), *Infant Development* (1952), and *Youth: The Years from Ten to Sixteen* (1956).

GESNERIA [jĕs-nēr′ē-ə], a genus of perennial evergreen plants in the gesneria family, Gesneriaceae, native to tropical America. One of the very few species of this genus in cultivation is *Gesneria longiflora*, a small-leaved plant grown chiefly for its tubular white flowers. Other genera of the gesneria family are well-known garden and greenhouse ornamentals, among them the African violets (*Saintpaulia*), gloxinias (*Sinningia*), and episcias (*Episcia*). Gesneriads, as members of the family are called, have rather thick, often hairy leaves and tubular flowers. Most gesneriads can be grown out-of-doors only in semi-tropical climates, but many do well as house plants if provided with a reasonably humid atmosphere and humusrich soil.

See also AFRICAN VIOLET; EPISCIA; GLOXINIA.

GESTALT [gə-shtält′] **PSYCHOLOGY,** the view that mental phenomena are organized wholes, that experience consists not in bundles of discrete stimuli but in undivided structures which are more than just the sum of their physical components. A melody is more than a collection of tones. In fact, the form or structure of experience (*Gestalt*, a German word, is often translated "form") is considered to be independent of the particular stimulus components that give rise to it. Thus, for example, a circle is a circle even though the particular stimulus is a ball, the mouth of a bottle, or a group of children holding hands.

This view was first elaborated by Max Wertheimer in Germany (1912). Wolfgang Köhler and Kurt Koffka were also major figures in the development of Gestalt theory, which arose in Europe, partly to combat Wilhelm Wundt's sensationism (analysis of experience into component sensations), at the same time that behaviorism was being enunciated in America. The influence of Gestalt psychology has waned, but many of its principles, such as organization of the perceptual field and relativity of sensory experience, have been recognized as important concepts.

LAWRENCE R. BOULTER, University of Illinois
See also BEHAVIORISM.

GESTAPO [gə-stä′pō], short form of *Geheime Staatspolizei*, the secret state police of Nazi Germany. Established in Prussia (Apr., 1933) by Hermann Goering, the Gestapo became in 1934 part of the national security police under Heinrich Himmler and was exempt from control by the courts. The responsible agency for the concentration camps, it was declared a criminal organization by the International Tribunal at Nuremberg in 1946.

GESTATION [jĕs-tā′shən], the period of pregnancy, or carrying of the young in the uterus, in mammals. Gestation is usually reckoned from the date of conception, or insemination of the egg, to the date of birth of the young. In the Virginia opossum, a marsupial, or pouched mammal, gestation lasts only about 12 days, and the partially developed young spend the remainder of a 70-day period of development within the female's pouch. In other mammals, such as those of the weasel family, the em-

Ass, 12 mo.	Giraffe, 14 mo.
°Bat, 2 to 6 mo.	Guinea Pig, 68 days
°Bear, 6 to 9 mo.	Hamster, 16 days
Beaver, 4 mo.	Horse, 11 mo.
Camel, 13 mo.	Lion, 108 days
Cat, 60 days	Man, 280 days
Chimpanzee, 8 mo.	Monkey, Rhesus, 164 days
Cow, 285 days	Mouse, domestic 19 to 21 days
°Deer, 203 to 215 days	Pig, domestic, 113 days
Dog, 62 days	Raccoon, 63 days
Elephant,	Rat, domestic, 21 to 22 days
Indian, 20 to 23 mo.	Reindeer, 8 mo.
Fisher, 11 to 12 mo.	Sheep, 5 mo.
°Fox, 50 to 60 days	°Whale, about 1 yr.
° Depending on species.	

bryo may develop partially and then cease development for months, resulting in a long gestation period.

GESUALDO [hā-swäl'thō], **DON CARLO,** Prince of Venosa (c.1560–1613), Italian composer, known for his original harmonies. Acting with the severity typical of royal blood in that period, he ordered his first wife, her lover, and her child murdered. Gesualdo's music, which has been revived in the 20th century, is characterized by brilliant chromatic coloring and dramatic force. The abrupt harmonic changes and strong contrasts are unsurpassed by any of his contemporaries, and are striking even to modern ears. His principal compositions were madrigals.

GETA [jē'tə], **PUBLIUS SEPTIMIUS** (189–212 A.D.), Roman Emperor (211–12). The son of Septimius Severus and Julia Domna, Geta received imperial titles well before Septimius Severus died at York. Returning from Britain, Geta and his elder brother Caracalla, co-Emperors, quarreled constantly until Caracalla in 212 murdered Geta.

GETAE [jē'tē], Indo-European people of Thracian stock, called Dacians by the Romans. Located on the lower Danube in 513 B.C., after 300 B.C. they controlled modern Rumania. Despite variable contests with Persians, Macedonians, Romans, and barbarian neighbors, the Getae preserved their independence until Dacia was reduced to a Roman province in 107 A.D. After the breakdown of Roman rule c.270 they joined the Goths.

GETHSEMANE [gĕth-sĕm'ə-nē], **GARDEN OF** (Heb., "oil vat"), name recorded by Mark (14:32) and Matthew (26:36) for the place where Judas betrayed Christ. Luke's account (22:39) locates the site on the Mount of Olives, east of Jerusalem; John (18:1) speaks of it as a garden on the route between Jerusalem and Bethany, where Jesus and His Disciples retired at night. It was probably a private olive grove on the western face of the Mount of Olives affording a panorama of Jerusalem.

GETTY, J. PAUL (1892–1976), U.S. industrialist, who built a fortune, mainly from oil interests, and controlled more than 200 business firms. At his death Getty's fortune was estimated at from $2 billion to $4 billion, making him perhaps the world's richest private citizen. He was born in Minneapolis, the son of an attorney who became highly successful in the oil business. J. Paul Getty, a noted art collector, established the Getty Museum at Malibu, Calif.

GETTYSBURG [gĕt'ĭz-bûrg], borough of southern Pennsylvania and seat of Adams County, 35 mi (56 km) southwest of Harrisburg. Founded in 1743, it received its name when Gen. James Gettys purchased the land now occupied by Gettysburg about 1790.

The area is of great historical interest. There are more than 2,000 monumemts and markers located here in memory of the Battle of Gettysburg and related events of the Civil War. The Eternal Light Peace Memorial, a 40-ft (12-m) limestone shaft surmounted by an eternal gas flame, was dedicated here by President Franklin D. Roosevelt in 1938.

THEODORE R. SPEIGNER

GETTYSBURG, BATTLE OF, a pivotal engagement of the American Civil War, fought (July 1–3, 1863) in and around the small southern Pennsylvania town of Gettysburg. Following the Chancellorsville campaign, Gen. Robert E. Lee, commanding the Confederate Army of Northern Virginia, decided to invade the North. His chief consideration was the impossibility of feeding his army on the Rappahannock and the availability of food in Pennsylvania. Furthermore, Lee had become concerned about dwindling Southern manpower reserves. He hoped that by invading Pennsylvania he might encourage the advocates of peace in the North and thus help to end the war before the South's shortage of men and material became intolerable. Finally, he hoped that a successful campaign would relieve Union pressure on besieged Vicksburg, Miss.

On June 10 R. S. Ewell's corps left Culpeper and set out for Pennsylvania via the Shenandoah Valley, followed by the corps of James Longstreet and A. P. Hill. By the 15th Ewell had swept north through the valley, and by the 28th all of Lee's army was in Pennsylvania. Meanwhile Joseph Hooker, commanding the Union Army of the Potomac, had guessed Lee's intentions and had begun to move north. By the 28th Hooker's army was near Frederick, Md. On that same day President Abraham Lincoln replaced Hooker with George G. Meade.

While the Federals were moving rapidly northward, Lee remained in almost complete ignorance of their whereabouts, because his cavalry, under J. E. B. Stuart, was sweeping around the Union army instead of keeping between it and Lee. When, on the 28th, Lee learned that the enemy was at Frederick, he ordered his forces to converge on Cashtown, 7 mi (11 km) northwest of Gettysburg. On July 1 the leading elements of the armies met on the western outskirts of Gettysburg. A heavy engagement ensued. After early reverses the Confederates drove the Union forces back to the heights south of the town. Lee suggested to Ewell that he try to take the heights, but the latter demurred, and an excellent opportunity was lost.

As the rest of Meade's troops arrived, the Union army took up positions on Culp's and Cemetery hills, just south of the town, then down along Cemetery Ridge to the vicinity of Little Round Top. Lee ordered Longstreet to attack Cemetery Ridge on July 2. However, because of Longstreet's slowness and the unexpected presence of strong Union forces at an early hour, the attack succeeded only in driving D. E. Sickles' corps back from the Emmitsburg Road. A hot fight for the key point of Little Round Top ended with the Federals in possession.

Lee intended to renew his attack on Meade's left but, because of objections by the argumentative Longstreet, shifted the attack to the center. From 1 to 2 P.M. on July 3 Southern artillery bombarded the Union center. A column of 15,000 infantry led by G. E. Pickett advanced across a half mile (.8 km) of open ground in a charge that has become a synonym for courage. Despite its gallantry Pickett's charge was beaten back with frightful losses, and the battle ended. The armies faced each other throughout July 4, and that night Lee began the retreat to Virginia. Meade pursued cautiously, and Lee was able to recross the Potomac on July 13–14.

Union casualties for the campaign totaled 28,000. Confederate losses probably were below 30,000. Lee's army

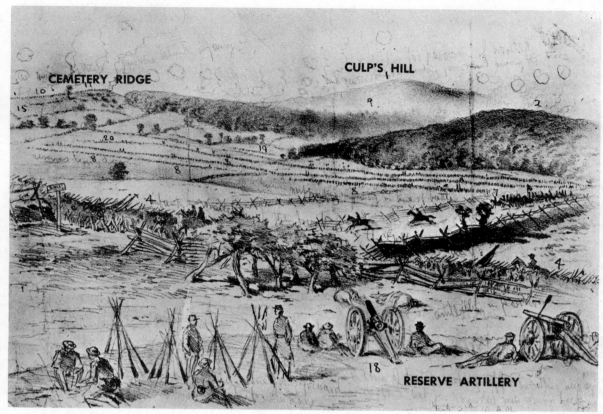

CEMETERY RIDGE

CULP'S HILL

RESERVE ARTILLERY

Section of an on-the-spot drawing, by Edwin Forbes, of Union positions at Gettysburg during the morning of July 3, 1863, showing the disposition of forces from the rear.

never exceeded 75,000. Meade had 100,000 troops, but only 90,000 were engaged. The effect of Lee's defeat has probably been exaggerated. Nevertheless, this was the last major Southern offensive.

Consult Montgomery, J. S., *Shaping of a Battle: Gettysburg* (1959); Stewart, G. R., *Pickett's Charge* (1959); Stackpole, E. J., and Nye, W. S., *Battle of Gettysburg* (1960).

LUDWELL H. JOHNSON, College of William and Mary

GETTYSBURG ADDRESS, speech delivered (Nov. 19, 1863) by President Abraham Lincoln at the dedication of the national cemetery on the Civil War battlefield at Gettysburg, Pa. Contrary to popular belief, the address was not written by Lincoln on the train to Gettysburg, but in Washington, D.C., with minor changes made at the dedication site. He was preceded on the rostrum by Edward Everett, who spoke for two hours. The President then read slowly from his prepared manuscript; when he had finished, he received only light applause, for the large audience was apparently tired by Everett's oration. The address, now renowned and widely quoted, both for its lofty sentiment and excellence of composition, was not, as is also commonly claimed, met by a conspiracy of silence. It was almost immediately discovered and widely acclaimed.

The Gettysburg Address

Fourscore and seven years ago our fathers brought forth on this continent a new nation, conceived in liberty, and dedicated to the proposition that all men are created equal.

Now we are engaged in a great civil war, testing whether that nation, or any nation so conceived and so dedicated, can long endure. We are met on a great battlefield of that war. We have come to dedicate a portion of that field as a final resting place for those who here gave their lives that that nation might live. It is altogether fitting and proper that we should do this.

But, in a larger sense, we cannot dedicate—we cannot consecrate—we cannot hallow—this ground. The brave men, living and dead, who struggled here, have consecrated it far above our poor power to add or detract. The world will little note, nor long remember what we say here, but it can never forget what they did here. It is for us the living, rather, to be dedicated here to the unfinished work which they who fought here have thus far so nobly advanced. It is rather for us to be here dedicated to the great task remaining before us—that from these honored dead we take increased devotion to that cause for which they gave the last full measure of devotion—that we here highly resolve that these dead shall not have died in vain—that this nation, under God, shall have a new birth of freedom—and that government of the people, by the people, for the people, shall not perish from the earth.

GETZ, STANLEY ("STAN") (1927–   ), jazz musician and tenor saxophonist, born in Philadelphia. He studied the double bass, the bassoon, and later the saxophone. He joined Stan Kenton in 1944 and then worked with Jimmy Dorsey, Benny Goodman, Randy Brooks, and Herbie Fields. He became known throughout the world as a result of his association with the Woody Herman band (1947–49). Later he led his own groups, which were built around his "cool" (vibrato-free) sound and delivery.

GEULINCX [*gŭ'lĭngks*], **ARNOLD** (1625–69), Belgian philosopher. An early supporter of Descartes, he lost his professorship at Louvain University, turned Calvinist, taught subsequently at Leiden, and died in penury. His posthumous *Ethica* (1675) and *Metaphysica* (1695) develop Cartesian themes, particularly that of occasionalism, and foreshadow the views of Malebranche, Spinoza, and Kant.

GEWANDHAUS [*gə-vänd'hoṳs*] **ORCHESTRA,** long-established Leipzig orchestra, taking its name from the Gewandhaus, or linen merchants' market hall, in which its concerts were held from 1781 until 1884. These concerts, which had previously been private (since 1743), were organized as a civic project in 1781 under J. A. Hiller (conductor from 1763). Since 1884 the concerts have been performed in a larger building. Notable conductors have included Hiller (1763–85), Felix Mendelssohn (1835–43), Arthur Nikisch (1895–1922), and Wilhelm Furtwängler (1922–28).

GEYSER [*gī'zər*], intermittent spring from which hot water and superheated steam are thrown into the air, of-

ten hundreds of feet. The water, seeping through cracks and crevices deep in the earth's crust, is heated by contact with hot rocks and gases. The water reaches temperatures higher than its normal boiling point because of the pressure from water at higher levels in the crust. As a result of normal circulation the superheated water moves nearer to the surface. The pressure is thereby reduced and some of the water becomes superheated steam, which forces the remaining water out of openings at the earth's surface. The interval of eruption is determined by the characteristics of the conduits, or passages, through which the water circulates.

Some notable localities where geysers occur are in New Zealand, Iceland, Tibet, and Yellowstone National Park in the United States. The famous Old Faithful geyser in Yellowstone Park erupts at regular intervals of about 65 minutes. The now extinct Waimangu geyser in New Zealand ejected water to a record height of 1,500 ft.

WARD S. MOTTS, University of Massachusetts
See also FUMAROLE; SPRING; VOLCANO.

GEYSERITE [*gī'zər-īt*], also known as siliceous sinter, variety of opal deposited around geysers and hot springs. The thermal waters carry dissolved silica, which is deposited when the water evaporates. Extensive deposits are found in hot-spring areas in many parts of the world, as at Yellowstone National Park, Wyo., and in New Zealand and Iceland.
See also GEYSER; OPAL; SPRING.

GEZER [*gē'zər*], ancient city of Biblical times, about 18 mi. northwest of Jerusalem, at the edge of the foothills along the coastal plain. It was the center of an important Canaanite city-state, founded about 3200 B.C., and was provided with massive fortifications. These were strengthened by King Solomon when Israel assumed control of Gezer in the 10th century B.C. (I Kings 9:15,16). It is the site of the first intensive excavation (1902–9) of an ancient Palestinian city.

G-FORCE, the apparent weight of a moving object relative to its actual weight at rest on the surface of the earth. For example, 2G indicates an effective weight equal to twice the actual weight. G-forces are due to the inertia of an accelerating body. A sitting man can withstand about 6G for 10 seconds before losing consciousness. However, a supine man can tolerate at least 14G for several minutes. Zero gravity is a different condition, in which a mass is apparently weightless. It occurs when an orbiting body is no longer subjected to propulsion forces.

GHALIB [*gä-lēb'*], pseudonym of Asadullah Khan (1796–1869), eminent Urdu poet. He was associated with the court of the last Mogul Emperor, Bahadur Shah, at Delhi until the Sepoy Mutiny of 1857; thereafter he led a retired life. In his Urdu and Persian divans (poetical works) he achieved rare intellectual acuity, converting old conventions into new symbols and combining obliqueness of expression with forceful wit. The first to use Urdu instead of Persian in corresponding with his friends, he has been called the founder of Urdu literary prose.

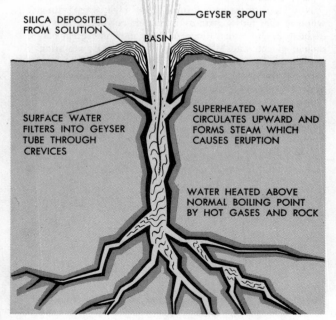

CUTAWAY DIAGRAM OF A GEYSER

SILICA DEPOSITED FROM SOLUTION

GEYSER SPOUT

BASIN

SURFACE WATER FILTERS INTO GEYSER TUBE THROUGH CREVICES

SUPERHEATED WATER CIRCULATES UPWARD AND FORMS STEAM WHICH CAUSES ERUPTION

WATER HEATED ABOVE NORMAL BOILING POINT BY HOT GASES AND ROCK

An adult education class, organized by the Ministry of Social Welfare, conducted outdoors in Nayagnia, a bush village in northern Ghana.
(MARC & EVELYNE BERNHEIM—RAPHO-GUILLUMETTE)

GHANA

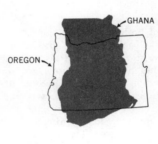

GHANA

OREGON

AREA	91,843 sq. mi.
ELEVATION	Sea level to 2,900 ft.
POPULATION	Approx. 7,800,000
PRINCIPAL LANGUAGES	Twi, Fanti, Dagomba, and English
PERCENTAGE OF LITERACY	20–25%
UNIT OF CURRENCY	cedi
NATIONAL ANTHEM	Lift High the Flag of Ghana
CAPITAL	Accra
PRINCIPAL PRODUCTS	Cocoa, bananas, coffee, palm oil, peanuts, kola nuts, maize, millet, rice; gold, diamonds, manganese, bauxite; fish

GHANA [gä'nə], republic of West Africa, on the Gulf of Guinea just a few degrees north of the equator. It is bounded on the north by the Republic of Upper Volta, on the west by the Republic of the Ivory Coast, and on the east by the Republic of Togo. Formerly a British colony (the Gold Coast, Ashanti, and the Northern Territories Protectorate), Ghana became independent in 1957, joined by neighboring (former British) Togoland. Ghana's total area is 91,843 sq. mi.

The Land

Physical Features. The 334 mi. of coast are mostly scrubland, much of which is extensively farmed, changing east of Accra to the open Accra plains. Near the mouth of the River Volta they turn to lagoons, which are particularly numerous in the neighborhood of Ada and Keta. At the western end of the coastal plain the forest belt comes close to the sea. This forest belt extends for some 170 mi. along the Western Region into Ashanti, forming the base of a rough triangle with its apex at the junction of the Afram and Volta rivers. A narrow belt of forest stretches north and east from the confluence of these rivers. Along the hills of the Volta region north of the forest belt, orchard bush appears, merging still farther north into parkland. There are no high mountains in Ghana. Half the country is less than 500 ft. above sea level. Broken into ridges and valleys, the forest belt rises from 600 ft. near Aburi and the Shai hills near the coast to over 2,000 ft. at Abetifi in the eastern region, just south of the Ashanti border. There are many streams and rivers, most of which are seasonal. The rivers in the open parkland of the north, with the exception of the Black and White Voltas, are dry for most of the year. Of the rivers flowing into the sea, only the Volta, Tano, and Ankobra have open mouths, but even these are impeded by shifting bars which curtail their navigation to shallow-draught river launches.

There are four vegetation zones: high forest, savannah-woodland, coastal scrub and grassland, and strand and mangrove. The high forest is made up of a large variety of plants which are arranged in a series of well-marked layers, or storeys. Where sunlight reaches the ground, small herbs, shrubs, and grasses grow. At 60 ft. appear trees with low branches and heavy crowns. Above this come trees with tall, straight trunks, usually with small crowns that form a thick canopy about 130 ft. high. Lastly are the very tall trees, reaching up to 200 ft. They are scattered and do not shut out light. Lianas entwine

603

GHANA

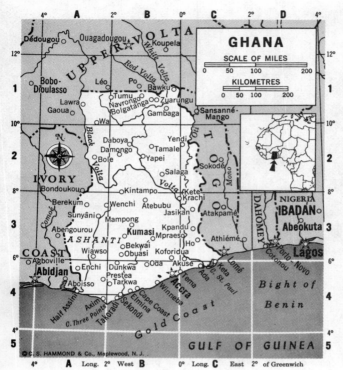

GHANA

SCALE OF MILES

0 50 100 200

KILOMETRES

0 50 100 200

© C. S. HAMMOND & Co., Maplewood, N. J.

A   Long. 2° West B   0° Long. C   East 2° of Greenwich

the trees, some of the vines climbing to the very tops of the highest trees.

The savannah-woodland, sometimes called the Guinea savannah-woodland, is the most extensive vegetation zone. With an area of about 65,000 sq. mi., it covers the whole of the region north of the high forest. Usually it consists of short trees, often widely spaced, with a carpet of grass. Some of the grasses attain a height of about 12 ft. From November to April, when the harmattan (dry, north-easterly wind) blows, the relative humidity is extremely low. This season is so extremely dry that the soil is baked hard, and much of the rain that falls at the beginning of the rainy season runs off before it can be absorbed.

The coastal vegetation consists either of dense scrub with hardly any grass or of grassland studded with clumps of bush and patches of scrub with a few trees, such as the baobab. Guinea grass is most common. In the moister western parts and also in the extreme east, fan palms and oil palms are prevalent. Along the seashore the vegetation is constantly bathed in spray and swept by moist breezes. The plant cover consists of succulent erect or creeping herbs, tufted plants, and grasses, which bind the sand with long, springlike shoots on partly buried horizontal stems. The lagoons and the beds of old lagoons, which are under water during the rains, are mainly associated with mangrove trees. These are not very extensive and do not grow tall. In the stagnant lagoon sections are found various water plants.

Climate. The eastern coastal belt is warm and comparatively dry; the southwest corner is hot and humid; the forest belt, warm and humid; and the north, hot and dry. Except in the north there are two rainy seasons, separated by a short and fairly dry period in July and

Below, a family compound in northern Ghana includes separate huts for each of the owner's wives. (MARC & EVELYNE BERNHEIM—RAPHO-GUILLUMETTE) The thatched hut is a granary, and a tree-trunk ladder leads to an adjacent roof. **Right,** two children in Accra. (FREDERICK AYER II—PHOTO RESEARCHERS)

August, with a longer dry season from December to February. In the north the rainy seasons tend to merge. Average annual rainfall in the coastal zone is 33 in.

The People

Population. Ghana has a population estimated at 7,800,000 with the highest density in the coastal areas, the Ashanti Region, and the two principal cities, Accra and Kumasi. According to tradition, the present Ghanaians are descended not from its earliest inhabitants but from migrating tribes. There are many small ethnic divisions in the territory, with over 50 different languages or dialects spoken. Among the more important linguistic groups are the Akans, including the Fanti, who live principally on the coast. The Ashanti live in the forest areas immediately to the north and the Guans on the plains of the Volta. The Ga and the Ewe-speaking peoples occupy the south and southeast, while the Moshi-Dagomba speaking tribes are found in the Northern Territories. The first migratory movement probably came down the Volta around the beginning of the 13th century.

Education. Primary schooling is free and compulsory, and secondary education is increasing. There are three universities and a number of teacher training colleges and technical institutes.

Economy

Basis. Per capita income in Ghana is over $200 per year, one of the highest in Africa. Ghana's economy is based upon production of a limited number of primary agricultural and mineral commodities. The basic crop is cocoa, of which Ghana is the world's leading producer. In a recent year the country produced around 425,000 tons, or about one-third of the world total. Since World War II, exports of cocoa beans have averaged about 70% of the total value of exports. Production is entirely in the hands of small-scale individual farmers, while marketing and export of the crop are controlled by a Cocoa Marketing Board established by ordinance in 1947. Other important agricultural products are shea nuts, coconuts, palm kernels, and palm oil. An expanding timber industry produces important quantities of mahogany and other forest products. Livestock-raising and fisheries are of increasing significance, although development of the former is handicapped by endemic cattle disease.

Mining remains the major industry of Ghana. It is next to agriculture in importance as a source of foreign exchange. Mining exports include gold, diamonds, bauxite, and manganese, but the total yearly value of these four does not match that of cocoa. Quarrying has become important domestically because of the many development projects using stone.

Gold reserves are found principally in the western and Ashanti regions, with some known deposits in the Northern Territories. No mining, however, is carried on in the north. Of the existing operations, one is a dredging outfit and the others are reef mines. The industry was plagued with rising costs in the 1960's, although gold prices had not increased. To forestall the closing of five marginal mines, the government of Ghana bought the shares of the stockholders, mostly foreign, and established the Ghana State Mining Corporation to control them.

University of Ghana, founded in 1948 and located at the edge of Accra, participates in the national adult education service.
(MARC & EVELYNE BERNHEIM—RAPHO-GUILLUMETTE)

Diamonds have been mined commercially in Ghana since 1920. Until recently, most of the production was in the hands of foreign companies, but the alluvial nature of the diamond deposits makes it possible for licensed Africans to mine small claims. Production of small operators, however, has progressively decreased since 1959, when 55% of total output was produced by them. All diamond sales must be transacted through the government diamond market in Accra.

Ghana's manganese reserves are of high and low grades. The African Manganese Co.,·Ltd., has been working the high-grade deposits since 1916, but the lower-grade ore has not been exploited. Production has increased steadily, but, until a 37% rise in 1961, price decreases more than matched this rise in volume. The United States and the United Kingdom are the principal markets for Ghana's manganese. Bauxite, significant at present, presumably will become even more important in the future. Total reserves have been estimated at 200,000,000 tons. Some deposits being worked in the western region north of Takoradi were opened up in 1941 by the British Aluminum Co. Larger deposits have been found in western Ashanti and the eastern region.

Ghana is making every effort to increase its manufacturing capacity. The Industrial Development Corporation (IDC), established in 1947, was formed specifically to develop industry by all means available. The corporation was operating 17 manufacturing enterprises by June 30, 1960, and the Industrial Cooperative Society, a branch of the IDC, was responsible for 9 more. The need for forcing these industries to support themselves became evident in Nov., 1961, and the IDC was dissolved. Each of its enterprises became self-supporting under the control of the Ministry of Industries.

After independence the government organized industry into five sectors: state enterprises, large-scale foreign private enterprise, operations owned jointly by the state and foreign private enterprise, co-operatives, and small-

605

scale Ghanaian private enterprise. Foreign private enterprises were welcomed if 60% of a company's net profit was reinvested in Ghana. After the first coup, in 1966, greater scope was given to private industry, and nonprofitable state enterprises were rigidly curtailed.

The first aluminum produced in Ghana entered the world market in Mar., 1967. Aluminum ingots were produced at the Valco smelter at Tema, which produces more than 100,000 tons of aluminum per year.

Power. No coal or petroleum reserves are known to exist in Ghana, but a refinery using imported petroleum has been constructed. Hydroelectric power is the one important potential source of energy. When the Volta River hydroelectric project began to produce in 1965, about 512,000 kilowatts became available for industrial use in the Accra-Akosombo-Tema area. Eventually the Accra-Sekondi-Kumasi triangle will be connected by a 161-kilovolt transmission system, and the Volta Dam's installed capacity should exceed 800,000 kilowatts. In the meantime, production of thermal electricity at Accra and Tema is increasing. All electricity production and transmission is owned and controlled by the state through the Electricity Division of the Ministry of Works and Housing.

The Ministry of Works and Housing also controls the water supply through its Water Supply Division. This division is making rapid strides in increasing the amount of pure water available, and development plans call for an increased supply sufficient to meet the estimated growth of demand.

Transportation. The International Airport at Accra is serviced by many major airlines. The frequency of flights of the different lines varies from once to about a dozen times weekly. Ocean service, passenger and cargo, is good. Some 30 lines serve the Ghanaian ports. The government operates the ports. Takoradi and Tema have deep-water harbors, but the surf ports at Accra, Cape Coast, and Winneba have been closed except for emergencies or contingencies.

The railroads are under the authority of the government's Railway Administration. The total trackage (all 3 ft. 6 in. gauge) is just under 800 mi., but the route mileage is about 200 mi. less. Part of it runs in a rough triangle between Accra, Takoradi, and Kumasi. A daily passenger train service runs between these three principal cities. The rest of the track is in branch lines. One branch line connects Accra and Tema.

Highways generally are good, considering the problems caused by the climate. Ghana has more than 20,000 mi. of roads, of which some 2,000 mi. are bitumen surfaced and about 1,400 gravel. The number of vehicles increased by one-third during the 1960's—an indication of the growing importance of road transport. The inland rivers, on the other hand, are almost useless as a means of transportation, for they are navigable only by canoe or other shallow-draft vessels. But a transportation system on Lake Volta is being developed.

Communications. Surface mail by ship is exchanged frequently, on an irregular schedule. There are several weekly air connections to London, and others to the United States. Mail is also exchanged overland daily with Togo and by air with Nigeria.

In Accra the old Fort James harbor, built by the English in the 17th century, today serves only Ghanaian fishing boats.
(MARC & EVELYNE BERNHEIM—RAPHO-GUILLUMETTE)

A cable station at Accra, run by Cable and Wire-less, Ltd., has a submarine cable with world connections and a radio telephone service to former British West African countries, the United Kingdom, and other countries. Improvement in internal telecommunications also is progressing rapidly.

Government

Since Jan. 13, 1972, when a coup d'état by young army officers—the second in six years—overthrew the duly constituted government of Prime Minister Kofi A. Busia, Ghana has been administered by a National Redemption Council under the leadership of Col. Ignatius K. Acheampong. The council, consisting of a dozen military and police officers, proclaimed that it would rule the country by "decrees having the force of law" and formally suspended the constitution, which had been in effect since the return to civilian rule in 1969. It also dissolved the National Assembly and issued a ban against all political parties and activities. The council promised the transfer of power to a democratically elected government as soon as circumstances made such a transfer possible.

History

Until the late 1400's the history of the Gold Coast (Ghana) was presented chiefly in traditions, tribal stories, and folklore. They frequently refer to migrations from the north, and the name of Ghana was revived largely from speculation of connections with the ancient kingdoms of the western Sudan. Ancient Ghana was a West African kingdom centered on a capital believed to have stood on the site of the ruins of Kaumbi Saleh, about 200 mi. north of Bamako in the Mali Republic. Since the earliest origins of present-day Ghanaians are largely unknown, the name may be more symbolic than historically significant.

The first fully authenticated contact between Europe and the Gold Coast dates from 1470, when a party of Portuguese landed. In 1482 the Portuguese built Elmina Castle as a permanent base. It had a lively trade in gold, hence the name Gold Coast. The first recorded English trading voyage to the coast was made by Thomas Windham in 1553. In the course of the next three centuries the English, Danes, Dutch, Germans, and Portuguese all controlled various parts of the coastal areas at different periods. In 1821 the United Kingdom government took over the control of the English private trading company operating the Gold Coast settlement. In 1844 the Fanti chiefs in the immediate neighborhood agreed, among other things, to submit cases of murder and other crimes to the Queen's judicial officers sitting with the chiefs.

From 1826 to 1900 the British fought a long series of campaigns against the Ashantis of the interior. Only in 1901 did they succeed in making Ashanti a colony and the Northern Territories a protectorate. The fourth territorial division eventually to form part of the nation, British Togoland, was a former German colony. After 1922 it was administered by Britain from Accra as a League of Nations mandate. In Dec., 1946, British Togoland became a United Nations Trust Territory, and in 1957, following a plebiscite, the United Nations agreed that the territory should become a part of Ghana when the Gold Coast achieved independence.

Constitutional progress was marked by continuous development in the Legislative Council, although until 1946 it was not the legislature for the whole country but only for the coastal area, then known as the "colony." Ashanti, until 1946, and the Northern Territories, until 1951, were administered directly by the governor. The constitution of 1951 provided for a greatly enlarged legislature comprised principally of members elected directly or indirectly by popular vote. An Executive Council was responsible for formulating policy, with a majority of African members drawn from the legislature.

The constitution, approved on Apr. 29, 1954, established a cabinet composed wholly of African ministers drawn from an all-African legislature chosen by direct vote. The Convention People's Party, in the elections that followed, won the majority of the seats in the new Legislative Assembly.

Independence. In May, 1956, Prime Minister Kwame Nkrumah's Gold Coast government proposed independence and changing the name of the country to Ghana. The British government agreed to a firm date for granting independence, providing that after a general election a reasonable majority in the Gold Coast Legislative Assembly approved. Held on July 12–17, 1956, the election resulted in the Convention People's Party (CPP) return to power with 71 of the 104 seats in the Legislative Assembly. On Mar. 6, 1957, full independence was granted.

After independence the CPP government under

Ship unloads at Sekondi-Takoradi on Gulf of Guinea. (EWING GALLOWAY)

A yam field in northern Ghana. Stones are placed on the earth mounds, which contain the young plants, to protect them from the sun. When the rains start, stones are removed. (BLACK STAR)

A prospector's diamonds are assayed. (GHANA INFORMATION SERVICES)

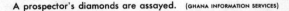

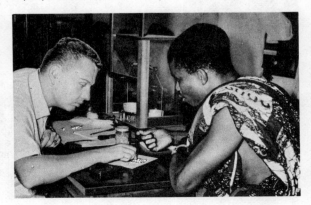

Nkrumah's leadership sought to develop Ghana as a modern unitary state along socialist lines. CPP control, however, did not go unchallenged. To stifle criticism, Nkrumah resorted to "emergency measures." By the Preventive Detention Act (1958), opponents could be imprisoned without trial for up to five years. Strict censorship was also imposed.

Republic. Prior to the adoption of a republican constitution, on July 1, 1960, Ghana had a ministerial government. The 1960 constitution vested great power in the president, while that of the National Assembly was diminished both as a result of the increased power of the presidency and the complete dominance of the CPP. In Jan., 1964, Ghana was made a one-party state, with the CPP as the single party. At the same time the president was empowered to remove members of the judiciary at his pleasure. Executive authority in the various regions was in the hands of regional and district commissioners, appointed by and responsible to the central government.

On Feb. 24, 1966, while Nkrumah was visiting Communist China, the Ghanaian army and police overthrew his government. Nkrumah and all his ministers were dismissed, the CPP and the parliament dissolved, and the constitution suspended. A National Liberation Council (NLC) was established as the new government, with Lt. Gen. Joseph A. Ankrah as chairman. The coup was generally welcomed by the Ghanaian people, who were pleased by the release of hundreds of political prisoners.

The NLC disclaimed any intention of ruling indefinitely and pledged an early return to civilian government. By 1968 it had drafted a new constitution, which was subsequently approved by a constituent assembly. Political activity in the country then resumed, and four parties emerged. The strongest of these proved to be the Progress party, led by Dr. Kofi A. Busia. He formed a government that assumed power on Oct. 1, 1969.

But neither the NLC nor the succeeding Busia regime, despite some austerity measures, was able to put the country's economy on an even keel. Nkrumah's legacy of foreign debts was crushing, and low world prices for cocoa aggravated the situation. Following a drastic devaluation of the cedi (Dec., 1971), the military again staged a coup d'état in Jan., 1972, charging the government with corruption and "general mismanagement." The constitution was suspended, parliament dissolved, and all political activities banned. The ruling National Redemption Council then placed the economy "on a war footing."

Consult Afrifa, A. A., *The Ghana Coup* (1966); Boateng, E. A., *Geography of Ghana* (2d ed., 1966); Fage, J. D., *Ghana: A Historical Interpretation* (1966); Genoud, Roger, *Nationalism and Economic Development in Ghana* (1968).

RICHARD P. STEVENS

GHANA, KINGDOM OF, ancient west African kingdom of the Sudan. During early medieval times it was an important source of the gold on which many European financial enterprises and currencies depended. Ghana was first described by Arab writers in the 8th century, although there is a possibility that it was a power in west Africa after the withdrawal of the Romans from North Africa. Ghana was conquered by North African Muslims in the 10th century. While it soon regained its political independence, Ghana lost its hold over many of its subject peoples. Two hundred years of decay followed. In 1235 Ghana became part of the empire of Mali.

Ancient Ghana was located northwest of the Senegal and northeast of the Niger River. Its territory was roughly circular, about 400 mi. in diameter. It has no connection with the contemporary state of Ghana, located about 1,000 mi. to the southeast. While the people of Ghana were farmers and fishermen, their technology was built upon iron tools that enabled Ghana to control surrounding peoples. Iron swords and lances prevailed over the ebony weapons of its neighbors, and iron was used to make agricultural implements.

Ghana had no fixed boundaries. Its territory was defined by the reach of the king's authority, operating through provincial officials who collected taxes and raised armies among the farmers who had settled in Ghana. Aside from this tribute, however, the king's subjects continued to follow their traditional ways of life.

Ghana's significance in Old World history derives from an advantageous location complemented by military power. Gold was found in the river valleys of the upper Niger and Senegal just to the south. It sustained the wealth and historic importance of Ghana and lent splendor to the royal court. Salt was found in the Sahara to the north. Salt was a necessity that was rare among the peoples of the Sudan and they eagerly exchanged it for gold. The kingdom was notable not only for its early use of iron, but for the establishment of an organized state, and for a highly developed system of trade and taxation in a period when these cultural features were rare.

HANS HOFFMANN

Kumasi fort, built by the British in 1898 to hold the city against the Ashanti tribes. (CHARLES MAY—BLACK STAR)